U.S. ARMY

A COMPLETE HISTORY

U.S. ARMY

A COMPLETE HISTORY

Colonel Raymond K. Bluhm, Jr., U.S. Army (Ret)
Editor-in-Chief

Dale Andrade
Major General Bruce Jacobs, U.S. Army (Ret)
John Langellier
Lieutenant Colonel Clayton R. Newell, U.S. Army (Ret)
Matthew Seelinger

THE ARMY HISTORICAL FOUNDATION

HUGH LAUTER LEVIN ASSOCIATES, INC.

THE ARMY HISTORICAL FOUNDATION

The Army Historical Foundation, a nonprofit charitable organization, was founded in 1983 by Generals Lyman Lemnitzer, Bruce Palmer, and Orwin Talbott, with the support of Secretary of the Army John Marsh and Army Chief of Staff General Edward Meyer. The foundation's goal is to promote greater appreciation for the contributions that America's Army—Active, Reserve, and National Guard—has made to the nation in more than 230 years of service. The motto of the Army Historical Foundation—"Preserve the Heritage, Educate the Future"—summarizes its mission. The foundation's top priority is the building of a national museum for the United States Army, America's oldest military service and the only branch of the American armed forces without its own national museum. The foundation also supports Army history by presenting annual Distinguished Writing Awards for outstanding books and articles on Army history; awarding small grants to museums within the Army museum system to assist them with exhibits and programs; providing funds for acquisition and preservation of artifacts, books, and documents for the Army's collections; and sponsoring public historical education and research assistance programs.

The Army Historical Foundation
2425 Wilson Boulevard
Arlington, Virginia 22201
(703) 522-7901; fax (703) 522-7929
ArmyHstFnd@aol.com
http://www.ArmyHistoryFnd.org

Published by Hugh Lauter Levin Associates, Inc.
© 2004 The Army Historical Foundation
Design: Charles J. Ziga
Project Editor: James O. Muschett
Graphics Editor: Vincent Hawkins
Photo Researcher: Melissa Payne
Technical Editor: Sandra J. Daugherty
Copy Editors: Deborah T. Zindell, Eric Minton
Design production: Chris Berlingo

ISBN 0-88363-113-x
Printed in China
Distributed by Publishers Group West
http://www.HLLA.com

CONTENTS

"BOOTS ON THE GROUND"

OUR ARMY...SERVING OUR NATION

"Let us have a respectable Army, and one such as will be competent to every contingency."
—George Washington

On 14 June 1775 the First Continental Congress placed the militia at Boston under its control and authorized the raising of ten additional companies of riflemen. From those humble beginnings, 229 years ago, our Army has well and faithfully served the American people. Today, just as those first Soldiers in Boston did before them, more than 1.2 million Active, Reserve, and National Guard Soldiers continue to give selflessly to our great Nation.

Our Army has a long and proud history filled with tradition. Members of the First Continental Congress in 1775 never envisioned the unprecedented range of missions today's Army would be called upon to conduct; from antiterrorist military operations, to humanitarian relief, to the support of domestic civil authorities, to peace operations, to the waging of large-scale war. The preeminent land force in the world, it continues to be respected by our friends and feared by our enemies. We set the standard. Soldiers, Department of the Army civilians, veterans, retirees, and all of their families can take pride in the fact that their service and sacrifices preserve the privilege of living and working in a free society.

Yesterday, today, and tomorrow our Soldiers remain the centerpiece of our Army. What makes a Soldier? Time. The time to transform the individual American's dedication to life, liberty, and the pursuit of happiness into the skills, values, and traditions that make the United States Army the envy of the rest of the world. More than any piece of equipment, our Soldiers account for the Army's many successes at home and abroad.

Our Soldiers are warriors of character. We are first and foremost Americans, reflecting the values of the American people, and we are very fortunate to be serving the greatest nation on Earth. Our Army is, has been, and will remain a values-based institution. Our values will not change and they are nonnegotiable. Soldiers exemplify these values every day and are the epitome of our American spirit.

American Soldiers remain indispensable. They are the weapon of choice and the heart of our Army. Our Soldiers are paramount and will remain the centerpiece of our thinking, our systems, and our combat formations. As General Creighton Abrams taught us, "People are not in the Army, they are the Army."

The phrase "Boots on the Ground" reflects more than two centuries of dedication by American Soldiers to preserving liberty where it matters most—in the day-to-day lives of people. It reflects the harsh realities of war and the undying commitment of our Nation to peace, goodwill, and freedom for all. Every day, noble American Soldiers put it all on the line, standing shoulder to shoulder with all the brave men and women who have sacrificed so much over the course of American history.

General Peter J. Schoomaker
Chief of Staff, United States Army

MILITIA AND FRONTIER SCOUTS

1607–1774

MILITIA AND FRONTIER SCOUTS

1607–1774

Colonel Raymond K. Bluhm, Jr., USA (Ret)

There was no Army in the beginning, nor was there a nation to defend. In the early 1600s there were only scattered groups of European colonists struggling for survival on an increasingly hostile shore.

As official expeditions, the Spanish crown provided a strong professional military presence to its colonies using detachments of royal troops. Not so the English, who were the primary colonizers of the North American Atlantic coast. Their colonial interest was primarily economic. Financed by groups of investors who expected a return on their money, the focus of these colonies was not on military matters, but on trading, farming, and finding the mineral riches rumored to abound. Some in these early colonial outposts did anticipate some type of self defense would be needed and came bearing what scanty arms and armor they could afford. And some brought men with military experience, but they were few. Fortunately, they usually fought an enemy armed with stone age weapons. Busy with its own European wars and budget problems, the British parliament refused for almost 100 years to provide any military assistance to its American colonies other than an occasional visit by Royal Navy men-of-war.

Faced with the responsibility for their own survival, the colonists evolved their own style of self defense, drawing heavily on their experience with local English village militias. In most colonies, all male members of the community considered old and fit enough, usually ages 15–60 years, were required, in theory, to be in the militia. It was considered a community duty and somewhat of an honor since it marked the person as an adult. Settlements like Jamestown and Massachusetts Bay fought prolonged conflicts with local native Americans. They built fortified towns and had a more active militia with regular musters, town armories, elected officers, and public safety as well as military duties. In other colonies, however, militias were slow to develop and members were lackadaisical.

The pattern of colonial warfare was usually a surprise attack by either side followed by retaliatory raids back and forth, not infrequently on towns or villages that had nothing to do with the initial attack, but who were a convenient target. Twice, unexpected Indian attacks came close to wiping out the Virginia colony. New England had a similar experience in the Pequot War. Thrown into the mix were also occasional attacks by pirates or raiders from a rival nation. Though faced with danger, there was always a conflict with personal needs. Colonists had to grow food, raise livestock, clothe and shelter themselves. The hours given to militia duty were hours away from these more productive pursuits.

A military force was also a competitor for community talent and resources. An effective militia meant organization, leaders, money for equipment and food on campaign, and training. This often meant an unwelcome tax burden. Colonial authorities, not always popular, also were leery of having large groups of armed men unsupervised by legal authority. They therefore kept militias under close control through appointment of key leaders by the colony and securing many of the weapons.

Over time, the basic militia unit became the village or regional company. These hometown units were the main line of a colony's defense. Higher

organizations, usually a regiment, were also formed to provide command and control. Massachusetts Bay, for example, formed three regiments in 1636.

The value of early warning was not ignored. As the colonists pushed in from the coast, the tiny outer settlements provided important alarms to threats, and were bases for the young men hired by the colony to "range" the forests full time as scouts and couriers. These men watched the trails for Indian war parties and later for French soldiers coming down from Canada to attack outlying farms and towns. And they led the way to the Indian and French villages for the retaliation that followed. These men were often formed into units that specialized in the forest warfare of raid and ambush. The most famous of these were the New Hampshire "snowshoe men," and later during the French and Indian War, Roger's Rangers.

Over time, the colonies gained experience with putting aside their rivalries and combining their limited military resources in a cooperative effort to face a common enemy. The first tentative steps at military cooperation taken during the Pequot and Abenaki Wars proved their value with the joint

expedition that captured Louisbourg from the French in 1745. By necessity, the Americans developed their own brand of military leaders who were schooled in the forests and ways of the frontier fighter.

The tradition of the small, full-time military force backed by a community-based, part-time citizen-soldier army, both under firm civil authority, remains a central theme in the military history of this country. From its earliest days this nation has been formed by its wars, and its soldiers who fought them.

Pages 8-9: *Rogers' versatile Rangers use stealth to their advantage as they row a whaleboat toward their epic victory over Abenaki enemies at Saint François during the French and Indian War. ("Rogers' Rangers," Mort Künstler)*

Above: *Colonel Henry Bouquet's Royal American and Highland troops employed forest fighting tactics to score a major victory 5 August 1763 against Delaware and Shawnee Indians, breaking the siege of Fort Pitt during Pontiac's Rebellion. ("One Mile to Bushy Run Station," Robert Griffing, Paramount Press, Inc.)*

MILITIA AND FRONTIER SCOUTS
1607–1774

"My inclinations are strongly bent to arms."
—George Washington, letter to Colonel William Fitzhugh, November 15, 1754

1565

September. **First Militia in America. St. Augustine, Florida.**
After establishing St. Augustine, the Spanish governor directs all civilian males in the settlement to become members of the "milicia," with the mission to protect the town.

1607

26 May. **First Powhatan Attack. Jamestown, Virginia.**
More than 200 Powhatan Indians attack the first permanent English settlement founded on the James River. Two settlers are killed. In reprisal, English ships bombard Indian villages along the river. A triangular fort is completed after a month of hard work.

September. **Militia Formed and Drilled. Jamestown, Virginia.**
Captain John Smith is voted the first military leader of the colony. He organizes the men into companies, works to instill military discipline, instructs them in musketry, and requires daily drill. Every man is expected to be "on call" and stand guard. Minor attacks and skirmishes with the Indians continue.

1610

August. **Jamestown Militia Expands.**
New colonists include 100 army veterans. Military discipline is enforced and all adult males are required to own and practice with muskets. Five expeditions are sent to seize Indian crops and destroy their camps. Conflict continues until Powhatan's daughter, Pocahontas, is captured in 1613 and kept hostage to ensure a truce. With no overt threat, military discipline quickly declines again.

Left: *Jamestown colonists built the triangular James Fort as a defensive measure against pirates and Indians. Out of 480 settlers, only 59 lived through the winter of 1609. (Sidney E. King, National Park Service—Colonial National Historical Park)*

Opposite: *Captain John Smith, who frequently went on scouting trips, was finally captured and brought before Chief Powhatan in 1643. His daughter, Pocahontas, begs to spare Smith from execution. (New York Public Library)*

ARMY UNITS DATING BEFORE THE AMERICAN REVOLUTION

Organized	Current Designation	Component
1636	182nd Infantry Regiment	Massachusetts ARNG
	101st Engineer Battalion	Massachusetts ARNG
1639	772nd Military Police Company	Massachusetts ARNG
1662	104th Infantry Regiment	Massachusetts ARNG
1672	169th Infantry Regiment	Connecticut ARNG
	102nd Infantry Regiment	Connecticut ARNG
	192nd Field Artillery Regiment	Connecticut ARNG
1735	201st Field Artillery Regiment	West Virginia ARNG
1736	Service Battery, 2nd Bn., 214th Field Artillery Regt.	Georgia ARNG
1741	126th Signal Battalion	Massachusetts ARNG
1742	116th Infantry Regiment	Virginia ARNG
1747	11th Infantry Regiment	Pennsylvania ARNG
1751	HQ & HQ Battery, 118th Field Artillery Regt.	Georgia ARNG
1755	169th Military Police Company	Rhode Island ARNG
1756	263rd Air Defense Artillery	South Carolina ARNG
	295th and 296th Infantry Regiments	Puerto Rico ARNG
1774	175th Infantry Regiment	Maryland ARNG
	Troop A, 1st Sqdn., 104th Cavalry Regiment	Pennsylvania ARNG
	Company A, 2nd Special Forces	Rhode Island ARNG

1620

11 November. **Plymouth Colony Established. Cape Cod Bay, Massachusetts.**
The small band of Pilgrims establish a settlement on the bay. Many lack weapons, but they have recruited Myles Standish, an experienced soldier. Within a year a fort is built, and by 1622 a four-company militia is training on a regular basis with muskets and swords. Later, the colony's General Court directs formation of a militia company in each town.

1622

22 March. **Surprise Indian Attack. Virginia.**
Powhatan Indians stage a large coordinated surprise attack. Over 340 colonists, almost one-third of the inhabitants, are killed. Surviving militiamen strike back in counter-raids, and sporadic warfare continues for 14 years.

1624

July. **Raid on Pamunkey Tribe, Virginia.**
Jamestown militia penetrate deep into Indian territory to confiscate crops. The Pamunkey resist and a two-day battle is fought. The superior firepower and armor of the militiamen give them the edge. Indian losses are heavy, while no colonists are killed.

1629

Salem Militia Formed. Massachusetts Bay Colony.
The colony organizes its first militia company. The Puritan settlers had arrived with arms and equipment for 100 men. By 1636 ten companies exist and mandatory musters are held.

1632

Virginia Militia. Jamestown.
Despite a truce, the assembly orders militia members to bring muskets to church every Sunday and to practice military drills after services. Militia commanders are appointed for each of the colony's eight counties.

1635

First Intercolony Naval Battle. Chesapeake Bay.
Intense rivalry and competition for fishing and trading rights lead to a ship-to-ship battle between Virginia and Maryland militia. Armed skirmishes between the two colonies continue for 12 years.

1636

25 August. **Pequot War Begins. Massachusetts Bay Colony.**
After Pequot warriors repeatedly attack trading ships, militia are sent to destroy Indian villages and crops on Block Island. The raid is only partially successful, so the militia attack a peaceful Pequot village nearby on the Connecticut River, starting a full-scale war.

September. **Siege of Fort Saybrook, Connecticut.**
In retaliation, the Pequots begin a siege of the fort. Some colonists are killed and others are captured and

tortured to death. The arrival of militia reinforcements does not disperse the Indians.

13 December. **First Militia Regiments. Massachusetts.**
The General Court reorganizes the 15 town militia companies into three regional regiments—the North, East, and South Regiments—each with a colonel appointed by the Court. The company officers are elected locally. Other colonies follow a similar pattern, and several create quick-reaction "minute companies" for emergencies. Four Massachusetts Army National Guard units trace their origins back to these regiments, making them the oldest units in the Guard. (Birthday of Army National Guard)

1637

18 April. **First Conscription. Massachusetts Bay Colony.**
The colony enacts the first conscription act. Every able-bodied man is subject to being drafted in an emergency, but little is done to enforce the act.

26 May. **First Joint Colony Military Operation. Mystic River, Connecticut.**
Militia from Massachusetts Bay, Plymouth, and Connecticut, together with Narragansett Indians, make a dawn attack against a large Pequot village. The surprised Pequots resist and force the militia back. Fire is set to the village and over 500 Pequot men, women, and children are killed. Pequot reinforcements arrive, but the militia rear guard holds while the rest withdraw to the ships.

13 July. **Swamp Fight. New Haven, Connecticut.**
Massachusetts and Connecticut militia trap Pequots in a swamp. Pequot women and children are given safe passage, but a group of about 80 warriors continues to fight until a militia attack the next morning destroys them.

13 September. **Maryland Indian War. Annapolis, Maryland.**
The Maryland Assembly declares war against the Susquahannock tribe, but the unprepared militia is unable to muster and war is postponed until the next summer.

1638

Artillery Unit Formed. Boston, Massachusetts.
The Ancient and Honorable Artillery Company, a volunteer militia group, is formed to study and practice gunnery.

Opposite, top: *The value of Indian allies to colonial militia was priceless. Here scout Squanto leads Plymouth militia toward a hostile village. ("The March of Miles Standish," The Granger Collection, New York)*

Opposite, bottom: *In 1622, Opechananough and his warriors killed about one-third of the Jamestown colonists. (National Park Service—Colonial National Historical Park)*

Right: *For a frontier scout and his hound, a clearing in the forest was a dangerous area to cross, leaving them vulnerable to ambush from the surrounding forest. ("Crossing the Open," H. David Wright)*

COLONIAL MILITIA FIREARMS— FROM MATCHLOCK TO FLINTLOCK

Above: *Holding the burning match and forked support staff, an early colonist prepares to fire his matchlock arquebus. (Peter Newark's Military Pictures)*

When the European colonists arrived in the New World, they brought the latest in weapons technology—handheld firearms. Although these weapons were clumsy and unreliable, they far outmatched the stone age weapons of the Native Americans who opposed the settlers.

In 1450 the matchlock, using the first mechanical device designed to discharge a firearm, had been developed. It featured a longer barrel for greater range, a shorter, curved stock for easier and more comfortable handling, and a pan to hold priming powder. An S-shaped device, called a "serpentine," held a smoldering cord, or "match." The serpentine pivoted at its center and was connected to a simple lever-style trigger that forced the match down into the pan to ignite the priming powder.

These "hook guns" (*arquebus* in French; *hackbut* in German) with the matchlock firing system became the first truly usable military small arm. The matchlock's inexpensive production kept it in military use until the 1700s.

By 1540 an improved mechanical ignition system was developed. Called the "wheel lock," it used sparks from striking iron pyrites against steel to ignite the priming powder. When the trigger was pulled the wheel turned, the pan cover opened, and the pyrite hit the wheel, producing the sparks that ignited the priming powder.

While the wheel lock was far superior to the matchlock, it was also a delicate design, expensive to produce, and unsuitable for hard use in the field. Consequently, it never replaced the more rugged matchlock as the standard infantry weapon.

The next major development was the "snaphaunce" from the Dutch word *snaphaan*. Designed around 1570, it was also a flint-and-steel system. A piece of sharpened flint was held in a clamp on one arm of the pivoting cock. A steel "frizzen" was mounted opposite the cock and above the pan. When the trigger was pulled, the pan cover opened and the cock struck and forced open the steel battery, creating sparks that fell into the exposed priming powder.

The final stage in the "true" flintlock system, or fusil, was developed in France about 1615, and had the capability for both the "half cock" (safety) and "full cock" (firing) positions.

The flintlock had several advantages over the matchlock. It was not as vulnerable to wet weather and no burning match meant that soldiers could stand closer together in a battle line, thus increasing the volume of firepower in a given space. It could be loaded fairly quickly, and a well-trained soldier could fire at least three rounds a minute.

The initial firepower superiority of the colonists was lost when firearms were traded to or captured by the Indians. Lack of a means to produce gunpowder, lead, and iron repair parts, however, limited the adverse consequences until the rival European powers began seriously arming their Indian allies for use against one aother in the various North American wars.

—*Vince Hawkins*

1640

9 May. Burger Guard Formed. New Amsterdam (New York City).

A law is passed in the Dutch colony requiring all males to be armed as part of a Burger Guard (town citizen guard). This unit is sponsored by the merchant guilds, and the officers are guild leaders. The Guard acts as police and night watchmen to patrol the streets. A small number of Dutch troops are also posted to the colony's fort.

1643

19 May. First Common Defense. United Colonies of New England.

Representatives of Plymouth, Massachusetts Bay, Connecticut, and New Hampshire form a loose defensive confederation they call the "United Colonies of New England." The purpose is to pool their limited military resources for a joint force employable anywhere within the confederation, to share military costs, and to plan and coordinate joint military activities. This is the first formal intercolony agreement for common defense in America, and it sets a model for the future.

Summer. Maryland Militia Defeated.

Maryland militia finally take the field, but the Indians avoid battle. A second campaign ends in disaster. The Indians, armed with muskets from rival colony New Sweden, defeat the Marylanders, who flee the battlefield, abandoning arms and leaving 15 militiamen in the hands of the Indians. In 1652 a peace treaty is negotiated.

7 September. Militia System Reformed. Boston, Massachusetts.

The Massachusetts assembly refines its militia system. Control is decentralized by giving more power to local authorities. The senior regional militia commanders are empowered to muster and move forces to meet threats without council orders. Militia company leaders are likewise authorized to act on their own authority, thus greatly reducing reaction time. Certain professions are exempt from militia duty, but all other able-bodied men 16 to 60 years old are required to assemble four to six days each year for training. Each town must form a company and elect its officers.

October. Delawares Attack Dutch. Pavonia, New Netherlands.

Pretending friendship, a band of Delaware Indians surprise and kill the detachment of militia at the fort and set fire to the town. Delaware tribes throughout the Connecticut River valley also attack farms and small villages. Settlers flee to the fort at New Amsterdam and the Indians lay siege.

October–December. Dutch Counterattack. New Netherlands.

Captain John Underhill, a veteran of the Pequot War, leads the colony's mixed force of Regulars and town militia in a strategy of harsh attrition. He marches

into the countryside, attacking Indians and destroying villages, livestock, and fields. Within a year the Indians end their siege.

1644

February. **Attack on Dutch. Stamfield, Connecuticut.**
Delaware Indians raid the town, killing 150 settlers and local militia defenders.

18 April. **Second Surprise Attack. Virginia.**
Powhatan warriors make another well-coordinated attack against the colonists. Caught by surprise, almost 500 settlers are killed in the Sunday morning assault.

June. **Militia Retaliates. Virginia.**
The Virginia militia strikes back with three attacks, the largest up the York River against the Pamunkey. Intermittent fighting continues, and the colony seeks assistance from England.

1645

June. **Colonial Rangers Hired. Virginia.**
Parliment cannot send aid, so the Colonial Assembly hires a company of full-time mounted scouts for a one-year term of service to "range" the frontier. In addition, a number of small forts are built on the western edge of the settled areas.

Above: *The European ties are apparent in the military uniforms and weaponry of Colonial militias. ("New Sweden & New Netherlands," David Rickman, Osprey Publishing)*

Right: *The fortified settlement speaks volumes about the hostile new world being settled. ("Plymouth, 1627," Cal Sacks, American Heritage Publishing Co.)*

Opposite: *Finnish and Swedish settlers landed in 1638, building Ft. Christina, now Wilmington, Delaware. ("The Landing of the Swedes and Finns," Stanley Arthur, University of Delaware)*

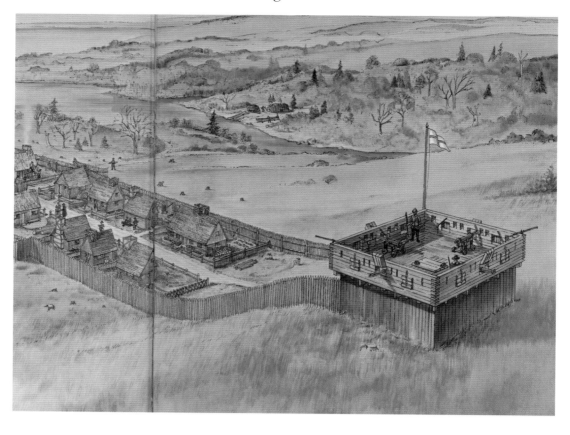

12 August. Militia Quick-Reaction Force. New England.
The United Colonies of New England enacts regulations to improve military readiness. The Bay Colony requires each militia company commander to designate 30 soldiers as a quick-reaction force that will be able to assemble with arms and equipment within a half-hour.

1646

March. Virginians Attack.
Governor Sir William Berkeley leads mounted militia in a preemptive raid to capture a hostile chief. The captive is brought to Jamestown, where he is eventually shot and killed by a guard. In October, a peace is finally concluded, but hostile acts continue.

1648

27 April. Dutch–Swedish Conflict. New Netherlands.
The Dutch build Fort Beversrede on the bank of the Schuylkill River opposite one of several forts built by the New Sweden colony. Each side attacks the other's fort. (Fort Beversrede is now Philadelphia.)

1655

Summer. The Peach War. New Netherlands.
A Delaware Indian woman is shot while taking peaches from an orchard. In short order, more than 1,000 Delawares attack New Amsterdam. More than 150 captives are taken by the Indians. Militia pursue the Indians, and within a few weeks most of the prisoners are rescued.

THE AMERICAN COLONIAL MILITIA

Right: *Starting in 1637, Massachusetts militia companies were required to muster and drill once a week as well as provide night security for their village. All men aged 16–60 were required to join. ("The First Muster," Don Troiani, National Guard Bureau)*

The militia units formed in the American colonies all shared a number of common characteristics. They followed the traditional English system of geographically based, local defense forces designed for short-term emergencies. In general, all free, white males aged 16–60 were required to serve. Initially militiamen had to provide their own weapons and equipment, usually pikes, swords, and, if possible, firearms. The typical militia company numbered around 60 soldiers. Company officers were chosen by popular ballot, and in turn, each company commander appointed the unit's noncommissioned officers. In some colonies unit musters were held as often as once per month, and a system of fines and punishments prompted compliance with militia laws. Others were less strict. Cavalry and artillery units were hard to raise and expensive to maintain and equip; therefore, the infantry remained the backbone of the militia system. The governors in each colony reserved the right to appoint militia generals and colonels and jealously protected their powers of overall command and control. Legislatures retained strict regulatory control over the militia's training and administration.

Militia units defended against attacks by Native Americans, pirates, and even other colonies, conducted reprisal raids, local law enforcement, and response to natural disasters. In 1645, Massachusetts created the first "minuteman" units in villages most exposed to Indian attacks. These elite, quick-response units were prepared to respond at any time of day or night. Minutemen were required to have their arms, ammunition, and equipment constantly ready, and were to rally at designated assembly points within 30 minutes of an alarm.

As Americans migrated westward toward the Appalachians, scattered settlements rested their security on frontier forts. Citizen-soldiers on horseback ranged between the forts, checking on settlers and monitoring Indian activities. These mounted "rangers" represented the earliest tradition of service by American Ranger forces. When England became embroiled in colonial wars with Spain and France, the colonies were required to raise units for service. Militia organizations created for extended operations were called "Provincial" units and largely drew their members from local companies. The greatest accomplishment of American Provincial militia forces was the capture of the French fortress of Louisbourg, Nova Scotia, in 1745.

—*Michael Doubler*

Right: *On the night of 19 December 1675, a small army of Rhode Island militia, guided by an Indian deserter, march through a snowstorm to assault a large Narragansett stronghold in the Great Swamp. Two companies prematurely assault the fortified town before the rest of the army is in position, suffering heavy losses, and are forced to pull back. A second wave, led by Captain Benjamin Church, takes the town in fierce fighting. The town is burned with great loss of Indian life. Militia losses are also heavy, including 14 militia commanders killed. ("English Take Philip's Fort," Library of Congress)*

1659

September. **Dutch–Esopus War. New Netherlands.**
The Esopus Indians assault the small fort at Wiltwyck. When invited Esopus leaders attend a peace conference, they are killed. The outraged Indians seize eight Dutch militiamen and burn them to death. The conflict continues until 1664. (Wiltwyck is now Kingston, New York.)

1673

7 August. **English-Dutch Conflict. New York.**
Dutch warships arrive to retake the former Dutch settlements lost earlier to the English colonists. New York is bombarded and surrenders on 12 August. The Dutch then move up the Hudson to retake other towns. Their victory is fleeting. In February 1674, all the Dutch American territories are passed back to the English by treaty and New Netherlands is absorbed into the New York colony.

1675

21–24 June. **King Philip's War Begins. Miles Garrison, Rhode Island.**
The Council of the United Colonies assembles a joint militia force after warriors of the Wampanoag tribe under Chief Metacom (also known as King Philip) attack Swansea, Massachusetts, and nearby settlements. Captain Benjamin Church leads the Rhode Island unit. The war against King Philip and his allied tribes spreads through New England.

28 June. **Skirmish at Miles Bridge, Massachusetts.**
A militia force under Captain Church is attacked near Swansea. The ill-trained militia make a poor showing against the smaller force of Indians.

29 June. **King Philip Attacks. Rhode Island.**
King Philip and his warriors attack settlers in the towns of Rehoboth and Taunton. The militia pursue them to the large Pocasset swamp and camp on the edge of the swamp.

1 July. **Conflict Between Colonies.**
Connecticut sends troops to assist the campaign against Philip. However, when New York militia occupy territory disputed with Connecticut, the Connecticut troops are recalled.

8 July. **Battle of Pocasset Swamp, Rhode Island.**
Captain Church becomes impatient and leads 20 volunteers into the swamp. The militiamen are trapped and hold off the 300 Indians in a six-hour fight. A boat finally arrives to rescue the militiamen.

19 July. **Second Battle of Pocasset Swamp.**
The militia make another foray into the swamp, but the lack of training and a misguided effort to imitate the rigid European tactical formations in the dense brush and trees bring disaster. Some 15 colonists are killed in action.

29 July. **Philip Escapes.**
While the militia are building a fort to starve out the Indians, King Philip and his warriors slip out of the swamp. Plymouth troops and allied Mohegans pursue Philip's band for two days, but lack of supplies hinders them and Philip escapes again.

July–August. **Indian War of 1675–76. Maryland.**
A trading dispute between Maryland Nanticoke Indians and a Virginia planter begins a series of thefts, killings, and reprisals. When Virginia militia go to Maryland to confront the Indians, a fight ensues and several innocent Susquahannocks are killed. In retaliation, a coalition of allied tribes attack settlers in both colonies.

August. **Philip Attacks Peace Delegation. Brookfield, Massachusetts.**
A detachment of militia is ambushed en route to a peace conference with the Nipmuck tribe. Nine militiamen are killed and the survivors are trapped for two days as the Indians burn the town.

25 August. **Battle of Sugar Loaf Hill, Massachusetts.**
Two companies of militia led by Captains Richard Beers and Thomas Lothrop battle Indians attempting to join King Philip. The militia suffer the worst of the fight.

August–September. **Virginia Militia Assembled. Williamsburg, Virginia.**
Colonel John Washington and Major Isaac Allerton are commissioned to investigate the July incident with the Nanticokes. Instead they assemble more than 700 men for action against the Indians and Maryland sends another 250 mounted troops.

1–5 September. **Towns Destroyed. Massachusetts.**
Indians burn the towns of Hadley, Deerfield, and Northfield. Captain Beers rushes his company to assist the Northfield garrison and is ambushed near Saw Mill Brook. He and most of his men are killed. A relief company arriving the next day finds the heads of Beers' militiamen on poles along the road.

9 September. **United Colonies Declare War.**
The United Colonies Council formally declares war against King Philip and his allies. Each member of the confederation is levied to provide militia for a 1,000-man army. As the force gathers, the council plans a preemptory attack on the Narragansetts and appoints Governor Josiah Winslow of Plymouth as the joint army commander.

18 September. **Battle of Bloody Brook. Deerfield, Massachusetts.**
Indians destroy a Deerfield militia company bringing supplies to Hadley. More than 60 men are killed, leaving the town defenseless.

September–October. **Village Attacked. Piscataway Creek, Maryland.**
A joint force of Virginia and Maryland militia surrounds the fortified main Susquahannock village near the Potomac River. Five chiefs come out under a flag of truce, but the talks become angry and the chiefs are killed. The village is then besieged for six weeks. Susquahannock warriors make nightly sorties, killing militia sentries before making a nighttime escape with their families. Governor Berkeley refuses to continue the militia mobilization and puts the money into a series of small local forts, angering the threatened frontier settlers.

16 October. **Battle at Salmon Falls, Maine.**
During early fall more than half a dozen Maine towns are attacked and burned. When a militia company tries to bring help to the town of Kittery, Indians drive them back to their garrison post at Salmon Falls. A request for help goes unanswered and when the militiamen venture out again, they are ambushed.

19–20 December.
Guided by an Indian deserter, Governor Winslow leads a small army through a snowstorm to assault a large Narragansett stronghold in the Great Swamp. An all-night march through the frozen swamp brings the militia to the fortified camp. Two militia companies foolishly attack before the rest of the army is in position. They suffer heavy losses and are driven back. Captain Benjamin Church, who suffers three

Above: *Battles in the forest frequently became a series of fierce hand-to-hand combats using knives and tomahawks with no quarter asked or given. ("Fight in the Forest," N. C. Wyeth, Collection of the Brandywine River Museum, Gift of Richard S. du Pont, 1975)*

wounds, leads another assault. Despite the fierce resistance, the town is taken and burned with great loss of Indian life. Militia losses are also heavy, including 14 militia commanders killed. On the difficult march back to camp 16 miles away, the militia lose more men to the cold and to Indians.

1676

21 February. **Battle of Medford, Massachusetts.**
A large force of King Philip's warriors defeats the 160-man Medford militia company. Half the town is burned and 20 civilians killed. Indians continue to raid and destroy homes within ten miles of Boston.

21 April. **Battle of Sudbury, Massachusetts.**
In reprisal for a night attack on his camp, King Philip sends almost 900 warriors against Sudbury. Militia units from nearby towns respond and a hard, day-long battle ensues. The Indians finally withdraw at nightfall.

May. **Bacon's Rebellion. Henrico County, Virginia.**
Self-appointed leader Nathaniel Bacon, Jr., gathers a group of angry Virginians for action against the continuing Indian raids. After convincing a tribe of friendly Indians to attack the Susquahannocks, Bacon then turns on them and attacks. The governor declares Bacon a "traitor" for raising an unauthorized armed force, then rescinds the order.

19 May. **Battle at the Connecticut River Falls. Massachusetts.**
A mounted unit of Massachusetts militia surprises and attacks a hostile Indian camp. The Indians counter-attack, inflicting heavy losses but losing even more men themselves.

June. **Church Raises Army. New England.**
The Council of the United Colonies commissions Benjamin Church to raise a new unified army of colonists and friendly Indians.

12 June. **Hadley Attacked Again. Massachusetts.**
King Philip attacks the town again with about 700 warriors. The defending militia, helped by friendly Pequots and Mohegans, successfully repel the attack.

Below: *King Philip was betrayed by Alderman, a Wampanoag informer, and killed. Without leaders, Indian resistance in the region was soon over. ("The Death of King Philip," Howard Pyle, Hoffenreffer Museum of Anthropology, Brown University)*

23 June. Bacon's Rebellion. Virginia.
Bacon appears in Jamestown with an armed force. He demands an official militia commission with authority to raise forces and fight any Indians in the colony. The frightened Virginia assembly agrees.

29 July. Bacon's Rebellion. Virginia.
Governor Berkeley revokes Bacon's commission and declares him a traitor. However, Bacon and his men have already attacked the peaceful Pamunkey tribe in the Great Dragon Swamp near the Rappahannock River, making them enemies.

July. Campaign by Church Successful. New England.
Militia forces in Massachusetts and Rhode Island score a number of successes and repel raids on several towns. Militiamen led by Church are victorious in skirmishes around Taunton, and he recruits many of his Indian prisoners into his army. In Maine, peace finally comes when the northern tribes, tired of the war, sign a treaty.

1 August. Capture of King Philip's Family. Massachusetts.
Church leads a raid on Philip's camp and captures Philip's wife and young son. Philip escapes, but his wife and son are imprisoned and eventually sold into slavery.

12 August. King Philip Killed. Assowamset Swamp, Massachusetts.
An Indian deserter leads Church and his men to Philip's camp in the swamp near Taunton. Moving at night, the militia surround the camp. When Philip tries to escape, he is shot and killed. His head is sent to Plymouth for display.

11 September. Philip's War Chief Captured. Massachusetts.
A determined search locates Philip's senior war chief Annawon in another camp. He is quickly captured and executed by Church. Other than a few final skirmishes, the war is over. Given the population at the time, it is America's most destructive war. The defensive coalition of colonies soon falls apart.

18 September. Bacon's Rebellion Ends. Virginia.
Nathaniel Bacon and his illegal militia force the governor to flee, but when they burn Jamestown, Bacon's men lose popular support. Within a few weeks an official militia force chases Bacon and his men to Yorktown, where Bacon dies of disease in October. Bacon's rebellion strengthens the colonists' belief in governmental control of military power among the citizens.

Above: *Two hundred Canadians and Abenaki Indians destroy the settlement of Schenectady, New York. ("Attack on Schenectady," Schenectady County Historical Society, NY)*

1688

April. Abenaki War (King William's War) Begins. Penobscot Bay, Maine.
Acting on royal order, a militia expedition is sent to the bay to destroy a French trading post operated by the French son-in-law of an Abenaki chief. Shortly after, settlers at Saco, Maine, take several Abenakis captive for killing cattle. Retaliatory hostilities by the Abenakis quickly commence against settlements.

1689

July. Abenaki War Expands. New England.
The conflict spreads as part of a larger French-English struggle. With English encouragement, more than 1,000 Iroquois warriors attack French settlements near Quebec, killing and taking hundreds of prisoners. Meanwhile, the French sponsor and lead Abenakis and their allies against towns in New Hampshire and Maine.

1690

8 January. **Schenectady Destroyed. New York.**
Over 200 Canadians and Abenaki Indians attack the town. The stockade gates are open and unguarded during the night when the raiders strike. In two hours more than 60 settlers are killed and 27 taken captive. Albany militia and Mohawk allies pursue the raiders to the gates of Montreal.

February–March. **Raids Across Border. New England.**
Two large French-Abenaki groups raid into New York, Maine, and New Hampshire, overwhelming the local militia.

8 March. **Salmon Falls Attacked. New Hampshire.**
A mixed group of 50 French, Indians, and Canadians breaks into the town stockade and a fortified house. Thirty-four settlers are killed, and others are taken captive.

April. **Renewed Common Defense. New York City.**
The French-Indian attacks stir the New England colonies to plan joint military action. They plan an ambitious scheme for a two-pronged campaign against Canada. Five colonies pledge men as do the allied Iroquois tribes. One force (commanded by Major Fitz-John Winthrop) is to march north from Albany against Montreal, while another (under Sir William Phips) sails up the St. Lawrence River and attacks Quebec.

11 May. **Capture of Port Royal. Acadia (Nova Scotia).**
Unable to afford a Quebec expedition, Massachusetts sends Phips on a coastal expedition with 14 ships and 700 militiamen against Port Royal, a French base for privateers. The outgunned French quickly surrender. A small garrison is left, and the expedition returns to Boston.

27–31 May. **Fall of Fort Loyal. Casco, Maine.**
A third French-Indian raiding party destroys Casco and pursues survivors to Fort Loyal. After a four-day siege, the outnumbered militia garrison surrenders under a French guarantee of safety. As the New

Englanders march out of the fort, the Indians attack and massacre more than 100 men and their families. A few survivors are taken to Quebec.

21 August. **Phips Expedition. Boston.**
Phips' success encourages Massachusetts to sponsor the Quebec expeditionary force. A fleet of 34 ships carrying approximately 2,000 New England militia under Major John Walley sails for Canada.

23 August. **Schuyler Strikes La Prairie. New York.**
A small party of volunteers led by Captain John Schuyler paddles up Lake Champlain and raids the French village of La Prairie. They are the only part of Winthrop's small army to see action. Understrength, low on supplies, and lacking canoes, Winthrop turns back.

16 October. **Attack on Quebec. Canada.**
Phips lands his militiamen two miles from the town. They are supposed to move overland and assault the west side of the town while the ships bombard from the river. The whole scheme fails. For several days the militia try unsuccessfully to break through French defenses. Limited supplies and ammunition are soon gone and several ships are damaged by the heavy cannon fire from the fort. Confusion reigns as militiamen rush to board the ships for the return home.

1691

1 August. **Battle at La Prairie. Canada.**
Captain Schuyler leads another raid against the French-Canadian settlement. The early dawn attack surprises the Canadians, who suffer a number of casualties. As Schuyler and his men withdraw to their boats, they are ambushed and must fight hard against the larger enemy force before finally breaking through. Forty-three militiamen and Iroquois are killed.

September. **Church Recalled to Duty. Casco Bay, Maine.**
Benjamin Church, now a major, is called from retirement to lead 300 Massachusetts militiamen against the Abenaki. The old soldier's tactics win no big victories, but he destroys several villages. In November the disheartened Abenakis agree to a six-month armistice, which they break within two months.

1692

5 February. **Attack on York, Maine.**
Abenakis join Canadians to attack York and slaughter or capture most of the inhabitants. Abenaki-Canadian attacks

continue for five years despite increased militia patrols. Deerfield, Massachusetts, a favorite target for Indian attacks because of its northern location, is hit repeatedly.

10 June. **Attack on Wells, Maine.**
Abenakis and Canadians attack the town and several sloops moored in the bay. The militia and settlers successfully defend themselves from several fortified houses.

August. **Fort William Henry Built. Pemaquid, Maine.**
Royal Governor William Phips orders the construction of a stone fort at the town and stations a militia garrison there as an advanced position against the Abenakis.

1696

14 July. **Fort William Henry Falls. Pemaquid, Maine.**
A French-Indian force sailing from Quebec meets little resistance in capturing Fort William Henry and the town. The French restrain the Indians, and only a few of the captives are killed. Massachusetts sends Major Church and his militia in a futile counterraid.

1699

7 January. **Abenaki War (King William's War) Ends. Casco Bay, Maine.**
The September 1697 Treaty of Ryswick ends the conflict in Europe, but it is not until now, 15 months later, that the Abenakis agree to peace in New England.

1702

10 September. **Queen Anne's War (War of Spanish Succession).**
The South Carolina assembly approves a preemptive attack on the Spanish at St. Augustine, Florida. The motive is to prevent French occupation. South Carolina militia and allied Chickasaw Indians are assembled, and the expedition is launched in December using English warships. Bombardment by the ships is unable to force the surrender of the fort, and a land assault also fails. The town is pillaged and burned, beginning ten years of warfare in America.

1703

1 March. **Massachusetts Militia Reorganized. Boston.**
The Assembly approves 120 pairs of "good snow shoes" for each of the four militia regiments for scouting during the winter. These duties are rotated among the companies, and a reserve reaction force is usually designated. The patrols are long, difficult, and dangerous, but they play an important role in securing the frontiers. Their exploits make the "snowshoe men" local heroes.

10 August. **Indian Attacks Resume. Maine.**
Encouraged by the French, the Abenaki make simultaneous attacks on the Maine settlements of Wells, Saco, Casco Bay, and others. The fort at Casco

holds out until relief arrives. Two months later Black Point and York are attacked.

1704

29 February. **Deerfield Attacked. Massachusetts.**
More than 350 French-Canadians and Indians attack the settlement. An alert militia sergeant is able to rally seven men in one of the fortified houses. Others do the same, but many townsfolk are killed or captured and the town is again burned. Militia pursue the raiders and inflict some casualties.

1–28 July. **Church Recalled to Duty.**
Benjamin Church, now a 65-year-old colonel, is called once again for his service. He sails from Boston with a group of 550 New England militiamen and successfully raids coastal settlements in French Acadia. The ever-aggressive Church hopes to lead his men on to attack Fort Royal, but the fort is too strong. This is the fifth and last expedition by the redoubtable old militia hero.

July. **Invasion of Florida. Western Florida.**
An army of Carolina militia and Chickasaw Indians marches into Spanish territory, destroying villages of the hostile Appalachee tribe and laying waste all Spanish missions they find. When they try to advance toward the French outposts in Louisiana, however, hostile Choctaws block the way.

1706

Summer. **Charleston Attacked. South Carolina.**
Militia manning fortifications around Charleston repulse a Spanish landing force brought by French privateers.

1710

16 October. **Port Royal Captured and Queen Anne's War Ends. Acadia.**
A force of English ships and provincial militia successfully captures the French fort of Port Royal and rename it Annapolis. By the next summer, all of Acadia, renamed Nova Scotia, is under English control. The 1713 Treaty of Utrecht finally ends the war, giving England many of the French territories, and another treaty is signed with the Abenakis.

Opposite: *Townsfolk in Deerfield, Massachusetts, did not expect an attack in the middle of winter. The French and Indian raiders surprised and quickly destroyed the town. (Fruitlands Museum, Prospect Hill, Harvard, Massachusetts)*

Right: *A new Tuscarora uprising in North Carolina was a result of settlements expanding into territory the Indians considered theirs, and threatened the peace throughout the southeast frontier in 1710. (The Granger Collection, New York)*

THE TUSCARORA WAR

Right: *The conflict between the expanding North Carolina settlements and the Tuscarora tribe lasted for several years. With the help of Colonel James Moore, the Tuscarora were finally defeated and a treaty signed. ("Preparing to Meet the Enemy," Robert Griffing, Paramount Press, Inc.)*

As the sun rose on 22 September 1711, more than 500 Tuscarora warriors struck without warning the small farms along the Neuse, Trent, and Pamlico rivers that comprised the main settlements in North Carolina. The Indians launched a war that would last two years and make the colony almost unlivable.

For years the Tuscaroras had suffered from colonists encroaching on their land, enslaving Indian women and children and cheating in trading. The last straw was the establishment of New Bern in 1710 and the arrival of more than 400 new settlers who took the most desirable land along the Neuse and Trent rivers.

The Tuscarora knew of fighting between supporters of Governor Edward Hyde and Thomas Cary, former chief executive of the colony, and worked with success to gather allies among other tribes. In the surprise attack, aimed at the isolated farms, 130–140 people were killed and 20–30 captured. As surviving settlers fled to fortified farms, William Brice formed a small force and, with help from militia sent by the governor, attempted a reprisal attack. It was a failure. In several skirmishes Brice's men were beaten by the Indians and forced to retreat.

Indian attacks continued until January 1712, when militia leader John Barnwell marched up from South Carolina. Leading an army of 33 colonials and about 500 Indian allies, Barnwell burned a path through Tuscarora territory, killing everything in his way until he reached the grateful North Carolinians on 11 February. Barnwell then led an attack on the main Tuscarora camp, called

"Fort Catechna." The Indian fortifications were well built and some of Barnwell's troops deserted, forcing him to negotiate a truce. The Indians released some prisoners, and Barnwell led his army back to New Bern.

The North Carolina Assembly was not satisfied. They wanted an end to the Tuscarora menace. In early April 1712, Barnwell, reinforced with more North Carolinians and friendly Indians, again attacked Fort Catechna. The results were the same, and Barnwell settled for another negotiated peace. This time the Tuscarora gave up all captives, stolen goods, and their corn. The Indians could no longer build forts and would confine themselves to land designated by Barnwell. Finally, they had to pay tribute to the governor. In return, the Tuscarora could live unmolested.

After Barnwell headed back to South Carolina, some North Carolinians captured and sold a number of Tuscarora Indians into slavery, breaking the treaty. The outraged Tuscarora renewed the offensive, burning homes and killing settlers throughout the summer and fall of 1712. An attack against the Indians was defeated with heavy casualties, and the governor again asked South Carolina for help. This time Colonel James Moore came with an army of more than 900 Yamassee Indians. In March 1713, his army seized a Tuscarora fort, killing approximately 400 and taking a similar number of prisoners. Those not killed or captured fled the area. This ended the uprising, and a final treaty was signed with the Tuscarora in April 1713.

—*Kevin M. Hymel*

1711

22 September. **Tuscarora War Begins. North Carolina.**
The abused Tuscarora tribe rises up against local settlers. Surprise attacks at New Bern and other settlements kill more than 200 settlers. The Tuscaroras, joined by other small tribes, exchange revenge raids with colonists for months, and the colony officials ask for assistance from South Carolina.

1712

January–February. **Tuscarora War. Neuse River, North Carolina.**
Colonel John Barnwell is sent by South Carolina with a small group of militia and 500 Indian allies to help New Bern. They destroy hostile Indian camps and skirmish with the Tuscaroras, easing the attacks on the settlements.

March. **Tuscarora Town Attacked. Fort Nohucke.**
Encouraged by his success, Barnwell attacks Fort Nohucke, the main town of the Tuscarora chief "Hancock." The assault fails and local militia flee the battle. Barnwell exchanges prisoners and returns to New Bern, where the town officials demand he go back and destroy the Indian camp. Barnwell convinces Hancock to sign a peace treaty, but within days Barnwell breaks it and then departs as Indian attacks resume.

1713

23 March. **Tuscaroras Defeated. Fort Nohucke.**
South Carolina again sends militia and more than 1,000 Indian allies to help North Carolina. They strike again at Hancock's fortified town, and after severe fighting the Tuscaroras are destroyed. Hundreds of warriors are killed and more than 400 captives are sold as slaves.

1715

15 April. **Yamasee War Begins. Savannah, South Carolina.**
Settlers' abuses of local tribes cause another short but bloody conflict. On Good Friday, war parties of Yamasee, Catawba, and Creek warriors attack settlements north of Savannah, killing more than 100 settlers. The militia is mustered and a campaign begins against the Yamasee towns. By fall, most of the surviving Indians have been driven south into Spanish territory.

Above: *Snowshoes enabled Rangers and other soldiers to maneuver despite heavy snows that immobilized other troops. ("Snowshoe Men, Massachusetts Bay, 1743," Eric Manders, Company of Military Historians)*

1717

Spring. **Dummer's War (Lovewell's War) Begins. Kennebec River, Maine.**
Expansion of New England settlements in the river valley ignites another ten years of Abenaki attacks.

23 August. **Attack on Norridgewock, Canada.**
Massachusetts militia attack the Abenaki base village of Norridgewock, killing seven chiefs and the local French priest, Father Sebastian Rale.

1725

April. **Snowshoe Patrol Ambushed. Saco Lake, Maine.**
Raids by Abenakis continue, and Captain John Lovewell, a well-known snowshoe man, leads his 75-man company into the forests scouting for Indians. They are ambushed and in the day-long battle 50 scouts, including Lovewell, are killed.

1727

Fort Oswego Built. New York.
To counter French presence, New York constructs Fort

Left: *To the surprise of the British, New England troops captured the heavily fortified French port of Louisbourg, Cape Breton, a base for French ships raiding the English colonies. ("Landing of New England Troops at Louisbourg, 1745," John Carter Brown Library, Brown University)*

Oswego on the eastern shore of Lake Ontario. It is the westernmost outpost of the colony and is manned by militia. The fort is an important base for frontier patrols and operations into Canada.

1728

9 March. **Attack on Yamasees. Florida.**
South Carolina militia cross into Spanish territory to attack a Yamasee village near St. Augustine.

1733

13 January. **Georgia Colonists Arrive. Charleston, South Carolina.**
Led by cofounder James Oglethorpe, the first 130 settlers for the new colony of Georgia arrive. Oglethorpe is an experienced soldier and within a few years has established a number of defensive forts—Fredericka, Augusta, and others. Oglethorpe is also made military commander for South Carolina and is sent Scottish Highlanders to strengthen his forces.

1740

January–July. **War of Jenkin's Ear Begins. Spanish Florida.**
War begins between England and Spain, and Oglethorpe leads an expedition of South Carolina and Georgia militia against the Spanish near his borders. Aided by friendly Creeks, Cherokees, and

Chickasaws, he captures two Spanish forts and then lays siege to St. Augustine. In July he is forced to withdraw when Spanish reinforcements arrive.

1741

17 April. American Regiment in Colombia. Cartagena, Colombia.
A British expeditionary force led by Admiral Edward Vernon begins its withdrawal. The ground forces land on 4 March, but poor planning and incompetence cause the operation to fail with heavy losses, mostly due to yellow fever. Of the 3,000 men recruited into the separate American Regiment, only 600 return home. One of the sickly survivors is Virginia Captain Lawrence Washington, who names his farm "Mount Vernon" after the admiral.

1742

5–7 July. Battle of Bloody Marsh. St. Simon's Island, Georgia.
Georgia militia under Oglethorpe successfully rout the advance party of a raiding Spanish army. Georgia rangers and Highlanders then infiltrate behind the main Spanish body and attack again. In the two engagements, more than 300 Spaniards are killed or captured. Oglethorpe then writes a bogus letter stating that reinforcements are on the way to him and arranges for the correspondence to be captured. Fearing the worst, the Spanish leave. During the year, Georgia militia defeat other Spanish raids on coastal settlements, and in 1743 Oglethorpe unsuccessfully attacks St. Augustine again.

Left: *Hiding, the Seneca scouts chose high ground in a stream as their resting point to avoid pursuit. The water easily hid their tracks from followers but they still had to be sure no trail was left behind. ("Seneca Scouts," Robert Griffing, Paramount Press, Inc.)*

Opposite: *On 9 July 1775, General Braddock crossed the second ford of Pennsylvania's Monongahela River along with his aides Washington and Orme. On the other side of the river, workers toiled to make the terrain passable for an army. ("The Crossing," Robert Griffing, Paramount Press, Inc.)*

1744

14 May. **King George's War Begins. Cape Breton Island, Nova Scotia.**
French troops from Louisbourg capture the small fort at the fishing town of Canseau. Several weeks later the fort at Annapolis Royal is also attacked, but Major Paul Mascarene and his Massachusetts militiamen refuse to surrender. When reinforcements arrive for the fort, the French withdraw.

1745

January. **Massachusetts Counterattacks. Boston.**
A joint New England force of more than 4,200 men with Royal Navy ships and supplies from seven colonies is assembled for an expedition against Louisbourg. Militia Colonel William Pepperell is given command.

30 April. **Landing at Louisbourg. Cape Breton Island.**
The New England force arrives in Gabarus Bay. The French are deceived by a feint and before they can recover, the real landing takes place several miles away. Light French resistance is swept away and camp is set up only two miles from the fort.

2 May. **Artillery Position Taken. Louisbourg.**
A scouting party finds the French have abandoned a key artillery position, leaving behind 30 spiked cannon. The French are surprised when their guns are put back in operation against them. During May, skirmishing occurs with French-Indian patrols while the New Englanders drag cannon overland to the heights north of the fort. Within several weeks, five artillery batteries are hammering the French. More than 9,000 cannonballs are fired at the fort.

23 May. **Island Battery Battle. Louisbourg.**
During the night an American landing party rows to an island near the fort to capture an artillery battery. However, surprise is lost when a drunken colonist begins cheering, and the attack is repulsed with heavy losses.

17 June. **Louisbourg Surrenders.**
The fort surrenders after another artillery position is built on 10 June and the bombardment of the fort increases. It is a great victory for the colonial militia and a source of pride in New England. The elation turns sour, however, when the militia receive none of the booty.

July–December. **More Border Warfare. New England.**
During July the French-Indian alliance raids militia posts in New Hampshire, Vermont, and Maine. In November a French-Indian force attacks and burns Saratoga, New York.

1746

April–August. **Fort Number 4. New Hampshire.**
The small fort is the northernmost of the colony, with only three women and 22 militiamen under Sergeant John Hawks as garrison. Beginning in April, Indian attacks force settlers to take refuge in the fort. Unable to sustain themselves, they abandon the fort.

1747

7 April. **Fort Number 4.**
The fort is reoccupied in March with 30 militiamen under Captain Phineas Stevens. On 7 April, a large French-Indian raiding party begins a siege. Offered surrender terms, Stevens convinces his men to hold out. After three days the attackers withdraw. Stevens is presented a dress sword for his actions. The fort is attacked again in 1749.

1748

January–September. **Frontier Warfare Continues.**
The war along the frontiers continues with French-Indian raiding parties hitting towns in New York, Connecticut, and New Hampshire. Indians also attack the Carolina backcountry, and two troops of South Carolina "rangers" are formed. In September, the Spanish raid Brunswick, but town militia drive them off.

Left: *After a long, dangerous journey George Washington delivers a letter from Virginia's Lieutenant Governor Robert Dinwiddie to the French army demanding that they leave the Ohio Valley. ("Domain of Three Nations," John Buxton, Paramount Press, Inc.)*

18 October. **King George's War Ends.**
The Treaty of Aix-la-Chapelle ends the war. Britain returns Louisbourg to the French, embittering the New England colonists.

1752

November. **George Washington Commissioned. Mount Vernon, Virginia.**
Twenty-one-year-old George Washington is appointed as one of the four District Adjutants of Virginia. The position is accompanied by a major's commission in the Virginia militia, with duties to supervise the military activities of his district and "teach the officers their duty and train the private men to the use of their arms."

1753

31 October. **Washington's Special Mission. Williamsburg, Virginia.**
Major Washington departs on a special mission from Lieutenant Governor Robert Dinwiddie. Washington and eight men travel more than 500 miles to the newly established French Fort Le Boeuf on the south side of Lake Erie and present a letter demanding that the French withdraw their troops from the region.

25–27 November. **Washington Holds Indian Council. Logstown, Pennsylvania.**
Washington camps near a small trading post on the Allegheny River and holds a council with local Indian leaders. During the council, French deserters arrive

and Washington learns of new French forts on the Wabash and Mississippi rivers. The French are claiming the entire Ohio territory, and giving the Indians wampum belts to signify allegiance to France.

4–7 December. Washington Makes Contact. Venango (Franklin, Pennsylvania).

Washington finds the French flag flying and a French captain in charge at the former Virginia trading post. The captain tells Washington that the letter must be delivered to a more senior officer. Bad weather prevents immediate departure and the French officers use the time to try to turn the Indians from supporting the English.

12–15 December. Washington Delivers Letter. Fort Le Boeuf (Waterford, Pennsylvania).

The French take Washington north to the fort, where he presents the letter. While he waits for a reply, the French try to recruit his Indian escort. Recognizing the danger, Washington complains, and the French finally produce a letter of reply.

16 December. Washington Returns.

Washington departs Fort Le Boeuf in a snowstorm. Traveling with only one companion, Christopher Gist, Washington makes the hazardous four-week return trip by canoe, horse, and foot. Washington almost drowns crossing an icy river and barely survives an ambush by Indians.

1754

16 January. Washington's Report. Williamsburg, Virginia.

After a round trip of almost 1,000 miles in 11 weeks, Major Washington delivers a full report to the Virginia council. He includes a recommendation to construct a fort where the Allegheny and Monogohela rivers merge to create the Ohio River. From this vantage point, called the Forks of the Ohio, the entire Ohio River valley can be controlled.

January–February. Virginia Expedition Prepares.

Approval is given to raise a militia regiment of six companies to eject the French and establish a Virginia presence in the disputed area. Washington is promoted to lieutenant colonel and made second-in-command of the regiment. The first company is soon sent ahead with workers to cut a trail. By mid-February the men are working on the fort they name Fort Prince George (now Pittsburgh, Pennsylvania).

March–April. Expedition Departs. Alexandria, Virginia.

Washington finds that men are slow to enlist and badly in need of training. On 2 April he departs with two understrength companies totaling about 180 men and officers, plus some regimental staff. By 10 April they reach Winchester, where another company and a few Indian scouts join them. They then march on to Willis Creek (Cumberland, Maryland) to await supply wagons and the rest of the regiment en route under Colonel Joshua Fry, the senior officer.

16 April. French Seize Fort Prince George.

The small group of Virginians building the fort are captured by a much larger French and Indian force. The French allow them to depart, then enlarge the fort, which they rename Fort Duquesne.

Below: *Colonel George Washington travels 500 miles on horseback to Fort Le Boeuf to deliver a warning to the French to stay out of the Ohio Valley in 1753. ("Washington on His Mission to the Ohio," Library of Congress)*

26 May. French and Indian War Begins. Great Meadows, Pennsylvania.

Two days after establishing a base camp at a large open area called Great Meadows, Washington learns that a party of 30 French and Indians is nearby and planning an attack. Washington leads a predawn march through the forest to the French camp. In a 15-minute fight, 12 French soldiers are killed, including the leader. One Frenchman escapes to Fort Duquesne and reports the attack. The French accuse Washington of murder and making an unprovoked attack.

29 May. Fort Necessity. Great Meadows, Pennsylvania.

Washington and his men fortify their camp with a log palisade, a trench, and a low earth berm around the perimeter. Inside the palisade a rough log storehouse is built. It is a poor location and subject to flooding. Washington christens the little stockade Fort Necessity.

9–29 June. Reinforcements Arrive. Fort Necessity.

The last two companies of the Virginia regiment arrive and Washington learns that Colonel Fry is dead and *he* is now commanding the regiment. An independent company of South Carolina militia marches in but refuses to help on the road without extra pay. Work on the road progresses and crews are more than ten miles beyond the meadow camp toward the French fort. On 29 June, Indian scouts alert Washington of a French force approaching, and he assembles all his men at the little fort.

3 July. French Attack. Fort Necessity.

More than 1,000 French and Indians attack the fort in a rainy four-hour battle. Thirty-one Virginians are killed, and many others are wounded and sick. Washington's supplies are low, his trench is flooded, and much of his powder is wet. At dark, the French commander calls a truce and offers terms. Washington, with no hope of reinforcement, signs the surrender paper not realizing that he is confessing to "murdering" a French officer in the May attack. At dawn on 4 July, Washington and the surviving militiamen march out of the fort. Two of his captains are retained by the French as hostages.

July–November. Washington Resigns. Williamsburg, Virginia.

Some councilmen blame Washington for the defeat. In the fall the governor decides to reorganize the militia, breaking the regiment into independent companies and eliminating rank above captain. Washington resigns rather than be demoted. He later inquires without success about a commission in the British army.

Above: *Colonel George Washington drills his companies of Virginia militia outside Fort Necessity, Pennsylvania, in July 1754 as they prepare for the expected French attack. ("Fort Necessity, 3 July 1754," Robert Griffing, Paramount Press, Inc.)*

15 March. **Washington Joins Braddock. Mount Vernon, Virginia.**
British Major General Edward Braddock, recently arrived commander in chief of the British forces in North America, offers Washington a staff position as a provincial captain. Washington agrees to serve only as an unpaid civilian without military rank; as a civilian aide he is not subordinate to the British officers. Braddock has two understrength British regiments, the 44th and 48th, which he fills with American recruits.

19 April. **Braddock Expedition. Alexandria, Virginia.**
The first elements of Braddock's 2,200-man force depart for Fort Duquesne followed by other units including the two Regular regiments. With the expedition are militia companies from Virginia, Maryland, and Carolina, horse-drawn artillery, various camp followers, and two young Virginia contract teamsters, Daniel Morgan and Daniel Boone.

1 June. **Monckton Expedition. Bay of Fundy, Nova Scotia.**
An expedition of New England Provincials plus some British Regulars led by Lieutenant Colonel Robert Monckton lands and begins operations against Fort Beausejour. By 17 June the job is done and England controls the entire region.

Above: *Members of this Virginia regiment marched with Colonel George Washington against the French. ("Soldier, Virginia Regiment, 1754," Don Troiani)*

Left: *The French established Fort Duquesne, a strong outpost at the critical junction of Pennsylvania's Monongahela and Allegheny rivers, controlling access to the Ohio River. (Cal Sacks, American Heritage Publishing Co.)*

Left: *Only a few miles from his objective, General Braddock and his army of British regulars and colonists were ambushed by French-led Indians. Braddock was mortally wounded, and Washington attempted to withdraw the panicked troops. (Wisconsin Historical Society)*

Below: *Colonel George Washington posed for this 1772 portrait during his tenure as the commander of Virginia's forces. (Washington and Lee University)*

10 June. **Advance Party. Little Meadows, Pennsylvania.**

When Braddock complains about the slow progress, Washington suggests putting a fast-moving detachment of 1,200 infantry and artillery troops ahead while the slow, heavy support wagons follow. Braddock agrees.

9 July. **Braddock's Defeat. Monongahela River.**

Braddock's force crosses the river, reforms, and continues toward Fort Duquesne ten miles away. Without warning, the advance guard hits a French-Indian force coming to intercept them. Volleys are exchanged and the French commander is killed, but the Indians react quickly, moving around both flanks of the British column and occupying a key hill. Braddock's front units suffer heavy losses and collapse, becoming entangled with rear units ordered forward. Many militia try to disperse to cover and are shot by panicked Regulars. More than 60 of 86 British officers are killed and more are wounded trying to form ranks on the road. Braddock is mortally wounded, and Washington rallies the surviving militia as a rear guard while the rest of the army retreats.

August–September. **Washington Promoted. Williamsburg, Virginia.**

The Virginia Assembly offers Washington the position of colonel and senior officer in the reestablished militia regiment. Washington is only 23 years old. His force is inadequate, the support from the Assembly is marginal, and the recruits are poor quality, but he accepts.

8 September. **Battle of Lake George. New York.**

A force of almost 4,000 American militia and Mohawks under William Johnson engage the French from Fort Carillon in three battles. Initially, an American party is ambushed after moving out of its partially fortified camp. The camp is then successfully defended against heavy French-Indian attacks. As the French withdraw, a relief party of New Hampshire and New York militia intercept them and inflict heavy

EYEWITNESS: THE DEFEAT OF GENERAL BRADDOCK

Left: *After taking a fatal wound to the chest and another round to the shoulder, Major General Braddock was carted off of the battlefield, 9 July 1755. He died of his injuries days later and was buried in a hidden grave near Fort Necessity, Pennsylvania. ("Braddock's Retreat," Alonzo Chappel, Chicago Historical Society)*

On 9 July 1755, shortly after crossing the Monongahela River, the advance guard of Major General Edward Braddock's expedition of British regulars, American militia, and Indians unexpectedly collided with French-led Indians and Canadians coming from Fort Duquesne (now Pittsburg, Pennsylvania) to intercept them. George Washington, a volunteer civilian aide to Braddock, witnessed the battle:

"We continued our March from Fort Cumberland to Frazier's (which is within 7 Miles of Duquisne) with't meet'g with any extrodinary event, hav'g only a stragler or two picked up by French Indians. When we came to this place, we were attack'd (very unexpectedly I must own) by abt. 300 French and Ind'ns; Our numbers consisted of abt. 1300 well arm'd Men, chiefly Regular's, who were immediately struck with such deadly Panick, that nothing but confusion and disobedience of order's prevail'd amongst them: The Officer's in gen'l behav'd with incomparable bravery, for which they greatly suffer'd, there being near 60 kill'd and wound'd. A large portion, out of the number we had! The Virginian Companies behav'd like men and died like Soldiers; for I believe out of 3 Companys that were there that day, scarce 30 were left alive: Captn. Peyrouny and all his Officer's, down to a Corporal, were kill'd; Captn. Polson shar'd almost as hard a Fate, for only one of his Escap'd: In short the dastardly behaviour of the English Soldier's expos'd all those who were inclin'd to do their duty to almost certain Death; and at length, in despight of every effort to the contrary, broke and run as Sheep before the Hounds, leav'g the Artillery, Ammunition, Provisions, and, every individual thing we had with us a prey to the Enemy; and when we endeavour'd to rally them in hopes of regaining our invaluable loss, it was with as much success as if we had attempted to have stop'd the wild Bears of the Mountains. The Genl. was wounded behind in the shoulder, and into the Breast, of w'ch he died three days after; . . . I luckily escap'd with't a wound tho' I had four Bullets through my Coat and two Horses shot under me. It is suppose that we left 300 or more dead in the Field; about that number we brought of wounded; . . . two thirds of both [?] received their shott from our own cowardly English Soldier's who gather'd themselves into a body contrary to orders 10 or 12 deep, wou'd then level, Fire and shoot down the Men before them."

—*Kevin M. Hymel*

casualties. One of the New Hampshire companies is commanded by Captain Robert Rogers, with John Stark as his deputy. Following the battle, Fort William Henry is constructed at the south end of the lake for use as a base against the French presence.

24 September. Rogers Assumes Scout Mission. Fort William Henry. New York.

Rogers and his men become Johnson's scouts, making frequent patrols into French-held territory. When most of the Provincials return home for the winter, Rogers stays with a small group. Throughout the fall and winter his patrols monitor the French-Indian activities.

1756

18 April. Battle of Great Cacapon. Virginia.

A patrol from the Virginia Regiment is ambushed by Indians while scouting near the Cacapon River. The captain and 16 of his men are killed.

23 May. American Ranger Company. Boston.

Governor William Shirley, commander in chief of the British forces in North America, is enthusiastic about Rogers and his techniques, and he establishes the Independent Company of American Rangers under Rogers. The company is supported by royal funds rather than the colony. Later, two more companies of militia veterans and one company of 50 Stockbridge Indians are formed and sent to join Rogers. Throughout the summer and fall, Ranger patrols and offensive raids constitute the only real positive activity against the French. Ranger companies are based on an island near Fort Edward and at Fort William Henry.

14 August. Fort Oswego Falls. New York.

A French-Indian army forces the surrender of the

1,800 American Provincials and militia holding the fort. Indians kill more than 30 of the wounded before French officers stop them.

1757

15–21 January. Battle of La Barbue Creek (Battle on Snowshoes). Lake Champlain.

Rogers leads a group of 74 Rangers on a six-day patrol. They intercept a French group traveling in sleighs on the frozen lake. En route back with seven prisoners, the Rangers are attacked. They battle for more than five hours until dark and then separate into small groups to slip away. The Rangers lose 29 men dead, wounded, or taken prisoner. Many of the captured Rangers are tortured to death by the Indians.

19–23 March. First Attack on Fort William Henry. New York.

The untested fort successfully holds out against a four-day siege by French troops and Indians who then withdraw. The French return four months later.

10 August. Massacre at Fort William Henry.

After four days of heavy cannon bombardment by a superior French-Indian force and no hope of relief, the fort surrenders with terms of safe passage. In addition to the Regulars, a large number of American Provincial soldiers and Rangers are in the fort. As the column of captives comes out, Indians rush into the fort to slaughter the wounded and sick, then attack the departing captives. In all, several hundred are killed and hundreds more taken as Indian prisoners for ransom.

24 December. Ranger Christmas Eve Raid. New York.

Rogers takes a patrol of 150 Rangers to the outskirts of Fort Carillon (Ticonderoga). They capture several

Right: *The capture of Fort Ticonderoga on 8 July 1758 was a major setback to the British control of the important upper New York lakes. The French overcame a British force five times larger to win their largest victory in the war. The British suffered over 60 percent casualties. The 42d Highland Regiment, the famous "Black Watch," bore the brunt of the assault and lost about 1,000 men. ("The Black Watch," courtesy of the Fort Ticonderoga Museum)*

French soldiers, snipe at the sentries, and burn outbuildings. The Rangers depart after dark, leaving a note to Major General Louis-Joseph de Montcalm, commander of French forces in North America, thanking him for the fresh meat.

1758

10–13 March. **Battle of Rogers' Rock. New York.**
A patrol of about 200 Rangers and volunteers is sent to scout French strength at Fort Carillon. On 13 March, a Ranger ambush is prematurely sprung and the Rangers are attacked by 700 enemy. Ranger losses are heavy, and Rogers barely escapes with his life.

5–8 July. **Attack on Fort Carillon. Ticonderoga.**
A force of British Regulars and 9,000 American Provincials and militia move up Lake Champlain to capture the fort. Rogers' Rangers and British light infantry lead the way. The frontal assault by the British Regulars is repulsed with heavy losses, making the British and Americans withdraw.

August–September. **Work on Forbes Road. Pennyslvania.**
Colonel George Washington works his 1st Virginia Regiment to cut a new road ordered for another attack against Fort Duquesne. Forts are built along the road, the last being at Loyalhanna (later Fort Ligonier), 50 miles from the objective. The Virginians then join the rest of the forces for the campaign.

12 October. **Attack on Fort Ligonier. Pennsylvania.**
A French-Indian force makes a spoiling attack against the British supply depot, hoping to disrupt the threat to Duquesne. Washington and his regiment help beat off the attack.

25 November. **Occupation of Fort Duquesne. Forks of the Ohio.**
As senior militia colonel, Washington leads the left-flank column as British Regulars and Americans advance on the fort, which they find abandoned. Brigadier General John Forbes renames it Fort Pitt. This is Washington's last campaign for England.

December. **Washington Resigns Again. Williamsburg.**
Colonel Washington arrives from Winchester and resigns his militia commission. For three years he has served on the Virginia frontier, building Fort Loudoun and establishing 16 blockhouses. He does not put his uniform on again for 16 years.

ROBERT ROGERS OF THE RANGERS

Robert Rogers was born in November 1731, the fourth boy in a Scotch-Irish farming family living near Methuen in the Massachusetts Bay Colony. His formal education was very limited, but enough for him to read and write. Rogers learned woodcraft from the few friendly Indians in the area, and was more interested in roaming the woods than farming.

At age 14, Robert Rogers joined a local militia company searching for Indian raiders from Canada. It was the beginning of a military career that continued for more than 30 years. Between campaigns Rogers rented his land and took employment as a surveyor and hunter to pay debts. He was described by contemporaries as being six feet tall, well proportioned, and athletic, with "great presence of mind, intrepidity [and] perseverance"—qualities that made him a superb leader.

When the conflict between England and France ignited in 1754, Rogers recruited more than 50 fellow New Hampshire men to form a militia company that was then sent to campaign with the British forces in New York. This earned him the rank of captain, and Rogers soon made a name for himself for daring scouting patrols deep into French territory. Unhindered by winter snows, he roamed throughout the Lake George-Lake Champlain area, bringing back prisoners or scalps and keeping British commanders informed of enemy movements.

In May 1756, Massachusetts Governor William Shirley gave Rogers command of a Provincial "Independent Company of Rangers," which was deployed to assist the British. In one mission that went bad, Rogers was shot in the hand, knee, and shoulder, and had his musket shot out of his hand. He survived the fight but lost his first men in battle. During his recovery he composed a tactical manual—he famous "Rogers' Rangers Rules"—for his type of operations.

Roger's success led to his promotion to major in 1758, and expansion of the Ranger force to nine companies. Officers of the Regular British army began applying many of Rogers' ideas in their use of light infantry. The Rangers did have their problems, and there were defeats. After the fierce "Battle on Snowshoes" with a French-Indian force on 13 March 1758, Rogers returned with only 54 of his original 181 men. His independent-minded men also resisted formal military regulations and once mutinied at a British fort. Rogers himself incurred numerous debts

Above: *Young Captain Rogers quickly proved his worth as a scout and leader against the French and Indians. He was given an "Independent Company of Rangers" and began to test his ideas for aggressive small unit operations. ("Rogers at Detroit, 1760," Gary S. Zaboly, courtesy of the collection of Timothy J. Todish and the artist)*

and came under criticism from jealous British officers. One, Sir Thomas Gage, was a bitter enemy.

After the war, Rogers received various appointments but was not paid. He was court-martialed by Gates and was plagued with personal debts and accusations of dishonesty. During trips to England to face charges, he was sentenced twice to debtor's prison. At the start of the American Revolution, Rogers offered his services to George Washington, who rebuffed him. Rogers then got British permission to raise the loyalist Queen's American Rangers and later the King's Rangers. There was no glory for Rogers, however, and he was forced to retire by 1777, facing more debts. By the time of his death in 1795, he had been in and out of debtor's prisons, divorced, and reduced to an alcoholic. It was a sad end for one of America's first and most daring militia warriors.

—Kevin M. Hymel

ROGERS' RANGERS STANDING ORDERS, 1757

The unparalleled success of Robert Rogers' company of Rangers in their actions against the French and Indians caused British commander Lord Loudoun (John Campbell, 4th Earl of Loudoun)to ask Rogers to write down his methods of operations so that they might be learned by the new light infantry forces that Loudoun and Thomas Gage were developing. In October 1757, Rogers wrote down a set of basic "rules." Listed below (in contemporary language) are 19 rules followed by his Rangers. Over time Rogers elaborated on the rules, but the basics have never changed and today are taught to American infantrymen and Rangers.

STANDING ORDERS:

1. Don't forget nothing.

2. Have your musket clean as a whistle, hatchet scoured, 60 rounds powder and ball, and be ready to march at a minute's notice.

3. When you're on the march, act the way you would if you were sneaking up on a deer. See the enemy first.

4. Tell the truth about what you see and what you do. There is an army depending on us for correct information. You can lie all you please when you tell the folks about Rangers, but don't ever lie to a Ranger or an officer.

5. Don't never take a chance you don't have to.

6. When we're on the march, we march single file, far enough apart so one shot can't go through two men.

7. If we strike swamps or soft ground, we spread out abreast so it's hard to track us.

8. When we march, we keep moving until dark so as to give the enemy the least possible chance at us.

9. When we camp, half the party stays awake while the other half sleeps.

10. If we take prisoners, keep 'em separate until we have time to examine them so they can't cook up a story between 'em.

11. Don't ever march home the same way. Take a different route so you won't be ambushed.

12. No matter whether we travel in big parties or little ones, each party has to keep a scout 20 yards ahead, 20 yards on each flank, and 20 yards in the rear, so the main body can't be surprised.

Above: *Rogers' amazing success with his Rangers gave birth to a new form of soldier training. (Hastings House Publishers)*

13. Every night you'll be told where to meet if surrounded by a superior force.

14. Don't sit down to eat without posting sentries.

15. Don't sleep beyond dawn. Dawn's when the French and Indians attack.

16. Don't cross a river by regular ford.

17. If somebody's trailing you, make a circle, come back onto your own tracks and ambush the folks that aim to ambush you.

18. Don't stand up when the enemy's coming against you. Kneel down. Hide behind a tree.

19. Let the enemy come until he's almost close enough to touch. Then let him have it and jump out and finish him with your hatchet.

—Kevin M. Hymel

Above: *On 25 November 1758, Colonel George Washington and his Virginians salute the raising of the British flag over the captured ruins of Fort Duquesne, Pennsylvania. It is renamed Fort Pitt. (The Granger Collection, New York)*

Below: *Captain John Gorham's company of "Indian Rangers of the Woods" was composed mostly of Native Americans and men of mixed blood. They were one of the units used by General Wolf in his attack on Quebec. (Frederick Ray, Company of Military Historians)*

1759

12 September. **Rogers' St. Francis Raid. Crown Point, New York.**
Major Rogers leads an expedition to raid the Indian town of St. Francis on the St. Lawrence River, more than 150 miles through the wilderness. The town is a major French-Indian base. After preparing equipment and drawing 30 days' rations, they depart by boat the night of 13 September.

13 September. **On the Plains of Abraham. Quebec.**
During the night the British slip ashore from the St. Lawrence River and gain the plateau outside the city. When the French sally out for open battle, they are defeated and surrender the city on the 17th. Six companies of American Rangers, including Joseph Gorham's company, participate in the campaign.

24 September–6 October. **Attack on St. Francis. Canada.**
Two days after landing and marching inland, Rogers learns that the French have discovered his boats, destroyed them, and are now in pursuit. After a conference of the officers, he decides to continue the mission. The Ranger raiders attack the village at 3 a.m. on the 6th, totally surprising the Indians. The village is burned with many Indian casualties, including women and children. Ranger losses are few and several English women prisoners are freed.

With Indian corn from the village as food for the return trip, the Rangers depart.

14 October–4 November. **Return from St. Francis. Wells River. New Hampshire.**
After eight days, the Rangers split into smaller groups and take different routes to the rendezvous at Wells River. Food is almost gone, and freezing rain and snow keeps game scarce. Pursuing French-Indian parties catch some of the Rangers. Rogers' group arrives at the river to find neither a relief party nor the expected supplies. Desperately hungry, one group resorts to eating bodies they find along a riverbank. As more Rangers straggle into the camp, Rogers and several others build a raft and float down the river to Fort Number 4. Barely surviving the river falls and rapids, they finally make contact on 31 October. On 4 November, Rogers takes supplies and leads search parties to locate survivors. In the raid itself only one man was wounded, but the return march cost 49 Rangers' lives.

9 December. **Cherokee War Begins. South Carolina.**
A long series of small raids and killings by both whites and Indians again leads to war with the Cherokees.

A delegation of Cherokee chiefs are seized at a meeting and held as hostages at Fort Prince George.

1760

19 January–February. **Cherokees Retaliate. Fort Prince George, South Carolina.**
The Cherokees attempt to sneak weapons into the fort in the hope of seizing the fort and freeing their chiefs, but the ruse fails. In February, the Indians offer to talk but kill the fort commander. In retaliation the hostage chiefs are shot, and Cherokees continue raiding across the southern frontier.

March–June. **Fort 96 Built. South Carolina.**
A hasty log stockade is expanded into a strong fort manned by South Carolina militia. In addition, local

Below: *In October 1759, with supplies diminished, Lieutenant Dunbar and his Rangers were caught by pursuing Indians and sustained heavy casualties while returning from their St. Francis raid. ("Dunbar's Massacre," Gary S. Zaboly)*

militia companies are assembled and seven companies of Rangers are formed for scouting and raiding duty. A British Regular regiment is sent from New York to assist, and a large but inconclusive engagement is fought with the Cherokees in June.

May–June. **Ranger Raid. Crown Point, New York.**
Leading an understrength force of Rangers, Rogers defeats two French forces near Lake Champlain. Rangers penetrate north to the St. Lawrence to attack several forts, with the loss of only one man.

8 August. **Cherokee War. Fort Loudoun (Vonore, Tennessee).**
For most of the summer the Cherokees besiege the garrison of 200 militiamen and their families. Finally, the fort commander is pressured by his men to surrender with promise of safe escort. Two days later, the column of walking militiamen and their families is attacked. Many are killed and the survivors taken captive.

8 September–November. **Montreal Surrenders. War Ends. Canada.**
Montreal surrenders, and the next day Rogers and two Ranger companies are sent up the St. Lawrence River to the Great Lakes to notify French outposts. On 29 November, they arrive at Fort Detroit, now Detroit, Michigan, and raise the British flag.

1761

May. **Cherokee War. Fort Prince George, South Carolina.**
A militia regiment plus a mounted scout detachment arrive to help fight the Cherokees. Francis Marion, William Moultrie, and Henry Laurens are among the arrivals. The scouts move into the countryside, skirmishing with the Indians and destroying Cherokee villages. The Cherokees finally agree to sign a treaty in December.

1763

Winter. **Pontiac's Rebellion Begins. Fort Detroit.**
With the encouragement of pro-French Canadians, several tribes in the Ohio-Great Lakes region unite against the English and Americans under Ottawa chief Pontiac. Pontiac attempts to overcome Fort Detroit's garrison from the inside, but his plan fails. The Indians then besiege the fort. By the end of May, seven other forts have been tricked and their garrisons killed.

2 June. **Fort Michilimackinac Captured. Michigan Territory.**
Ojibwa Indians pretend to chase a lacrosse ball into the fort's open gate. Once inside they rush the militia garrison and capture the fort. Four more forts in the Ohio territory are destroyed during June.

31 July. **Battle of Bloody Creek. Fort Detroit.**
A mostly Regular British force defending the fort

Opposite, top: *The Pennsylvania Regiment was not uniformed at first, but by February 1757, a uniform was approved with green coats, red jackets, and buckskin breeches. ("Pennsylvania Regiment 1756–1758," Eric I. Manders, Company of Military Historians)*

Opposite, bottom: *The Indians' wrath was nothing to trifle with. Frontiersmen and their settlements were constantly on the defense. (Sidney E. King, Colonial National Historical Park)*

Right: *Chartered in 1741 by wealthy men of Boston who were interested in the military, The Independent Company of Massachusetts was an approved unit outside the colony's militia. John Hancock was a company officer. ("The Independent Company of Massachusetts," H. Charles McBarron, Jr., Company of Military Historians)*

attempts a night sortie against the Indians besieging the fort and are defeated. American Provincial units participating include the Queen's American Rangers under Captain Joseph Hopkins.

5 August. **Battle of Bushy Run. Pennsylvania.**
A mixed force of Highland Regulars, Royal Americans, and Provincial Ranger companies bringing supplies to Fort Pitt are attacked near the small creek. Led by the experienced Indian fighter Colonel Henry Bouquet, they hold behind a barricade of flour bags, then counterattack, defeating the Indians. After the initial victories, Pontiac's supporters lose interest and seek accommodation, forcing Pontiac to a treaty in October.

1771

16 May. **Battle of the Alamance Creek. North Carolina.**
Governor William Tryon leads 1,200 North Carolina militia in a small action that defeats armed rebels from the backcountry called "Regulators."

1774

15 May. **Lord Dunmore's War. Virginia.**
Shawnee Indians attack settlements along the Ohio River. Virginia militia mobilize and two groups, one led by Virginia governor John Murray, 4th Earl of Dunmore and one by militia Colonel Andrew Lewis, are formed to move against the Ohio Indian villages.

26 August. **Militia Protest. Worchester, Massachusetts.**
Deteriorating relations between England and its American colonies cause Parliament to disband Massachusetts militia units suspected of disloyalty. In defiance to Parliament, more than 2,000 Massachusetts militiamen assemble with their

21 September. Fairfax Independent Company. Fairfax County, Virginia.
George Washington chairs a committee forming a volunteer independent company of militia. The company adopts a uniform with a dark blue coat faced with buff, buff waistcoat and breeches. Washington wears this uniform when he attends the Continental Congress, and it eventually becomes the uniform of officers of the Continental Army.

21–26 October. Militia Reorganization. Concord, Massachusetts.
The Provincial Congress of Massachusetts establishes a Provincial army to replace the old militia. A Committee of Safety is appointed to act as the senior military headquarters, and another committee organizes logistic support. All militia companies are directed to elect officers who will in turn elect regimental officers and staffs. Officers loyal to the king are replaced. Men aged 16 to 60 are recruited to fill out the units. Once formed, each regiment is to provide one-quarter of its men as volunteers for 50-man "minuteman" companies.

officers on the village common and parade with their weapons.

1 September. British Raid. Charlestown, Massachusetts.
British General Thomas Gage sends troops to bring in gunpowder stored in a nearby magazine. The powder is secured and another detachment brings in two small cannon from Cambridge. Alarmed by rumors of fighting, several thousand local militiamen gather, causing Gage to fortify the narrow neck of land connecting Boston to the mainland.

5 September. First Continental Congress. Philadelphia.
Fifty-six representatives from all of the American colonies except Georgia gather for the first session of the Continental Congress. The delegates discuss the need for common defense and action against British repression.

8 September. British Raid. Charlestown, Massachusetts.
A detachment of Gage's British Regulars is rowed from Boston to the harbor defense artillery battery located on the edge of bay. Their mission is to bring the cannon back to Boston, but to their surprise, they find the guns and ammunition gone and the fort stripped. A week later four more cannon disappear from the Boston common.

Opposite, top: *The 60th Royal Americans were recruited in the colonies. The 2d and 3d Battalions were at the surrender of Louisbourg and Quebec while the 1st was at the capture of Fort Duquesne, Pennsylvania, and fought in the Carolinas. ("The 60th (Royal American) Regiment of Foot," Frederick E. Ray, Jr., Company of Military Historians)*

Opposite, bottom: *The Shawnee Indian warrior, usually loyal to the British, was a very deadly opponent to whomever met the wrong end of his war club. ("Shawnee Warrior," Don Troiani)*

Left: *As colonial hostility grew toward England, detachments of British regulars were sent through the downtown streets of Boston to display the authority and power of England. (The Granger Collection, New York)*

Each man has to supply his own weapon, but powder and pay are to be provided. Although reluctant to give up control over their local militia companies, most towns and districts comply, and gathering of arms and training of the new units quickly begins.

10 October. **Battle of Point Pleasant. Ohio.**
The forces of Shawnee chief Cornstalk and Colonel Andrew Lewis battle all day near the mouth of the Kanawha River. Neither leader has enthusiasm for further fighting, and a truce is declared on 26 October.

14 December. **Seizure of Royal Arsenals. Fort William and Mary, New Hampshire.**
Major John Sullivan leads a group of Massachusetts militia in a surprise raid on the fort, capturing it with all weapons and powder. In Rhode Island, militia remove 44 cannon from Fort George at Newport. The Rhode Island assembly also distributes arms to its militia companies and orders the men to stand ready.

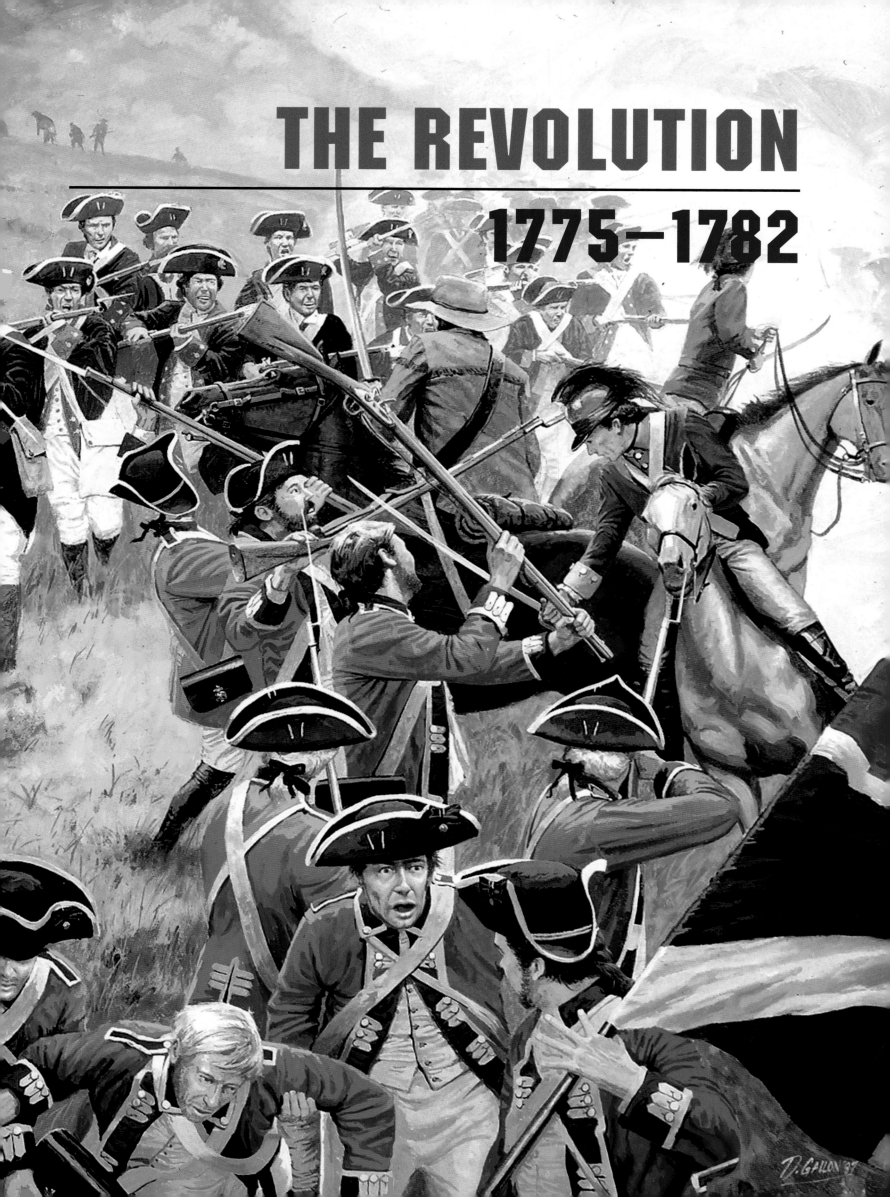

THE REVOLUTION

1775–1782

THE REVOLUTION
1775–1782

Colonel Raymond K. Bluhm, Jr., USA (Ret)

When the Continental Congress reconvened on 10 May 1775, open warfare already existed with England. The British attempt in April to seize the arms hidden at Concord had ended in a bloody retreat with losses on both sides. The makeshift army of local militiamen outside Boston was growing daily by hundreds from adjacent colonies who accepted, more or less, the leadership of the senior Massachusetts militia officer, Artemus Ward. The night before Congress met, a joint colonial expedition captured the British garrison and the heavy cannon at Fort Ticonderoga, New York.

The first problem facing Congress was to bring order out of the patchwork force around Boston. Composed of "first response" militia from four different colonies, it would have a very short life. On 14 June 1775, Congress resolved to create its own force. It approved the recruiting of ten companies of riflemen—eight from Pennsylvania and one each from Virginia and Maryland. The delegates also agreed to place the militia at Boston under congressional authority for six months. The next day George Washington was selected as the commander of this new army. On 17 June, as Washington and Congress worked out an army organization, General Ward's strongpoint on Breed's Hill overlooking Boston was attacked and captured.

An experienced militia officer, Washington knew he faced daunting challenges. His strategic mission was one of defense—to keep the British from re-establishing control over the colonies. To do this, he had to have a dependable army capable of holding its own against, if not defeating, the British regulars, and a logistical base of support. For the British to win, they had to destroy the American army; for the Americans to win (i.e. cause the British to leave), Washington had to inflict as much punishment as possible, yet avoid a decisive battle that could destroy his army. After several near disasters, it was clear that short-term militia could not do this; an army of American Regulars was needed—the Continentals.

The course of the war flowed from north to south. The first actions took place in New England and north into Canada, which many hoped would be the 14th state. The British were forced out of Boston but captured New York City. Battles were fought throughout New York, New Jersey, and Pennsylvania for six years. Washington suffered several tactical defeats, but each time he slipped away to strike back where least expected. A British effort to split New England with invading columns from Canada ended with the first major British defeat at Saratoga in 1777. As fighting continued, American leaders became more

proficient, and with the help of training from von Steuben, the veteran Continental Line equaled the British troops.

Virginian George Rogers Clark took the fight into the far west, where he surprised the British garrisons at outposts in the Illinois country and secured the Ohio and upper Mississippi Valleys for the future United States. However, with British support, the Indians continued their long-running conflict with Americans. It was primarily a militia war since few Continentals could be sent to help.

Frustrated, the British went south, hoping to take advantage of the strong Loyalist support in some areas of North and South Carolina. Their initial success was lost with the arrival of Nathanael Greene as Washington's southern commander. His fight-and-run tactics exhausted the British forces and sent them to seek resupply at Yorktown, Virginia. Seeing their chance, Washington and his French allies quickly turned Yorktown into a trap, and another British surrender, in 1781.

In late 1782, peace negotiations were underway in Paris. In the north, Washington concentrated his Main Army to keep the British contained in New York. Raids and skirmishes continued in the south as Greene's Southern Army besieged the British who were holding Charleston and gradually squeezed the British into a few other enclaves on the coast.

The long war was ending.

Pages 52–53: *Only the willingness of the British commander, Lord Cornwallis, to fire artillery into his own troops mixed with advancing American Continentals saved him from defeat at the Battle of Guilford Courthouse, South Carolina, 15 March 1781. ("Turning Point at Guilford," Dale Gallon)*

Above: *Washington and his staff watch as the ragged Continentals march into winter quarters at Valley Forge, Pennsylvania. ("Washington at Valley Forge," W. Trego, Valley Forge Historical Society)*

THE REVOLUTION
1775–1782

"These are the times that try men's souls. The summer soldier and sunshine patriot will, in this crisis, shrink from the service of their country; but he that stands it now, deserves the love and thanks of man and woman."
—Thomas Paine, *The Crisis*, December 1776

1775

January. **British Army Assembles. Boston, Massachusetts.**
Major General Thomas Gage, British military commander in chief, assembles a force of 4,000 infantry and 450 royal marines. Periodically he sends them through the countryside as training, to look for arms and to show the flag.

26 February. **British Foray. Salem.**
A British regiment lands to seize militia cannon reported here. Armed minutemen and militia block the way and the British depart empty-handed.

23 March. **Militia Mobilization. Richmond, Virginia.**
Aroused by events in Massachusetts, the unofficial Virginia Convention of Delegates debates its course of action. Patrick Henry is the leading voice for armed action against the British and serves for a time as colonel of the 1st Virginia Regiment.

30 March. **British Probe. Massachusetts.**
A brigade of 1,200 British Regulars march out of Boston and along the Charles River. The local militia are alerted and take defensive positions at the river crossings. The British turn away rather than confront the Americans.

April. **Provincial Army Formed. Concord.**
The unofficial Provincial Congress asks other New England colonies for men to expand its "Provincial Army" into a 30,000-man New England army. In addition to infantry, the new regional army would have six companies of artillery, armed with the cannon taken from the forts. Concord is a major supply point for the new force. By the end of July, New Hampshire, Connecticut, and Rhode Island have sent detachments.

18 April. **Concord Expedition. Boston.**
A provisional brigade of 700 British infantrymen is organized for a "powder" raid on Concord. On the night of the 18th the men are shuttled in longboats

Left: *Boston silversmith and militia courier Paul Revere rides toward Concord to warn Samuel Adams and John Hancock that British troops were en route to arrest them. ("Paul Revere," A. Lassell Ripley, courtesy of UnumProvident Corporation)*

ARMY BATTLE STREAMERS—AMERICAN REVOLUTION

Lexington, 1775

Ticonderoga, 1775

Boston, 1775–1776

Quebec, 1775, 1776

Charleston, 1776, 1780

Long Island, 1776

Trenton, 1776

Princeton, 1777

Saratoga, 1777

Brandywine, 1777

Germantown, 1777

Monmouth, 1778

Savannah, 1778, 1779

Cowpens, 1781

Guilford Court House, 1781

Yorktown, 1781

from Boston across the Charles River. No significant resistance is expected, so the mixed force of light infantry, grenadiers, and marines has no artillery, no rations, and only 36 rounds of musket ammunition per man. The embarkation is disorganized and slow, giving American alarm riders time to carry warnings to the countryside.

19 April. Battle of Lexington.
When the leading British detachment reaches Lexington, they find a battle line of 75 militia and minutemen drawn up on the village green. Captain John Parker, the senior militia commander, has no specific orders to stop the British, and his uncertain men begin to move aside. As the British advance, a shot, perhaps

two, is fired. Control is lost and the British soldiers fire a volley into the American ranks. Both sides fire and then the British move forward with bayonets. In a matter of minutes eight Americans are dead, 11 wounded; one British soldier is wounded. The British re-form and continue on toward Concord, six miles away.

Battle of Concord Bridge.
Colonel James Barrett, Concord militia commander, removes the weapons and supplies stored in the town, then orders his men across North Bridge to a ridgeline. As he waits, reinforcements from the nearby towns join his company. Six British companies go to North Bridge. Suddenly, the Americans on the ridge see smoke rising from the

Left: *Minutemen were the first local militia to respond to the alarm bells as the British regulars advanced into the Massachusetts countryside. (Russell Freedman, The Granger Collection, New York)*

Below: *At Lexington, the battle line of American militia held its fire until the "shot heard round the world." ("Battle of Lexington," W. B. Wollen, National Army Museum, London, England)*

town. Alarmed that the British are burning the town, the militia move toward the bridge. As they approach, the British open fire and four or five Americans go down. Volleys are exchanged, killing and wounding men on both sides before the British turn and run back to the town. The Americans move into the hills around the town.

Pursuit to Boston.
As hundreds of men of the Provincial Army gather near Concord, Colonel Barrett directs them to positions along the Lexington road. By noon, the British are marching back to Boston. At Meriam's Corner, barely a mile from Concord, the British column is fired on by the militia, beginning a 16-mile

gauntlet of ambushes. Despite the British use of light infantry flankers and rear guards, Americans come within easy musket range of the retreating men, fire with deadly effect, then race ahead to fire again. Brigadier General William Heath arrives to command the Americans in the running battle. More than 2,000 Americans dog the British column, and another 2,000 wait in ambushes at woodlines, ridges, and bridge crossings. In the tiny village of Menotomy (now Arlington, Massachusetts) almost every house and stone wall conceals American snipers who inflict almost half the British casualties. Finally, after 7 p.m., the British column reaches Charlestown Neck. The day cost the British 73 dead, 174 wounded, and 26 missing. American losses are 49 killed, about 41 wounded, and five missing.

20–30 *April*. Provincial Army Organized. Cambridge.

Artemus Ward, General of the Massachusetts Provincial Army, takes command of the 15,000–20,000 militiamen surrounding Boston. He assigns regiments to Heath and Major General John Thomas with responsibility to hold the American lines. Thinking their duty done, many militia officers and their men are returning home. Alarmed, the Committee of Public Safety requests all Massachusetts towns to send men for eight months (April to December) of paid service. As news of the battles spreads, individuals and units from other colonies arrive and are merged with the Massachusetts army, forming a de facto New England army. Included are the Rhode Island brigade of Brigadier Nathanael Greene, a New Hampshire regiment under Colonel John Stark, and the Connecticut regiment of veteran Brigadier General Israel Putnam, who is made Heath's second in command. This multi-colony force is referred to as the "Army of Observation."

2 May. Ticonderoga Campaign. Cambridge.

Connecticut Captain Benedict Arnold, recently arrived with his company, convinces the Committee of Public Safety to commission him a colonel in its Provincial Army and sponsor his plan to capture Fort Ticonderoga and its heavy guns. The fort has a small garrison and is in bad repair. Arnold learns that Ethan Allen, from New Hampshire Grants (now Vermont), is already on the way with his irregular "Green Mountain Boys."

Above: *American militia exchanged musket fire with the British at Concord Bridge. Failing to find either the weapons or American leaders they sought, the British withdrew toward Boston under heavy fire from growing numbers of Americans. ("Concord Bridge," A. Lassell Ripley, courtesy of UnumProvident Corporation)*

THE MILITIA IN THE AMERICAN REVOLUTION

During the American Revolution, the Continental Army and the militia represented the two sides of a double-edged sword, and victory would have not been possible without both. The Continental Army shouldered the main burden of confronting British Regulars with militia units fighting alongside. In addition, the militia controlled the countryside, battled loyalist militia, and performed other important auxiliary functions.

The militia's most widely recognized accomplishments occurred before the founding of the Continental Army. Starting in late 1774, militia units in New England demonstrated against British raids to seize suspected American weapons caches. The most famous raid came on 19 April 1775, when Massachusetts minutemen confronted British troops at Lexington and Concord and fired the "shot heard 'round the world." Two months later at Bunker Hill, New England militiamen fighting from defensive positions inflicted ghastly casualties on the British before finally being forced to withdraw. The militia's greatest contribution was to provide a reservoir of manpower. Continental line regiments—units raised by the states for service with the Continental Army—drew heavily from militia membership to fill their ranks. Militia units fought in a large majority of the Revolution's 1,331 recognized engagements. When Washington assembled his army in early 1776, nearly half of the troops were militia.

The militia's record in head-on battle with British Regulars was mixed. Militia unreliability and routs at a number of battles soured relations with the Continentals. Militiamen fought best from prepared defenses or when deployed alongside seasoned Continentals. However, under the inspired leadership of men like John Stark, Daniel Morgan, Francis Marion, Thomas Sumter, and Andrew Pickens, American militiamen also scored a number of victories. The battle of Bennington, Vermont, was one of the few times militiamen alone defeated European professional troops in open combat. In Virginia, North Carolina, and South Carolina the militia fought a bloody but successful guerrilla war against loyalist forces that eventually prompted a British withdrawal from the entire region.

The militia also performed a number of important auxiliary functions. Militia patrols harassed

Above: *The need for self defense made formation of a local militia company mandatory, and prominent citizens were usually selected to lead the unit whether they had military experience or not. Being selected as an officer was looked upon as both an honor and a civic duty. ("Colonel Joseph Crockett's Western Battalion," Peter Copeland, Company of Military Historians)*

British outposts, attacked enemy foraging parties, quashed pro-British activities, and monitored enemy movements. Other activities included suppressing Indian uprisings, repelling British maritime raids, enforcing local laws, garrisoning forts, guarding prisoners of war, transporting supplies, and patrolling against slave insurrections.

An unintended consequence of the militia's part in gaining American independence was to secure for itself a permanent place in the military establishment of the United States. Article I, Section 8 of the U.S. Constitution outlines the three enduring missions of the militia: "to execute the Laws of the union, suppress Insurrections, and repel Invasions."

—*Michael Doubler*

9 May. **Ticonderoga: First U.S. Army Campaign. New York.**

Arnold rushes to Lake Champlain and demands that Allen serve under him. The two finally settle on a dual-command arrangement. Before dawn on the 10th, Arnold, Allen, and 83 men row across the lake and rush into the fort, surprising the few sentries. They locate the post commander and Allen demands that the fort surrender "in the name of the Great Jehovah and the Continental Congress." Fifty soldiers and more than 100 cannon and other supplies are captured. A garrison is left at the fort, and Arnold and Allen depart, but there is no means to move the guns.

12 May. **Capture of Crown Point. New York.**

Lieutenant Colonel Seth Warner takes a detachment of Green Mountain Boys from Ticonderoga down Lake Champlain and captures the fort at Crown Point without a fight. The Americans now control the southern portion of the lake, providing a base for operations against Canada.

15–16 May. **Congressional Army Proposed. Philadelphia, Pennsylvania.**

On the 15th, the Second Continental Congress forms a committee that includes George Washington, a Virginia delegate, to study the defense of New York. The next day Richard Henry Lee, also a delegate from Virginia, makes a motion that Congress raise its own army, but disagreement prevents action.

17–18 May. **Capture of St. John's. Canada.**

Arnold sails to the north end of Lake Champlain and descends the Richelieu River to the British fort at St. John's. With 50 men he captures the small garrison, plus boats and supplies, then withdraws. Allen takes another group toward the fort, but he runs into a British relief force and must withdraw. On the 18th Arnold's men capture a British supply sloop that they rechristen *Enterprise*, starting a long line of famous U.S. ships to carry the name.

27 May. **Skirmishes on Hog and Noodle Islands. Boston Bay, Massachusetts.**

A detachment under Stark is sent to Hog and Noodle Islands to seize livestock and British supplies. A warship with royal marines arrives and minor fighting occurs on the islands, but the ship runs aground and is abandoned. The next morning militiamen wade to the ship and take supplies, including cannon, then set her afire. Putnam, already a respected veteran leader, is promoted to major general.

Above: *American militia place successive ambushes along the route of the British retreat from Concord, with losses to both sides. (North Wind Picture Archives)*

(Below: *The American rifleman was the proud, but independent defender of his own home and his community, making Washington's goal of a more formal disciplined army difficult. ("The Rifleman," H. David Wright)*

14 June. **Congress Raises First Army. Philadelphia.**
The Continental Congress votes to raise ten companies of riflemen, two each from Maryland and Virginia and six from Pennsylvania. These are the first units of the future United States Army. Congress also takes responsibility for all the New England forces gathered around Boston and those being mobilized. A committee, including Washington and Philip Schuyler of New York, is formed to draft regulations for the new army, officially named the "Continental Army." (Birthday of the U.S. Army and Infantry)

15 June. **Selection of Commander in Chief.**
John Adams works behind the scenes to have Virginia delegate and former militia colonel George Washington offered the commission and position as "General & Commander in Chief of the American Forces." Despite some opposition, Adams prevails.

16 June. **Washington Accepts Command.**
Washington accepts the commission, but he refuses a salary, asking only that his expenses be paid. Congress begins organizing the Continental Army, authorizing types and strengths of units and positions for an engineer, adjutant general, paymaster, commissary general, and quartermaster. (Birthday of Adjutant General Corps, Corps of Engineers, Finance Corps, and Quartermaster Corps)

17 June. **Battle of Breed's/Bunker Hill. Charlestown, Massachusetts.**
During the night of 16 June, Ward sends Colonel

William Prescott with 1,100 militiamen to fortify Bunker Hill. Putnam persuades Prescott that nearby Breed's Hill is a better military position. Colonel Richard Gridley, Ward's chief engineer, stakes out a square earth redoubt 136 feet on a side and the troops begin digging. By dawn, they have the earthwork overlooking the harbor almost completed. The British are surprised and decide to land and capture the position by a flank envelopment. Prescott receives some reinforcements, including Stark's regiment, which takes positions on the beach and hillside to the left. Major General Dr. Joseph Warren also arrives at the redoubt. He is senior but defers to Prescott as commander. The British light infantry tries to advance along the beach, but Stark's men stop them, inflicting heavy British casualties. The British assaults in the center and right flank meet a fierce volume of musket fire and fall back, but American ammunition is almost gone. A third British attack is made directly on the redoubt. After one American volley, the British break in and rout the defenders. Prescott escapes, but Warren is killed. He is the first American general officer to die in combat. Putnam's and Stark's men fight a rear guard-action.

20–30 June. **First Continental Army Review. Philadelphia.**
On 20 June, Washington receives orders from Congress to "take charge of the army of the united colonies." He conducts his first official military function with a review of Philadelphia's militia companies. Authorization for four major generals and eight brigadier generals is approved, but Congress reserves the authority to select the officers. Artemus Ward, Charles Lee, Israel Putnam, and Philip Schuyler are named as major generals—Ward as Washington's second in command. Brigadier generals are selected on the 22nd, with positions allocated to states depending on the number of troops contributed. Washington requests Horatio Gates for his Adjutant General. On the 23rd Washington departs for Cambridge with a mounted escort and his new staff. On 30 June, Congress approves 69 Articles of War to regulate the behavior and discipline of the Army.

Above: *Under Major General Joseph Warren and Colonel William Prescott 1,100 minutemen repulsed the British regulars twice before having to abandon the position on Breed's Hill, more popularly known as "Bunker Hill." (". . . the whites of their eyes!" National Guard Heritage Print)*

Above: *An untalented, but politically connected Horatio Gates was appointed Washington's second-in-command. His schemes to replace Washington caused frequent problems in the Continental Army. (Charles Wilson Peale, Independence National Historical Park)*

22 June. Morgan's Rifle Company. Frederick County, Virginia.

Daniel Morgan is commissioned a captain in the new Continental Army. He quickly recruits one of the Virginia companies. The men are mounted and they start the 600-mile ride to Cambridge. Additional rifle companies form under George Read, Michael Cresap, Hugh Stevenson, Thomas Price, and others. By mid-July, a total of 13 rifle companies have been authorized.

2–10 July. Washington Takes Command. Cambridge.

After a 12-day journey, Washington arrives late on 2 July. The next day he formally assumes command of the Continental Army and reviews three regiments. On the 4th he issues General Order #1, formally announcing that the militia units there are now under the authority of Congress as the new "Continental Army." Some officers resign rather than accept the change. Washington organizes the new army into three "grand divisions" under Ward, Putnam, and Charles Lee. He tours the camps and is shocked to find only 14,000 men fit for duty and almost no ammunition. Washington also establishes the first American Army system of rank insignia. He directs

all sergeants to wear a strip of red cloth sewn on the right shoulder; corporals, wear green strips.

12 July. Fort Charlotte. South Carolina.

State militia capture the British fort on the Savannah River in the first action of the war in the state.

18 July. Schuyler Takes Command. Fort Ticonderoga. New York.

Major General Schuyler arrives at the fort and finds it in bad shape, with few supplies and a weak, undisciplined garrison. Several days later, Congress designates Schuyler as commander of the New York (Northern) Department, beginning a system of regional commands that continues during the war.

27 July. Medical Corps Established. Philadelphia.

Congress authorizes a wartime hospital for the army. Dr. Benjamin Church, a supposed Massachusetts "revolutionary" but really a British spy, is appointed Director General and Chief Physician of the Hospital of the Army. (Birthday of the Army Medical Corps and the Medical Department)

29 July. Chaplains and Judge Advocate Established. Philadelphia.

Congress authorizes pay for a chaplain in each regiment and appoints Colonel William Tudor as the first Judge Advocate. (Birthday of the Chaplains Corps and the Judge Advocate General Corps)

2 August. Rifle Companies Arrive. Cambridge.

Morgan arrives with his rifle company. Cresap's 1st Maryland Rifles are already in camp. Although valued for their shooting and fighting skills, the rifle companies are unruly and a disciplinary problem.

Opposite, bottom: *The elite Philadelphia Light Horse Troop escorted General Washington from Philadelphia to Cambridge, Massachusetts, to take command of the Continental Army. (James Claypoole, Mr. and Mrs. B. Mastai Collection)*

Right: *On 3 July 1775, Washington took command of the newly formed Continental Army at the main American camp in Cambridge, Massachusetts, overlooking the British forces in Boston. ("Washington Takes Command")*

14 August. **First Army Quartermaster Appointed.**
Washington appoints Thomas Mifflin as the first Quartermaster General, responsible for camps, transportation, movement of troops, and other logistical matters. Joseph Trumbull is already serving as Commissary General for procurement of rations and general supplies. A separate Commissary of Artillery is also appointed to handle the special artillery logistical requirements.

28 August. **Canadian Expedition. Ticonderoga.**
Brigadier General Richard Montgomery, Schuyler's deputy, departs for Canada with a hurriedly organized expedition of 1,200 men. Scouts in Canada report strong anti-British feelings among the Canadians, and Montgomery sees an opportunity to capture the towns along the St. Lawrence River. Schuyler is ill, but he follows the next day with another 500 men. Ethan Allen accompanies the expedition.

5 September. **Army Commands First Continental Warship.**
The fishing schooner *Hannah*, captured by Army troops in August and now mounting four 4-pounder cannon, sets sail to help blockade British troops in Boston. *Hannah*, commanded by Army officer John Broughton, is considered to be the first Continental combat ship and remains in service until October. It is the beginning of what will become the most powerful naval force in the world—the U.S. Navy.

5–16 September. **Attack on St. John's. Canada.**
From Ile Aux Noix, Montgomery and Schuyler lead columns toward the St. John's fort. Mohawks and Canadian Loyalists ambush them, and the Americans withdraw. A second effort also fails. Schuyler becomes ill, and on the 16th he turns command over to Montgomery and returns to Ticonderoga.

10 September. **Prospect Hill Mutiny. Massachusetts.**
The independent-minded frontiersmen of rifle regiments, called "shirtmen" because of their loose hunting shirts, are a source of frequent discipline problems. When a sergeant of Thompson's Rifle Battalion is arrested and confined in the camp, his friends march with loaded weapons to free him. The guard is reinforced by 500 men, and other regiments assemble as reserve. Washington, Lee, and Greene order the riflemen to ground their weapons, and march them back to camp. A court-martial fines 33 men; the ringleader also receives six days' confinement.

12 September. **Arnold's Column. Cambridge.**
Washington approves a proposal by newly promoted Colonel Benedict Arnold to take a second group overland to attack Quebec City. Arnold departs the next day with 1,000 men, including Morgan's company. Morgan is put in charge of all the riflemen and leads the way. The expedition is ill prepared; Arnold has badly underestimated the distance (350 miles) and the difficulties. He has planned on a 20-day march; it takes 45 days, and the men nearly starve.

Above: *Poor planning and harsh elements in Maine and Canada nearly defeated Colonel Benedict Arnold and his men before they could reach the St. Lawrence River, as part of the 300-mile march to Quebec. ("Benedict Arnold's March to Canada," Knoedler Galleries, New York)*

15 September. **Capture of Fort Johnson. Charleston, South Carolina.**
Provincial militia seize the fort that guards the entrance to Charleston Bay. This brings an important port under American control.

18–25 September. **Montgomery's Force. St. John's, Canada.**
Montgomery blocks the Richelieu River and places St. John's under siege. Ethan Allen is sent ahead to recruit Canadian volunteers. He meets Major John Brown, who has also been recruiting Canadians, and the two plan an attack on Montreal. On 25 September Allen's group is attacked by a British-Canadian force and the new recruits are routed. Allen is captured and sent to England in chains.

4 October. **Dr. Church's Treason. Cambridge.**
Dr. Church is court-martialed and found guilty of "criminal correspondence with the enemy." Church is the first confirmed traitor to the American army. He is confined until 1777 and then permitted to leave the country. Dr. John Morgan replaces Church and makes major improvements in medical care, encouraging use of experimental inoculation to combat smallpox and requiring competency examinations of medical personnel.

18 October. **Capture of Chambly. Canada.**
The town is captured by a combined American-Canadian unit. They seize more than 80 British prisoners and several tons of badly needed ammunition and gunpowder.

24–25 October. **Defense of Norfolk. Virginia.**
A British naval force sails into Hampton Creek to destroy the town, but the defending militiamen force the landing parties to withdraw. American marksmen kill sailors on the ships, and in the confusion two ships run aground and are captured.

2 November. **Capture of St. John's. Canada.**
The British garrison surrenders after 55 days. To save his resources, Montgomery paroles all the prisoners; he then begins preparations to march on Montreal.

4–8 November. **Continental Army Reorganized. Philadelphia.**
With the majority of the Continental Army enlistments expiring in January, Washington orders some units extended by two weeks, causing grumbling and desertions. Congress sets enlistments at a minimum of one year. The Army is to reorganize on

Opposite, bottom:
American forces captured Montreal, Quebec, one of the few successful campaigns to add a fourteenth colony to the new United States. ("Montreal, 25 September 1775," H. Charles McBarron, Army Art Collection, NMUSA)

Right: *Both militia and Continental Army units proudly carried distinctive flags or colors as symbols of the unit's spirit and to facilitate identification on the smoky battlefield. ("Continental Army Flags," J. Charlton Jones)*

1 January into 26 (later 27) infantry regiments with separate artillery. Regiments will have eight companies, each with 728 officers and men. For the first time a standard Army uniform is prescribed—brown coats, with each regiment to have collar, cuffs, and lapels of a different color.

5 November. **Militia General Appointed Continental Navy Commander.**
Brigadier General Esek Hopkins, Rhode Island Militia, is appointed the first Commander in Chief of the Continental Navy by the Continental Congress.

9–15 November. **Arnold's Force Arrives. Quebec. Canada.**
Arnold's exhausted and starving force reaches the St. Lawrence River. Only 675 men remain of the original 1,000. On the 13th, they cross the river; two days later Arnold parades his men in front of the town, trying unsuccessfully to bluff the defenders into surrendering.

13–15 November. **Occupation of Montreal. Canada.**
The British army abandons the city to Montgomery. His men pursue the retreating British and capture two ships on the St. Lawrence.

17 November. Knox Appointed. Cambridge.
Colonel Henry Knox replaces Colonel Richard Gridley as commander of the Continental Regiment of Artillery. Gridley continues as the Army's Chief Engineer. When Knox proposes a plan to bring the guns from Ticonderoga to the American lines around Boston, Washington agrees; Knox departs several days later. (Birthday of the Field Artillery and Air Defense Artillery)

19 November. Defense of Fort Ninety-Six. South Carolina.
The patriot militia garrison at the fort is attacked by Loyalists and besieged for two days before a truce.

29 November. Continental Army Schooner Captures British Ship.
By hiding their true identity, a small group from the Continental Army schooner *Lee* is able to board and capture the British brigantine *Nancy* off Boston harbor. *Nancy* is carrying a large amount of arms and powder that is quickly sent to Washington's camp. *Lee* is commanded by Captain John Manley.

5 December. Knox Expedition. Ticonderoga.
Knox arrives on the 5th and begins removing the cannons. Three days later Knox begins boating the guns down Lake Champlain. With the arrival of freezing temperatures, Knox uses 40 sleds pulled by oxen to haul the 43 cannon, three howitzers, and 14 mortars over the snow-covered mountains.

8–9 December. Siege of Quebec.
Montgomery leaves Brigadier General David Wooster

with a detachment in Montreal and joins Arnold outside Quebec. Shelling of the city begins on 9 December but has little effect. Montgomery realizes they have little time. Enlistments of the New England men expire at the end of the year and several disgruntled commanders refuse to serve with Arnold.

9 December. Battle of Great Bridge. Norfolk.
American militia defeat loyalists and royal marines, who withdraw to Norfolk and evacuate the town by ship.

30 December. Enlistment of Blacks. Cambridge.
Washington authorizes official enlistment in the Army of "free negroes" who are with his forces around Boston, and Congress approves on 16 January. However, many states specifically prohibit blacks from militia service. Rhode Island, an exception, begins recruiting a black regiment in 1778. The regiment, which also eventually includes whites, wins a high reputation as a fighting unit.

30–31 December. Battle of Quebec.
In a blinding snowstorm, the Americans make a night attack on the city. Montgomery is killed at the start of the attack, and his column withdraws. Arnold, leading

Opposite, top: *In a show of determination and expertise, Colonel Henry Knox and his men successfully drag the cannons over the snow-clad mountains from Fort Ticonderoga to Boston. Their arrival gave Washington the firepower he needed to force the British out of Boston. ("Ticonderoga," Tom Lovell, Dixon-Ticonderoga Co.)*

Opposite, bottom: *The American night assault on Quebec is made under cover of a snowstorm but fails in the face of determined British-Canadian resistance, confusion, and the loss of key leaders. ("Attack on Quebec," North Wind Picture Archives)*

Right: *Hurrying to rendezvous with forces under Colonel Benedict Arnold for a surprise attack on Quebec, Major General Richard Montgomery falls, mortally wounded, still holding his sword. ("Death of Montgomery," detail, Alonzo Chappel, Chicago Historical Society)*

the second column, is wounded at the first barricade. He passes command to Daniel Morgan, a junior captain. Without reinforcements, however, the Americans are trapped in the Lower Town, and more than 420 are forced to surrender. Montgomery is buried in the city, never knowing he had been promoted to major general. He is the first general of the Continental Army to die in battle, and the first to die on foreign soil. Morgan spends eight months in prison before being exchanged. Arnold blockades the city, but he receives no reinforcements.

31 December. **Army Strength.**
The Army ends the year with: Continentals: 27,443; short-term militia: 10,180.

1776

1 January. **Continental Army Reorganized. Cambridge.**
The Continental Army is reorganized. The new 1st through 27th Continental regiments fill slowly with the one-year enlistees, meaning that short-term militia units must still be used. The men of a Continental regiment are generally from the same state except for the 1st Continental, which has the original rifle companies. Washington's command at Cambridge becomes the "Main Army," which he organizes into three divisions and six brigades. Washington also raises the new "Union" or "Cambridge" flag of the United Colonies at his

headquarters. It has red and white stripes and a British "union jack" in the upper corner.

6 January. **Hamilton's Battery. New York City.**
New York approves formation of an artillery company (battery). Nineteen-year-old Alexander Hamilton applies to command it and passes proficiency tests. He is commissioned a captain on 14 March and given the command. The unit is transferred to the Continental Army on the 17th. (Now designated Battery D, 1st Battalion, 5th Artillery, it is the oldest continually serving Regular U.S. Army unit.)

9 January. **Continental Army Strength. Cambridge.**
Of the 8,212 men on the Main Army rosters, only 5,582 are present and fit for duty. Washington writes to the New England states requesting 13 more militia regiments to serve 60 days. Congress authorizes Schuyler to recruit three regiments in the Northern Department, including two of Canadians, designated the 1st and 2nd Canadian Regiments.

10 January. **Arnold Promoted. Philadelphia.**
Congress promotes Benedict Arnold to brigadier general in recognition of his personal heroism and leadership on the march to Quebec and the assault on the city.

17 January. **Arrest of Sir Johnson. Albany, New York.**
Schuyler effectively ends loyalist support in the area by forcing Sir John Johnson, the New York Tory commander, to disarm and disperse the Mohawk Indians and loyalist militia he is assembling on his estate. Johnson is taken to an Army post and confined.

24 January. **Knox Arrives. Cambridge.**
Knox arrives with the cannon he brought more than 300 miles from Ticonderoga on boats and sleds. He has not lost even one, although several had to be retrieved out of icy rivers.

27 February. **Battle of Moore's Creek Bridge. North Carolina.**
The 1st North Carolina Regiment under Colonel James Moore, reinforced with other troops, defeats a larger group of Highland loyalists. The patriots inflict heavy losses and capture many, weakening loyalist strength in the state.

2–10 March. **Fortifying Dorchester Heights. Dorchester, Massachusetts.**
Washington plans to lure British troops out of Boston and then seize the town by an amphibious assault. He orders the placement of cannon in concealed batteries on Dorchester Heights within range of Boston. For three nights American guns fire on Boston, then cease firing before dawn and are hidden. During the third night, infantry fortify the Heights under cover of the noise. Chief Engineer Gridley uses "chandeliers"—

prefabricated wooden frames covered with earth—to save time. Overnight the new cannon are in place. The British prepare to boat over and assault the Heights as Washington prepares his own amphibious assault force. Both operations are disrupted by a fierce three-day storm, and the British decide to abandon Boston. The last troops leave on the 15th.

12 March. Commander's Guard Formed. Cambridge.

Washington requests four candidates from each of the 24 Main Army regiments. The men must be native-born Americans and 5'9"–5'10" tall. From these he selects 50 men for an elite Commander in Chief's

Guard under Captain Caleb Gibbs. The men will serve as his personal escort and headquarters guard and will perform special missions.

May. Naval Service. Delaware Bay.

The Pennsylvania militia artillery company of Captain Thomas Proctor serve as gun crews aboard the Continental Navy ship *Hornet,* where they fight in the engagement with the British frigate *Roebuck.*

2–8 May. Wooster Relieved. Quebec.

Major General John Thomas arrives in Quebec and relieves the inept Wooster, who had taken over from Arnold in April. Thomas finds a poorly positioned American army with only 250 effective soldiers. When the British sally out of Quebec on 6 May, Thomas begins a fighting retreat back toward Montreal. Smallpox breaks out among the Americans, and Thomas is infected.

19 May. The Cedars. Canada.

This small American outpost west of Montreal surrenders after two days of siege by a British-Indian force. Several American relief columns are ambushed and defeated.

Opposite: *The American assault parties become lost in the Quebec streets and are either killed or captured by the British-Canadian defenders. ("Barricade in Quebec," Sydney Adamson, Library of Congress)*

Above: *First raised by Washington at Cambridge, this flag, known as the Grand Union, is the first national flag to officially fly over the new Continental Army. (Photo, Mr. and Mrs. B. Mastai Collection)*

Right: *Washington confers with his engineers to select the best location for siege positions around Boston. ("Washington at Boston," Frank T. Merrill, John Hancock Mutual Life Insurance Company)*

16 June. Battle of Chambly. New York.
Arnold commands the American rear guard in a delaying action at Chambly while the survivors of the Northern Army retreat to Crown Point.

26 June. Hickey Plot to Kill Washington. New York City.
Thomas Hickey, an enlisted member of the Commander in Chief's Guard, is court-martialed and found guilty of mutiny and sedition. At least ten members of the Guard joined with Tories in a conspiracy to kill Washington. Hickey had approached one of the headquarters cooks to poison Washington's food, but the cook exposed the plot and the group was arrested. Hickey—the first Continental Army soldier to be executed—is hanged in the center of the city on the 28th.

1 June. Sullivan Arrives. St. John's, Canada.
Brigadier General John Sullivan arrives with reinforcements and takes command from the dying Thomas. Sullivan a counterattack by 2,000 men to seize Trois Rivieres, unaware it is garrisoned by 6,000 British Regulars.

8–14 June. Attack on Trois Rivieres. Canada.
The Americans become lost in the dark, but Colonel Anthony Wayne's group routs a superior British force. The main attack, however, is repulsed. The retreating Americans find their boats gone, and they break into small groups to escape in the swamps. Brigadier William Thompson is taken prisoner—the first American Army general to be captured—and more than 600 men are lost. Arnold barely gets out of Montreal and across the river with 300 men on the 9th, and Sullivan evacuates his camp only an hour before the British arrive. The Americans begin a long withdrawal back to Lake Champlain.

12 June. Board of War and Ordnance. Philadelphia.
Congress sets up a five-member congressional committee to supervise a Board of War and Ordnance that will be appointed to manage the American war effort. The board is the forerunner of the War Department and later the Department of Defense.

Above: *The life of the Revolutionary War prisoner on both sides of the conflict was hard and often fatal from disease. Americans kept on British prison ships were especially vulnerable. (Charles Allen Munn Collection, Fordham University Library)*

28 June. **Battle of Fort Sullivan. South Carolina.**
On 4 June, a British fleet arrives and attacks Fort Sullivan, the key to Charleston's defenses. Colonel William Moultrie has only 26 cannons to reply to the 100 guns of the warships. The American gunners cause heavy losses to the ships with little damage to themselves due to the fort's sand and palmetto log construction, which absorbs the British shot and shell. When the flagpole is hit, Sergeant William Jasper, 2d South Carolina Regiment, races out to repair the pole and reraise the blue "Palmetto" flag. At sunset, the battered British ships depart, ending the British threat for three years. (The fort is later renamed Fort Moultrie.)

July. **Frontier Warfare. Southern Department.**
Armed and encouraged by British agents, bands of Cherokees begin raiding settlements. In Virginia, five militia companies defend Eaton's Station while Fort Lee on the Watauga River survives a two-week siege. When other Cherokee bands hit Carolina and Georgia settlements, the militia responds by destroying Indian villages.

4 July. **Independence Declared. Philadelphia.**
The 2nd Continental Congress approves the Declaration of Independence. Washington announces it to his army at a mass formation on the evening of 9 July.

5–7 July. **Crown Point Abandoned. New York.**
Major Generals Schuyler and Gates arrive as the remnants of the Northern Army reach Crown Point. Only 5,000 of the returnees are fit for duty. Crown Point is in such poor condition that it is abandoned. The British halt at the northern end of the lake to build a fleet of boats. To counter this threat, Gates authorizes Arnold to build an American fleet. Within days, workers are gathered and construction begins.

22–29 August. **Battle of Long Island. New York.**
A British force lands on Long Island against scattered resistance from American detachments under Putnam. The British slip behind the American lines during the night of 26 August and capture many Continentals—including Major Generals William Alexander (Lord Stirling) and John Sullivan—in heavy fighting. The rest flee to Brooklyn Heights. Washington realizes the danger of being cut off and, during the night of the 29th, slips his army across the river to Manhattan.

September. **Continental Army. Philadelphia.**
Anticipating the loss of many of the one-year soldiers at the end of the year, Congress changes the enlistments in the Continental Army to "the duration of the war." This is unpopular and recruiting is difficult, leaving many units understrength.

7 September. First Army Submarine. New York.
Army Sergeant Ezra Lee takes a one-man submarine, *Turtle*, to attack HMS *Eagle* off Staten Island. The attack fails when something prevents the attachment of the explosive mine. Lee is forced to release the mine and withdraw. Two more attempts are tried during the month, with neither successful. *Turtle* is finally sunk.

15 September. Battle of Kips Bay. Manhattan Island.
Howe lands troops above New York City, scattering the militia. Putnam quickly marches his division out of the city to confront the British and to avoid being cut off. He arrives to find a furious Washington trying unsuccessfully to rally the militia. Even with Putnam's men, the Americans are unable to re-form and must retreat to Harlem Heights. Washington is almost captured in the withdrawal as the British occupy the city.

16 September. Battle of Harlem Heights.
A patrol of Major Thomas Knowlton's Rangers encounters a larger British force and is forced to retreat with the British in pursuit sounding fox horns—an insulting reference to a "chase." Washington sends reinforcements, and a sharp fight develops that ends with the British forced back. The small victory heartens the Americans, but Washington knows he must maneuver out of the closing British ring.

Above: *Having lost Boston, the British were determined to take control of New York in the Battle of Long Island on 27 August 1776. ("Battle of Long Island," National Guard Heritage Print)*

Below: *The Continental Army's* American Turtle *was the first submarine ever used in combat. For reasons unknown, it failed in this and two subsequent attempts against British men-of-war and was finally scuttled. ("The* American Turtle," *U.S. Navy Historical Center)*

Opposite: *The Battle of Long Island was a disaster for the American forces, and Washington was barely able to save portions of his army. New York and Long Island remained in the possession of the British until 1784. (The Granger Collection, New York)*

22 September. Nathan Hale Hanged. New York City.
Captain Nathan Hale of Knowlton's Rangers is hanged after being discovered the previous day in disguise behind British lines. Washington had requested a Ranger officer for the mission and Hale volunteered. Posing as a schoolmaster, Hale spent ten days wandering British camps before being arrested and exposed by a Tory cousin.

11–14 October. Battle of Valcour Island. Lake Champlain.
In the first "fleet" action of the United States, Brigadier General Benedict Arnold leads his small Army flotilla of 15 assorted schooners, galleys, and gunboats into action near Valcour Island against a British invasion force of 53 ships and gunboats and an army of 13,000 men. Arnold is outgunned but positions his boats in a narrow channel between the island and lake shore, handicapping the larger British boats and drawing them in. The two fleets battle until nightfall. After dark, Arnold leads his silenced fleet through the British blockade and escapes. The next day a running battle is fought as the British ships gradually close on the fleeing Americans. Arnold finally beaches and burns his last boats and takes the survivors to Ticonderoga. His defense of the lake has delayed a British invasion until spring.

18–22 October. Main Army. New York.
As Washington is evacuating his army north to White Plains, Colonel John Glover's 14th Continentals delay a British landing at Pell's Point that threatens Washington's flank. Farther north, at Mamaroneck, on the 22nd, Colonel John Haslet's Delaware Regiment defeats Major Robert Rogers' regiment of Queen's American Rangers. Rogers had offered his services to Washington at the start of the war, but Washington turned him away. Washington leaves a 2,800-man garrison under Colonel Robert Magaw at Fort Washington on the northern end of Manhattan to deny the Hudson River to British ships.

18 October . Kosciuszko Commissioned. Philadelphia.
Congress grants former Polish Army officer Thadeusz Kosciuszko a commission as a colonel of engineers. He goes north to assist in defending Ticonderoga.

28–31 October. Battle of White Plains. New York.
The British move against Washington at White Plains, making the main attack against the key American right flank on Chatterton's Hill. Hamilton's lone battery helps hold back the attacks until the supporting militia panic, and the hill is lost. Despite a desperate resistance by Haslet's and Charles Webb's Continentals, the Americans must withdraw north. Washington splits his

EYEWITNESS: BATTLE OF VALCOUR BAY, 1776

Right: *The Battle of Valcour Bay, 11–13 October 1776, was yet another example of the aggressive military skill of Benedict Arnold. Though not a victory, the battle delayed the British advance for months. His later act of treason was a hard blow to Washington. (U.S. Navy Historical Center)*

In the second year of the Revolution, British forces were pushing down Lake Champlain. Brigadier General Benedict Arnold, one of the most aggressive and capable American commanders, led a flotilla of hastily built gunboats and galleys to confront and hopefully delay the larger British fleet. Arnold carefully selected his battleground in the narrows along Valcour Island, where the British superiority in numbers would be diminished.

"Yesterday morning at eight o'clock, the enemy fleet… appeared off the Cumberland Head. We immediately prepared to receive them. . . . At eleven o'clock they ran under the lee of Valcour and began the attack. The schooner, by some bad management, fell to leeward and was first attacked; one of her masts was wounded, and her rigging shot away. The captain thought prudent to run her on the point of Valcour, where all the men were saved. They boarded her and at night set fire to her. At half past twelve the engagement became very warm. Some of the enemy's ship's and all her gondolas beat and rowed up within musket-shot of us. They continued a very hot fire with round and grape-shot until five o'clock, when they thought proper to retire to about six or seven hundred yards distance, and continued the fire until dark. The *Congress* and *Washington* have suffered greatly; the latter lost her first lieutenant killed, captain and master wounded. The *New York* lost all her officers, except her captain. The *Philadelphia* was hulled in so many places that she sunk in about one hour after the

engagement was over. The whole killed and wounded amounts to about 60. The enemy landed a large number of Indians on the island and each shore, who kept up an incessant fire on us, but did little damage. The enemy had to appearance, upwards of one thousand bateaus, prepared for boarding. we suffered much for want of seamen and gunners. I was obliged myself to point most of the guns on board the *Congress*, which I believe did good execution. The *Congress* received seven shot between wind and water, was hulled a dozen times, had her mainmast wounded in two places and her yard in one. The *Washington* was hulled a number of times, her mainmast shot through, and must have a new one. Both vessels are very leaky and want repairing.

On consulting with General Waterbury and Colonel Wigglesworth, it was thought prudent to return to Crown Point, every vessel's ammunition being nearly three-fourths spent. At seven o'clock Colonel Wigglesworth, being in the *Trumbull*, got underway, the gondolas and small vessels followed, and the *Congress* and *Washington* brought up the rear. The enemy did not attempt to molest us. Most of the fleet is this minute come to anchor. . . . The enemy's fleet is underway to leeward and beating up. As soon as our leaks are stopped, the whole fleet will make the utmost dispatch to Crown Point, where I beg you will send ammunition and your further orders for us."

—*Kevin M. Hymel*

Right: *A Revolution-era cannon was usually manned by at least five men. Here, two men reload the gun while another stands by with the burning fuse and a fourth holds his thumb over the touch-hole to prevent a premature firing. (Don Troiani)*

Below: *Continental cavalry was limited to a few regiments of light dragoons, which carried a smaller flag or color than did infantry. (J. Carlton Jones)*

army, leaving large detachments under Lee and Heath while he takes the rest of the army over the Hudson to New Jersey.

15–30 November. **Battle of Fort Washington. New York.**
The British turn south and attack Colonel Robert Magaw's isolated fort from three directions, overwhelming Magaw. It is a serious loss of men and cannon for Washington's dwindling army. On the 20th, the British cross to New Jersey and move on Washington's headquarters at Fort Lee. An American patrol gives warning, allowing Washington and most of his army to escape. Almost 2,000 American militia leave as their enlistment expires. Washington marches his army south and reaches Trenton ahead of the British in early December. He crosses the Delaware River and orders all boats seized.

26 November. **Continental Artillery Regiments Approved. Philadelphia.**
Congress approves formation of Colonel Charles Harrison's Continental Artillery Regiment (later 1st Continental Artillery) and assigns it to the Southern Army. The men will be recruited in the summer of 1777. Lieutenant Colonel John Lamb's and Colonel John Crane's Continental Artillery Regiments (later 2d and 3d) will be approved in January 1777 and assigned to the Main Army and Northern Department, respectively.

12 December. **Continental Dragoons Formed. Philadelphia.**
Congress gives extraordinary emergency powers to Washington to conduct the war while they adjourn to meet in Baltimore. The first Continental cavalry unit,

a regiment of light dragoons later designated 2d Dragoons, is authorized to be raised by Elisha Sheldon, who is made Lieutenant Colonel/Commandant of Cavalry. Several mounted state militia units already serve with the army. Colonel Theodoric Bland's mounted Virginians transfer to Continental service in March 1777 and are designated 1st Dragoons because of their previous service. (Birthday of the Cavalry/Armor Branch)

13 December. **Major General Lee Captured. New Jersey.**
Relations between Washington and Charles Lee, his next senior general, are strained after White Plains. Lee writes several letters highly critical of Washington proposing he (Lee) be given command of the army, with even greater dictatorial powers. Lee ignores Washington's orders to return to the Main Army and stays in northern New Jersey, where he is captured by a British patrol on the 13th. Lee is held until exchanged in April 1778. Sullivan takes command of Lee's men and rejoins Washington.

Opposite: *A fanciful depiction of mortally wounded Hessian Colonel Johann G. Rahl's surrender to Washington following his defeat at the battle of Trenton, New Jersey. (Alonzo Chappel, Chicago Historical Society)*

Above: *Although only part of his force arrived in time, Washington still was able to overcome the resistance of the surprised Hessian garrison in Trenton, New Jersey, after the famous crossing of the Delaware River on Christmas. ("Trenton, 26 December 1776," H. Charles McBarron, Army Art Collection, NMUSA)*

Below: *Formed out of Essex County, Massachusetts, militia, Colonel John Glover's regiment was always dependable. They became the 14th Continental Regiment. ("Glover's Marblehead Regiment," H. Charles McBarron, Company of Military Historians)*

25–26 December. **Battle of Trenton.**
Washington leads a surprise night attack across the Delaware River during a winter storm. Two detachments turn back, but the third, led by Washington, crosses successfully with artillery. Among his men are Colonel John Stark, Major Aaron Burr, and Lieutenants John Marshall and James Monroe. The Hessian garrison resists and there is some sharp fighting before Knox's artillery convinces them to surrender. Captain William Washington and Monroe are among the few Americans wounded. Washington makes a difficult recrossing of the river, taking the captured supplies and prisoners.

27–29 December. **Emergency Powers Extended. Baltimore, Maryland.**
Congress extends the term of Washington's emergency powers, promotes Henry Knox to brigadier general, and adds 16 regiments of Continental infantry. The new regiments are identified by the names of their commanders, not numbers. Permission is also given to recruit two more light dragoon regiments. To encourage enlistments, the term of Continental service is relaxed to three years.

30 December. **Second Crossing. Trenton.**
Washington recrosses the Delaware River seeking a battle. He persuades the New England militia regiments whose enlistments are expiring, to stay with him for six more weeks.

31 December. **Army Strength.**
The Army ends the year with: Continentals: 46,891; one-year militia: 26,060; short-term militia: 16,700 (est.).

1777

2–3 January. Battle of Trenton/Princeton.
After a day-long series of actions, both armies camp around Trenton, but at 1 a.m. on the 3rd the Continental Army slips past the British and marches on Princeton 12 miles north. When Brigadier General Hugh Mercer's brigade engages a British detachment, Mercer is killed and his men start to break until Washington leads a counterattack. Some British fight from the Princeton College buildings until Hamilton's artillery battery fires directly on them. The Americans break off and depart for their winter camp at Morristown.

6 January–March. Winter Quarters. Morristown.
The American winter quarters are in the hills around the town, where Washington can watch British movements. During the winter his army undertakes a program of inoculations against smallpox. Washington orders active patrolling and foraging raids against the British. Despite a new enlistment bonus of $20 and 100 acres of land, recruiting is slow. The militia's six-week extension ends and many depart. Lee, still a British prisoner, gives them a plan for winning the war by gaining control of the middle states. Fortunately, the British ignore him, and Lee's treason remains unknown for many years.

2–4 February. Fort McIntosh. Satilla River, Georgia.
A Tory force from Florida besieges the small fort for two days, forcing the little garrison of 3d South Carolina Continentals to surrender.

9–19 February. Officers Promoted. Baltimore.
Congress promotes nine colonels to brigadier general, including John Glover and Anthony Wayne. Five new major generals—William Alexander (Lord Stirling), Thomas Mifflin, Adam Stephen, Arthur St. Clair, and Benjamin Lincoln—are also selected, apportioning the selectees among the states. Connecticut, Benedict Arnold's state, already has two generals, so Arnold, who is more senior than some selected, is not promoted. He angrily submits his resignation, but Washington persuades him to withdraw it.

11 April. Surgeon General Replaced. Philadelphia.
Congress appoints Dr. William Shippen to replace John Morgan as the Director-General of Hospitals and Physician in Chief to the Army. Morgan, apparently a difficult man, had been dismissed in January without official explanation.

May. Gambling Prohibited. Morristown.
Washington issues a General Order forbidding gambling. Weapons, powder, and clothing arrive from France and Washington reorganizes the 9,000-man Main Army into five divisions, with Major Generals

Greene, Alexander, Sullivan, Stephen, and Lincoln as commanders. On 29 May Washington moves his army out of winter camp and toward Princeton.

2 May. Arnold Promoted. Philadelphia.
Congress promotes Arnold to major general in recognition for his "gallant conduct" in helping repulse a British attack on Danbury, Connecticut, in April. However, his promotion is not backdated, and Arnold remains junior to those promoted in February, which embitters him.

17 May. Thomas' Swamp. Florida.
British Regulars, Tories, and Indians attack and rout a small militia detachment at Thomas' Swamp. The Indians massacre half the American prisoners.

14 June. United States Flag Adopted. Philadelphia.
Congress approves the first official flag of the United States with stars in the canton rather than the "union" used on the flag of 1775. No guidance is provided as to how the stars—one per state—are to be arrayed.

20 June. Corps of Invalids.
Congress authorizes a Continental Army Corps of Invalids under Major Lewis Nicola. The Corps is composed of men unfit for active field duty but still suitable for guard, recruiting, and other light duties.

The Corps proves to be especially useful in garrison duty at West Point.

26 June. Battle of Woodbridge. New Jersey.
Alexander and his outnumbered division fight a delaying action at Woodbridge that checks a British effort to outflank Washington. Frustrated, the British withdraw to Staten Island.

2–7 July. Attack on Ticonderoga. New York.
After moving down Lake Champlain in June, the British army under Major General John Burgoyne began an assault on the fort by placing cannon on Mount Defiance overlooking the fort. This forces St. Clair, the American commander, to abandon the fort. Before dawn on 6 July, the American sick and wounded are loaded onto boats and sent to Fort Anne near Skenesboro. The rest of the army slips away except the rear guard, who disobey orders and stop to rest at Hubbardton. British troops arrive and hard fighting occurs. The Americans, under Colonel Seth Warner, are winning until Hessians arrive and turn the battle.

8 July. Fort Anne. Skenesboro.
Militia help with the wounded and then join the Continentals in halting the British pursuers. After a two-hour fight, the Americans retreat.

9 July. **British General Captured. Newport, Rhode Island.**
Forty Rhode Island militiamen land at night and abduct Major General Richard Prescott, the British general commanding forces in the state. He will be exchanged for Charles Lee.

22 July. **Senior Engineer Appointed. Philadelphia.**
Congress assigns Le Begue de Presle Duportail, a French officer commissioned Colonel of Engineers on 8 July, as the Continental Army's senior engineer. He becomes an invaluable aide to Washington, and in November is made a brigadier general and Chief of Engineers.

27–30 July. **Fort Edward. New York.**
Although Washington sends Generals Arnold and Lincoln with reinforcements, Schuyler's army can only delay the British advance. Fort Edward is abandoned as the Americans continue to retreat.

31 July. **Lafayette Commissioned. Philadelphia.**
Nineteen-year-old Gilbert du Motier, Marquis de Lafayette, is made a major general—the youngest general officer ever commissioned in the American army. He joins Washington's staff.

2–19 August. **Attack on Fort Stanwix. New York.**
British force begins siege operations against the fort. Colonel Peter Gansevoort has only 750 men in the garrison, and he sends for help. Arnold volunteers to lead a relief force and Schuyler approves. Congress already blames Schuyler for the loss of Ticonderoga and has ordered Gates to the Northern Department. Gates arrives at the Bemis Heights headquarters on the 19th and takes command from Schuyler, who

Above: *Like most generals of the time Washington did not have a professional military staff. He usually made his plans himself and kept them secret until the last moment. (John Ward Dunsmore, Sons of the American Revolution)*

departs and later writes Congress to demand a court-martial.

6–23 August. Battle of Oriskany.
A relief force under Colonel Nicholas Herkimer is ambushed six miles from Fort Stanwix. The surprised Americans battle fiercely and Herkimer, mortally wounded, continues to direct his men. During the fighting, a group from the fort burns the Indian camp. Rain slows the fighting, and when the Indians find their food and supplies destroyed they leave, letting the Americans withdraw. When Gansevoort refuses to surrender, the British return to Oswego.

13–16 August. Battle of Bennington. Vermont.
After a skirmish at Sancoick's Mill, Brigadier General John Stark's state militia defeats a large Hessian foraging force at Bennington. Stark leads a double envelopment to defeat the German position. Stark had resigned from the Continental Army in February when Congress did not promote him and has a state commission to command the militia.

28 August–3 September. British Army Harassed. Middle Department.
Detachments of Continentals and Pennsylvania militia harass and delay the British army as it marches toward Philadelphia from its landing at Elk River. Heavy skirmishing takes place at Elkton, Maryland, and Wilmington and Cooch's Bridge, Delaware.

1 September. Frontier Warfare.
More than 400 Indians attack isolated Fort Henry (now Wheeling, West Virginia), but the garrison holds off the attack despite the loss of almost half its men. Reinforcements arrive the next day, and the Indians withdraw.

11 September. Battle of Brandywine Creek. Pennsylvania.
Washington's Main Army is along the creek between Philadelphia and the British army. While the Hessians divert American attention at Chadd's Ford, the British cross and outflank the Continentals. A shift of American units to meet the threat lets the Hessians penetrate the center. They capture the American artillery and turn the guns around. The furious fight lasts almost two hours as the Americans are pushed back. Lafayette is wounded, and the battle ends with darkness.

15 September. DeKalb and Pulaski Commissioned. Philadelphia.
Congress commissions Baron Johann DeKalb (a German) as major general and Count Casimir Pulaski (a Pole) as brigadier general. Pulaski had served bravely as a volunteer aide to Washington at Brandywine and at Washington's recommendation, Congress approves Pulaski as Commander of the Horse (chief of American dragoons). DeKalb joins the army at Valley Forge.

18 September. Army Saves Liberty Bell. Philadelphia.
As the British advance, Congress prepares to move to Lancaster, Pennsylvania, to avoid capture. The Liberty Bell is secretly sent in an army baggage wagon to Allentown, Pennsylvania, where it is hidden.

19 September. Battle of Freeman's Farm. New York.
Gates' army has fortified Bemis Heights under the direction of Arnold and Kosciuszko, blocking Burgoyne's route. When three British columns advance, Arnold convinces Gates to send him with Morgan's provisional rifle corps and Major Henry Dearborn's light infantry against the center column near Freeman's farm. At the farm, long-range American rifle fire kills many British officers and noncommissioned officers in the open fields. A major

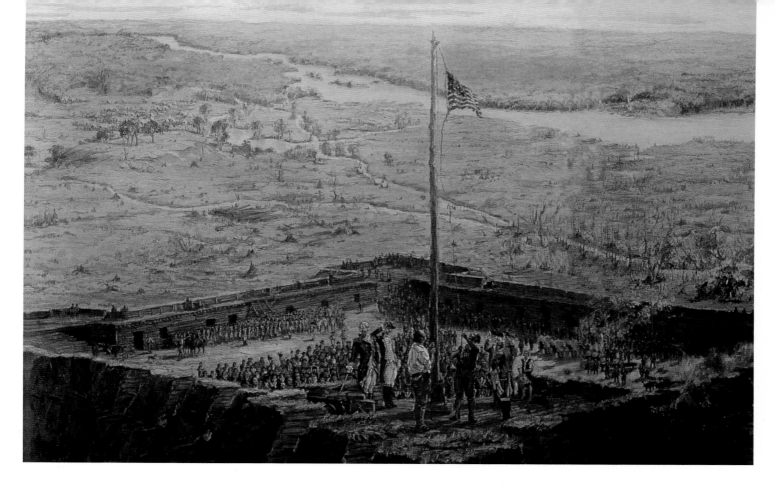

engagement builds and Gates orders a withdrawal, which Arnold ignores until he is forced to retire. Burgoyne goes into fortified positions to wait for promised reinforcements. In his official report, Gates refuses to mention Arnold's role and relieves him from command.

20–23 September. **Battle of Paoli. Pennsylvania.**
When Anthony Wayne camps his division at Warren's Tavern, the British make a midnight bayonet attack

Above: *Fort Stanwix was an important outpost controlling a major travel route from the Hudson River to Lake Ontario. Failure to capture it doomed the western British advance from Canada and contributed to the British defeat at Saratoga. (Rome Historical Society, New York)*

Below: *During the fighting at the battle of Brandywine, Pennsylvania, Brigadier General Marquis de Lafayette was wounded by a British musket ball in the leg. (Library of Congress)*

that overruns the American camp. Wayne's surprised men fight back and are able to save their cannon before retreating.

4 October. Battle of Germantown.
The Continental Army attacks the British camp at dawn, forcing the British regiments back. However, thick morning fog and smoke confuse the maneuvering American units, causing them to fire on one another. A British strongpoint in a stone house further hinders the attack, and Washington orders a withdrawal.

5–6 October. Hudson River Forts. New York.
The British make simultaneous attacks on Forts Clinton and Montgomery along the Hudson River, hoping to help Burgoyne. The outnumbered Americans hold for a short time, then abandon both forts.

7–13 October. Battle of Bemis Heights.
Morgan's infantry engages an advancing British force. Arnold, relieved of his command, is ordered by Gates to stay in his tent. Instead, he rides into the fighting, rallies the faltering American left flank and leads it in a headlong charge that captures two British positions. Arnold's left leg is badly injured again, and Gates submits court-martial charges.

13–17 October. Surrender at Saratoga.
Stark, promoted to Continental Army brigadier general on 4 October, uses his brigade to block a British escape to the north. Trapped, Burgoyne surrenders his army to Gates on the 17th. Gates informs Congress directly, ignoring Washington and further straining relations between the two generals. Gates then requests Congress release him from field duty for reasons of health. On the 17th Congress also reorganizes the Board of War to consist of three men not serving in Congress. Within a few weeks, Gates is named as President of the Board, with Colonel James Wilkinson as secretary.

5 November. Conway Plot. Whitemarsh, New Jersey.
Washington learns that Brigadier General Thomas Conway has written a letter highly critical of him to

Above: *Tattered and torn by the elements and enemy, the Continentals press forward. ("The Nation Makers," Howard Pyle, Brandywine River Museum, Purchased through a grant from the Mabel Pew Myrin Trust, 1984)*

Left: *The British defeat the Americans at the Battle of Brandywine. But their spirited resistance shows the continued improvement in the Continental Army. ("Battle of Brandywine," Rick Reeves)*

Gates. Washington writes a simple two-sentence letter to Conway. Without replying, Conway submits a letter of resignation to Congress, which is sent to the newly established Board of War.

15–20 November. Forts Mifflin and Mercer. Delaware River.
Forts Mifflin and Mercer block the British from using the river to reach Philadelphia. Fort Mifflin is finally leveled after six days of heavy bombardment from British warships and shore batteries, with American losses of more than 300 men. The 40 surviving soldiers set fire to the ruins and escape. Greene orders Fort Mercer abandoned and burned.

13–14 December. Conway Promoted.
Congress ignores Conway's resignation letter and promotes him to major general over 23 senior brigadiers, angering many Continental officers. Conway is given the new position of Inspector General of the Army, reporting directly to Gates on the Board of War rather than to Washington.

19 December. Valley Forge. Pennsylvania.
The Continental Army goes into winter quarters. The men build log shelters but lack food and other supplies. By spring more than 2,000 soldiers are dead of cold and disease. An anonymous pamphlet, *Thoughts of a Freeman*, highly critical of Washington's leadership, is circulated in the Congress and the Army. At winter quarters near Trenton, the four regiments of light dragoons train under Pulaski for offensive operations at a riding school for men and horses.

31 December. Army Strength.
The Army ends the year with: Continentals: 46,891; militia: 26,060; short-term militia: 23,800 (est.).

1778

2 January. Clark Expedition. Williamsburg, Virginia.
George Rogers Clark presents the Virginia Assembly with a plan to capture British outposts and eliminate support for Indians raiders in the Kentucky-Illinois territory. Clark is made a colonel of the Virginia militia, authorized to raise seven rifle companies to implement the plan. His goal is to capture Detroit.

25 January. West Point Fortified. New York.
Washington orders fortifications built at West Point on the Hudson River. Now the home of the U.S. Military Academy, it is the oldest American military post in continuous occupation by U.S. soldiers.

9–23 February. Conway Conspiracy. Valley Forge.
Washington writes scathing letters to Gates and prominent congressmen about Conway's disloyalty, bringing the scheming into the open. Gates blames his aide, Wilkinson, who challenges Gates to a duel. Gates apologizes on the "field of honor," and Conway resigns in April. Baron Friedrich Wilhelm von Steuben arrives in camp on February 23rd as volunteer aide to Washington.

2 March. **Quartermaster Named. Valley Forge.**
Congress reorganizes the Army's logistical system and Washington asks Nathanael Greene to be Quartermaster General. Greene reluctantly accepts the position.

8 March. **Soldiers Serve on Ships. Barbados.**
An entire infantry company from the 1st South Carolina Regiment is killed when the frigate *Randolph* blows up during a sea battle with a British warship off the Barbados coast. The Continentals were serving as marines aboard the ship, a frequent practice.

19 March. **First Drill. Valley Forge.**
Von Steuben conducts the first drill training for the Continental Main Army. He selects and personally drills 100 men as a demonstration company, then uses them to train others. His drill regulations, known as the "Blue Book," are written with the help of Alexander Hamilton and eventually adopted for the Army. Von Steuben emphasizes the role of officers as trainers of their men and develops a new battle formation of two ranks rather than three, thus giving the American battle lines more firepower.

28 March. **Pulaski Legion. Valley Forge.**
Frustrated by his conflicts with American officers, Count Pulaski resigns as Commander of Horse and receives permission to raise a small "independent corps" of light infantry and lancers, to be called the "Pulaski Legion," for use in raids and scouting.

10 April. **Army Pensions. Valley Forge.**
Washington writes to the president of the Congress,

Henry Laurens in support of pension and widow benefits for Continental officers. Congress, afraid of a professional army, debates the proposal hotly and approves a modified version in May. The efforts of Greene and Commissary-General Jeremiah Wadsworth improve the flow of supplies, and new recruits arrive at the camp.

5 May. **Von Steuben Made Inspector General. Valley Forge.**
Congress appoints Von Steuben a major general and Inspector General (IG) of the Army. Details of the position's duties, responsibilities, and relationship to the chain of command are left unspecified, causing problems with some commanders. The next day, Continentals demonstrate their new drill proficiency with a grand review. The Main Army is at 13,000 men, the strongest in months, and is well trained. On 20 May, Major General Charles Lee, exchanged in April, arrives in camp looking for a command.

27 May. **Clark Expedition. Corn Island, Ohio River.**
Clark arrives and discovers that only three of the seven companies have been recruited. The Continental garrison at Fort Pitt is too small to send men, leaving him a mostly Virginian militia force. Undaunted, Clark fortifies Corn Island and begins training. When he explains the mission, some militia desert.

27 May. **Marechausse Corps Formed. Philadelphia.**
Formation of a small unit of Army military police is approved to assist the Provost Marshal in keeping order in camp and preventing desertion. Its members include four official executioners. The unit is organized

GEORGE ROGERS CLARK

One of the lesser known giants of the Revolution is George Rogers Clark, yet his victory in the western theater of the Revolution secured the critical Ohio and Mississippi river valleys for the new United States. Clark was a Virginian, born 19 November 1752 near Charlottesville. As a boy he received little formal education, but his close relationship with neighbor George Mason helped him to become widely read. Taught surveying by his grandfather, Clark made his first surveying expedition down the Ohio River at age 19. Long-distance expeditions molded Clark into a first-class woodsman and frontier fighter. In 1774, at age 21, Clark served as a militia captain during Lord Dunmore's War, fighting against the Shawnee Indians.

When the Revolution began, Clark successfully petitioned Governor Patrick Henry and the Virginia legislature to accept Kentucky as a county of Virginia. Clark was made commander of the county's militia with the rank of major and charged with its defense. In 1778 Clark's daring plan to capture the Illinois territory from the British won Henry's approval. Clark was promoted to lieutenant colonel with authority to recruit 200 men for three months. By February 1779, in a daring, hardship-filled expedition, Clark and his small force had taken the key British forts in the area. They successfully secured them against British and Indian counterattacks. The only prize that escaped him was Detroit. He planned three different expeditions but was never given the resources to carry them out. At the war's end, Brigadier General Clark's hold on the territory ensured its transfer to the United States. His campaign was the only successful American invasion of enemy-held territory.

Clark and his men had received no pay during the war, forcing Clark to spend his own money on supplies. His petition to Virginia for $20,000 in back pay and expenses was unsuccessful, and he never received the land Virginia granted his regiment. Nearly destitute, Clark served as Kentucky's Indian commissioner. In 1786 Clark led his last military expedition against the Wabash Indians in the Northwest Territory. It failed due to the mutiny of the Kentucky militia. That same year, Clark fell victim to the intrigues of James Wilkinson, an ambitious schemer who maligned Clark and caused his removal. At 35, Clark was discredited, unemployed, and in debt.

In 1803 Clark built a cabin at Clarksville (Indiana) and ran a grist mill. There he entertained his younger brother, William, who was on his way to explore the Louisiana Territory. In 1809 Clark suffered a stroke with partial paralysis, followed by an accident that resulted in the amputation of his right leg. These injuries, combined with arthritis contracted during his campaigns, left him crippled and almost speechless. In 1812, Virginia finally granted him a $400 annual pension and a sword. Clark died 13 February 1818 at age 65, in his sister's home near Louisville, Kentucky. His last, whispered words were, "Come on, my brave boys! St. Vin----."

—*Vince Hawkins*

Above: *The undaunted leadership of George Rogers Clark secured the Illinois-Ohio territory for the struggling United States, opening the route for future expansion into what became the Northwest Territory. ("George Rogers Clark," John Wesley Jarvis, Virginia State Library)*

Left: *Baron Von Steuben volunteered to serve in America's new army without pay or compensation. He was given the task of training the Continental Army to stand up to the British regulars, who would have to be defeated on the open field of battle if victory was to be earned. Many of his ideas on the use of junior officers and NCOs to train their men can be seen in the Army today. (Jack Keay, Marshall Cavendish Corporation)*

1 June. Congress also authorizes a Corps of Miners and Sappers, consisting of three companies for the Main Army, but it is not formed until August 1780.

29 May. Frontier Warfare. Kentucky.
A small blockhouse is saved from a surprise Indian attack by the efforts of two men who defend the door until the rest of the militia garrison awaken. One, a slave, Dick Pointer, is bought by the Virginia Assembly and given his freedom as a reward for his heroism.

1 June. Cobbleskill Raid. New York.
The town is sacked and burned by Tories and Mohawks. Most of the defending Continental soldiers and settlers are killed.

16–18 June. Philadelphia Liberated. Pennsylvania.
After Saratoga, the British consolidate their forces in New York City, and on the 16th they begin moving out of Philadelphia. Arnold, appointed American military commander of Philadelphia, arrives on the 18th.

24–28 June. Clark Expedition. Illinois Country.
Clark leaves a small detachment behind to guard supplies, loads 175 men on flatboats, shoots the rapids, and heads down river. The men row day and night for four days, then land and march overland 120 miles to Kaskaskia, Illinois.

28 June. Battle of Monmouth. New Jersey.
Charles Lee is given command of the leading American units with orders to attack the British near the Monmouth Courthouse. Lee's vague instructions cause confusion and a retreat. Washington rushes forward, angrily berates Lee, and relieves him. Taking personal command, Washington rallies the troops to fight the British to a draw. During the long artillery duel "Molly Pitcher" (Mary Hays) works an artillery piece for her wounded husband.

3–4 July. Wyoming Valley Massacre. New York.
Forty Fort is attacked by over 1,200 Tories and Indians. When the garrison refuses to surrender, the town is set afire. Despite warnings, the 450 militia and Continentals rush out and are ambushed in the woods. Almost all are killed or captured and tortured to death.

4 July. Lee's Court-Martial. New Jersey.
After the Monmouth battle, Lee writes two insulting letters to Washington and demands an immediate inquiry. Washington arrests Lee and the court-martial lasts until August. Lee is found guilty of disobedience, misbehavior, and disrespect and is suspended from the Army for a year. He continues to write angry letters, and Congress officially discharges him in January 1780.

4–20 July. Capture of Kaskaskia and Vincennes. Illinois Country.
Clark and his men cross the Kaskaskia River during the night. They find the town undefended and the gates to the fort open. The British commander is captured, and Clark's men patrol the town streets. The next day a mounted detachment is sent to demand the surrender of other towns in the area. Although the inhabitants far outnumbered his men, Clark cleverly creates the impression that his "Long Knives" are the advance of a larger army. On 20 July, Vincennes, Clark's last objective, surrenders peacefully.

August. Frontier Warfare. Fort Pitt, Pennsylvania.
Brigadier General Lachlan McIntosh arrives with two regiments of Continentals—the 8th Pennsylvania and 14th Virginia—and assumes command of the fort. McIntosh builds and garrisons Forts McIntosh and Laurens farther west as support bases.

1 August. French Arrive. Rhode Island.
French Admiral Comte d'Estaing arrives with his fleet and lands the first French troops. The plan is to capture Newport in a coordinated operation using American land forces under Sullivan and the French warships, but relations between Sullivan and the French are difficult.

15–29 August. Battle of Newport. Rhode Island.
While waiting for French support, Sullivan bombards Newport and readies his army. D'Estaing refuses to cooperate and departs with his fleet and troops. Discouraged, Sullivan's militia desert, forcing him to withdraw. The British follow and attack the retreating Americans. Finally Greene, holding Sullivan's right flank, counterattacks, sending the British-Hessian force back to their fortifications.

7–16 September. Defense of Boonesboro. Kentucky.
Militia under Major Daniel Boone defend the stockade for nine days against a determined attack by Shawnees and Chippewas. The Indians finally depart

Opposite, bottom: *The Provost Company of Light Dragoons was the military police force of the Continental Army, with the mission to patrol rear areas, secure headquarters, and round up deserters and stragglers. ("Provost Company," Frederick Chapman, Company of Military Historians)*

Right: *Major General Charles Lee's poor leadership almost loses the Battle of Monmouth, New Jersey, before an angry Washington arrives to rally his men. It is said that "Washington swore like an angel." (H. Charles McBarron, Company of Military Historians)*

AMERICAN WOMEN AND THE CONTINENTAL ARMY

Left: *Not infrequently, women "camp followers" served as water carriers for artillery gun crews. "Molly Pitcher" (Mary Hays) and her courage in stepping forward to fill her wounded husband's place at his cannon became an American legend. ("Molly Pitcher," Fraunces Tavern Museum)*

Although social expectations limited the scope of women's contributions to the war effort, Revolutionary-era women aided their country in a wide variety of ways, many of which have been forgotten by history. Women were unable to join local militias or enlist in the Continental Army, but many accompanied their soldier husbands to war as "camp followers," the customary term used for all non-military persons accompanying an army. Jemima Warner, the wife of Private James Warner, a member of Thompson's Pennsylvania Rifle Battalion, went with her husband on Colonel Benedict Arnold's expedition to capture Quebec during the winter of 1775–76 because she was worried about his health. During the trek north, Private Warner became so ill that he dropped out of the column and died within hours. His wife covered his body with leaves, picked up his musket, and traveled 20 miles to catch up with the others. On 11 December 1775, during the siege of Quebec, the widowed Jemima Warner was killed by enemy fire.

Margaret Cochran Corbin was with her husband John, a matross (artilleryman) with Proctor's Pennsylvania Artillery, during the defense of Fort Tryon on 15 November 1776. When John Corbin was killed, Margaret continued to serve the cannon until she was wounded. When the British eventually captured the fort, Margaret was sent to a hospital in New York City. In 1777, she went to Philadelphia and was assigned to the Continental Invalid Corps until formally mustered out of the Army in 1783. She was given an annual military pension of half her dead husband's pay. Corbin was the first woman to receive a government pension for war-related activities.

Women who accompanied their husbands to war typically found less dramatic chores that needed to be done. Many worked as cooks, laundresses, seamstresses, and nurses, for either rations or pay. Army regulations authorized a certain number of women (usually three to six per company) to draw rations for themselves and their children for these services. Life with the Army was far from easy. Sarah Osborn's husband insisted that she accompany him when he enlisted as a commissary sergeant with the Third New York Regiment. Sarah cooked for her husband's unit and was present at the Battle of Yorktown. A dissatisfied nurse named Alice Redman petitioned the Maryland Council of Safety in 1776, complaining that she was paid $2 a month and had 16 men to cook for and take care of. Her rations did not include tea or coffee, which she longed for, and she was obliged to use part of her salary to buy brooms and soap to keep her ward clean.

Toward the end of the war, Deborah Sampson Gannett disguised herself as a man and enlisted in the 4th Massachusetts as Robert Shurtliff. The majority of Deborah's 18 months of service took place after the Battle of Yorktown, when fighting between local Patriot and Tory forces was still going on near West Point. When Deborah was wounded in the leg by Tory guerrillas, she was forced to see a doctor. When he discovered her to be a woman, Deborah was honorably discharged. Years later, Deborah petitioned the federal government for a pension, which was granted.

—*Judi Bellefaire*

Right: *Militia Major Daniel Boone escaped from Shawnee captivity just in time to warn Fort Boonesboro of the immanent attack from the Indians. This is a sketch of the fort. (James R. Stuart, State Historical Society of Wisconsin)*

Boone's Fort

when the tunnel they are digging under the stockade wall collapses in heavy rains.

1 October. **Schuyler Court-Martial. Pawling, New York.**
Philip Schuyler's court-martial for the loss of Ticonderoga begins. After a short trial, Schuyler is acquitted but no longer has a command. He resigns in April 1779.

11 November. **Defense of Fort Alden. New York.**
Tories, Senecas, and Mohawks attack Cherry Valley. Despite warnings from scouts, the commander, Colonel Ichabod Alden, is killed in the attack. His 7th Massachusetts Continentals under Major Daniel Whiting defend the fort, but the town is burned.

17 December. **Vincennes Retaken. Illinois Country.**
A force of 800 British Regulars, Indians, and Canadians from Detroit surprise the American detachment and capture Fort Sackville.

December. **Attack on Savannah. Georgia.**
In mid-December British forces land and march on Savannah. They outflank the American positions and take the city on the 29th. Large amounts of supplies

and ammunition are lost. Major General Benjamin Lincoln, the new American commander in the south, arrives too late to help.

31 December. **Army Strength.**
Washington has placed his army into winter quarters in New York, New Jersey, and Connecticut. The Army ends the year with: Continentals: 32,899; militia: 4,353; short-term militia: 13,800 (est.).

1779

6–29 January. **Fort Morris. Georgia.**
The fort's garrison is forced to surrender to a much larger British force. On 29 January, Augusta is occupied without a fight by Tories from South Carolina.

3 February. **Charges Against Arnold. Philadelphia.**
Congress receives accusations of dishonesty and profiteering against Benedict Arnold, along with reports that he is associating with wealthy Tories. Washington defends him, but Arnold demands an inquiry.

Left: *On 25 February 1779, after an epic winter march, George Rogers Clark captures Fort Sackville at Vincennes on the Wabash River. It is a major victory in securing the region for the United States ("Vincennes," H. Charles McBarron, Company of Military Historians)*

Below: *Seeking revenge for the attack on his camp at Paoli, Pennsylvania, General Anthony Wayne leads his light infantry in a similar night bayonet attack to seize the British defenses at Stony Point, New York. (Constantino Brumidi, Office of the Architect of the Capitol)*

3 February. **Battle of Beaufort. South Carolina.**
Brigadier General William Moultrie and a militia force successfully defend Port Royal Island against a landing party of British troops.

5 February. **Clark Marches on Vincennes.**
Clark takes a small detachment of 170 men on an incredible three-week, 180-mile march through icy streams and flooded prairies to recapture Fort Sackville. Clark orders his officers to lead the way and threatens to shoot any man who turns back.

10–14 February. **Battle of Kettle Creek. Georgia.**
South Carolina and Georgia militia led by Colonel John Pickens attack Tories at Carr's Fort. Pickens learns of a larger Tory force approaching and breaks off the fighting to intercept them. He circles behind the Tories and launches a surprise assault that defeats them.

18 February. **Congress Issues Plan for Inspector General Duties. Philadelphia.**
Congress establishes the Army Inspector General as a noncommand staff position reporting to Washington. Von Steuben continues his training program and sets up a system of inspectors for the entire Army.

23–25 February. **Fort Sackville Retaken. Vincennes.**
Clark's demand for unconditional surrender is refused, so the Americans surround the fort, picking off

defenders. After several days, two Indians are caught returning from Kentucky with American captives and fresh scalps. Clark has them tomahawked and scalped in front of the fort. The British surrender, and the American flag is again raised over Vincennes.

29 March. Slaves Proposed for Army Service. Philadelphia.

A large number of African-Americans are serving in the New England army units. To raise critical manpower in the south, Congress writes to the South Carolina and Georgia assemblies suggesting that 3,000 slaves be enlisted into the militia. The owners would be paid and, if the slaves gave good service, they would be granted their freedom and $50 at the end of the war. The proposal is rejected by both states.

1 April. Frontier Warfare. Kentucky.

Indians continue to raid the American settlers and outposts in the south. Colonel Evan Shelby leads 900 Virginia and South Carolina militia in a month-long campaign, destroying the hostile Indian villages along the Clinch, Powell, and Tennessee rivers.

21 April. Frontier Warfare. New York.

An expedition of Continentals under Colonel Gose Van Schaick completes a 180-mile march to destroy the main village of the Onondaga Indians. Twenty Indians are killed and some are taken prisoner.

9–11 May. Fort Nelson. Norfolk, Virginia.

A British naval expedition attacks Fort Nelson, which guards Norfolk, Portsmouth, and the American shipyards in the area. The small garrison evacuates the fort and flees. The British seize large quantities of supplies and weapons and burn or take 137 ships.

Right: *Light infantry troops under Marquis de Fleury pull down the British flag after capturing Stony Point, New York. Initially commissioned as an engineer, de Fleury also served with dragoons and as a trainer. ("The Fort's Our Own," Dale Gallon)*

20 June. Battle of Stono Ferry. South Carolina.
Lincoln leads Continentals and Carolina militia on a dawn assault against the British fortifications on James Island. The Americans meet strong resistance and must withdraw.

2 July. Battle of Pound Ridge. New York.
British light dragoons and mounted Tory rangers attack the 2nd Continental Dragoons in their camp. Badly outnumbered, the Continentals retreat until local militia arrive to help drive the British from the field.

15–16 July. Battle of Stony Point.
Major General "Mad" Anthony Wayne leads his provisional light infantry corps in a night bayonet attack to retake the fort at Stony Point. In the dark, the British outposts are fooled by a feint while American columns move silently past them. Wayne, with the main assault, is slightly wounded as the Americans break into the fort and capture it in hand-to-hand fighting.

11 August. Brodhead Expedition. Fort Pitt, Pennsylvania.
Colonel Daniel Brodhead, the fort commander, leads 600 Continentals and militia against the hostile Indians in the Allegheny Valley. Brodhead's force returns to Pitt a month later after traveling some 400 miles and destroying ten villages.

13 August. Penobscot Expedition. Castine, Maine.
Without consulting Washington, Massachusetts sends militia to attack the British base at Penobscot. The poorly planned effort ends in disaster when British reinforcements arrive. The militia burn their boats and flee into the woods, losing over 400 men.

18–19 August. Battle of Paulus Hook. New Jersey.
Major Henry ("Light Horse Harry") Lee leads Virginians, Marylanders, and his own dismounted dragoons in a night attack on the British fort. Despite getting lost, Lee and his men successfully breach the British defenses with bayonets, seize the fort, and withdraw.

19–29 August. Sullivan Expedition. Tioga, Pennsylvania.
After months of slow progress, Major General Sullivan begins a campaign against the Iroquois on the New York-Pennsylvania frontier with an army of almost 4,000 Continental infantry, artillery, and militia. On the 29th, scouts discover a British force waiting in ambush near Newtown. The Americans outflank the enemy, forcing them to retire.

11–12 May. Attack on Charleston. South Carolina.
British forces pursue Colonel Moultrie to Charleston and demand the city's surrender. When a mounted attack by Pulaski and his legion fails, command of the city's defense is given to Moultrie, who refuses to surrender. An American relief column forces the British to withdraw.

23 May. Arnold's Treason. Philadelphia.
Arnold, bitter at the delay of his hearing, sends a letter to the British offering his services. The British are delighted, and a series of letters is exchanged in which Arnold negotiates his price.

1 June. Attacks on Stony Point and Verplanck's Point. New York.
In preparation for a campaign up the Hudson River to capture West Point the British attack the forts guarding the river. The unfinished blockhouse at Stony Point is easily taken, and across the river, a heavy bombardment of Fort Lafayette forces it to surrender.

4–14 September. **Sullivan Expedition. New York.**
En route to the main Iroquois town, the advance party led by Lieutenant Thomas Boyd is ambushed. Boyd is captured, interrogated, and tortured. His remains are found in the town the next day. Sullivan burns the town and more than 40 others, destroying an estimated 160,000 bushels of corn and beans.

2 October. **Continental Army Uniform. Morristown, New Jersey.**
An Army General Order establishes blue as the basic color of the Continental Army uniform coat and specifies trim colors for units: artillery and artificers, scarlet facings and lining; light dragoons, white facing and lining; infantry, white lining with white, buff, red, or blue facings for different states. Except for short periods, the Army has had a blue uniform ever since. Today it is a formal dress uniform.

9–20 October. **Siege of Savannah. Georgia.**
American and French troops attack British positions around the town but are turned back with heavy losses. Pulaski is fatally wounded by grapeshot while leading a charge and d'Estaing is wounded. Discouraged, the French depart, forcing Lincoln to retreat back to Charleston.

5 December. **Main Army in Winter Quarters. Morristown.**
The Continental Army settles in after a difficult march. Many units arrive without their baggage, leaving the soldiers unprepared for the severe weather. As tools and equipment appear, log huts are built. It will be the most trying winter the Army and Washington will endure.

23 December. **Arnold's Court-Martial. Middlebrook.**
Arnold's court-martial finally convenes, with Arnold acting as his own defense counsel.

31 December. **Army Strength.**
The Army ends the year with: Continentals: 27,699; militia: 5,135; short-term militia: 12,350.

Opposite: *The Continental Army uniforms provided little camouflage, but they proudly displayed the colors of the red and blue that will mark Army uniforms for many years. (National Park Service)*

Below: *One of the first tasks facing troops preparing a winter camp is the construction of the huts and other buildings that would shelter them until the next campaign. (Don Troiani, National Park Service)*

1780

---

1 January. **West Point Mutiny. New York.**
About 100 Massachusetts men at West Point mutiny and leave for home, claiming their enlistments are up. When they are brought back, the ringleaders receive only light punishment.

9 January. **Main Army Supply Problems. Morristown, New Jersey.**
Food is scarce at the Continental Army's winter encampment. Against Washington's orders, soldiers begin to forage for themselves in the countryside. He decides to reorganize the requisition system, dividing the states into districts and requiring a set amount of supplies from each. Officers are dispatched to ensure collection and transport of the supplies to camp. By the end of the month, this system has somewhat eased the supply situation.

14 January. **Staten Island Raid. New York.**
Major General Alexander (Lord Stirling) takes a force of 2,500 men across the frozen Hudson River by sled to attack the British on Staten Island. They are

discovered and forced to spend the night in the snow and sub-zero temperatures before withdrawing.

26 January. **Arnold's Court-Martial. Middlebrook.**
The court-martial board finds Arnold guilty of two minor charges concerning misuse of property. The penalty is a written reprimand from Washington. Washington delays as long as possible, but finally on 6 April, he writes a mild letter of reprimand. Arnold is outraged at both the court and the punishment.

11 February–1 April. **Siege of Charleston.**
A British force lands and marches on Charleston, capturing Fort Johnson on 6 March. As Lincoln and his small garrison work on the city's fortifications, detachments of Continentals slip in—the Virginians come 500 miles in 28 days—but at the same time equal numbers of militia leave.

8–10 April. **Siege of Charleston, South Carolina.**
The British fleet runs past Fort Moultrie's guns into the bay. On land, the first British parallel trench is completed, cutting the city off on three sides. Lincoln refuses a demand for surrender, and the British begin the next parallel closer to the last American defenses.

14 April. **Siege of Charleston. Monck's Corner.**
Brigadier Isaac Huger with remnants of mounted units, guards the last American line of supply to Charleston. A British pre-dawn charge captures the crossroads, trapping Lincoln and his army.

24–26 April. **Siege of Charleston.**
A dawn sortie of Virginia Continentals captures the closest British trench, but they are forced back after two days. The British resume digging day and night.

6 May. **Lenud's Ferry. Santee River.**
British dragoons surprise Americans regrouping at this crossing. Lieutenant Colonel William Washington and others are forced to flee into the swamps.

8–12 May. **Siege of Charleston.**
American positions are bombarded with cannon and musketry. On the 12th, the city council asks Lincoln to surrender. The British terms require a humiliating surrender with no honors of war. Almost 2,600 Continentals and militia are captured, including Lincoln and six other generals. Colonel Abraham Buford's detachment of Virginia Continentals is the last Continental unit left in the south.

25 May. **Mutiny of Connecticut Line. Morristown.**
Unpaid for five months and poorly fed, two regiments of the Connecticut Line leave camp and solicit neighboring units to join them. Pennsylvania troops are called out, and the mutineers return to camp. A few leaders are confined, but most of the men are pardoned.

26 May. **Cahokia Attacked. Illinois.**
Colonel George Rogers Clark learns of an impending British attack and brings reinforcements to Cahokia from Fort Jefferson on the Ohio River. The next day a large force of Indians and Tories makes an unsuccessful attack.

29 May. **Battle of Waxhaws. South Carolina.**
Buford's Continentals are surprised by Lieutenant Colonel Banastre Tarleton and his mounted legion of dragoons, but Buford refuses surrender. The British overrun the Americans and Buford raises a white flag, but Tarleton refuses to "give quarter" (i.e. show mercy), even to the wounded, and many are killed. The phrase "Tarleton's quarter" comes to mean "no mercy."

7 June. **Battle of Connecticut Farms. New Jersey.**
Hearing of the American morale problems, the British commander in New York decides to attack. Stiff resistance by Colonel Elias Dayton's 2d New Jersey Continentals and local militia forces a withdrawal.

21 June. DeKalb Arrives. Hillsboro.
Major General Johann DeKalb arrives with Brigadier General William Smallwood's Maryland brigade and Brigadier General Mordecai Gist's brigade of Maryland and Delaware regiments. They have made a hard forced march from the Main Army at Morristown but are too late to help Charleston.

23 June. Battle of Springfield. New Jersey.
Greene reinforces the troops facing New York, turning back a British attack and forcing them to withdraw to Staten Island.

10 July. French Army Arrives. Rhode Island.
A French fleet arrives bringing Lieutenant General Jean de Vimeur (Comte de Rochambeau) and 6,000 French troops. The next day he comes ashore with his officers to arrange the landing of the French army.

25 July. Gates Takes Command. Coxe's Mill, North Carolina.
Major General Horatio Gates assumes command of the small southern American army and orders a march against the British at Camden. He ignores the poor physical condition of the men and the lack of rations.

20 June. Battle of Ramsur's Mill. North Carolina.
Colonel Francis Locke leads North Carolina militia in a surprise attack on a camp of Tories. The fighting is close and confused, but Locke's men prevail. This defeat badly weakens loyalist support in the area.

30 July–1 August. Partisan Warfare. South Carolina.
Colonel Isaac Shelby and South Carolina Brigadier Thomas Sumter lead their men in attacks against two British outposts.

Above: *Major General Johann DeKalb became an American hero when he died of eleven wounds in an unsuccessful attempt to hold the American right flank at the Battle of Camden. (Charles Wilson Peale, Independence National Historical Park Collection)*

Right: *The 2d Rhode Island Regiment fought bravely at the 1777 Battle of Springfield, helping turn back a British attempt to break out of New York. (Don Troiani, National Park Service)*

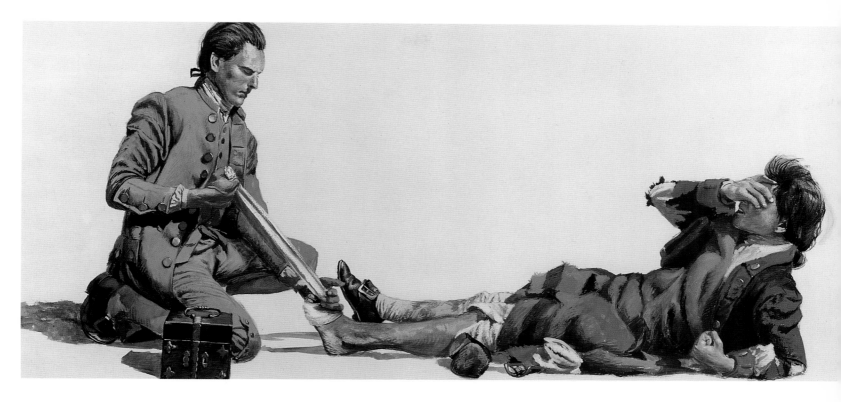

1 August. Frontier Warfare. Kentucky.
Clark leads 1,000 militia with some small artillery across the Ohio River against the Shawnees. Daniel Boone and other well-known Kentuckians are in the ranks. Clark and his men reach the deserted Shawnee "capital" called Chillicothe and destroy it, then march on to Piqua, where they battle Shawnees and drive them from the field. The town is destroyed, and Clark takes the militia back to Kentucky.

5 August. Arnold's Treason. West Point.
Arnold assumes command at West Point, a key position guarding the upper Hudson River. He asks Washington for this assignment with plans to betray it, and has been negotiating with the British for an annual spying salary and a bonus for delivering the fort.

6–15 August. Battle of Hanging Rock. South Carolina.
On the 6th Sumter attacks a Tory camp near Hanging Rock. After initial success, the militia discipline disappears as the men loot Tory rum. A counterattack forces Sumter to withdraw.

15–16 August. Battle of Camden.
A meal of molasses and cornmeal gives Gates' men serious diarrhea, but he puts them on a night march toward the advancing British. The two armies bump into one another in the dark. At daylight Gates places all his militia on the left flank, opposite the British Regulars, while his Continentals are on the right or in reserve. Gates gives a few preliminary orders, then moves to the rear and takes no part in the battle. Under British pressure, the militia break and Gates flees on horseback. The two veteran Continental regiments of Smallwood and DeKalb fight as long as possible, but they are overwhelmed. DeKalb falls, mortally hurt with eleven wounds. It is the worst American defeat of the war, with more than 800 dead and 1,000 captured.

24 September. Arnold Escapes. West Point.
British Major John Andre, returning to New York in disguise after meeting with Arnold, is stopped by three local militiamen. Andre carries a pass signed by Arnold, but other papers are found in Andre's boot. Lieutenant Colonel John Jameson sends the captured documents to Washington, who is nearby, but he also sends a report to Arnold, his commander. Arnold receives the note as he breakfasts with several of Washington's staff. He excuses himself, gets a horse, and slips away to a British ship. Greene is placed in temporary command at West Point. Andre is held as a spy, court-martialed, and hanged on 2 October.

2 October. Morgan Returns. Hillsboro, North Carolina.
When passed over for promotion to brigadier in 1779, Colonel Daniel Morgan left the Army and refused to return. He has now come to help in response to a plea from Gates. Morgan is given command of a

Above: *Medical knowledge was poor and a surgeon's tools were crude. With no concept of infection, often the only answer to a limb injury was amputation. (Don Troiani, National Park Service)*

Left: *The Battle of Kings Mountain on 7 October 1780 destroyed the Tory base of support in western South Carolina. ("Battle of King's Mountain," Company of Military Historians)*

provisional corps of light infantry, plus the few surviving dragoons under Lieutenant Colonel William Washington.

7 October. Battle of King's Mountain. South Carolina. In response to a threat to "lay waste to their country with fire and sword," militia companies under Colonels Isaac Shelby, John Sevier, and William Campbell cross the mountains into South Carolina looking for British Major Patrick Ferguson and his 1,000-man Tory legion. Ferguson moves to the crest of King's Mountain, believing the steep slopes will protect his camp. The militia attack up the mountain from different directions, and repeated bayonet charges by the Tories fail to disperse them. Ferguson soon falls, hit by at least six musket balls. When the Tories try to surrender, many frontiersmen cry "Tarleton's quarter" and shoot some prisoners before the officers gain control.

13–14 October. Greene Given Command. Philadelphia. On the 13th, Morgan is promoted to brigadier general. The next day Congress approves Major General Nathanael Greene as commander of the Southern Department. Greene leaves immediately for North Carolina, not even waiting to see his wife. En route, he visits Thomas Jefferson, and they develop an idea for lightweight boats transported on wagons. Greene leaves Von Steuben in Virginia as senior military commander, tasked to send supplies south to the army.

16–19 October. Frontier Warfare. New York. A large Indian-Tory raiding party devastates the Schoharie Valley and attacks Middle Fort. Without artillery, they are unable to capture the fort, but the frightened post commander still tries to surrender until he is stopped by a militiaman who threatens to shoot him. Colonel John Brown and a small

NATHANAEL GREENE, "THE FIGHTING QUAKER"

Called Washington's most trusted officer, Nathanael Greene was self taught in military tactics, but he had a superior gift for it. Born 7 August 1742, the Rhode Islander lacked a formal education, though he was literate and used every opportunity to read while he worked at the family ironworks.

When Greene was expelled from the Quaker Church in 1774 for attending a military parade, he joined the militia as a private. By May 1775 he was a militia brigadier general leading the Rhode Island units sent to Boston. A month later he received a Continental commission as a brigadier. Greene favorably impressed George Washington, and in the summer of 1776, Congress selected the 34-year-old Greene for major general.

He missed the Battle of Long Island due to illness but returned to defend New Jersey from British invasion. On Christmas night 1776, Greene commanded part of Washington's forces that crossed the Delaware and surprised Hessian troops at Trenton. A week later at Princeton, Greene was in the thick of the fighting again.

During the summer months of 1777, Greene took part in every major conflict in the north. When the British attacked at Brandywine River and flanked Washington's army, Green's division marched over four miles of broken country in less than 50 minutes to establish a new defensive line. But at Germantown, his troops became lost in an early morning fog and arrived too late to the battlefield.

Greene spent the winter as the army quartermaster at Valley Forge. Though it was a thankless job, he did much to bring order out of the chaotic supply system. The next summer, he returned to command and fought in the Battle of Monmouth and the Rhode Island campaign.

After the American defeat at Camden, South Carolina, Washington sent Greene south to take command. Realizing he had to take back the initiative, Greene split his small army, sending one group northwest under Brigadier General Daniel Morgan. To offset his lack of strength, Greene used the light forces of Francis Marion, Henry Lee, and Thomas Sumter to conduct guerrilla warfare.

After Morgan won the Battle of Cowpens in January 1781, Greene evaded Cornwallis for 200 miles, then, after resupply and rest, turned on the British. At Guilford Court House, North Carolina, on 15 March 1781, his men battled Cornwallis' regulars toe to toe before finally retreating.

Greene continued to fight to liberate South Carolina and Georgia. He was repulsed at Hobkirk's Hill in South Carolina but brushed it off, saying, "We fight, get beat, rise, and fight again." He attacked again at Eutaw Springs in September. The British claimed a victory but lost heavily and retreated to Charleston.

After the war Greene returned to Rhode Island, but eventually took up residence in a beautiful plantation in Savannah, a gift from the state of Georgia. He died there in June 1786.

Greene fought in almost every major campaign of the war, a proven master of both conventional and unconventional warfare. He understood that the key to winning the war was to maintain the existence of the army. George Washington is said to have commented to Greene after the Battle of Brandywine, "You, sir, are my favorite officer."

—*Kevin M. Hymel*

Above: *Nathanael Greene enlisted as a private, and the following year, he was a general. A natural military leader, Greene became the senior American commander in the south. (Independence Hall, Pennsylvania)*

American units. Champe is foiled when Arnold embarks his men on ships for operations in Virginia on 11 December. After several weeks Champe returns to American lines.

21 October. **Continental Army. Philadelphia.**
Congress agrees to provide Continental officers with a pension of half pay for life, and an end-of-service payment for soldiers. It is a major accomplishment for Washington. With the three-year enlistments of 1777 due to expire, Washington is desperately trying to maintain a core of Continentals. The system of setting quotas of men and supplies for each state is not working.

26 October. **Raid at Tearcoat Swamp. South Carolina.**
Local partisan leader Colonel Francis Marion leads a successful attack on a group of Tory militia, capturing horses and supplies.

9 November. **Battle at Fishdam Ford.**
Sumter's camp is attacked at night by British infantry and dragoons. The Americans defend their position, inflicting severe casualties on the British.

20 November. **Battle at Blackstocks Plantation.**
Sumter turns on British dragoons and mounted infantry who are chasing him. A British counterattack gains temporary success, but heavy losses and

detachment from Fort Paris are defeated trying to intercept the raiders. Destruction continues until the 19th, when militia and Oneida Indian allies force the attackers out of the valley.

20 October. **Sergeant Major Champe. New York.**
Washington asks Major Henry Lee for a volunteer from his Partisan Corps (Lee's Legion) for a secret mission to abduct Arnold and bring him back for court-martial. Sergeant Major John Champe accepts the mission. After dark, Champe "deserts" to the British lines. He convinces the British of his sincerity and is accepted for service in one of Arnold's loyalist

Above: *William Washington and his dragoons drove the British dragoons from the field, sealing the American victory at the Battle of Cowpens in 1781. (North Wind Picture Archives)*

Right: *Captain Henry "Light Horse Harry" Lee of the 5th Virginia Light Dragoons was promoted through the ranks quickly and became one of the best-known American light cavalry leaders of the war in the south. (Charles Wilson Peale, Independence Hall National Historical Park Collection)*

Opposite: *The defeat and flight of Major General Horatio Gates at the Battle of Camden caused Washington to send Major General Nathanael Greene to command the Southern Army. ("The Meeting of Greene and Gates," Howard Pyle, Wilmington Society of Fine Arts)*

American flank attacks end the battle. Sumter is seriously wounded, and both sides withdraw.

21–22 November. **Raid at Brookhaven. New York.**
Major Benjamin Tallmadge leads his 2d Continental Dragons in a dismounted raid on a fortified British outpost. The Americans attack at dawn, capturing the garrison without loss. It is the last significant action of the war in the north.

30 November. **Light Horse Harry Promoted. Philadelphia.**
Congress promotes 23-year-old Lee to lieutenant colonel and redesignates his legion as the 2d Partisan Corps for scouting and raids behind enemy lines. This is the fourth partisan unit in the Army.

3 December. **Greene Takes Command. Charlotte, North Carolina.**
Greene formally takes command from Gates. The supply situation is grim and only about 1,500 men are fit for duty. Greene appoints new staff officers and assigns them tasks. Colonels Kosciuszko, Edward Carrington, and Edward Stevens are sent to map the roads and rivers. Discipline is tightened—one guilty soldier is publicly hanged. Greene writes to Marion and personally visits the wounded Sumter, proposing exchanges of intelligence and coordination of operations. Greene breaks his forces into two

elements; he commands one, Morgan the other, forcing the British to also divide.

4 December. **Rugeley's Mill. South Carolina.**
William Washington's dragoons surround a group of Tory militia in a fortified stone barn. Washington has no artillery, but he puts a log on wagon wheels and pulls it forward, threatening to fire at the barn. One hundred Tories surrender.

16–20 December. **Southern Army Splits.**
Morgan marches north to conduct operations in the Catawba area. Two days later, Greene moves near Cheraw to resupply and rebuild his force. He tells Kosciuszko to begin work on the lightweight boats.

28–30 December. **Southern Army Offensives. South Carolina.**
Lee joins forces with Marion to attack the British at Georgetown, and then Fort Watson on the Santee River. Two days later, Washington's dragoons destroy a large detachment of Georgia Tories at Hammond's Store.

31 December. **Army Strength.**
The Army ends the year with: Continentals: 21,015; militia: 5,811; short-term militia: 16,000 (est.).

1781

1 January. Continental Army Reorganized.
A reorganization plan for the Continental Army calls for 49 infantry regiments, the Canadian Regiment, four artillery regiments, four legionary corps, two partisan corps, and a regiment of artificers (repair experts). More officers and enlisted men are approved in each regiment. Special units such as the Corps of Engineers, Corps of Invalids, and the Marechausse remain unchanged. All other units must disband and transfer their personnel. Every regiment except the Canadian Regiment is assigned to a state to provide provisions and replacements. Washington retains the authority to select officers (colonel and below) for retirement.

1 January. Mutiny of the Pennsylvania Line. Morristown, New Jersey.
Several regiments of the Pennsylvania Line mutiny in protest to living conditions, late pay, and the terms of service. Wayne is unable to stop the uprising, and several officers and mutineers are killed. The rebels march to Princeton, where they demand a meeting with delegations from Pennsylvania and Congress. British agents encourage the men to desert, but the agents are seized and turned over as a sign of loyalty.

Negotiations result in review panels, and about half of the protesters are released from the Army. The rest must remain "for the duration of the war," but they are given leave until 15 March, with promises of back pay and better provisions when they return. The promises are not kept.

1–7 January. Arnold's Raid. Virginia.
Benedict Arnold, now a British Provincial brigadier general, arrives with a force of 1,600 British Regulars and Tories. He sails up the James River, lands, and marches into Richmond on the 5th without resistance. He burns the city, sends raiders to other towns, then

Right: *War hero Peter Francisco used his huge size and long sword to wreak havoc with the British who tried to capture him. After his war service, he was appointed to sergeant-at-arms of the Virginia House of Delegates. (Anne S. K. Brown Military Collection, Brown University Library)*

withdraws to Portsmouth. Von Steuben calls in many of the frontier detachments to help.

Mid-January. **Detroit Campaign. New York City.** Washington approves a plan by Thomas Jefferson to have Clark attack Detroit and directs that Continental artillery and infantry units assigned to Fort Pitt assist Clark. Clark asks for a Continental commission, but Congress refuses. To give him seniority, Jefferson makes Clark a Virginia brigadier general, and Clark returns to Louisville.

16–17 January. **Battle of Cowpens. South Carolina.** Morgan takes his men to an open meadow called "the cowpens" and sends word for the militia to assemble there. As the men camp on the night of the 16th, Morgan tells the militia to fire only two well-aimed shots, then retire and reform in the rear. The next day, Morgan places militia as skirmishers and in a second line. His main third line is Maryland and Delaware Continentals and veteran Virginia militia. Washington's dragoons and mounted Georgia militia are in reserve. When the British make a frontal assault, the militia shoot twice, then run for the rear, most re-forming as reserve. The American position almost collapses when a shift on the right flank is misunderstood as a general retreat. Morgan and his officers regain control at the critical moment. The

Continentals turn to blast the British at close range and then charge with the bayonet. At the same time, the militia rejoin the battle as Washington's dragoons hit the British right flank. The British infantry drop their weapons as Tarleton's men flee. Tarleton engages Washington in a dramatic mounted duel before riding off.

20–27 January. **New Jersey Mutiny. Pompton, New Jersey.** A portion of the New Jersey Brigade mutinies, seeking the same concessions the Pennsylvania received. On Washington's orders, Major General Robert Howe marches his New England division to the New Jersey camp, arriving the night of the 26th. He places three cannon in plain view and orders the New Jersey troops to assemble without arms. The two ringleaders of the mutiny are shot immediately by a firing squad of other mutineers, and one man is reprieved.

30 January–1 February. **Greene Withdraws. South Carolina.** Morgan's men rejoin Greene's army and all quickly march north. The British pursue as fast as possible, burning supplies to improve mobility but also causing a food shortage. The chase continues with Greene always slipping away, frequently using the lightweight boats he has. An ill Morgan is replaced by veteran

Continental Colonel Ortho Williams. Greene crosses into Virginia on 14 February. He resupplies, then sends Lee and Pickens back to harass the British, under Lord Cornwallis, who are suffering severely from lack of provisions. On the 23rd, Greene returns to North Carolina with his Continentals.

25 February. Battle of Haw River. South Carolina.
Lee and Pickens locate a detachment of 300 mounted Tory militia. While Pickens' men hide, Lee and his dragoons pose as part of Tarleton's Legion. The American's green uniform coats are almost identical to Tarleton's. The Americans have the advantage of surprise and quickly rout the Tories, killing more than 90 without an American lost.

25 February. **Lafayette Comes to Virginia.**
Washington gives Lafayette command of a new corps composed of the light infantry companies from all the Main Army regiments and sends him to Virginia to assist Von Steuben.

1 March. **Articles of Confederation Ratified. Philadelphia.**
The Articles create a new "government" officially titled "The United States of America." Congress retains the Continental Army as its national army. The Articles include a statement of state responsibility to maintain a trained and armed militia.

15 March. **Battle of Guilford Courthouse. North Carolina.**
Greene bolsters his core of Continentals with militia. He is determined to fight and he selects Guilford Courthouse as his battlefield. Greene deploys his men as Morgan had done at Cowpens, but it does not work. When the British attack, the militia fire and run, but they do not reform as a reserve—they flee the battle. The American second line is forced back and the flanks begin to collapse. The British assault again but are stopped by Maryland and Delaware Continentals, who counterattack with bayonets. As a general melee takes place in the center of the field, Cornwallis orders British artillery fired into the struggling mass, killing many on both sides but also driving the Continentals back. Greene makes an orderly withdrawal. The British, too weak to follow, march to Wilmington for resupply.

April–May. **Frontier Warfare. New York.**
War parties move out of Canada and Fort Oswego to raid settlements and forts in the upper Mohawk Valley. Cherry Valley is attacked in April and two companies of Continentals bringing supplies to Fort Stanwix are captured. Major General William Heath, commander of the Department, has only 2,500 men to protect more than 2,500 square miles of territory.

April. **Brodhead Expedition. Fort Pitt, Pennsylvania.**
In large part to thwart Clark's proposed campaign against Detroit, Colonel Brodhead organizes and leads an expedition of 300 volunteers against the Delaware town of Coshocton. The town is attacked in a heavy rain, surprising the Indians. About 30 are captured; the male captives are killed and the rest brought back to Fort Pitt. Many of the militia then go home.

Opposite: *Light Horse Harry Lee led his 2d Partisan Corps (Lee's Legion) in surprise attacks on isolated Tory and British outposts. (Don Troiani)*

Right: *General Nathanael Greene turned his troops and faced the full force of Cornwallis' pursuing British Regulars at the Battle of Guilford Courthouse. ("Guilford Courthouse," H. Charles McBarron, Company of Military Historians)*

15 April. **Fort Watson. South Carolina.**
Lee and Marion join forces again to capture Fort Watson. At the suggestion of Colonel Hezekiah Maham, the Americans build a tall wooden tower from which riflemen can shoot over the stockade into the fort. Without protection from the musket fire, the British surrender.

18–30 April. **Arnold's Tobacco Raids. Virginia.**
Arnold sails up the James to attack Williamsburg, and then Petersburg. Virginia militia under Continental Colonel J. P. Muhlenberg, a Lutheran minister, hold the British at bay for most of the day, but they are finally forced back by artillery fire. An effective American rear guard inflicts numerous casualties on the pursuing British. On 20 May, Cornwallis arrives from Wilmington to take command, and Arnold returns to New York.

Battle of Hobkirk's Hill. South Carolina.
Greene camps a few miles from Camden, intending to attack a nearby British force. The British commander strikes first, surprising the Americans. Greene counterattacks with the 1st Maryland Continentals, but they become disorganized and fall back. The militia units give way also, and Greene must again retreat. The British occupy the American camp, but they have taken heavy losses and cannot control the countryside. Two days later they withdraw to Charleston.

1–21 May. **Partisan Attacks. South Carolina.**
American forces led by Lee, Marion, and Sumter capture isolated British and Tory outposts one by one—

Orangeburg on the 11th; Fort Motte on the 12th, using flaming arrows; Fort Granby on the 15th; and Fort Galphin on the 21st.

5 June. **Augusta Retaken. Georgia.**
Lee and his men join the Americans besieging Augusta. A small fort is captured on the 23rd, but Fort Cornwallis holds out until a Maham tower (a tower of logs with a protected platform) is used with a small cannon. This convinces the garrison to surrender.

18 June. **Assault on Ninety-Six. South Carolina.**
Since 22 May, Army engineer Kosciusko has been directing a classic siege against the fortified Tory post. In mid-June, news arrives of a British relief force, so Greene orders a direct assault against the main defenses, which have a dry moat and steep earthen walls. After an artillery bombardment, the American assault teams break into the moat. They struggle for an hour under deadly crossfire but cannot get over the walls and must withdraw, leaving their dead and wounded. Greene withdraws the next day.

6 July. **Battle of Green Springs. Virginia.**
After a long march, Wayne's Pennsylvania brigade has joined Lafayette's corps. Wayne, in charge of the advance body, engages a small British force, not realizing more troops are hiding nearby. Lafayette discovers the trap, but he is too late to warn Wayne. The British attack and Wayne reacts with a counterattack that stops the British line. Lafayette then forms a rear guard to cover Wayne's withdrawal. The British continue on to Yorktown to establish a base for resupply.

10 July. **Frontier Warfare. Sharon Springs Swamp, New York.**
Thick brush hides American militia as they deploy in a crescent formation around a camp of Tories and Indians. A small decoy group draws the enemy into the center, then signals the militia to open fire and charge with bayonets. After a short fight, the Tories and Indians flee.

7–16 August. **Detroit Campaign. Ohio River.**
Clark has been waiting for Colonel Archibald Lochry to arrive with more troops, but he can delay no longer and departs on the 7th. Lochry arrives with a small group of Pennsylvania militia on the 16th and sends messengers to catch Clark. Tories and Indians capture the messengers and begin to stalk Lochry's group.

14 August. **De Grasse Arrives. New York.**
Washington learns that Admiral de Grasse is on the way to Chesapeake Bay with his fleet and will remain until mid-October. Washington quickly decides to campaign in the south with about half the Main Army (1,400 men) and 5,000 French troops. If coordinated with de Grasse's presence, they can trap Cornwallis in Yorktown. Heath is tasked with implementing a deception plan to cover Washington's movements. On the 21st, the allied armies begin moving as if to attack New York, but at Princeton they turn south and march

Right: *General Washington receives the salute of passing Continental troops. He wears the blue ribbon sash of the Army's commander. ("General George Washington, Commander-in-Chief, Continental Army 1777," Don Troiani)*

quickly for Maryland ports. As many troops as possible, plus siege guns and other heavy equipment, will boat down the bay.

24 August. **Detroit Campaign. Ohio River.**
When Lochry's group comes ashore to camp, they are attacked. All the Americans are killed or captured. The British and Indians then follow Clark to Louisville, but do not find an opportunity to strike. At Louisville, Clark learns a new governor has canceled the expedition.

6 September. **March to Yorktown.**
American units with heavy equipment reach Maryland's Head of Elk port and embark for Virginia. Other units sail from Baltimore and Annapolis. Passing through Philadelphia, unpaid soldiers openly confront nervous congressmen. Congress agrees to borrow enough French funds from Rochambeau to provide a month's pay.

New London Raid. Connecticut.
Benedict Arnold lands near New London with a raiding force of British and Tories. He burns the unfortified town and sends detachments against nearby Fort Trumbull and Fort Griswold. Trumbull's garrison

moves to Fort Griswold, which holds out for 40 minutes before being overrun. After the surrender, many of the American captives are bayoneted. Arnold and his raiders return to New York.

8 September. **Battle of Eutaw Springs. South Carolina.**
Greene advances against the British at the springs. He again places militia in the front rank, and they stand up well, exchanging volleys for a long period. When they retreat, North Carolina Continentals advance, but they also are forced back. Lieutenant Colonel Washington and his dragoons become ensnarled in thick brush, where he is wounded and captured. Virginia and Maryland Continentals reform the American line and drive the British back through their camp, where many troops stop to plunder the British tents. The British stop and fire into the milling Americans. Both sides suffer heavy losses. Greene withdraws once more, and the British retire to Charleston.

15–30 September. **Yorktown Siege.**
The French and American armies, almost 16,000 men, conduct a Grand Review. Washington organizes three divisions commanded by Lafayette, Lincoln, and Von

Steuben. Rochambeau has seven regiments plus siege artillery and support troops. On the 24th the men and equipment arrive from Annapolis. Cornwallis has about 6,000 men, some of whom are stationed across the York River in Gloucester. By the evening of the 28th the allies are in position around Yorktown.

30 September–1 October. Yorktown Siege.

Artillery is rolled into position for the allied bombardment. Washington also sends French troops, including Lauzun's Legion, across the York River to keep Tarleton in Gloucester.

3 October. Gloucester Siege.

Lauzun's Legion clashes in a cavalry battle outside Gloucester. Infantry from both sides join the fight and the British withdraw behind their positions, where they remain.

5–9 October. Yorktown Siege.

After dark the Continental Corps of Miners and Sappers under Washington's chief engineer, Brigadier General Louis Duportail, begins the first siege trench. Work continues in a heavy rain through the next night. As a section of trench is completed, it is occupied by infantry units. More artillery is emplaced, and on the 9th Washington fires the first siege gun.

10 October. Dragoon Raid. Treadwell's Neck, New York.

A detachment of Continental dragoons commanded by Major Lemuel Trescott captures Fort Slongo. There are no American casualties.

13–14 October. Yorktown Siege.

Two British positions, Redoubts 9 and 10, endanger the completion of the second trench line, only 300 yards from the British lines. An American and French assault is organized to make simultaneous night attacks. Lieutenant Colonel Alexander Hamilton demands the honor of leading the American light infantry attacking Redoubt 10. Lieutenant John Mansfield volunteers to command the "forlorn hope" at the point of the assault. During the night of the 14th, the bayonet attacks are made. After a quick fight the two redoubts are secured. Artillery is moved forward, permitting the allied guns to fire point-blank into the British lines. An attempt to evacuate Gloucester fails, and on the 16th, Cornwallis's officers advise surrender.

Below: *Francis "Swamp Fox" Marion and his South Carolina militia, along with William Washington and the Continental Dragoons, use flaming arrows to set fire to the Motte house, which is occupied by British troops. ("The Capture of Fort Motte," Mort Künstler)*

Right: *Careful planning went into the selection and preparation of the trenches and artillery sites for the siege of Yorktown, Virginia. Detachments of infantry were sent forward to assist the engineers who laid out the positions. ("Digging Trenches at Yorktown," Mort Künstler)*

Below: *An artillery battery depicts an enlisted man (behind cannon), mounted artillery field officer, artillery company officer (saluting), and four enlisted artillerymen. ("Artillery, 1777–1783," H. A. Ogden, U.S. Army Quartermaster General)*

19 October. **Surrender at Yorktown.**
After several negotiation meetings, Cornwallis's army marches to a large field and lays down its arms and flags. Brigadier Charles O'Hara attempts to give Cornwallis's sword to Rochambeau, who directs him to Washington. Washington in turn points to Lincoln, his deputy, who suffered the humiliating surrender at

Charleston. Tarleton and his men surrender at Gloucester. In total, more than 7,000 prisoners are taken. One of Washington's aides is sent to Philadelphia with the news of the surrender. He arrives at 3 a.m. on the 22nd. There is no money in the U.S. Treasury to pay his travel expenses, so some congressmen each donate a dollar to reimburse him.

21 October. **Griffin Mutiny. South Carolina.**
Maintaining discipline continues to be a problem in the Southern Army. During a lecture by officers about lax discipline to a formation of Maryland Continentals, a drunken soldier, Timothy Griffin, appears and shouts disrespectful comments, encouraging the men to ignore the officers. He is arrested and shot the next day for encouraging mutiny.

24–30 October. **Frontier Warfare. Johnstown, New York.**
Militia under Colonel Marinus Willett catch 700 Tories and Indians withdrawing from an attack on Johnstown. He has pushed his 400 men hard in a rainy night-and-day march. Willett immediately attacks, personally leading a frontal assault. When the Tories retreat, Willett pursues and three days later strikes the Tory rear guard at Jerseyfield. Tory leader Walter Butler is killed and the Tories flee.

30 October. **First Secretary at War.**
Major General Benjamin Lincoln is appointed
Secretary at War by Congress. His War Office has a
staff of four, and replaces the Board of War.

5–10 November. **Forces Relocate. Yorktown.**
On the 10th, the Yorktown trenches are filled in and
the allied armies disperse, but British forces still hold
New York, Charleston, Savannah, and other towns.
The French remain in Virginia; Major General Arthur
St. Clair takes Continentals to reinforce Greene in the
Carolinas; and Washington moves the Main Army
back north.

1 December. **Charleston Besieged. South Carolina.**
After some light fighting, Greene drives the British and
Tories back into the town, where they are boxed in.

22 December. **Lafayette Departs. Boston.**
Lafayette, on leave from the Army, sails back to
France. His commission as a major general ends in
November 1783.

31 December. **Army Strength.**
The Army ends the year with: Continentals: 13,292;
militia: 7,298; short-term militia: 8,750 (est.).

January–March. **Deliberations with Congress.
Philadelphia.**
Washington spends the winter in discussions with
Congress concerning the future of the Continental
Army. Anxious to reduce expenses, a Congressional
committee recommends reducing the number of Army
regiments and officers, but Washington is able to
retain the current size.

7–8 March. **Gnadenhuetten Massacre. Ohio.**
Almost 100 peaceful Indians, mostly women and
children living at the Moravian Mission town of
Gnadenhuetten, are gathered up by Pennsylvania
militia and brutally massacred. This action only
further inflames more Indian raids.

Below: *Flying the white flag of surrender, General
Cornwallis gives up the fight against George Washington
and his superior forces. ("Surrender at Yorktown," John
Turnbull, The Granger Collection, New York)*

Right: *After the victory at Yorktown, large British forces still remained in New York and parts of the south. Washington had to continue to hold his army together and train for any eventuality until peace was declared. ("Forging an Army," Rick Reeves)*

April. **Main Army Headquarters. Newburgh, New York.**
On the 1st, Washington opens his headquarters and assembles most of the Main Army in the area. Food and clothing supplies improve, but there is no money for pay.

Gornell Mutiny. South Carolina.
Encouraged by British agents, a mutiny is plotted among disgruntled soldiers of Greene's Southern Army. Their plan includes the kidnapping of Greene. The mutiny is discovered and the ringleader, Sergeant Gornell, is tried and executed.

23 April. **Army Reduced. Philadelphia.**
Congress reverses one of the key 1780 reforms of the Army by reducing the number of officers in each regiment. It also reduces staff and eliminates many positions supporting the Army in the field.

22 May. **King George Washington. New York.**
Disgusted with the Confederation Congress, a small group of Continental Army officers consider restoration of a monarchy with Washington as king. Colonel Lewis Nicola sends Washington a letter proposing that Washington use the Army to seize power. Washington is shocked and strongly rejects the idea.

4–6 June. **Crawford's Defeat. Ohio.**
Colonel William Crawford leads mounted Pennsylvania militia from Fort Pitt against the Indian towns in northern Ohio. On the 4th, near the Indian town of Upper Sandusky, they become encircled by

Indians and Tories with three small artillery pieces. The Americans begin withdrawing in the dark but panic and lose discipline. Many are cut off and killed. Crawford and a small group are captured, marched to another town, and tortured to death.

20 July. **Great Seal Adopted. Philadelphia.**
Congress adopts the first Great Seal of the United States. The eagle from the seal becomes a common part of the Army uniform.

7 August. **First Army Award. Newburg, New York.**
The first American Army decoration, the Badge of Military Merit—later renamed the Purple Heart—is established by Washington for meritorious service. Three are presented in 1783. In addition, Washington authorizes all enlisted soldiers who have "served more than three years with bravery, fidelity, and good conduct" to wear a chevron on the left sleeve of the uniform coat. Two chevrons are worn for six years' service.

7 August. **More Army Reductions. Philadelphia.**
Congress directs a further Army reduction by disbanding low-strength units and reassigning the men. By 1 January the number of regiments allotted to each state will be cut and some reduced to battalion size.

16–19 August. **Battle of Blue Licks. Licking River, Kentucky.**
On the 16th, Bryan's Station is attacked by a large force of Shawnees and Tory Rangers. The small garrison holds out until reinforcements arrive. A group of 200 militia under Major Hugh McGary, including

Daniel Boone, pursues the raiders and catches them the next day at Blue Licks Springs. In the ensuing battle, 70 Kentuckians are killed or captured. Among the dead is Boone's son, Israel.

27 August. Ambush at Combahee Ferry. South Carolina.
A detachment of American light infantry and dragoons is ambushed at the ferry crossing. Colonel John Laurens, former aide to Washington and son of a president of Congress, is killed.

29 August. Fair Lawn Fight. South Carolina.
A militia force led by Francis Marion surprises and defeats 200 British dragoons camped near Savannah. It is Marion's last combat action in the war.

11–13 September. Frontier Warfare. Wheeling, West Virginia.
Almost 300 Indians and Tories attack Fort Henry for two days but are held off by a determined defense.

5 October. Gates Returns. Main Army Camp, Newburg, New York.
Major General Horatio Gates returns to duty and again becomes the center of anti-Washington plotting.

Above: *The Army Badge of Merit was created by Washington to honor enlisted men who had distinguished themselves. Its design later was the basis for the Purple Heart Medal. (American Military Insignia)*

Right: *John Laurens, former aide to Washington, and son of the president of the Continental Congress, was killed on 27 August 1782 at Cambahee Ferry in South Carolina. (South Carolina Historical Society Collection)*

3–10 November. Frontier Warfare. Ohio.
Clark leads an expedition against the Shawnees in retaliation for the Blue Licks defeat. He tries unsuccessfully to lure the Indians into a fight, and after several days returns to Kentucky.

4 November. John's Island. South Carolina.
Captain William Wilmot, 2d Maryland Continentals, is killed in a skirmish with a British foraging party. Most likely he is the last American soldier to die in an official action of the Revolution.

30 November. Peace Treaty. France.
In Paris, the American and British representatives sign a provisional treaty that ends all hostilities pending final agreement by the governments. The Indians are not parties to the treaty.

14–24 December. British and French Depart.
On the 14th the British garrison and thousands of loyalists sail from Charleston to New York. The British had already evacuated Savannah in July, taking the Georgia Tories with them. On the 24th the French army leaves Boston for the West Indies.

31 December. Army Strength.
The Army ends the year with: Continentals and militia: 14,256 (est.).

U.S. ARMY UNITS DATING FROM THE AMERICAN REVOLUTION

Organized	Current Designation	Component
1775	Battery B, 3d Battalion, 197th Field Artillery Regiment	New Hampshire ARNG
	HQ & HQ Detachment, 192d Engineer Battalion	Connecticut ARNG
	109th Field Artillery Regimen	Pennsylvania ARNG
	Company A, 1st Battalion, 69th Infantry Regiment	New York ARNG
	Battery A, 1st Battalion, 159th Field Artillery Regiment	New York ARNG
	Service Battery, 1st Battalion, 156th Field Artillery Regiment	New York ARNG
	198th Signal Battalion	New York ARNG
1776	1st Battalion, 5th Field Artillery Regiment	U.S. Army
	Detachment 1, Troop B, 1st Squadron, 713th Cavalry Regiment	South Carolina ARNG
1777	103d Engineer Battalion	Pennsylvania ARNG
1778	1st Squadron, 150th Armored Cavalry	West Virginia ARNG

Left: *A platoon of Continentals forms into the two-rank formation taught by Baron Von Steuben. This placed more muskets into action than the customary British three ranks. (Don Troiani, National Park Service)*

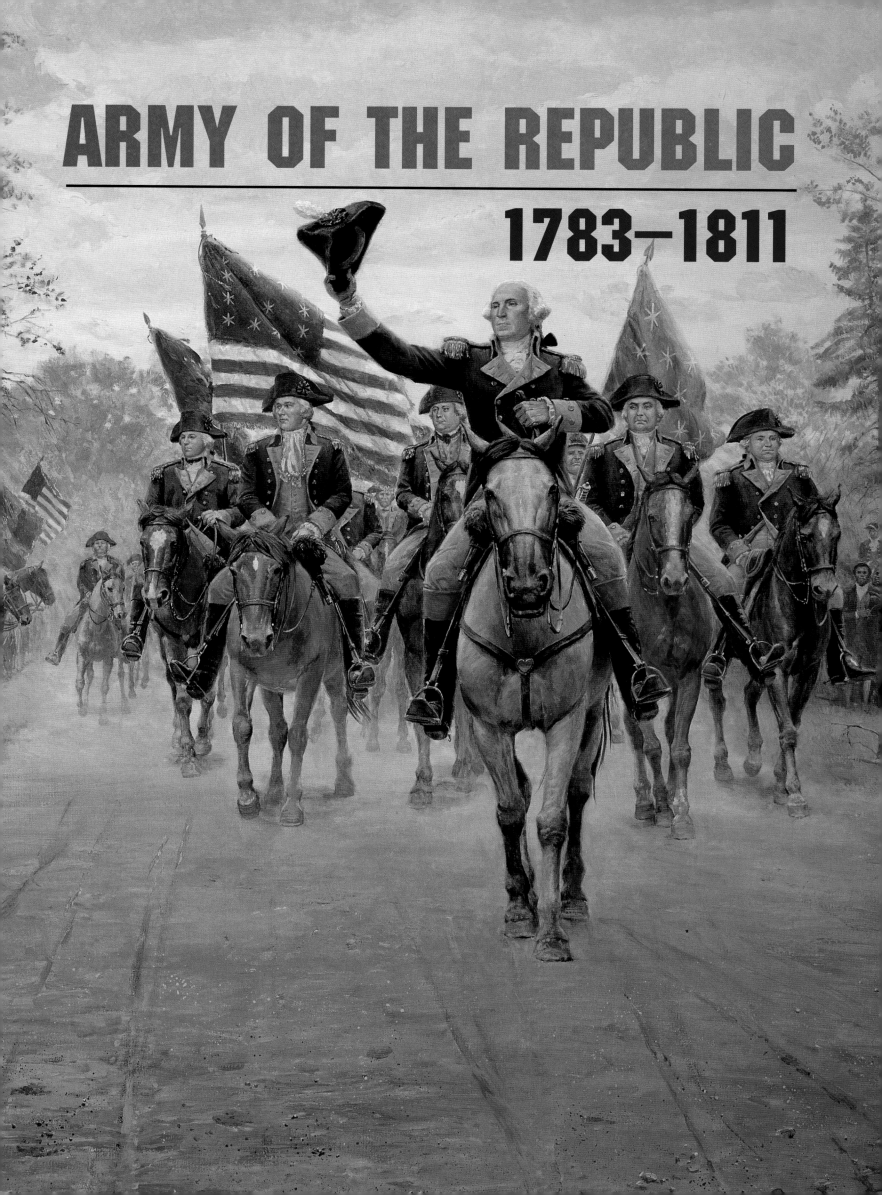

ARMY OF THE REPUBLIC

1783–1811

ARMY OF THE REPUBLIC

1783–1811

Colonel Raymond K. Bluhm, Jr., USA (Ret)

As peace negotiations brought the war to its closing months, anger over long-standing congressional failure to meet promises of adequate pay and support to the Continental Army almost sparked an uprising by some officers, who proposed direct action. Through his personal intervention, Washington was able to establish the concept of a non-political military as a bedrock principle of the American Army.

Following declaration of peace in April 1783, most of the Continental Army was put on leave and finally discharged in November. Washington returned his commission and was home in time for Christmas dinner. The end of the war brought the end of the Continental Army but only began the history of the Army.

In June 1784, the Army reached its lowest point— a single detachment of about 80 men headed by a captain. Later a regiment of 700 one-year enlistees was approved. Josiah Harmar was made lieutenant colonel and "Commander of the Army" in August with three missions: to guard the weapons left from the war; to occupy the military posts on the frontiers the British were to turn over; and to control and protect the settlers moving into the Ohio Valley. These last two tasks took the Army into its first major Indian war.

The men and money for the U.S. Infantry Regiment were provided by state quotas from Congress, which some states ignored. In addition,

dishonest contractors provided substandard food and uniforms, or even defaulted, leaving soldiers starving and in rags. In 1785, Congress gave Henry Knox responsibility for army, navy, and Indian affairs, but his hard work met with limited success. The Army's new forts and efforts to establish American authority over the Northwest Territory brought increased conflict with the Indians who were supplied with arms by British agents.

Ratification of the Constitution in 1788 brought a division of responsibility for military matters between the Congress and the new executive branch. Washington appointed Knox as his Secretary of War, and the existing Army was adopted by the new government. Congress now had the power to mandate support and taxes from the states and responded to pleas from western settlers by increasing the size of the Army to include a battalion of artillery, though recruiting the men was another matter.

In September 1790, Harmar launched a campaign against hostile Indian tribes that ended in his defeat. In response, Congress expanded the Army to two regiments and replaced Harmar with Major General Arthur St. Clair, who the next year led the under-strength regiments and militia into the worst disaster of Army history—half the Army were casualties. A new Army commander, Major General Anthony Wayne, finally led a well-trained and reorganized Army called "Legion of the United States" to a 1794 victory at Fallen Timbers, which brought a temporary peace. Other conflicts with Indians and holdout British agents continued on the southern border with Florida and in the West.

The Army mission to explore the immense Louisiana Territory purchased from France in 1802 started with the extraordinary Lewis and Clark expedition and continued for the next 100 years. Detachments of Army troops, scientists, and topographical engineers from the new military academy at West Point probed, mapped, explored, and marked the growing nation from Canada to Mexico.

A tiny Army of barely 3,000 officers and men provided frontier law and order, protected both settlers and Indians, secured coastal and land borders, and led the country west into its new territories.

Above: *On 23 December 1783, General George Washington resigned his commission before the Continental Congress in Annapolis, Maryland. ("Washington Resigning His Commission," John Trumbull, courtesy Architect of the Capitol, Washington, D.C.)*

Pages 116–117: *On 4 October 1794, General George Washington takes charge of the "Army of the Constitution," with 11,000 militiamen serving in the federalized force. Washington is reviewing the troops at Carlisle, Pennsylvania. ("Washington at Carlisle, 1794," Mort Künstler)*

ARMY OF THE REPUBLIC

1783–1811

"To be prepared for war is one of the most effectual means of preserving peace."
—President George Washington, first annual address to Congress, 8 January 1790

Above: *Washington and Von Steuben frequently walked the camps inspecting the troops. (The Granger Collection, New York)*

1783

January. **Status of the Army.**
The Main Army under General Washington is gathered in camps in New York, while Nathaniel Greene's Southern Army besieges Charleston, South Carolina. Minor clashes continue with British and Tory patrols. In the west, Fort Pitt remains a major American base. Three officers petition Congress requesting remedy of problems of pay and officer retirement. State units with less than 500 men are disbanded and men with remaining service are used to fill understrength regiments. Washington, concerned about the morale of his army, remains in camp at Newburg, New York, rather than visit Mt. Vernon.

March. **Armistice.**
Congress receives the news that a preliminary peace treaty has been signed, and official military activity halts.

10–12 March. **Newburg Addresses. Main Army camp, Newburg.**
On the 10th an unsigned "address" to the officers circulates in camp listing the failures of Congress to provide support. The secret writer (Major John Armstrong, aide to General Gates) proposes defiance and refusal to fight unless the grievances are resolved. A mass meeting of the officers is called. A second unsigned address appears on the 12th suggesting Washington approves of the proposed actions. Washington forbids the unauthorized meeting and calls his own meeting of the officers for Saturday, 15 March. He also forwards the papers to with a letter asking support for the soldiers to Alexander Hamilton, his former aide, who is now a delegate in Congress.

15 March. **Officer Meeting. Newburg.**
The officers gather in a large hall and Washington gives a prepared statement asking for continued loyalty, then he begins reading a letter from a congressman. He stops and puts on a pair of

the first shots were fired at Lexington. Washington also orders a prayer of thanksgiving be given by the unit chaplains, and an extra ration of liquor issued to every man to toast "the United States of America."

2 May. **Proposal for a "Peace Establishment." Philadelphia.**
Hamilton heads a congressional committee on military affairs and asks Washington for ideas on the postwar army. Washington proposes a small Regular army of five regiments (four infantry and one artillery); a well-trained, organized, and armed militia; a system of arsenals; and a military academy. Congress takes no action.

3 May. **Badges of Military Merit Presented. Newburg.**
Washington presents the first Army award, which he calls the Badge of Military Merit, to two noncommissioned officers of the Continental Army—Sergeants Elijah Churchill (2d Legionary Corps), and William Brown (5th Connecticut Regiment). A third badge is later awarded to Sergeant Daniel Bissell, Jr. (2d Connecticut Regiment). These are the only Badges of Military Merit ever given.

13 May. **First American Veterans Society Formed. Fishkill, New York.**
At the suggestion of Major General Henry Knox, a

spectacles, which most have never before seen him wear, with only a comment that reminds them of his own personal sacrifices in the war. He finishes and leaves. A resolution pledging their support to civil authority is passed without opposition by the shamed officers. Within a few days Congress changes the half-pay retirement to full pay for five years, paid in government securities—but takes no actions to implement it.

12–15 April. **Revolutionary War Hostilities End. Philadelphia.**
Congress approves the draft treaty and issues a proclamation ending hostilities.

19 April. **Washington Announces the End of Hostilities. Newburg.**
The Congressional Proclamation is read to the Army at evening formations. It is exactly eight years since

Above: *After the surrender at Yorktown, the focus of conflict shifted to the southern theater under the direction of Nathaniel Greene. ("The American Soldier, 1783," H. Charles McBarron, Army Art Collection, NMUSA)*

ARMY BATTLE STREAMERS— INDIAN WARS

MIAMI 1790-1795

Miami, 1790–1795

Tippecanoe, 1811

Above: *Washington created the Military Badge of Merit for exemplary enlisted soldiers. ("Newburgh, May 1783," H. Charles McBarron, Army Art Collection, NMUSA)*

group of Continental Army officers form the first American veteran's society, known as the Society of the Cincinnati. Washington is elected its first president.

2 June. **Continental Army Released from Duty.**
Washington begins placing virtually the entire Army on leave. Departing soldiers receive no back pay, but they are permitted to take their muskets. Promissory notes for three months' pay are issued. A small number of infantry and artillery units of men with three-year terms remain on duty. Major General William Heath at West Point. Another detachment under Lieutenant Colonel William Hull is temporarily sent to western New York to maintain civil order when mobs protest taxes and land claims.

6 June. **Washington's Guard Furloughed. Newburg.**
The Commander-in-Chief's Guard is furloughed and the protection of Washington is given to a New Hampshire detachment. In addition, a small mounted detail from the Marechaussee Corps remains as

couriers and escort. Both groups are discharged in November.

15 June. **Soldiers Blockade Congress. Philadelphia.**
More than 300 furloughed Pennsylvania soldiers, armed and angry at receiving no pay, surround the statehouse where Congress is meeting. The congressmen adjourn early, two days later Congress moves to Princeton, New Jersey, where Washington and his few remaining troops provide greater security.

17 August. **Washington Departs Army Headquarters. Newburg.**
Turning over field command of the Army to Knox, Washington departs to meet with Congress and to prepare his last reports and papers.

30 September. **Stark Promoted.**
On furlough, Brigadier John Stark is finally recognized with a brevet promotion to major general.

18 October. **Congress Orders Army Officially Discharged.**
Congress directs that all the furloughed officers and men "be absolutely discharged" from the Army on 3 November. The exact number of soldiers who served in the war as militia or Continentals is unknown, but the largest force Washington ever led in the field was only 17,000. Annual records 1775–1783 give a total over 376,000, but many men served two or three enlistments. Verified American battle casualties were 4,044, but no doubt were higher, with another 6,004 wounded. Deaths from disease, weather, and other causes were also high, but numbers are unknown.

29 October. **Lincoln Resigns.**
With no war and no army, Secretary at War Major General Benjamin Lincoln resigns. The position remains vacant for almost two years.

2–3 November. **Farewell Address. Rock Hill, New Jersey.**
Washington issues his last General Order in the form of a farewell address to his officers and men. All but three of the Continental Army's general officers are discharged. Only Washington, and Major Generals Henry Knox and Frederick von Steuben remain on duty.

5–15 November. **Army in North Discharged.**
Public announcements are published to tell the furloughed soldiers in the Northern Department that they are discharged. The remaining 500 Continental infantry and 100 artillerymen, many from the 4th

Massachusetts, are formed into Jackson's Continental Regiment under Colonel Henry Jackson near New York City. On the 15th, the furloughed Continentals in the Southern Army and Western Department are discharged. Security of the western frontiers now falls entirely on state militias and the settlers.

17–25 November. **British Depart New York City.**
The British garrison and more than 7,000 loyalists depart to waiting warships. British troops leave on the 25th as Washington leads his remaining troops into the city. In December, the last British troops depart Staten Island and Long Island.

4 December. **Washington Bides His Officers Farewell. New York City.**
At Fraunces Tavern Washington meets with his closest officers. He emotionally embraces each, and then takes a barge to New Jersey to begin his trip to meet the Congress in Annapolis.

23 December. **Washington Returns His Commission. Annapolis.**
Arriving about noon, Washington goes to the statehouse where Congress is meeting. He makes a brief statement and returns his commission as General and Commander-in-Chief of the American Forces to Thomas Mifflin, President of the Congress. He then departs for Mount Vernon, arriving in time for Christmas Eve dinner. Major General Henry Knox succeeds Washington as senior officer of the Army.

1784

1 January. **Status of the Army.**
Only Jackson's Continental Regiment, about 700 infantry and artillerymen, remains of the Continental Army. The regiment is split between West Point and Fort Pitt.

14 January. **Continental Congress Ratifies Treaty of Paris.**
The draft treaty is formally ratified, ending the Revolution. Under its terms, the British are to evacuate all their forts south of the Great Lakes. The Kentucky and Illinois territories captured by George Rogers Clark are confirmed as U.S. territory.

15 April. **Von Steuben Resigns from the Army.**
Major General von Steuben resigns. He has served without pay as the Army's Inspector General and military advisor to Washington. In gratitude, Congress awards him a gold-hilted sword and a pension. He settles in New York and dies on his farm in 1794.

Above: *Epaulets replaced earlier means of identifying officers. A lieutenant of 1781 is shown here with the epaulet on his left shoulder. ("The American Soldier, 1781," H. Charles McBarron, Army Art Collection, NMUSA)*

2 June. **Army Reduced Again.**
Despite continued British presence and Indian raids in the west, Congress directs the disbanding of Jackson's Continental Regiment, keeping only 80 privates and a few officers under Captain John Doughty. A 55-man detachment from the 2d Continental Artillery, Alexander Hamilton's former unit, guards West Point. The remaining 25 men are posted to Fort Pitt.

June. **U.S. Infantry Regiment (First) Established.**
Congress approves formation for 12 months of a 700-man U.S. Infantry Regiment (also called First American Regiment) with eight infantry and two artillery companies. Its mission is to occupy the former British military posts, protect the western frontiers, and guard military storage. A private will receive $6.66 a month, a sergeant $15. New York, Pennsylvania, New Jersey, and Connecticut are asked to provide men, but New York refuses. It takes many weeks to recruit the detachments.

20 June. Knox Resigns. West Point.
Major General Henry Knox, the last serving Continental Army general, resigns his commission and returns to Boston. Colonel Jackson is discharged and his regiment officially disbanded, leaving Captain Doughty as the Army's senior officer.

12 August. Harmar Appointed Army Commander.
Veteran officer Josiah Harmar is approved as "lieutenant colonel-commandant" of the new U.S. Infantry Regiment and also named "Commander of the Army." Harmar's pay is $50.00 a month plus $20.00 for living expenses. He travels to Pittsburgh to join the recruits forming there. The regiment is the start of a new American Army. Today, the 3d Infantry (The Old Guard), traces its lineage to this unit.

Winter. U.S. Infantry Regiment Activities. Fort Pitt.
Harmar keeps the 200 men of his regiment busy working and conducting patrols to keep law and order among the growing number of settlers. Abandoned Fort McIntosh (Pennsylvania), 30 miles down the Ohio River, is rebuilt and garrisoned.

1785

1 January. Status of the Army.
Only the undermanned U.S. Infantry Regiment at Fort Pitt and its small artillery detachment at West Point are on active service.

21 January. Treaty Signed with Indians. Fort McIntosh.
As the Army's senior officer, Harmar meets with chiefs of several tribes and tells them that the British are defeated and the land south of the Great Lakes now belongs to the Americans. Some land will be provided to the Indians if they agree to give up claims to eastern Ohio. A treaty is signed, but Shawnee raids continue.

8 March. Knox Appointed Secretary at War.
Congress appoints Henry Knox as Secretary at War to head the Congressional Board of War. Knox has an annual salary of $2,450, three clerks, and a messenger. His responsibilities include army, naval, and Indian affairs, as well as land grants. Army officers often serve as Indian Agents or Peace Commissioners with the authority to negotiate and draft treaties.

January. **Army Strength Drops.**
Harmar's regiment is down to about 200 one-year enlistees, mostly Continental Army veterans. Despite letters from Secretary at War Knox, the states fail to fill their quotas. Several federal arsenals with stored weapons are left to local militia for safekeeping. War parties under Blue Jacket (Shawnee) and Little Turtle (Miami) continue raids into Kentucky.

Summer. **Clark's Last Campaign. Kentucky.**
In response to the raids by Indians crossing from north of the Ohio River, local leaders ask George Rogers Clark to command a militia expedition into the Northwest Territory. Clark reluctantly accepts and spends the summer organizing while scouts watch Indian activity.

Opposite, top: *Photograph of the regimental color of the U.S. 1st Infantry Regiment, 1791. (West Point Museum)*

Left: *Known as the "Father of American Artillery," Henry Knox became the second Secretary of War. (James Harvey Young, Army Art Collection, NMUSA)*

Below: *In June 1783, Captain John Doughty became the Army's highest ranking officer after the discharge of all but 80 men from service. (Janet R. M. Fitzgerald after Thomas B. Woodburn, Army Art Collection, NMUSA)*

12 April. **New Call for Troops.**
Aware that most enlistments in the U.S. Infantry Regiment will have expired by the end of the summer, Congress requests the same states to recruit another 700 men, this time for a three-year enlistment. The response is poor.

25 July. **Quartermaster Department Abolished.**
Congress abolishes the Army Quartermaster department, giving responsibility for provision of food and clothing to civilian contractors. The system fails miserably; contractors default or cheat, leaving the soldiers ill-clothed and often starving.

Fall. **New Forts Built. Northwest Territory.**
Ordered to remove squatters and Indians from the federal lands, Harmar builds and garrisons three forts farther down the Ohio River—Fort Finney at Great Miami River; Fort Steuben (Steubenville); and Fort Harmar (Marietta). The largest, Fort Harmar, is made regimental headquarters. Captain John Hamtramck raises Fort Steuben in record time by offering a prize of six gallons of whiskey for completing the first building.+

Left: *Starting in Massachusetts in 1786, the Shay Rebellion quickly spread in Massachusetts. It was one of the first popular challenges to the concept of a central federal authority for the new nation. (The Granger Collection, New York)*

Opposite: *In 1784, the American Army was reduced to one infantry regiment, yet was still expected to protect the nation's frontiers. ("The American Soldier, 1786," H. Charles McBarron, Army Art Collection, NMUSA)*

July. **Army Strength.**
Knox reports to Congress that the Army has only 518 men in its ranks.

September. **Indian Campaign. Indiana-Ohio Territory.**
Clark organizes two militia columns—one under his command and one led by Colonel Benjamin Logan. Clark plans to attack the Miami Indian villages along the Wabash River with 1,200 men while Logan takes 800 men against the Shawnees.

26 September. **Shays' Rebellion. Springfield, Massachusetts.**
The governor sends 600 militiamen to protect the state courts from "Regulators," many of whom are unpaid veterans angry over taxation and devalued currency. Daniel Shays leads the largest group. Secretary Knox travels to the area, concerned about the security of the weapons in the Springfield Arsenal.

October. **Clark's Indian Campaign. Northwest Territory.**
Clark's men are undisciplined, and supplies are scarce. Two days out from Vincennes, half the force mutinies and deserts. Clark turns back, barely avoiding a large Indian ambush. Logan's column destroys several Shawnee towns but unfortunately kills a friendly chief, further inflaming the Indians. The Indian raids continue, and settler defense is left to local militia companies.

20 October. Army Expanded.
Congress increases the Army by 1,340, with quotas given to six states. Only two artillery companies are recruited; these are combined with the two artillery companies of the U.S. Infantry Regiment to form a separate artillery battalion under Major John Doughty. Congress also modifies the Articles of War to lessen the severity of punishments. Flogging is limited to 100 strokes, and rights of the accused are improved.

26 December. Regulators Assemble. Worchester, Massachusetts.
Shays assembles 1,200 men and marches to Springfield where, together with another band, they disrupt court activities. The state militia guarding the arsenal is outnumbered and Governor James Bowdoin calls an emergency 30-day mobilization of 4,400 more men.

1787

January. **Status of the Army.**
Congress again limits Army enlistments to only one year. Recruiting is difficult, and Army strength remains below its 840 authorization.

18–19 January. **Lincoln Called to Help. Boston.**
The governor asks retired Major General Benjamin Lincoln to assist in the Regulator emergency. Lincoln joins the assembled militia force and prepares to march against the rebels.

25–27 January. **Regulators Attack Arsenal. Springfield.**
The Regulators attempt to seize the government arsenal but are driven off when the militia opens fire with a cannon, killing three rebels. On the 27th, Lincoln and his militia force arrive at the arsenal, but Shays and his men are gone.

4 February. **Shays' Rebellion Defeated. Petersham, Massachusetts.**
Lincoln's militia attacks Shays' rebels, killing several and dispersing the rest, ending the rebellion. More than 140 rebels are eventually captured for trial; Shays flees the state. Lincoln and the militia are soon released.

June. **Fort Knox Constructed. Vincennes, Indian Territory.**
Major John Hamtramck and three companies of the U.S. Infantry Regiment abandon Fort Steuben. By barge and on foot they move west to Vincennes to build a new fort, to be named Fort Knox. During the summer the regiment loses its first man to Indians.

13 July. **St. Clair Appointed Northwest Territory Governor.**
Retired Major General Arthur St. Clair is appointed Territorial Governor and Superintendent of Indian Affairs for the Northwest Territory, with the authority to raise a militia. The Army is charged with preserving peace and order in the territory, protecting surveyors, removing Indians, and evicting squatters.

31 July. **Harmar Promoted. Fort Pitt.**
Congress promotes Colonel Harmar to brevet brigadier general, making him the only general officer in the Army. He continues to command the regiment, which has few other officers.

3 October. **Army Strength Extended.**
Concerned over the Regulator rebellion and the increasing number of hostile Indian incidents in the Northwest, Congress approves the Army's manpower of 840 for three more years.

1788

1 January. **Status of the Army.**
The Army is depleted by deaths and desertions, and recruiting remains a problem. Tiny garrisons guard West

Point and the Springfield Arsenal, while the rest of the Army serves as peacekeepers in the Northwest Territory.

June. **St. Clair Arrives. Fort Harmar, Northwest Territory.**
A few weeks after St. Clair assumes his position as Territorial Governor, he invites senior Indian chiefs to a council. It ends when Indians attack the Army guards of nearby government supplies. Attacks on other supply convoys soon follow.

2 October. **Army Clothing and Pay Withheld.**
The civilian contractor hired by the War Department fails to deliver adequate clothing to the Army posts. On-hand supplies are given to the small number of recruits, but serving soldiers receive nothing. Congress again fails to provide pay, leaving the Army unpaid since January 1787.

1789

1 January. **Army Strength.**
Army strength remains below 840 men. The tiny U.S. Infantry Regiment continues its struggles in the Ohio Valley, while other detachments guard West Point and other arsenals.

30 April. **Washington Inaugurated.**
George Washington is inaugurated as the first President and Commander-in-Chief of the Army and

Navy and of militia called to federal service under the Constitution. He has power to nominate, and with Senate consent, appoint the officers of the Regular armed forces. Appointment of militia officers remains with the states.

August. **Kentucky Militia Raid. Northwest Territory.**
Major John Hardin leads a group of 200 Kentucky militiamen on a retaliatory raid against the Wea tribe.

7 August. **Department of War Established.**
In its first military affairs act, Congress transfers the War Office to the Executive Branch and renames it the "Department of War." Its head is renamed "Secretary of War" but retains responsibilities for both military and Indian affairs. The bill to establish the department is behind those for the foreign affairs and treasury departments, thus the Secretary of War is ranked third in cabinet seniority.

8 August. **Secretary of War Report.**
Knox makes his first report to the President, listing the Army rolls as carrying only 672 men—76 guarding West Point and the Springfield Arsenal, and 596 stationed at posts in the Ohio Valley.

12 September. **Knox Remains Secretary of War.**
Washington retains Henry Knox as Secretary of War in the new Executive Branch.

29 September. **Congress Adopts the Army.**
Congress adopts the existing army as "the establishment for the troops in the service of the United States" under the Constitution. Congress also provides an oath of allegiance to the Constitution and authority for the President to mobilize the militia in event of Indian attacks, and modifies the Articles of War. The United States Army is organized into a Regiment of Infantry and a Battalion of Artillery. All companies, however, have only 60 privates, plus officers and noncommissioned officers. No staff is provided.

Fall. **Harmar Moves Army Headquarters. Northwest Territory.**
Harmar relocates the headquarters of the Regiment of Infantry to the recently built Fort Washington, near Cincinnati.

1790

January. **Secret Army Expedition.**
During the year, Secretary Knox orders a secret mission to explore the Missouri River. Harmar sends Lieutenant

John Armstrong, but he is unprepared for such a trip and must return after reaching the Mississippi. Still below its 840 authorization, the Army must abandon some small forts.

30 April. **Congress Reorganizes the Army.**
Congress authorizes an increase in the size of infantry and artillery companies, and adds an Army surgeon and medical assistants, for a total Army of 1,273 officers and men. A three-year enlistment term is set for both officers and men. Pay scales are slightly improved, and a pension of up to $5.00 a month is provided for soldiers injured in the line of duty. However, no system is set up to recruit the additional men.

July. **Little Turtle's War. Fort Washington.**
Harmar is directed to organize two punitive expeditions against the hostile Indians. He will lead one from Fort Washington while Major Hamtramck takes the other from Fort Knox. St. Clair uses the new federal authority to call for Pennsylvania and Kentucky militia quotas of 500 and 1,000 men, respectively: Only 1,133 militiamen show up. They have little equipment and many are "hardly able to bear arms."

24–30 September. **First U.S. Army Campaign. Fort Washington.**
Harmar musters only 320 from his regiment to bolster the unruly Kentucky militia. Supplies are also lacking.

Urged to action by St. Clair, Harmar sends militia under Colonel John Hardin ahead to Turkey Creek. Harmar follows on the 30th with his Regulars and the supply train.

14–17 October. **Hardin's Raid. Northwest Territory.**
On the 13th, Harmar's scouts learn the Indians are abandoning their towns, and Harmar's force destroys the villages known as Miami Town. On the 17th, Colonel John Trotter is ordered to make on a three-day scout of the surrounding area. After a halfhearted effort he returns the next day.

19 October. **Harmar's First Defeat. Miami River.**
Harmar relieves Trotter of command and sends Hardin out with mounted militia. Almost a third of his militia desert, but Hardin continues on with about 140 men. Near a swamp they are ambushed and panic, disrupting a detachment of Regulars sent to help. A small band of nine militiamen and 30 Regulars led by Captain John Armstrong make a desperate stand. Only Armstrong and seven others survive. At dark Hardin retreats back to Harmar's location.

21–23 October. **Cornfield Ambush. Miami Town.**
As Harmar withdraws, his scouts report Indians gathering near Miami Town. Major John Wyllys and Hardin are sent with a detachment of Regulars and 400 militia to attack. The Miamis lure the militia into another ambush. Wyllys and his 60 Regulars are left to

EARLY ARMY DISCIPLINE

The first disciplinary regulations for the Army were the *Articles of War*, approved by Congress on 30 June 1775. They were based on the British version but included specific differences and underwent several changes to adjust them to the emerging American army. The *Articles* described the types of offenses and the corresponding punishments. For minor offenses, such as profanity, indecency, or irreverence in church, the penalty was a monetary fine or confinement. Being drunk on guard duty, dueling, missing formation, unauthorized firing of weapons, or absence without leave brought corporal punishment. More serious offenses, such as mutiny, disobeying orders, striking an officer, cowardice, desertion, or treason, were punishable as sentenced by a court-martial, to include death.

The *Articles* also established the level, regimental or general, and the membership of the courts-martial board. Regimental courts-martial usually handled the lower classes of offenses, while general courts martial were reserved for offenses of severe criminality or disloyalty and were composed of no less than 13 field officers. The Judge Advocate General would prosecute; the death sentence was ordered only when two-thirds of the court agreed. A death sentence had to be approved by the Commander-in-Chief or Congress. Regimental courts-martial had three to five officers. The sentence of this court, specifically regarding corporal punishment, had to have the regimental commander's approval.

General Washington, fully understanding the necessity for strict discipline, usually backed the sentences and included the findings of the courts martial in the *General Orders to the Army*. Discipline was a major problem throughout the war, and the *General Orders* are replete with his displeasure over the conduct of officers and men.

Corporal punishment was most often prescribed and was normally carried out by the musicians. Flogging, the most common method, was authorized by Congress and approved by public opinion. The *Articles of September 1776* authorized a total of 100 lashes that could be spread out over two days. The offender was tied between two halberds planted in the ground and flogged with a cat-o'-nine-tails. The "gauntlet" was another favored method. The offender was stripped to the waist and forced to walk slowly between two lines of soldiers with switches, each man giving one severe blow. To "ride the wooden horse" the offender was seated on a narrow-edged wooden plank, his hands tied behind him and two muskets tied to his dangling feet to keep him from "falling off." With "cobbing" the offender was forced to lie across a barrel and receive a set number of blows from a large oak paddle with holes drilled in it.

Corporal punishment was inflicted only on enlisted men. Officers were fined, made to forfeit pay, or cashiered for their offenses, although death by hanging or firing squadcould be imposed. While various forms of corporal punishment continued to be used throughout the Civil War, flogging was abolished on 5 August 1861. On 3 May 1951 Congress replaced the *Articles of War* with the modern *Uniform Code of Military Justice*.

—*Vince Hawkins*

Above: *Punishment by flogging for even minor offenses was not a rare occurrence in the U.S. Army of the 1800s. The commander could spread a large number of lashes over several days so as not to injure the soldier too badly. ("Flogging a Soldier," Michael Haynes)*

has cost more than 400 American lives. The militia loudly blame Harmar for the disaster. Harmar considers courts-martial of Trotter and other militia officers but does nothing. Encouraged by the victories, the Indians increase their attacks.

December. **War Department Moves. Philadelphia.**
The War Department moves with the rest of the national government from New York back to Philadelphia where it remains until it relocates to the new capital city in 1799.

1791

January. **Harmar Retains Command of the Army.**
Despite his October defeat, Harmar remains the Army commander. Combat losses, sickness, and desertions leave the Army badly weakened, and only a meager flow of shoddy supplies and bad food reaches the frontier posts. Dunlap's Station in the Northwest Territory is attacked by 200 Shawnees. The small fortified station, with 88 defenders, is besieged for a week.

fight alone. Before Harmar arrives with a relief force, Wyllys is overrun; only ten survive. A seriously wounded Harmar withdraws with low food and heavy casualties on the 23rd.

3 November. **Harmar's Retreat. Fort Washington.**
Harmar's battered army straggles to the fort, exhausted from their 340-mile march. The unsuccessful campaign

3 March. **Congress Strengthens the Army.**
Congress authorizes a second infantry regiment of 995 men. The U.S. Infantry Regiment is redesignated as the 1st Regiment of Infantry and the new unit becomes the 2d Regiment. A $6 bounty for enlistment in the Regulars helps recruiting, but arms and equipment are lacking. Congress also authorizes a major general as Army commander, a brigadier general

Above: *The battalion of artillery was broken into smaller detachments to garrison forts and supply the infantry. ("U.S. Battalion of Artillery, 1786–1794," H. Charles McBarron, Company of Military Historians)*

Right: *Women, children, and others often traveled with the Army from one destination to another. Many were family members of the soldiers, others mere fortune-seekers. ("Camp Followers," Old Niagara Association)*

20–23 May. Militia Raid. Northwest Territory.
With St. Clair's approval, militia Brigadier Charles Scott leads a force of 800 Kentucky volunteers in a raid against the Kickapoo villages along the Wabash River. Continental Army officer James Wilkinson, now a Kentucky militia brigadier, goes along.

July. New Troops Arrive. Fort Washington.
A few six-month levies begin to arrive from Fort Pitt. St. Clair places quotas on local settlements to fill out two levie regiments. Supplies are still a major problem. The contractor is dishonest and Quartermaster General Samuel Hodgsdon is incompetent. The delivered equipment is broken or worn out, and the ammunition is moldy.

1–21 August. Wilkinson Raid. Fort Washington.
Wilkinson leads a second raid of mounted Kentucky militia against the Indian town of L'Anguille, a main Miami village. After 20 days and the loss of two men killed, Wilkinson returns.

7–29 August. St. Clair Moves. Northwest Territory.
Feeling pressure for action, St. Clair marches his small army six miles. The march clearly shows the troops' lack of training and discipline. On the 16th, young Ensign William Henry Harrison joins the 1st Regiment of Infantry.

as deputy, an adjutant general, a chaplain, and a quartermaster general. In addition, Congress approves raising 2,000 six-month volunteer "levies" commanded by a "Major General of Levies." Former Continental officer Richard Butler is given the position, the only officer to ever hold the title.

4 March. St. Clair Appointed Major General.
Territorial Governor Arthur St. Clair is made a major general and replaces Harmar as Army commander. St. Clair is to lead a July expedition of 3,000 Regulars and militia against the hostile tribes to establish "a strong and permanent military fort" as the base for future operations. Harmar demands a court of inquiry on his defeat.

15 May–June. St. Clair Takes Command. Fort Washington.
St. Clair arrives with detailed guidance from Washington. He finds only 85 men of the 1st Regiment present for duty. Drawing men from the other forts, he is able to assemble 427 Regulars. The levies and the new recruits for the two Regular regiments are slow to arrive.

Opposite, top: *Arthur St. Clair became the Army's Commanding General on 4 March 1791. In 1791, he led the U.S. Army into one of its greatest disasters. ("Arthur St. Clair," Charles Wilson Peale, Army Art Collection, NMUSA)*

Opposite, bottom: *President Washington selected Anthony Wayne to lead and rebuild the Army. He became its Commanding General in 1792. ("Anthony Wayne," Peter Frederick Rothermel, Army Art Collection, NMUSA)*

Right: *The Army of the 1790s was organized as a legion: a composite unit bringing together several different types of fighters under one commander. ("The American Soldier, 1794," H. Charles McBarron, Army Art Collection, NMUSA)*

15–24 September. **Harmar's Court of Inquiry. Fort Washington.**
Major General Richard Butler convenes the court of inquiry. After hearing witnesses and deliberating for nine days, the court exonerates Harmar. However, his reputation is ruined and he resigns in January 1792.

19 September–October. **Fort Hamilton Built. Ludlow Station.**
St. Clair marches the army 18 miles to the Great Miami River, where two weeks are spent constructing Fort Hamilton. It is the first of the series of forts to secure his route into hostile territory. New recruits arrive, including the still forming 2d Regiment, but desertions are also increasing.

4–13 October. **Campaign Begins. Fort Hamilton.**
St. Clair and his army depart on the 4th, leaving a small garrison and some artillery to guard supplies. After 30 miles, St. Clair begins construction of a second fort. He has about 2,300 men—the understrength 1st and 2d Regiments of Infantry; about 800 six-month volunteers organized into two Regiments of Levies; and another 600 militiamen, some mounted. Efforts to enforce discipline are futile and desertions continue. Hundreds of livestock and more than 200 women and children accompany the column.

Left: *The star-shaped Fort McHenry was key to the defense of Baltimore Harbor and represented the latest concepts for harbor defenses of the time. (National Park Service, Fort McHenry)*

Opposite, bottom: *Soldiers of various sub-legions were distinguished by different colored plumes on their caps. ("Infantry of the Legion of the U.S., 1794," H. Charles McBarron, Company of Military Historians)*

14–23 October. **Fort Jefferson Built. Northwest Territory.**
Despite wet, freezing weather, the fort is completed and named Fort Jefferson. Living conditions are miserable. Many soldiers have no winter clothing. On the 17th, the last flour ration is issued. Officer's rations are reduced to half, and the whiskey ration runs out. Desertions rise and morale falls. On the 22nd, James Wilkinson accepts appointment as a lieutenant colonel and commander of the new 2d Regiment of Infantry. In swearing his oath of allegiance to the United States, he fails to mention that he is also paid Agent No.13 for the Spanish king.

24 October. **The Army Advances. Fort Jefferson.**
Leaving behind a small garrison, St. Clair marches his ragged army six miles and camps again, waiting for a resupply train. The weather is cold, with alternating rain, hail, and snow daily. As enlistments expire, small groups of men head for the rear. Patrols sight Indians and find numerous Indian campsites. Security is tightened and the men are ordered to remain clothed at night with their muskets at hand.

30 October. **Militia Deserters Threaten Supplies.**
After marching only seven miles, the army camps in a dense forest. A group of 60–70 militia desert with plans to plunder the expected supply train. St. Clair sends Major Hamtramck with his best unit, the 1st Regiment, back to protect the supplies.

31 October–3 November. **Army Advances to Wabash River.**
The loaded pack train arrives on its own. The next several days are spent building a fortified supply dump and preparing a trail, then St. Clair marches another eight miles north. It is sunset on the 3rd when the troops arrive at the campsite, and they are too tired to dig entrenchments. The camp is laid out in a rough rectangle facing the shallow Wabash River on the west. In the main camp are the artillery, 2d Infantry, several units of levies, and mounted militia. Kentucky militia and more levies are posted across the river, 200–300 yards away, as security.

4 November. **St. Clair Defeated. Wabash River.**
Sentries report Indians during the night, but Butler does not tell St. Clair, who is ill. The troops muster into battle ranks before sunrise but are soon dismissed. Militia Colonel William Oldham ignores orders to send out morning patrols. Suddenly, hundreds of warriors erupt from the trees across the river, driving the militia through the main camp. The Indians then charge the main line, which holds by musketry and bayonet, forcing the Indians around the flanks to the rear of the camp. During the four-hour battle, the 2d Regiment makes three bayonet charges, but each time the Indians return closer. The artillery fires, but the guns are aimed too high. The Shawnees and gunners fight hand to hand among the cannon until most of the artillerymen are dead. Butler is shot twice and dies in his tent. He is

first of four American generals killed in the U.S.-Indian Wars. St. Clair fights on foot, rallying his reserve. The women fight alongside the men; few survive. St. Clair finally orders the camp abandoned, leaving behind the badly wounded and the supplies. He leads a breakout charge; those who make it out head for Fort Jefferson. The rest perish—men, women, and children. Of approximately 1,400 Regulars, levies and militia, 918 have been killed, 276 wounded. Almost half of the entire U.S. Army is dead or wounded—it is the worst relative defeat in Army history.

4–8 November. **St. Clair's Retreat. Fort Jefferson.**
Most survivors reach the fort by evening, but St. Clair orders them to keep moving since there is no food at the fort, and attack is imminent. The 1st Regiment is at the fort and acts as a rear guard. By the 8th, the remnants of St. Clair's army have arrived at Fort Washington. The militia is released, and the levies are discharged without pay. St. Clair sends Major Ebenezer Denny to report the disaster to Knox in Philadelphia.

19 December. **Washington Informed. Philadelphia.**
Denny reports the news to Knox, who goes to the President. Washington is outraged. Congress is shocked and orders a committee to investigate the defeat.

1792

January. **Harmar Resigns.**
Harmar resigns from the Army. When St. Clair visits Washington, Washington agrees to a congressional investigation, but he also requests St. Clair's resignation.

January. **Wilkinson's Expedition. Northwest Territory.**
Wilkinson leads a Regular and militia force for a retaliatory raid against the Miami villages. The weather is freezing, with heavy snow, and by the time the men march the 100 miles to the fort, the idea of a raid is forgotten. The Regulars return, while a detachment of militia rides to the St. Clair battlefield to gather abandoned equipment and bury the human remains.

5 March. **Legion of the United States.**
St. Clair resigns his Army commission. Congress authorizes an increase in the Regular Army to 5,120. The two infantry regiments and artillery battalion are authorized more men. In addition, three more infantry regiments and four troops of dragoons, all enlisted for three years, are approved. Pay and ration allowances

are increased. Washington is given authority to organize this force and with the advice of Knox directs the creation of "The Legion of the United States." He also selects former major general Anthony Wayne to be commander. A brigadier position is approved to command each of four sublegions and James Wilkinson is nominated for one.

27 March–8 May. **Congressional Investigation of St. Clair.**
The House committee concludes that St. Clair's defeat was due to inadequate forces; gross mismanagement by the quartermaster and contractors; and the lack of discipline and experience in the troops. St. Clair receives no blame in the final report and is permitted to continue as governor until 1802.

8 May. **1792 Militia Act.**
Congress passes a Militia Act "to establish a uniform militia throughout the United States." It includes compulsory universal service for all free, white male citizens between 18 and 45 years of age. Within six months of enrollment, each man must have his own weapons and equipment. Implementation is left to each state, resulting in a wide variance of results. The act also provides for "volunteer" artillery and mounted units equipped and uniformed at the members' expense.

June. **Wayne Takes Command. Pittsburgh.**
Major General Wayne, new Legion commander and commander-in-chief of the Army, makes his headquarters at Fort Fayette, near the center of the town. Since it is a small post, he orders the Legion to encamp nearby.

June. **Army Negotiators Murdered. Northwest Territory.**
Colonial John Hardin and Captain Alexander Trueman, acting as official peace commissioners, are invited to a meeting by the Miami tribes. After being welcomed, they are killed without warning.

4 September. **Legion of the United States Is Formed. Fort Fayette.**
Wayne organizes the Legion into four sublegions (1st–4th), each authorized 1,280 men. A sublegion has two battalions (four companies each) of infantry armed with muskets, one battalion of rifleman, a company of dragoons, and a company of horse artillery. The 1st Regiment becomes the 1st Sublegion; and the decimated 2d Regiment is the 2d Sublegion. One of the junior infantry officers in the new 4th Sublegion is Lieutenant William Clark, younger brother of George Rogers Clark.

30 September. **Chickamauga Indian War Begins. Nashville, Tennessee.**
Defense of the southern settlements is up to the loal militia. When a combined force of Chickamauga, Creek, Cherokee, and Shawnee warriors attack

Buchanan's Station near Nashville, local militia successfully defend the settlement. Lawyer Andrew Jackson is appointed a militia captain and adjutant of a mounted regiment that is frequently called to action during the two-year conflict.

30 November. **Wayne Drills the Legion. Legionville, Northwest Territory.**
To ease discipline problems, Wayne relocates the Legion camp 22 miles down the Ohio River from Pittsburgh. Wayne emphasizes hard training, issuing Von Steuben's "Blue Book" of drill to officers and requiring frequent musket practice. Marksmanship is encouraged by an extra whiskey ration to the best shots. Discipline is strict for both troops and camp followers. Several men are shot or hanged for capital crimes, and washerwomen who litter the camp area are dunked in the icy river.

THE LEGION OF THE UNITED STATES

The Legion incorporated infantry, dragoons, and artillery into a single combined-arms unit of 5,120 men at full strength. Revolutionary War hero "Mad" Anthony Wayne accepted the major general position, becoming commander of the Legion and the senior officer of the Army. Lieutenant Colonel James Wilkinson, commander of the 2d Infantry, accepted a brigadier position, but no other qualified men volunteered. The final Legion organization was completed in 1793 and Wilkinson was made Wayne's deputy. The four sublegions were led by senior majors promoted to "lieutenant colonel-commandant." These were John Hamtramck, David Strong, Henry Gaither, and Jonathon Clark.

Each sublegion was authorized two battalions of infantry, one battalion of riflemen, one company of light dragoons, and one of artillery, totaling 1,280 men. Due to a lack of recruits, only two battalions of riflemen were ever formed. This was partially offset with establishment of an elite light (rifle) infantry company in each infantry battalion. In 1794, additional artillerymen were also authorized. The 1st and 2d Infantry Regiments were redesignated 1st and 2d Sublegions respectively, while the 3d and 4th Sublegions were formed from newly enlisted men.

A highly competent, imaginative, and strong-willed commander, Wayne set about making the Legion into an effective fighting force. Over the next two years he oversaw every detail of the Legion's training, determined that it would be a well disciplined, reliable unit before it fought a single battle. Every company commander received von Steuben's famed *Blue Book* and was expected to personally supervise its use so that tactical drills could be executed with equal expertise on either parade ground or battlefield. Wayne strictly enforced a rigid discipline. He instructed the troops in individual marksmanship, bayonet use, and field fortifications.

Understanding the value of high espirit de corps, Wayne ordered on 11 September 1792 that every sub-legion would have its own distinctive color for cap bindings and plumes. The 1st Sublegion had white, the 2d red, the 3d yellow, and the 4th green. For special ceremonies, the 1st and 3d sublegions wore their hair tinted black, while the 2d and 4th had white powered hair. Each sublegion also received its own flag. His men became known as "Wayne's Legion."

For a variety of reasons, including the awkward rank structure, the legion concept was not totally accepted. Despite Wayne's successful use of the Legion in the Fallen Timbers campaign in 1794, the legion concept was dropped. Under the Act of 30 May 1796 Congress replaced the Legion with a more traditional regimental structure, but the rank of colonel remained absent until 1802.

—*Vince Hawkins*

Above: *Wayne made his Legion a well uniformed and drilled unit with strict discipline. Training was hard but the results were indisputable. ("Legion of the U.S.," Darby Erd)*

5 December. Washington Reelected.
George Washington is elected to a second term as President and Commander-in-Chief of federal military forces.

1793

February. **Sublegion Commanders Selected. Camp Legionville.**
Wilkinson accepts a brigadier commission. Wayne and Wilkinson deeply dislike each other, but Wilkinson is now Wayne's deputy. The Legion is not authorized colonels, so four of the Legion's senior majors are made sublegion commanders with the rank of lieutenant colonel-commandant. Total authorized Legion strength 258 officers and 5,156 noncommissioned officers and men.

April-7 October. **Wayne Begins His Campaign. Hobson's Choice, Northwest Territory.**
Wayne moves the Legion downriver and establishes a camp near Fort Washington which he names "Hobson's Choice." Hard training continues for both the foot and mounted troops while Wilkinson tries to undermine Wayne with both superiors and subordinates. Wayne, in turn, ignores his deputy. On 7 October, Wayne breaks camp and begins his offensive campaign. Great care is taken to post security on the march, and entrenchments are dug each night. Roving mounted patrols frustrate the Indians following the army.

14 October. **Fort Greenville. Northwest Territory.**
Six miles north of Fort Jefferson, Wayne halts and sets up winter camp. He uses the time to harden and train his troops. Construction begins on a large, 50-acre fort that Wayne names Fort Greenville (now Greenville, Ohio).

17 October. **Indian Ambush.**
A supply train bound for Fort Greenville with a Legion escort is attacked. Two officers and several men are killed. The Indians take all the horses, a serious blow to the faltering transportation system. More than 1,700 horses are needed; fewer than 300 are available.

24 December. **Wayne Builds Fort Recovery.**
While Wilkinson hosts a Christmas Eve dinner at Fort Jefferson, Wayne takes eight companies of the Legion to the site of St. Clair's defeat. He orders burial details to search the snow for overlooked remains and abandoned arms and supplies. Work also begins on a new fort on the battlefield. When it is completed several weeks later, Wayne christens it Fort Recovery.

1794

January. **Status of the Army.**
Army forts penetrate deep into hostile territory, but providing garrisons strains Legion's manpower. By June strength is down to 3,578. During the year the "Springfield" musket produced at the Springfield Arsenal is adopted as the infantry musket.

27 March. **First System of Coastal Forts.**
American coastal defenses was left to the states, and little has been done. The 1794 Naval Act acquires land for coast fortifications, and Army officers are sent to survey sites. Construction begins on 24 coastal forts, including one at Baltimore harbor to be named Fort McHenry. These defenses, which are initially open earthen parapets with Revolutionary War cannon, become known as the "First American System." With periodic modernization, they are used until the 1950s.

2 April. **Army Arsenal System Expanded.**
Congress approves money for two more arsenals. A site at Harper's Ferry, VA is chosen for one. Eli Whitney, who has attracted favorable attention in the War Department with his production techniques and efforts to machine-make muskets with totally interchangeable parts, is offered the senior position, but turns it down.

9 May. **Corps of Artillerists and Engineers Formed.**
To garrison the new coast defense forts, Congress authorizes 764 more sergeants and privates for a new Corps of Artillerists and Engineers, which also incorporates the Legion's artillery battalion. The Corps is organized into four battalions, each with four companies. Each company is authorized two "cadets" at a sergeant's pay. Washington establishes a school for artillerists and engineers at West Point where most of the Corps is posted. The total authorized artillery strength is 992 plus 56 officers.

12 June. **Army Rebuilds Fort Massac. Northwest Territory.**
Major Thomas Doyle, with a Legion infantry company and some artillerymen, rebuids this abandoned fort on the strategic Ohio River for use against the Indians on both sides of the river.

30 June–1 July. **Indians Attack Fort Recovery.**
Chiefs Little Turtle and Blue Jacket attack the fort with more than 1,200 warriors. A detachment of 140 Legion riflemen and dragoons camped outside are hit first and fall back to the fort. The small garrison, mainly Captain William Eaton and his 4th Sublegion company, holds the walls. Cannon recovered from the St. Clair battlefield help throw back the attackers with many casualties. The Indians make an unusual night attack but again are beaten off. Another dawn attack penetrates the stockade, but Eaton's men repulse the assault and the Indians finally withdraw.

American losses are 30 wounded and 22 officers and men killed.

16 July–8 August. **Whiskey Rebellion. Allegheny County, Pennsylvania.**
Angry grain farmers attack a tax inspector, who is defended by militia and Legionnaires from Fort Fayette. Several rebels and a militia officer are killed and some soldiers wounded. On 4 August, Washington proclaims the rebel activities as treason, giving him authority to call up militia. He orders the rebels to disperse peacefully and offers amnesty in exchange for swearing loyalty to the United States. At the same time Washington calls up 12,950 militiamen from four states.

August. **Legion Begins Campaign. Northwest Territory.**
Reinforced by Kentucky militia with Chickasaw and Choctaw scouts, Wayne marches the Legion into Indian country, destroying villages and fields. His force comprises about 3,500 men. Heavy patrols protect the main body, which travels 12 or fewer miles a day and building fortified camps each night. On the 8th, Wayne to build Fort Defiance, a fort strong enough to defy "the English, Indians and all the devils in hell," as his forward base.

15–18 August. **Wayne Advances.**
Wayne crosses the Maumee River and marches the Legion along it. About ten miles from British-held

Fort Miami, Indians appear under a flag of truce. Wayne ignores them and continues his advance. On the 18th, U.S. scouts are ambushed and one is captured. Under torture he tells the Indians that Wayne plans to attack the next day. The Indians prepare for battle and move to predesignated positions in a massive tangle of brush and fallen trees. Instead of advancing, however, Wayne halts for two days and builds Fort Deposit to protect his extra supplies.

20 August. **Battle of Fallen Timbers.**
Taking only two days' rations, a blanket, weapons, and ammunition, the Legionnaires advance along the river. Wilkinson commands the left (1st and 3d Sublegions), screened by light infantry and mounted Kentucky volunteers. Hamtramck leads the right (2d and 4th Sublegions) with dragoons near the river. Mounted groups cover Wayne's rear and lead the way. About five miles from Fort Miami, Ottawa warriors suddenly charge, scattering the advance party. The charge is premature and ruins the planned ambush by a larger group of Indians and Canadian militia. Hamtramck's men fire one volley and charge with fixed bayonets. In 45 minutes of hand-to-hand fighting, the Legion drives the Indians from the trees, sending the survivors fleeing to the fort for help, but t.he British refuse. Wayne's losses are 33 killed and 100 wounded. When the British rebuff his demands to evacuate the fort, Wayne taunts them for several days, then withdraws to Fort Defiance.

24 August. **Whiskey Rebellion.**
Reports of continued resistance and the doubtful loyalty of some Pennsylvania militia units causes Washington to ask for more Virginia militia. He also calls on two faithful old soldiers—Daniel Morgan to command the Virginians and Virginia governor Henry Lee to command the entire federalized militia force.

6 September. **Chickamauga War Ends. South of the Ohio.**
Against War Department orders, militia attack the Indian towns of Nickjack and Running Water. Major James Ore leads the raid of 550 mounted infantry, inflicting significant casualties on the Indians, bringing their chiefs to peace terms and ending the war.

9 September–4 October. **First Federal Militia Call-up.**
Under the new Constitution, Washington issues orders to Pennsylvania, New Jersey, Maryland, and Virginia to assemble, supply, and deploy a force of 15,450 militia. All four states have problems providing their quota and many lack weapons and equipment. Exceptions are the "volunteer" militia units, who have their own equipment and are enthusiastic about the expedition. One of those enlisting in the Virginia militia is Meriwether Lewis.

12 September–22 October. **Legion Builds Fort Wayne.**
The Legion marches to Miami Town (the site of the Harmar's defeat) clears land, and builds another Fort Wayne. On the 22nd, Hamtramck and six companies move into the new fort. The Legion now mans forts from the Ohio River to the Great Lakes, ending the campaign.

4–20 October. **First Presidential Field Command. Carlisle, Pennsylvania.**
Washington and Hamilton (Knox is on vacation) take charge of the "Army of the Constitution." Washington organizes two "wings," the right (Morgan) at Carlisle and the left (Lee) at Cumberland. The federalized force numbers about 11,000 militiamen. On the 10th, the first Carlisle column marches west. Washington rides to Cumberland, where Lee is training his men, then returns to Philadelphia. This first field command for an American President as Commander-in-Chief is also Washington's last.

22–31 October. **The Constitution Army Moves West.**
Lee marches parallel to Morgan on his north. The plan is to unite near Parkinson's Ferry on the Monongahela River. Both wings experience severe weather problems while crossing the mountains due to rain and ice.

2–17 November. **Whiskey Rebellion Ends.**
Lee sends patrols in search of insurgent "whiskey men," but few can be found. In predawn raids on the 13th, Lee's troops arrest about 200 suspects. Others come in voluntarily. Some 20 men are finally taken to Philadelphia for trial. Washington orders that a force be retained in the area for six months, and volunteers are organized into a provisional unit under Morgan. On the 17th, Lee and the other militia units return home.

31 December. **Knox Steps Down.**
Henry Knox resigns as Secretary of War. He has served as Commander of the Army and Secretary of War under both the Articles of Confederation and the Constitution. Knox becomes a gentleman farmer and dies in 1806.

1795

2 January. **New Secretary of War Appointed.**
Timothy Pickering is appointed to be the second Secretary of War. He served as Washington's Adjutant General and on the Board of War during the Revolution. In the west, Captain Zebulon Pike becomes commander of Fort Massac. His wife and young son, Zebulon M. Pike, are with him.

March. **Jay Treaty Ratified.**
Congress ratifies John Jay's Treaty by which the British agree (again) to withdraw from all their military posts remaining south of the Great Lakes. The Army has the responsibility to insure compliance and effect transfer of the forts.

Opposite, top: *William Eaton, former Army officer and envoy to Tunisia, is one of the key witnesses in the trial against Aaron Burr. (Historical Society of Pennsylvania)*

Opposite, bottom: *James McHenry served as Secretary of War from 1796 until 1800. (H. Pollack, Army Art Collection, NMUSA)*

Above: *In December 1796, James Wilkinson took Anthony Wayne's place as senior officer of the Army. (Charles Willson Peale, Army Art Collection, NMUSA)*

1 May. **Meriwether Lewis Joins the Legion.**
Former Kentucky militiaman Meriwether Lewis joins the 2d Sublegion as an infantry ensign.

June. **Morgan's Force Disbands. Pittsburgh.**
Morgan releases most of his 1,200 men and departs for home. Daniel Morgan's 40 years of military service, which began in 1755 with Washington on the Braddock expedition, are finally over.

16 June–3 August. **Treaty of Greenville. Fort Greenville.**
Wayne meets with senior Indian chiefs representing 12 tribes. The Jay treaty, by which the British withdraw entirely to Canada, stuns the Indians. On the 3rd, a treaty is signed officially ending hostilities in the area.

24 June. **Regiment of Artillerists and Engineers Organized. West Point.**

Lieutenant Colonel Stephen Rochefontaine, a former French officer, takes command of the regiment. He organizes four battalions and sets up a rudimentary school for training the officers and cadets. The instruction includes the study of basic gunnery, military fortifications, and von Steuben's drill. Discipline is a problem at times, and several duels are fought between the officers. As men are trained they are transferred to the forts being constructed. By 1798, only two officers, a cadet, and 76 enlisted men remain at the school.

11 July. **Fort Detroit Transferred. Northwest Territory.**

Captain Moses Porter and his 65-man company of Artillery and Engineers take possession of the fort from the British.

6 November. **Meriwether Lewis Is Court-Martialed. Fort Greenville.**

Ensign Lewis is court-martialed for insulting and fighting with other officers while intoxicated. He is found not guilty. Wayne transfers Lewis to the elite "Chosen Rifle Company" commanded by Lieutenant William Clark.

10 December. **Pickering Resigns.**

Timothy Pickering resigns as Secretary of War.

14 December. **Wayne Departs. Fort Greenville.**

Wayne issues an order bidding a "temporary adieu to the Legion" and departs for Philadelphia to meet with Congress. Wilkinson assumes command of the Legion.

THE CORPS OF DISCOVERY

When Captain Meriwether Lewis and Lieutenant William Clark were preparing for their great expedition across the North American continent, they knew they would need a trustworthy group of strong, well-trained, and determined men to accompany them.

President Jefferson authorized Lewis to pick volunteers from the noncommissioned officers and men of the Army regiments stationed at the western posts, as well as to enlist others he saw as necessary to the expeditions success. Civilians could also be hired as needed, and both money and a letter of credit were issued to help pay those chosen. Lewis initially estimated that about a dozen men would be sufficient, but by the time the group had reached the Mississippi, Lewis and Clark agreed that more were needed.

In early August 1803, Lewis wrote to Clark about the importance of selecting the right men, explaining "their qualifications should be such as perfectly fit them for the service, otherwise they will rather clog than further the objects in view." The first couple of candidates joined Lewis in Pittsburg along with temporary crews hired to help take the boats down the Ohio. Lewis planned a "Corps of Discovery" of two teams. One, the "return party," would travel up the Missouri to the river's falls and then take the large keelboat and first scientific samples back to St. Louis and await his return. The second, smaller team would continue on to the Pacific. The time until the actual start up the Missouri would be used to evaluate the volunteers for selection to the Corps.

As word of the expedition and the promise of pay and a land grant spread, a number of volunteers came forward. The 26 men who were finally selected came from various backgrounds, each contributing specific skills to the expedition. Four men were selected to be sergeants, leading squads ranging in size from eight to eleven men. When one sergeant died of appendicitis during the trip, the men voted to select his replacement. The average age of the sergeants at the start was 29 years.

One sergeant was an experienced carpenter. Of the 22 privates, three were blacksmiths, two skilled hunters, two boatmen, one an interpreter, and one a tailor, but everyone shared in the tasks throughout the trip. The average age of the privates was also 29. Three were punished at different times for drinking, fighting, or absence without permission. For repeated offenses one private was transferred to the return party despite his promises to reform.

The men of the Corps were encouraged to keep their own journals of the expedition, and several did. After the expedition, five of the privates reenlisted and three fought in the War of 1812. Five went into the trapping and fur-trading business and did well. Four were killed in wars or in altercations with Indians.

The success of the two-year, cross-continent adventure speaks highly of the ability of Lewis and Clark to correctly judge the high character of the men they selected and is a testament to their dedication and teamwork.

—*Kevin M. Hymel*

Above: *Captain Meriwether Lewis and Lieutenant William Clark hand selected the best men for their journey. Originally, Lewis believed that twelve men would suffice. (Michael Haynes)*

27 January. **McHenry Becomes Secretary of War.**
James McHenry is appointed the third Secretary of
War. McHenry served as a regimental surgeon during
the Revolution, was a prisoner and ended the war as a
staff officer for Washington and Lafayette.

30 May. **Legion Ordered Abolished.**
Congress eliminates the Legion structure, returning
the Army to a regimental organization effective 31
October. One reason is to correct the top heavy
Legion rank structure, which has six brigadier
positions but no colonels or lieutenant colonels.

1 July. **William Clark Resigns. Fort Washington.**
First Lieutenant William Clark resigns from the Army
and returns to Kentucky. His friend Lewis remains in
the Army, and is often employed as a long-distance
courier.

July–14 August. **Wayne Returns West. Fort
Washington.**
Wayne returns and Wilkinson takes leave. Rumors
abound of Wilkinson's deals with the Spanish, and he
plans to divert attention by pressing charges of
improper conduct and incompetence against Wayne.
Wayne ignores him and embarks on an inspection of
the frontier posts. On 14 August, Wayne arrives at Fort
Detroit, now commanded by Colonel John
Hamtramck. Wayne's health is not good, and he stays
for three months.

11 September. **Last British Fort Transferred. Fort
Mackinac, Northwest Territory.**
Major Henry Burbeck and a company of Artillerists
and Engineers take possession of this last British fort
to be transferred.

1 November. **Army Reorganized.**
The Army reorganizes into four separate regiments of
infantry, two companies of light dragoons, and the
Corps of Artillerists and Engineers. The infantry of 1st
Sublegion is redesignated the 1st Infantry; 2d Sublegion
becomes the 2d Infantry; 3d Sublegion the 3d Infantry;

and 4th Sublegion the 4th Infantry. Only two generals—a major general and a brigadier—are authorized. Two staff positions—a paymaster general and a quartermaster general—are authorized. Excess officers and men are released with six months' pay and subsistence allowance.

15 December. Anthony Wayne Dies. Presque Isle, Pennsylvania.

Wayne crosses Lake Erie and arrives at the fort in mid-November. Worn out and ill, "Mad" Anthony Wayne dies in bed in the fort's quarters. As he has requested, he is buried in full uniform at the foot of the fort's flag pole. His body is later moved to the family plot in Pennsylvania. Brigadier General James Wilkinson now is senior officer and commander of the Army.

1797

February. Captain Eaton's Secret Mission. Philadelphia.

While Captain William H. Eaton waits for his resignation to be approved, he is sent to help Secretary of State John Pickering. Eaton is tasked to uncover the espionage activities of Dr. Nicholas Romayne, a physician in New York City. Eaton pretends to be a court-martialed captain seeking revenge by selling information on American forces along the Florida-Georgia border. When Romayne makes an offer, Eaton pulls a pistol and seizes the doctor along with incriminating documents from his desk. With an Army escort, Eaton takes his prisoner to Philadelphia and turns him over to Pickering.

3 March. Judge Advocate Created.

Congress authorizes a Judge Advocate for the Army for the first time since the Revolution. Captain Campbell Smith assumes the duties on 2 June.

4 March. Adams Inaugurated. Philadelphia.

John Adams becomes the second President and Commander-in-Chief of the Army. In the bitter political fighting between Federalists and Jefferson Republicans, Army commissions and promotions are used as political patronage.

March—May. Eaton Has Another Mission. Philadelphia.

Adams fears a Spanish move against the southern states. He asks Eaton to undertake a mission of disinformation. Eaton, posing as a debt-ridden Army officer with a sincere concern for peace, cultivates the deputy-minister of the Spanish legation. Over several

Opposite: *Cockade and gilt eagle for the chapeau of an Army general officer, circa 1800–1812. (Smithsonian Institution, National Museum of American History)*

Above: *Alexander Hamilton served as Army Inspector General. Although he became senior officer, political pressure kept him from officially being named commander. ("Alexander Hamilton," P. T. Weaver, Army Art Collection, NMUSA)*

weeks, Eaton tells the minister of secret American forts and forces standing by should Spain attack. To add credibility, Eaton refuses Spanish money and job offers. By summer, Spain proposes a treaty of friendship with the United States and Adams rewards Eaton, finally discharged, with the post of Counsel-General to Tunis. When Eaton returns in 1805 he is a national hero, having led a rag-tag army of U.S. Marines, mercenaries and Arabs to victory in Tripoli.

May–June. Problems Along the Southern Frontier. Southwest Territory

Incidents with Indians and concerns about Spanish intentions cause Adams to increase the number of Army troops in the south. Colonel Thomas Butler, with seven companies of the 4th Infantry Regiment, some artillery, and a company of dragoons, is sent to Knoxville. Captain Isaac Guion with a detachment of the 3d Infantry Regiment and artillerymen, is also sent south.

27 April. Quasi-War. Regiment of Artillerists and Engineers Formed.
Congress increases Army strength and purchases arms and munitions. In addition to the Corps of Artillerists and Engineers, a separate regiment with three battalions is authorized. In May, a fourth battalion is approved. Congress also authorizes enlistment of a "Provisional Army" of 10,000 men for three years' service. In addition, the President may accept the service of any volunteer unit that agrees to arm and equip itself, and may select the officers for both the Volunteer and Provisional units.

3 May. Department of War Gives Up Navy Responsibilities.
The Department of the Navy is created, taking responsibility for naval matters from the War Department. The War Department retains responsibility for Indian Affairs, land grants, and Army matters.

3–7 July. Washington Returns As Commander. Mount Vernon.
George Washington accepts a commission as the Army's first lieutenant general, with the title of General-in-Chief of the Army. He stipulates that he is to receive no pay nor have any duties until he actually takes the field. The Senate approves on 7 July. After bitter political infighting, Alexander Hamilton and Charles C. Pinckney are appointed as major generals. Wilkinson remains a brigadier. Hamilton is made Inspector General and second-in-command of the Army.

7 June. Army Pay.
Congress directs that soldier's pay cannot be more than two months late, but this is impossible on the frontier. Soldiers plant gardens and raise livestock to ease the supply burdens. Wilkinson, however, finds many soldiers have become full-time laborers and farmers. He issues an order forbidding the practice, but many ignore it.

24 June. Quasi-War With France.
War with France appears imminent. Congress issues state quotas for 80,000 militia men. Money is also provided for Army engineers to strengthen harbor fortifications against potential French attacks.

4 July–October. Fort Adams Built. Tennessee.
Captain Guion arrives with his detachment to build a fort on Chickasaw Bluffs overlooking the Mississippi River. The fort is not completed until October when Major William Kersey arrives with more of the 3d Regiment. Guion goes on to Natchez to establish order until territorial authorities are set up. (Chickasaw Bluffs is now Memphis, Tennessee.)

16 July. Quasi-War. Regular Army Expanded.
Congress adds 39 officers and 704 enlisted men to the Army regiments. Also authorized, but never formed, are 12 new infantry regiments and six troops of light dragoons. Army pay is raised by one dollar and rations are increased. Four civilian instructors and an officer are approved for the artillery school at West Point.

September. New Fort Built. Loftus Heights. Mississippi Territory.
The Army constructs Fort Adams on the Heights. This fort is only six miles from Spanish territory and controls the traffic along the river. On a leisurely inspection trip of southern posts, Wilkinson and his party reach Natchez by barge on 27 September and visit the fort.

1799

January. **New Army Uniforms and Insignia Adopted.**
Hamilton and Pinckney recruit and organize the expanded army. Responsibility for purchase of army supplies is given to the War Department. Changes to the Army uniform are made during the year. The commanding general (Lieutenant General Washington) is to wear two epaulettes with three stars; major generals wear two stars and brigadiers one star. Field officers (colonels, lieutenant colonels, and majors) wear two plain epaulettes; company-grade officers (captains and below) wear only one. Infantry and artillery wear blue coats with red facings while the dragoons wear green coats with white. All soldiers wear a black cockade with a small white or gold eagle in the center on their hats.

2–3 March. **Army Reorganized.**
A Medical Department headed by a physician general officer is created. The Corps and the Regiment of Artillerists and Engineers are redesignated as 1st and 2d Regiments of Artillerists and Engineers, respectively. The ranks of ensign (infantry and artillery) and coronet (dragoons) are replaced by second lieutenant and former lieutenants become first lieutenants Pay and some allowances are increased, but the daily whiskey ration is reduced; and the Army staff is increased.

14 December. **Washington Dies. Mount Vernon.**
Washington dies at age 67, still officially on Army service. The title and the rank of lieutenant general that Congress established for him personally are abolished. Major General Alexander Hamilton is now senior officer in the Army, but for political reasons he remains titled Inspector General.

1800

January. **Status of the Army.**
When the threat of war recedes, plans for expansion of the Army die. The arsenal at Harper's Ferry develops a rifled musket of caliber .62, making it one of the first mass-produced firearms for the Army.

5 January. **McHenry Recommends Schools.**
Secretary of War McHenry recommends the creation of a military academy with five subordinate schools to train both Army and Navy personnel. No action is taken.

30 March. **First Army Metal Branch Insignia.**
The Army approves a metal insignia for the dragoons.

Opposite, top: *The first metal branch insignia—a Dragoon cap badge, circa 1800. (Smithsonian Institution, National Museum of American History)*

Above: *Samuel Dexter, Secretary of War 1800–1801, was responsible for President Washington's eulogy in December 1799. (Walter M. Brackett, Army Art Collection, NMUSA)*

It is the first branch insignia adopted by the Army. Metal insignia for other branches does not appear until the War of 1812.

7 May. **Harrison Appointed Territory Governor.**
Congress divides the Northwest Territory, appointing former Army captain William Henry Harrison governor of the western Indiana Territory. As governor he is commander of the territorial militia. St. Clair retains the eastern Ohio Territory.

13 June. **Dexter Replaces McHenry as Secretary of War.**
President Adams appoints Samuel Dexter to be fourth Secretary of War. Dexter is the first Secretary without any military experience.

June. **Department of War Moves to Washington.**
The national government to Washington City and temporary offices for the War Department are set up near the President's House.

15 June. **Temporary Forces Discharged.**
Congress orders all new recruits released with three months' pay and money to get home. The Army drops to

3,429 men—116 dragoons, 1,501 artillerists and engineers, and 1,812 infantrymen. Both Hamilton and Pickering resign their commissions, leaving Wilkinson the Army's only general officer and again its commander.

1801

January. Status of the Army
In the South, the small Army has increasing problems with squatters on Indian lands. Along the Atlantic coast, many of the 14 defense forts are completed, but they have only small 24-pound and 32-pound cannon as primary weapons.

20 February. Jefferson Writes Lewis. Washington City.
President-elect Jefferson offers Captain Meriwether Lewis a position as his private secretary. As a boy, Lewis lived near Jefferson, and in 1792 he had written Jefferson volunteering to serve on a western expedition. Jefferson offers a salary of $500, retention of Army rank, and right to promotion. Lewis receives the letter on 7 March and readily accepts.

4 March. Jefferson Inaugurated.
Thomas Jefferson becomes the third President and Commander-in-Chief. As part of his "midnight appointments," Adams filled vacant Army officer positions with Federalists. Jefferson, who favors a smaller Army anyway, seeks to purge the Federalist influence.

5 March. Dearborn Appointed Secretary.
Dexter resigns and Jefferson appoints Henry Dearborn as fifth Secretary of War. He is a veteran of the Revolution with extensive experience.

1 April. Lewis Assumes Position.
Lewis begins his duties as Jefferson's private secretary. A first task is to evaluate the political affiliation (Federalist or Republican) of all Army officers and their professional fitness. Jefferson and Dearborn use the report in selecting officers to retain or discharge.

30 April. Army Hair Regulations Changed.
The old style of long hair tied in a queue with a ribbon at the back of the head is eliminated for a shorter cut. Many old soldiers resist the change. One colonel is court-martialed for refusing to cut his hair, but he dies before the sentence is enforced. Army tradition says he is buried with his queue sticking out of the coffin in defiance. Other uniform changes are introduced, including full-length trousers and round, top-hat style caps.

10 June. Artillerymen Serve at Sea.
Two batteries of U.S. Army artillery are assigned to serve with the U.S. fleet as gun crews during the war with Tripoli.

Opposite, top: *Henry Dearborn replaced Samuel Dexter as Secretary of War in 1801. Dearborn later succeeded James Wilkinson as Commanding General of the Army in 1812. ("Henry Dearborn," Walter M. Brackett, Army Art Collection, NMUSA)*

Opposite, bottom: *Grand-nephew of Benjamin Franklin, Jonathan Williams was appointed inspector of fortifications and superintendent at West Point. ("Jonathan Williams," Thomas Sully, U.S. Military Academy Library, West Point, New York)*

Right: *President Jefferson signed the bill approving the creation of the U.S. Military Academy in March 1802. The academy began instruction in July. ("Cadets of the U.S. Military Academy, 1802." H. Charles McBarron, Company of Military Historians)*

June–December. **Army Builds the Natchez Trace.**
Wilkinson is appointed peace commissioner and is sent to make treaties with the tribes on the southeastern frontier. The Chickasaws and Choctaws agree to permit the Army to build a rough trail from Natchez to Nashville and to station small detachments along the trail.

14 December. **First Superintendent at West Point.**
Major Jonathan Williams, 2d Regiment of Artillerists and Inspector of Fortifications, arrives to command the small school of application. He will be the first superintendent of the new military academy when it opens the following July.

1802

1 January. **Status of the Army.**
The Army comprises two companies of dismounted dragoons, two regiments of artillerists and engineers, and four regiments of infantry. Although 5,438 positions are authorized, rosters show only 248 officers, 9 cadets, and 3,794 enlisted men on duty. Ten officers fill general staff positions.

March. **Jackson Appointed Militia General. Knoxville, Tennessee.**
Andrew Jackson, lawyer and part time militiaman, is made major general and commander of the Tennessee

militia. In one of his first actions Jackson orders the arrest of a settler for murdering an Indian.

16 March. Army Strength Cut. Military Academy Founded.

President Jefferson establishes a military academy but also drastically reduces the Army. The dragoon regiments are eliminated, and the infantry is cut to two regiments. Brigadier General Wilkinson remains the senior Army officer, but his pay and staff are reduced. The rank of colonel is restored, but more than 70 officers are discharged with only three months' pay. Many are bitter.

1 April. Separation of Artillerists and Engineers.

The 1st and 2d Regiments of Artillerists and Engineers are disbanded. The artillerymen are reformed into the Regiment of Artillery. For economy, no horses are authorized—men or oxen must drag the cannon. The engineers become the Corps of Engineers, with seven officers and ten cadets, all stationed at West Point to "constitute a military academy." No enlisted men are authorized in the Corps until 1808.

4 July. Military Academy Opens. West Point.

The U.S. Military Academy officially opens. The superintendent and senior Corps of Engineers officer is Major Jonathan Williams. The first students are ensigns and cadets assigned to the Engineer Corps and the Artillery Regiment, and they wear their normal uniforms to class. Cadets receive "warrants" from the President and a sergeant's pay. The artillery company commander, Captain George Izard, remains the post commander because Secretary Dearborn has ruled that Engineers may command only members of their own Corps. Williams resigns over this policy in June 1803.

12 October. First Graduates of the Military Academy. West Point.

The first two graduates of the new military academy, Joseph G. Swift and Simon M. Levy, are commissioned as second lieutenants in the Corps of Engineers. Both officers had been attending courses of instruction at West Point prior to the creation of the new school.

3 December. Distinctive Uniform Approved for Engineers.

The Corps of Engineers receives permission to wear a distinctive uniform. The coat is a deep blue with a gold-embroidered velvet stand-up collar and cuffs. A unique embossed button with a bastion, eagle and the Corps motto "Essayons," which Engineers wear to the present day, is also adopted.

1803

18 January. Jefferson Proposes Western Expedition.

In a confidential message to Congress, President Jefferson requests $2,500 to fund an expedition up the Missouri River as far as the Pacific to strengthen American claims on the Columbia territory. He asks that the appropriation be hidden in a general budget line for "extending the external commerce" to "cover the undertaking from notice." The territory does not belong to the United States and Spanish authorities who control it for the French reject Jefferson's request for safe passage. He asks Lewis to plan and lead the expedition.

9 March. **Troops Ordered to Chicago River. Fort Detroit.**
Hamtramck is ordered to send troops across Lake Michigan to the mouth of the Chicago River to build a fort. By August, Captain John Whistler (grandfather of future painter James Whistler) is there with a detachment of 1st Infantry, and construction is underway. When the fort is completed in the spring, it is named Fort Dearborn (now Chicago, Illinois).

March. **Efforts to Improve Militia.**
Congress passes a series of acts to purchase arms and equipment for 80,000 militiamen, if called up. In addition, Army food is is improved, the whiskey ration (wine or beer optional) is restored, and additional clothing is issued.

15 March. **June. Lewis Gathers Equipment.**
Captain Lewis draws advance pay and funds for supplies. He orders 15 new Model 1803 .54-caliber rifled muskets from the Harper's Ferry arsenal. These will be the first standard Army-issue musket. Lewis also gathers equipment, 4,200 rations (including dried soup), tools, trading materials, and mapping and scientific instruments. He visits experts in astronomy, medicine, botany, zoology, and cartography, learning as much as possible in a few weeks. On the 19th, Lewis writes his old Army friend, William Clark, inviting him to join as co-commander with the promised rank, pay and benefits of a captain, plus a veteran's land grant. Lewis then directs the Army to transport the supplies to Pittsburgh, and returns to Washington for final discussions.

4 July. **Lewis Receives Orders. Washington.**
Jefferson gives Lewis detailed instructions for a secret code (based on the word "artichoke") and a letter of general credit. Lewis has authority to select enlisted men from Army garrisons along the way. Some men will go only part_way to help transport supplies; others will travel the entire distance. Lewis departs the next day for Pittsburgh.

29 July. **Clark Joins the Expedition. Pittsburgh.**
Lewis receives Clark's letter of acceptance, but the expedition is behind schedule. Lewis had problems transporting his supplies to Pittsburgh. The specially designed 55-foot-long, eight-foot-wide, galley-style keelboat is weeks late, and the water level of the river is dropping.

31 August. **Lewis Begins.**
Within hours of completion, the keelboat is loaded and Lewis is moving down the Ohio with a hired

crew. He also has two soldiers for the expedition, and a $20 Newfoundland named "Seaman." Clark is waiting at the Clarksville home of his older brother, George Rogers Clark, with his personal slave, York, and more volunteers.

14 October. **Lewis and Clark Meet. Clarksville, Indiana Territory.**
Lewis meets Clark for the first time in seven years. The trip has been hard. Many times the keelboat had to be lifted over rock ledges or towed by oxen due to the low water. Lewis writes Jefferson that the expedition will have to camp for the winter.

15 October–28 November. **Corps of Discovery Formed.**
At Clarksville nine men are sworn in as the first enlisted members of the Corps of Discovery. On 11 November, the expedition arrives at Fort Massac, where they rest. Lewis hires a local guide, George Drouillard, and two soldiers from the Massac garrison join. On the 13th, they move into the powerful Mississippi, and after two weeks of hard work they reach Fort Kaskaskia. About a dozen men volunteer from the garrison of 1st Infantry and Artillerists.

December. **Corps Makes Winter Camp. Dubois (Wood) River.**
The Corps camps on the river, across the Mississippi from the Missouri River. Lewis crosses to St. Louis for supplies and information. The Spanish governor refuses Lewis permission to continue until the territory is formally transferred to the U.S. Meanwhile, Clark supervises camp construction. He modifies the keelboat, arming it with a small cannon and two blunderbusses mounted on swivels. More men arrive, but only four are acceptable. Lewis sends the first sample specimens back to President Jefferson and receives letters of instruction.

20 December. **Lower Louisiana District Transferred. New Orleans.**
Brigadier General Wilkinson assists in the transfer of the lower Louisiana Territory to the United States. Wilkinson is accompanied by three artillery companies from Fort Adams under Lieutenant Colonel Constant Freeman. Wilkinson sends small detachments to replace the various Spanish garrisons. In many cases, junior officers in command of the distant posts wield both civil and military authority over their areas.

1804

January. **Status of the Army**
The moving allowance for unmarried and married officers of the same rank is the same. A colonel can move 750 pound; a lieutenant, 200 pounds. Reimbursement for living expenses is $1.00–$1.25 a day. Many officers must sell personal property when they are transferred; others resign rather than go into debt. To make ends meet, many soldiers engage side businesses such as distilling whiskey, farming, real estate, and fur trading.

9–10 March. **Formal Transfer of Upper Louisiana.**
On 9 March, Captain Amos Stoddard, Regiment of Artillery, commander of Fort Kaskaskia, acts as agent for the French, accepting the transfer of the Upper Louisiana District from the Spanish lieutenant-governor. The next day, Stoddard lowers the French flag and raises the American flag over the fort, signifying final transfer to the United States. An artillery company acts as honor guard, and Captain Lewis is an official witness. Stoddard, a French speaker, remains acting governor until July. Detachments of the 1st Infantry are sent to take over the other Spanish outposts in the area.

31 March. **Permanent Corps of Discovery Chosen. Wood River.**
The 25 men picked to make the full trip of the expedition are divided into three squads, each under a sergeant. The rest are a "return crew" who will go as far as the first winter camp, then return with specimens and dispatches. Discipline problems arise when the bored men slip away to a local whiskey peddler, get drunk, and fight.

Opposite, top: The compass used by William Clark during the expedition. (Smithsonian Institution, National Museum of American History, Behring Center)

Opposite, bottom: Stars and Stripes are hoisted over New Orleans to replace the French Tricolor, representing the transfer of the lower portion of the Louisiana Territory from France to the U.S. (The Granger Collection, New York)

Right: *Lewis and Clark sail west on their large keelboat as the Corps of Discovery embarks on its journey. ("Lewis and Clark 1804," L. Edward Fisher, Missouri Bankers Assoc.)*

20 April. **Westernmost Fort Transferred. Natchitoches, Louisiana Territory.**
Captain Edward Turner and a company of the 1st Infantry occupy the former Spanish fort, which they rename Fort Claiborne.

May. **Wilkinson Betrays Lewis and Clark. Washington.**
Wilkinson informs the Spanish ambassador that a secret American expedition is departing St. Louis to explore the Louisiana Territory. Within weeks Spanish cavalry begin searching the Platte and Missouri River valleys for the Corps of Discovery.

6 May. **Clark's Commission. St. Louis.**
Lewis receives a letter from Secretary Dearborn with Clark's commission. It is not a captain's commission, but one as a lieutenant in the artillery, with a captain's pay. Clark accepts it, and Lewis assures him that they will continue as "captains and co-commanders". They agree to say nothing to the men, and Clark never officially protests. He is finally promoted to captain by Congress in 2000, 196 years later.

14–20 May. **Lewis and Clark Expedition Begins.**
Clark takes the Corps of Discovery up the Missouri River on the afternoon of the 14th. Two days later the keelboat and two pirogues arrive at St. Charles, where they wait for Lewis. While they wait, Clark permits many of the men to attend a dance in the town. Several guards from the boats leave their posts without permission and get drunk. All are punished with a flogging. Private John Collins receives 100 lashes, the others only 25. Lewis arrives on the 20th with two more men, and the next afternoon all set off again. The Corps will be gone two years.

21 May–29 June. **Lewis and Clark. Missouri River.**
The Corps passes the home of Daniel Boone, and on the 25th, La Charette, the last white settlement. The river is difficult, with high water, bad weather, insects and deadly "sawyers" (large sunken logs). At times the only way forward is to tow the boats by hand. Collins is court-martialed again on 29 June for stealing whiskey and getting drunk on guard. He's given another 100 lashes. Courts martial and punishments are usually carried out by the enlisted men themselves.

July. **First Indian Students at the Military Academy. West Point.**
Before departing St. Louis, Lewis recommends the sons of prominent local Indian families for appointment to the new military academy. Six are sent in July; five of them graduate in 1806. One, Lorimier

Left: *The Corps of Discovery encountered a number of Indian tribes and attempted to establish peaceful relations between the Indians and the westward-expanding United States. ("Into the Unknown," James K. Ralston, United States National Park Service, Jefferson National Expansion Memorial)*

Chouteau, a half-Indian, serves for three years. Another, Charles Gratiot, serves for 32 years, becomes a brevet brigadier and Chief of the Engineer Corps.

3 August. **First Meeting with Indians. Council Bluffs.** The Corps encounters Otos Indians on 2 August. After a demonstration of drill and musketry Lewis makes a long speech and distributes gifts. The Indians ask for gunpowder and whiskey, which Lewis provides sparingly. That night, Private Moses Reed deserts and a search party brings him back. He is court-martialed and sentenced to running a gauntlet between two lines of men four times. Later in the month a council is held with the Yankton Sioux.

20–26 August. **Death of Sergeant Floyd. Missouri River.** On the 20th, Sergeant Charles Floyd, one of the most reliable Corps members, dies from a burst appendix. He is the first U.S. Army soldier to die west of the Mississippi and is buried on a bluff overlooking the river. The men select Patrick Gass to be Floyd's replacement. Later that day Private George Shannon fails to return from a hunting trip and cannot be found.

23–25 September. **Meeting the Teton Sioux. Bad River.** The Corps comes upon two villages of Teton Sioux and arranges for a council. After the usual demonstrations, the seven Indian chiefs are shown the boats. They are belligerent and demand a large number of gifts, then try to seize a pirogue. Each side braces to fight, but a chief intervenes and asks the Americans to

stay longer. It is agreed, and the Corps spends several uneasy days nearby before moving to stay with the Arikaras for several days.

16 October. **Army Escorts Scientific Expedition. St. Catherine's Landing, Mississippi Territory.** An expedition of civilian scientists departs north up the Ouachita River (in present-day Arkansas) with an Army escort composed of a sergeant and 12 enlisted men. This is the first U.S. exploration of the area. They are gone four months and return without incident.

20 October. **First Encounter with a Grizzly Bear. Missouri River.** Private Pierre Cruzatte is the first of the Corps to meet a grizzly bear. He wounds the bear, then drops his rifle and tomahawk and runs for his life. He barely escapes.

27 October–31 December. **Winter Camp with the Mandans. Fort Mandan.** The Corps reaches the Mandan villages and is welcomed in a friendly fashion. Lewis calculates they have traveled 1,609 miles. A small stockade with log cabins, which they call Fort Mandan, is built near one of the villages. The men hunt and encounter both friendly and hostile groups of Indians. Toussaint Charbonneau, one of the French traders living with the Indians, is hired as a translator. He is assisted by one of his Indians wives, a Shoshone named Sacagawea. (Fort Mandan is in North Dakota.)

MAJOR GENERAL ANTHONY WAYNE

His undaunted courage and ferocity in battle won him the sobriquet "Mad Anthony." His intelligence, skill, and resourcefulness as a commander earned him a reputation as one of America's foremost generals.

Anthony Wayne was born 1 January 1745 in Waynesborough, Pennsylvania. Wayne farmed and had a successful tannery. In 1774 he was elected to the Pennsylvania legislature and also served on the Committee of Public Safety.

In September 1775 Wayne raised a unit of volunteers and received a commission as colonel of the 4th Pennsylvania Battalion on 3 January 1776. He served in the abortive Canadian Expedition and was wounded at the Battle of Trois Rivières on 8 June. On 21 February 1777, Wayne was promoted to brigadier general and in April joined Washington's army at Morristown.

Given command of the regiments of the Pennsylvania Line, Wayne led a skillful defense at Chadd's Ford during the Battle of Brandywine on 11 September. Ten days later at Paoli, he was hit by a surprise British night attack, resulting in accusations of negligence. He demanded a court-martial and was cleared of all charges. At Germantown on 4 October, Wayne was wounded again while leading his men in a furious bayonet assault. In June 1778, Wayne led the initial assault against the British at Monmouth, New Jersey, then resolutely held the American center against repeated counterattacks.

In June 1779 Wayne received command of the newly formed Light Corps. He won fame leading this corps in a night attack against Stony Point, New York, on 16 July. For this victory Wayne was awarded a gold medal by Congress. In December, Wayne retired and returned home.

Recalled to duty in May 1780, Wayne subsequently harassed British posts along the Hudson River. In July, he was badly repulsed at Bull's Ferry. On 1 January 1781, the Pennsylvania Line mutinied in protest of no pay and bad conditions. Utilizing his reputation with his men, Wayne helped quell the mutiny.

That May, Wayne and his Pennsylvanians joined General Lafayette in Virginia. At Green Spring on 6 July, Wayne's force was nearly destroyed in a British trap. Following the British surrender at Yorktown, Wayne went to reinforce General Greene's southern

army. Arriving in January 1782, Wayne was almost immediately sent on the Georgia Expedition against the Creeks and Cherokees. By August he had forced the British to evacuate Savannah and the Indians to negotiate a treaty. Wayne was brevetted major general on 30 September 1783, then retired.

On 5 March 1792, President Washington reappointed Wayne a major general and Commander of the Army with instructions to end Indian resistance in the Northwest Territory. Wayne took command of the new Legion of the United States, restructuring and rigorously training it before opening his campaign and decisively defeating the Indians in the Battle of Fallen Timbers. His successful negotiation of the 1795 Treaty of Greenville, opened the Northwest to settlement.

In ill health, Wayne died at the Army post at Presque Isle, Ohio, on the evening of 15 December 1796 at age 51. A soldier to the last, Wayne had requested his body be buried at the foot of the post flagpole.

—*Vince Hawkins*

Above: *Major General Anthony Wayne, a Revolutionary War hero, restored the confidence and pride of the Army with his victory at the Battle of Fallen Timbers. (North Wind Picture Archives)*

1805

January. **Status of the Army.**
Army strength has dropped to a low of only 175 officers, 12 cadets, and 2,389 enlisted men.

11 January. **William Hull Named Governor.**
Congress creates the Michigan Territory, with its capital at Detroit. William Hull, a Revolutionary War hero and a major general in the Massachusetts militia, is named governor.

11 February. **Lewis is a Midwife. Fort Mandan.**
Lewis assists with the birth of Sacagawea's child. He administers a dose of ground rattlesnake rattle mixed with water, which seems to ease the delivery, and a healthy baby boy is born. Temperatures average below zero, but food and shelter are adequate.

26 March. **Wilkinson Appointed Governor. Washington.**
The Louisiana Purchase is divided into two sections—the Territory of Orleans (its capital at New Orleans) and the Louisiana Territory (its capital at St. Louis). Brigadier General Wilkinson, in addition to commanding the Army, is appointed governor of the Louisiana Territory.

7 April. **Corps of Discovery Detachment Returns to St. Louis. Fort Mandan.**
Corporal Richard Warfington leads the return group back using the keelboat loaded with specimens, samples, letters, and a lengthy report to Jefferson. As soon as the keelboat departs, the Corps, now consisting of Lewis, Clark, 28 enlisted soldiers, Charbonneau, Sacagawea, and her baby, head west in pirogues and canoes

19 April. **Williams Reappointed Academy Superintendent. West Point.**
Williams returns to the academy as a lieutenant colonel and head of the Engineer Corps, with responsibility for construction of all the coastal forts. The duty keeps Williams away for lengthy periods, with adverse effects on the academy.

27 April. **Eaton's Expedition. North Africa.**
Former Army Captain William Eaton, Consular Envoy to Tunis, leads a small force of Arabs and U.S. Marines across the desert from Egypt to "the shores of Tripoli" to capture the city of Derna.

3 June–14 July. **Corps Finds A New River. Marias River.**
The river divides and Lewis takes a group up the north fork (Marias River) while Clark goes south.

When they meet on the 8th, they decide to go south. On the 13th, they reach the first falls and are dismayed to find there are five. The difficult portage around the falls and rapids takes almost a month, requiring the men to pull the 1,000-lb. boats by hand more than 18 miles. This puts them behind schedule.

23 July. First Army Fort West of the Mississippi River. Louisiana Territory

At the direction of the War Department, Wilkinson selects the site for Fort Bellefontaine just northwest of St. Louis. The fort, constructed by troops of the 1st Infantry under Lieutenant Colonel Jacob Kingsbury, serves as both a military post and a government "factory" for commercial trading with the Indians.

25 July–8 August. Three Forks. Missouri River.

The Corps arrives at the convergence of three rivers. They name one the Jefferson River and follow it until it forks again. They follow the middle fork, which they name the Beaverhead River. Progress is slow. On the 8th, Lewis decides to take three men overland to find Indians and horses.

12–18 August. Corps of Discovery Crosses Continental Divide. Lemhi Pass.

Lewis and his small party follow an Indian in hopes of finding the Shoshones. Carrying a small American flag, they cross a ridge expecting to see a slope toward the Pacific Ocean. Instead, Lewis stares at "immence ranges of high mountains still to the West of us." He

Opposite: *A common part of conferences with the Native Americans was the smoking of a ceremonial pipe. This depicts such an event during one of the many meetings held by Lewis and Clark. The passing of the pipe symbolized friendship among parties. ("Peace Pipe," John F. Clymer, courtesy Mrs. John F. Clymer and the Clymer Museum of Art)*

Right: *Soldier labor was often the only means available to construct Army facilities. Soldiers with building skills were prized assets in constructing the dozens of forts and barracks. ("The American Soldier, 1805," Charles McBarron, Army Art Collection, NMUSA)*

is looking at the Bitterroot Range. On the 13th, he finds the Indian camp. During the first council on the 17th, Sacagawea recognizes the Indian leader as her brother. All ride to meet Clark and establish Camp Fortunate as a base. Food is scarce, but they have horses and proceed on.

9 September. Upper Mississippi Expedition. Fort Bellefontaine.

Wilkinson sends First Lieutenant Zebulon Pike with a keelboat and a party of 20 soldiers of the 1st Infantry to explore the source of the Mississippi River. An additional mission is to establish U.S. authority over the Indians and British traders operating in the area.

11–22 September. Corps of Discovery in the Bitterroot Mountains.

The Corps departs its valley camp, Traveler's Rest, and climbs into the mountains. Several colts are killed for meat. On the 16th, the first snow (six to eight inches) inches falls. Many of the men are sick, so Clark goes ahead. He finds a Nez Perce village and sends food back.

25 September. Upper Mississippi Expedition. Mississippi River.

Pike stops at Sioux villages along the river, dispensing gifts and holding council. On the 24th he reaches the falls marking the boundary between the Sioux and Chippewa. On an island in the river, Pike negotiates the first Indian treaty signed in the new Louisiana Territory. For presents worth $200, 60 gallons of whiskey, and a promise of $2,000 more, Pike receives rights to 155,520 acres. He then continues north in the face of an early winter.

October. Wilkinson Expedition. Missouri River.

Wilkinson sends his son, First Lieutenant James B. Wilkinson, and a 40-man detachment from the 2d Infantry up the river to trade and establish a trading fort at the Platte River. They travel some 300 miles and are attacked by hostile Indians. One man is killed, and the expedition withdraws to St. Louis.

7 October. Corps of Discovery Heads Downriver. Clearwater River.

The new canoes are completed and loaded. Health and food are improved, and the Corps pushes off for the Columbia River and the Pacific.

16 October. Pike Reaches Swan River. Little Falls.

Pike and his men construct a log house and palisade on the Swan River. Pike leaves a Sergeant Kellerman in charge and travels by sled with a small detail to Leech Lake, which he mistakenly identifies as the source of the Mississippi. He also visits trading posts in the area, informing them they are now in U.S. territory.

7–15 November. Lewis & Clark Reach Coast. Columbia River.

As they paddle downriver, the fog parts and Lewis and Clark see the Columbia River estuary, which they mistake for the Pacific (still 20 miles away). For a week they struggle to survive a severe storm that threatens

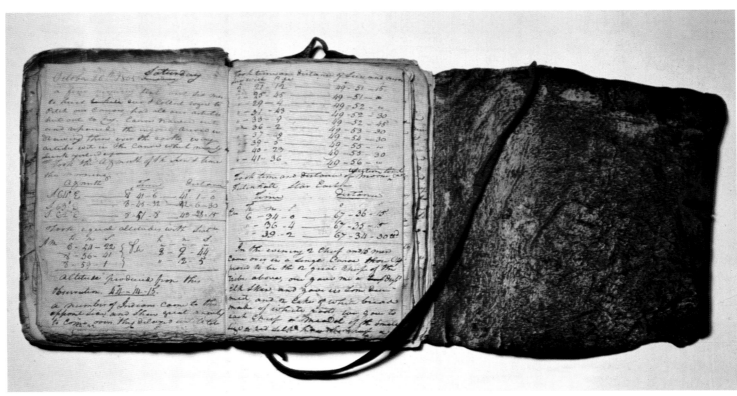

Opposite: *Lieutenant William Clark's elk-skin-bound journal of the Corps of Discovery's trek to the pacific. (Missouri Historical Society, St. Louis, The Clark Family Collection, William Clark Papers)*

Right: *Sergeant Charles Floyd was the only member of the Corps who died during the journey. His comrades in the Corps of Discovery buried him on a bluff overlooking the Missouri River. ("Funeral of Sergeant Floyd," Michael Haynes)*

to destroy the canoes. At last, on the 15th, they round Point Ellice and land on a sandy Pacific beach. Clark estimates they have come 4,162 miles.

7 December. **Winter Camp. Fort Clatsop.**
After exploring the coast area, the Corps builds a small fort, completing it in time for Christmas dinner. They name it Fort Clatsop after the local tribe and spend the winter, hunting, fishing, gathering samples, and preparing for the return.

1806

January. **Status of the Army.**
Army strength hovers at 2,729. The Army adopts the British system of honorary or "brevet" rank for the first time. This permits an officer to wear and have the privileges of a higher rank, usually as a reward for bravery or service, but without an increase in pay. A brevet may also be awarded for other services.

February. **Pike Returns. Little Falls.**
Pike returns and discovers the sergeant has been entertaining the locals and consumed or traded most of the supplies, including Pike's personal keg of whiskey. The sergeant is court-martialed and reduced in rank. Pike returns with his men to St. Louis on 30 April.

23 March–April. **Corps of Discovery Begins Return Trip. Fort Clatsop.**
The Corps begins its return. Lewis is able to buy one

canoe but must steal a second one. Relations with the Indians are not good. Petty theft is frequent, including one attempt at dognapping Seaman, who is recovered after a two-mile chase. Food is scarce, and a common meal of both Indians and the Corps is roast dog.

10 April. **Articles of War Revised.**
Congress revises the Articles of War. Two levels of court-martial—general and garrison or regimental—are set composed of different boards of officers. Each level can impose a different degree of punishment. Court-martial boards for militia members are to be composed of militia officers.

19 April–2 June. **Red River Expedition. Orleans Territory.**
Thomas Freeman, a civilian surveyor, and naturalist Peter Curtis begin an exploration up the Red River with an Army escort of 19 soldiers led by Captain Richard Sparks, 2d Infantry, and Lieutenant Enoch Humphreys, Artillery. On 19 May, they reach the fort at Natchitoches, where they are told a large Spanish force is waiting to intercept them. Sparks is not intimidated. Reinforced with another 21 men and with additional supplies, they continue on.

30 June–3 July. **Corps Recrosses Bitterroot Mountains.**
Nez Perce guides help the Corps cross the Bitterroot Mountains. Earlier, deep snow had forced them back. Back again at Traveler's Rest, Lewis and Clark decide to split the Corps into several smaller groups and explore the region in more detail. Each group takes a

different route to the planned rendezvous on the Yellowstone River.

15 July. Pike's Arkansas River Expedition. Fort Bellifontaine.

Wilkinson sends Pike to explore the southwestern boundary of the Territory. Pike takes 23 men, including Wilkinson's son to escort some Osage Indians returning from a visit to Washington. Pike's party travels up the Missouri to the Osage River, then to the village where they stay until 3 September.

26 July–17 August. Lewis Fights the Blackfeet. Two Medicine River.

Lewis and his three men meet eight Blackfoot Indians. They eat and camp together peacefully until dawn, when the Indians attempt to steal guns and horses. Two Indians are killed; the rest flee. By 12 August the Corps is reassembled, and they travel back to the Mandan villages where Sacagawea, her husband, and baby remain. At his request, Private John Colter is discharged.

29 July. Sparks Confronts the Spanish. Red River.

Captain Sparks' scouts discover the Spanish. As the Americans prepare defensive positions, a squadron of Spanish dragoons appears. After a conference under a flag of truce, Sparks agrees to return downriver.

September. Army Escort Attacked. Upper Missouri River.

Arikaras attack an Army party escorting a group of Mandans returning from Washington. Three soldiers are killed and several wounded. These are likely the first Army combat casualties west of the Mississippi.

3 September–28 October. Pike Meets the Pawnees. Republican River.

Pike visits the main Pawnee village for talks and learns that Spanish soldiers are searching for him. The first week of October, Pike reaches the Arkansas River, where Lieutenant Wilkinson and five men are detached to return to St. Louis. It takes them 73 days of hard struggle to reach the Mississippi. Pike continues west looking for the headwaters of the Arkansas.

23 September. **Corps of Discovery. Mission Completed. St. Louis.**
Traveling almost 50 miles a day down the Missouri, the Corps arrives at St. Louis about noon on the 23rd. Lewis works on his report to President Jefferson. His earlier reports sent back the first year have already been released by Jefferson and published.

September–8 October. **Burr's Letter to Wilkinson. New Orleans.**
En route to New Orleans. Wilkinson stops at Natchez. Without authority, he meets with the Spanish and agrees to establish a 100-mile-wide buffer zone along the Sabine River to protect Spanish territory. On 8 October, Wilkinson receives a letter from former Vice-President Aaron Burr. In the letter, Burr outlines his plan to recruit an armed force, seize towns (including New Orleans), and then attack Mexico. He hopes to create a new country and asks Wilkinson to be his deputy.

21–22 October. **Wilkinson Betrays Burr. Natchez.**
Wilkinson writesto Jefferson, detailing Burr's letter but pretending not to know who sent it. Wilkinson reassures the President that he is taking all precautions to protect American interests. An Army lieutenant carries the letters to the President. Wilkinson also writes to the Spanish, offering the same information for $150,000 in gold. They refuse. Wilkinson submits a voucher to the War Department for the expense of sending the messenger to the Spanish—and he is repaid.

October–November. **Pike Sees Peak.**
Pike's expedition climbs Cheyenne Mountain and on 15 November sights another mountain, possibly "Pike's Peak." They camp at a huge gorge (Royal Gorge), which they identify as the head of the Arkansas River, then travel in a direction they think will take them to the Red River. With little food and only summer clothing, the men suffer terribly as severe weather settles in. In mid-December, they encounter what Pike identifies as the Red River.

25 November. **Wilkinson Sounds Alarm. New Orleans.**
Wilkinson declares a civil emergency and without legal authority begins arresting suspected Burr supporters in town and at Fort Adams. He ignores the civil courts and issues orders for local forces to prepare defenses against the arrival of Burr's force.

27 November. **Jefferson Issues Warning.**
On the 27th, Jefferson issues a nationwide warning against the plot, and he orders state militias, the Army, and federal and state officials to stop the conspiracy.

November–December. **Pike and Pawnees. Orleans Territory**
Pike's small group is surrounded by 60 heavily armed Pawnees. The Indians rough them up, taking equipment and personal items before the expedition can get away.

Opposite, top: *The Corps of Discovery escape a bear attack. ("Hasty Retreat," John F. Clymer, Courtesy Mrs. John F. Clymer, Clymer Museum of Art)*

Opposite, bottom: *Lewis and Clark at the juncture of the Missouri and Marias rivers in June 1805. ("Decision," Robert F. Morgan, Courtesy of the Montana Historical Society John Reddy photographer)*

Right: *Lewis leads the Corps up the Jefferson River. ("Up The Jefferson," John F. Clymer, Courtesy Mrs. John F. Clymer, Clymer Museum of Art)*

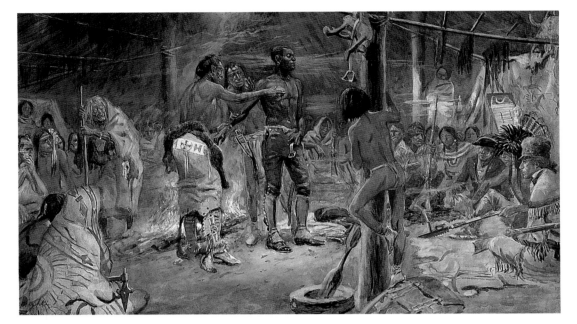

Left: *As the Corps of Discovery moved west, they had many encounters with various Indian tribes. William Clark's personal slave, York, piques the curiosity of one such tribe. ("York," Charles M. Russell. Courtesy of the Montana Historical Society, John Reddy, photographer)*

1807

January. **Status of the Army.**
The Army remains organized under the Peace Establishment Act of 1802. Total authorized strength is 241 officers and cadets and 3,046 enlisted men. Actual on-hand strength is much less.

4 January–7 February. **Pike's Expedition in Trouble. Orleans Territory.**
Food is gone, and many of Pike's men have frozen feet. On the 4th, Pike realizes he has gone in a big circle—they are back at the gorge. The expedition struggles south again. On the 22nd, two men with frozen feet stay behind in a small shelter. The rest continue into the San Luis Valley. At the Conejos River on 6 February they build a small stockade, and volunteers go back for the two left behind. All return, alive but badly injured.

18 February. **Army Arrests Burr. Fort Stoddard.**
Lieutenant Edmund P. Gaines, 2d Infantry, is alerted that Aaron Burr is nearby. Burr, under his third federal indictment for treason, is attempting to escape to Spanish territory. Gaines, with a small detail, intercepts Burr and brings him to the fort. Burr is later sent to Richmond for trial.

26 February. **Spanish Arrest Pike. Rio Grande River.**
A large Spanish cavalry patrol arrests Pike and his men and takes them to Santa Fe for questioning. Pike maintains that he never intended to cross into Spanish territory and thought he was at the Red River. The Spanish then take the Americans to their headquarters at Chihuahua, Mexico. Pike's journal is confiscated and not returned to the United States until 1910.

Opposite, below: *After climbing to the summit of the Bitterroot Range, Meriwether Lewis expected to find lower mountains and an easy route to the Pacific ahead of him. He was amazed to see the higher Rocky Mountains waiting ahead. ("Lewis' First View of the Rockies," Olaf Seltzer, Gilcrease Museum, Tulsa, Oklahoma)*

Right: *Traveling through the mountains proved so difficult for the Corps of Discovery that Lewis and Clark split the team for the trip home. ("Lewis and Clark in Bitterroot Mountains," John F. Clymer, courtesy Mrs. John F. Clymer and the Clymer Museum of Art)*

28 February–4 March. **Lewis and Clark Rewarded.**
In addition to a land grant of 1,600 acres and cash, Lewis and Clark receive prominent jobs. Both officers resign from the Regular Army. Lewis is appointed governor of the Territory of Louisiana, while Clark is made the territory's Superintendent of Indian Affairs and a brigadier of the militia.

April. **Pike Released. Mexico.**
After interrogation, Pike and his men are released and told to return to American territory. They arrive at Natchitoches on 1 July. The expedition brings valuable information about the southern plains, but Pike, a supporter of Wilkinson, is suspected of involvement in the Burr treason. He is questioned by Secretary Dearborn and found guiltless. During his absence Pike had been promoted to captain.

June. **Wilkinson at Burr Hearing. Richmond, Virginia.**
Burr tries to discredit Wilkinson's testimony with charges Wilkinson illegally arrested civilians in New Orleans and obtained statements without authority. Judge John Marshall dismisses the charges. Burr and others are indicted for treason and placed on trial in August. One of the observers is a young law student named Winfield Scott.

July. **Winfield Scott Joins Militia. Petersburg, Virginia.**
On 6 July, President Jefferson calls for mobilization of militia in response to the British attack on the Chesapeake. Scott, who is not even enrolled, finds a militia uniform and rides off to serve as a volunteer in a Petersburg cavalry unit. He distinguishes himself by capturing a boatload of British sailors who have come ashore for supplies.

22 December. **Embargo Act. Washington.**
When Congress passes an Embargo Act prohibiting importation of goods produced in England, the Army is tasked with assisting civil authorities in stopping smuggling along the border with Canada. Civilian resentment is strong. Army property is destroyed and soldiers insulted and assaulted.

1808

January–March. **Army Engineers Strengthen Coast Defenses.**
The Army has 2,775 men scattered in small detachments. Army engineers strengthen coastal forts and add a few heavy guns, but the Army's artillery is basically immobile, untrained for field duty. In March, Congress votes to keep the emergency militia authorization at 80,000.

Left: *Lewis and Clark encountered some of the worst rapids of their trip during their journey down the Columbia River. ("Angry River," John F. Clymer, courtesy Mrs. John F. Clymer and the Clymer Museum of Art)*

12 April. **Regular Army Expanded.**
Congress adds 6,000 Regulars and eight new regiments —five infantry regiments (3d–7th), a regiment of riflemen, a regiment of light dragoons, and a light artillery regiment—for five years. The "light" or "flying" artillery is a new French concept using mobile, horse-drawn guns and mounted crews in direct support of the infantry. Positions for two more brigadier generals are approved, with pay of $104 a month; allowances for rations, forage, travel, and quarters are increased. An artificer and 18 enlisted men are added to the Corps of Engineers. Regular officers do not seek positions in the new regiments, fearing discharge if the Army is again reduced. Lieutenant Zachary Taylor is one of the officers of the new 7th Infantry.

19 April. **Jefferson Declares Insurrection in New England.**
State and federal agents attempting to enforce the trade embargo along the U.S.-Canadian border encounter strong local resistance. Jefferson declares the area in a state of insurrection. In June, a company from the Regiment of Artillerists, serving as infantry, is sent to help. For the rest of the year Regulars and militia, at times riding aboard naval vessels, skirmish with smugglers.

May–July. **Light Artillery Regiment Test. Fort McHenry, Maryland.**
Appointment of officers to the new Light Artillery Regiment is slow, and Secretary Dearborn is skeptical. On 8 May, 22-year-old Winfield Scott receives a commission as a captain, Light Artillery,

with instructions to recruit and train a company in Petersburg. As a test, Captain George Peter, the regiment's senior officer, is ordered to prepare a gun carriage, wagons, horses and equipment for one six-pounder cannon. After training, he is to march to Washington, and conduct demonstrations of the new light artillery concepts. Peter's test is successful, and funds are provided for a full regiment. Each company is armed with two six-pounder cannon and two 5 1/2-inch howitzers. Peter leads his proud men, dressed in new uniforms and wearing tall leather caps with red and blue feather plumes, in a Fourth of July parade through Washington.

September. **Western Forts Constructed. Louisiana Territory.**
Troops from the 1st Infantry are sent deeper into the new territory to construct forts. Captain Eli B. Clemson begins Fort Osage about 300 miles up the Missouri. A company of mounted St. Charles militia help garrison the post. More 1st Infantry under Lieutenant Alpha Kingsley begin construction of Fort Madison (now Fort Madison, Iowa), which suffers periodic harassment by Sac and Fox Indians.

2 December. **Army Ordered to New Orleans.**
Secretary Dearborn directs Wilkinson to take command of U.S. forces in New Orleans and directs the 3d, 5th, and 7th Infantry regiments, part of the 6th, the Rifle Regiment, Light Dragoons and several Light Artillery companies (including Peter's and Scott's) to assemble there as soon as possible.

ZEBULON M. PIKE

As a soldier for all of his adult life, Zebulon M. Pike accomplished many difficult missions for his country in the early 1800s. Pike, however, will always be remembered for the peak that bears his name in Colorado. Zebulon Montgomery Pike was born in Lambeton (now, Trenton), New Jersey in 1779. His father was a career soldier, and Pike was raised on a succession of frontier Army posts. He followed his father into the Army at age 15. Serving first as a cadet with an infantry regiment, he became a second Lieutenant in the 2d Infantry Regiment in 1799. He spent his free time learning military history and tactics, mathematics, French, and Spanish—skills he would rely on during his treks west.

In 1805 Pike was picked by Major General James Wilkenson to command an expedition to discover the source of the Mississippi River. Leaving St. Louis in August 1805 with 20 soldiers on a keelboat, the expedition made it to present-day Little Falls, Minnesota. Pike continued on with a few men as far north as Lake Leech (in what is now Minnesota), which he mistakenly thought was the source of the Mississippi.

After two months back in St. Louis, Pike was sent out to find the headwaters of the Arkansas and Red rivers, which marked the southwestern borders of the Louisiana Territory. His less public mission was to scout Spanish settlements and military presence in the area. The new expedition left in July 1806 and traveled up the Missouri and Osage rivers, crossed Kansas and

entered what is now Colorado. As winter winds began to blow, Pike and several others climbed the highest peak they had discovered. The men were not equipped for such an effort but finally reached the top. It was not "Pike's Peak" but most probably Cheyenne Mountain.

Pike continued his exploration, eventually crossing into Spanish territory, where he and his men were arrested by a Spanish patrol and taken into Mexico. They were eventually released and retuned to Louisiana in 1807. On his return, Pike learned he had been promoted to captain in August 1806. Three years later, he published his story of the two journeys in *Account of Expeditions to the Sources of the Mississippi and Through the Western Parts of Louisiana.* It was accepted at that time for soldiers on active duty to write and publish books on their experiences to augment their meager salary.

Pike gained leadership experience during tours with several infantry regiments prior to the War of 1812, making a reputation as an aggressive and competent leader. Pike was promoted to colonel in July 1812 and given command of the 15th Infantry on the northern front near Niagara. He drilled his men hard and experimented unsuccessfully with the use of long pikes by rear ranks of the regiment to fend off cavalry and bayonet attacks. In March 1813, Pike was promoted to brigadier general, serving as both Adjutant General and Inspector General.
On 27 April 1813, Pike led an amphibious attack against York, Upper Canada (now Toronto). The attack was sluggish until Pike crossed the river and led his men against the town, personally storming one of the redoubts. As he prepared to take another, the Canadians inside exploded a large powder magazine, killing friend and foe alike. Pike was fatally struck by flying debris and was evacuated by boat. He lived long enough to learn that the town had been taken and died with his head on the captured flag.

Although he died as a soldier leading his men in battle, Zebulon Pike will best be remembered as an explorer, among those led the way West.

—*Vince Hawkins*

Above: *Lieutenant Zebulon M. Pike was both a soldier of courage and an explorer who led expeditions into Colorado and Canada. ("Zebulon M. Pike," Rembrandt Peale, New York Sate Office of Parks, Recreation, and Historical Preservation)*

24 December. Peter's Winter March. Baltimore.
Captain Peter and his company begin a 16-day overland march to Pittsburgh to board river barges for the trip to New Orleans. Scott's company is ordered to travel by ship from Norfolk.

1809

January. Status of the Army.
The Army strength authorization is 5,712 with more than half in New Orleans. Each regiment leaves behind an officer and a small detail to continue recruiting. The Army adopts a uniform of single-breasted blue coats without regimental color facings, tightly tailored white trousers, and stovepipe hats with cockades on the left side. Pay is low, and both officers and enlisted men still engage in unofficial businesses to supplement their frequently late salary.

15 February. New Brigadier Generals Selected.
Two new brigadier general officer positions are authorized. Wilkinson, the Army's senior general, is a Virginian, so to maintain regional balance, Revolutionary War veterans Wade Hampton of South Carolina and Peter Gansevoort of New York are selected.

4–7 March. Madison Becomes President.
James Madison is sworn in as fourth President and Commander-in-Chief. On the 7th, he appoints William Eustis as Secretary of War. Eustis served during the Revolution and Shays' Rebellion as a contract surgeon with the Army.

1 April–22 June. Wilkinson Orders Relocation. New Orleans.
Scott and his artillery company arrive on the 1st. When Wilkinson arrives later, he finds half the men sick and unfit for duty. Wilkinson ignores orders to move north to Fort Adams. On 29 May, he orders the army to an unhealthy swampy area called Terre aux Boeufs, 12 miles south of the city. Major Pike arrives on 1 June with 500 men to begin camp construction, but it is hopeless. The area floods; the men are hot and miserable. The food is rotten and the water bad, and uniforms rot with mildew. The death rate and sick lists increase. Scott is so disgusted he submits a letter of resignation and returns to Virginia. Peter also resigns.

22 June. Wilkinson Ordered to Move. Terre aux Boeuf.
Reports of conditions at Terre aux Boeuf cause Eustis to send Wilkinson a direct order to move the army to high ground at Fort Adams near Natchez. Barely 600 men are fit for duty; but Wilkinson still delays.

Above: *Lewis and Clark explored the Columbia River and Pacific coast, making contact with a number of Indians. ("Lewis and Clark on the Lower Columbia," Charles Russell, Amon Carter Museum, Fort Worth, Texas)*

Right: *On the trip home, Lewis and Clark often fashioned their own rafts. ("Crossing the Lewis Fork," John F. Clymer, courtesy of Mrs. John F. Clymer and the Clymer Museum of Art)*

July. **Scott Withdraws Resignation. Petersburg.**
In late July, Scott writes to the Secretary of War retracting his letter of resignation, which is still pending action, and requesting a return to his regiment. After some delay, the War Department concurs.

September. **Army Finally Moves. Fort Adams.**
Wilkinson finally moves, but he fails to properly plan, resulting in the deaths of almost 300 sick soldiers. By the end of October only 414 men are fit for duty. Penny-pinching Eustis orders all the light artillery horses sold to save the cost of hay; refuses permission to rent buildings for shelter or to buy extra food for the sick; and must personally approve any purchase over $50. Wilkinson is relieved of command by Brigadier General Wade Hampton and ordered back to Washington.

November. **Scott Court-Martialed. Fort Adams.**
Scott returns in early November as the senior captain in the regiment. Brigadier General Wilkinson is still in town. Another officer accuses Scott of making derogatory remarks about Willkinson in public, and court-martial charges are ordered against Scott.

1810

January. **Status of the Army.**
The regimental recruiting system is not working, and new recruits are few. Authorized strength of the two "old" regiments is 2,765, but the seven "new" regiments have only 4,189 total.

Above: *Lieutenant William Clark leads the way on the last leg of the trip home. ("Clark on the Yellowstone," J. K. Ralston, First Interstate Bank, Livingston, MT)*

Left: *A triumphant Corps of Discovery paddles into St. Louis, completing their journey to the Pacific and back. ("Return of the Corps of Discovery," Stanley Meltzoff, Exxon Mobil)*

Left: *On 30 September 1809 William Henry Harrison concludes a treaty with several tribes to purchase about three million acres of land on the Wabash and White rivers to enable further settlement in the Northwest. ("The Prophet," Stanley Aruthurs, Delaware Art Museum, Wilmington, Louisa du Pont Copeland Memorial Fund)*

Opposite: *After being arrested by the Spanish, Zebulon Pike was taken to Santa Fe and later to Mexico. He was released and returned to Louisiana in 1807. ("Pike at Santa Fe," Frederick Remington, Library of Congress)*

10 January. **Scott Court-Martialed. Fort Adams.**
A court-martial board hears the charges of misconduct and embezzlement against Scott, who defends himself. He defeats most of the charges; however, he is found guilty of "un-officer conduct" and sentenced to suspension from all pay and allowances for 12 months. Hampton, while sympathetic, upholds the sentence. Scott returns to Virginia, but before going he fights a pistol duel with his accuser; both miss. Meanwhile, Wilkinson has returned to Washington to face two congressional inquiries.

27 October. **Army Troops Sent Into West Florida. Baton Rouge.**
The American settlers in the Spanish territory of West Florida revolt and take control of Baton Rouge, the capital. They ask for assistance, and President Madison sends Army troops to annex the territory for the United States.

1811

January. **Status of the Army.**
The War Department is composed of Secretary Eustis and seven civilian clerks, while the Army staff has only three officers. Coastal defenses consist of 24 forts and 32 enclosed batteries and fortifications of stone or brick. These carry 750 cannon of different sizes which require over 12,000 men to serve properly. The Army has 10,000 authorized, but actual strength is only 5,956. A few graduates of West Point are serving as junior officers, but promotion by seniority is slow. Only 18 cadets are commissioned in 1811.

11 January. **Scott Requests Return to Duty. Petersburg, Virginia.**
Scott spends much of his time studying military history. When the regiment commander dies, Scott writes to Eustis asking, as senior regimental captain, promotion to major to replace the commander. Scott is restored to active status with pay, but he receives neither promotion nor orders and sits at home.

15 January. **Secret Legislation on Florida.**
Congress secretly authorizes the President to take control of East Florida if requested by "local authority," or if there is threat of occupation by "any foreign government." Secretary of State James Monroe sends two militia officers, Brigadier George Mathews and Colonel John McKee, to the Army post at Point Petre (Peter) on the Georgia-East Florida border. They are empowered to negotiate transfer of East Florida or to find another way to accomplish the same thing. The post and its small arsenal are garrisoned by elements of the Rifle Regiment under Lieutenant

Colonel Thomas A. Smith with a detachment of the Light Dragoons.

1 June. **Wilkinson Court-Martialed. Washington.**
Wilkinson faces eight charges with 25 specifications for his actions in the Burr affair. At the same time, Congress is investigating the Army deaths at Terre aux Boeuf.

July. **Harrison Meets Tecumseh. Vincennes, Indiana Territory.**
Territorial Governor Harrison meets again with Shawnee Chief Tecumseh, who rejects the 1809 Treaty of Fort Wayne and is working to build a coalition of tribes from Michigan to Georgia. They have met several times previously concerning Indian attacks on settlers, and Harrison now threatens military action. Secretary Eustis orders the 4th Infantry, with 600 men under Colonel John Boyd at Pittsburgh, and a company of the Rifle Regiment to Fort Washington.

Only 300 men are to go on to Vincennes. Angry, Harrison changes the orders and directs all the Regulars and the entire Indiana Territorial militia to mobilize and join him.

19 September. **Harrison Moves North. Vincennes.**
Using boats to transport supplies, Harrison marches his men north along the Wabash River toward Prophetstown, Tecumseh's main village, located near the Tippecanoe River.

October. **Scott Receives Orders. Petersburg.**
Scott receives orders to Baton Rouge. On arrival, he is appointed to chair a court martial of Colonel Thomas Cushing, who is accused of failing to follow orders and of prying into Hampton's correspondence. Cushing, a friend of Wilkinson's, is found guilty but does not resign and later becomes Adjutant General of the Army.

EYEWITNESS: BATTLE OF TIPPCANOE

In November 1811, General William Henry Harrison, the governor of the Indiana Territory, led 1,000 Regulars and militia to an area seven miles north of today's Lafayette, Indiana, in preparation to attack a large Shawnee village known as Prophetstown. Before sunrise on 8 November, Issac Taylor, a volunteer militia rifleman, woke up in a drizzling rain to fight for his life.

"In a few moments I heard the crack of rifle fire. . . . I had just time to think that some sentinel was alarmed and had fired his rifle without a real cause, when I heard the crack of another rifle, followed by an awful Indian yell all around the encampment. In less than a minute I saw the Indians charging our lines most furiously and shooting a great many rifle balls into our camp fires, throwing the live coals into the air three feet high. At this moment my friend Warnock was shot by a rifle ball through his body. He ran a few yards and fell dead on the ground. Our lines were broken and a few Indians were found on the inside of the encampment. In a few moments they were killed. Our lines closed up and our men in their proper places. One Indian was killed in the back part of Captain Geiger's tent, while he was attempting to tomahawk the Captain.

"The sentinels, closely pursued by the Indians, came to the lines of encampment in haste and confusion. Daniel Pettit was pursued so closely and furiously by an Indian . . . that to save his life he cocked his rifle as he ran and turning suddenly round, placed the muzzle of his gun against the body of the Indian and shot an ounce ball through him. The Indians made four or five most fierce charges on our lines, yelling and screaming as they advanced, shooting balls and arrows into our ranks. At each charge they were driven back in confusion, carrying off their dead and wounded as they retreated.

"Colonel Owen . . . one of General Harrison's volunteer aides, fell early in action by the side of the General. . . . Colonel Davies was mortally wounded early in the battle, gallantly charging the Indians on foot with his sword and pistols. . . . Captain Spencer and both his lieutenants were killed. . . . Just after daylight the Indians retreated across the prairie toward their town, carrying off the wounded. . . . An almost deafening and universal shout was raised by our men. 'Huzza! Huzza! Huzza!'

"The morning light disclosed the fact that the killed and wounded of our army, numbering between eight and nine hundred men, amounted to one hundred and eight. Thirty-six Indians were found near our lines. Many of the dead were carried off during the battle. Ours was a bloody victory, theirs was a bloody defeat.

We received rations for two days on the morning after the action . . . no more rations until the next Tuesday evening, being six days afterwards. . . . We performed the solemn duty of consigning to their graves our . . . soldiers, without shrouds or coffins."

—*Kevin M. Hymel*

Above: *General William Henry Harrison learned to soldier under Anthony Wayne. He later was appointed a territorial governor, and his military victories over the Indians helped elect him President of the United States. (Army Art Collection)*

1–27 October. **Fort Harrison Constructed. Indiana Territory.**

Harrison builds a base for his operations. By the end of the month a blockhouse and outworks are completed and with a bottle of whiskey broken over the main gate christened "Fort Harrison" (now Terre Haut, Indiana). Leaving supplies and his sick with a small garrison, Harrison, reinforced with 76 mounted Kentucky riflemen under Major Joseph H. Daviess, moves ahead.

6–7 November. **Battle of Tippecanoe. Indiana Territory.**

As Harrison's army approaches Prophetstown, Indians appear and propose a conference the next day. They are sent by Tecumseh's brother, an Indian mystic called "The Prophet," who is in charge during

Right: *Commanding General William Eustis, a former Army surgeon, helped care for the wounded at Bunker Hill. (Walter M. Brackett, Army Art Collection, NMUSA)*

Below: *U.S. Army officers are depicted in their formal dress uniforms. This style of uniform was a transition from the cutaway jacket to the straight breasted coat. ("U.S. Army Officers Social Full Dress," H. Charles McBarron, Company of Military Historians)*

Tecumseh's absence. Harrison halts about a mile west of the village and forms his men into a narrow rectangular defensive formation on a piece of slightly raised ground. All 950 Americans stay on full alert during the night. Ammunition is distributed, sentries posted, and bayonets fixed. At about 4 a.m. on the 7th, the Indians attack the northern end of the camp. Many Indians burst into the center of the camp, and the fighting is hand-to-hand in the dark. A special group of warriors infiltrate to kill Harrison. He is not identified, but Major Daviess, dressed in a distinctive white overcoat is killed. Three times the Indians charge and are driven back. At dawn as the Indians fall back to regroup, Harrison counterattacks. The surprised Indians break and are pursued by the mounted troops. The battle lasts more than two hours, leaving 66 soldiers killed or mortally wounded and 151 less seriously wounded. It is the first combat action for both the 4th Infantry and the Rifle Regiment.

December. **Congress Improves the Military.**
On the 24th, Congress lifts the 1809 freeze on recruiting and authorizes six companies of rangers for frontier serve. Other military legislation is prepared for the next year.

THE WAR OF 1812

1812–1815

THE WAR OF 1812

1812–1815

Colonel Raymond K. Bluhm, Jr., USA (Ret)

The Paris Treaty of 1783 did not bring peace for the Army. The hostile acts by the British on the open seas and the continued support by its agents to Indians resisting American expansion brought another war in June 1812.

The undermanned Army found itself in a complex conflict with fighting on four fronts: the Canadian-Great Lakes border; the southern Gulf territory; the Northwest Territory; and along the east coast. It was also a time of transition for Army leadership. The old heroes of the Revolution were not up to the new campaigns and a fresh generation of fascinating soldiers stepped onto the scene. Men like Jacob Brown, Winfield Scott, Zebulon Pike, Zachary Taylor, Edmund Gaines, William Harrison, and Andrew Jackson emerged as the new Army leaders. The few junior West Point officers were also starting to make contributions, primarily in fortifications and artillery.

To meet the crisis, Congress ultimately approved 44 Regular infantry regiments plus artillery, dragoons, and a frontier force of Rangers, but low pay and poor living conditions made it difficult to recruit men. In addition, President James Madison was authorized to raise short term Volunteer units and 100,000 militiamen. Funds were also provided to purchase horses and equipment for the light artillery regiments.

In an unconventional attempt to secure the southeast border, President Madison sponsored a group of American rebels in an effort to overthrow the Spanish authorities in East Florida. Despite the support of a small flotilla of U.S. Navy boats and Army dragoons, the effort stalled and finally died.

The first American military operations along the border with Canada did not go well. In mid-July 1812, an American force crossed from Fort Detroit into Canada with little results. In response, the British sent Indian allies under Tecumseh to strike deep against the extended American supply lines. Throughout the Northwest the tiny Army garrisons were besieged by Indians. Forts Detroit and Dearborn soon fell and their garrisons were massacred.

Another American invasion was defeated at Queenstown in September when militia refused to fight, a not uncommon problem due to bad leadership and poor discipline. Unreliability of militia units frequently left the Regular regiments as the core of the American forces. The war revealed the deterioration of the old militia system and the need for reform of the citizen-soldier concept.

American and British Regulars continued to fight new battles on the northern front in 1813 and 1814 with mixed results as another threat developed in the southeast. The conflict with the Red Stick faction of the Creek tribe was in full blaze, but Andrew Jackson commanded the theater of operations with an iron hand. He put down a series of militia mutinies in his force and led them on to finally destroy the main Red Stick village.

A British invasion across Lake Erie was beaten back at Plattsburg, New York, in August 1814, ending major fighting in the north, but several days later British raiders landed in Maryland to attack Washington, D.C. The defensive force of local militia broke in confusion, leaving the capital to be plundered. Fortunately, a successful defense of

Baltimore by the artillerymen of Fort McHenry ended the British offensive and indirectly gave the United States its national anthem.

Barely four months later in January 1815, Jackson led militia and Regulars to defeat a British army marching on New Orleans. A treaty already signed and on the way from Belgium ended the war with Britain. The Army, however, still faced hostile Indians in Florida, the southeast, and western plains. This conflict would last for another 80 years.

Above: *Photograph of the Star-Spangled Banner taken before the current restoration project by the Smithsonian. (Smithsonian Institution, National Museum of American History)*

Pages 172–173: *At Chippewa, Upper Canada, on 5 July 1814, a British commander expected the Americans to be untrained troops he would easily defeat. But Winfield Scott's well-trained brigade advanced under heavy fire— and the enemy commander realized his error in judgment. "Those are Regulars, by God!" he exclaimed. ("The Battle of Chippewa," H. Charles McBarron, Army Art Collection, NMUSA)*

THE WAR OF 1812

1812–1815

"We, Sir, are ready . . . except that we have no suitable ensign to display over the (main) Fort, and it is my desire to have a flag so large that the British will have no difficulty in seeing it from a distance."
—Major George Armistead, Corps of Artillery, Commander, Fort McHenry, 1813

1812

January. **Status of the Army.**
The Army has 5,608 men, including 65 West Point graduates, on duty. Senior Army leadership is three brigadier generals—James Wilkinson, Wade Hampton, and Peter Gansevoort. The 1st, 4th, and 7th Infantry Regiments garrison forts throughout the Northwest Territory. Fort Michilimackinac, 300 miles north of Detroit, has only an artillery company of 62 men. The other regiments are in the south. Despite curriculum improvements and stricter standards for acceptance, the Military Academy is struggling. No new cadets have been admitted since January 1810.

2–12 January. **Army Expansion Acts Passed.**
Congress approves more regiments: ten infantry (8th–17th); two light artillery (2d and 3d); the 2d Regiment of Light Dragoons; and six frontier companies of United States Rangers—all to serve five years. Army leadership is increased to two major generals and seven brigadier generals.

27 January. **Henry Dearborn Appointed Commanding General.**
Henry Dearborn, former Secretary of War, is the first chosen to be a major general, making him the Army's senior officer.

February–March. **Army Increased.**
Congress authorizes President James Madison to call 30,000 federal Volunteers into service, but the states select the Volunteer officers. Funds are also provided to buy horses for the three light artillery regiments, making them fully mounted for the first time since 1809.

14–22 February. **Wilkinson Found Not Guilty. Washington.**
Brigadier General James Wilkinson is acquitted of complicity in the Burr affair for lack of proof. The congressional investigations also adjourn and Wilkinson is sent back to command in New Orleans.

March. **New Generals and Staff Appointed.**
Thomas Pinckney becomes the second major general. Dearborn commands only the Northern Department (Military Districts One–Five), while Pinckney commands the Southern Department (Military Districts Six–Eight). Three of the new brigadier positions are filled by Joseph Bloomfield, James Winchester, and Thomas Flournoy. Morgan Lewis is appointed as the new brigadier Quartermaster General, and a position for Commissary General of Purchases is created to buy army supplies. However, authority of the position is vague, and it is months before the office is staffed.

Above: *Morgan Lewis, Army Quartermaster General. ("Morgan Lewis," R. Burlin, courtesy the Society of the Cincinnati, Anderson House, Washington, D.C.)*

ARMY BATTLE STREAMERS

CANADA 1812-1815

War of 1812

Canada, 1812–1815

Chippewa, 1814

Lundy's Lane, 1814

Bladensburg, 1814

McHenry, 1814

New Orleans, 1814–1815

Indian Wars

Creeks, 1813–1814

14–17 March. **Patriots' War. Point Petre (Peter), Georgia.**
Brigadier General Mathews, agent of President Madison, finds the Spanish have no intention of giving up East Florida. Using dissatisfied Florida residents and American supporters in Georgia, Mathews organizes an army of 250 "Patriots" who are secretly armed and supplied by the Army arsenal at Point Peter just across the St. Mary's River. With U.S. Navy support, the Patriots cross into East Florida and seize the Spanish fort at Fernandina. On the 17th, after several days as the "local authority," the Patriots turn the fort over to Mathews and Lieutenant Daniel Appling and his company from the Rifle Regiment. Backed by Lieutenant Colonel Thomas A. Smith with more Riflemen and Light Dragoons, the Patriots march on St. Augustine.

April. **American Strategy against Canada.**
Madison requests 1,200 Ohio militia to reinforce the Detroit garrison. The 4th Infantry is ordered to Dayton and Captain Zachary Taylor's company of 7th Infantry recruits is sent to Fort Harrison. Madison and Dearborn plan a four-pronged effort against Canada: across Lake Champlain toward Montreal; across the Niagara River against York; from Sackets Harbor against Kingston; and from Detroit into western Canada. On the 8th, Michigan territorial governor William Hull is confirmed as the Army's eighth brigadier general. He is to assemble an "Army of the Northwest" in Ohio and march to Detroit. His requests for increased naval and logistical support are ignored.

10 April. **Militia Call-Up.**
Congress gives Madison authority to mobilize up to 100,000 militiamen for six months. The Militia Act of 1792 requires all adult, able-bodied, free white males to enroll in their local, state-funded militia company and to be available for mandatory state or federal service. Requirements for periodic drills are frequently ignored. In emergencies, temporary state or federal "volunteer" units are formed. Secretary of War William Eustis sends manpower quotas to the 17 states, directing the governors to assemble and equip the men. Three governors refuse, saying the order is unconstitutional.

23 April. **Corps of Artificers Formed.**
Congress authorizes a Corps of Artificers under the new Quartermaster General. The corps and its supervisor are contracted to perform civilian engineering, construction, and special skilled jobs such as carpenter, blacksmith, and mason for the Army. The corps does not have military rank, but officers wear a unique uniform with shoulder "wings" and stars to denote position. A company of Army "bombardiers, sappers, and miners" is also formed by adding officers and enlisted men to the Corps of Engineers.

29 April. **Military Academy Improved. West Point.**
Congress adds professors and engineer officers to the Military Academy faculty, establishes a library, and gives the President authority to appoint the

superintendent. The total number of cadets in the Army is set at 250, and they are assigned to the academy rather than directly to units.

14 May. Ordnance Department Formed.

Congress authorizes a Department of Ordnance with a colonel as Commissary-General of Ordnance and a number of deputy assistants. (Birthday of the Ordnance Corps)

1–26 June. Northwest Army. Urbana, Ohio.

On the 1st, Hull's Northwest Army, composed of three Ohio militia regiments, begins its march for Detroit. At Urbana, Hull signs a treaty with local tribes allowing his troops to cross Indian country. The 4th Infantry arrives on the 9th and requires several days to recover from its forced march. While waiting, Hull sends men ahead to cut a road through the forest and prepare blockhouses at 20-mile intervals. On the 15th, the main body, about 2,000 men, resumes its march despite protests from Ohio militia, who have not been paid. There is no pay to give, and a formation of the 4th Infantry ends the protests. On the 26th, old dispatches arrive telling Hull war is imminent and to speed his march. He caches some heavy baggage and puts the rest along with his sick and some families on the steamboat *Cuyahoga*.

18 June. War is Declared.

Congress declares war against Great Britain.

26 June. Army Increased Again.

Congress approves eight more Regular Army infantry regiments (18th–25th) each with ten 90-man companies. Authorized Army strength is raised to 35,603; actual strength is now only 6,744. Few men enlist despite bonuses of cash and land. More Army brigadier positions are approved and appointments

made in July—Thomas Cushing, John Armstrong, Alexander Smyth, and John Chandler (to replace the deceased Gansevoort).

June–July. **Scott and Pike Promoted.**
Winfield Scott arrives in Baltimore, where he learns he is a lieutenant colonel and second in command of the new 2d Artillery Regiment forming at Fort Mifflin. Zebulon Pike is promoted to colonel and commander of the 15th Infantry. Another young officer joining Dearborn is Lieutenant Sylvanus Thayer, Engineers, West Point class of 1808, who is destined to become the "Father of West Point."

5 July. **Hull Arrives at Detroit.**
En route to Detroit, the *Cuyugoa* is captured by the British. Hull's official reports are taken as well as many medical supplies, equipment, and tools. On the 5th, Hull and his men arrive at Detroit. More than 100 sick have been left with garrisons along the way, but within a few days several hundred Michigan Territorial Militia arrive, giving Hull about 2,000 men. At Detroit is Hull's only warship, the brig *Adams*, under command of Captain Henry Brevoort, 2d Infantry.

9–12 July. **Hull Invades Canada. Sandwich, Canada.**
A letter from Secretary Eustis announces the war and authorizes Hull to begin offensive operations. On the 12th Hull takes his army across the Detroit River into Canada, captures the village of Sandwich without a fight and establishes a base. Mounted patrols probe toward Fort Malden. Almost 200 Ohio militia refuse to go to Canada and stay behind.

16 July. **First Land Fight of the War. Canard River, Canada.**
A reconnaissance patrol led by militia Colonel Lewis Cass penetrates 12 miles to a guarded bridge on the Canard River. Cass splits his force of Ohio militia and Captain Josiah Snelling's company of 4th Infantry and attacks, forcing the British-Canadian-Indian defenders to retreat. Cass withdraws the next day. Without heavy artillery and lacking confidence in his militia to attack a fortified position like Fort Malden, Hull limits his activity to local patrols.

17 July. **Fort Michilimackinac Falls. Mackinac Island, Michigan Territory.**
Early on the 17th, the small American garrison is surprised by a British-Indian force. Outgunned and outnumbered, the fort surrenders without firing a shot.

3–19 August. **Dearborn's Truce. New York.**
Without approval, Dearborn unwisely accepts a British

offer of a two-week truce, permitting the British to shift forces to Detroit. The mobilization of 1,000 New York volunteers is slow. Dearborn places militia Major General Stephen Van Rensselaer in command of the "Army of the Center" while he focuses on eastern operations.

4–7 August. **Battle of Brownstown. Michigan Territory.**
Alliance of several large tribes to the British cuts Hull's supply line to Ohio. He sends a detachment of Ohio militia to escort a supply train waiting at the Raisin River. Near Brownstown, a small British-Indian force under Tecumseh ambushes the escort party. When the escort commander tries to withdraw to a better position, his entire force flees. Seventeen soldiers are dead, 12 are wounded, and more of Hull's papers are left behind. Hull withdraws to Detroit when he learns British reinforcements have arrived at Malden.

Above: *Brigadier General William Hull marched the 4th Infantry Regiment to reinforce Detroit. Heavy fighting and casualties were in their future. (H. Charles McBarron, West Point Museum Collection)*

Above: *Shown wearing the 1813–1814 uniform are an ensign who has the duty of carrying the regimental standard and an enlisted man. The regimental color had a practical use on the battlefield for identification and as a symbol of the regiment. ("Ensign and Private with Regiment Standard, 25th Infantry, Fall 1813–Spring 1814," Don Troiani)*

9 August. **Battle of Monguagon. Michigan Territory.**
Hull sends the 4th Infantry under Lieutenant Colonel James Miller, reinforced with artillery and militia, to link up with the supply train. Miller hits a British-Indian roadblock at the abandoned Indian town of Moguagon, about 14 miles south of Detroit. Determined action by the 4th forces the British and Indians to finally retreat through a heavy rainstorm. American losses are 18 killed and 64 wounded, including Miller, who halts the advance. Hull recalls the force.

14 August. **Militia Morale Low. Fort Detroit.**
Morale, especially among the militia, is very bad, and some plot mutiny. On the 14th, Hull orders a force of 350 Ohio militia to make a third attempt to reach the supply train. The men are slow to depart and do not travel far.

15–16 August. **Hull Surrenders. Fort Detroit**
In the fort are many civilians and military families, including Hull's own. On the 15th, Hull receives a surrender demand from the approaching British commander, saying there may be difficulty in controlling the Indians once a battle begins. Hull refuses the demand and orders the Ohio militia to return. When the British cannon open fire from across the river in Canada, the Michigan militia desert en mass. The British bombardment continues through the night and next morning, with American artillery firing in reply. On the 16th, 700 British regulars and Canadians plus Indians with Tecumseh cross the river and surround the fort. As they move to assault positions, Hull raises a white flag and he surrenders the 2,500-man garrison. Disgusted, Lieutenant William Partridge breaks his sword over his knee and throws it at Hull's feet. All the militia are paroled, but the American Regulars are held as prisoners of war.

15 August. **Fort Dearborn Abandoned.**
The fort is held by Captain Nathan Heald with 55 men of the 4th Infantry and 12 militiamen. In compliance with Hull's order to destroy supplies and withdraw, they evacuate the fort and move along the Lake Michigan shore with their families, a few civilians, and Miami Indian scouts—about 100 people. Less than two miles from the fort, the column is attacked by 500 Potawattomi Indians. Heald forms his men and assaults the Indians on the top of a small ridge, where the soldiers stubbornly fight with muskets and bayonets until more than half are dead. Ensign George Ronan (West Point, class of 1811) is killed in the hand-to-hand fighting. He is the first Academy graduate to die in combat. Most of the women and children are killed. Wounded, Heald accepts surrender terms, and the few survivors are taken captive. Only 18 return at the end of the war. The fort is burned and not rebuilt until 1816.

4–9 September. **Indians Attack Forts. Indiana Territory.**
Active patrols by U.S. Ranger companies and militia have kept the frontier fairly quiet. However, the loss of Detroit, Chicago, and Mackinac opens the way for rearmed Indian war parties to come south. As Brigadier General William Henry Harrison tries to assemble men and supplies, Indian attacks begin. On the 4th, Fort Harrison is attacked by 400 Shawnees under Tecumseh. Captain Zachary Taylor and his 50 7th Infantry Regulars fight a stubborn defense. They lose one of the fort's two blockhouses but hold back further assaults. On the 5th, 200 Winnebagos hit the 1st Infantry company at Fort Madison, north of St. Louis. The next day attacks begin on Fort Wayne, where the garrison of 1st Infantry repulses two major assaults. The Indians keep the forts under siege for days before they are driven off. Taylor receives a brevet promotion to major for his actions.

12 September. **Patriots' War. Twelve-Mile Swamp, East Florida.**
Responding to the Spanish plea for help, former slaves and Seminoles attack a resupply wagon train escorted by 20 Georgia Volunteers and U.S. Marines. The Americans fight off the attack but must abandon the supplies to the enemy.

17 September–October. **Harrison Takes Command. Ohio.**
William Henry Harrison, now a Kentucky militia major general, is given command of the "North Western Army" with the mission to retake Detroit. As Harrison works to organize his army, he sends small retaliatory raids against hostile villages in Ohio and Indiana.

20–21 September. **Rifles Raid British Supplies. Gananoque, Canada.**
Captain Benjamin Forsyth leads his Rifle Regiment company into Canada to raid a British supply depot. Traveling by boat, they surprise and rout a larger Canadian militia force and carry away barrels of flints, gunpowder, and cartridges. Forsyth is promoted to major in January.

24 September–3 October. **Patriots War. Battle of Alachua. East Florida.**
About 100 Georgia Volunteers marching on the Indian town of Alachua are intercepted by Seminoles, and a bitter two-hour battle is fought. The Georgians build a barricade and hold out for six days. Lack of food finally forces them to withdraw, taking their wounded on crude stretchers. Fighting more skirmishes with Seminoles, the Georgians meet a relief column and are taken back to their base.

4 October. **Canadian Raid Repulsed. Ogdensburg, New York.**
Artillery batteries under New York militia Brigadier Jacob J. Brown turn back an amphibious raid by a British-Canadian force. Lieutenant Colonel Winfield Scott arrives at Buffalo with two companies of the 2d Artillery and is sent to guard a shipyard at Black Rock, a small harbor on the Niagara River.

9 October. **Artillerymen Seize Ships. Fort Erie, New York.**
Captain Nathan Towson leads 50 volunteers from the 2d Artillery on a midnight raid across the Niagara River to seize two British brigs (one is the former *Adams*) anchored near Fort Eire. Both ships carry American prisoners of war. After initial success, the raiders' escape is disrupted by winds and river current.

Scott brings reinforcements, and a daylong fight develops. The old *Adams* is burned, but all prisoners and raiders return.

13 October. **Battle of Queenstown Heights. Queenstown.**
In predawn darkness the first wave of an American assault force of 1,200 militia and Regulars crosses the Niagara River to seize Queenstown. Artillery support, including Scott's 2d Artillery, is provided from the American side of the river. Despite poor planning and rough weather, the first boats successfully land 225 men under heavy fire from the town and from cannon on the nearby heights. After Lieutenant Colonel Solomon Van Rensselaer, the senior commander, is badly wounded, Captain John E. Wool, 13th Infantry, takes charge. Wool leads his company and others up the steep bluff in a flanking attack that captures the heights. The British try several times to retake the guns. More Americans land, but with daylight, Fort George cannon fire on the boats. Major General Stephen Van Rensselaer sends Scott over to take command. With the help of Captain Joseph Totten, Engineers, a rough defensive position is built on the heights. American wounded are sent back on the boats, but ammunition is short

Above: *On 16 August 1812, Brigadier General William Hull surrendered Fort Detroit to the British without major resistance following several days of bombardment. He was later court-martialed for this action. (National Archives)*

and as the fighting intensifies, more militiamen slip away to the boats. From across the river fresh militia watch the battle but refuse to cross, and many boatmen desert, leaving those fighting on the Canadian side stranded. When Scott gives the order to withdraw, there are no boats. Under British fire, Scott, Totten, and another officer go forward with a flag of truce. Indians try to kill them, but British soldiers intervene. A total of 958 Americans are captive, 120 Americans dead or mortally wounded, and 120 others wounded. An unknown number are also dead or wounded at Fort Niagara where the Americans lose an artillery duel with Fort George. At the British headquarters, two Indians try again to kill Scott and he defends himself with a sword.

16 October. **Van Rensselaer Resigns. Fort Niagara.**
Major General Van Rensselaer, disgusted at the militia cowardice and angry at Brigadier Alexander Smyth's refusal to send his Regular brigade from Fort Niagara to support the attack, resigns. Dearborn appoints Smyth as the new commander of the Army of the Center, with orders to continue the campaign to invade Canada.

17–30 October. **Attack on Kickapoos. Kickapoo Town, Illinois Territory.**
A series of attacks by Illinois Kickapoos prompts Territorial Governor Ninian Edwards to mobilize his territorial militia. Edwards leads a combined force of 360 U.S. Rangers and Illinois militia to destroy a Kickapoo village near Lake Peoria, killing 20 warriors.

19 November. **Prisoners Seized. Quebec, Canada.**
A parole is arranged, but British officers interrogate the American prisoners. When a number of Irish-American soldiers are seized, Scott, the senior American, protests. He orders the rest of the men to remain silent, preventing further impressments.

19–23 November. **Dearborn Attempts Attack. Plattsburg, New York.**
Dearborn advances against Montreal with seven regiments of Regular infantry, artillery, light dragoons,

Left: *The war along the Niagara River was often characterized by artillery duels between American and British forts on opposite sides of the river. (Army Art Collection, NMUSA)*

and militia. After light skirmishing on the 20th, the militia refuse to advance. Disgusted, Pike takes his 15th Infantry into Canada where they successfully attack a Canadian outpost. Returning, Pike's men mistakenly fire on an American militia unit, inflicting some casualties are suffered before the mistake is discovered. Dearborn returns to Plattsburg. On the 21st, Fort Niagara and Fort George engage in another artillery duel. During the fighting, Betsy "Fanny" Doyle, wife of one of the artillerymen, serves with one of the gun crews after her husband is wounded.

28–30 November. Smyth Launches Attack. Niagara River.

Detachments of Smyth's Army of the Center, under Lieutenant Colonel Charles Boerstler and Captain Sampson King, cross the river before dawn to prepare the way for the main force. Participating are the newly recruited elements of five Regular regiments (12th, 13th, 14th, 20th, and 23d Infantry). Boerstler enjoys initial success, seizing a bridge, but then withdraws. King and 60 of his men are stranded when all the boats are taken back. However, they attack and seize two British batteries before being captured. Smyth sends Colonel William Winder with 250 men to help, but Winder runs into resistance and also retreats. Smyth tries again on the 30th. As the rain soaks the men waiting in the boats, he cancels the operation for the winter. Disgusted, the militia go home. Militia Brigadier Peter B. Porter accuses Smyth of cowardice, and challenges him to a pistol duel; both men miss. Smyth departs on leave and is dropped from the Army rolls in March 1813.

3 December. Secretary of War Eustis Resigns.

Eustis resigns under sharp criticism from Congress, and Secretary of State James Monroe assumes the duties. Eustis, who disliked the Military Academy and the Engineer Corps, has reassigned cadets and staff until only one faculty officer remains and all the cadets are gone. Under Monroe, six cadets begin training.

17–18 December. Battle of Mississinewa River. Indiana Territory.

Despite cold and deep snow, Lieutenant Colonel John B. Campbell, 19th Infantry, attacks the Miami villages along the river. His force of 600 men includes a company of the 19th, one of 2d Light Dragoons,

Above: *The Seminole ambushes of supply wagon trains even with escorts forced an American withdrawal to the St. Johns River. ("Swamp Ambush, St. Augustine, FL. 11 September 1812," Colonel Charles H. Waterhouse, USMCR (Ret), Marine Corps Art Collection)*

Left: *Fort Harrison was typical of the early log Army posts along the frontier in the Old Northwest. ("Fort Harrison, 1815," Library of Congress)*

a regiment of Kentucky dragoons, Pennsylvania militia, and scouts. He destroys several deserted villages and gathers a few prisoners, then builds a fortified camp for the night. Before dawn on the 18th, Indians make a strong attack. Campbell uses the scouts as a reserve, sending them to threatened points of his perimeter. At daylight, the dragoons charge the Indians, causing them to flee. Campbell suffers only eight killed and 48 wounded, but more than 300 are injured by frostbite on the return march.

20 *December.* Harrison Orders Advance. Ohio.
Harrison orders Brigadier General James Winchester to the Maumee Rapids. Cold weather has frozen the swamps and mud, making movement possible but also increasing the hardships of the men. Winchester's original force of 2,500 from the 17th Infantry and three Kentucky militia regiments is at half strength from illness and desertions. They reach the rapids on 10 January and begin work on a hasty defensive position. Harrison orders reinforcements forward to join Winchester, but travel is slow.

1813

January. Status of the Army.
Recruiting is not filling the regiments. To encourage enlistments a $16 bonus is given, pay is increased (privates from $5 to $8 a month), flogging is suspended,

and the enlistment term is changed from five years to "duration" or lesser terms. Some troops enlist for only a year. On the 29th, Congress approves an increase for one year to 25 infantry regiments, adds six major generals and six brigadier generals, and increases the officers in each regiment and the Corps of Engineers. For the first time eight Topographical Engineers are authorized. This brings authorized Regular strength to 58,354, but at the end of the January only 19,036 are present. More federal Volunteers are approved, including a Regiment of Sea Fencibles (infantry) intended for use in company-size units for seacoast defense.

7 *January.* Jackson's Army. Nashville, Tennessee Territory.
Andrew Jackson, now a major general of U.S. Volunteers, departs for New Orleans with 2,500 Volunteers he has raised. Ice and bad weather make it a difficult trip.

7 *January.* Patriot War. Tennessee Militia Attack. East Florida.
Some 250 Tennessee volunteers led by Colonel John Williams join Lieutenant Colonel Thomas A. Smith and his Regulars in a three-week campaign to destroy Seminole villages in north central Florida. Almost 400 houses are burned and hundreds of horses and cattle taken, breaking the strength of the Seminoles in the area.

10 *January*. Scott Returns. Washington.
Winfield Scott, a paroled prisoner, arrives in
Washington. He is asked to make a formal report to
the President on the
Queenstown battle and the
status of American prisoners.

13 *January*. Armstrong Appointed.
Brigadier General John Armstrong is nominated to be
Secretary of War. Armstrong, a Continental Army
veteran, wrote the infamous Newburg Addresses and is
not well regarded. He is barely confirmed.

**18–23 *January*. Battle of Raisin River. Frenchtown,
Michigan Territory.**
Civilians in Frenchtown ask for protection and
Winchester's bored militia, camped at the Maumee
River, press for action. Without authority, on the 18th
he sends troops forward, surprising and routing the
Canadian-Indian force occupying the town. The next
day, Winchester arrives with 350 more men of the 17th
Infantry but without a resupply of ammunition.
Despite receiving warnings, he orders neither
fortification nor resupply. In the predawn dark of the
21st, the British and Indians counterattack but are
initially repulsed. The 17th Infantry, camped outside
the town, is caught in a crossfire. When a militia sortie
fails, the Americans on the right break, taking heavy
casualties from the Indians, who capture Winchester
and strip him to his undershirt. When the British
offer terms, Winchester orders his men still holding
the town to surrender. Leaving 70–80 seriously
wounded Americans behind, the British take 500
prisoners north. On the 23rd, Indians massacre the
wounded and burn the town. In all, about 400
Americans are dead. "Remember Raisin River"
becomes an American battle cry. (Frenchtown is now
Monroe, Michigan.)

**23 *January*–1 February. Harrison Retreats.
Maumee Rapids.**
About 30 survivors from Frenchtown straggle into
Harrison's camp. Worried, Harrison burns the camp
and withdraws 15 miles. On 1 February he pulls further
back to the Maumee Rapids, where he builds Fort
Meigs. This strongly designed fort is one of the first
planned by a West Point-trained engineer, Captain
Eleazar D. Wood, class of 1806.

**6–7 *February*. Forsyth's Rifles Free Prisoners.
Elizabethtown, Canada**
Major Forsyth leads 200 Riflemen and militia in a
night raid across the frozen St. Lawrence River. They
capture the small British detachment and free a

number of American prisoners. The raiders take the
freed prisoners plus 120 muskets and escape back to
Ogdensburg. Forsyth later receives a brevet promotion
to lieutenant colonel for his actions.

21–22 *February*. British Counterraid. Ogdensburg.
Angered by Forsyth's raid, the British commander
brings 800 Canadian militia and Indians to attack the
town. Forsyth's men put up a stout defense, fighting
house to house, but the Rifles, outnumbered and
almost surrounded, finally retreat from the town.

3 *March*. Army Expansion and Promotions.
Congress increases the Army to 44 infantry regiments
(26th–44th) and adds one regiment of artillery (3d).
Many of the new regiments are never recruited, but
additional general officer positions and new units open
promotions. James Wilkinson, still in New Orleans, is
promoted to Regular Army major general along with

OLD HICKORY

British General Sir Edward Pakenham was confident his men could overwhelm the ragtag collection of American Regulars, militiamen, Indians, free blacks, and pirates who defended the Rodriguez Canal that lay between him and New Orleans.

What Pakenham had not considered was the iron determination of the American commander, 47-year-old Major General Andrew Jackson. Jackson was a born fighter who dueled for honor and bore scars from a British soldier's sword during the American Revolution. Having recently defeated the Creek Indians, he declared upon hearing that the British were approaching New Orleans, "By the eternal they shall not sleep on our soil!"

Jackson was born in Wexham Settlement, South Carolina, to Irish immigrants. He was the youngest of three sons, and his father died before he was born, leaving his mother to raise the three boys. Ignoring his mother's hope that he would become a minister, 13-year-old Andrew joined a local militia company to fight in the American Revolution. He participated in the battle of Hanging Rock, fought near Charleston in 1780. A year later he and his brother Robert were captured by the British. When Jackson refused to shine a British officer's boots, the officer struck him with his sword, leaving life-long scars on his head and fingers. His mother arranged for the release of the two brothers, but Robert died on his way home while Andrew had contracted smallpox as a prisoner. Jackson's mother died soon after of cholera, leaving young Andrew an orphan at the age of 14.

After the war, Jackson lived with various relatives until 1784 when he began studying law, becoming an attorney in North Carolina three years later. He eventually moved west, becoming a prosecutor and lawyer in Tennessee. Years later he served as a delegate from Tennessee during the state's acceptance into the union, and as an undistinguished United States congressman and senator. He became involved in some land speculation deals that almost put him in prison. He participated in three duels: one to decide the result of who would become the head of the Tennessee militia; one over a horse-race wager, which left Jackson with a bullet in his chest; and one that left him with a bullet in his arm.

When war with Great Britain broke out in 1812, Jackson led the state militia against a hostile "Red Stick" faction of the Creek Indians who were being encouraged and supplied by British agents. Through outstanding leadership and harsh discipline, Jackson led his men through the wilderness, winning victories at the battles of Tallushatchee and Talladega. He crushed the Red Sticks at

the Battle of Horseshoe Bend, effectively removing them from most of present-day Georgia and Alabama. His success in battle earned him the rank of major general.

With the Creeks suppressed, Jackson turned to the British, who hoped to capture Mobile and New Orleans. When the British attacked Camp Bowyer, Mobile's main defensive work. He ordered the line defended, and he attacked three weeks later, capturing Pensacola. With the overland campaign stymied, Jackson rushed to New Orleans to prepare its defense. Organizing his men, Jackson hit the British landing force in a night battle and then retreated to a defensive position flanked to the south by the Mississippi River and to the north by a swamp. The British attacked at dawn across open fields. When the smoke of battle lifted, Jackson had won the day.

Although the draft treaty ending the war had already been signed, nothing could take away from Jackson's victory. He became one of the most popular men in the United States and rode his military success into the White House for two terms. The old soldier died in bed 8 June 1845.

—*Kevin M. Hymel*

Above: *Portrait of Andrew Jackson. (Anne S. K. Brown Military Collection, Brown University Library)*

Left: *These surgeon's amputating tools were a necessity in successfully treating serious wounds where amputation was the only alternative to potential infection and certain death. (Historical Collections, National Museum of Health and Medicine, Armed Forces Institute of Pathology)*

William Henry Harrison, Wade Hampton, and Morgan Lewis. New brigadiers include Zebulon Pike, George Izard, William Winder, and two militia colonels, Duncan McArthur and Lewis Cass. Izard's promotion opens the way for Scott, who becomes a colonel at age 26 and commander of the 2d Artillery. In April he takes his regiment north to Fort Niagara.

15 March. Jackson Ignores Orders. Natchez, Mississippi Territory.

When Jackson arrives with his Volunteers, he finds orders from Secretary Armstrong to immediately discharge the men, without pay or supplies. Outraged, Jackson refuses to abandon his men, a number of whom are sick and have no means to return home. Jackson personally leads the return march to Nashville through the harsh winter weather, ensuring that all sick and injured are transported. His men give him the nickname "Old Hickory."

April. Army Officers Command Ships. Vergennes, Vermont.

U.S. Navy Lieutenant Thomas Macdonough is building an American fleet on Lake Champlain, but he lacks experienced sailors. He appeals to the Army and militia units stationed nearby, and appoints several Army officers with sailing experience as ship captains. When the Secretary of the Navy learns of this, he sends Macdonough a letter (which Macdonough wisely ignores) stating that regulations forbid such a practice. More than 200 soldiers serve on the ships.

2 April. Army Fighting Smugglers. Americus, New York.

The Army is used to enforce the Federal Embargo Acts prohibiting importation of British goods. These Acts are very unpopular and usually ignored. When Lieutenant Loring Austin and a detachment of 50 troopers of 1st Light Dragoons arrest 13 smugglers in the town, local officials release the men and press civil charges against Austin. Brigadier General Pike sends bail money to free the officer.

12–15 April. Mobile Occupied. Fort Charlotte, West Florida.

Wilkinson directs Colonel John Bowyer to move his 5th Infantry from Fort Stoddert against the Spanish at Mobile. Bowyer and his men arrive on the 12th to find American gunboats already in Mobile Bay. The Spanish commander of Fort Charlotte negotiates surrender and turns the fort over to Bowyer on the 15th without firing a shot. A new fort, Fort Bowyer, is begun southeast of the city at the entrance to the bay.

27 April. Battle of York. York, Canada.

The ill Dearborn selects Pike to lead an all-Regular force of 1,700 men in an amphibious assault across Lake Ontario to attack York. Pike plans it in detail. On the 27th, Forsyth and the Rifles are the first wave and fight their way ashore. Pike and his staff lead the second wave. The British garrison gives a stiff fight before retreating. As the British withdraw, they blow up a large powder magazine, causing more than 200 American casualties, including Pike. He lives long enough to receive the captured British flag. The Americans plunder the town, take military supplies, burn one ship, and take another. On 8 May they depart to attack Fort George.

28 April–9 May. First Siege of Fort Meigs. Maumee River, Ohio.

The two Regular infantry regiments, the 17th and 19th,

are overrun and their cannon spiked, but the Kentuckians break ranks to pursue the fleeing British and are overwhelmed by a counterattack. The Kentuckians lose 200 killed and 500 taken captive; only 150 escape to the boats. When the rest of the brigade arrives by foot, Colonel John Miller leads his 19th Infantry in a sortie out of the fort to make linkup. Unable to continue the siege, the British depart. Harrison leaves Clay in command and moves to Fort Stevenson, near the lake, to continue the campaign. Harrison's engineer, Captain Wood, receives a brevet promotion to major for his distinguished service during the battle.

29 April–6 May. **British Raid Towns. Upper Chesapeake Bay.**
A British fleet sails up Chesapeake Bay, attacking towns weakly defended by local militia. Only Fort Defiance, at the upper end of the bay, is able to repulse the raiders on the 29th. A British party ascends the Susquehanna River a short distance to burn warehouses.

1 May. **Army Regulations and Uniforms.**
Secretary Armstrong publishes *Rules and Regulations of the Army of the United States,* which lays out officers' duties, rules for promotion, uniform regulations, pay tables, instructions for recruiting, and other topics. The book remains the Army's administrative handbook for

Above: *As a young officer in 1783, John Armstrong, Secretary of War 1813–1814, penned the infamous "Newburgh Letters" suggesting the Army take action against Congress. ("John Armstrong," Daniel Huntington after John Vanderlyn, Army Art Collection, NMUSA)*

Right: *When supplies failed to arrive, the poorly clothed men of the Kentucky Militia made makeshift coats of blankets to keep warm. ("Kentucky Militia, River Raisin, January 1813," H. Charles McBarron, Company of Military Historians)*

Opposite: *A gun crew of the 2d Regiment Artillery is seen here loading their cannon to fire yet another blast. ("2d U.S. Regiment of Artillery, 1812-1813," H. Charles McBarron, Company of Military Historians)*

destroyed" by sickness, bad living conditions, and lack of uniforms. Half the militia are gone, the other half due to leave. In early April, Harrison brings 300 militia reinforcements and orders a Kentucky brigade led by Brigadier General Green Clay to come. On the 28th, 2,500 British, Canadians, and Indians led by Tecumseh surround the fort. The fort is bombarded by British cannon for four days. On the 5th, part of the Kentucky brigade arrives on flatboats, taking the British by surprise. Several British artillery batteries

book remains the Army's administrative handbook for many years, but a common field manual for operations is still lacking. The first *Army Register* is also printed, listing all Regular and Volunteer officers and authorized units. New uniforms are ordered for both infantry and artillery with simple dark blue trousers and coats without red trim. Severe shortages of blue cloth limit distribution, however, leaving many units to find substitutes. The Rifle Regiment keeps its unique green uniforms. Tall leather "tar-bucket" caps with pom-poms are prescribed except for general officers who wear the "chapeau-bras" or "cocked hat." The country is divided into nine military districts with a brigadier responsible for each district, including recruiting.

13–27 May. **Capture of Fort George. Fort Niagara.**
Colonel Winfield Scott arrives with his 2d Artillery Regiment on the 13th. He is given the additional job of adjutant general (chief of staff) to Dearborn and directed to plan an attack on Fort George. Scott plans a 2,500-man joint amphibious operation with Navy Commodore Isaac Chauncey for the 27th, preceded by a two-day cross-river artillery bombardment of British positions. On the foggy morning of the 27th, Scott leads the first assault wave ashore at Newark, Canada, near the fort. He has Forsyth's Riflemen, the 2d Artillery fighting as infantry, and two companies of the 15th Infantry. The Americans are met head-on at the beach, but with the help of cannon fire from Navy ships and the arrival of succeeding waves, the British are forced back. When Scott learns that fuses are set to blow up the powder magazines in the fort, he takes two companies and dashes into the fort just as one of the magazines explodes. He is thrown off his horse, breaking a collarbone, but he recovers and with another officer extinguishes the other fuses. Scott then remounts and pursues the British until ordered back.

15 May. **Patriot War Ends. Withdrawal of Troops. East Florida.**
When the Senate refuses to approve the annexation of East Florida, Secretary of State Monroe orders Pinckney to withdraw all U.S. forces by 15 May. St. Augustine never surrenders, and within a year the Patriot movement collapses.

29 May. **Battle of Stony Point and Sackets Harbor. New York.**
A British force attacks Sackets Harbor, the main U.S. naval base on Lake Ontario. A mixed force of militia, Regular infantry, and Light Dragoons led by Dragoon Commander Lieutenant Colonel Electus Backus, holds while Brigadier General Jacob Brown, the area commander, deploys more militia and Regulars with

batteries of the Light and 3d Artillery. Most of the militia break under the British attack, but one small company stubbornly remains with the Regulars. The British make several unsuccessful attacks and finally withdraw. American losses are 23 killed, including Backus, and 114 wounded.

1 June. **Johnson's Mounted Kentucky Rifles. Ohio Territory.**
A new regiment of mounted Kentucky militia led by Colonel Richard Johnson arrives for duty with Harrison. It is a well-trained and disciplined force of 1,000. Wearing top hats with plumes and black hunting shirts with red fringe, the men normally ride to battle, then fight as dismounted infantry with rifles, pistols, and tomahawks. Harrison uses them to counter Indian raids in the Raisin River area.

5 June. **British Attack Hampton. Hampton, Virginia.**
A British landing force attacks the town. After a short fight the local militia withdraw, leaving the town to be sacked and burned by the British.

6 June. **Battle of Stony Creek. Canada.**
Dearborn orders pursuit of the British by Brigadier William Winder's brigade of Regulars (5th, 13th, 14th, and 16th Infantry). Winder locates the British, and Brigadier John Chandler's brigade (9th, 23d, and 25th

Infantry) is sent to assist. Chandler is senior and takes command, but fails to set proper security. Before dawn, the British attack the surprised American camp with bayonets. In the confused fighting the Americans defend themselves fiercely. Both American generals are captured, but the British suffer heavy losses and withdraw. Colonel James Burn, surviving senior American officer, orders a retreat without waiting to bury the dead or strike tents. Dearborn fears a British attack and withdraws to Fort George, where he requests relief from duty "to a place where my mind may be more at ease." He is reassigned to command the defenses of Boston, and Lewis becomes acting department commander.

24 June. **Battle of the Beaver Dams. Thorold, Canada.**
Lieutenant Colonel Charles G. Boerstler is given command of a task force of companies from four Regular infantry regiments, a company of light artillery, and Light Dragoons, plus a few militia—altogether about 600 men. His mission is to destroy a British outpost about 16 miles from Fort George. Boerstler's column is ambushed by 200 Indians and British Regulars in a heavily wooded area known as Beaver Dams. The Americans fight tenaciously but are almost out of ammunition. Boerstler is wounded and still in command when a British officer shows a flag of truce. He tells Boerstler that a force of 2,200 surrounds him and the only way to prevent a massacre is to surrender. Boerstler asks for terms to protect the wounded. It is agreed, and almost 500 Americans are taken prisoner. Boerstler realizes too late that he was tricked.

27 June. **Defenses of Baltimore. Fort McHenry, Maryland.**
Maryland militia Major General Samuel Smith is charged with the defense of Baltimore. He is unhappy with the Fort McHenry commander and on the 27th, the deputy, Major George Armistead, 3d Artillery, takes command. He and Smith work to strengthen the fort and the other defensive positions in the area. One of the items Armistead desires is a large flag for the fort. He contracts Mrs. Mary Pickersgill, a Baltimore seamstress, to make the large flag that becomes "Old Glory."

10 July. **Raid on York. Canada.**
Scott and 250 Regulars are landed by Commodore Chaunce at the undefended town. They take prisoners, free some American captives, and confiscate military supplies. They consider an attack on the British supply depot at Burlington Heights but find it too strongly defended.

15 July. **Dearborn Departs. Fort George, Canada.**
Dearborn, relieved from command on the 6th, departs to supervise defenses in New York. His repeated requests for a board of inquiry are ignored. Wilkinson, told to report to Dearborn in March as his deputy, is still en route from New Orleans. He now becomes the Niagara department commander. Scott leaves the command staff and returns to his artillery regiment.

20–28 July. **Second Siege of Fort Meigs. Ohio.**
The British return with 1,500 troops and Indians. Instead of a direct attack, an attempt is made to lure Brigadier Clay to send troops out of the fort into an ambush by staging a mock battle with a phantom American column. The ruse fails and the British again withdraw.

27 July. **Creek War. Battle of Burnt Corn Creek. Mississippi Territory.**
Colonel James Caller leads Mississippi militia in a surprise attack on a Creek Indian pack train bringing arms from Spanish Florida. The Indians are part of the hostile "Red Stick" faction attacking settlers and fighting a tribal war with Creeks friendly to Americans. The militia scatters the Indian escort, but a counterattack by the main Red Stick force drives off the militia.

29 July–2 August. **Attack on Fort Stevenson. Sandusky River, Ohio.**
Harrison learns the British plan to attack Fort Stevenson. Harrison orders the understrength fort evacuated, but 21-year-old Major George Croghan, certain his 160 Regulars from the 17th and 24th Infantry can hold, convinces Harrison to let them stay. The attack opens on 1 August with an ineffective cannon bombardment followed by a frontal assault that ends in disaster when the fort's lone six-pound

Opposite: *After his injury in the explosion, the victorious Pike was taken to an American ship where he died, his head pillowed on the captured British flag. ("Death of Zebulon Pike," The Granger Collection, New York)*

Right: *The powder explosion at York (today's Toronto) killed 42 British soldiers and 52 American troops; 180 more were injured. (Historic Fort York, Toronto, Canada)*

cannon "Old Betsy" is used. The British withdraw and Croghan receives a brevet promotion to lieutenant colonel.

10 August. **Maryland Militia Defend Town. St. Michaels, Maryland.**
A British naval force attacks the small Chesapeake Bay town at night but is driven off by the local Maryland militia. The town conducts the first American "blackout," and deceives British gunners about the town's location by hoisting lanterns in trees along the shore.

20 August–4 September. **Wilkinson Takes Command. Sackets Harbor.**
Wilkinson arrives on the 20th with orders for an offensive against Montreal. He plans two converging columns—one of 7,000 men boated from Fort Niagara to Sackets Harbor, and the other Major General Wade Hampton's partially trained 4,000-man division from Plattsburg. More than 300 boats, mostly open bateaux, are used to transport the Niagara army. Wilkinson leaves Scott in command of Fort George, but when militia under Brigadier George McClure arrive, Scott takes the 2d Artillery on an unsuccessful forced march to join Wilkinson.

30 August. **Creek War. Fall of Fort Mims. Mississippi Territory.**
At noon about 800 Red Sticks make a surprise attack, rushing through the open main gate and firing through stockade loopholes. The 300 settlers, friendly Creeks, and Mississippi Territorial Militia fight from

building to building until they are burned out. Only six defenders fight their way out of the massacre.

3 September. **Fort Madison Attacked. Louisiana Territory.**
After a year of periodic probes, Sac Indians mount a major attack. The garrison holds out, but supplies are almost gone and the decision is made to abandon the fort. During the night the garrison dig a trench from a corner block house to the river bank, where boats are hidden. As they slip away, the last soldier sets the fort afire. All make it safely down the Mississippi to St. Louis.

10 September. **Soldiers Reinforce Navy. Put-In-Bay, Lake Erie.**
Harrison has sent experienced seamen from his army, plus 100 expert Kentucky riflemen, to bolster the crews of Commodore Oliver H. Perry's fleet. The riflemen act as sharpshooters in the rigging of the ships. On the 10th Perry defeats the British fleet, taking control of the lake.

25 September–1 October. **Harrison Invades Canada. Detroit River.**
Harrison's army has been reinforced by Johnson's regiment plus another 3,000 Kentuckians led by Governor Isaac Shelby. On the 25th, Johnson is sent north toward Detroit. Two days later a joint Army-Navy operation ferries 4,500 men across Lake Erie to a site below Fort Malden. The British abandon the fort and retreat up the Thames River with Tecumseh and his followers. Harrison arrives opposite Detroit and sends most of his Regulars to occupy the abandoned

town. On 1 October, he takes a force of about 3,500 in pursuit of the British using Johnson's mounted Kentucky militia to lead the way.

4–5 October. Battle of Thames River. Moraviantown, Canada.

The quick American advance captures many slow-moving British supply boats and wagons. On the 4th, Tecumseh tries to delay the pursuit at the small town of Chatham, but his warriors withdraw after a brief skirmish. Outside Moraviantown, the British choose a defensive position. The 41st Foot is placed on the left next to the river with a cannon, and Tecumseh's Indians are on the right, anchored by a large swamp. Johnson sees the 41st is deployed in open ranks and thus vulnerable to a mounted charge. A skeptical Harrison agrees and Johnson attacks, sending the battalion of his brother James straight up the road headlong into the 41st while he takes the other battalion through a wooded area to hit the Indians' flank. The 41st is overrun by the mounted charge, but the other battalion has a hard time in the brush and many dismount for hand-to-hand fighting with Tecumseh's Indians. Tecumseh is killed (Johnson takes credit) and the Indians scatter. American losses are 15 killed and 30 wounded. Harrison captures almost all the British weapons and supplies and returns to Detroit.

11 October. Creek War. Jackson Marches. Mississippi Territory.

Secretary Armstrong appoints Major General Thomas Pinckney to command the campaign. Four separate columns of troops will enter Red Stick territory: the East Tennessee Militia under Major General John Cocke, West Tennessee militia under Andrew Jackson, Georgia militia under Major General John Floyd, and Mississippi Volunteers led by Brigadier Ferdinand L. Claiborne. Volunteers include Davy Crockett and friendly Creeks and Cherokees recruited by Chief Pathkiller. Jackson, his arm in a sling from a near-fatal dueling wound, marches his force south toward the Red Stick villages near the Coosa River, where he plans to build a fort.

21–26 October. Battle of Chateauquay River. Spears, Canada.

By the 21st, Hampton is marching down the Chateauquay River to join Wilkinson on the St. Lawrence. Near Spears, 1,500 Canadian militia block the way. During the rainy night Hampton sends a flanking detachment across the river, but the men become lost and are fired on by both sides. When they finally attack, the Canadians are prepared and the effort stalls. The next day Hampton receives confusing orders to prepare winter quarters, and he withdraws to Plattsburg, New York. Meanwhile, rough winter weather delays Wilkinson's move down the St. Lawrence. He puts a division under Brigadier John P. Boyd on the Canadian shore to protect his flank where a British force of 800 shadows his rear guard.

3 November. **Creek War. Battle of Tallushatchee. Mississippi Territory.**

Jackson sends 1,000 mounted militia and Indians forward under Brigadier John Coffee to attack the Red Stick village of Tallushatchee. Coffee encircles the village while a small decoy party approaches directly. The Indians rush out to attack the decoy and are trapped. In the desperate fight Coffee's men suffer five dead and 40 wounded. More than 180 Indians are killed, and 84 women and children are taken captive. One orphaned Indian child is adopted and raised by Jackson. The village is destroyed and Fort Strother is built nearby as a base, but food and supplies are short.

7–9 November. **Creek War. Battle of Talladega. Mississippi Territory.**

Friendly Creeks ask Jackson to help their town, under siege by Red Sticks. He takes 2,000 infantry and mounted troops and at 4 a.m. advances with two columns, militia on the left, Volunteers on the right, to surround the Red Sticks. A small detachment under Colonel William Carroll acts as bait, advancing and then falling back. More than 1,000 Red Sticks charge into the center of the closing columns. Some militia panic, but Jackson's reserve plugs the gap, and the militiamen rally. Only a few Red Sticks escape the trap. Jackson's men lose 17 killed and 82 wounded. Jackson buys provisions from the grateful Creeks with his own money and returns to the unprotected fort.

10–11 November. **Battle of Chrysler's Farm. Canada.**

The British approach Boyd's rear guard on the Canadian side of the St. Lawrence, and he attempts to drive them back, but he forgets to take artillery or ammunition resupply and sends his four units piecemeal into battle. Each attack is beaten back for a total of 400 casualties. The 21st and 23d Infantry cover the American withdrawal over the river. Although this is not a victory for the Americans, high British losses end the chase.

November–Winter Quarters. **French Mills, New York.**

Shortly after Chrysler's Farm, Wilkinson reaches St. Regis, New York, where Hampton is supposed to meet him. Instead, he learns Hampton has returned to Plattsburg, put many men on leave, and left for Washington. Wilkinson ends the campaign and moves to French Mills for winter quarters. An incompetent Quartermaster General Department, dishonest contractors, and Wilkinson's disinterest in his men result in another disastrous winter. The army is six months behind in pay with inadequate shelter and little food. In ten weeks 200 die, and a third of the Northwest Army is rendered unfit.

13 November. **Creek War. Claiborne Expedition. Mississippi Territory.**
Brigadier Claiborne begins a punitive expedition against the Red Stick towns of Econochaca or "Holy Ground," a sanctuary that Red Stick prophets have protected with an invisible "magical barrier." Claiborne, a veteran of Wayne's Legion, moves his force of 1,200 Mississippi Volunteers and Regulars of the 3d Infantry up the Alabama River, establishing a string of forts to protect his rear.

17–18 November. **Jackson's Army Mutinies. Fort Strother, Mississippi Territory.**
Jackson has two brigades of one-year Volunteers and one of state militia. No supplies or reinforcements have been received, and the starving men are angry. On the 10th many of the militia begin to leave. When Jackson deploys the Volunteers across the road and threatens to shoot, the militiamen return to camp. The next day some Volunteers try to leave, and Jackson uses the militia to stop them. Jackson promises that if supplies do not arrive in two days, he will take the men home. No supplies arrive and Jackson tells his men that if only two men agree to stay, he will stay with them. To his surprise 109 men step forward. They protect the fort while the rest go for supplies. Twelve miles from the fort the men meet the supply wagon train and have a feast. When Jackson orders them back to the fort, they balk, and one company starts for home. Jackson places Coffee with a mounted detachment across their path and loudly orders Coffee

to shoot anyone who refuses to turn back. After some tense moments, the company turns back, but on his return to camp Jackson finds a whole brigade in mutiny. He grabs a musket and places himself in their way, saying he will shoot the first man who steps forward. As the men hesitate, first Coffee and another officer, then several loyal companies fall in beside Jackson, ending the mutiny. Later, it is discovered Jackson's musket is broken.

29 November. **Creek War. Battle of Autosse. Mississippi Territory.**
After leaving his base on the Chattahoochee River, Major General Floyd uses his force of Georgia militia and Creeks to surround the Red Stick town of Autosse and a second nearby village. The Red Sticks fight hard, but with the help of several small artillery pieces, Floyd's men are victorious.

9–12 December. **Creek War. Another Mutiny. Fort Strother.**
On the 9th, Jackson hears that the men of the Volunteer Brigade, whose enlistments end the next day, plan to leave that night. He musters the brigade on the parade ground facing two artillery guns and crews, and tells the brigade that as long as he is alive, he will not permit them to leave until reinforcements arrive. Then, standing in front of the guns, Jackson orders the artillerymen to light their matches. After several minutes, officers come forward and pledge the loyalty of the brigade. Reinforcements arrive on the

THE MILITIA IN THE WAR OF 1812

The Militia Act of 1792 required all free, able-bodied men ages 18–45 to serve in their enrolled state militia and to provide their own weapons and equipment. No federal monies were authorized for pay, equipment, training, or any other purpose. The raising and training of militia formations was the responsibility of each state under an Adjutant General who was accountable to the governor for the training, discipline, and administration of the state militia system. The same system applied to territories awaiting acceptance as states.

Unfortunately, the Militia Act contained no sanctions for noncompliance, and in the following years the quality of militia units diminished greatly. Still, citizen-soldiers performed important service west of the Appalachians. Militiamen augmented Regular troops during struggles with Native Americans. The militia's role in the Whiskey Rebellion of 1794 established an important precedent for the exercise of the new constitutional power of the President to mobilize the militia to enforce federal laws. In 1808, Congress approved an annual federal allotment to the states of $200,000 for the purchase of arms.

The War of 1812 revealed glaring deficiencies in the militia system and raised serious questions regarding the sharing of the responsibilities for the common defense between the federal government and the states. In New England antiwar sentiment was strong; and several governors refused to call out the militia except to defend their own state. Despite the official "seniority" of Regular officers, Army and militia generals frequently bickered over command arrangements. On a number of occasions, militia units refused to cross into Canada to attack British positions even to help engaged American units.

Under competent and aggressive leaders, however, militiamen could perform well. William Henry Harrison was such a leader. In October 1813, Harrison led a mixed army of Regulars and militiamen into southern Ontario and smashed the British at the Battle of the Thames River. The following year militiamen assisted Regulars in defending Fort McHenry and blocking the land approaches to Baltimore.

The militia's most dramatic display of combat prowess came at the Battle of New Orleans under the command of Andrew Jackson in January 1815. In the popular mind, the battle took its place alongside Bunker Hill as a demonstration of the natural abilities and fighting spirit of American citizen-soldiers. For Harrison and Jackson, their exploits as militia leaders propelled them to national fame and eventually the presidency.

Ironically, the sense of success in the War of 1812 led to the demise of the enrolled militia system. Glaring militia deficiencies were forgotten as most Americans convinced themselves that mandatory militia service was no longer required and that dedicated volunteers would always respond when called. Drill periods and the cost of purchasing arms and equipment were viewed as unwelcome anachronistic burdens. The enrolled militia system fell apart from neglect, and by the 1840s several states had either rescinded their militia laws or no longer enforced them.

—*Michael Doubler*

Above: *Maryland state militia mustered to defend Baltimore in 1814 included artillery units like the 1st Maryland Artillery Regiment depicted here. ("Maryland Volunteer Militia Artillery, 1814," H. Charles McBarron, Company of Military Historians)*

12th, but they have only a few days left before discharge. Disgusted, Jackson sends his Volunteers and the new men home. To defend the fort he now has just the militia, whose terms are up on 4 January.

19–29 December. **British Take Fort Niagara. New York.**
In early December, McClure abandons Fort George and burns nearby Newark, Canada. Seeking revenge, the British attack Fort Niagara on the night of 18–19 December with more than 500 troops and Indians. They surprise the sentries, enter an open gate, and assault the garrison. Some militia hold out in two fortified buildings, but eventually they are overcome. More than 80 are killed, and 244 are captured. The British then ravage the countryside for two weeks. On the 29th, they scatter the militia defending Black Rock and Buffalo and burn the towns. (In 1994, Fort Niagara's captured flag is purchased in England and returned to the fort.)

23–24 December. **Creek War—Battle of Econochaca. Mississippi Territory.**
During the morning Claiborne's expedition arrives at the Red Stick town, where only warriors remain. They have made no defensive preparations, placing their faith in the magical ring. When they see Claiborne's

men advancing on the town without pause, most warriors flee, leaving Chief Weatherford and a few others to put up a short fight before also running. Claiborne burns the town and continues on to destroy another village after a minor skirmish. Claiborne returns home, releases his Volunteers, and resigns on 17 January. The 3d Infantry remains to garrison the forts along the Alabama River.

1814

January. **Status of the Army.**
Authorized strength of the Army is 57,351, but many regiments exist only on paper. To improve recruiting, the enlistment bonus is increased to $124 cash, and in many regiments terms of service of up to five years are offered. The largest concentration of Regulars is in the north under Wilkinson. Pinckney is senior officer in the south.

14–24 January. **Creek War—Battles of Emuckfaw and Enotachopco Creeks.**
On the 14th, Jackson receives 850 new, untrained militia recruits. He marches them into the field with 200 Indian allies against the heavily fortified Red Stick

town of Tohopeka. As they rest along Emuckfaw Creek on the 22nd, Jackson's force is attacked by 900 Creeks. Two counterattacks led by Coffee finally drive off the Indians. As the militia cross Enotachopco Creek on the 24th en route back to Fort Strother, they are attacked again. Jackson tries to maneuver, but the rear guard panics. Only Jackson's personal leadership rallies the men to beat off the attack. At the fort, Jackson begins a strenuous training program of drill, hard discipline, and physical labor. A few weeks later the 39th Infantry under Colonel John Williams arrives, followed by more Volunteers.

24 January. **New Generation of Generals.**
A new generation of younger Regular officers move into senior Army positions. Jacob Brown and George Izard are promoted to major general. Five new brigadiers are also selected: Thomas Macomb, Edmund P. Gaines, Daniel Bissel, and Thomas A. Smith—all Regulars with an average age of 36 years—and Winfield Scott, at 28 the youngest general in the Army.

27 January. **Creek War. Battle of Calabee Creek. Mississippi Territory.**
Brigadier John Floyd's force of 1,700 Georgia Volunteers and friendly Creeks is surprised in their camp by 1,800 Red Sticks. The Indians penetrate the camp in chaotic hand-to-hand fighting. Floyd is able to get his artillery into play, and a bayonet counterattack scatters the Red Sticks, who retreat into the swamp. Floyd has lost 22 killed and withdraws to Fort Mitchell to tend to his wounded.

10 February. **More Regiments Authorized.**
Congress approves four more infantry regiments (45th–48th) and increases the number of soldiers per company to 90 in all infantry regiments. As usual, recruiting is difficult and the new regiments never approach authorized strength.

14–27 March. **Creek War. Battle of Horseshoe Bend. Mississippi Territory.**
After weeks of training, Jackson has a tough, disciplined army. On the 14th, he leads 2,700 militia and Regulars of the 39th Infantry with 600 Cherokees and Creeks against the heavily fortified Red Stick stronghold of Tohopeka. The town is in a bend of the Tallapoosa River, with the river on three sides and a strong earth and timber breastwork on the fourth. Jackson's offer to evacuate the women and children is refused, and he begins a bombardment by his two small field guns. Coffee's brigade and the Indians occupy the riverbank, while the 39th and the militia deploy in front of the village. Without orders, Cherokees and scouts cross the river and attack the rear of the village. Seeing an opportunity, Jackson orders the militia and the 39th to charge the breastworks. The 39th is first over the wall. In the hand-to-hand fight through the burning village, Major Lemuel Montgomery is killed and Lieutenant Samuel Houston suffers three serious wounds. The trapped Red Sticks make a desperate stand, but they are crushed in the five-hour battle. American losses are estimated at 47 killed and 159 wounded. The Creek and Cherokee allies lose 23 killed. Jackson orders the American dead buried in the river to prevent scalping of the bodies.

28 March–17 April. **Creek War. Jackson Destroys Towns.**
Jackson makes a three-week march of destruction through Red Stick territory. On the 17th, he arrives at the junction of the Coosa and Tallapoosa Rivers, where he constructs Fort Jackson while patrols search for remaining Red Sticks. Many surrender or escape to Florida. Jackson refuses to talk peace until Chief Weatherford, who led the Fort Mims attack, surrenders. After several days Weatherford suddenly appears alone at Jackson's tent, giving himself up. Impressed by the courage of the chief, Jackson arranges a truce.

30 March. **Battle of La Colle Mill. Canada.**
Major General Wilkinson makes a poorly planned advance into Canada and attacks a strongly fortified British position around a stone mill. His light cannon

Left: *Dressed in the tall leather cap and short jacket of the period, this Regular infantryman is biting the end off a waxed paper cartridge in preparation to firing his rifle. ("Regular Infantryman, 1813," H. Charles McBarron, copyright Parks Canada)*

Opposite: *On 5 October 1813, American troops forced the withdrawal of General Proctor. The Americans catch up with the British forces and defeat them at the Thames River, Canada. ("Battle of Thames," The Granger Collection, New York)*

have no effect on the stone walls, and the infantry, struggling through deep snow, are unable to advance. Wilkinson is unable to make progress and withdraws to Plattsburg, where he finds orders relieving him of command and ordering him to Washington to face yet another court-martial, this time for drunkenness and neglect of duty.

March. New Army Leadership.
Major General Jacob Brown assumes command of the Army of the North, replacing Wilkinson. He organizes two "divisions"—the "Right" under Izard at Plattsburg and the "Left" under himself. Brown gives Scott a brigade in the Left Division and responsibility to train the entire command. Scott institutes a strict training program of ten hours a day, first focusing on basic soldiering, then progressing to complex battle

drill. Discipline is also tough. Scott has four deserters shot in front of the brigade. Regulation blue uniform jackets ordered earlier for Scott's men fail to arrive and gray jackets normally used for militia are substituted.

2 April. First Weather Records.
Dr. James Tilton, Physician and Surgeon General of the Army, directs each army surgeon and medical staff to maintain a daily diary of the local weather and "medical topography." These are the first organized meteorological records in America.

18–19 April. Creek War Ends. Fort Jackson.
Major General Pinckney is appointed region commander and peace treaty commissioner. He orders Jackson to garrison the forts in the area and to take the rest of his men back to Tennessee for discharge. Newly

mobilized militia replace the fort garrisons as enlistments expire. On the 19th Jackson receives a commission as a brigadier general in the Regular Army, command of the 7th Military District, and a brevet promotion to major general.

25 *April.* Hull Court Martial. Washington.
Dearborn sits as president of Hull's court-martial for treason and cowardice. Hull is found guilty of cowardice and sentenced to be shot. President Madison approves the finding but remits the death penalty. Hull is cashiered from the Army and dies in poverty in 1825. He is the only Army general officer sentenced to be shot.

11 *May.* Harrison Resigns.
Angry with Secretary Armstrong, Harrison resigns, and his Regular major general position is given to Jackson. In June, Jackson is sent to Fort Jackson to replace Pinckney as peace commissioner. Command of the Northwest Army at Fort Detroit falls to Brigadier Duncan McArthur. His army is little more than a garrison force for the fort, with few resources and little activity.

12 *May.* Units Consolidated.
Per the Act of 30 March, the 1st, 2d, and 3d Artillery Regiments are consolidated to form a single Corps of Artillery, with 12 independent battalions of four companies each. The Regiment of Light Artillery remains separate. The 1st and 2d Light Dragoons are consolidated into the 1st Light Dragoon Regiment. Three new Regiments of Riflemen (2d–4th) are authorized for five years or "duration." Green wool cloth is expensive, so the Rifle regiments are issued dark gray uniforms, with long green hunting shirts for summer. The Riflemen also receive new cap badges showing a hunting horn with the regimental number in its center. The horn in one form or another remains the symbol of the infantry and rifle regiments for many years.

30 *May.* Battle of Sandy Creek. Lake Ontario, New York.
A detachment of Rifles and Indians under Major Daniel Appling ambushes seven boats of British sailors and marines trying to capture the cannon and munitions being guarded by Appling. After some minutes of heavy fire, Appling orders his men, whose rifles have no bayonets, to charge the British, who

EYEWITNESS: THE BATTLE OF HORSESHOE BEND

On 27 March 1814 Major General Andrew Jackson led 3,300 U.S. Army Regulars, militia, and Indian allies against a hostile faction of Creek Indians known as "Red Sticks" under Chief Menawa. More than 1,000 Red Sticks were well dug-in behind an eight-foot palisade and earth rampart at a loop-like bend in the Tallapoosa River near today's Davits, Aabama. After the battle, Jackson submitted the following description of the action.

"Early on the morning of the 27th having encamped the preceding night at a distance of six miles from them—I detailed Gen. [John] Coffee with the mounted men and nearly the whole of the Indian force, to pass the river at a ford about three miles below their encampment, and to surround the bend in such a manor that none of [the Red Sticks] should escape by attempting to cross the river. With the remainder of the forces I proceeded along the point of land which leads to the front of the breastwork; and at half past ten o'clock A.M. I had planted my artillery on a small eminence . . . from whence I immediately opened a brisk fire upon its centre. With the musquetry and rifles I kept up a galling fire whenever the enemy shewed themselves behind their works, or ventured to approach them. This was continued with occasional intermissions, for about two hours, when Capt. [William] Russell's company of spies and a part of the Cherokee force, headed by their gallant chieftain, Col. Richard Brown, and conducted by the brave Col. [Gideon] Morgan, crossed over the extremity of the peninsula in canoes and set fire to a few of [the] buildings which were there situated. They then advanced with great gallantry toward the breastwork, and commenced firing upon the enemy who lay behind it.

"Finding that this force, notwithstanding the determined bravery they displayed, was wholly insufficient to dislodge the enemy and that General Coffee had secured the opposite banks of the river, I now determined upon taking possession of their works by storm. . . . The regular troops, led on by their intrepid and skillful commander Col. [John] Williams, and by the gallant Major [Lemuel] Montgomery were presently in possession of the nearer side of the breastwork; and the militia accompanied them in the charge with a vivacity and firmness which could not have been exceeded and has seldom been equalled by troops of any description. A few companies of General [George] Doherty's Brigade on the right, were led on with great gallantry by Col. [Samuel] Bunch—the advance guard, by the Adjutant General Sitler, and the left extremity of the line by Capt. [John] Gordon of the Spies and Capt. [James] McMurry, of Gen. [Thomas] Johnson's Brigade of West Tennessee Militia.

"Having maintained for a few minutes a very obstinate contest, muzzle to muzzle, through the portholes, in which many of the enemy's balls were welded to the bayonets of our musquets, our troops succeeded in gaining possession of the opposite side of the works. The event could no longer be doubtful. The enemy, altho many of them fought to the last with a kind of bravery which desperation inspires, were at length entirely routed and cut to pieces. The whole margin of the river which surrounded the peninsular was strewn with the slain. Five hundred and fifty seven were found by officers of great respecability whom I ordered to count them; a very great number who were thrown into the river by their surviving friends, and killed in attempting to pass by General Coffee's men stationed on the opposite banks."

—Kevin M. Hymel

Above: *The horseshoe bend of the Tallapoosa River that contained the Red Stick village is shown in this photograph. (Courtesy National Park Service)*

quickly surrender. More than 140 captives are taken, and the cannon are delivered safely to the fleet at Sackets Harbor.

2 June. Taylor Expedition. Mississippi River.
Major Zachary Taylor, promoted in May, leads an expedition of 24th Infantry up the Mississippi in a show of American authority. He builds Fort Johnson (Warsaw, Illinois) on bluffs overlooking the river, then continues upriver. On the 2nd, he captures the British outpost at Prairie du Chien and begins building Fort Shelby. A company-size garrison of about 200 men under Lieutenant Joseph Perkins is left to occupy the fort when Taylor moves on.

22 June. Battle of Craney Island. Norfolk, Virginia.
British landing parties attempt to capture the harbor defense batteries protecting Norfolk. Since April, work parties supervised by Engineer Captain Sylvanus Thayer have toiled to improve the fortifications. The British landing barges are engaged by the repositioned artillery batteries and suffer numerous losses, forcing a withdrawal. Two days later the British attack Hampton across the bay and ravage the town.

28 June. Death of Rifleman Forsyth. Odelltown, New York.
Brevet Lieutenant Colonel Benjamin Forsyth of the 1st Rifle Regiment is killed while directing his men in a successful ambush of a large British-Indian force. Appling, now a lieutenant colonel, replaces him.

3 July. Expedition to Capture Fort Mackinac. Michigan Territory.
Lieutenant Colonel George Croghan, breveted after his defense of Fort Stephenson, departs Detroit with an expedition of 700 men to recapture Fort Mackinac. His force includes a regiment of Ohio militia and five companies from the 24th, 17th, and 19th Infantry and the Corps of Artillery.

3–4 July. Americans Invade Canada. Niagara River.
Brown takes his Left Division across the river in rainy predawn darkness to attack Fort Erie. He has 1,028 Regulars of Scott's and Ripley's brigades, four companies of light artillery, and some Light Dragoons and Riflemen. Also in the force are Pennsylvania Volunteers and Indians. The unfinished and undermanned fort surrenders before sundown. The next morning Brown marches north toward Montreal with Scott's brigade in the lead. Scott moves quickly, using his artillery to defeat British efforts at delay. By

Above: *Lieutenant Sam Houston leads his men of the 39th Infantry over the Indian barricades to destroy the Red Stick village at Horseshoe Bend. (Ed Elvidge, courtesy National Park Service)*

dusk Scott is camped within a mile of the Chippewa River and the main British battle line.

5 July. **Battle of Chippewa. Chippewa River, Canada.**
Scott is forming his brigade for a delayed Fourth of July review when Brown alerts him to a British attack. Scott deploys his three regiments, positions his artillery, and advances to meet the British. The British commander expects the gray-clad Americans to break under his artillery fire, but they maneuver and fire without falter. Watching, he exclaims, "Those are Regulars, by God!" Scott's 25th Infantry outflanks and breaks the British right. When the British left advances, Scott splits his force by giving Major Henry Leavenworth the 9th and 22d Infantry and Major John McNeill the 11th. Scott orders them to incline their units toward the center, catching the advancing British in a deadly crossfire. Scott then orders a bayonet charge. The British give way and withdraw over the river, leaving more than 400 casualties behind. Scott has 44 killed and 224 wounded.

7–24 July. **Brown Pursues British. Chippewa, Canada.**
Brown advances over the river, forcing the British to retreat toward Fort George. Scott leads the pursuit to the fort, but without heavy guns and naval support, nothing more can be done. Concerned about overextending his army, Brown retires south of the Chippewa River, followed by a reinforced British force.

11 July. **British Invade Maine. Eastport, Maine.**
The British begin diversionary attacks along the Atlantic coast. On the 11th, 1,000 troops land at Eastport, forcing the 85-man militia garrison to surrender Fort Sullivan.

17–20 July. **British Capture Fort Shelby. Prairie du Chien, Illinois Territory.**
A force of 700 British Regulars with artillery, militia, and Indians attack Fort Shelby. The fort's supporting gunboat, *Governor Clark*, is damaged by the British artillery and departs. After a two-day bombardment, outnumbered and out of ammunition, Lieutenant Perkins negotiates safe passage for his men and surrenders the fort on the 20th.

19–21 July. **Fort Shelby Reinforcements Attacked. Mississippi River.**
Concerned about Fort Shelby, Brigadier Benjamin Howard, District Commander at St. Louis, has sent reinforcements under Captain John Campbell. Campbell has his 33-man company of 1st Infantry and 66 U.S. Rangers in three gunboats with several Army families. On the 19th, while struggling with a strong storm and river damage, the boats are driven ashore and attacked by more than 400 British and Indians. When Campbell's boat is set afire, another boat rescues the passengers while fighting off boarding Indians. Using the swivel guns on the boats and their muskets, the two surviving boats succeed in getting out of range. They return to St. Louis with more than 30 killed or wounded, including several women and children. En route back they are joined by the *Governor Clark* with news of the attack on the fort.

25–26 July. **Battle of Lundy's Lane. Canada.**
In late afternoon Major Leavenworth spots British movement near Lundy's Lane on a ridgetop north of the river. Scott's brigade is sent to investigate and is caught in an open area under heavy British fire. Scott refuses to retreat and advances Major Thomas Jessup's 25th Infantry through woods on the right while sending for help. Jessup emerges on the British left flank, capturing several hundred prisoners and a British major general. It is almost dark when Brown arrives with more troops. He places Scott's brigade in reserve and puts Brigidier Eleazar Ripley's brigade in the line. Of his original 1,300 men, Scott has only 400 left. Ripley's men drive the British infantry back. Ordered to capture the British artillery with his 21st Infantry, Colonel James Miller replies "I'll try, sir!" He succeeds, and his reply becomes the motto of the regiment. Three British counterattacks are thrown back by hand-to-hand fighting in the dark. Scott and

Opposite: *A member of the U.S. Light Dragoons is depicted on outpost duty. ("Trooper, U.S. Light Dragoons, 1812," H. Charles McBarron, copyright Parks Canada)*

Right: *While there were no enlisted engineers, each infantry regiment had men skilled as "pioneers" to do the basic combat engineer tasks. They would often direct infantry work parties. The corporals were identifiable by the epaulets on their right shoulders. ("Pioneers, 25th U.S. Infantry Regiment, 1814," Frederick P. Todd, Company of Military Historians)*

Leavenworth lead their small unit into the center of the melee. Scott, already injured, is wounded again and carried away barely conscious. Brown is also hit. As he is being evacuated, Brown makes a comment that Ripley understands as an order to return to camp. After midnight on the 26th, the Americans leave the battlefield. An angry Brown orders Ripley to reoccupy the battlefield, but the British have advanced in strength and Ripley must withdraw again. Killed, wounded, and captured on both sides are almost 900 men. Within a few days, Ripley returns the army to the U.S. side of the Niagara River, leaving a garrison at Fort Erie on the Canadian shore. Brown replaces Ripley with Brigadier Edmund P. Gaines.

3 August. **Battle of Conjockta Creek. New York.**
About midnight, some 600 British light infantry cross the Niagara River to destroy American supplies at Black Rock and Buffalo. They are stopped at Conjockta Creek by 240 men from the 1st Rifle Regiment under Major Lodowick Morgan, whose men have destroyed the bridge and occupy well-selected blocking positions. After suffering more than 30 casualties, the British turn back. Morgan is killed in another skirmish on 13 August. Within a month the aggressive 1st and 4th Rifles suffer 20 percent casualties in small actions.

4 August. **Battle of Fort Mackinac. Mackinac Island, Michigan Territory.**
The navy squadron carrying Lieutenant Colonel Croghan's expedition arrives off Fort Mackinac. The landing areas near the fort are unsuitable, so Croghan lands on the far side of the island. Marching overland, Croghan and his men run into a British-Canadian-Indian force dug in across the trail. When Croghan tries to outflank the position, his men stumble into an Indian ambush. He gives up the attack and sails back to Detroit.

ORIGINS OF THE WEST POINT GRAY

As British Major General Phineas Riall watched the gray-clad Americans cooly deploying under the fire of his artillery at Chippewa, he realized the troops were not the New York militia he was expecting and exclaimed, "These are Regulars, by God!" He had reason to be surprised. American Regulars normally wore blue, not gray.

In the early days of the War of 1812, the American Army changed to an all-dark-blue uniform. Many units, however, did not receive the new uniforms or wore out the initial issue in the hard campaigning as the war dragged on. Adequate amounts of the expensive blue cloth were hard to provide and the Army quartermaster was forced to use whatever cloth could be found. Even when the blue uniforms were produced, the Army's contract transportation frequently delayed, misshipped, lost or outright stole many items. Gray cloth used for work clothes and cheaper militia uniforms was less expensive and more available, so it was used as an alternative.

In the summer of 1814, thousands of gray uniform jackets were shipped to Winfield Scott's brigade of Regulars along the northern New York border with Canada, and to the U.S. Military Academy at West Point. When Riall first saw the gray uniforms on the Americans advancing toward him across the battlefield, he immediately assumed they belonged to the poorly trained American militia volunteers. He was wrong. It was Scott's well-disciplined Regulars who won the battle.

The shipment of uniforms that arrived at West Point also had a historic impact. It has determined the Academy's basic uniform color for almost 200 years. The academy Superintendent, Captain Alden Partridge, fashioned his own uniform from the gray cloth and wore it on almost every occasion, earning him the name "Old Pewter." But stories relating the victory at Chippewa as the reason for the choice of West Point gray are myth.

The first mention of gray as the official West Point color comes from an 1815 letter from Brigadier General Joseph G. Swift, Inspector General of the Military Academy, to Secretary of War William Crawford. In the letter, Swift explained that the cadet uniform at the Academy "has been Grey for the last fifteen months," and that "cloth of this colour looks well while it remains whole and of the price of the Uniform $18 to $20, better suits the finance of the Cadets than one of Blue would." It was availability, practicality, and economy, not admiration for battlefield victories, that motivated the high command to promote West Point gray.

Swift's letter, however, was overlooked by the Secretary until the war was finished and finer details of building a peacetime army could be addressed. On 4 September 1816, it became official. Crawford issued a general order that "a Coatee of grey sattinett, single breasted" would become the "strictly adhered to" uniform of West Point cadets, "and any deviation will be considered a military offense." From then on, after four years in a gray uniform, Academy graduates could "put away cadet gray and don Army blue" as the Regular soldiers so feared by the enemy.

—*Kevin M. Hymel*

Above: *The cadets of West Point donned gray uniforms instead of the standard Army blue because of the availability and affordable price of gray cloth. ("Superintendent Partridge and Cadets, Summer Dress, 1815," Frederick T. Chapman)*

Mid-August. **Izard Ordered West. Plattsburg, New York.**

Secretary Armstrong believes Sackets Harbor is the next British target. He orders Major General Izard, the area commander, to reinforce the town with 4,000 troops. This leaves Plattsburg, the actual British objective, vulnerable. Izard disagrees without success. Before departing on the 26th, Izard puts men to work building fortifications and leaves behind Brigadier Thomas Macomb with detachments from the eight Regular infantry regiments, the 1st Rifle Regiment, and a company of the Light Artillery—about 1,500 men, plus sick, wounded, and prisoners.

13–15 August. **British Attack Fort Erie. Fort Erie, Canada.**

The British open fire on Fort Erie with heavy guns brought from Fort George. The fort is defended by Gaines' brigade of two Regular infantry regiments reinforced with detachments from 1st and 4th Rifles, Light Dragoons, five other infantry regiments, and artillery. Army engineers directed by West Point graduate Brevet Lieutenant Colonel William McRee have so greatly strengthened the fort that the two-day British bombardment does little damage. On the 15th, the British make a major ground assault. Two attacks are thrown back, but a large force captures one exterior bastion and holds it for two hours until a powder magazine explodes, killing most of the British attackers. The ground assaults stop, but the bombardment continues.

20–24 August. **Battle of Bladensburg. Bladensburg, Maryland.**

Brigadier William H. Winder assembles Maryland and District of Columbia militia and detachments from the 12th, 36th, and 38th Infantry and the 1st Light Dragoons at Bladensburg, east of Washington. Their mission is to block a British force of 4,000 that landed from the Patuxant River. Secretary Armstrong believes Baltimore, not Washington, is the British objective and delays reinforcing Winder. President Madison and his cabinet ride out to watch and advise Winder, and Secretary of State James Monroe leads one group of dragoons to scout the approaching British. On the 23rd, mounted militia skirmish with the British, and Winder orders several bridges over the Anacostia River burned. Along the west bank of the Anacostia River opposite Bladensburg, Winder deploys his 6,000 men in three successive positions, holding the Regulars in reserve. Unknown to Winder, Monroe later moves the units, placing them too far apart to support one another. About noon the British attack, crossing one remaining bridge or wading the river and scattering the first line of militia. The British Congreve rockets especially unnerve the militia. Pressed on the flanks, the militia in the second and third positions collapse, retreating in disorder. Several units try to hold, including a U.S. Navy artillery and Marine detachment, but they are too few. American losses are light, only 10–12 killed and 40 wounded. but the withdrawal turns into a disorderly rout. It is the last time an American President personally commands soldiers in combat.

24–25 August. **Washington Burned.**

Winder withdraws his few troops toward Georgetown, while American officials evacuate official papers, military supplies, and themselves. President Madison and Monroe cross the Potomac to Virginia. They spend the night then return to Maryland. After setting fire to the public buildings and several residences, the

British make a night withdrawal to Benedict, Maryland, and rejoin their ships. The attack galvanizes public support, and enlistments jump.

26 August. Fort Warburton Destroyed. Maryland.
While Washington is attacked by land, seven British warships sail up the Potomac River. Only Fort Warburton (now Fort Washington), opposite Mount Vernon, defends the river, and it is undergunned and manned by only 60 artillerymen. Earlier requests for heavier guns were denied as too expensive. When British ships appear on the river and lob a few shells into the fort, the garrison evacuates and blows up the powder magazine.

27 August–6 September. Alexandria Occupied. Virginia.
As the British destroy Fort Warburton, a civilian delegation appears from Alexandria (located a short distance upriver) offering a truce to save the defenseless town. A high ransom is negotiated, and the British sail to the town wharf to load their ships. When a brigade of Virginia militia approach, city officials ask them to wait outside town. Other Virginia militia regiments arrive in the area and join with sailors from the Washington Navy Yard to emplace heavy guns and artillery in hasty positions along the river.

30–31 August. Battle of Caulks' Field. Chestertown, Maryland.
A small British flotilla along Maryland's Eastern Shore diverts American forces from the Washington raiders. After several small raids, the British commander decides to attack the camp of Lieutenant Colonel Philip Reed's 21st Maryland Regiment. Reed, a Continental veteran, has trained his men well. When his scouts report the landing party, Reed forms his men and engages the British in successive positions with both artillery and infantry. In the fighting the British commander is mortally wounded, and they withdraw to their ships. Only three Americans are lost against 32 British killed and wounded.

31 August–3 September. British Invade New York.
A British force of 10,000 troops crosses the Niagara River and marches for Plattsburg. Macomb calls for militia reinforcements and strengthens his positions on the bluffs dominating the south side of the Saranac River across from Plattsburg. Directing the work are two Corps of Engineer officers, Major Joseph Totten (West Point, 1802) and Lieutenant R. E. DeRussy. At a crossroads nine miles from Plattsburg, the British send two brigades left along the shore of Cumberland Bay, while the rest continue on the Beekmantown Road.

5–6 September. Battle of Plattsburg. Beekmantown Road.
Macomb sends Major John E. Wool and 250 Regulars of the 29th Infantry to help delay the advancing British. At daybreak Wool's men open fire on the British column. Wool's backup force of New York militia panics and flees at the sight of their own red-jacketed dragoons, who are mistaken for British. Joined by a detachment of the Light Artillery with two guns, Wool's men fight a series of delaying engagements through Plattsburg to the Saranac River. Almost all the militia has deserted so Macomb distributes his Regulars in the three earthen forts—Forts Brown, Scott, and Moreau—two blockhouses, and the trenches. On the shore road, Captain John Sproull's militia and Major Appling with 110 men from the 1st Rifles receive cannon-fire support from ships in the bay. With this help, they are able to delay for a while at the Dead Creek bridge, but eventually both also withdraw across the river. The British halt in town to consolidate. When they begin using houses for shelter, Macomb orders red-hot cannon balls fired. A long-range exchange of cannon fire continues as more British forces arrive.

5–6 September. **Battle of Credit Island. Mississippi River.**

Major Zachary Taylor is leading a second expedition to retake Fort Shelby. The 350-man detachment of 7th Infantry, Rangers, and militia is traveling in eight boats. Taylor halts the boats near several islands to wait out a storm, not knowing that more than 1,200 British and Indians, including Sacs led by Black Hawk, are nearby with some small artillery. On the morning of the 5th, Indians open fire from one of the islands and Taylor's men drive them away. When Taylor's boats come under artillery fire, he withdraws to the Des Moines River, where a temporary fort is built, which he names Fort Johnson. The fight is the last major action of the war in the west.

Opposite: *The Corps of Artillery was formed by the consolidation of 1st, 2d, and 3d Artillery Regiments. ("U.S. Corps of Artillery, 1814-1821," H. Charles McBarron, Company of Military Historians)*

Right: *Shown are officers and men of the Rifle Regiment in their various field uniforms. ("American Soldier, 1814," H. Charles McBarron, Army Art Collection, NMUSA)*

10 September. Battle of Plattsburg.

At 2 a.m. Captain George McGlassin leads a raiding party of 60 volunteers from the 15th Infantry across the river to attack a British rocket battery. Tied together with ropes, the men wade the river and assault the position with bayonets, scattering the 300 British soldiers. The raiders destroy the rockets and withdraw without losing a man. McGlassin later receives a brevet promotion to major.

11 September. Battle of Plattsburg.

At 7:30 a.m. the British fleet arrives in the bay to engage Macdonough's ships. Many of his officers, gun crews, and ship-borne infantry are Army volunteers. Captain White Youngs, 15th Infantry, is the senior Army commander. When the naval battle begins, the British also launch a ground attack with an artillery bombardment. One column attacks over bridges in the town. Another, with more than 7,000 men, flanks Macomb's position by wading a ford upriver and driving the Vermont defenders back against the rear of the American positions. Macomb's escape route is blocked and the British are preparing to advance when they are ordered to immediately withdraw. Macdonough has soundly beaten the British fleet and without its support the British commander fears being cut off. In the haste to depart for Canada, large amounts of supplies are abandoned. American Army killed and wounded are about 100 men.

11–12 September. Battle of Fort McHenry. Baltimore.

Militia Major General Samuel Smith has been working on Baltimore's defenses for more than a year. When Winder, the Army District commander, appears, he is ordered to serve under Smith. About 15,000 militiamen from Maryland, Virginia, and Pennsylvania are around the city. The main defense for the harbor is Fort McHenry, commanded by Major George Armistead, Corps of Artillery. He has a garrison of artillerymen and detachments from the 12th, 14th, 36th, and 38th Infantry regiments. The infantry and two companies of U.S. Sea Fencibles are placed in the outer works facing the river to defeat any landings. Captain Frederick Evans commands the guns in the fort, which include a number of heavy naval cannon taken from a French warship. Smaller fortifications sit on both sides of the harbor entrance to provide supporting fires. These are manned by militia, marines, and sailors. A large chain mounted on logs stretches across the inner harbor entrance, and behind it is a line of old sunken ships.

11–12 September. Battle of North Point. Maryland.

The British fleet lands 4,000 troops at North Point before dawn, and the advance brigade moves quickly toward Baltimore. About noon, the British halt to rest about seven miles east of the city, unaware that Brigadier John Strickler's 3d Maryland Brigade of 6,000 well-trained militiamen waits ahead. When a skirmish develops, the British commander rides up to observe the action and is killed. Command passes to his deputy who advances against the American line. He send a regiment to turn the American left and Strickler tries to block the move with the 51st Maryland but is too late. The 51st collapses, taking other units with it, and the British center charges. After a ten-minute struggle the American line breaks. Strickler orders a withdrawal to his second defensive line, where he prepares for the next attack. The British have also had heavy casualties and delay

ALEXANDER MACOMB

Above: *Alexander Macomb enrolled in the New York state militia at the age of 16. He became the Commanding General of the Army in 1828. ("Alexander Macomb," Thomas Sully, Army Art Collection, NMUSA)*

Alexander Macomb was a major figure in the U.S. Army during the War of 1812 and then later as a reforming commanding general of the Army.

After his birth in Detroit in April 1782, Macomb's family moved to New York. Teenage Alexander obtained a Regular Army commission as a "cornet" of Light Dragoons on 10 January 1799 and served until discharged in June 1800. He rejoined the Army in February 1801 as a second lieutenant of the 2d Infantry Regiment and was assigned to the staff of Brigadier James Wilkinson, the Army's senior officer.

In October 1802, Macomb was promoted to first lieutenant in the new Corps of Engineers and sent to study at the United States Military Academy at West Point. He was one of the first graduates and stayed until promoted to captain and assigned to work on U.S. fortifications along the Georgia and Carolina coasts. A talented and hard-working officer, he was promoted to major in 1808 and lieutenant colonel in July 1810.

Looming war in 1812 forced Congress to expand the woefully understrength Army with new regiments.

Macomb requested field duty and on 6 July was made colonel of the new 3d Artillery Regiment. He recruited and trained the men for the unit, and the regiment was soon on the northern frontier at Sackets Harbor, New York.

During 1813 Macomb participated in the campaigns against Canada, including the capture of Fort George. He became known as one of the new generation of Army leaders with energy, leadership, and organizational skills sorely lacking in older, more senior officers. In recognition of his service Macomb was promoted to brigadier general on 24 January 1814 and placed in command of the forces at Plattsburg, New York, where he made his greatest contribution of the war. Macomb and his Plattsburg garrison of 4,000 men were the target of a well-planned British campaign to seize control of Lake Champlain. His determined defense helped turn back a British invasion force of 15,000, winning him a gold medal from Congress and a brevet promotion to major general.

After the war, Brigadier General Macomb was placed in command of the western Illinois and Michigan territories, building forts, constructing roads, and providing security for the settlers moving into the area. When the Army was cut back in March 1821, Macomb was reduced to colonel but made Chief, Corps of Engineers.

When Major General Jacob Brown, General in Chief of the Army, died in February 1828, selection of a replacement became deadlocked between Winfield Scott and Edmund Gaines. President Adams picked Macomb and promoted him to major general. This infuriated Scott, who had been Macomb's superior. He demanded Macomb's arrest and even appealed to Congress for action, all to no avail.

During his tenure as Army commander, Macomb worked hard to enhance the prestige and authority of his position and improve Army organization, in particular bringing the independent Army departments under centralized control. At one point he court-martialed the Adjutant General for insubordination. He effectively handled a number of border crises, including suppression of local warring factions along the Northern frontier in 1838, where a border dispute with Great Britain threatened to explode. Although now overshadowed by Winfield Scott, Macomb's contributions to the Army were no less significant. He died of apoplexy in Washington, D.C., on 25 June 1841.

—*Kevin M. Hymel*

their advance as the day ends in a heavy rain. Concerned about his men's ability to fight in the dark, Strickler withdraws to the main defensive positions on Hampstead Hill. Meanwhile, the British ships work their way to within a few miles of Fort McHenry, attempting to flank the fort and support a British land.

13–14 September. **Battle of Fort McHenry. Baltimore.**
The British advance again early on the 13th, but seeing the strength of the American positions, decide that only a night attack supported by naval cannons can succeed. The British warships engage Captain Evans' artillerymen in Fort McHenry in a gunnery duel but cannot move forward because of the chain blocking the harbor entrance. Shortly after 9 a.m. all the British ships move out of range of the fort except the "bomb" ships, which continue lobbing their large, high-angle mortar shells into the fort. About 3 p.m. the warships move in again but are driven off. Realizing an attack on the city cannot succeed, the British make a night withdrawal while continuing to bombard the fort. By 7 a.m. on the 14th the land force is embarked and the warships depart. The fort has suffered more than 400 direct hits from the mortars but only minimal loss of life. Overhead floats the large American flag raised at first light by Major Armistead to replace the smaller flag flown during the night. Francis Scott Key,

who is detained on a British ship, sees the flag through the dawn mist and fog and is inspired to write a poem entitled "The Star Spangled Banner."

16 September. **British Attack Fort Bowyer. Mobile Bay, West Florida.**
A British landing party, supported by several warships, attacks Fort Bowyer at the entrance to Mobile Bay. Major William Lawrence defends the fort with 160 men of the 2d Infantry and a detachment of Corps of Artillery. The attack is beaten off with relatively heavy British losses, including one ship.

17 September. **Brown Leads Sortie. Fort Erie, Canada.**
British cannon have continuously bombarded Fort Erie since August. Brigadier Brown, though still recovering from his wounds, takes over when Gaines is injured. Brown directs a major sortie against the British artillery positions. Moving at dusk through a heavy rain, 1,000 New York militia and 600 Regulars surprise and capture two of the positions, spiking the guns. Efforts to take a third position are unsuccessful, and Brown withdraws into the fort. American casualties are more than 500, including the engineer Major Eleazar Wood, who was leading a detachment of 21st Infantry, and Lieutenant Lewis G. A. Armistead, younger brother of the hero of Fort

McHenry. The British, who suffer even more casualties, give up the siege and return to Chippewa.

Mid-September. **Militia Mutiny. Tennessee Territory.**
Problems erupt among militia units called up to replace fort garrisons. The units demand release after three months' service, ignoring the law of April 1812 that made the term of federal call-up six months. More than 200 militia deserters from Fort Jackson are arrested at Jackson's order and brought to Mobile for court-martial in December.

20–27 September. **Militia Call-up. Mobile, West Florida.**
Reports indicate a large British force is en route to the Gulf and may use Pensacola as a base. Major General Jackson asks the governors of Tennessee, Mississippi, and Kentucky to mobilize militia units and move them to the forts near Mobile and New Orleans. Orders are also sent to the Regular units in the District to bring all available men and recruits. Officers acting as Indian Agents are authorized to talk to the Cherokee, Choctaws, Chickasaws, and friendly Creek chiefs to raise Indian volunteers. Lieutenant Colonel William MacRae, senior officer in New Orleans, prepares the city's fortifications for action.

27 September. **Armstrong Replaced.**
President Madison, angry over the Bladensburg debacle, asks for Armstrong's resignation as Secretary of War. Secretary of State James Monroe temporarily takes the position.

October. **Taylor Withdraws. Fort Johnson, Illinois Territory.**
With winter approaching, Captain Taylor withdraws his detachment, destroys Fort Johnson, and returns to St. Louis with his men.

October. **Winder Replaced. Washington.**
Brigadier Winfield Scott replaces Winder as commander of the politically sensitive Tenth Military District around Washington. Scott also must chair a board of inquiry into Winder's actions. With the peace treaty in December, charges against Winder are forgotten.

5–16 October. **Coffee's Brigade Arrives. Camp Gaines, Mississippi Territory.**
When Brigadier John Coffee arrives at the rendezvous for his Tennessee Volunteers, he finds that instead of ten companies, he has more than 21. He organizes a two-regiment brigade, and on the 5th he takes it south in response to Jackson's call. By the 16th, Coffee's

Opposite: *The long brutal Battle of Lundy's Lane lasted past dark and ended in hand-to-hand fighting. Almost 900 are killed, wounded, or captured on both sides. ("Battle of Lundy's Lane," The Granger Collection, New York)*

Below: *When Scott and his brigade encounter British forces positioned at Lundy's Lane, Scott refuses to withdraw and instead sends his regiments forward to attack. ("Battle of Lundy's Lane," National Archives of Canada)*

mounted brigade of 2,000 is at Camp Gaines, on the Mobile River, having traveled more than 220 miles in ten days.

October–November. **McArthur Raid. Detroit, Michigan Territory.**
Brigadier Duncan McArthur leads a mounted detachment of 650 volunteers and 70 Indians on a raid into Canada. They move up the Thames River to Oxford, then circle south to Lake Erie and finally return to Detroit. McArthur's rear-area destruction ties down large numbers of British and Canadian militia, delaying operations against Detroit until spring.

5 November. **Americans Withdraw. Fort Erie, Canada.**
The new northern commander, Major General George Izard, destroys Fort Erie and withdraws to the U.S. side of the Niagara River. He is concerned about reports of British reinforcements and being cut off from support during the winter.

3–9 November. **Jackson Attacks Pensacola. East Florida.**
Jackson leads 4,500 men in a unauthorized invasion of East Florida. In addition to Coffee's brigade, Jackson has the 3d Infantry under Major Joseph Woodruff; a provisional battalion from the 39th and 44th Infantry under Major Henry Peire; 700 Choctaws led by Major Uriah Blue; Tennessee Rangers; Mississippi Dragoons; and some artillery. By the 7th they are at Pensacola, which is protected by several forts and by British warships in the harbor. When Major Peire is sent forward with a white flag of truce to offer terms, he is fired upon by the Spanish. Jackson attacks the next

morning right into the city, surprising the Spanish, who surrender after a brief resistance. On the 8th, the two forts guarding the bay entrance are blown up by the departing British. The invasion cost seven killed and 11 wounded, including two Choctaws.

22 November–1 December. **Jackson Goes to New Orleans.**
Before Jackson moves to New Orleans, he learns that Brigadier James Winchester, recently returned from captivity, is en route to be his deputy. He orders Winchester to secure the Mobile area and places the 3d and 39th Infantry in the town, the 2d Infantry at Fort Bowyer, and Coffee with mounted militia at Baton Rouge. Jackson then departs with the 44th

Opposite, below:
Photograph of a U.S. militia drum, circa 1812. (Army Collection, NMUSA)

Right: *Photograph of a flintlock pistol commonly used by officers and cavalry, circa 1812. (Army Collection, NMUSA)*

Infantry to join the 7th Infantry and Corps of Artillery troops in New Orleans.

8 December. **Final Raid Against the Red Sticks. West Florida.**
In accordance with a 16 November order from Jackson, Major Blue takes 1,000 mounted Tennessee militia and Choctaws in a sweep into West Florida to search out hostile Red Stick, Creek, and Seminole villages. Blue has some success and returns by mid-month with prisoners.

22–23 December. **British Invade Louisiana. Lake Borgne, Louisiana.**
On the 22nd, British Regulars land less than 10 miles from New Orleans and capture a small militia outpost. They then move inland three miles to Villere Plantation, where another detachment of local militia is captured. Jackson recalls Coffee and his men from Florida and sends Major Thomas Hinds with Mississippi Dragoons to scout the British position. Most of the New Orleans defenders are local militia, including two battalions of free Negros and a unit of Choctaw Indians. Jackson also has the understrength 7th and 44th Infantry regiments. Disgusted with the slow support from the state, Jackson declares martial law, requisitioning tools and supplies and drafting citizens to help.

23–24 December. **Jackson Attacks. Villere Plantation, Louisiana.**
Jackson takes action before more British reinforcements arrive. During the foggy evening of the 23rd, he attacks the British camp with a combined force of 1,340 Regulars of the 7th and 44th Infantry and militia and Coffee's dismounted brigade. U.S. Navy ships in the river provide cannon support. In a confused night fight, the British rally and stop Jackson's advance, but Coffee's men, pushing deep into the British rear, come close to winning the battle. British counterattacks finally succeed, and Jackson

withdraws behind earthworks along the dry ditch known as the Rodriguez Canal, five miles south of New Orleans. He has lost 213 men but has convinced the British that they should wait for more troops.

24 December. **Treaty Signed. Ghent, Belgium.**
U.S. negotiators sign a draft peace treaty and send it to the United States for ratification. The ship will not arrive at New York until 11 February.

28 December. **Battle of New Orleans—First Attack.**
Using additional troops landed on the 25th, the British advance against Jackson's defensive line that stretches almost a mile from the Mississippi on his right to a thick swamp on the left. Logs, earth, and large cotton bales coated with mud have been used to build breastworks and protect four batteries of cannon. Next to the river, a small bastion projects foward, permitting cannon to fire across the front of the breastworks. After British cannon destroy one of the American ships on the river, two columns of infantry are sent in a probing attack. They are thrown back, and the British wait for heavier artillery to arrive. The American artillery spends the next days firing at any British target within range, while at night small groups of infantry slip close to the British lines to snipe.

1815

January. **Status of the Army.**
Strength of the Regular Army is 62,674—3,495 officers and 59,179 enlisted. U.S. Rangers and Indian raiders continue to skirmish in the upper Mississippi Valley. The main focus of Army activity is New Orleans and the Gulf area, where British troops have arrived with orders to capture strategic ports and to block American access to the Mississippi River.

1–2 January. **Battle of New Orleans. Artillery Duel.** At midmorning on a foggy New Year's Day, newly emplaced British heavy cannons open fire, surprising the Americans, who are forming for a review. Jackson's artillery replies, and the artillery battle lasts almost four hours. Captain Enoch Humphry's Corps of Artillery crews in Battery No.1 and Dominic You's volunteers in Battery No.3 are especially accurate. The British positions are badly battered, and at dark their artillery pulls back. American gunners suffer three guns damaged and 34 men killed or wounded. The next day 2,250 militia, mostly from Kentucky, join Jackson, but only 700 have weapons and a search for muskets begins. Jackson prepares three successive defensive lines and bends the far left of his first line, where Coffee has command, back at an angle as flank protection. The Choctaw battalion screens Coffee front.

5 January. **Army Tactical Board Formed. Washington.** Congress directs the Army to form a board of five officers to develop a standardized system of tactical instructions. Experience has shown the problems of trying to coordinate units trained with different tactical concepts. Brigadier Winfield Scott is appointed to head a Board of Tactics, and he asks

Opposite: *Forced to retreat, Brigadier Stricker and his 3d Maryland Brigade fell back to the second line of defenses at Hampstead Hill near Baltimore. ("Militia on Hampstead Hill," Maryland Historical Society, Baltimore, MD)*

Right: *The Battle of North Point started favorably for the Americans. Although soon forced to withdraw under strong British pressure, the 3d Maryland Brigade's resistance inflicted heavy casualties, delaying the British advance. ("Battle of North Point," Don Troiani, National Guard Bureau print)*

Colonel Joseph Swift, Chief of Engineers, to join him. When the board adjourns at the end of February, it has drafted a 360-page tactical manual titled *Rules and Regulations for the Field Exercise and Maneuvers of Infantry*. This is the first official U.S. Army field manual since Von Steuben's "Blue Book" during the Revolution.

7–8 January. Battle of New Orleans—Third British Attack.

Reinforcements increase the British force to about 8,000 men, and during the night of the 7th, heavy artillery is moved closer to the American positions. A strong detachment is also ferried across the Mississippi to attack the weakly defended American west-bank battery. The river current carries the British boats farther downstream than expected, disrupting the coordinated attack planned for both sides of the river. At 6 a.m., in the predawn dark and fog, the assault begins on Jackson's 3,500 Regulars and militia on the east bank. One reinforced British brigade makes the main attack on the American left, nearest the swamp. By chance, that is the strongest American position. Another brigade of 1,200 attacks the American right. As the morning fog lifts, the American cannon on both banks blast the British formations, followed by the rifles and muskets of the infantry. By 8:30 a.m. the British commander and many officers are dead and the attacks

are shattered. The British on the west bank capture the battery, but too late, and they are withdrawn. Total American losses are 13 killed, 39 wounded, and 19 missing. Almost 300 British Regulars lie dead on the battlefield and another 1,200 are wounded. A 12-hour truce is arranged the next day to permit the British to recover their casualties. No follow-up American attacks are made although after the truce artillery is fired into the British camp, which is secretly being evacuated.

9–18 January. Attack on Fort St. Phillip. Plaquemines Bend, Louisiana

British bombard Fort St. Phillip located at a strategic river bend 70 miles south of New Orleans. Two Corps of Artillery companies and two of the 7th Infantry hold the fort. After lobbing more than 1,000 shells at the defenders, the British depart. Two Americans are killed, seven wounded.

13 January. British Attack Point Petre. Georgia.

A British landing party of 700 marines and soldiers is ambushed and delayed by Captain Abram A. Massis and 80 men from the 1st Rifles and 42d Infantry. This gives the American artillerymen in the coastal battery time to spike their guns and escape.

23 January. Jackson Returns to New Orleans.

Jackson leaves the 7th Infantry to hold the defensive

positions and marches the rest of his force into the city for celebrations. He retains the militia until confirmation of the treaty is received. He also keeps New Orleans under martial law until March, much to the displeasure of local authorities and citizens.

8–12 February. British Attack Fort Bowyer Again. Mobile Bay, East Florida.

As a first step to take Mobile, a British force is landed to capture the fort. For two days they move infantry and artillery into position under heavy fire from the fort. The garrison is about 370 men of the 2d Infantry and Corps of Artillery led by Major William Lawrence. But the incomplete fort, designed as a coastal defense battery, is isolated, its landward defenses are limited, and it lacks adequate covered protection. On the 13th, after three days of bombardment and faced with an impending assault from trenches only yards from his walls, Lawrence agrees to surrender. However, the attack on Mobile never occurs. Also on the 13th, a British ship arrives with news of the draft peace treaty. Offensive operations are halted and prisoners are exchanged. Confirmation of the ratified treaty arrives on 14 March and the next day the British begin their departure.

4–17 February. War of 1812 Ends.

A copy of the proposed treaty arrives in Washington on the 4th, and Congress ratifies it on the 15th. President Madison announces the official end to the war at 11 p.m. on Friday, 17 February, but it takes weeks for the news to reach the distant frontier outposts. Most militia and Volunteers are released almost immediately, but when Canadians initially refuse to give up Fort Mackinac, Americans continue to occupy Fort Malden. During the war about 2,260 American soldiers and two brigadier generals were killed in action and more than 4,500 soldiers wounded. The number of deaths from illness is not known but far exceeds these figures. The exact number of prisoners is also unknown but includes five American generals captured. Of the 120 West Point graduates by 1815, 100 have served during the war, of whom approximately 25 percent were killed or wounded. Notably, none of the fortifications designed by the new West Point engineers was ever captured. The last hostile action in the west is on 24 May between a Ranger company and Indians in the Illinois Territory.

21 February. Militia Mutineers Executed. Mobile.

All 205 militiamen arrested for mutiny were found guilty by the court-martial board of militia officers.

The six ringleaders of the Tennessee militia mutiny are shot by a firing detail. Less harsh penalties are given the others.

2 March. **Monroe Relinquishes Secretary of War Position.**
James Monroe steps down as Secretary of War. Scott is considered for the position; though flattered, he discourages the suggestion and the position remains vacant. Secretary of the Treasury Alexander J. Dallas is made acting secretary.

3 March. **Army Reduction.**
After extensive debate, Congress directs a total restructuring of the Army effective 1 May. Army strength is set at 10,000 Regulars, plus the Corps of Engineers. President Monroe exempts officers, noncommissioned officers, and musicians from the limit, lifting the Army to 12,383. Major general positions are cut from eight to two and brigadiers from 16 to four. All other generals are discharged or reduced to colonel. A board of six generals—Major Generals Brown and Jackson and Brigadier Generals Macomb, Gaines, Scott, and Ripley—is formed to implement the reductions. The number of infantry regiments is cut from 44 to eight by combining old regiments and renumbering. The Ordnance Department, Rifle Regiment, Regiment of Light Artillery, and Corps of Artillery are retained but reduced in size. The Light Dragoons are disbanded leaving the Army without cavalry for more than 30 years. More than 1,700 of the 2,271 serving officers must be released or reduced and thousands of enlisted men discharged from the regiments. Some, like Zachary Taylor, resign when they are reduced. Pay is reduced to prewar levels and officers leaving the service are given three months' severance pay.

1 May. **Army Reorganization.**
The country is organized into two regional military divisions, each with a major general and two brigadiers. There is no overall Army commander; each division commander reports directly to the Secretary of War. The six members of the Board are retained as the six authorized generals. Seniority is set alphabetically by date of rank, making Major General Brown senior to Jackson. Macomb is senior among the brigadiers, followed by Ripley, Gaines, and Scott.

22 May. **Senior Commanders Designated.**
Jackson is given command of the Southern Division, which extends up the Mississippi to include the Illinois Territory. Brown has the Northern Division.

15 June. **Generals Discharged.**
Major Generals Pinckney, Izard, Dearborn, and Wilkinson are honorably discharged. Court-martial charges against Wilkinson were dropped.

17 June. **Barbary War—Army Fights at Sea. Cape de Gata, Spain.**
Captain Samuel B. Archer and his Company H, Corps of Artillery, are serving as gun crews aboard Commodore Stephen Decatur's flagship, the U.S.S.

Opposite: *Jackson placed his 3,500 men in three successive lines of defense. A strongly defended left flank was anchored on the Mississippi while on the right lay a thick cypress swamp. This forced the British assault to the center of Jackson's defense. ("Battle of New Orleans," Army Art Collection, NMUSA)*

Right: *The 7th U.S. Infantry Regiment earned their nickname "Cotton Balers" for their role in defending the American line, partly constructed using large cotton bales. ("Cotton Bailers," Dale Gallon)*

Guerriere, when Decatur captures the Algerian flagship and sails into the harbor of Algiers to demand release of American prisoners. One of the Army officers is Lieutenant James Monroe, nephew of the President; he is wounded while directing guns on the

quarterdeck. Army artillerymen also serve on other ships of Decatur's squadron.

9 July. **Scott Departs for Europe. New York.**
Scott is one of several young officers sent to observe European armies. By chance, as he is departing, Scott meets the returning survivors of the soldiers taken captive and imprisoned after Queenstown in 1812.

1 August. **Crawford Appointed Secretary of War.**
President Monroe appoints William H. Crawford as Secretary of War. Crawford is a lawyer with no military experience, but Congress has retained an Adjutant and Inspector General and an Adjutant General on the Army general staff to help.

September. **Rifle Regiment Moves to Missouri.**
Colonel Thomas A. Smith, reduced from general officer but retained on duty, is made commander of the consolidated Rifle Regiment. He leads his men and their families west to their new post near St. Louis, where the regiment is tasked with frontier duty.

2 December. **First Foreign Cadets. West Point.**
The first two foreign cadets, brothers from Latin America, arrive to begin studies at West Point. They begin a tradition of attendance by foreign cadets that has built valuable relationships with the military and leaders of many countries.

Above: *Francis Scott Key, author of the poem that became the lyrics of the National Anthem, watched the bombardment of Fort McHenry from a British prison ship on which he was detained. ("By Dawn's Early Light," Percy Moran, Maryland Historical Society)*

Left: *At dawn, Major Armistead has the smaller size "storm" flag that had flown over Fort McHenry during the rainy night replaced by the huge 42-foot-by-30-foot "Star-Spangled Banner." ("The Flag is Full of Stars," Dale Gallon)*

ARMY LINEAGE AND THE 1815 REORGANIZATION

Lineage of Army units is very important in determining the history, battle honors, and campaign credits of the units. The Army lacked a formal system for recognizing and recording battle honors until 1861. Previously, the honors of a unit were retained in the oral history passed along by its soldiers. When Regular units are consolidated, their history and honors pass to the new unit; however, when a unit is disbanded, as happened to all but one of the Continental Army units, it is normally permanently removed and its history ends. Today, units are usually inactivated rather than disbanded and when reactivated assume the same lineage and honors.

Most of the regiments of the Regular Army until the Civil War were born in the reorganization of March 1815. Within a few months, the Army of more than 62,600 shrank to barely 12,000 men in a complicated reorganization.

The War Department made no effort to maintain any association between the old regiments and the new ones. The Army's two senior commanders, Major General Jacob Brown, Northern Department, and

Major General Andrew Jackson, Southern Department, modified implementation for the units in their departments. In general, they sought to minimize disruption by consolidating companies, even from different regiments, that were located near one another.

Eight new infantry regiments were created and the eight most senior Army colonels became the regimental commanders. Regimental numbers were then assigned according to the colonel's date of rank. Final infantry organization looked like this: Colonel Daniel Bissell: 1st Infantry (2d, 3d, 7th, and 44th); Hugh Brady: 2d Infantry (6th, 16th, 22d, 23d, and 32d); John Miller: 3d Infantry (1st, 5th, 17th, 19th, and 28th); William King: 4th Infantry (14th, 18th, 20th, 36th, and 38th); James Miller: 5th Infantry (4th, 9th, 13th, 21st, 40th, and 46th); Henry Atkinson: 6th Infantry (11th, 25th, 27th, 29th, and 37th); James McDonald: 7th Infantry (8th, 24th, and 39th); and Robert Nicholas: 8th Infantry (10th and 12th). With the exception of the 8th Infantry, these regiments are represented in the Army today.

The four Rifle Regiments were grouped into a single Rifle Regiment under Colonel Thomas A. Smith. The excess men from seven disbanded infantry regiments were used to fill the Light Artillery Regiment. The Regiment of Light Dragoons was disbanded and its men, along with those from four infantry regiments, were transferred into the Corps of Artillery. Excess officers and enlisted men were discharged.

The Army also introduced the system of identifying companies alphabetically, A–I and K. The letter "J" is not used to avoid confusion with the letter "I." In Brown's Northern Division, company designations were decided by the rank of the captain, the most senior having Company A, the next senior B, and so on. In the south, Jackson did the same except that the two elite light companies in each infantry regiment were permanently designated as A and B.

—*Ray Bluhm*

Above: *As the Army transformed through the early 1800s, so did its battle dress. This image shows the variation in uniform from one Regiment to the next. ("Those Are Regulars, By God 1814–1815," Darby Erd)*

BUILDING A NATION

1816-1848

BUILDING A NATION

1816–1843

Colonel Raymond K. Bluhm, Jr., USA (Ret)

The 30-year period between the end of War of 1812 and the start of the hostilities with Mexico in 1846 was not one of peace or inactivity for the small Regular Army. Much of the Army's energies were spent dealing with Native American issues. Charged by Congress with conducting Indian Affairs, the Army found itself with two conflicting missions: to maintain peace with and among the various Indian tribes, and at the same time to enforce the congressionally mandated Removal Act of 1830 to resettle Indians west of the Mississippi—an action widely disliked in the Army and which was resisted by some tribes. This long conflict between the continually compressed Indians and the expanding United States broke into open warfare in 1817 and 1835 with the Seminoles in Florida, and in 1831 with the Sac-Fox in Illinois and Wisconsin.

The Regular Army also faced challenges to its status and function within American society. With peace in 1815 came renewed congressional budget cuts and questions as to the need for a standing army. There was a steady decline in public interest in serving in the military, Regular or militia, especially in the eastern states, eroding the concept of a quickly "expandable" militia-based army in emergencies. Desertions were also a constant problem. To improve recruiting, the Army initiated its first centralized recruiting system, selecting quality officers and soldiers for temporary recruiting duty to replace the old regimental teams. Many young male immigrants arriving from overseas received their first wages from an Army paymaster, albeit months late. From 1835 to 1836, 23,530 men enlisted, some for several short terms. Of these, roughly 13,000 served in Florida.

At the same time, the role of the Regular soldier as a nation builder expanded. The engineering graduates of West Point were tasked with river and harbor improvements, road building, canal and railroad surveys, and defensive fortifications along the coast and northern borders. Other junior officers led scientific expeditions up American rivers or out onto the plains into the heart of the new western territory and sought to find its ill-defined southern and northern borders. With the creation of an Artillery School of Practice in 1824 and a similar Infantry school in 1827, the Army took the first steps in building a system of professional development schools.

To act as a buffer between the Indians and arriving settlers, a line of forts was built running from Fort Snelling, Minnesota, in the north, to Fort Jesup, Louisiana, in the south, along the western frontier and connected by a military road. But by the mid-1840s demands to protect travelers on the Santa Fe and Oregon trails pushed Army presence increasingly west. To increase its mobility and capability to deal with the fast-moving, horse-mounted Indians, the Army formed regiments of dragoons in 1833 and in 1836 introduced mules to replace wagon horses and oxen.

The two bitter wars with the Seminoles took a toll on the Army from both combat losses and disease. The wily enemy, daunting swamps, and unhealthy conditions caused a number of officers to resign rather than serve there. In 1836 only 103 company grade officers were left in the Army. The unrelenting and dogged pursuit of the renegade Seminoles by Colonel William Worth finally brought an uneasy peace in 1842.

Peace, in turn, again brought congressional budget cuts, even as tensions with Mexico were increasing. The expensive horses of one of the dragoon

regiments were taken away, the light artillery batteries were dismounted, and Army strength was cut to fewer than 9,000 officers and men. The Army regiments that had gathered in Florida were reduced in size and again dispersed in small detachments to garrison frontier outposts. Yet, within the Army, a core of dedicated professionals remained, many of them graduates of the revitalized academy at West Point. They recruited, trained, and endured peacetime garrison life while in the West tensions with Mexico increased.

Above: *Life at Fort Scott was like that of a small frontier village. It included officers, enlisted soldiers, military families, tradesmen, and travelers. ("People at Fort Scott," Don Troiani, HFC Commissioned Art Collection)*

Pages 220–221: *The westward expansion of America presented many challenges for the nation and introduced many new roles for the Army. Here, a Dragoon is on escort duty for a wagon train to protect the settlers from Indian attack. (Hugh Brown, HFC Commissioned Art Collection)*

BUILDING A NATION

1816-1843

"The ax, pick, saw and trowel has become more the implement of the American soldier than the cannon, musket or sword."
—Lieutenant Colonel Zachary Taylor, 4th Infantry, 18 September 1820

1816

January. **Status of the Army.**
The Army, reduced to 10,000 men in March 1815, has declined below that since the end of the war. Major Generals Jacob Brown and Andrew Jackson and the four brigadiers—Alexander Macomb, Edmund P. Gaines, Winfield Scott, and Eleazer W. Ripley—are the Army's senior leaders. Many units are still reorganizing and moving to new posts. Work is progressing on the 18 planned arsenals as the Army begins road-building projects in the southeast.

April. **Brigadier Smith Takes Command. Illinois Territory.**
Brevet Brigadier General Thomas A. Smith, senior

commander at St. Louis, arrives at Cantonment Davis with the Rifle Regiment. He leaves a small garrison and takes the 8th Infantry and the Rifle Regiment north to Rock Island to construct Fort Armstrong, then continues north with the Rifles to Prairie du Chien.

24 April. **Army General Staff Increased.**
Seven positions are added to the general staff, including an inspector general and three topographical engineers.

May. **Troops Begin Building Detroit. Fort Meigs Road.**
Secretary of War Crawford directs Brigadier General Macomb, at Detroit, to begin construction of a 70-mile-long road connecting to Fort Meigs, Ohio. Major John Anderson, Corps of Engineers, is sent to survey the route. Both the 5th Infantry from Detroit and 3d Infantry from Fort Wayne start work. The troops receive extra pay of 15 cents a day and an extra whiskey ration. The road takes over two years to complete.

17 May. **Zachary Taylor Reinstated in Army.**
Zachary Taylor, who took a discharge rather than be reduced in rank, is reinstated as a major of the 3d Infantry at $50 a month plus allowances.

June. **Camp Crawford/Fort Scott Constructed. Flint River, Georgia.**
Brigadier General Gaines sends Lieutenant Colonel Duncan L. Clinch with a detachment of 4th Infantry to build a fort, later named Fort Scott, on the Flint River as border protection against hostile Creeks and Seminoles crossing from East Florida. The fort is completed in September. The supply route is by boat through Spanish territory past the "Negro Fort," a former British outpost occupied by hostile Indians and former slaves.

Left: *Such fancy uniforms helped with recruiting but also served a practical purpose by helping leaders identify units in the confusion of the smoky battlefield. The artist was a British spy gathering information on the American Army. (C. H. Smith, courtesy John Langellier)*

ARMY BATTLE STREAMERS—INDIAN WARS

SEMINOLES 1835-1842

Seminoles, 1817–1818

Black Hawk, 1832

Seminoles, 1835–1842

Creeks, 1836–1837

Seminoles, 1855–1858

---

20 June. **Rifle Regiment Reoccupies Fort Shelby. Prairie du Chien.**
The Rifle Regiment begins constructing Fort Crawford overlooking the town, firmly reestablishing American control along the upper Mississippi.

4 July. **Third Infantry Arrives at Fort Dearborn. Chicago.**
Three companies of the 3d Infantry begin reconstruction at the destroyed fort. A government trading post and Indian affairs office are also built.

27 July. **Negro Fort Destroyed. Prospect Bluff, Spanish East Florida.**
After a resupply ship is fired on, Gaines is ordered to destroy Negro Fort. Clinch is sent with several ships and a small landing force of 4th Infantry and Creek allies. A heated cannonball causes the fort's powder magazine to explode, destroying the fort and killing about 300 defenders.

August. **Fort Howard Established. Green Bay, Illinois Territory.**
The United States sends a strong force—four companies of 3d Infantry, two companies of Riflemen, and a detachment of artillery—from Fort Mackinac under Colonel John Miller to establish Fort Howard at the mouth of the Fox River. Major Zachary Taylor becomes commander in 1817.

22 October. **Crawford Steps Down as Secretary of War.**
Crawford becomes Secretary of the Treasury and

George Graham, Chief Clerk of the War Department, is appointed as acting Secretary of War.

1817

January. **Status of the Army.**
Major Generals Brown and Jackson continue to share leadership of the Army, but relations between the War Department and Jackson are strained. Army strength continues to fall; only 8,000 Regulars are fit for duty. The War Department undertakes extensive road-building projects in the south and northwest, linking the border posts.

4 March. **James Monroe Inaugurated.**
James Monroe, veteran of the Continental Army, is inaugurated as fifth President and Commander-in-Chief of the Army. The Secretary of War position remains vacant until August.

22 April. **Jackson Confronts War Department Over Chain of Command.**
Jackson, angered by War Department transfer orders sent directly to one of his officers, forbids obedience to any order that does not come through him. When members of Congress level charges of insubordination, Jackson threatens to resign. Jackson is finally appeased when President Monroe agrees to route future orders through the commander except in emergencies.

June. **Report on Health Status of the Army. Northern Department.**

Army Hospital Surgeon Joseph Lovell completes a report on the poor condition of the troops stationed in that department. The report, with recommendations for corrections, is published in the fall and becomes the basis for major reforms in the Medical Staff and the health system of the Army.

June. **Jackson's Military Road.**

The Army begins building a road running more than 200 miles from Nashville to New Orleans. When completed in January 1820, it has 35 bridges and 392 causeways. Army engineer graduates from West Point play a significant role in its success.

28 July. **Sylvanus Thayer Becomes Academy Superintendent. West Point.**

Captain Sylvanus Thayer is appointed the fifth superintendent of the U.S. Military Academy. His appointment resolves a conflict between the faculty and the previous superintendent, Captain Alden Partridge. Thayer introduces strict discipline and tough academic standards. There are 213 cadets enrolled, and he weeds out those not qualified.

September. **Fort Smith Established. Arkansas River.**
Jackson directs Majors Stephen H. Long and William Bradford to build a fort on the Arkansas River at the border of the Osage Indian lands. The two travel up the Arkansas about 450 miles and select a site for the post, named Fort Smith. Its purpose is to prevent conflict between the Osage and the Cherokees being moved from their homes east of the Mississippi.

8 October. **Calhoun Appointed Secretary of War.**
John C. Calhoun is appointed tenth Secretary of War. He is a reformer with ideas for improving the Army and national defense. He finds there are only 8,221 men in the Army.

21 November. **First Seminole War Begins. Fowltown, Georgia.**
In response to a threat made against settlers, Brigadier General Gaines sends Major David E. Twiggs with 250 troops of the 1st, 4th, and 7th Infantry to arrest Chief Neamathla and senior leaders of the Mikasukis tribe at the village of Fowltown. When the Indians resist, Twiggs attacks. Five Indians are killed, but the chief escapes. Evidence is found of British complicity, and the village is burned. Indian reprisals begin quickly.

30 November. **Seminoles Make Retaliatory Attacks. Apalachicola River.**
An Army resupply boat coming upriver carrying 40 soldiers of the 4th and 7th Infantry with their families to Fort Scott is attacked by Creek and Seminole Indians. The commander, Lieutenant Richard W. Scott, and 33 men, seven wives, and four children are killed. Several days later three boats with 120 soldiers are also attacked on the river and pinned down for hours until a rescue party arrives.

23 December. **Gaines Retakes Amelia Island. East Florida.**
Gaines takes a small force and recaptures Amelia Island. The island, located just south of the Georgia border, had been seized from the Spanish earlier in the year by pirates and slave traders.

26 December. **Department of War Orders Expedition. Nashville.**
Secretary Crawford sends Jackson to Fort Scott to take personal command of operations against the Seminoles. Jackson is authorized to call for militia support from nearby states.

1818

January. **Status of the Army.**
During the year the Medical Corps adopts a heraldic coat of arms—the first coat of arms in the Army. Despite efforts to improve, the regimental recruiting system is failing to provide sufficient numbers of acceptable recruits. Army strength is at 640 officers and 7,580 enlisted men. Thayer reduces the Corps of Cadets to 181. Other reforms in the curriculum, methods of instruction, and grading are also introduced.

January. **Jackson Raises Volunteers. Nashville, Tennessee.**
Jackson asks militia officers who served with him in the Creek War to raise 1,000 volunteer "gun men" for action against the Seminoles. As he rides to Fort Scott, the volunteers join him.

9–10 March. **Jackson Takes Command. Fort Scott.**
After a 46-day forced march of 450 miles from Tennessee, Jackson arrives at the fort with about 1,000 volunteers. Some 500 Regulars of the 1st, 4th, and 7th Infantry and a battalion of Corps of Artillery are already there. It was a difficult march, with little food. Without waiting for his supply wagons, Jackson assembles more militia and Creek allies, issues three days' rations, and marches south toward the old Negro Fort.

Above: *This depiction shows the difference between the uniforms of "line," or combat unit officers, and those assigned to the staff of a general officer. ("General, Staff, and Line Officers, Light Artillery 1813–1821," H. A. Ogden)*

Opposite: *The infantry summer uniform in Florida was made of a light-colored linen, much cooler than wool. ("4th U.S. Infantry Regiment, Summer Uniform, 1835–1842," H. Charles McBarron, Company of Military Historians)*

15–26 March. **Fort Gadsden Built. Prospect Bluff, East Florida.**
Without clear authority to be in Florida, Jackson's force arrives at the old fort on the 15th. He orders it rebuilt and Lieutenant James Gadsden, his Army engineer, directs its construction. Jackson is so pleased with the work he names it Fort Gadsden. On the 26th he marches to St. Marks, where Spanish authorities and British agents are supporting the Seminoles and bands of escaped slaves.

1–9 April. **Jackson Captures St. Marks. East Florida.**
En route to St. Marks, Jackson is joined by 1,500 militia and friendly Creeks, giving him more than 4,000 men. Jackson seizes St. Marks on the 6th, leaves a garrison, and continues 100 miles farther east through the swamps to attack the Seminole villages of Chief Billy Bowlegs along the Suwanee River.

4 April. **Congress Changes Flag Design.**
Congress sets the design of the U.S. flag to have 13 stripes and a star for every state. Army units do not carry this flag in the field, but use it to designate post and forts. A "national flag" with an eagle on a dark blue field is carried by units along with a regimental flag—red for artillery, light yellow for infantry.

8 April. **First Army Surgeon General Appointed.**
As part of his Army reforms, Secretary Calhoun creates the position of Army Surgeon General, with a salary of $2,500 per year. Dr. Joseph Lovell, a serving physician and activist for medical reforms, is appointed to the position. Like all Army medical positions, this is a civilian appointment with military rank.

12 April. **Captive Army Wife Freed. Natural Bridge, East Florida.**
Resistance is light, with small skirmishes as the Indians flee ahead of Jackson's advance. In one action a detachment of militia and Creeks kill 37 Seminoles and rescue the sole surviving Army wife from the boat attack in November.

15–29 April. **Seminole Towns Destroyed. Suwanee River.**
Dividing his force into three groups, Jackson advances on the main Seminole towns. A rear guard of several hundred Seminoles and Negroes delays Jackson permitting inhabitants to escape. Two British agents are captured with letters and other evidence of complicity in the Indian attacks. Lieutenant Gadsden leads a detachment to capture the agents' schooner, which is then used to transport sick and wounded. Jackson makes a five-day march back to St. Marks, where the British agents are court-martialed and executed.

May. **Army Quartermaster General Appointed.**
Colonel Thomas S. Jesup, acting Adjutant General of the Army, is promoted to brigadier general and made Quartermaster General of the Army, a position he will hold for 42 years. Respected for his organizational ability, he is also given field command.

24–27 May. **Jackson Takes Pensacola. West Florida.**
Jackson moves against the Spanish at Pensacola. When the Americans appear on the 24th, the Spanish governor flees to a nearby fort. Jackson's forces occupy the town after a brief exchange of fire, and he sends other units to destroy nearby Seminole villages. The artillery company bombards the fort until it surrenders on the 27th. Before he departs for home, Jackson appoints Colonel William King military governor of Pensacola and Gadsden as port tax collector. Jackson reports to the Secretary of War that "the Seminole War may now be considered at a close." There is

public controversy over his actions, and the captured territory is returned to Spain within a year.

24 July. First Graduation of Thayer System Cadets. West Point.

Twenty-two cadets are graduated after successful completion of examinations, following a year of instruction in the revised and strengthened course implemented by Thayer. For the first time commissions and thus seniority as lieutenants are awarded in order of academic merit.

30 August. Yellowstone River Expedition. Fort Bellefontaine, Missouri Territory.

Lieutenant Colonel Talbot Chambers loads some 350 men of the Rifle Regiment aboard six keelboats and moves up the Missouri as the advance party of the Army's Yellowstone River Expedition. An initiative of Secretary Calhoun, the expedition's purpose is to establish a permanent Army post near the mouth of the Yellowstone River. They travel about 80 miles beyond Fort Osage before winter ice forces them to stop until spring.

11 September. War Department Orders Farming.

A General Order is issued to the western Army posts directing the garrison commanders to initiate extensive agricultural programs to provide food and livestock beyond that needed for food. It is both an economic and a health improvement measure. Most posts, however, comply with such enthusiasm that within a few years Inspector General George Croghan is complaining that military duties and training are being ignored. Despite his reports of adverse military impact, the War Department continues the farming program until 1833.

31 October. First Seminole War Ends.

The First Seminole War officially ends with the withdrawal of the last of the U.S. troops out of Florida. Approximately 1,100 Regulars and 7,000 militiamen were employed in the war, with 47 killed and 36 wounded.

1819

January. Status of the Army.

Army strength is reported as 7,676. As a peacetime Army, the men are mainly engaged in construction work, both military and civilian. Forts are being built, roads surveyed and cut, and frontiers patrolled. Arsenals at Baton Rouge and Detroit are completed as the Ordnance Department experiments with artillery improvements. Stretched thin, the small Army mans more than 70 posts and coastal forts.

Norwich Military Academy Founded. Northfield, Vermont.

The first military training of college students begins at what will become Norwich University. It is the beginning of the Army Reserve Officer Training Corps (ROTC), which today provides the majority of Army officers.

March–May. Army Units Relocated West. Missouri Territory.

To establish U.S. presence and deal with continuing Indian attacks, the 5th and 6th Infantry are sent to join the Rifle Regiment in Missouri. Lieutenant Colonel Henry Leavenworth moves his 5th Infantry across the Great Lakes to Fort Howard at Green Bay, and then to the Mississippi River to board boats. The 6th Infantry marches from Plattsburg, New York to Pittsburgh, then boats to Fort Bellefontaine near St. Louis. The moves, which include men, equipment, and families, take three months or more.

14 June–21 July. Army Yellowstone Expedition. St. Louis.

On 14 June Chambers leads five armed keelboats with 270 Riflemen up the Missouri River as the first of the second phase of the expedition. They are followed on 21 June by the scientific group under Major Stephen H. Long of the Topographic Bureau in the steamboat *Western Explorer*. This group is composed of both civilian scientists and military topographers. On 4–5 July, eight companies of the

6th Infantry follow in keelboats and three steamboats. This is the first use of steamboats on the river.

August. **Northernmost Army Post Established. Missouri Territory.**
Sixteen boatloads of the 5th Infantry under Leavenworth arrive at the juncture of the Mississippi and Minnesota rivers, where they build a temporary fortified camp on land purchased from the Indians by Zebulon Pike in 1804.

29 September. **Yellowstone Expedition Builds Camps. Council Bluffs.**
Construction is started on a fort on the river bottoms to house the almost 1,200 men on the expedition. It is named Camp Missouri. The Long group camps a few miles away at Camp Engineer. Army engineers also make a survey for a 330-mile road back to Missouri in November. Troops begin work on it in the spring.

1820

January. **Status of the Army.**
Army strength is 641 officers and 8,047 men.

March. **Abolition of West Point Proposed.**
A resolution is proposed in Congress to abolish the

U.S. Military Academy as a "retreat for the pampered sons of the rich." No action is taken, but investigations are made of Thayer's program to improve the quality of candidates and to eliminate cadets who do not meet the standards of academic excellence and conduct that he is introducing.

April. **Yellowstone Expedition Funds Cut. Council Bluffs.**
Congress cuts funds, causing Calhoun to halt the plans for the entire expedition to continue on to the Yellowstone. Chambers is told to build a major post where he is. A site is found on high ground, and Fort Atkinson is built. Long's scientific detachment also scales back its plans. He must content himself with exploring the Platte and Arkansas Rivers.

May. **Fort Snelling Built. Missouri Territory.**
Leavenworth moves the 5th Infantry to a better site and begins construction of a permanent fort that becomes Fort Snelling. It is named after the next commander, Colonel Josiah Snelling, who completes the fort.

24 July. **Yellowstone Expedition Divides.**
After exploring the area along the base of the Rockies, and making the first ascent of Pike's Peak, the group splits. Captain John R. Bell takes a detachment of the scientific group down the Arkansas River, while Major Long and the rest follow what turns out to be the Canadian River back to civilization.

12 December. **Calhoun Submits Army Reduction Report to Congress.**
In compliance with a congressional request for a plan to reduce the Army to about 6,000 men, Secretary of War Calhoun submits his own proposal based on the concept of an "expandable" Army. By keeping the same or a slightly higher number of regiments and companies with fewer soldiers, the Army could be quickly increased for war by adding more privates without needing more officers.

1821

January. **Status of the Army.**
Army strength is 712 officers and 8,230 men of an authorized 12,383.

2 March. **Congress Directs Another Major Army Reorganization.**
Congress rejects Calhoun's plan and reduces Army authorized strength to 6,126 officers and men. Infantry

companies have only 51 enlisted men, and the 8th Infantry and the Rifle Regiment are disbanded. The artillery is merged with Ordnance and reorganized into four artillery regiments, each with eight dismounted or "foot" companies and one light battery. General officer positions are also cut. Two of the four brigadier positions are dropped and the geographic commands are reduced to two—the Eastern and the Western Departments. The Medical Department is also reduced. Cadet positions are removed from the regiments and placed at West Point to be trained by the Corps of Engineers. A separate group of ten topographical engineers is approved, as well as a Purchasing Department (for commissary supplies) and a Pay Department. This act sets the structure of the Army for the next 11 years.

27 March. Insignia and Uniform Changes.

All company officers now wear a leather bell-crown hat and silver bullion shoulder "wings" on the uniform coat instead of the single epaulet. Captains wear a silver (infantry) or gold (artillery) chevron above each elbow, lieutenants a silver or gold chevron below the elbow. Enlisted men wear worsted shoulder wings (white or yellow). Sergeants wear a worsted chevron above (sergeants major) or below (sergeants) each elbow. Corporals wear a chevron on only the right lower arm. Field grade officers retained their bullion shoulder epaulettes and chapeaus.

1–15 June. Brown Designated Army General-in-Chief.

Jacob Brown remains the one major general. On the 15th he is designated General-in-Chief of the Army, with offices in Washington. Andrew Jackson resigns

from the Army to be governor of the new Florida Territory. Alexander Macomb, the senior brigadier general, is reduced to colonel but appointed Chief Army Engineer, a prestigious post, and he keeps his brigadier's pay. Winfield Scott and Edmund Gaines, though junior to Macomb, keep their brigadier stars. The fourth brigadier, Eleazer Ripley, resigns. Scott takes command of the Eastern Department, and the Western Department goes to Gaines. It is agreed they will switch commands in two years, but the dispute over seniority between the two officers continues for years.

Opposite: *("U.S. Military Academy, 1816–1817," H. Charles McBarron, Company of Military Historians)*

Above: *("Regimental Officers, Engineer and Cadet, 1821–1832," H. A. Ogden)*

Left: The Western Engineer *was the first steamboat to successfully explore the Missouri River as part of the Yellowstone expedition. ("Engineer Cantonment, February 1820," Titian R. Peale, American Philosophical Society Library)*

Left: *At the large meeting held at Council Bluffs in October 1819, Major Stephen Long sternly berated the gathered Pawnees for their attacks on white traders. He is shown here in his Corps of Engineer uniform along with one of the expedition scientists and an infantry private. ("The American Soldier, 1819," H. Charles McBarron, Army Art Collection, NMUSA)*

Opposite: *Stephen H. Long (1784–1864) graduated from Dartmouth College and entered the Army as an engineer. After several explorations in the West, he was detached to assist railroads with route surveys. In 1861 he was promoted to colonel and made head of the Corps of Topographical Engineers. ("Major Stephen H. Long," Charles Wilson Peale, Independence National Historical Park)*

1 July. **Florida Becomes U.S. Territory.**
Governor Jackson formally accepts Florida from the Spanish. Detachments from Army regiments are sent to occupy key forts and other locations.

August–November. **Seventh Infantry Moves to Western Frontier.**
Men of the disbanded 8th Infantry, including Lieutenant Colonel Zachary Taylor are absorbed into the 7th Infantry, which is being transferred from Georgia to the southwestern frontier. Taylor arrives with several 7th companies near Natchitoches, Louisiana, on 19 November to construct a temporary camp.

1822

January. **Status of the Army.**
Army strength is 530 officers and 5,746 enlisted men.

Spring. **Army Surgeon Studies Digestive System. Fort Mackinac.**
Post Surgeon William Beaumont treats a Canadian trapper, Alexis St. Martin, for a gunshot wound to the abdomen. The wound does not close completely, letting Beaumont observe the human digestive process for the first time. Beaumont begins a long-term medical research study with St. Martin that

lasts several years and results in a major contribution to medicine.

March–June. **Taylor Establishes Cantonment Jesup. Louisiana.**
Lieutenant Colonel Taylor selects a site for a new Army fort between the Sabine and Red Rivers, about 12 miles from Natchitoches. Named Fort Jesup after the Army's Quartermaster General, it is garrisoned by four companies of the 7th. Taylor has serious conflicts with the regimental commander and is reassigned back to the 1st Infantry in July.

6 May. **Army Directed to Enforce Restrictions Concerning Indians.**
To stop the flow of liquor to the Indians, Congress directs Indian Agents and the Army to search the goods and packages of traders. Post commanders are given detailed orders for seizure of contraband and legal proceedings against violators. Frontier settlers are restricted from cutting timber on Indian lands.

July. **First Centralized Army Recruiting Begins.**
Army recruiting continues to be a problem; only 54 infantrymen have been recruited, and the artillery regiments have done only slightly better. As a test Major General Brown directs Scott to set up three centralized recruiting stations in his department separate from the regimental teams.

6 July. **Fort Brady Constructed. Sault Ste. Marie, Michigan Territory.**
Colonel Hugh Brady directs a detachment of 250 soldiers of the 2d Infantry in the construction of this fort, which is key to the defense of the northwest. It is the third of Calhoun's planned forts.

December. **Army Recruiting.**
The new recruiting system brings significant results, signing up more than 600 men in less than six months. The system eventually becomes formalized as the General Recruiting Service. Talented officers such as Zachary Taylor receive tours of recruiting duty, helping to improve the system. Recruits are not promised duty with specific units but are assigned according to Army needs. With processing, some initial training, and travel, it is a year before many recruits actually sign in at their new units.

1823

January. **Status of the Army.**
The Army reports having 512 officers and 4,699 enlisted

men. To increase enlistments, Scott opens up three more centralized recruiting stations.

22–23 June. **First Army Western Campaign. Fort Atkinson.**
In response to Arikara attack on a group of traders, Colonel Henry Leavenworth takes six companies of his 6th Infantry, some light artillery with two six-pounders, scouts, and local militia on a campaign against the tribe. This is the Army's first major action against Indians west of the Mississippi River.

9 July. **Second Long Exploration. Fort Snelling.**
Major Stephen Long departs the fort to explore the source of the Minnesota River, locate the 49th parallel (which forms the boundary with Canada), and determine the extent of British presence in the area. Taking a small escort from the fort's 5th Infantry garrison, Long and his scientists accomplish their mission, placing a stake at the parallel marked "US" on one side and "GB" on the other. By the time he returns to Philadelphia in October to prepare his reports, Long has traveled more than 5,400 miles.

9–14 August. **Fight at Arikara Towns. Missouri Territory.**
After a 700-mile journey by keelboat, Leavenworth's force of about 1,100 men engages the Arikaras and pushes them into their two fortified towns. After the light artillery bombards the Indians for several days, Leavenworth attempts to negotiate a truce. Negotiations end when the Indians escape during the night of the 14th.

THE SOLDIER'S LIFE: 1815–1845

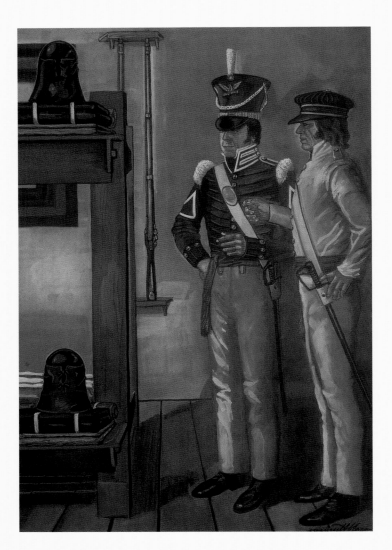

Recruitment during peacetime was difficult due to the low pay and requirements for enlisting. Recruits had to be between 21 and 35 years of age (though some much younger men lied about their ages to get in), at least 5 feet three inches to 5 feet six inches in height, of sound physical and mental constitution, and able to speak English. Enlistments were for five years, except between 1833 and 1838 when they were lowered to three years. The majority of recruits during this period were from northern cities with 40 percent or more being immigrants, mostly Irish and German. The average age was 24 to 25 years, with a third or more being illiterate. Many joined the Army to escape family ties, debt, prison, or inability to make a living, or simply for the promise of adventure.

Unless stationed in permanent quarters in the east, enlisted soldiers usually quartered in temporary wooden buildings, adobe huts, or tents. Soldiers discovered they had to construct the posts and quarters themselves. The bedsteads were wooden, the men sleeping two and sometimes four to a bed. Blankets were issued, along with straw to use as a mattress. In the late 1850s the Army began using a single iron bedstead.

The rations were meager. Breakfast consisted of bread, salt pork or beef and, after 1832, coffee and sugar. Other meals included beans, vinegar for seasoning, and possibly a vegetable. Until 1830, all soldiers received a whiskey ration. Rations could be augmented by purchases from the sutlers, and most posts maintained vegetable gardens. At times the War Department ordered frontier garrisons to farm to save on food and transportation costs. The 6th Infantry at Fort Atkinson, Nebraska, turned their post into a gigantic farm, having by 1822 some 517 acres planted in various vegetables, with 382 cattle and 600 hogs. Finally, in 1890, a pound of vegetables was added to the daily ration.

Uniforms were issued in three sizes only and were of poor quality. If a soldier wanted his uniform tailored or of better cloth, he had to pay for it himself. Pay was supposed to be delivered every two months, but it was often delayed. In 1815, a private received five dollars a month and a sergeant major nine (the prewar rates). Only three pay raises were given prior to the Civil War, so that in 1854 a private got $11 a month and a senior sergeant received $21.

The Army had no standardized training program before 1860. Training was haphazard and the responsibility of the post commanders and regimental noncommissioned officers. Marksmanship training was limited, and many soldiers regularly discharged their weapon only when coming off guard detail.

The average soldier spent most of his time on work details. Besides building and repairing their own posts and quarters, soldiers blazed and cleared trails, and built military roads, bridges, and causeways. Off-duty activity depended on the post. There were entertainments such as hunting, fishing, card playing, gambling, and the occasional dance. Some posts had libraries, and many engaged in amateur theatrics, choirs, and music. Regimental bands were approved in 1832.

—*Vince Hawkins*

Above: *Daily inspections by senior NCOs was a normal part of a soldier's life and critical to maintaining equipment as well as healthy living conditions in the crowded barracks. (Army Art Collection, NMUSA)*

Left: *Built in the early 1820s when relations with British Canada were still very tenuous, Fort Snelling occupied a key strategic position to control Indians and travel in the upper Mississippi River valley. ("Fort Snelling," J. C. Wild, Minnesota Historical Society)*

1824

January. **Status of the Army.**
Army strength is 525 officers and 5,424 enlisted men. Brown expands the concept of the General Recruiting Service to the Western Department, and the War Department selects the officers detailed to recruiting duty. For many officers and their families it is a welcome two-year break from frontier hardships.

March–April. **Army Pushes Forts West.**
The Army establishes two new forts to patrol the southwestern frontier, populated by settlers, Osage Indians, and the displaced Cherokees and Choctaws being moved into the area. In March, two companies of the 7th Infantry are sent to a site about five miles from the Red River to construct Fort Towson. A month later the garrison of Fort Smith relocates up the Arkansas River to establish Fort Gibson.

24 May. **First U.S. Army Professional School. Fortress Monroe, Virginia.**
Secretary of War Calhoun establishes the Army's first professional school, the Artillery School of Practice. Ten companies of artillery representing the four regiments form the administrative staff and training cadre. West Point graduates assigned to the artillery are sent to the school for a year of training before joining their regiments.

Right: *On the frontier, death could come to a soldier from accident, disease, or enemy action. Burials during a patrol or campaign were simple affairs far from the home garrison, and the locations soon forgotten. Depicted is a group of dragoons giving final honors to a comrade. (Hugh Brown, HFC Commissioned Art Collection)*

Above: *General Jacob Brown (1775–1828) defeated the British at Chippewa and Lundy's Lane. A brave and highly regarded soldier, he became the commanding general of the Army in 1821. ("Jacob Jennings Brown," John Wesley Jarvis, Corcoran Gallery of Art)*

31 May. **Army Engineers Survey C&O Canal.**
As directed by Congress, the Army Corps of Engineers begins the land survey for the Chesapeake and Ohio Canal. The canal is completed in 1850.

1825

January. **Status of the Army.**
Army strength is 532 officers and 5,247 enlisted men. During the year the Army approves a soft cloth forage cap for wear by company officers in place of the heavier leather "tar-buckets."

7 March. **Barbour Made Secretary of War.**
James Barbour is appointed as 11th Secretary of War, replacing Calhoun.

9 November. **Army Strength.**
The Secretary of War reports that the Army has 3,237

infantry, 1,921 artillery, and 430 new recruits, a slight drop in strength.

1826

January. **Status of the Army.**
A "Cavalry Tactics" Board is convened during the year, with Brigadier General Scott as president. Several militia generals serve with him. They develop detailed regulations for mounted units and artillery, including equipment, training, tactical formations, and maneuvers.

4 March–August. **New Camp Established. Fort Bellefontaine.**
Brigadier Atkinson and Major General Gaines are tasked to find a suitable site to replace Fort Bellefontaine. They find a location overlooking the Mississippi, about ten miles south of St. Louis. The land is purchased in July and four companies of 1st Infantry under Major Stephen W. Kearny arrive from Bellefontaine to start building.

19 September–23 October. **Jefferson Barracks Established.**
Colonel Henry Leavenworth brings four companies of the 3d Infantry to help build the new fort, temporarily called Cantonment Miller. On 23 October, it is designated as "The Jefferson Barracks" and the "Infantry School of Practice." All new infantry second lieutenants are to attend, as are units coming west. The Barracks becomes one of the largest and most important Army posts west of the Mississippi and remains active until 1946.

1827

January. **Status of the Army.**
Army strength is 540 officers and 5,269 enlisted men.

2 March. **Command Pay Instituted.**
Congress establishes a $10 per month "command pay" for officers commanding a company. The senior lieutenant could receive the pay during the absence of his captain.

7 March. **Leavenworth Directed to Establish Fort. Jefferson Barracks.**
On War Department orders to locate a new fort farther west, Colonel Leavenworth and a small escort party travel up the Missouri River to the edge of Indian Territory, where he selects a site on high ground above the river.

17 April–June. **Cantonment Leavenworth.**
Four companies of the 3d Infantry under Captain William Belknap travel to join Leavenworth. On their arrival Leavenworth plants a pole and raises a flag establishing Cantonment Leavenworth. The new post has the mission to protect the fur trade and trading caravans on the Santa Fe Trail. In June, Fort Atkinson is closed and the garrison of 6th Infantry moves to Leavenworth.

20–28 June. **Infantry School of Practice. Jefferson Barracks.**
Major General Brown makes an inspection visit to the post, which now houses 22 companies from the 1st, 3d, and 6th Infantry regiments. The many Barracks buildings are not finished for several years. This construction effort, plus the other demands, prevents the Infantry School of Practice from becoming a true training center, although Majors Kearny and Twiggs, charged with giving instruction, do their best.

26 May. **Private Perry (Poe) Enlists.**
Edgar Allan Poe enlists in the Army as Edgar A. Perry. He is discharged in 1829 as a sergeant major, and the next year, using his real name, enters West Point as a cadet. He is dismissed after a year for disciplinary infractions.

24 June. **The Winnebago War. Fort Snelling.**
Indians attack settler families and two Army keelboats in response to rumors that two Winnebagos held in the fort jail have been killed by soldiers. Michigan Territorial Governor Lewis Cass mobilizes companies of militia, sending some to reoccupy abandoned Fort Crawford. He also alerts Indian Superintendent William Clark and Brigadier Atkinson with the 6th Infantry at Jefferson Barracks. Among the 6th's officers is newly commissioned Second Lieutenant Albert Sidney Johnson.

16 June. **Adjutant General Authorizes Use Of Brevet Rank.**
The Adjutant General issues an order that officers holding brevet rank are considered to be on duty and have command commensurate with that rank only when they are commanding the number of troops associated with that rank. This order causes great anger among officers with brevets but no chance to command.

15–29 July. **The Winnebago War: Army Forces Mobilize. Illinois Territory.**
Atkinson brings a force of 580 men on steamboats upriver to Prairie du Chien. Other troops converge on

Drawn by A. Rider   *Eng. by C. G. Childs*

Above: *Organized before the Revolutionary War, the Philadelphia Troop of Light Horse, an independent militia unit, took a new name after the adoption of the Constitution: The Philadelphia City Cavalry. ("2d Troop, Philadelphia City Cavalry, 1823," J. H. Nesmith, Company of Military Historians)*

the area. Major John Fowle brings four companies of 5th Infantry from Fort Snelling, and Major William Whistler leads a detachment of 3d Infantry from Fort Howard. Additional militia, some mounted, are assembled by Illinois Territorial Governor Ninian Edwards at Peoria and Galena, while Cass attempts to convene a council to prevent open warfare.

3–22 September. **Winnebagos Surrender. Prairie du Chien.**
Winnebagos bearing a white flag and two American flags appear at the camp of Major Whistler. With the group are two Indians who had attacked a family. Shortly after Atkinson arrives, other wanted Winnebagos turn themselves in. On the 9th a provisional treaty is made in which the United States promises to appoint a commission to look at Indian grievances. All troops return home except Major Fowle and his men, who are sent to rebuild and occupy Fort Crawford.

Left: *After Canadian trapper Alexis St. Martin received a gunshot wound to the gut, Army Surgeon William Beaumont was able to study the digestive system of the human body. ("Surgeon William Beaumont," Dean Cornwell, National Archives)*

Opposite: *After exploring the Rocky Mountains, a returning party of Army explorers and scientists including artist Samuel Seymour made camp near a band of Kiowa Indians. Seymour made this painting of the camp and trading between the two groups. ("Kiowa Camp," Samuel Seymour, Yale University Library)*

1828

January. **Status of the Army.**
Army strength is 546 officers and 5,176 enlisted men. To further strengthen American presence in the north, a new post called Fort Winnebago is ordered built at the portage between the Fox and Wisconsin rivers. Major Twiggs and troops from the 3d Infantry are given that task. The 1st Infantry leaves Baton Rouge and is split between Forts Crawford, Snelling, and Winnebago.

24 February. **Army General-in-Chief Dies.**
Major General Jacob Brown, Army General-in-Chief, dies after several strokes and declining health. He is buried on the 27th in the Congressional Cemetery, Washington, D.C. The personal animosity and rivalry between Scott and Gaines flare into a bitter political competition to be Brown's successor.

23 May. **Porter Appointed Secretary of War.**
President Adams appoints Peter B. Porter as the 12th Secretary of War. Porter, a former Army officer, had commanded a brigade at Chippewa and Lundy's Lane in the War of 1812.

29 May. **Macomb Appointed Army's Commanding General.**
President Adams breaks the deadlock between Scott and Gaines by promoting Alexander Macomb to Regular Army major general and appointing him commanding general of the Army. Scott refuses to recognize Macomb as his senior and demands Macomb be arrested for "presumption of command." Scott also submits his resignation, which is held in abeyance at the War Department; he is ordered back to his post at Jefferson Barracks.

7 July. **Corps of Engineers Begins B&O Railroad Survey.**
The Army Corps of Engineers is directed by Congress to survey a route for the Baltimore and Ohio Railroad, providing the country's first passenger rail service.

14 December. **Scott Relieved of Command.**
Scott's ranting about Macomb's promotion results in President Adams relieving him of command of the Western Department and placing him on an "awaiting orders" list. Brevet Brigadier Henry Atkinson, Colonel, 6th Infantry, assumes the command. Scott appeals to friends in Congress without result.

Right: *In 1816, the Army felt that a fort at Prairie du Chien was essential. Fort Crawford, named after William H. Crawford, was built on the site of the former Fort Shelby. ("Fort Crawford," Henry Lewis, Wisconsin Historical Society)*

1829

January. **Status of the Army.**
Army strength is 540 officers and 4,989 enlisted men. During the year the Army publishes new *U.S. Infantry Drill Regulations* developed by Scott. The training concept is based on three levels of training—the soldier, the company, and the battalion.

2 March. **New Artillery Regulations Published.**
The Army publishes a new artillery regulation, *A System of Exercise and Instruction of Field Artillery.* For the first time the terms "field," "light," and "horse" artillery are used.

4 March. **Andrew Jackson Inaugurated.**
Andrew Jackson is inaugurated as the seventh President and Commander-in-Chief of the Army.

Above: *When the Army reorganization of 1821 consolidated the Corps of Artillery and the Light Artillery Regiment, their uniforms also changed. The coats still retained the yellow artillery buttons and colored trim but became tighter and the pants were loosened. ("U.S. Artillery Units, Winter Uniform, 1825–1832," H. Charles McBarron, Company of Military Historians)*

Right: *This leather "bell" cap worn by a militia officer in the early 1800s was a copy of that worn by the Regulars. (Don Troiani Collection)*

Opposite: *While Secretary of War from 1825 through 1828, James Barbour (1775–1842) established the Army's Infantry School of Practice. ("James Barbour," Henry Ulke, Army Art Collection, NMUSA)*

Hero of both the War of 1812 and the Creek Indian War, Jackson has extensive military experience.

9 March. Eaton Made Secretary of War.

President Jackson appoints John H. Eaton to be 13th Secretary of War. Eaton had served with Jackson during the Creek War and in Florida. Eaton offers Scott an extended furlough to Europe with his family to consider the resignation threat. Scott accepts and departs in May.

4–14 May. First Army Trading Caravan Escort. Jefferson Barracks.

Attacks by Kiowa and Comanche Indians on trading caravans along the Santa Fe Trail bring a request for Army help. Captain Bennet Riley is ordered to escort a large Santa Fe trading caravan to the border of Spanish-Mexican territory, then wait and escort the caravan back. He departs the Barracks by steamboat on the 4th for Cantonment Leavenworth with four companies (170 men) of the 6th Infantry.

5 June–1 July. Comanches Attack Riley. Missouri Territory.

Riley and his men escort the caravan to the border, then make camp on Chouteau's Island in the Arkansas River to await the traders' return. Almost immediately, hostile Comanches begin attacking the sentries and raiding the camp to steal horses and cattle.

18 July. Taylor Assumes Fort Command. Fort Crawford, Michigan Territory.

Lieutenant Colonel Zachary Taylor assumes command, replacing Major Stephen W. Kearny. The garrison is four companies of the 1st Infantry, totaling 183 officers and men, plus their families. The Post Surgeon, William Beaumont, is conducting his study of the digestive tract with his Canadian patient, Alexis

St. Martin. Taylor is tasked with building a new fort above the river flood plain.

13 August. **New Orders Concerning Brevet Rank.**
Officers are given brevet promotions after ten years of honorable service. To eliminate the confusion, a new order is issued stating that an officer with a brevet rank cannot command at that rank unless specifically authorized by the War Department. Duels among officers, often over seniority, are not uncommon.

8 November. **Riley Returns. Cantonment Leavenworth.**
Riley and his men return after spending the summer on the Mexican border. They have suffered four soldiers killed in Comanche raids, bad weather, and boredom. This is the Army's first experience facing the mounted tribes, and Riley's detailed report emphasizes the disadvantage of dismounted infantry.

23 November. **Scott Reinstated in Command.**
When Scott returns from Europe he withdraws his resignation. On the 23rd he is given command of the Eastern Department, resuming the rotation of commands with Gaines.

1830

January. **Status of the Army.**
Army strength is 625 officers and 5,324 enlisted men.

28 May. **Indian Removal Act Passed.**
Congress passes the Indian Removal Act requiring the Indian tribes east of the Mississippi River to sign agreements to move to designated areas west of the river. The Army is tasked with forcing the Indians to sign, gathering and transporting the Indians, protecting them from the western Indians, and creating a line of forts to supervise the new Indian frontier. Army detachments are sent west to establish new camps. The 3d Infantry leaves Jefferson Barracks for the Choctaw Nation and the Red River area.

27 September. **Treaty of Dancing Rabbit Creek Mississippi.**
Secretary of War Eaton and former militia general John Coffee complete negotiations with the Choctaws to move the Indians to new lands west of the Mississippi River. Colonel George Gibson, the Commissary General of Subsistence, supervises the Indians' move to the river. The Army is responsible to settling the Choctaws west of the river. Most of the emigration is completed by the summer of 1833.

1831

January. **Status of the Army.**
Army strength is 627 officers and 5,324 enlisted men.

8 February. **War Department Renames Posts.**
By general orders, the War Department directs all existing "permanent" Army cantonments and fortifications to be renamed forts.

Spring. **Black Hawk War Begins. Illinois.**
A band of Sac-Fox Indians led by Black Hawk crosses the Mississippi River to their traditional lands in Illinois. Under agreements of an 1805 treaty, the land is being sold to white settlers. Black Hawk ignores warnings and takes his band to an area near the Rock River. When John Reynolds, the new Illinois governor, threatens to mobilize militia and drive the Indians out, Brigadier Edmund Gaines, commander of the Western Department, comes to Rock Island from Jefferson Barracks with troops of the 6th Infantry and some artillery to meet with Black Hawk. In the tense meeting, Black Hawk renounces the treaty and refuses to leave Illinois. Gaines asks for militia support before taking action.

Above: *In 1827, when Colonel Henry Leavenworth selected a site on the bluffs overlooking the Missouri River for a new Army post, little did he realize that it would become a major gateway to the West and the home of the future Army staff college. ("The Landing–1827," Jerry D. Thomas)*

18 June. **Secretary of Navy Acts as Secretary of War.**
Eaton resigns after a bitter personal battle to have his wife, a former barmaid, accepted by Washington society. Secretary of Navy Levi Woodbury acts as Secretary of War for six weeks. President Jackson, who supported Eaton, appoints him governor of the Florida Territory.

25–30 June. **Black Hawk Forced to Leave. Rock River, Illinois.**
The Illinois militia assembles on the 25th and the next day move against the Sac-Fox village with Gaines' 6th Infantry Regulars. The deserted village is destroyed. Another meeting with Black Hawk is held, and the peace faction of his band convinces him to sign an agreement on the 30th to return west of the Mississippi.

1 August. **Cass Made Secretary of War.**
President Jackson appoints Lewis Cass as 14th Secretary of War. Cass was an Army officer in the War of 1812, serving as colonel of the 27th Infantry. He ended the war as a brigadier general.

1 November. **Secretary of War Calls for Mounted Troops.**
In his annual report to Congress, Secretary Cass calls for the establishment of a mounted force "on the frontier south of the Missouri." The increasing number of Indian incidents lend weight to his proposal.

1832

January. **Status of the Army.**
Army strength is 613 officers and 5,256 enlisted men spread among 44 Army forts, arsenals, and posts.

5 April. **Ordnance Department Reestablished.**
Congress reestablishes a separate Ordnance Department of 308 officers and men headed by a colonel. Colonel George Bomford is the first to head up the reestablished department.

6–11 April. **Black Hawk Returns to Illinois.**
Encouraged by false promises of British support and anticipating help from the Winnebagos, Black Hawk returns to Illinois on 6 April with a band of about 500 mounted warriors and 1,500 women, children, and elderly. The Indians make no hostile acts. Brigadier General Henry Atkinson is in the area with six companies (about 200 men) of the 6th Infantry. Black Hawk refuses his request for a meeting, and Atkinson requests reinforcements.

16 April. **Illinois Militia Mobilizes.**
Governor Reynolds assembles about 1,700 Illinois volunteers at Beardstown on the Illinois River and marches them to the Mississippi to receive supplies from St. Louis. They are organized under militia Brigadier Samuel Whiteside into a brigade of three regiments. One of the companies elects Abraham Lincoln to be its captain. Farther north, Colonel Henry Dodge of the Michigan Militia gathers a force of mounted rangers.

1 May. **Bonneville Expedition. Fort Osage.**
Captain Benjamin L. E. Bonneville, on a two-year leave from the Army, leads a privately funded 110-man expedition into the central and western Spanish and Indian territories. Although his self-proclaimed purpose is to investigate possibilities for a fur trade business, he receives and follows detailed instructions from the Secretary of War to gather information on terrain, weather, and Indians. He is gone for three years.

7–8 May. **Taylor Assumes Regimental Command. Fort Armstrong, Illinois.**
Taylor is promoted to colonel in April. This entitles

Right: *The Grand Council at Prairie du Chien in August 1825 attempted to end inter-tribal wars among the nine tribes by an agreement that would set specific boundaries for their land. ("Grand Council at Prairie du Chien," J. O. Lewis, Library of Congress)*

Below: *The uniforms for enlisted men of several Army branches are identified by the color of their jacket trim and the insignia on their leather caps. ("Enlisted Men: Artillery, Infantry, Dragoons, 1835–1850," H. A. Ogden)*

him to a monthly salary of $75.00, $5.00 for two servants, and $12.00 for horse forage. He takes command of the 1st Infantry at its Fort Armstrong headquarters on 7 May. The next day Atkinson places Taylor in charge of all ten Regular companies—the four of the 1st and the six from the 6th Infantry—and the dismounted militia.

9–10 May. Atkinson Moves Against Black Hawk. Rock River, Illinois.

Atkinson orders Whiteside to take the mounted militia up the south side of the river to locate Black Hawk's camp. Taylor's slower force will march along the north bank, escorting the boats with supplies. The two groups are to meet at Dixon's Ferry.

11–14 May. "Stillman's Run." Sycamore Creek, Illinois.

As Whiteside advances he is joined by a mounted battalion of Illinois militia under Majors Isaiah Stillman and David Bailey. After passing through Dixon's Ferry, Reynolds orders Stillman to attack Black Hawk's band. On the 14th, as Stillman approaches Black Hawk's camp, an Indian truce party appears with a white flag. When other Indian scouts are spotted, the militia suspect a trap and open fire, killing several Indians. The militia pursue the Indians into an ambush hastily prepared by Black Hawk. Most of the surprised militia flee back to Dixon's Ferry, while a small group of 12 makes a valiant but fatal effort as rear guard. All are killed, and Lincoln's company is detailed to bury the dead.

19–29 May. Pursuit of Black Hawk. Illinois, Michigan Territory.

Taylor's Regulars and the surviving militia begin searching for Black Hawk's band, which has hidden its trail and moved north into the Michigan Territory (now Wisconsin). Their terms ended, Atkinson must release all but 300 of the militia. Reynolds issues a call for 2,000 new volunteers. Lincoln reenlists as a private

Congress Enlarges the Army.
Congress increases the Medical Department to 69 surgeons and assistants. It also creates a battalion of Mounted Rangers with 25 officers and 660 enlisted men in six companies. The men are to be one-year volunteers and provide their own arms, equipment, and horses for $1.00 a day. Henry Dodge receives a commission as a major to lead the battalion. Captains include Nathan Boone (Daniel Boone's son).

16 June–July. **Scott Given Command of Illinois Field Operations.**
President Jackson is unhappy with Atkinson's apparent lack of action and angry at Brigadier Edmond Gaines, who commands the Western Department. On 16 June Jackson directs Brigadier Winfield Scott, commander of the Eastern Department, to go to Illinois and take charge of the war. Jackson also orders the War Department to send more Regulars, and soon nine companies of artillery serving as infantry and nine companies of infantry are dispatched.

1–10 July. **Scott and Cholera Arrive in Fort Dearborn. Chicago.**
Four steamships carrying Scott, 1,000 Regulars, and supplies depart Buffalo on the 1st. As they pass Detroit, some of the men become infected with Asiatic cholera. By the time the ships arrive at Fort Dearborn on the 10th, they are virtual hospitals. More than 50

in a 20-day mounted company, then reenlists again in a "spy" (scout) company. Atkinson brings two companies of the 3d Infantry from Fort Winnebago.

June. **Atkinson Reorganizes and Resumes Pursuit. Rock River.**
Fresh troops give Atkinson more than 3,400 militia and 700 Regulars. He reorganizes the militia into three brigades, each with a "spy" or scout battalion. Small skirmishes occur sporadically, and attacks by Black Hawk and 200 warriors near Galena cause militia to be diverted to defend the town. On the 15th, the Michigan Rangers under Dodge engage and kill 11 hostile Indians on the Pecatonica River.

11 June. **Eagle Adopted as Insignia for Colonels.**
General Order 50 designates a silver American eagle as the insignia for rank of colonel. The insignia is embroidered on an epaulet worn on each shoulder. Prior to this, colonels wore a metallic-gold fringed epaulet on each shoulder. A silver-embroidered hunting bugle similar to the old Rifle Regiment insignia is also added to the tails of infantry officers' coats. Many use it also as a cap insignia, and eventually it becomes the infantry insignia.

Opposite, top: *Major General Peter B. Porter became Secretary of War under John Quincy Adams in July 1828. ("Peter Buell Porter," Daniel Huntington, Army Art Collection, NMUSA)*

Opposite, bottom: *("Captain, U.S. Artillery, 1832," Colonel James D. Campbell collection)*

Right: *The Army was often called upon to escort wagon trains along the Oregon and Santa Fe trails. (Hugh Brown, HFC Commissioned Art Collection)*

men have died, and almost 100 more are sick. The alcoholic ship's doctor refuses to help, leaving care of the men up to Scott. He takes great personal risk of infection in seeing to their welfare, doing everything possible to stop the disease. More than 200 die.

18–21 July. **Battle of Wisconsin Heights. Michigan Territory.**
On the 18th a militia brigade with a detachment of mounted Michigan men led by Colonel Henry Dodge finds Black Hawk's trail heading west toward the Wisconsin River. They catch Black Hawk near the river on the 21st. The Indians skillfully fight a delaying action in the river bottoms, keeping the militia at bay. During the night, they escape across the river on makeshift rafts.

27–31 July. **Pursuit of Black Hawk Resumes. Michigan Territory.**
A picked force of 1,300 men, including mounted militia and 400 Regulars under Taylor, crosses the river on the 28th and takes up the pursuit. After three days of forced march, Atkinson's force is within 20 miles of Black Hawk's band, which has reached the banks of the Mississippi River.

1–2 August. **Battle of Bad Axe. Bad Axe River, Michigan Territory.**
As the Indians are crossing the Mississippi, the steamboat *Warrior* appears, carrying troops. Black Hawk raises a white flag and offers to surrender, but the boat captain suspects a trick and orders the troops to open fire. The fighting continues until the

steamboat departs, leaving 23 Indians dead. In the morning, Taylor's Regulars and most of the militia attack the Indian camp. In fierce fighting the Indians are pushed against the river just as the steamboat returns. Black Hawk escapes, but his band is destroyed. About 150 Indians are killed and 50 captured. Atkinson loses 24 men killed or wounded. After the battle, the wounded and prisoners are put on the steamboat and taken to Fort Crawford.

7–25 August. **Black Hawk War Ends. Fort Crawford.**
The militia are released from duty when Scott and his staff arrive on the 7th. On the 25th Black Hawk is captured by Winnebagos and turned over to the Army. Scott has Colonel Taylor send his adjutant, Lieutenant Jefferson Davis, to escort Black Hawk and other Sac-Fox prisoners to Jefferson Barracks, where they are put in irons. Black Hawk is later imprisoned for a short time in Fortress Monroe. Jefferson Davis leaves the Army in 1835 and marries one of Taylor's daughters. During the Black Hawk War and the actions against the Sac-Fox, five Regular enlisted men were killed and one wounded. Militia forces suffered one officer and four enlisted men killed and four oficers and 31 enlisted wounded

August. **Mounted Rangers Deployed on the Frontier.**
The first four Ranger companies are sent to Fort Armstrong and employed to patrol the northern Illinois-Michigan Territory border areas, where hostile Winnebagos and Pottawatomie are still causing problems. When the cholera epidemic hits the fort, 15 Rangers die of the disease.

political developments in South Carolina and to find a way to reinforce federal forces. Anger over federal tariff laws and slavery issues has caused radicals to talk of leaving the union. The South Carolina governor has mobilized 25,000 volunteers against possible federal intervention. Scott arrives on 26 November on the pretext of making an annual inspection of coastal defenses and arsenals. He reports that improvements are needed and requests reinforcements. Five artillery companies and 16 cannon are sent from Fortress Monroe. All Regular officers in the area must renew their oath of allegiance to the Constitution, and suspect officers are reassigned. A "sprained ankle" lets Scott stay the winter in Georgia to monitor developments.

1833

September. **Scott Negotiates Indian Treaty. Fort Armstrong.**
Scott assembles the Sac-Fox chiefs plus Winnebagos, Sioux, and Menominees. The ceremonies take weeks. At the end the United States has gained most of what is now Iowa and Wisconsin.

14 September–November. **Rangers On Patrol. Fort Gibson, Arkansas River.**
Captain Jesse Bean and his company of mounted Rangers arrive on the 14th. Three weeks later they make a long patrol into the Pawnee and Comanche territory. After two days on the trail the Rangers are joined by a party of tourists, including authors Washington Irving and Charles J. Latrobe. Both write books based on their experiences with the Army. In November, the Ranger companies of Captains Boone and Lemuel Ford also arrive at Fort Gibson.

5 November. **Whiskey Ration Ends.**
At the urging of the Surgeon General, General Order No. 100 ends the daily whiskey ration in the Army, replacing it with a sugar and coffee ration. However, alcoholism among both officers and enlisted men continues to be a problem.

November–December. **Nullification Crisis. Charleston, South Carolina.**
President Jackson sends Scott to quietly observe

January. **Status of the Army.**
Army strength is 659 officers and 5,443 enlisted men. Health and sanitation are major concerns as Army posts suffer periodic outbreaks of cholera and other diseases.

January–March. **Nullification Crisis. Charleston, South Carolina.**
Scott works to ease tensions. In one instance he sends a detachment of artillerymen under Major Samuel Ringgold to help fight a sugar-refinery fire threatening Charleston. In March 1833 the Clay compromise bill ends the crisis and Scott returns to New York.

February. **Mounted Rangers Arrive. Fort Leavenworth.**
Captain Matthew Duncan's company of mounted Rangers arrive at the fort. As soon as weather permits, they join with a company of the 6th Infantry for escort duty along the Santa Fe Trail.

March. **Congress Acts to Improve Morale and Stop Desertions.**
The Secretary of War reports a significant problem with desertions. Each deserter represents a loss of $81.60. Congress acts to improve morale by reducing the enlistment term from five to three years, increasing pay (a private goes from $5 to $6 per month), and approving a reenlistment bonus of two months' pay. Whipping is also reinstated as a punishment for desertion.

2 March. **First Regiment of Dragoons Established.**
The Battalion of Mounted Rangers is discontinued. In its place, Congress authorizes the 1st Regiment of Dragoons, with 749 officers and men. Henry Dodge is

Opposite: John H. Eaton became Secretary of War on 9 March 1829. He began compensation pay for discharged soldiers who served honorably, and made the Topographical Engineers a separate bureau. ("John Henry Eaton," Robert Walter Weir, Army Art Collection, NMUSA)

Right: Chief Black Hawk twice led his band of Sac-Fox Indians back across the Mississippi into the old tribal lands in Illinois, sparking fights with the white settlers in the area. ("Black Hawk," George Catlin, National Collection of Fine Arts, Smithsonian Institution. Art Resource/NY)

Below: During the Black Hawk War, most of the frontiersmen and farmers that comprised the Illinois Militiamen lacked a uniform and wore civilian work or hunting clothes. ("Illinois Militia, Black Hawk War, 1832," H. Charles McBarron, Company of Military Historians)

promoted to colonel of the regiment. Stephen W. Kearny is promoted from the infantry to dragoon lieutenant colonel. Captain Edwin V. Sumner and Lieutenant Philip St. George Cooke also transfer from the infantry and three Ranger captains, including Nathan Boone, join the dragoons. Dodge supervises the Ranger companies in the west until August, while Kearny and others recruit and assemble the dragoons at Jefferson Barracks, which is designated as the regimental headquarters. The 1st Dragoons is later

redesignated the 1st Cavalry Regiment. Its units are the oldest continually serving cavalry in the Army.

4 July. **1832 Uniform Regulations Become Effective.** Officers now wear a knee-length double-breasted coat with facings of the branch colors prescribed during the Revolution. Cocked hats are again worn and all officers and sergeants wear epaulets with regimental numbers on both shoulders. Below colonel, rank is distinguished by the size and material of the epaulets.

20 November–14 December. **Dragoons Move to Fort Gibson. Arkansas Territory.** Horses and recruits arrive at Jefferson Barracks in late fall. After training both, Colonel Dodge leads the first five dragoon companies on a 500-mile winter march to Fort Gibson. Despite the harsh weather, they establish a new camp since the fort cannot accommodate them. Recruiting for the last five companies continues through the winter and spring. In June they march west to join the rest of the regiment.

1834

January. **Status of the Army.**
Army strength is 666 officers and 5,747 enlisted men.

29 January–22 March. **First Use of Army Troops in Labor Disputes. Williamsport, Maryland.**
Regular Army troops are deployed to restore peace when armed violence occurs between rival groups of workers on the Chesapeake-Ohio Canal. Two companies of the 1st Artillery are ordered to Williamsport from Forts McHenry and Washington. It is the first time Regular troops are used in a domestic labor dispute.

17 June–4 July. **Leavenworth Leads First Dragoon Expedition. Fort Gibson.**
Following a formal review, Brevet Brigadier General Henry Leavenworth leads eight companies of dragoons out on their first long patrol—a distance of more than 500 miles—to scout the upper Red River Valley and negotiate treaties with the Indians in that area. Artist George Catlin accompanies the regiment. Traveling in summer temperatures of more than 114 degrees, the horses and men cannot keep the pace, and are ill. On 4 July, Leavenworth and 200 men are left at the Washita River with the wagons and heavy supplies

while Dodge moves ahead. He takes six companies with ten days' rations tied to their saddles.

30 June. **Indian Department Established.**
Congress establishes the Indian Department within the War Office.

22 July–15 August. **Dodge Holds Indian Councils. Red River Valley.**
Dodge leaves behind two more companies and continues on in terrible heat, reaching the villages on 22 July. He meets with the Pawnees and Comanches until the 25th, then returns to the Washita camp to find that Leavenworth had died on the 21st from injuries suffered in a riding accident. Leavenworth is buried along with other dragoons who died of illness. He is the first Army general to die west of the Mississippi. The regiment returns to Fort Gibson on 15 August. More than 100 enlisted men die from the effects of the trip.

1835

January. **Status of the Army.**
Army strength is 666 officers and 5,746 enlisted men. In the Florida Territory, there are only about 600 Army Regulars, mostly 4th Infantry commanded by Colonel Duncan Clinch, with a few "foot" companies of 2d and 4th Artillery. The main Army posts are Fort King (Ocala), Fort Drane, and Fort Brooke (Tampa).

29 May. **Dodge Leads His Last Patrol.**
Colonel Dodge takes three companies of 1st Dragoons,

about 125 officers and men, up the Platte and South Platte rivers. They then swing south past Bent's Fort, going almost to Pueblo. As he travels, Dodge holds frequent councils with Indians, emphasizing peaceful trade and travel. On the return trip, Dodge uses the Santa Fe Trail to arrive at Fort Leavenworth on 16 September after a trip of 1,600 miles.

22 August. **Bonneville Expedition Returns.**
Captain Bonneville reports back and is told that he has been dropped from Army rolls as a deserter. Despite the fact that Bonneville sent two excellent field reports back (only one actually arrived), Secretary Cass refuses to reinstate him. Bonneville sends letters of protest to the President and in April 1836 Jackson returns his rank. Bonneville's maps and journals add important knowledge of the areas, including routes over the mountains discovered by a detachment he had sent into California. His journals are edited and published by Washington Irving.

November. **Army Prepares to Enforce Seminole Removal. Florida Territory.**
Brigadier General Clinch notifies Seminole leaders that they must assemble their groups for relocation as was agreed in treaties of 1832 and 1833. If they do not, the Army will gather them by force. Clinch has 14 companies of infantry and foot artillery and begins positioning these troops. Among the officers is Lieutenant George G. Meade, 3d Artillery.

18–25 December. **Battle of Black Point. Black Swamp, Florida Territory.**
Hostile Seminoles attack cooperative Indians, causing the governor to mobilize 500 mounted militiamen. When the militia wagon train of baggage becomes separated from the main group, it is attacked by Seminoles led by Osceola, a leader of Indian resistance. The militia suffer six killed and eight wounded. Scouts locate the Indian camp several days later and attack with little result. Indian raids on sugar plantations increase south of St. Augustine.

23–27 December. **Fort King Reinforcements. Fort Brooke, Florida Territory.**
Major Francis L. Dade departs with a column of eight officers, a surgeon, a guide, and 100 men from Company C, 2d Artillery and Company B, 3d Artillery, to reinforce Fort King. They are "foot" artillery trained to fight as infantry and they bring along a six-pound artillery piece pulled by horses. Dade volunteers to lead the group to permit Captain George W. Gardiner, commander of Company C, to remain at the fort with his sick wife. At the last minute Gardiner joins the group.

Opposite, top: *Lewis Cass was a Regular officer who served almost five years as Secretary of War. He recommended a public armory for fabrication of cannons and an establishment of a regiment of dragoons. ("Lewis Cass," Daniel Huntington, Army Art Collection, NMUSA)*

Opposite, bottom: *The Ordnance Regimental Crest's flaming bomb and crossed cannon are among the oldest emblems still used in the Army. (U.S. Army Ordnance Museum)*

Above: *Benjamin Bonneville graduated from West Point and served on the western frontier where he took leave and made a somewhat mysterious expedition into Indian territory, supposedly to start a fur trade business. (Denver Public Library Western Collection)*

28 December. **Ambushes Begin Second Seminole War. Florida Territory.**
Seminoles ambush and kill Mr. Wiley Thompson, chief Indian Agent, and Lieutenant Constantine Smith as the two men are walking outside Fort King. At the same time, about 50 miles away near Wahoo Swamp, a larger band of Seminoles attacks Major Dade's detachment. Dade and many of the men are killed in the first volley. The surprised artillerymen throw up a hasty barricade, gather their wounded, and defend themselves with their

muskets and the small cannon for several hours. Despite a heroic defense, they are overrun. Only three soldiers survive; two later die of wounds.

29–31 December. **Battle of Withlacoochee River.**
Brigadier Clinch leads an attack on the Seminole camp near the river. He has about 250 Regulars from the 1st, 2d, and 3d Artillery, and 4th Infantry under Lieutenant Colonel Alexander Fanning, and 560 mounted militia led by Colonel Richard Call. On the 30th, they reach the river and the Regulars cross using a single canoe. On the far bank they reform and move to an open area, where the Indians open fire. Bayonet charges hold the Seminoles at bay while the troops fall back across the river. They have lost four killed, 51 wounded. Their terms over, the militia go home.

1836

January. **Status of the Army.**
The strength of the Army is 7,151—680 officers and 6,471 enlisted men—which is close to its authorized 7,194. Under General-in-Chief Major General Macomb, the Army has seven regiments of infantry, four regiments of artillery, one regiment of dragoons, some engineers, and staff officers. The Army garrisons 53 different posts and forts, usually with one company each. Under Macomb are three brigadier generals—Scott, Gaines, and Jesup (Quartermaster General). Fourteen other officers hold the brevet rank of brigadier. The majority of the junior officers are graduates of West Point. Most of the enlisted men are recent immigrants with little education.

17 January. **Militia Battle Seminoles. Florida Territory.**
Volunteer St. Augustine Guards engage a band of Seminoles and are forced to retreat with almost half their force casualties. Indians have burned 16 plantations by the end of the month. Numerous other small fights occur during the month between militia and Indians with losses on both sides.

21 January. **Winfield Scott Ordered to Take Florida Command.**
Thoughout the Western and Eastern Departments share Florida, Scott is given overall command of the operations there. A letter is sent to Gaines telling him to remain in New Orleans, but before the letter arrives, he leaves for Florida with troops. Colonel Abraham Eustis, commander at Charleston, is also ordered to gather troops and sail for St. Augustine as soon as possible.

February. **Sixth Infantry Sent to Texas Border. Jefferson Barracks.**
Concerned about developments in Texas, Secretary Cass orders the entire 6th Infantry to Fort Jesup, Louisiana, to strengthen the American presence.

9–22 February. **Gaines and Scott Land in Florida.**
Brigadier General Gaines lands at Tampa with six companies of the 4th Infantry and a regiment of Louisiana volunteers. He is joined by Florida militia and quickly marches for Fort King, where he expects to find supplies. On the 20th, Gaines' men reach the site of the Dade ambush and take time to bury the remains. Two days later, they arrive at the fort and discover the extra food is not there. Within a few days Gaines heads back toward Tampa. Meanwhile, Scott lands at Picolata on the St. Johns River, but he has no troops. Incensed at Gaines' presence, Scott prepares his own campaign plan.

26–27 February. **Siege at Withlacoochee River. Florida Territory.**
As Gaines' force of about 980 men ford the river on the 28th, Indians on the other side open fire. Lieutenant James F. Izard, leading the advance party of 4th Infantry, is mortally wounded. Heavy musket fire pours into the men all day, and Gaines orders a log breastwork built, which he names Camp Izard. By the next day, almost 1,100 Seminoles surround the camp. Gaines is able to send two letters to Clinch asking for

help. Repeated attacks and an attempt to burn the fort fail, so the Indians settle into a siege. Food is desperately low, and the men kill horses and mules for food.

1–8 March. **Clinch Disobeys Scott to Help Gaines. Fort Drane.**
On the 1st Scott orders Clinch not to help Gaines, but Clinch disobeys. He takes supplies from his farm and on the 5th heads for Camp Izard with reinforcements and food. Scott later reverses his order, but Clinch is already en route. The Seminoles ask for talks, but as Gaines meets with them on the 6th, Clinch's force arrives and opens fire, sending the Indians into the swamp. At Tampa, militia mobilized for three months at Scott's call are arriving from Georgia, South Carolina, and Alabama.

9–28 March. **Gaines Returns to Louisiana.**
Gaines issues Order No. 7 on 9 March declaring a victory. He turns Camp Izard over to Clinch and departs Florida for New Orleans. When he arrives on the 28th, he finds orders directing him to take command of the western border, where another crisis, caused by the Texan revolt against Mexico, is building.

25–31 March. **Scott Begins His Campaign. Camp Izard.**
Scott plans to have three columns converge on the Seminole villages in the Withlacoochee Cove area. Communication among the three is to be a cannon fired periodically during the day. The commanders are ordered to begin moving on the 25th. Colonel William Lindsay, 2d Artillery, commands the center column of 1,250, mostly Alabama and Florida volunteers, who are spirited but undisciplined. The left column, commanded by Brevet Brigadier Abraham Eustis, comprises 1,400 men of the 1st Artillery and militia units from South Carolina. Scott travels with the right flank column, which is under Clinch. It is supposed to drive the Seminoles into the other two groups. The column reaches Camp Izard on the 28th, and the next morning the men begin crossing the river. The Indians wait to open fire until the rear supply trains begin crossing. Other Seminoles shoot from an island in the river until bayonet charges clear the way. A heavy fight occurs on the 31st with 15 casualties, but the Louisiana militia earn the respect of many by their willingness to stay in the fight. The center column has to fight Indians for most of its march and build a fortified position, Fort Alabama, to guard its rear. Three days late arriving at his starting position, Lindsay is out of food and must return to Fort Brooke. Eustis has

Above: *Mounted Ranger companies were Regular units that formed an early warning system against Indian war parties from the Pawnee and Comanche tribes. (H. Charles McBarron, Company of Military Historians)*

similar problems, having to cut a way through dense thickets and fight several hot actions. He reaches his starting point five days late. Low on supplies and out of contact, Eustis also turns for Fort Brooke. The campaign is a failure.

April. **Border Tensions Over Texas Revolt. Fort Jesup, Louisiana.**
Reinforced by the 6th Infantry, Gaines maintains a strong American military presence. The retreat of the Texan army following the defeats at the Alamo and Goliad has encouraged the Cherokees in the area to consider supporting the Mexicans. Gaines has instructions not to cross the Sabine River unless the Indians become involved. Without federal authority, Gaines also calls for volunteers from Louisiana, Alabama, Mississippi, and Arkansas. The Texan victory at San Jacinto on 21 April calms the situation.

1 April. **Scott Renews Operations.**
With the Seminoles now split into small bands, Scott sends units out to search. Eustis sweeps the Pease Creek area while Lindsay and Clinch move along both

banks of the Withlacoochee in opposite directions. The Seminoles elude the searchers and for 12 days a band attacks a camp of Georgia militia and a few Regulars, while others try to overrun Fort Alabama. On 12 April Seminoles surround an isolated blockhouse and keep the garrison of Florida militiamen under siege for 48 days. Scott is accused of ignoring the militiamen. On the 14th Indians assault a burial party at Fort Barnwell. The fort commander, Major William Gates, a graduate of the first class at West Point, is court-martialed for cowardice for not recovering the bodies. He is found guilty, and his name is stricken from the rolls of the Army. Gates appeals and is reinstated in January 1837. In an unusual night attack on 20 April, Seminoles try to surprise sentries at Fort Drane but are held off until Clinch brings relief on the 24th.

27 April. **Destruction of Fort Alabama. Thlonotosassa Creek.**
Militia Colonel William Chisolm leads Alabama militia and Regulars from the 4th Infantry and 2d Artillery to destroy the abandoned fort. Near the fort they are ambushed by a large Seminole force. While the artillery engages the Indians, Chisolm leads a bayonet charge across the creek, scattering the ambushers. Five soldiers are killed and 24 wounded. Chisolm leaves a booby-trapped powder barrel in the fort. Twenty minutes after the troops depart, the fort is destroyed by a large explosion. Within a few weeks the militia enlistments end and they are released.

April. **Creeks Resist Forced Move. Alabama-Georgia.**
Violence breaks out when the Creeks, who are preparing to leave their lands and emigrate west of the Mississippi, discover that the transportation contract was given to a company that swindled them in the past. Georgia militia attack a Creek camp, and bands of Creeks kill scattered farm families. More than 1,103 Regulars and 9,000 Georgia and Alabama militia begin moving into the Creek territory.

21 May. **Change of Florida Command. Florida.**
Secretary Cass orders Scott north to direct the Creek removal. Scott, frustrated by the lack of military success, is ready to depart. Clinch has resigned, leaving Eustis the next senior Regular officer. Scott turns military command over to him. Quartermaster Brigadier Thomas S. Jesup is actually the next senior Army general, but he is also fully occupied with the Creeks. Florida Governor Richard K. Call, who served under Jackson in the Creek War, requests command of military operations.

STEPHEN WATTS KEARNY

When Stephen Watts Kearny died in 1848, it was the culmination of a remarkable 36-year career as a professional Army officer. A strict disciplinarian, he was also capable, energetic, and fiercely determined—the archetypical frontier officer.

Kearny was born 30 August 1794 in Newark, New Jersey. He joined the Regular Army as a first lieutenant, 13th Infantry, on 12 March 1812, and in October found himself fighting in Canada at the Battle of Queenstown, where he was wounded and captured. Later paroled, Kearny was promoted to captain in April 1813. He was retained in the 1815 reorganization but transferred to the 2d Infantry, joining the regiment on the Missouri frontier.

In 1819, Kearny accompanied the Army's Yellowstone Expedition, helping establish Camp Missouri (later Fort Atkinson, Nebraska) on the Missouri River. The following summer he went with another expedition north toward Camp Cold Water (later Fort Snelling, Minnesota). In 1823 Kearny received a brevet promotion to major. Two years later he was a member of a second Yellowstone Expedition; he then went to St. Louis to help build Jefferson Barracks. In 1828 Kearny was commander at Prairie du Chien; he was promoted to Regular major in the 3d Infantry in May 1829. In 1831, Major Kearny was given responsibility for rebuilding Fort Towson (Oklahoma) on the border with the Choctaw Indian Territory.

In March 1833, Kearny was promoted to lieutenant colonel and second-in-command of the new Regiment of Dragoons. The next year he survived a disastrous expedition into the southern plains. On 4 June 1836, Kearny was promoted to colonel and made commander of the redesignated 1st Regiment of Dragoons. A believer in a well-trained unit, Kearny drilled his men hard at Fort Leavenworth, turning them into a crack regiment. Finding the existing manuals not applicable for operations on the open plains, he wrote his own—*Carbine Manual*, or *Rules for the Exercise and Maneuvers for U.S. Dragoons*. In 1845, he took the 1st Dragoons on a long patrol west along the Oregon Trail as far the South Pass through the Rockies, then returned by the Santa Fe Trail.

War with Mexico brought Kearney promotion to brigadier general and orders to form "The Army of the West" with his 1st Dragoons and mounted militia and to capture Santa Fe and California. By mid-August Kearny occupied Santa Fe peacefully, then took the dragoons on to California. On 6 December, he attacked a larger force of Mexicans at San Pasqual, California, losing many men and receiving two wounds.

Despite a dispute over authority with the senior Navy officer, Commodore Robert Stockton, Kearny led a joint Army-Navy force to victory in two battles, San Gabriel on 8 January and La Mesa on 9 January; this brought California under full American control. Kearny then marched back to Fort Leavenworth, where he preferred charges against Captain John C. Fremont for having supported Stockton.

In April 1848, Kearny was sent to command at Vera Cruz, Mexico, where he fell victim to yellow fever. Transfer to Mexico City did not help his health. He returned to Jefferson Barracks in July, and on 30 August, he was promoted to brigadier general. Still in ill health, he died on 31 October at age 54.

—*Vince Hawkins*

Above: *Stephen W. Kearny was a hard-driving leader who molded his 1st Dragoon Regiment into a crack unit that was often the only authority on the western frontier. ("Steven Kearny," Kansas State Historical Society, Topeka, KS)*

23 May. **Second Regiment of Dragoons Established.**
Congress approves establishment of the 2d Regiment of Dragoons. This adds another 749 officers and men to the Regular Army's authorized strength. Lieutenant Colonel David E. Twiggs is promoted out of the 4th Infantry to be the regiment's colonel. The detachment of 1st Dragoons in Florida is redesignated as Company D, 2d Dragoons, and recruiting teams are sent out to fill the other nine companies. Congress also authorizes 10,000 volunteers with enlistments for six or 12 months.

26–28 May. **Scott Plans Operations Against Creeks. Milledgeville, Georgia.**
Scott meets with his commanders and makes an elaborate plan using multiple columns advancing through Creek territory from different directions. Supplies are not sufficient, however, slowing implementation. Jesup departs to assemble his force of Alabama militia and await the signal to advance.

1–7 June. **Fort King Abandoned; Fort Drane Attacked. Florida Territory.**
Troop strength is badly weakened by fevers and illness. Only 166 men in the six companies at Fort King are fit for duty, so the post is abandoned. Fort Drane comes under continuous Indian attack until Captain Lemuel Gates drags a howitzer out the front gate and fires it at the Seminoles. Gates then leads a bayonet charge, driving them away.

9 June. **Fort Defiance Garrison Sorties. Micanopy, Florida.**
With 70 men, Major Julius F. Heilman counterattacks 250 Seminoles surrounding the fort. He uses foot detachments of the 2d and 3d Artillery to engage the Indians, while sending mounted 2d Dragoons under Lieutenant Thompson B. Wheelock around the flank. The Dragoons charge the Indians, while an artillery crew pushes a six-pounder cannon forward in the center, firing as they advance. The Indians disappear into the forest.

10–28 June. **Jesup Ends Creek Conflict. Alabama-Georgia.**

Without waiting for Scott's signal, Jesup marches with the Alabama militia. Twice Scott orders him to stop, but Jesup is afraid his militiamen will desert unless there is action. He attacks and seizes the main Creek camp on the 16th, taking the chief and 300 Creeks captive. This ends Creek resistance but infuriates Scott. On 28 June, Scott receives a letter ordering him to come to Washington immediately. He expects to be commended on his work.

20 June. **Wool Sent to Direct Cherokee Move. Tennessee.**

Army Inspector General Colonel John E. Wool is sent to command the Tennessee militia slowly assembling the Cherokees. He is sympathetic to the Indians' plight, and when he tries to protect them from mistreatment in Alabama, charges are brought against him by the governor for interfering with civil authority. The court vindicates Wool, but the forced move of the Indians drags on.

21 June. **Governor Call Given Florida Military Command.**

Secretary Cass gives Governor Call authority to command all military forces in Florida. This is unusual. Call is only a territorial militia brigadier, yet he will command militia from other states as well as 1,000 Regulars. Before he can start his campaign, Call must recruit more federalized volunteers. Among the units formed is the Creek Volunteer Regiment. A number of Regulars apply for the senior leader positions. Two West Pointers, Captain John F. Lane, 2d Dragoons, and Captain Harvey Brown, 4th Artillery, are selected as regimental commander and deputy. Joining them is David Moniac, who is made a regimental major. The first Creek Indian graduate of West Point, he served in the 6th Infantry until 1822.

July. **Tensions Rise on Texas Border.**

Fears of renewed conflict grow when Mexico refuses to recognize the new Texas Republic and rumors of an Indian uprising spread. Brigadier General Gaines

Right: *An illustration of the uniforms of staff and line officers in the early 1830s. With slight variations, these types of headwear were used until 1850 when the* chapeau de bras *and the tall leather caps were to be phased out. ("Staff and Line Officers, Cadets, 1832–1835," H. A. Ogden)*

moves troops near the border and on 10 July sends a Lieutenant Colonel William Whistler with a squadron of 2d Dragoons and six companies of the 7th Infantry to occupy Nacogdoches in territory disputed with Mexico. Nothing happens and they are withdrawn in December.

2 July. Creeks Begin Migration West. Fort Mitchell, Georgia.
The first increment of Creeks departs, with many of the resisting warriors chained and guarded by Regulars. The others soon follow. The Creek warriors who are in Florida in the Volunteer Regiment fighting Seminoles are unable join their families until the following year.

18 July–22 July. Taylor Takes 1st Infantry South. Fort Crawford.
Texas is fighting its war of independence and there is concern the conflict may spread. Colonel Zachary Taylor loads his 1st Infantry companies, their families, and personal possessions on river steamers and sails down the Mississippi to Jefferson Barracks, where the rest of the regiment comes aboard, bringing the regiment together for the first time. Their destination is Fort Jesup, Louisiana, a post Taylor helped build in 1822. His paymaster, Major William S. Harney, is promoted to lieutenant colonel in August and transfers to 2d Dragoons.

19 July. Battle of Welika Pond. Micanopy, Florida.
A train of 22 wagons is sent to evacuate the sick and wounded from Fort Drain. It is escorted by a detachment of 62 men from the 2d Dragoons, 1st, 2d, and 3d Artillery led by Captain William S. Maitland. The wagons are ambushed by a band 200 Seminoles under Osceola near Fort Defiance. The escort fights desperately until a relief party arrives. The men then charge the Indians, pushing them back. Five soldiers are killed and six wounded.

July–August. Actions Continue Against Seminoles.
Numerous small combat actions occur as both sides harvest crops for food. On 27 July and 21 August there is fighting at Ridgley's Mill and Fort Drane by the foot artillerymen and dismounted dragoons. As usual, the Indians remove their dead and wounded. Army battle casualties are small; more serious is the high number of sick. Bad food and water, measles, and tropical fevers ravage all the fort garrisons and civilian refugees during the summer months.

21 August. Osceola Camp Attacked. Fort Defiance.
Major B. K. Pierce learns that Osceola is near Fort Drane. He gathers a force of 2d Dragoons and artillerymen from the 1st, 3d, and 4th Artillery. For mobility he mounts two men on each horse. The column attacks before dawn; their mounted charge catches the Seminoles by surprise. Pierce battles the Indians for more than an hour; then, outnumbered, he withdraws with losses of one killed and 16 wounded. He evacuates Fort Defiance on the 24th.

11–30 September. Tennessee Brigade Arrives. Tallahassee.
A Tennessee militia brigade arrives on the 11th, giving Governor Call the first of the men he requested. He marches them to the Suwanee River and, after a delay, finally crosses on the 29th. Call then sends a small group downstream to bring supplies he expects from Navy boats. The main force marches to old Fort Drane, but finds no Indians. On the 30th, the 750-man Creek Volunteer Regiment marching south from Georgia, skirmishes with Seminoles in northern Florida.

8–19 October. More Small Unit Fighting. Withlacoochee River.

On the 8th, Major Pierce with 200 Regulars joins Call. As Call's force tries to cross the Withlacoochee on the 13th, they receive heavy musket fire and are forced back. Low on food, Call looks for the expected naval supplies but finds nothing since the boats are stuck downriver. He finally heads back to Fort Drane on the 17th. On the 19th, the Creek Regiment arrives at Call's camp after a hard march. Shortly after arriving, Colonel Lane dies in his tent from an accidental or self-inflicted gun shot and his deputy, Brown, takes command.

3 October–November. Court of Inquiry on Scott. Frederick, Maryland.

Scott is shocked to find a War Department court of inquiry awaiting him to look into the charges and counter-charges between himself and Gaines. Each officer accuses the other of causing the failure of the spring campaign against the Seminoles. The court clears Scott and censures Gaines for his malicious language during the hearings and for lack of aggressiveness in Florida.

5 October. Attorney General Made Acting Secretary of War.

Attorney General Benjamin F. Butler is appointed by President Jackson to temporarily supervise the War Department.

4–18 November. Call Renews His Campaign. Withlacoochee River.

On the 4th, acting Secretary Butler writes to Governor Call that he is replaced by Brevet Major General Thomas S. Jesup. Unaware of this, Call launches his next campaign. He leads 2,500 men back across the Withlacoochee, but it is too late—Osceola's camp is empty. Wide sweeps are made on both sides of the river. Militia find a second large camp on the 17th and the Tennessee brigade charges in, wading to their waists in swamp. The Seminoles leave 20 dead and most of their supplies. One militiaman is killed and ten wounded. The next day scouts find another 600 Seminoles. Call attacks with a double flanking tactic that routs the Indians, leaving 25 of them dead at the cost of three soldiers killed.

21 November. Battle of Wahoo Swamp.

Call moves against a prepared Seminole position on the edge of an open field bordering a swamp. He deploys him men in a line almost a mile long, with the Tennessee Brigade on the right, companies from the 1st, 2d, 3d, and 4th Artillery with Florida militia in the center, and the Creek Volunteer Regiment on the left. The soldiers advance to within 50 yards of the Seminoles, then fire single volley and charge with the bayonets. In heavy fighting the Seminoles are driven back across a stream. Major Moniac is killed leading his Creeks in pursuit. Both sides spend the rest of the day firing across the stream. At dusk Call withdraws and the next day marches away for resupply.

December. **Second Dragoons Arrive in Florida.**
Five companies of the new 2d Dragoon Regiment
arrive by ship at Savannah, where they receive horses,
mount up, and ride for Florida. As the men are
recruited for the other four companies, they go to
Jefferson Barracks, where the Major Kearny equips
and trains them.

2–9 December. **Governor Call Replaced. Volusia,
Florida Territory.**
On the 2nd, Call receives Cass's letter relieving him of
command. He protests to Jackson to no avail. Jesup,
who arrived in Florida in September but stayed out of
Call's campaign, now takes over. His instructions are
to drive the Seminoles out of their strongholds.

12 December. **Jesup's Campaign Begins. Florida Territory.**
Jesup plans to keep his forces together rather than
splitting them up. The Tennessee Brigade departs for
home after building Fort Armstrong on the Dade
battlefield. Jesup is left with 350 Alabama Volunteers,
250 Marines, and 450 Army Regulars, plus some sailors
to help garrison forts. He divides Florida into two
zones. Command of the northern zone goes to Brevet
Brigadier Walker K. Armistead, an Engineer. He is to
secure the area while Jesup takes the main force in
search of Seminoles in the southern zone.

January. **Status of the Army.**
Of its authorized 7,957 strength, the Army has
6,283—672 officers and 5,611 enlisted men. Almost
half are in Florida with the 2d Dragoons, 1st–4th
Artillery and 4th Infantry regiments. Others are
maintaining coastal defenses, guarding arsenals,
manning frontier posts, or assembling the Creeks for
removal. Many West Point graduates, the only
trained engineers in the country, are engaged in
building roads or on loan to railroad companies
making railroad route surveys.

10–27 January. **Jesup Changes Tactics.**
Jesup's force finds several bands of Seminoles as it
sweeps the area. On the 10th, troops capture 52
Seminoles and on the 17th a militia detachment kills a
key Indian leader. Six days later another chief is
surprised and killed with four warriors near Lake
Apopka, and more captives are taken. The largest
action occurs at Hatcheelustee Creek on the 27th,
when the brigade under Colonel Archibald
Henderson, the U.S. Marine Corps Commandant,
successfully attacks a large band of Seminoles. By the
end of the month, Jesup has changed his tactics. He is

now using small, faster-moving detachments to react to reports brought in by his scouts.

3–18 February. **Battle of Lake Monroe. Camp Monroe.**
On the 3rd, Jesup meets with some Seminole chiefs. They agree to a truce and promise to hold council on the 18th, but on the 8th Colonel Alexander Fanning's detachment of dragoons and foot artillery is surprised by more than 500 attacking Seminoles and almost overrun. The Regulars defend themselves with the help of cannon fire from Navy boats on the lake. Captain Charles Mellon, 2d Artillery, is killed in the action. A fort built on the site is named for him. Another small engagement is fought about 60 miles west of the lake with little result. No Seminole chiefs appear on the 18th.

4 March. **Van Buren Inaugurated as President.**
Martin Van Buren becomes the eighth President and Commander-in-Chief of the Army.
6 March. **Seminoles Sign Treaty. Fort Dade.**
After days of negotiations with Jesup, three Seminole leaders sign a treaty agreeing to end hostilities and to assemble at designated locations, and then be moved west of the Mississippi. They are told they may take "their Negroes" with them, which angers southern slave owners seeking to recover escaped slaves. Within days Seminoles come to the assembly camp at Tampa.

7 March. **Poinsett Appointed Secretary of War.**
Joel R. Poinsett is appointed as the 15th Secretary of War by President Van Buren. He will serve under two Presidents. Later his name will be given to the pointsettia plant, which he brings from Mexico after serving there as U.S. Ambassador.

19 May. **Army Major Commands Changed.**
The two major geographic commands of the army are modified by Secretary Poinsett. The Eastern and Western Departments are redesignated as "divisions" with the Mississippi River as the boundary between the two. This is done in part to clarify the command in Florida. Brigadier General Gaines retains the Western Division, Scott the Eastern Division.

2 June–July. **Osceola "Frees" Seminole Refugees. Tampa.**
During the night of 2 June, Osceola and 200 warriors remove the Indians from the Tampa camp, destroying Jesup's treaty. Faced with an embarrassing failure, Jesup is offered the chance to return to his quartermaster duties in Washington. He refuses and plans more operations. An immediate problem is troop health. Fevers and sickness leave fewer than 100 men of the

Opposite: *Although surprised and outnumbered, the ambushed men of Dade's command built a crude log breastwork in a futile effort to defend themselves. Only three escape the trap. ("Do Your Best...," Jackson Walker)*

Below: *Henry Dodge served in the Michigan militia until commissioned as an officer of the Mounted Rangers, as shown in this sketch. When the Rangers become the 1st Dragoons, Dodge is appointed the regimental colonel. ("Colonel Henry Dodge," Kansas State Historical Society, Topeka, KS)*

five battalions of Alabama and Georgia Volunteers fit for duty, and they have fewer than 50 horses.

5 August. **Lieutenant Robert E. Lee Arrives. St Louis.**
First Lieutenant Robert E. Lee and his assistant, 2d Lieutenant Montgomery C. Meigs, both Corps of Engineers, arrive in St. Louis. Lee's job is to improve the Mississippi for boat travel through the river's rapids and to alter the flow of the river so it removes the silt built up in the harbor at St. Louis. Two weeks later Lee goes upriver to survey the two sets of rapids. He returns in October and completes the project plans in December, then departs on leave until May, leaving Meigs in charge.

September. **Jesup's Second Campaign Plan.**
Jesup requests reinforcements. He wants to build a force of more than 6,000 Regulars to secure essential forts, perform escort duty, and serve in seven mobile columns that will operate independently in assigned areas. Secretary Poinsett sends Taylor's 1st Infantry and the 6th Infantry under Colonel Henry Atkinson, but few of the expensive-to-maintain mounted troops.

Jesup is authorized to recruit state volunteers, including Indians, to fill out his needs. He also requests new equipment such as Dearborn wagons, rubber pontoons and boats, shotguns, Mackinaw boats, and "portable" (dehydrated) soup.

8–10 September. **Night Attack on Seminole Camp. Mosquito Inlet.**
Moving at night, Brigadier General Joseph M. Hernandez leads a 170-man detachment of his Florida Volunteers, 2d Dragoons, and 3d Artillery in a surprise dawn raid on a large Seminole camp. They surround the camp and capture all but one of the Indians. They successfully repeat the tactic the next night at a second camp, capturing several key Indian leaders. Dragoon Lieutenant John W. S. McNeil and one Seminole are the only fatalities.

September–October. **Indians Recruited to Fight Seminoles. Fort Leavenworth.**
Army efforts to recruit Indians to replace the expired Creek regiment are partially successful when 91 Shawnees and 87 Delaware sign up for a six-month

term. Each tribal group is organized into two companies under Regular officers and shipped to Florida, where they join Taylor's command.

October. **Jesup Opens His Fall Campaign. Florida Territory.**
The last four companies of 2d Dragoons arrive after riding overland 1,200 miles from Jefferson Barracks in just 55 days. Many state volunteers also enlist, and with these additional troops Jesup begins his new campaign. Colonel Taylor, with 1,400 men, is given the Pease River area, while other detachments move to suspected Seminole locations.

21–22 October. **Osceola Seized at Conference. Fort Peyton.**
Osceola agrees to talk under a white flag on the 21st. Jesup sends Hernandez with a detachment of volunteers and 2d Dragoons. Hernandez has orders not to let Osceola remain free. When it is clear after lengthy discussions that Osceola is not going to

surrender, Hernandez signals his men and the Indians are seized. By December, Jesup has nine Seminole leaders and a number of warriors in prison.

29 November. **Seminoles Escape. Castillo, St. Augustine.**
During the night two chiefs and 18 other Seminoles pry out some window bars and escape from the prison.

14 December. **More Seminole Chiefs Captured. Fort Mellon.**
When a delegation of Cherokee chiefs fails to convince resisting Seminoles to come to the assembly camps, Jesup orders the imprisonment of four Seminoles chiefs who came in under a flag of truce.

25–28 December. **Battle of Lake Okeechobee.**
Colonel Zachary Taylor's detachment of 800 Regulars and Volunteers captures an Indian near the lake on the 25th. The prisoner points out a Seminole defensive position on a small hammock across a wide bog of mud

Right: *General Gaines is a jealous rival of Winfield Scott. Without orders, he takes troops into Florida and is almost defeated. To avoid conflict with Scott, Gaines is sent to the southwestern frontier. ("Major General Edmund P. Gaines," Colonel James D. Campbell Collection)*

and water covered with five-foot-tall sawgrass. More than 400 Seminole warriors are waiting behind log breastworks with lanes cut for musket fire. Colonel Richard Gentry, with his Missouri Volunteers and scouts, is put in the front rank, followed by a second rank of the 4th and 6th Infantry. Taylor holds the 1st Infantry and some 4th Artillery men in reserve. Moving through knee-deep mud, the Volunteers and 6th Infantry take heavy fire and losses. Gentry is killed and all but one of the officers and most of the sergeants of the 6th go down, including Lieutenant Colonel Thompson with his third and fatal wound. With the front heavily engaged, Taylor sends the 1st Infantry to attack the Indian flank. After three hours of battle, the Seminole defense collapses. Taylor has lost 26 killed and 112 wounded. Seminole losses are 25 killed and wounded and 180 captured. On the 27th the troops march to Fort Gardner, bringing their wounded on make-shift litters. The Missouri Volunteers are angry with Taylor for placing them in the front rank; they complain to Congress, but Taylor is defended by Secretary Poinsett and promoted to brevet brigadier general.

26 December. Fight at Wacasassa River.
Georgia Volunteers engage in a hot but indecisive firefight with Seminoles at the Wacasassa River in northern Florida. On the St. John's River, Jesup builds a new log fort for use as a supply depot; he names it Fort Christmas.

1838

January. **Status of the Army.**
Army authorized strength is 7,834—642 officers and 7,192 enlisted men; of these, 4,636 are in Florida. During the year, the War Department buys horses to mount the "light "batteries of the four artillery regiments authorized by Congress in 1821. Captain Samuel Ringgold's Battery C, 3d Artillery is the first to be equipped. A fellow officer of the 3d, Lieutenant Robert Anderson (later commander at Fort Sumter) translates a French manual on light artillery, which is used to develop American regulations. During the year the Ordnance Department tests the Jenks breech-loading rifle but rejects it because of powder fouling the barrel.

4 January–21 March. **Scott Sent to Resolve Canadian Crisis. New York.**
Brigadier General Scott is sent to the U.S.-Canadian border to help settle an international crisis caused by the cross-border activities of anti-Canadian revolutionaries called "Patriots." The rebels cross into Canada to raid and then are pursued by the Canadians into American territory, angering sympathetic locals. Colonel William Worth, the district commander, has few troops, so Scott calls for militia support from New York. He travels widely and speaks out publicly to

undermine popular support for the rebels. Faced with mobilized opposition on both sides of the border, the rebels surrender to Scott on 21 March.

15 January. Fight In the Everglades. Jupiter Inlet, Everglades.

A mixed detachment of 1st Artillery, Volunteers, and sailors under Lieutenant Levi N. Powell, U.S. Navy, has the mission of searching the Everglades. It is a hot, unseasonably dry winter and they are forced to drag their boats overland through the swamps. Near the inlet they capture an Indian woman who leads them to a Seminole camp, where Levi makes an impetuous charge. The attack is met with a blast of musketry and Powell is forced to make a fighting withdrawal, losing five killed and 15 wounded.

24 January. Battle of Lockahatchee River.

About noon, scouts report that more than 200 Seminoles are hiding on a hummock ahead of Jesup's troops. He orders an immediate attack, sending companies of 2d Dragoons and Tennessee Volunteers wading through the cypress swamp with the foot artillerymen of the 3d Artillery. On the flanks, companies of the 4th Artillery open fire with cannon and Congreve rockets. The Indians fall back over a creek and the Tennessee attack starts to falter, when

Jesup gallops up, dismounts, and with pistol in hand leads the way over the stream. A musket ball hits his glasses and cuts his face, but the attack continues and the Indians fade away. Seven soldiers are dead and 31 wounded. Indian losses are unknown.

8 February–21 March. Jesup Attempts Peaceful Solution.

Halting his southward march for resupplies of shoes—more than 400 men are barefoot—Jesup also meets with several Seminole leaders. He agrees to ask the War Department to allow the Seminoles to remain in the unsettled southern portions of Florida, if the Indians will gather their people at the Army's camp. Jesup writes two letters to Secretary Poinsett and sends them off, while the troops enjoy the truce. Samuel Colt arrives in mid-March, trying to sell the Army on purchase of his new revolvers and rifles, which the officers test and most reject due to misfires. On 15 March, Jesup receives a sharp denial of the Seminoles' proposal from Poinsett. Jesup calls a meeting to announce the response, but the Indians refuse to come. On the 21st, Jesup orders Colonel Twiggs to use his 2d Dragoons to disarm all the Indians in the camp and take them into custody. This nets more than 500 Seminole captives. In this same period Taylor's men capture chief Holatoochee and 40 more warriors.

Opposite: *Gaines' men build a hasty log breastworks to fight off the attacking Seminoles. He names it "Camp Izard" after one of the officers killed. Gaines and his men survive only because Colonel Clinch arrives with fresh troops and food. ("Battle at Camp Izard," Jackson Walker)*

Right: *After the Dade massacre and other attacks, calls to muster militia went to South Carolina, Louisiana, Alabama, and Georgia. Part of Georgia's quota of 3,000 for Federal service were the Macon Volunteers. ("The Macon Volunteers, April 1836," Jackson Walker. National Guard Bureau print)*

Above: *Fighting in the Florida swamps was often conducted as ambushes and close hand-to-hand combat between small groups. ("From Right, Left and Centre," Jackson Walker)*

Opposite: *The lack of money for horses and equipment meant that for years the men of the "foot Artillery" were trained and served as infantry as a normal part of their service. ("Private, 3d U.S. Artillery Regiment, Spring 1836," Don Troiani, Don Troiani Collection)*

22–23 *March.* Everglades Battle.
A detachment of sailors and men from the 1st, 3d, and 4th Artillery under Lieutenant Colonel James Bankhead engages Seminoles holding positions on a swamp hummock. Bankhead uses a double envelopment, but due to deep water, one flank must move in rowboats to attack. Fearful of being surrounded, the Indians disperse.

April. Harney's Special Mission.
Jesup gives Lieutenant Colonel Harney the mission of capturing Old Sam, one of the few remaining Seminole chiefs. Harney picks 50 dragoons and 50 men from the 3d Artillery and sets off into the swamps. On the 24th, an Indian camp is attacked in a two-and-a-half-hour battle, but Old Sam is not found. A company of the 4th Artillery fights a separate engagement on the 29th near Micanopy.

1 May. Lee Resumes River Projects. St. Louis.
Now Captain Robert E. Lee returns with his family and begins contracting for the work on the river rapids and the diversion dams for the harbor. When Congress fails to authorize money to finish, Lee gets the city to loan money to complete the dams. A four-mile channel is also opened through the rapids. He continues working in St. Louis until July 1840.

8 May–October. Army Moves Cherokees. Georgia-Tennessee.
Scott's troops gather the last Cherokees for removal. The 3d and 4th Artillery, 4th Infantry, and six companies of 2d Dragoons are sent from Florida to help. In Order No. 35 Scott directs his men to give consideration to the Indians during the move, but that is often ignored. He organizes assembly centers, and as groups are gathered they are sent with an officer and several physicians but are otherwise unguarded and under the supervision of their own Indian leaders. The last and largest group of Cherokees starts later in the year than planned. Unseasonably harsh weather and delays cause many Indians to perish of illness, poor food, and exposure during the 1,200-mile march called the "Trail of Tears."

15 May. Zachary Taylor Assumes Florida Command.
Jesup turns the campaign over to Brigadier General Zachary Taylor and returns to Washington to resume his duties as Army Quartermaster General. Taylor, already known as "Old Rough and Ready," has 1,833 Regulars and about 500 Volunteers in his Florida command.

June–August. Dragoons Engage Seminoles. Kenahapa Prairie, Florida Territory.
On 17 June detachments of the 2d Dragoons skirmish with Seminoles while searching the prairie area in north Florida. Continuing their patrols, the dragoons have another fight near Fort Norton, Georgia, on 16 August.

5 July. Topographical Engineers Corps and 8th Infantry Established.
Topographical engineers are reorganized into a separate corps of 36 officers under Colonel John J. Abert. The 8th Infantry Regiment is also authorized, and each infantry company is increased by adding a sergeant and 38 privates, increasing a regiment's strength from 547 to 937. Each artillery regiment receives a fourth company, and each company adds 16 privates. All officers (except generals) and soldiers receive an extra daily food ration after five years of service. A private's pay is raised to $8 per month and a sergeant major's to $17, but $1 per month is held back until the end of the soldier's enlistment to prevent desertion. For ten years of service, 106 acres of land is promised to every enlisted man, but within days Congress reduces the pay again and withdraws the land grants.

Summer–Fall. **First Topographical Corps Exploration. Fort Snelling.**
Lieutenant John C. Fremont accompanies scientist Joseph N. Nicollet on the first western expedition sponsored by the new Topographical Corps. The explorers travel west as far as the Minnesota–South Dakota border, and then return with observations on the geography and plants in the area. The 8th Infantry is sent to Sackets Harbor, New York, as soon as its companies are recruited.

5–31 December. **Scott Sent to Calm Northern Border.**
On 5 December, Scott is again sent north to calm relations with Canada. A group of Patriots has crossed from Detroit and raided Windsor, Canada. Several were captured and executed by the British, outraging sympathetic Americans. Avoiding the use of troops, Scott travels east through the American border towns, calming the excited citizens.

1839

January. **Status of the Army.**
The Regular Army is authorized at 12,539. The Senior Army leaders are Major General Alexander Macomb, commanding general, and Brigadier Generals Gaines and Scott, commanding the Western and Eastern Divisions, respectively. Brevet Brigadier General Zachary Taylor has field command in Florida. His troops have built or reconstructed 53 forts, 8,000 feet of bridging, and almost 1,000 miles of new roads.

January. **Scott Sent to End Aroostook War. Maine.**
A long-standing conflict between Maine and New

Brunswick over ownership of the border Aroostook area threatens to escalate into war. President Van Buren gives Scott the mission of restoring peace. Before leaving Washington, Scott successfully lobbies for a six-month militia call-up and authority to spend up to $10 million to settle border claims with Canada.

15 February. **Poinsett Approves Taylor's Plan.**
Taylor receives approval for his plan to divide northern Florida into 20-mile- (later 18-mile-) square areas. A small fort with a 20-man garrison, half of them mounted, will be located in the center of each square, with connecting roads and trails throughout each square for rapid movement and patrolling. He estimates it will take the equivalent of four full regiments to implement the plan.

20 March. **Seminoles Ambush Army Boat. Miami River. Florida Territory.**
A boat of 2d Infantry is ambushed on the river by a large band of Seminoles. The commander, Captain Samuel A. Russell, directs the men to land and attack.

Russell falls after being hit five times, and a Lieutenant Woodruff takes command, organizing a fighting withdrawal.

5–25 March. Scott Ends Aroostook War. Augusta, Maine.

Scott arrives in Augusta on 5 March with his adjutant, Captain Robert Anderson, and aide, Lieutenant Erasmus D. Keyes. He charms the Maine legislature and receives approval to be their negotiator. By chance, the senior British general in Canada, an enemy in 1813, is now a personal friend of Scott's. The two generals soon reach agreement, and the "war" is over. Scott's reputation is so high that he considers proposals to be a candidate for President in the approaching election, but he eventually declines.

Spring. **Second Nicollet-Fremont Expedition. St. Louis.**

Secretary Poinsett and Colonel Abert sponsor a second, larger Topographical Corps expedition led by Nicollet, with Fremont again as an assistant. This time the group follows the Missouri River to Fort Pierre, north to Devils Lake, then south on the Minnesota River to the Mississippi. The scientific studies and geographic information are published and used by the Corps.

22 May. **Army Commanding General Declares Victory. Fort King. Florida Territory.**

Major General Macomb, Commanding General of the Army, who arrived earlier in the month, meets with Seminole leaders. He promises to permit the Indians to settle peacefully along the Kissimmee River if they

Left: *Indicated only by the red silk sash around his waist, this officer is speaking with a friendly Indian scout while his enlisted men wait in the background. The soldiers are wearing the leather forage cap that could be folded flat for storage. ("The American Soldier, 1839," H. Charles McBarron, Army Art Collection, NMUSA)*

Right: *David Moniac was a Creek Indian and West Point graduate. He left the Army in 1822 but returned to command the Creek Mounted Volunteers against the Seminoles. He was killed while leading his men at the battle of Wahoo Swamp in November 1836. ("Tribal Duel," Jackson Walker)*

will cease hostilities and bring in their followers by 15 July. A truce is agreed and a treaty signed. Macomb issues a General Order announcing "victory" and several days later departs for Washington.

Summer. **Army Improves Training. Camp Washington, New Jersey.**
Scott organizes a "Grand Camp of Instruction" near Trenton for Regular troops in his Eastern Division. They are brought together for drill and training that includes maneuvers with the companies of light mounted artillery, one from each artillery regiment. Two companies—Company C (Captain Samuel Ringgold) and Company E (Captain Braxton Bragg, 3d Artillery)—are to become famous.

July–November. **Non-Treaty Seminoles Resume Fighting. Florida Territory.**
Non-treaty Seminoles ignore the truce and resume attacks. On 21 July a company of the 6th Infantry battles Indians near Fort Andrews. Two days later 160 Seminoles make a surprise attack and overrun a camp of 2d Dragoons under Lieutenant Colonel Harney,

who barely escapes. Eighteen dragoons are killed, and several of the men captured are tortured to death. On 29 August, a 17-man detachment of the 6th holds off 50 Indians near Fort Andrews. In September elements of the 6th and the 3d Artillery have separate skirmishes with Seminoles on the 10th and 27th. The last fight of the year occurs on 25 November when the 3d Artillery engages Seminoles near Picolata.

1840

January. **Status of the Army.**
Regular Army strength is 716 officers and 8,988 enlisted men. There are 186 officers and 2,815 deployed in Florida with the 1st, 2d, 4th, 6th, and 7th Infantry Regiments, 2d and 3d Artillery, and 2d Dragoons. The 3d Infantry is in southwest Texas on patrol and road construction duty, while the 5th and 8th Infantry are posted on northern and western borders with the 1st Dragoons and 1st and 4th Artillery. A few artillery detachments also man coastal defenses.

January–April. **Seventh Infantry Tracks Seminoles. Florida Territory.**

The cool season brings more activity, but Taylor is sick and worn out. On 26 February, he asks permission to turn over the command on 1 May. In three small skirmishes, elements of the 7th Infantry engage Seminole bands. Near Fort King on 28 March, a patrol of 16 men led by Captain Gabriel J. Rains is ambushed by more than 90 Indians. Rains leads a charge of 12 survivors out of the ambush but is badly wounded and must be carried to the fort. Taylor agrees to test the use of bloodhounds to track the Seminoles, but the highly controversial experiment is a failure. During the month of April, sweeps made by the 2d Dragoons, 1st, 6th, and 7th Infantry, and 3d Artillery result in six engagements.

1–6 May. **Taylor Turns Over Command.**

On 1 May, Taylor departs for Louisiana. Colonel David Twiggs takes temporary command until Brevet Brigadier General Walker K. Armistead assumes formal command on 6 May. Armistead was top graduate of the second West Point class (1803) and former Chief Engineer. He reports his army's strength to be 214 officers and 3,403 enlisted men, of whom 564 are sick. In addition, he has 1,500 Florida militiamen. He continues Taylor's campaign, trying to force the remaining Seminoles into southern Florida.

2–28 May. **Winnebagos on Rampage. Wisconsin Territory.**

The 8th Infantry under Colonel William J. Worth is sent from Sackets Harbor, New York to Camp McKeon, Wisconsin, after a band of Winnebago Indians leaves the reservation and attacks settlers in the region.

May–September. **Troops Continue Hunt for Seminoles. Florida Territory.**

On 19 May, a lieutenant and five men of the 2d Infantry are killed in a Seminole ambush. Nine other small-scale encounters take place over the summer. In June, Captain Benjamin L. E. Bonneville leads a 7th Infantry patrol deep into Big Swamp, catching a large band of Seminoles by surprise. Lieutenant Colonel Bennett Riley disguises his 2d Infantry men as Indians and uses guerrilla tactics in successful attacks against Indian camps. Harney does much the same with his dragoons.

October. **More Regular Troops Assigned to Florida.**

The War Department, determined to end the war, sends reinforcements. The 8th Infantry completes its task with the Winnebagos and is sent by steamboat to help with the Seminoles. A few weeks later, the 3d Infantry arrives at Fort King from Texas, where it has been building roads and clearing rivers. Also arriving at Fort Pierce to join Company A, 3d Artillery, is newly commissioned Second Lieutenant William T. Sherman.

November. **Peace Initiative by Armistead Fails.**

Armistead meets with Seminole leaders to negotiate a peaceful removal. The talks last two weeks while the Indians receive government supplies; then, to Armistead's dismay, they disappear. Fighting resumes, and Armistead divides his command into three regional districts for better control.

3–24 December. **Dragoons Conduct Major Operation. Fort Dallas.**

Lieutenant Colonel William Harney leads a 90-man detachment out of Fort Dallas (now Miami) and into the everglades. He has 16 canoes carrying 21 dragoons armed with new Colt rifles and 69 men from the 3d Artillery. They are dressed and painted like Indians despite Armistead's orders not to do that. Harney seeks retaliation for the night attack his men suffered 18 months before by attacking the camp of the Seminole chief responsible. The attack is successful; several braves

FLYING ARTILLERY

Left: *Captain George Peter's battery of light "flying" artillery was considered an expensive experiment in its day. All the cannoneers rode horseback rather than walk. ("Captain Peter's Battery, 1st American Light Artillery," Colonel Harry C. Larter, Jr., Collection of Major Charles West)*

The term "flying artillery" refers to a light artillery battery or company in which all the cannoneers ride on horseback, as opposed to being "mounted," which has some men riding on the limbers. In 1808 Congress authorized a regiment of mounted light artillery. Only one company, Captain George Peter's, was equipped, and in 1809 it was dismounted like the rest of the regiment to save money. During the War of 1812, five batteries of the light regiment were remounted and used in the northern campaigns, but then the 1815 Army reorganization eliminated the light artillery completely. In 1821, a light artillery company was authorized in each of the four artillery regiments (1st–4th), but none were mounted until September 1838, when Secretary of War Joel R. Poinsett directed they be equipped as planned.

Captain Samuel Ringgold's Company C, 3d U.S. Artillery, was the first to be equipped; he placed all his men on horses, making it a true "flying" light artillery company. The remaining three companies were initially "mounted" light artillery with men riding horses as well as the caissons and limbers into action. A second light company was formed in the 3d Artillery in 1845.

In 1839 a "camp of instruction" for the light artillery was established at Trenton, New Jersey, using material translated by Lieutenants Daniel Tyler and Robert Anderson from French regulations and manuals. Ringgold preferred British methods and trained his company in that manner. A revised American artillery manual issued in 1843 incorporated elements of both.

The two primary theories Ringgold emphasized for the "flying" artillery were speed and precision. The first was accomplished with a new "family" of American artillery weapons. Changes in gun-carriage design permitted the gun and limber to be hooked together for traveling, reducing the number of men and horses required in the battery. Mounted on the light field carriages were the Model 1840 light smoothbore brass six-pound gun and the 12-pound howitzer. The six-pounder's rate of fire depended largely on how quickly the gun could be relaid after firing. A well-trained crew could average two to three rounds per minute in battle conditions depending on the type of round. The second theory, precision, was accomplished by practicing to perfection Ringgold's standardized loading and firing drill.

The Mexican War provided the ultimate "field test" for Ringgold's theories. In battle after battle American mounted artillery companies raced across the field, dominating the action. The heavier Mexican guns were no match for the maneuverability and firing speed of the American guns. Ringgold's guns unlimbered beyond effective Mexican infantry range, loaded, and fired on the enemy's batteries "before they could touch off their first shots."

During the action, Ringgold's horse was struck by an enemy shell that mangled both of Ringgold's thighs. Mortally wounded, Ringgold died three days later, never knowing of General Taylor's report that credited his flying artillery guns with winning the battle.

—*Vince Hawkins*

are killed and the chief and three other braves are captured and hanged. After two weeks of more searching, Harney returns to the fort.

1841

January. **Status of the Army.**
Army strength is 733 officers and 9,837 enlisted men. Most of the Army is deployed in Florida. During the year, several improvements are made to Army weapons. The Ordnance Department begins inspecting the production of Army cannons in the civilian factories, resulting in better quality. The Model 1841 rifle is also introduced. It is the first to use a percussion cap rather than a flint and needs less powder, reducing the recoil. Production of flintlocks ends.

2–4 March. **Second Infantry Surprises Seminoles. Fort Brooks. Florida Territory.**
Lieutenant William Alburtis springs a counter-ambush on Seminoles lying in wait near the fort by circling to the rear of the Indians and attacking them. Two days later a Seminole band attacking a train is driven off in tree-to-tree fighting and a charge by the infantrymen.

4 March. **Harrison Inaugurated as President.**
William Henry Harrison, a former officer in Wayne's Legion and a major general during the War of 1812, becomes the ninth President and Commander-in-Chief. He dies after one month in office.

5 March. **Bell Appointed Secretary of War.**
John Bell is made the 16th Secretary of War by President Harrison. Bell is concerned over the expense of the Seminole War, which is costing $92,300 a month, not including the pay of the Regulars in Florida. He begins looking for ways to reduce forces and costs.

6 April. **John Tyler Inaugurated President.**
Vice President John Tyler becomes the tenth President and Commander-in-Chief. Tyler served as a captain in the Virginia militia during the War of 1812.

1 May–4 June. **Sherman Escorts Indians. Fort Pierce, Florida Territory.**
On 1 May Lieutenant Sherman is sent out with ten men to escort Seminole Chief Coacoochee and a small group of Indians to the fort for talks. After weeks of no progress, the fort commander seizes the Indians on 4 June for transport to Louisiana. They are later released after promising to bring in the rest of their band.

31 May. **Worth Replaces Armistead.**
At his own request Armistead is reassigned. On the 31st Colonel William Worth becomes commander of the forces in Florida, termed the Army of the South and composed of about 4,800 Regulars. Worth reduces costs by removing civilian teamsters, guides, and others from the Army payroll, angering local officials already complaining about Army interference with merchants.

June. **Worth Initiates New Campaign.**
Worth concentrates on eliminating the Seminoles' sources of food. He emphasizes continuous pressure throughout the summer planting and growing season by use of many small, fast-moving detachments. In addition, settlers are encouraged to move into former Indian areas under supervision of junior officers and with support of Army rations and security. Taking personal charge, Worth aggressively campaigns during the hot summer, sparking many small skirmishes.

25 June. **Major General Macomb Dies. Washington.**
Major General Alexander Macomb, Commanding General of the Army, dies at age 59 of apoplexy (stroke). He began his military career at age 16 in the New York militia. Commissioned as a coronet in 1799, he was one of the first to receive formal training at West Point.

Opposite: *Robert E. Lee, shown here as an engineer captain, spent the first years of his military career planning and supervising construction of fortifications and handling other engineer projects such as flood control and harbor improvement. ("Captain Robert E. Lee," Washington, Custis, Lee Collection, Washington and Lee University)*

Right: *In 1837, Osceola was captured under a flag of truce and imprisoned by General Jesup. He died in prison within a year. ("The Captive Osceola, October 1837," Jackson Walker)*

5 July. **Scott Becomes Commanding General of the Army.**
Promoted to major general with date of rank 25 June, Winfield Scott is approved as the senior officer of the U.S. Army. He is 55 years old and has been a Regular since 1808. John E. Wool fills the vacant Regular brigadier position. Scott has finally surpassed Gaines, his rival, who decides not to resign.

5 August. **First Infantry Regiment Departs Florida.**
The 1st Infantry departs for Jefferson Barracks after three and a half years in Florida. The regiment has lost six officers and 135 enlisted men to disease and combat in the war.

13 September. **Bell Resigns as Secretary of War.**
John Bell resigns as secretary and Albert M. Lea, Chief Clerk of the War Department, supervises the department for a month.

10 October. **Eighth Infantry Survives Storm. Punta Rassa, Florida.**
During the night, a terrific storm hits the Florida coast where four companies of the 8th Infantry are camped. The high tide floods the area and the next morning, nothing remains—except the 200 men who sit waiting on the limbs of several large oak trees. There are no casualties, and every man has kept his musket.

12 October. **Spencer Made Secretary of War.**
John C. Spencer is appointed 18th Secretary of War by President Tyler.

17 October. **Second Dragoons Return North.**
Five companies of the 2d Dragoons depart Florida, including Company D, which has been fighting more than five years. They are ordered west to Forts Towson (Indian Territory) and Jesup (Louisiana), with Jesup as the regimental headquarters. A later experiment with arming two of the companies at Fort Jesup with lances is unsuccessful.

20 December. **Patrols in Big Cypress Swamp. Florida Territory.**
The 8th Infantry spends most of the month wading through water or dragging boats over hammocks, destroying crops, and searching deserted Seminole villages. On the 20th they have a sharp fight with about 20 Indians, losing two men. The Indians are dispersed and the bodies of the two soldiers are weighted and sunk in a pond.

1842

January. **Status of the Army.**
Army strength is 754 officers and 10,415 enlisted men. Major General Winfield Scott is the Army's

Left: *Colonel Richard Gentry, commander of the Missouri Volunteers, along with many of his men and almost every officer and sergeant of the 6th Infantry, are killed or wounded during the attack at Lake Okeechobee. ("The Gentry Lane," Jackson Walker)*

commanding general, while brigadiers Edmund Gaines and John Wool, the Army Inspector General, command the Western and Eastern Divisions respectively. Colonel William Worth commands the Army's regiments in Florida, but many of his men are sick; more than 200 have died of disease in the previous eight months.

25 January. Second Infantry Battles Near Dunn's Lake. Florida Territory.

Struggling for six weeks through the swamps, 102 men of the 2d Infantry, led by Major Joseph Plympton, surprise Seminoles camped near the lake. In a 90-minute battle the infantrymen drive the Indians from their log fortifications and secure the hummock.

February–March. Sixth Infantry and Third Artillery Depart Florida.

On 14 March, Colonel Worth reports to Scott that fewer than 200 Seminoles remain and that more Army troops can be withdrawn from Florida. Shortly, two more regiments leave. The 3d Artillery departs Florida after almost six years. They have lost 11 officers and 158 enlisted men to disease and combat. The 6th Infantry, which lost 10 officers and 129 enlisted men, goes to Jefferson Barracks; it stays only a month before being sent to Fort Towson on the Red River in Indian Territory.

19 April–May. Battle of Big Hummock. Pelikakaha, Florida Territory.

On 19 April, 40 Seminole warriors led by Chief Hallack-Tustenugge are found on a fortified swamp hammock. Colonel Worth personally directs a frontal assault by companies of the 2d, 4th, and 8th Infantry through the mud and tall sawgrass, while a detachment of 2d Dragoons moves to the Indians' rear. After a period of heavy firing, the Indians flee, leaving their food and equipment. Ten days later Hallack comes to Worth's camp requesting talks. After several days of feeding the Indians, Worth invites Hallack to talk at Fort King. Before departing for the fort, Worth leaves orders to wait three days, then, if no other orders arrive, to seize the waiting Indians. At the same time, at the fort, Hallack is also taken. In all, 43 warriors and 71 women and children—almost half of the Indians estimated to remain in Florida—are taken prisoner.

May. Second Infantry Leaves.

The 2d Infantry departs after five years with losses of two officers and 131 enlisted men from disease and combat. Its companies are sent to posts on the Great Lakes frontier. The remaining five companies of 2nd Dragoons leave in May. The regiment suffered seven officers dead, two killed in combat. Twenty enlisted men are dead in combat, 172 from disease.

EYEWITNESS: FREMONT'S FIRST EXPEDITION, 1842

In 1842 Lieutenant John C. Fremont, Army Corps of Topographical Engineers, was chosen to lead an expedition to explore better routes for settlers to use in crossing the Rocky Mountains to the Oregon territory. He took the 23-man party to present-day Wyoming and the eastern edge of the mountains. On 15 August, he spotted what he thought was the highest peak in the range, a mountain that would become known as Fremont Peak, and went ahead with a small group to climb it. They rode on mules until the slope became too steep and dismounted.

From this point our progress was uninterrupted climbing. Hitherto I had worn a pair of thick moccasins, but here I put on a thin pair, which I had brought for the purpose, as now the use of our toes became necessary to a further advance. . . . Our cautious method of advancing in the outset had spared my strength; and, with the exception of a slight disposition to headache, I felt no remains of yesterday's illness. In a few minutes we had reached a point where the buttress was overhanging. . . . Putting hands and feet in the crevices between the blocks, I succeeded in getting over it, and, when I reached the top, found my companions in a small valley below.

Descending to them, we continued climbing, and in a short time reached the crest. I sprang upon the summit, another step would have precipitated me into an immense snow field five hundred feet below. . . . As soon as I gratified the first feeling of curiosity I descended, and each man ascended in his turn, for I would only allow one at a time to mount the unstable and precarious slab, which it seemed a breath would hurl in the abyss below. We mounted the barometer in the snow of the summit, and fixing a ramrod in the crevice, unfurled the national flag to wave in the breeze where never a flag waved before.

Having now made what observations our means afforded, we proceeded to descend. We had accomplished an object of laudable ambition, and beyond the strict order of our instructions. We had climbed the loftiest peak of the Rocky Mountains, and looked down upon the snow a thousand feet below, and standing where never human foot had stood before, felt the exultation of first explorers.

—Kevin M. Hymel

---

17 May. **Last Combat Actions of the War. Fort Wacahoota.**
Two companies of the 7th Infantry engage a band of Indians near the fort. The same day another company of the 7th skirmishes with Seminoles at Clay's Landing on the Suwanee River. These are the last two official combat actions of the war.

10 June–August. **First Fremont Expedition. Kansas City, Missouri.**
Lieutenant John C. Fremont leads an Army expedition of 30 men, including Army Scout Kit Carson, to explore the Oregon Trail. By August they are at South Pass mapping routes for emigration through the Rocky Mountains.

20 July. **Seventh Infantry Departs Florida.**
The 7th Infantry is reassigned. During its three years of fighting in Florida, the 7th lost four officers and 116 enlisted men to illness and combat.

August. **Scott Initiates Army Reforms.**
Major General Scott issues General Order No. 53, which requires due judicial process for offenses and prohibits arbitrary punishments by officers and noncommissioned officers. Scott also reduces the Army staff and discourages the awarding of brevet promotions.

14 August. **Worth Declares Seminole War is Over.**
With authority given him in May by the Secretary of War, Worth issues Order No. 28, declaring the war ended (again). Worth takes a 90-day leave and is promoted to brevet brigadier general backdated to 1 March. He places Colonel Josiah H. Vose, 4th Infantry, in charge of gathering the last Indians and coordinating final arrangements. Things do not go smoothly, however, and white-Indian incidents threaten to renew hostilities.

23 August. **Congress Cuts Army Strength.**
Congress directs a reduction in Army strength. Ten privates are eliminated from each company, cutting

TOPOGRAPHICAL ENGINEERS

Topographical engineers have been an essential part of the Army since the Revolution. In 1777 Robert Erskine accepted an appointment as General George Washington's geographer with the specific mission "to Survey the Roads and take Sketches of the Country where the army is to Act." When Erskine died in 1780, two geographer positions were established, one each with the northern and southern departments of the Army. Even at this early date, the topographical engineers, or "topogs" as they came to be known, functioned as a distinct group of engineers. After the Revolution, Congress retained one to serve as surveyor of public lands in compliance with the Land Ordinance of 1785. On 3 March 1813, Congress authorized eight topographical engineers and eight assistants for the Army General Staff.

In the Army reduction following the War of 1812, only two topographical engineers were retained to complete surveys of Lake Champlain and the northern frontier. In 1816 Congress increased the number to ten. Despite recognition of their valuable service, the topographers were not members of the Corps of Engineers nor had they separate branch status.

In 1818, the Topographical Engineers were combined with the Corps of Engineers into a single Engineer Department. The topographers became part of the Topographical Bureau. They were responsible for compiling maps, caring for surveying instruments, and collecting and preserving specimens from scientific expeditions. Topographer officers led surveying and scientific expeditions into the west and handled the boundary surveys; one served in military operations against the Seminole Indians. With the General Survey Act of 1824, they became heavily involved in improving river navigation and performing other civil works.

By 1834 the massive number of work projects forced a shift in their duties from surveying to engineering and construction. That year the topographers took over coastal lighthouse construction, and in 1836 the Coast Survey was reestablished. In 1838 topogs began assisting the railroads with surveying and construction supervision.

On 5 July 1838, Congress authorized a separate Topographical Engineer Corps of 36 officers but no enlisted personnel. The new Corps assumed responsibility for all major river and harbor improvements, began road-building projects, worked on boundary surveys, and embarked on several public works projects in Washington, D.C.

At the outbreak of the Mexican War the Corps had 42 officers. Of these, 26 served with the armies in Mexico with duties of observation, reconnaissance, preparing defenses and fortifications, and mapping. Twelve of the officers who served in Mexico had become generals by the Civil War. The more notable of these were John C. Fremont, Stephen W. Kearny, George G. Meade, John Pope, and Joseph E. Johnston. In 1863 the independent status of the Topographical Engineer Corps ended when it merged with the Corps of Engineers. Of the 72 officers who served with the Topographical Corps during its short span from 1838 to 1863, all but eight obtained their commissions from the U.S. Military Academy.

—*Vince Hawkins*

Above: *Topographical engineers were authorized by the War Department to conduct mapping surveys and to explore routes for roads and later railroads. (Topographical Engineer insignia, U.S. Army Regulations, 1851)*

Army strength by about 1,400. Overall Army authorized strength is 8,600 officers and men. The number of regiments is not cut, but the 2d Dragoons are to be dismounted and converted to a rifle regiment. The number of horses in each of the 1st Dragoon companies is reduced to only 40.

August–October. **Vose Departs with Fourth Infantry.**
Colonel Vose is given permission to take his 4th Infantry Regiment to Jefferson Barracks. The regiment, in Florida since the 1820s, was engaged in combat during the entire war; one of its officers, Major Dade, was among the first to fall. The 4th lost six officers and 128 enlisted men.

1 November–31 December. **Worth Renews Efforts to End Hostilities.**
Worth returns from leave and talks with the leaders of the remaining small bands of Seminoles and Creeks. Cash rewards bring in a few Indians, and others are captured; all are shipped west. Lieutenant Colonel Ethan Allen Hitchcock, 3d Infantry, and grandson of Ethan Allen, continues pursuit of fugitive Indians in the field. Hitchcock convinces one of the largest groups to give up, and they are shipped out in January. Only a few hundred remain hidden in the Everglades. The total count of Indians and Negroes removed is less that 6,000. In all, the Army suffered 290 wounded and 1,466 deaths, including 328 killed in action. The Volunteers had 55 men killed and 267 wounded. Many more died of disease, but no records were kept.

1 December. **Son of Secretary of War Hanged**
Midshipman Philip Spencer, son of the Secretary of War, is hanged for mutiny by the captain of the brig *Somers.*

1843

January. **Status of the Army.**
Army strength is 781 officers and 9,847 enlisted men, but many enlistments are due to expire soon and new recruits will not be accepted until the Army has dropped to its approved size.

3–8 March. **Secretaries of War Change.**
Spencer resigns on 3 March and five days later is replaced by James M. Porter as 18th Secretary of War.

13 March. **Second Dragoons Dismounted. Jefferson Barracks, Missouri.**
General Order No. 22 directs the demoralized 2d Dragoons to turn their remaining horses over to the 1st

Above: *On an Army post, the parade ground was the center of activity, with ceremonial functions, reviews, dress parades, band concerts, changing of the guards, and posting of colors for reveille and retreat. ("Watching Parade, Fort Scott, 1842–1853," Jerry D. Thomas)*

Dragoons. The bitter dragoons keep their uniforms and traditions, but they are to be armed with rifles and must begin retraining as infantry.

22 April. **Third Infantry Arrives. Jefferson Barracks.**
Lieutenant Colonel Hitchcock arrives with the officers and men of the 3d Infantry. Included are Second Lieutenants George Sykes and Don Carlos Buell, who joined the regiment in Florida. Only the 8th Infantry is left in Florida. In its two years of combat, the 3d has lost 70 officers and men.

May–July. **First Dragoons Patrol Western Prairies.**
Captain Nathan Boone leads a patrol of 62 1st Dragoons out of Fort Gibson and along the Arkansas River, then on the Santa Fe Trail, where he meets three companies under Captain Philip St. George Cooke. Cooke is escorting trader caravans along the trail, protecting them from both Indians and Texas bandits. Boone then explores the Canadian and Washita Rivers before returning on 14 July.

30 May–June. Fremont Leads Second Expedition. St. Louis.
A second Army expedition under Fremont departs for Oregon. After crossing the mountains at South Pass in June, Fremont's group swings north to the Snake and Columbia Rivers.

30 September. Lieutenant Grant Reports for Duty. Jefferson Barracks.
Brevet Second Lieutenant Ulysses S. Grant reports for his first duty assignment. An expert horseman, he arrives on his own mount expecting to be assigned to the dragoons. Instead, he is posted to the 4th Infantry, where he becomes close friends with Second Lieutenant James Longstreet.

25 October. Fremont Reaches Oregon Territory.
Lieutenant Fremont leads his expedition into the small village of Walla Walla, completing his survey of the Oregon Trail.

Above: *In his 1829 inaugural address, President Andrew Jackson set a policy to relocate about 100,000 American Indians to the west side of the Mississippi. The Army was given the distasteful job of gathering the Indians and escorting them to their new lands. ("Trail of Tears," Robert Lindneux, Woolaroc Museum, Bartlesville, OK)*

Right: *As the only U.S. mounted troops in most of the West, dragoons spent long days on scouting patrols, explorations, and escort duties. (Hugh Brown, HFC Commissioned Art Collection)*

EYEWITNESS: SECOND SEMINOLE WAR

During the Second Seminole War, First Lieutenant George A. McCall served with the 4th Infantry, part of Major General Edmund P. Gaines' force in Florida, and for a time acted as the general's aide-de-camp. McCall later served with distinction in both the War with Mexico and the Civil War and retired as a general officer in 1863. A voluminous and articulate letter writer, Lieutenant McCall recounts the campaign in Big Cypress Swamp in the following letter:

Fort Brooke, Tampa, 27 February 1842.

My Dear E,

Give me joy: I am out of the "Big Cypress" at last; and in good health. . . . I was ordered here with my company, which with one other of the 4th Regiment now constitutes the garrison of this place. Four companies of our regiment will probably be here during the summer. The 6th Regiment has left for Jefferson Barracks, and the 2nd Infantry and 3rd Artillery will go in a month or two to the North or East. All this, you see, is favorable to the closing of the war. If Assinoah comes in, he will bring in about 120 souls, and then there will be but 190 or 200 left. When our regiment will get out, and where we shall go, I can form no conjecture.

I must go to bed, for now I have a bed! I slept last night in a bed, and in a house for the first time since I left fort Gibson on the 15th September last.

God bless you.
G.A.McC.

P.S. As the transport which is to carry the mail will be detained till tomorrow, I will give you a resumé of our late campaign.

We marched to the Big Cypress, a most formidable swamp, extending diagonally across the peninsula from northeast to southwest, seventy-five miles, with an average width of thirty miles. The troops numbered 800 men, and were commanded by Major William G. Belknap, 8th infantry. The campaign lasted 52 days, during which period we made seven explorations of its depth, or, as they were called, 'scouts,' averaging seven days each; in other words, we were marching through water from six inches to three feet deep, 48 days. Three times we passed entirely through or across its widest parts. On the seventh

scout, no more than 200 men of the 800 could be mustered for duty; fevers, diarrhea, and swollen feet and ankles—the latter attributed by the surgeons to constant marching in the water—having laid up in the hospital three-fourths of the command. My own health being unaffected, enabled me to march in command of two of the four companies on this last fruitless expedition.

On all of these marches, I carried my seven days' rations in a bag rolled in my blanket and strapped across my shoulders, together with an extra flannel shirt (the only wear on such tramps) and pair of socks, besides my double gun—swords being worse than useless. Adieu, my dearest E.

—Vince Hawkins

Above: *In reality, few officers on campaign in the field would have been able to maintain the fine appearance of this captain for very long. Uniforms were very expensive and cleaning facilities crude or non-existent. (Collection of Colonel James Campbell, Jr.)*

WAR WITH MEXICO

1844–1848

WAR WITH MEXICO

1844–1848

Colonel Raymond K. Bluhm, Jr., USA (Ret)

I
n 1844 the ill-defined southern and western edge of the 1802 Louisiana Purchase that joins U.S. and Mexican territory is a source of increasing tension between the two nations. Mexicans see the presence of U.S. Army expeditions and the increasing number of American settlers in the area as signs of U.S. ambitions for further expansion. They are not entirely wrong. Many prominent Americans, including President Polk, believe in "Manifest Destiny" and see the Army as the instrument to achieve it.

The Army has been patrolling trails, contacting Indians, and probing the West with expeditions for some time, occasionally into Mexican territory. In January 1844 Lieutenant John Fremont enters California with an Army expedition, then slips out ahead of Mexican patrols. When Mexico threatens to invade the Republic of Texas, Colonel Zachary Taylor is ordered to form an "Army of Observation" at Fort Jesup, Louisiana. After Texas joins the Union, Taylor begins moving troops into the border area, ending up in 1846 eye to eye with Mexican forces over the Rio Grande River. Small incidents occur, but it is the ambush of a dragoon patrol and incursions into Texas by large Mexican detachments that finally ignite real fighting. While Congress debates war, Taylor fights and wins the first two battles on Texas soil. A week after a formal declaration, Taylor crosses the river into Mexico. At about the same time, Fremont, who has returned to California, receives mysterious orders from a presidential courier that apparently authorize him to seize California.

To support the war, Congress increases the Regular Army and initially authorizes the mobilization of 50,000 short-term Volunteers. More increases in Regulars and Volunteers are approved later, but the Mexican Army remains much larger. The American Army, however, has a growing corps of well-trained junior officers, especially in artillery and engineers, from West Point who add much to the quality of the force.

Within a few months, either by plan or chance, U.S. troops are invading Mexico from multiple directions. Taylor is fighting his way south toward Monterrey, and a column of 1st Dragoons and mounted Missouri Volunteers led by Colonel Steven Kearny are riding west to take control of New Mexico. Kearny enters Santa Fe without firing a shot and soon goes on to California, where in July, unknown to him, the independent Bear Flag Republic has been set up with Fremont's help. Soon after Kearny departs, the Missouri Volunteers under Colonel Alexander Doniphan march south into Mexico as an independent force to capture Chihuahua.

A second large army composed of most of the remaining Regulars and thousands of Volunteers is placed under Major General Winfield Scott. He captures the port of Vera Cruz in March 1847 with a large amphibious invasion and then advances inland to seize Mexico City. After a series of hard-fought battles, Scott's army occupies the city in September. A difficult and brutal guerrilla war against the American outposts and supply line to the coast continues until U.S. troops withdraw a year later. As with all wars of the period, the majority of losses are from disease rather than enemy action.

As the Volunteer regiments return home they are immediately released from service. Some have done very well, others have not, and some were returned early to get rid of them. Congress reduces the Regular Army to its prewar size and regiments are once again split up to garrison the frontier outposts.

The Regular Army that ends the Mexican War in 1848 is very different in many respects from its previous self. It started the war after the years in the

Florida swamps as an undermanned, but hard-bitten, veteran Indian-fighting force. Most operations were by detachments and the majority of junior and mid-level leaders had never seen, much less led or planned the support of, a force larger than their own company. Very few had even seen their full regiment. At all levels the officers and NCOs are now more experienced. They have assaulted fortifications, suffered enemy artillery fire, fought through towns, placed artillery batteries, maneuvered units large and small in the face of the enemy, and waged large campaigns over extended distances. They have also served with the Volunteers and seen all the weaknesses and strengths of American citizen-soldiers.

The officer ranks of Taylor's and Scott's armies are filled with the men who would in less than 15 years lead even greater armies against each other. Winning the war in Mexico was the Army's last great contribution to the geographic growth of the nation, almost doubling its size. The war was also the training ground for the Civil War that would almost destroy the growing nation.

Pages 278–279: *In September 1847, Gideon Pillow's brigade fights its way through a grove of trees outside Mexico City. Their objective is visible over the tree line—the Castle at Chapultepec. ("Pillow's Attack Advancing Through the Woods," James Walker, Army Art Collection, NMUSA)*

Above: *Captain Charles A. May's squadron of 2d Dragoons slashed through the enemy lines in an attack that climaxed the opening campaigns of the Mexican War at Resaca de la Palma, Texas, 9 May 1846. ("Remember Your Regiment," Army Art Collection, NMUSA)*

WAR WITH MEXICO

1844–1848

*"Brave Rifles! Veterans! You have been baptized in fire and blood
and have come out steel."*
—Major General Winfield Scott, Mexico City, 1848

1844

January. **Status of the Army.**
The Regular Army has four generals—Major General Winfield Scott, Commanding General, and Brigadiers Edmund Gaines, John Wool, and Thomas Jesup (Quartermaster General). Another 801 officers and 8,130 enlisted men serve in two technical corps (officers only in the Engineers and Topography), eight staff departments, and 14 line regiments: 1st–8th Infantry; 1st–4th Artillery; and 1st and 2d Dragoons. As Regular units return from Florida, they are reassigned, usually along the western frontier. None of the generals are West Point graduates, but five field-grade and most of the company-grade officers are graduates.

Above: *Quartermaster General Thomas S. Jesup, identified at center by the blue plume on his hat, is seen inspecting a saddle. Jesup had no enlisted men in his personnel; civilians were employed instead. ("Staff Officers, U.S. Army," H. Charles McBarron, Company of Military Historians)*

3–18 January. **Fremont Expedition. Sierra Nevada Mountains.**
Lieutenant John C. Fremont's expedition with chief guides Kit Carson and Thomas "Broken Hand" Fitzpatrick makes its way south along the eastern edge of the Sierra Nevadas. On the 11th they reach the shore of Pyramid Lake, named after a unique rock formation. Supplies are low and many horses are lame. On the 18th, Fremont decides to turn west and make a hazardous winter crossing of the mountains to California.

30 January. **Porter Resigns as Secretary of War.**
James Porter resigns and on 15 February is replaced by William Wilkins. Wilkins, a lawyer, has no previous military experience.

4–5 February. **Fremont Tries Crossing Mountains.**
Ignoring his guides, Fremont moves into the Sierra Nevadas. The expedition is soon scattered over 20 miles, with the horses floundering in neck-deep snow. While the others rest and prepare a path, Fremont and Carson take a small party to scout ahead. From Carson Pass, they see California but cannot go forward.

10–24 February. **Fremont Reaches California.**
The expedition packs down the snow and lays branches to make a path for the horses. Food is gone, so Fremont's dog and young horses are killed and eaten. On the 14th, while the men descend the western slope, Fremont falls into an icy stream and is saved by Carson. On the 24th, the exhausted and starving expedition arrives at Sutter's Fort, where they recover for two weeks.

March. **2d Dragoons Remounted. Fort Jesup, Louisiana.**
On the 4th Congress approves remounting the 2d Dragoons. Colonel David Twiggs proclaims a holiday and issues extra liquor. Two celebrating officers climb up on the post howitzer and a "mounted salute" is fired, setting the trousers of one officer afire. Following the 1833 tradition of the first dragoon regiment, each company is mounted on

ARMY BATTLE STREAMERS—WAR WITH MEXICO

PALO ALTO 1846

Palo Alto 1846	Cerro Gordo 1847
Resaca de la Palma 1846	Contreras 1847
Monterey 1846	Churubusco 1847
Buena Vista 1847	Molino del Ray 1847
Vera Cruz 1847	Chapultepec 1847

different color horses. The regiment begins wearing a yellow band on its caps.

April–May. **Fremont Leaves California.**
Mexican patrols search for Fremont and his men. They cross the Mojave Desert on the Old Spanish Trail, arriving at Mountain Meadows by 13 May. They are stalked by Indians most of the way and kill two but lose one of their own men in skirmishes.

22 April. **Military Regions Reorganized.**
The Army's Eastern and Western Divisions, discontinued in 1842, are reestablished with Regulars Wool and Gaines as commanders. The nine departments are distributed between the divisions, with brevet brigadier generals as commanders.

23–27 April. **Taylor Sent to Southwestern Frontier. Fort Smith.**
When Colonel Zachary Taylor is ordered to command the 1st Military District at Fort Jesup, he assumes his brevet rank of brigadier general. Major William W. S. Bliss is assigned as his deputy. On the 27th, secret orders direct Taylor to form "The Army of Observation" and take it to the Sabine River. Although the district is in Gaines' Western Division, he is not informed. Taylor has an independent command.

Above: *Despite his lack of military experience, William Wilkins (1779–1865) was selected to replace James Porter when he resigned the position of Secretary of War. ("William Wilkins," Robert Walter Weir, Army Art Collection, NMUSA)*

Above: *("2d Infantry Regiment, Winter Full Dress, 1841–1851," H. Charles McBarron, Company of Military Historians)*

Right: *Instilling military discipline and bearing into raw recruits is a never-ending but critical responsibility of the Army's noncommissioned and junior officers. The frequent breakdown of the militia system during peacetime brought many untrained militiamen into the Army. ("Drilling the Volunteers" U.S. Mexico at War, by Donald S. Frazier, © 1998 Gale Group. Reprinted by permission of Gale Group)*

April–August. **Troops Join Taylor. Fort Jesup.**
Eight companies of the 3d Infantry and eight of the 4th Infantry, a total of 290 men, arrive from Jefferson Barracks. They are followed by 376 remounted 2d Dragoons under Colonel Twiggs. The troops patrol the southwestern border areas.

August–September. **Dragoons Visit Indian Villages. Fort Leavenworth.**
As a show of strength, a large detachment of 1st Dragoons is sent to the villages along the Platte River. Twelve wagons and two 12-pounder howitzers are taken. Painter Charles Deas accompanies them. Councils are held with the Pawnees, Otos, and Potawatomis. Farther north, a company of 50 1st Dragoons from Fort Des Moines makes a similar circuit through the Iowa Territory, where conflicts are breaking out between the Sioux and displaced tribes from the east.

6 August. **Fremont Returns. St. Louis.**
After exploring for 14 months and traveling thousands of miles, Fremont's party returns to St. Louis.

30 November. **Western Defense Line Completed.**
Fort Wilkins, located on Lake Superior, is finished. It is the northernmost outpost in the outer chain of defensive western frontier forts started in the Tyler administration. The completed defensive forts are connected by a military road that now stretches from Canada to Fort Washita near the Texas border.

1845

January. **Status of the Army.**
Of 12,539 authorized, Army strength is only 813 officers and 7,760 enlisted men. Sporadic efforts are made to improve training, including attempts at larger unit training using the two regiments at the Jefferson Barracks infantry school. During the year, Major Samuel Ringgold's manual for light artillery, *Instruction of Field Artillery, Horse and Foot,* is adopted by the War Department. Infantry training is still conducted per Scott's *Infantry Tactics; Or, Rules for the Exercise and Maneuvers of the United States Infantry,* published in 1840. Officers have to buy their copies. The term "squadron" is adopted by the dragoons, indicating a unit of two or more companies.

MAJOR GENERAL ZACHARY TAYLOR

Due to his stocky, muscular build, an iron constitution, and preference for comfortable, unpretentious uniforms, Zachary Taylor's soldiers called him "Old Rough and Ready." His impeccable honesty, integrity, and compassion won him the respect and admiration of both his men and his enemies. Zachary Taylor was born at Montebello, Virginia, on 24 November 1784 and grew up near Louisville, Kentucky. In 1806, Taylor joined the Army as a short-term volunteer, and in 1808 he was appointed a first lieutenant in the 7th Infantry. In 1810 he was promoted to captain.

During the War of 1812 Taylor recruited and trained troops, fought Indians from Indiana to Missouri, built Fort Johnson on the Des Moines River, and ended up as a major in command of old Fort Knox. Following command of Fort Winnebago, Wisconsin, Taylor was promoted to lieutenant colonel of the 4th Infantry at New Orleans on 20 April 1819. He spent the next decade on the frontier building forts and roads, recruiting, and handling Indian affairs.

On 4 April 1832, Taylor was promoted to colonel and given command of the 1st Infantry, stationed at Fort Crawford. During the Black Hawk War, Taylor fought with distinction at Bad Axe River on 2 August 1832. In 1837, Taylor was sent to command the Army forces in Florida. In December, he defeated the Seminoles in a bitter action at Lake Okeechobee on Christmas Day. He was brevetted brigadier general for his victory, but after two years of inconclusive skirmishing he was unable to end the war. He requested a change of command, and on 21 April 1840 he returned to duty on the southwestern frontier.

Taylor's military career reached its zenith during the Mexican War. It made him a national hero and carried him to the White House. In 1845, Taylor was sent to Texas with 4,000 men; he made his forward post at Fort Texas (later Brown) opposite Matamoras. After hostilities began Taylor defeated an invading Mexican army more than twice the size of his own at Palo Alto on 8 May. He defeated them again the following day at Resaca de la Palma, then crossed the Rio Grande and occupied Matamoras. In July he was brevetted major general.

In September, reinforced by thousands of volunteers, Taylor moved toward Saltillo. On the 21st he launched an assault against the fortified city of Monterrey. When his attack bogged down, he negotiated an armistice that allowed the Mexican garrison to withdraw; he then entered the city. President Polk, however, terminated the armistice and ordered the advance to continue. In mid-November, Taylor took Saltillo but was then ordered to send most of his Regular troops and Volunteers to reinforce General Winfield Scott's campaign in central Mexico. With only 4,600 men, Taylor continued his advance until 21 February 1847, when he came upon a force of nearly 20,000 men under General Santa Anna at Buena Vista. Refusing an offer to surrender, Taylor stood his ground, repulsing the enemy in a desperate two-day battle. This victory effectively ended the war in the northern provinces, although Taylor remained in Mexico until November, when he returned to the United States and assumed a regional command.

Taylor was elected as the 12th President in March 1849. On 4 July 1850, he fell gravely ill; he died in the White House on 9 July 1850.

—*Vince Hawkins*

Above: *For his success on the battlefield in the War of Mexico, the already popular General Zachary Taylor was the choice for President of the United States in 1847. ("Zachary Taylor," White House Historical Association, White House Collection 64)*

Above: *During their expedition leading through the South Pass of the Oregon Trail, the 1st Dragoons made first contact with several Plains Indian tribes. (Hugh Brown, HFC Commissioned Art Collection)*

Right: *There are few descriptions of the 3d Infantry Regiment's undress uniform. ("3rd Infantry Regiment, Undress Uniform, 1846–1851," H. Charles McBarron, Company of Military Historians)*

4 March. **Polk Inaugurated President.**
James K. Polk becomes the 11th President and Commander-in-Chief of the Army. He has served as a major in the Tennessee militia.

6 March. **Marcy Made Secretary of War.**
William L. Marcy is appointed 20th Secretary of War by President Polk to replace Wilkins. Marcy saw action in the War of 1812 with a New York militia regiment.

18 May–24 August. **Oregon Trail-South Pass Expedition. Fort Leavenworth.**
Colonel Stephen W. Kearny leads four companies of 1st Dragoons, about 250 men, on a show of force through Indian country. Second Lieutenant Richard S. Ewell, just

returned from a year on recruiting duty, rides with Company A. Taking 19 wagons, 50 cattle, and 25 sheep, the regiment rides west along the Oregon Trail to Fort Laramie, stopping periodically for Kearny to hold councils with Sioux, Cheyenne, and Kiowa leaders. The whole unit returns on the Santa Fe Trail, a patrol of 2,200 miles in 99 days, without losing a man.

3 June–11 August. Dragoons Meet the Sioux.
Captain Edwin V. Sumner leads a squadron of 1st Dragoons into Sioux territory, holding the first councils with leaders of various Sioux tribal groups.

15 June–July. Taylor's Army Ordered to Texas. Fort Jesup.
Taylor's Army of Observation is ordered to move to the Texas coast. On 4 July Texas accepts annexation into the United States, with the Rio Grande as its claimed southern border. Taylor sends his infantry to New Orleans for embarkation and departs on the first steamer with the 3d Infantry. The other regiments soon follow. Captain Braxton Bragg's light company from the 3d Artillery is also ordered to join the force. Seven companies of 2d Dragoons depart 25 July with 60 wagons to ride more than 500 miles overland to join Taylor. Five companies of Texas Rangers also join.

20 June–12 August. Third Fremont Expedition. St. Louis.
Lieutenant Fremont leads his third Army western expedition with orders to survey the region around the Arkansas and Red Rivers. He has 55 men—many are

Below: *A rare daguerreotype of a U.S. horse artillery battery on campaign. U.S. artillery proved more mobile and tactically superior to that of the Mexicans. ("Major Lucien Webster's Mounted Artillery," Beinecke Rare Book and Manuscript Library, Yale University, New Haven, CT)*

August. Army of Occupation. Nueces River.
Taylor camps near Corpus Christi and renames his force "The Army of Occupation." It remains here for almost eight months. Taylor calls for volunteers from four southern states. Ten companies of "foot" artillery serving as infantry arrive and are formed into a Battalion of Artillery. The dragoons ride in on the 27th.

August. Gaines Calls up Volunteers. Louisiana.
Without authority, Gaines, excited by war rumors, calls for mobilization of several regiments of Louisiana volunteers. He is reprimanded by the War Department, starting a long, bitter feud by mail with Secretary Marcy. Two companies of New Orleans artillery are sent to Taylor, but the rest are released.

12–16 August. Fremont and Abert Expeditions. Bent's Fort, Indian Territory.
On 12 August, a group led by Lieutenant James W. Abert, son of Colonel John J. Abert, Chief of the Topographical Engineers, is detached from Fremont for a three-month scientific expedition south into Kiowa and Comanche territory. Four days later, Fremont, acting unauthorized or possibly on secret orders, takes the rest of his expedition toward the Mexican province of California.

September–December. Taylor's Army Increases.
The 5th, 7th, and 8th Infantry regiments and some companies of foot artillery arrive, giving Taylor about 3,900 men. He organizes into three brigades—1st

veterans of the last expedition. Each man receives a new Hawkins rifle, two pistols, a knife, and a horse or mule, and equipment. By 2 August the group is at Bent's Fort, where Kit Carson and other scouts join.

July. Army Senior Officers Unprepared for War.
The Adjutant General reports that of the 18 Regular Army colonels authorized, only six are with their regiments. Of the others, four are too old and feeble; six are detached for other duty; and one is under arrest for drunkenness. Taylor's replacement with the 6th Infantry has yet to arrive.

26–31 July. Taylor Lands in Texas. Nueces Bay.
On the 26th, Taylor lands on St. Joseph's Island and shuttles his men to the mainland. He sends scouts, among them Topo Engineer Lieutenant George G. Meade, looking for suitable camp sites. The only wheeled transportation are 20 four-mule wagons, but there are no mules. Regimental quartermasters like Lieutenant Ulysses Grant, 4th Infantry, are tasked to purchase and break the mules to harness.

Brigade (8th Infantry and Artillery Battalion under Colonel William Worth); 2d Brigade (5th and 7th Infantry commanded by Lieutenant Colonel James McIntosh); and 3d Brigade (Colonel William Whistler with 3d and 4th Infantry). Taylor keeps the three light artillery batteries (Captain Bragg, Major Ringgold, and Lieutenant James Duncan), the 2d Dragoons (Colonel David Twiggs), and the Texas Ranger companies under Twiggs' direct control. Drill and training are initially enforced, but over time discipline erodes as camp followers and local traders set up brothels and bars on the outskirts of the camp. In late fall, Taylor sends his engineer officers to identify routes toward the Rio Grande.

September–November. **Fremont Expedition.**
The Fremont expedition travels west, fording the Colorado River and reaching the Great Salt Lake in October. Fremont spends two weeks exploring the area, then crosses the Great Salt Desert.

Opposite, top: *Fort Scott dragoons made periodic visits to the Pawnee Indians along the Platte River to try to end their conflict with the neighboring Sioux Indians. ("Dragoons Bound for Pawnee Country, 1844," Gary Hawk, Historic Preservation Association of Bourbon County, Kansas)*

Opposite, bottom: *After serving in a New York militia in the War of 1812, William Marcy (1786-1857) was appointed to the position of Secretary of War on 6 March 1845. ("William Learned Marcy," Henry Ulke, Army Art Collection, NMUSA)*

Above: *Fort Laramie was typical of American outposts in the Wyoming Territory. ("Fort Laramie," Yale University Library, New Haven, CT)*

December. Army of Occupation.

Taylor's men build makeshift shelters, but the poor-quality tenting is inadequate to protect them from the wet and freezing weather. Almost a quarter of the men are too sick for duty. The officers organize theaters and produce plays, one starring Lieutenant Grant in a lead female role. In addition, the officers quarrel about the seniority of Regular verses brevet rank. Worth, a Regular colonel but a brevet brigadier, demands seniority over Twiggs, a more senior colonel. Taylor favors Twiggs; when President Polk agrees, Worth submits his resignation and leaves for Washington in April. When Worth hears news of fighting on 9 May, he withdraws his resignation and Scott sends him back to Texas.

5–31 December. Fremont Enters California.

On the 5th Fremont and his detachment pass through what later will be known as Donner Pass and descend the Sierras. By 8 December, they are only a few miles from Sutter's Fort, where Fremont and Carson seek supplies and mules. They depart on the 14th to look for the rest of the expedition, which crossed the mountains by another route. Sutter reports the presence of Fremont to the Mexican authorities.

January. Status of the Army.

Army strength has dropped to 8,613. Taylor has more than 4,300 men, but he is short of officers. Many field-grade officers are too old and infirm to take the field; other officers are assigned away from their units, like Lieutenant William T. Sherman, 3d Artillery, on recruiting duty in Pittsburgh. Majors and captains fill in, leaving many companies led by lieutenants. Only scattered companies remain on the frontiers and coastal defenses. Colonel Joseph G. Totten, Chief Engineer, is seeking approval for a unit of enlisted engineers and has sent Captain Alexander J. Swift to study engineer units in the French army.

15–27 January. Fremont Names "Golden Gate."

Fremont returns to Sutter's Fort. He explores the San Francisco Bay area, which he describes as "a golden gate" in a letter to his wife. On the 27th he arrives in Monterey, California's military headquarters, and receives approval for a temporary stay.

3 February–1 March. Taylor's Army Moves South. Texas.

Taylor is ordered to move to the Rio Grande River and occupy positions opposite Matamoras, deep in the disputed territory. Insufficient wagons and draft animals limit the army to only 20 days' supplies. The other supplies and heavy weapons must go by ship. The 2d Dragoons and Ringgold's battery lead the way on the 8th.

22 February–9 March. Fremont Violates Agreement. California.

Fremont travels south toward Monterey from his camp near San Jose. The expedition now numbers 60 men. On the 5th Mexican authorities order Fremont to leave immediately. Instead he goes to Gavilan Peak, builds a log fort, and raises the American flag for the first time in California. By the 8th, Mexican troops are gathering below the fort. Fremont avoids a fight by slipping away during the night.

19–20 March. Taylor Faces First Mexican Forces. Arroyo Colorado.

Mexican troops wait on the other side of the lagoon as engineers scout the fords. Taylor positions Ringgold's and Duncan's guns to cover the crossing and orders the brigades to close up. On the 20th, Worth leads four light companies across and the Mexicans withdraw.

Opposite: *The well-armed dragoons usually carried an 1843 cavalry carbine with a snap attachment permitting it to be clipped to the wide shoulder belt when not in use. ("Trooper, 1st Regiment of U.S. Dragoons, 1846–1847," Don Troiani, www.historicalartprints.com)*

Right: *American troops advance through the hilly country of Mexico. Using his engineers like Robert E. Lee, Scott was able to outflank many Mexican defensive positions, keeping the Mexicans off balance. ("March Around Lake Chalco," James Walker, Army Art Collection, NMUSA)*

28 March–24 April. Taylor Advances to Rio Grande.
Marching in four columns abreast, Taylor moves toward Matamoras. The supply train is sent to Point Isabel to meet the ships with the heavy equipment. An American flag is raised and a fortified camp set up. On 1 April, two dragoons are captured by Mexicans but released. A number of soldiers desert, enticed by Mexican promises of money and land. On 10 April, Colonel Trueman Cross, Taylor's chief quartermaster, is murdered by bandits. An American patrol is ambushed nine days later and Lieutenant Theodore Porter, son of Commodore David Porter, is killed. A Mexican demand to withdraw is refused by Taylor.

25 April. Mexican Ambush Opens Hostilities. Carricitos Ranch, Texas.
Two companies of 2d Dragoons, about 60 men, under Captain Seth B. Thompson are sent to investigate reports of Mexican cavalry crossing the Rio Grande. About 20 miles from the American camp, Thompson leads his squadron into a large enclosed pasture. A Mexican brigade of cavalry and infantry hidden nearby surrounds the pasture, firing on the dragoons. The dragoons return fire while several try to jump the high chaparral fence. Captain William Hardee attempts an escape to the river, but all efforts fail. Ten dragoons are killed and four wounded. The dragoons surrender and are taken across the river; they are released three weeks later. Taylor reports that the war has started and sends a call to the Louisiana governor for four regiments of infantry.

28–31 April. Attack on Texas Rangers.
Mexican patrols probe toward Point Isabel. One patrol attacks Captain Samuel Walker's company of Texas Rangers. Five Rangers are killed and four captured. On 31 April, the 5,700-man Mexican Army of the North begins crossing into Texas as Taylor strengthens the defenses of his camp and builds an extensive earth fortification named Fort Texas (later Brown).

May. Military Academy Graduates Largest Class. West Point.
The class of 1846 is the largest the academy has graduated to date. The 59 new second lieutenants include John Gibbon, A. P. Hill, his roommate George B. McClellan, Thomas J. Jackson, George E. Pickett, Jesse L. Reno, George Stoneman, and Samuel D. Sturgis. Because the Army is limited to only 168 Regular second lieutenants, graduates going to filled regiments receive brevet commissions until a space opens. Transferring between regiments for promotion is common. Fifty-three of the class are assigned to fight in Mexico and four will be killed. Twelve members will become Union general officers; ten will become Confederate generals.

1–7 May. Mexicans Attack Fort Texas.
Taylor leaves Major Jacob Brown in command of a garrison of 7th Infantry, a 2d Artillery company with four 18-pounders, and Bragg's light company of 3d Artillery. He marches the rest of his army to protect Point Isabel. Two days later Mexicans surround the

Above: *General Zachary Taylor is shown in his camp at Walnut Springs with a group of his officers in the opening days of the war. His horse, "Old Whitney," awaits the general in the background. ("Zachary Taylor at Walnut Springs," William Garl Brown, Jr., National Portrait Gallery, Smithsonian Institution/Art Resource, NY)*

Opposite: *("Indiana Volunteer Infantry Regiments, 1846–1847," H. Charles McBarron, Company of Military Historians)*

fort and begin a week-long bombardment; the American guns return fire. Major Brown is mortally wounded on the 6th and command goes to Captain Edgar Hawkins, who refuses a demand to surrender. Despite the impact of 2,800 Mexican cannon shells, the fort holds out until Taylor returns.

3–11 May. **Gaines Illegally Mobilizes Volunteers. New Orleans.**
When Taylor's request for reinforcements arrives, Gaines orders Regulars from Jefferson Barracks and Pensacola to New Orleans, and calls for Volunteers

from four states in addition to Louisiana. By late on 7 May, four companies of the 1st Infantry and two companies of Volunteer artillery from New Orleans arrive at Point Isabel. In addition, about 4,500 Louisianans sign up for six months' service. Gaines mobilizes more than 15 regiments. The War Department, which has no money for such a force, orders Gaines to cancel his call to arms. A court of inquiry finds that Gaines exceeded his authority. When he argues, Gaines is made Eastern Division commander in New York, far from the theater of operations.

8 May. **Battle of Palo Alto. Texas.**
Taylor marches on the 7th with 2,228 men, a supply train of 200 wagons, and two 18-pounder cannons. About noon on the 8th, his scouts find the Mexican battle line blocking the road at Palo Alto. Taylor places Twiggs with the heavier force on the right and Lieutenant Colonel William G. Belknap's 1st Brigade on the left. Mexican attempts to flank the right are blocked by the 5th Infantry and 3d Infantry, which form squares to repel the cavalry. At the same time,

CITIZEN SOLDIERS IN THE MEXICAN WAR

The demise of the enrolled militia system following the War of 1812 raised serious questions regarding the nation's future needs for military manpower. Two important institutions arose in the early 19th century that provided America with new sources of uniformed manpower for the next 100 years.

State citizen-soldiers banded together to create volunteer militia companies that supplanted the former system of mandatory militia service. Volunteer militia companies drew together those with an affinity for the military lifestyle and often formed along ethnic or occupational lines. Militiamen provided their own weapons, uniforms, and equipment and created elite units of infantry, cavalry, and artillery. Companies usually met for training one night per week and conducted 14-day encampments each summer. Volunteer militia companies were as much social as military organizations and participated in ceremonies and charitable events. Militiamen understood that they were always available for state service under the command of local officials and the governor. When ordered into federal service, militiamen were limited to nine months

of duty, and opinions differed regarding geographic limits on their employment.

The second category of troops authorized was federal Volunteers. In simplest terms, Volunteer regiments were citizen-soldier units recruited by the states for national service, frequently from the ranks of its militia. Unlike the militia, Volunteer units did not exist in peacetime. The states had the responsibility for raising Volunteer regiments, but for uniforms, arms, and equipment the states looked to the federal government. Volunteer company officers were chosen by the men of the unit. While the governors had the authority to appoint officers above the rank of captain, the President reserved the right to appoint general officers. In contrast to the militia, Volunteer units were organized for one year of service with no geographic bounds on their employment.

The U.S. Army that fought in the Mexican War had three components: Regulars, militiamen, and Volunteers. Altogether, the nation mobilized 116,000 troops of all types for service. Of the total manpower effort, nearly three-quarters were temporary citizen-soldiers. Militiamen performed important service by manning a security zone along the southwestern border with Mexico, and some entire militia units agreed to enlist in a federal Volunteer regiment. The most renowned militia-based Volunteer regiment of the war was the Mississippi Rifles commanded by Colonel Jefferson Davis that distinguished itself at the battle of Buena Vista.

Dozens of state Volunteer regiments were recruited for federal service, giving the United States the sustained manpower to fight its first extended foreign war. Approximately 73,500 Volunteers served in 1846–48, and their regiments played a major role in the fighting. During the 1847 offensive against Mexico City, a manpower crisis paralyzed operations when the 12-month enlistment of several Volunteer regiments expired. More than one-third of the army was sent home. Congress responded by requiring new Volunteer regiments to serve for the duration of the war and stipulating that Volunteer regiments in the future would be mustered into service for three years.

When the Mexican War ended, Volunteer regiments were disbanded and the men returned to their local communities.

—Michael Doubler

Ringgold moves his mounted batteries forward with the 4th Infantry, placing heavy fire on the Mexicans. On the left, Duncan's expert use of his guns halts another Mexican attack. Together with the 8th Infantry and some dragoons, Duncan's fire collapses the Mexicans. Taylor advances his 18-pounders down the road, where they use canister to blast the attacking cavalry. As darkness falls, the Mexicans withdraw a short distance. American losses are only five killed and 48 wounded, but they include Ringgold, who is mortally wounded.

9 May. Battle of Resaca de la Palma.

The Artillery Battalion and 18-pounders secure the wagon train while Taylor advances with fewer than 2,000 men. Captain George A. McCall, commanding a provisional battalion of the light infantry companies in a screen ahead, finds the Mexicans in a strong position behind a partially flooded ravine with thick chaparral on both flanks. Taylor sends the 8th and 5th Infantry to the left and the 3d and 4th Infantry to the right. The thick brush and terrain break the battle into confused small-unit actions. On the road, Lieutenant Randolph Ridgely moves Ringgold's battery well forward and batters the Mexicans with grapeshot. Taylor sends Captain Charles May and his squadron of 2d Dragoons to capture a Mexican artillery battery, but they cannot hold the position. Taylor then orders the 8th Infantry to retake and hold the guns. When

the 4th Infantry breaks through on the left flank, capturing their headquarters, the Mexican line collapses and the troops flee across the river. American losses are 49 dead, 83 wounded.

9–10 May. Fremont Meets Gillespie. Klamath Lake, Oregon.

Fremont meets with Lieutenant Archibald Gillespie, U.S. Marine Corps, who carries letters and instructions from the President. From these Fremont understands that he is to take action to win California from Mexico. That night 20 Klamath Indians attack the American camp, killing three men. Fremont vows retribution and spends several days ambushing Indians in the area before returning to California.

13–28 May. War Officially Declared on Mexico.

Congress passes a War Act and mobilization acts on 13 May giving Polk approval to raise 50,000 Volunteers, but the enlistment terms are confusing and cause future problems. The men must furnish their own uniforms and horses, are paid at Regular Army rates, and elect their own company-level officers. Higher ranks including the generals are federally appointed militia officers. A number of former Regular officers return as Volunteers—Henry Clay, Jr., Meriwether Lewis Clark (son of explorer William Clark), Albert Sidney Johnston, Jubal Early, and Jefferson Davis. Scott is given command of the new

Right: *Captain Charles May led his squadron of 2d Dragoons in a dramatic charge at Resca de Palma that captured and temporarily held a Mexican battery. (Army Art Collection, NMUSA)*

Below: *As Marine Lieutenant Archibald Gillespie meets with Lieutenant John C. Fremont to pass on a secret message from the President, their camp is stalked by hostile Klamath Indians. ("Fremont Meets with Gillespie," Col. Charles Waterhouse, USMC (Ret), Marine Corps Art Collection)*

forces. The number of privates authorized in Regular artillery, infantry, and dragoon companies is increased to 100. A Company of Sappers, Miners, and Pontoniers of 100 enlisted men is approved. Three officers from the Corps of Engineers—Captain William H. Swift and Lieutenants Gustavus W. Smith and George B. McClellan—are selected to lead the unit. It later becomes Company A, U.S. Engineers.

15–19 May. Mobilizations Orders Issued.
Secretary of War Marcy sends the call to the state

governors, who are asked to form units of Volunteers from their militia. Scott plans for a ratio of three-to-one cavalry to infantry regiments and orders the Army's nine staff departments to purchase and position arms, supplies, and transportation at assembly points and along routes of movement. At the same time the officers on duty with the Army's General Recruiting Service are directed to increase their efforts to fill the Regular regiments.

19 May. Regiment of Mounted Riflemen Established.
On 19 May, a Regiment of Mounted Riflemen with ten companies is approved. Polk appoints many of the officers from among civilian political supporters. Scott's criticism of this causes the Mexican field command to be withdrawn. Persifor F. Smith is colonel of the regiment and John C. Fremont, promoted to lieutenant colonel, is second-in-command but never serves with the regiment. To train the new recruits, a lieutenant from West Point is assigned to each company. The same field (fatigue) uniform is prescribed as for dragoons except a letter "R" and dark blue trousers are worn with a crimson sash for officers and noncommissioned officers. Armed with the Model 1841 rifle and saber, the regiment is intended to protect settlers on the Oregon Trail. Instead, it is soon bound for Mexico. It later becomes the 3d Cavalry.

18–22 May. **Taylor Enters Mexico. Matamoras.**
Taylor's troops cross the Rio Grande. Captain Croghan Ker, 2d Dragoons, takes possession of Matamoras and raises the American flag. Taylor orders protection of civilians, churches, and property. Lieutenant Colonel John Garland leads a detachment of dragoons and Texas Rangers to attack the Mexican rear guard on the 22nd, losing several men. As the Volunteers arrive, Taylor finds a mixture of three-month and six-month units. The Volunteers lack discipline and frequent fights break out; poor sanitation leads to high rates of sickness. Most are returned home by July.

29 May. **Additional General Officers Approved.**
To command the expanded Army, Congress approves a third Regular Army major general and two more brigadier positions.

30 May–19 June. **California in Rebellion. Sutter Buttes, California.**
Fremont's camp at the Buttes becomes the gathering site for rebellious American settlers, but he refuses to take an active part in making two raids or leading the rebels. Under pressure from his men, Fremont disbands his official exploration group and many join the rebels. Publicly, Fremont remains aloof from the rebel capture of the town of Sonoma. Official prisoners are taken to Fremont, who finally acts and jails them in Sutter's Fort.

May–June. **Kearny Forms Army of the West. Fort Leavenworth.**
With orders to capture New Mexico and California,

Colonel Steven W. Kearny gathers a force of about 1,750 men, which he titles "Army of the West." In addition to his 1st Dragoons, Kearny assembles the 1st Missouri Mounted Volunteers (Colonel Alexander W. Doniphan); the St. Louis Volunteer Artillery (two light companies led by Major Meriwether Lewis Clark); the Missouri Volunteer Infantry Battalion; the Leclede Rangers; a company of Indian scouts; and some Topographical Engineers. Second-in-command is Captain Philip St. George Cooke. He is told supplies will be shipped to California and waiting for him in ports held by the U.S. Navy.

6 June–29 July. **Army of the West Marches.**
As soon as units are ready, Kearny sends them west to rendezvous near Bent's Fort. The first to leave on the 6th are the 1st Dragoons. Doniphan's regiment is next, followed by the other units. It is a difficult march. Bad food and water, scurvy, and accidents cause several deaths and injuries, but the march toughens the men and by 29 July all are at the camp. A battalion of Mormon Volunteers is still organizing.

11 June–23 September. **Wool Given Separate Command.**
Brigadier General John E. Wool receives orders to go to Texas and form a command to seize the Mexican town of Chihuahua. He turns the Eastern Division over to Gaines and goes to San Antonio, where he assembles some 3,400 Regulars and Volunteers—the 1st and 2d Illinois Regiments (Colonels John Hardin and William Bissell); the Arkansas Mounted Volunteers (Colonel Archibald Yell); and the Independent Company of Kentucky Mounted Volunteers (Captain John Williams). He also has a squadron of five companies of 1st and 2d Dragoons (Lieutenant Colonel William S. Harney); three companies of 6th Infantry (Major Benjamin Bonneville); Company B, 4th Artillery, and two Engineers, one of whom is Captain Robert E. Lee. Volunteer Brigadier James Shields is named Wool's deputy. They work during the summer to train the Volunteers and gather equipment. On 23 September the advance party of Wool's Division of the Center marches for the Rio Grande

June. **Taylor Ordered to Take Monterrey, Mexico.**
Taylor receives orders to seize Monterrey. He is also informed of Wool's separate column and mission. Taylor decides to capture Camargo, about 120 miles west, for use as a supply point and then use the San Juan River valley to approach Monterrey from the north.

Opposite: *An 1821 reorganization of the artillery specified that one company from each of the four artillery regiments would be equipped and designated as light artillery. These companies were considered as Army elite. ("Duncan's Light Battery,' A Company, 2d U.S. Artillery Regiment, 1847," Harry Larter, Company of Military Historians)*

Right: *Men of the 1st Dragoons of Kearny's "Army of the West" are seen here in front of the barracks at Fort Leavenworth preparing to depart for Santa Fe, and for some, ultimately, California. ("Army of the West," Don Stivers)*

26 June. **Additional General Officers Approved.**
To command the expanded Army, Congress approves eight new generals, three Regulars, and five Volunteers. On 29 June, Taylor receives the new Regular major general position, while Kearny and Twiggs become the brigadiers. J. P. Henderson and William O. Butler are the first Volunteer major generals to be appointed.

29 June. **Experimental Rocket and Howitzer Company.**
The Ordnance Department creates an experimental Howitzer and Rocket Company led by Major George H. Talcott. The Hale rockets are improved versions of the Congreve rockets used by the British in the War of 1812. The two- and three-inch-diameter rockets have three fins and stabilizing sticks to keep on course and are launched from a trough. Improvements in cannon after the war cause the rockets to be later discarded. The bronze 12-pounder mountain howitzers can be broken into two loads for two mules.

4–12 July. **Fremont Assumes Command. Sonoma.**
At a public meeting on the 4th, California is declared the independent "Bear Flag Republic" and Fremont is appointed head of the California army. Returning to

Sutter's Fort, Fremont learns on the 6th of the capture of Monterey and Yerba Buena by U.S. naval forces under Commodore John D. Sloat. He raises the American flag over the fort, and then goes with his men to Monterey.

6 July–19 September. **Taylor Advances. Monterrey.**
The 7th Infantry leads the march west to Camargo, which proves to be of no value. It is unhealthy and is more than 500 miles by river inland. Taylor waits several weeks to accumulate supplies and men. He releases the 60-day Volunteers, but a number of Volunteer units remain. He creates four divisions: 1st (Twiggs); 2d (Worth); the all Volunteer Field Division (Major General Butler); and the Texas Division (Texan Volunteers under Major General James P. Henderson). On 19 August Taylor uses steamboats to bridge the Rio Grande and marches to Cerralvo, 60 miles away. Almost 4,000 Volunteers are left behind to garrison captured towns. Thirty days later Taylor is outside Monterrey with about 6,200 men.

15–29 July. **Commodore Stockton in Command. Monterey, California.**
Commodore Robert F. Stockton, U.S. Navy, arrives

detachment under Stockton and together they enter the town without firing a shot. The Mexicans have fled.

2–22 September. **Fremont Named Military Governor of California.**
Stockton appoints Fremont military governor and directs recruitment to fill the California Battalion. Stockton writes letters to President Polk describing the state of affairs and his actions, then gives them to Kit Carson to carry overland to Washington. A revolt against the Americans in Los Angeles erupts on the 22nd, forcing the garrison to flee in a ship.

12 September. **Scott Denied Command in Mexico.**
Scott's requests for reinstatement as field commander are denied by Marcy. Some Volunteer units in Mexico are becoming notorious for lack of discipline and mistreatment of Mexican civilians. Scott proposes changes to the Articles of War to give court-martial authority for crimes in Mexico usually handled in the United States by civil courts.

Above: *Colonel Steven W. Kearny, a wounded veteran of the War of 1812 and an experienced Indian fighter, personified the professional Army leader required for the independent campaigns far from home posts. ("Stephen Watts Kearny," Missouri Historical Society, St. Louis)*

Right: *This young militiaman is a member of an artillery regiment, but from the musket he holds, he is more likely to be used in a more common infantry role as "foot artillery." (Collection of Michael F. Bremer, Woodbridge, New Jersey)*

and assumes command. Fremont is made a "major" and his men are mustered into the Army as volunteers in the California Battalion. They sail south to San Diego and land with some marines on the 29th. Preparations are made for an assault on Mexican forces at Los Angeles.

2–22 August. **Capture of Santa Fe. New Mexico.**
Kearny marches his "Army of the West" to Santa Fe. As he approaches Santa Fe, a surrender demand is sent ahead and when Kearny arrives on the 18th, the Mexican army is gone. He claims the town without a fight on the 22nd and announces its annexation to the United States. His army has marched 856 miles in less than 60 days.

13 August. **Los Angeles Captured.**
Marching north, Fremont links up with a navy-marine

20–24 September. **Battle of Monterrey. Mexico.**
Monterrey is guarded by strong forts and 7,000 defenders. A reconnaissance finds the western side vulnerable, so Taylor sends Worth with 1,600 men to capture two western hills while the main force pushes from the east. On the 21st, a Mexican cavalry attack on Worth is repulsed by Hays' Texans and Duncan's light artillery. The next day Texans lead the attack, which secures one hill after a daylong battle. In the east, Colonel John Garland's brigade suffers heavy fire from two large forts and then bogs down in house-to-house fighting despite cannon brought into the streets by Lieutenants John B. Reynolds and George H. Thomas. Garland withdraws, but three companies of 4th Infantry sent to help are hit by deadly fire and lose almost a third of their officers and men. Brigadier General John Quitman's brigade of Volunteers, helped by the 1st Infantry, finally captures one of the eastern forts. During the rainy night, Worth sends a picked detachment up the slope of the second hill. At 3 a.m. Lieutenant Colonel Thomas Childs leads a surprise attack that takes the fort. A howitzer is dragged up the hill and used to blast the Mexicans out of a fortified bishop's palace. On the 23rd, Quitman's men on the east and Worth's on the west wage a bitter house-to-house battle into the town center, chopping and blasting holes through house walls to advance. The next day Mexican officers and Taylor negotiate a surrender and eight-week armistice, allowing Mexican forces, including the San Patricio Battalion of American deserters, to withdraw. American losses are 120 killed, 368 wounded, and 43 missing. Twenty-eight cannon are captured. Secretary Marcy sends an angry letter telling Taylor to cancel the armistice.

September–October. **Army of the West. Santa Fe.**
With the area secure, Kearny appoints Doniphan military governor of the territory. During his short tenure Doniphan drafts a constitution and legal code. He is the first U.S. Army Military Governor. More Volunteers arrive—the 2d Missouri Mounted Rifles under Colonel Sterling Price and an independent battalion with artillery. Kearny directs Doniphan to secure a peace with Indian leaders, then reinforce Wool at Chihuahua. On 26 September, Kearny departs for California with two small mountain howitzers and five companies of 1st Dragoons, many mounted on mules. A battalion of 500 Mormon infantrymen, still en route, is to follow him. Doniphan sends detachments on long marches into the mountains to meet with Navaho, Apache, Zuni, and Ute leaders.

October. **Scott's Vera Cruz Plan. Camargo.**
President Polk and Secretary Marcy decide the only

Above: *Santa Fe surrendered to the American forces as Kearny's Army of the West approached. He claimed the territory for the U.S. and established a civil-military government that was soon challenged by local insurgents. ("1846, Brigadier General Stephen Kearny's New Mexican Campaign," Copyright Stock Montage, Inc.)*

way to bring Mexico to terms is to capture Mexico City. Reluctantly, they ask Scott for advice and on the 27th he gives them a five-page campaign plan. He proposes Tampico and the island of Lobos as staging areas and Vera Cruz as the entry point for American forces. Taylor has made a similar proposal. Marcy sends orders to Taylor to take Tampico.

6 October. **Kearny Meets Carson. New Mexico.**
Near Socorro, Kearny meets Kit Carson with Stockton's dispatches. Carson tells Kearny that California is secure. With a difficult trail ahead and scarce water, Kearny decides to send the majority of his force back to Santa Fe. He retains two companies (120 men) and two cannon, puts supplies on pack mules, and returns the wagons with the other dragoon companies. Cooke is given a brevet promotion to lieutenant colonel and sent back to bring the Mormon Battalion. Their task is to improve the trail to California. Carson agrees to guide Kearny through the snow-covered mountains to California.

U.S. REGIMENT OF MOUNTED RIFLES

On 19 May 1846, Congress authorized the creation of a regiment of United States Mounted Rifles. Although originally intended for garrison and outpost duty on the Oregon Trail, the regiment was ordered to duty in Mexico as soon as it was raised. The companies of the regiment were quickly recruited and organized at Fort McHenry, Columbus, Ohio, and Jefferson Barracks, Missouri. While pay and allowances for the Rifles was to be the same as the U.S. Dragoon regiments, there were certain distinctions between the Rifle regiment and the regular cavalry establishment.

Like the dragoons, the Rifle regiment was organized into ten companies with a company strength of 64 privates. In 1847, this was increased to 70, equaling the dragoons. The Rifles were to have an "R" stamped on their uniform buttons instead of a "D," and their trousers were to be dark blue with a black stripe bordered in yellow down the side instead of the sky-blue trousers worn by the dragoons. Officers wore a crimson waist sash (dragoons wore orange sashes) and a distinctive eagle device with an "R" in its center on their forage caps. As the regiment was intended to fight on both horse and foot, they were armed with Model 1840 sabers, M1841 ("Mississippi") rifles, and flintlock pistols. In 1847 the War Department purchased 1,000 six-shot Whitneyville-Walker Colt revolvers to replace the flintlocks, but only 220 of these arrived before the war's end.

The majority of officers appointed by President James K. Polk to command the regiment were civilians and western democrats, much to the chagrin of General Winfield Scott, who found the civilian appointees completely incompetent and unsuited to command. Notable exceptions to this were the regiment's commander, Colonel Persifor F. Smith, who was quickly promoted to brigadier general, and his replacement, Colonel Edwin V. Sumner, who had been one of the original captains of the Regiment of Dragoons. The regiment's lieutenant colonel was John C. Fremont and its major was William W. Loring.

Soon after organizing, the Rifles were sent to join General Zachary Taylor in northern Mexico, then were transferred by sea to General Scott's army at Vera Cruz. During the passage most of the regiment's horses were lost overboard. The remainder were given to the 2d Dragoons, and the Rifles served as dismounted infantry. By May 1847, enough suitable horses had been procured to mount two companies, C and I. While the two mounted companies operated against Mexican

guerrillas, the other companies continued as light infantry, fighting with distinction throughout General Scott's campaign and leading the fight to seize one of the gates into Mexico City. When Scott rode into the Grand Plaza to take formal possession of Mexico City, he saw that a group of Mounted Rifles had raised their flag ahead of him. Doffing his hat and bowing from the saddle, Scott addressed them with, "Brave Rifles! Veterans! You have been baptized in fire and blood and have come out steel!"

Following the war, the Mounted Rifles were reorganized. So many of the men took advantage of Congress' promise—to terminate enlistments at war's end of any Regular who signed up for duty against Mexico—hat the regiment had to be recruited from scratch. On 10 May 1849, Lieutenant Colonel Loring led the new regiment on a 2,000-mile march to its duty station in California. The regiment reached the West Coast in the middle of gold-rush fever and the temptation of riches caused many of the recruits to desert. By 1851, the regiment was so reduced that it had to recruit anew. Following this third reorganization the Rifles were assigned to Texas until December 1855, when they were transferred to New Mexico. On 3 August 1861, the Regiment of Mounted Rifles was redesignated the 3d U.S. Cavalry, and continues to serve today as the 3d Armored Cavalry Regiment.

—*Vince Hawkins*

Opposite: *A U.S. mounted rifleman handles his M1841 "Mississippi Rifle." ("Halls of Montezuma," Don Prechtel)*

Above: *Samuel Ringgold trained Company C, 3d Artillery, as "flying artillery" with men mounted on horses so they could move with and support the infantry. Here, his men prepare to fire upon the Mexican positions during the Battle of Palo Alto. ("Ringgold's Battery at Palo Alto, 8 May 1846," William T. Trego, Courtesy John Langellier)*

9–31 October. Wool's Division. Rio Grande.

Harney's dragoons and the two engineers ford the river on the 9th. The next day Captain Lee puts in a pontoon bridge using four boats. Before crossing the main body on the 12th, Wool issues an order directing proper treatment of Mexican civilians. Stringent enforcement will keep incidents in his command to a minimum. By the 31st, Wool is at Monclava, where he is ordered to stay during the armistice.

9–19 October. The Mormon Battalion. Santa Fe.

The battalion arrives with wagons and families, and Cooke assumes command. Leaving the families behind, Cooke leads the battalion for California.

3 November. Congress Establishes 10th Military Department.

Congress establishes the 10th Military District to encompass the Oregon Territory and whatever territory the United States may occupy in California. No commander is named.

13 November–5 December. Taylor Captures Saltillo.

Taylor has orders to go east to capture Tampico, but when the armistice ends he leads Worth's division southwest to Saltillo, a key road junction. The city with its supplies is taken without resistance. Taylor ignores orders to hold at Monterrey and keeps Worth in place. Meanwhile, his troops are changing. The 2d Infantry arrives, but the Texans are released. Wool sends his aide, Lieutenant Irwin McDowell, to Taylor with a letter suggesting that instead of going to Chihuahua he bring his men east to join Taylor. With reports of Mexican offensive preparations, Taylor agrees and orders Wool to the town of Parras, closer to Worth.

Above: *At the Battle of Palo Alto, General Zachary Taylor told his men "that their main dependence must be in the bayonet," but American artillery bore the brunt of the battle forcing the Mexicans to retreat. ("Battle of Palo Alto," Carl Nebel, Courtesy Special Collections Division. The University of Texas at Arlington Libraries, Arlington, TX)*

Right: *Shot through the legs, Major Ringgold collapses and dies at the front of the Battle of Palo Alto, where his artillery sometimes advanced before the infantry. ("Death of Major Ringgold," Sterling Library, Yale University, New Haven, CT)*

23 November. **Scott Selected for Mexico Command.** Unhappy with both Scott and Taylor, President Polk has considered giving a commission and senior command to Senator Thomas Hart Benton. Benton wants the rank of lieutenant general, not used since Washington's death. When Polk finds no political support for Benton, he calls Scott to the White House on the 19th and gives him command of the campaign. Scott is ecstatic, not yet realizing that Polk will continue to search for another commander. Scott goes to New York to make family farewells. Before departing for Mexico, he sends Captain Francis M. Dimond to Havana to hire agents to infiltrate Mexico; within weeks several are on their way.

28 November. **Patterson Ordered to Tampico. Camargo.** Polk and Marcy are angry at Taylor for ignoring orders. On the 28th, Major General Robert Patterson, commanding Taylor's rear supply area, receives letters

from Marcy to seize Tampico. Patterson begins preparations, but in fact, Tampico is already occupied by the American Navy. News of that reaches Washington and the Army Adjutant General attempts to telegraph Scott in New York—the first use of the telegraph by the Army.

6 December. **Battle of San Pascual. California.** Kearny crosses into California and confirms earlier information that Mexican-led insurgents have retaken Los Angeles and other towns. On the 5th, he is joined by Major Archibald Gillespie, U.S. Marine Corps, with 35 sailors and marines; at dawn the next day they advance to the village of San Pascual, where a larger

Mexican mounted force is encountered. The dragoons charge the Mexicans, shots are exchanged, and the Mexicans withdraw with the dragoons in pursuit. Outside of town, Mexican lancers turn on the surprised dragoons, killing 21. Kearny and 17 others are wounded. Kearny moves his weakened force into a defensive position about ten miles away.

11–12 December. Kearny Arrives at San Diego.

A small relief force arrives on the 11th and brings Kearny to San Diego. The Army troops combine with Stockton's force and Kearny becomes Stockton's field commander for operations against Los Angeles. Farther north and out of contact, Fremont, now a lieutenant colonel, is gradually working his way south, capturing Mexican insurgents with his California Battalion and reasserting American control in the towns.

13–16 December. Worth Asks for Reinforcements. Saltillo.

Unaware of Patterson's orders, Taylor starts Brigadier General Twiggs' division toward Victoria. On the 16th, Taylor receives a plea from Worth for reinforcements to face an expected Mexican attack. Taylor sends Quitman's brigade on to Victoria and returns to Monterrey with the rest of the troops. Wool also marches east to join Worth.

14–31 December. Battle of Brazito. Texas.

Doniphan leaves Santa Fe on the 14th with his 1st Missouri regiment and several companies of Volunteers. Colonel Sterling Price, his regiment, and Major Meriwether Clark's light artillery battalion are left to secure New Mexico. Doniphan marches 250 difficult miles over the desert. To conserve water, the units are separated by two days along the trail. They rejoin at the Brazito River on the 25th, in time to defend against 1,200 Mexican infantry and cavalry. Doniphan refuses a threat of "surrender or no quarter" and his men fire a volley that breaks the Mexican charge. Doniphan's counterattack scatters the Mexican infantry. Only seven Americans are wounded. Doniphan enters El Paso on the 27th.

21–24 December. Patterson Marches to Tampico. Matamoras.

Patterson departs on the rough trail to Tampico. The trail converges at Victoria with the road from Monterrey being used by Quitman. Patterson has 4,000 Volunteers and the recently arrived engineer company, which is tasked with moving ahead of the main body of troops and improving the trail. Due to illness and deaths, only two officers, Smith and McClellan, and 45 of the 100 enlisted engineers are fit for duty. Work details provided from the line units are organized by Smith into shifts and encouraged to speed, making impressive progress.

29 December. Quitman Enters Victoria. Mexico.

The Mexican Army abandons the town before Quitman's brigade arrives and the Americans occupy the city peacefully. Taylor, returning from Monterrey, and Patterson's column arrive six days later.

1847

January. Status of the Army.

Actual strength is recorded as 10,690 officers and men, but many are ill. Winfield Scott, the Army's commanding general, and Zachary Taylor are both in Mexico. Most of the Army is committed to the war in California or Mexico except a few scattered infantry

Right: *As the Mormon Battalion advanced behind Kearny's detachment, it was tasked to improve the trail into a road suitable for wagons to travel to California. The men are shown here cutting a ramp into a stream bank.* ("Mormon Battalion, 1846," copyright by Intellectual Reserve, Inc., courtesy of The Museum of Church History and Art)

and artillery companies in frontier and coastal forts. Uniform regulations change to permit noncommissioned officers to wear chevrons on their field uniforms with the points up, while dress uniform chevrons point down. A new lozenge (diamond) is added to distinguish first sergeants. Enlisted men may also wear a chevron, point up, below the elbow on the dress uniform for every five years of service. A red stripe on the service chevron indicates wartime service.

3–16 January. Scott at Camargo. Mexico.

Major General Winfield Scott goes to the rear base to meet Taylor, but Taylor, angry at what he sees as Scott's presumption of command, is far south at Victoria. Scott sends orders to Worth, Twiggs, and Patterson to prepare their units to march, and by the 16th all are on the road. Worth is sent north to Brazos to embark on ships for Lobos. Twiggs and Patterson march to Tampico to do the same. Scott is assembling almost 9,000 men, leaving Taylor with only the Volunteer force at Wool's command near Saltillo and part of Butler's Field Division.

8–9 January. Battles of San Gabriel River and La Mesa. Los Angeles.

After training Stockton's sailors in land tactics, the 600-man Army-Navy-Marine force led by Kearny marches south. On 8 January, the Americans arrive at the San Gabriel River, where a Mexican force of about equal size is positioned along the other side. Advancing in a hollow square, Kearny's men fight off cavalry attacks, wade the river, and disperse the Mexican infantry, which has been weakened by artillery fire. Only two Americans are killed. The next day Kearny advances to La Mesa, where another Mexican force is quickly routed. On the 10th, Los Angeles is again in American hands.

13 January. Scott's Plans Intercepted by Santa Anna.

Some of Scott's dispatches are captured. Santa Anna realizes Taylor's weakened situation and decides to attack him. Wool increases patrols by detachments of mounted Volunteers. Two sleeping patrol groups are captured by the Mexicans.

13–17 January. Kearny-Fremont-Stockton Conflict. Los Angeles.

Fremont negotiates a treaty with the Mexicans on the 13th and then rides to Los Angeles to meet Stockton and Kearny. Kearny, who has a letter from the Secretary of War giving him full authority in California, dislikes Fremont, dating to the mountain howitzer matter in 1843. On the 16th, Kearny sends letters refuting Stockton's authority to appoint civil officials and ordering Fremont to report to him. Stockton replies that a California government now exists, and he intends to ignore Kearny. When Fremont sees Kearny on the 17th, he supports Stockton. Fremont also says Stockton is appointing him governor of California. Stockton writes the proclamation that day. Kearny is outraged but bides his time. The Mormon Battalion and other forces loyal to him are expected soon.

19 January–5 February. **Taos Revolt. New Mexico.**
Resistance to American occupation flares into an uprising. Rebellious Indians and New Mexicans murder Governor Bent and other Americans in Taos while other locations are also attacked. Price recalls his scattered detachments and marches from Santa Fe toward Taos with about 350 1st Dragoons and Volunteers with four howitzers. A rebel force near Santa Cruz is scattered by a mounted charge on 24 January. The same day a company skirmishes with rebels near Mora, suffering four killed. Price outflanks a strong rebel position on the Embudo Road five days later and marches on through deep snow. He arrives at Taos on 3 February, where more than 1,200 rebels are entrenched. Price shells the town without effect. A ground assault on the 4th forces the insurgents to surrender or flee. Price has seven killed, including a dragoon captain, and 45 men wounded. The victory secures New Mexico for the United States.

February. **Army's First Steamboat. Louisville.**
A contractor finishes the General Jesup, first of six steamboats ordered by the Quartermaster Corps. Work on the boats is supervised by Lieutenant Colonel Stephen Long, who also repairs the Corps of Engineers fleet of snag boats for river clearance and builds a new dredge.

1–27 February. **Doniphan Marches on Chihuahua. El Paso.**
Clark's battalion of six light artillery pieces arrives on the 1st after a harrowing march through blizzards and sandstorms. Doniphan sends the company of Chihuahua Rangers ahead as scouts, and then on the 8th he starts the first units of his force of 924 soldiers on the road south. A large wagon train of more than 400 wagons is accompanying the expedition. Doniphan organizes the civilian teamsters and traders into an ad hoc battalion. Moving 12 to 25 miles a day, the spread-out column moves deeper into the desolate Mexican countryside. Groups of Apache Indians appear on the flanks, looking for an opportunity to

steal horses or cattle. On the 25th a large prairie wildfire almost destroys the wagons and supplies.

11 February. **Regular Army Adds Regiments.**
Congress authorizes ten new Regular Army units to serve for the duration of the war—one dragoon regiment (3d Dragoons), eight infantry regiments (9th–16th Infantry), and a Voltigeur and Foot Rifleman Regiment. (The Voltigeur is a French concept to improve infantry mobility by pairing a mounted and a dismounted rifleman on a single horse for relatively short distances.) The regiment never receives horses or its distinctive gray uniforms. It remains a foot infantry unit in the standard sky-blue jacket and trousers trimmed with white. Very few Regular officers transfer to the new regiments, called the "New Establishment," since it is expected they will be inactivated at the end of the war. Not until August are officer appointments made, recruits enlisted, and the units en route. Many positions are given to Democrats as political favors; William Polk, brother of the President, becomes a major in the 3d Dragoons.

13 February. **Kearny's Authority Confirmed. Monterey.**
Orders arrive confirming Kearny's full authority as commander of the 10th Military Department and

senior American officer in California. He also issues proclamations making himself governor and establishing other civil government posts with the capitol at Monterey. At the end of the month he orders Fremont to bring him all official documents and to disband the California Battalion. Fremont ignores the orders.

14–20 February. **Taylor Advances to Agua Nueva.**
Taylor moves his army, about 4,800 men, 17 miles south to Agua Nueva. He rebuffs Wool's suggestion to withdraw to a defensive position near the St. Juan de la Buena Vista ranch. On the 20th, a patrol under May observes Mexican cavalry moving past the American camp. They also spot a larger Mexican force of 15,000 approaching up the road. May's report is confirmed by Texas Ranger Captain Ben McCulloch, who has ridden in disguise through the Mexican camp.

19–21 February. **Scott Lands and Proclaims Martial Law. Tampico.**
Scott lands on the 20th. He issues a proclamation placing areas of Mexico under American control under martial law. This permits court-martial of soldiers who commit crimes against Mexican civilians. Taylor is experiencing increasing attacks against his lines of communication, and retaliation by his Volunteers is often brutal, further alienating the population. On the 21st Scott sails for his assembly area at Lobos Island and finds few troops have arrived.

21 February. **Taylor Prepares for Battle. Buena Vista.**
Taylor withdraws his forces to Buena Vista as recommended by Wool. The Arkansas regiment left to load the Army's supplies and bring the wagons panics when Mexican lancers approach, leaving dragoons to burn the wagons. Taylor leaves Wool in command and takes an escort of dragoons and Davis's 1st Mississippi Regiment back to Saltillo to protect it from the Mexican cavalry. Wool places Company B, 4th

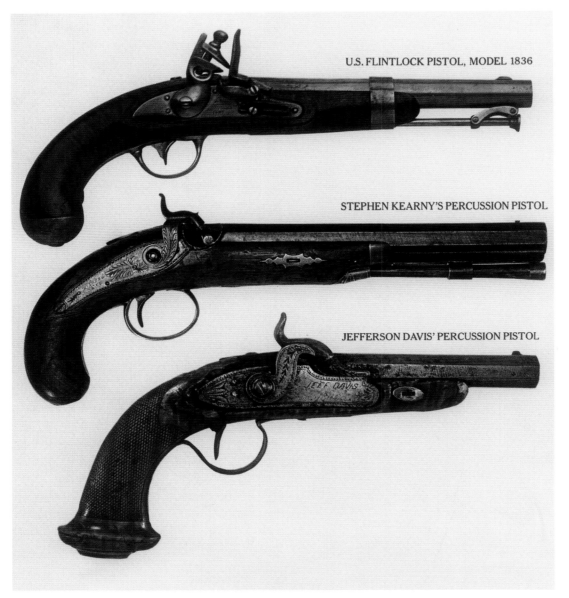

U.S. FLINTLOCK PISTOL, MODEL 1836

STEPHEN KEARNY'S PERCUSSION PISTOL

JEFFERSON DAVIS' PERCUSSION PISTOL

Left: *Both old flintlock and newer percussion pistols were used as personal weapons by officers. (Time–Life Books)*

Opposite: *This dark blue flag is the regimental color carried by the 6th U.S. Infantry Regiment during the war. The battle honors were added after the war and were not authorized to be placed on flags until 1861. (West Point Museum Collection)*

Artillery, 3d Indiana, and 1st Illinois on the right to block the road to Saltillo. The 2d Kentucky and 2d Illinois with Company C, 3d Artillery, and Company E, 4th Artillery, hold the center. The 2d Indiana and a section of three howitzers under Lieutenant John Paul Jones O'Brien are on the left.

22 February. **Battle of Buena Vista—First Day.**
Taylor returns early on the 22nd in time to refuse a demand to surrender. Santa Anna then sends light troops onto the mountain slope overlooking the American right in an attempt to turn that flank. Dismounted Kentucky cavalry and Indiana riflemen hold the flank in a daylong fight. At dark Taylor returns to Saltillo, leaving Wool to reposition the troops during a rainy night.

23 February. **Battle of Buena Vista—Second Day.**
A morning Mexican attack along the road is turned back, with heavy losses and an American counterattack pushes the Mexicans back. However, on the left, an advance by two Mexican divisions crumples the 2d Indiana's line. Taylor arrives and sends Davis's 1st Mississippi and the 3d Indiana as reinforcements. They rally the retreating troops and form a concave line that catches the advancing Mexicans in a cross-fire and stops them. Meanwhile, Mexican cavalry break through and attack the Arkansas and Kentucky Volunteers guarding the American rear area. The two units are hit hard but hold with the help of May and his dragoons. An American counterattack in the center runs headlong into another Mexican assault force, catching many of the American units are out of position. O'Brien's artillerymen make a stubborn fighting withdrawal, retreating only as far as each gun recoils, then loading and firing again. One gun is captured when the crew is killed, and another is disabled, but he continues to cover the infantry until he is wounded and overrun. Lieutenant George Thomas works his section of guns in support and is joined by Bragg, bringing up the rest of his battery at a wild gallop. The deadly artillery fire combines with the arrival of the Indiana and Mississippi regiments to tip the battle for the Americans, and the Mexicans withdraw. Taylor has lost 272 killed and 387 wounded, but has inflicted casualties of more than 20 percent on Santa Anna.

25–28 February. **Battle of Sacramento River.**
Doniphan's Missouri Volunteers barely survive a prairie wildfire on the 25th. Two days later scouts find a Mexican force of 3,000 with artillery in fortifications guarding the ford over the Sacramento River. The road goes into a deep gully, then rises to a small

plateau and passes in front of the Mexican position. On the afternoon of the 28th Doniphan marches his three-mile-long column directly down the road, then suddenly swings to the right off the road and enters the gully to flank the Mexican position. The Volunteers then use picks and shovels to quickly build a ramp for the horses, wagons, and cannon, emerging on the plateau into battle formation. Batteries from Clark's battalion push forward to engage advancing Mexican lancers, blasting them into retreat. The Americans advance as Clark's guns continue to engage the Mexican artillery and cavalry. Doniphan leads an all-out assault, taking the men over the Mexican breastworks in hand-to-hand combat. Some of Clark's gunners rush into the positions and turn captured guns on the retreating Mexicans. Mounted Missourians pursue fleeing Mexicans down to the river. Doniphan has three men killed, eight wounded. Estimated Mexican losses are more than 200, plus wagons, weapons, thousands of pounds of supplies, and a large herd of livestock. On 2 March Doniphan's men march into Chihuahua to the tune of "Yankee Doodle" played by Major Clark's band.

1–3 March. **Scott Organizes for the Invasion. Lobos Island.**
By March most of Scott's 13,000 troops are on the island. Many of the transports and 65 of the specially designed landing boats are ready. He organizes three divisions—1st (Worth), 2d (Twiggs) and 3d (Patterson)—plus a cavalry brigade (Harney) and a battalion of heavy siege artillery (Colonel James Bankhead). On 3 March, the invasion fleet with Scott in the lead ship sails south to rendezvous with Commodore David E. Conner's flotilla.

3 March. **Artillery Regiments Gain Companies.**
Congress authorizes the four artillery regiments to be increased from ten to 12 companies, but most continue, serving as infantry. Some of the first companies to arrive in Mexico are used as individual replacements, but by the end of the year most regiments have 12 companies, each with about 95 men.

7–9 March. **Landing at Vera Cruz. Collada Beach.**
Scott takes a boat with his staff for a reconnaissance of the landing area and is brought under close Mexican cannon fire. With him are his engineers—Captain Lee and Lieutenants Meade, Joseph E. Johnston, and P. G. T. Beauregard. With good weather on the 9th, Worth loads his 5,500-man brigade into the landing boats and leads the assault wave ashore to martial music played by regimental bands on the transport ships. There is no resistance and Scott's entire force is ashore by dark.

10–27 March. **Capture of Vera Cruz.**
Scott places his three divisions in an arc around the town, cutting it off on the landward side. When his heavy mortars fail to arrive, Scott gets Conner to send heavy cannon ashore to comprise a siege battery manned by sailors. Lee supervises placement of the guns and on the 23rd a general bombardment by five batteries begins. After two days, the Mexicans ask to discuss terms and on the 27th surrender. Scott

Above: *Missouri militia colonel Alexander Doniphan led the second detachment of Kearny's army to Santa Fe and then into Mexico, defeating the Mexicans at the Sacramento River. ("Alexander W. Doniphan," Missouri Historical Society, St. Louis)*

Left: *Two dismounted mounted riflemen move forward while a third holds their horses. While necessary, this took every third of fourth man off the firing line. ("Mounted Companies, U.S. Regiment of Mounted Riflemen, 1847," H. Charles McBarron, Company of Military Historians)*

emphasizes adherence to his orders for proper treatment of the Mexicans and, to help win their friendship, attends a Catholic service in full dress uniform with his staff. Worth is appointed military governor of the city.

25 March–14 April. **Fremont Concedes to Kearny. Monterey.**
In a face-to-face confrontation, Fremont finally agrees to disband the California Battalion and obey Kearny's orders. Mason comes to Los Angeles to assume command from Fremont. Relations are so bad that Fremont challenges Mason to a duel with shotguns at 20 paces, but Kearny orders it stopped.

8 April. **Scott Marches Toward Mexico City.**
Scott is anxious to move inland before the season for yellow fever arrives along the coast, but he lacks the wagons and mules necessary to carry sufficient supplies from the port to an advancing army. No help is arriving from the United States. Deciding he must move, he sends Twiggs' division west on the National

EYEWITNESS: THE BATTLE OF SACRAMENTO

During the Mexican War, Colonel Alexander Doniphan led his 1st Missouri Mounted Regiment through a hard march to Mexico. At Sacramento his smaller force won a stunning American victory.

"As we form, the enemy's artillery opens on us, and, at that instant, Weightman's clear voice is heard—'Form battery, action front, load and fire at will'; and our pieces ring out the death-knell of the enemy; now comes the friendly struggle between our gunners, who shall pour in the deadliest and quickest fire, and beautifully are those pieces served, mowing lane after lane through the solid columns of the Mexicans. In the center of the battery, their horses bounding at every discharge, stand Clark and his officers. As the balls fly through the opposing ranks, and the shells tear their columns, shout after shout is heard from our men. Further to our right sits Colonel Doniphan on his beautiful chestnut charger, with his leg crossed over the saddle, steadily whittling a piece of wood, but with his eye glancing proudly over the ranks of his little band. As the cannonading becomes hotter, he quietly says: 'Well, they're giving us hell now boys!' and passes coolly to the left of our position, untouched by the copper hail that pours around him.

"And here we are (at a distance too great for anything but cannon), sitting on our horses dodging Mexican balls as they come humming through our ranks, first striking the ground and midway, and so becoming visible. It was surprising the skill which we soon obtained in this employment. After a few shots, we could tell to a foot where the copper messenger would alight; although, a few minutes before, joke after joke was passing among us, the silence was now almost unbroken, for nothing acts so well, by way of a safety valve to a man's courage, as having to sit on horseback half an hour and dodge cannon balls. As yet we know of no injuries amongst us, but suddenly, a German close by, blurts out 'I'se Kilt,' and, tumbling off his horse, rolls up his trowsers [sic], showing a severe contusion on his leg, caused by a stone thrown up by the ricochet of a cannon-ball; round the limb goes a handkerchief, and up mounts the man again. At that moment a groan bursts from the line to my left, and a man is borne dying from the ranks, while off goes the head of Lieutenant Dorn's horse. Hot work on all sides. . . .

"A shell explodes directly in the ranks of the enemy—they draw back behind their entrenchments—and we immediately advance until within four hundred yards—again the deadly shower opens from our ranks, fiercely returned. The order to charge rings through our line—Colonel Mitchell, on his favorite white charger Roderick, waves his sabre as he leads us on; rumbling and crashing behind us comes Weightman with his howitzers, leaving the rest of the battery in position to cover the advance. Dashing past us goes Major Owens, waving his hand in an exulting manner, and shouting out, 'Give it to them, boys! They can't withstand us'—and away he goes: falling, in two minutes a corpse, struck in the forehead by a grape-shot while storming the redoubts. And being so close to the gun that the fire actually burns his clothes. Rapidly is our charge made; but just fairly under way, it is about to be ruined! A countermanding order, as if from Doniphan, is given by a drunken officer whose rank (alone) requires respect. In surprise we suddenly halt within a few yards of the redoubts, and are fully exposed to the whole of the enemy's fire. 'For God's sake, advance!' roars out our sutler Pomeroy, who was fighting in the ranks—our hesitation vanishes, and away we instantly dash forward, gallantly led by Mitchell and Gilpin, while Weightman fires his howitzers loaded with canister, with great effect, and again advancing, wheels them to the right and left, throwing in another charge of grape and canister and raking the whole line of the enemy's position. To our left is a battalion of brave cavalry, from Durango, who have arrived on the field only half an hour before—'tis their last fight—they are terribly cut to pieces, and are forced to retreat. A piece of their artillery, being dismounted, they attempt to 'snake,' by fastening their lassos to it, and drag it along the ground, but they are overtaken and made prisoners and the gun is ours. Our men, pouring over the embankments, actually push the Mexicans out."

(*A Campaign in New Mexico with Colonel Doniphan*, by Frank S. Edwards, a volunteer with the Missouri artillery. University of New Mexico Press, 1996, reprinted from 1847.)

—*Kevin M. Hymel*

Above: *This view gives a sense of the broken terrain and the difficulty both sides had in maneuvering forces during battle. ("Battle of Buena Vista," Library of Congress)*

Opposite: *General Winfield "Old Fuss and Feathers" Scott. ("Winfield Scott," Giusseppina Vannutelli, Army Art Collection, NMUSA)*

Road as the lead element in the march on Mexico City. The 1st Infantry is left to garrison the city.

11–18 April. **Battle of Cerro Gordo.**
The advance guard of Mounted Rifles is stopped by heavy rifle and artillery fire from Mexican positions overlooking the road. Artillery and infantry hold three small hills south of the road while others are on two hills—La Atalaya and El Telegrafo (the largest hill)—on the north. This is the main Mexican army of 12,000, with its camp and reserves near Cerro Gordo behind the hill. Lieutenant Beauregard makes a recon of the Mexican positions and Patterson postpones an attack until Scott arrives. On the 13th, Scott sends more engineers, including Captain Lee, to find a way around the Mexican defenses. Lee is almost captured but finds a trail to move troops and cannon to the

north. Scott plans to send Twiggs' division in a turning movement around the Mexican far left flank, while Brigadier General Gideon Pillow's brigade, also Volunteers, makes a secondary attack against the three southern hills. Work parties prepare the trail without being detected, but on the 17th Twiggs' marching men are spotted and come under fire from La Atayala. Twiggs diverts a brigade under Harney to take La Atalaya while sending his other two brigades on to the north. With support from Lieutenant Jesse Reno's mountain howitzers, the Mounted Rifles, 3d and 7th Infantry, and 1st Artillery clear La Atalaya but foolishly continue on against El Telegrafo, where they are stopped and forced to take cover. That night Scott changes his plan. He directs Twiggs to take El Telegrafo but also to continue the flanking movement with Colonel Bennett Riley, reinforced with Shields' Volunteers. The next morning heavy fighting renews as the Regulars climb El Telegrafo and fight into the Mexican works, forcing the defenders to flee. Captain John B. Magruder, 1st Artillery, turns the Mexican guns and bombards the camp. At the same time, Shields and Riley appear in the Mexican left rear, causing a general retreat. When Shields is wounded, Colonel Edward Baker, 4th Illinois, leads the charge

WINFIELD SCOTT

From the opening shots of the War of 1812 to the outbreak of the Civil War, Winfield Scott's name was synonymous with the United States Army. He served 14 Presidents and wrote the first comprehensive set of Army regulations to upgrade U.S. military professionalism. Ordered wherever military or diplomatic trouble loomed, Scott stood head and shoulders above his peers, both physically (at 6 feet 4 inches), and professionally.

Of humble origins, Scott worked his way up to be the Army's highest-ranking officer through his talents for war and self-promotion. He was born near Petersburg, Virginia, on 13 June 1786, and found his true calling in 1807 when he joined a local cavalry troop. Commissioned a captain of light artillery and sent to New Orleans in May 1808, he had conflicts with other officers and was suspended from duty for some months. As the War of 1812 approached he was promoted to lieutenant colonel and took his regiment to join General Stephen van Rensselaer's army at Niagara in October. During the Battle of Queenston Heights on 13 October, Scott crossed the Niagara River to join the Regular troops already fighting there, but the militia reinforcements refused to go over. With the senior officer wounded and evacuated, Scott took charge and defended the heights from several attacks before being overwhelmed and taken prisoner.

Eventually exchanged, Scott emerged as one of the few American heroes of the fiasco. The defeat taught him the invaluable lesson of taking a defensive-position initiative on the battlefield. From then on Scott always sought the offensive. At Fort George, Ontario, on 27 May 1813, he launched an amphibious assault, capturing the fort and routing the British. At age 28, Scott was promoted to brigadier general, and at the battle of Chippewa on 5 July 1814, his well-drilled brigade flanked the British army. He did so again at Lundy's Lane on the 25th.

Scott retained his rank in the postwar reduction and spent time observing armies in Europe before returning to duty as one of the two Army department commanders. Unfortunately, his vanity, propensity for taking quick personal offense, and a sharp tongue brought him into a life-long bitter feud with his equally quarrelsome peer, Edmund Gaines.

Scott later served as senior commander for six months in Florida during the Second Seminole War until recalled to a hearing on his conflict with Gaines. His success in cooling tensions along the Canadian border in 1838 restored his image, and he became commanding general of the Army in 1841.

Initially kept out of the Mexican War for political reasons, Scott finally got his chance in March 1847 when he led an amphibious landing to capture Vera Cruz. He then marched inland and defeated the Mexican army under General Santa Anna in a series of battles, finally taking Mexico City in September. During the campaign, Scott kept tight discipline and enforced his regulations to protect the Mexican civilians. His policy paid off—many Mexican villagers came to tolerate the Americans at least as much their own troops. After the fall of Mexico City, a delegation even offered Scott the presidency of Mexico, which he declined.

The elderly Scott had no active role in the Civil War before stepping down in 1862, but his plan for strategic victory over the South, the so-called Anaconda Plan, brought Union victory. His example of leadership in Mexico shaped many Army leaders, north and south, including Robert E. Lee, George B. McClellan, P T. G. Beauregard, and Ulysses S. Grant.

—*Kevin M. Hymel*

into the Mexican camp. Meanwhile, Pillow's attack south of the road becomes confused and fails. Before it can be untangled, the Mexicans withdraw, pursued by dragoons and a light artillery battery. American losses are 63 killed and 368 wounded out of 8,500. Mexican losses are uncertain, but 199 officers and 2,837 enlisted are captured, along with Santa Anna's wooden leg and 83 artillery pieces. Scott enters Jalapa the next day.

25 April. Doniphan Departs Chihuahua.
Orders arrive from Taylor on the 23rd, telling Doniphan to join him at Saltillo. Doniphan's first element leaves two days later. The trail is rough, rutted, and dusty, and it crosses 75 miles of desert, but the wagons and troops try to make 25 miles a day. Several men die of typhoid.

May. Taylor Goes on Defensive.
Secretary Marcy allocates the ten new regiments between Taylor and Scott, giving Taylor an infantry brigade of four regiments and the new 3d Dragoons. Taylor requests permission for an offensive campaign before the enlistments of his 12-month Volunteers end in May, but it is not approved. Within weeks the Volunteers depart, forcing him to assume a defensive posture in the north. Bored troops and inactivity soon breed discipline problems.

6 May. Volunteers Depart Scott's Army. Jalapa.
The one-year enlistments for many of Scott's Volunteers expire in June. Almost none of the men want to reenlist, so Scott sends seven regiments back to Vera Cruz to depart, leaving him only 7,000 men. The same day, Worth captures Puebla, 60 miles away, where some American prisoners are freed. Scott appoints Worth as military governor.

12–13 May. Missourians Battle Apaches.
Apache raiders strike during the night on 12 May, taking several dozen horses, and Captain John Reid takes a patrol in pursuit. They join with friendly Mexican ranchers and the joint force tracks the 40 Apaches to a water hole. Reid and several Mexicans decoy the Apaches into an ambush. The two sides charge each other repeatedly in a wild melee at close range before the Indians finally ride away. Several Missourians are wounded and 15 Apaches are dead. Eighteen Mexican women and children are freed and more than 500 horses recovered.

22 May–6 June. Doniphan's Men Head Home.
On the 22nd the 1st Missouri column reaches Wool's camp. The issued cannon are turned in, but Wool lets the Volunteers keep the captured Mexican guns. The next day the Volunteers ride to Monterrey, where Taylor gives

orders for official release from service. By 6 June, the last of Doniphan's Missouri Volunteers are on steamers for home. After a march of more than 2,100 miles, Doniphan is bringing almost 90 percent of his men back.

31 May. Kearny Returns with Fremont. Monterey, California.

Kearny appoints Colonel Richard Mason as commander of the 10th Military Department, then begins the overland return to Washington. With him are Lieutenant Cooke and Fremont, who is unaware that Kearny plans to press court-martial charges against him. Nineteen of Fremont's original party return also.

4 June. Scott Withdraws His Rear Security. Jalapa.

Scott must rebuild his army. He recalls all the garrisons left for security along his route of supply to Vera Cruz, cutting himself off from his base of supply, and concentrates his army at Puebla. Worth's poor governance of Puebla, however, is causing major problems, Scott convenes a court-martial to investigate the complaints, and Worth receives an official reprimand.

26 June. Indians Attack Wagon Trains. Pawnee Ford, Indian Territory.

Small detachments of dragoons are attempting to protect the Army's line of supply from Santa Fe to Monterrey. On 26 June, Lieutenant John Love and a detachment of 80 1st Dragoons come to the aid of two supply trains under Indian attack. Five dragoons are killed and six wounded. Secretary Marcy orders the formation of a battalion of five companies from Fort Leavenworth to be stationed along the trail.

August. Reinforcements Arrive for Scott. Puebla.

The troops are diverted from Taylor and detachments of the new regiments (9th, 11th, 12th, 14th, 15th Infantry, and 3d Dragoons) and a few recruits begin to arrive. Several supply trains and columns of troops are attacked by guerrillas. In July, a brigade under Pillow marches in, followed in August by 2,500 men led by Brigadier General Franklin Pierce. They also bring money for the troops, who have not been paid in eight months, forcing soldiers to loot to augment their rations. Scott's army tops out at about 14,000; 10,738 of them are fit for duty.

6–7 August. Scott Marches on Mexico City. Puebla.

Unofficial peace negotiations come to nothing, freeing Scott to begin offensive operations. While his staff engineers scout the roads, Scott organizes four divisions—1st Division with six regiments (Worth); 2d Division with six regiments (Twiggs); 3d Division with five "new" infantry regiments and the Voltigeurs (Pillow); and a 4th Division (Quitman) with the three

Opposite: *Colonel Jefferson Davis led his regiment of red-frocked Mississippi Rifles forward in a charge that scattered the advancing Mexican lines at a critical moment during the Battle of Buena Vista. (The Mississippi Rifles," Ken Riley, National Guard Heritage print)*

Right: *The Army's one-of-a-kind experimental Rocket and Howitzer Battery is shown here firing at the besieged city of Vera Cruz. Success with the rockets was less than hoped due to lack of a reliable means of guiding the rockets. ("Vera Cruz, Rocket and Howitzer Battery," Don Stivers)*

remaining Volunteer regiments and a detachment of marines. Each division has at least one company of horse-drawn artillery. The 3d Division also has the Howitzer and Rocket Company. The three dragoon regiments are in a separate brigade under Harney, which on the 7th leads the army toward Mexico City. Scott leaves a garrison of about 400 under Colonel Thomas Childs to secure Puebla's supply depots and hospitals.

11–17 August. **Advance on Mexico City. Yalta.**
On the 11th, Scott's lead elements arrive at Ayolta, overlooking Mexico City about 15 miles away. Engineers including Mason, Lee, Beauregard, and McClellan are sent to determine the best approach to the city. With only four days' rations left, Scott must act. On the 15th, Scott learns of a southern road to the crossroads at San Agustin that will bear the artillery and wagons and turns the army onto it. Despite portions of the road being under water, only three days later the army occupies the town, only nine miles south of Mexico City.

19–20 August. **Battle of Contreras.**
Engineers again scout the roads north and west. Worth finds a strong Mexican position at San Antonio blocking the road north. Scott orders him to halt while

engineers and work details from Pillow's division improve a trail found by Lee and Beauregard leading to another north-south road farther west. The trail cuts through an extensive lava bed and emerges at Contreras. Strong Mexican units have moved into the same area, and the engineers are soon under heavy fire. Pillow reacts with artillery and sends Riley's brigade forward, unwittingly placing it between two large Mexican forces. He follows up with another brigade and the 15th Infantry, then neither he nor his adjutant, Captain Joseph Hooker, seem to know what next to do. On his own initiative, Brevet Brigadier Persifor Smith leads his brigade forward and assumes command of the exposed troops. Seeing an opening, Scott shifts more forces to the west. When Smith learns of a trail found by Engineer Lieutenant Zealous B. Tower that circles behind the Mexican position near Contreras, he takes three brigades of 4,500 men on a stormy night march that gets them into position by dawn. A surprise dawn attack destroys the Mexicans in 17 minutes. Two cannon lost by O'Brien at Buena Vista are recaptured, along with five generals and more than 800 prisoners.

20 August. **Battle of Churubusco.**
Scott uses the Contreras road to circle north around the lava field to the river crossing at Churubusco, north of San Antonio. He finds two strongpoints—the

stone Convent of San Mateo and the fortified gateway at the bridge—guarding the crossing. Four brigades attack the convent with great difficulty through cornfields and irrigation ditches. East of the lava field, Worth uses a brigade to outflank and rout the defenders at San Antonio. He continues north to join Pillow in an attack on the bridge. Worth's 6th, 5th, and 8th Infantry regiments are pushed back several times before the bridge is captured. Finally, after the 3d Infantry climbs the convent walls and corners the defenders in the buildings, a white flag is accepted. A

detachment of 1st Dragoons led by Captain Philip Kearny and Lieutenant Richard S. Ewell pursues the Mexicans almost to the city gates. They capture an artillery position but then must retreat, during which a grapeshot mangles Kearny's left arm. Scott's losses in the two days of fighting are 137 killed and 865 wounded, but Santa Anna has lost 10,000 killed, wounded, or captured. Among the prisoners are 72 American deserters of the San Patricio Battalion.

Above: *With artillery support, the Regiment of Voltigeurs and 11th Infantry are able to finally seize the fortified buildings on the road to Mexico City known as the Molino del Ray. ("Battle of Molino del Ray," James Walker, Army Art Collection, NMUSA)*

Left: *General Zachary Taylor directs artillery fire during the battle of Buena Vista. ("A Little More Grape, Captain Bragg," Lithograph by Currier, 1847, Picture History)*

8 September. Battle of Molino del Ray.
Worth attacks before his artillery is in position, and the initial assault on Molino del Ray by Colonel John Garland's brigade of foot artillery is turned back with heavy losses. After repeated assaults Lieutenant Colonel Joseph E. Johnston's Voltigeurs and the 11th Infantry finally break through a wall and fight building to building until the Mexicans withdraw. Fighting at the Casa is also fierce, but shelling finally drives the Mexicans out. In the two hours of fighting Worth's losses are 116 killed and almost 700 wounded. More than 2,000 Mexicans are killed or wounded.

12–14 September. Assault on Chapultepec.
The castle of Chapultepec sits on a rocky hill guarding two causeways to the city gates. American artillery bombards the castle and its defensive works on the 12th and the morning of the 13th. Scott then orders a main attack by two divisions from the west—Pillow's division with Worth in support on his left, while Quitman's division moves on the right along a causeway toward the east end of the hill. Pillow's brigades fight their way through a grove of trees at the base of the hill and up the slope. The attack falters at the walls when the assault parties with the scaling ladders fail to appear, and Pillow asks Worth for reinforcements. Quitman's men are also stopped by artillery defending the causeway. Quitman sends Smith's brigade to flank the position while also sending Shield's' brigade with ladders to assist Pillow. Worth's men and the ladders appear at about the same

Above: *The American assault surges over the walls on Chapultepec Castle, with the Voltigeurs the first to place their colors on the wall. ("Storming of Chapultepec, 13 September 1847," copyright Stock Montage, Inc.)*

Right: *Major General Scott was a believer in drill, discipline, and formal reviews. Here, he pays honor to the men who had brought him success in the Mexican campaign. ("Scott Reviews Army of Occupation," Decatur House, Washington, D.C.)*

21 August–7 September. Armistice. Tucubaya.
Santa Anna asks for an armistice and Scott agrees. The time is spent resting the army and obtaining supplies. After two weeks of no progress in the talks and reports that Santa Anna is violating the truce by improving defenses, Scott ends the armistice. Worth is ordered to attack the next morning with his entire division to seize Molino del Ray and Casa Mata, a complex of fortified buildings where a gun foundry is suspected.

22 August. Fremont Arrested. Fort Leavenworth.
Kearny watches as a lieutenant reads the court-martial charges to Fremont. He is under arrest and must report to the Adjutant General in Washington.

Above: American artillery (perhaps Lieutenant James Longstreet's Battery) is shown moving forward to support infantry advancing past the captured Chapultepec (right) on the road to Mexico City. ("Attack on Mexico City," James Walker, Army Art Collection, NMUSA)

time, and the American assault surges over the castle walls. Johnston leads Voltigeurs forward while Lieutenant James Longstreet carries the 8th Infantry colors up the hill. When he's wounded he hands the flag to Lieutenant George Pickett, who takes it over the wall. Lieutenant Lewis Armistead is wounded as he leads men of the 6th Infantry up the hill. The troops from the three divisions become intermixed as they scramble into the castle. By 9:30 a.m. the Stars and Stripes has been raised. With the castle taken, Quitman leads the Mounted Rifles in a rush along the southern causeway to capture Belen Gate, while Worth, supported by Jackson's gun section, pushes toward the strongly fortified San Cosme Gate. Lieutenant Grant drags a mountain howitzer into a church belfry to engage the gate's defenders, and Lieutenant Henry Hunt brings more artillery into action. By dusk Worth's and Quitman's men are in the city, but they halt as darkness falls. Early in the morning of the 14th, a delegation comes to Scott to say Santa Anna and his army have fled the city. Within hours Scott, in full dress uniform with gold epaulets, rides into the main city plaza escorted by dragoons. Quitman is appointed military governor of the city. The task for Scott now becomes establishing security and military government of the occupied country.

13 September–12 October. Siege of Puebla.
In an attempt to cut off Scott from his base at Vera Cruz, Mexican forces infiltrate and surround the town and demand its surrender. Colonel Childs refuses and his small garrison in three strong points resists the attempts to take the town. Santa Anna arrives on the 22nd with more men, but Childs refuses to give up. Relief columns are held up by heavy rain and guerrilla attacks. A reinforced brigade under Brigadier Joseph Lane, including 2d Lieutenant A. P. Hill, 1st Artillery, fights its way from Vera Cruz. At Huamantla, Lane's advance guard of Texas Rangers is ambushed and Captain Samuel Walker is killed. On the 12th Lane's brigade arrives at Puebla to break the siege.

September–December. Scott Sets Up Occupation.
Scott leaves the Mexican officials in their positions, opens Mexican courts, orders respect for religious ceremonies, and reforms the tax system. He reorganizes his army into three brigades and designates a geographic area for each to control. In setting his own command accounts, he finds an excess of $100,000. He sets the money aside and it is later used to establish a Soldiers' Home in Washington, D.C., for retired enlisted men of the Regular Army.

October–November. **Fighting a Guerrilla War. Aqua Frio.** Despite the fall of Mexico City, the countryside is not secure. Army wagon trains and small detachments are attacked along the roads and in the villages. In October, Scott stations Army units to garrison key villages for security; he places emphasis on building relations with the local civilians. Harsh sentences also fall on Americans found guilty of mistreating Mexican civilians; several soldiers are hanged for offenses. Lane attacks a guerrilla force at Attics on 19 October, chasing them from the town. Later in October he raids a guerrilla camp at Tlaxala, taking 20 captives. A detachment of 2d Dragoons is ambushed on 2 November by 150 guerrillas near Aqua Frio. Fighting dismounted, the 23 dragoons hold out, losing three killed and two wounded but killing the Mexican leader. Lane leads another raid on Tlaxala, taking 13 prisoners and recovering 21 stolen wagons. On the 23rd and 24th, Company D, the 3d Dragoons fight off two more attacks. Lane leads a raid on a guerrilla base, freeing 23 American prisoners and killing more than 60 Mexicans.

1 November. **Wounded Evacuated from Mexico City.** On the 1st, Colonel Harney and a 350-man detachment escort more than 400 wagons of sick and wounded eastward. It is the first wagon train back since the army left Puebla in August.

2 November. **Fremont Court-Martial Begins. Washington Arsenal.** A board of 13 officers convenes to hear the charges and testimony in the Fremont case. Fremont faces three charges: mutiny, refusing a lawful command, and conduct prejudicial to military discipline. The trial lasts until January.

25 November. **Taylor Departs Mexico. Matamoras.** Taylor passes command to Wool and departs the next day on a six-month leave. He arrives in New Orleans on 3 December to a hero's welcome. Although still in official command of his army, he never returns to Mexico.

1848

18 January–10 February. **Lane Leads the Counter-Guerrilla War.**
Guerrilla and bandit activity continue in Central Mexico. Lane takes a mixed force of Mounted Rifles, Texas Rangers, and 3d Dragoons on a search to capture Santa Anna. They have several skirmishes but fail to find him.

31 January. **Fremont Dismissed from Army. Washington.**
Fremont is found guilty of all three charges and sentenced to be dismissed from the Army. The court's findings are sent to President Polk for approval. He does not approve the mutiny verdict and offers Fremont a chance to return to duty with the Mounted Rifles. Fremont declines unless all charges are lifted. Polk does not reply, and Fremont resigns from the Army on 15 March.

2 February. **Treaty of Guadalupe-Hidalgo.**
President Polk signs the treaty ending the war with Mexico. It is ratified 10 March, ending the war.

EYEWITNESS: LIEUTENANT GRANT AT MEXICO CITY, 12 SEPTEMBER 1847

Tom Jones

At this stage of the war, sencond Lieutenant Ulysses S. "Sam" Grant was serving as quartermaster for the 4th Infantry, part of Brigadier General William J. Worth's division. However, Grant frequently got into action by attaching himself to a front-line unit. On one such occasion during Worth's attack on the San Cosme gate of Mexico City, Grant played a unique role in assisting the American advance. He recalled:

"Worth's command gradually advanced to the front now open to it. Later in the day in reconnoitering I found a church off to the south of the road, which looked to me as if the belfry would command the ground back of the *garita* (gateway) San Cosme. I got an officer of the voltigeurs, with a mountain howitzer and the men to work it, to go with me. The road being in possession of the enemy, we had to take the field to the south to reach the church. This took us over several ditches breast deep in water

and grown up with water plants. . . . The howitzer was taken to pieces and carried by the men to its destination. When I knocked for admission a priest came to the door, who, politely, declined to admit us. With the little Spanish then at my command, I explained to him that he might save property by opening the door, and he certainly would save himself becoming a prisoner, for a time at least; and besides, I intended to go in whether he consented or not. He began to see his duty in the same light that I did, and opened the door, though he did not look as if it gave him special pleasure to do so. The gun was carried to the belfry and put together. We were not more than two or three hundred yards from San Cosme. The shots from our little gun dropped in upon the enemy and created great confusion. Why they did not send out a small party and capture us, I do not know. We had no infantry or other defenses besides our one gun.

"The effect of this gun upon the troops about the gate of the city was so marked that General Worth saw it from his position. (This was mentioned in the reports of Major Lee, Colonel Garland, and General Worth) He was so pleased that he sent a staff officer, Lieutenant Pemberton—later Lieutenant-General commanding the defenses of Vicksburg—to bring me to him. He expressed his gratification at the services the howitzer in the church steeple was doing, saying that every shot was effective, and ordered a captain of voltigeurs to report to me with another howitzer to be placed along with the one already rendering so much service. I could not tell the General that there was not room enough in the steeple for another gun, because he probably would have looked upon such a statement as a contradiction from a second lieutenant. I took the captain with me, but did not use the gun."
(Personal Memoirs of Ulysses S. Grant, by Ulysses S. Grant)

While Grant's gun was doing its service, his best friend in Mexico, Lieutenant Calvin Benjamin, was mortally wounded. That evening, learning the news, Grant hurried to Calvin's side in time to have his friend die in his arms.

—*Vince Hawkins*

Several days after notification of the signing, a delegation of senior Mexicans asks Scott to accept a $1 million position as dictator of Mexico for six years. He turns them down.

17–25 February. **Lane Pursues Guerrillas.**
Colonel Lane takes his antiguerrilla force on another sweep against guerrillas operating north of Mexico City. On the 25th he finds a large Mexican force near Pachuca and attacks it, capturing or killing more than 50 guerrillas.

18 February. **Scott Relieved of Command. Mexico City.**
A battle between Scott and some of his generals as to who did what to win the war is just starting. Scott places Worth, Pillow, and Duncan under arrest for contempt and disrespect. Polk drops the charges against Worth and Duncan and changes the court to one of inquiry. He orders Scott relieved of command in Mexico and back to Washington. Major General William O. Butler becomes commander and organizes the drawdown of American troops.

Left: *Illustrated here is a selection of the infantry, dragoon, and artillery uniforms worn during the Mexican campaign. (Voltigeur, Infantry, Dragoon, Artillery, Campaign Uniform, 1841–1851," H. A. Ogden, Dover Publications)*

Opposite: *An artillery piece has been moved forward and is used to fire point blank range at a fortified gate during a final assault on Mexico City. ("Assault on Mexico City," James Walker, West Point Museum Collection, U.S. Military Academy, West Point, New York)*

9 March. **Price Attacks After Treaty is Signed.**
Believing a Mexican army is coming north to attack,
Price gathers several companies of Regulars and
Volunteers and marches south from Santa Fe. When
he finds no enemy, he decides to attack Chihuahua,
where a Mexican force is located. He occupies the
town on 7 March, dismissing as a trick repeated
messages from the Mexicans that a peace treaty has
been signed. Price advances to Santa Cruz de Rosales.
He bombards the town with artillery, then attacks. His
men fight into the center of the town by dusk, when
the Mexican commander surrenders. Of his 665 men,
Price has four killed and 19 wounded. The Mexicans
report more than 40 soldiers and civilians killed. This
is the last battle of the war.

21 March–21 April. **Court of Inquiry. Mexico City.**
A court of inquiry convenes to hear the testimony on
the charges and countercharges. Scott is ready to drop
the matter, but Pillow demands the inquiry and
witnesses are called until 21 April, when the court
decides to recess and reconvene in the United States.
When it finally ends on 1 July, Pillow is found
faultless.

1 May–2 August. **Americans Withdraw from Mexico.**
When Scott arrives in Vera Cruz, he refuses space on a
fast steamer so that wounded and sick soldiers may
depart first; he leaves on a sailing brig, arriving in New
York on 20 May. Troops are withdrawn to Mexico City
from their occupation posts, and on 30 May American
troops begin evacuating the city. On 1 June all General
Court-Martial prisoners, including the remaining San
Patricios, are released. In a final ceremony on the 12th,
Worth turns the city over to Mexican officials and
marches his division for Jalapa, where troops are held to
avoid yellow fever until their ships are ready. Most sail
for New Orleans or Pass Christian, Mississippi, where
hospitals are set up for the sick and wounded. As the ten
"new" regiments (9th–16th Infantry, 3d Dragoons, and
Voltigeurs) arrive from Mexico, they are sent to
demobilization posts and discharged.

30 May. **Surgeon General Lawson Promoted.**
Army Surgeon General Thomas Lawson is promoted
to brevet brigadier general for meritorious conduct
during the war. He is the first Army medical officer
promoted to general.

19 June. Peacetime Army Organization.
Congress decides to keep the Army at its prewar 1846 strength, with the exception that the number of privates and some staff are reduced. Strength overages are to be reduced through attrition, and officers are permitted to keep their wartime promotions but are returned to their original units. Many of the light batteries are dismounted to save money. Congress approves a death award of three months' pay to the families of enlisted men who died in the war.

1 July. Taylor Appointed to Western Division.
Brevet Major General Zachary Taylor assumes command of the Western Division at Baton Rouge. Although he is the Whig candidate for President, Taylor remains on active duty. He retains the position until he resigns from the Army on 31 January 1849.

6 July. Lax Wartime Discipline Tightens.
In an effort to tighten standards of military appearance, which have become lax during the war, General Order 25 is issued directing "cropped hair," no

whiskers below the lower ear tip, and no moustaches—except in the cavalry regiments. The Army also reports it has 8,866 officers and men, with 7,500 fit for duty.

18 July. Dragoons Sent to California.
As part of the redistribution of Regular units, some detachments go to California. Brevet Lieutenant Colonel John Marshall Washington, 4th Artillery, is given command of a group composed of three companies each from 1st and 2d Dragoons and Company C, 3d Artillery. They march to Santa Fe, arriving in early October. Two of the 2d Dragoon companies under Major Lawrence P. Graham then continue west to Los Angeles, arriving on 9 January 1849, after almost starving in the desert.

2 August. Last American Troops Depart Mexico. Vera Cruz.
The 1st Artillery is the last regiment to depart on 1 August. The next day quartermaster soldiers with horses and equipment depart on the last steamer for New

Orleans. Losses to the Regular Army during the war were 1,010 killed in action, 4,899 dead from disease, and 2,745 wounded. The Volunteers suffered 711 combat deaths, 6,256 from disease, and 1,357 wounded. More than 9,000 men are listed as deserters.

7 August. Regiment of Mounted Rifles Reconstituted. Jefferson Barracks.

After the Mounted Rifles arrive at the Barracks on 24 July, a legal technicality in the terms of enlistment in the regiment forced discharge of the entire regiment on 7 August and reenlistment of those willing to do so. Many of the men sign up again, as do former 3d Dragoons and new recruits. The regiment is given its original mission to secure the Oregon Trail and preparations begin.

31 August. Army Geographic Commands Realigned.

The United States has acquired another 529,017 square miles to administer and defend. The War Department forms the 11th Military Department in the Western Division, incorporating the Oregon Territory. The boundaries of the old departments are adjusted and veterans such as Worth, Twiggs, Kearny, Wool, and others are named for the commands. In October, a Pacific Division is created to include both California and Oregon, with Brevet Major General Persifoer Smith in command.

7 September. Scott Moves Army Headquarters. New York.

For personal and political reasons Scott moves the Army headquarters from Washington to New York. He also takes command of the Eastern Division.

7 November. Zachary Taylor Elected President.

Major General Zachary Taylor, a serving Regular officer, is elected President. It is the first and only time that has happened. Since Taylor still commands the Western Division, Scott does not feel it is appropriate to have a President-elect technically as his military subordinate. Scott temporarily gives up his position as Army Commanding General, retaining only command of the Eastern Division. Taylor resigns from the Army on 31 January.

Opposite: *The Mexican War continued the tradition of joint Army-Navy operations that has long been the hallmark of American campaigns overseas. ("Scott Landing at Vera Cruz," U.S. Department of Defense)*

Above: *A victorious General Winfield Scott and his staff ride into the plaza of Mexico City. ("Scott Enters Mexico City," Carl Nebel, courtesy Special Collections Division, University of Texas at Arlington Libraries, Arlington, TX)*

GARRISONING THE WESTERN FRONTIER

1849–1860

GARRISONING THE WESTERN FRONTIER

1849–1860

Lieutenant Colonel Clayton R. Newell, USA (Ret)

When Mexico ceded California and New Mexico to the United States after the Mexican War, the Army found itself playing key roles in bringing the new acquisitions under national control as it subdued Native American tribes in the area, protected the waves of settlers that swept across the Great Plains, and explored, mapped, and surveyed the western frontier. Expending considerable effort and resources between the end of the Mexican War and the beginning of the Civil War, the Army established more than 80 new posts in the West, most of them built by soldiers. Few of these posts remain today. Some, such as Fort Bliss, Texas, and Fort Riley, Kansas, are still important Army installations; others remain as towns that survived after the posts were abandoned, but most simply faded away when the Army moved on to other places.

Many of the Army's western forts were evacuated in 1861 when the bulk of the Regular Army withdrew to fight in the Civil War. All of the posts in Texas were evacuated when Brigadier General David Twiggs, the department commander, surrendered them to Confederate forces early in 1861. Only two regiments—the 5th Infantry in the Southwest and the 9th Infantry in California—remained in the West to represent federal authority during the war, and they occupied only a portion of the western posts.

The frontier posts posed new challenges for the Army. Before the Mexican War there were only 56 military posts in the United States and they were generally located along the Gulf of Mexico, the Mississippi River, and the Great Lakes, where they were accessible by water. But in the West there were few navigable waterways, and keeping the far-flung posts supplied required moving wagon trains long distances through hostile territory that posed significant challenges from the environment and the Native Americans who lived there. Army duty in the West was difficult. Indians posed a threat to the isolated posts, and providing military escorts to protect supply trains, immigrant parties, and work details required long periods in the field away from even the rudimentary comforts of the small forts and camps. As the Army sent more men west, the posts were improved to raise the standard of living. By 1853, Jefferson Barracks, Missouri, included rectangular wooden buildings with comfortable quarters for officers and enlisted men, and by 1860 the Army had developed recruiting depots and was experimenting with replacement training camps. After 1850, the Army was able to adequately man most of its posts in the West, although usually at less than authorized strength.

There are no streamers on the Army Flag for campaigns in the West between the Mexican and Civil Wars, but there was considerable fighting. While the United States government negotiated more than 60 treaties and agreements with various Indian tribes between 1849 and 1860, there were still frequent violent clashes between Native Americans and soldiers throughout the period. The Office of Indian Affairs listed 22 distinct conflicts during the 1850s. The Army was at the forefront of implementing a national policy of displacing Native Americans to accommodate the needs of white settlers. When the Indians resisted being moved from their traditional homelands, the Army met force with force to settle the issue. When a tribe agreed to a treaty, however, the Army became responsible for protecting them from hostile Indians and disgruntled settlers. The

result was a dynamic tension between the Native Americans and the new residents, with the Army in the middle carrying out its dual responsibilities of protecting settlers and looking out for the interests of Indians.

In conducting its duties on the western frontier, the Army relied heavily on what today would be considered junior officers—captains and lieutenants. But because the seniority system kept officers in lower grades for many years, most were experienced soldiers. Many company-grade officers who spent their formative years in the west building forts, fighting Indians, and protecting settlers, used their experience to good advantage and rose to senior positions in both armies during the Civil War. While they are best remembered for their accomplishments

as general officers in opposing armies, they also made notable contributions as the U.S. Army garrisoned the western frontier.

Pages 324–325: *In the wake of the war with Mexico, U.S. troops were assigned to duties in a vastly increased area of operations where distances usually meant horse soldiers enjoyed an advantage over infantry. ("Dragoons in the Mountains," Don Troiani, www.historicalartprints.com)*

Above: *In addition to dragoons wielding sabers and carbines, men of the Regiment of Mounted Rifles carried then state-of-the-art rifled muskets, which allowed them greater range. ("Mounted Rifles," Don Troiani, www.historicalartprints.com)*

GARRISONING THE WESTERN FRONTIER

1849–1860

"All posts through an Indian country should be placed on, or near the great thoroughfares where aid and protection can be had by the traveler in case of necessity."

—Colonel Joseph K. F. Mansfield

1849

January. **Status of the Army.**
The forces raised to fight the war with Mexico are released as soon as possible. Only 15 regiments remain, plus about 651 men in the Engineer and Ordnance Departments. The total number of authorized troops is almost 3,000 men less than the Army had in 1815. In addition, the Army is hit with gold rush fever. The discovery of gold in California causes widespread desertions, especially among soldiers being sent to the far West. In the first eight months of the year, the companies in California lose almost 500 men out of 1,200 to the gold fields. Recruiting is almost impossible, and actual strength is about 10,000 officers and men.

12 February–12 April. **Route Reconnaissance. Texas.**
Lieutenants Henry C. Whiting, Engineers, and Martin L. Smith, Topographical Engineers, are sent

with nine men to find a road route between San Antonio and El Paso. They survive the 1,600-mile trip through Indian country without incident.

28 February. **Army Boundary Explorations.**
Major William H. Emory, Topographical Engineers, is named chief astronomer for the survey party organized to establish the boundary between the United States and Mexico in accordance with the Treaty of Guadalupe-Hidalgo. His assistants are Lieutenants L. F. Hardcastle and Amiel Weeks Whipple.

2 March. **Judge Advocate of the Army Created.**
Congress establishes the Judge Advocate of the Army. The position had been abolished in the 1802 reduction of the Army.

3 March. **Indian Affairs Established.**
Congress creates the Department of the Interior, which takes responsibility for Indian affairs from the War Department. As a result, one federal agency, the Interior Department, makes treaties with Indian tribes while another, the War Department, has to enforce them.

3 March. **Fort McIntosh Built. Texas.**
Second Lieutenant Egbert Ludovicus Viele, 1st Infantry, establishes the post on the Rio Grande at Laredo to guard the frontier and prevent Indians from moving between Mexico and the United States. Named for Colonel James S. McIntosh, 5th Infantry, who died of wounds received at the Battle of Molino del Rey, the post is abandoned in 1858. It is rebuilt after the Civil War and used as an Army post until 1946. Since 1947 it has been the home of Laredo Community College.

8 March. **New Secretary of War.**
George W. Crawford becomes the Secretary of War. A lawyer from Georgia, he has no military experience prior to accepting the post and resigns when President Zachary Taylor dies in 1850. He will chair the Georgia secession convention in 1861.

ARMY BATTLE STREAMERS— INDIAN WARS 1849–1860

SEMINOLES 1855 -1858

Seminoles, 1855–1858

13 March. **Fort Inge Established. Texas.**
Captain Sidney Burbank, 1st Infantry, establishes a post on the Leon River near the present town of Uvalde as part of the frontier defensive system. Named for First Lieutenant Zebulon M. P. Inge, 2d Dragoons, who was killed in the Battle of Resaca de la Palma, it is occupied by Confederate troops during the Civil War. In 1866 federal troops return and occupy it until it is abandoned in 1869.

18 March. **Fort Croghan Built. Texas.**
Brevet Second Lieutenant Charles H. Tyler, 2d Dragoons, establishes the post on Hamilton Creek at the present town of Burnet. Part of the frontier defensive system, the fort is named for Colonel George Croghan, an inspector general, who died in 1849. The fort is abandoned in 1853.

27 March. **New Post on Brazos. Fort Graham, Texas.**
The 2d Dragoons of Captain Ripley A. Arnold set up a post on the Brazos River northwest of the present town of Hillsboro as part of the frontier defense system. Named for Lieutenant Colonel William M. Graham, 11th Infantry, who was killed in the Battle of Molino del Rey, it is abandoned in 1853.

27 March. **Eagle Pass Post Established. Fort Duncan, Texas.**
Captain Sidney Burbank, 1st Infantry, establishes the post on the Rio Grande at Eagle Pass. Named for Colonel James Duncan, an inspector general, it is evacuated in 1861 and garrisoned by Confederate troops. Federal troops reoccupy the fort from 1868 until 1883, when the Army and the land owners are unable to agree on a fair price for the site. In 1894 the Army acquires the land, and the post is occupied again for a short time following the Mexican Revolution before being abandoned in 1916.

4 April. **Army Explores Santa Fe Trail. Fort Smith, Arkansas.**
Captain Randolph Barnes Marcy and Lieutenant James Hervey Simpson, along with two companies of the 5th Infantry and a company of the 1st Dragoons, begin a three-month expedition to survey a southern wagon trail and potential rail route to Santa Fe.

13 *April*. Fort Ripley Built. Minnesota.
Colonel George M. Brooke, 5th Infantry, selects a site along the Mississippi River in 1848 to control and protect the Winnebago Indians on their reservation and to protect the area from Sioux and Chippewa. The fort is named for Brigadier General Eleazar W. Ripley, who served in the War of 1812. After a fire in January 1877 destroys the officers' quarters and storehouses, the Army abandons the post.

10 *May*. Mounted Rifles March for Oregon. Jefferson Barracks, Missouri.
Colonel William W. Loring departs for Oregon with the reconstituted Regiment of Mounted Riflemen. They are to establish posts along the Oregon Trail to protect settlers moving west. The regiment has been reorganizing and training since resolution of its enlistment problems after returning from the Mexican War.

10 *May*. Scott Back in Command of the Army.
Major General Winfield Scott resumes command of the Army. President James Polk vacated the office when he agreed to let Scott command Army forces in the Mexican War. After the war, Scott commands only the Eastern Department until Zachary Taylor officially retires from the Army and is inaugurated as President.

15 *May*. Fort Vancouver Built. Oregon Territory.
Captain John S. Hathaway, 1st Artillery, takes over a Hudson's Bay Company fort named for Captain

Above: *In addition to typical military assignments, the U.S. Army undertook many expeditions to chart the American West as follow-up to what Lewis and Clark had done nearly a half-century earlier. ("Scouts in the Tetons," John Mix Stanley, Gilcrease Museum)*

George Vancouver, an English navigator and explorer. In 1859 Vancouver Arsenal is established at the post; the name is changed to Vancouver Barracks in 1879. The Army abandons the barracks in 1946; it is now a historical monument.

6 *June*. Dragoons Build Fort Worth. Texas.
Captain Ripley A. Arnold, 2d Dragoons, places the fort on the Trinity River at the present city of Fort Worth to protect the area from Indians. Named for Colonel William Jenkins Worth, 8th Infantry, the department commander, the fort is abandoned in 1853.

27 *June*. Army Explores Sacramento River. Benicia, California.
Captain William H. Warner, Topographical Engineers, begins a reconnaissance from the Upper Sacramento River over the Sierra Mountains to the Humboldt River.

7 *July*. Fort Lincoln Built. Texas.
First Lieutenant James Longstreet, 8th Infantry, establishes the post on the Rio Seco near the present town of Old D'Hanis. Built to protect the settlement

of D'Hanis, the post is named for Captain George Lincoln, 8th Infantry, who was killed in the Battle of Buena Vista. The post is abandoned in 1852.

15 August. **Conrad Becomes Secretary of War.**
Charles M. Conrad, a Louisiana lawyer and politician with no military experience, becomes the Secretary of War for President Millard Fillmore. He resigned from the U.S. House of Representatives to accept the position. In 1851, as an economic move, he directs frontier post commanders to plant vegetable gardens, but the practice is soon abandoned as impractical at most forts. During the Civil War he serves in the Confederate Congress; he resumes the practice of law in New Orleans after the war.

16 August. **Navajo Expedition Santa Fe, New Mexico Territory.**
Lieutenant Colonel John M. Washington leads a punitive Army expedition against the Navajo Indians. Lieutenant James H. Simpson, Topographic Engineers, accompanying the expedition, is the first white man to discover and describe the Indian pueblos in Chaco Canyon. On the return march he examines some of the most important archaeological sites in the Southwest, including Pueblo Bonito, Zuni, and Inscription Rock.

Above: *Secretary of War George Washington Crawford assumed his duties on 8 March 1849 but left his post in less than a year. (Daniel Huntington, Army Art Collection, NMUSA)*

Below: *Dragoons of Company D appear in front of Fort Snelling, Minnesota, in a range of uniforms, from the colorful European-inspired full dress to mixed civilian-military garb often worn in the field. ("Company D, 1st Regiment of U.S. Dragoons," David P. Geister, Company of Military Historians)*

28 August. **Fort Steilacoom Built. Oregon.**
Captain Bennett H. Hill, 1st Artillery, establishes the post at the present town of Steilacoom. Second Lieutenant George Tallmadge, 4th Artillery, supervises construction of the fort, which is named for a small stream near the post. The fort is abandoned in 1874, and part of the land is given to the Territory of Washington for use as the Western State Hospital for the Insane. The rest of the land is transferred to the Interior Department in 1884.

31 August. **Navajo Expedition. Tunisha Valley, New Mexico Territory.**
Lieutenant Colonel Washington and James S. Calhoun, Indian agent for New Mexico, meet with Navajo chiefs to discuss a treaty. After the council Washington demands the return of a stolen horse, which prompts the Navajos to flee. Musket and artillery fire from Washington's forces kill six of the Indians. After pursuing the Navajos into their stronghold in Canyon de Chelly, Washington and Calhoun convince the Navajo tribal chiefs to sign a treaty.

September. **Army Explorer Killed. Goose Lake, California.**
Captain William H. Warner, Topographical Engineers, is killed by Pit River Indians when they ambush his expedition.

8 September. **Fort Bliss Established. Texas.**
Captain Jefferson Van Horn, 3d Infantry, establishes the post as part of the frontier defense system. It is located close to the Mexican border to deal with Indians, protect travelers along the route to California, and guard against raids from Mexico. It is named for Captain William Wallace Smith Bliss, Major General Zachary Taylor's son-in-law and adjutant general during the Mexican War. The post is evacuated in 1861 and largely destroyed by Confederates, but California troops reoccupy it in 1862 and begin rebuilding. The post occupies several more sites until the Army purchases the present location in 1890 and occupies it in 1893. It remains an active Army post.

11 September. **Army Explores Colorado River. Mission San Diego de Aleada, California.**
Lieutenant Amiel Weeks Whipple, accompanied by First Lieutenant Case J. Couts and his company of 1st Dragoons, departs to chart the location of the Gila and Colorado Rivers. Some 17 days later the party reaches the Colorado River.

October. **White Family Massacre. Point of Rocks, New Mexico.**
Ute and Jicillara Apache warriors attack the wagon train of J. M. White and kidnap his wife and daughter. Guided by Kit Carson, Captain William Grier leads his company of 1st Dragoons in pursuit and catches the Indians about a month later. Mrs. Smith was killed before she could be rescued, and the little girl was never seen again.

2 October. **Army Exploration Continues. Camp Calhoun, California.**
Lieutenant Couts establishes the camp on the Colorado River for Whipple's survey team. It is named for John C. Calhoun, Secretary of War from 1817 to 1825.

8 October. **Mounted Rifles Arrive. Oregon Territory.**
Colonel Loring, with five companies of the Regiment of Mounted Rifles and 175 wagons, arrives at the new regimental headquarters at Oregon City after a 2,016-mile march from Missouri. Four other companies have been detached along the Oregon Trail to establish posts at Fort Laramie and Fort Hall. The regiment is the first military unit to travel the entire length of the Oregon Trail.

26 October. **Fort Gates Built. Texas.**
Captain William R. Montgomery, 8th Infantry, establishes the post on the Leon River, about six miles from the present town of Gatesville, as part of the frontier defense system. Named for Captain Collison R. Gates, 8th Infantry, a veteran of the Mexican War who died in 1849, the post is abandoned in 1852.

Right: *Captain Howard Stansbury's assignment to chart the Great Salt Lake in 1849–1850 was typical of the Army's scientific expeditions. Their exploits were often recorded in illustrations for official reports. (Smithsonian Institution)*

1850

January. Status of the Army.

On-hand strength of the Army is 10,763 officers and men in regiments across the country at more than 100 different posts and forts. The 1st Infantry garrisons four forts in the Southwest. Some regiments seem destined never to settle down. The 7th Infantry is moved four times in less than six months. Rumors of riches in the gold mines of California cause major problems with desertions. Patrols led by regimental officers scour the Oregon and California hills for bands of deserters.

1 March. New Frontier Fort. Fort Merrill, Texas.

Captain Samuel M. Plummer, 1st Infantry, builds the post on the Nueces River. Part of the frontier defense system, it is named for Captain Moses E. Merrill, 5th Infantry, who was killed at the Battle of Molino. It is abandoned in 1855.

12 April. First Infantry Battles Indians. Laredo, Texas.

Companies G and I, 1st Infantry, fight off an Indian attack near Laredo, suffering eight men killed or wounded.

21 May. Fort Dalles Built on Columbia River. Oregon Territory.

Captain Stephen S. Tucker, Mounted Rifles, builds the post on the Columbia River near the present town of The Dalles. "The Dalles" comes from the French word "dalle," which describes river rapids flowing swiftly through a narrow channel over flat, basaltic rocks, as the Columbia River does in that area. The post is not regularly garrisoned after 1861, although it is used as a quartermaster depot to distribute supplies. The military land is transferred to the Interior Department in 1877.

17 June. Army Strength Increased.

Congress authorizes a slight increase to 74 enlisted men for each company stationed on the frontier, although the size of light artillery companies remains at 64. This brings the total authorized strength to 12,927 officers and men; actual strength is much lower. Almost 8,000 of the men present are stationed in Texas, New Mexico, California, and Oregon. The same legislation makes the enlistment period five years.

27 June. Army Explores Utah Territory.

Captain Howard Stansbury and Lieutenant John W. Gunnison complete the first survey of the Great Salt Lake area. They map a key route used by stage coaches, the Pony Express, and the Union Pacific Railroad. The expedition spends the winter at Salt Lake, where Stansbury makes a thorough survey that includes the western shores for the first time. At the same time Gunnison maps Utah Lake and writes the first objective study of the Mormons ever done by an outsider.

2 June. Fort Dodge Built. Iowa.

Captain Samuel Woods, 6th Infantry, establishes the post on the Des Moines River at the present town of Fort Dodge. Named for Colonel Henry Dodge, 1st Dragoons, the post is abandoned in 1853; William Williams, former post sutler, purchases it and lays out the town of Fort Dodge.

8 August. Dragoons Build Fort Atkinson. Kansas.
Lieutenant Colonel Edwin V. Sumner, 1st Dragoons, establishes the post to control the Indians and protect the Santa Fe Trail. Located on the Arkansas River close to the present Dodge City, the post is named for Colonel Henry Atkinson, 6th Infantry, who died in 1842. Because it was built of sod, it is popularly known as Fort Sod or Fort Sodom. It is used occasionally as a camp until Fort Dodge, Kansas, is established in 1865, then abandoned in 1854 because of the high cost of supplying it.

22 August. Fort Arbuckle Built. Indian Territory.
Near the Canadian River, Captain Randolph B. Marcy, 5th Infantry, establishes a fort to protect travelers on the route to New Mexico and California and the local Chickasaw Indians. Named for Colonel Matthew Arbuckle, 7th Infantry, the post is relocated in 1851 to the site of a Kickapoo Indian village about five miles from the Washita River. The post is evacuated in 1861 and occupied by Confederate Texas troops, then reoccupied by the 6th Infantry and 10th Cavalry after the Civil War. The Army abandons it in 1870, at which time it reverts to the Chickasaw Nation.

Above: *Shown here are typical firearms issued to the Army in the 1850s, including: (top) the smoothbore cavalry musketoon; (middle) a U.S. percussion-cap musket M1842; and (bottom) a Hall carbine M1843. (Photograph by Ed Castle, National Museum of American History, Smithsonian Institution)*

16 September. U.S. Military Academy Expands.
Congress authorizes the professors of engineering, philosophy, mathematics, ethics, and chemistry annual pay of $2,000; the professors of drawing and French each receive $1,500. The superintendent receives no less than the highest paid professor.

28 September. Army Pay Increased.
Congress grants officers serving in California and Oregon an additional $2 a day to help defray the higher living expenses in the West. Enlisted soldiers serving in the West are entitled to double pay, although the government retains half of that until the soldier receives an honorable discharge. Veterans of the Mexican War receive an additional $2 a month, and a five-year enlistment warrants a monthly bonus of $1.

6 November. Fort Built on Alcatraz Island. California.
Located in San Francisco Bay, the island is declared a military reservation by executive order. In 1853 First Lieutenant Zealous Bates Tower, Corps of Engineers, begins constructing fortifications, and the post is garrisoned in December 1859. It becomes a U.S. military prison in 1907 and a federal penitentiary for incorrigible civilians in 1934.

27 November. Fort Yuma Established. California.
Captain Samuel P. Huntington establishes the post on the site of Camp Calhoun. In 1851 it is moved to a low hill across the river from the present town of Yuma,

A SOLDIER'S LIFE IN THE FRONTIER ARMY

Everyday life for a soldier on the western frontier was best described as one of "glittering misery." The daily routine—one of poor food, rough quarters, low pay, extreme weather, endless work details, and boredom—was punctuated only by the daily guard mounting, weekly dress parades, and the occasional expeditions against Indians or bandits.

The garrison day started with reveille at 5:30 a.m. On campaign, wake-up could be as early as 3 a.m. The day was ruled by the soldier's "clock," the fife and drum, or later the bugle, with different "calls" to various duties. Roll was taken on average three times a day. Depending on the unit commander, drill could also be thrice daily and included the manual of arms, field exercises, and occasional target practice. "Fatigue" calls included police detail (cleaning the post), caring for animals, construction and maintenance of the post, wood and water details, kitchen detail, and road and bridge building. Escort duty and regular patrols were made away from the post. After the lowering of the flag at "Retreat," the last call, *Tattoo*, was played at about 9 p.m. All this for $7.00 a month (in 1854; $13.00 in 1866), rations, and longevity pay.

Unofficial positions such as unit carpenter, tailor, or barber excused the men from drill and work details and allowed them to augment their pay by earning extra money. This was especially the case with officers' orderlies whose cooking skills could earn them an additional $10 to $15 a month. Weekly dress parades were often a source of enjoyment, especially for families in a headquarters post where the regimental

band provided music. The hum-drum garrison life was such that some soldiers longed for field campaigns, for a short period, as a change.

Sergeant Eugene Bandel described his life in 1859 at Camp Prentiss, California, in a letter to his parents:

"At daybreak I am awakened by the drums and fifes. I get up, read the roll call of the company . . . and then go back to bed again. Towards six o'clock I arise once more, dress, etc. In the meantime the company clerk . . . has completed the sick list and the morning report. At seven the drums beat the sick call. The sergeant, or corporal, who has been assigned the duty for that particular day, takes the sick list and marches the sick who are in quarters (not in the hospital) to the tent of the doctor. At half past seven comes the call to breakfast, though, to be sure, the soldiers have usually eaten by that time. After signing the morning report, I then take it to the captain of the company, who also signs. After this it is delivered to the office of the adjutant. . . . The call to guard muster beats at eight. I inspect the detail for the company and march them to parade. At nine the drums beat for drill. The company is then formed and for one hour is drilled in marching and the manual of arms. After this, as a rule, my labors for the day are over until towards evening, with the exception of the summons for orders which beats at eleven o'clock. . . . After that I am my own master until five-thirty, since the different calls during the day, such as the signal for noon meal, and the like, do not necessitate my presence. Then, to be sure, one hour is devoted to exercise. At sundown the drum beats the signal for retreat. I read the roll once more, announce the various details for the following day, and leave the company. *Tattoo* beats at half past eight. Once more I call the roll and then am glad that I am one day nearer my discharge."

—*Vince Hawkins*

Above: *Troops stationed in the West lived in open-bay barracks often in spartan conditions. (Hugh Brown, National Park Service, Harpers Ferry Center Commissioned Art Collection)*

Arizona, to protect the southern route for settlers and control the Yuma Indians. The Army establishes a quartermaster depot there in 1864 and abandons the post in 1883 when the railroad makes the depot unnecessary. The military reservation is transferred to the Interior Department in 1884. Fort Yuma Indian School and the Mission of St. Thomas now occupy the site.

Winter. Army Explores Southern California.
Lieutenant George H. Derby, Topographical Engineers, is designated to make a reconnaissance of the country from the Gulf of California to Fort Yuma, California.

1851

January. Status of the Army.
The previous year saw at least 11 significant conflicts with the Indians, most involving the 2d Dragoons. The pay increases have helped retain and recruit a few more men and actual Army strength is at 914 officers

Above: *Frontier forts were used as places for Indians to receive the supplies promised by the U.S. government in return for signing treaties. ("Fort Union and Distribution of Goods to the Assiniboines," John Mix Stanley, Denver Public Library, Western History Collection, Z-8897)*

Right: *On 15 August 1850 Charles Magill Conrad became Secretary of War. (Daniel Huntington, Army Art Collection, NMUSA)*

and 9,594 enlisted men. The use by officers of shoulder straps with the insignia of rank is common. Mustaches are permitted only in the cavalry. All of the Light Artillery are now dismounted, with most of their horses turned over to the dragoons.

January. Engineers Plan Coastal Defense.
Joseph G. Totten, Chief Engineer of the Army, recommends increasing the number of coastal fortifications to 186, including 28 for the Texas Gulf Coast and the Pacific states.

12 April. **Yuma and Mojave Uprising. Baja, California.**
Lieutenant Thomas Sweeny leads men of the 2d Infantry to burn two Cocopas Indian villages, leading to the surrender of some 150 warriors who agree to help fight the Yuma Indians.

24 June. **Fort Belknap Built. Texas.**
Lieutenant Colonel William G. Belknap, 5th Infantry, for whom the fort was named, selects the site, although Captain Carter L. Stevenson, 5th Artillery, has been there since 13 June. Located on the Salt Fork of the Brazos River, the post protects travelers on the route from Fort Smith, Arkansas, to Santa Fe, New Mexico. The Army abandons the post in 1859 due to a shortage of water, but Confederate troops occupy it during the Civil War. After the war the Army uses it as a temporary base to protect the mail line and for operations against Indians. It is abandoned for lack of water in 1867.

6 July. **Fort Mason Built on Comanche Creek. Texas.**
Captain Hamilton Merrill, 2d Dragoons, establishes the post near Comanche Creek to protect the German settlements in the area. Named for Second Lieutenant George T. Mason, 2d Dragoons, who was killed at La Rosia, it is abandoned in 1859 but occupied on occasion until 1861, when it is evacuated. It is reoccupied after the war and abandoned again in 1869.

16 July. **Mounted Rifles Returned. Jefferson Barracks.**
Desertions and other losses have depleted the regiment so badly that it is returned to the Barracks for reorganization and outfitting. Once it is retrained, the regiment is sent to Texas.

26 July. **Headquarters Put at Fort Union. New Mexico Territory.**
Lieutenant Colonel Edwin V. Sumner, 1st Dragoons, establishes the post on the mountain branch of the Santa Fe Trail. Sumner, the department commander, wants the fort to be the new department headquarters because he considers Santa Fe to be a "sink of vice and extravagance." It is also to deter the Ute and Jicarilla Apache Indians, protect the Santa Fe Trail, and provide a supply depot. The largest post in the Southwest, it functions as a military garrison, territorial arsenal, and military supply depot. As railroads move into the area, the post loses its importance, and the arsenal closes in 1882. In 1956 Fort Union becomes a national monument.

14 September. **Fort Orford. Oregon Territory.**
Second Lieutenant Powel T. Wyman, 1st Artillery, establishes the post at the head of Trichenor Bay at Port Orford because of hostile Indians in the area. Soldiers build the post using lumber shipped from San Francisco and local cedar logs. The post is abandoned in 1856, and the buildings are moved to Fort Umpqua.

18 September. **First Army Fort in Arizona. Fort Defiance.**
Major Electus Backus, 3d Infantry, establishes the post

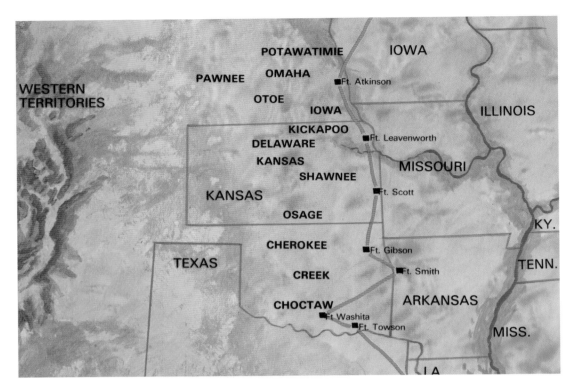

on a site selected by Lieutenant Colonel Sumner. The first U.S. Army post in Arizona, it is located at the mouth of Canon Bonita. The Army abandons the post in 1861, but it is reoccupied by Kit Carson and the 1st New Mexico Infantry in 1863 as a base for operations against Navajos. In 1868 it becomes the headquarters for the Navajo Indian Agency.

23 September. **Fort Fillmore. New Mexico Territory.**
Lieutenant Colonel Dixon S. Miles, 3d Infantry, establishes the post as part of the frontier defensive system. Located on the Rio Grande near Mesilla, it is named for President Millard Fillmore. Abandoned in 1861, it is briefly occupied by Confederate troops from Texas. In 1862 Union soldiers of the 1st California Volunteers occupy the fort just before it is finally abandoned.

14 November. **Fort Phantom Hill Built. Texas.**
Major John J. Abercrombie, 5th Infantry, establishes the fort between the Elm and Clear Forks of the Brazos River to protect the route from Fort Smith, Arkansas, to Santa Fe, New Mexico. Abandoned by the Army in 1854, it serves as a station on the Butterfield Overland stage route until the Civil War and is used occasionally as a subpost after 1867.

1852

January. **Status of the Army.**
During the year regiments continue to be moved around the country. The 4th Infantry is sent from its posts in Michigan to Oregon as a replacement for the Regiment of Mounted Riflemen.

5 February. **Fort Terret. Texas.**
Lieutenant Colonel Henry Bainbridge, 1st Infantry, establishes a post on the North Fork of the Llano River as part of the frontier defense system. Named for First Lieutenant John C. Terret, 1st Infantry, who was killed at the Battle of Monterrey, it is abandoned in 1854.

6 February. **Third Infantry Battles Apaches. New Mexico.**
Company K, 3d Infantry, fights a band of Apaches and loses three men. The regiment continues an expedition against tribes near the Gila River.

26 February. **Fort Rosecrans. California.**
Although the military reservation is established on Ballast Point in 1852, work does not begin on an earthwork to protect the entrance to San Diego Bay until 1873. The fort, named for Brevet Major General William S. Rosecrans in 1899, is transferred to the Navy Department in 1959.

14 March. **Fort McKavett. Texas.**
Major Pitcairn Morrison, 8th Infantry, places a fort on the San Saba River at the present town of Fort McKavett as part of the frontier defense system. Named for Captain Henry McKavett, 8th Infantry, who was killed at the Battle of Monterrey, it is abandoned in 1859. After the Civil War it is rebuilt under the direction of Colonel Ronald Mackenzie, 4th Cavalry, and abandoned in 1883.

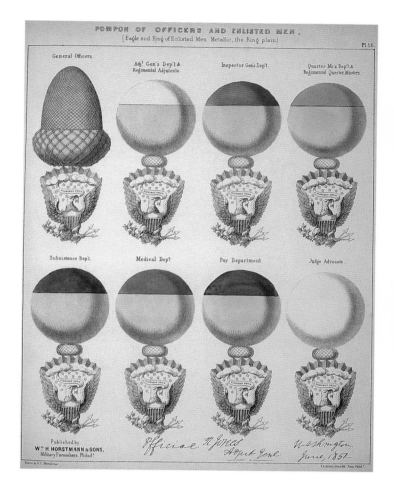

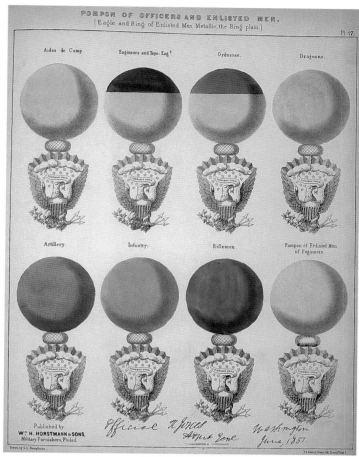

18 May. Fort Ewell. Texas.

Lieutenant Colonel William W. Loring, Mounted Riflemen, establishes the post on the Nueces River. Named for Captain Richard S. Ewell, 1st Dragoons, it is built of adobe, and Captain William Grigsby Freeman, 4th Artillery, deems it a very uninviting spot in his 1853 inspection. It is abandoned in 1854.

Above: *The Army uniform regulations of 1851 established an elaborate color-coded system for the pompons worn on caps in order to distinguish branches. (John P. Langellier)*

Below: *A Saxony-blue pompon topped the 1851-pattern enlisted caps for infantrymen, while a matching band was sewn above the visor. (U.S. Army Center of Military History, NMUSA)*

26 May. Fort Reading. California.

First Lieutenant Nelson H. Davis, 2d Infantry, establishes the post on Cow Creek near the present town of Redding. Named for Major Pierson B. Reading, a paymaster in the California Volunteers during the Mexican War and a pioneer California settler, the fort protects the mining district. The garrison is withdrawn in 1856, but the post is occasionally occupied until 1867. The Army abandons it in 1870, and the buildings are sold. In 1881 the military reservation is returned to the public domain.

16 June. Scott Named as Presidential Candidate. Baltimore, Maryland.

The Whig party nominates Major General Winfield Scott, Commanding General of the Army, as its presidential candidate. Scott remains commanding general and loses the election to Franklin Pierce in November.

20 June. **Fort Clark. Texas.**
Captain William Edgar Prince, 1st Infantry, builds the post on Las Moras Creek near the present town of Brackettville as part of the defensive system that protects the road between San Antonio and El Paso. Named for Major Roger B. Clark, 1st Infantry, who died in 1847, the post is surrendered in 1861 to Confederates, who occupy it briefly. In 1866 Captain John A. Wilcox, 4th Cavalry, reoccupies the post, and it remains active until 1946.

22 June. **Fort Massachusetts. Utah Territory.**
Established by Major George A. H. Blake, 1st Dragoons, the post is the first U.S. Army post in the present state of Colorado and the farthest north in the Department of New Mexico. It protects settlers in the San Luis Valley and guards the approach to New Mexico through the Sangre de Cristo Pass. Located north of the present town of Fort Garland, it probably receives its name because the department commander, Colonel Sumner, is a native of Boston. Fort Garland replaces the post in 1858.

5 July. **4th Infantry Hit By Cholera. Panama.**
Part of the route for eight companies of the 4th Infantry being transferred from New York to the Pacific Coast is via railroad over the Isthmus of Panama. The regiment is struck by cholera and jungle fever. Before they reach California, 107 men have died.

August. **Recruiting Bounty Abolished.**
Despite recruiting problems, the War Department abolishes the $2 bonus for bringing in a new recruit.

14 August. **Fort Burgwin. New Mexico Territory.**
Second Lieutenant Robert Ransom, 1st Dragoons, plans and builds the post just south of Taos to protect the wagon road between Santa Fe and Taos. Named for Captain John H. K. Burgwin, who died of wounds received in the Taos uprising in 1847, the post is abandoned in 1860. A century later, the remnants of the post are uncovered and reconstructed. It is now the Fort Burgwin Research Center, part of Southern Methodist University.

31 August. **Army Gets Bonus Pay.**
Congress extends the $2-a-day bonus to all officers serving on the western frontier.

1 September. **Lee Goes to U.S. Military Academy. West Point, New York.**
Brevet Colonel Robert E. Lee becomes the superintendent of the Military Academy. Some of the cadets he trains will serve under or against him in the Civil War.

8 September. **Fort Conrad. New Mexico Territory.**
Major Marshall S. Howe, 2d Dragoons, establishes the post as part of the defensive system intended to restrain hostile Indians and protect the north-south route along the Rio Grande. Named for Charles M. Conrad, the Secretary of War, the post is abandoned in 1854.

16 October. **Fort Jones. California.**
Second Lieutenant Joseph B. Collins, 4th Infantry, sets the post on the Scott River at the present town of

Fort Jones. Named for Colonel Roger Jones, an adjutant general, it protects the gold mining district. The Army abandons the post in 1858, and the military reservation is transferred to the Interior Department in 1870.

28 October. **Fort Chadbourne. Texas.**
Captain John Beardsley, 8th Infantry, builds a fort on Oak Creek close to the present town of Fort

Above: *Troops assemble at Fort Scott, Kansas, wearing field gear and packs in preparation for a campaign. (National Park Service, Harpers Ferry Center Commissioned Art Collection, Keith Rocco/Tradition Studios)*

Below: *Jefferson Davis became Secretary of War during a period of westward expansion and growing strife. Just a few years after leaving the War Department, he would become the president of the Confederate States of America. (Daniel Huntington, U.S. Army Art Collection, NMUSA)*

Chadbourne to protect the route between Fort Smith, Arkansas, and Santa Fe, New Mexico. Named for Second Lieutenant Theodore L. Chadbourne, who was killed in the Battle of Resaca de la Palma, the post is surrendered to the Confederacy in 1861. It is reoccupied by federal troops in 1867 but abandoned shortly thereafter when the water supply fails.

26 November. **Recruit Training Moved. New York.**
The depot for instruction of new recruits is moved from Fort Wood on Bedloe's Island to Fort Columbus in New York Harbor.

1853

30 January. **Fort Humboldt. California.**
Captain Robert C. Buchanan builds the fort on a bluff overlooking Humboldt Bay to protect the area from Indians. The fort, a supply depot for other Army facilities in northern California, is abandoned in 1867 and transferred to the Interior Department in 1870.

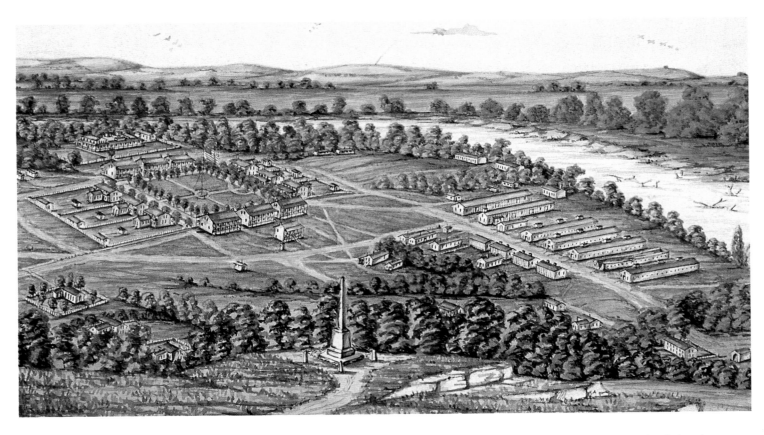

March. **Scott Moves Army Headquarters. New York City.**
Winfield Scott, commanding general of the Army, moves his headquarters from Washington, D.C., to New York when Franklin Pierce, who had defeated Scott in the 1852 presidential election, takes office.

7 March. **Davis Becomes New Secretary of War.**
Jefferson Davis becomes the Secretary of War. A graduate of the U.S. Military Academy, he resigned from the U.S. House of Representatives in 1846 to command a Mississippi regiment during the Mexican War, and after the war he served in the U.S. Senate. While Secretary of War, he obtains four new regiments for the Army and sponsors the U.S. Army Camel Corps. After leaving office he is again elected to the U.S. Senate, but he resigns in 1861 when Mississippi secedes from the Union. After a brief period as a major general in the Mississippi militia, he becomes the president of the Confederate States of America.

29 March. **Army Builds Capitol Building.**
Army Engineers begin completion of the north and south wings of the U.S. Capitol under the supervision of Lieutenant Montgomery C. Meigs. Best known for

Above: *Fort Riley, Kansas, was one of the remote western garrisons guarding the frontier. Today it is one of the largest and most important Army posts. (Collection of The New-York Historical Society, neg. #47330, accession #1925.193)*

his service as the quartermaster general of the Army during the Civil War, Meigs designs and builds the Washington Aqueduct and a number of buildings in Washington, D.C., including the Pension Building, which is restored in 1985 to become the National Building Museum.

29 April. **Fort Ridgely. Minnesota.**
Captain Samuel Woods, 6th Infantry, establishes a fort on the Minnesota River near New Ulm to protect the frontier from Sioux Indians. The post is named for three officers from Maryland who died during the Mexican War: First Lieutenant Henderson Ridgely, 4th Infantry; First Lieutenant Randolph Ridgely, 3d Artillery; and Thomas P. Ridgely, 2d Artillery. The Army abandons the post in 1867 and transfers the military reservation to the Interior Department in 1870. It is now a Minnesota state park.

17 May. **Fort Riley. Kansas.**
Captain Charles S. Lovell, 6th Infantry, places a post on the Kansas River at a site selected by Colonel Thomas T. Fauntleroy, 1st Dragoons. Lovell believes it will replace Forts Leavenworth, Scott, Atkinson, Kearny, and Laramie by improving efficiency and reducing costs. First called Fort Center because it is close to the geographical center of the continental United States, it is later named for Colonel Bennett Riley, 1st Infantry, who died in June 1853. The post continues to be in operation.

June. **Sioux Attack. Fort Laramie. Utah Territory.**
A group of Miniconjou Sioux seize a ferry operating on the Platte River, and one of them fires on Army Sergeant Raymond, who recaptures the boat. Second Lieutenant Hugh Fleming, with 23 men, goes to the Indian village to arrest the offender. The Indians refuse to give up the suspect and fire on the soldiers, who return fire. In the resulting skirmish, three Indians are killed, three are wounded, and two are taken prisoner. The Miniconjou Sioux are incensed by this action, but after a full explanation by First Lieutenant Richard B. Garnett, the post commander, there are no further hostilities.

June. **Army is Below Strength.**
The authorized size of the Army is 13,821, but the actual strength is 10,417. Of the 8,342 officers and men assigned to the western frontier, only 6,918 are at their assigned posts, for an average of 124 soldiers for each of the 54 posts in the western commands.

23 June. **Army Explores the Plains. Fort Leavenworth, Kansas.**
Captain John W. Gunnison begins an expedition to explore the 38th parallel through Kansas, Colorado, and Utah as a possible railroad route. A detachment of the Regiment of Mounted Riflemen accompanies him, along with several civilian scientists.

15 July. **Army Searches for Rail Routes. Fort Smith, Arkansas.**
Lieutenant Amiel W. Whipple leads a party west along the 35th parallel to survey a possible railroad route. The expedition of some 70 men includes

Above: *An infantry drummer (left) and first sergeant (right) in the 1851-pattern dress uniform flank an infantry private in the uniform as it had evolved by 1857. ("The Regulations of 1851, and Variations," Darby Erd)*

Below: *A youthful infantry second lieutenant of the early 1850s and his lady pose for a portrait. (U.S. Army Military History Institute, Carlisle Barracks, PA)*

soldiers, teamsters, herders, and scientists. Whipple explores the Southwest for more than eight months, eventually reaching Los Angeles, California, on 21 March 1854. Although no transcontinental railroad follows his route, an 1856 federal wagon road program improves the trail he surveyed.

August. **Army Strength Falls. Fort Jones, California.**
While inspecting the post, Inspector General Joseph K. F. Mansfield reports that Company E, 4th Infantry, has only 34 names on its roll out of an authorized strength of three officers, eight noncommissioned officers, and 74 privates. The company's captain, Ulysses S. Grant, has recently resigned his commission. The remaining officers present include the company commander, Lieutenant J. C. Bonneycastle, Lieutenant George Crook, and Lieutenant John B. Hood, a recent graduate of the U.S. Military Academy who is awaiting a regimental vacancy.

28 September. **Fort Lane. Oregon.**
A post is established on the Rogue River by Captain Andrew J. Smith, 1st Dragoons, to protect the Indian reservation of the same name. It is named for

U.S. ARMY WEAPONS

The decade following the Mexican War, 1850–1860, witnessed major changes in weapons technology. These developments were made possible by advances in chemistry, metallurgy, and ballistics.

During the Mexican War, the smoothbore flintlock musket was still the standard U.S. Army infantry weapon. Relatively unchanged since the eighteenth century, the flintlock's limited range left the infantryman at a severe disadvantage against artillery. This changed with the Army's adoption of the .58-caliber rifle musket, officially designated Model 1855. The rifle musket incorporated several new advances. It used a percussion cap, which drastically cut down on the number of misfires and allowed the weapon to be fired in wet weather. The bore was rifled, which greatly improved the range over that of smoothbore flintlock, giving it a range of 800 to 1,000 yards as compared to the flintlock's average 100 yards. It remained fitted for a bayonet.

Of equal importance to the rifle musket was an improvement in its ammunition. Adoption of the sub-caliber Minié bullet enabled the rifle musket to be loaded faster and easier than previous rifles using round balls, without detracting from the rifle's superior range. The Minié bullet had an expanding hollow base. When fired, the base of the bullet expanded, causing it to fit tightly in the grooves. This allowed for maximum spin, better trajectory, and consistent accuracy at longer ranges. The rifle musket enabled the infantryman to accurately hit targets at ranges similar to that of the standard artillery piece.

There were significant improvements in breech-loading rifles and carbines. In 1855, U.S. cavalry regiments replaced their standard-issue musketoons with a variety of rifled, breech-loading, percussion carbines. Many U.S. and foreign models were tested until 1858, when the .52-caliber Model 1852 Sharps carbine was ordered. All of these versions used a type of "trap-door" breech-loading system and fired a paper- or linen-wrapped cartridge. The Sharps was loaded by dropping the trigger guard to open the breech. After the round was inserted, the trigger guard was returned, closing the breech block and cutting the cartridge for ignition. A breech-loader carbine could fire up to ten rounds a minute, three times the capability of the infantry's rifle musket, at ranges of up to 600 yards. A few carbine models using metal cartridges began to appear in the 1860s.

By the early 1850s, the mounted units had adopted the popular Colt .36-caliber Model 1851 "Navy" six-shot cap-and-ball pistol. This weapon was highly regarded on the frontier as it gave the necessary firepower to defeat the close-combat tactics of the Indians. Although mounted and artillery units were still issued sabers and swords, the advantages provided by the breech-loading carbine and the six-shot pistol heralded the demise of the edged weapons.

The standard Army artillery field guns were the bronze, smoothbore, muzzle-loading Model 1840–41 six-pounder gun, and the 12-pounder mountain howitzer. In 1857, the bronze 12-pounder "Napoleon" was adopted, becoming the standard Army field gun until the 1880s. Technological advances also improved the artillery. Percussion and friction primer systems replaced lit fuses while newly developed compressed gunpowder increased the range of the projectiles. Advancements in metallurgy enabled the manufacture of more reliable cast iron guns and greater ease in rifling, which resulted in the Chambers (1849), Treadwell (1855), and Parrott (1861) rifled guns. By 1863, these were replaced by the more effective cast-iron three-inch Ordnance Gun. Although breech-loading rifled cannons had been developed in England in the mid-1850s and were used to some extent during the Civil War, breech-loading artillery was not employed by the U.S. Army until the late 1880s.

—*Vince Hawkins*

Above: *During the 1840s and 1850s Samuel Colt's revolver gained popularity with the U.S. Army and civilians alike, such as this .44-caliber six-shot "Dragoon" model. (Photograph by Ed Castle, National Museum of American History, Smithsonian Institution)*

Right: *The unique Regiment of Mounted Rifles provided the mobility of the cavalry combined with the firepower of the infantry. They were trained to fight either on horseback or on foot, as the situation required. ("United States Mounted Infantry, 1853," James T. Jones, Company of Military Historians)*

Brigadier General Joseph Lane, the first territorial governor of Oregon. Abandoned in 1856, the military reservation is transferred to the Interior Department in 1871.

October. **Jefferson Barracks Expands. Missouri.**
The depot for the collection and instruction of recruits for the mounted regiments of the Army is moved from Carlisle Barracks, Pennsylvania, to Jefferson Barracks. Men employed in enlisting and drilling recruits are deducted from the authorized strength of the regiments.

26 October. **Mounted Rifles Attacked. Sevier River, Utah Territory.**
Captain John W. Gunnison and a detachment from Company A, Mounted Rifles are attacked by a party of Piaute Indians, who kill the captain and all but four

others. It is two days before the main body reaches the massacre site, at which time Lieutenant E. G. Beckwith, 3d Artillery, assumes command of the expedition and leads the survivors to a winter camp at Salt Lake City.

11 October. **Military Academy Changes Curriculum. West Point.**
Secretary of War Davis disregards the advice of the academy faculty and directs the change of the curriculum from five to four years.

24 December. **Fort Thorn. New Mexico.**
A fort to guard the road between El Paso and Santa Fe and the road to San Diego is established by Captain Israel B. Richardson, 3d Infantry, on the Rio Grande near the present town of Hatch. Named for First Lieutenant Herman Thorn, 2d Infantry, who

drowned in the Colorado River in 1849, the post is on the edge of an extensive marsh. When it is abandoned in 1859 much of the property, including doors and window casings, is removed and taken to Fort Fillmore, New Mexico, although the hospital and one of the storerooms are left to be used by travelers. Confederate troops occupy the post in 1861, and the 1st California Volunteers are there briefly in 1862.

27–31 December. **Third Artillery Shipwrecked. Cape Hatteras, North Carolina.**
The majority of the 3d Artillery (with families and dependents—some 600 people) sets sail from New York for a new posting in California. Off Cape Hatteras the ship encounters a fierce storm and is disabled. The leaking ship drifts aimlessly for days with its machinery broken and its sails blown away. Another vessel appears and succeeds in rescuing 108 people before the lines are broken and the sinking troop ship disappears in the storm. On 31 December, the ship is resighted and the rest of the survivors taken off. More than 200 are dead. The next year the regiment is sent again, some sailing without mishap and others going overland.

30 December. **Gadsden Purchase. Mexico City.**
James Gadsden signs a treaty with Mexico that adds 45,535 square miles of territory in southern Arizona and New Mexico to the southwestern part of the United States. The purpose of the purchase is to allow for the construction of a southern route for a transcontinental railroad, which is never built although the Army provides assistance by surveying potential routes.

Above: *Chevrons were color coded for each of the branches in the 1851 U.S. Army regulations. (U.S. Army Center of Military History)*

January. **Status of the Army.**
Army strength is 10,417—956 officers and 9,456 enlisted men. Army senior leadership is now one Regular major general (Winfield Scott) and three Regular brigadier generals (Thomas Jessup, John E. Wool, and David E. Twiggs). The 2d Infantry is relocated from Carlisle Barracks to Fort Leavenworth and other forts.

21 February. **Army Explores Sierra Nevada.**
Lieutenant Edward B. Beckwith, 3d Artillery, receives permission to explore a route through the Sierra Nevada Mountains. He locates two passes suitable for a railway, but because he is not an engineer, his recommendations are overlooked when the Secretary of War evaluates the routes. However, the first transcontinental railroad eventually follows the route he recommends.

5 March. **Apache Uprising. Fort Union, New Mexico.**
Lieutenant Colonel Philip St. George Cooke, 2d Dragoons, commander of Fort Union, defeats a band of Jicarilla Apaches led by Lobo Blanco, the third ranking chief and the man responsible for the White family massacre in 1849. Lobo Blanco is killed in the fight.

26–30 March. **Battle of Cieneguila. Taos, New Mexico.**
Lieutenant John W. Davidson and his Company I, 1st Dragoons, ride into an ambush set up by Chacon, first chief of the Jicarilla Apaches, to avenge Lobo Blanco's

death. The Dragoons, outnumbered by four to one, fight for three hours before they are able to retreat, leaving 22 dead. By the time Davidson and the remnants of his company reach Taos, only two men have not been hit by an arrow or a bullet.

1 April. **Fort Craig. New Mexico.**
Captain Daniel T. Chandler, 3d Infantry, places a fort on the Rio Grande near the present town of San Marcial where it can protect the north-south route along the Rio Grande. Named for Captain Louis S. Craig, 3d Infantry, who was murdered by deserters in California in 1852, the fort is abandoned and transferred to the Interior Department in 1885.

8 April. **Battle of Rio Caliente. New Mexico.**
Scouts of Lieutenant Colonel Philip St. George Cooke, leading a column of 250 men of the 1st and 2d Dragoons and 2d Artillery serving as infantry, discover an ambush set by the Jicarilla chief Chacon. Cooke initiates a preemptive attack, causing the surprised Indians to flee in disorder. The brief battle claims one soldier dead and one wounded. The Apaches have five killed and six wounded, but in the confusion following the fight, 17 Apache women and children get lost in the wilderness and die of exposure.

14 April. Recruiting Incentive.
The War Department restores the $2 payment for new recruits. The payments continue until the Civil War.

4 August. Army Pay Raised.
Congress raises enlisted pay by $4 a month. A soldier enlisting for a second time receives an additional $2 a month and a subsequent enlistment for five years adds another $1.

10 August. Fort Tejon. California.
First Lieutenant Thomas F. Castor, 1st Dragoons, establishes the post near the Tejon Indian Reservation near the present town of Lebec. The post commands the passes in the vicinity and controls hostile Indians while protecting those on the reservation. In 1858 the fort becomes a station on the Butterfield Overland stage route, and soldiers provide military escorts through the passes. The post is evacuated in 1861 but reoccupied by California Volunteer troops in 1863. The Army abandons it in 1864 and it becomes part of Rancho Tejon, the original Mexican grant.

Above: *U.S. sailors load Egyptian camels for their long journey to Texas, where the Army would deploy them on a trial basis. (Harvard College Library)*

19 August. Grattan Massacre. Fort Laramie, Wyoming.
A Miniconjou Sioux named High Forehead kills a cow near the fort and the cow's owner complains to the post commander, Lieutenant Hugh Fleming. Brevet Second Lieutenant John L. Grattan, 6th Infantry, is sent with an interpreter, 28 enlisted men, and two small cannons to arrest High Forehead. The reports are conflicting, but it appears Grattan trains the cannon on the teepee of Chief Conquering Bear, the head of the Sioux nation, and orders the chief to produce the guilty Indians or he will open fire. The Indians refuse and the subsequent cannon fire kills Conquering Bear. The soldiers are killed almost instantly, and the angry Indians, incensed at the death of their chief, plunder a nearby trading post and kill a mail carrier.

7 October. Fort Davis. Texas.
Lieutenant Colonel Washington Sewell, 8th Infantry, occupies the site just north of the present town of Fort Davis. Named for Secretary of War Jefferson Davis, the post protects the San Antonio–El Paso road and controls Comanche and Apache Indians. It is evacuated in 1861 and occupied briefly by Confederate troops. Bands of Mexicans and Indians largely destroy the fort during the Civil War, but Lieutenant Colonel Wesley Merritt, 9th Cavalry, rebuilds it in 1867. The Army abandons the post in 1891.

Right: *The two regiments of dragoons authorized during the 1830s continued to serve as a mobile force after the Mexican War at garrisons from the cold northern Plains to the deserts of the Southwest. ("Dragoons in Winter," Don Troiani, www.historicalartprints.com)*

1855

January. Status of the Army.

The Army has grown slightly to a total of 10,745 officers and men. Army arsenals continue the conversion of old smoothbore muskets to a new Model 1855 rifle using a percussion cap with a standardized caliber of .58 minié projectile. During the month Dragoons and Riflemen have three clashes with Apaches.

15 February. Scott Made Commanding General of the Army.

Congress passes a special act making Winfield Scott Commanding General of the Army and a brevet lieutenant general retroactive to 20 March 1847, when he fought the Battle of Vera Cruz in the Mexican War. Scott is the first officer since George Washington to hold three-star rank, but the rank is not made a permanent part of the Army's rank structure.

3 March. Army Camel Corps Established.

Congress appropriates $30,000 for the Army to experiment with camels. Second Lieutenant George H. Crossman, a veteran of the Seminole Wars, believes they are well adapted for grassy or sandy plains and rough, rocky terrain. With the support of Secretary Davis, camels are purchased and tested with fair success. The U.S. Army Camel Corps uses them as pack animals on expeditions as far west as

California. The animals are sold during the Civil War, but wild camels wander the American desert for years, with the last authenticated sightings occurring in the early 1900s.

3 March. Army Strength Increased.

Congress authorizes four new regiments—the 1st and 2d Cavalry and the 9th and 10th Infantry. The infantry regiments are formed using a rifle-regiment type organization of about 840 men. A school of instruction is established at Jefferson Barracks for training the new cavalry soldiers, who are recruited largely in rural areas where the population is most familiar with horses. The infantry regiments each receive 20 men selected from the permanent party and the best recruits at Fort Columbus, New York, and Newport Barracks, Rhode Island, to provide a trained cadre for new soldiers.

26 March. 9th Infantry Regiment. Fort Monroe, Virginia.

The 9th Infantry is organized, and Lieutenant Colonel George Wright becomes its colonel. In November the regiment moves to the Pacific Coast to conduct operations against Indians, build roads, and construct new posts.

26 March. 2d Cavalry Organized. Jefferson Barracks.

The 2d Cavalry is organized under the command of Colonel Albert Sidney Johnston. Robert E. Lee, an engineer, is designated the regiment's lieutenant

U.S. ARMY CAMEL CORPS

When Congress appropriated $30,000 on 3 March 1855 for the purpose of "importing camels for Army transportation and for other military purposes," Secretary of War Jefferson Davis finally had his wish after four years of trying. Thus began one of the most unusual experiments in Army history—the U.S. Camel Corps.

Davis assigned West Point graduate Major Henry C. Wayne and Navy Lieutenant David D. Porter to travel to the Middle East and purchase camels. Wayne was in charge of the purchasing, while Porter commanded the Navy store ship *Supply* to transport the animals. After months of searching to find healthy animals and suitable men, *Supply* landed at Powder Horn, Texas, on 13 May 1856, with 34 camels and five native drovers. Most of the camels were the one-hump Middle Eastern Arabian type, renowned for their swiftness, along with a few of the Asian Bactrian, or two-hump type, used for their strength and load-carrying abilities. After a second purchasing voyage, Porter arrived at Indianola, Texas, on 10 February 1857, with 41 camels and eight drovers, bringing the Corps' total to 75 camels and 13 Arabian and Egyptian drovers.

In August 1856, the Corps moved to Camp Verde, Texas, roughly 65 miles north of San Antonio. Major Wayne was replaced in January 1857 by Edward Fitzgerald Beale. After months of acclimating the camels to their new environment, their heavy packs, and training the skeptical soldier handlers, the Corps

was ready for a field test. On 25 June 1857, Beale left Camp Verde for Fort Defiance, New Mexico, with 25 camels, around 100 horses and mules, a dozen wagons, 44 soldiers, and two drovers to survey for a wagon road from Fort Defiance to the Colorado River. After a slow start, due primarily to months of inactivity, the camels began keeping up with the wagons and eventually passed them on the rough trail. On 31 August, the expedition left Fort Defiance on its mission; by 20 October they had crossed the Colorado River, having covered some 1,200 miles without the loss of a single camel. The expedition then traveled to Fort Tejon, California, where the camels remained until 1863.

Beale's official report praised the camels for their superior endurance and their ability to travel long distances with heavy loads. In January 1858, he used camels to test the same route under winter conditions, and in April he surveyed a route for a road from Fort Smith to the Colorado River.

In April 1859 an exploratory expedition with 24 camels set out from Camp Verde to survey the area between the Pecos and Rio Grande Rivers. This expedition was also successful, and a second expedition was sent out in the summer of 1860. Comprising 20 camels and 25 pack mules, the expedition surveyed the areas between the El Paso Road and the Rio Grande, and from Camp Stockton to Fort Davis for possible roadways. Both expeditions proved the usefulness of camels in desert terrain, but Congress ignored requests to buy more.

The advent of the Civil War ended the Camel Corps. The camels and drivers were forgotten. Camels at Fort Tejon were sold at auction in 1863, and those at Camp Verde, Confederate "captives" for a while, were sold in 1866. Purchased by circuses, miners, and ranchers, many of the camels were eventually turned loose in the desert. The unemployed drovers faded into the local population.

The last known Army camel died in April 1934, but "camel sightings" in the southwestern desert continued for many decades.

—*Vince Hawkins*

Above: *During Jefferson Davis' tenure as Secretary of War, the Army conducted a short-lived experiment to utilize camels in the "Great American Desert."*

colonel. After procuring horses in Kentucky, the regiment moves to Texas, where it serves until 1861. Lee's wife and family remain in Virginia.

April. **Army Observers in Europe.**
A group of officers including Captain George B. McClellan return from travels to the Crimea and a number of European countries where they have been to observe warfare and take notes on other armies. They submit a detailed report. In addition, McClellan designs an advanced saddle that becomes the Army standard for many years.

28 April. **Battle of Poncha Pass. Colorado.**
Colonel Thomas T. Fauntleroy, 1st Dragoons, with two companies of Regulars and two of Volunteers, surprises some 150 Ute warriors at night as they dance wildly around a blazing bonfire. After approaching to within 150 yards, the soldiers open fire, quickly dropping about 40 dancers while the remainder flee into the nearby hills. The brief encounter ends the Utes interest in further fighting.

4 May. **Fort Stanton. New Mexico.**
Lieutenant Colonel Dixon S. Miles, 3d Infantry, camps on the Rio Bonita to control Mescalero Apaches. Named for Captain Henry W. Stanton, 1st Dragoons, who was killed by Apaches, the post is abandoned in 1861, but Colonel Kit Carson, 1st New Mexico Infantry, reoccupies the fort a year later. The post is transferred to the Interior Department in 1896. Fort Stanton later becomes America's first federal tuberculosis hospital and the first German internment camp during World War II.

28 May. **1st Cavalry Formed. Louisville, Kentucky.**
Colonel Edwin V. Sumner organizes the 1st Cavalry Regiment. The officers of the include Lieutenant Colonel Joseph E. Johnston, Major John Sedgwick, Captain George B. McClellan, and Lieutenant J. E. B. Stuart.

7 June. **Fort Pierre. South Dakota.**
Major Albermarle Cady, 6th Infantry, sets up the post, purchased from Benard Pratte and Company. Located on the Missouri River about three miles from the present town of Pierre, it is found unsatisfactory because of insufficient grass, timber, and hay. The Army abandons the post in 1857 and ships some of the construction material to Fort Randall, South Dakota.

29 July. **Battle of Solomon Fork. Solomon River, Kansas Territory.**
Colonel Edwin V. Sumner leads two companies of the 1st Cavalry and two of the 2d Dragoons against a band of some 300 Cheyenne who had washed in a "magical

Above: *The uniform regulations of 1851 prescribed orange as the branch color for dragoons. ("2d U.S. Dragoon Regiment, 1853–1854," H. Charles McBarron, Company of Military Historians)*

Left: *In 1855 Army General Orders prescribed a stiff felt hat with turned-up brim on one side, plumes, and a regimental number for the two new cavalry regiments. (Museum of American History, Smithsonian Institution)*

lake" to protect themselves from bullets. When Sumner orders his soldiers to charge with drawn sabers, it causes the Indians to flee because their "magic water" works only against bullets, not blades. During the fight, Lieutenant J. E. B. Stuart is wounded by a bullet in his chest.

15 August. New Army Uniforms.
The Army replaces the uniform cap that has been worn for almost 50 years with a stiff felt hat. The brim of the new headgear is folded up on the right side and fastened with a brass eagle. Black feathers ornament the hat's left side; field officers have three feathers, company officers two, and enlisted soldiers one.

20 August. Fort Lancaster. Texas.
Captain Stephen D. Carpenter, 1st Infantry, establishes the post on Live Oak Creek near the Pecos River to guard the San Antonio–El Paso road. It is evacuated in 1861 and not reoccupied.

24 August. Blue Water Creek Expedition. Fort Kearny, Nebraska.
Colonel William S. Harney departs with 600 soldiers from the 2d Dragoons, 6th Infantry, the 10th Infantry, and the 4th Artillery, on an expedition against the Sioux to retaliate for the massacre of Brevet Second Lieutenant John L. Grattan and his force of 29 men a year earlier.

3 September. Battle of Blue Water Creek. Ash Hollow, Nebraska.
Colonel Harney attacks the Sioux village of Little Thunder on Blue Water Creek, killing 86 Indians and capturing 70 women and children. The Army loses four soldiers killed, seven wounded, and one missing. Leaving Ash Hollow, Harney proceeds to Fort Laramie for a council with Sioux chiefs. He threatens the Indians with continuing military action if any further depredations occur.

8 September. Fort Grattan. Nebraska.
Colonel Harney builds a small earthwork immediately after the Battle of Blue Water Creek to protect settlers and the monthly mail passing between Fort Kearny and Fort Laramie. Named for Lieutenant Grattan, the post is abandoned less than a month later.

30 September. Fort Cascades. Washington.
Captain Granville O. Haller, 4th Infantry, establishes the post on the Columbia River near the present Bonneville Dam to protect the movement of people and supplies along the river. Named for the lower rapids in the river, the fort includes two blockhouses with garrisons a few miles away. The post is abandoned in 1861 and relinquished to private owners.

13 October. 10th Infantry. Carlisle Barracks, Pennsylvania.
The newly organized 10th Infantry, commanded by Colonel Edward B. Alexander, departs the post to occupy posts west of the Mississippi River.

16 October. **Indian Protection. Fort Lane, Oregon.**
Captain Andrew Jackson Smith, 1st Dragoons, opens the post to protect Indians menaced by white mobs. Before he can admit all of them, settlers kill 23 Indians, including old men, women, and children.

31 October. **Battle of Hungry Hill. Fort Lane, Oregon.**
Leading 250 Regulars from the 1st Dragoons, 4th Infantry, 3d Artillery, and volunteers, Captain Smith attacks a band of 75–150 warriors on Hungry Hill but is unable to dislodge them after a day-long battle. The next morning the Indians attack the dragoons but they hold, ending the battle in a draw.

15 December. **Seminole Campaign. Great Cypress Swamp, Florida.**
Hostilities open when Seminoles, who had kept the peace for a number of years, are frustrated by increasing inroads by white settlers and attack an Army camp. The event that triggers the uprising comes when surveyors vandalize crops belonging to Billy Bowlegs, a Seminole leader.

December. **Indian Clashes.**
During the year the Army has experienced more than 19 significant combats with Indians, the most conflict it has seen in many years.

Opposite: *The majority of troops serving in the small Army of the 1850s served at garrisons dispersed west of the Mississippi to the Pacific Coast. ("Friendly Indians Feeling to Fort Benton," 1859, John Mix Stanley, Courtesy of The Anschutz Collection, Denver, CO)*

Right: *Massive smoothbore cannon guarded ports and key waterways. "Heavy" artillery regiments manned, and ordnance personnel maintained, the weapons; all were protected within forts built by Army engineers. ("Artillery, Ordnance, and Engineers, 1851–1858," H. A. Ogden)*

1856

January. **Status of the Army.**
Army strength grows as a result of the formation of the four new regiments. The year starts with an actual strength of 15,752 officers and men.

2 January. **Camp Cooper Texas.**
Major William J. Hardee, 2d Cavalry, places a fort on the Clear Fork of the Brazos River near the Comanche Indian Reservation to protect the El Paso–Red River Trail. Named for Colonel Samuel Cooper, an adjutant general, the camp is surrendered to Confederates in 1861 and never reoccupied.

26 March. **Battle of the Cascades. Fort Cascades, Washington.**
About 100 Yakima, Klikitat, and Chinook warriors attack settlers near the fort and capture one of the post's outlaying blockhouses. When word of the attack reaches Fort Vancouver, Second Lieutenant Philip H. Sheridan, 4th Infantry, gathers 40 men and heads for the fort by steamboat. At about the same time, Colonel George Wright leaves Fort Dalles with 250 men of the 9th Infantry on two steamboats. On 28 March, the columns unite, drive the Indians from the besieged blockhouse, and restore order.

May. **Camp Naches. Washington.**
Colonel George Wright establishes this post on the Naches River as a base of operations for the Indian campaign of 1856. The fortifications are large wicker baskets of willow filled with dirt, prompting settlers to refer to it as the "basket fort." The post is abandoned at the end of the campaign.

26 May. **Battle of Big Meadows. Oregon.**
Captain Andrew Jackson Smith, 1st Dragoons, waits at Big Meadows, expecting a band of Indians under Old John to surrender in accordance with an agreement made on 21 May. Warned of possible attack, Smith establishes defensive positions on a small knoll for the dragoons, infantry, and small howitzer under his command. The Indians attack at about 10 a.m. the next morning and the battle continues through the day. After a night of sniping at the soldiers, Old John resumes the attack on the 28th. By afternoon a third of the soldiers are dead or wounded and water and ammunition are perilously low. A company of the 4th Infantry, led by Captain Christopher C. Augur, reaches the beleaguered position and strikes the Indians from the rear, driving them off. The battle convinces most of the Indians to surrender, but Old John holds out until 30 June before giving himself up.

26 June. **Fort Randall. South Dakota.**
First Lieutenant George H. Paige, 2d Infantry, builds a fort on the Missouri just north of the boundary with Nebraska to replace Fort Pierre. It maintains peace among the Sioux, Ponca, and other tribes and protects settlers moving into the area. Named for Lieutenant Colonel Daniel D. Randall, deputy paymaster, the post is abandoned in 1892.

27 June. **Battle of Gila River. Mount Graham, Arizona.**
A company of 1st Dragoons under Captain Richard E. Ewell surprises a large camp of Coyotera Apaches in what they believe is a secure camp. Ewell's Dragoons

attack the panicked Indians, killing or wounding 40 warriors and capturing 45 women and children. Two officers and seven enlisted men are wounded in the brief encounter.

26 July. Fort Hoskins. Oregon.
To control and protect Indians near the Siletz Agency, Captain Christopher C. Augur, 4th Infantry, establishes a fort on the Luckiamute River. It is one of three forts that monitor the Grand Ronde Reservation. Forts Umpqua and Yamhill are the other two. Second Lieutenant Philip Sheridan, 4th Infantry, supervises the construction of a blockhouse near the fort. Named for First Lieutenant Charles Hoskins, 4th Infantry, who was killed at the Battle of Monterrey, the post is abandoned in 1865.

28 July. Fort Umpqua. Oregon.
Captain John F. Reynolds, 3d Artillery, selects the site and Captain Joseph Stewart, 3d Artillery, builds a fort on the Umpqua River. The post is one of three established to monitor Indians at the Grand Ronde and Siletz agencies. In 1862, Colonel Justus Steinberger, 1st Washington Infantry, arrives for an inspection and finds the fort's commissioned and noncommissioned officers out on a hunting trip. His report and the reduction in Indian activity cause the fort to be abandoned later that year.

31 July. Fort Lookout. South Dakota.
Captain Nathaniel Lyon, 2d Infantry, establishes the fort on the Missouri River near a Columbia Fur Company trading post to control local Indians. When it is abandoned in 1857, the buildings are dismantled and shipped down the Missouri River to Fort Randall, South Dakota.

August. Cavalry Raid Cheyenne. Fort Kearny, Nebraska.
Captain George H. Stewart sets out with Company K and elements of two other 1st Cavalry companies to find the Cheyenne Indians who shot a mail coach driver with an arrow. When he finds a camp of about 80 Indians, he attacks, killing 10 and wounding 10.

8 August. Fort Simcoe. Washington.
Major Robert S. Garnett, 9th Infantry, establishes a base in the Simcoe Valley for operations against Indians and to protect settlers in the area. Abandoned in 1859, the buildings are transferred to the Interior Department to be used as the headquarters for the Yakima Indian Agency.

26 August. Fort Bellingham. Washington.
Captain George E. Pickett, 9th Infantry, establishes the post at the present town of Bellingham in response to an appeal by local settlers. Considered a temporary post, it protects the Whatcom coal mining district until it is abandoned in 1860.

30 August. Fort Yamhill. Oregon.
Brevet Second Lieutenant William B. Hazen, 4th Infantry, places an Army garrison in a blockhouse built by local settlers who fear Indian uprisings might spread to the nearby Grand Ronde Reservation. Named for its location near the Yamhill River, this is one of three posts established to control local Indians. After the post is abandoned in 1866, the blockhouse is moved to the Indian Agency and used as a jail.

Right: *In 1856, Colonel Edwin Sumner employed his dragoons to disperse a crowd threatening voters in Topeka, Kansas Territory, during a period when the area experienced the sectional violence that erupted in a civil war five years later. (Harvard College Library)*

23 September. Fort Walla Walla. Washington.
The fort is established by Major Edward J. Steptoe, 9th Infantry, at the present town of Walla Walla to control hostile Indians and protect transportation routes in the area. It is garrisoned irregularly until 1867, when it becomes a depot for wintering public animals. The Army abandons the post in 1911; it is now a Veterans Administration hospital.

26 October. Fort Townsend. Washington.
As protection from Indians, Captain Granville O. Haller, 4th Infantry, establishes a post on Port Townsend Bay. It is abandoned in 1861 and becomes a marine hospital. The Army occupies the post again in 1874, but the garrison is evacuated after a fire in 1895.

November. **Apache Expedition. New Mexico Territory.**
After a Navajo Indian agent disappears and is presumed killed by Mogollon Apaches, Colonel Benjamin Bonneville embarks on a punitive expedition and kills any Apaches he finds, including friendly Mimbres.

Above: *As with his predecessor, Secretary of War John Buchanan Floyd was a southerner and suspected by some of favoring succession. (Daniel Huntington, U.S. Army Art Collection, NMUSA)*

Opposite: *A dragoon, garbed in a Mexican War-era field uniform, boldly charges with carbine or muskatoon in hand. (Don Troiani, www.historicalartprints.com)*

27 November. **Presidio Calabasa. Arizona.**
After the Gadsden Purchase, Major Enoch Steen occupies the stone buildings of a Mexican post with four companies of 1st Dragoons. The name is changed to Camp Moore for Captain Benjamin D. Moore, who was killed at the Battle of San Pascual during the Mexican War. It is abandoned in 1857 when Fort Buchanan is established.

1857

January. **Status of the Army.**
By 1857 there are 178 companies at or en route to western stations, bringing the Army's authorized strength to 17,875. The Army is attempting to learn from its experiences. The new edition of *Regulations of the Army of the United States* includes the concept developed during the Mexican War of using a division to combine the combat arms under a single commander. According to the regulations, a division is to consist of two or three brigades of infantry or cavalry and troops of other corps, including artillery and engineers. Brigades are to have two or more regiments, although there is no indication of how many "troops of the other corps" should be included. The regulations specify that divisions and brigades be designated by numbers rather than the names of the commanders, although the names of commanders are to be included on reports.

21 February. **Officers' Army Pay Increased.**
Congress increases officer base pay by $20 a month.

4 March–23 April. **Seminole Campaign Ends. Big Cypress, Florida.**
Eight companies of 5th Infantry and a company of 4th Artillery corner the largest band of Seminoles in the swamp. After a final fight, 165 of the Seminoles agree to leave Florida, although about 120 remain in the state.

6 March. **New Secretary of War.**
John B. Floyd becomes the Secretary of War. He has no prior military experience. A Virginian, he disagrees with the federal government's decision to send supplies to Fort Sumter, South Carolina. He is asked to resign for accepting and paying drafts from government contractors for future services. Floyd leaves office in December 1859 amid claims that he has transferred arms to U.S. arsenals located in southern states in anticipation of the approaching war.

7 March. **Fort Buchanan. Arizona.**
To control Apache Indians and protect travel routes

through southern Arizona, Major Enoch Steen, 1st Dragoons, establishes the post and names it for President James Buchanan. Located between the present towns of Patagonia and Sonoita, the post is evacuated and burned in 1861 when a Confederate force from Texas occupies Arizona. The Army does not regarrison after the Civil War.

27–28 May. **Rogue River Expedition. Big Meadows, Oregon.**
Takelma and Tututni chiefs agree to surrender but instead attack Captain Andrew Jackson Smith's force of 30 infantry and 50 dragoons with some 200 warriors. On the second day of the battle, Army reinforcements arrive and rout the Indians.

28 May–December. **Mormon Expedition. Fort Leavenworth, Kansas.**
In Utah members of the Mormon community are attacking wagon trains, have massacred at least one group of settlers, and are resisting federal authority. An Army expedition to restore order is gathered and the first detachment, composed of the 5th and 10th Infantry with two pieces of artillery, departs for Utah. Colonel Albert S. Johnston, expedition commander,

follows a few days later with eight companies of the 2d Dragoons.

7 June. **Camp Hudson. Texas.**
Named for Second Lieutenant Walter W. Hudson, 1st

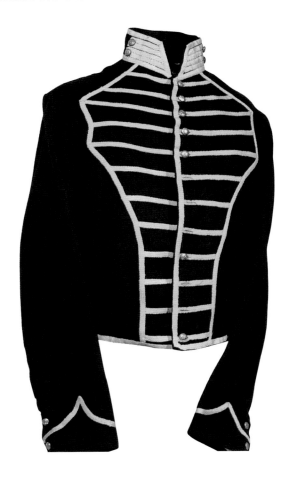

Right: *The 1854-pattern cavalry trumpeter's jacket featured prominent yellow worsted lace on the chest to set off these mounted musicians from their comrades. (Center of Military History, NMUSA)*

Infantry, who died of wounds received in action with Indians near Laredo, the post is built by First Lieutenant Theodore Fink, 8th Infantry, on the Devils River. It is evacuated in 1861 and reoccupied after the Civil War before being abandoned in 1868.

11 June. **Fort Bragg. California.**
First Lieutenant Horatio Gates Gibson, 3d Artillery, places the post inside the Mendocino Indian Reservation near the present day town of Fort Bragg. It is named for Captain Braxton Bragg, 3d Artillery, which causes some agitation for changing the name when he leaves the U.S. Army to join the Confederacy in 1861, but the designation remains until the post is abandoned in 1864.

17 July. **Army Camel Corps. Fort Davis, Texas.**
Former U.S. Navy Lieutenant Edward F. Beale leads the Army Camel Corps through Fort Davis on their way to Arizona. Secretary Floyd is enthusiastic about the experiment and requests funds to purchase more camels, but nothing is done.

28 August. **Fort Abercrombie. North Dakota.**
Lieutenant Colonel John J. Abercrombie, 2d Infantry, establishes the first permanent U.S. Army fort in the present state of North Dakota. Located at Graham's Point north of the confluence of the Bois de Sioux

and Otter Tail Rivers, it is named for its founder. It guards wagon trains and steamboat traffic on the Red River and is a supply base for wagon trains headed to the Montana border. The Army abandons it in 1878 and sells the buildings to settlers.

5 October. **Election Supervision. Kansas.**
Soldiers supervise elections and protect voters in the territory, permitting the free election of an antislavery state legislature.

12 October. **Fort Ter-waw. California.**
First Lieutenant George Crook, 4th Infantry, suggests the name, which reportedly means "beautiful place" in the local Yurok Indian language, for the fort he establishes on the Klamath Indian Reservation. During the winter of 1861–1862 the Klamath River floods the post four times and washes away 17 of its 20 buildings, prompting the Army to abandon the site.

November–December. **Mormon Expedition. Utah Territory.**
As the Army expedition advances, the Mormons destroy all food and forage ahead of it and succeed in capturing or destroying parts of the Army supply trains, leaving Johnston's force in great need of supplies. Faced with increasingly harsh weather, Johnston puts the expedition in winter quarters at Fort Bridger. On 24 November, he

EYEWITNESS: SABER CHARGE AT SOLOMON'S FORK

In 1857, in response to repeated attacks on civilian wagon trains in the Platte River region, the U.S. Army launched an expedition against the southern Cheyennes. On 29 July, the 1st U.S. Cavalry, under the command of Colonel Edwin Vose "Bull" Sumner, encountered a force of more than 300 Cheyenne warriors drawn up for battle at the south fork of the Solomon River. Trooper Robert M. Peck, "E" Company, a participant, describes the only large-unit saber charge against hostile plains tribes:

"When the Cheyennes were almost in rifle-shot they were outflanking us both right and left. . . . A large party of the Indians had crossed the river, and, after passing our right, was about to recross and come up on our pack train in the rear. They were also turning our left, all the while keeping up that infernal yelling. Noticing that the Cheyennes were turning our left, the colonel ordered Captain Beall (the left company) to deploy his company to the left and head them off. He seemed to have determined to offset the disparity of numbers by a bold dash that would create a panic in the enemy's ranks, and roared out, 'Sling—carbine!' then immediately, 'Draw—saber!' and we knew the old man was going to try a saber charge on them.

"I noticed with some surprise that when the command 'Draw—saber' was given (which I then thought was a serious mistake in the colonel) and our three hundred bright blades flashed out of their scabbards, the Cheyennes, who were coming on at a lope, checked up. The sight of so much cold steel seemed to cool their ardor. The party that had started to cross the river after passing our right also hesitated, and Captain Beall . . . easily turned back those that were turning our left flank. I then said to myself, 'I guess "Old Bull" knows what he is doing, after all; he knows that the Indians will not stand a saber charge.' And so it proved.

"The Indians had almost ceased their yelling, had slowed down almost to a walk and were wavering. We had kept a steady trot, but now came the command in the well-known roar of 'Old Bull,' 'Gallop—march!' and then immediately 'Charge!' and with a wild yell we brought our sabers to 'tierce point' and dashed at them.

"All their chief's fiery pleading could not hold them then, for every redskin seemed suddenly to

remember that he had urgent business in the other direction, but as they wheeled to run sent a shower of arrows toward us, by way of a 'parting shot' as it were. Few of the missiles, however, took effect. They scattered as they ran, some going to the north, some east, but by far the greater number struck across the river and went south; and these, as we afterwards discovered, were heading for their village, which was about fifteen miles south of the Solomon, on the next creek.

"It was a running fight, mostly a chase, for about seven miles, when the colonel had 'Recall' sounded, calling us back to the Solomon where the fight began.

"It was estimated that about 30 Cheyennes were killed, though they were scattered over the country so far and wide that it was almost impossible to count the dead correctly. Cade and Lynch were all the killed, but under the tent-fly were twelve wounded. None of the wounded were mortally hurt."

—*Vince Hawkins*

Above: *A dragoon trumpeter in the prescribed uniform of the 1854–1857 period. ("Bugler, Dragoon Regiment," Don Troiani, www.historicalartprints.com)*

Above: *The Regiment of Mounted Rifles retained the dual cavalry-infantry capability needed to counter the bands of hostile Indians encountered on the southwestern plains, mountains, and deserts. ("Mounted Rifles," Don Troiani, www.historicalartprints.com)*

sends a detachment led by Captain Randolph B. Marcy south over the mountains to get supplies from Fort Massachusetts in New Mexico, almost 700 miles away. Marcy and his volunteer detachment of 40 enlisted men and 25 civilian packers fight their way through deep snow and subzero weather for 51 days.

1858

9 January. **Army Explores Grand Canyon.**
Lieutenant Joseph Christmas Ives begins an expedition to explore the Colorado River in a 54-foot paddle boat. Upon reaching the mouth of the Black Canyon, the head of navigation for the river, Ives and his men move overland to become the first party in recorded history to explore the floor of the Grand Canyon.

13 January. **Marcy Arrives. Fort Massachusetts, New Mexico.**
Barely surviving their hazardous journey and subsisting on meat from worn-out mules, Captain Marcy and his small band arrive at the fort with the loss of only one man. They remain only long enough to gather and pack the needed supplies, then head back. They are joined by a detachment of Mounted Rifles as escorts because of reports that the Mormons plan to ambush the returnees. They arrive unharmed at Fort Bridger in February.

Left: *Captain John Buford gained years of experience leading a troop of cavalry in the West before assuming greater responsibilities as a Union cavalry commander during the Civil War. (USAMHI, Carlisle Barracks, PA)*

ALBERT SIDNEY JOHNSTON

Standing over six feet tall, with muscular build, a square jaw, and piercing dark eyes, Albert Sidney Johnston was the very model of a frontier soldier. During a military career that spanned more than 25 years, he served in three different armies.

Born in Washington, Kentucky, on 2 February 1803, Johnston graduated eighth in his class from West Point in 1826. Brevetted a second lieutenant, he served a year at Sackett's Harbor, New York, before joining the 6th Infantry at Jefferson Barracks, Missouri, in June 1827 as a Regular lieutenant. Johnston had several years of garrison duty, including a atour as regimental adjutant during the Black War, before his wife's illness forced him to resign in April 1834; he then took up farming. Following his wife's death, Johnston went to Texas in 1836, volunteering as a private soldier for the Mexican War. He was soon appointed adjutant-general and, on 31 January 1837, became commander of the Texas army. His rapid rise incurred jealousy, and he was seriously wounded in a duel. In 1838, Johnston was appointed secretary of war for the Republic of Texas. He led a vigorous campaign against Indian raiders, but his actions against the Cherokees earned him Sam Houston's displeasure; on 1 March 1840, Johnston resigned.

During the Mexican War, Johnston was commissioned a colonel of the 1st Texas Rifle Volunteers, serving with distinction at Monterrey. After the war he returned to farming, but in 1849 financial ruin led him back to the Army, where he accepted a Regular commission as a major and the position of paymaster. In 1855, Johnston was appointed colonel of the newly raised 2d Cavalry. His operations against the Comanches added to his reputation, and in 1856 he was appointed commander of the Department of Texas. In mid-1857, Johnston led an expedition against insurgent Mormons in Utah. After a series of negotiations his army marched into Salt Lake City without opposition in June 1858. He was brevetted brigadier general and remained in command in Utah through 1860. In January 1861, Johnston was appointed commander of the Department of the Pacific, with headquarters in San Francisco, California.

With Texas' secession from the Union, Johnston reluctantly submitted his resignation on 10 April 1861. While waiting for approval and for his replacement to arrive, Johnston was offered the Army's second-

ranking position under Lieutenant General Winfield Scott, but he refused. Instead, Johnston, a friend of Jefferson Davis, returned to Richmond, Virginia, where he became a Confederate general on 31 August 1861. Davis appointed him commander of the Western Department, and Johnston began recruiting and training the Army of the Mississippi.

At first, Johnston's forces were able to defend the Mississippi River and the borders of Kentucky, but in early 1862, Union troops forced Johnston to retreat. In succession he lost Forts Henry and Donelson, opening the way into the South. This was followed by the fall of Nashville and a retreat back to Corinth, Mississippi. On 6 April 1862, he launched a surprise attack against Union forces encamped at Shiloh Church, Tennessee. While personally leading an assault against the Peach Orchard, Johnston was severely wounded by a bullet fired from his own men that severed an artery behind his right knee. Disregarding the seriousness of the injury, and having sent his personal surgeon to care for the wounded, Johnston bled to death before help could arrive.

Johnston was temporarily entombed in New Orleans, but in January 1867, Texas claimed him and his body was returned to Austin.

—*Vince Hawkins*

Above: *During his colorful career Albert Sidney Johnston held many posts, ranging from secretary of war for the Republic of Texas to the first colonel commanding the 2d U.S. Cavalry Regiment. (National Archives)*

8 May. **Third Seminole Campaign Ends. Florida.**
The United States declares the wars against the Seminoles officially over.

15–18 May. **Yakima Expedition. Fort Walla Walla, Washington.**
About 1,000 Yakima warriors intercept a column of 158 men commanded by Lieutenant Colonel Edward J. Steptoe, 9th Infantry. The Indians attack and kill two officers, but the rest of Steptoe's command escapes.

June. **Mormon Expedition Concludes. Utah.**
In the spring, Colonel Johnston's command is reinforced by detachments of the Mounted Rifles and 3d Infantry, bringing its strength to about 5,500 men, and in June he advances into the Salt Lake Valley. The presence of this large army helps bring negotiations between Mormon leaders and federal authorities in Utah to a peaceful resolution to the conflict. Brigadier General William S. Harney also arrives to set up a regional military department. Colonel Johnston returns to his 2d Cavalry Regiment and is awarded a brevet promotion to brigadier general in November.

18 June. **Changes to U.S. Military Academy. West Point, New York.**
Congress authorizes the superintendent of the Military Academy the local rank and pay of a colonel of engineers, and the commandant of cadets that of a lieutenant colonel. Secretary of War Floyd returns the length of the course back to five years.

24 June. **Fort Garland. Colorado.**
To curb Utes and Jicarilla Apaches, Captain Andrew W. Bowman establishes a fort in the San Luis Valley close to an important Indian trail between the Rio Grande valley and the Arkansas River. The fort is named for Colonel John Garland, 8th Infantry, the department commander. The Army abandons the post in 1883. It is now a state historical monument near the present town of Fort Garland.

11 August. **Fort Taylor. Washington.**
Colonel George Wright, 9th Infantry, establishes the post on the Snake River as a base of operations in the campaign against Spokane, Coeur d'Alene, and Palouse Indians. Built of basalt rock, it is named for First Lieutenant Oliver Hazard Perry Taylor, 1st Dragoons, who was killed in a fight with Spokane Indians. The post is abandoned at the close of the campaign.

1 September. **Battle of Four Lakes. Yakima Plain, Washington.**
Colonel George Wright, leading a column of some

Above: *In 1858 Army regulations called for a new black felt hat looped up on the side to provide a jaunty look that was more suited to the parade ground than campaigning. ("1st U.S. Dragoon Regiment, 1858–1861," H. Charles McBarron, Company of Military Historians)*

600 soldiers from the 1st Dragoons, 3d Artillery, and 9th Infantry, and supported by 30 Nez Perce scouts and 400 pack mules, encounters a large force of warriors from a number of Northwest tribes. Deploying his dismounted infantry and artillery soldiers, Wright forces the Indians out of their positions in wooded hills. Once they are on an open plain, he sends Major William N. Grier, 1st Dragoons, and four mounted companies charging into the fray. The warriors break in the face of the assault. Wright has no casualties, and about 60 Indians are killed.

8–24 September. **Navajo Uprising. Fort Defiance, Arizona.**
After a Navajo murders an officer's black servant on 12 July, the Indians fail to turn over the suspect and hostilities commence with a punitive expedition. Lieutenant Colonel Dixon S. Miles takes Company G, 3d Infantry, into the traditional Navajo base in Canyon de Chelly. After a week, Miles returns to the fort, claiming more than a dozen Navajo casualties.

15–25 September. Wichita Expedition. Fort Belknap, Oklahoma.
Captain Earl Van Dorn departs with four companies of his 2d Cavalry and one company of the 5th Infantry in search of Comanche and Kiowa Indians. His force also includes 135 Indian auxiliaries from the Brazos Reservation. He establishes Camp Radziminski on Otter Creek near the present town of Tipton. Named for a first lieutenant of the 2d Cavalry who died of tuberculosis, the camp is abandoned in 1859.

28 September. Fort Quitman. Texas.
Captain James V. Bomford, 8th Infantry, builds an adobe fort on the Rio Grande to protect the stage line and east-west route along the river. Named for Major General John Anthony Quitman, who died in 1858, it is usually in poor repair. Confederate troops occupy it until 1862; then the 2d California Cavalry takes control of it until 1863. It is abandoned in 1877.

1 October. Wichita Expedition. Rush Springs, Oklahoma.
Captain Van Dorn defeats a band of Comanches under Buffalo Hump. During the fighting 56 Comanche warriors and two women are killed, and another 25 or so die later of wounds. Van Dorn is wounded and five soldiers are killed. The soldiers burn 120 lodges and capture 300 horses.

Above: *Lieutenant Kirby Smith of the elite Corps of Topographical Engineers takes a solar reading as part of his duties at Camp Floyd, Utah Territory, in 1858. (Library of Congress)*

4 December. Fort Gaston. California.
Captain Edmund Underwood, 4th Infantry, establishes the post on the Trinity River to control and protect the Indians on the Hoopa Valley Reservation. Named for Second Lieutenant William Gaston, who was killed during the expedition against the Spokane Indians, the post is abandoned and transferred to the Interior Department for use by the Indian Agency in 1892.

1859

January. Status of the Army.
Reported strength in June 1858 shows 17,498—1,099 officers and 16,399 enlisted men—the highest point for the Army in ten years. Since that time, however, the Army's strength has declined steadily and now hovers at slightly more than 16,000. Almost all are west of the Mississippi.

23 March. Fort Stockton. Texas.
The post is established on Comanche Creek by First Lieutenant Walter Jones, 1st Infantry, to protect the San Antonio-El Paso stage route. Named for Commodore Robert H. Stockton, U.S. Navy, the post is evacuated in 1861, briefly occupied by Confederate troops, and reoccupied by the 9th Cavalry in 1867. It is abandoned in 1886.

19 April. Fort Mojave. Arizona.
The fort is built by Major William Hoffman on the Colorado River across from the present town of Needles, California, to control the Mojave and Piaute

Indians and protect the settlers' route to California. It is abandoned in 1861, then regarrisoned; it remains open until 1890, when it is transferred to the Interior Department for an Indian school. The Indian Service discontinues the school in 1935 and destroys the buildings.

30 April. **Comanche Expedition. Camp Radziminski.**
Captain Van Dorn takes six companies of 2d Cavalry—some 500 officers and enlisted men—in search of Comanche Indians who are raiding in the area. After four days on patrol, they capture a small Indian boy who is forced to reveal the location of his village.

13 May. **Battle of Crooked Creek. Oklahoma.**
Captain Van Dorn finds a Comanche village with men, women, and children. After separating the Indians from their horses, the soldiers attack the camp, killing 49 warriors and capturing others. Two soldiers and four Indian auxiliaries are killed and nine soldiers wounded. Lieutenant Fitzhugh Lee is struck in the chest by an arrow with such force that it pierces his lung and protrudes out of his back, but he manages to survive the wound.

Summer. **Army Explores the Great Basin. Utah.**
Captain James Hervey Simpson makes an extensive reconnaissance across the Great Basin from Camp Floyd, Utah, to Carson City and Genoa at the base of the Sierra Nevadas. His route is used for wagons and stagecoaches, but it is not suitable for a railroad.

Summer. **Army Explorations. Santa Fe, New Mexico.**
Captain John M. Macomb, Topographical Engineers, leads a party northward along the Old Spanish Trail to the Colorado Plateau and the junction of the Green and Grand Rivers. The reports produced by members of the expedition help complete knowledge about the drainage system of the Colorado River.

15 June. **Fort Colville. Washington.**
As a base for the northwest boundary commission conducting the surveys to locate the U.S.-Canadian border, Captain Pinkney Lugenbeel, 9th Infantry, establishes a post on Mill Creek. Named for a Hudson's Bay Company trading post on the site, the military reservation is transferred to the Interior Department in 1887.

27 July. **Army Occupies San Juan Island. Puget Sound, Oregon Territory.**
The border between the United States and Canada is not clearly defined among the islands of the Sound. Captain George E. Pickett is sent with a 68-man

company of the 9th Infantry and a lone cannon to occupy San Juan Island and establish U.S. ownership. When he is ordered off the island by British officials backed by several warships, Pickett refuses, saying he will fight to remain.

August. **Confrontation with British. San Juan Island.**
Captain Pickett is reinforced by more companies—one of the 9th Infantry, three from the 4th Infantry, four from the 3d Artillery, and some engineers. While the British maintain their distance, reports of the situation reach the War Department and General Scott decides to come west to settle the matter.

Fall. **Fort Piute. California.**
Fort Beale is established by Captain James H. Carleton to protect military and civilian travelers between San Bernardino and Fort Mojave. It is named for Edward F. Beale, who is conducting the Camel Corps experiment. During the Civil War the post is garrisoned by detachments of California Volunteers. In 1866 local concern for protection causes the Army to reopen the post, at which time it becomes Fort Piute.

1 October. **Fort Cobb. Indian Territory.**
Major William H. Emory, 1st Cavalry, establishes the post near the present town of Fort Cobb to protect the Wichita Indian Agency. In 1862, Osage, Shawnee, Delaware, and Caddo Indians attack the post, kill

Above: *By the end of the 1850s, the two cavalry regiments wore a mixture of uniforms and carried a variety of weapons typical of the transitional nature of the times. ("2d U.S. Cavalry Regiment, 1858–1861," Frederick Todd, Company of Military Historians)*

Right: *From its beginning in 1842, professional military instruction was provided at The Citadel. Here, cadet artillerymen as they appeared as the Civil War loomed on the horizon. ("Citadel Cadet Battery, Charleston, South Carolina," H. Charles McBarron, Company of Military Historians)*

Below: *Pre-Civil War militia units on both sides often appeared in elaborate dress uniforms that did not necessarily reflect their military prowess. ("Cincinnati Rover Guard, 1853," Frederick Chapman, Company of Military Historians)*

most of the garrison, and set fire to the buildings. After the Civil War, Colonel William B. Hazen, 38th Infantry, moves Kiowa and Comanche Indians from Kansas to Fort Cobb. Major General Philip Sheridan briefly uses the post as his headquarters at the start of his campaign against the Plains Indians. In 1869 the post is abandoned and the Kiowa and Comanche Agency moves to Fort Sill, Oklahoma.

5 October. **John Brown Raid. Harper's Ferry, Virginia.**
Lieutenant Colonel Robert E. Lee, 2d Cavalry, who is home to Virginia on leave, is assisted by Lieutenant J. E. B. Stuart in directing a detachment of U.S. Marines in the capture of abolitionist John Brown and his followers. Brown and his men attacked the Harpers Ferry federal arsenal to seize weapons for sponsoring a slave revolt in the south. After a trial, Brown is hanged for treason on 2 December.

20 October–10 November. **Scott Arranges Negotiations. San Juan Island.**
Lieutenant General Scott arrives and proposes a joint military occupation until a negotiated agreement can be reached. The U.S. armed presence is reduced and Captain Pickett is placed in command of the small garrison on the southern half while British marines occupy the north. This ends the trouble. Captain Pickett resigns in 1861 to become a Confederate general. His deputy, Lieutenant James Forsyth, becomes a Union general officer. The entire island ultimately belongs to the United States.

22 October. **Fort Larned. Kansas.**
First Lieutenant David Bell, 1st Cavalry, establishes the post on the Pawnee River to protect the Santa Fe Trail and provide a central point for distributing annuities to the Indians. Named for Colonel Benjamin F. Larned, paymaster general, the Army abandons the post in 1878 and transfers it to the Interior Department in 1883.

January. **Status of the Army.**

There are increasing strains in the Army as the officers and men watch the growing succession crisis in the east. Many officers are from the South, and they are torn between their oaths and loyalty to their units and comrades from the North, and their ties to family and home states. Army strength hovers at slightly over 16,000 men.

30 April. **Navajo Uprising. Fort Defiance, Arizona.**

Attacked by more than 1,000 Navajo, the small garrison of soldiers from Companies B, C, and E, 3d Infantry, drive off the Indians.

3 May–September. **Army Explorations. St. Louis, Missouri.**

Major H. A. Blake, 1st Dragoons, with 13 officers and 292 recruits, departs to open a wagon road between Fort Benton, Indian Territory, and Walla Walla, Oregon. The command reaches the Coeur d'Alene Mission in Idaho in September after covering 3,000 miles by water and 600 by land.

21 June. **First Army Signal Officer Appointed. Washington, D.C.**

Congress names Albert J. Myer, an Army surgeon, to be the Army's first Signal Officer. In March 1863, it established a separate Signal Corps. This is the Signal Corps birthday.

September–November. **Navajo Expedition. Fort Defiance, Arizona.**

Major Edward R. S. Canby, 10th Infantry, leads an offensive against the Navajos with nine infantry companies from four regiments (5th, 7th, 8th, and 10th) and six companies of Mounted Rifles and 2d Dragoons—a total of about 600 soldiers. After a month in the field, during which the column engages in at least nine fire skirmishes and is harassed by Navajo warriors almost every day, Canby returns to the fort. The Navajos have lost more than 30 warriors, 1,000 horses, and 3,000 sheep. Although there was no large battle, the large number of soldiers moving through their territory prompt the Navajo tribal elders to initiate peace overtures.

November. **Apache Uprising. Fort Buchanan, New Mexico.**

A band of Pinal Apaches raids the ranch of John Ward, who tells the fort commander that Chiricahua Apaches led by Cochise were responsible.

Above: *Military Surgeon Albert Myer was appointed as the Army's first Chief Signal Officer in 1860. (U.S. Army Signal Center and Fort Gordon, GA)*

12 December. **Commanding General of the Army.**

Lieutenant General Winfield Scott, Commanding General of the Army since 1841, transfers his headquarters back to Washington, D.C., from New York City, where he had moved because of his differences with a succession of Secretaries of War.

31 December. **Army Stationing.**

On the eve of the Civil War, the Regular Army consists of ten infantry regiments, four artillery regiments, and five mounted regiments of three different types (two of cavalry, two of dragoons, and one of mounted riflemen). There is a total of 197 companies in the 19 regiments, but only 18 of them are east of the Mississippi River, and they are all artillery; eight of those are training at Fort Monroe, Virginia. The Army's other 179 companies are scattered across the western half of the continent in small, isolated garrisons.

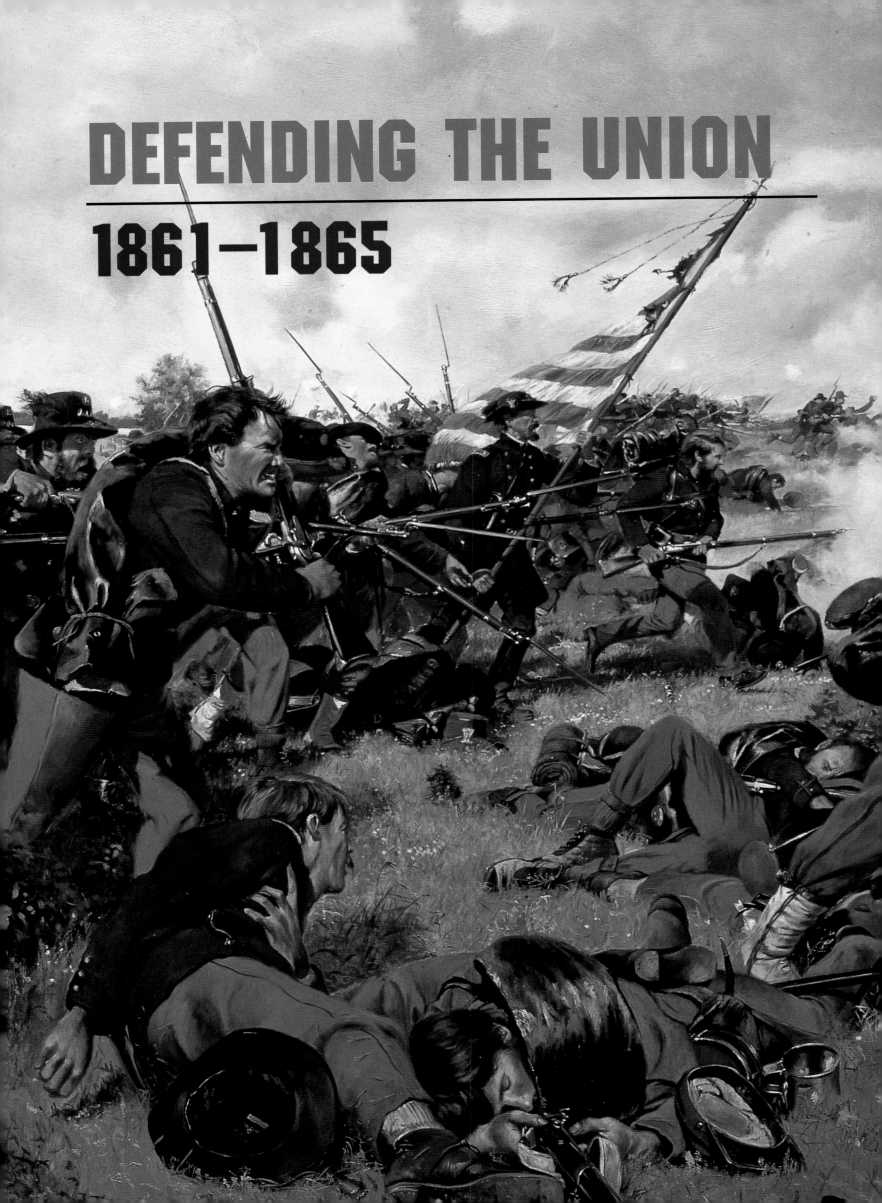

DEFENDING THE UNION

1861–1865

DEFENDING THE UNION

1861–1865

Matthew Seelinger

The Civil War remains one of the most important events in American history and the history of the U.S. Army. In terms of sheer numbers of men who served, and of those killed and wounded, the Civil War greatly exceeded all American conflicts to that point. Not until World War I would American troops fight in such massed armies again. In all, more than 2,666,999 men served in the Union Army, the vast majority of them serving in Volunteer units raised by the states. The Union Army possessed only a small number of Regular units with veteran officers (including many West Point graduates) and enlisted men. Most soldiers served in temporary units raised in their home states. Few of these citizen-soldiers would receive adequate training before being thrust into battle. Fortunately for the Union Army, the Confederate Army was no better trained. The war's early battles reflected the participants' inexperience. As the war dragged on, however, armies became veteran and battle-hardened. This, coupled with increasingly advanced weaponry, brought battle casualties to staggering levels. In all, the U.S. Army lost 361,538 dead during the war. While disease still killed more soldiers than bullets, more than 110,000 federal troops died in action or of wounds. All told the war took in excess of 620,000 American lives.

The Civil War brought industrial warfare to the U.S. Army. The North's superior industrial capacity proved to be one of the most important factors in winning the war. The South simply could not produce the necessary amounts of small arms, artillery, and other materiel required to win the war. Furthermore, the Civil War also marked the first time America employed the doctrine of strategic or "total" war—

Union armies not only attempted to destroy the enemy forces in the field but also destroyed the South's industrial base. As a result, much of the South's key cities and manufacturing centers lay in ruins by the end of the war.

Two inventions of nineteenth century industry, the railroad and the telegraph, were also used with great effect for the first time in American warfare. The railroad greatly facilitated the transport of men and equipment, and control of the rail system often meant victory. The telegraph also was used extensively and allowed much faster communication between the high political command in Washington, D.C., and the armies in the field.

New, modern weapons, however, had the greatest effect on the battlefields of the war. The Civil War marked the first mass employment of rifles in American military history. While rifles had existed for many years, the development of the Minié ball made wide-scale use of rifles practical. Instead of inaccurate, short-range smoothbore muskets, soldiers on both sides used rifles with devastating effect. The greater accuracy and improved range of the rifled musket made frontal assaults suicidal. Breech-loading and repeating rifles, used by considerable numbers of Union troops by the end of the war, only increased the carnage.

Rifling, improved shells, and fuses also improved the range and accuracy of artillery, permitting the placing of artillery behind battle lines, but increased problems with directing fire. Rifled muskets killed or wounded many more men than artillery. But when employed in defensive positions, artillery could wreak considerable destruction upon infantry formations, particularly when canister rounds were used.

Unfortunately for the soldiers of both sides, the accepted tactics and lack of adequate means for command and control on the battlefield still required massed formations of troops marching toward enemy positions. In the final year of the war, soldiers of both sides dug elaborate systems of trenches and other field works as protection from enemy fire, much as the soldiers of World War I would do 50 years later.

A number of skilled general officers emerged during the war to lead the Union to victory, but in the early years of the war, the Union Army was plagued with poor leadership. Almost a third of the Army's officers, including Robert E. Lee, eventual commander of all the Confederate armies, resigned their commissions and returned to their home states in the South. The Army's commanding general, Winfield Scott, was elderly and in poor health. George B. McClellan demonstrated his expertise at organizing and training troops but failed as a battle commander. John Pope, Ambrose Burnside, and Joseph Hooker all suffered humiliating defeats. Others like Don Carlos Buell and William Rosecrans eventually proved ineffective.

In 1863, Ulysses S. Grant emerged as the general officer who could bring victory to the Union with the help of Philip H. Sheridan, George G. Meade,

George H. Thomas, and William Tecumseh Sherman. Younger officers such as Wesley Merritt, George Crook, Nelson A. Miles, George Armstrong Custer, and Emory Upton, gained extensive combat experience in the war and later played influential roles in the postwar Army.

The war, while a devastating upheaval that took hundreds of thousands of lives, served to define and strengthen the nation. It also fixed the Army's importance in the history of the United States.

Pages 368-369: *Union and Confederate forces met each other on hundreds of battlefields in a bloody Civil War, such as the clash between Corporal Francis A. Waller of the 6th Wisconsin, who killed a Confederate color bearer at Gettysburg on 1 July 1863. ("Fight for the Colors," Don Troiani, www.historicalartprints.com)*

Above: *Union Volunteers had to endure long hours of drill to learn the basics of the mass formations used during the war. Once they did, they could respond automatically despite the noise and confusion of the battlefield. ("Military Drill Scene," James Walker, Alexander McCook Craighead Collection, West Point Museum, U.S. Army Military Academy, West Point, New York)*

DEFENDING THE UNION
1861–1865

"I shall fight it out on this line if it takes all summer."
—Lieutenant General Ulysses S. Grant, 11 September 1864

1861

January. **Status of the Army.**
The Army has only 16,367 Regulars of the 18,122 authorized—there are no Volunteers or militia. Of the 197 companies in the Army's 19 regiments, 18 artillery companies are at the ten posts east of the Mississippi. The rest—30 artillery, 50 mounted, and 99 infantry companies—are spread in 79 western frontier or Pacific coastal forts. Of 1,105 Army officers, dozens of officers have already resigned, including Brigadier Joseph E. Johnston, Quartermaster General of the Army. To protect Washington, Major General Winfield Scott brings the 2d Artillery company and Engineer Company A from West Point. Also en route are units from Plattsburg, New York, and Forts McHenry and Leavenworth, as well as units expelled from the South. As they arrive, the Regulars are posted to protect key federal buildings. South of the city, Engineer Captain George W. C. Lee, son of Lieutenant Colonel Robert E. Lee, directs the rebuilding of the Fort Washington defenses on the banks of the Potomac.

9 January. **Supply Ship Fired Upon. Charleston Harbor, South Carolina.**
The steamship *Star of the West*, attempting to resupply Fort Sumter, is fired upon by two South Carolina artillery batteries, one manned by cadets from the Citadel. The unarmed ship withdraws.

18 January. **Holt Appointed Secretary of War.**
President James Buchanan appoints Joseph Holt as the 25th Secretary of War. Holt is pro-Union but has no previous military experience.

10–20 January. **Troops Secure Southern Forts. Florida.**
Pensacola is evacuated by First Lieutenant Adam Slemmer, who takes his 47 men of the 1st Artillery to occupy Fort Pickens, located on nearby Santa Rosa Island. Refusing to surrender, he holds out until another company arrives in February. On the 14th, Fort Taylor at Key West is secured. Four days later Fort Jefferson on the Dry Tortugas is garrisoned. These few installations in the South are to remain in Union hands and become critical to the successful Union blockade.

February. **St. Louis Arsenal Secured. St. Louis, Missouri.**
Captain Nathaniel Lyon brings his company of 2d Infantry from Jefferson Barracks to secure the federal treasury, the arsenal, and its arms. He is later reinforced by Captain James Totten's 2d Artillery company from Kentucky. The city remains in federal hands.

4–14 February. **Apache Uprising Begins. Apache Pass, Arizona.**
Second Lieutenant George N. Bascom takes a detachment of 7th Infantry to meet with Chiricahua Apaches led by Chief Cochise. Bascom demands the return of a rancher's stepson recently captured by Apaches and angrily reacts to Cochise's truthful denials of involvement by seizing the Indians. Cochise escapes, but at least one Apache is killed and others held. In retaliation, Cochise raids a stage station and

ARMY BATTLE STREAMERS—CIVIL WAR

SUMTER 1861

Sumter, 1861	Fredericksburg, 1862	Spotsylvania, 1864
Bull Run, 1861	Murfreesborough, 1862–1863	Cold Harbor, 1864
Henry and Donelson, 1862	Chancellorsville, 1863	Petersburg, 1864-1865
Mississippi River, 1862–1863	Gettysburg, 1863	Shenandoah, 1864
Peninsula, 1862	Vicksburg, 1863	Franklin, 1864
Shiloh, 1862	Chickamauga, 1863	Nashville, 1964
Valley, 1862	Chattanooga, 1863	Appomattox, 1865
Manassas, 1862	Wilderness, 1864	
Antietam, 1862	Atlanta, 1864	

wagon train, killing several but offering to trade prisoners. A detachment of 1st Dragoons arrives from Fort Buchanan on the 14th to help Bascom and in scouting the area finds the mutilated bodies of the three white prisoners. Bascom hangs the Apache hostages, and a bloody conflict begins.

13 February. **Capital Protected from Southern Mobs.**
Mobs of southern supporters enter Washington in an attempt to disrupt the counting of the electoral ballots and invalidate Abraham Lincoln's election. Regular troops are called out to block the streets and guard the congressional galleries.

18 February. **Twiggs Surrenders Forces in Texas. San Antonio.**
Major General David E. Twiggs surrenders all troops, equipment, and facilities in the Department of Texas to Texas militia with the agreement that the 102 officers and 2,328 enlisted men can withdraw. Only about 1,200 make it out before Fort Sumter is fired upon, and those still in Texan hands are made prisoner. Twiggs is dismissed from the Army two weeks later and eventually becomes a major general in the Confederate Army.

Opposite: *General Winfield Scott, who commanded the Army at the outset of the Civil War, talks to a West Point cadet. ("General Officer, Cadet and Staff," Henry A. Ogden, Dover Publications)*

Above: *Secretary of War Joseph Holt was the Army's first Judge Advocate and prosecutor in the Lincoln assassination trials. (Louis P. Spinner, Army Art Collection, NMUSA)*

4 March. Abraham Lincoln Inaugurated.
Abraham Lincoln is inaugurated as the 16th President of the United States and Commander-in-Chief. His only military experience was a short time as an Illinois militia captain during the Black Hawk War.

5 March. Cameron Appointed Secretary of War.
Simon Cameron is appointed the 26th Secretary of War. Cameron, who has no military experience, was promised a cabinet position by Republican leaders.

12–14 April. Fort Sumter Bombarded. Charleston Harbor.
Major Robert Anderson refuses to surrender. Confederate artillery under P .G. T. Beauregard, now a Confederate brigadier general, opens fire on the fort. Anderson, who had been Beauregard's artillery instructor at West Point, orders his garrison of 1st Artillerymen to return fire. The first cannon lanyard is pulled by Captain Abner Doubleday. After 34 hours of bombardment, Anderson is running out of provisions and must surrender. He evacuates his six officers and 78 enlisted men on the morning of 14 April. Neither side suffers any fatalities during the bombardment, but one private dies in an accidental explosion during the 100-gun salute that accompanies the surrender, and another is mortally wounded.

15 April. Call-Up of State Militias.
President Lincoln issues a call for 75,000 state militia troops for three months' service. Eventually, more than 90,000 men respond, but offers by four governors to send mounted troops are refused by the War Department due to expense.

18 April. Federal Arsenal and Armory Evacuated. Harpers Ferry, Virginia.
As Virginia militia approach the federal arsenal, First Lieutenant Roger Jones and his 42 soldiers set fire to the facility and retreat. Much of the installation is destroyed, but the Rebels recover 4,000 muskets and

milling machinery. In Washington, five companies of Pennsylvania Volunteers are the first to arrive after Lincoln's call for militia.

19 April. Massachusetts Troops Attacked. Baltimore, Maryland.

On the way to Washington, the 6th Massachusetts Infantry is attacked by a prosecessionist mob. Four soldiers and 12 civilians are killed in the ensuing melee.

20 April. Robert E. Lee Resigns from the Army.

Recalled from the 2d Cavalry in Texas in February for reassignment, Lieutenant Colonel Robert E. Lee resigns his commission. He has turned down an offer to command all federal forces because his home state, Virginia, seceded from the Union on 17 April. Lee is soon appointed to command the state's forces.

23–30 April. Federal Troops Captured. Texas.

On 23 April, Texas militia captures a company of the 8th Infantry near San Antonio. Two days later, Major Caleb Sibley, commanding officer of the 3d Infantry, surrenders the regiment to Confederate forces at Saluria. Starting on the 23rd, Lieutenant Colonel William H. Emory withdraws his 1st Cavalry out of the forts they garrison, assembles 11 companies with 150 dependents, and marches for Fort Leavenworth just ahead of Southern militia. Scott orders other Regular units in the western territories also to move to the fort.

3 May. Additional Troops Called-Up.

Using his emergency powers, President Lincoln calls for an additional 42,000 three-year Volunteers and 22,714 Regulars. The Volunteers are divided into 40 regiments—39 infantry and one mounted (1st New York). Governor Richard Yates of Illinois convinces the Army to accept five companies of Illinois cavalry. The Regulars are organized into the 11th–19th Infantry, 5th Artillery and the 3d Cavalry Regiments. These infantry regiments use a new concept of three battalions—two for tactical field use and one for recruiting and training.

3 May. Scott's Anaconda Plan.

Major General Scott proposes a strategy for fighting a war against the Confederacy. Later known as the "Anaconda Plan," it initially is ridiculed, but Scott's overall plan eventually becomes a key concept in the Union's victory.

10–12 May. Riots in St. Louis, Missouri.

Riots erupt in St. Louis as Lyon, now a brigadier general of Missouri Volunteers, surrounds a camp of southern sympathizers and marches captured militiamen through the city's streets. Two soldiers and 28 civilians are killed.

13 May. Baltimore Occupied.

Without authority, Brigadier Benjamin Butler marches his troops into the city to occupy Federal Hill. Ten days later Butler is sent to command Fort Monroe, Virginia.

24 May. **Death of Colonel Elmer Ellsworth. Alexandria, Virginia.**
Moving before dawn, Union troops cross the "Long Bridge" to take control of Alexandria. There is no formal resistance, but while removing a Confederate flag from a hotel, Colonel Elmer Ellsworth, commander of the 11th New York (Fire Zouaves), is shot and killed by the hotel's proprietor. Ellsworth is the first Union officer killed in the war. His body lies in state at the White House for several weeks.

3 June. **Battle of Philippi. (West) Virginia.**
George B. McClellan, newly appointed major general of Volunteers and commander of the Department of Ohio, rushes troops by train to western Virginia to reinforce pro-Union forces. They march several miles to surprise and rout the Confederates at Philippi. The battle is dubbed the "Philippi Races."

10 June. **Battle of Big Bethel. Virginia.**
A Union force of 2,500 from Fort Monroe, commanded by Brigadier Ebenezer Pierce, attacks a smaller force of Confederates under Colonel John B. Magruder at Big Bethel Church, eight miles northwest of Hampton. Union forces attack piecemeal and are soon driven back. Federal casualties are 76 killed, wounded, and missing; Confederate losses number less than a dozen.

11 June. **Southerners Depart the Army.**
Lieutenant Colonel Edward R. S. Canby, 10th Infantry, becomes the Department of New Mexico commander when Colonels William W. Loring and

George Crittenden, Majors Henry Hopkins Sibley and James Longstreet, Captain Richard S. Ewell, Lieutenant Joseph Wheeler, and other officers resign. In California, Brigadier General Albert S. Johnston resigns as head of the Department of the Pacific, turning it over to Brigadier George Wright. He has only a few companies of 9th Infantry to secure the whole Pacific coast and begins recruiting Volunteer units. Eventually 17,000 Californians will serve.

15–17 June. **Union Forces Take Missouri Capital.**
Federal troops under Brigadier Nathanial Lyon march unopposed into Jefferson City and pursue the fleeing prosecessionist governor and his militia. On 17 June, Lyon's troops rout Missouri State Guard forces at Boonville.

17 June. **Grant Appointed Illinois Colonel. Springfield, Illinois.**
Governor Yates appoints Ulysses S. Grant colonel and commander of the 21st Illinois Volunteer Infantry Regiment. Grant has been seeking active duty for weeks. After several weeks of training, the regiment is ordered to march to Missouri.

18 June. **Lincoln Observes Hot Air Balloon. Washington, D.C.**
President Lincoln observes Thaddeus S. C. Lowe's ascent in the hot air balloon *Enterprise*. From 500 feet, Lowe sends Lincoln the first air-to-ground telegraphic message. Four days later, Lowe is making ascents to observe enemy troops and, with Major Leyard Colburn, making the first aerial map. In August,

Opposite: Answering the call for troops, members of the 7th New York board a train bound for Washington, D.C. (7th Regiment Fund, New York)

Right: *General Irvin McDowell's experience as an instructor at West Point helped earn him command of Union forces around Washington. McDowell's poor performance at Bull Run caused his relief. (National Archives)*

Below: *Chicago's Colonel Elmer E. Ellsworth raised a colorful regiment of United States Zouave Cadets. ("Zouave Cadets," H. Charles McBarron, Company of Military Historians)*

Confederates fire a rifled cannon at Lowe's balloon, the incident marks the first use of antiaircraft artillery.

4 July. **Lincoln Requests More Troops.**
President Lincoln asks Congress to authorize 400,000 more three-year Volunteers. Instead, on 22 July, Congress authorizes 500,000, mostly infantry.

5 July. **Skirmish at Carthage. Missouri.**
A Federal force numbering just more than 1,000 men under Colonel Franz Sigel joins the campaign to drive Confederate forces from Missouri. Sigel's troops battle the Missouri State Guard near Carthage. The outnumbered Federals fight well, but they are eventually forced to withdraw.

11 July. **Battle of Rich Mountain. Virginia.**
On 6 July, Major General McClellan, with 30,000 troops, begins advancing against 10,000 Confederates led by Brigadier General Robert S. Garnett. McClellan orders Brigadier General William S. Rosecrans to attack Rich Mountain with 2,000 men on 11 July to force the Rebels from their positions. Rosecrans' attack is successful and quickly drives Garnett east. Federal casualties are relatively light— fewer than 100 killed and wounded.

16–21 July. **First Battle of Bull Run (First Manassas).**
Brigadier General Irvin McDowell, Union commander in Washington, is ordered to take the offensive. Most of his 35,000 troops are untested militia and require more training. On 16 July, he marches toward Manassas Junction where a Confederate force numbering 21,000 commanded by P. G. T. Beauregard waits along Bull Run. Realizing that a Union attack is imminent, Confederate Brigadier Joseph E. Johnston loads his 12,000 troops onto trains and transports them from the lower

MANPOWER IN THE CIVIL WAR

The American Civil War required an unprecedented mobilization of military manpower. Regulars were men who enlisted for service in the few standing units created by Congress as a permanent force. Terms of enlistment varied but by the 1860s were usually three years. To augment this core force were Volunteers and militia. Volunteers were also federal troops but raised by the states to serve in temporary units to meet military emergencies. Militia were state forces controlled by the governor; they normally served only within their home state. They could also be called to short-term national duty in time of emergency. Regulars, militiamen, and Volunteers all served during the war, but Volunteers were the bulk of both the Union and Confederate armies.

In 1861, the U.S. Regular Army numbered 16,367 officers and men organized into 19 regiments. However, the Army was widely dispersed in small outposts of company- or smaller-sized garrisons scattered throughout the nation. At the beginning of the Civil War, the Regular Army suffered a serious blow when 313 officers—nearly one-third of the officer corps—resigned to join the Confederacy. The War Department decided to keep the Regular Army units together as a reliable reserve rather than to disperse the officers and men as training cadres for Volunteer regiments.

After the attack on Fort Sumter, President Lincoln ordered 75,000 militiamen into federal service for 90 days to put down the insurrection. Militia companies formed the basis for the earliest Volunteer regiments formed on both sides. Northern militia rushed to Washington, D.C., to defend their capital. After a while, the militia's influence waned, but militia units still performed valuable service in garrisoning forts, protecting borders, guarding prisoners of war, and turning out en masse for local defense whenever enemy armies or raiding parties posed a threat.

Following the debacle at First Bull Run, the President called for 500,000 federal volunteers for up to three years of service. It was the first of a series of federal call-ups that eventually brought nearly 2.7 million men into the Union Army. The Union Army attained its maximum strength of just under one million men in the spring of 1865 while Confederate manpower peaked at 464,500 soldiers in late 1863.

The creation and expansion of the mass, citizen-soldier armies of the Civil War occurred quickly. Many of the militia-based regiments that had responded to the first call-up reformed as three-year

Volunteer regiments and became the backbone of Union field forces. The North raised the equivalent of 2,047 regiments: 1,696 infantry, 272 cavalry, and 78 artillery. The number of Confederate regiments is estimated at 750–1,000.

The typical Civil War infantry regiment consisted of ten companies and had a total strength of about 1,000 soldiers. The states recruited and organized Volunteer regiments in numerical order from specific geographic regions, and unit colors bore the regiment's number and state affiliation. State governors appointed the field-grade officers in each regiment while company officers were selected by popular ballot or given commissions in recognition of their recruiting skills. Company commanders selected noncommissioned officers based on their knowledge, experience, or leadership abilities.

Civil War armies had a voracious appetite for manpower, and both sides eventually resorted to conscription. In April 1862, the Confederacy enacted the first national draft laws in American history. Less than a year later, the North resorted to the draft as well. The real effect of conscription was to spur enlistment in Volunteer regiments. Only 6 percent of Union and 20 percent of Confederate troops entered the military through conscription.

—*Michael Doubler*

Shenandoah Valley to Manassas Junction. On the morning of 21 July, the battle initially goes well for McDowell's troops as they cross Bull Run and outflank the Confederate left. As the battle intensifies around Henry House Hill, however, Johnston's reinforcements arrive and the Union lines crumble. Pursued by Confederate cavalry, the exhausted Federals make a panicked retreat back to Washington. Federal losses are 460 killed, 1,124 wounded, and 1,312 missing; the Confederates lose 387 killed, 1,582 wounded, and 13 missing. Throughout the war, the Union will tend to name battles after a prominent body of water within the battlefield; the Confederates will use the nearest town.

22 July. **McClellan Summoned to Command.**
Lincoln relieves McDowell and gives McClellan command of what will become the Army of the Potomac. On that same day, Congress authorizes the creation of military boards (essentially the Army's first efficiency boards) to review Volunteer officers and remove those found to be unqualified. A bill also is introduced in the Senate calling for another 500,000 three-year Volunteers.

25 July. **Fremont Takes Command in the West. Missouri.**
Famed Army explorer and former Republican presidential candidate John C. Frémont, wearing the rank of a Regular major general, arrives in St. Louis to assume command of the Department of the West, created for him in July. He has military responsibility for the territory from Illinois to the Rocky Mountains.

August. **First Army Hospital Train. St. Louis, Missouri.**
A train is used to move wounded Union soldiers from the Wilson's Creek battlefield to hospitals in St. Louis. The men are laid in rows on the floor of the cars without bedding for the 110 mile journey. By the end of the war, an efficient hospital system is in operation by the U.S. Military Railroad, moving over 220,000 sick and wounded to rear area hospitals.

5 August. **Flogging Abolished.**
Congress abolishes flogging as a form of punishment in the Army. Flogging had been abolished in 1812 but was reinstated a few years later. Privates' pay is increased from $11 to $13 a month.

6 August. **Regular Army Cavalry Reorganized.**
The five Regular mounted regiments are renamed according to seniority and given similar organizations. The 1st and 2d Dragoons become the 1st and 2d

Cavalry; the Mounted Rifle Regiment becomes the 3d Cavalry; the 1st and 2d Cavalry become the 4th and 5th Cavalry; and the 3d Cavalry, formed in May, becomes the 6th Cavalry. The regiments retain these designations today.

7 August. **Grant Promoted to Brigadier. Missouri.**
Grant receives a promotion to brigadier general of Volunteers and is given command of the District of Southeastern Missouri. Captain John Pope, a Topographical Engineer, is also promoted to brigadier and assigned under McClellan.

Opposite: *Men of the 7th New York in the gray uniform they wore early in the war. ("7th New York," Fritz Kredel,* Soldiers of the American Army, 1775–1954*)*

Above: *Elmer Ellsworth's colonel's uniform coat reveals the fatal shotgun blast that took his life at the hands of a Confederate sympathizer. (New York State Military Museum)*

10 August. Battle of Wilson's Creek. Missouri.
At Wilson's Creek, ten miles southwest of Springfield, Union forces under Lyon meet a larger army of Confederates. While outnumbered roughly 15,000 to 5,000, Lyon's Army of the West initially fares well. At midmorning, however, a Confederate counterattack smashes Sigel's brigade on the Union left. Already wounded, Lyon is shot in the chest while leading an attack on Bloody Hill and dies minutes later. Major Samuel D. Sturgis, a brigade commander, assumes command and orders a retreat; the Confederates are too exhausted to pursue. The Union defeat jeopardizes Federal control of Missouri.

25 August. First Army Battle Honor Awarded.
In recognition for their actions at Wilson's Creek, Major General Fremont orders the word "Springfield" emblazoned on the colors of the regiments who fought there. This is confirmed by Congress in December 1861, and on 22 February 1862, War Department General Order 19 directs placing upon regiment colors and battery guidons the names of battles in which the unit participated. It is the beginning to today's campaign/battle honor streamer system.

26 August–11 October. Fighting in Northwestern Virginia.
General Robert E. Lee arrives to coordinate Confederate forces. He wins a minor victory at Kessler's Cross Lanes on 26 August, but the rest of the campaign is a failure. The Federal victories at Carnifex Ferry (10 September) and Cheat Mountain (12–15 September) put most of northwestern Virginia firmly in Union hands. Brigadier William S. Rosecrans is appointed commander of the Department of Western Virginia on 11 October.

27 August. Surrender of Union Forces. Fort Fillmore, New Mexico Territory.
An attempt on 25 July by Major Isaac Lynde to defeat an approaching Texan militia force fails. Lynde decides to abandon the fort and withdraw to Fort Stanton, 140 miles across the desert. Bad planning and lack of water doom the effort. The smaller force of Texans easily overtake the column, and Lynde surrenders his seven companies of the 7th U.S. Infantry and three companies of 3d Cavalry without firing a shot. Lynde is dismissed from the Army without a hearing but is permitted to retire after the war.

27–28 August. Amphibious Operation at Hatteras Inlet. North Carolina.
A joint Army-Navy operation under Major General Butler is launched against Forts Hatteras and Clark. The force of gunboats and transports carrying 900 troops arrives on 27 August. Under a naval bombardment troops land and easily take both forts on the 28th, capturing more than 700 Confederates.

September–November. Apache Uprising. New Mexico Territory.
Colonel Christopher ("Kit") Carson is sent with five companies of the 1st New Mexico Cavalry to reopen Fort Stanton and use it to conduct operations against the Mescalero Apaches, who are raiding in the area. By mid-November, many Apaches have given up and are gathered at the fort.

5– 6 September. Grant Captures Paducah. Kentucky.
During the night, Brigadier General Grant moves two regiments of infantry and an artillery battery by steamboat from Cairo up the Ohio River and at dawn lands them at Paducah, which is virtually undefended. The town is a strategic key to control of the Ohio as well as opening the way up the Cumberland and Tennessee Rivers for access into the south.

13 September. **Navajo War Restarts. Fort Lyon, New Mexico Territory.**
A dispute between an Army lieutenant and a Navajo chief over a horse race results in violence. The fort fires on Navajos camped nearby, and the Navajos retaliate by resuming raids throughout the territory. In December the fort is abandoned.

13–20 September. **Siege of Lexington. Missouri.**
A force of 6,000 Confederate Missouri State Guards march on Lexington, a Union stronghold on the Missouri River. Defending the town are 3,500 Federals under Colonel James A. Mulligan. Confederates surround the town and bombard Union positions. On the morning of 20 September they attack, advancing behind mobile breastworks made of dampened hemp. Mulligan surrenders later that day.

24 September–1 October. **Balloon Corps Established.**
The Army establishes the U.S. Balloon Corps after seeing the use of Lowe's balloons to direct the first aerial-directed artillery fire on the 24th at Chain Bridge, Virginia. The Corps will have seven balloons and see substantial action during the Peninsula, Fredericksburg, and Chancellorsville campaigns.

9 October. **Raid on Fort Pickens. Santa Rosa Island, Florida.**
Regulars of the 1st and 2d Artillery and 3d Infantry with the 6th New York Volunteer Infantry repel a Confederate raid on Fort Pickens.

21 October. **Battle of Ball's Bluff. Leesburg, Virginia.**
McClellan orders Brigadier General Charles P. Stone to send a force across the Potomac River to engage Confederates near Leesburg. After crossing the river, the Union troops, under the operational control of Colonel Edward A. Baker, quickly run into trouble. A Confederate attack drives the Federals back over the steep banks of Ball's Bluff and into the river. Baker is killed along with nearly 50 other soldiers, and hundreds more are captured or drowned. Confederate losses are minimal. The action at Ball's Bluff results in the creation of the Joint Committee on the Conduct of the War, a congressional committee with broad powers over the entire war effort. Stone is arrested on 28 January 1862 and held imprisoned without charges for seven months.

21 October. **Skirmish at Camp Wildcat. Southeastern Kentucky.**
Some 7,500 Confederates attack a Union camp at Wildcat Mountain. The 5,400 Federals in the camp, commanded by Brigadier General Albin F. Schoepf, use field fortifications and the rugged terrain to repel the Confederates. Casualties number 50 killed and wounded on each side.

1 November. **McClellan Replaces Winfield Scott.**
In response to a letter of resignation the previous day, Lincoln replaces the ailing 75-year-old Scott as General-in-Chief of the Army. Scott has led the Army since 1841. Lincoln selects Major General

Fremont, Brigadier General Grant takes 3,500 Federals by riverboat from his headquarters at Cairo, Illinois, down the Mississippi to attack Confederates at Belmont. Grant lands his men north of Belmont the next day. The initial attack surprises the Rebels, and their camp is quickly captured. Another Rebel force crosses the river and launches a counterattack supported by artillery. Grant extricates his force, loads it onto transports and returns to Cairo. It is Grant's first battle of the war.

8 November. **Skirmish at Ivy Mountain. Floyd County, Kentucky.**
Union forces led by Brigadier General William Nelson engage a Confederate force at Ivy Mountain and quickly drive the Rebels back into Virginia.

20 December. **Action at Dranesville, Virginia.**
In a sharp action in northern Virginia, Brigadier General Edward O. C. Ord's brigade of Pennsylvania Volunteer infantry, supported by cavalry and artillery, clashes with Rebel cavalry led by Brigadier General J. E. B. Stuart. The Federals drive off the Rebels and inflict nearly 200 casualties.

1862

January. **Status of the Army.**
Army strength stands at 575,917 Regulars and Volunteers. Major General McClellan continues to organize and train a massive Army of the Potomac for the eventual spring invasion of Virginia. Major General Winfield Scott Hancock is attempting to concentrate Regular troops from the western frontier at Fort Leavenworth and to replace them with Volunteer regiments to meet Confederate advances and the continuing Indian attacks.

10 January. **Battle of Middle Creek. Kentucky.**
After their defeat at Ivy Mountain, Confederate forces move back into eastern Kentucky. A Union brigade under Colonel James A. Garfield (the future President) is sent to deal with them. On 10 January, Garfield attacks the Confederates at Middle Creek and forces them back into Virginia. Casualties are light on both sides.

15 January. **Edwin M. Stanton Appointed Secretary of War.**
Edwin M. Stanton is appointed as the 26th Secretary of War, replacing Simon Cameron, who is accused of excessive patronage and corruption. Cameron also embarrassed Lincoln by publishing a recommendation

George B. McClellan, who has been angling for the position since July. McClellan immerses himself in the task of organizing the Army as Scott retires to New York.

2–9 November. **Frémont Relieved. St Louis.**
When Frémont ignores warnings from President Lincoln to curb radical abolitionist statements and activities, and has other charges made against him, Lincoln replaces him as commander of the Western Department. Major General David Hunter arrives on the 3rd to take temporary command. A week later the department is expanded to include Kansas and New Mexico, and Major General Henry W. Halleck is given command. Frémont returns east to await a congressional inquiry into his conduct.

4–7 November. **Joint Army-Navy Operation. Port Royal Sound, South Carolina.**
On 4 November, a Union naval squadron, accompanied by 13,000 soldiers under the command of Brigadier General Thomas W. Sherman, arrives off Port Royal Sound. Confederate-held Fort Walker (Hilton Head Island) and Fort Beauregard (Phillips Island) are captured by nightfall on 7 November.

6–7 November. **Battle of Belmont. Belmont, Missouri.**
On 6 November, following a plan earlier approved by

Opposite: *Major General George B. McClellan replaced Scott as commanding general. He reorganized and restored the Army of the Potomac, but proved unequal to the task of making it a fighting and winning army. (Alexander Laurie, West Point Museum, U.S. Army Military Academy, West Point, NY)*

Right: *Private George C. Platt valiantly struggles to save the regimental standard from being captured on 3 July 1863 during the Battle of Gettysburg. ("Medal of Honor–6th Cavalry, 1863," Don Stivers)*

to arm slaves. Stanton immediately begins to reform contracting procedures.

19 January. Battle of Mill Springs. Logan's Cross Roads, Kentucky.

As a Union force of 4,000 under Brigadier General George H. Thomas advances south toward the Cumberland River, a Confederate force of similar strength attacks in the midst of a heavy downpour. The initial Rebel assault is checked by Colonel Speed Fry's 4th Kentucky Infantry. The Confederate attack soon stalls and Crittenden withdraws his troops across the Cumberland, but he is forced to abandon his artillery and large amounts of supplies.

27 January. Lincoln Issues General War Order Number 1.

Impatient with McClellan's lack of action, President Lincoln issues General War Order Number 1, calling for "a general movement of the Land and Naval forces of the United States against the insurgent forces" on 22 February. Four days later, Lincoln issues Special War Order 1, specifically directing McClellan and the Army of the Potomac to advance on Richmond. McClellan ignores the order.

2–6 February. Fort Henry and Fort Heiman Captured. Tennessee.

On 2 February, Grant and his two-division Army of the West Tennessee board Navy steamboats to attack Forts Henry and Heiman along the Tennessee River. On the morning of the 4th, the troops disembark on both banks of the river. The Rebels quickly abandon Fort Heiman, while Union gunboats bombard Fort Henry. On the 6th, Fort Henry's commander surrenders. The capture of the forts gives the Union control of the upper Tennessee River.

7–8 February. Amphibious Assault on Roanoke Island. North Carolina.

Under the protection of naval gunfire, Brigadier General Ambrose Burnside lands 15,000 troops on the southern end of Roanoke Island and quickly overwhelms the Confederate defenders. The capture of Roanoke Island nets 2,500 prisoners and opens the North Carolina coast to federal attack.

11 February. United States Military Rail Road Established.

In an effort to centralize control of the railways for military purposes, Secretary of War Stanton establishes the United States Military Rail Road (USMRR) and appoints former railway official Daniel McCallum as superintendent. By the end of the war it is the largest railroad system in the world, extending more than 2,100 miles. The last train dispatched by the USMRR carries Lincoln's body back to Springfield in April 1865.

13–16 February. Fort Donelson Captured. Tennessee.

Grant turns to Fort Donelson on the Cumberland River, which is larger and better defended than Fort Henry. On 13 February, his two divisions, led by John McClernand and Charles F. Smith, probe the defenses

but are driven back, and the supporting naval bombardment has little effect. The Confederate commander attempts a breakout toward Nashville on the morning of 15 February. The attack goes well at first and throws the Federals into confusion, but soon loses momentum and fails. Grant, absent during the initial assault, returns and orders a counterattack. Early the next morning Confederate leaders and troops flee, leaving Brigadier Simon Bolivar Buckner to surrender the fort to Grant, who demands, "No terms except an unconditional and immediate surrender can be accepted." The Federals capture 11,500 prisoners and large amounts of arms and supplies. Grant is promoted to major general of Volunteers effective the 16th and made Commander, District of West Tennessee.

16–21 February. **Battle of Valverde. New Mexico.**
A Confederate force of 2,500 under now General Henry Sibley continues the invasion of the southwest. He faces his brother-in-law, Union Colonel Edward Canby, who already is facing hostile Utes, Navajos, and Apaches. Well-fortified Fort Craig blocks the Confederate advance, and Canby has reinforced the garrison with companies of Regulars from the 5th, 7th, and 10th Infantry and the 1st, 2d, and 3d Cavalry, plus 1,600 New Mexico and Colorado Volunteers and militia. Efforts to draw Canby out fail until a movement by Sibley to bypass the fort results in a

battle at a river ford on the 21st. Initial Union success is overturned by confusion and militia cowardice, and Sibley withdraws back into the fort. Losses on both sides are about equal.

22 February. **U.S. Military Telegraph Created.**
Secretary of War Stanton establishes the U.S. Military Telegraph (USMT). The bureau is a civilian office directly under the War Department to oversee military telegraphic communications. By the end of the war it provides direct communication to almost all Union field commanders.

24 February. **First Confederate State Capital Falls. Nashville.**
Union forces, under the overall command of Major General Don Carlos Buell, march into Nashville, the capital of Tennessee. It is the first to fall to federal troops.

7–8 March. **Battle of Pea Ridge. Northwestern Arkansas.**
Confederate forces gather in northwestern Arkansas in an attempt to defeat Brigadier General Samuel L. Curtis's Army of the Southwest and advance back into Missouri. Curtis's 11,000 troops clash with 18,000 Confederates near a rocky plateau called Pea Ridge on 7 March. When Rebel artillery pounds the Union lines, Curtis orders counterfire and much of the Rebel

Opposite: *Early in the war Union forces began attacking and capturing southern coastal forts as part of the Union total blockade plan. ("Landing at Hatteras Island, 6 August 1862," Alfred Waud, Franklin D. Roosevelt Library, Hyde Park, NY)*

Right: *Both sides probed each other to gauge strength and possible weak spots to exploit with direct assault. ("Attack on the Picket Post, 1862," Albert Bierstadt, The Century Association, New York City)*

Below: *Edwin Stanton, lawyer turned Lincoln's Secretary of War, assumed office in 1862. He established a Bureau of Colored Troops and convinced Lincoln to release political prisoners from military control. (Army Art Collection, NMUSA)*

artillery is quickly silenced. Curtis then orders his troops to advance, and the Confederates withdraw. Union losses are 1,384 killed, wounded, and missing.

11 March. **Halleck Appointed to Department of the Mississippi.**
Major General Halleck is appointed commander of the Department of the Mississippi, giving him command of Union forces between Colorado and the Appalachians—11 states, three territories, the Indian Territory, and Grant's district in Tennessee. On that same day, Major General Fremont, cleared of charges, is given command of the Mountain Department in western Virginia.

11–17 March. **McClellan Relieved as General-in-Chief.**
Angry with McClellan's delays, Lincoln issues War Order Number 3, which relieves McClellan as general-in-chief but keeps him in command of the Army of the Potomac. McClellan organizes his army into five corps—I Corps (McDowell), II Corps (Major General Edwin V. Sumner), III Corps (Major General Samuel P. Heintzelman), IV Corps (Major General Erasmus Darwin Keyes), and V Corps (Major General Nathaniel P. Banks). On the 17th McClellan begins moving the Army of the Potomac south to Fort Monroe for his peninsula campaign. With the assistance of his military advisors, Lincoln serves as Army general-in-chief for the next four months.

EYEWITNESS: BATTLE OF SHILOH, 6–7 APRIL 1862

Private George R. Hutto served in the 6th Indiana Volunteer Infantry, which was part of the Union Army of the Ohio under Major General Don Carlos Buell. Buell's units began arriving at Pittsburg Landing from Nashville during the evening of 6 April to reinforce Grant's hard-pressed Army of the Tennessee that had been surprised that morning by a major Confederate attack. The 6th Indiana arrived in time to help break the final Confederate attack late on 7 April, ending the battle. In the letter below to his uncle almost two weeks after the battle, Private Hutto describes his experience. (Note: Original spelling and grammar have been retained.)

April 21st '62
Shilo Battlefield
Tennessee
Uncle J. P. Hutto,

It is with much pleasure that I take my pen in hand to inform you that I am well at present and hope this will find you the same. We left Nashville March 28th and reached Savana after Ten days hard and dirty marching and got on the boat *Tigres* and went up to the Pitsburg landing and was ordered off the boat and as soon as we formed in line of battle we was put on the double quick to the battlefield which place we reached about 1 o'clock PM on the 7 of April.

We was in the battle about 3 hours and then we repulsed the enimie and affected a complete rout of the Enimie but it was so late that we coud not follow them that night but the next day we followed them six miles and our cavlry and theirs had a sermish and killed some 40 of them and we could not get to attact them so at night we returned to our camp on the battlefield and remain there yet. we were ten days with out our tents and it rained a good deal but we have got out tents now and fare a good deal better but it rains a good deal here but it is warm and it is not so bad as if it was cold like it is in Ind. The Rebels never came to see about their dead or cripled and we had their dead all to bury and their cripled to attend to and we buried theirs mostly face down and the boy(s) said that the reason they burried them that way sose they could dig deeper if they wanted to.

I would have written to you sooner but we have bin a marching all the time and have not had any chance to rite to you. I will rite as often as I can but I have a poor chance to rite but I will do the best I can and I want you to rite soon and often. I am anxious to here from you. I dus me so much good to here from you or any of my friends. So no more at present. Write soon and often.

Yours Truly
George R. Hutto

Above: *Skirmishers keep enemy forces at a distance and provide a warning of approaching attacks. ("Skirmish Line," Gilbert Gaul, West Point Museum, U.S. Army Military Academy, West Point, NY)*

Right: *Northern infantry became the mainstay of Lincoln's army. By war's end they typically wore four-button, dark blue sack coats and kepis or "bummer's caps," having abandoned the many fanciful outfits worn during the early days of the Civil War. ("U.S. Regular Infantry," Henry A. Ogden, Dover Publications)*

13 March. **Battle of New Bern. North Carolina.**
After taking Roanoke Island, Burnside moves to the town of New Bern on the Neuse River. On 13 March, Union troops have a brief battle with Confederate defenders, who quickly retreat. Union losses are fewer than 500. For his victories along the North Carolina coast, Burnside is promoted to major general of Volunteers.

23 March. **Battle of Kernstown, Virginia.**
A Union division under Brigadier General James Shields comes under attack by Confederates led by Major General "Stonewall" Jackson just south of Winchester. The initial attack drives the Federals back, but reinforcements arrive and Jackson breaks off the engagement, retreating south to Newton. While the battle is a tactical victory for the Union, the Confederates benefit strategically.

26–28 March. **Battle of La Glorietta Pass. New Mexico Territory.**
A Rebel force of 1,400 Texans moves into New Mexico Territory and clashes with an equal number of Union Volunteers under Colonel John P. Slough at La Glorietta Pass. While neither side achieves a decisive victory, the Confederates are forced to retreat to Texas when Major John Chivington attacks the poorly guarded Confederate wagon train and destroys all their supplies.

6–7 April. **Battle of Shiloh. Pittsburg Landing, Tennessee.**
On 3 April, Grant marches his 40,000-man Army of the Tennessee to Pittsburg Landing on the Tennessee River. His men camp around Shiloh Church, about nine miles inland, with few scouts and pickets deployed. As a result, an army of 40,000 Confederates approaches Shiloh undetected and attacks early on 6 April. By the time Grant arrives from his

headquarters, at Savannah, Union forces have been forced back in confusion. He rallies his commanders and orders divisions under Brigadier Generals W. H. L. Wallace and Benjamin Prentiss to hold their positions in the center at all costs. Prentiss's division holds an area along a sunken road that becomes known as the "Hornet's Nest." Wallace is mortally wounded, and Prentiss is forced to surrender what is left of his division. The Confederates are finally stopped by Union artillery. During the night Buell's Army of the Ohio reinforces Grant, and a Union counterattack in the morning reclaims the lost ground. A final Confederate assault fails, and they retreat. Union casualties are 1,745 killed, 8,408 wounded, and 2,855 missing. Grant is criticized for being surprised, and rumors spread that he was drunk in his headquarters. Halleck replaces Grant as commander, Western District of Tennessee, with Major General George H. Thomas and names Grant second-in-command of the department, a position with no authority.

5 April–4 May. Siege of Yorktown.

McClellan's army advances to Yorktown, which is defended by 13,000 well-entrenched Rebels. McClellan decides to initiate siege operations and brings up heavy artillery. He plans to assault the Rebel positions on 6 May after a massive artillery bombardment, but before the attack is launched the Confederates slip away. As Union troops enter Yorktown, they encounter land mines, or "subterra shells," and booby traps for the first time. These were developed by Confederate Brigadier Gabriel J. Rains, a West Point graduate.

7 April. Island Number 10 Captured. Missouri.

After Union Major General John Pope's Army of the Mississippi takes New Madrid, Pope focuses on the Rebel stronghold, Island Number 10, which defends a sharp bend in the Mississippi. After engineers cut a canal through swamps to bypass the island's strongest defenses, Pope runs gunboats and transports past the Rebel batteries and lands troops to trap the Confederates. After a heavy bombardment from Union gunboats, aided by a balloon with two artillery officers, Island Number 10's commander surrenders.

10–11 April. Fort Pulaski Recaptured. Georgia.

After the Confederates reject a Union demand for surrender, Major General Hunter orders Union batteries on Tybee Island to bombard Fort Pulaski. Fort Pulaski is considered one of the strongest coastal forts in America, but its masonry walls crumble under the shells of rifled artillery and on 11 April, the fort surrenders.

12 April. The Great Locomotive Chase. Georgia and Tennessee.

Twenty Union soldiers, disguised as Southerners and led by James J. Andrews, commandeer a Confederate locomotive named the *General* at Big Shanty, Georgia. The Federals plan to destroy rails, telegraph lines, and bridges along the way until they reach Union lines. Confederates, however, pursue in another locomotive. When the *General* runs out of fuel, the raiders flee into the woods. All are quickly captured and imprisoned. Andrews and seven others are later executed. Six raiders eventually are exchanged; these soldiers are the first to receive the Medal of Honor, on 25 March 1863 in Washington.

Right: *During the Battle of Shiloh, Union artillery helped defend a contested portion of the battlefield called the Hornet's Nest. ("The Hornet's Nest," T. Lindsay, Cincinatti Museum Center - Cincinnati Historical Society Library)*

Below: *Brogans were the essential footwear of hard-marching infantryman. There is little difference between left or right shoe—this concept of specificity was not common until late in the war. (Courtesy Don Troiani, www.historicalartprints.com)*

21 April. **First Use of a Machine Gun. Yorktown, Virginia.**

Men of the 56th New York Volunteers open fire for the first time with a "coffee mill" gun during the attack on the town. Operated by turning a crank to produce rapid fire, the 50 or so guns purchased by the Army proved unsafe and mechanically unreliable. They were soon discarded.

25 April. **Surgeon General Appointed.**

First Lieutenant William A. Hammond, a medical inspector in the Department of Western Virginia, is promoted to brigadier general and named Army Surgeon General. His appointment will have a profound positive effect on the Army's medical system, but his promotion over the heads of several more senior medical officers angers many of the Medical Department's leaders.

29 April–30 May. **Halleck Moves Against Corinth. Mississippi.**

Major General Halleck gathers three armies—Armies of the Tennessee, Ohio, and Mississippi—at Pittsburg Landing and slowly begins to slowly move south to capture Corinth. On 1 May, William T. Sherman, commander, 5th Division, Army of the Tennessee, is promoted to major general, U.S. Volunteers. Halleck decides to conduct siege operations rather than attack the entrenchments. During the night of 29–30 May, the Confederates evacuate the town. Colonel Philip H. Sheridan, promoted on 25 May from his position as Halleck's quartermaster captain, pursues with his 2d Michigan Cavalry. Each side suffers approximately 1,000 casualties during the operation.

1 May. **Union Troops Occupy New Orleans. Louisiana.**

Union troops under Major General Butler occupy New Orleans after city officials surrender. Butler becomes the city's military governor and on 7 June, after several incidents against his troops, issues General Order #28 stating that Southern women who show disrespect to Union soldiers will be treated as prostitutes.

4–5 May. **Battle of Williamsburg. Virginia.**

The Federals catch the Rebel rear guard at Williamsburg on 4 May. Confederate Major General James Longstreet establishes a defensive line around a redoubt known as Fort Magruder and fends off attacks

Above: *Following a battle, almost any shelter was pressed into service as a field aid station. Suitable ambulances and a system of regimental and field hospitals were not in place at the start of the war. ("Island of Mercy, Pay Mill at Antietam," Keith Rocco, Private Collection)*

Below: *New York City College Class of 1848 medical school graduate William A. Hammond became the Union's surgeon general, sponsoring many new improvements. (Army Medical Library)*

from three Union divisions under Brigadier Generals Joseph Hooker, William F. "Baldy" Smith, and Philip Kearny. Confederate reinforcements arrive, but Brigadier General Hancock's flanking force repulses their assaults. The Confederates withdraw during the evening and continue their retreat toward Richmond.

8 May. Battle of McDowell.

In the west, Major General Frémont sends 6,000 Union troops under Brigadier Robert H. Milroy east from the Allegheny Mountains into the Shenandoah Valley. They meet Jackson's 9,000 Confederates in positions on Sitlington's Hill near McDowell. Although outnumbered, the Federals attack. The rugged ground provides excellent cover for Milroy's troops, and they inflict heavy losses on the exposed Confederates, but they are unable to drive the Rebels from the field. After nightfall, the Federals withdraw east toward Monterey; Jackson pursues them for the next two days.

23 May. Battle of Front Royal.

Jackson surprises a Union outpost commanded by Colonel J. R. Kenly at Front Royal on 23 May. In a brief battle, the Confederates take most of the 1,063 Federals prisoner and capture large amounts of arms and supplies.

May 24. First Army Mobile Telegraph.

The Army develops a wagon-mounted telegraph, which permits instant military communications between major headquarters during field operations for the first time.

Right: *The Union's Military Telegraph was one of several technological advances that marked the Union Army's transition into an Industrial Age force. ("Signal Telegraph Train Used at Fredericksburg," Alfred Waud, Library of Congress)*

25 May. **Battle of Winchester.**
As Banks withdraws north to Winchester, Jackson quickly follows. At dawn the battle commences just south of the town. Banks' troops are quickly overpowered and make a disorderly retreat through the town and across the Potomac. Lincoln orders McDowell and Fremont to send divisions to the Shenandoah Valley to deal with Jackson.

27 May. **Battle of Hanover Court House.**
In a brief, sharp engagement, Brigadier General Fitz John Porter's division from V Corps attacks a North Carolina brigade that threatens McClellan's flank. The Confederates are overpowered and driven from the field. Porter's Federals inflict more than 300 casualties and take more than 700 prisoners.

31 May–1 June. **Battle of Fair Oaks (Seven Pines).**
McClellan deploys the Army of the Potomac on both sides of the Chickahominy River, leaving III and IV Corps isolated on the south bank at Fair Oaks. They are attacked by Confederates in brutal fighting, but McClellan is able to reinforce his embattled left with Major General John Sedgwick's division from II Corps. The Rebel attack continues on 1 June with little result, and General Robert E. Lee, the new Confederate commander, orders a withdrawal. Both sides claim victory.

8–9 June. **Battles of Cross Keys and Port Republic.**
After skirmishing with elements of Jackson's army on

6 June near Harrisonburg, Fremont attacks Confederates bivouacked around Cross Keys on 8 June. His uncoordinated attack is beaten back. On that same day, Colonel Samuel S. Carroll leads a Federal cavalry raid on Port Republic, takes several of Jackson's staff officers prisoner, and nearly captures Jackson himself. On 9 June, Union forces are attacked northeast of Port Republic. They fight valiantly but are driven from the field when more Rebels arrive from Cross Keys. In two battles over two days, Union forces suffer 181 killed, 836 wounded, and 685 missing.

12–15 June. **Pursuit of Stuart.**
Federal troops pursue Confederate Brigadier General J. E .B. Stuart and his 1,200 cavalrymen as they reconnoiter the Army of the Potomac. Among the Union pursuers is Brigadier General Philip St. George Cooke, Stuart's father-in-law.

25 June. **Battle of Oak Grove (King's Schoolhouse).**
In the first of what come to be known as the Seven Days Battles, McClellan orders Hooker to march his division, with support from Kearny's division, up the Williamsburg Road to drive the Confederates away from Oak Grove. This will bring Union siege guns into range of the Richmond defenses. The Federal attack over swampy ground makes little progress and ends at nightfall. It is McClellan's last offensive move against Richmond.

ROLE OF WOMEN IN THE CIVIL WAR

Initially, Americans assumed that the only way women could help in the war effort was by preparing food, clothing, and bandages for soldiers. Before long, however, both the Union and Confederate armies realized that their small medical departments were incapable of caring for the increasing numbers of sick and wounded soldiers. Both armies turned to the only source of professionally trained nurses available, convent-trained Catholic nuns. More than 200 Catholic nuns served on battlefields and in military hospitals.

But there were not enough nursing nuns, so the military turned to civilian women. The Union Army appointed Dorothea Dix to be superintendent of contract nurses. Dix wanted her nurses middle-aged and plain so that the chances of distractive romantic liaisons with soldiers would be limited. Hannah Ropes, a 53-year-old mother of four, was typical of the women hired by Dix. In 1863, Ropes died of typhoid she contracted from a patient. One volunteer, "Mother" Mary Ann Bickerdyke, nursed the participants of 19 battles. She was the only nurse for the 2,000 Union casualties at Lookout Mountain and Missionary Ridge. Another volunteer, Clara Barton, also nursed on whatever battlefields she could get to. Twice, hospitals where she worked were bombarded by enemy shells. Noticing the scarcity of basic medical supplies, Barton took it upon herself to obtain them. After the war, Barton used her formidable organizational skills to establish the American Red Cross.

The Confederate Army was placing civilian nurses on the payroll by 1863. Kate Cumming, a native of Mobile, Alabama, was inspired to nurse because she hated Yankees and wanted to do her part for her country. Sally Tompkins established a military hospital in Richmond, Virginia, which became renowned for its low casualty rate. Tompkins' success, which has been attributed to her insistence on cleanliness and proper diet, prompted the Confederate Army to grant her a commission as a captain.

At least seven women physicians worked with ill and wounded soldiers during the Civil War, including Dr. Mary Walker, the only woman to receive the Medal of Honor. A volunteer physician and contract surgeon, Walker was known for her willingness to cross enemy lines to aid soldiers and civilians. During one of her forays, she was captured by Confederate soldiers and held as a prisoner of war for several months.

In a less traditional role, perhaps hundreds of young women disguised themselves as men so they

could fight on the battlefield. Calling herself Lyons Wakeman, Rosetta Wakeman joined the 153d New York State Volunteers. The unit guarded Washington, D.C., for two years before it marched 700 miles to participate in the Louisiana Red River Campaign. Wakeman fought her first battle at Pleasant Hill on 9 April 1864 and eventually died of dysentery.

Jennie Hodgers enlisted in the 95th Illinois Infantry as Albert Cashier and participated in the Vicksburg and Mobile campaigns. Her service became known 50 years later when she applied for a pension, which resulted in an official inquiry.

Several courageous women risked their lives gathering military intelligence. Elizabeth Van Lew, the daughter of a wealthy Virginia family, was educated in Philadelphia, where she learned to abhor slavery. When the war started, she used her social connections to obtain information of interest to the Union Army, and devised a code by which to pass it along. Her messages were read by Generals Benjamin Butler and George Meade and Secretary of War Edwin Stanton.

The former slave Harriet Tubman served the Union Army as a scout and intelligence gatherer in the Beaufort, South Carolina, area between 1863 and 1864, reporting to Major General David Hunter.

—*Judy Belifaire*

Above: *Women filled many roles during the war, one of the most appreciated that of nurse and hospital attendant. Some did disguise themselves as men and served in the ranks. ("Campaign Sketches: The Letter for Home," Winslow Homer, S. P. Avery, Miriam and Ira D. Wallach Division of Art, Prints and Photographs, New York Public Library)*

Right: *The 13th Pennsylvania Reserves acquired a nickname from the practice of requiring early recruits to prove their marksmanship by presenting the tail of a buck they had shot during a hunt. At several major engagements where the unit fought, this ability with a musket was crucial. ("The Bucktails," Dale Gallon)*

Below: *Thaddeus Lowe goes aloft in his balloon* Intrepid *to observe Confederate actions in the distance. Balloons saw limited use and were soon abandoned. (Library of Congress)*

26 June. Battle of Mechanicsville.

Lee attacks Porter's isolated V Corps north of the Chickahominy River. Porter's troops, entrenched behind Beaver Dam Creek and around Mechanicsville, drive off the Rebels. Federal casualties are light, but Confederates losses total 1,500. Despite winning another tactical victory, McClellan orders Porter to withdraw to Gaines' Mill, five miles away, and abandons his plan to take Richmond by siege.

26 June. Army of Virginia Formed.

To improve control over Union forces in northern Virginia, the Army of Virginia is formed, realigning troops and commanders of three departments into three corps—I Corps (Fremont—Mountain Department); II Corps (Banks—Department of Shenandoah) and III Corps (McDowell—Department of Rappahannock). Major General Pope is appointed commander, but he is junior to all three officers and his appointment is resented. Fremont refuses to serve under Pope and resigns from the Army. He is replaced by Major General Sigel. Pope combines his cavalry into two brigades, one of them under Brigadier John Buford. Two other corps and several divisions join Pope later.

27 June. Battle of Gaines' Mill. Virginia.

The Army of the Potomac is attacked again by Lee's Confederates, who launch a number of uncoordinated assaults against Porter's entrenched V Corps with little success. At 7:00 p.m., Lee orders a general attack, and Porter's lines finally buckle. Brigadier Cooke sends the two brigades of his Cavalry Reserve Division to attack the advancing Rebels. In a desperate charge the 2d U.S. and 5th U.S. Calvary suffer heavily. Federal casualties are 893 killed, 3,107 wounded, and 2,836 missing. McClellan, believing he is outnumbered and outflanked, withdraws toward the James River.

28 June. First Division Patch.
To distinguish his officers from those of other units, Major General Philip Kearny directs that the officers of his 3d Division, III Corps, Army of the Potomac, wear a red piece of cloth on the tops of their caps. The practice soon spreads to the enlisted men.

29 June. Battle of Savage's Station.
On the afternoon of 29 June, 14,000 Confederates hit Major General Sumner's II Corps, which is serving as McClellan's rear guard. The battle ends in stalemate. The Confederates suffer more than 400 casualties. Union losses are 919 killed and wounded. Another 2,500 Federals are taken prisoner when the Rebels capture a field hospital.

30 June. Battle of White Oak Swamp (Glendale).
McClellan pulls back to White Oak Swamp and places his army in defensive positions. Lee orders an attack, and after savage fighting, the Federals begin to withdraw toward Harrison's Landing. Darkness falls before the battle reaches a decisive conclusion.

Casualties are heavy on both sides; 1,800 Federals are taken prisoner, including Brigadier Generals George A. McCall and John F. Reynolds.

July. Creation of Taps. Harrison's Landing, Virginia.
Brigadier General Daniel Butterfield, a brigade commander in the Army of the Potomac, works with bugler, Musician Oliver W. Norton of the 83d Pennsylvania Volunteers, to refine a bugle call that Butterfield has been composing. Butterfield orders the call played that night to his men instead of the official "Lights Out." The call becomes known as "Taps" and is now used by all services.

1 July. Battle of Malvern Hill.
In the final action of the so-called Seven Days Battles, McClellan's 80,000 troops are entrenched with 250 cannon on the long, high ridge with streams protecting the flanks. The Rebels open with artillery, but most of their guns are quickly silenced by Union counterbattery fire. The Confederate assault led by Major Generals Magruder and D. H. Hill is beaten

back with heavy losses. McClellan abandons the campaign to take Richmond, much to the disgust of many of his subordinate generals.

2 July. **Morrill Act Passed.**
Congress passes the Morrill Act, which sets aside federal land for engineering and agricultural colleges. The legislation, sponsored by Representative Justin Morrill (R-Vermont), requires colleges created by the act to include military instruction as part of the curriculum. This marks the origins of the Reserve Officer Training Corps (ROTC).

4 July. **Letterman Appointed Medical Director.**
Dr. Jonathan Letterman is appointed medical director, Army of the Potomac. His ideas for improving the ambulance and evacuation system, training of medical personnel, positioning of medical supplies forward, and development of field hospitals are eventually adopted by all the Army and result in saving many lives.

11–17 July. **Halleck Appointed General-in-Chief.**
Lincoln brings Major General Halleck from the Department of the Mississippi to be general-in-chief of the Army. Grant resumes his position as commander, District of Western Tennessee, with authority over Union forces in the area. He quickly begins planning offensive operations.

12 July. **Medal of Honor Approved.**
Lincoln signs legislation creating the Medal of Honor. Originally intended to honor enlisted soldiers, it is later awarded to officers as well as enlisted men. A total of 1,198 Army Medals of Honor will be granted to Union soldiers for valor during the war.

15 July. **Apache Uprising: Battle of Apache Pass. Arizona.**
As the brigade of California Volunteers known as the "California Column" marches east, its advance guard under Captain Thomas Roberts is ambushed in the pass by a large force of Apaches under Cochise and Mangas Coloradas. Roberts' men beat off the attack with the help of two mountain howitzers. Colonel James H. Carlton, the brigade commander, orders Fort Bowie built in the pass to secure it.

17 July. **Congress Authorizes Recruitment of Black Troops.**
Although recruitment of black soldiers began unofficially in the Army's Department of the South in April 1862, Congress officially authorizes the recruitment of African-American troops with the

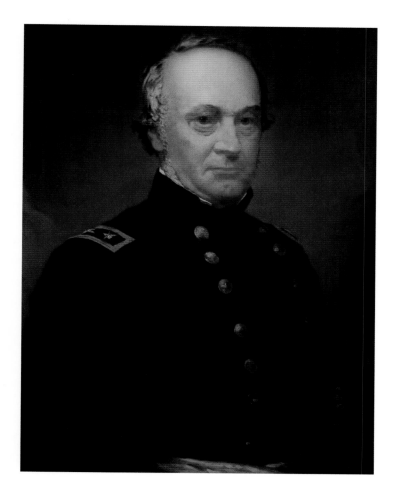

Opposite: *The 5th New York Volunteer Infantry fought valiantly at Gaines Mill. ("The Red Devils at Gaines Mill," Don Troiani, www.historicalartprints.com)*

Above: *Major General Jacob Henry Halleck proved to be an excellent Chief of Staff, but a less than inspiring field commander. (Jacob H. Lazarus, West Point Museum, U.S. Military Academy, West Point, NY)*

passage of the Second Confiscation Act. Congress also issues a new organization for cavalry regiments, changing the "company" to "troop" and giving 12 troops to each regiment.

4 August. **Militia Act of 1862 Approved.**
President Lincoln signs the Militia Act of 1862 calling for a draft of 300,000 militia for nine months. In practice, no one is drafted by the act, but it stimulates three-year Volunteer and nine-month militia enlistments.

5 August. **Battle of Baton Rouge. Louisiana.**
A Confederate force led by Major General John C. Breckinridge, a former vice president of the United States, attacks the 2,500 Federals who have occupied the town since July. The Confederate attack goes well until they come under fire from Union gunboats. Breckinridge elects to withdraw when he loses his

naval support. Union forces suffer 383 killed, wounded, and missing, with Brigadier General Thomas Williams, the Federal commander, among the dead.

6–9 August. Battle of Kirksville. Missouri.
Colonel John McNeil and 1,000 Federal troopers catch 2,500 Confederates at Kirksville. Over the next three days, Union troops secure the town, destroy Colonel Joseph C. Porter's command, and solidify federal control of northeastern Missouri.

9 August. Battle of Cedar Mountain. Virginia.
Banks' II Corps, Army of Virginia, is attacked by Jackson's 22,000 men at Cedar Mountain. Banks deploys his 12,000 men in front of the mountain, with artillery in the nearby hills. After an artillery duel, the Federals, unaware that they are outnumbered, attack and shatter the Rebel left flank. Jackson rallies his men as Major General A. P. Hill's division arrives and the Confederates win the field.

18 August. Buford Hits Stuart. Veriersville, Virginia.
The 1st Michigan Cavalry of Buford's brigade, Army of Virginia, surprises the headquarters of Stuart. Stuart barely escapes, leaving his famous plumed hat behind.

18–28 August. Sioux War: Sioux Attack Fort Ridgely. Minnesota.
Resentful Sioux on the Redwing Reservation kill almost 400 settlers and their families. Militia Lieutenant

Thomas P. Gere takes 46 men of the 5th Minnesota Infantry to rescue survivors. At a Red River ferry his detachment is attacked—only 23 men return. On the 20th, a Sioux war party of 400 warriors led by Little Crow begins a two-day siege of the fort. The garrison drives off the initial Indian attack with artillery and repels a second, more powerful assault the following day. Indian losses are more than 100; only three defenders are killed. Former governor Henry Hastings Sibley is commissioned a colonel in the state militia and given the task of putting down the Sioux uprising. He is able to raise a new regiment, the 6th Minnesota Infantry, and reach Fort Ridgely on the 28th.

25 August. Recruitment of Blacks Begins.
The War Department officially begins recruiting black soldiers, with an initial limit of 5,000 men for guard and labor duties.

29–30 August. Second Battle of Bull Run (Manassas). Virginia.
In the early evening of 28 August, elements of Pope's Army of Virginia make contact with Jackson's corps near the old Bull Run battlefield. The next day Pope orders several attacks against Jackson's line, which lies behind a railroad cut. While inflicting heavy casualties, the Union assaults cannot break the Rebel line. Furthermore, Pope fails to learn that Longstreet's corps has arrived on the battlefield. A Confederate realignment slightly to the rear gives Pope the mistaken impression of a retreat. In the late morning, he attacks again but is driven off. Longstreet then hits the exposed Union left, surprising the Federals and driving them back. By nightfall, Pope's army is centered on Henry House Hill, a mile back from his original positions. Pope, with loses of 9,931 killed or wounded and 3,895 missing, makes an orderly withdrawal the next day.

29–30 August. Battle of Richmond. Kentucky.
Confederates march into central Kentucky, threatening Cincinnati. Major General Nelson, the Union commander in Kentucky, sends two brigades totaling 6,500 raw recruits to hold Richmond while he gathers reinforcements. When the veteran Confederate forces attack, they overwhelm the green Union troops. Nelson is wounded and the Federals hastily retreat toward Louisville, allowing the Confederates to advance to the Ohio River.

1 September. Battle of Chantilly (Ox Hill). Virginia.
Jackson's corps, led by Stuart's cavalry, moves past Pope's army as it retreats toward Washington, threatening to cut it off. Two Union divisions—1st

Opposite: *Louisianans numbered among the more than 180,000 African-Americans who rallied to the Union cause.* ("Corps D'Afrique," Fritz Kredel, Soldiers of the American Army, 1775–1954)

Right: *Conflicts with Indians stretched Union resources in the West.* ("Night Attack with Apaches," Don Troiani, www.historicalartprints.com)

Below: *The Army Medal of Honor was intended for enlisted men who displayed exceptional valor.* (Quintet Publishing Ltd., London)

Division, III Corps, commanded by one-armed Major General Philip Kearny, and 1st Division, IX Corps, under Brigadier General Isaac Stevens, move to block Jackson near Chantilly. They attack twice during a driving thunderstorm, but the Confederates hold their

positions, killing Stevens, and then Kearny when he blunders into a Georgia regiment. The Federals suffer 1,300 casualties, the Confederates only 800.

1–3 September. **Sioux War: Battle of Birch Coulee. Minnesota.**
Sibley sends a detachment of 150 men to the reservation, including a mounted company, to bury the dead. At dawn on the 2nd they are attacked by several hundred Sioux. The survivors of the first attack scrape holes in the ground and defend themselves. A relief party of three companies is stopped and surrounded before it can link up; it also digs in. Sibley personally takes all the remaining troops and leads them in a successful breakthrough, ending the battle. In the eastern Dakota Territory, Fort Abercrombie also experiences Sioux attacks from the 3rd to the 6th.

4–15 September. **Confederates Capture Harper's Ferry. Maryland.**
As Lee's Army of Northern Virginia crosses into Maryland, he sends Jackson to capture the arsenal at Harper's Ferry, guarded by Colonel Dixon S. Miles with 14,000 troops, many of them raw recruits. Confederate artillery begins to bombard the town on 14 September. A Federal relief column led by VI Corps commander Major General William B. Franklin is blocked at Crampton's Gap, and Union resistance ends the next morning after 219 are killed or wounded, including Miles. Before dawn, Colonel Benjamin F. Davis slips his 8th New York Cavalry out through Confederate lines. In their escape they capture one of Lee's reserve ammunition trains,

taking 97 wagons and more than 200 Rebels. The 12,500 Federals taken prisoner in town constitute the largest surrender of U.S. troops until the defeat at Bataan in 1942. Jackson captures dozens of wagons, artillery pieces, and large quantities of small arms and supplies.

3–5 September. **Porter and Franklin Relieved.**
Two Union corps commanders, Major Generals Franklin and Fitz John Porter, are relieved of command to stand investigation into their performance at Second Bull Run. For better control, McClellan divides his army into three "wings" under major generals: Right Wing—Center Wing—Sumner; and Right Wing—Franklin, who is restored by McClellan to duty.

12 September. **Union Army of Virginia Discontinued.**
Pope is relieved of command 2 September and transferred to the Department of the Northwest in Minnesota to fight Indians. On 12 September, the Army of Virginia is disbanded, its I, II, and III Corps becoming the XI, XII, and I Corps, Army of the Potomac.

14 September. **Battle of South Mountain.**
Brigadier General Alfred Pleasanton's cavalry brigade clashes with Lee's eastern wing at Turner's Gap on South Mountain. Union reinforcements arrive, including Major General Jesse Reno's IX Corps and Hooker's I Corps. The fighting continues past dark until the Confederates withdraw. Casualties are heavy on both sides. Among the dead is Reno, shot while scouting the lines at sundown.

14–17 September. **Battle of Munfordville. Kentucky.**
A small Union force guarding a railroad bridge over the Green River is attacked by an advance force of Rebels from General Braxton Bragg's Army of Mississippi on 14 September. The Federals under Colonel John T. Wilder initially drive off the Rebels and are reinforced, but Bragg surrounds Wilder. On 17 September, Wilder asks for a parley, but upon seeing the powerful Rebel artillery positions, he immediately surrenders.

17 September. **Battle of Antietam (Sharpsburg). Maryland.**
In a stroke of luck, McClellan obtains a copy of Lee's battle plan, Order Number 191. Despite this, McClellan hesitates, allowing the Confederates time to consolidate and establish a defensive line with just more than 38,000 troops behind Antietam Creek. On 17 September, McClellan, with approximately three corps (75,000 soldiers), orders Joseph Hooker's I Corps

Opposite: *Field commanders usually gathered late at night after troops were settled to decide on actions for the next day. ("Strategy," © Don Spaulding, by arrangement with Mill Pond Press, Inc.)*

Right: *Capture of this bridge occurred late in the day and contributed little to the outcome of the battle. ("Battle of Antietam: Burnside Bridge," James Hope, Antietam National Battlefield, MD)*

to attack the Confederate left. The Union attack presses through Miller's cornfield against Jackson's Confederates, who put up savage resistance, and Hooker orders up artillery to clear the Rebels from the field. As the Federals approach the Dunkard Church, Hooker is wounded and the Rebels retake Miller's cornfield. Shortly after I Corps is driven back, Major General Joseph Mansfield's XII Corps attacks from the East Woods and recaptures the cornfield, but Mansfield is mortally wounded. A division of Sumner's II Corps loses more than 2,000 men in 20 minutes while trying to clear the West Woods. At the center of the battlefield, D. H. Hill's Rebels occupy a sunken farm road and fortify it with fence rails. Sumner sends his two remaining divisions against the Rebel center. Brigadier William H. French's 3d Division is beaten back with heavy losses, but Major General Israel B. Richardson's 1st Division drives the Confederates from their positions in a sunken road (later nicknamed "Bloody Lane") and repels several counterattacks with heavy casualties on both sides, including Richardson. McClellan now has an opportunity to split Lee's army in half, but he decides not to press the attack or commit his V and VI Corps reserves. On the Union left, Burnside's IX Corps belatedly crosses the creek and pushes toward Sharpsburg. They collide with A. P. Hill's division and are driven back, bringing the battle to a close. It is the bloodiest single day of the war, and the costliest day in American military history. Federal casualties are 2,010 killed, 9,416 wounded, and 1,043 missing; Confederate losses are 2,700 killed, 9,024 wounded, and 2,000 missing. McClellan wires Washington he has won a great victory, but he allows Lee to retreat unmolested.

18 September. **Western Commanders Change. Fort Union, New Mexico Territory.**
Brigadier General Canby is recalled for duty in the east. He is replaced as commander of the Department of New Mexico by Carlton, who was recently promoted to brigadier.

19 September. **Battle of Iuka. Mississippi.**
When a Confederate army of 14,000 troops occupies Iuka on 14 September, Grant sends Major General Rosecrans' reduced Army of the Mississippi and Major General Ord's 2d Division to retake it. Local civilians, however, provide intelligence on Union movements, and Rosecrans is late in arriving. When Rebels attack Rosecrans on 19 September, the wind and topography prevent Ord and Grant from hearing the battle and reinforcing Rosecrans. In a hard fight one mile southwest of Iuka, Rosecrans loses 144 killed, 598 wounded, and 40 missing, but the next day the Rebels evacuate Iuka.

19–23 September. **Battle of Wood Lake. Minnesota.**
Colonel Henry Sibley leads four Minnesota state regiments up the Red River against the Dakota Sioux. Early on the 23rd, a 3d Minnesota foraging party leaves the camp near Wood Lake and stumbles across 200 Indians who have crept into ambush positions. In the ensuing battle, fire from several howitzers and a charge by the Renville Rangers break the Sioux and they flee. Sibley captures 2,000 Sioux men, women, and children over the next few weeks. Major General Pope, newly arrived at his headquarters in St. Paul, approves a military commission that tries and sentences 307 Dakota Sioux to hang; President Lincoln reduces the

Opposite: *Union troops advancing through the cornfield at Antietam were greeted with a withering blast of Confederate musket fire. ("Through the Cornfield," Keith Rocco)*

Below: *Brigadier General James Carleton led the California Column from the West Coast to retake the New Mexico Territory from the Confederates. (Museum of New Mexico, Santa Fe)*

number to 40. Sibley is commissioned as a brigadier general of U.S. Volunteers and named commander of the Military District of Minnesota.

27 September. First Black Regiment Organized. New Orleans.

The 1st Louisiana Native Guards, consisting largely of free blacks, becomes the first regiment of black soldiers mustered into the Army. Over the next two months, the Army musters two additional Louisiana Native Guard regiments and a regiment of heavy artillery of African-Americans.

29 September. Union General Murders Fellow General. Louisville, Kentucky.

Union Brigadier General Jefferson C. Davis fatally shoots his commander, Major General William Nelson, in the lobby of a hotel as the result of Davis's long-simmering personal grudge over assignments he considered trivial. Davis is indicted but released on bail, and he continues active Army service. He receives brevets for gallantry and ends the war as a corps commander. The charges are dropped in 1864.

3–4 October. Battle of Corinth. Mississippi.

Upon learning a Confederate army is approaching, Rosecrans moves his small army into defensive fortifications around Corinth. The battle begins midmorning on 3 October, and by nightfall the Confederates have pushed the Federals into their inner line of fortifications. The following day, in sweltering heat, Rosecrans repels several vicious assaults until the Confederates withdraw toward the northwest. On 5 October, Union troops catch the retreating Rebels at the Hatchie River and take 300 prisoners.

7–8 October. Battle of Perryville. Kentucky.

Major General Buell marches his Army of the Ohio to the outskirts of Perryville to halt a Rebel invasion of Kentucky. Buell was relieved a few days before, but Major General George Thomas declines to accept the command on the eve of battle and the order is revoked. Skirmishing begins on the 7th; the main battle erupts the following day. Although outnumbered, the Confederates strike the Union center, nearly destroying Major General Alexander McCook's I Corps. McCook's men are driven back, but they establish new lines and hold. Brigadier General Sheridan's 11th Division repels a final Rebel assault and, with the help of reinforcements, drives the Confederates through the streets of Perryville. Both sides suffer heavy casualties. The Confederates withdraw during the night, ending the invasion. Buell, however, fails to pursue. He is relieved again on 24 October and his command is given to Rosecrans, who renames it the Army of the Cumberland. Buell returns home to await orders; none come, and he resigns in 1864.

28 October. First Combat Action of Black Troops. Island Mounds, Missouri.

During a battle at Island Mounds, the 1st Kansas Colored Volunteer Infantry becomes the first unit of black soldiers to participate in combat operations. The regiment loses 10 killed and 12 wounded in the Union victory.

5–6 November. Cavalry Skirmish at Chester Gap. Virginia.
Brigadier General Alfred Pleasanton and 1,500 Federal cavalrymen scatter 3,000 Confederate troopers led by Stuart. The next day McClellan organizes a cavalry division of two brigades with Pleasanton in command.

7 November. McClellan Relieved. Rectortown.
McClellan is relieved as commander of the Army of the Potomac and replaced by Major General Burnside. McClellan goes home to New Jersey to await orders. He receives none, resigns, and runs as a Democrat against Lincoln in 1864.

7 December. Battle of Prairie Grove. Arkansas.
Brigadier James Blunt's 7,000-man 1st Division, Army of the Frontier, faces a Confederate force of 11,000. Blunt calls for reinforcements, and two divisions led by Brigadier General Francis Herron begin a forced march from Springfield, Missouri. The battle begins just after midnight on 7 December. Herron's men attack the Confederates along a ridge overlooking Prairie Grove but cannot drive them from their positions, and Blunt's flank attack is unsuccessful. The battle is a draw and the Confederates withdraw during the night.

13 December. Battle of Fredericksburg. Virginia.
In mid-November, Burnside begins moving the 120,000-man Army of the Potomac south toward Richmond. He plans to cross the Rappahannock River at Fredericksburg and get behind Lee's main force to the west. The Union plan goes awry when pontoons for bridging the Rappahannock fail to arrive in a timely manner. The delay allows Lee to move his forces to Fredericksburg and establish fortified positions manned by nearly 80,000 troops. Before dawn on 11 December, Union engineers begin constructing the delayed pontoon bridges, but Rebel sharpshooters hidden in the town drive them off. Federal artillery across the river on Stafford Heights bombards the town, reducing much of it to rubble. Union infantry then cross in boats and clear out the snipers. The bulk of Burnside's army crosses on 12 December and occupies the town. On 13 December, Union forces begin attacking the Confederate positions. On the left, units from Major General Franklin's grand division, led by Brigadier General George G. Meade, suffer heavy casualties but breach the Rebel defenses. Franklin, however, fails to support the breakthrough, and the Federals are driven back. At the center of the line, the brigades of Sumner's grand division attack the strong Confederate defensives on Marye's Heights. Union forces launch a number of courageous but futile charges across open ground that leave Union dead and wounded piled up before a stone wall at the base of Marye's Heights. By the end of the day, more than 12,000 Federals lie dead and wounded;

Confederate losses are just over 5,000. After two days of skirmishing, Burnside withdraws back across the Rappahannock during a torrential downpour.

20 December. **Raid on Holly Springs. Mississippi.**
Grant's plans to take the Confederate stronghold of Vicksburg are dealt a significant setback when Rebel cavalry raid the Union supply depot at Holly Springs. The Rebels take most of the Union garrison prisoner and capture or destroy the large quantities of supplies Grant had gathered to support his planned offensive.

27–29 December. **Battle of Chickasaw Bluffs. Mississippi.**
As part of Grant's plan to take Vicksburg, Major General Sherman's XIII Corps probes the Rebel defenses along Chickasaw Bluffs on 27 December. The Confederates are outnumbered, but their defenses are virtually impregnable. On 29 December Sherman orders a major attack against the bluffs. The Federals reach the base of the bluffs but can advance no further. The attack is over by mid-afternoon, with heavy Union casualties. On 1 January, Sherman abandons the effort and withdraws.

31 December. **Battle of Parker's Crossroads. Tennessee.**
Northeast of Jackson, Tennessee, Brigadier General Nathan Bedford Forrest and his force of Rebel cavalry engage Colonel Cyrus L. Dunham's brigade. Forrest's artillery pounds Dunham's men and drives them back. As he demands Dunham's surrender, another Union brigade under Colonel John W. Fuller arrives and

Opposite, top: *A Union cavalry sergeant escorts a Federal supply train. ("The American Soldier, 1863," H. Charles McBarron, Army Art Collection, NMUSA)*

Opposite, bottom: *The industrial might of the North was felt in the massive flow of weapons and munitions, as with this ordnance awaiting distribution. (Library of Congress)*

Above: *("The Battle of Fredericksburg, 13 December, 1862," Carl Rochling, Philadelphia Museum of Art and Commissioners of Fairmont Park, PA)*

strikes the Confederate rear. Forrest gathers his command and withdraws from the field, abandoning much of the booty captured from earlier raids. More than 300 Confederates are captured; Union losses are 237 killed and wounded.

31 December–2 January. **Battle of Stones River (Murfreesboro). Tennessee.**
Rosecrans is ordered to pursue Braxton Bragg into Tennessee, destroy his army, and take Chattanooga. The 45,000 men of Rosecrans' Army of the Cumberland clash with Bragg's 35,000 along Stones River near Murfreesboro. At dawn on 31 December, two Confederate corps surprise the Union right wing under Major General McCook. His men are forced back with heavy casualties. Sheridan's 3d Division puts up stiff resistance and staves off disaster on the Union right. Rosecrans also displays personal valor helping to establish new defensive positions. The battle then shifts toward a salient held by Union infantry under Major

JOHN WILDER AND HIS "LIGHTNING" BRIGADE

In December 1862, Major General William S. Rosecrans reorganized the Union Army of the Cumberland in preparation for an offensive against Murfreesboro, Tennessee. For his performance at the battle of Shiloh, Colonel John Thomas Wilder, commanding the 17th Indiana Infantry Regiment, was appointed to command the 1st Brigade, 5th Division, XIV Corps. The brigade consisted of his 17th Indiana, the 72d and 75th Indiana, and 98th Illinois Infantry Regiments with the 18th Indiana Battery, commanded by Captain Eli Lilly. Assigned to protect Union supply lines in Kentucky from enemy cavalry raiders, Wilder quickly realized the near impossibility of effectively engaging a mounted enemy with dismounted infantry. As an experiment, Wilder mounted a detachment of the 17th Indiana on mules. It was too little, and Wilder expanded the idea to mount his whole brigade—a concept similar to the old Regiment of Mounted Riflemen.

General Rosecrans approved, and in February 1863 gave Wilder the authority to proceed. The 75th Indiana, not wishing to become mounted, was replaced by the 123d Illinois Infantry. Not one to wait for government process, Wilder quickly "appropriated" mounts from Rebel sympathizers in Tennessee; by March the entire brigade was mounted. The brigade, a mounted unit, was required by Army regulations to be issued cavalry uniforms, but Wilder's men considered themselves "mounted infantry," and they removed the yellow cavalry piping.

To make his brigade truly effective Wilder sought a better weapon than the standard muzzle-loaded infantry rifle. His answer came in March 1863 when Christopher Spencer visited Army units trying to sell his repeating rifle. The Spencer repeater used copper rim-fire .52-caliber cartridges that could be quickly loaded with seven rounds in a tubular magazine inserted through the stock. A special box carried ten extra magazines, giving the soldier 70 rounds. Wilder once again circumvented government "red tape." He took out a loan from his bank in Indiana to purchase 2,000 of the rifles. Each man in the brigade signed a note for $35.00, with Wilder cosigning, to buy his own Spencer rifle.

In April, Captain Lilly's battery was augmented by a "Jackass Battery," four 12-pound mountain howitzers carried by mules. With their six three-inch Rodman rifled cannon, the battery now boasted five sections, a total of 10 guns. The brigade got its first real chance to try out its new weapons on 24 June 1863 at Hoover's Gap, Tennessee. As the lead element of XIV Corps, Wilder was ordered to advance cautiously on foot. Instead, Wilder charged through the gap, driving the enemy back and taking positions a mile inside the gap. Wilder's brigade then held its position against counterattacks by two brigades as the Spencer rifles and Lilly's battery inflicted heavy casualties. Major General George H. Thomas, the Army commander, told Wilder, "You have saved the lives of a thousand men by your gallant conduct today. I didn't expect to get the gap for three days," and named the unit "Wilder's Lightning Brigade."

In July, the 92d Illinois Infantry joined the brigade to help spearhead the Union advance on Chattanooga. At Chickamauga on 18–20 September, the brigade gave its most exemplary service. Wilder's brigade stubbornly defended Alexander's Bridge over Chickamauga Creek against a Confederate corps. On the 19th, the brigade successfully covered the Union flank, repelling repeated heavy assaults. The "Lightning Brigade" withstood attacks by an enemy division again on the 20th, buying time for Thomas to form a new line at Snodgrass Hill. It was Wilder's intention to charge mounted through the enemy and cut a path to join Thomas, but the order was countermanded and Wilder reluctantly ordered his brigade to cover the Army's withdrawal to Chattanooga.

Following the battle, Wilder took a leave of absence, and on 28 September the brigade, now under the command of Colonel Abram O. Miller, was assigned to the 2d Division, Cavalry Corps. In November the brigade was split up, half being sent to duty in Alabama and Mississippi, the other half remaining in Tennessee. In July 1864, the brigade reunited, Lilly's battery being replaced by the Chicago Board of Trade Battery. In August, Colonel Wilder was brevetted a brigadier general of Volunteers. He resigned from the service on 4 October and command of the brigade returned to Colonel Miller.

The "Lightning Brigade" continued to perform exceptionally throughout the rest of the war, repeatedly demonstrating the effectiveness of mounted infantry armed with rapid-firing weapons. On 23 May 1865, the brigade headed for Nashville, where from June to August its regiments were mustered out of service.

—Vince Hawkins

General Thomas and supported by artillery. Bragg launches three attacks against it but is driven back with heavy losses. Rosecrans strengthens his lines and brings up more ammunition. On 2 January, Confederates renew attacks on the Union lines. The assaulting Rebel brigades, decimated by massed artillery, lose 1,700 men. Union forces then counterattack, cross Stones River, and end the battle. The Union loses 1,677 killed, 7,543 wounded, and 3,686 missing.

1863

January. **Status of the Army.**
The Union Army's ranks have swelled to 918,354 men, mostly U.S. Volunteers. The Regular Army, still authorized only 39,273, remains a relatively small part of the Union forces. Other than a few companies of 9th Infantry in posts on the Pacific coast and the 5th Infantry, all the Regulars are in the east.

1 January. **Confederates Capture Galveston. Texas.**
Federal troops occupying Galveston, commanded by Colonel I. S. Burrell, repel a Rebel attack. Rebel gunboats, however, drive off the U.S. naval support, forcing Burrell to surrender. The Confederates will hold Galveston for the remainder of the war.

Above: *Union engineers built bridges and provided other combat support that proved essential to the Union's success during the Civil War. ("The American Soldier, 1862," H. Charles McBarron, Army Art Collection, NMUSA)*

Left: *Union ordnance personnel provided much-needed support to Union combat forces. ("Sergeant of Ordnance," Don Troiani, www.historicalartprints.com)*

9–11 January. **Battle of Arkansas Post. Arkansas.**
Major General McClernand, temporary commander of Army of the Mississippi, leads a joint Army-Navy expedition against Confederate positions at Fort Hindman and Arkansas Post along the Arkansas River. McClernand lands his men downstream from the Rebels on 9 January and marches overland while gunboats bombard the Rebel earthworks. The Federal attack quickly captures the fort and supporting works on 11 January.

20 January. **The Mud March. Rappahannock River, Virginia.**
After the disaster at Fredericksburg, Burnside marches the Army of the Potomac up the Rappahannock in another effort to cross the river and reach Lee's left flank. Icy rains, however, turn the roads into a quagmire. The movement is soon abandoned and the men return

to their winter camps near Falmouth. Soldiers dub the maneuver the "Mud March." Morale in the Army of the Potomac sinks to its lowest point in the war.

23–26 January. Burnside Is Relieved.
Burnside has lost the confidence of many of his commanders and men. He drafts an order to court-martial eight "disloyal" senior officers and tells Lincoln it must be approved or he will resign. Instead, Lincoln selects Major General Hooker to command Army of the Potomac and sends Burnside to the Department of the Ohio. Generals Franklin and Sumner are also reassigned.

27 January. Battle of Bear River. Idaho Territory.
Withdrawal of the Regular Army units protecting the telegraph lines, the stage and mail roads, and prospectors and settlers leaves them victim to frequent attack by hostile Shoshones, Bannocks, and Utes. Volunteer units attempt to fill the gap. In early January, scouts report the camp of hostile Shoshone Chief Bear Hunter along the Bear River. Colonel Patrick E. Connor and his 1st California Cavalry march out of Fort Douglas, moving at night through deep snow to try to surprise the village. The Indians are waiting in prepared positions in a dry ravine and repulse a frontal attack. Connor sends detachments to flank the ravine, trapping the Indians. Shoshone casualties are heavy—224 warriors killed and 164 women and children taken prisoner. Connor's regiment suffers 21 dead and 46 wounded; 75 others

suffer frostbitten feet. This reduces the number of Indian attacks in the area, and many chiefs come in to talk peace.

5 February. Army of the Potomac Reorganized.
Major General Hooker abolishes Burnside's grand division structure and reorganizes the Army of the Potomac into nine corps—I Corps (Brigadier General Reynolds); II Corps (Major General Darius N. Couch); III Corps (Major General Daniel E. Sickles); V Corps (Major General Meade); VI Corps (Major General Sedgwick); IX Corps (Major General William E. Smith); XI Corps (Major General Sigel); XII Corps (Major General Henry W. Slocum); and Cavalry Corps (Major General George Stoneman). For the first time, the majority of the Army's cavalry is brought under a single commander. Some weeks later, Hooker directs Colonel George H. Sharpe to form a Bureau of Military Information—the first formal Army intelligence organization. Sharpe later becomes Grant's chief of intelligence.

3 March. Congress Passes Conscription Law.
Congress passes the Enrollment Act, a conscription law based on its constitutional power to "raise and support armies." A military obligation is imposed on all able-bodied men between the ages of 20 and 45. Several provisions, however, weaken it. Enrollees are not required to come forward; instead, enrollment officers canvass residences looking for eligible men, and men may hire a substitute or pay a $300 fee to

avoid military service. Overall, the Act stimulates enlistments, and only 6 percent of the soldiers serving in the Union Army by the war's end are conscripts. The Confederacy also enacts conscription laws.

3 March. **Signal Corps Established; Engineer Corps Reorganized.**
The Signal Corps is made a separate branch of the Army, with a Chief Signal Officer at the rank of colonel, along with other officers and enlisted personnel. Major Albert J. Meyer, a former surgeon who has been serving as the Army's signal officer since 1860, is appointed Chief Signal Officer. The Corps of Topographical Engineers, a separate branch since 1831, is consolidated with the Corps of Engineers.

21 March. **Creation of Corps and Division Badge System.**
To help renew sagging morale of the Army of the Potomac, Major General Joseph Hooker directs his chief of staff, Brigadier General Daniel Butterfield, to develop a system of badges to help soldiers identify with their units. A General Order is issued laying out a different design for each corps with different colors for each division. The concept spreads to the other Union armies and is the basis for the modern Army unit patches. A system of unit flags also is created.

12–14 April. **Red River Campaign. Louisiana.**
Major General Banks commences an expedition with his XIX Corps to sever Port Hudson's supply lines via the Red River. With 15,000 men Banks occupies Fort Bisland on 12 April On the 14th, Brigadier General Cuvier Grover's 4th Division clashes with Rebels at Irish Bend, forcing the Confederates up Bayou Teche.

17 April–2 May. **Grierson's Raid. Tennessee, Mississippi, and Louisiana.**
Leaving on 17 April from La Grange, Tennessee, Union Colonel Benjamin H. Grierson leads a force of three Volunteer cavalry regiments—6th and 7th Illinois and 2d Iowa—and Battery K, 1st Illinois Light Artillery (a total of about 1,700 men) on a 16-day raid. Riding and raiding for 800 miles behind Rebel lines through three states, the raiders kill or capture 600 Rebels, wreck large quantities of railroad lines, and capture 3,000 small arms and 1,000 horses and mules. Grierson's force loses only three killed, seven wounded, and nine missing.

26 April–3 May. **Streight's Raid. Alabama and Georgia.**
Under orders from Rosecrans, Colonel Abdel D. Streight leads a brigade of 1,700 cavalrymen, many

Opposite: *Burnside's plan to outflank the Confederate positions behind Fredericksburg turns into chaos when heavy rains turn roads into quagmires and creeks into rivers. ("The Mud March," Giovanni Ponticelli, West Point Museum, U.S. Army Military Academy, West Point, NY)*

Above: *Major General Ambrose Burnside became better known for his "sideburns" than for his military victories against the Confederates. (Library of Congress)*

unmounted, on a raid from Tuscumbia, Alabama, into Georgia to cut the Georgia Railroad. Streight is quickly discovered and pursued by Forrest. After fighting delaying actions at Sand Mountain and Hog Mountain, Streight is deceived into surrendering his force near Rome, Georgia, on 3 May.

30 April–1 May. **Battle of Port Gibson. Mississippi.**
On 30 April, Grant's Army of Tennessee, led by McClernand's XIII Corps and a division from XVII Corps, crosses the Mississippi below Vicksburg and advances on Port Gibson. The battle against the 8,000 Confederate defenders begins 1 May. It is a difficult fight before the Rebels withdraw. Union casualties are 131 dead, 719 wounded, and 25 missing. The Confederates evacuate Grand Gulf, which Grant converts into his supply base.

1–4 May. **Battle of Chancellorsville. Virginia.**
On 12 April Major General Hooker sends Major

UNION ARMY FLAGS

U.S. Artillery Regimental Colors

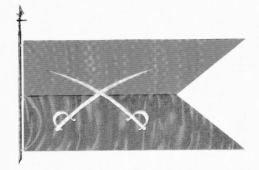

George Custer's Troopers

HQ Army of the Ohio

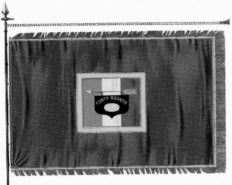

HQ Army of the Tennessee

HQ IX Corps

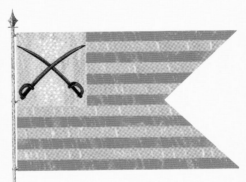

HQ First Cavalry Division

HQ Army of the Potomac

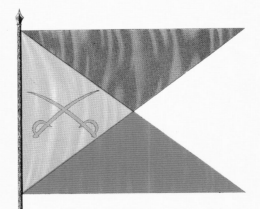

HQ Cavalry Corps

Infantry Regimental Colors

Right: *The 22d Iowa Infantry made a heroic, but fruitless attack against the Confederate positions at Vicksburg, Mississippi, on 22 May 1863. (Library of Congress)*

Below: *Using a system devised by Colonel Albert Myer, chief Union signal officer, signalmen in tall signal stations could send messages quickly over many miles using flags by day and torches by night. (Military Archive and Research Services)*

General Stoneman and his cavalry on a diversionary raid. The raid, hindered by swollen rivers, accomplishes little and leaves Hooker without a mounted screen. Then on the 30th, Hooker marches 130,000 men of the Army of the Potomac across the Rappahannock and Rapidan rivers and around Lee's left flank to Chancellorsville. Lee leaves troops to guard the Fredericksburg crossings and marches west to Chancellorsville, where the two armies clash on 1 May. In a risky but brilliant plan, Lee divides his force, retaining some 13,000 men to hold Hooker's force in place and sending Jackson on a flanking march around the Union right. Hooker discounts the movement, thinking it is a withdrawal. In the early evening of 2 May, Jackson's troops emerge from the woods on the right of Major General O. O. Howard's XI Corps and smash into it, sending it into panicked retreat. After heroic efforts, Union lines are stabilized at nightfall. While conducting a late reconnaissance, Jackson and his staff are accidentally fired upon by North Carolina troops; two staff officers are killed and Jackson is seriously wounded (he dies eight days later). Heavy fighting continues around Chancellorsville on 3 May as Hooker reforms in a defensive perimeter. At Fredericksburg, Major General Sedgwick's VI Corps crosses the river, seizes the heights, and marches toward Lee's rear. Lee counterattacks at Salem Church, stopping Sedgwick's advance. Early on 5 May, Hooker withdraws across the Rappahannock. Casualties on both sides are high. Union losses are 1,606 killed, 9,762 wounded, and 5,919 missing; Confederate losses are 1,665 killed, 9,081 wounded, and 2,108 missing.

12 May. **Battle of Raymond. Mississippi.**
Grant continues toward Vicksburg from the east, but a force of 4,000 Confederates blocks his path. On 12 May, two divisions of Major General James B. McPherson's XVII Corps clash with Rebel troops

outside of Raymond. McPherson launches a number of uncoordinated assaults, which are easily repelled. The outnumbered Confederates finally retreat toward Jackson.

14 May. Battle of Jackson.

Grant now advances on Jackson, Mississippi's capital and an important rail center. It is defended by only 6,000 men under Joseph E. Johnston. After a brief battle, Sherman's XV Corps takes Jackson and cuts the rail line to Vicksburg.

16 May. Battle of Champion Hill.

As Grant continues west, a Confederate army of about 22,000 men that has come out of the Vicksburg defenses to attack the Union supply lines meets McClernand's XIII Corps at heavily wooded Champion Hill, about halfway to Vicksburg. An intense battle erupts and McPherson's XVII Corps comes into action as the hill changes hands three times before the tide of battle turns and the Rebels withdraw to the Big Black River. Union casualties are 410 killed, 1,844 wounded, and 187 missing; Confederate losses are 381 killed, 1,018 wounded, and 2,441 missing.

17–18 May. Battle of Big Black River.

McClernand's XIII Corps reaches the Big Black River. A Union attack breaks the Confederate defense

and sends them fleeing across the river; many are trapped when their panicked comrades burn the two bridges. McClernand's men take 1,700 prisoners and suffer fewer than 300 casualties. Union engineers quickly push four pontoon bridges across the river, and the Army of the Tennessee closes around Vicksburg by dark on the 18th.

18–22 May. Assaults on Vicksburg.

Believing the 30,000 Rebel defenders demoralized, Grant decides to take the city's elaborate system of fortifications by direct assault and launches attacks by his three corps on 19 and 22 May; they are repulsed with heavy casualties, and losses in Sherman's XIII Corps are particularly severe. Siege operations then begin with Union engineers digging trenches and preparing underground mines under the Confederate lines while artillery bombards the city around the clock. Grant also calls for reinforcements, and his army quickly grows to 77,000.

22 May–9 July. Siege of Port Hudson. Louisiana.

The siege of heavily fortified Port Hudson begins on 22 May when Major General Banks positions his XIX Corps of 30,000 troops along the landward side of the town. Port Hudson has a garrison of 7,500. After launching two unsuccessful and costly attacks against the Rebel defenses on 27 May and 13 June, Banks resorts to a siege until Major General Franklin Gardner surrenders on 9 July. Union losses are heavy—approximately 10,000, almost half from sickness.

22 May. **Bureau of Colored Troops Established.**
The War Department creates the Bureau of Colored Troops to organize and supervise units of black troops, first called United States Colored Volunteers, and later, United States Colored Troops (USCT). Led by Major George L. Stearns, the bureau recruits and organizes 186,017 black soldiers into 120 infantry regiments, 12 heavy artillery regiments, one light artillery regiment, and seven cavalry regiments.

May–June. **Army of the Potomac Reorganizes.**
The casualties at Chancellorsville, loss of 54 regiments through expiration of enlistments, and infusion of new recruits make a reorganization necessary for the Army of the Potomac. Hooker shuffles divisions, brigades, and regiments in an effort to balance and standardize units, and he replaces several commanders. The Cavalry Corps is compressed from three to two divisions. The artillery is reassigned from the divisions into corps brigades and a reserve, all under Brigadier Henry J. Hunt, the army's chief of artillery.

9 June. **Battle of Brandy Station. Virginia.**
Concerned about Confederate troop movements, Hooker orders Pleasanton to take his Cavalry Corps and a brigade of infantry on a reconnaissance toward Culpeper. In the early morning of 9 June, Pleasanton's forces clash with Stuart's Confederate cavalry corps at Brandy Station. The result is the largest cavalry battle in American military history. Although the Union troopers surprise the Confederates in their camps, the Rebels fight to a draw. After a 12-hour battle, Pleasanton withdraws, having proven the Union cavalry is at least equal to Stuart's. Union casualties are 69 killed, 352 wounded, and 486 taken prisoner; Rebel losses total 523. Hooker begins shifting the Army of the Potomac north as Pleasanton continues to try to penetrate Stuart's screen, resulting in sharp cavalry fights at Aldie, Middleburg, and Upperville.

14–15 June. **Second Battle of Winchester.**
The north-bound Confederates eliminate a Federal garrison at Martinsburg, then rout a Union force of 7,000 at Winchester. Nearly 4,000 Union troops are killed, wounded, or captured, and large quantities of arms and supplies fall into Confederate hands. Rebel casualties are minimal.

28 June. **Hooker Is Replaced.**
Major General Hooker offers to step down and Lincoln accepts, replacing him with Major General

Above: *This Union first sergeant was barely old enough to shave, yet he has the unmistakable demeanor of someone prepared to take care of himself and his men. (U.S. Army Military History Institute, Carlisle Barracks, PA)*

Meade as commander of the Army of the Potomac. Meade has little time to adjust to his new command. One of his first acts is to promote three young captains—George A. Custer, Elon Farnsworth, and Wesley Merritt—to brigadier general of U.S. Volunteers; each is given a cavalry brigade. Hooker goes to Washington to await orders.

1–3 July. **Battle of Gettysburg. Pennsylvania.**
On 1 July, elements of the Army of the Potomac and the Army of Northern Virginia clash west of town. Union cavalry of Brigadier General Buford's brigade hold off advancing Confederates. Reinforcements arrive under I Corps commander Major General Reynolds, who is killed in the fighting. The Confederates push the men of I Corps (Doubleday) and XI Corps (Howard) east through town to high ground, where they establish strong defensive positions on Culp's and Cemetery Hills. Late in the

day Meade arrives with III Corps (Sickles) and XII Corps (Slocum) and the army engages in a fishhook-shaped battle line running south from Culp's and Cemetery Hills, along Cemetery Ridge to Little Round Top. Meade's II Corps (Hancock) and V Corps (Sykes) hurriedly arrive the morning of 2 July. The same day Major General Sickles jeopardizes the Union line by advancing his III Corps troops forward into an exposed salient at the Peach Orchard, the Wheat Field, and Devil's Den. Longstreet's corps attacks late in the afternoon and pushes Sickles' men back in a bloody struggle. Only skillful leadership by Meade prevents total disaster. While scouting around unoccupied Little Round Top, Brigadier General Gouverneur K. Warren, Chief Engineer, recognizes it as a weak spot and rushes V Corps troops to the hill. Fighting rages as the Rebels repeatedly charge up the slopes only to be driven back. A desperate defense by the men of Brigadier Strong Vincent's 3d Brigade, 1st Division, including the 20th Maine, breaks the assaulting force. Later, Confederates renew attacks on Culp's Hill and Cemetery Hill in the north, but the assaults fail. Lee decides a massed attack on 3 July against the Union center along Cemetery Ridge held by Hancock's II Corps will break through. A supporting attack by Ewell on Culp's Hill earlier in the day is easily repulsed, and another attack by Stuart's cavalry is checked by Brigadier David Gregg's

Federal troopers east of town. After a massive cannonade, three divisions of Rebels begin their attack from Seminary Ridge at 3:00 p.m. Relatively few reach the Union lines before being driven back. A final, almost suicidal charge by Brigadier Elon Farnsworth's cavalry brigade brings the battle to a close. Of 93,000 Federals engaged, Meade's losses are 3,149 killed, 14,503 wounded, and 5,616 missing; Lee's reported losses are at least 4,637 killed, 12,391 wounded, and 5,846 missing. Meade does not vigorously pursue the defeated Rebels, much to the dismay of Lincoln.

2–26 July. **Morgan's Raid. Kentucky, Indiana, and Ohio.**
On 2 July, Confederate Brigadier General John Hunt Morgan leads 2,500 Rebel troopers on a raid into Kentucky, crosses the Ohio River into Indiana, and heads toward Ohio. Eventually, cavalry from Burnside's Department of the Ohio catches Morgan's force on the 26th at Salineville, Ohio, and forces Morgan to surrender.

3–4 July. **Vicksburg Falls.**
On 3 July, the Confederate commander, Lieutenant General John Pemberton, meets with Grant to discuss terms of surrender. Grant first demands unconditional surrender but eventually allows the Rebels to surrender and sign paroles. On 4 July,

Opposite: *Pleasanton's Union cavalry caught J. E. B. Stuart's cavalry corps by surprise, and fought them in the largest cavalry battle in American history. ("Brandy Station Review," Don Troiani, www.historicalartprints.com)*

Right: *General John Buford's cavalry temporarily held up Lee's advance forces as they marched on Gettysburg. ("Buying Time," Dale Gallon)*

Below: *Meade takes command of the Army of the Potomac. (Courtesy of The Civil War & Underground Railroad Museum of Philadelphia)*

Union soldiers march into the town. At the cost of fewer than 5,000 casualties Grant has taken 29,495 prisoners and hundreds of cannon and has broken Confederate control of the Mississippi. On the 4th

Congress promotes him to Regular Army major general, making him third senior Army general behind Halleck and John E. Wool. It is his first Regular rank since resigning as a captain in 1854.

10–18 July. **Assault on Fort Wagner. South Carolina.**
After an attack on Fort Wagner fails, Union Brigadier General Truman Seymour organizes another assault for 18 July with Brigadier General George S. Strong's brigade in the lead. Colonel Robert Gould Shaw volunteers his 54th Massachusetts Volunteer Infantry, comprising only black troops, to lead the attack. After a heavy artillery bombardment, the 54th and following regiments attack after sundown. A few Federals break into the fort before being driven back with heavy casualties. Among the Union dead are Gould and Strong. For his bravery, Sergeant William H. Carney, the 54th's color bearer, is awarded the Medal of Honor; he is the first African-American to earn the medal.

13–17 July. **Draft Riots. New York City.**
Riots against the draft break out on 13 July, and Federal troops, some of whom had just fought at Gettysburg, are ordered to New York to restore order. Calm returns by 17 July, but not before more than 100 people have died in the rioting, many of them blacks murdered by rioters. The draft is suspended for one month in the city.

21–22 August. **Quantrill's Raid. Lawrence, Kansas.**
Confederate Captain William Quantrill leads 450 guerrillas on a raid against the staunchly pro-Union town. His men burn most of the town and murder 180

"THE SUPERB" HANCOCK

Named after an American military hero, Winfield Scott Hancock earned him the sobriquet "the Superb" and the thanks of a grateful Congress for his performance on the battlefield. An energetic, industrious, and exceptionally capable commander, Hancock showed valor and determination in action. Grant said of him, "His personal courage and his presence with his command in the thickest of the fight, won him the confidence of troops serving under him."

Hancock was born 14 February 1824 in Montgomery Square, Pennsylvania. His mother named him after General Winfield Scott, the hero of the War of 1812. At age 16 he entered West Point, graduating 18th in a class of 25 in 1844, with a commission as second lieutenant in the 6th Infantry. After two years on the western frontier, he went with the 6th Infantry to join Scott's army in Mexico. His actions there won him brevet promotion to first lieutenant for his gallantry.

Hancock then served in numerous regimental staff posts, being promoted to captain in November 1855. He saw action during the Third Seminole War (1855–1858), helped quell disorder in "Bleeding Kansas" (1859–1860), and then briefly served as chief quartermaster in the Southern District, California. At the outbreak of the Civil War he was recalled east to serve with the newly formed Army of the Potomac. On 23 September 1861, he was appointed brigadier general of Volunteers and put to work organizing and training the army. Given command of the 3d Brigade in W. F. Smith's division, Hancock saw his first action of the war at Williamsburg on 5 May 1862, when he led a crucial flank attack for which McClellan called him "superb." At Antietam on 17 September, Hancock was given command of the 1st Division, II Corps, when its commander was killed. For his performance he was promoted to major general of Volunteers on 29 November.

In December, Hancock fought with great valor at Fredericksburg. Six months later, in May, at Chancellorsville he employed a skirmish line to cover his division's front in a skillful rear-guard action that enabled the army to withdraw across the Rappahannock. His deployment of one man every three yards in skirmish order is considered a classic maneuver. Hancock was given command of the II Corps.

At Gettysburg on 1–3 July, Hancock reached the pinnacle of his military career and justified the description "superb." On the first day, as the senior surviving Union officer, he assumed command of the advance engaged elements of the Army of the Potomac

and deployed them in strong defensive positions. On the second day, his corps stabilized and held the Union left against enemy attempts to turn that flank. On the third day, despite being severely wounded in the thigh, Hancock refused to leave the field until his II Corps had repulsed the main Confederate charge. In August he was made brigadier general of the Regular Army.

After months of recuperation from his wound, Winfield Hancock resumed command, fighting at the battles of Wilderness, Spotsylvania, North Anna, and Cold Harbor. In June, during the Petersburg siege, his wound reopened and he was forced to relinquish field command. He was recalled to Washington on 26 November to organize the 1st Veteran Volunteer Corps. On 21 April 1866, Hancock received the thanks of Congress and on 26 July was made a Regular major general.

Hancock then held a series of senior commands. During the 1880 presidential election Hancock took leave to stand as the Democratic candidate and was narrowly defeated by James A. Garfield, another Civil War Army veteran. On 9 February 1886, Hancock died at his headquarters on Governor's Island, New York.

—*Vince Hawkins*

Above: *Winfield Scott Hancock. (U.S. Army Military History Institute, Carlisle Barracks, PA)*

men. In response, Union commander Brigadier General Thomas Ewing issues orders to remove anyone not loyal to the Union from four western Missouri counties, and to destroy the property of any Southern supporter.

15 September. Army Chief of Ordnance Retires.
Brigadier General James W. Ripley retires as Chief of Ordnance. A veteran of the War of 1812, Ripley had steadfastly refused to consider weapons like the repeating rifle and Gatling gun. His departure opens the way for Army testing and adoption of more advanced weapons.

17 September. Youngest Recipient of Medal of Honor.
Musician Willie Johnston, age 12, a drummer boy with 3d Vermont Infantry, is awarded the Medal of Honor for his bravery during the Seven Days Battles (25 June–1 July 1862). He is the youngest person to receive the medal.

19–20 September. Battle of Chickamauga. Georgia.
Rosecrans marches the Army of the Cumberland past Chattanooga into Georgia. On the 19th, a division of Major General George H. Thomas's XIV Corps attacks the main Confederate army near Chickamauga Creek. Rosecrans shifts units to help as Thomas's men receive three major assaults on the 19th, suffering heavy casualties. The Confederate attacks are renewed the next day with little success until Rosecrans mistakenly opens a hole in the Federal lines. The Rebels pour into the gap, collapsing the entire Union left wing. Only the actions of Thomas, who earns the nickname "The Rock of Chickamauga," save the Union army from disaster. As troops of XX and XXI Corps stream past in panic, Thomas forms his XIV Corps in a strong defensive position on Snodgrass Hill and refuses to budge. Without orders, Major General Gordon Granger marches his Reserve Corps to help Thomas. To avoid being cut off, Thomas finally makes a skillful night withdrawal, blocking the mountain pass to Chattanooga. Union casualties are 11,413 killed or wounded and 4,757 missing. Rebel casualties are even heavier.

24 September–3 October. Reinforcements Sent to Rosecrans.
XI Corps (Howard) and XII Corps (Slocum), Army of the Potomac, are dispatched from Virginia to reinforce Rosecrans. Major General Hooker is given command of the two corps. In a major rail movement organized by Colonel Daniel C. McCallum, director of the U.S. Military Railroad, the 20,000 men of the two corps are moved by two different routes in 13 days, their heavy equipment following. Sherman is already on his way from Mississippi with his army. On the 28th, the XX and XXI Corps are consolidated into a new IV Corps under Granger. The two former commanders, McCook and Crittenden, are ordered to a court of inquiry into their behavior during the battle.

Above: *At Gettysburg, Captain John Bigelow's 9th Massachusetts Battery handled their six bronze Napoleon 12-pounders with incredible bravery and skill. ("Retreat by Fire," Don Troiani, www.historicalartprints.com)*

4 October. **Battle of Bristoe Station. Virginia.**
In attempt to cut off Meade's III Corps at Bristoe Station, A. P. Hill attacks the Federal center along Broad Run. Unaware that the Union II Corps is emplaced nearby behind a railroad embankment, Hill's infantry is caught in a deadly crossfire and suffers 1,900 casualties before withdrawing across the Rappahannock. Union casualties are just more than 500.

9–23 October. **New Union Commanders.**
Responding to a telegram on 9th, Grant travels by train from Vicksburg to meet Secretary of War Stanton. On the 18th as they ride to Louisville, Grant is told that the Departments of Ohio, the Cumberland, and the Tennessee are being consolidated into a new centralized command—the Military Division of the Mississippi. Grant is given General Order 337 creating the command and appointing him its commander with "headquarters in the field" effective the 16th. Grant now controls the Army of the Tennessee, Army of the Cumberland, and Army of the Ohio (Burnside) as well other military units. He sends a telegram ahead on the 19th replacing Rosecrans with Thomas. His most pressing problem is Chattanooga, where the Army of the Cumberland is besieged and in danger of starving—Grant arrives there on the 23rd. Rosecrans departs to command the Department of Missouri.

26–28 October. **The Cracker Line. Chattanooga.**
With Grant's approval, Thomas implements an operation to open a supply route into the city from the west in coordination with Hooker's troops, who have been protecting rail lines above the city. A night river crossing under Thomas's Chief Engineer, Brigadier W. F. Smith, is successful, permitting his engineers to lay a prepared pontoon bridge for infantry. Hooker pushes east against Confederate positions on Raccoon Mountain. Within 48 hours the way is clear, although Confederate cavalry continue efforts for days to cut the new supply line

17 November–5 December. **Siege of Knoxville.**
Longstreet's corps lays siege to Knoxville on 17 November and attempts to take the city by assault on 29 November. The defenders, led by Major General Burnside, have heavily fortified the town, and the Rebel attack is repulsed. On 5 December, Sherman's XIV Corps ends the siege and he enters the city.

23–25 November. **Battle of Chattanooga. Tennessee.**
A surprise Union attack captures Orchard Knob on the 23rd, then a combined force under Hooker captures Lookout Mountain the next day. On the 25th, Sherman, with his recently arrived XII Corps, attacks Confederate positions on Missionary Ridge and Tunnel Hill, but he stalls and Grant orders Thomas to reinforce the assault. Four divisions of Thomas's men attack abreast, overwhelm a series of Rebel rifle pits and then, without orders, continue the assault up the

Right: *At the Battle of Chickamauga, Major General George H. Thomas' determination not to retreat earned him praise and a nickname to match his steadfastness. ("Thomas, Rock of Chickamauga," Keith Rocco, Private Collection)*

Below: *During the battle of Chickamauga, the 21st Ohio Infantry made a determined stand against a large Confederate attack at Horseshoe Ridge. ("To the Last Round," Keith Rocco, Private Collection)*

steep slope, routing the Confederate defenders. Seven Union color bearers are presented the Medal of Honor for their actions; leading the 24th Wisconsin with their flag is the regiment's young adjutant, Lieutenant Arthur MacArthur, who also receives the medal. Union casualties are 5,815 killed, wounded, and missing; Confederate losses are 6,667.

1861

January. **Status of the Army.**
The Army has grown to 970,905 soldiers, and capable leaders such as Grant, Sherman, Meade, and Thomas are in command. A looming problem is that many Union soldiers' three-year enlistments end during the year.

6–15 January. **Navajo War: Canyon de Chelly Campaign. New Mexico Territory.**
In response to Brigadier General Carlton's December order to initiate an winter campaign against the Navajos, Colonel Carson takes 389 officers and men into the canyon, a traditional Navajo stronghold. Carson rides in from the west while two more companies approach from the east. A fight in the canyon on the 12th results in 11 Navajos warriors killed. The discouraged Navajos surrender on the 15th. Carson orders the Navajo homes and fields destroyed and the Indians taken to a reservation. By the end of the year most of the surviving tribe is gathered there.

February. **Rank of Lieutenant General Revived.**
Congress passes a bill establishing the rank of lieutenant general in the Regular Army. The last one to hold that rank was George Washington. Scott's rank had been a brevet only.

9 February. **Escape from Libby Prison. Richmond, Virginia.**
Colonel Thomas E. Rose (7th Pennsylvania Infantry) leads 109 Union officers by tunnel out of Libby Prison in the largest prisoner escape of the war. Only 59 of the escapees reach Union lines; Rose is among the 48 recaptured.

20 February. **Battle of Olustee (Ocean Pond). Florida.**
After taking Jacksonville earlier in the year, a force of 5,000 Federals under Brigadier General Seymour moves inland to destroy enemy railroads and property. The Federals make contact with a Confederate force of equal size. The Confederates attack the slow-moving Federals and force Seymour's troops back to Jacksonville.

22 February. **Battle of Okolona. Mississippi.**
A force of 7,000 Union cavalrymen led by Brigadier General William ("Sooey") Smith runs into 2,500 Rebels commanded by Major General Nathan Bedford Forrest at West Point, Mississippi. When the cautious Smith withdraws, Forrest attacks Smith's rear guard at Okolona and routs the Federals. Only a desperate charge by the 4th Missouri Volunteer Cavalry prevents Forrest from overrunning the entire Union force. Federal casualties are 319 killed, wounded, and missing; Forrest loses a handful of men.

28 February–2 March. **Kilpatrick-Dahlgren Raid. Richmond, Virginia.**
In an effort to free Union prisoners, Brigadier General H. Judson Kilpatrick launches a cavalry raid on 28 February. With 3,500 troopers Kilpatrick leads one column, while Colonel Ulric Dahlgren heads a second column. Upon reaching Richmond on 1 March, Kilpatrick grows cautious and halts, leaving Dahlgren unsupported. The next day Rebel cavalry ambush Dahlgren's men. Dahlgren is killed and nearly 100 Federals are taken prisoner. The Confederates claim to find papers on Dahlgren's body that call for the burning of Richmond and the assassination of Confederate president Jefferson Davis and his cabinet. Authenticity of the papers is still a question.

March. **Federal Troops Used as Strikebreakers. Cold Springs, New York.**
A labor strike at the Parrott Armaments Works, producer of Parrott cannons, threatens the Union war effort. Two companies of troops are sent. Martial law is declared and strike leaders arrested. They are held seven weeks, ending the strike. It is the first time federal troops are used in a labor dispute.

9 March. **Grant Promoted and Named Commanding General.**
Congress approves the nomination by President Lincoln of Grant to lieutenant general and names him

Opposite: *Generals Grant and Thomas are shown at Orchard Knob observing the unauthorized, but spectacularly successful, attack to the top of Missionary Ridge. (Lithograph, from a painting by Thure de Thulstrup, Library of Congress)*

Right: *The bridge over Potomac Creek was one of the largest railroad spans built by the Union forces. An engine and boxcar test the strength of the new structure. (Association of American Railroads)*

to replace Halleck as commanding general of the Army. Halleck will remain in Washington as the Army's chief of staff. Major General William T. Sherman takes Grant's place in command of the Division of the Mississippi on the 18th.

23 March. Army of the Potomac Reorganized.
Meade reorganizes his army, reducing it from five corps to three, and reshuffling many of the divisions and brigades, combining some and establishing others. Both Major Generals Winfield Scott Hancock and John Gibbon return after recovering from their Gettysburg wounds and resume command.

8 April. Battle of Sabine Crossroads (Mansfield). Louisiana.
Major General Banks is given command of 30,000 troops with naval support and is ordered to advance his Army of the Gulf up the Red River. After capturing Alexandria, Louisiana, Banks leads 20,000 troops toward Shreveport. On 8 April, Banks' force clashes with a much smaller force of Rebels led by Major General Richard Taylor (son of Zachary Taylor) at Sabine Crossroads. The aggressive Rebels smash two Union lines until Brigadier General Robert A. Cameron halts the Confederate advance. After sunset, the Federals withdraw to Pleasant Hill.

9 April. Battle of Pleasant Hill (Blair's) Landing.
Fighting erupts at Pleasant Hill Landing by Taylor, but his flank attack fails, and the Federals are able to hold their positions. The battle is inconclusive, but Banks retreats back down the Red River, ending the Union campaign.

12 April. Fort Pillow Massacre. Tennessee.
Union-held Fort Pillow comes under attack by Major General Forrest and a large force of Rebel cavalry. The garrison, commanded by Major Lionel F. Booth, is 557 men of the 13th Tennessee Cavalry and the 6th Battery (USCT). Booth is killed and Forrest demands that the fort's acting commander, Major William F. Bradford, to surrender. When he refuses, the Confederates storm the defenses and quickly take the fort. Among the 500 prisoners are approximately 250 black soldiers. Forrest's men murder Bradford and many of the prisoners, black and white.

5–6 May. Battle of the Wilderness. Spotsylvania County, Virginia.
Grant, now commanding all of the Union armies, establishes his field headquarters with Meade's Army of the Potomac. Fighting begins on 5 May when Major General Warren's V Corps encounters Lee's Rebel forces in an area of tangled brush and woods called the Wilderness. The battle centers on two roads—the Orange Turnpike and the Orange Plank Road. Despite heavy Union attacks, particularly by Hancock's II Corps and Sedgwick's VI Corps, the Confederates hold. On 6 May, the Union attack resumes and makes good progress until fresh Confederate troops arrive, counterattack, and drive the Federals back. Casualties for both sides are staggering—Union losses are 2,246 killed, 12,037 wounded, and 3,383 missing; Confederate casualties total 10,800. Hundreds of badly wounded soldiers unable to move are burned to death when the battle sparks a forest fire. Grant does not retreat, but shifts Meade's army south toward Spotsylvania Court House to flank Lee's right.

7 May. Atlanta Campaign Begins. Northwestern Georgia.

Major General William T. Sherman, with a total strength of 110,000 soldiers in his three Union armies, launches his campaign to take Atlanta. He is opposed by some 70,000 Rebels of the Army of Tennessee.

8–21 May. Battle of Spotsylvania Court House. Virginia.

The Army of the Potomac's advance is stopped by strong Confederate defensive positions near the courthouse. After several days of skirmishing and probing, Grant orders an assault on 12 May against a salient called the "Mule Shoe." Led by Hancock's II Corps, the Federals focus their attack on a portion of the salient that becomes known as the "Bloody Angle." A furious battle rages for the next 24 hours as both sides feed fresh troops into the melee. The Confederates withdraw to a new line at the base of the salient, which the Federals attack on 18 May with little success. By 21 May, the battle is over. Casualties are very heavy for both sides—18,000 Union troops killed, wounded, or missing and Confederate casualties estimated at 10,000. Among the dead is Major General John Sedgwick, the popular Union VI Corps commander.

9 May. Battle of Cloyd's Mountain.

Brigadier General George R. Crook leads his 2d Infantry Division into southwest Virginia to cut the Virginia and Tennessee Railroad. He has a brief but savage battle near Cloyd's Mountain before overwhelming the Confederates and capturing their artillery. One of the Union heroes is Colonel Rutherford B. Hayes, the future president, commander of the 1st Brigade.

11 May. **Battle of Yellow Tavern.**
Major General Sheridan leads 12,000 of the Cavalry Corps south toward Richmond. They battle Stuart's 5,000 Rebel cavalrymen at Yellow Tavern, six miles north of Richmond. The battle rages for much of the day, but the Federals, with superior numbers and overwhelming firepower, gain the upper hand. During an assault on the Rebel lines, led by Brigadier General Custer's 1st Brigade, Stuart is mortally wounded.

15 May. **Battle of New Market.**
In the Shenandoah Valley, Major General Franz Sigel and his army of 9,000 men meet a smaller force of Confederates at New Market. In a daylong battle, Sigel's Federals are defeated and forced north to Cedar Creek. Union casualties are 93 killed, 482 wounded, and 256 missing; Rebel losses are 42 killed, 522 wounded, and 13 missing. Among the Confederate dead are 10 cadets from the Virginia Military Institute (VMI) Corps of Cadets. Sigel is replaced as commander of the Department of West Virginia by Major General David Hunter.

16 May. **Battle of Drewry's Bluff.**
Major General Benjamin Butler, commander of the Army of the James, marches his 35,000 troops up the James River toward Richmond. On 16 May he clashes with a mixed forced of 18,000 Rebels assigned to the defenses of Richmond at Drewry's Bluff. The battle eventually ends in a stalemate and Butler withdraws. Union casualties are 390 killed, 2,380 wounded, and 1,390 missing.

23–27 May. **Battle of the North Anna River.**
Grant keeps Meade moving south. Federal troops are able to pierce the Rebel North Anna River line and threaten Lee's entire army. During the night of 23–24 May, Lee redeploys his forces in an inverted "V" with its apex along the North Anna. Grant believes Lee is retreating and attacks, not realizing the Rebels are strongly entrenched. Elements of Burnside's IX Corps and Hancock's II Corps suffer heavy casualties.

ULYSSES S. GRANT

During the Battle of the Wilderness, one of the Union generals expressed concern to the Army commander that Lee would send his Confederate army to cut them off. At this, the commander, Ulysses S. Grant, retorted, "Go back to your command, and try to think about what we are going to do ourselves, instead of what Lee is going to do." That calm, bulldog determination marked Grant's life.

Born in 1822 as a son of an Ohio farmer, Hiram Ulysses Grant attended West Point, graduating without distinction in 1843. At the academy, for uncertain reasons, his name became Ulysses S. Grant, which he retained. Grant joined the 4th Infantry at Jefferson Barracks (Missouri), and went with the regiment into combat in the Mexican War, where he won two brevet promotions. After the war Grant saw little opportunity in the much-reduced Army and resigned in 1854. He was unsuccessful as a civilian, however, trying his hand as a farmer, bill collector, firewood peddler, and finally clerk in his father's store in Galena, Illinois. The Civil War changed all that.

After Fort Sumter in 1861, Grant worked as a civilian aide in the Illinois Adjutant General's office until being commissioned a Volunteer colonel and commander of the 21st Illinois Infantry. He and his regiment took a small part in several actions in Missouri. Promoted to brigadier general of Volunteers in August, Grant moved his headquarters to Cairo, Illinois. From there he launched expeditions against Confederate positions, capturing Paducah, Kentucky, in September and Forts Henry and Donelson, Tennessee, on the Tennessee River by February 1862. At Fort Donelson Grant offered, "No terms except unconditional and immediate surrender can be accepted." Capture of the fort, containing some 15,000 troops, was a major Union success.

In April 1862, Grant's Army of the Tennessee, camped at Shiloh Church, was surprised and almost destroyed, but he recovered the next day and drove the Confederates from the field. Union and Confederate losses were enormous, resulting in Grant's temporary relief of command.

Grant returned to command in July and made his next target Vicksburg, Mississippi, a key fortified city overlooking the Mississippi River. After long months of unsuccessful maneuvering, including an unsuccessful attempt to bypass the town via canal, Grant embarked on a daring strategy. In April 1863, he marched south on the west bank of the Mississippi and crossed the river. Cutting loose from his supply line, Grant marched east to capture Jackson, then turned west to besiege Vicksburg. On 4 July the city surrendered. The Confederacy had been split in half, and Grant's victory won him a promotion to major general.

Grant, now commanding three Union armies, set out to relieve the beleaguered Union troops in Chattanooga, Tennessee. Directing attacks on Confederate strongpoints on Orchard Knob, Lookout Mountain, and Missionary Ridge on 23–25 November, he broke the siege and pushed the Confederates deeper into the south. In March 1864, Congress approved Grant to be a lieutenant general and the commanding general of the Army.

Although responsible for coordinating all the Union armies, Grant made his field headquarters with Meade's Army of the Potomac. Grant realized the key to victory was the destruction of Lee's Army of Northern Virginia. The campaign commenced with the Battle of the Wilderness on 5 May. Despite setbacks, Grant refused to withdraw, sending Meade's army forward to clash again at Spotsylvania and Cold Harbor. After each battle, Grant kept moving to Lee's right flank, driving the Confederate closer to Richmond. By June, Grant had Petersburg, a strategic railroad junction south of Richmond, under siege. For ten months Grant kept his stranglehold on the city, draining the resources of the Confederate Army.

Finally, in late March 1865, Grant ordered an assault all along the line. Petersburg fell and Grant pursued the desperate retreat of Lee's army west, cutting it off near Appomattox Court House, Virginia. There the two men met on 9 April to arrange the surrender of Lee's army. Grant's generous terms did much to help heal the nation.

Grant's popularity led to his election as President for two terms, 1868 to 1877. Unfortunately, he left that office beset by scandals involving members of his administrations. His civilian career as an investment broker was destroyed by dishonest partners who left Grant deep in debt just as he was diagnosed with throat cancer. In a final display of his dogged courage, the dying Ulysses Grant forced himself to complete a memoir still regarded as one of the finest in American history. He died just weeks after its completion in 1885, but his work ensured the financial future of his family.

—*Kevin M. Hymel*

3 June. Battle of Cold Harbor.
Grant sends Sheridan and his troopers to capture the strategic crossroads at Cold Harbor. The Union cavalrymen seize the position on 31 May. Over the next two days, the Federals probe the Rebel lines, but the main Union attack is delayed until 3 June. The attack, led by Hancock's II Corps, Major General Horatio Wright's VI Corps, and Major General William F. Smith's XVIII Corps, fails, with major losses. Grant refuses to call a truce until 7 June; by then, many wounded have succumbed. Total Union casualties are 13,000 killed, wounded, and missing.

5–11 June. Battle of Piedmont. Shenandoah Valley.
As Hunter marches an army of 12,000 troops south toward Staunton, he engages a force of 5,600 Rebels near Piedmont. The Confederates are routed and Hunter's men march on to Staunton, where they destroy the railroad and supply depots. On 11 June, they reach Lexington and burn VMI.

9 June. Siege of Petersburg. Virginia.
Meade's forces, including a division of U.S. Colored Troops, make the first assaults against the formidable defenses of Petersburg. Over the next several days, more Union troops arrive, but they are unable to break the Rebel lines. After two more assaults later in the month, the Army of the Potomac settles into a siege that will last ten months.

10 June. Battle of Brice's Cross Roads. Mississippi.
Sherman gives Brigadier General Samuel Sturgis an expeditionary force of 8,100 troops to march into Mississippi and attack Forrest's headquarters at Tupelo. Forrest learns of the Federal movement and meets Sturgis at Brice's Cross Roads, just north of Tupelo. Despite being outnumbered two-to-one, Forrest routs Sturgis, capturing 22 artillery pieces and hundreds of supply wagons. Despite the defeat, Sherman presses on with his campaign into Georgia.

11–12 June. Battle of Trevilian Station. Virginia.
In late May, Sheridan sets out with his Cavalry Corps to destroy the railroad between Richmond and Charlottesville. He battles Rebel cavalry led by Major Generals Wade Hampton and Fitzhugh Lee near Trevilian Station in a bloody two-day battle. Sheridan withdraws and abandons his effort to reinforce Hunter's army in the Shenandoah Valley. Union losses are 735 killed, wounded, and missing; Confederate casualties are estimated at 1,000.

Above: *Major General William T. Sherman's men must endure weeks of hard fighting on the outskirts of Atlanta before the Confederates withdraw from the city. ("Battle of Atlanta," detail, Department of Parks, Atlanta, GA)*

17–18 June. **Battle of Lynchburg. Virginia.**
Hunter crosses the Blue Ridge with 18,500 troops and attacks Lynchburg on 17 June. The first Union attacks are repulsed. Union assaults on 18 June are again easily repelled, and though he has more men, Hunter withdraws into West Virginia. Union losses are 700 killed, wounded, and missing.

27 June. **Battle of Kennesaw Mountain. Georgia.**
At 9:00 a.m., after an hour-long bombardment of Rebel lines around Kennesaw Mountain, Sherman orders a series of assaults against strongly fortified Rebel positions. The attacks are repulsed and the assault is called off. Sherman loses 3,000 men killed, wounded, and missing.

9 July. **Battle of Monocacy. Maryland.**
With Lieutenant General Jubal Early advancing his Rebels toward Washington, Major General Lew Wallace organizes a 6,000-man scratch force of veteran infantry, cavalry, untested militia, and a few artillery pieces, placing them behind Monocacy Creek. Though

greatly outnumbered, the Federals hold their positions and inflict heavy casualties. By the afternoon, however, Wallace is in danger of being cut off and orders a retreat after losing more than 1,800 men killed, wounded, or missing. Wallace has delayed Early enough to allow VI Corps to rush to the defenses of Washington.

11–12 July. **Fighting on the Outskirts of Washington.**
Early's Rebels reach the Washington suburbs on 11 July and clash with Union forces at Fort Stevens the following day. After a brief battle, Early withdraws his troops. Among those witnessing the fighting is President Lincoln, who peers over the fort's wall to get a better view. Future Supreme Court Justice Captain Oliver Wendell Holmes, Jr., not realizing it is the President, yells, "Get down, you damn fool, before you get shot!" Lincoln obeys the order.

13–15 July. **Battle of Tupelo. Mississippi.**
Sherman orders Major General Andrew J. Smith to take 14,000 troops and attack Forrest at his base at Tupelo. The two sides make contact on 13 July and

heavy fighting occurs the following day. Smith's entrenched men repulse three Rebel attacks, inflicting many casualties. Smith, however, fails to realize this and begins to withdraw. Forrest leads another unsuccessful attack on Smith's rear guard on 15 July and is wounded. Union casualties number 674 killed, wounded, and missing.

20 *July*. Battle of Peachtree Creek. Georgia.
Major General Thomas sends his Army of the Cumberland across Peachtree Creek on 20 July and is attacked by General John B. Hood's Rebel army. Thomas easily repels the Rebel attack. Hood loses 4,796 killed, wounded, and missing; Federal losses are 1,779.

23–24 *July*. Second Battle of Kernstown. Virginia.
After withdrawing into Virginia, Early strikes Crook's 9,500 Federals at Kernstown. On 24 July, main fighting rages around Opequon Church. The outnumbered Union troops are forced to withdraw, with Colonel Hayes' brigade covering much of the retreat to Bunker Hill. Federal casualties are 1,185 killed, wounded, and missing. Grant decides to end the Rebel threat in the Shenandoah. He orders the VI and XIX Corps west, with Sheridan in overall command with orders to neutralize enemy forces and destroy the Shenandoah's value to the Confederacy.

22–28 *July*. Fighting Around Atlanta.
During an intense battle on 22 July, both sides suffer heavy casualties. Union losses are more than 3,600 killed, wounded, or missing, including Major General McPherson, commander of the Army of the Tennessee. He is the only Union Army commander to be killed in action in the war. Major General John A. Logan replaces him. On 28 July, four Rebel divisions attack Major General O. O. Howard's XV Corps west of Atlanta at Ezra Church. His men inflict heavy casualties on the attackers with minimum losses.

30 *July*. Battle of the Crater. Virginia.
In an effort to penetrate the Confederate lines at Petersburg, Union officers dig under the Rebel

Opposite: *The 1st Maine Heavy Artillery spent the first part of the war manning defensive forts around Washington, D.C. They taste combat for the first time when they are sent in as infantry in an attack on the strong Confederate positions at Petersburg, Virginia. ("The Forlorn Hope—1st Maine Heavy Artillery at Petersburg, June 1864," Don Troiani, www.historicalartprints.com)*

Below: *Private Henry H. Hardenburg seizes a Rebel flag, earning him the Medal of Honor. ("Medal of Honor," Keith Rocco)*

Above: *George A. Custer carries his personal flag while leading a charge of his Michigan brigade of the 1st Division, Cavalry Corps. ("Bravado," © Don Spaulding, by arrangement with Mill Pond Press, Inc.)*

positions at Elliot's Salient and detonate a huge mine. Much of the work is done by the 48th Pennsylvania Infantry, a regiment with many coal miners. The mine, comprising 8,000 pounds of black powder, explodes on the morning of 30 July, killing some 300 Rebels and opening a 170-foot gap. The follow-on attack, however, goes awry. Instead of advancing around the huge blast crater, troops from Burnside's IX Corps pour into it and become trapped. The Rebels quickly recover and inflict heavy casualties. A division of black troops led by Brigadier General Edward Ferrero supports the initial assault. They fan out around the crater as instructed, but are soon pinned down. By 1:00 p.m., the Rebels have regained control of the crater. Union forces suffer nearly 4,000 casualties. Burnside is put on leave without orders and retires in April 1865.

23 August. Fort Morgan Captured. Mobile Bay, Alabama.
After a daylong bombardment, Fort Morgan, the largest Rebel fort in Mobile Bay, falls to Union troops led by Major General Granger.

18–21 August. Battle of Globe Tavern. Virginia.
Grant orders Warren's V Corps to extend the siege lines west of Petersburg and cut the Weldon Railroad. While dismantling tracks near Globe Tavern on 18 August, Union forces are attacked. Both sides rush reinforcements to the area, and on the following day, major fighting occurs. A Confederate double envelopment nearly destroys the Union force, and only a strong counterattack by Warren prevents total disaster. Fighting continues over the next two days with little change in each side's positions. Casualties are heavy.

25 August. Battle of Reams' Station.
As Hancock's II Corps destroys the Confederate rail system south of Globe Tavern, Confederates strike and send the Federals into a disorderly retreat. In addition to keeping a rail link open to Petersburg, the Rebels take more than 2,000 prisoners, while suffering just more than 700 casualties.

2 September. Atlanta Falls.
The Confederates withdraw from the city, destroying the railroad rolling stock and ordnance stores. The ensuing explosions and fires destroy much of Atlanta. Sherman, recently promoted to major general in the Regular Army, leads his XX Corps into Atlanta on 2 September. Since the campaign began in early May, Sherman's three armies have suffered nearly 37,000 casualties.

19 September. Third Battle of Winchester. Virginia.
Sheridan, now commanding all Union troops in the Shenandoah Valley, attacks Early's Confederates around Winchester in the third major battle of the war fought there. Sheridan has superior numbers and focuses 25,000 troops against the Rebel center. The Confederates, however, inflict heavy casualties before Sheridan's overwhelming numbers force them to withdraw south toward Strasburg. Among the dead is Colonel George S. Patton, 2d Virginia Infantry, grandfather of the famous World War II general.

22 September. Battle of Fisher's Hill. Virginia.
Sheridan pursues Early to Fisher's Hill near Strasburg. As Crook's VIII Corps flanks the Rebel line, Brigadier General James Ricketts leads VI Corps in a frontal attack. Crook surprises the Rebels while Ricketts' men charge uphill, routing the defenders. Union casualties number just more than 500 killed, wounded, and missing. After the conclusion of the battle, Union forces begin a scorched-earth campaign in the Valley that locals refer to as "the Burning."

CIVIL WAR MEDICINE

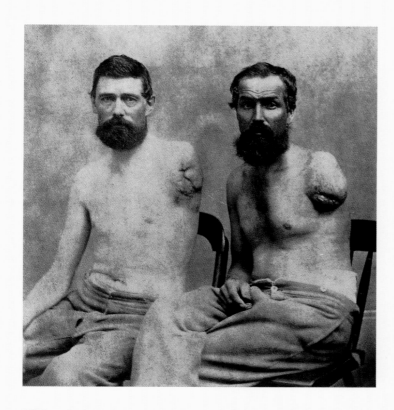

The technology for curing could not keep up with the technology for killing in the Civil War. With soft, heavy bullets that would penetrate a man, wounds to the body and head were usually fatal, while for shattered arm or leg bones, the safest option was quick amputation. After horrific battles, wounded men were brought to the over-worked surgeon's tent where unsanitary saws and knives awaited. With a practiced doctor, the procedure usually was quick. Lucky patients received a small dose of ether. A gulp of whiskey was often an alternative.

Conditions within even the largest base hospitals were crude. Without knowledge of germs or infection, the war was fought, as a Union surgeon commented, "at the end of the medical middle ages." At the beginning of the war, the Union had only 16 Army hospitals. By the end of the war it was running 350, the Confederacy 154.

Disease was the biggest killer of the war. For every soldier who died in battle, two died of disease. Thousands more were sick in infirmaries. The problems began early as recruits exposed each other to the measles, mumps, and other diseases. Men from the country were more susceptible to diseases than their city-dwelling comrades. Men from the midwestern states suffered a 43 percent higher mortality rate than those from the Northeast. Once the armies began to train and fight, other diseases, mostly from lack of sanitary discipline, exposure, and poor diets, tore through the ranks.

In the early battles, regimental musicians often removed wounded from the battlefield. But they were unskilled and often unreliable. Many men left the ranks to help their friends, reducing the unit's fighting strength. Between the first aid stations at the front, and the hospitals in the rear, there was no organized transportation system. To remedy this situation, Union Major General George McClellan approved an ambulance corps for the Army of the Potomac in 1862, an idea proposed by Surgeon Jonathan Letterman.

Other aid came in the form of the U.S. Sanitary Commission, a civilian agency that helped the Army Medical Bureau with health problems. The commission established depots for the distribution of food, clothing, and medicine to the Army. It gave lodging to recovering or furloughed men. It sent sanitary inspectors to camps to advise on proper hygiene; sent doctors, nurses, medicine, and bandages to the battle front; and chartered ships to evacuate wounded.

Groups like the Western Sanitary Commission, the Roman Catholic Sisters of Charity, and the YMCA also contributed to better health for the Union Army. Confederate wounded fared worse than their Northern counterparts, suffering a higher mortality rate of sick and wounded.

Probably the greatest advancement in the field of Civil War medicine was the employment of women in the ranks of nurses, both North and South. While many had to overcome the prejudices of male doctors who felt that rooms of wounded and dying men were no place for a lady, by the end of the war about 3,200 women served as Army nurses in the North. While most served far behind the lines in hospitals, some, like Clara Barton and Mary Ann Bickerdyke, saved lives on the battlefield.

—*Kevin M. Hymel*

Above: *Two wounded veterans graphically reveal the common treatment of amputation practiced by military surgeons of the era. (Library of Congress)*

27 September. **Battle of Pilot Knob (Fort Davidson). Missouri.**
Union forces slated to reinforce Sherman are diverted to deal with a large Confederate force under Major General Sterling Price. The Union garrison of Fort Davidson, commanded by Brigadier General Ewing, is attacked by Price. The Rebel assaults are repulsed, with heavy losses. Ewing's Federals slip out of the fort during the night and escape, but not before destroying anything of value to the Rebels.

Fall. **Confederate Prisoners Enlisted.**
To meet continued shortages of troops in the west, the War Department creates a program to enlist Confederate prisoners who swear an oath of loyalty for duty against the Indians. Referred to as "galvanized yankees," the men are in organized into six regiments—the 1st–6th U.S. Volunteers—with Regular U.S. officers. The first regiment deploys to frontier posts in Minnesota and the Dakotas before the end of the year. The regiments are disbanded in 1866 as more Regular units are shifted west.

2 October. **Battle of Saltville. Virginia.**
Brigadier General Stephen G. Burbridge advances 5,200 Federals, including the 5th U.S. Colored Infantry, to destroy the nearby Confederate salt works. The Federals' attack on 2 April is driven back. Burbridge withdraws the following day, leaving his wounded on the field. Confederate partisans, led by Champ Ferguson, kill more than 100 wounded black soldiers, and their actions become known as the "Saltville Massacre." Major General Breckinridge, the Confederate theater commander, orders Ferguson arrested. Ferguson is hanged after the war.

5 October. **Battle of Allatoona Pass. Georgia.**
When the Union supply depot and railroad at Allatoona Pass are threatened, Brigadier General John M. Corse's 4th Division, XV Corps, is sent to reinforce the garrison. On 5 October a fierce battle with Major General Samuel G. French's Rebel division pushes Corse's troops into Star Fort, their main fieldwork. Despite being wounded, Corse holds out until the Confederates withdraw. Union casualties are 706 killed, wounded, and missing.

19 October. **Battle of Cedar Creek. Virginia.**
By mid-October, Sheridan believes the Shenandoah Valley is secure and travels to Washington for a strategy meeting, placing VI Corps commander Horatio Wright in command of Army of the Shenandoah. On the morning of 19 October, Confederates make a surprise attack at Cedar Creek, driving Federals back. Sheridan hears the sounds of heavy fighting and rushes to the battlefield. He rallies his men and orders his cavalry to counterattack. The assault, led by Brigadier George A. Custer and his 3d Division, smashes the Confederate left flank. The Confederates buckle and retreat south. Sheridan's victory all but secures the Shenandoah for the Union.

23–24 October. **Battles of Westport and Mine Creek. Missouri and Kansas.**
At Westport on 23 October, a Confederate force under Major General Sterling Price attacks 20,000 Union troops under Major General Samuel R. Curtis, the commander of the Department of Kansas. Curtis's troops defeat the Confederates in a two-hour battle. The next day, two brigades of pursuing Union cavalry, one led by Lieutenant Colonel Frederick W. Benteen, catch up with the retreating Confederates. They make a furious charge headed by the 4th Iowa Cavalry, routing the two Confederate cavalry divisions facing them.

15 November. **Sherman's "March to the Sea" Begins. Georgia.**

Sherman begins marching a 60,000-man army east toward the Atlantic coast with the goal of destroying the Rebel war effort and cutting the Confederacy in two. His troops will live off the land as they march through Georgia. Furthermore, they will be out of communication with the Union high command in Washington until they reach the coast.

25 November. **Battle of Adobe Walls. Texas.**

Major General Carlton, territorial commander, responds to raids by Kiowa and Comanche bands on wagon trains using the Sante Fe trail by sending Colonel Kit Carson with 350 men of his regiment and the 1st California Cavalry and 75 Ute Indian scouts in pursuit. Carson locates a Kiowa camp near an abandoned fur-trading post called Adobe Walls. His surprise attack on the 25th destroys the camp, but hundreds of Comanches rush from a nearby camp and surround Carson's detachment. Using mountain howitzers and smoke from a grass fire, Carson is able to withdraw.

29 November. **Sand Creek Massacre. Colorado Territory.**

Militia Colonel John Chivington attacks a camp of peaceful Cheyenne and Arapaho Indians with 700 troops of the Colorado militia, supported by artillery. After a brief battle, Chivington orders wounded and prisoners killed. More than 200 Indians, including women and children, lie dead and the rest flee. The massacre is condemned and Chivington comes under investigation from Congress. He is discharged from the militia but escapes any further punishment.

Opposite: *The Union plan to use an underground mine to blast through the Confederate defensive lines around Petersburg turned into a bloody disaster when Union troops became trapped in the bomb's crater. ("The Battle of the Crater," Tom Lovell, Greenwich Workshop)*

Below: *The Minnesota Sioux uprising of 1864 was a foreshadowing of the conflicts the Army would face on the western plains once the Civil War was over. ("The 8th Minnesota Infantry Mounted in the Battle of Tatt-Kouty," Carl L. Boeckmann, Minnesota Historical Society)*

30 November. **Battle of Franklin. Tennessee.**
Major General John M. Schofield and his Army of
the Ohio are attacked by a Confederate army of
38,000 at Franklin. Schofield has 32,000 men in
strongly fortified defensive positions. A Confederate
frontal assault is a bloody failure; six Confederate
generals are killed or mortally wounded and another is
taken prisoner. Schofield loses 189 killed, 1,033
wounded, and 1,104 missing.

15–16 December. **Battle of Nashville.**
In heavy fog, Major General Thomas sends the troops of
the Army of the Cumberland against Hood's
Confederates, and by nightfall the Rebel lines have
collapsed. On the following day a Federal division
commanded by Brigadier General John McArthur
captures a hill anchoring Hood's left, and the Rebel line
disintegrates. Federal troops take more than 4,000
Confederate prisoners; another 1,500 Rebels are killed or
wounded.

21 December. **Savannah Captured. Georgia.**
After marching 300 miles in just over a month and
leaving a trail of destruction, Sherman's army reaches
Savannah. The city falls on the 21st after Confederate
defenders withdraw.

1865

1 January. **Status of the Army.**
The strength of the Union Army has reached
1,000,692 officers and men. The Army is well supplied
with arms, ammunition, food, clothing, and other
supplies. A new, younger set of general officers lead
the Army, and for the first time they are all West
Point graduates. The Army's commanding general,
Lieutenant General Ulysses S. Grant, remains in the
field with the Army of the Potomac outside
Petersburg. The others are Major Generals Henry
Halleck, William T. Sherman, George G. Meade,
Philip H. Sheridan, and George H. Thomas.

12–15 January. **Fort Fisher Captured. North Carolina.**
Brigadier General Alfred H. Terry leads a joint Army-
Navy force in the largest amphibious operation of the
war. Terry's force of 58 ships and 8,000 troops arrives
on 12 January and immediately begins bombarding the
fort. On the 15th, a combined force of soldiers, sailors,
and marines captures the fort. Union casualties are just
more than 1,600 killed, wounded, and missing; Union
troops take Wilmington on 22 February.

Opposite: *Deadly improvements in weaponry during the 1860s often required defensive tactics rather than massed infantry formations. ("Reverse the Trenches," Keith Rocco)*

Right: *Major General Philip H. Sheridan rallied his men during a heroic ride to the Cedar Creek battle-field south of Winchester, Virginia. (Army Art Collection, NMUSA)*

19 January–17. February. Sherman Turns North.
On the 19th, Sherman swings his forces north into South Carolina with the goal of linking with Meade in Virginia. Columbia, the capital of South Carolina, falls to Sherman on 17 February. Within a week most of South Carolina is in Union hands.

2 March. Battle of Waynesboro. Virginia.
Sheridan's two cavalry divisions catch a Rebel force near Waynesboro. Led by Custer's 3d Division, the Federals rout the Confederates, killing or capturing almost all of them. With the Shenandoah

Valley secure, Sheridan marches across the Blue Ridge to join Grant.

3 March. Freedmen's Bureau Established.
Congress creates the Bureau of Refugees, Freedmen, and Abandoned Lands, an autonomous agency within the War Department designed to protect freed slaves and Unionist Southern whites. In May, Major General O. O. Howard is appointed to head the bureau.

19 March. Battle of Bentonville. North Carolina.
In the last major battle of the war outside of Virginia,

Sherman's 60,000 Federals clash with General Johnston's Rebel Army of Tennessee at Bentonville. The Confederates put up a tough fight, particularly against Major General Henry Slocum's Army of Georgia, but eventually withdraw in the face of superior numbers.

22 March–20 April. **Wilson's Raid. Tennessee, Alabama, and Georgia.**
Brigadier General James H. Wilson launches a raid from Tennessee with 14,000 cavalrymen and infantry. In Alabama, he defeats Forrest at Selma on 2 April and destroys Rebel arms factories and supplies. Wilson's troops occupy Montgomery on 12 April, then march into Georgia and reach Macon on 20 April.

25 March. **Battle of Fort Stedman. Virginia.**
The Confederates make an assault against Fort Stedman, a Federal position near the Confederate lines, in an attempt to break out from Petersburg. The initial attack goes well and the fort is captured. A counterattack by Brigadier General John F. Hartranft's 3d Division, IX Corps, soon halts the effort and 1,900 Confederates surrender.

30 March–1 April. **Battle of Five Forks.**
In a three-day battle, Union forces led by Warren and Sheridan rout a force of Confederate infantry and cavalry at the crossroads of Five Forks and cut the Southside Railroad, Lee's main supply route.

3 April. **Richmond Falls.**
Confederate government and troops evacuate the city and the mayor opens it to Union troops at 8:15 am. Retreating Rebel forces burn stores of equipment and other material to prevent it from falling into enemy hands. The resulting fires devastate much of the city.

6 April. **Battle of Sayler's (Sailers) Creek.**
Union forces vigorously pursue Lee's army, resulting in a pitched battle at Sayler's Creek. The Federals, led by Sheridan, Custer, and Wright, rout the Confederates and capture several thousand prisoners, including Ewell and five other generals. Confederate casualties total 7,700, while Union losses are just more than 1,100.

6–7 April. **Fighting Around High Bridge and Farmville. Virginia.**
Union troops extinguish a fire on the High Bridge set by the Rebels, cross the Appomattox River, and march

Left: *Only the use of a prairie fire and the covering fire from his mountain howitzers enabled Kit Carson to disengage his outnumbered troops from attacking Comanches. ("Battle of Adobe Wells, 25 November, 1864," Nick Eggenhofer, Fort Union National Monument, National Park Service, Waltrous, NM)*

Opposite, bottom: *A plainly dressed Ulysses S. Grant confers with his staff. ("Lieutenant General, Major General, Brigadier General and Staff," Henry A. Ogden, Dover Publications)*

toward the Rebel supply base at Farmville. Major General Andrew A. Humphreys' II Corps drives the Rebels away from their resupply operation. On the night of 7 April, Grant sends a proposal for Lee's surrender; Lee refuses.

9 April. Lee Surrenders. Appomattox Court House, Virginia.

Trapped, Lee agrees to meet to negotiate surrender of his Army of Northern Virginia. Grant and Lee meet in the McLean House at Appomattox Court House to discuss terms. The terms are generous: Lee's officers are allowed to keep their horses, side arms, and personal baggage; rifles and artillery are to be surrendered; and all officers and men are to be paroled and allowed to return home peacefully as long as they obey the laws and authority of the federal government. Lee agrees and Grant orders rations for Lee's hungry troops.

14 April. Lincoln Assassinated.

While attending a play at Ford's Theater, President Lincoln is shot by John Wilkes Booth, actor and Southern sympathizer, who flees through Maryland to Virginia. Lincoln is moved across the street. Secretary of War Stanton sets up a command post and declares martial law in the city. Lincoln dies the next day. Booth and another conspirator are caught by Union cavalry hiding near Port Tobacco on 26 April. During the capture Booth is shot and killed.

14 April. U.S. Flag Raised Over Fort Sumter.

Four years after the war started, Army and Navy personnel raise the U.S. flag over Fort Sumter, scene of

Above: *A Union artillery battery struggles through the snow while heading for its winter encampment. Such weather usually brought a temporary cessation of fighting. ("To Winter Quarters," Alan Fearnley)*

the war's first shots. Robert Anderson, the officer who surrendered the fort and now a brigadier general on the retired list, raises the same flag that flew over the fort the day he ordered it lowered.

17–26 April. Sherman and Johnston Agree to Armistice. North Carolina.

Sherman and Joseph E. Johnston meet at Bennett Place, where the two sign an agreement calling for an armistice, with proposed surrender terms that give a general amnesty and recognize the existing state governments. The agreement infuriates Secretary Stanton, who demands that Sherman call for the complete surrender of Johnston's army. On 24 April, Halleck orders Sherman to begin attacks on the Rebels in 48 hours. Sherman and Johnston finally sign terms similar to those signed at Appomattox.

20 April. Halleck Reassigned.

Partly as a result of the dispute with Sherman, Grant removes Halleck as chief of the Army staff and sends him to Richmond as commander of the Military Division of the James. During his short tenure,

Halleck is responsible for reconstruction in Virginia. He issues orders preserving the surviving official records of the Confederacy and permits selling of condemned Army horses and mules to Southern farmers. In August, Halleck is reassigned to the Division of the Pacific.

27 April. Sultana Disaster. Mississippi River.

Following their release from Confederate prison camps, more than 2,000 Union soldiers, along with dozens of other passengers, crowd onto the old side-wheel steamer *Sultana* for the journey home. Just north of Memphis, the ship's boilers explode, setting the *Sultana* ablaze. More than 1,700 burn to death or drown in the catastrophe, the worst maritime disaster in U.S. history.

1 May. Union Army Begins Demobilization.

War Department General Order 79 issues demobilizing orders for the 1,052,038 Regulars and Volunteers of the Union Army. Corps and divisions are to move intact to nine assembly areas, then to camps where muster rolls, pay rolls, and other administrative matters are handled. From the camps the men return with their units to their home states or camps of organization for individual release. In Washington, nine Army officers are appointed to conduct the trial of the Lincoln conspirators.

4 May. Confederates in Alabama and Mississippi Surrender. Alabama.
Lieutenant General Richard Taylor surrenders his troops to Major General Edward R. S. Canby at Citronelle. There is still fighting in Missouri.

10–11 May. End of Hostilities Declared.
President Andrew Johnson proclaims that the war is over. Partisan William Quantrill is killed in Kentucky, but other skirmishes against Confederate guerrillas continue for several months. On the 11th, men of the 4th Michigan Cavalry capture Jefferson Davis in Georgia. He is sent to Nashville, and later imprisoned at Fortress Monroe, Virginia.

12–13 May. Battle of Palmito Ranch. Brownsville, Texas.
In a last battle of the war, Colonel Theodore H. Barrett violates orders and attacks a small force of Confederates

Opposite: *On 9 April 1865, Lee met Grant to surrender the Army of Northern Virginia. ("The Surrender," Keith Rocco, Appomattox Court House National Park, National Park Service)*

Above: *A Union survivor contemplates the ultimate sacrifice made by a fallen comrade. ("A Trooper Meditating Beside a Grave," Winslow Homer, Josyln Art Museum, Omaha, NE)*

Left: *In 1907 the War Department authorized the Civil War Campaign Medal for Union troops who served between 15 April 1861 and 9 April 1865. (Quintet Publishing Ltd., London)*

Above: *Brigadier General Joshua Chamberlain is selected by Grant to receive surrendered arms and flags. As Confederate General John B. Gordon's vanquished Confederates pass, Chamberlain orders his veterans to give a salute. Of this 12 April event Chamberlain wrote: "It was a scene worthy of a pilgrimage." ("Last Salute," Don Troiani, www.historicalartprints.com)*

Below: *As Grant and Lee discuss terms, Union soldiers begin to share their rations with starving Confederates. (National Archives)*

Opposite: *With the Civil War's conclusion hundreds of thousands of Union citizen soldiers could resume lives with their families. ("Last Leave," Mort Künstler)*

at Palmito Ranch. After another day of fighting, the Union troops withdraw. Casualties are minimal.

23–24 May. Grand Review of the Army.

Led by Major General George G. Meade, the Army of the Potomac marches in a grand review down Pennsylvania Avenue in Washington on 23 May. President Johnson, Lieutenant General Grant, government officials, members of Congress, and thousands of cheering civilians watch. On the following day, the western armies, led by Sherman, make the same march through Washington. No U.S. Colored Troops participate in the review.

2–23 June. Surrender of Confederate Trans-Mississippi Department. Texas.

In Galveston, Major General Canby accepts the surrender of General Kirby Smith. On the 23rd, Brigadier General Stand Watie, the Cherokee leader of Rebel troops in the Indian Territory, comes into Doakesville and surrenders; he is the last Confederate general to give up.

6 July. General Order Authorizes Arrest of Civilians.

Grant issues a General Order to Union officers empowering them to arrest civilians charged with crimes against federal personnel or against blacks.

7 July. Lincoln Conspirators Hanged. Washington, D.C.

Four of the convicted conspirators in the Lincoln assassination—Mary Surratt, Lewis Paine, David Herold, and George Atzerodt—are hanged in the yard of the Washington Arsenal, now Fort Lesley J. McNair. Samuel Mudd, Michael O'Laughlin, Edman Spangler, and Samuel Arnold are also convicted but not hanged.

11–26 July. Battles With Sioux Continue. Fort Laramie, Indian Territory.

Sioux raids have been continuing since spring. A detachment of the 7th Iowa Cavalry skirmishes with a band Sioux on the 11th, killing 20 or more warriors. Another detachment pursues the Sioux, but has their horses run off and the abashed troopers must walk back to the fort. Sioux then attempt to overrun the Platte Bridge Station defended by men of the 11th Ohio and 11th Kansas Cavalry and the 6th U.S. Volunteers, but are beaten off. The 6th is a unit of "galvanized yankees," former Confederate prisoners who agreed to parole for service in the west.

10 November. Henry Wirz Executed. Washington, D.C.

Captain Henry Wirz, the Confederate commandant of the Andersonville prisoner-of-war camp in Georgia, is hanged after his conviction of war crimes by a court-martial. Horrible living conditions at Andersonville led to the deaths of more than 10,000 Union prisoners.

31 December. Demobilization of the Army.

By the end of 1865, the Army has shrunk to 199,153 Regular and Volunteer officers and men.

THE ARMY IN THE WEST

1866—1897

THE ARMY IN THE WEST

1866–1897

Lieutenant Colonel Clayton R. Newell, USA (Ret)

When the Civil War ended in 1865 the Union Army was the most powerful military force in the world, but it was quickly demobilized as the nation sought to put the war behind it and get on with settling the western part of the country. Although the size of the wartime military establishment was dramatically reduced immediately after the war, the Regular Army received a significant increase in size from its prewar strength. In 1860 the authorized strength of the Regular Army was 18,122 officers and men; in July 1866 Congress set its post-war size at 54,302 a substantial increase, although Reconstruction duties in the South took about a third of the Army's strength. As the only federal agency with enough personnel to handle the job, the Army assumed responsibility for an wide variety of tasks in the South when the Civil War ended. In 1867 Congress divided the area into five military districts each commanded by a major general to oversee the civil functions performed by the Army, which included running schools, operating railroads, building bridges, supervising banks, and administering the judicial system. During the process of establishing local governments and supervising elections, the number of Army troops required in the South decreased as states were readmitted to the Union. Of the 39,847 officers and enlisted men present for duty in 1867, 17,809 were stationed in the South, about a third of which were in Texas. By 1870 only 8,951 officers out of the Army's total strength of 29,902 officers and men were in the South. The Army's role in Reconstruction finally ended in 1877.

As the requirements of Reconstruction diminished and threats to settlers in the west declined, Congress periodically reduced the authorized strength of the Army. Although the trend was a continued decrease in size, there were occasional increases to meet threats in the West. In 1867 the President authorized companies on the western frontier to have 100 privates rather than 64, allowing the Regular Army to attain a strength of 56,815, the largest it would reach until the Spanish-American War, but it steadily declined thereafter. When the 7th Cavalry met with disaster on the banks of the Little Bighorn River in 1876 Congress authorized a temporary increase of 2,500 cavalry soldiers. These increases aside, the companies that garrisoned the far-flung western posts were chronically understrength. In 1881, for example, cavalry troops averaged 46 privates while artillery and infantry companies had 28 and 29 privates respectively. Soldiers who were sick, performing other duties, or in the stockade further reduced the number available for duty.

As the Army focused its attention on the West the number of new settlers grew by one million between 1860 and 1870 and increased by another two an a half million by 1880. The Army established additional posts as necessary to accommodate the constantly changing environment on the frontier and closed others when they were no longer needed. Between 1866 and 1894 there were 65 new posts in the West to guard settlers' migration routes, protect railroad workers and miners, and provide tangible evidence to the remaining hostile Indians that the white settlers were there to stay. Even with the new posts, however, the total number of military installations steadily decreased as the West became less dangerous. In 1867 there were 286 military posts in the United States, 134 of which were in the states that had been part of the Confederacy. By 1870 the

number of garrisoned posts was reduced to 202, only 54 of which were in the southern states. In the 1880s, as the threat from hostile Indians decreased and railroads provided the capability to rapidly concentrate forces at crisis points in a timely manner, the Army adopted a policy of consolidating smaller garrisons into larger facilities, further decreasing the number of western posts. In 1880 there were 111 posts in the West. That was down to 82 in 1889 and dropped by another 20 by 1890.

With the tide of white settlers threatening to overwhelm the Native Americans, there were only a handful of tribes that had the capability and the will to resist. In the Great Plains these included the Sioux, Cheyenne, Arapaho, Comanche, and Kiowa. In the Rocky Mountains there were the Nez Perce, Ute, and Bannock. The Paiute and Modoc held out in the Northwest, and the Apache in the Southwest. Altogether there were no more than 100,000 Indians who were ready to actively oppose the Army as it moved back to the western frontier, it took 25 years

and thousands of determined soldiers to subdue them. Although the Army flag carries nine streamers for campaigns against the Indians in the West, they do not represent all of the clashes between soldiers and Indian tribes during the period. As the instrument of national policy charged with protecting both white settlers and Native Americans, the Army conducted more than a thousand actions, large and small, against Indian warriors on the western frontier between 1866 and 1891.

Pages 438–439: *In a highly romanticized painting, post-Civil War cavalry troopers gallop with carbines at the ready. Usually skirmishes were less dramatic and were fought on foot. ("Pursuit and Attack," John Grandee, Army Art Collection, NMUSA)*

Above: *Sergeant Thomas Shaw of Troop K, 9th U.S. Cavalry, received a Medal of Honor for his heroic actions in 1881 against the Apaches. ("Edge of the Storm," D. J. Neary/U.S. Cavalry Museum, Ft. Riley, KS)*

THE ARMY IN THE WEST
1866–1897

"There are two classes of people, one demanding the utter extinction of the Indians, and the other full of love for their conversion to civilization and Christianity. Unfortunately, the army stands between them and gets the cuff from both sides."

—General William Tecumseh Sherman

1866

January. Status of the Army.
The Army is in the process of mustering out the more than one million volunteers that manned the Union Army. By June, 1,001,670 men are discharged by the Quartermaster Department. At the end of the year only about 11,000 volunteers, mostly U.S. Colored Troops, remain in the service. General Ulysses S. Grant is the commanding general of the Army. He wants a Regular Army of about 80,000, but neither the Secretary of War, Edwin M. Stanton, nor Congress agree with him.

24 January. Medal of Honor Awarded. Washington, D.C.
Dr. Mary E. Walker, a nurse with the Union Army, becomes the first woman to be awarded the Medal of Honor.

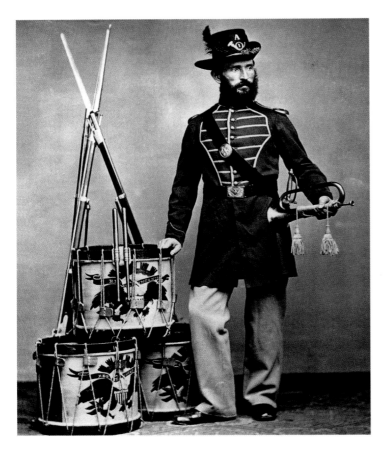

1 February. Reward for Deserters.
The Army posts a $30 reward for deserters. Regular Army deserters are offered an amnesty if they turn themselves in before 15 August. They would be returned to duty without punishment but must make up time lost. In spite of these measures there are 13,608 desertions between October 1866 and September 1867. With the end of the Army's occupation of the south, desertions drop significantly. There are 7,271 deserters for the fiscal year ending 30 June 1873, but only 1,678 in 1874.

13 May. Fortifying the Bozeman Trail. Fort Kearny, Wyoming.
Colonel Henry B. Carrington leads the 18th Infantry up the Bozeman Trail to establish a series of forts with 200 mounted infantry armed with new Spencer seven-shot repeating rifles. The expedition prompts Chief Red Cloud to take up arms against the new posts, and his resistance leads to the Laramie Treaty in 1868.

15 June. Fort Buford Built in Sioux Country. North Dakota.
Captain William G. Rankin, 31st Infantry, establishes the fort on the Missouri River to protect travelers and navigation on the river. Named for Major General John Buford, the post is in the heart of buffalo country, which upsets the Sioux.

10 July. Fort Sanders Protects Railroad and Stage Routes. Wyoming.
Captain Henry R. Mizner, 18th Infantry, establishes a post near the town of Laramie to protect the Denver-Salt Lake stage route, emigrants traveling west, and crews working on the Union Pacific Railway. Named for Brigadier General William P. Sanders, who died of wounds during the Civil War, the fort is abandoned in 1882.

13 July. Fortifying the Bozeman Trail. Wyoming.
Colonel Henry B. Carrington, 18th Infantry, establishes Fort Phil Kearny as part of the defense system on the Bozeman Trail. Located near the present

ARMY BATTLE STREAMERS—

APACHES 1873

Indian Wars, 1866-1897

Comanches, 1867–1875

Modocs, 1872–1873

Apaches, 1873

Little Big Horn, 1876–1877

Nez Perces, 1877

Bannocks, 1878

Cheyennes, 1878–1879

Utes, 1879–1880

Apaches, 1885–1886

Pine Ridge, 1890–1891

Opposite: *In the years following the Civil War, uniforms issued during that conflict continued as regulation wear for soldiers, including trumpeters. (National Museum of American History, Smithsonian Institution)*

Below: *Brigadier General Nelson Miles, a cavalry captain, other officers, and troopers in field uniform worn during the 1880s for Southwest campaigns. (Henry A. Ogden, Quartermaster General)*

town of Buffalo, it is named for Major General Philip Kearny, who was killed during the Civil War. The post was abandoned in 1868 in compliance with the Laramie Treaty of 1868 that eliminated the forts along the Bozeman Trail and temporarily ended fighting with the Sioux under Red Cloud.

13 July. Changes at the Military Academy.
Congress allows an officer of any arm to be detailed as superintendent of the U.S. Military Academy at West Point, New York. Prior to the legislation the position was always held by an engineer officer. The change began transforming the Academy into a general education institution for officers from all Army branches. The change prompts a group of engineer officers to form the Essayons Club, which becomes the Engineer School of Application in 1885.

28 July. Congress Sets Regular Army Strength.
Congress establishes the size of the Regular Army at 54,302 officers and enlisted men organized into 60 regiments, 45 infantry, ten cavalry, and five artillery. The new regiments include two of cavalry and four of infantry for black soldiers, although they have white officers.

12 August. Fort C. F. Smith Fortifies the Bozeman Trail. Montana.
Captain Nathaniel C. Kinney, 18th Infantry, establishes the northernmost of three forts built to protect the Bozeman Trail on what is now the Crow Indian Reservation. It is named for Major General Charles Ferguson Smith and abandoned in 1868 in compliance with the Laramie Treaty.

21 August. Fort Bayard to Protect Miners. New Mexico.
First Lieutenant James M. Kerr, 125th U.S. Colored Infantry, establishes a fort near the base of the Santa Rita Mountains to protect miners in the Palo Altos mining district. Named for Brigadier General George D. Bayard, who died of wounds during the Civil War, it was abandoned in 1900 and the buildings transferred to the Surgeon General. It is now a Veterans Administration hospital.

THE POST-CIVIL WAR ARMY: FORMING THE FUTURE

After the Civil War the government quickly reduced the Union Army, and by 30 June 1866 more than one million men had been discharged. However, on 28 July 1866, Congress increased the Regular Army to 54,851 officers and men. This unusual action was a result of the requirement to maintain order and enforce reconstruction in the South and renewed problems with Indians in the West.

The Act added four cavalry and 27 infantry regiments while leaving the number of artillery regiments at five. Two of the cavalry regiments and four of the infantry regiments were to "be composed of colored men." These became the famed Buffalo Soldiers. The total of infantry regiments went from 19 to 45, which included the 10 regiments (1st–10th Infantry) that existed before the war. These regiments retained their ten companies during the war.

The nine Regular regiments added in 1861 had four eight-company battalions. These regiments now went to ten companies without adding any battalions. The lost battalions merged into a new regiment and were given two more companies, making them also ten-company regiments. With minor changes, these regiments remain in the Army today. In addition, eight totally new regiments were formed, the four "colored" mentioned above, and four "veteran reserve corps."

The four black infantry regiments—the 38th, 39th, 40th, and 41st—had white officers, and the enlisted soldiers were mainly veterans of the U.S. Colored Troop units that had been disbanded. The Army also recruited 1,000 Indian scouts to be distributed among Regular Army units as needed. Scouts enlisted for three years and drew the pay and allowances of cavalry soldiers. If they furnished their own horses and horse equipment they received an additional 40 cents a day.

The act also dealt with personnel issues. The term of enlistment for soldiers was set at five years for cavalry and three for infantry and artillery. The number of officers included one general, one lieutenant general, five major generals, and ten brigadier generals. Army officers who held brevet rank from the Civil War could wear the insignia and use the title of their highest grade but were only entitled to "command, pay, and emolument" of their permanent rank in the Regular Army. No person who had served in any capacity in the Confederacy was permitted to hold any position or office in the Army.

The Act's 38 sections dealt with a wide variety of other issues, two of which had long-lasting impact on the Army. It abolished the sutler system that had been the main provider of subsistence items to soldiers, and authorized the Army's Subsistence Department to provide articles for sale at cost to officers and enlisted men, beginning 1 July 1867. Since then Army commissary stores have provided foodstuffs and related grocery store items at discounted prices to members of the armed forces and their family members.

The act also allowed detail of 20 officers to colleges having an enrollment of at least 150 male students "for the purpose of promoting knowledge of military science among the young men of the United States." Together with the 1862 Morrill Act that provided for military instruction in land-grant colleges, these two acts laid the foundation for the Reserve Officers' Training Corps, which today provides the majority of Army officers.

—*Lieutenant Colonel Clayton R. Newell, USA (Ret)*

Above: *The prescribed standard carried by cavalry regiments in the post–Civil War era through 1887 was of blue silk with painted eagle motif. This relic was carried in its pack train by the ill-fated 7th Cavalry at Little Bighorn. (Little Bighorn Battlefield National Monument, National Park Service)*

Right: *The defeat at Little Bighorn prompted a legion of artists to depict surrounded and outnumbered cavalry troopers ready to receive a final, fatal enemy onslaught. ("The Last Stand," Frederic Remington, Woolaroc Museum, Bartlesville, OK)*

21 September. **Black Regiments Activated.**
The 9th Cavalry is organized at Greenville, Louisiana, under the command of Colonel Edward Hatch, and the 10th Cavalry is organized under the command of Colonel Benjamin H. Grierson at Fort Leavenworth, Kansas. Both units have white officers.

6 November. **Fort Lowell. New Mexico.**
Established on the Chama River near the town of Teirra Amarilla, the fort protects the area against the Ute Indians. Named for Brigadier General Charles R. Lowell, who died of wounds during the Civil War, the post is abandoned in 1869 when the Utes are considered pacified. In 1872 an agency for Utes and Apaches moves into buildings at the fort. The last rations are issued there in 1881.

21 December. **Fetterman Massacre. Fort Phil Kearny, Wyoming.**
Colonel Henry B. Carrington, 18th Infantry, sends Captain William J. Fetterman to rescue a wagon train of wood when it is attacked by Sioux some six miles from the fort. Carrington instructs Fetterman not to go too far from the fort, but he takes offensive action and leads his detachment of 80 soldiers and civilians into a trap set by 1500–2000 Sioux warriors led by Red Cloud. Fetterman's force is wiped out in less than an hour.

1867

January. **Status of the Army.**
The War Department adopts Lieutenant Emory Upton's Infantry Tactics for drill. For the first time, the Army has tactics designed for American soldiers, a significant advance from the regulations Von Steuben developed during the Revolutionary War. Upton, lieutenant colonel of the 25th Infantry, based the new drill on his experience with troops during the Civil War. By August, some 50,000 Springfield rifle-muskets have been altered to fire a breech-loaded metallic cartridge.

2 March. **Soldiers Get a Pay Raise.**
Congress authorizes a increase in Army pay. Officers below the rank of major general receive a raise of one-third and field and mounted officers are entitled to the same compensation as cavalry officers of like grade. Enlisted soldiers are given the same pay as the volunteers at the end of the Civil War, but the increase is for three years only.

30 March. **United States Buys Alaska.**
The United States agrees to purchase Alaska from Russia for $7.2 million.

April. **Raid on Apaches. Fort Whipple, Arizona.**
Captain J. M. Williams, 8th Cavalry, leads 85 soldiers on raids along the Verde River, killing some 50 Apache Indians.

7 April. **Hancock Indian Council. Fort Larned, Kansas.**
General Winfield Scott Hancock summons Cheyenne chiefs to a council but bad weather results in a low turnout. The next day he goes to a Cheyenne and Sioux village to deliver a stern message to more chiefs, but the Indians flee prompting Hancock to comment that "This looks like the commencement of war."

19 April. **Hancock Burns Indian Village. Pawnee Fork, Kansas.**
General Hancock orders an abandoned Cheyenne and Sioux village burned to convince the Indians that he is serious about stopping their raiding.

14 June. **Fort Stevenson Built to Protect Indians. North Dakota.**
Major Joseph N. G. Whistler, 31st Infantry, establishes the fort on the Missouri River as a base for supplies and to protect river traffic and Indians at the Fort Berthold Indian Agency. Named for Brigadier General Thomas G. Stevenson, who was killed during

the Civil War, the post was abandoned in 1883 and turned over to the Fort Berthold Agency for use as a school.

18 June. **Sioux Checked by Fort Ransom. North Dakota.**
Captain George H. Crossman, 10th Infantry, establishes the post on the Cheyenne River to keep the Sioux in check. Named for Brigadier General Thomas E. G. Ransom, the post is abandoned in 1872 when Fort Seward is established.

30 June. **Transportation Routes Get Protection. Montana.**
Major William Clinton, 13th Infantry, establishes Fort Shaw on the Sun River to protect the route between Fort Benton and Helena and prevent the movement of Indians. Named for Colonel Robert G. Shaw, 54th Massachusetts Infantry, it is abandoned in 1891.

17 July. **Fort Totten. North Dakota.**
Captain Samuel A. Wainwright, 31st Infantry, establishes the post on Devils Lake to enforce getting Indians on reservations and to protect settlers traveling from Minnesota to Montana. Named for Brigadier General Joseph G. Totten, chief engineer of the Army, the post is abandoned in 1890 and becomes

Opposite: *On 21 August 1867, men of the 10th U.S. Cavalry, a Regular Army regiment, joined with troopers of the 18th Kansas Volunteer in an attack against Kiowa and Cheyenne warriors. ("Battle of Prairie Dog Creek," Ralph Hines, National Guard Bureau)*

Right: *Infantrymen dispatched to cut wood at Fort Phil Kearny in present-day Wyoming take cover on 2 August 1867 behind wagon beds that serve as makeshift defense works. Their single-shot breech-loading Springfield rifles allowed them to repel a superior enemy force. ("Good Marksmanship and Guts," H. Charles McBarron, Army Art Collection, NMUSA)*

becomes the headquarters for the Fort Totten Indian Agency and an industrial school.

21 July. Fort D. A. Russell Protects Railway Workers. Wyoming.

Colonel John D. Stevenson, 30th Infantry, establishes the post near the present city of Cheyenne to protect railway workers. Named for Brigadier General D. A. Russell, who was killed during the Civil War, the name of the post is changed to Fort Francis E. Warren, the first governor of the state of Wyoming. It is now an Air Force base.

19 July. Post Named for Fetterman. Wyoming.

Major William McEntyre, 4th Infantry, establishes Fort Fetterman on the North Platte River where the Bozeman Trail leaves the river and turns north. Named for Captain William J. Fetterman, the fort protects settlers' routes and controls Indian activities. The Army sells the buildings in 1882 and transfers the military reservation to the Interior Department in 1884. For a time the old post is the nucleus of a cattle town, which eventually disappears.

31 July. Supply Point Established. Texas.

Lieutenant Colonel Samuel D. Sturgis, 6th Cavalry, establishes Fort Griffin near the Clear Fork of the Brazos River to replace Fort Belknap. The post is a supply point for buffalo hunters and protects cattle trails and settlers' routes in the area. Named for Colonel Charles Griffin, 35th Infantry, the site is now a state park.

1 August. Hay Field Fight. Fort C. F. Smith, Montana.

Lieutenant Sigismund Sternberg with 19 soldiers and six civilians equipped with converted breech-loading Springfield and several repeating rifles hold off a much larger force of Sioux warriors with three killed and three wounded. Fortified behind a barrier of a low log corral, the force withstands six hours of attacks before a relief column arrives to disperse the warriors.

2 August. Wagon Box Fight. Fort Phil Kearny, Wyoming.

Captain James W. Powell, 27th Infantry, and a work detail of 31 soldiers armed with breech-loading rifles use wagon boxes as a fort to hold off 1,500 mounted Sioux and Cheyenne warriors. Fortified behind wagons, the force holds off the Indians for four and a half hours until relief arrives and disperses the warriors with howitzer fire. Army losses are three killed and two wounded.

16 August. **Fort Harney. Oregon.**
Lieutenant Colonel George Crook, 23d Infantry, establishes a camp near the present town of Burns for operations against Indians. After a series of name changes the camp is designated a fort and named for Brigadier General William S. Harney. The Army abandons the post in 1880.

27 August. **Post Protects Passes. Montana.**
Captain Robert S. LaMotte, 13th Infantry, establishes Fort Ellis near Bozeman to protect settlers and miners. Located to block Indian raids through Bozeman, Bridger, and Flathead passes, it is named for Colonel Augustus Van Horn Ellis, 124th New York Infantry, who was killed at Gettysburg. The Army abandons the post in 1886.

18 October. **United States Takes Possession of Alaska. Sitka, Alaska.**
Major General Lovell H. Rousseau, accompanied by Major Charles O. Wood, 9th Infantry, and companies of the 9th Infantry and 2d Artillery accept possession of Alaska from a Russian naval captain. The Army has responsibility for Alaska except for customs, commerce, and navigation, which the Treasury Department handles.

26 November. **Frontier Defense System. Texas.**
Captain Benjamin T. Hutchins, 6th Cavalry, establishes Fort Richardson near Jacksboro as part of the defense system to control Indians and protect the cattle trade. Named for Major General Israel B. Richardson, who died of wounds during the Civil War, the post is abandoned in 1878.

December. **Last Unit of Colored Troops Released.**
The 125th U.S. Colored Infantry, organized in Kentucky in 1865, is mustered out of federal service. It is the last regiment of U.S. Colored Troops in the Army.

4 December. **Fort Concho. Texas.**
First Lieutenant Peter M. Boehm, 4th Cavalry, establishes an outpost of Fort Chadborne on the middle branch of the Concho River as part of the defense system from El Paso to the Red River. Captain George G. Hunt, 4th Cavalry, later establishes a permanent post at the present town of San Angelo when Fort Chadborne is closed. Named for the river on which it was located, the Army abandoned the post in 1889.

1868

January. **Status of the Army.**
The War Department curtails recruiting activities and reduces the enlisted strength of all infantry and dismounted artillery companies to 50 men. The Army records only about 14,000 enlistments by October. During the year, the Army opens two schools. The Artillery School at Fort Monroe, Virginia, which

Left: *With a Sharps carbine at the ready, a cavalry company first sergeant, identified by the diamond insignia, appears in the field uniform of the 1860s, which consisted of surplus from the Civil War. ("First Sergeant," Don Stivers)*

closed on the eve of the Civil War, resumes operation, and a Signal School of Instruction opens at Fort Greble in Washington, D.C. It moves to Fort Whipple (later Fort Myer) in 1869 and remains in operation until 1885.

29 April. Laramie Treaty Briefly Ends Sioux Fighting. Fort Laramie, Wyoming.

Lieutenant General William T. Sherman and Sioux chiefs sign a treaty that agrees to most of Red Cloud's demands. As a result, the Army abandons its posts along the Bozeman Trail. Known as the Fort Laramie Treaty, it holds for a number of years but is eventually undone by white encroachment on Indian lands for a railroad and gold.

May. Grant Named Candidate.

The Republican party names General Ulysses S. Grant, commanding general of the Army, its candidate for President. He remains in his Army position while campaigning and wins the election in November.

4 May. Border Post Established. Arizona.

Captain Stephen G. Whipple, 32d Infantry, establishes Camp Crittenden, named for Colonel Thomas L. Crittenden, 32d Infantry. Located near the source of the Sonita River, the camp controls Apache Indians, protects settlers, and guards the border with Mexico. The Army abandons the camp in 1873 because it is considered an unhealthy site.

1 June. Schofield Appointed Secretary of War.

John M. Schofield becomes the Secretary of War. He is a graduate of the U.S. Military Academy and served in the Civil War, rising to the rank of brigadier general in the Regular Army. After serving as Secretary until March 1869, he returns to Army duty and is promoted to major general. He serves in various command positions until 1888, when he becomes commanding general of the Army.

30 June. Bozeman Trail Post Replaced. Wyoming.

Major Richard I. Dodge, 30th Infantry, establishes Fort Fred Steele on the North Platte River as part of the protective system for the Union Pacific Railroad and the Overland Trail. Named for Colonel Frederick Steele, 20th Infantry, the post is a partial replacement for the forts abandoned along the Bozeman Trail in compliance with the Laramie Treaty. The Army abandons the post in 1886.

17–25 September. Battle of Beechers Island. Republican River, Colorado.

A group of 50 Army scouts under Major George A. Forsyth holds off a Cheyenne and Ogallala Sioux war party of 600–700 warriors under Chief Roman Nose from a sandy island in the Arikaree Fork of the Republican River. Forsyth and some 20 scouts are wounded and Lieutenant Frederick H. Beecher and three scouts are killed. Roman Nose is killed in the fighting. After eight days of fighting, a company of the 10th Cavalry, a black regiment, led by Captain Louis H. Carpenter, comes to their rescue.

Above: *On a sandy high point in the middle of a meandering stream, a few Regular Army officers and a group of well-armed civilian scouts held off overwhelming odds in one of the most dramatic engagements fought in the West. ("Battle of Beecher's Island," Robert Lindneux, Courtesy Colorado Historical Society)*

15 November. **Comanche Campaign Opens. Fort Bascom, New Mexico.**
Major Andrew W. Evans, 3d Cavalry, departs with six companies of cavalry, one company of the 37th Infantry, and a battery of mountain howitzers in search of a Comanche raiding party.

18 November. **Post Established to Support Winter Campaigning. Oklahoma.**
Captain John H. Page, 3d Infantry, establishes Camp Supply near the present town of Fort Supply to support Major General Philip Sheridan's upcoming winter campaign. Designated a fort in 1878, it is abandoned in 1894 and turned over to Oklahoma, becoming the Western State Hospital for the mentally ill in 1903.

23 November. **Sheridan Begins Winter Campaigning. Camp Supply, Oklahoma.**
Major General Philip Sheridan, commanding the Department of the Missouri, institutes a winter campaign to locate elusive Indian bands. The campaign begins when the 7th Cavalry under the command of Lieutenant Colonel George A. Custer sets out early in the morning in search of Indians.

27 November. **Battle of the Washita. Oklahoma.**
Custer leads the 7th Cavalry in a successful attack on Black Kettle's Cheyenne camp on the Washita River in Indian Territory, killing 103 Indians, including 93 women, old men, and children. Black Kettle and his wife are among the dead. A larger camp of Kiowa, Arapahoe, Cheyenne, and Comanche Indians close by initiates a new battle that comes near to disaster for the 7th. They are saved when the regimental quartermaster drives a wagon load of ammunition through the Indians to resupply the beleaguered cavalrymen. Some 50 Indians are killed and about the same number wounded. Some 50 women and children are captured along with supplies and ponies. Major Joel H. Elliott and Captain Louis M. Hamilton, grandson of Alexander Hamilton, and 19 soldiers die in the battle; 13 are wounded.

5 December. **Fort Omaha. Nebraska.**
Captain William Sinclair, 3d Artillery, establishes the post within the present city limits of Omaha. First called Camp Sherman for Lieutenant General William T. Sherman, the name is changed to Omaha in 1869. The garrison is withdrawn in 1895 when the post is replaced by Fort Crook. The Army retains the military reservation when it is unable to get a reasonable price for the property.

EYEWITNESS: BATTLE OF BEECHER'S ISLAND

On 17 September 1868, Brevet Colonel George A. Forsyth and his newly formed 50-man scout unit were attacked by more than 700 Sioux and Cheyenne warriors along the Arickaree Fork of the Republican River in Colorado. Forsyth's command withstood an eight-day siege before being relieved by a company of the 10th Cavalry on 25 September. He describes the battle:

"As my scouts were to serve as soldiers, I organized the command as a troop of cavalry. Our equipment was simple: a blanket apiece, saddle and bridle, a lariat and picket-pin, a canteen, a haversack, butcher-knife, tin plate, and tin cup. A Spencer repeating rifle, . . . a Colt's revolver, army size, and 140 rounds of rifle and 30 rounds of revolver ammunition per man—this carried on the person. Each man, officers included, carried seven days' cooked rations in his haversack.

"At early dawn, as I was standing by a sentry near one of the outposts. . . . It had begun to be light enough by this time to see dimly surrounding objects within a few hundred yards, when suddenly Grover . . . placed his hand on my shoulder and said, 'Oh, heavens, general, look at the Indians!'

"The ground seemed to grow them. The command was ordered to lead their horses to the little island just in front of us, to form a circle facing outward, securely tie their horses to the bushes just outside the circle. . . . throw themselves on the ground, and entrench themselves as rapidly as possible.

"No sooner were the charging warriors fairly under way than a withering fire was suddenly poured in upon us . . . and then came a sudden lull. Sitting upright in my pit as well as I was able, I shouted, 'Now!' and 40 good men and true sent their first of seven successive volleys into the ranks of the charging warriors.

"Crash! On they came, answering back the first volley with a ringing war-whoop. Crash! And now I began to see falling warriors, ay, and horses too; but still they sweep forward with yet wilder yells. Crash! They seem to be fairly falling over each other, both men and horses down in heaps, and wild shrieks from the women and children on the hills proclaim that they too see the slaughter of their braves; but still they come. Crash! They have ceased to yell, but yet come bravely on. What? No! Yes, down goes their medicine-

man; but Roman Nose still recklessly leads the column. But now I can see great gaps in their ranks, showing that our bullets have tolled heavily among them. Crash! Can I believe my eyes? Roman Nose is down! He and his horse lie dead together on the sand, and for an instant the column shakes; but a hundred yards more and they are upon us! Crash! They stagger! They draw half rein! They hesitate! They are breaking! Crash! The Indians divide each side of the little breastwork, throw themselves almost beneath the off side of their chargers, and with hoarse cries of rage and anguish break for either bank of the river, and scatter wildly in every direction, as the scouts, springing to their feet with a ringing cheer, pour in volley after volley from their revolvers almost in the very faces of their now demoralized and retreating foe."

In the engagement, Forsyth was thrice wounded; Lieutenant F. H. Beecher and Surgeon Moore were killed. The command lost four killed and 15 wounded. As Forsyth said, "It was no ordinary command, this company of 50 scouts."

—*Vince Hawkins*

Above: *Civil War veteran George Forsyth commanded the besieged defenders of Beecher's Island. (National Archives)*

1869

January. Status of the Army.
In March Congress reduces the number of infantry regiments to 25, cutting the Army's authorized strength to 37,313. Part of the reorganization combines the four black infantry regiments, which have been understrength since their organization into two new units. The 38th and 41st become the 24th Infantry, and the 39th and 40th join to be the 25th Infantry. Both of the new regiments serve in the West. Because of the confusion about brevet ranks and seniority, Congress requires officers to wear the uniform and insignia of their Regular Army rank rather than brevet ranks received during the Civil War, and brevet ranks are no longer considered senior to regular ranks.

7 January. Base of Operations Established. Oklahoma.
Major General Philip Sheridan establishes Fort Sill as a base for conducting operations against the Kiowa and Cheyenne Indians. Located at the junction of Cache and Medicine Bluff Creeks, the post is named for Brigadier General Joshua W. Sill, who was killed during the Civil War. The fort plays a central role in controlling the southern Plains Indians, and after 1876

Above: *The 21st Infantry Band played as part of the 10 May 1869 "golden spike" ceremony, when ribbons of steel at last linked the United States from coast to coast. (National Park Service)*

the garrison protects Indians in the area. The post remains active as the Army's field artillery school.

18 February. Light Artillery School Authorized. Fort Riley, Kansas.
The School of Instruction for Light Artillery is the Army's first school to open since the end of the Civil War. There is no theoretical instruction, and the school is discontinued in March 1871.

4 March. Grant Inaugurated President.
Grant becomes the eighteenth President of the United States. His administration institutes the so-called Peace Policy for dealing with hostile Indians, frustrating some Army commanders on the Western frontier who would like to follow a harder line.

8 March. Sherman Replaces Grant as Commanding General of the Army.
William Tecumseh Sherman becomes the commanding general of the Army, succeeding Grant and receiving the four-star rank of general. At the same time Philip Sheridan is appointed a lieutenant general. Sherman remains commanding general until 1 November 1883, becoming the second longest serving commanding general of the Army. Only Winfield Scott held the office longer. Sherman begins the tradition of being politically neutral while in office. While commanding general he establishes a system of Army schools.

13 March. **Grant Appoints Rawlins Secretary of War.**
John A. Rawlins becomes Secretary of War. During
the Civil War he served with Ulysses S. Grant as his
aide de camp and principal advisor. At the beginning
of the war he was a major in the 45th Illinois Infantry,
but by 1865 he was a major general in the Regular
Army. After serving only six months as Secretary,
Rawlins dies of tuberculosis while still in office.

6 April. **Alaska Expedition Begins. San Francisco,
California.**
Captain Charles W. Raymond, an Engineer officer,
boards the brig *Commodore* to sail to Sitka, Alaska,
and conduct an expedition along the Yukon River. At
Sitka he meets his escort, Private Michael Foley of the
9th Infantry.

6 April. **Winter Campaigning. Fort Hays, Kansas.**
Lieutenant Colonel George Custer's column arrives at
the post, ending Sheridan's winter campaign.

10 May. **Transcontinental Railroad Completed.
Promontory Point, Utah.**
A battalion of the 21st Infantry commanded by Major
Milton Cogswell serves as the honor guard for the
ceremony that links the Central Pacific and Union
Pacific railroads. Continuing on to the Presidio of San
Francisco, the battalion becomes the first military unit
to cross the continent by rail.

9 June. **Republican River Expedition. Fort
McPherson, Nebraska.**
Major Eugene Carr, 5th Cavalry, leads eight troops of
cavalry and three companies of Pawnee scouts, a total
of 500 men, in search of Tall Bull and his band of
Cheyenne.

28 June. **Protection for Indians and Miners. Wyoming.**
First Lieutenant Patrick Henry Breslin, 4th Infantry,
establishes Camp Augur at the present town of
Lander to protect the Bannock and Shoshone Indians
and settlers in the Sweetwater mining district. Named
for Brigadier General Christopher C. Augur, the post
is abandoned in 1871 when Fort Washakie is
established.

July. **Expedition to Find Military Routes. Camp
Halleck, Nevada.**
Lieutenant George M. Wheeler begins a five-month
expedition in eastern Nevada. He seeks a route for a
military road for moving troops from the Pacific
Department to posts in Arizona and Nevada to
monitor Mormon settlements and protect mining
camps.

Above: *William Tecumseh Sherman replaced Ulysses
Grant as commanding general of the Army. (Daniel
Huntington, Army Art Collection, NMUSA)*

4 July. **Alaska Expedition Claims British Fort. Fort
Hamilton, Lower Yukon.**
Captain Charles W. Raymond, Private Foley, and 11
others board two whaleboats towed by a small river
steamer and head up the Yukon River. After 27 days
they arrive at Fort Yukon, a British trading post
located almost exactly on the Arctic Circle. Raymond
uses astronomical observations to prove that the post
is on American soil and takes formal possession of the
fort, ordering the British traders to leave.

8 July. **Fort Pembina Meets Local Defense Request.
North Dakota.**
Captain Lloyd Wheaton, 20th Infantry, establishes a
fort near the town of Pembina on the Red River of the
North when the Minnesota legislature petitions
Congress for protection because of Indian unrest in
the Red River Valley. The post is abandoned in 1895
after a large fire.

11 July. **Battle of Summit Springs. Colorado.**
Major Eugene Carr, 5th Cavalry, and his 500 men,
guided by Army scout William "Buffalo Bill" Cody,
surprise and attack Tall Bull's village near Summit
Springs. The chief and 52 others are killed, while Carr
suffers but one wounded soldier. The surviving
Indians retire to a reservation.

Left: *Among the Army outposts on the Pacific coast abandoned as troops were pulled east to fight the Civil War was Fort Bragg, California, named after Braxton Bragg for his notable service in the Mexican War. ("Fort Bragg," Alexander Edouart, Army Art Collection, NMUSA)*

25 October. **Belknap Becomes Secretary of War.**
William W. Belknap becomes Secretary of War. He served in the Civil War, where he was commissioned a major in the 15th Iowa Infantry in 1861, rose to command the 4th Division in XVII Corps, and mustered out in 1865 as a major general. A lawyer by profession, he is a collector of internal revenue in Iowa when President Ulysses S. Grant names him to replace John M. Rawlins. Impeached for taking money in return for appointing post traders, he resigns in 1876. The Senate tries Belknap after he leaves office, but there are not enough votes to convict.

1870

January. **Status of the Army.**
During the year Congress approves new pay scales for officers ranging from $1,400 for an infantry second lieutenant to $3,500 for a colonel. Enlisted pay increases to $13 a month for a private and $22 for line sergeants. A sergeant major receives $36 a month. Congress also reduces the number of enlisted soldiers in the Army to 30,000 and provides for retirement after 30 years of service.

16 May. **Fort Apache. Arizona.**
Major John Green, 1st Cavalry, establishes the post near the present town of Fort Apache to control Coyotero Apaches. The Army abandons the post in 1924 and turns it over to the Indian Service for use as a school.

19 May. **Medal of Honor Awarded to Black Soldier. Fort McKavett, Texas.**
Sergeant Emanuel Stance, 9th Cavalry, leads a scouting party in pursuit of a band of Apaches who have stolen some horses. The day after the troopers recover the horses Stance observes several Indians about to fire on two government wagons, so he immediately orders his men to attack, causing the Apaches to retreat. For his actions Stance receives the Medal of Honor on 9 July, only six weeks after the engagement, becoming the first black soldier after the Civil War to be so honored.

27 May. **Fort Built for Interior Department. Idaho.**
Captain James E. Putnam, 12th Infantry, establishes Fort Hall at the request of the Interior Department to control the Shoshoni and Bannock Indians reservations. Located near the town of Blackfoot, it is named for a Hudson's Bay Company fort. The Army abandons the post in 1883 and transfers it to the Interior Department for use by the Indian Service.

30 June. **Upton Appointed Commandant of Cadets.**
Lieutenant Colonel Emory Upton, 25th Infantry, becomes the commandant of cadets at the Military Academy. His writings argue for numerous reforms in the Army, the best known of which, *The Military Policy of the United States*, is published in 1904, after his death by suicide in 1881. Circulated within the Army before its publication, it made the case for a strong Regular Army, advocating a professional army based on the German model.

August. **Seminole-Negro Scouts Recruited. Fort Duncan, Texas.**

Lieutenant John L. Bullis, 24th Infantry, recruits a group of Seminole Negro Indian scouts. Most are descendents of runaway slaves who had taken refuge among the Seminole Indians in Florida. They serve along the Southwest border of the United States, usually with one of the Army's four black regiments.

20 August. **Fort Stambaugh Protects Miners. Wyoming.**

Major James S. Brisbin, 2d Cavalry, establishes the post to protect miners when the boundaries of the Shoshone Indian Reservation were drawn near the Sweetwater mining district. Located between Atlantic City and the Oregon Trail, the post is named for First Lieutenant Charles B. Stambaugh, 2d Cavalry, who was killed by Indians in Wyoming. The Army abandoned the post in 1878.

22 August. **Yellowstone Expedition. Fort Ellis, Montana.**

Lieutenant Gustavus C. Doane and five enlisted men accompany a scientific expedition to Yellowstone. By the last week in August the expedition reaches Lake Yellowstone, where they become the first white men to see what is now Yellowstone National Park.

1 November. **Army Begins National Weather Service.**

The Signal Corps establishes a congressionally mandated national weather service. A group of 22 Signal Corps observer-sergeants are organized to report observations by telegraph daily. By 1873, the Signal Corps is issuing some 70 weather bulletins a day and almost as many weather maps. The Signal Corps staffs offices across the country with trained observers who provide meteorological data for weather forecasts.

1871

January. **Status of the Army.**

The Army has 26,848 enlisted men and 2,105 officers in the Army for a total of 28,953, well below authorized strength.

January. **Fort Washakie Named for Shoshone Chief. Wyoming.**

Captain Robert A. Torrey, 13th Infantry, establishes the post near the present town of Fort Washakie to protect the Shoshone Indians. Originally called Camp Brown, the name is changed in 1878 to honor Chief Washakie, a Shoshone leader. The Army plans to abandon the post in 1899, but the chief, then 90 years old, objects. In 1909 the post is turned over to the Interior Department to become the headquarters for the Shoshone Agency.

3 May. **United States Geographical Survey Begins. Camp Halleck, Nevada.**

First Lieutenant George Montague Wheeler, an Engineer officer, assembles a party of 30 men to

Right: *Although they rode into battle on horses, in most instances cavalrymen in the American West dismounted to fight on foot in an extended skirmish line as prescribed by the tactics of the time. ("On the Skirmish Line," Charles Schreyvogel, National Cowboy & Western Heritage Museum, Oklahoma City, OK)*

explore and map the area south of the Central Pacific Railroad tracks. In addition to topographical data and accurate maps, Wheeler gathers information about the numbers, habits, and disposition of Indians in the area, sites suitable for military operations and routes for roads or railroads. Assisted by Lieutenants D. A. Lyle, 2d Artillery, and D. W. Lockwood, Corps of Engineers, Wheeler organizes his force into several survey parties, which work independently. They meet in Death Valley, California, in July, where they endure temperatures up to 120 degrees. This effort begins the United States Geographical Surveys Beyond the 100th Meridian.

2 July. Army Expedition Contributes to Yellowstone National Park. Chicago.

Captain J. W. Barlow and a small party of engineers and explorers depart on a mission to construct and accurately map of the head-waters of the Yellowstone River. Traveling by train, stagecoach, and wagon they reach Yellowstone Lake on 29 July. He describes the "superbly beautiful" geysers "scattered so lavishly" along the river "surrounded by with high enclosing hills clothed with rich foliage." His report, published by the U.S. Senate, contributes to the establishment of Yellowstone National Park in 1872.

16 September. Grand Canyon Expedition Begins. Camp Mojave, California.

Lieutenant George M. Wheeler and a party of civilians that include an artist and photographer, a sergeant, five enlisted soldiers from C Company, 12th Infantry, and more than a dozen Mojave Indian guides start up the Colorado River in three boats. When they enter Paiute country, the Mojave guides become nervous about entering a stronghold of their traditional enemies. Wheeler manages a truce between the tribes and the expedition continues upriver toward the Grand Canyon.

20 October. Grand Canyon Expedition Rescued. Diamond Creek, Arizona.

Wheeler's expedition, down to its last bits of food and the boats leaking, meets the rescue party that had been summoned earlier. In his report Wheeler proposes a broad plan to complete the engineer map of the western part of the country that eventually leads to a change in how the surveys were made.

1872

January. Status of the Army.

The Army convenes a board to examine and test weapons. After examining more than 100 firearms, the Army adopts the single-shot Model Springfield breechloader that fires a center-fire .45-caliber cartridge. During the year the Adjutant General's Department adopts the topographic engineer shield as a branch insignia. The shield symbolizes the Adjutant General's role of speaking for the commander, and 13 embossed stars replaced the initials T. E. on the upper

Opposite: *In the unfortunate instance when soldiers became Indian captives, they could face a horrible fate of torture and death. ("Missing," Frederic Remington, Thomas Gilcrease Institute of American Art, Tulsa, OK)*

Right: *Among the Army explorations of the American West in the post-Civil War years was the Wheeler Expedition, the first to make its way through the Grand Canyon in the early 1870s. (National Archives)*

shield. In the Southwest, Cochise, a Chiricahua Apache chief, leads his followers in a series of violent raids against white settlers and the Army. After keeping the Army at bay for months in his stronghold in the Chiricahua Mountains, he received assurances that he and his tribe could remain in their traditional homeland and surrendered to Brigadier General Oliver O. Howard to live on a reservation near the post.

3 April. **Captain Jack Leaves Reservation. Lost River Gap, Oregon.**
Major Elmer Otis holds a conference with the Modoc leader Captain Jack and other leaders of the tribe to persuade them to return to the reservation peacefully. Captain Jack had led his band off the reservation in 1870 when they were harassed by other Modocs. The meeting produces no progress.

12 April. **Oregon Superintendent Asked to Move Modocs. Oregon.**
The commissioner of Indian Affairs asks the superintendent of Indian Affairs in Oregon, T. B. Odeneal, to get Captain Jack and his band of Modocs back to the reservation.

30 April. **Fort Tularosa Protects Apache Reservation. New Mexico.**
Captain Frederick W. Coleman, 15th Infantry, establishes the post to protect the newly opened Apache reservation. When the Indian Bureau moves the agency headquarters the post is reestablished at Horse Creek some 18 miles away. The post is abandoned in 1874 when the Indians were moved to Ojo Caliente, Arizona.

27 May. **Protecting Railroad Workers. North Dakota.**
Captain John C. Bates, 20th Infantry, establishes Fort Seward on the James River near the present town of Jamestown to protect Northern Pacific Railroad workers. Initially called Camp Sykes for Colonel George Sykes, 20th Infantry, the name is changed in 1873 to honor William H. Seward, the Secretary of State. The Army abandons the post in 1877.

14 June. **Fort Abraham Lincoln. North Dakota.**
Lieutenant Colonel Daniel Huston, 6th Infantry, establishes the post on the Missouri River near the town of Bismarck to protect engineers and workers building the Northern Pacific Railroad. Initially named for Colonel Henry Boyd McKean, 81st Pennsylvania Infantry, it is changed to honor the President. The post is abandoned in 1891. The area is now a state park and part of the post has been restored.

6 July. **Odeneal Directed to Move Modocs. Oregon.**
The commissioner of Indian Affairs directs T. B. Odeneal, the superintendent of Indian Affairs in Oregon, to move Captain Jack and his band to the Klamath reservation, using force if necessary.

26 July. Stanley Survey in Sioux Territory. Fort Rice, North Dakota.
Colonel D. S. Stanley takes a party of 33 officers, 553 enlisted men, 13 Indians, and five scouts along with two Gatling guns and a brass cannon to begin a survey east of Bozeman, Montana. Earlier civilian attempts to survey the route had been interrupted by hostile Sioux in the area. The party is under almost constant harassment from a band of Hunkpapa Sioux.

27 July. Support to Stanley Survey. Fort Ellis, Montana.
Major Eugene M. Baker, 2d Cavalry, leads a force along the Yellowstone River to meet Stanley's party from Fort Rice. This group too has challenges from Indians. Early in the morning of 14 August Indians are detected sneaking into the camp. Baker, who has been playing cards and drinking all night, is unable to assume command. His subordinates form a skirmish line and drive off the would-be raiders. Two men are killed in the short fight, which becomes known as the Battle of Poker Flat. The Army is foiled by the Indians and is unsuccessful in providing assistance to the railroad survey in 1872.

28 November. Modoc Campaign Heats Up. Fort Klamath, Oregon.
A cavalry troop under Captain James Jackson departs for Captain Jack's camp on Lost River, arriving there the next day. While the soldiers attempt to disarm the Indians, a Modoc warrior named Scarfaced Charlie and an unidentified Army sergeant engage in a verbal argument that leads to shooting. Neither is hit but a general exchange of gunfire ensues as the Modocs flee to the Lava Beds in California. The encounter leaves

one soldier killed and seven wounded with two Modoc killed and three wounded. As the Modocs move south, a group led by Hooker Jim kills 18 settlers on November 30.

28 December. Battle of Skull Cave. Salt River Canyon, Arizona.
Army troops led by Captains William M. Brown and James Burns attack a band of Indians at the Battle of Skull Cave, killing 76 Yavapai Apaches.

1873

January. Status of the Army.
Congress grants burial rights in national cemeteries, a responsibility of the Army's Quartermaster Department, to all honorably discharged Civil War veterans. It also appropriates one million dollars for headstones at national cemeteries. The Secretary of War, after being presented with a number of options, decides to use marble or other durable stone for the markers. The design he selects, with minor modifications, is still in use.

17 January. Captain Jack Holds Off Army Forces. Lava Beds, California.
Colonel Frank Wheaton, 21st Infantry, with about 400 men, half of them Regulars, attack Modoc positions in thick fog, but the troops cannot see the Indians and make no progress in the rugged terrain. At the end of the day the Army forces withdraw with losses of 35 killed and 25 wounded. Captain Jack's band of some 150 Modoc Indians, including women and children, suffer no casualties.

Left: *The meager $13 a month paid to privates in the frontier Army was delivered by traveling paymasters at irregular intervals. Possible robberies were to be prevented by details of enlisted men sent to guard the payroll. ("Paymaster's Escort," Rufus Zogbaum, George M. Langellier, Jr., Collection)*

Right: *Because of their valor at Red River, Texas, on 29 September 1872, ten troopers of the 4th U.S. Cavalry received the Congressional Medal of Honor. ("Heroes of Red River," Don Stivers)*

Spring. **Custer Supports Railroad Survey. Fort Rice, North Dakota.**

The 7th Cavalry under Lieutenant Colonel George A. Custer prepares to provide an escort for Colonel D. S. Stanley's expedition to assist the Northern Pacific Railroad survey. In addition Custer is to intimidate the Indians, find locations for new military posts, and make a scientific assessment of the Yellowstone country. With the 7th Cavalry are four companies of the 17th Infantry, five from the 22d Infantry, and a battalion that includes companies from the 8th and 9th Infantry along with 30 Indian scouts. The entire expedition numbers some 1,900 men and 250 wagons. The steamer *Key West* with Colonel George A. Forsyth, the veteran of Beecher Island in 1868, carries supplies up the Yellowstone River to establish a depot for the expedition at the mouth of the Powder River. The scientific party includes civilian specialists in zoology, botany, paleontology, and geology as well as a number of British noblemen, a photographer, an artist, and a taxidermist.

27 March. **Attack on Apaches Prompts Return to Reservation. Turret Peak, Arizona.**

An Army column led by Captain George M. Randall, 23d Infantry, surprises an Apache camp and kills 23 Indians. Many of the Indians report to reservations after the fight.

6 April. **Yavapai Surrender to Crook. Camp Verde, Arizona.**

Some 300 Yavapai under Chalipun surrender to Brigadier General George Crook. By fall more than 6,000 Apache and Yavapai are on reservations in Arizona and New Mexico.

11 April. **Captain Jack Kills Canby. Lava Beds, California.**

Brigadier General Edward R. S. Canby, commander of the Department of the Pacific, with about 1,000 men moves to besiege the Modoc stronghold. In spite of earlier warnings that Captain Jack is planning an attack, Canby and three civilian commissioners arrange a parley with Modoc. When Captain Jack kills Canby and other Indians kill one commissioner and

wound another, the siege is resumed. Canby is the only Regular Army general killed by Indians in the United States.

15 April. Modoc Position Attacked. Lava Beds, California.

Colonel Alvin C. Gillem, 1st Cavalry, uses howitzers and mortars to support attacks against Modoc positions, but for three days most of the Modoc warriors hold off the attack with only one casualty, a boy who is killed when he tries to open a cannon shell with an ax. Several Modoc women reportedly die of sickness. Army losses are seven killed and 13 wounded.

26 April. Modocs Surprise Army. Lava Beds, California.

Captain Evan Thomas with five officers, 66 enlisted soldiers, and 14 Warm Spring Scouts are having lunch near the Lava Beds when they are attacked by 22 Modoc warriors led by Scarfaced Charley. Some of the troops flee, and those who stay to fight are either killed or wounded. Five officers and 13 enlisted men are killed and 16 wounded. The disaster leads to

Above: *Soldiers of the post-Civil War army played an important role in the westward expansion of America. In the fast-moving situations they encountered in protecting settlers from Indians, soldiers frequently found it essential to be able to improvise, as is the case of these infantrymen using their infantry rifles and equipment to carry out a mission better suited to cavalry. ("Guarding the New Frontier," Don Stivers)*

Colonel Gillem being replaced by Brigadier General Jefferson C. Davis.

10 May. Modocs in Disarray. Dry Lake, California.

Modoc warriors attack an Army camp, killing five, two of whom are Warm Spring Indian Scouts, and wounding another 12 soldiers. The Modocs lose five killed, including Ellen's Man, a prominent leader. The deaths lead to dissension among the Modocs, and a group led by Hooker Jim surrenders and agree to help capture Captain Jack.

18 May. Cross-Border Operation. Santa Rosa Mountains, Mexico.

Colonel Ranald S. Mackenzie, 4th Cavalry, leads a force of cavalry and infantry across the Rio Grande into Mexico in pursuit of a band of Apache raiders. Finding a camp of Kickapoos and Lipas, Mackenzie leads a charge that kills 19 warriors. After capturing some 40 women and children and 65 ponies, he destroys the camp and the equipment before moving back across the border.

4 June. Captain Jack Captured. Langell's Valley, California.

With their source of water cut off, the Modocs are forced into the open where Captain Jack and all of his followers are captured. On 4 July, the prisoners arrive at Fort Klamath, Oregon, and four days later, after a trial by the peace commission, six Modoc are found guilty of murdering members of the commission.

Right: *A twelve-pound mountain howitzer and its artillery gunner poised to shell Modoc Indians in their protective positions among the Lava Beds. (National Archives)*

12 June. **Army Expedition Seeks Yellowstone Route. Fort Bridger, Wyoming.**
Captain W. A. Jones, Corps of Engineers, leads a party that includes a geologist, a botanist, an Army surgeon, a chemist, and Lieutenant S. E. Blount of the 13th Infantry as an astronomer to make a reconnaissance for a military road from the Union Pacific Railroad line to Yellowstone National Park. He locates a route through Togwoheap Pass that connects the park with the railroad, and his report, published in 1885, provides extensive new scientific information about the area.

4 August. **Custer Holds Off Sioux. Tongue River, Montana.**
Lieutenant Colonel Custer, moving well ahead of the main body of Colonel Stanley's expedition, surprises a band of about 250 Sioux warriors setting up an ambush. Custer dismounts his cavalry and meets the Indian charge with a disciplined volley of fire. After a three-hour battle Custer orders a daring charge that sweeps the Indians from the field.

11 August. **Custer Holds Off Sioux Again. Bighorn River, Montana.**
After pursuing the Sioux that attacked him on 4 August, Custer is resting his cavalry when some 500 Indians cross the river to attack. Custer seizes the moment, orders the regimental band to play "Gerry Owen," and charges the approaching Indians. As before, the attacking cavalry surprise the Indians and

they flee the field. After the battle, the expedition has no more serious trouble from the Sioux, although the Indians do not appear to be particularly intimidated as had been the plan.

3 October. **Captain Jack and Others Hanged. Fort Klamath, Oregon.**
Four of the six Modoc Indians found guilty of murder—Captain Jack, John Schonchin, Black Jim, and Boston Charley—are hanged. The remainder of the Modoc—39 men, 64 women, and 60 children—are sent to Indian Territory as prisoners of war. In 1909 those that desire to return to the Klamath Reservation are allowed to do so.

1874

January. **Status of the Army.**
In July General William T. Sherman, commanding general of the Army, announces the end of Grant's "Peace Policy" and instructs Lieutenant General Philip Sheridan to aggressively pursue hostile Indians. In October, Sherman moves his headquarters to St. Louis, Missouri, after a series of disagreements with the Secretary of War, William W. Belknap.

16 June. **Army Strength Reduced.**
Congress reduces the enlisted strength of the Army to 25,000. This causes the Army to eliminate its recruiting efforts. Noncommissioned officers and

meritorious soldiers can reenlist but only if they sign up at the posts where their enlistment expire. When strength falls below 25,000 in the middle of November, restricted recruiting resumes.

2 July. **Black Hills Expedition Begins. Fort Abraham Lincoln, North Dakota**
With civilian prospectors searching for gold in the Black Hills, sacred to the Sioux and part of their reservation, Lieutenant Colonel George A. Custer and the 7th Cavalry begin a reconnaissance into the area. His command includes ten companies of cavalry, two companies of infantry, three Gatling guns, and a Rodman cannon as well as a detachment of Indian scouts and guides. Custer's band plays "Gerry Owen" as the 1,000 men and 100 wagons depart the post. The scientific party includes Captain William Ludlow, Corps of Engineers, and civilian specialists in geology, topography, and paleontology.

17 July. **Fort Reno Protects Indian Agency. Oklahoma.**
Lieutenant Colonel Thomas H. Neill, 6th Cavalry, establishes a fort near the present town of El Reno to protect the Darlington Indian Agency. Named for Major General Jesse L. Reno, who was killed during

Above: *The 1874 discovery of gold in the Black Hills by Custer's army expedition opened the floodgates of prospectors to the region and ignited a war with the Lakota (Sioux) and their allies against the settlers and prospectors. (National Archives)*

the Civil War, the post is abandoned in 1908 and becomes a remount station. In 1938 it is the Reno Quartermaster Depot and in 1949 the military reservation becomes the Fort Reno Livestock Research Station.

27 July. **Army Prepares Southern Plains Operations. Fort Leavenworth, Kansas.**
Brigadier General John Pope orders companies from the 6th Cavalry and 5th Infantry to assemble at Fort Dodge, Kansas, and 8th Cavalry units to congregate in New Mexico. The intent is to begin operations against southern Plains Indians.

30 August. **Red River War Opens. Tule Canyon, Texas.**
Colonel Nelson A. Miles, 5th Infantry, leads a force of the 6th Cavalry and 5th Infantry in a five-hour running battle over 12 miles in pursuit of a Cheyenne war party. The Indians make a final stand along the slopes of Tule Canyon. Although Miles forces the Indians to retreat, he cannot follow them because his provisions are exhausted.

30 August. **Reports of Gold in the Black Hills. Fort Abraham Lincoln, North Dakota.**
Custer's expedition to the Black Hills returns with mixed reports. Captain Ludlow doubted on the presence of any significant amount of gold, and the geologist barely mentions it in his report. But Custer's dispatches have included dramatic statements that "gold has been found at several places" and "almost

every panful of earth produced gold in small, yet paying quantities." Bolstered by Custer's enthusiasm, prospectors continue to swarm into the Black Hills.

9–12 September. **Lone Wolf Attacks Supply Train. Washita River, Texas.**
Lone Wolf, Satanta, and Big Tree lead 250 Kiowas and Comanches in an attack on an Army supply train. After a three-day siege Major William R. Price rescues the train.

26 September. **Indian Camp Destroyed. Palo Duro Canyon, Texas.**
Colonel Ranald S. Mackenzie, 4th Cavalry, leads a column of cavalry soldiers in an attack on the winter camp of Kiowa, Comanche, and Cheyenne. The attack separates the Indians from their horses and belongings, forcing them onto the reservation.

23 December. **Fort Yates is Agency Headquarters. North Dakota.**
Established on the Missouri River at the present town of Fort Yates, it is the headquarters for the Standing Rock Sioux Indian Agency and designated as such until 1878, when it is named for Captain George W. Yates, 7th Cavalry, who was killed at the Little Bighorn. It is abandoned as a military post in 1903 but remains the headquarters of the Standing Rock Reservation.

1875

January. **Status of the Army.**
The Army strength is 22,796 enlisted men and 2,068 officers for a total of 24,864. As part of the Army's program of establishing better communications in the west, a 4th Infantry detachment under Lieutenant Adolphus W. Greely completes the first telegraph line into what is now the state of Oklahoma.

3 February. **Fort Elliot Keeps Indians on Reservation. Texas.**
Major Henry Cary Bankhead, 4th Cavalry, establishes the post near the headwaters of Sweetwater Creek to keep Indians on their reservations. Originally a sub-post of Fort Sill, Oklahoma, it is named for Major

Right: *Before the creation of the National Park Service, the U.S. Army dispatched cavalrymen to protect the early national parks from poachers and other intruders who might spoil the pristine wilderness of such sites as Yellowstone. ("Necessary Details of Troops," H. Charles McBarron, Army Art Collection, NMUSA)*

Joel H. Elliott, 7th Cavalry, who was killed on the Washita River. The Army abandons the post in 1890.

6 March. **Cheyenne Surrender. Darlington Agency, Oklahoma.**
Some 820 Cheyenne surrender to Indian agents in one day. This is one of a number of mass surrenders that marks the end of the Red River War.

25 April. **Expedition to Confirm Gold in the Black Hills. Cheyenne, Wyoming.**
With prospectors pouring into the Black Hills and the Sioux growing ever more restive, the Army supports another expedition to look for gold in the area. A group of civilian scientists that includes 11 professional miners receive an escort of 400 soldiers supported by 75 wagons. After an extensive four-month geological

and mineralogical survey the expedition confirms the presence of gold.

1876

January. Status of the Army.

The War Department modifies the regimental tables of organization so that the authorized size of the Army is reduced to 27,442, a number that would not significantly change until the Spanish-American War. The Secretary of War directs the inspector general of the Army to report to the commanding general on all subjects pertaining to military control and discipline. Inspectors general in the field are to report to local commanders, which means they are no longer considered spies from a higher headquarters. This relationship continues today.

8 February. Sheridan Initiates Operations to Subdue Sioux.

From his headquarters of the Division of the Missouri, Lieutenant General Philip Sheridan directs several columns converging on the Yellowstone River to trap the Sioux and force their return to the reservations. One column under Major General George Crook moves north from Fort Fetterman, Wyoming, in late May with about 1,000 troops. At the same time two columns under Brigadier General Alfred H. Terry march up the Yellowstone. Terry moves from Fort Abraham Lincoln, North Dakota, with one column of more than 1,000 men to the

mouth of Powder River. The second column, numbering about 450 men under Colonel John Gibbon, is marching from Fort Ellis, Montana, to the mouth of the Bighorn River.

March. Army Strength Falls.

Captain Henry C. Corbin, 24th Infantry, testifies before Congress that the largest company in his regiment can muster only seven able-bodied soldiers. His testimony reflects the situation of the Army in the West, where most units were badly under strength.

8 March. Taft Appointed Secretary of War.

Alphonso Taft becomes Secretary of War. He has no military experience prior to his appointment. After only a few months in office he is appointed attorney general of the United States. His son, William Howard Taft, becomes the 27th President of the United States in 1909. At Taft's request, General William T. Sherman agrees to move his headquarters back to Washington, D.C., from St. Louis, where he had moved it in 1874.

16 March. Little Bighorn Campaign Begins. Powder River, Montana.

Colonel Joseph J. Reynolds, 3d Cavalry, surprises a Cheyenne-Sioux camp, but a planned attack miscarries, and his column withdraws, leaving two dead soldiers behind.

22 May. **Cameron Replaces Taft as Secretary of War.**
James D. Cameron becomes Secretary of War. He has
no military experience, although during the Civil War
he supervised the movement of Union troops over one
of his father's railroads. After less than a year in office
he leaves to take a seat in the U.S. Senate vacated by
his father. In 1878 he marries General William T.
Sherman's niece.

17 June. **Battle on the Rosebud. Rosebud River,
Montana.**
Crook's troops fight an indecisive engagement with a
large band of Sioux and Cheyenne under Crazy Horse
and Sitting Bull and then move back to the Tongue
River to wait for reinforcements. Meanwhile, Terry is
on the trail of the same Indian band. He sends
Lieutenant Colonel George Custer with the 7th
Cavalry up the Rosebud to locate the war party and
move south of it. Terry, with the rest of his command,
continues up the Yellowstone to meet Gibbon and
close on the Indians from the north.

25 June. **Custer Defeated. Little Bighorn River,
Montana.**
Custer and the 7th Cavalry proceed up the Rosebud
and discover 4,000 to 5,000 Indians, including about
2,500 warriors, camping along the banks of the Little
Bighorn River. Custer divides his forces to strike the
camp from several directions. While Captain
Frederick W. Benteen and 125 men swing farther
south, Major Marcus A. Reno with another 125 men
ford the river and attack the south end of the village.
Reno is forced to withdraw, allowing the Indians to
concentrate on Custer's command. They surround him
on broken terrain east of the Little Bighorn and kill
his force of 211 men. Meanwhile, the combined forces
of Benteen and Reno are able to withstand further
attacks. When the Indians learn of Terry's approach
from the north, they leave.

5 July. **Officer Instructors at Colleges Increased.**
Congress increases the number of officers from the 20
to 30 that the President can detail as instructors at
civilian colleges. This arrangement was first approved
in 1866.

15 August. **Congress Reacts to Little Bighorn Battle.**
Prompted by the disaster at the Little Bighorn,
Congress authorizes adding 2,500 cavalry soldiers to
the Army, but no new units are added to the force
structure. The additional privates became part of
existing cavalry companies. This emergency increase is
eliminated in 1877, when the maximum enlisted
strength of the Army is once again set at 25,000.

Above: *Alphonso Taft (1810–1891) spent only three months
as Secretary of War before being appointed Attorney
General. (Daniel Huntington, Army Art Collection,
NMUSA)*

9 September. **American Horse, Sioux War Chief Killed.
Slim Buttes, Montana.**
Captain Anson Mills, 3d Cavalry, and 150 troopers
surprise and attack a Sioux camp, killing war chief
American Horse and forcing the Indians to surrender
or flee.

12 October. **Fort McKinney Supports Little Bighorn
Campaign. Wyoming.**
Captain Edwin Pollock, 9th Infantry, establishes the
post as part of a series of depots to support an
expedition led by Colonel Ranald Mackenzie, 4th
Cavalry, to pursue Sioux Indians. Initially called
Cantonment Reno because of its proximity to the
abandoned post of the same name, it is named for
First Lieutenant John A. McKinney, who was killed
by Indians. The fort becomes a center for controlling
Indians in the cattle country east of the Bighorn
Mountains. The Army abandons the post in 1894 and
the next year the buildings and part of the land were
given to Wyoming, which made it the State Soldiers'
and Sailors' Home in 1903.

Above: *The defeat of the 7th Cavalry at Little Bighorn became part of Western lore, and many artists have imagined what the regiment's final moments were like. Archeological studies have answered some questions and raised others. ("Custer's Last Stand," Mort Künstler)*

14 November. **Expedition to Find Crazy Horse. Fort Fetterman, Wyoming.**
A column of about 2,200 men under Colonel Ranald Mackenzie leaves in search of Crazy Horse. The force includes 11 troops of cavalry, 15 companies of infantry, and 400 Indian scouts. Supporting the soldiers are 300 civilians with 168 wagons and 400 pack mules.

25 November. **Cheyenne Village Destroyed. Powder River, Montana.**
In below-freezing weather, companies of the 2d, 4th, and 5th Cavalry under Colonel Ranald S. Mackenzie surprise the Cheyenne village of Dull Knife and Little Wolf and destroy it after a fierce fight. Six soldiers are killed and 11 wounded. The Indians lose 40 killed and all of their food, clothing, and shelter.

1877

January. **Status of the Army.**
The last Army troops leave the South, ending the federal military occupation that began in 1865.

President Rutherford B. Hayes uses Army troops in railway strikes that spread to more than a dozen states. Federal soldiers have very little contact with mobs but their presence tends to contribute to restoring order. Signal Corps observer-sergeants report strike conditions in their area to Washington.

8 January. **Crazy Horse Attacks Miles. Wolf Mountain, Montana.**
More than 500 Sioux and Cheyenne led by Crazy Horse attack Colonel Nelson Miles' camp during a snowstorm. Alerted ahead of time, Miles and his men defeat the attack. Casualties are light on both sides.

12 February. **Fort Huachuca Built for Operations Against Apaches. Arizona.**
Captain Samuel M. Whiteside, 6th Cavalry, establishes the post to protect settlers. Located 15 miles north of the Mexican border, it sees little use after Geronimo is captured in 1886 and is transferred to the state of Arizona in 1949 for use by Army National Guard troops and the state Fish and Game Commission. Reactivated in 1951, it now houses Army signal and intelligence facilities.

12 March. **McCrary Appointed Secretary of War.**
George W. McCrary becomes Secretary of War. A lawyer and politician from Indiana, he has no prior military experience. During his tenure federal troops

EYEWITNESS: BATTLE AT THE ROSEBUD

In 1876, the U.S. Army deployed a massive expedition against the free-roaming bands of Plains Indians, most notably the Sioux. Three Army columns moving from Montana and Nebraska converged on the Bighorn River country known to be a favorite Indian hunting area. The largest columns under Brigadier General George Crook, totaling over 1,325 men, was the first to encounter the enemy. On 17 June, while camped along the Rosebud River, Crook's column was surprised by an estimated force of 1,500 Sioux and Cheyenne warriors led by Crazy Horse. Trooper Phineas Towne recounts his role in the desperate battle:

"General Crook gave orders to saddle up. . . . After we had saddled and formed into line, my troop, F, Third Cavalry, was placed on the left flank of the command, and it with two other troops were detailed as skirmishers and were ordered to make a flank movement to our left and gain the hills, where we dismounted, leaving each fourth trooper to hold the horses. We then formed a skirmish line on foot, which was commanded by Lieutenant-Colonel Royall.

"After perhaps two hours, we were ordered to fall back and remount our horses to take a new position (our horses were held in check in a ravine) as it was impossible to hold our present position against such overwhelming odds. I must say that I never saw so great a body of Indians in one place as I saw at that time. . . . It seemed that if one Indian was shot five were there to take his place. If we had remained in our first position we would all have been killed, and I consider that we retreated in the right time.

"I had not gone more than one third of the distance from our position to where the horses were when I overtook three other soldiers of my own troop carrying a sergeant by the name of Marshall, who had been shot through the face. I knew that time was precious and none to lose. . . . Glancing back, I saw the hostiles coming over the hill. I said to the others, 'Quick, here they come!'

"At that instant my comrades, to save themselves, dropped the wounded sergeant and hastened to their horses. . . . Grasping him with all my strength, I carried my comrade until it was useless to carry him any farther, for he was dead. I then laid him down and left him and hurried to get away.

"I don't think I had gone more than ten yards when I was surrounded by about 20 or more of the most murdering looking Indians I ever saw. You can talk of seeing devils; here they were in full form. . . . It was enough to strike terror to anyone's heart.

"I knew that my time had come, I knew that I would be taken prisoner. I fought, but it was fighting against terrible odds. There I was down in that ravine, alone in the midst of a lot of murderous savages.

"Taking my carbine from me and throwing a lariat over my head and tightening it about my feet, I was helpless. This was all done in an instant, while I struggled and fought in vain, until I was struck on the head with something which rendered me unconscious and caused me to fall. As I went down a bullet struck me in the body.

"I think that when the bullet struck me I regained my consciousness, because I realized I was being dragged at a lively pace over the ground by a pony at the other end of the lariat.

"After I was dragged in this manner for some distance, my captors were charged by one of the troops of cavalry, and to save themselves from capture abandoned me and made their escape. Thus I was enabled to regain my liberty."

—*Vince Hawkins*

Above: *Guy V. Henry survived life-threatening wounds to continue a distinguished career as a cavalry officer. (Wyoming State Archives)*

withdraw from the reconstruction governments in South Carolina and Louisiana. He resigns in 1879 to accept a seat on the U.S. Court of Appeals for the Eighth Circuit.

3 April. **Prisoners Sought. Piedras Negras, Mexico.**
Lieutenant Colonel William R. Shafter, 24th Infantry, leads a column of black cavalry and infantry across the Rio Grande to demand the release of two Mexican prisoners who had assisted the Army. The prisoners had been removed earlier by Mexican authorities, and Shafter's incursion creates a diplomatic crisis between the United States and Mexico.

Below: *In a scene reminiscent of the clash at Wounded Knee, cavalry troopers in overcoats engage in a brisk fight during the dead of winter. ("Through the Smoke Sprang the Daring Young Soldier," Frederic Remington, Amon Carter Museum, Fort Worth, TX)*

16 April. **Fort Sherman. Idaho.**
Lieutenant Colonel Henry Clay Merriam, 2d Infantry, establishes the post to protect settlers. First designated for its location on Lake Coeur d'Alene, it is renamed for General William T. Sherman in 1887. The Army abandones the post in 1900.

20 April. **Geronimo Arrested. Ojo Caliente Reservation, Arizona.**
Indian agent John Clum arrests Geronimo and sends him to the San Carlos reservation.

5 May. **Crazy Horse Surrenders. Nebraska.**
Crazy Horse, war leader of the Oglala Lakota Sioux, and some 1,000 men, women, and children surrender.

7 May. **Sioux Chiefs Lame Deer and Iron Star Killed. Muddy Creek, Montana.**
Colonel Nelson Miles, leading a force of cavalry and

infantry, surprise Lame Deer's Sioux camp. Lame Deer and Iron Star attempt to surrender, but when they believe an Indian scout is aiming at them shots are fired and both men are killed. The Sioux have 14 killed in the fighting, and Miles loses four killed and seven wounded.

1 June. **McCrary Authorizes Cross-Border Operations.**
George W. McCrary, Secretary of War, issues an order that allows the Army to cross the Rio Grande into Mexico when in direct pursuit of "a band of marauders."

13 June. **Nez Perce Kill Settlers. Wallowa Valley, Washington**
Angry at mistreatment, Nez Perce warriors kill four settlers and flee north under Chief Joseph. Brigadier General Oliver O. Howard follows the Indians.

14 June. **First Black Graduate of the U.S. Military Academy.**
Lieutenant Henry O. Flipper becomes the first black cadet to graduate from the U.S. Military Academy. He is assigned to the 10th Cavalry.

17 June. **Confrontation with Nez Perce. White Bird Canyon, Washington.**
Captain David Perry, 1st Cavalry, with two troops of

Above: *Occasionally military columns were able to locate an Indian village, which was most vulnerable to attack in the early hours of the morning while its inhabitants slept. ("Attack at Dawn," Charles Schreyvogel, Thomas Gilcrease Institute of History and Art, Tulsa, OK)*

Regulars and a group of volunteers attempt to meet with Nez Perce Indians under a flag of truce, but civilian volunteers open fire, beginning a fierce fight. Perry loses 34 dead while the Indians have but three wounded.

25 June. **Fort Missoula Eases Residents' Concerns. Montana.**
Captain Charles C. Rawn, 7th Infantry, establishes a fort near the town of Missoula when residents express concern that moving the Salish Indians from the Bitterroot Valley to the Jocko Indian Reservation might cause an uprising. The post is garrisoned occasionally and remains an Army installation.

4 July. **Fort Custer Helps Control Sioux. Montana.**
Lieutenant Colonel George P. Buell, 11th Infantry, establishes the post on a bluff where the Bighorn and Little Bighorn rivers converge. Built to control the Sioux, it is named for Lieutenant Colonel George A. Custer. The Army abandons the post in 1898.

Above: *Keeping the far-scattered garrisons in the West supplied proved a costly and sometimes dangerous mission. ("Attack on the Supply Wagons," Frederic Remington, Private Collection)*

11 July. Howard Attacks Nez Perce Village. Clearwater, Idaho.

Brigadier General Oliver O. Howard and a force of 400 men attack a Nez Perce village and the fighting continues until dark. The next morning Captain Marcus P. Miller maneuvers a battalion of the 4th Artillery that is fighting as infantry into position to break the Indian defenses. The Army has 13 dead and 27 wounded, while the Nez Perce escape with light casualties.

August. Northern Cheyenne Unhappy on Reservation. Oklahoma.

More than 940 hostile Northern Cheyenne arrive at the Cheyenne and Arapaho Indian Agency, where they are quartered with the more peaceful Southern Cheyenne. About 375 of the Northern Cheyenne led by Dull Knife, Wild Hog, and Little Wolf will not affiliate with the Southern Cheyenne.

9 August. Nez Perce Village Surprised. Big Hole River, Montana.

Colonel John Gibbon surprises a Nez Perce camp. Looking Glass attacks but is driven off after the Indians kill two officers, 22 enlisted men, and six civilians. The Nez Perce have 89 killed, many of whom are women and children.

19 August. Nez Perce Capture Army Mules. Camas Meadows, Washington.

Some 200 Nez Perce warriors skirmish with Army troops and make off with 150 mules.

2 September. Victorio Leaves Reservation. San Carlos Reservation, Arizona.

Victorio, an Apache chief, leads a band of 310 followers from the reservation.

5 September. Crazy Horse Killed. Camp Robinson, Nebraska.

Crazy Horse, war leader of the Oglala Lakota Sioux, is killed while resisting confinement at the post guardhouse. He is buried in an unknown grave on the Plains and remembered as the greatest of all Sioux leaders.

13 September. Nez Perce Elude Trap. Canyon Creek, Montana.

Colonel Samuel D. Sturgis, 7th Cavalry, attempts to trap a band of Nez Perce, but they successfully elude the cavalry and escape.

30 September. Miles Parleys With Chief Joseph. Bear Paw Mountain, Montana.

Troops under Colonel Nelson A. Miles catch the Nez Perce following a long and bloody pursuit over 1,700 miles. After a day of fighting Miles holds a parley with Chief Joseph. They come to no agreement and both sides exchange sporadic gunfire for the next five days.

THE CUSTER BROTHERS: GLORY ENOUGH FOR TWO

As boys they were renown for their horseplay and practical jokes, traits they continued as grown men. They spent all their adult lives in the Army, much of it serving together. On a hot Sunday in June 1876, they died side by side.

George Armstrong and Thomas Ward Custer were both born in New Rumley, Ohio. George, the eldest of five children, was born on 5 December 1839; his younger brother, Thomas on 15 March 1845. George entered West Point in 1857, but due to the outbreak of the Civil War graduated early in June 1861. Assigned as a second lieutenant to the 2d U.S. Cavalry, George saw his first action at Bull Run in July. In September of that same year, Tom enlisted as a private in the 21st Ohio Volunteer Infantry.

For the next two years, circumstances kept the brothers apart, George fighting in the east while Tom served in the western theater. In 1862 George served on General George B. McClellan's staff, then transferred to General Alfred Pleasanton's cavalry staff, fighting at Antietam and Fredericksburg. Tom's unit engaged primarily in construction and occupation duties before fighting at Nashville and Stone's River. In June, en route to Gettysburg, George was promoted from captain to brigadier general of volunteers and given command of a Michigan cavalry brigade. George fought with distinction, earning a brevet to Regular major. Tom fought at Chickamauga, then served as escort for Generals George Thomas and U.S. Grant during the battles for Missionary Ridge.

In 1864, his three-year service concluded, Tom reenlisted as a corporal. Continuing on escort duty, Tom saw action at Kennesaw Mountain and Jonesboro, Georgia. During the same period, George's brigade fought at Yellow Tavern, Winchester, and Fisher's Hill, Virginia. In October 1864, George arranged for Tom to receive a second lieutenant's commission with the 6th Michigan Cavalry, and a transfer to his staff.

In March 1865, George was brevetted brigadier general of Regulars and given command of the 3rd Cavalry Division. Following the victory at Five Forks on 1 April, George led a relentless pursuit of the Army of Northern Virginia. At Namozine Church on 3 April, Tom captured an enemy flag, earning himself a Congressional Medal of Honor. Three days later, at

Sailor's Creek, Tom took another enemy flag despite being shot in the face. Only his brother's threat of arrest made Tom leave the field to receive treatment for his severe wound. Tom's heroism earned him a second Medal of Honor, making him the first U.S. soldier to receive this distinction.

Following the war, George was assigned to occupation duty in Texas and Tom was discharged in January 1866. In July, George received an appointment as lieutenant colonel of the newly raised 7th Cavalry and in November Tom joined the 7th as a first lieutenant. He served as quartermaster and alternately commanded seven of the regiment's companies. He participated in every major campaign and expedition and was promoted to captain in 1875.

In January 1876 a massive campaign was launched against the Sioux and Cheyenne. On 25 June, George, Tom, their youngest brother Boston, a civilian observer, and five companies of the 7th were annihilated at the Little Bighorn River. In one of the worst disasters in U.S. military history, the Custer family suffered the loss of three brothers and a brother-in-law. In 1877 the bodies of George and Tom were exhumed from the battlefield and separated— George was reinterred at West Point and Tom at Fort Leavenworth, Kansas.

—Vince Hawkins

Above: *George and Tom Custer, along with their younger brother, nephew, and brother-in-law, died together on 25 June 1876. ("Into the Valley," Michael Schreck)*

5 October. **Chief Joseph Surrenders. Bear Paw Mountain, Montana.**
Looking Glass is killed in fighting with the Army. After talking again to Miles, Chief Joseph surrenders with the famous speech that ended, "From where the sun now stands, I will fight no more forever." Although he and his people are sent to Oklahoma, he is later allowed to move to a reservation in Washington.

1878

January. **Status of the Army.**
The Regular Army consists of 2,153 officers and 28,254 enlisted men in ten regiments of cavalry, five artillery, and 25 infantry in addition to staff and service troops. This organization remains unchanged for decades.

Below: *George Crook remarked it took diamond dust to polish a diamond, meaning that the best way to fight an Apache was to employ other Apaches as scouts and allies. ("Apache Scouts Listening," Frederic Remington, Private Collection)*

30 May. **Bannocks Kill White Settlers. Camas Prairie, Idaho.**
A Bannock Indian kills two white men shortly after a group of Bannocks, Paiutes, and Shoshones arrive at their traditional root-digging area and find that most of the roots had already been eaten by hogs. Some of the Indians returned to their reservations, but about 200 warriors under Buffalo Horn launch an offensive.

8 June. **Bannock Chief Killed. Silver City, Idaho.**
A raiding party of Bannock warriors who had killed some ten white men meet significant resistance and Buffalo Horn is killed in the fighting. After withdrawing west the party is joined by Paiute, Oyte, and Egan Indians, increasing their strength to about 450 fighters.

23 June. **Bannocks Escape Cavalry. Steens Mountain, Oregon.**
Captain Ruben Bernard, 1st Cavalry, leading three troops of cavalry, surprises the Indians in their camp, driving them into defensive positions. After exchanging fire during the day, the Indians make good their escape, leaving the camp and its contents behind.

8 July. **Howard Forces Bannocks South. Birch Creek, Oregon.**
Scouts for Brigadier General Oliver O. Howard discover the Bannocks in entrenched positions. After heavy fighting, the soldiers manage to outflank the Indians and force them to flee south.

28 August. **Fort Meade Controls Sioux and Protects Miners. South Dakota.**
Major Henry M. Lazelle, 1st Infantry, establishes the post near the town of Deadwood to control the Sioux and protect the Black Hills mining district. Named for Major General George G. Meade, the buildings have been a Veterans Administration hospital since 1944.

9 September. **Northern Cheyenne Leave Reservation. Fort Reno, Oklahoma.**
Unhappy with agency life, 89 Northern Cheyenne warriors led by Dull Knife and Little Wolf accompanied by almost 250 women and children abandon their lodges and escape. The Army dispatches troops from several posts to intercept them, but the Indians elude their pursuers and continue north, raiding settlements along the way.

27 September. **Cheyenne Continue North. Smoky Hill River, Kansas.**
Army troops overtake the fleeing Northern Cheyenne on Punished Woman's Fork, where the Indians await their pursuers in strong entrenched positions. The Army commander and one Indian are killed and three enlisted men wounded in the attack. The Cheyenne escape and continue moving north.

15 October. **Fort Lewis Built to Protect Indian Reservation. Colorado.**
Lieutenant Colonel Robert E. Crofton, 13th Infantry, establishes a fort at Pagosa Springs, and Lieutenant General Philip Sheridan moves it near Durango and the Southern Ute Reservation in 1879. Named for Lieutenant Colonel William H. Lewis, 19th Infantry, who was killed by Indians, the Army abandons the post in 1891.

23 October. **Dull Knife Surrenders. Fort Robinson, Nebraska.**
Dull Knife, with 149 Indians, including Old Crow and Wild Hog, surrenders to a cavalry patrol. Little Wolf and his followers refuse to surrender, and escape.

1879

January. **Status of the Army.**
Congress authorizes the Secretary of War to produce

Above: *A trooper ready for campaign contrasts sharply with the finery of a corporal in the European-inspired cavalry dress uniform of the 1870s. ("Soldiers of 7th Cavalry," Fritz Kredel,* Soldiers of the American Army 1775-1954*)*

Army supplies at the prison at Fort Leavenworth as long as they can be made economically and properly.

29 January. **Army Privates Relieved from Mandatory Cooking Duties.**
Congress repeals the long-standing statute that requires the privates in a company to be detailed to cook for ten days. The new law gives company commanders more discretion in selecting the soldiers who do the cooking, but it is another 20 years before Congress authorizes two enlisted cooks with sergeants' pay for each company and battery.

2 January. **Cheyenne Conduct Hunger Strike. Fort Robinson, Nebraska.**
Dull Knife refuses to return to Indian Territory. The post commander cuts off all food and water to the Indians to force their departure. After a week with no water or rations Dull Knife attempts to leave but half are killed before the Army grants the remainder permission to join the Sioux at the Pine Ridge reservation.

6 March. **Fort Cantonment. Oklahoma.**
Colonel Richard I. Dodge, 23d Infantry, establishes the post near the present town of Canton after settlers in Kansas demanded protection from Northern

Cheyenne Indians. In 1882 the post is transferred to the Interior Department, which contracts with the Mennonites to operate a school for Plains Indians. The federal government assumes responsibility for the school in 1898, which operates until 1949.

27 March. Little Wolf Surrenders. Little Missouri River, Montana.

Lieutenant William Philo Clark, 2d Cavalry, and two troops intercept Little Wolf and his followers near the telegraph line from Fort Robinson to Hat Creek. Little Wolf's band surrenders without fighting and gives up all their arms along with some 250 ponies. The 33 warriors, 43 women, and 38 children march with the troops to Fort Keogh, where Little Wolf and the men sign on as scouts for the Army.

9 May. Fort Assiniboine Blocks Sitting Bull. Montana.

Colonel Thomas H. Ruger, 18th U.S. Infantry,

Above: *Cavalry troopers form into line as their first sergeant prepares them to move out in the field. ("Top," Don Stivers)*

establishes the post, which is named for the Assiniboine Indians. Located on Beaver Creek near the town of Havre, it prevents Sitting Bull and his warriors from returning from Canada. The Army abandons the post in 1911.

14 June. Bicycle Corps Rides to St. Louis. Fort Missoula, Montana.

In a mobility test the experimental 25th Infantry Bicycle Corps commanded by Lieutenant James A. Moss begins a 900-mile ride to St. Louis, Missouri. After a successful but strenuous ride, they complete the trip in 40 days.

7 August. New System of Target Practice Adopted.

The Ordnance Department adopts a regulated method of target practice and provides each soldier with 20 rounds of ammunition per month. Prizes and furloughs are to be awarded to the best shots.

4 September. Victorio Leads Apache Attack. Ojo Caliente, Arizona Territory.

Apaches under Victorio attack a camp of the 9th Cavalry and disappear into Mexico. The soldiers of the

9th Cavalry continue to fight Victorio's Apaches back and forth across the border for the next two years.

10 September. **Indian Agent in Dispute With Utes. White River Agency, Colorado.**
Nathan C. Meeker, the Indian agent, has a dispute with Northern Utes and requests Army assistance.

16 September. **Army Troops Move to Assist Agent. Fort Steele, Wyoming.**
Major Thomas T. Thornburgh, 4th Infantry, and a column of 200 men deploy to assist Meeker at the White River agency.

29 September. **Meeker Killed; Utes Take Captives. Milk Creek, Colorado.**
Thornburgh agrees to talk to the Utes, but a gesture of greeting is mistaken for a threat and shots are fired beginning a two-day battle, which turns into a siege. Reinforcements are too late to save Thornburgh, who is killed along with ten soldiers. The Utes have 23 warriors killed. The Indians later kill Meeker and nine of his employees at the White River Agency. They then took Meeker's wife and daughter and another woman and two children captive.

11 October. **Utes Surrender Captives. White River Agency, Colorado.**
In anticipation of a major offensive against the Utes, Colonel Wesley Merritt, 5th Cavalry, assembles 700 soldiers at the agency and as many more are on the way to help rescue Mrs. Meeker and the other captives. Colonel Ranald Mackenzie, 4th Cavalry, has 1,500 infantry and cavalry at Fort Garland, Colorado, and Colonel Edward Hatch, 9th Cavalry, is at Fort Lewis, Colorado, with another 500 soldiers. As it turns out, Indian agents obtain the release of the women and children without the use of force, ending the campaign.

10 December. **Ramsey Becomes Secretary of War.**
Alexander Ramsey becomes Secretary of War. A lawyer and politician, he has no military experience when he is appointed to replace George W. McCrary. Ramsey leaves the office when James Garfield becomes President.

1880

January. **Status of the Army.**
The total strength of the Army is 26,411, with 24,259 enlisted men and 2,152 officers. President Rutherford B. Hayes rescinds the 1 June 1877 order that allowed Army troops to pursue hostile Indians across the Mexican border. Mexican president Proforia Diaz agrees to cooperate with the U.S. to capture the Apache chief Victorio.

22 April. **Protection for Indian Agency. Nebraska.**
Major John Jacques Upham, 5th Cavalry, establishes Fort Niobara on the Niobara River a few miles from the present town of Valentine to control the Spotted Tail Agency. Abandoned in 1906, the military reservation is now a wildlife refuge.

29 July. **Black Cavalry Pursues Victorio. Fort Quitman, Texas.**
Colonel Benjamin H. Grierson, 10th Cavalry, leads a force of cavalry and infantry to find the Apache chief, Victorio, who was crossing the Rio Grande from Mexico to conduct raids in Texas. The soldiers of the 10th Cavalry and 24th Infantry force Victorio to retreat back across the Mexican border.

Above: *A cavalryman's reliable pistol was much more favored than an awkward saber for close-in fighting from horseback. ("The Trooper," Frederic Remington, Private Collection)*

Left: *The search for hostile Indians kept troops in the saddle despite sandstorms and blazing sun in summer, and bitter winter cold. ("The Quest," Frederic Remington, Courtesy of The Anschutz Collection, Denver, CO)*

22 August. **Fort Maginnis. Montana.**
Captain Daingerfield Parker, 3d Infantry, establishes a fort on Ford's Creek about 20 miles from Lewiston to protect settlers, cattlemen, and transportation routes. Named for Major Martin Maginnis, 11th Minnesota Infantry, Montana's delegate to Congress, the post is abandoned in 1890.

15–16 October. **Victorio Killed by Mexican Army. Tres Castillos, Mexico.**
Colonel George P. Buell combines his Regular infantry and cavalry with Mexican irregulars commanded by Colonel Joaquin Terrazas to find the Apache chief Victorio, but as they close in on the Apaches, Terrazas orders Buell and the U.S. troops out of Mexico. When the Mexican troops engage the Apaches, Terrazas kills Victorio.

1881

January. **Status of the Army.**
Major George N. Sternberg discovers the germ causing pneumonia. He also does research on cholera, yellow fever, and other diseases, becoming known as the "father of American bacteriology." Sternberg goes on to become the Surgeon General of the Army.

5 March. **Lincoln's Son Appointed Secretary of War.**
Robert Todd Lincoln, eldest son of President Abraham Lincoln, becomes Secretary of War. He entered Harvard Law School in 1864 but left to serve on Ulysses S. Grant's staff, where he held the rank of captain. After the war he completed his law studies at the University of Chicago. During his tenure he recommends increasing the pay of privates as a way to reduce the rate of desertion. He is the ambassador to the United Kingdom from 1889 to 1893 and later becomes president and chairman of the board of the Pullman Palace Car Company.

7 May. **Greely Begins Alaska Expedition. Fort Conger, Alaska.**
First Lieutenant Adolphus W. Greely leads a 25-man contingent to Alaska to establish a meteorological station. After establishing Fort Conger on Lady Franklin Bay, conducting detailed meteorological and geophysical observations and exploring the interior, the expedition becomes stranded in Alaska for three years.

7 May. **Infantry and Cavalry School Founded. Fort Leavenworth, Kansas.**
In May, General William T. Sherman establishes the School of Application for Infantry and Cavalry. Instruction included "everything which pertains to Army organization, tactics, discipline, equipment, . . . and generally everything which is provided for in Army regulations." Reading, writing, geography, algebra, geometry, and trigonometry were all part of the course as well as a reading list of books on the "science and practice of war." In 1886 it is redesignated The United States Infantry and Cavalry School. It continues to function today as the Army's Command and General Staff College.

19 July. **Sitting Bull Surrenders. Fort Buford, North Dakota.**
Sitting Bull and 45 warriors, 67 women, and 73 children ride into the post and surrender. Ten days later they are transported to Fort Randall, South Dakota, aboard the steamer *General Sherman,* where they are guarded by the 25th Infantry.

30 August. **Geronimo Leaves the Reservation. Fort Apache, Arizona.**
While at the San Carlos reservation Geronimo comes under the influence of Nakaidoklini, a prophet who preaches Indian supremacy and separation from the whites. Colonel Eugene A. Carr, 4th Cavalry, arrests the prophet at his village on Cibicu Creek, but on the way back to the post the column is attacked by Apaches trying to rescue the medicine man. During the melee a soldier shoots and kills Nakaidoklini. The altercation prompts Geronimo to lead a band of Indians away from the reservation.

September. **Controlling Ute Indians. Utah.**
Captain Hamilton S. Hawkins, 6th Infantry, establishes Fort Thornburgh to control Ute Indians and protect their agents after removal of the Uncompahgre and White River Utes from Colorado to a new agency in Utah. Named for Major Thomas T. Thornburgh, 4th Infantry, who was killed by Utes in 1879, the post is abandoned in 1883.

1882

January. **Status of the Army.**
Desertion is the Army's biggest personnel problem in the West. Robert T. Lincoln, the Secretary of War, noted in his annual report that for every two recruits who enlist in the Army, one soldier deserts. Mexico and the United States agree to reasonable pursuit of Indian raiders by the troops of each country across the boundary.

19–23 April. **Apaches Kill Police Chief. Horseshoe Canyon, Arizona.**
An Apache war party kills the police chief at the San Carlos reservation and compels the Warm Spring Apaches to join the resistance. Lieutenant Colonel George A. Forsyth pursues the raiders, engages them at Horseshoe Canyon, and continues the pursuit across the border into Mexico. After Forsyth joins Captain Tullius C. Tupper, 6th Cavalry, they meet a Mexican infantry unit and are ordered out of the country.

9 June. **Fort Hancock Guards the Mexican Border. Texas.**
Established on the Rio Grande at the present town of Hancock, the post protects the area from Indians and Mexican bandits from across the river. Named for Major General Winfield Scott Hancock, the military reservation is transferred to the Interior Department in 1895.

17 July. Battle of Big Dry Wash. East Clear Creek, Arizona.
Captain Adna R. Chaffee, 6th Cavalry, leading troops of the 3d and 6th Cavalry, outflanks and surprises an ambush planned by White Mountain Apaches. His men inflict such heavy losses that the surviving Indians return to their reservation, ending further raiding.

1883

January. Status of the Army.
The Quartermaster Department has settled debts for 46 of 50 railroads the Army operated during the Civil War. The Attorney General and Secretary of War resolve the last four over the next five years. To preserve uniforms, the Army begins to produce and issue coats and trousers made from canvas that can be worn when troops are performing fatigue details.

21 March. Apaches Raid Across the Border. Fort Huachuca, Arizona.
Chato crosses the Mexican border with 23 warriors to

Above: *Son of the sixteenth President and veteran of the Union Army, Robert Todd Lincoln served as Secretary of War. (Daniel Huntington, Army Art Collection, NMUSA)*

Right: *Army engineers spent nearly four decades completing the Washington Monument in the mid-1880s. ("I Deliver to You This Column," H. Charles McBarron, Army Art Collection, NMUSA)*

spend a week raiding. They kill 11 people without being sighted by any of the hundreds of soldiers and civilians looking for the Apaches.

1 May. Army Battles Apaches in Mexico. San Bernardino Springs, Arizona.
An expedition commanded by Captain Emmit Crawford, 4th Cavalry, and Lieutenant Charles B. Gatewood that includes Indian scouts, cavalry, and 350 pack mules moves into Mexico in search of Geronimo and his followers. On 15 May Crawford's Indian scouts attack the encampment of the Apache leaders Chato and Benito, killing nine warriors and destroying 30 lodges. After the battle the Indians begin to return to the San Carlos Reservation in Arizona.

August. Greely Expedition Stranded. Fort Conger, Alaska.
Relief ships fail to reach First Lieutenant Adolphus W. Greely's expedition. He and his men break camp and make their way south by boat to Cape Sabine, where they spend the winter. Their supplies are very low.

1 November. Sheridan Appointed Commanding General of the Army.
Lieutenant General Philip Henry Sheridan is appointed commanding general of the Army, succeeding Sherman. He serves in that post until 5 August 1888 but does not receive his fourth star until June of that year.

Above: *Patrols in the remote reaches of deserts, mountains, and plains kept frontier troops in the field for generations. ("In the Shadows," Mort Künstler)*

January. **Status of the Army.**
The infantry rifle is provided with a rear sight, which enables the firer to correct for the drift of the bullet in flight. Congress establishes the enlisted rank of Post Quartermaster Sergeant, the first time enlisted men are directly assigned to the Quartermaster Department. Eighty men are assigned to the Department and given a distinguishing insignia, a crossed quill and key authorized in October 1883 that becomes the first Quartermaster insignia.

March. **Geronimo Returns to the Reservation. San Carlos Reservation, Arizona.**
Almost a year after he agreed to return to the reservation Geronimo arrives at the agency and begins to foment unrest among the Apaches.

June. **Greely Expedition Rescued. Cape Sabine, Alaska.**
First Lieutenant Adolphus W. Greely and six others from his expedition are found starving but alive. Initially criticized, he is eventually cleared and credited with having performed courageously.

1885

January. **Status of the Army.**
The Army has 24,705 enlisted men and 2,154 officers on its roles for a total strength of 26,859. The Army begins making its own artillery tubes at Watervliet Arsenal. The Washington Monument, recently completed by the Army Corps of Engineers, is dedicated.

4 March. **Ulysses S. Grant Reappointed General.**
Former President Ulysses S. Grant is reappointed a general in the Army and placed on the retired list, which enables him to receive pay to alleviate his impoverished financial condition.

3 March. **Board Authorized to Study Coastal Defenses.**
Congress authorizes a board of officers to design a plan for coastal defenses.

5 *March*. **Endicott Becomes Secretary of War.**
William C. Endicott becomes Secretary of War. A
lawyer who has served on the Massachusetts Supreme
Court, he has no military experience prior to taking
office.

17 *May*. **Geronimo Terrorizes Border. White River
Reservation, Arizona.**
Geronimo and about 150 Chiricahua Apaches leave the
reservation and begin terrorizing the border region.
Army cavalry and Apache scouts under Brigadier
General George Crook take up pursuit of the renegades.

13 *July*. **Expedition to Find Geronimo Unsuccessful.
Sierra Madre Mountains, Mexico.**
Captain Wirt Davis, 4th Cavalry, and Lieutenant
Matthias W. Day cross into Mexico with a troop of
cavalry and 100 Indian scouts to search for Geronimo
while Brigadier General George Crook deploys some
3,000 troops to patrol the border country. Davis and

Above: *Members of Company I, 25th U.S. Infantry,
display pride in the profession of arms at their posting
in the 1880s to Fort Snelling, Minnesota. (National
Archives)*

Day have several close encounters with Apaches, but
are unsuccessful in finding Geronimo's band.

23 *July*. **Death of Ulysses S. Grant. Mount McGregor,
New York.**
Ulysses S. Grant dies in a cottage he and his family
had taken for the summer to avoid the heat so he can
continue work on his memoirs. By this time his throat
cancer is so advanced that he has to write notes on
slips of paper to complete the manuscript. With the
help of Mark Twain the memoirs are published after
Grant's death, becoming a great success and earning
almost half a million dollars for his family.

8 *August*. **Grant Laid to Rest. New York City.**
Ulysses S. Grant is laid to rest at Riverside Park after
funeral services on 4 August at Mount McGregor,
New York. Three U.S. Presidents ride in the parade
and former Union and Confederate generals ride
together in carriages during the funeral procession.

November. **Josanie Leads Apache Raid. Southern
Arizona and New Mexico.**
In spite of Crook's border patrols of 3,000 soldiers, for
about four weeks about a dozen Apache warriors led

ARMY MULES: SHAVETAILS AND BELL-RINGERS

For 125 years the mule was the "workhorse" of the U.S. Army, replacing even the much-vaunted horse as the most important animal in service. Used in every conflict during that time, the mule became such an indispensable part of Army life that it became both the mascot and the symbol of the Army.

The first documented large-scale use of mules in the Army came during the Second Seminole War in 1835. Up to that point horses and oxen moved Army supply wagons, since mules were comparatively expensive and the Army knew little about them. During the Mexican War mules were used to great effect by every major command. Many of the animals came from the Mexican Army, which relied on harness and pack mules for transporting supplies over terrain unsuitable for oxen or horse drawn wagons.

By the end of the 1850s the Quartermaster Department recognized the superiority of the mule for transport service and developed a system of four- and six-mule wagons, established a set of regulations for harness mules, and was experimenting with pack mules. Civilian breeders had an important and thriving business supplying mules to meet the Army's needs. During the Civil War roughly one million mules were purchased for the Army and were such a vital part of Union Army logistics that President Lincoln signed General Order No. 300 forbidding the exportation of mules from the United States.

It was General George Crook, the "father of the pack train," who created the company pack train system that became the model for the Army and which remained virtually unchanged for nearly eighty years. Crook's company pack train relied on experienced civilian packers, introduced the smaller Mexican mule into the Army and used the aparejo, the light-weight, highly efficient Mexican pack saddle. With pack trains supplying the cavalry, and using Indian scouts, the Army was finally able to defeat the highly mobile Indian tribes dominating the western frontier.

In 1898 the Indian Wars ended and the Army sold all its four- and six-mule wagons and harness mules, keeping only five company pack trains. The Spanish-American War necessitated rebuilding the mule supply trains and initiating new developments, such as the first mule-packed mountain artillery units used during the Philippine Insurrection. During the Chinese relief expedition in 1900, the U.S. Army

garnered great admiration for the speed, efficiency, and expertise demonstrated by its mule-born supply train. In General Pershing's pursuit of Pancho Villa in 1916, mule pack trains successfully competed against mechanized supply trucks.

During World War I, mules again proved their worth against mechanization, keeping the front-line troops fully supplied by going where the trucks could not. The AEF's greatest victory, the Meuse-Argonne offensive, would have been impossible without the 90,000 animals that moved its weapons and supplies. In World War II mules were important in achieving victory in both European and Pacific theaters. They proved vital to supply operations in Tunisia, Sicily, and Italy. In the Pacific, mules were the primary source of supply for the Chindits, Marauders, and the MARS units, and for the first time mules were airlifted to the front lines.

Although the Army sent no mules to Korea they were still used. Captured Chinese and Korean mules were considered a prize possession by the units that had them. On 15 December 1956, the last two operational mule units, the 35th Quartermaster Pack Company, and Battery A, 4th Field Artillery Pack Battalion, were deactivated at Fort Carson, Colorado. Although no longer carried on the U.S. Army's TO&E, mules continue to be used by Special Forces, from the Vietnam War to current operations in Afghanistan.

—*Vince Hawkins*

Above: *Although at times difficult to handle, Army mules provided logistical support even in the most hostile terrain. (Arizona Historical Society, Tucson, AZ)*

Above: *Philip H. Sheridan succeeded Sherman as commanding general of the Army. (William F. Cogswell, Army Art Collection, NMUSA)*

by Josanie raid settlements in New Mexico and Arizona, killing 38 people, and safely return to Mexico. None of the patrols sight the raiders.

9 November. **Railroad Completed. Cajon Pass, California.**
The last spike is driven for the California Southern Railroad. It was surveyed and its work crews protected by Army troops.

1886

January. **Status of the Army.**
The Endicott Board, headed by the Secretary of War, William Endicott, proposes fortifying 28 principal harbors in the United States with earthworks and masonry fortifications with 2,362 guns and emplacements. Congress appropriates funds for the coastal fortifications and establishes the Board of Ordnance and Fortifications to oversee coastal defense programs in 1888. By the Spanish-American War only 151 guns have been installed.

9 January. **Geronimo Agrees to Talk to Crook. Aros River, Mexico.**
Captain Emmett Crawford discovers an Apache camp

in Sonora, Mexico. Geronimo and his followers flee but send a message saying they are ready to surrender. Two days later, as they prepare for Geronimo's surrender, Crawford's forces come under attack by Mexican irregulars and Crawford is killed. First Lieutenant Marion P. Maus is able to open talks with Geronimo and the other chiefs, arranging a meeting between them and Brigadier General George Crook in "two moons."

25 March. **Geronimo Almost Surrenders. Canon de los Embredos, Mexico.**
Brigadier General George Crook meets with Geronimo. Two days later the Apache chiefs make surrender speeches, but after Crook departs and telegraphs the news to Washington the Indians change their minds and flee. As a result, Crook is immediately replaced by Brigadier General Nelson A. Miles.

5 May. **Search for Geronimo Is Fruitless. Fort Huachuca, Arizona.**
General Miles sends Captain Henry W. Lawton, 4th Cavalry, and a surgeon, Leonard Wood, in pursuit of Geronimo. Lawton's command includes his troop of 4th Cavalry, a detachment of the 8th Infantry, and 20 Apache scouts. The expedition spent four months searching for Geronimo with no success.

20 July. **Brief Encounter with Apaches. Mexico.**
Lawton's column of cavalry, infantry, and Apache scouts surprises Geronimo. Although the Apaches elude capture, by the end of August they indicate a willingness to surrender.

17 August. **Fort Yellowstone Guards New Park. Wyoming.**
Captain Moses Harris, 1st Cavalry, establishes the post in Yellowstone Park to protect it from vandalism, enforce game laws, and guard the natural wonders of the area. Originally named Camp Sheridan for Lieutenant General Philip Sheridan, it is designated Fort Yellowstone in 1891 and abandoned in 1918.

20 August. **Agent Receives Support to Control Utes. Utah.**
Major Frederick W. Benteen, 9th Cavalry, establishes Fort Du Chesne at the junction of the Du Chesne and Uintah rivers to control the Uncompahgre and White River Utes who are resisting their agent. The post is abandoned in 1910; the buildings became the headquarters for the Uintah and Oray Indian Reservation.

24 August. Geronimo Agrees to Surrender to Miles. Bavispe River, Mexico.
Lieutenant Charles B. Gatewood meets with Geronimo, who agrees to surrender, but only to Brigadier General Nelson Miles in person.

4 September. Geronimo Surrenders. Skeleton Canyon, Arizona.
General Nelson meets with Geronimo, who finally surrenders as promised. Four days later the Apaches are loaded aboard trains and sent to Florida, where they remain until 1894 when they are moved to Fort Sill, Oklahoma. Geronimo dies there in 1919.

1887

January. Status of the Army.
The Army and Navy General Hospital at Hot Springs opens with a capacity for 16 officers and 64 enlisted men. It is the only general hospital in use between the Civil War and the Spanish-American War. Through the efforts of the National Guard Association, Congress doubles the $200,000 annual federal grant for firearms for the militia that has been in effect since 1808. Adolphus W. Greely, well-known for his expedition into the Arctic, is promoted to brigadier general and appointed chief of the Signal Corps.

29 January. Cavalry and Light Artillery School Authorized. Fort Riley, Kansas.
Congress authorizes the Army to establish a permanent school for drill and instruction of cavalry and light artillery. Construction of facilities takes five years before the school can open.

1 March. Army Hospital Corps Established.
Congress establishes the Army Hospital Corps to provide a professional cadre of enlisted soldiers in the medical field. Prior to creation of the corps, hospital orderlies were detailed from line units.

26 July. Regimental Level Training. Buffalo, New York.
For the first time since 1866 a regiment is in one place to conduct exercises as an entire unit when the 12th Infantry assembles at Buffalo.

20 October. Fort Logan Authorized as Part of Post Reduction Program. Colorado.
On 17 February Congress approved building a military post near Denver as part of a policy of reducing the number of small posts and concentrating troops near rail lines. The state donates land at no cost to the

Above: *The Army officer dress uniform of the 1880s featured a high-collared tunic with branch color chest cords and a plumed leather helmet. (National Park Service)*

federal government, and Major George K. Brady, 18th Infantry, with two companies begins building temporary quarters on 25 October. Named for Major General John A. Logan, the post is still in operation.

1888

January. Status of the Army.
Brigadier General Thomas Lincoln Casey begins planning and supervising construction for what is now the main building for the Library of Congress. In June, Congress awards Philip Sheridan, commanding general of the Army, the four-star rank of general.

14 August. **Sheridan Dies in Office; Replaced by Schofield.**

Major General John McAllister Schofield is appointed commanding general of the Army, succeeding Sheridan, who died in office on 5 August. Schofield remains a major general throughout his tenure.

Below: *Perhaps the last true Indian campaign against a determined and capable enemy was against the Apaches and their leader Geronimo. ("Bringing in Geronimo," Mort Künstler)*

January. **Status of the Army.**

The Army occupies some 134 posts scattered across the country with a total strength of about 25,000 officers and men. The largest garrison is 700 men. The Quartermaster Department settles the last claim for payment from civilian firms for items furnished to the Army during the Civil War. The 21st Infantry assembles to conduct maneuvers as a regiment, only the second such exercise since 1866.

Right: *In a little-known example of Army experiments to improve mobility, a group from the 25th U.S. Infantry set out on bicycles to Yellowstone National Park in 1896 to test the military utility of this lightweight form of transportation. (National Archives)*

5 March. **Proctor New Secretary of War.**
Redfield Proctor becomes Secretary of War. He served with Vermont troops in the Civil War and commanded a regiment at Gettysburg. During his tenure he revises the military justice code and institutes a system of efficiency reports and examinations for officers. He will leave office in 1891 to serve in the U.S. Senate.

1890

January. **Status of the Army.**
The total strength of the Army is 27,089 with 24,921 enlisted men and 2,168 officers. Congress adds one pound of vegetables to the daily ration for soldiers. The Secretary of War is to determine the proportion of fresh potatoes, onions, cabbage, beets, turnips, carrots, and squash or canned tomatoes that goes into the ration.

16 June. **Officer Promotions Modified.**
Congress passes legislation that allows officers below the grade of brigadier general to be promoted with their branches. Officers could therefore be transferred within a branch without the loss of rank that was previously linked to regimental promotion. Promotions for all officers below the rank of major begin to be made by examination to develop a minimum level of professional competence.

10 September. **Fort Sam Houston Named for Texas Hero. Texas.**
After the Mexican War the Army maintained a depot in San Antonio, and the city served as the headquarters for the Texas Department. In 1870 the city donated land for a permanent post, and in 1876 construction began on the San Antonio Quartermaster Depot. Further construction for permanent facilities for the department headquarters and 12 cavalry companies followed over the next decade, becoming known as the Post of San Antonio. It is designated Fort Sam Houston in 1890 to honor the man who played a prominent role in Texas history. The post remains active today.

1 October. **Weather Service Established.**
Congress transfers the Weather Service to the Department of Agriculture to "increase the efficiency and reduce the expenses of the Signal Corps of the Army." The legislation also provides the Signal Corps with one major, four captains, and four lieutenants in addition to the Chief Signal Officer.

20 November. **Ghost Dance Sweeps Sioux. Pine Ridge, South Dakota.**
In North and South Dakota the Sioux so enthusiastically embrace a new Ghost Dance religion preached by Indian prophet Wovoka that residents request additional military protection against possible

GENERAL JOHN CROOK: INDIAN FIGHTER

John Crook was an 1852 graduate of West Point and was first assigned to exploration and frontier defense duties in the new Northwest, where he took part in several Indian campaigns as a captain. He gained a reputation as a tough fighter in the Civil War, commanding a Union cavalry division at Chickamauga. He pursued Confederate General Joseph Wheeler into Tennessee, defeating him at Farmington. He conducted actions against the Confederate railroad in Virginia and participated in the battles of Winchester, Fisher's Hill, and Cedar Creek in the Shenandoah campaign. He also led his cavalry in the Petersburg campaigns, ending the war as a brevet major general.

After the war, Crook reverted to his Regular rank of lieutenant colonel and was sent to Boise, Idaho, to fight in the Paiute War in 1867. Already knowledgeable about Indian fighting, he studied the Indian ways until one officer commented, "He knew the Indians better than the Indian did." His dogged persistence and incredible stamina in pursuit of the Indians wore them down. He also employed Indians as scouts and fighters and personally led attacks, moving his army in the summer heat and winter snow. The Paiute chiefs finally sued for peace in 1868.

Next, Crook was sent to Arizona where he campaigned against the Apaches under Cochise. Using Indian scouts and pack mules for mobility, he kept his troops in the field in search of the elusive band. Knowing when they were most vulnerable, he launched attacks in the winter of 1872 when food was scarce for the Apaches. He engaged the Indians in some 20 assaults, leaving the warriors weakened and demoralized. By the summer of 1873 Indian resistance was broken. Crook's Tonto Basin campaign, as it was known, was a flawless counter-guerrilla action with decisive results, and he was promoted to brigadier general in 1873 for his success.

In 1875 he took command of the Department of the Platte and soon found himself fighting in the Great Sioux War of 1876. Crook's biggest setback of the war came at the Battle of Rosebud, where he was surprised by Sioux and Cheyenne Indians and forced to retire. His troops were part of a larger three-pronged Army offensive against the Indians, and while Rosebud was a defeat, it was overshadowed eight days later when Lieutenant Colonel George A. Custer's 7th Cavalry Regiment, another element of the attack, was almost annihilated on the Little Bighorn.

Crook then led a vengeful campaign against the Sioux, finding and destroying their village at Slim Buttes.

In 1882, Crook was sent back to Arizona to put down an uprising by Chiricahua Apaches under Geronimo, who had raided Arizona and New Mexico from a base in the Sierra Madre mountains in Mexico across the border. Crook led an expedition into Mexico, using his proven methods of Indian scouts and pack mules. After only one engagement he found Geronimo and negotiated his return to a reservation in Arizona. But peace did not come easy, and Geronimo and some of his followers escaped the reservation in 1884. Crook pursued again. Despite deadly encounters with Mexican authorities, Crook met with Geronimo to discuss surrender, but Geronimo fled. Before Crook could pursue again, he was replaced with General Nelson A. Miles and returned to the Department of the Platte.

Crook was promoted to major general in April 1888 and given command of the Division of the Missouri. He died suddenly two years later. Despite being one America's greatest Indian fighters, in his last years he joined the Indian Rights Association to try to protect the Indians relocated to Florida.

—*Kevin M. Hymel*

Above: *George Crook, "The Grey Fox," was both friend and foe to Native Americans within his Department of the Platte. (Little Bighorn Battlefield National Monument, National Park Service)*

violence. Major General Nelson Miles encourages the arrest of Indian leaders, and cavalry and infantry move to the reservations.

29 November. **Army-Navy Football.**
The first Army-Navy football game is played at West Point, New York; Navy wins with a score of 24–0.

15 December. **Sitting Bull Killed. Standing Rock Reservation, South Dakota.**
After feuding with the reservation's Indian agent, Sitting Bull is killed when Indian policemen attempt to arrest him. Big Foot, another Sioux chief, escapes arrest and leads his band toward the Pine Ridge Agency.

28 December. **Tragic Last Army-Indian Confrontation. Wounded Knee, Montana.**
The 7th Cavalry under Colonel James Forsyth locates Big Foot and about 350 Miniconjous who are on the way to counsel the rebellious Sioux to surrender. Forsyth escorts them to Wounded Knee Creek, where about 500 soldiers and four small cannon surround an Indian village with some 350 people. The intent is to disarm the Indians. Neither side anticipates a fight. The next day the soldiers surrounded the camp and began to disarm the Indians. A scuffle develops into fighting with weapons, and some 200 Indians including Big Foot and women and children are killed or wounded when the soldiers open fire with Hotchkiss guns. The Army has 25 killed and 39 wounded. It is the Army's last engagement with Indians that can be considered a battle.

30 December. **Miles Concentrates Forces Against Sioux. White Clay Creek, Montana.**
Sioux ambush a patrol of the 7th Cavalry and the 9th Cavalry comes to its relief. Major General Nelson Miles concentrates 3,500 soldiers around the reservation, and the Sioux surrender the next month.

1891

January. **Status of the Army.**
First Lieutenant John J. Pershing, who will command U.S. forces in France in World War I, becomes the professor of military science and tactics at the University of Nebraska. He is assigned there until 1895, during which time he studies law, receiving his degree in 1893. In the latter part of the year the Army helps quell disturbances along the Mexican border caused by a large band of outlaws who operate on both sides of the international boundary.

Above: *Commanding General of the Army John M. Schofield recommended the establishment of military bases on Hawaii. (Stephan William Shaw, Army Art Collection, NMUSA)*

15 January. **Sioux Surrender. White Clay Creek, Montana.**
The Sioux formally surrender and end the Pine Ridge Campaign when Kicking Bear gives his rifle to Brigadier General Nelson Miles. It is the last campaign in the Indian Wars.

February. **Mandatory Retirement.**
Congress passes a law compelling officers to retire at the age of 64.

1 March. **Indian Scout Units Authorized.**
The War Department authorizes enlisting a company of Indian Scouts for each of the 26 regiments of white cavalry and infantry regiments serving west of the Mississippi River. Officials hope it will divert Indians from the warlike tribes to legitimate activities. Over the next six years 1,071 Indians enlist or reenlist in the

companies. In 1897, the War Department will conclude that the units "never reached a degree of substantial success as useful soldiers."

5 March. **Elkins Appointed Secretary of War.**
Stephen B. Elkins becomes Secretary of War. He served in the 77th Missouri Infantry in the Civil War, during which, with the help of the future outlaw Cole Younger, he escaped from Quantrill's Raiders. After the war he became a successful businessman who founded the town of Elkins, West Virginia, where he had extensive land and mining interests. While Secretary, he recommends renewing the rank of lieutenant general and giving pay raises to noncommissioned officers. After leaving office in 1893 he is elected to the U.S. Senate, where he serves until his death in 1911.

3 October. **New Drill Regulations Adopted.**
The War Department issues three separate sets of drill regulations for infantry, cavalry, and artillery.

Above: *Hardtack, coffee, and bacon was usual fare in the West. ("Cavalryman's Breakfast on the Prairie," Frederic Remington, Amon Carter Museum, Fort Worth, TX)*

1892

January. **Status of the Army.**
The Artillery School begins publishing *The Journal of the United States Artillery*. First Lieutenant William A. Glassford travels to Paris to purchase a balloon for the Signal Corps. The balloon, named the *General Myer* to honor the first chief of the Signal Corps, is exhibited at the World's Columbian Exposition in Chicago. When the fair closes in 1893 the balloon is shipped to Fort Riley for use by the signal detachment there. The Signal Corps also constructs a field telegraph line between Separ, New Mexico, to an international boundary marker to support the International Boundary Commission in New Mexico. It is used to transmit chronometric signals from an observatory in El Paso, Texas, to determine longitude of the marker.

23 April. **Congress Authorizes Fort Logan H. Roots. Arkansas.**
Located on the Arkansas River near Little Rock, Congress authorizes the post, but construction does not start until 1893. In 1897 it is named for Captain Logan

Holt Roots. First garrisoned in 1896, construction halts in 1898 when the troops are moved to Puerto Rico during the Spanish-American War, although a small force remains at the post until World War I. It has been a Veterans Administration hospital since 1921.

14 July. Army Troops Intervene in Miners Strike. Coeur d'Alene, Idaho.
Federal troops restore order and establish martial law when striking silver miners clash with strike-breakers. Troops are also used to enforce court injunctions in other situations around the country.

1893

January. Status of the Army.
A group of officers founds the Infantry Society, which became the United States Infantry Association in 1894 and begins publishing the *Infantry Journal*. The Army adopts the Danish .30-caliber Krag-Jorgensen rifle with a five-round magazine to replace model 1873 Springfield. Late in the year the Signal Corps completed a permanent telegraph line between Forts Ringgold and McIntosh in Texas, but maintenance was a challenge because local residents used the insulators for target practice.

9 January. School for Cavalry and Artillery Opens.
The school of instruction for drill and practice for the cavalry and light artillery opens at Fort Riley, Kansas. Authorized by Congress in January 1887, the opening was delayed until appropriate facilities were constructed. The year-long course concentrates on practical training for units.

5 March. Lamont Named Secretary of War.
Daniel S. Lamont becomes Secretary of War. He was a military secretary with the rank of colonel for New York governor Grover Cleveland in 1883, and when Cleveland was elected President Lamont served as his private secretary from 1885 to 1889. While Secretary he recommends that the land being used by Apaches be acquired for their permanent use and their status as prisoners be ended.

24 June. Army Medical School Opens.
Brigadier General George M. Sternberg, the Surgeon General, opens the U.S. Army Medical School to instruct candidates for the Medical Corps in Army procedures and medical practice. One of the first part-time teachers is Walter Reed, who later heads the 1900–1901 yellow-fever commission in Cuba that discovers the mosquito that carried yellow fever, an accomplishment that changes life in the tropics. Another Army physician, William Gorgas, uses Reed's research to fight malaria and make building the Panama Canal possible.

3 November. Military Instructors at Colleges Increased.
Congress authorizes the Army to detail up to 100 officers for assignment as instructors to colleges.

1894

January. Status of the Army.
Late in the year Congress rules that men enlisting in the Army must be citizens of the United States or have declared their intention to become citizens. They also have to be less than 30 years of age and able to speak, read, and write English. The Signal Corps' balloon

Above: *A special field uniform including an "Irish frieze" overcoat was prescribed for Indian scouts beginning in 1890. The crossed arrows insignia was adopted in World War II by the 1st Special Service Force and later by the Army Special Forces. ("United States Scouts, Campaign Uniform, 1890," Company of Military Historians)*

detachment transfers from Fort Riley, Kansas, to Fort Logan, Colorado, where conditions are better suited to aeronautics. The Signal Corps acquires responsibility for the War Department library, including Mathew Brady's Civil War photographs purchased in 1875 when Brady was experiencing financial difficulties.

Above: *Escorting supplies or wagon trains of arriving immigrants was a common task for the frontier Army. This mundane duty was tiresome and boring, yet it could turn instantly deadly for everyone if an attack or flash flood should occur. ("Distant Thunder," Frank McCarthy)*

3 July. **Army Troops Intervene in Rail Strike. Chicago, Illinois.**
Federal troops enforce a court injunction that forbids the American Railway Union from interfering with interstate commerce and delivery of mail when strikers at Pullman Company turn violent.

8 July. **Regulars Fire on Mob. Hammond, Indiana.**
A small detachment of Regulars opens fire on a mob much larger than their numbers, killing at least one and wounding a dozen or more rioters. On 20 July the Federal troops keeping order during the strike are withdrawn.

1895

January. **Status of the Army.**
The Quartermaster Department organizes into four divisions—Supply and Transportation; Construction and Repair; Correspondence and Examining; and Mail and Records. During 1895 the Army recruits 7,780 men, of whom 5,518 are citizens. Many of the 2,262 foreign-born recruits serve for long periods without being naturalized.

5 October. **Miles Replaces Schofield as Commanding General of the Army.**
Major General Nelson A. Miles becomes the commanding general of the Army. He was a brevet brigadier general at the end of the Civil War and served throughout the West, where he gained a reputation as one of the Army's most successful Indian fighters. In 1900 he is promoted to lieutenant general, and he retires from active service in 1903.

1896

January. **Status of the Army.**
The strength of the Army is 24,869 enlisted men and 2,169 officers for a total of 27,038. Late in the year, when gold is discovered in Alaska, the Army is called upon to police and explore the area. The 14th Infantry and elements of other infantry and cavalry regiments spend two years surveying routes and estimating resources of the territory.

31 July. **Troops Keep Order. Jackson Hole, Wyoming.**
Major Adna Chaffee takes a squadron of the 9th Cavalry and a battalion of the 8th Infantry by train to Market Lake Idaho, and then on to Jackson Hole to prevent an outbreak of hostilities when civilians kill three Bannock Indians, one of whom was a child. The presence of Regular Army troops maintains calm, and the issue is resolved in the courts.

1897

January. **Status of the Army.**
Even though railroads now carry much of the materiel needed at Western posts, wagons continue to be an important part of the Army's logistical system. In the fiscal year ending on 30 June the Quartermaster Department moves 32,647 tons of supplies by wagon and 48,745 by rail. Stagecoach lines carry 967 Army passengers and just over a ton of stores.

Above: *The mounted color guard of the 10th U.S. Cavalry Regiment is shown in the dress uniform of the final decades of the nineteenth century. Yellow became the cavalry branch color in 1851. ("10th U.S. Cavalry Regiment, 1896," Harry C. Lauter, Jr., Company of Military Historians)*

5 March. **Alger Becomes Secretary of War.**
Russell A. Alger, Civil War veteran who enlisted as a private, rose to become a brevet major general of volunteers, and was elected commander of the Grand Army of the Republic in 1889, becomes Secretary of War. He is criticized for the department's poor performance during the Spanish-American War and resigns in 1899 at President McKinley's request.

31 May. **Last Indian Scouts Discharged.**
The Army discharges 53 members of L Troop, 7th Cavalry, ending the Army scout program. A number of the Indian Scouts, however, enlist in other units and continue to serve many more years as members of the Regular Army.

ARMY OF EMPIRE

1898–1913

ARMY OF EMPIRE

1898–1913

John Langellier

In the final years of the nineteenth century, the Army concluded its frontier constabulary duty. While still manning a string of defenses along the American coasts, the Army faced the challenges of the United States becoming an international power. With the explosion of USS *Maine* in Havana Harbor, the Army became engaged around the world.

In 1898, the United States entered the world scene with a burst of enthusiasm that rallied popular support to President William McKinley's call to arms against Spain. Nearly one million men stepped forth to join the colors, but just over a tenth of this number actually would don a uniform. Among them was Harvard-educated Theodore Roosevelt, who resigned his post as Undersecretary of the Navy to become the deputy commander of the 1st Regiment of Volunteer Cavalry (the Rough Riders); he embodied a powerful, vocal group that sought overseas expansion even at the cost of war. Roosevelt and his like-minded contemporaries eagerly enlisted, hastily trained, and haphazardly equipped for the war. In Cuba they would face a foe of superior numbers awaiting them in defensive positions that the enemy had been able to prepare for generations.

Despite these shortcomings, as V Corps steamed south, it was the first time that such a large body of American soldiers had gathered since the Civil War. Once ashore they moved against Santiago 18 miles away. Some 4,000–5,000 Cuban insurgents under rebel leader Calixto García reinforced the U.S. troops, who greeted their new Spanish-speaking comrades in arms with "Viva Cuba libre," to which came the reply, "Vivan los Americanos."

Sharp fighting soon followed, but more American troops fell to disease than to Spanish infantry and artillery. Even as Cuba was secured, Commanding General of the Army Nelson A. Miles made a hasty invasion of Puerto Rico. This veteran, and Congressional Medal of Honor recipient, raced against time, fearful that his landing force would not seize this strategic island before the Spanish capitulated, and thus retained control of Puerto Rico. His rapid progress overpowered the Spanish garrisons in time to claim the prize as part of the negotiations with Madrid.

Admiral George Dewey's destruction of the Spanish fleet in Manila Bay opened the way for Army forces to land and take Manila, angering many Filipinos who saw the Americans as replacements for their former Spanish masters. Under the leadership of Emilio Aquinaldo, an insurrection erupted in the Philippines. Even when that ended in 1902, a bloody, protracted ten-year guerrilla war continued in the islands with Muslim fundamentalists who employed guile and fanatical suicidal attacks.

The Army was called to other parts of the world at the same time. In 1900 American soldiers found themselves in China to quell the Society of Harmonious Fists, or "Boxers." This Chinese grassroots movement to drive out the "foreign devils" from their country gained the support of the Empress and most of her top advisors. An international coalition responded, including the Americans who sought to rescue the members of the American and other legations who were surrounded in Peking. The 15th Infantry would stay many years in China to

maintain the "open door" policy espoused by Washington.

The lessons learned in both the Civil War and the clash with Spain stimulated the Army during this period in its search for greater professional sophistication and improved technology. Not long after the Chinese rebellion had been quelled, an expanded Army began operating under a newly established general staff led by progressive Secretaries of War, Chiefs of Staff of the Army, and other influential reformers and expansionists who created a modern martial organization, in large part based on Emory Upton's rediscovered and previously unpublished writings. With Upton providing a similar intellectual underpinning to that the U.S. Navy had found in Alfred Thayer Mahan, the U.S. Army was on a new course. Technological advances in armament, transportation, communication, and even aviation combined with improved war planning, intelligence, logistical operations, and military education ensued during the dynamic decade and a half that followed the outbreak of the Spanish-American War. The period between 1898 and 1913 proved one of the most critical eras in the evolution of the Army.

Pages 492–493: *During the Spanish-American War, the 1st Volunteer Cavalry led by Colonel "Teddy" Roosevelt captured the public's imagination and helped him become President years later. ("Charge of the Rough Riders up San Juan Hill," by Frederic Remington, Frederic Remington Art Museum, Ogdensburg, NY)*

Above: *Lieutenant Thomas E. Selfridge became the Army's first aviation casualty when he crashed while flying with Orville Wright during the period when the Army began its pioneer efforts at aviation. (David Craig)*

ARMY OF EMPIRE

1898–1913

"It has been a splendid little war; begun with the highest motives, carried on with magnificent intelligence and spirit, favored by that fortune which loves the brave."

—John Hay, U.S. Ambassador to the Court of St. James, to Colonel Theodore Roosevelt, 1st U.S. Volunteer Cavalry, May 1898

1898

January. **Status of the Army.**
The Regular Army remains a constabulary force of approximately 27,400 officers and enlisted men. Most are assigned to 25 infantry regiments, ten regiments of cavalry, and five regiments of artillery, all of which are broken into small detachments from Alaska to Florida. Eight staff departments headed by brigadier generals help manage and supply the Army, while the Corps of Engineers is engaged in both civil and military works. Major General Nelson A. Miles, Civil War veteran and hero of the Indian wars, is the Army's commanding general. Major Generals Wesley Merritt and John R. Brooke are the other two senior officers and command the two main military regional departments. Reduced funding has delayed the planned modernization of the coastal artillery batteries. One unusual Army mission underway at congressional direction is the transport by Lieutenant

D. B. Devore of more than 900 reindeer from Lapland to Alaska to help feed miners who are reported to be starving.

15 February. **USS *Maine* Explosion Triggers Spanish-American War. Cuba.**
USS *Maine* explodes in Havana Harbor, killing 266 crewmen. Although the destruction of the ship probably was the result of an internal explosion, "jingoists" among the general public, press, and politicians bent on war against Spain call for a military response. "Remember the Maine" becomes their rallying cry.

18 February. **Military Peacekeeping Force to Alaska.**
The Army establishes a safety zone in Alaska to protect miners and property during the gold rush in that territory. The 14th Infantry is assigned the mission of patrolling the zone.

8 March. **Expansion of U.S. Artillery.**
Congress enacts legislation to add two new Regular regiments of artillery (6th and 7th) to the Army.

11 April. **United States to Declare War on Spain.**
President William McKinley requests that Congress declare war on Spain.

15 April. **Invasion Force Gathers.**
Orders are issued for the concentration of troops at several Gulf of Mexico ports, but the orders are soon rescinded because the locations are found to be unsuitable. Troops are directed to two other locations—Camp Alger at Falls Church, Virginia, and Camp Thomas at Chickamauga Park, Georgia. Some 22 infantry regiments and six regiments of cavalry along with ten batteries of field artillery are gathered. Plans are to form eight corps (I–VIII), each under a major general. VI Corps is never formed. The War Department's Office of Military Information is tasked to compile background information on each of the campaign areas for the commanders.

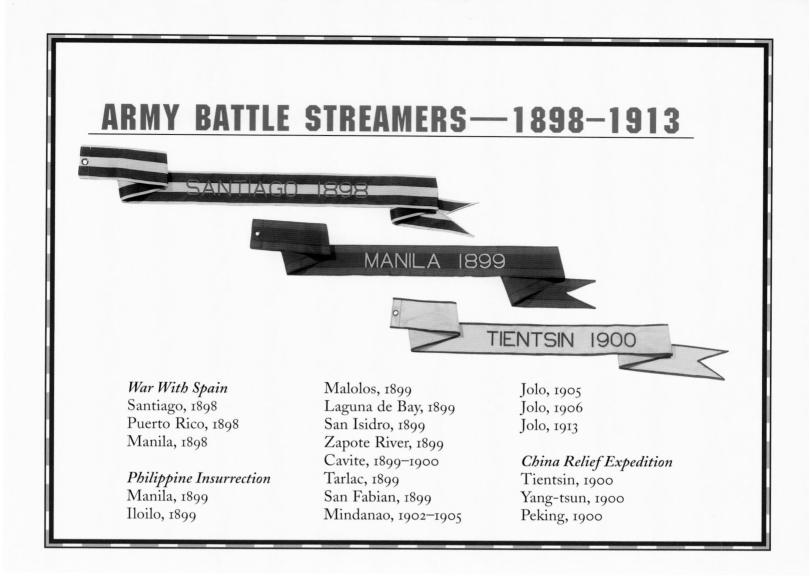

ARMY BATTLE STREAMERS—1898–1913

SANTIAGO 1898

MANILA 1899

TIENTSIN 1900

War With Spain
Santiago, 1898
Puerto Rico, 1898
Manila, 1898

Philippine Insurrection
Manila, 1899
Iloilo, 1899

Malolos, 1899
Laguna de Bay, 1899
San Isidro, 1899
Zapote River, 1899
Cavite, 1899–1900
Tarlac, 1899
San Fabian, 1899
Mindanao, 1902–1905

Jolo, 1905
Jolo, 1906
Jolo, 1913

China Relief Expedition
Tientsin, 1900
Yang-tsun, 1900
Peking, 1900

19 April. **Congress Authorizes Armed Intervention in Cuba.**
A joint resolution of Congress authorizes the President to undertake armed intervention in Cuba against Spanish forces.

22–23 April. **Volunteers Called for War Against Spain.**
A mobilization act passed by Congress calls for 125,000 volunteers to be enlisted, and the recruitment of another 10,000 men into a special force deemed as "possessing immunity from diseases incident to tropical climates" (mostly African-Americans, based on an erroneous belief that this group was inured to tropical diseases because of their heredity and background). The next day approval is given to almost double the Regular Army to 65,000 for the duration of the war.

25 April. **Official Declaration of War With Spain.**
Despite diplomatic efforts by President William McKinley and others to avert conflict, Congress declares that a state of war has existed with Spain since 21 April.

26 April. **Reorganization of Regular Army Regiments.**
Congress approves a third battalion for Regular infantry regiments, adding four companies to each regiment. Two companies exist on paper but were not filled previously, while two new companies (L and M) are added. Company strength also is increased to 100. At West Point, 59 cadets graduate from the United States Military Academy. Many join commands

Opposite: *Depicted in this 1898 print are a dashing cavalry officer with saber and an artillery officer with field glasses. ("Men of the Army and Navy," Howard Chandler Christy)*

Right: *An accurate artistic rendering of an infantry officer in the typical field uniform worn at the outset of the Spanish-American War. ("Men of the Army and Navy," Howard Chandler Christy)*

heading for the Spanish-American War, including Second Lieutenant Clarke Churchman, who will be wounded at San Juan Hill, and Second Lieutenant Charles H. Munson, who dies on board a ship en route to the Philippine Islands.

1–30 May. Disease Claims Lives Before Fight Begins.
Eighty officers and 2,520 enlisted men die from disease in the mobilization camps prior to departure for overseas duty, mainly from poor sanitation and food. Chaos reigns in the camps due to poor planning and general lack of discipline in many Volunteer units.

19 May. Signal Corps Intercepts Spanish Communications.
With authority from President McKinley, the Army Signal Corps, under Chief Signal Officer Brigadier General Adolphus W. Greely, takes control of the nation's telephone and telegraph lines following the declaration of war. Of special concern are terminals near the Army's mobilization camps. Censorship is imposed on U.S. and foreign commercial companies

Above: *These two "shavetails" of the 10th U.S. Infantry probably had little more than shooting range experience when the United States declared war on Spain. (Frontier Army Museum, Fort Leavenworth, KS)*

Right: *The Rough Riders donned brown canvas fatigue clothing, while volunteers reported in heavy blue wool uniforms when William McKinley called the nation to arms in 1898. ("Cuban Expedition, 1898," Fritz Kredel)*

prohibiting coded messages or any information on the military, and incoming traffic is monitored. On 19 May, Captain James Allen sees a message in Tampa stating the Spanish fleet has just arrived in Santiago harbor. This information is passed to the U.S. Navy, which had lost track of the Spanish fleet a week before, and action is taken to blockade the harbor, trapping the fleet. This not only sets the stage for the destruction of that fleet, but also changes the War Department's land campaign objective from Havana to Santiago.

25 May. Troops Depart for the Philippines. California.
Most of Brigadier Thomas M. Anderson's 2d Division, VIII Army Corps, sails via chartered ships from San Francisco for the Philippine Islands. The expedition consists of the 1st California and 2d Oregon Volunteer Infantry and a battalion of the 14th U.S. Infantry. It is the vanguard of the 14,000 men who mobilized in Camp Merritt, a disease-ridden camp named for the corps commander, Major General Wesley Merritt, and located in Golden Gate Park. Priority of Navy transports has been given to the Cuba expedition, and lack of civilian ships forces the rest of VIII Corps to be sent in groups about three weeks apart.

28 May. Regular Officers Retain Rank.
To provide experienced officers for the Volunteer units, Congress authorizes Regular officers to transfer to the Volunteers without having to relinquish their

Right: *Rough Rider Lieutenant Colonel Roosevelt is shown watching the loading of supplies, weapons, and troops to be transported from Florida to Cuba. The logistical demands overwhelmed the Army's capabilities in 1898. ("Embarking for Cuba," Charles Johnson Post, Army Art Collection, NMUSA)*

Regular rank and grade. During the war 387 Regular officers will serve with Volunteer regiments.

1 June. Signal Corps Cuts Spanish Communications. Cuban Coast.

A chartered ship with newly promoted Volunteer Lieutenant Colonel Allen, three Signal Corps sergeants, and ten volunteers from the 1st Artillery arrives off the Cuban coast with the mission to locate and cut the three underwater telegraph cables running to Spain. One cable is found and cut, but repeated artillery fire finally forces their ship to leave.

14 June. Troops Sail for Cuba. Tampa, Florida.

Some 17,000 U.S. troops are forced to wait for a week aboard their 32 transports, where they live in primitive sanitary conditions and in sultry heat without ice or fresh food before they finally sail for Cuba. The popular tune "There'll Be A Hot Time in the Old Town Tonight" characterizes the enthusiasm and privations of the force as it steams southward.

18 June. Summary Court-Martial Authorized.

In an effort to streamline military justice, Congress authorizes summary courts-martial of enlisted personnel by one officer with specific limited punishments.

22 June. Opening Salvos of the Spanish American War. Cuba.

After hearing the shelling of Daiquiri by the U.S. Navy, the Army's V Corps lands amid chaos but without resistance from the more than 200,000 Spanish troops on the island. There are no boats suitable for them, so the horses and mules are forced to jump into the water and swim for shore. The corps consists of 18 Regular and two Volunteer regiments of infantry, ten squadrons of Regular and two of Volunteer cavalry serving dismounted, a mounted squadron of Regular cavalry, four light batteries and two batteries of siege artillery, and a machine-gun company, all commanded by Civil War veteran and Medal of Honor recipient Major General William "Pecos Bill" Shafter.

24 June. Battle of Las Guasimas. Cuba.

The Cavalry Division commanded by Volunteer Major General "Fighting Joe" Wheeler, a former Confederate general, attacks through thick jungle and seizes Spanish positions at Las Guasimas Ridge. The dismounted cavalrymen of the 1st and 10th Cavalry and 1st Volunteer Cavalry ("Rough Riders") do well. Captain Allyn Capron, Jr., Troop L of the Rough Riders, along with his first sergeant, Hamilton Fish, a Columbia University alumnus and athlete, proceed with several other of his troops to take the point. They encounter deadly fire from the Mauser rifles of the Spanish. Both Capron and Fish fall as two of the first casualties. Assistant Surgeon James Robb Church, 1st U.S. Volunteer Cavalry, also performs gallantly, voluntarily and unaided carrying several seriously wounded men from the firing line to a secure position, in each instance the target of intense fire and great danger— actions for which he will receive the Medal of Honor.

28 June. U.S. Forces Begin Move on Santiago. Cuba.
Major General Shafter learns from Cuban sources that some 8,000 Spanish troops have slipped out of the town of Manzanillo and are making their way to join Spanish forces to the east. This intelligence spurs Shafter to press the attack against Santiago.

30 June. American Expedition Lands. Philippines.
After a miserable trip aboard cramped transports, the 2,400 men of Anderson's 2d Division land at Cavite, south of Manila. He puts them to work unloading since the docks cannot accommodate the ships.

30 June. Heroics in Cuba.
At Tayabocoa, Cuba Private Dennis Bell, Troop H, 10th U.S. Cavalry, voluntarily goes ashore to rescue wounded comrades after previous attempts have failed to reach the men. The following year his heroism is acknowledged with the presentation of the Medal of Honor. Three other soldiers from the 10th Cavalry—Private William H. Thompkins, Troop G, and Privates George H. Wanton and Fitz Lee, both of Troop M, also will be presented the Medal of Honor for similar valorous actions.

Above: *The Regulars of the 1st and 10th Cavalry leading the American advance ran into the first serious Spanish opposition at Las Guasimas. ("Charge of the 1st and 10th Regular Cavalry, 1898," Howard Chandler Christy, West Point Museum, West Point, NY)*

1 July. Battles of El Caney and San Juan Hill. Cuba.
Major General Shafter orders a simultaneous assault on the three Spanish positions—El Caney on the right by one division and Kettle Hill and San Juan Hill straight ahead by two others. Army Regulars and Volunteers attack together to capture the heights, where forts and trenches are manned by the determined Spaniards. The hard fighting at El Caney costs Brigadier General Henry W. Lawton's 2d Infantry Division four officers and 127 enlisted men dead and 25 officers and 335 enlisted wounded. Pushing through thick brush and jungle, Regular and Volunteer infantrymen in the other two divisions also battle a formidable foe before carrying Kettle Hill and San Juan Hill. Involved in the fighting are the Regulars of the 6th, 9th, 13th, and 16th Infantry along with Rough Riders and troopers of the 1st, 6th, and 10th Cavalry. An artillery battery of Gatling guns is also brought forward in support. In all, eight men participating in the assault will receive the Medal of Honor. Total losses in taking the two hills is 15 officers and 127 enlisted men killed and 69 officers and 945 enlisted wounded. During the battle, the Signal Corps air balloon is brought forward to observe the Spanish positions with less than sterling success. The balloon's lines become entangled in the brush, and the balloon's placement along the same trail being used by the advancing troops attracts heavy and well-directed Spanish fire, causing casualties.

EYEWITNESS: SAN JUAN HILL

On 1 July 1898, Major General William R. Shafter's V Corps found its advance on Santiago City, Cuba, blocked by Spanish forces occupying the San Juan Heights in defensive positions with block houses, forts, entrenchments, rifle pits, and barbed wire fences. Kettle Hill, a small knob in the valley in front of the heights and at El Caney, a position on the American right, were also fortified. Shafter's plan was to simultaneously assault both El Caney and the San Juan Heights. One infantry division would attack El Caney at dawn and secure the American right. Once they were engaged the dismounted troopers of Major General Joseph Wheeler's cavalry division would attack Kettle Hill while a second infantry division assaulted the steep San Juan Heights. Corporal John Conn, 24th Infantry Regiment, described the action:

"After we had advanced about a mile, we began to meet the wounded coming to the rear, and thought seriously of the situation, and then in a short time the road was almost choked with the wounded and stragglers. Our progress was very slow so when we got into the zone of the small arms firing it was about 11:30 o'clock. It was terrible. There were wounded lying all alongside and in the road, and the air seemed alive with bullets and shells of all descriptions and caliber. You could not tell from what direction they were coming; all that we could understand was that we were needed further in front, and we could not shoot, for we could not see anything to shoot at. We advanced until we were assured by our divisional commander that our mettle was about to be tested; that he was depending on his boys of the 24th to make history, and that the fate of his record and possibly of the nation depended on the quality of the mettle mentioned.

"We piled up all our extra baggage and our blanket rolls, nothing but our arms, ammunition and canteens being needed and, fully stripped for fighting, we advanced with our regimental chaplain's last words ringing in our ears: 'Acquit yourselves like men and fight.' We were right in it then, in good shape—lots of music and very few drums. From the appearance we passed two or three regiments lying in the road (71st New York Volunteers), so that we had to stumble over them and pick our way through them to advance . . . until we were in the desired position, and it was terrible—just one continual roar of small arms, cannon and bursting shells; but our position was comparatively secure on account of the river bank.

"The orders from our colonel were: '24th Infantry move forward 150 yards.' With a last look at our arms and ammunition—and yes a little prayer—we started, and such a volley as they sent into us! It was then that Sergeant Brown was shot almost at the river bank. We had to cut and destroy a barbed wire fence. How or by what means it was destroyed no one scarcely knows; but destroyed it surely was, and in that angry mob, nearly all the officers having been disabled, there was no organization recognized. Men were crazy. Someone said: 'Let us charge," and someone sounded 'Let us charge' on a bugle. When that pack of demons swept forward the Spaniards stood as long as mortals could stand, then quit their trenches and retreated. . . . When we gained the hill they were in full retreat. It seems now almost impossible that civilized men could so recklessly destroy each other."

—*Vince Hawkins*

Above: *Lieutenant Colonel Theodore Roosevelt with his "Rough Riders" (1st U.S. Volunteer Cavalry) in a victory photo after the famed battle for the San Juan Heights. The ebullient "T. R." was recommended for the Congressional Medal of Honor for his actions, but it was not awarded until the 1990s. (National Archives)*

3 July. Spanish Fleet Takes to High Seas. Cuba.
The Spanish squadron attempts to escape from Havana Harbor, but the American fleet destroys it at sea, while 3,500 haggard reinforcements from Manzanillo join their comrades in Santiago for the final fight against the Americans.

7 July. Hawaii Annexed.
A joint resolution of Congress annexes the Hawaiian Islands, which will provide a strategic harbor for the U.S. Pacific Fleet and a staging area for American ground forces in the region. In Cuba, Shafter's forces seal off the last possible route of retreat for the Spanish defenders of Santiago.

14 July. Black Troops Volunteer for Hospital Duty. Cuba.
African-American troops of the 24th Infantry volunteer to nurse U.S. soldiers suffering from malaria and yellow fever. More than half of these 60 men succumb to the diseases they have volunteered to combat.

15 July. Insignia Authorized to Designate Major U.S. Units.
Following the practice established during the Civil War, Army corps and divisions are authorized

designation badges. Some resurrect badges from that war; others design new badges for wear on their uniforms and caps.

17 July. U.S. Forces Victorious. Cuba.
The Spanish surrender Santiago, and Major General Shafter's forces enter the city. In Paris, Spanish representatives indicate a desire to negotiate a truce, and American representatives are sent.

18 July. New Transport Organization Authorized.
The Division of Transportation is created in the Quartermaster Department to exercise command and control of all rail and water transport for the Army.

21 July. U.S. Forces Sail for Puerto Rico. Cuba.
Lieutenant General Nelson A. Miles debarks with his troops from Guantánamo for the campaign in Puerto Rico.

25 July. Army Lands in Puerto Rico and Philippines.
Miles' expeditionary force comes ashore at Guánica, Puerto Rico. It is the last time the senior general of the Army leads troops in the field. At Cavite in the Philippines, Major General Merritt arrives with the third and final increment of his force, bringing the VIII Corps to a total of 10,946 officers and men. Merritt

makes contact with Emilio Aguinaldo, self-proclaimed president of an independent Philippine Republic, who has been leading the fight against the Spanish.

27 July. Miles Receives Reinforcements. Puerto Rico.
Ships carrying some 3,300 reinforcements consisting of the 16th Pennsylvania and 2d and 3d Wisconsin Volunteer Infantry of the I Corps arrive to join Miles' campaign, but the commander of these troops, Major General James H. Wilson, receives orders not to land. Rather, his sea transports are dispatched east to participate in the anticipated action at Ponce, where Brigadier General Theodore Schwan's Regulars of the 11th and 19th Infantry, along with his cavalry and artillery, are seeking to link up with Miles.

29 July. VIII Corps Moves Into Position. Philippine Islands.
Negotiations with Aguinaldo's commanders permit Merritt to move his troops through the Filipino lines and into attack positions on the outskirts of Manila. Major J. Franklin Bell, Merritt's intelligence officer, is sent ahead to find a route for the attack.

1 August. Miles Troops Advance. Puerto Rico.
Miles' lead element captures the town of Marroyo. The Spanish garrison at Guayma capitulates the next day.

3 August. Miles Forces Continue to Grow.
Another 3,700 infantrymen of the 3d Illinois, 4th Ohio, and 4th Pennsylvania Volunteers, commanded by Brigadier General Peter C. Hains, add even more might to Miles' campaign when they come ashore at Arroyo. A few days later the arrival of Major General John R. Brooke's 2,000 artillerymen and cavalry troopers helps make the outcome of the contest inevitable.

9 August. Wilson's Troops Advance.
An Army column under Major General Wilson bound for Coamo breaks through a gorge fortified and defended by the Spanish. Other U.S. Army columns also move to seize towns.

12 August. The Spanish Sign Peace Accords. Madrid, Spain.
Spanish officials sign the peace protocols they have received from Washington, setting the stage for formal peace negotiations to begin in Paris.

13 August. Manila Is Taken. Philippine Islands.
Purposefully excluding Aguinaldo's waiting army from any role, Merritt sends the brigades of Brigadier Arthur MacArthur and Francis V. Greene in an early-morning assault on the city. A prearranged deal with Spanish authorities limits their resistance in the face of overwhelming forces. Advancing in a pouring rain, the men receive some naval gun fire support from the American ships in the bay and take the center of the city with only a little trouble from defenders in a blockhouse in MacArthur's sector. American losses are

Opposite: *Lieutenant John H. Parker's six-gun Gatling Gun Detachment provided welcome support at San Juan Hill in one of the first instances of rapid-fire weapons being employed in direct support of an attack. ("Gatlings to the Assault," H. Charles McBarron, U.S. Army Art Collection, NMUSA)*

Right: *Captain Alan Capron's battery provided artillery support against the Spanish emplacements at El Caney on 1 July 1898. (Library of Congress)*

five killed and 38 wounded. The Filipinos are outraged at the deception and several tense situations and scattered gunfire occur when they attempt to force Americans out of some areas. Naming Merritt as military governor of the city, the War Department refuses to consider a joint occupation, leaving VIII Corps now inside the city surrounded by Aguinaldo's army.

25–26 August. Merritt Departs.
In ill health and feeling his age, Major General Merritt requests replacement on 25 August. The next day he receives orders to go to Paris to take part in the U.S.-Spanish peace negotiations. His second-in-command, Brigadier General Elwell S. Otis, takes over. Otis, nicknamed "Granny," is widely disliked, and Merritt's departure is followed by a wave of requests from other officers asking for reassignment. Adding to Otis's problems is the ever-present conflict between the discipline demanded by the Regular officers and the "part-time" citizen soldier attitude of many Volunteers. State Volunteer units also frequently bring with them internal hometown political or other partisan conflicts that erode unit cohesion.

31 August. U.S. Army's Expansion.
The Volunteer army raised for war against Spain attains its highest troop strength at 216,029 soldiers. Volunteers and Regular army forces combine for a total of 275,000 men under arms. This number stands in sharp contrast to the average strength of the Army for the three previous decades. Of these men some 379 were killed in action, another 1,604 sustained wounds, and nearly 4,000 more perished from disease and other causes.

30 September. Last Indian Uprising. Minnesota.
A protest by a band of Chippewas living near the Lake Leech Agency turns violent when a detachment of 20 soldiers from the 3d Infantry arrives to try to restore order. Gunfire breaks out and 80 reinforcements from the 3d Infantry are sent under Captain Melville C. Wilkinson. The infantrymen are surrounded and fight for two days before the Indians break off the fight. Wilkinson and six soldiers are dead and 14 men wounded. Within a few days, a larger force of 3d Infantry arrives and peace is restored. It is the last battle of the Indian Wars.

7 October. **Khaki Combat Uniforms Adopted.**
The Army drops its traditional two-tone blue woolen campaign uniform and adopts a khaki color for field uniforms for the first time.

16 November. **Regulations Launch Transport Corps.**
The Secretary of War approves regulations governing, and formation of, the newly established Army Transport Service reporting directly to the Quartermaster General of the Army. Two home ports—San Francisco and New York—are designated, each with an Army officer as General Superintendent in charge of all Army shipping routed to and from that port. He has an officer as assistant as well as a medical officer; all others are civilian employees.

10 December. **Peace Treaty Signed with Spain.**
The Treaty of Peace is signed with Spain giving Puerto Rico, Cuba, and the Philippines to the United States. It is ratified by the Senate 11 April 1899. Volunteer enlistments are already ending, and many waiting to be shipped overseas are released from duty.

26 December. **Troops Arrive at Mindoro. Philippines.**
The 1st Separate Brigade, led by Brigadier Marcus P. Miller, arrives in transports off the island of Mindoro with the mission from Otis to occupy the port city of Iloilo. Miller finds armed Filipinos in the city and

Opposite: *Most cavalrymen sent to Cuba had to leave their horses behind and fought dismounted alongside the infantry. ("The Rough Riders," Mort Künstler)*

Above: *Thousands of American troops fell prey to diseases ranging from measles to yellow fever. The Army Medical Corps administered to them, although often under the most primitive conditions. ("Field Hospital Back of the Lines," Charles Johnson Post, Army Art Collection, NMUSA)*

decides to keep his men on the ships and negotiate a peaceful landing if possible. The effort is futile and after 94 days the ships return to Manila.

1899

January. **Status of the Army.**
The largest Army of Regulars and Volunteers since the Civil War begins the year committed to two theaters of conflict on opposite sides of the globe. Overall strength has dropped with the release of some Volunteers, but still almost half of the 155,772 officers and enlisted serving in the Army are deployed outside the United States: 43,159 in Cuba, 6,372 in Puerto Rico, and 21,790 in the Philippine Islands.

.4–5 February. **War Breaks Out with Filipino Army. Philippines.**

Relations between the American forces and the Philippine Republican Army camped on the outskirts of Manila are hostile. The Filipinos are frustrated at the failure to recognize their independence and angry at biased treatment by their former American allies. Open warfare finally breaks out on the night of 4 February, after a 1st Nebraska Volunteer sentry, Private William Grayson, fires at a Filipino patrol when they ignore his challenge. His shots are answered and within hours the fighting is general. Both sides are unprepared.

5 February. **VIII Corps Attacks.**

Brigadier General MacArthur uses his division to expand the American positions on the north and captures a fortified a ridge overlooking the city. The 20th Kansas Volunteer Infantry, led by Colonel Fredrick Funston, is one of the leading units in the assault. In the south, Brigadier General Anderson's 1st Division's attacks suffer from some initial confusion but finally succeed in taking the village of Pasay. The battle has been fought over a 16-mile front and involved most of 13 American regiments. Losses are 44 killed and 194 wounded, mostly men in the 14th Infantry and 3d Artillery.

Above: *Volunteer gunners from Utah blast away at enemy positions in the Philippines. They man some of the first breech-loading field pieces adopted by the United States— the 3.2-inch "bag gun." ("The Utah Light Battery," Donna Neary, National Guard Bureau)*

10 February. **MacArthur Captures Caloocan.**

Taking the offensive again, MacArthur sends his troops, supported by naval gunfire, into the fortified town of Caloocan, seizing the railroad terminus with several engines and hundreds of railcars. This action pushes the American perimeter three to six miles out of Manila.

2 March. **Volunteers Authorized for the Philippines.**

The unexpected outbreak of a rebellion prompts Congress to make several increases in the Army. The Regular Army size is increased by almost 3,000 by adding officers and men to the existing regiments. In addition, 35,000 two-year Volunteers could be raised to fill four new Volunteer regiments of cavalry (11th–14th), and five regiments of Volunteer infantry (26th–30th). State designations are not used and Volunteer officers have federal, not state, commissions—a major change from the old militia system. Other items include requiring an examination for all second lieutenants before appointment, raising the pay of cooks, and increasing the number of cadets at West Point.

17–31 March. **U.S. Forces Win Major Victory. Philippines.**

After reorganizing VIII Corps into a defensive force to hold the improved positions around Manila and a field force to attack Aguinaldo's army, Major General Otis begins a campaign to capture the Philippine Republic's capital of Malolos and to destroy its army. Using MacArthur's 2d Division as the striking force, Otis plans a sweeping movement with two brigades around the Filipinos' left flank, then uses a third

Right: *The White House communication room run by Captain Benjamin F. Montgomery (left at desk) and men from the Signal Corps provided rapid communication between Washington and the U.S. forces deployed to Cuba. (Library of Congress)*

Below: *Elihu Root served as a reformist Secretary of War from 1899 through 1904, and later as Secretary of State before being elected a U.S. senator in 1909. (Raimundo de Madrazo, Army Art Collection, NMUSA)*

brigade in a frontal attack to drive the Filipinos into the waiting brigades. The plan is too ambitious and unrealistic given the terrain and jungle. Strong Filipino resistance and other factors soon cause Otis to change his plans and use MacArthur's flanking move as the main assault. Fighting across several rivers and through fortified towns, the American Regulars and Volunteers finally take the burning town of Malolos, Aguinaldo's first capital.

21 April. **Insignia for Electricians.**
General Order No. 80 prescribes a forked-lightning insignia for the newly created noncommissioned officer specialty of artillery electrician sergeant, a new skill that is in keeping with advances made in coastal artillery during the period.

27 April. **20th Kansas Volunteers Go Into Action. Philippine Islands.**
Volunteer Colonel Fredrick Funston leads a raiding party of the 20th Kansas Volunteer Infantry across the Rio Grande del Pampanga River in small crafts to outflank the enemy. They succeed in defeating an enemy who outnumbers them. Funston and two of his men, Private Edward White and Private William B. Trembley, receive the Medal of Honor. Between 1899 and 1913 another 68 men, including two members of the Philippine Scouts and nine doughboys from the 1st North Dakota Volunteers, would be presented the Medal of Honor for extraordinary valor.

30 June. **Experimental Electric Vehicles.**
The chief signal officer reports the purchase of three electric vehicles for trial as trucks to haul three-quarter-ton signal equipment, and one for the transport of officers. After two years of testing the inability of the vehicles' batteries to retain their charges for sufficient periods ends this pioneering experiment and leads to the adoption of gasoline-powered motor transport instead.

Left: *Colonel Franklin Bell's daring leadership of the 36th Volunteer Infantry in the Philippines earned him the Medal of Honor and subsequent rapid advancement in the Army. ("I Would Rather Die at the Front," Rick Reeves)*

Opposite: *Men from the North Dakota and Oregon volunteers rush to secure a burning bridge at San Isidro, Luzon, 6 May 1899. ("Soldiers in the Sun," Donna Neary, National Guard Bureau)*

July. **Volunteers Depart. Philippines.**
Strength of VIII Corps declines as the enlistment terms of many Regulars and Volunteers comes to an end. By the end of the month 8,000 Volunteers have sailed for home. With sickness and other problems, only 20,000 men are reported for duty in Luzon. New recruits are on the way but do not arrive until September.

1 August. **Root Appointed New Secretary of War.**
Elihu Root becomes Secretary of War. After his admission to the state bar he practiced law and became a prominent figure in New York political circles, which paved the way for his serving as Secretary of War until 31 January 1904. Root institutes a series of key reforms within the Army, in part inspired by the writings of the late Brigadier General Emory Upton. These include an increase in the permanent strength of the Regulars, the creation of a General Staff, rotation of officers between staff and line, less reliance on seniority in selection of leadership, joint planning between the land and sea forces, an improved reserve program with special attention to the National Guard, and the reorganization of the military school system.

September–October. **Dry Season Campaign. Philippines.**
Taking advantage of the dry season, various American columns drive the Filipinos out of a series of towns, clearing the central plain of Luzon and pushing the Filipino insurgents deeper into the hills. During the year, a small force of 3d Cavalry and some Macabebe scouts under Volunteer Brigadier General Samuel B. M. Young have been in pursuit of Aguinaldo. Young captures a number of towns and finds and releases American prisoners but has been able to come only as close as Aguinaldo's rear guard on several occasions.

11 November. **Battle of San Jacinto. Philippines.**
Men of the 33d U.S. Volunteer Regiment fight through a vicious planned ambush to emerge victorious over Filipinos near San Jacinto. While Volunteers fire from rice paddies to pin the main enemy positions, Major Peyton C. March leads his battalion in turning the enemy's left flank and attacking them from the rear. Losses for the 33d are 21 men killed or wounded.

13 November. **Further Victories Over Insurgents. Philippines.**
After a two-month campaign, soldiers of the 36th Volunteer Infantry from MacArthur's division march into Tarlac, the last capital of the Philippine Republic. The Filipino enemy abandons conventional warfare to carry on the fight for independence as guerrillas. Brigadier Joseph Wheeler, who arrived in the Philippines in August after his Cuban service, is serving as one of MacArthur's brigade commanders. Concerned about Wheeler's recklessness, MacArthur finally assigns Wheeler's brigade to assist in maintaining the logistics lines.

9 December. Volunteers Engage Guerrillas. Philippines.
During a three-hour engagement on the island of Luzon, a battalion of the 34th U.S. Volunteers, commanded by Lieutenant Colonel Robert L. Howze, destroys a brigade of Filipino guerrillas.

18 December. Lawton Killed in Action. Philippines.
Major General Henry W. Lawton, the popular senior field commander in VIII Corps, is killed by a rifle bullet while walking the firing line in the midst of a small action near San Mateo. Visible even in the rain and mist with his white raincoat and pith helmet, the tall general made a conspicuous target.

1900

January. **Status of the Army.**
Total strength is fewer than 100,000, with only 22,785 officers and enlisted remaining in the U.S. Although deployment to Cuba has dropped to 9,500, 3,385 remain in Puerto Rico and the force in the Philippines is almost 64,000. Combat activity continues on many of the islands, including Samar, Leyte, and Jolo, as the American occupation is expanded. As territory is brought under control, the senior Army officer is named as military governor of the area.

7 January. **Intense Fighting Tests Volunteers. Philippines.**
The 1st Battalion, 28th U.S. Volunteer Infantry, fights a two-hour battle with an entrenched Filipino force at Patol Bridge, Cavite, killing more than 100 of the enemy. The U.S. soldiers suffer only eight wounded. On the same day at Barrio Lumim on Luzon, the 2d and 3d Battalions, 28th U.S. Volunteer Infantry, defeat a numerically superior rebel force in a three-hour engagement.

24 March. **New Force Created. Puerto Rico.**
The Army organizes a local unit, the Puerto Rico Battalion, in San Juan to help with security.

27 April. **U.S. War Dead Returned. New York Harbor.**
The U.S. Army transport *Crook* docks with caskets bearing the remains of 747 military personnel. By 30 June, some 1,222 bodies from the Spanish-American War—13.63 percent of them unidentified—will have been returned to the United States.

15 May. **MacArthur Replaces Otis. Philippines.**
Volunteer Major General Arthur MacArthur replaces Major General Otis as commander of American forces and as governor-general of the islands. He has about 63,000 troops in his command.

LIEUTENANT GENERAL ARTHUR MacARTHUR

Arthur MacArthur was only 18 when, as a lieutenant with the 24th Wisconsin Infantry, he found himself and his comrades under fire from the Confederates at Missionary Ridge in Tennessee. The men had taken a line of enemy trenches, but when they received fire from further up the hill, they started a charge. No orders were given. As they charged, MacArthur grabbed the regiment's colors as the man carrying it was wounded. Shouting, "On Wisconsin!" the young officer led the charge and planted the flag on the crest of the hill. For his actions MacArthur was awarded the Medal of Honor and was promoted to major.

Born in Massachusetts on 2 June 1845, MacArthur moved with his family to Milwaukee, Wisconsin, as a boy and grew up there. In August 1862, 17-year-old MacArthur was commissioned as a second lieutenant in the 24th Wisconsin Volunteer Infantry. Fighting in the western theater, he distinguished himself in two battles before Missionary Ridge. By January 1864, he was a major and leading the 24th in combat at Resaca, Kenesaw Mountain, Jonesboro, and Franklin, where he was wounded in hand-to-hand fighting. MacArthur was promoted to lieutenant colonel at the age of 19; his men called him the "boy colonel of the west."

MacArthur mustered out of the Army after the war but returned in 1866 as a Regular lieutenant in the 17th Infantry, serving 20 years in the southwest frontier. It was during this time, in 1880, that his wife "Pinky" gave birth to a third son, Douglas. The baby would grow to be more famous than his father, eventually outranking him and earning his own Medal of Honor.

After the outbreak of the Spanish-American War, MacArthur was made a brigadier general of Volunteers and assigned to the Philippines as a brigade commander. He distinguished himself in fighting around Manila in February 1899 and then led the occupation of Luzon Island, crushing organized resistance.

But the war was not over. The Filipino insurrectos began a guerrilla war, sniping at U.S. soldiers and fighting small engagements before melting back into villages. In January 1900, MacArthur became the commander of all U.S. troops in the Philippines. In May he was made the military governor of the islands. He initiated new laws and democratic reforms, created schools and hospitals, and

dug wells. He founded the Philippine Scouts, who fought alongside U.S. soldiers and would prove themselves invaluable 41 years later when the Japanese invaded the islands.

When the Philippines were placed under civilian control in 1901, MacArthur, now a Regular major general, returned to the United States, where he served in a number of departmental commands. He served as an observer with the Japanese army during the Russo-Japanese War of 1904. In 1906 MacArthur was promoted to lieutenant general, becoming the ranking general of the Army. He retired in 1909 and died in 1912 while addressing the survivors of his Civil War regiment. After he collapsed while delivering a speech to the men, they draped the regiment's flag, which he had carried up Missionary Hill, over his body.

—*Kevin M. Hymel*

Above: *Major General Arthur MacArthur, military governor of the Philippines, was a strong-willed soldier who clashed with the Secretary of War about how the islands should be governed. (MacArthur Memorial and Archive, Norfolk, VA)*

Right: *Battery F (Reilly's Battery), 5th U.S. Artillery, in action, on 5 August 1900, at Peitsang, were part of the international relief force dispatched in the wake of the Boxer Rebellion. (National Archives)*

26 May. **Communications and Education.**
The Signal Corps begins construction of the Washington-Alaska telegraph cable.

5 June. **U.S. Patrol Fights Guerrillas. Philippines.**
An 18-man patrol from the 28th Volunteer Infantry engages Filipino rebels at Payapay, killing 14. Company A's commander dies in the action.

6 June. **Lieutenant General Rank Restored.**
Congress revives the title of lieutenant general for the senior major general commanding the Army. Major General Nelson A. Miles, Army commanding general since 1895, is the first to be so honored.

20 June. **The Boxer Rebellion Gains Strength. China.**
The siege of the foreign legations by the violent anti-foreigner "Boxers" in Peking begins, endangering the lives of the Americans there. An international relief force is formed including the United States, which alerts troops in the Philippines as well as on the West Coast for deployment. Volunteer Brigadier General Adna R. Chaffee is selected to lead the all-Regular American force that will be composed of the 9th and 14th Infantry, two troops of the 6th Cavalry, and a battery of the 5th Artillery.

8–13 July. **American Expeditionary Force Arrives. Taku, China.**
The 9th Infantry, under Colonel Emerson H. Liscum, is the first unit to arrive. The regiment travels from the Philippines with all equipment and several months of supplies in a record 19 days. Liscum, with two

battalions of the 9th, immediately marches 40 miles to join the International Relief Force at Tientsin.

13 July. **Ninth Infantry at Tientsin. China.**
The men of the 9th take part in an assault on the walled city. Positioned in the open for 15 hours, the 9th suffers 22 wounded and 18 killed, including Colonel Liscum. Liscum took the regimental colors from a fallen color bearer, only to receive a mortal wound himself. On the same day, Captain Andre W. Brewster of the 9th, while under fire, rescues two of his men from drowning. Two years later his heroism will be recognized with the presentation of the Medal of Honor. Another officer of the 9th U.S. Infantry, First Lieutenant Louis B. Lawton, carries a message and guides reinforcements across a wide-open space under heavy fire, during which he is wounded three times. He, too, will receive the Medal of Honor for his actions, as will Private Robert Von Schlick, Company C.

16 July. **Volunteers Keep Fighting. Barrio de Talaug, Philippines.**
A force of 120 men from the 28th U.S. Volunteer Infantry on Luzon successfully assaults an entrenched position of more than 400 rebels in a four-hour battle.

17 July. **Joint Army-Navy Action.**
Infantrymen of the 28th Volunteers, supported by the U.S. Navy gunboat USS *Villalobos*, rout a large rebel force at Taal, Batangas, in the Philippines.

EYEWITNESS: THE RELIEF OF PEKING

In late 1899 elements of the Imperial Chinese government incited a secret organization, the I Ho Chuan ("Fists of Righteous Harmony"), to violence against foreigners in an uprising known as the "Boxer Rebellion." On 20 June 1900, the Boxers began a siege of the International Legation compound in Peking. On 14 August, an international relief force including U.S. troops broke the siege. Private Harry J. Dill, 14th U.S. Infantry Regiment, was there:

"We started on 4 August, and on the 14th forced the first wall and planted the stars and stripes, the first foreign flag to wave over Peking in the present war. The flag was planted by a bugler of E Company [Calvin P. Titus] after the color bearer had been killed.

"On the 5th and 6th we had stiff fights with the Chinese [at Peit-tsang and Yang-tsun respectively], the engagement on the latter date being especially severe. They had four batteries of artillery throwing shrapnel, and 3,000 other men engaged. The Americans, the 14th Infantry and 5th Artillery, did all the work in routing them, and the 14th's loss was 14 killed outright and 56 wounded. Some of the latter died subsequently.

"At 3 o'clock on the morning of the 6th we started from Pei-tsang, the town we had helped the Japs capture on the 5th, and after a march of between 14 and 15 miles through a country ankle-deep in sand and with a broiling sun pouring down (and the officers wouldn't allow us to get water), went into the fight. The advance guard sighted the enemy ahead and we were deployed in line of battle. For the next two hours we were under as heavy a fire as was probably ever poured upon any body of troops. The rifle balls were coming like rain, throwing up little puffs of dust, and the shrapnel was dropping everywhere. I saw one shell knock over 16 men, though only seven were injured. A part of it carried away a piece of my hat brim. We advanced with a yell and were for nearly three-quarters of an hour in the open where we encountered an awful fire. We pressed on, however, and carried the trenches at the point of the bayonet. Some of the men were overcome by the heat and a few went raving insane.

"The Japs are America's best friends. They are as bold as lions. The Russians are not much account.

They were driven back at the city wall, which we carried with not half as many men. The Germans are fighters from the heart. We joined the Japs in capturing Tung-Chou, a walled city about 15 miles from Peking. Our troops on the 15th took the second wall and four gates, let out the missionaries and would have forced the secret city [Forbidden City] had we not been recalled.

"The hardships of the campaign were all forgotten when we saw the people of the legations. They actually cried with joy. They did not look as though they had suffered, being in good health and actually fat. On the other hand our poor boys looked like skeletons. They had marched through all kinds of country under a broiling sun for 10 days, sometimes without food. At night it was almost freezing cold and we sometimes slept in mud puddles.

"Our total loss in the advance was between 80 and 90 killed and wounded, without counting several more who died from heat and sickness."

—*Vince Hawkins*

Above: *Men of the 9th U.S. Infantry encamped in Peking after the relief of the city. (Library of Congress)*

26–29 July. More Relief Troops Arrive. China.
The 14th Infantry, 6th Cavalry, and 5th Artillery arrive along with General Chaffee and march to Tientsin. Within a few days the international force moves to relieve the Boxer siege that has been renewed against the foreign legations in Peking.

2 August. Hopeful Note Bolsters Morale of Besieged Legations.
A 30 July letter from Lieutenant Colonel J. S. Mallory, 41st Volunteer Infantry, arrives at the besieged legations stating: "A relief column of 10,000 is at the point of starting for Peking, more to follow. God grant they may be in time."

5–6 August. Relief Force Advance Continues.
Chinese resistance at the Pei-Ho River and the next day at Yang Ts'un is overcome by the Allied force, but costs the Americans seven killed and 65 wounded. Allied troops capture the Hsiku Arsenal and Peitsang before halting to encamp at Tao-Wa-Se, China.

13–14 August. Assault Against Peking.
Musician Calvin Titus, 14th U.S. Infantry, clambers

Above: *Private Calvin Titus, trumpeter of the 14th Infantry, scaled the wall of Peking, leading the way for U.S. relief forces into the city. ("I'll Try, Sir," H. Charles McBarron, Army Art Collection, NMUSA)*

up the high walls of Peking to help open the main gate to the outer city. His action shows the way up to others who join him and they succeed in driving defenders away, opening the gate and placing the American flag on the wall. For his heroism Titus later obtains an appointment to the United State Military Academy, where he receives the Medal of Honor.

15 August. U.S. Redlegs Blast Chinese Gate.
First Lieutenant Charles P. Summerall's two-gun section of Battery F (Reilly's Battery), 5th U.S. Artillery, is called forward with the 14th Infantry to assault a series of three gates leading into the inner city. Summerall nonchalantly walks up to the first gate and marks an "X" in chalk as an aiming point for the guns, which then blast a hole for the infantry. While observing the Boxer positions, Captain Henry J. Reilly, the battery commander, is killed. Elements of the 14th U.S. Infantry have seized the outer walls and prepare to storm the final gate into the inner Forbidden City when they are recalled. As the allies confer for several days, the Boxers and their Royal supporters flee the city, and the siege is broken.

28 August. First Victory Parade.
After defeating the Boxers, Chaffee's troops participate in the Allied victory parade in the Forbidden City.

Above: *Men of Battery F, 5th U.S. Artillery, pay tribute to their fallen commanding officer, Captain Henry J. Reilly, who was killed during the attack on Peking. (Collection Jean S. and Frederic A. Sharf)*

17 September. **Regulars and Volunteers Assault Outpost. Philippines.**
Doughboys of the 15th U.S. Infantry and 37th Volunteer Infantry sustain heavy losses as they capture a fortified guerrilla village on Luzon.

3 October. **American Relief Force Departs. China.**
With the Boxers defeated, Chaffee begins the withdrawal of the American Relief Force back to Manila. He leaves about 2,100 men—one infantry regiment, a squadron of the 6th Cavalry, Battery F, 5th Artillery, and some support troops—behind as a security force for the railroad.

21 October. **Mounted Patrol Ambushed. Looc, Luzon, Philippines.**
While on a three-day mounted patrol, 20 men from the 2d Battalion, 28th U.S. Volunteer Infantry, are ambushed by a rebel force of 400. Captain George W. Beigler leads the patrol in a four-hour running battle along the jungle road. The rebels suffer 75 killed and wounded, with only four casualties among the Volunteers. Beigler receives the Medal of Honor for his actions.

8 December. **Troopers Repel Attackers. Lake Taal, Philippines.**
A detachment from Troop M, 1st U.S. Cavalry, engages in a running fight against an estimated 200 Filipinos, whom they disperse after a two-and-one-half-hour engagement.

1901

January. **Status of the Army.**
Army strength is about 101,000, with less than 25 percent in the United States. More than 67,000 are serving in the Philippines. The Adjutant General comments that there is not one Regular regiment of infantry in the country. There is concern in Congress as well.

31 January. **Eradication of Yellow Fever. Cuba.**
The U.S. Army Medical Corps concludes its first yellow fever experiment to determine the cause of the disease.

2 February. **Congress Authorizes Increased Army Strength.**
Congress passes legislation approving significant changes in the Army. The Army Nurse Corps is established with 202 members, and approval is given to recruit Philippine Scouts and the Puerto Rico Regiment under American Army officers. Also approved are a reorganization of the artillery, an

ARMY NURSES IN THE WAR

When the Spanish-American War started in 1898, the Army believed that its Hospital Corps could cope with the expected numbers of sick and injured soldiers. No one anticipated the severe toll tropical diseases would take on American troops, and military authorities were quickly forced to seek the help of civilian women. Soon after the start of the war, the Army placed 1,500 civilian nurses under contract. The contracts stipulated that the nurses would work wherever they were assigned. Although the majority of these women were sent to military hospitals in the United States, many found themselves on the way to Cuba, Guam, and even the Philippines.

The war was short; however, the American Army in the Philippines suffered numerous casualties in putting down a follow-on rebellion by Filipino natives anxious for immediate independence. Among the first 17 contract nurses to arrive at the First Reserve Hospital in Manila in December 1898 was Chief Nurse Mona B. Fraser. On reporting to the commanding officer in Manila, Fraser was told, "Nurses are not needed. No provision has been made for them, and no quarters are available, so you may as well go back on the same ship." Fraser persuaded the commander to allow the nurses to stay one month to see if they could improve conditions at the hospital. The hospital was under tents, and the women worked 12–15 hour days bathing patients, washing bed linen, and reorganizing the hospital kitchen. Their efforts must have appeased the hospital commander, because they were still at the hospital "when the shot which started the Philippine Insurrection was fired 4 February 1899 [and] wounded boys were brought in in (sic) droves." Luckily, that month more contract nurses arrived, enabling Fraser to begin sending nurses to small field hospitals farther inland.

One of the new arrivals was Miss Estelle Hine, who arrived on the ship *Ohio*. She wrote that the ship anchored a few miles out in Manila Bay and the nurses boarded small launches for transportation to the city. Instead, however, "we were met by small boats from the shore saying that there had been an attack on Manila and the fighting was still in progress." The nurses returned to their ship and remained aboard for a week before they were allowed into the city. Their first night there, "we were kept awake by firing on all sides of the city, the booming of bamboo as whole districts of native shacks were burned by our troops,

and the constant pacing of sentries."

By 1900, more than 100 contract nurses were in the Philippines working in military hospitals. Helena Maria Gottschalk (later Arendt) was stationed at one of these field hospitals. She remembered, "Moro snipers fired on the hospital at night, forcing us to cover the windows with blankets or whatever was available, despite the tropical heat." Nurses were frequently assigned transport duty, accompanying badly wounded soldiers to San Francisco for medical care. In October 1899, Chief Nurse Mona Fraser endured a miserable trip home with five wounded soldiers when their ship ran into a storm that stayed with them until they reached the West Coast. Shortly after Fraser's return to Manila, she succumbed to malaria and had to return to San Francisco.

On 2 February 1901, the day the Army Nurse Corps was established, the contracts of the Army nurses serving in the Philippines were annulled, and the nurses signed up for three years' duty with the Army. These nurses and their colleagues in Army hospitals in the United States were the first women to serve as official members of the U.S. Army.

—*Judi Bellafaire*

Above: *U.S. Army nurses also were on hand for the first time to attend to the medical needs of the men felled in combat by the enemy—or more often by diseases that plagued them even before they left the United States. (Bettmann Corbis)*

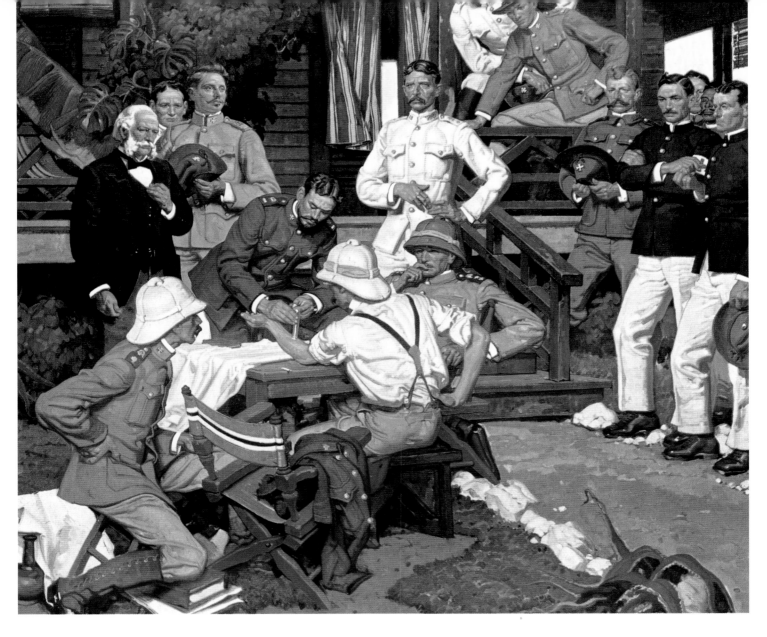

Above: *Major Walter Reed and other Army surgeons worked hard to make advances in the treatment of tropical diseases, which proved more of a threat to U.S. forces than enemy bullets. (Daniel Cornwell, National Archives)*

increase in cavalry regiments to 15 (11th–15th), and five more regiments of infantry (26th–30th). Enlisted strength could be increased at the discretion of the President. The act prescribes 17 inspectors general for the IG's Department and requires rotation of staff officers to line positions. Finally, it approves a lieutenant general to be the senior officer of the Army, making Nelson Miles' rank permanent. Six major generals and 16 brigadiers are also approved. On the same day, Benjamin O. Davis, Sr., becomes the first African-American soldier to be commissioned from the ranks as an officer in the Regular Army. He later will be the first African-American promoted to brigadier general.

6 February. **Walter Reed Makes Medical Breakthrough. Cuba.**
Army Medical Corps Surgeon Major Walter Reed proves that the Stegomyia mosquito transmits yellow fever, pointing the way for control of the disease.

26 February. **Filipino Positions Taken. Mindanao, Philippines.**
A 60-man patrol from 3d Battalion, 28th Volunteers, travels up the Agusan River on gunboat USS *Calamines* and makes a surprise attack on rebel positions at Bacona and Can Mataeo, capturing two cannon.

23 March. **Emilio Aguinaldo Captured. Luzon, Philippines.**
Posing as a prisoner of war, Colonel Fredrick Funston travels with a group of Americans and disguised Macabebe scouts into the enemy-held jungles. His ruse succeeds, allowing him to capture Emilio Aguinaldo and escape to a waiting ship.

1 May. **1st Cavalry Troopers Face Insurrectionists. Philippines.**
Troop K, 1st Cavalry, drives an estimated 250 Filipinos from three separate positions on Mount Solo during sharp fighting.

1 July. **Reorganization of Forces. Puerto Rico.**
The Puerto Rico Battalion is reorganized as the Puerto Rico Provisional Regiment of Infantry with battalions and placed on the Regular Army list.

3 July. **10th Cavalryman Receives Medal of Honor.**
Nearly four years after leaving cover at Santiago, Cuba, to brave a hail of Spanish fire and rescue a wounded comrade, Sergeant Major Edward L. Baker, Jr., of the 10th Cavalry is presented with the Medal of Honor.

23 September. **Filipino Guerrillas Overrun U.S. Troops. Balangiga, Samar, Philippines.**
Forty-eight soldiers of Company C, 9th U.S. Infantry, perish when they are attacked during breakfast by Filipino guerrillas operating in the area. A few survivors fight their way to boats and escape.

November. **Army War College Formed.**
Headquarters of the Army issues General Order No. 155 establishing the Army War College in Washington, D.C., for the advanced education of senior officers.

17 November. **Climbing Cliffs to Overtake Guerrillas. Caducan River, Philippines.**
Major Littleton Waller's troops scale cliffs along the river to overtake a Filipino guerrilla headquarters operating along its banks.

1902

January. **Status of the Army.**
Army strength is fewer than 83,000 officers and enlisted. Mandatory release of the Volunteers serving in the Philippines at the end of their terms the previous summer has dropped the Army there to 36,000, permitting guerrillas to continue to operate in many areas.

1 January. **New Publication Begins.**
The Coast Artillery Journal is established.

3 March. **Artillery Consolidation Initiated.**
The coast, or heavy artillery, and light artillery, or field artillery, are combined into a single Corps of Artillery. This branch will be the largest in the Army for a time.

17 March. **Corps of Engineer Receive Distinctive Uniform.**
The Adjutant General's Office issues General Order No. 27 calling for an entirely new full-dress uniform for officers of the Corps of Engineers. This outfit will be a precursor of a major change in the U.S. Army uniform for all branches that will be adopted later in the year.

22 March. **Aides de Camp Insignia.**
The Army and Navy Register notes that Howard

Chandler Christy, an artist who achieved fame for his illustrations of the Spanish-American War and later would be noted for his patriotic World War I posters, has designed a new insignia for wear by general officers' aides-de-camp. The same basic pattern remains in use after more than a century.

20 May. **Military Government Ends. Havana, Cuba.**
Major General Leonard Wood concludes his term as military governor of Cuba, handing over control of the island to the first elected president of the country. Wood began his career as a surgeon, participated in the campaigns against Apache leader Geronimo, and was the original colonel of the 1st Volunteer Cavalry until his promotion to brigadier general of Volunteers early in the Spanish-American War. Concurrent with the end of Wood's tenure as governor, U.S. troops begin to withdraw from the island.

2 June. **Uniforms for Nurses.**
The Adjutant General's Office issues General Order No. 49, which prescribes the uniform for the Army Nurse Corps.

Below: *The Army's smart, new full-dress uniforms incorporated the appropriate branch color, in this case red, for the enlisted Coast Artillerymen shown in their fort. ("Coast Artillery, Enlisted Men, 1902–1907 (Full Dress)," H. A. Ogden)*

26 June. **Artillery Badge Authorized.**

The Adjutant General's Office publishes General Order No. 94 prescribing a special qualification gunner's insignia for artillerymen, and a badge for men designated as first-class artillery gunners.

30 June. **New Pay Scale Initiated.**

Army foreign service pay is established for the first time. The rate is set at 20 percent of pay proper.

4 July. **End of Philippine Insurrection Proclaimed.**

President Theodore Roosevelt prematurely announces the end of the Philippine Insurrection. In a little over three years there were 2,811 separate combat actions recorded.

14 July. **Major Uniform Change Introduced.**

General Order No. 81 introduces new uniform changes that include olive drab service uniforms, branch collar insignia for all enlisted personnel, reduced-size chevrons from previous patterns worn points up rather than points down (as had been regulation since 1851), and russet-colored footgear to be worn with certain uniforms. This last change ushers in the era of the so-called "Brown Shoe Army."

September. **First Joint Service Exercises Held. New England.**

For the first time, exercises are held on the New England coast combining Regular artillery and militia with Navy battleships.

Above: *The .30-caliber M-1903 Springfield represented a major improvement in accuracy and range over earlier Army-issue rifles. (Salamandar Picture Library, London)*

Right: *The new uniform regulations of 1902 also introduced the olive drab color for service and field dress. ("The American Soldier, 1903," H. Charles McBarron, Army Art Collection, NMUSA)*

21 January. **National Guard Created.**

Congress passes Public Law 57-33, known as the "Dick" Act for its sponsor, Congressman Charles W. Dick. It revises the 1792 Militia Act and provides for federal and state support to create a National Guard from the old "organized militia" units with the goal in five years of having them at the same standards of organization, armament, and discipline as the Regular Army. The rest of the "militia" are regarded as a general manpower pool.

THE MILITIA SYSTEM MODERNIZES

The bloodletting of the American Civil War dampened enthusiasm for membership in the Volunteer militia in the years following that conflict. However, by the late 1870s the potential for labor strife and veterans' kinder memories of military service had revived interest in the militia. The Great Railroad Strike of 1877 required the use of Regulars and militiamen to quell violent labor protests. Afterwards, business leaders viewed a volunteer militia as the protector of capitalism and the established order.

The post-bellum period saw a number of important changes to the militia system. In 1879, militia leaders founded the National Guard Association to champion legislation favorable to state soldiers. The regiment, rather than the company, became the basic unit for militia organizations. Pennsylvania and New York organized the nation's first standing militia combat divisions in peacetime. Large, imposing armories appeared in major cities and became the focus for both martial and community activities. Several states officially adopted the name "National Guard" for militia and specified the Army's field uniform as standard garb. By the late 1890s, more than 100,000 militiamen were serving in state regiments.

Like previous conflicts, the Spanish-American War utilized field forces composed of Regulars, militiamen, and federal Volunteers. After Congress declared war on Spain in April 1898, the War Department concentrated on mobilizing forces for operations in the Caribbean and the Southwest Pacific. The Regular Army numbered approximately 30,000 soldiers at the time, and President William McKinley issued calls for as many as 200,000 Volunteers. However, the militia's growing influence could not be ignored. The War Department agreed to accept National Guard units for service before creating new Volunteer regiments. To avoid any possible restrictions on their employment, Guard regiments enlisted as individuals for active duty. Entire regiments of state soldiers were accepted for duty, but too many militiamen lacked proper uniforms, weapons, and training. The miserable mobilization camps for which the war became notorious did little to prepare Guardsmen for combat.

Before the conflict ended, the Army had successfully exerted its power in the Caribbean and the Philippines. For the main effort against Cuba, the Regular Army formed the core of the expeditionary force. Militia-based regiments constituted the bulk of

the invading troops that quickly captured Puerto Rico. The ground campaign in the Philippines resulted in the archipelago's quick capture, but Moro nationalists fueled a growing independence movement that resulted in a prolonged insurrection. National Guard units fought effectively against the guerrillas, but calls to bring the troops home grew louder as time passed. The Army offered individual Guardsmen an opportunity to remain on active duty by volunteering in new regiments and brought the original militia regiments home by August 1899.

The Spanish-American War sparked a series of reforms that changed the American military. New global responsibilities resulted in a permanent expansion of the Regular Army. Militia champions won support in Congress and the War Department for reforms that transformed the militia into the modern National Guard.

The Militia Act of 1903 completely altered past militia practices. Guard units received increased federal funding and equipment, and in return, they were subject to Army standards and inspections. The Act required Guardsmen to attend 24 drill periods and five days of summer camp each year. The participation of Guard members during national emergencies became compulsory. Guard units were subject to federal call-ups for nine months. At first their service was restricted to within U.S. borders, but amendments to the Act five years later removed all time and geographic limits on the Guard's employment.

—*Michael Doubler*

Above: *During 1912 maneuvers that brought Regular and Guard troops together, Guardsmen gained experience with new Army technologies, including receiving instructions by wireless message during field exercises. (National Archives)*

14 February. General Staff and Chief of Staff Created.
In response to sweeping reforms called for by
Secretary of the Army Elihu Root, Congress approves
the Army general staff of 45 officers and creates the
office of Chief of Staff of the Army.

April–May. **Pershing Destroys Moro Fort. Philippines.**
Captain John J. Pershing leads a detachment in
an assault against the fort of the rebellious Moro
Sultan of Bacclod, destroying it and scattering
the Moros. Pershing's detachment is later fired on
by Taraca Moros as those forts are also attacked
and destroyed.

11 June. **U.S. Military Academy Class of 1903
Graduates. West Point, New York.**
Secretary of War Elihu Root presents diplomas to 64
graduates of the United States Military Academy,
including the top man in the class, Douglas
MacArthur.

23 June. **New Rifle Begins Long Career. Springfield,
Massachusetts.**
The M-1903 Springfield .30-caliber magazine rifle is
adopted by the U.S. Army as a replacement for the

Above: *(Left) Major General Samuel B. M. Young was
the Army's last commanding general and first Chief of
Staff. (Marion Porter Sharpe, Army Art Collection,
NMUSA). (Right) Adna Romanza Chaffee became Chief
of Staff in 1904. (Cedric Baldwin Egeli, Army Art
Collection, NMUSA)*

Krag-Jörgensen and remains in service for nearly a
half century.

8 August. **End of An Era.**
Lieutenant General Nelson A. Miles, Commanding
General of the Army, retires from active service after
42 years. He is succeeded by newly promoted
Lieutenant General Samuel B. M. Young.

15 August. **Military Intelligence Capabilities Improved.**
The Division of Military Information (forerunner
to the Intelligence Division) transfers from the
Adjutant General's Office to the Office of the Chief
of Staff.

16 August. **Army's First Chief of Staff.**
After one week as Commanding General, Lieutenant
General Samuel B. M. Young becomes the U.S.
Army's first Chief of Staff. During the Civil War,
Young enlisted as a private in the 12th Pennsylvania
Cavalry, and by war's end he wore the eagles of a
colonel. In 1866 he secured a commission as a second
lieutenant with the 12th U.S. Infantry. Over the
next three-and-a-half decades he advanced steadily,
reaching the rank of major general in February 1901,
and then served as the first president of the Army War
College. He oversees the creation of the Army
General Staff and recommends establishment of a
general service corps, but he serves only six months
in the position.

Right: *The large Army maneuver exercise of 1904 was part of an increased effort to improve tactical and logistical skills resulting from the lessons learned during the Spanish-American War. (National Archives)*

Below: *William Howard Taft would serve as Secretary of War, and later in other important national posts, including President of the United States. (William Valentine Schevill, Army Art Collection, NMUSA)*

1904

January. Status of the Army.

Army strength hovers around 70,000 officers and men;t only 15,000 continue to serve in the still unsettled Philippines, and a few thousand remain in China. During the year, the Army organizes into five regional divisions under major generals, with departments headed by brigadiers. These headquarters are responsible for all military activities in their area.

9 January. Chaffee Becomes New Chief of Staff.

Adna Romanza Chaffee, one of the first troopers to enlist in the 6th U.S. Cavalry when the regiment was formed in 1861, becomes Chief of Staff of the Army. He advocates higher allowances for quarters and improved canteen (a combination post exchange and enlisted club of the era) services to improve morale and discipline, and calls for an increase in officer strength to offset the impact of diversions from troop duties.

11 January. New Secretary of War Assumes Office.

William Howard Taft is appointed Secretary of War. In 1900, President William McKinley dispatched Taft to establish a civil government in the Philippines. In this capacity he clashed with the military governor of the islands, Major General Arthur MacArthur. His main focus is oversight for Army activities connected with the building of the Panama Canal. He also continues his interest in the Philippine Islands.

28 January. Medal of Honor Changes.

Secretary of War Taft approves a new design and a lapel rosette for the Army Medal of Honor. On 22 November, to protect the pattern from being copied or abused, Major General George L. Gillespie obtains Patent Serial No. 197,369. By 19 December, Gillespie has transfered the patent "to W. H. Taft and his successor or successors as Secretary of War of the United States."

Army schools, including those for the Engineer Corps and Signal Corps, will be located at the fort.

July–September. **Army Conducts Exercises.**
The Army is busy during the summer months with a series of field exercises undertaken with the National Guard. Exercises take place in several western states under direction of Regular officers, and one is staged on the old Civil War battlefield at Manassas, Virginia.

September–November. **Scouts Suffer Defeat. Philippines.**
Members of the Pulahanes religious sect annihilate two Philippine Scout units and their American Army officers on the island of Samar.

1905

11 January. **New Medals Authorized.**
Congress authorizes a medal for the Certificate of Merit, which had been created on 3 March 1847 for U.S. Army privates and expanded to include noncommissioned officers in 1854, for distinguished service in battle or peacetime, for heroism involving saving life or property at the risk of one's own life, or for other services deemed deserving by the President. Campaign badges also were prescribed for the first time to acknowledge service in the Civil War, Indian Wars, Spanish-American War, and Philippine campaign. American artist Francis D. Millet designed the motifs that appear on the medals.

12 January. **China Service Acknowledged.**
General Order No. 5 calls for the creation of a China Campaign Medal for veterans of the Boxer Rebellion and a Philippine Campaign Medal for soldiers who have served in the Philippine Islands.

27 January. **Army Engineers Engage in Internal Improvements.**
The U.S. Army Corps of Engineers begins work as part of the Alaskan Road Commission.

1–24 May. **First Actions Against the Moros. Philippines.**
The U.S. Army conducts the first of three campaigns to quell radical Muslim Moro tribesmen on Jolo Island. The Moros rebel against American efforts to curtail slavery and tribal feuding.

25 August. **Army Signal School Established. Kansas.**
As part of Secretary Root's education plan, a school to train junior Signal Corps officers is created at Fort

23 April. **Reorganization of the Adjutant General's Department.**
The Adjutant General's Department is redesigned as the Military Secretary's Department, while the Adjutant General's Office consolidates with the Record and Pension Office to become known as the Military Secretary's Office.

24 April. **New Medal of Honor Policy.**
Future Secretary of State Cordell Hull, a congressman from Tennessee, introduces an act to change the issuance of the Medal of Honor, requiring all claims to be accompanied by official documents detailing the action for which the medal is being awarded. The law also calls for the purchase of 3,000 of the medals based on a new design—a silver five-pointed star, heavily electroplated in gold.

4 May. **Purchase of Panama Canal Property.**
The United States assumes the rights and property of the French Panama Canal Company for the sum of $40 million.

27 June. **Changes in Army Education.**
The War Department issues General Order No. 115 consolidating the seven Army Service Schools into one system at Fort Leavenworth, Kansas, largely because of the influence of Colonel Arthur L. Wagner, a powerful proponent of military education. Later in the year a Staff College is formed to serve as a bridge between the War College and the Infantry and Cavalry School (later renamed School of the Line). Eventually several

Above: *(Left) Philippine Campaign Medal. (Right) China Campaign Medal.*

Right: *Troops inspect Moro dead after the Battle of Bud Dajo, 5 August 1906, one of the many hard-fought engagements during the guerrilla war in the Philippines. (from* America at War: The Philippines, 1898–1913, *by A. B. Feuer, Copyright 2002, reproduced with permission of Greenwood Publishing Group, Inc., Westport, CT)*

Below: *Major General James Franklin Bell was a major proponent of military education who rose to Chief of Staff. (Adrian Lamb, Army Art Collection, NMUSA)*

Leavenworth. Much of the work is experimental, with research into electrical and acoustical signaling, photography, and engineering. Instruction in signals is also incorporated into the curricula of the other Army schools for officers.

16–22 October. Raid on Moro Chief. Philippines.

A hand-picked raiding party of officers and men from the 22d Infantry and Philippine Scouts, led by Captain Frank R. McCoy, succeeds in surprising a notorious

Moro chief in his camp near the Malang River. The chief is killed and his band dispersed.

1906

January. Status of the Army.

Army strength remains at fewer than 70,000 officers and enlisted. A recent study of U.S. coastal defenses shows that while defenses are adequate against large ships, there is very little that can be done against an amphibious invasion using smaller ships, and the Chesapeake Bay is totally undefended.

16 January. Bates Becomes Chief.

Lieutenant General John C. Bates begins a brief three-month assignment as Chief of Staff of the Army before retiring from active duty. He is the last Civil War veteran to serve in the position.

6–8 March. Second Campaign Against the Moros. Jolo Island, Philippines.

The Army wages the second Jolo campaign in response to attacks by Muslim groups attempting to drive the United States out of the Philippines. A principal action is the destruction of the Moro fort of Bad-Dajo by a detachment of the 6th Infantry. In heavy fighting Lieutenant Gordon Johnson and a few men scale the Moro stockade and attack the defenders from the inside, forcing the survivors to flee.

Army troops of the 22d Infantry, 6th Cavalry, detachments of artillerymen and Engineers and local National Guardsmen to maintain order and provide disaster relief in San Francisco after it is hit with a devastating earthquake and fire. Fort Mason and the Presidio are used as refugee camps. More than a million rations are rushed to the stricken city and distributed to the people.

25 June. **Ordnance Corps Expanded.**
Congress expands the number of officers authorized for the Ordnance Corps and approves a brigadier general position for its chief. Picatinny Arsenal at Dover, New Jersey, is opened, providing the Army with its own source of powder production for the first time.

29 June. **Philippine Service Acknowledged.**
By Act of Congress (Public Law 360, 59th Congress), implemented by War Department General Order 124 dated 9 July 1906, a medal is created for soldiers "who followed the flag" in the Philippine Islands.

25 July. **African-Americans and Filipino Forces Stand Fast. Philippines.**
On Samar, African-American soldiers of the 24th Infantry and native troops of the Philippine Constabulary beat off a series of assaults by hundreds of Pulahane religious zealots armed with bolo knives.

3 August. **Army Returns to Cuba.**
An Army expeditionary force soon named the "Army of Cuban Occupation" is dispatched after a request for assistance from the elected government that is threatened by an internal insurrection and resigning. President McKinley sends William H. Taft to head a provisional government and provides five regiments of infantry, two regiments of cavalry, and several batteries of artillery to restore and maintain order. The island remains under U.S. control and the troops stay until 1909.

13–14 August. **Racial Violence Ends Military Careers. Texas.**
A few minutes after midnight, gunfire erupts near Brownsville. Local civilians accuse men of the 1st Battalion, 25th Infantry, from Fort Brown of the incident, which leads to court-martial proceedings and the wholesale dismissal of all but a few of the African-American infantrymen in the three companies.

20 September. **"Black Jack" Pershing Promoted.**
Captain John J. Pershing is promoted ahead of 862 senior officers to become a brigadier general.

16 April. **Bell Becomes Chief of Staff.**
Major General James Franklin Bell is sworn in as Chief of Staff of the Army. He is the second chief to wear the Medal of Honor. Unlike his recent predecessors, he is not promoted to lieutenant general. During his four influential years in this assignment, Bell spearheads legislation to increase pay, manpower strength, technical services, and reserve forces; he also promotes military aviation.

18 April. **Army Aid in Wake of Disaster. San Francisco.**
Brigadier General Fredric Funston mobilizes Regular

Above: *Regulars and National Guardsmen in the San Francisco area responded to the earthquake and subsequent fire that devastated the city in April 1906. ("The American Soldier, 1906," H. Charles McBarron, Army Art Collection, NMUSA)*

Pershing's detractors claim his unprecedented jump in rank came from the power of his father-in-law, Senator Francis E. Warren, the head of the U.S. Senate's military affairs committee. Pershing has made a name for himself in his successful handling of some of the most difficult areas of Moro resistance in the Philippines. He also had the good fortune to come into close contact with President Theodore Roosevelt and served as a military attaché in Japan and in an assignment as an observer in the Russo-Japanese War.

December 30. **Identification Tags Adopted.**
The War Department issues General Order No. 204 beginning the U.S. Army's use of metal "dog tags" for identification. Previous unofficial employment of such devices could be traced as far back as the American Civil War.

1907

January. **Status of the Army.**
The Army continues to be scattered around the world, stretching thin its fewer than 69,000 officers and men. Some companies report only eight men present for duty. One regiment is escorting a renegade band of Ute Indians back to their reservation in South Dakota after they left to protest poor government support.

The Coast Artillery and Field Artillery are reestablished as separate branches of the Army on 25 January.

February–March. **Panama Canal's Construction.**
The resignation of the civilian chief engineer in 1906 has left the Panama Canal uncompleted. President Theodore Roosevelt selects Lieutenant Colonel George W. Goethals, U.S. Army Corps of Engineers, to be the new head of the project as Chief Engineer and Chairman of the Panama Canal Commission. With Goethals is a group of other Army officers from the Engineers and Medical Departments. Colonel William C. Gorgas, Medical Corps, who is made head of the Sanitation Department, makes major contributions to the elimination of yellow fever in the area.

2 March. **Adjutant General's Department Revived.**
Congress reestablishes the Adjutant General's Department but abolishes the position of lieutenant general. It will not be reinstated until World War I.

1 August. **Birth of Army Aviation.**
The Office of the Chief of the Signal Corps issues an order to form an "Aeronautical Division" that is "to have charge of all matters pertaining to military ballooning, air machines, and all kindred subjects." Ten balloons are in service by the end of the year.

Above: *These modest brick quarters at Fort Myer, Virginia, have housed the Army Chiefs of Staff since 1 June 1908. ("Quarters One," Valeria P. M. Bell, Army Art Collection, NMUSA)*

23 December. **Airplanes for the Army.**
Army Chief Signal Officer Brigadier General James Allen calls for bids based on Specification No. 486 to produce a military aircraft capable of carrying two passengers and flying for one hour at a minimum speed of 40 miles per hour.

1908

21 January. **Lighter-Than-Air Army Aviation.**
The Signal Corps issues Specification 483 setting out requirements for contractors who wish to bid on a dirigible that would be lifted by hydrogen and carry two passengers with a total weight of 350 pounds at an optimum speed of 20 miles per hour but no less than 16 miles per hour. The craft is to be able to remain aloft for at least two hours.

1 March. **New Quartermaster School. Philadelphia.**
The Quartermaster School is founded at the Philadelphia Quartermaster Depot.

8 March. **Wright Brothers Receive Contract.**
After receiving 41 bids for military aircraft, the Signal Corps awards a contract to Orville and Wilbur Wright, who respond that they will be able to deliver the plane within 200 days.

23 April. **Army Medical Reserve Established.**
Congressional legislation creates a Medical Reserve Corps of several hundred doctors with military commissions ready to expand the capability of the Army's medical department in time of war. They will be first lieutenants but rank below other Regulars of the same rank. By 30 June, 160 physicians are recommended. The successful program is expanded in 1909 and again in 1913.

11 May. **Congress Increases Army Budget.**
Congress approves the first changes in the rate of pay for the Army since 24 July 1876. The base pay of a private is set at $15 per month in lieu of the previous $13, while a corporal makes $21 and a sergeant first class (Signal) or first sergeant receives $45. New lieutenants get $1,700 a year; major generals receive $8,000. In addition, money is provided to improve coastal defenses. The 1902 Dick Act is modified so there is no penalty for avoiding militia service, but supply and organization of the National Guard is required to meet Regular Army standards within two years.

14 May. **Tests for Physical Fitness Imposed.**
Army officers serving in the field must demonstrate to a medical officer that they can ride a horse 30 miles a

day for three days. Officers in the Coast Artillery must show they can walk 50 miles in three days. All officers below field grade must have an annual physical exam. Officers failing these tests will be referred to a retirement board.

1 July. **Luke Becomes Secretary of War.**
Tennessee-born Luke Edward Wright becomes Ssecretary of War with President William Taft's inauguration. Wright enlisted at the age of 15 in the Confederate Army and became a second lieutenant before the Civil War concluded. In 1901, he became vice-governor of the Philippines and governor general in 1904. He is an early proponent of military aviation.

20 July. **Army Receives Dirigible. Virginia.**
Thomas Baldwin delivers Signal Corps Dirigible No. 1 to the Army at Fort Myer.

12 August. **Dirigible Tests. Virginia.**
Official test flights of Dirigible No. 1 begin at Fort Myer.

9 September. **Wright Airplane Tests.**
As part of the trials for the Wright Flyer being considered for final acceptance, Lieutenant Frank P. Lahm goes aloft for six-and-a-half minutes over Fort Myer to become the first military passenger to fly on an airplane.

17 September. **First Army Aviation Death. Virginia.**
Coast Artillery Second Lieutenant Thomas E. Selfridge is killed in a crash while airborne over Fort Myer with pilot Wilbur Wright, thereby becoming the first military airplane fatality in history. On the plane's fourth circuit around the course, a propeller slicesd a bracing wire, bringing the fragile plane to the ground. The War Department postpones further testing until the summer of 1909.

1909

January. **Cuban Occupation Ends. Cuba.**
The last troops of the Army of Cuban Occupation formally withdraw as the government is returned to Cuban civil authorities.

3 March. **1906 Brownsville Incident Investigated.**
Congress orders an investigation into the facts of the incident involving the three companies of 25th Infantry who were dishonorably discharged after being accused by townspeople of "shooting up" Brownsville, Texas, in August 1906. Clear evidence is found of rampant racial bias in the town. The case of each man is reviewed; many are exonerated and permitted to return to the Army.

12 March. **Dickinson Becomes Secretary of War.**
Jacob McGavock Dickinson replaces Luke Wright as Secretary of War. Dickinson enlisted as a teenager

Right: *The "old" inspects the "new" in this symbolic snapshot of a mounted trooper checking over the Wright Flyer at Fort Myer. Airplanes and machine guns were two of the technological advances that spelled the demise of horse cavalry. (National Archives)*

Signal Corps contract. They remain aloft for one hour, 12 minutes, and 40 seconds to establish a new record and exceed the time required by the government specifications.

2 August. **Wright Airplane Accepted.**
U.S. Army officials accept the Wright Flyer as its first aircraft for $25,000. The Wright brothers also receive a $5,000 bonus for exceeding the specified speed when their flying machine averages 42.5 miles per hour.

26 October. **Army Pioneer Airplane Pilots. Maryland.**
The first solo flights are by the U.S. Army's original pilots, cavalry Lieutenant Frank P. Lahm and engineer Second Lieutenant Fredric E. Humphreys. They take off from a leased field adjacent to Maryland Agricultural College in College Park. Their first flights last a scant three minutes, 13 seconds each. They ultimately log in total flight times of just over three hours each.

1910

2 March. **Foulois Makes Solo. Texas.**
Signal Corps Lieutenant Benjamin Foulois makes his first solo flight at Fort Sam Houston. For a time he is the only pilot in the Army when Lieutenants Lahm and Humphreys both return to duty with their respective branches.

22 April. **Wood Becomes Chief of Staff.**
Former U.S. Army surgeon Leonard Wood becomes a lieutenant general and Chief of Staff of the Army. As a proponent of national preparedness, he is instrumental in the establishment of the Plattsburg, New York, officers camp, which is designed to train businessmen and professionals during a four-week course in military basics. He makes improvements to the Army General Staff while also pressing for greater numbers of officers.

June. **First Aluminum Canteen.**
As part of the adoption of a major new design for field equipage, the Army begins using the first aluminum canteen and cup with a folding handle.

11 July. **First Weapons Test from Aircraft. Sheepshead Bay, New York.**
Lieutenant Jacob E. Fickel fires a 1903 Springfield rifle from a military plane for the first time as a foreshadowing of aerial combat capabilities. Two years later, in June 1912, Captain Charles F. Chandler will demonstrate an even more lethal aviation weapon

with the Confederate Army, becoming a private in the cavalry at age 14. During his tenure he proposes legislation to permit the admission of foreign students to West Point. He also recommends an annuity retirement system for civil service employees. Seeking to eliminate the devastation to the ranks by alcoholism and venereal disease, he asks Congress to pass legislation to stop the pay of soldiers rendered unfit for duty because of illness.

26 May. **Army Dirigible Pilots Go Aloft. Virginia.**
Army pilots make their first flight in Dirigible No. 1 at Fort Myer.

11 June. **Class of 1909 Graduates. West Point.**
At West Point early Army aviator Dana H. Crissy, George Smith Patton, Jr., and Chinese student Ting Chia Cer are among the 103 cadets who receive their diplomas.

27 July. **Wright Airplane Passes Requirements. Virginia.**
Once again Wilbur Wright takes Lieutenant Lahm as a passenger to fulfill the endurance test required by the

Above: *Former medical officer Leonard Wood had proven his leadership on the battlefield and was selected to be Chief of Staff. (Charles J. Fox, Army Art Collection, NMUSA)*

when he fires a Lewis machine gun from a Wright Model B piloted by Lieutenant De Witt Milling.

1911

1 January. **New Publication.**
The Field Artillery Journal is established.

15 January. **First Aerial Bombing.**
First Lieutenant Myron S. Crissy drops a live bomb for the first time from an Army airplane from a height of 1,500 feet.

3 March. **Congress Funds Improvements.**
The U.S. Army Dental Corps is established. A $125,000 special congressional appropriation also allows the Army Signal Corps to purchase new equipment for aeronautical training and reconnaissance. In addition, one Regular officer may now be assigned to train each National Guard regiment or battalion-sized separate unit, and 200 line officers are added to the strength. When the number of West Point graduates is not sufficient to fill second lieutenant quotas, civilians may be accepted after passing an examination.

29 March. **Return to Heavy-Caliber Pistol.**
The U.S. Army adopts the M-1911 .45-caliber automatic pistol, beginning its use as one of the longest-lived issue small arms in Army history. Its larger caliber provides more stopping power than the various Colt .38 revolvers adopted in 1892, and holds

more cartridges than the Colt M-1909 that was chambered for the .45-caliber cartridge.

March–May. **Unrest Along U.S.-Mexico Border.**
As a result of internal Mexican conflict, the border is very unsettled. The Army decides to make a show of strength and provide training by assembling a large "maneuver division" in Texas. Large numbers of troops, including 36 companies of coast artillery, are given deployment orders. The railroads are swamped and units are unprepared to deploy, so the division is never filled. However, many officers for the first time are dealing with moving and supplying large numbers of troops and learning valuable lessons. The border tensions continue. On 13 April, Captain Julien E. Gaujot, Troop K, 1st U.S. Cavalry, crosses the field of

Above: *Twice during the twentieth century Henry J. Stimson served as Secretary of War. (Julius Gari Melchers, Army Art Collection, NMUSA)*

Left: *The .45-caliber M-1911 Colt automatic pistol replaced most other Army handguns. Its magazine allowed for quick reloading and carried more rounds than old revolvers. Its .45-caliber slug had considerable stopping power. (Salamandar Picture Library, London)*

The U.S. Army establishes the School of Fire at Fort Sill; it will be redesignated the Field Artillery School in 1919.

15 July. **Typhoid Fever Research.**
Captain W. W. Russell, U.S. Army Medical Corps, conducts research that leads to the adoption of a compulsory typhoid vaccination for Army personnel.

August–September. **Army Fights Forest Fires.**
Large numbers of the Regular Army are used during the fire season to fight large forest fires that ravage Montana, Idaho, Washington, and Oregon.

8 September. **Campaign Hat Adopted.**
The Army adopts a new campaign hat, sometimes known as the "Montana Peak," a version of which remains in use by male drill instructors, some law enforcement agencies, and the National Park Service, as well as becoming a symbol of the U.S. Forest Service's "Smokey the Bear."

22 December. **Moros Suffer Defeat. Jolo, Philippines.**
Captain John J. Pershing surrounds Bud Dajo, a major stronghold of the rebellious Moros, and forces them to surrender.

1912

January. **Status of the Army.**
Army strength has grown slightly, up from the 84,000 in June 1911 to now approaching 92,000. Despite a new federally imposed fine of $500, signs can still be seen saying "No Soldiers Allowed" at the entrances to public places. The Army is spread over 49 posts in 24 states with an average garrison of fewer than 700 men.

14 January. **Skirmishes With Moros. Philippines.**
Captain E. G. Peyton leads two troops of cavalry and two companies of Philippine Scouts in a sweep of Jolo Island. His detachment succeeds in rounding up the worst of the Moro bands with the loss of only two wounded.

February. **Adjutant General Relieved By Secretary Stimson.**
Major General Fred C. Ainsworth, Adjutant General of the Army since 1898, is relieved of his duties by Secretary Stimson for insubordination. Ainsworth has had continuing conflict with Chief of Staff Wood over Wood's efforts to make administrative reforms. When Wood and Stimson accept findings in a report

fire at Aqua Prieta to obtain the permission of the rebel commander to receive the surrender of the surrounded forces of Mexican Federals and escort such forces, together with five Americans held as prisoners, back to the safety of his lines.

22 May. **Stimson's First Stint as Secretary of War.**
Henry Lewis Stimson becomes Secretary of War, and continues to enlarge the troop and administrative reorganizations initiated by Elihu Root. He is a strong advocate for a peacetime force based upon divisional rather than regimental organization, and he presses for the authority of the Secretary of War and the Army Chief of Staff over the Army bureau chiefs, who prior to the Root reforms could undermine their authority by dealing directly with Congress.

Above: *A dapper young major shows off his new "Montana Peak" campaign hat and handsome olive drab overcoat prescribed by regulations in 1911. (Frontier Army Museum, Fort Leavenworth, KS)*

PHILIPPINE SCOUTS: COMRADES IN ARMS

On 2 February 1901 Congress authorized the enlistment of 5,000 Filipinos for service in the U.S. Army. Designated Philippine Scouts, the Filipinos were organized into 50 companies of 100 men each. An effort was made to organize the companies by province and language. The units were to be segregated, their officers being selected from among either white American noncommissioned officers serving in the Philippines or those Filipinos who had graduated from West Point.

This was not the first time local Filipinos had been used by the U.S. Army. In January 1901 a four-company battalion of Cagayan Native Scouts was recruited for six months' service in northern Luzon, and in September several companies of Macabebe Scouts were also inducted into service.

In 1904 the Scouts were organized into four-company battalions with company strength at 110 men. Stationed in the regions with the most guerrilla action, the Scouts proved instrumental in suppressing the insurrection, and were highly effective in subduing the more fanatical tribes such as the Pulajaniis and the Muslim Moros.

During World War I the Scouts were increased to nearly 8,000 men. In the period 1919–1920 the battalions were reorganized and designated the 43d, 45th, and 57th Infantry, the 24th and 25th Field Artillery, and the 26th Cavalry Regiments. On 10 April 1922, the Philippine Division was organized. A "square" division, it consisted of the 23d and 24th Infantry Brigades with two regiments each, the 12th Artillery Brigade of four regiments, plus service and support units. By October, budget cuts left only the 23d Infantry Brigade (45th and 57th Regiments) and the attached 26th Cavalry Regiment still active.

With divisional focus on individual and unit training, the Scouts slowly evolved into a well-disciplined and skilled formation. In 1923, the Philippine Scouts were officially integrated into the Regular U.S. Army. By 1925 annual field exercises and division maneuvers were being conducted to practice War Plan Orange, a defensive plan designed to make maximum use of the islands' small garrison.

By the outbreak of World War II, the Scouts had been increased to 12,000 men. On 20 December 1941, the main Japanese invasion force landed on Luzon. The Japanese expected a quick campaign to conquer the Philippines, but got instead a bloody, desperate, five-month-long struggle that delayed their timetable of conquest in south Asia and cost them more than 20,000 casualties. The Scouts performed valiantly, and through a series of delaying actions and fierce counterattacks slowed the Japanese advance, making them pay dearly for every foot of ground.

On 9 April 1942, the remnants of the Philippine Division, surrounded by superior enemy forces, were ordered to surrender. They had lost some 6,000 casualties during the campaign. Thousands more died during the Bataan Death March and in Japanese prison camps. Those Scouts who escaped capture went into the mountains and fought as guerrillas until liberated in 1945.

On 6 April 1946, the Scouts were reactivated as the 12th Infantry Division (Philippine Scouts) with 36,000 Filipinos enlisting for three years' service. The division was to replace those U.S. garrison forces withdrawing from the Philippines. Unfortunately, the new Scouts did not have the same service heritage as their predecessors, and the division was gradually dismantled as enlistments expired. By 28 February 1950, only 373 Scouts remained awaiting discharge or retirement.

—*Vince Hawkins*

Above: *Lieutenant Matthew A. Baston and a group of Macabebe scouts, who in 1899 were some of the first Filipinos to serve with U.S. forces. (National Archives)*

disapproved by Ainsworth, he writes an insulting memo. Stimson orders charges for a court-martial, but Ainsworth is finally permitted to retire.

11 February. USS Maine Raised.
The U.S. Army Corps of Engineers raises U.S.S. *Maine* from Havana Harbor.

23 February. Army Aviator "Wings" Introduced.
The U.S. Army establishes the new rating of "Military Aviator" for which a special gold device consisting of a spread eagle, crossed flags representative of the Signal Corps that controls early aviation, and a placard reading "Military Aviator" will be adopted.

1 June. Altitude Record Established.
Lieutenant Henry E. "Hap" Arnold, United States Military Academy 1907, sets a world high-altitude record of 6,540 feet. More than four decades later he will become the only man in Army aviation history to wear five stars as general of the Air Force.

5 June. The Beginning of National Guard Military Aviation.
Lieutenant Colonel Charles B. Winder, Ohio Army National Guard, becomes the first Guard pilot.

12 June. Footgear Improvements. Fort Leavenworth. Kansas.
The "Munson Last" is adopted as standard for the

Above: *Early Army pilots received this certificate to attest to their attainment of the skills required for military aviators in the early days of Army aviation. (National Archives)*

production of Army footgear as one of the recommendations of a board to improve military issue. On 31 July, the namesake of this design, Lieutenant Colonel Edward Lyman Munson of the Medical Corps, publishes the proceedings of the three-person board that recommended this model of military shoe.

5 July. Trio of Army Aviators Receive New Badge.
Three U.S. Army officers become the first to qualify as "Military Aviators" and receive the newly minted special gold badge.

12 August. Ground and Air Operations Tested.
The Army employs aircraft for the first time in maneuvers with ground forces.

24 August. Congress Reorganizes Army.
Congress consolidates the Quartermaster, Pay, and Subsistence Departments into the Quartermaster Corps, with an authorization for a major general and 183 officers as opposed to the 223 officers previously in the separate organizations. In addition, it passes the "Manchu Law," which states that officers who have not served two years of line duty during the previous six years had to be returned immediately to troop duty for two years before further staff duty was allowed. This caused great turmoil, especially among the service school faculties and department staffs. Another aspect of the legislation provided that a soldier who enlisted for three years would also have four years as a "reserve," but no money is provided for reserve pay except in time of war. After two years, only 16 men will have signed up.

12 November. Air-Sea Efforts.
The Signal Corps obtains its first "flying boat," a two-seat Curtiss-F airplane.

1913

January–February. Status of the Army.
Slightly more than 90,000 officers and enlisted are serving, more than 6,000 of them patrolling the U.S.-Mexican border. To manage its affairs, the Army is administratively divided into six geographical departments—Eastern, Central, Western, Southern, Philippine, and Hawaiian. If the Army takes to the field, it is to be organized into divisions and brigades. In February, border tensions cause deployment of the troops designated for the 2d Division to Texas. More than 11,000 men are assembled in a week—a much improved performance over earlier exercises.

5 March. Expansion of Military Aviation. California.
In anticipation of possible border problems with
Mexico, the U.S. Army forms the 1st Provisional Aero
Squadron, to be stationed in San Diego. On the same
day Lindley Miller Garrison becomes Secretary of
War. He focuses on military preparedness in response
to the border unrest and the outbreak of the First
World War in Europe. Garrison called for a federal
reserve to serve as a ready source of expansion for the
regular Army.

**26 March. Army Corps of Engineers Assumes Flood
Control Mission.**
Devastating floods in Ohio and Indiana result in the
assignment of flood control to the U.S. Army Corps
of Engineers, supported by troops from line units and
National Guardsmen.

**9 June. New School for Foot Soldiers. Fort Sill,
Oklahoma.**
The U.S. Army opens the School of Musketry,
forerunner of the Infantry School.

13–15 June. Moro War Ends. Jolo, Philippines.
Brigadier General John J. Pershing leads an assault
on Bud Bagsak, the last Moro insurgent stronghold,
capturing it and successfully ending the uprising and
the third Jolo campaign. Pershing's performance
during the years he fights in the Philippines prompts
one contemporary to describe him as "cool as a bowl
of crushed ice" when engaged in even the most
heated combat.

Above: *John J. Pershing took personal command of the 8th
Infantry and Philippine Scouts in the Battle of Bagsak,
11–15 June 1913. Destruction of the fort ended the last
Moro stronghold. ("Knocking out the Moros," H. Charles
McBarron, Army Art Collection, NMUSA)*

THE EXPEDITIONARY ARMY

1914–1919

THE EXPEDITIONARY ARMY

1914–1919

Major General Bruce Jacobs, AUS (Ret)

These are the years of "the World War Era." Spanning only five years, this period marks an indelible line of demarcation for an army that had grappled fairly unsuccessfully with reformation and modernization in the decade and a half since the Spanish-American War. It is only with the advent of the World War Era that the realities of military unpreparedness finally catch up with all concerned—the War Department, Congress, the Executive Branch—and with the nation's industrial managers who will be called upon to produce results that may resemble miracles on the one hand or abject failure on the other.

In this remarkable era several million civilians become soldiers. The United States Army will never again be quite the same as before the World War Era. Even though the nation might revert to the days of a small and poorly nourished army—as indeed it would in the interwar years of 1920–1940—the institutional Army, shaken to its core by the events of 1914–1919 ceases to be a frontier-oriented scattering of centurions. Gone forever is the clan of warriors who turned the pages of history into the twentieth century.

Neither the Army nor the nation effectively used the years from the end of the War with Spain to the entry of the United States into the World War to produce a military structure capable of conducting large-scale operations in support of American national interests. Perhaps there was no reason to, but the fact remains that when the U.S. entered the war, the tactical organization of the Army was still in the hands of theorists. The adoption of the modern machinery of war was a leisurely process influenced by the lack of any commitment to urgency.

Only when the war ended would it became clear, in retrospect, that America found it necessary to rely

upon its allies for significant assistance in spite of its own vaunted industrial base. The nation learned important lessons about industrial mobilization. Although many Liberty engines would be produced, no U.S.-made war planes flew over France; no U.S.-manufactured tanks appeared on the battlefield; nor any heavy field artillery or trench mortars. It was not until mid-1918 that troops deploying from the United States were equipped with Browning machine guns of U.S. origin. This devastating reflection comes from no less a reliable source than the final report of the commander of the American Expeditionary Force, General John J. Pershing.

But the World War Era proves beyond the shadow of a doubt the ability of the Army to adapt quickly to new circumstances; and it established for all time an appreciation for the tenacity and the courage of young Americans called upon to go to war.

The Army's professional leadership—its skills honed in the thickets of the Philippines, in the cane fields of Cuba, the sun-drenched jungles of Puerto Rico, the hot and arid plains of the great American Southwest, and on the nation's northern rim—would not fail the nation. Its genius, starting with a small but well-trained and disciplined Regular Army, was in its ability to organize itself for modern, large-scale warfare. Owing at least in part to the deployment of the 1916 Punitive Expedition to the Mexican Border in reply to Pancho Villa's raid on Columbus, New Mexico, it gained experience in mobilization and rapid reaction. On the border, it integrated the mobilized National Guard into its training structure. Subsequently it trained and schooled the raw levies who came to the colors by means of the draft. In the end it created an Expeditionary Army of 42 divisions along with requisite corps and army troops.

The new National Army of 1917–1919 was a reflection of the demanding character of its field commander, the iron-jawed General John J. Pershing. Although the phrase had not yet come into the Army's lexicon, Pershing demonstrated "zero tolerance" toward deviations from his tough standards in training and discipline.

Under Pershing, the Army's senior lieutenants and captains of "the old army" become the colonels of the expeditionary force. The field grade officers of the Army's peacetime garrisons become the field commanders who would lead the divisions. What emerges is a great citizen army, predominantly men taken from civilian life who will be the heart and soul of the long-awaited AEF that enables the Allies to turn the tide of battle. The Army will forever be influenced by this influx of civilian soldiers. And the experience will produce millions of American men who have had their eyes opened to the world beyond American continental limits.

Pershing's American Expeditionary Force represented—up to that time and for many years to come—the largest movement in history of U.S. troops to foreign destinations. By the time the Armistice was signed on 11 November 1918 to put an end to hostilities, American forces served in France, Belgium, Great Britain, Italy, in Northern Russia, in Siberia, in Luxembourg, and in the Occupation of Germany. More than two million Americans served in the AEF.

Thus are the seeds sown for the evolution of a new army culture, which starts to take shape in this era, an era in which the U.S. shows itself as a player on the world scene. And where this might once have been a stage best served by ostentatious naval demonstration such as the international voyage of the Great White Fleet during the presidency of Theodore Roosevelt, this is an era typified more by the soldier in olive drab. And those who serve abroad in this era are the first to perceive—in the faces of liberated and rescued people—the foreshadowing of future reliance on America's "coming to the rescue" in time of crisis.

After 18 months in "the Great War" the curtain comes down on an intensely significant American epoch that concludes with national—indeed universal—aspirations expressed in the forlorn hope that mankind just concluded "the war to end war." The Army demobilizes rapidly and returns millions in uniform to civilian life. The nation, and its army, settles down to peacetime pursuits. The U.S. rapidly departs from Europe, declines to enter the League of Nations, and settles into an uneasy isolationism.

An American literary figure and former ambulance driver in France, Malcolm Cowley, will make the prescient observation as the doughboys of the wartime AEF fade away: "They would go back into civilian life almost as if they were soldiers on a long furlough."

Pages 534–535: *Men from the 23d Infantry, 2d Division, man a 37mm gun as they assault the German lines. The regiment would earn six campaign streamers as a result of such actions. (National Archives)*

Above: *This painting captures the surreal style of combat that often arose when men of the AEF met the enemy face to face with fixed bayonets in the forests of France. (N.C. Wyeth, Farnsworth Art Museum, Portland, ME)*

THE EXPEDITIONARY ARMY
1914–1919

...Send the word, to beware
We'll be over, we're coming over
And we won't be back
'Til it's over over there!

Popular song, 1917—George M. Cohan

1914

1 January. Civil Administration In Moro Province. Mindanao, Philippines.

The Army turns over reins of the Moro Province to a civilian administration. This is expected to end the protracted guerrilla campaign by the tribes people who inhabit central and western Mindanao and who regard imposition of U.S. law as a challenge to Islam. The region is now the Department of Mindanao and Sulu. In fact, Army and constabulary forces encounter sporadic Moro attacks over the next several decades.

7 January. First Air Unit Approved. San Diego, California.

The Army's Chief Signal Officers gives official approval to organization of the 1st Aero Squadron, U.S. Army, to consist of 20 officers, 90 men, and eight airplanes. The unit had been formed as a "provisional squadron" at Texas City, Texas, in the summer of 1913.

23 March. Horses Lost in Stable Fire. Fort Riley, Kansas.

A fire sweeps through Number Three Stables with a loss of 29 schooled horses, 4 polo ponies, and 6 private mounts owned by cavalry officers. Among the few horses to survive is Vestibule, a thoroughbred stallion given to the Army by August Belmont.

2 April. Wotherspoon Becomes Chief of Staff.

Major General William W. Wotherspoon is selected to replace Leonard Wood as the Army's sixth chief of staff. Wotherspoon served in the Indian Wars, led Apache scouts, and fought Filipino insurgents. He had been instrumental in creating an independent Army War College.

25 April. Tensions Hasten Graduations. Fort Riley.

Student officers in cavalry and field artillery courses are graduated hurriedly and sent to their regiments owing to the "situation" on the border with Mexico.

28 April. South of the Border. Tampico, Mexico.

President Woodrow Wilson, aroused by the seizure of U.S. sailors in Tampico and by the inability or unwillingness of the Huerta (Mexican) government to punish anti-U.S. activities, orders Army troops to assist U.S. sailors and Marines in establishing law and order in the volatile seaport town.

2 May. Army Hero Takes Command. Vera Cruz, Mexico.

Brigadier General Frederick Funston, a recipient of the Medal of Honor for heroic action in the Philippines, is placed in command of all American forces and named the American military governor for the duration of the occupation. Funston commands a force that includes 3,607 soldiers and 3,446 Marines.

Left: *William W. Wotherspoon transferred from the U.S. Navy and became the chief of staff of the Army in 1914. (Thomas W. Orlando, Army Art Collection, NMUSA)*

ARMY BATTLE STREAMERS—
MEXICAN EXPEDITION & WORLD WAR I

Mexico 1916–1917

Cambrai, 1917	Somme Offensive, 1918
Somme Defensive, 1918	Oise-Aisne, 1918
Lys, 1918	Ypres-Lys, 1918
Aisne, 1918	St. Mihiel, 1918
Montdidier-Noyon, 1918	Meuse-Argonne, 1918
Champagne-Marne, 1918	Vittoria Veneto, 1918
Aisne-Marne, 1918	

5–6 May. **Daring Raid. Outside of Vera Cruz, Mexico.**
Dispatched on a daring intelligence mission, Captain Douglas MacArthur conducts a daring nighttime reconnaissance deep into Mexican lines and returns to the U.S. position in possession of three commandeered railroad locomotives. He is recommended for the Medal of Honor.

28 June. **Assassination Triggers World War.**
Archduke Franz Ferdinand is murdered at Sarajevo. 28 July, Austria-Hungary declares war on Serbia. 31 July, Russia engages in full mobilization. 1 August, Germany declares war on Russia. 3 August, Germany declares war on France. 4 August, Great Britain declares war on Germany. 6 August, Austria-Hungary declares war on Russia. 12 August, France declares war on Austria-Hungary. 13 August, Great Britain declares war on Austria-Hungary. 16 August, British

Expeditionary Force lands in Europe. 25 August, Japan declares war on Germany. 27 August, Japan declares war on Austria-Hungary.

18 July. **Army Readies Its Wings.**
With responsibility for all U.S. Army aircraft including military balloons, the War Department, with the approval of Congress, creates the Aviation Section within the Army Signal Corps. The aviation section is allotted spaces for 60 officers and 260 enlisted men and specifies that new pilot-trainees will be "unmarried lieutenants of the line, not over 30 years of age."

3 August. **Conclusion of Canal Venture. Panama Canal Zone.**
The Corps of Engineers announces that work on the Panama Canal is completed six months ahead of

Left: *After six years of labor and moving millions of tons of earth, the Army Corps of Engineers concluded its historic work on the Panama Canal in 1914. ("Steam Shovel in the Culebra Cut," William Pretyman, Army Art Collection, NMUSA)*

Opposite, below: *Former superintendent of the U.S. Military Academy General Hugh Scott (1853–1934) later became the Army's chief of staff. (Robert Oliver Skemp, Army Art Collection, NMUSA)*

schedule—and under budget. It is the most formidable and most difficult canal construction project ever undertaken by any U.S. organization. Recognition is given to the work of Colonel William C. Gorgas for his success in eliminating malaria and yellow fever, keys to the success of the ambitious American strategic achievement.

4 August. **President States U.S. Position on War.**
President Woodrow Wilson proclaims the neutrality of the United States.

10 August–6 September. **Businessmen Get Training. Plattsburg, New York.**
In a novel experiment that is expected to provide a "reserve" of men trained for leadership in wartime, the Army sounds reveille at the first camp for training volunteer civilian businessmen. It is destined to be a model for future camps. Previous training camp programs have concentrated on college men.

October. **U.S. Cavalry Reinforces Mexican Border Positions. Naco, Arizona.**
Naco, astride the Mexican-Arizona border, is under siege by revolutionaries of Pancho Villa. The conflict threatens to spill over the border and the 10th Cavalry, reinforced by elements of the 9th Cavalry, is sent to protect the American town. The troopers build earthen defensive positions. Wild firing kills one soldier and wounds 18.

19–26 November. **Cross-Country Flight.**
The Army Air Service conducts a landmark cross-

country flight: Fort Sill, Oklahoma, to Fort Sam Houston, Texas, a distance of 429 miles.

23 November. **Funston Mission Ends. Vera Cruz, Mexico.**
The mission of General Frederick Funston to confront the Huerta government comes to an end as the U.S. Army's 5th Brigade departs. Huerta is now reported living in Spain and the new Mexican president is Venustiano Carranza. U.S. recognition of Carranza enrages Francisco (Pancho) Villa and other Mexican dissidents.

24 December. **First Air Raid Hits England.**
U.S. military officials study implications of the first German air raid on England.

1915

9 January. **Chief of Staff Meets Pancho Villa. Naco, Mexico.**
Major General Hugh Scott, impatient with lack of diplomatic progress, goes to meet with Pancho Villa. Villa ends the armed conflict around the town that resulted in Americans being killed.

1 March. **Proposal for Military Training. Washington, D.C.**
Lively discussion ensues as Captain George Van Horn Moseley of the War College Division (General Staff) submits a plan for universal military training that is presented to the Military Committee of the U. S. Senate.

Right: *The 1916 Punitive Expedition launched against Pancho Villa included the mobilization of the 1st Aero Squadron. The squadron's Curtis R-2 biplanes handled the communications along the 140-mile line of the expeditionary force. Occasional scouting missions added a new dimension to reconnaissance. ("Black Jack's New Scouts," James Dietz)*

13 April. **Fliers to Border Patrol. Brownsville, Texas.**
Lieutenants Thomas D. Milling and B. Q. Jones are ordered from the 1st Aero Squadron to report for duty with the border patrol to seek out positions held by Mexican insurgent, Pancho Villa. They proceed by rail with one airplane, necessary accessories, and eight men. The detachment reaches Brownsville on 17 April and sets up its camp at the west end of the cavalry drill field. First reconnaissance mission is flown 20 April.

22 April. **Gas Used in Europe War.**
The U.S. learns that the German Army uses asphyxiating gas against French and British forces in the northern part of the Ypres Salient.

7 May. Lusitania **Incident Angers U.S. Coast of Ireland, Atlantic Ocean.**
German U-Boat *U-20* torpedoes and sinks Britain's RMS *Lusitania*, a merchant vessel en route to New York from Liverpool. The ship sinks in 18 minutes, taking 1,195 lives including 123 Americans. German submarine warfare targeting merchant ships inflames U.S. public opinion, jeopardizing President Woodrow Wilson's neutrality policy.

30 June. **Assignments Announced. Fort Riley, Kansas.**
Lieutenant George S. Patton, Jr., is relieved of duties as Master of the Sword, Mounted Service School. Patton's tenure at Fort Riley is notable for his having graduated the first- and second-year courses and for his authorship of *Saber Regulations, 1914*. He is scheduled to join the 15th Cavalry at Fort Bliss, Texas.

29 July. **Air Squadron Relocated. Fort Sill, Oklahoma**
With orders to take part in fire control operations for the field artillery, the 1st Aero Squadron arrives at its new station under the command of Captain Benjamin D. Foulois. One section, with accompanying field artillery batteries, is quickly dispatched to Brownsville, Texas, to join the Army's border patrol.

10 August. **Scott Meets Villa Again. El Paso, Texas.**
Major General Hugh Scott meets with Pancho Villa again. Scott convinces Villa to drop demands for a large "loan" from American mining companies in northern Mexico, and to return other American property Villa has taken.

Left: *Chief of Staff of the Army Hugh Scott met with Pancho Villa (in civilian garb to Scott's left) in an unsuccessful effort to halt the Mexican civil war that was spreading into the border area with Texas. (National Archives)*

Below: *Troopers of the 13th Cavalry pose ready with their Benét-Mercie M1909 .30-caliber "automatic machine rifle," which they used with deadly effect against Villa's men when they attacked Columbus, New Mexico. (National Archives)*

16–17 August. **Flood Disaster. Texas City, Texas.**
As the area is inundated by flood waters in the wake of a severe summer storm, soldiers of the 27th Infantry Regiment come to the rescue of the community. The regiment is currently stationed in Texas City.

1 November. **Guard Takes to Skies. Mineola, New York.**
The 1st Aero Company, New York National Guard, is organized under Captain Raynall C. Bolling as the "Aviation Detachment, First Battalion, Signal Corps, National Guard, N.Y." It starts out with 4 officers, 40 enlisted men, and seven aircraft provided by the Aero Club of New York City.

9 November. **Continental Army Proposal by Secretary of War.**
Lindley M. Garrison, Secretary of War, briefs the President and then launches his campaign to effect an army reorganization that is intended to create a force of 400,000 volunteers to become known as the Continental Army. This force is proposed to replace the National Guard as the first-line reserve for the army. This becomes a bitter controversy. Congress indicates disfavor. President Wilson first supports the proposal, then changes his mind.

THE NATIONAL GUARD 1916–1918

In August 1914, as Americans watched anxiously while Europe plunged into World War I, a sharp debate ensued over the best means for expanding the Army. Arguments favoring an expanded role for the National Guard prevailed. The National Defense Act of 1916 specifically designated the National Guard as the Army's primary reserve, while authorizing an expanded Regular Army and Army Reserve. All state militia units were officially designated as "National Guard," and the President received authority to mobilize the Guard for the duration of a national emergency. The number of annual drill periods increased from 24 to 48 with pay provided for all drills. Summer camp was extended from 5 to 15 days.

Only two weeks after passage of the act, units of the National Guard were ordered to active duty to defend the southwestern border against incursions from Mexico. A civil war raged in Mexico, and Mexican revolutionaries conducted deadly cross-border raids against American ranchers. President Woodrow Wilson ordered a punitive expedition of 10,000 Regulars under Brigadier John J. Pershing into northern Mexico to track Pancho Villa down. The President also asked the governors of Texas, New Mexico, and Arizona to provide Guardsmen for border protection, and by 11 May, 5,260 Guardsmen were headed for the troubled areas. By the early spring of 1917, the border crisis had abated and most Guardsmen headed home.

The European crisis was not over, however, and exhausted Allied leaders pleaded for American reinforcements. Much of America's initial combat power would have to come from the Guard. At the declaration of war in April 1917, 66,594 Guardsmen were still serving along the Mexican border. By August, more than 379,700 Guardsmen in sixteen divisions were organizing for combat at mobilization camps.

The National Guard's 26th "Yankee" Division, composed of troops from New England, arrived in France on 28 October, followed in early November by the 42d "Rainbow" Division. General Pershing, the AEF commander, insisted that his troops receive thorough training before entering the trenches. Individuals and then small units were placed in the front line to gain experience while Pershing held off

Allied pressure to use American troops as replacements.

In March 1918, however, a huge German offensive prompted Pershing to commit American units. From then on Guardsmen figured prominently on the Western Front. The 26th and 42d Divisions went into action soon followed by the 28th "Keystone" Division. Four Guard divisions—26th, 28th, 32d, and 42d—took part in the allied counter-offensive in July. In September, the AEF cleared the St. Mihiel Salient and then attacked the heavily defended German sector in the Argonne Forest.

The regiments of the 93d Division, composed of African-Americans, were deployed separately as part of a French division, the 369th Regiment winning particular praise for its fighting valor.

Of the 43 American divisions sent to France, 18—about 40 percent of the entire AEF—were National Guard. Overall, 433,478 Guardsmen served in World War I, suffering 103,721 killed and wounded, approximately 43 percent of American casualties. When asked, the German High Command considered eight American divisions especially effective; six of those were National Guard.

—*Michael Doubler*

Above: *The citizen-soldiers of the Army National Guard suffered the same privations and dangers at the front as their Regular comrades. ("The Engineer," H. T. Dunn, Smithsonian Institution)*

1916

10 February. **Garrison Rebuffed, Resigns.**
Lindley M. Garrison (appointed 5 March 1913) tenders
President Wilson his resignation as Secretary of War.
Assistant Secretary of War Henry S. Breckenridge
also resigns.

24 February. **Army Planning Is Questioned.**
Acting Secretary of War Hugh L. Scott asks the War
College Division whether any War Department plans
exist for action in the event "of a complete rupture"
with Germany.

9 March. **Baker Heads Army. Washington, D.C.**
A distinguished lawyer from Cleveland, Ohio, the
Hon. Newton D. Baker, is named by President Wilson
to be Secretary of War. Baker replaces the controversial
Lindley M. Garrison, who fails in his proposal ("the
Continental Army") to eliminate the National Guard
as a cornerstone of military mobilization.

9 March. **Villa Strikes U.S. Town. Columbus,
New Mexico.**
A force of approximately 500 Mexican irregulars led
by Francisco (Pancho) Villa attacks the town and

nearby Camp Furlong, the base camp of the 13th
Cavalry Regiment. U.S. casualties are 11 civilians and
9 soldiers. The surprised soldiers and townspeople
drive off the attackers, killing many of Villa's men.
The cavalrymen chase Villa's men across the border
and pursue them for several days.

15 March. **Pershing in Command. Mexican Border.**
The Mexican president rules that Americans may
pursue Villa in Mexico but insists that Pershing's
forces may penetrate no farther than the northern
province of Chiahuahua. The Punitive Expedition of
three brigades crosses the border to take up the
pursuit. Pershing's small headquarters "family" includes
his new aide, Lt. George S. Patton, Jr.

28–29 March. **Villistas Routed. Guerrero, Mexico.**
The 7th Cavalry regiment makes a 17-hour forced
march, surprising a force of 500 of Villa's men. The
cavalrymen charge, routing the Villistas and killing
35 to 40.

1 April. **Radio Link Established. Mexico**
In order to make best possible use of the six airplanes
available on the border, the Army establishes a radio-
telegraph communications link between Namiquipa
and El Valle to do away with the need for employing

aircraft on this dangerous route. The Signal Corps soon has 19 radio stations on the air helping to link army forces in Mexico.

5 *April*. Aero Squadron on the Move. San Geronimo, Mexico.
Foulois moves his squadron headquarters to San Geronimo. Previously the squadron had been located at Casas Grandes, Mexico, with aircraft flying out of Colonia Dublan.

8 *April*. Pershing Moves South. Colonia Dublan, Mexico.
With nearly 7,000 troops now under his command Pershing is reported to be more than 400 miles into Mexican territory. With the Mexican railroads denied to him Pershing turns to new motor transport companies to haul food, clothing, weapons, and ammunition from stores assembled at Columbus, New Mexico.

12 *April*. Cavalry Attacked by Rebels. Santa Cruz de Villegas. Mexico.
A detachment of the 13th Cavalry is attacked while moving through the town. The troopers fight their way to a nearby ranch and hold off their attackers until a relief force arrives.

13 *April*. Mexican Ultimatum Ignored. Parral, Mexico.
The U.S. consul at the Mexican town of Chihuahua forwards an ultimatum issued by the governor of Chihuahua stating that U.S. troops at Parral must be withdrawn. General Pershing replies that he takes his orders from the President of the United States.

16 *April*. The Lafayette Escadrille is Formed. Luxeuil-les-Bains (Vosges), France.
At this air base near Switzerland, American volunteers from French flying units are brought together to form Escadrille No. 124, soon to be better-known as the Lafayette Escadrille of the French Army.

5 *May*. Apache Scouts See Action. Ojos Azules, Mexico.
Apache Scouts accompanying a six-troop force of the 11th Cavalry regiment under the command of Major Robert Lee Howze (Medal of Honor, 1901) encounter and attack a larger group of Villa's men, killing 60 of the enemy without suffering a loss.

Opposite: *The 1916–1917 Mexican expedition was a watershed in Army history with the first operational use of new technology such as biplanes and combustion engine vehicles. ("On the Border," James Dietz)*

Below: *In one of the final mounted actions fought by American horse soldiers, troopers of the 11th U.S. Cavalry charged with .45-caliber pistols against Villistas in Mexico. ("The Last Charge," Don Stivers)*

9 May. Southwestern Guardsmen Answer Call to Border.
National Guardsmen from southwestern states—Texas, New Mexico, Arizona—are called into federal service for border protection. Within 48 hours 5,260 state troops head for the border.

13 May. Lafayette Pilots See Action. Alsace Region, France.
The French Army announces the *Escadrille Américain* is in action; it now has seven Americans rated for cockpit duty.

18 May. Escadrille Nails First Enemy Plane. Thann, Alsace region.
Sergeant Kiffin Yates Rockwell brings down the escadrille's first plane, a German on reconnaissance, in his first combat sortie. The downed airplane crashes behind enemy lines, but a friendly observation post reports Rockwell's victory. Before becoming a pilot, Rockwell, a native of Asheville, North Carolina, was wounded at La Targette, north of Arras, as a soldier in the French Foreign Legion.

3 June. Army Reorganization.
Congress establishes The Army of the United States (AUS). This designation is used to refer to all Regular Army and National Guard and reserve personnel when on federal active duty. In addition, the Veterinary Corps is established with an initial strength of one officer and 16 enlisted men for every 400 animals in the Army. An Officers' Reserve Corps (ORC) is to be recruited and trained.

Above: *Marching many dusty miles without ever bringing Pancho Villa to bay, men of the 16th U.S. Infantry pass through a Mexican village where they are wary of being attacked. (National Archives)*

Left: *Dust storms, soaring temperatures, and scarce water often contributed to the American soldier's miseries in Mexico. (National Archives)*

21 June. **Patrol Is Attacked. Carrixal, Mexico.**
A force of several hundred Mexicans attack two troops of the 10th Cavalry regiment on a reconnaissance patrol. Two officers and 10 "Buffalo Soldiers" are killed, as well as 75 Mexicans.

18 June. **Mobilization of the Guard is Stepped Up.**
A wider mobilization of National Guard troops is ordered to enable the Army to expand operations along the Mexican Border. The first Guard unit to reach the border (30 June) is the 1st Illinois Infantry.

13 July. **First Guard Airmen Mobilized. Mineola, New York.**
In anticipation of duty on the Mexican Border, New York's pioneering 1st Aero Company is mustered into federal service. (On 2 November 1916, after getting 25 pilots qualified as military aviators, the 1st Aero Company, N.Y. National Guard, is mustered out without ever having reached the border.)

28 August. **Major Foulois Reports.**
In his report covering operations of the 1st Aero Squadron for the period of 15 March through 15 August, Foulois notes that despite severe difficulties with equipment, 540 flights had been made in Mexico and the U.S., totaling 346 hours and covering 19,533 miles.

28 August. **Italy in War on Allied Side.**
Italy declares war on Germany.

31 August. **Guard Troops' Numbers Increase Rapidly.**
The Army's end-of-the-month reports show that 111,954 Guardsmen are now on duty in the southwest, including the two organized divisions from New York and Pennsylvania. The Guard force includes 60,000 horses and mules for cavalry, artillery, and supply units.

18–19 November. **Guard Cross-Country Flight. Mineola, N.Y., to Princeton, N.J.**
New York's 1st Aero Company, with seven JN-4s, is led by Captain Raynall C. Bolling in pioneering non-stop, cross-country flight from the Mineola, N.Y., airfield to Princeton, N.J. Fliers attend a football game, remain in Princeton overnight, and return to Mineola.

1917

28 January. **Pershing Assembles Expedition. Colonia Dublan, Mexico.**
Pershing orders his command to assemble at Palomas, Chihuahua, so that the U.S. force will march across

Above: *Former foes joined the Army pursuit of Villa in Mexico. U.S. cavalryman First Sergeant Chicken rode with fellow Apache scouts at Ojos Azules during Pershing's excursion south of the border. (National Archives)*

the border together. The Punitive Expedition of 11,500 soldiers organizes for its withdrawal from Mexico and the Army also plans for return of National Guard units to home states.

31 January. **Submarine Warfare Threat Increases.**
Germany announces unrestricted submarine warfare in specified zones. President Wilson is to seek authority to arm merchant ships.

2 February. **Old Rough Rider Seeks Command. Oyster Bay, New York**
Former President and ex-commander of the Rough Riders in the Spanish-American War Theodore Roosevelt makes a request to lead a division of volunteers to the western front on the Allied side. On 3 February Secretary of War Baker declines Roosevelt's offer. Roosevelt reiterates his request on 7 February. Secretary Baker repeats his refusal on 9 February.

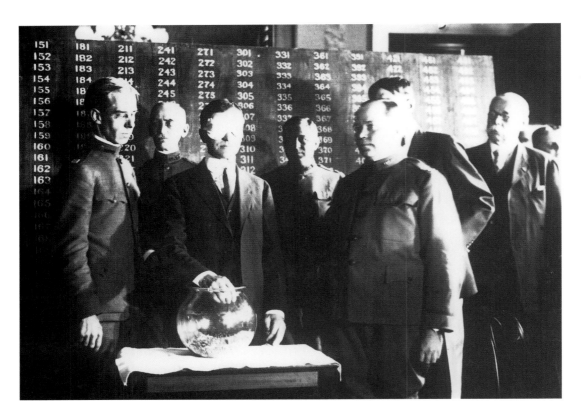

Left: *Secretary of War Newton Baker draws the first lot for the selective service—draft number 258. (National Archives)*

Below: *Artist James Montgomery Flagg's recruiting poster featuring a convincing Uncle Sam became one of the most famous patriotic icons to emerge from World War I. (Army Art Collection, NMUSA)*

3 February. **Rift with Germany. Washington, D.C.** U.S. severs diplomatic relations with Germany.

5 February. **Troops Leave Mexico.**
In response to orders from Southern Department Commander, Major General Frederick Funston, all American forces are back on U.S. soil and the Punitive Expedition is officially closed out.

11–15 March. **Revolution in Russia Ousts Czar.**
The revolution in Russia leads to abdication of the czar, pressure for Russian withdrawal from the Allied side in the war.

6 April. **U.S. Joins Allied Effort.**
President Woodrow Wilson goes before Congress and requests a declaration of war, which joins the U.S. to the Allies (England, France, Italy, Japan, et al.) in the struggle against Germany and the Central Powers. The U.S. Regular Army numbers fewer than 200,000 men at this point; it has no tanks, no immediate capability for producing artillery, and fewer than 50 qualified military aviators in its ranks.

28 April. **Congress Adopts Draft Bill.**
As a major step toward raising a wartime army, Congress passes the Selective Service Act and sends it to President Wilson for his signature.

1 May. **Call for Railway Engineers.**
Recruiting offices unveil posters that prove to be prophetic: "First to France—Join the Engineers."

Company A, 11th Engineers (Railway), will soon lead the debarkment of Army elements at Boulogne, France. Soon the 11th, 12th, and 14th Railway Engineers will be in action on the Western Front.

OVERSEAS IN UNIFORM: ARMY WOMEN DURING WORLD WAR I

When the United States entered World War I in 1917, the 400 nurses of the Army Nurse Corps were the only women in Army uniform. By the end of the war, the corps had expanded to more than 21,000, with approximately half serving in Army hospitals overseas, predominantly with the American Expeditionary Force in Europe.

Army nurses arrived in France in May 1917, well before American troops, and were sometimes assigned to British casualty clearing stations very near the front lines. Nurse Helen McClellan spent eleven weeks at a clearing station near St. Sixte's Convent, Belgium. One night, around 10:15 p.m., enemy planes bombed the camp. Pieces of shrapnel ripped through the tent McClelland shared with another Army nurse, Beatrice McDonald. Said McClelland, "Even with my eyes closed I saw the flashes from the explosion. My uniform hanging on the bedpost was full of holes. My mattress was full of shrapnel." McDonald was hit in the eye, and in the midst of the attack McClelland left cover and ran to help her friend. This action earned her the Distinguished Service Cross, one of three awarded to Army nurses during the war. McDonald lost the sight in her eye but returned to duty as soon as she was able.

Although several Army nurses were wounded by enemy fire, none died from their wounds. Two nurses en route to Europe aboard SS *Mongolia* were killed when the ship's guns misfired. The vast majority of Army nurse casualties occurred from the massive influenza epidemic that swept around the world in 1918 and 1919, during which millions of people died. The "swine flu" was highly contagious and flourished in crowded military hospitals and bases. More than 260 Army nurses died when influenza they contracted from their patients turned into pneumonia. Following the armistice, the Army accepted the service of 18 African-American nurses and used them in the U.S. to care for German POWs and African-American soldiers.

During World War I, the Army discovered that it needed women in roles other than nursing. In 1918, General Pershing, AEF commander in Europe, noticed that soldiers at headquarters were having trouble using the French telephone system to relay orders to units in the field. Pershing believed that American women telephone operators could do a better job, so he asked the Army to send women with switchboard experience to Signal Corps units in Europe. The Army hired the women under contracts and the first 33 set sail for

France on 1 March 1918. By late April, a total of 233 were in Europe. Organized into Women's Telephone Units, they became known as the "Hello Girls." They were assigned to AEF headquarters and in 75 French towns, handling calls relating to troop movements, artillery, and supplies. In several instances the women went forward to operate communications equipment immediately behind the front lines. In September 1918, during the attack at St. Mihiel, six operators were assigned to headquarters only five miles away.

The Quartermaster Corps contracted American women for France. More than 68 skilled stenographers, typists, indexers and cataloguers, statisticians, topographical draftswomen, and librarians were assigned in Tours, France, between August 1918 and August 1919. The women were scattered throughout the supply, personnel, graves registration, inspection, finance, and salvage divisions and the troop train meal service.

Within months, many of these divisions sent memorandums to headquarters requesting additional women, but their pleas were ignored, and the Army's female contract workers were ordered home during the summer of 1919.

—*Judi Bellefaire*

Above: *The Army Nurse Corps, founded fewer than 20 years before, came into its own during World War I when technological advances in weaponry brought about massive casualties. (National Archives)*

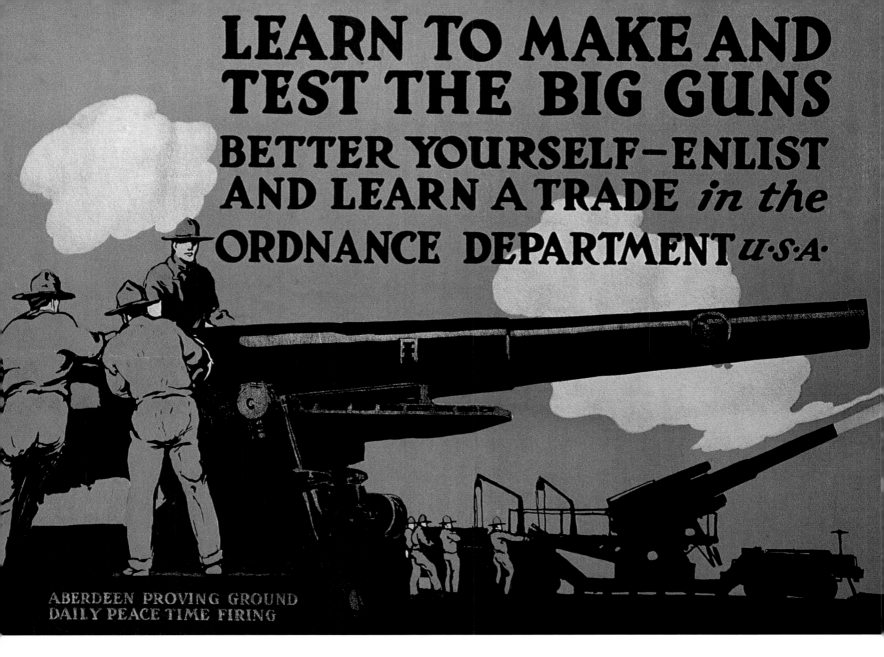

LEARN TO MAKE AND TEST THE BIG GUNS
BETTER YOURSELF—ENLIST AND LEARN A TRADE *in the* ORDNANCE DEPARTMENT *u·s·a·*

ABERDEEN PROVING GROUND
DAILY PEACE TIME FIRING

2 May. **Pershing is Placed on Alert. Fort Sam Houston, Texas.**
Major General John J. Pershing, commander of the Southern Department, is informed by the War Department that he may be designated to command an overseas expeditionary force destined for France and he is summoned to a meeting in Washington.

18 May. **Draft Law is Signed.**
The Selective Service Act providing a draft for military manpower is signed by the President. As the government proceeds to develop draft machinery, the new law is challenged on Constitutional grounds as the U.S. Supreme Court opinion is awaited.

18 May. **Roosevelt "Releases" His Volunteers. Oyster Bay, New York.**
President Wilson says, "I shall not avail myself, at any rate at the present stage of the war, of the

Above: *The need to produce and maintain heavy artillery brought about a call for volunteers to enlist in the Ordnance Corps as the Americans mobilized for World War I. (Gary A. Borkan Collection)*

authorization conferred by the act [of Congress] to organize volunteer divisions. To do so would . . . contribute practically nothing to the effective strength of the armies now engaged against Germany." Upon being advised of the President's decision, Colonel Roosevelt immediately issues a statement to his colleagues "to disband and abandon" all further efforts in connection with the volunteer divisions, leaving the men free to make other arrangements to serve.

24 May. **First to be First.**
The Army designates the new First Expeditionary Division, Regular Army, to lead the American Army to France. Troops for the division are summoned from locations near the Mexican border, Brownsville (Texas), Douglas (Arizona), El Paso (Texas) and from Forts Sam Houston, Ringgold, and Bliss; from Washington Barracks; and from Fort Oglethorpe, Georgia. The division is to assemble in France under the command of Brigadier General William L. Sibert, who earned distinction as an engineer officer in the construction of the Panama Canal.

Right: *The first doughboys debark in France on 26 June 1917 at St. Nazire. (Anne S. K. Brown Military Collector, Brown University)*

Below: *In June 1917, John J. Pershing, wearing four stars to denote his position as the AEF's commander, landed at Bordeux, France, to take charge of his growing forces. (National Archives)*

26 May. **Commander of AEF Receives Orders.**
Major General John J. Pershing is designated Commander-in-Chief of the American Expeditionary Force (AEF), slated to fight in France. The Secretary of War gives Pershing orders approved by President Wilson: "You are directed to cooperate with the forces of the other countries employed against the enemy; but in so doing, the underlying idea must be kept in view that the forces of the United States are a separate and distinct component of the combined forces, the identity of which must be preserved."

28 May. **Pershing Gathers Staff for France. Governor's Island, New York.**
The staff which is to serve under General Pershing in France assembles and prepares to sail aboard S.S. *Baltic.* The initial AEF headquarters complement includes 57 army officers, 2 Marine Corps officers, 67 enlisted personnel, 36 field clerks, 3 interpreters, and 3 newspaper correspondents.

5 June. **Ten Million Men Register for Draft.**
The first draft registration is conducted making use of civil election machinery and it is estimated that 10 million American men are in the manpower pool for possible service.

7–9 June. **1st Division Takes Shape and Ships Out. Hoboken, New Jersey.**
The 1st Infantry Brigade (16th, 18th Infantry Regiments) and 2d Infantry Brigade (26th, 28th Infantry Regiments) are formed and prepare to leave for France. Division headquarters and infantry elements depart Hoboken 14 June. Artillery and other elements of the division are to sail on 31 July.

13 June. **Over There! Boulogne, France.**
After a brief stop in England, Pershing and members of his AEF staff land in the Pas-de-Calais region to begin planning to enter combat alongside the Allies.

14 June. **President's Flag Day Speech. Washington, D.C.**
President Wilson, in his Flag Day speech, declares that the initial soldiers of the new AEF will be followed by more soldiers as rapidly as possible and that these soldiers will not be held in the U.S. for training. Training areas in France are being negotiated by Pershing.

23 June. **Ambulance Volunteers In the Army Now.**
In a swift response to a plea from Marshal Joffre, who needs every able-bodied Frenchman on the firing line, the War Department directs formation of the "United States Army Ambulance Service" with ambulance sections organized for direct attachment to French combat divisions. Manpower is to come from Norton-Harjes/American Field Service units already in France and new units to be recruited in the U.S. Camp Crane, Allentown, Pennsylvania, is designated as the primary mobilization and training center. Eventually 184 officers and 4,858 soldiers serve in 113 ambulance sections at the front.

26 June. **Vanguard of AEF Arrives. St. Nazaire, France.**
The first American Troops, including infantry elements of the new 1st Division, land in France after crossing the Atlantic. The last divisional elements will reach St. Nazaire on 22 December. The arrival of doughboys has an immediate effect of raising the morale of dispirited French civilians, who have now endured three years of horrific warfare. The grateful French will construct a monument to mark this occasion. It will be destroyed by the invading Germans in 1941 and rebuilt by the French in 1989.

4 July. **Ceremonial Words Spoken. Paris, France.**
Concluding a ceremony with General Pershing at the tomb of Marquis de Lafayette, Colonel C. E. Stanton, speaking for Pershing, makes the memorable remark: *"Lafayette, nous voici!"* ("Lafayette, we are here!")

4 July. **Liberty Engine for U.S. Air Fleet.**
The first test model of a new aircraft engine design by the Packard Motor Car Company is inspected and

Above: *General Tasker Bliss (1853–1930) played many important roles during his distinguished career, including service as the Army's chief of staff from 23 September 1917 to 18 May 1918. ("Tasker Howard Bliss," Frank Ingoglia, Army Art Collection, NMUSA)*

Left: *James Montgomery Flagg appealed to men who wanted to enter the ranks of the Regular Army. (Gary A. Borkan Collection)*

approved just 33 days after the first drawings were produced. There will be 15,131 of these engines produced by war's end.

5 July. Now It's the 1st Division, AEF. Gondrecourt, France.

Assigned to the 1st Training Area (Gondrecourt), the First Expeditionary Division is renamed the 1st Division, AEF—the name it will carry with great distinction for many years to come. It is to undergo training with the French 47th Division (Chasseurs).

5 July. Camp Hospital No. 1 is Open. Gondrecourt, France

Army Camp Hospital No. 1 is established by the redesignation of Field Hospital No. 13, until now in the 1st Division. It is located in temporary wooden barracks, of French construction, with a bed capacity of 300, to serve the 1st Training Area.

5 July. Army Supply Line. Paris, France

The Line of Communication (later to be the Service of Supply) is established as an integral part of the AEF under Brigadier General R. M. Blatchford. A network of base sections and other subordinate commands are to be established to control the movement of men and supplies from the ports to training areas and to the front.

14 July. U.S. Medic Wounded. British Sector. Near Arras, France

First Lieutenant Louis J. Genella, Medical Corps, hit by shellfire, is the first American wounded in the World War. He is serving with British medical forces.

16 July. Division Artillerymen in Training Area. Le Valdahon, France.

With all of the division's artillery elements now in France, the 1st Field Artillery Brigade is formed under Brigadier General Peyton C. March and the redlegs commence training at the French Army artillery ranges at Le Valdahon (Doubs).

19 July. Signal Corps To Film the War.

The Signal Corps, which has been taking pictures since the 1880s, is assigned responsibility for Army photographic services. By 1 November 1918 the Signal Corps has taken over 30,000 still pictures and 750,000 feet of motion picture film. The AEF is impressed with the French and British use of carrier pigeons as an effective means of communication and requests that pigeon specialists be commissioned in the Army. By war's end the Signal Corps has deployed more than 15,000 pigeons in the AEF.

24 July. Pershing, Haig Confer. Headquarters, British Expeditionary Forces.

General Pershing holds a meeting with British Field Marshal Haig.

5 August. 1st Aero Squadron to France. Columbus, New Mexico.

Now under the command of Major Ralph Royce, the 1st Aero Squadron says farewell to the Mexican Border as it heads for Avord and, later, Issoudon, to continue training in France.

14 August. AEF Leadership Takes Shape. Washington, D.C.

President Wilson sends to the Senate the names of 184 officers whom he has designated to be general officers in the new National Army, the name given to the Army's wartime component. Thirty-seven on the list are new major generals; the remainder gain one-star rank.

Above: *The mass casualties suffered during World War I taxed the resources of Army medical personnel who fought to save the lives of the wounded. ("American Soldier, 1918," H. Charles McBarron, Army Art Collection, NMUSA)*

14 August. **"Rainbow" Division on Duty. Camp Mills, New York.**
The 42d Division is formed with National Guard units from 26 states and the District of Columbia, leading to its designation as the "Rainbow" Division. It is anticipated that it will be the first Guard division to be sent overseas. The War Department assigns Brigadier General William A. Mann, former head of the Militia Division of the War Department, as its commander. Colonel Douglas MacArthur is named the division chief of staff.

28 August. **Commander of Troops. Paris, France**
General Pershing prepares to relocate his headquarters and assigns Colonel William H. Allaire, the provost marshal, as commander of U.S. troops in Paris. This command is directed to monitor and register all enlisted personnel, U.S. civilians, and officers below grade of brigadier general visiting the French capital.

1 September. **Pershing in the Field. Chaumont, France.**
Pershing moves out of Paris and establishes his AEF headquarters at Chaumont (Haute-Marne), where it will remain for the duration of the war. The headquarters sets up shop in the French army's old Damrémont caserne.

Above: *Men of the 347th Field Artillery tackle an obstacle course to prepare them for the rigors of fighting they will face at the front. (National Guard Bureau)*

4 September. **Soldiers Die in Hospital Bombing. Dannes-Camiers, France.**
Four U.S. soldiers, all members of U.S. Base Hospital No. 5, die when the enemy bombs the British hospital to which they are attached. They are the first soldiers of the AEF to be killed by enemy fire.

5 September. **Engineers Suffer Battle Casualties. Gouzeaucourt, France.**
Two members of the U.S. 11th Engineer Regiment are the first battle casualties of an American unit at the front. Sergeant Matthew R. Calderwood and Private William Branigan are wounded by shellfire while working on a railway project with the British.

22 September. **Scott Leaves Post as Chief of Staff.**
Major General Hugh L. Scott (appointed 17 November 1914) retires but is immediately recalled to active duty to inspect the battlefront in France. He later commands the 78th Division at Camp Dix, New Jersey.

23 September. **Bliss Is the New Chief of Staff.**
With promotion to full (four-star) general, Tasker H. Bliss, an artilleryman, is named the Army's chief of staff.

27 September. **National Guard Artillerymen. Camp Coetquidan, France.**
The 101st Field Artillery, the first regimental-size element of the National Guard in France, arrives at this French Army artillery center in the vanguard of the 26th (New England) Division.

Right: *Men of Company G, 16th U.S. Infantry, fall out in their olive drab service uniforms, including the campaign hat that proved impractical for combat in the trenches. (National Archives)*

Below: *Intensive stateside training was conducted frequently with the assistance of officers and NCOs back from line service. New soldiers, with gas masks in place but without helmets, prepare to go "over the top" during a trench warfare training exercise. (National Archives)*

2 October. **March Commands AEF Artillery.**
Major General Peyton C. March is named to command the Army artillery in France. He is succeeded in command of the 1st Field Artillery Brigade by Brigadier General Charles P. Summerall.

6 October. **Pershing Confirmed as Full General.**
General John J. Pershing, AEF commander, is confirmed in four-star rank as Army strength reaches 90,000 men in France.

7 October. **AEF Shipping News.**
The AEF sends the War Department its proposed "Priority Schedule" to determine the order of shipment for troops from the United States to France. The initial plan calls for the movement of 1,328,448 soldiers in six phases. Each of first five phases is to include a combat Army corps of six divisions plus corps troops. The sixth phase is to include [field] Army troops and manpower for rear area and tank corps projects.

9 October. **U.S. Commander in England. London.**
Major General George T. Bartlett, a Coast Artillery officer, assumes command of American Troops in England.

10 October. **Anti-Aircraft Troops. Langres, France.**
Training begins for the first anti-aircraft troops in the AEF. Langres (Haute-Marne) also will be home to the school for trench mortar training.

12 October. **Three-Hundred-Bed Camp Hospital Opens. Le Valdahon, France.**
The hospital accompanying the 1st Field Artillery Brigade is redesignated Army Camp Hospital No. 12. The hospital, which can accommodate 300 patients,

occupies a French military hospital situated in three stone buildings and a number of huts. It will remain in this location for the duration of the war.

18 October. **Army Transport Service for AEF.**
The Transport Service, under a director general who reports to the commanding general, Services of Supply, is created. The new organization is to control all port operations; construct and operate railways, and be responsible for the utilization of canals throughout the U.S. sectors. Brigadier General William F. Atterbury is named to fill this post.

21 October. **Doughboys Into Trenches. Sommervillier Sector, (Lorraine) France.**
Soldiers from the 1st Division occupy positions in the front trenches for the first time as each of four infantry regiments sends a battalion into lines alongside French troops.

23 October. **Artillery in Action. Sommervillier Sector (Lorraine), France.**
Equipped with French 75mm guns, the first rounds of American artillery are fired into German lines by Battery C, 6th Field Artillery, in support of a defensive force organized by the 2d Battalion, 16th Infantry Regiment, 1st Division.

24–25 October. **Disaster on the Italian Front. Caporetto, Italy.**
Austro-German forces inflict a crushing defeat on the Italian Army near Caporetto and begin their advance toward Venice. This necessitates the diversion of

French and British divisions to the Italian front—and increases pressure on Pershing to provide U.S. troops to help man French and British trenches. Pershing persists in his policy that Americans will serve in the front lines, but as elements of an independent (American) army.

25 October. **Infantry School of Arms. Fort Sill, Oklahoma.**
First Lieutenant Edward C. Allworth, 60th Infantry, is among 210 lieutenants reporting as students for a one-month course of training. A year later Captain Allworth will earn the Medal of Honor for gallantry in action at the Meuse River with the 5th Division.

26 October. **2d Division Created. Bourmont, France**
With regiments newly arrived in France, the AEF forms the U.S. 2d Division under the command of Major General Omar Bundy. Uniquely, the division structure is built around an Army infantry brigade and a Marine Corps brigade. The division is to train in the Bourmont area while its artillery organizes and trains at Le Valdahon.

30 October. **Power Shortages Worry Washington.**
Federal officials fear wartime demands are bringing on power shortages that can adversely impact the heavily industrialized Niagara (N.Y.) region and rapidly spread elsewhere. Secretary Baker calls on Army engineers to take the lead in a newly formed Power Section in the War Industries Board. Colonel Charles Keller, West Point, 1890 (later, a general officer in France), becomes Joint National Power Administrator.

Opposite: *African-Americans from the 369th Infantry were assigned to duty with French forces, and thus usually wore the helmets, carried the weapons, and used the equipment provided by the allies. (National Archives)*

Right: *The men of the AEF were not the only ones to suffer during the First World War. Many French villages fell prey to the destruction as well. ("American Troops Advancing," Harold Brett, Army Art Collection, NMUSA)*

31 October. **Yankee Division Joins AEF. Neufchateau, France.**
The 26th Division headquarters opens on French soil. Having commandeered shipping at the port of embarkation, the impetuous "Yankee" Division led by Major General Clarence Edwards—ostensibly headed for Camp Greene, North Carolina—joins the AEF ahead of schedule, and ahead of the 42d (Rainbow) division! It is the first fully organized division in France. It numbers 28,000 officers and men.

2–3 November. **Raid on U.S. Trenches. Bathelémont-les-Bauzemont, France.**
German troops raid trenches manned by the 1st Division, killing three soldiers of the 16th Infantry—the first of the 50,510 U.S. battle deaths in the war. In this incursion, the first American prisoners are taken.

7 November. **Bolsheviks Seize Power in Russia.**
Bolshevik leader Lenin takes power. Allies brace for
the appearance on the Western Front of German Army
forces no longer needed in the east in the wake of the
overthrow of the Russian Imperial Government.

20 November–4 December. **Railway Troops At the
Front. Picardy Region, France.**
British forces with tanks in support launch an attack
near Cambrai, the first major offensive in which U.S.
troops participate. Three U.S. engineer regiments are
serving with the British: 11th Engineers engaged in
front-line operations put down an average of 1.4 miles
of track per day, while under fire and taking casualties;
the 12th Railway Engineers deliver ammunition to
British artillery; the 14th Railway Engineers operate
light railways in support of the British VI Corps.
During the war, the Corps of Engineers deploys
60,000 railway troops to France. "Cambrai 1917" is the
first U.S. campaign streamer in the war. The Cambrai
battle ends on 4 December.

28 November. **General Staff College. Langres, France.**
Field grade officers in the AEF have the opportunity
to obtain a senior service school education with the
establishment of the General Staff College at Langres.
Also at Langres is the First Army Tank School, with
Major George S. Patton, Jr., as its chief. Other schools
for a variety of special needs are scattered throughout
eastern France.

7 December. **U.S. vs. Austria-Hungary.**
The United States announces it is at war with
Austria-Hungary.

12 December. **Elements of the Colored Division
Embarks. Camp Stuart, Virginia.**
The infantry elements of the 93d (Provisional)
Division are ordered to Hoboken, New Jersey, to
begin their journey to France.

14 December. **Bullard Commands the 1st Division.**
Major General Robert Lee Bullard, an infantryman
since his graduation from West Point in 1885, is
designated to command the 1st Division.

26 December. **The President Takes Over Railroads.**
Traffic tie ups with enormous implications for impact
upon overseas shipping prompt President Wilson to
announce his decision to put U.S. railroads under
governmental control.

31 December. **Railroads Under Government Control.**
U.S. railroads transition from private ownership to
governmental control. The Director General of Railroads
is William McAdoo, the President's son-in-law. The
government takeover enables the War Department the
opportunity to establish the Purchase, Storage and
Traffic Division—creating a centrally controlled military
transportation directorate for railroads and ocean
transportation—which is soon under Major General
George W. Goethals of Panama Canal fame.

Above: *American field artillery haul their 75mm guns
into action. (Army Art Collection, NMUSA)*

Opposite: *With the establishment of divisions and higher
headquarters, the American Expeditionary Force adopted
shoulder sleeve insignia as a means of identification and to
build unit esprit. (U.S. Army)*

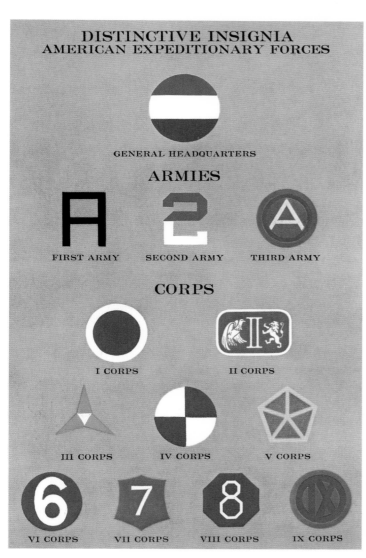

GENERAL HEADQUARTERS

ARMIES

FIRST ARMY · SECOND ARMY · THIRD ARMY

CORPS

I CORPS · II CORPS

III CORPS · IV CORPS · V CORPS

VI CORPS · VII CORPS · VIII CORPS · IX CORPS

DIVISIONS

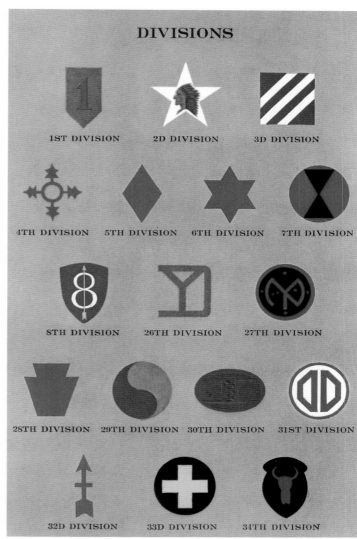

1ST DIVISION · 2D DIVISION · 3D DIVISION

4TH DIVISION · 5TH DIVISION · 6TH DIVISION · 7TH DIVISION

8TH DIVISION · 26TH DIVISION · 27TH DIVISION

28TH DIVISION · 29TH DIVISION · 30TH DIVISION · 31ST DIVISION

32D DIVISION · 33D DIVISION · 34TH DIVISION

DIVISIONS

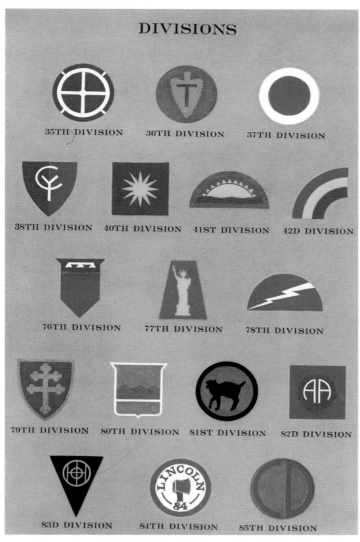

35TH DIVISION · 36TH DIVISION · 37TH DIVISION

38TH DIVISION · 40TH DIVISION · 41ST DIVISION · 42D DIVISION

76TH DIVISION · 77TH DIVISION · 78TH DIVISION

79TH DIVISION · 80TH DIVISION · 81ST DIVISION · 82D DIVISION

83D DIVISION · 84TH DIVISION · 85TH DIVISION

DIVISIONS

86TH DIVISION · 87TH DIVISION · 88TH DIVISION · 89TH DIVISION

90TH DIVISION · 91ST DIVISION · 92D DIVISION · 93D DIVISION

SPECIAL UNITS

SERVICES OF SUPPLY · ADVANCE SECTION S.O.S. · CHEMICAL WARFARE SERVICE

DISTRICT OF PARIS · AMBULANCE SERVICE · RESERVE MALLET · TANK CORPS

RAILHEAD · A.E.F. NORTH RUSSIA · REGULATING STATION

now has 547 officers, 229 field clerks (forerunner of the rank of warrant officers; see entry for 9 July 1918), 3,471 soldiers, and 22 interpreters.

31 December. **Agreement with British on Training.** General Pershing confers with his British counterpart and agrees to a plan to move six U.S. divisions to France in British ships with designated divisions to be trained behind British lines. The plan calls for the affiliation of U.S. battalions with British brigades. It is expected that a U.S. II Corps will be formed to facilitate this proposal.

1918

January–March. **Yanks in the Trenches. Western Front, France.**
Battle-weary French Army units start to see some respite from front-line duty as early-arriving U.S. divisions are pronounced ready for duty in the trenches. The 1st Division relieves a French division in a sector north of Toul in January; the 26th enters the line with the French northwest of Soissons in February; the 42d Division goes into the lines east of Lunéville in February; and toward the middle of March, the 2d Division enters the lines with the French southeast of Verdun. AEF elements are also providing support to units of the British army.

2 January. **Wound Recognition. Headquarters AEF.**
The Army authorizes the wound chevron for wear on the left uniform sleeve by soldiers wounded in action.

31 December. **U.S. Strength in France Grows.**
General Pershing's headquarters reports there are 174,664 American troops on the ground in France. Only the 1st Division, however, can lay claim to having actually served at the front. Headquarters AEF

Above: *The overseas cap and steel helmet were two new additions to the American soldier's kit once they reached Europe in 1917. ("Staff and Pioneer Infantry, 1918," Fritz Kredel,* Soldiers of the American Army, *1775–1954)*

Right: *Fighting in Alsace, men of the 32d Division aim their 37mm gun. (National Archives, U.S. Army Signal Corps)*

DEVELOPMENT OF THE ARMORED FORCE

The U.S. Army's introduction to the tank and the concepts of armored warfare began during World War I. Having seen the effectiveness of British and French tank units as an infantry support weapon, General Pershing decided this new weapon would be a vital asset for his AEF. In late 1917, he requested production of American tanks but meanwhile organized the Tank Corps, AEF, on 26 January 1918. Less than a month later, the War Department organized a separate Tank Corps under the Corps of Engineers in the U.S.

Initially, the AEF Tank Corps was planned to have several brigades, totaling more than 2,000 light and heavy tanks. As the Army had no tanks, French and British tanks were obtained, and in the fall of 1918 the AEF Tank Corps had three light tank battalions in action supporting the American divisions: the 331st, 344th, and 345th. The 301st Heavy Tank Battalion went into combat in September with the 27th Division. The results were mixed and the need for improved infantry-tank tactics and coordination was recognized.

As usual, the Army was drastically reduced at the end of the war just as American tanks were being delivered. In 1920, the combined Tank Corps was abolished, its units assigned to the infantry divisions "as a part of the infantry." Further tank development was then placed under the Chief of Infantry, whose office continued to view the tank as primarily an infantry support weapon.

In 1927, the Secretary of War ordered the test of a mechanized force and in 1928 the Experimental Mechanized Force was created. The force was a combined arms unit, with light and heavy tanks, motorized infantry, and truck-towed artillery and support elements. Due to outdated equipment the experiment was unsuccessful and ended within three months. The concept remained alive, however, and Army Chief of Staff Charles Summerall ordered the creation of a Mechanized Force in 1930. This new mechanized unit demonstrated capabilities beyond infantry support but was again short lived.

In 1931, Chief of Staff Douglas MacArthur disbanded the Mechanized Force and directed all combat arms to mechanize. The infantry would retain its tanks, but the cavalry and artillery would also utilize mechanized vehicles to fulfill their stated missions. To

Above: *The introduction of armor not only helped break the stalemate in the trenches, but also introduced a new type of warfare. ("The Light Tank in Action," G. M. Harding, Smithsonian Institution)*

circumvent the 1920 regulations, the cavalry's tanks were designated "combat cars." In 1938, the Army's first armored unit, the 7th Cavalry Brigade (Mechanized), composed of two mechanized cavalry regiments (1st and 13th), a truck-born infantry regiment (6th), and a motorized artillery regiment was created.

When World War II broke out, the Army was impressed with the concentrated German panzer divisions. On 10 July 1940, the U.S. Armored Force was created, with the 7th Mechanized Cavalry as core of the 1st Armored Division, and the three infantry tank regiments combining to become the 2d Armored Division. These formed the I Armored Corps.

Hard lessons learned in North Africa in 1941 led to a reorganization of U.S. armored divisions. In March 1942, brigade organization was replaced by two Combat Commands (A&B), which were "task organized," allowing greater flexibility. On 2 July 1942, the Armored Force was redesignated the Armored Command and by September headquarters for three new Armored Corps' (II, III, IV) were created.

In 1943, Lieutenant General Lesley J. McNair, Commander of Army Ground Forces, redesignated the armored corps as standard corps of both infantry and armor divisions. He reduced the strength of the armored divisions to provide separate tank battalions to every infantry division and increased the number of tank destroyer battalions. By the war's end in Europe, the Army had 16 armored divisions, 65 independent tank battalions, and some 61 tank destroyer battalions. The offensive power and combined arms concepts successfully demonstrated by the Combat Commands are still in use in today's Army.

—*Vince Hawkins*

7 January. The High Court Upholds the Draft Law. Washington, D.C.
The United States Supreme Court answers challenges, confirms the constitutionality of the Selective Draft Law, and rejects that "it creates involuntary servitude in violation of the Thirteenth Amendment."

9 January. African-American Regiments Join French Forces.
Pressed for manpower assistance, General Pershing assigns the 369th, 370th, 371st, and 372d Infantry Regiments from the U.S. 93d Division to the French Army. The four are all-black National Guard regiments representing New York, Illinois, Ohio, Massachusetts, New Jersey, Tennessee, and the District of Columbia.

9 January. Last Skirmish. Atascosa Canyon, Arizona.
Troop E, 10th Cavalry, fights what is likely the last skirmish against Indians and after a 30-minute

Above: *Lieutenant Reed M. Chambers, flying with the 94th Aero Squadron, shot down two Fokker D-7s to become an ace. The aviator earned the Distinguished Service Cross for heroism in aerial combat. ("Two Down to Glory," William S. Phillips, National Guard Heritage series)*

exchange of rifle fire, captures a small band of Yaqui Indians who have crossed the U.S. border from Mexico. There are no U. S. casualties. The Indians are tried in Federal District Court in Tucson and are sentenced to 30 days in the Pima County jail.

13 January. Line of Communications Headquarters Moves. Tours, France.
Headquarters, Line of Communications (soon to become the Services of Supply), moves from Paris to Tours (Indre-et-Loire).

15 January. The AEF Announces U.S. I Corps. Neufchâteau, France.
General Headquarters AEF orders the organization of the U.S. Army I Corps to prepare to assume duties of command and control of Army forces in action. 20 January Major General Hunter Liggett is ordered from the 41st Replacement Division to take command of the new Army corps.

17 January. "Relief and Reassignment Blues." Blois (Loir-et-Cher), France.
The Casual Officers' Depot at Blois is set up as a central distribution point for unassigned officers fresh from the U.S. It is also a collecting place for officers

Right: *Deadly machine guns were among the terrors of crossing no-man's land. ("Storming Machine Gun," George Harding, Army Art Collection, NMUSA)*

Below: *Peyton C. March commanded the first active artillery brigade of the AEF to land in France. More than a year later, March returned to the United States to assume duties as the acting chief of staff of the Army. (Nicodemus D. Hufford, Army Art Collection, NMUSA)*

from lieutenants to major generals deemed unsuited for combat. "Reclassification" becomes a dreaded word in the officer corps; this picturesque Loire valley town and APO 762 is soon infamous as "the end of the line" for officers who do not measure up to the stern demands of the AEF.

5 February. **First Shoot-Down by U.S. Near Saarbrucken, Germany.**
Army aviator, Lieutenant Stephan W. Thompson of the Signal Corps air service, becomes the first American pilot to shoot down an enemy plane.

5 February. **Yankee Division with French. Chemin des Dames Sector, France.**
The 26th Division moves into the area held by the French Sixth Army, north of battle-torn Soissons. The division is gaining battle experience by serving alongside French troops. Yankee Division troops go into the trenches by company, by battalion, and finally with entire regiments. The 101st Infantry moves into front-line positions, the first National Guard infantry regiment to see action.

5 February. **Transport is U-Boat Victim. Coast of Ireland.**
After ten months of uninterrupted safe passage of transports from the U.S. to France, the British troopship *Tuscania* is sunk by German submarine *U-77*, with the loss of 230 troops and crew members out of 2,397 on board. Victims of the incident are identified as members of the 32d Division, Guardsmen from Michigan and Wisconsin.

8 February. **Stars and Stripes Unfurled. Paris, France.**
The first issue of *Stars and Stripes*, the U.S. Army's newspaper, appears—"by and for the soldiers of the

Left: *Men of the 3d Infantry Division take part in the defense of the Marne to prevent the Germans from crossing this strategic river that was only 40 miles from Paris. ("The Rock of the Marne," H. Charles McBarron, Army Art Collection, NMUSA)*

Below: *The 38th Infantry Division's Brigadier General, Ulysses G. McAlexander, received the Distinguished Service Cross for his leadership at the Marne. (U.S. Army Military History Institute, Carlisle Barracks, PA)*

AEF." Soldier editors and reporters are assigned to the eight-page publication, which is to appear weekly. The cost is 50 centimes.

12 February. Soldier Serial Numbers.
The Army begins using service numbers to identify enlisted soldiers in the AEF. (When the system is extended to officers in 1921, Pershing receives number O-1).

16 February. Doughboys Take a Break. Aix-les-Bains (Savoy), France.
Five hundred doughboys, given a brief respite from the trenches, are the first U.S. soldiers to enjoy a new AEF holiday program. They are greeted with music provided by Lieutenant Jim Europe and the famed 369th Infantry Band from the Harlem Hellfighters' Regiment.

16 February. Balloon Goes Up. France
The Army's 2d Balloon Company is deployed over the front lines. During the war 5,866 U.S. balloon ascents will be made.

16 February. School To Train Aerial Observers. Chatillon-sur-Seine, France.
The 89th Aero Squadron under the command of Major J. T. McNarney arrives and starts work on a flying field for the II Corps Aeronautical School to train aerial observers for combat duties. A location 150 miles southeast of Paris is chosen for its proximity to the II Corps Artillery School at Montigny-sur-Aube.

18 February. Adieu Lafayette Escadrille.
The Lafayette Escadrille ceases to exist in deference to America's entry into the war. In all, 180 American pilots saw combat in 93 different squadrons under the French flag prior to the U.S. entry. Approximately one-third are listed as killed in action. Ninety Escadrille fliers enter the U. S. Army; many become members of the 103d Aero Squadron (organized 31 August 1917).

Right: *An Army medical aid station graphically portrays the devastation of a gas attack, with hundreds of victims being tended to by medical personnel. (National Archives)*

26 February. **First U.S. Gas Casualties. Western Front, France.**
American units suffer their first German gas attack. They are taken by surprise, and some units report high casualties.

3 March. **Russians Have Treaty with Germans.**
The Treaty of Brest-Litovsk is signed; Russia is no longer fighting against the Germans.

11 March. **First DSC to Pilot.**
Army aviator Lieutenant Paul Baer takes on seven German planes and shoots one down. He is the first Army flier awarded the Distinguished Service Cross.

12 March. **Black Regiment Trains with the French. Givry-en-Argonne, France.**
Colonel William (Big Bill) Hayward leads the 369th Infantry, destined to win fame as the "Hellfighters From Harlem" to its assignment with the French 16th Division. Soon the regiment is fighting alongside this French division in the Champagne-Marne Defensive.

13 March. **2d Division Moves Out. Sommedieu Sector, near Verdun, France.**
The 2d Division, less its artillery, moves into a new sector where it is to begin front-line service with the French X Corps, French 2d Army, on the west face of the St. Mihiel salient. The artillery is expected to join the division 22 March. The division will remain with the French until 13 May.

16 March. **The 3d Division Joins the AEF. Châteauvillain, France.**
Less its artillery and engineers, the 3d Division, led by Major General Joseph T. Dickman, assembles in the 9th Training Area to ready itself for combat. Engineers are already in action with British on the Amiens defense line (see 21 March, below).

21 March–April 6. **Offensive Smashes into British Sector. Picardy, France.**
The German Imperial Army unleashes its first great offensive of 1918 along a 50-mile front, striking at the British in the Picardy region, between the Oise and Scarpe rivers. Within eight days the British 5th Army is penetrated to a depth of 37 miles; French divisions are ordered to the British front and Pershing offers to send U.S. troops into battle.

21 March–6 April. **Engineers on the British Front. Somme River, Péronne, France.**
Elements of the 6th Engineer Regiment, in action in France in advance of its parent 3d Division, serves with engineers of the British 5th Army as part of the force designated to hold the Amiens defense line. When the British are forced back, this line becomes the front line. The 6th Engineer detachment is in contact with the enemy near Warfusée-Abancourt and holds firm to its positions until its relief on the morning of 3 April. 6th Engineers casualties total 78, including 25 killed in action. The threat subsides as the Somme defensive campaign ends on 6 April.

21 March. **American Divisions Preparing for Action.**
The AEF reports that General Pershing now has 300,000 U.S. troops on French soil.

21 March. **Regiment Stripped for Replacements. Rayaumieux, France.**
An omen of things to come in creating an AEF replacement system, all of the privates and captains in

the 128th Infantry Regiment, 32d Division, are ordered to join the under-strength 1st Division. Many noncommissioned officers ask to be reduced to the ranks so they can accompany their men. None of these requests is granted.

22 March. Structure for Tank Forces Approved. Bourg (Cher), France.

Upon receipt of approval from the War Department of its plan for formation of a U. S. Army Tank Corps, the AEF starts a tank training center (light tanks) at Bourg. A training center for heavy tanks is established at Camp Bovington in Wool, England. Manpower for the Tank Corps is drawn from the AEF at large and equipment is obtained from the French and British. The Tank Corps is placed under the command of Brigadier General Samuel D. Rockenbach, VMI 1889.

23 March. Artillery Shells Strike Paris.

Enemy success in the initial phase of the offensive brings German Army heavy artillery ("Big Bertha") within striking distance of Paris. Shells fired from a distance of 75 miles fall in the city limits.

23 March. The Second Army Corps Gets Organized. Pas-de-Calais Region, France.

After some delay resulting from the German offensive, AEF general headquarters approves the fielding of the U.S. Army II Corps for control of American troops with the British. Corps headquarters opens in British 1st Army Area. No U.S. commander is immediately designated as the corps adjusts to supervise training.

26 March. General Foch In Top Command.

French General, soon to be Marshal, Ferdinand Foch is given responsibility for coordinating French and British forces; on 3 April this mandate is extended to responsibility for strategic direction of the French, British, and American armies on the western front. The German onslaught is halted before it can seize Amiens, which would have separated the British and French armies and might have forced the British entirely out of northern France.

26 March. Bolling Death Reported. Amiens, France.

The death, at the hands of German officers, of Colonel Raynall C. Bolling, is reported at AEF Headquarters. The former commander of New York's 1st Aero Squadron is on a ground reconnaissance mission when he meets his fate. He is, to this point, the highest ranking officer killed in the war. (On 1 July 1918 the principal aviation facility for Washington, D.C. and the War Department is officially dedicated as Bolling Field.)

31 March. YD Relieves 1st Division. Toul Sector, France

Rain mixed with snow is falling as the 26th Division arrives and immediately starts the relief of the 1st Division and French troops. The Yankee Division occupies a front extending nearly 18 kilometers. The relief of the 1st Division is completed 3 April.

Right: *In a recreation of a battle, doughboys brave smoke simulating an enemy gas attack much like what took place in actual combat. (National Archives, U.S. Army Signal Corps)*

Below: *Arrayed in combat gear, including an officer in his raincoat that came to be known as a "trench coat," men of the 21st Field Artillery, 5th Division, are ready to man their guns. (Tom Jones, Company of Military Historians)*

9 April. **Second German Offensive Underway. Armentieres, France.**

The Battle of the Lys River is aimed at British troops along a 12-mile front south of Ypres. American medical and engineer units and air service squadrons take part in bitter fighting. The campaign concludes 27 April.

10 April. **32d Division Rebuilds for Combat.**

The Michigan-Wisconsin 32d Division transfers its duties as a replacement division to the 41st Division, quickly rebuilds its depleted infantry ranks, and prepares to move to the front as a combat division.

28 April. **Rickenbacker in Action.**

The former race car driver turned Army Signal Corps pilot, Captain Edward V. Rickenbacker, downs his first enemy plane, one month after he joins the 94th Aero Squadron. He will be the top American ace, with 26 confirmed kills. Rickenbacker reached France in 1917 as a chauffeur assigned to General Pershing's headquarters.

15–16 May. **Army Starts Inter-City Air Mail. Washington, D.C.**

Army aviators inaugurate air mail service between the nation's capital and New York City as Lieutenants George L. Boyle and H. P. Culver draw the coveted assignment. Boyle flies off the Mall with President Woodrow Wilson in the cheering audience. Culver, prepositioned in Philadelphia, is standing-by to take the mail from there. But Boyle crashes on a Maryland farm. Culver retrieves the mail and flies on to New York City. The Army pilots are flying modified Curtiss JN-4 "Jennies."

19 May. **Bliss Leaves Washington Post.**

After eight months General Tasker H. Bliss leaves the post of chief of staff. He is soon named to serve as the

War Department's representative to the American Section of the Supreme War Council at Versailles, France.

20 May. **March is Army Chief. Washington, D.C.**
With promotion to full general, Peyton C. March, previously the Army artillery commander in France, is designated the Army chief of staff. He is the third officer to hold this position in the 11 months since the U.S. entry into the war. March announces that shipment of troops to France is his top priority "even if they have to swim."

27 May. **German Offensive in French Sector. Chemin des Dames, France.**
The Third Battle of the Aisne gets underway as the Germans seize Chemin des Dames positions and cross the Aisne River around noon, taking bridges that the French are unable to destroy, and catching French defenders unready. By evening Germans are south of the Vesle. Early on 29 May the enemy captures Soissons. Now advancing swiftly toward the Marne River, they are in position to threaten Paris. French

Above: *Battery C, 6th Field Artillery, provides artillery support during fighting on the Lorraine front in Beaumont, France, 12 September 1918. A spent shell casing can be seen in the air as a new shell goes into the breech. (National Archives)*

reserves are mustered. U.S. 2d and 3d Divisions are alerted, and the French government considers a move to Bordeaux.

28 May. **Over the Top! Cantigny, France.**
Major General Bullard's 1st Division completes its move from Seicheprey (St. Mihiel region) and takes over an active portion of the battle line west of Montdidier. A determined attack by the 18th and 26th Infantry Regiments enables the division to seize Cantigny in the first substantial offensive action undertaken by U.S. troops in France.

30 May. **Reinforcing the French. Marne River.**
The 3d Division, less artillery and engineers, is deployed with the French Group of Armies of the North to defend the passages of the Marne River from Château-Thierry to Daery, 35 kilometers to the east. The motorized 7th Machine Gun Battalion joins the French 12 kilometers southeast of Château-Thierry; the remainder of the division moves by rail to Montmirail (25 kilometers southeast of Château-Thierry) to defend the Marne crossings.

31 May–5 June. **Rock of the Marne. Marne River.**
The 7th Machine Gun Battalion at Château-Thierry helps to thwart German attempts to cross the Marne. As infantry units from the 3d Division arrive they quickly reinforce French units holding the south bank

EYEWITNESS: RICKENBACKER'S FIRST "KILL"

In March 1918, the second squadron of the United States Air Service, the 94th "Hat-in-the- Ring" Squadron, was activated in France. One of the pilots in the 94th was Lieutenant Edward Vernon "Eddie" Rickenbacker. A noted race car driver, Rickenbacker enlisted and served as General Pershing's chauffeur and mechanic before transferring to the 94th. By the end of the war Rickenbacker was a captain, commander of the 94th Squadron and America's leading fighter "ace," with 25 confirmed aerial victories. On 6 November 1930, Rickenbacker received the Congressional Medal of Honor for his wartime service. In 1960 his 26th victory was officially confirmed. In his memoirs, *Fighting the Flying Circus*, Rickenbacker described his first "kill" on 29 April 1918.

"Precisely at five o'clock Captain [James Norman] Hall received a telephone call from the French headquarters at Beaumont stating that an enemy two-seater machine had just crossed our lines and was flying south over their heads.

Captain Hall and I had been walking about the field with our flying clothes on and our machines were standing side by side with their noses pointing into the wind. Within the minute we had jumped into our seats and our mechanics were twirling the propellers.

In five minutes we were above our observation balloon line . . .Yes! there was a scout coming towards us from north of Pont-à-Mousson . . . I knew it was a Hun the moment I saw it, for it had the familiar line of their new Pfalz . . .The Hun was steadily approaching us, unconscious of his danger, for we were fully in the sun . . .We had at least a thousand feet advantage over the enemy and we were two to one numerically . . . The Boche hadn't a chance to out fly us. His only salvation would be in a dive toward his own lines.

These thoughts passed through my mind in a flash and I quickly decided what tactics I would pursue . . . I would maintain my altitude and work toward a position on the other side of the Pfalz, hoping to cut off his retreat.

No sooner had I changed my line of flight than the German saw me clear of my sun cover . . . Surprised by discovering Hall just ahead of him, the Pfalz . . . banked around to the right and started for home—just as I had expected him to do. In a trice I was on his tail. Down, down we sped with throttles full open . . .The Boche had no heart for evolutions or

maneuvers . . . I was gaining upon him every instant and had my sights trained dead upon his cockpit before I fired my first shot.

At 150 yards I pressed my triggers. The tracer bullets cut a streak of living fire into the rear of the Pfalz tail. Raising the nose of my airplane slightly the fiery streak lifted itself like the stream of water pouring from a garden hose. Gradually it settled into the pilot's seat. The swerving of the Pfalz course indicated that its rudder no longer was controlled by a directing foot. At two thousand feet above the enemy's lines I pulled up my headlong dive and watched the enemy machine continuing on its course. Curving slightly to the left the Pfalz circled a little to the south and the next minute crashed onto the ground just at the edge of the woods a mile inside their own lines. I had brought down my first enemy airplane and had not been subjected to a single shot!"

—*Vince Hawkins*

Above: *One of the first "aces" in United States history, Captain Eddie Rickenbacker made the transition from race car driver to daring combat pilot. (National Archives)*

of the river to a distance of eight kilometers from Château-Thierry. The heroic defense by the 3d Division earns it an enduring nickname: "Rock of the Marne." But the German offensive has created a salient into the Allied lines—a triangle whose points are at Reims, Château-Thierry, and Soissons.

1 June. **Soldiers and Marines On the Scene. Château-Thierry, France.**
The 2d Division moves into positions northwest of Château-Thierry with its center at Lucy-le-Bocage. The division establishes its line across the main route to Paris. It repulses all attacks and effectively halts the German advance in that direction.

2 June. **"Captain Harry!" Angers, France**
The headquarters, 129th Field Artillery, 35th Division, receives War Department Special Orders 103, which announces "to be captain: First Lieutenant Harry S. Truman . . ." Truman writes to Bess: "I am back with the regiment and a sure enough captain." He is assigned to take command of the fractious Battery D from Kansas City, Missouri.

6 June. **Battle in Belleau Wood. Château-Thierry Sector.**
In an epic struggle, the 2d Division's soldiers and Marines strike a blow at strong enemy defensive positions; in a brutal battle the divisions take ground held by the Germans at Bouresches, Vaux, and Belleau Wood.

9 June. **German Offensive, Continued.**
Opening the fourth phase of its 1918 offensive the German Army crashes into the French sector between Noyon and Montdidier with two armies moving toward Compiègne. The enemy fails to reach his objectives. The campaign is over 13 June.

Above: *Supplying troops in the trenches presented a challenge including navigating the mud-soaked French roads with mule-drawn wagons and under-powered trucks as seen in this September 1918 traffic jam. (National Archives, U.S. Army Signal Corps)*

Below: *Long before the World War II Marine "code talkers," Choctaw Indian doughboys with the 36th Division provided secure communications that could not be translated by German listening posts. (Richard L. Hayes Collection, Chicago)*

Right: *The AEF manned only foreign-produced tanks such as this French Schneider with its main side-mounted 75mm gun. (National Archives, U.S. Army Signal Corps)*

Below: *Charles Livingston Bull's symbolic poster portrayed dueling eagles as a dramatic means to recruit potential AEF pilots. (Gary A. Borkan Collection)*

13 June. **Army Ambulance Sections to Italy.**
Thirty Army Ambulance Sections, each with 25 ambulances, are sent to the allied front in Italy.

15 June. **II Corps Commander is Named. British Sector.**
As the British Army's Somme Offensive gets underway, Major General George W. Read takes command of the U.S. II Corps, which is soon to exercise command over the U.S. 27th, and 30th Divisions; during the forthcoming campaign, II Corps will also command British and Australian divisions.

16–17 June. **Pancho Villa Revisited. Juarez, Mexico.**
A force composed of soldiers of the 24th Infantry and 5th and 7th Cavalry cross into Mexico to drive Pancho Villa out of Juarez. In a major fight, several hundred of Villa's men are killed.

17 June. **Enemy Intelligence Analysis of Yanks As Fighters.**
Intelligence gleaned from captured documents indicates there is no longer any doubt within the German high command as to the fighting ability of the American soldier. German corps opposing the 2d Division: "The 2d American Division can be rated as a very good division . . . the various attacks of the marines [2d Marine Infantry Brigade] were carried out smartly and ruthlessly . . . our fire did not materially check the advance of the infantry. The nerves of the Americans are still unshaken."

28 June. **Chemical Warfare Service.**
The Chemical Warfare Service is created, an expansion of the mission of the former Gas Service, AEF. 13 July the First Gas Regiment is created from the 30th Engineers. (This becomes the Chemical Corps in 1945 and the date is designated the birthday of the Chemical Corps.)

4 July. **Illinois Yanks with British. Hamel, France**
Corporal Thomas A. Pope, his company advancing behind tanks, goes forward alone when the unit is halted by enemy machine-gun fire. He rushes a

JOIN THE
ARMY AIR SERVICE
BE AN AMERICAN EAGLE!
CONSULT YOUR LOCAL DRAFT BOARD. READ THE ILLUSTRATED BOOKLET AT ANY RECRUITING OFFICE, OR WRITE TO THE CHIEF SIGNAL OFFICER OF THE ARMY, WASHINGTON, D.C.

machine-gun nest and kills several of enemy gun crew with his bayonet. Standing astride the gun, he holds off the others until reinforcements arrive. His outfit, Company E, 131st (the old 1st Illinois from Chicago) Infantry, 33d Division, is serving with the British to gain battle experience. Pope's fight will be recognized (1919) with the presentation of the Medal of Honor—the first for an Army action in France.

4–17 July. I Corps Order of Battle.
Major General Hunter Liggett's I Corps, now west of Château-Thierry, is composed of the American 1st, 2d, 3d, 4th, 26th, 28th Divisions and the French 167th Division.

7 July. Corps Gets New Number, Commander. Remiremont, France.
Headquarters AEF notifies Major General William M. Wright, in command of the III Corps, that his Corps is redesignated V Corps and that he will receive a new Corps staff.

9 July. Warrant Officers Are Official.
In establishing the Army Mine Planter Service as an element of the Coast Artillery, the Army introduces the rank and grade of warrant officer. The warrant officer lineage traces back to 1896 with the authorization for headquarters clerks, subsequently designated Army field clerks. (Warrant Officer rank was previously used in the U.S. Navy).

13 July. Corps Commander Designated. Meaux, France.
Major General Robert Lee Bullard is III Corps Commander. 15 July the corps headquarters moves into the French 10th Army zone west of Soissons.

14 July. Quentin Roosevelt Is a Casualty. France.
Lieutenant Quentin Roosevelt, one of the sons of former President Theodore Roosevelt, is killed in action soon after shooting down an enemy aircraft as a pilot in the 95th Pursuit Squadron.

15 July. American Divisional Manpower Twice the Enemies'.
There are 26 American divisions in France, making Allied front-line strength superior to the Germans' for the first time. Twelve American divisions are engaged

in combat operations or training in "quiet" sectors. Due to major differences in structure 12 U.S. divisions are numerically equivalent to 24 German, French, or British divisions. General Foch tells commanders the time is near for attack on the western face of the Marne salient.

15–18 July. Last Phase of the German Offensive.

The German Army focuses its Battle of the Marne offensive against the French Fourth Army east of Reims. American troops of the 3d and 28th Divisions distinguish themselves in critical defensive operations. Germans exploit a crack in the French line and cross the Marne but are driven back by noon on 16 July. Elements of the 28th Division are in the line with French divisions on either flank of the 3d Division, which stands firm in the face of intense artillery fire and repeated attacks in the eastern part of its sector. The U.S. I Corps front is held by a French division and the 26th (Yankee) Division, which relieves the 2d Division between Vaux and Torcy. By 18 July the German High Command abandons the offensive (U.S. Champagne-Marne campaign) and withdraws.

17 July. Troops to Northern Russia.

U.S. troops are ordered by President Wilson to prepare for movement to northern Russia "to guard military stores" and support British forces opposing the Bolsheviks, who are consolidating results of the October (1916) Revolution. Army elements for the Russian expedition are taken out of the 85th Division, which is in England awaiting orders to France.

18 July. French to Reduce Aisne-Marne Salient.

In quick reaction to the German defeat in the Champagne-Marne campaign, an Allied counterattack is launched against the Aisne-Marne Salient. The French 10th Army makes the main effort from south of Soissons moving east toward the Vesle River and Reims. The early morning attack takes the enemy by surprise. The 1st and 2d Divisions with the 1st Moroccan

Division between them successfully spearhead an attack that penetrates three miles into the enemy's positions by 8 a.m. To the south, elements of the U. S. 4th Division, with the French Sixth Army, advances two miles by nightfall. Farther south, the 26th Division captures two important villages formerly held by the enemy. German high command orders a "gradual" withdrawal from all positions south of the Marne.

19–30 July. **Action in the Aisne-Marne Campaign.**
The 1st and 2d Divisions overpower fresh German troops. The 2d Division advances to the Soissons-Château-Thierry highway and is relieved during the night by the French after an advance of six miles in which doughboys and Marines take 3,000 enemy prisoners and capture 75 guns. On 20–21 July the 1st Division seizes Bercy-le-Sec, which falls after an advance of seven miles. During the night of 21–22 July the 1st Division is relieved after five days of hard fighting, with 3,500 prisoners taken and 68 guns. Fighting with the French Sixth Army (21 July) the 4th and 26th Divisions continue the advance. The 26th is reinforced with the 56th Infantry Brigade from the 28th Division. The Yankee Division continues the pursuit

Above: *Not all combat took place in the trenches. Men of the AEF occasionally faced the perils of street fighting. ("Soldiers Firing," George Harding, Army Art Collection, NMUSA)*

until 24 July when it is halted near La Croix Rouge Ferme (Red Cross Farm) after a 10-mile thrust. The 3d Division crosses the Marne, captures Le Charmel (25 July), crosses the Ourcq River (28 July) and seizes Rochères. It is relieved 30 July after three major engagements during which it covers ten miles. Review of the U.S. effort in the region shows nine divisions engage during the campaign, putting a total of 310,000 troops into the field, sustaining nearly 67,000 casualties.

23 July. **VI Corps is Organized. Neufchâteau, France**
Major General Omar Bundy is designated temporary commander of U.S. VI Corps. Initially the corps is to supervise training and assume administrative control of divisions in its area of responsibility.

25 July. **Luke Among New Pilots. Saints, France.**
Lieutenant Frank Luke, 21-year-old aviator from Phoenix, Arizona, is one of nine replacement pilots reporting to the 27th Aero Squadron. Luke is destined to earn immortality as the "balloon buster" and he will be the second U.S. ace behind Captain Eddie Rickenbacker.

25 July. **AEF Regiment Heads for Italy. Marseille, France**
The U.S. 332d Infantry, detached from the 83d Division, assembles in southern France en route to the Italian front. A small U.S. force including the 331st Field Hospital is to serve with British Army forces in Italy.

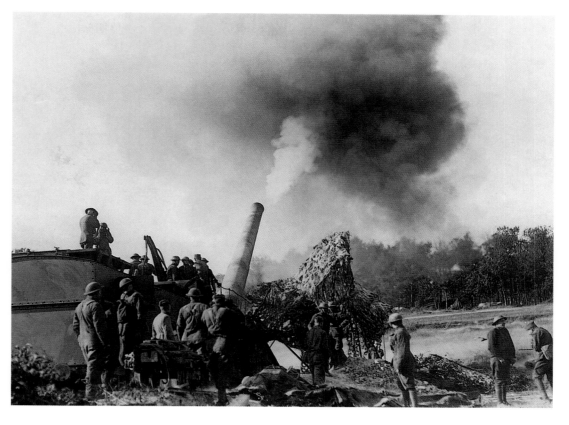

Right: *An AEF Coast Artillery crew fires a French 340mm gun, which lobbed its lethal shell up to 20 miles. (National Archives)*

Below: *Officers and men alike lived in primitive conditions. ("Captain's Command Post," J. Andre Smith, Army Art Collection, NMUSA)*

28 July–5 August. **Reduction of Marne Salient.**
The 42d Division, in relief of the 26th Division at La Croix Rouge Ferme, now crosses the Ourcq and engages in heavy fighting north of the river. It takes objectives in its zone and continues its pursuit toward the Vesle until relieved (3 August). It is reinforced with the 47th Infantry Regiment from the 4th Division. The

32d Division enters the line to the right of the 28th Division and the two National Guard divisions (now filled out with many draftees from other states) continue the attack to the Vesle. With the relief of the 28th near Bois des Grimpettes (3 August), the 32d and the 4th Divisions (which relieves the 42d Division) are now the only remaining American divisions still in the line. The 32d takes Fismes on the southern bank of the Vesle. The 4th and 32d continue the push with the help of the 6th Infantry Brigade, 3d Division. A bridgehead is established north of the river. The French command announces the Aisne-Marne Salient no longer exists and the conclusion of this campaign marks a major defeat for the enemy.

29 July. **Pershing Sends Harbord to Top Logistics Task. Tours, France.**
Major General James G. Harbord arrives to take over the sprawling and loosely organized Services of Supply. Having given up command of the 2d Division in response to General Pershing's need for a strong hand at the helm, the old cavalryman makes the network of ports, bases, supply dumps, schools, and personnel depots a model of efficiency.

7 August. **March Orders Consolidation. Washington, D.C.**
An order is issued by General March, Chief of Staff, consolidating all forces into "one army," the objective being to eliminate friction between the Regular Army, National Guard, and National Army (a wartime Army

Left: *Despite many new sophisticated weapons that became available during World War I, doughboys still had to employ the bayonet, bullets, and rifle butts against determined German foes. ("Men of Iron," Don Troiani)*

component). Secretary Baker tells him, "there is no order which it gives me more pleasure to sign than this."

10 August. **U.S. First Army In the Field. Chaumont, France.**
AEF commander General Pershing activates the U.S. First Army. This establishes a senior American field command. It brings most U.S. divisions under American command and is seen as an important step in Pershing's vision as to how the AEF will fight the forthcoming campaigns of the war. The 1st Army immediately begins preparations for reduction of the St. Mihiel salient.

14 August. **Graves Commands in Siberia. Vladivostok, Siberia.**
Major General William S. Graves, former commander of the 8th Division, arrives from Camp Fremont, California, to take command of American Expeditionary Forces in Siberia. Graves announces a policy of "strict neutrality" for U.S. soldiers.

15 August. **Troops Move in the Far East. Vladivostok, Siberia.**
Fresh from tropical duty in the Philippines, the U.S. 27th and 31st Infantry Regiments land in Siberia, where they find a city still recovering from the effects of recent fighting in which Soviet Red Army troops have been routed. The 27th and 31st Infantry constitute the backbone of the "AEF Siberia," which is destined to participate in what is sometimes called "perhaps the strangest adventure in our country's history."

16 August. **"The Country Has But One Army." Headquarters, AEF.**
Pershing reiterates admonishment that "distinctive appellations" (Regular Army, Reserve Corps, National Guard, National Army) will be discontinued and that "the single term, the United States Army, will be exclusively used." "This country," Pershing's message to the troops declares, "has but one army, the United States Army".

18 August. **Another Combat Corps, A New Commander. France.**
Major General Joseph T. Dickman, commander of the 3d Division in the critical battles at the Marne and Château-Thierry in June and July, is designated commander of the new IV Corps. The corps occupies a defensive sector in Lorraine with control of the 1st, 82d, and 90th Divisions.

18 August. **U.S. Divisions Aid French. Oise-Aisne Offensive.**
The 32d, 77th, and 28th Divisions participate with the French in breaking through German defenses in the opening hours of the Oise-Aisne offensive. The 32d (Red Arrow) Division's seizure of Juvigny is hailed as critical to success. By 4 September the Germans are withdrawing from the Vesle and Aisne rivers. The battle will continue, but U.S. divisions get orders to join the 1st Army for the battles to take place in the Meuse-Argonne.

21 August. **Tank Corps Deploys for Battle.**
Brigadier General Samuel D. Rockenbach, chief of the Tank Corps, pronounces the 326th, 327th, 344th,

and 354th Tank Battalions ready for action in the coming St. Mihiel operations.

30 August–11 September. **First Army Gets Ready.**
The First Army occupies a defensive sector in Lorraine. Holding the assigned sector of the front are the I Corps, IV Corps, and French II Colonial Corps. In order to assure closer cooperation (i.e., artillery and aviation support) Pershing places the 1st Army under the nominal direction of General Pétain as commander of the French Group of Armies of the East and Northeast.

3–4 September. **Doughboys in Hot Pursuit. Vesle River Front, France**
With the 28th and 77th Divisions in pursuit, the German Army, no longer in possession of the Aisne-Marne salient, continues its withdrawal away from the Vesle River. The 28th Division is relieved (8 September), then the 77th is relieved (16 September). Both divisions are quickly ordered to join the First Army for the coming Meuse-Argonne campaign.

4 September. **Michigan Draftees in Russia. Murmansk, Russia.**
The U.S. Army's role in the North Russian Expeditionary Force arrives and deploys to assist the British in the protection of supply dumps and the Murmansk railroad. The U.S. force is built around the 339th Infantry Regiment and a battalion of the 310th Engineers is detached from the 85th Division. The troops are predominantly draftees from Michigan.

7 September. **U.S.-Japanese Joint Operation. Ussuri Valley, Siberia.**
The 27th Infantry Regiment, following a Japanese

division, drives Bolsheviks out of the valley and enters the city of Habarovsk on the Amur river. The Stars and Stripes flies alongside the Japanese Rising Sun banner at the newly taken railroad station.

12–16 September. **All-American Attack. St. Mihiel Offensive, France.**
The new 1st Army launches the first all-American operation and wipes out the triangle-shaped salient 16 miles into allied positions under Germans control over four years. The main attack is by US I and IV Corps with V Corps in the secondary attack role. On 13 September patrols from 26th Division (V Corps) make contact with elements of the 1st Division (IV Corps) near the town of Vigneulles, effectively closing the jaws of the salient. Enemy troops who fail to withdraw beyond this point are captured or killed. Victory is complete by 16 September and movement of U.S. troops to the Meuse-Argonne area is immediately begun. Newly arriving divisions go into the line to consolidate the sector for the Allies.

13 September. **Charge! Call For Cavalry. Vicinity Viéville-sous-les-Côtes, France.**
The only cavalry regiment in the AEF, the 2d U. S. Cavalry, forms an impromptu mounted squadron for pursuit of retreating enemy forces in the St. Mihiel breakthrough. The squadron captures many prisoners. Leading the squadron in absence of the commander, who is ill, is Troop F commander, Captain Ernest N. Harmon, who will earn great distinction as an armored commander in World War II. During the battle, the 304th Tank Brigade under Major George S. Patton, Jr., conducts the first American tank attack.

Above: *African-Americans of the 369th New York fought with valor as part of the French 161st Division. ("The Black Rattlers," Don Stivers)*

16 September. Casualties on the Northern Front. Obozerskaya, Northern Russia

U.S. soldiers suffer their first casualties in fighting Russian Bolsheviks.

17–25 September. Pershing's Army Poised For Major Move.

The 1st Army occupies a defensive sector in Lorraine and plans for a major attack toward Mézières and Sedan in what is destined to become the great Meuse-Argonne offensive.

19 September. Lieutenant Luke is Grounded.

Lieutenant Frank Luke is grounded for his own good after 17 furious days of combat in which he knocks down 14 defended enemy balloons and 4 aircraft. His commanding officer, Major Harold Hartney, takes him out of action and sends him on leave to Paris for six days. On 29 September he takes to the air and disappears. It is learned that he crash-lands near Murvaux, France, and is killed in a gun battle with German troops.

20 September. II Corps Joins the Fight. Pérrone, France.

The U.S. II Corps joins the British Fourth Army in the line northwest of St.-Quentin, where it is preparing to attack the Hindenburg line in the continuing Somme offensive. Major General Read, corps commander, dispatches the 30th Division to relieve the 1st Australian Division.

21 September. First Army New Headquarters Site. Souilly, France.

With the relief of the French 2d Army, the American 1st Army opens its headquarters at Souilly (Meuse) and extends its zone northward.

24 September. The Order of Battle Takes Shape.

The 29th Division arrives in the 1st Army zone from the French 7th Army. The 1st Division arrives and is placed in Army reserve. The 1st Army's right is held by the IV Corps (Dickman) with the French 69th Division, and the American 90th, 78th, 89th, and 42d Divisions. On the Army left is the French II Colonial Corps, which includes the U.S. 26th Division. Adjacent to the French XVII Corps is the U.S. III Corps (Bullard) with the 33d, 80th, and 4th Divisions; the V Corps (Cameron) deploys the 79th, 37th, and

91st Divisions. The left corps sector is held by I Corps (Liggett) with the 35th, 28th, and 77th Divisions. Corps reserves are the 3d, 32d, and 92d Divisions. Army reserves include the 1st, 29th, and 82d Divisions. The French 8th and 4th Armies are, respectively, right and left of the American 1st Army as the eve of battle approaches.

25 September. New York Division Into Battle. British Front, France.

Going into battle on the British front, Major General John F. O'Ryan leads the 27th (New York) Division in the relief of the British 18th and 74th Divisions as the U.S. II Corps-Australian Corps continues its attack aimed at breaching the Hindenburg line. Major General Edward M. Lewis, a Regular, now commands the 30th (North Carolina, South Carolina, and Tennessee).

25–26 September. Pershing Unleashes U.S. Offensive. Meuse-Argonne, France.

At 2:30 a.m. 2,700 guns fire an intimidating artillery preparation all along the Army front. At 5:30 a.m. the artillery phases into a rolling barrage as the infantry pours out of the trenches and heads across no man's land. Doughboys of the III, V, and I Corps smash at the enemy's front between the Meuse River and the Argonne Forrest. The long-awaited major U.S. offensive by the 1st Army is underway.

26 September. Patton Leads Tank Brigade. Cheppy, France.

Major (soon to be Colonel) George S. Patton is wounded commanding the 304th Tank Brigade in action. Despite his wounds he remains on the battlefield until he turns over his command. He is later awarded the Distinguished Service Cross for this incident.

26 September–October 3. Enemy Resistance is Strong. Meuse-Argonne, France

Of the nine U.S. divisions in the initial assault, only five have previously experienced offensive combat, and four of the nine are supported with unfamiliar division artillery. The attack starts in the face of heavy fog over the entire front. Except for Montfaucon, satisfactory progress is made the first day. V Corps advances west of Montfaucon; III Corps drives to east of Montfaucon; I Corps on the Army's left penetrates the Aire River and pushes into the Argonne Forest. But at Montfaucon German defenders resist fiercely. On 27 September, fighting resumes and Montfaucon falls around noon. On 28 September, with increased artillery and tank support U.S. doughboys gain 1-1/2 miles along the front and encounter the German third line of defense, the Hindenburg Line. Heavy enemy artillery

fire is encountered. On 29 September positions are organized for defense while preparing for swift resumption of the battle. Pershing replaces several of the inexperienced divisions. The Army makes good use of 821 airplanes under its control. Intelligence confirms the shift of seven German divisions from other fronts to this crucial battlefield. Rumors abound that the enemy high command is urging its government to make peace overtures to the Allies.

28–30 September. Black Doughboy Regiment in Oise-Aisne Offensive.

The 370th Infantry Regiment, with the French XXX Corps, mans the line between Vauxaillon and Canal de l'Oise à l'Aisne. It stays with this French command until the armistice.

29 September. Assault On Hindenburg Line. British Front, France.

U.S. II Corps in the assault under British Fourth Army makes its main effort against the formidable

Below: *Although no official canine program existed, dogs were used to carry messages, keep guard duty, or even warn of a gas attack. ("The Dog that Saved a Regiment," Gayle Porter Hoskins, Denver Art Museum)*

Hindenburg Line on an 8,000-yard front parallel to the St.-Quentin Canal and the Bellicourt Tunnel and captures Bellicourt, enters Nauroy and heights above Bois de Malakoff. The 27th and 30th Divisions reach their objectives, are relieved on 1 October by Australian divisions, and withdraw to Pérrone to reorganize.

1 October. **SOS Sets Records. Tours, France.**
The Service of Supply (SOS) announces record-breaking figures disclosing that in September the American base ports handled 767,648 tons—a daily average of 25,588 tons. Troops are disembarking at the rate of 10,398 every day. American railway service in France has over a thousand locomotives and over 10,000 freight cars on the rails.

2 October. **The Lost Battalion. Argonne Forest, France.**
Elements of the 308th and 307th Infantry Regiments (The Lost Battalion) under Major Charles W. Whittelsey gain their objective and are cut off as other forces fail to keep pace. The German commander calls for a U.S. surrender but New Yorkers of the 77th Division hold out defiantly for five days in the ace of a fierce attack. Their last carrier pigeon, "Cher Ami," is used to fly a note to divert friendly artillery fire, which is hitting their positions. When the action is reviewed Whittelsey and two of his officers will be presented the Medal of Honor.

4–12 October. **Continuing the Meuse-Argonne Battle.**
The attack resumes at daybreak as the First Army faces the outpost zone of the Hindenburg Line. In the attack V Corps is in the center and III Corps has its right flank on the Meuse river. On the left, the I Corps attack pushes deeper into the Argonne. On line, right to left (i.e., from the Meuse) are the 33d, 4th, and 80th Divisions (III Corps), 4th and 33d Divisions; 3d and 32d in line with the 91st in transit from the line into reserve (V Corps); and the 1st, 28th, and 77th Divisions (I Corps). The 35th and 42d Divisions and the 183d Infantry Brigade of the 92d Division is in Army reserve. Important gains are made. On the second day the 28th and 82d Divisions smash at high ground in the vicinity of Château-Chéhéry to eliminate the threat to U.S. positions in the Argonne. This is coordinated with an attack by the 77th Division. Flank attack is successful and the main force links up with the "Lost Battalion." 9 October brings signs of withdrawal by the Germans as U.S. troops take control of the Argonne and assist the French in operations east of the Meuse river. The V Corps, in the center, employs the 3d and 80th Divisions to penetrate the Hindenburg Line. This is soon exploited further by the 4th Division. The battle abates somewhat (12 October) as the First Army pauses to catch its breath.

5 October. **Major League Infielder is Killed in Action.**
Captain Eddie Grant, a veteran National League infielder who was with the New York Giants prior to joining the Army, is among the casualties in the 77th

Right: *A sketch of cavalrymen serving with the AEF. These horse soldiers saw little action in combat but typically did provide reconnaissance and courier services. (Captain Harry Townsend, National Archives, U.S. Army Signal Corps)*

Division unit in the fight to reach the Lost Battalion. Grant, commander of Company H, 307th Infantry, was temporarily in command of the 2d Battalion when he was struck down.

6 October. **II Corps Commands Front. Tincourt-Boucly, France.**
With its advance headquarters in the Bois de Buire, II Corps relieves the Australian corps and assumes command of the front held by the 30th Division with the 27th Division in corps reserve.

8 October. **A Legend: Sergeant York. Chéhéry, Argonne Forest, France.**
A Tennessee draftee, Sergeant Alvin C. York takes over as leader of an 82d Division patrol. His skill as a sharpshooter results in the capture of nearly 150 German soldiers. The one-time conscientious objector is later presented the Medal of Honor and is enshrined as a national icon.

12 October. **Second U.S. Army in the Field. Old St. Mihiel Front.**
Two weeks into its major offensive in the Meuse-Argonne, Headquarters AEF announces that the new U.S. 2d Army is operational and in the field under the command of Major General Robert L. Bullard. 15 October the Second Army has 7th, 37th, 79th, 92d, and two French divisions holding the new front line, which is the base of the old salient from Port-sur-Seille to Fresnes-sur-Woeuvre. The 28th Division is in reserve.

14–16 October. **Doughboys Advance with the French.**
The French XVII Corps, including the American 29th and 33d Divisions with the 26th Division in reserve, continues operations driving north on the east side of the Meuse. The U.S. III Corps, V Corps, and I Corps (10 divisions plus four in 1st Army reserve) oppose 17 enemy divisions with six in reserve. The attack starts strongly with important gains by the 3d and 5th Divisions and seizure of dominating positions by the 82d and 77th Divisions. During the following days (15, 16 October) Côte de Châtillon, a stronghold in the Hindenburg Line, is taken by the 42d Division.

16 October. **First Army Command Turnover.**
General John J. Pershing relinquishes personal command of the 1st Army to Major General Hunter Liggett. Pershing becomes commander of the American Group of Armies in addition to his duties as commander-in-chief, AEF. Liggett's place at the helm of I Corps is taken by Major General Joseph T. Dickman, who moves over from IV Corps.

18 October. **Women's Corps is Abandoned.**
In a reversal of an earlier announcement, the proposed Women's Overseas Corps (WOC) is being abandoned in favor of a new Army Service Corps to consist of draftees classified as "limited service," men who would otherwise not be considered as eligible for overseas duty.

18 October. **British General Compliments Yanks.**
In recognition of the first occasion, in the British

Left: *Men of the 6th U.S. Infantry Regiment celebrate the 11 November 1918 armistice on the Meuse-Argonne front. (National Archives)*

sector, with the American II Corps in battle on its own, General Sir Henry Rawlinson, commander British Fourth Army, offers his congratulations "on your victory today." In nine days the U. S. pushed from Bellicourt to Le Cateau on the western bank of the Selle river, an advance of over 32 kilometers. In the process 15 large villages are liberated and 3,400 German prisoners taken by the 27th and 30th Divisions.

18 October. **AEF Old-timers Add a Stripe. Chaumont, France.**
The third service stripe—one for each six months overseas—is making its appearance in the AEF. It is estimated that only 1,718 hardy old-timers of the huge wartime force will have completed 18 months service in France by the end of this month. There are 117,072 members of the expeditionary force now entitled to two service stripes.

19 October. **Wildcats' Insignia Official.**
Headquarters AEF approves the wearing of shoulder sleeve insignia (patches) for major units. This gives official permission to the 81st Division whose men adopted the figure of a wildcat while en route to France. By year's end all AEF divisions will have approved shoulder sleeve insignia—many of them still in use to this day.

20 October. **6th Division Redlegs Reinforce the 89th. Romagne, France.**
Artillerymen of the 6th Division leave Le Valdahon's training ranges behind as they are hurriedly moved to the front in support of the 89th Division, which is to play a leading role in the coming Meuse-Argonne operation. The heavy (155mm) guns of the 11th Artillery join the guns of the 58th Field Artillery Brigade.

21–31 October. **AEF Ready To Renew Attack. Meuse-Argonne, France**
General Pershing directs the 1st Army to prepare for a general offensive. Preparation includes authorization for local operations to ensure favorable jump-off lines. These attacks are highly successful and involve offensive actions by the 3d, 5th, 29th, 32d, and 89th and 90th Divisions; also the 26th Division, operating east of the Meuse. As the battle unfolds changes are made in the order of battle on the Meuse-Argonne front as worn-out divisions are relieved and others placed in the battle line.

8 October–11 November. **In Action on the Vosges Front.**
In the rugged terrain in the Vosges Mountains, north of the Swiss border, three infantry regiments of the 93d Division continue to fight as integral parts of French divisions. Other U.S. divisions—notably the

EYEWITNESS: THE LOST BATTALION

On 2 October 1918, as part of the Meuse-Argonne Offensive, the U.S. 77th Infantry Division advanced through the Argonne Forest. The 1st Battalion, 308th Infantry Regiment, was ordered to take and hold the Charlevaux Road astride Hill 198. Led by Major Charles Whittlesey, the battalion penetrated deep into enemy lines and dug in on a steep slope near the road. With its flanks unsupported, the battalion was cut off and surrounded. For the next seven days the 1st Battalion repulsed repeated German attacks, spurning demands to surrender. The "Lost Battalion" went into the Argonne with 554 officers and men—it came out with 194. One survivor, Private Ralph E. John, Company "A," 308th, recounts the ordeal:

"We had had orders to advance straight north, but on this day we ran into fierce machine gun fire in thick woods . . . so our commander who was Major Charles W. Whittlesey, turned the outfit towards a hill on our right. We made it over the top of this little hill in fine shape and as the enemy fire had been so intense and as it was getting dark fast, we were commanded to dig in for the night . . . Major Whittlesey sent men back to get orders and find out how the advance was to be made for the day, and they quickly returned advising they couldn't get through. He knew then that we had been entirely cut off from support and were surrounded by the Germans.

There were a lot of German soldiers on the hill in front of us . . . They seemed to know that we were surrounded and felt that they could handle us with machine guns and potato masher bombs. Our men had not come up for relief for the night and we had practically no eats at all, just a few cans of corn willy and hardtack and no water at all.

We soon began to search the dead men for food and ammunition . . . But our food was almost entirely gone and the men had to have water. The Germans were trying every way to get at us, using potato mashers, machine guns and trench mortars in bitter attacks. But we had dug in and the Major was not going to give ground . . . There was so many dead around us, that the smell was unbearable. Right after noon on the third day . . . there came one of the worst barrages I have ever seen . . . Soon we realized that it

was our own artillery that was bombing us. That artillery fire that afternoon was the worst attack of the whole siege. Major Whittlesey released the last carrier pigeon along about the middle of the afternoon and when that pigeon took off, it carried a prayer from every man there. It seemed the absolute last hope of any relief.

When they stopped so we could get out a little, such a mess you never did see. Some of our men were dead, others dying and moaning for help. Some were already buried and others just in pieces . . . The most terrible thing of all . . . was the fact that we could do next to nothing for the wounded. We had no first aid to take care of them. What little supplies each of us had carried, had long since been used, even shirts, socks and underwear had been torn into rags for bandages. Everybody living was like a living scarecrow.

But shortly after dark, following terrible fighting and shooting to the rear of us . . . a bunch of our own boys broke through . . . I don't think I'll ever be as glad to see anyone as I was that bunch of men."

—*Vince Hawkins*

Above: *Major Charles W. Whittlesey commanded elements of three battalions from the 77th Infantry Division that were surrounded by the Germans. In five days of fighting, his force fell from 554 officers and men to only 194 doughboys, after many savage enemy assaults on their position. ("The Lost Battalion," Frank E. Schoonover, Anne S. K. Brown Collection)*

81st, 88th, and 92d—hold sectors with the French Seventh Army in the Vosges.

22 October. Heavy Blows Hit the Enemy Hard. Meuse-Argonne, France.
As the 1st Army drive is launched, the 3d Division reports capture of the Bois de Forêt; the 5th Division takes the Cunel Heights; the 89th seizes the northern and eastern part of Romagne Heights as U.S. troops maintain momentum in the face of fresh enemy divisions.

27 October. Advance by Yanks Helps the French. Meuse-Argonne, France.
The 78th Division on the 1st Army's left flank makes gains at Grandpré, which facilitates the advance of the right flank of the French Fourth Army.

27–28 October. Yanks Seize Bridgeheads in Italy. Piave River, Italy.
The American 332d Infantry, the only U.S. combat element in Italy, assists in the establishment of several bridgeheads. The regiment is composed of draftees from Ohio.

28 October–4 November. Doughboys Pursue Austrians. Piave River, Italy.
In action with the Italian 31st Division (British 14th Corps) the U.S. 332d Infantry pursues the Austrians to the Tagliamento River and consolidates gains as armistice with Austria goes into effect 4 November.

31 October. A 24-Hour Delay For Yanks. Meuse-Argonne, France.
The French request postponement of the resumption of the offensive until 1 November.

31 October–1 November. First Army Heads for Sedan. Meuse-Argonne, France.
On the eve of the resumption of the main attack by the 1st Army the U.S. forces are aligned at the front with III Corps (5th and 90th Divisions with the 32d in reserve) nearest to the Meuse; V Corps (89th and 2d Divisions in the line with the 1st and 42d in reserve); and I Corps (80th, 77th, and 78th Divisions in the line and the 6th and 82d in reserve). The 42d is transferred to I Corps reserve soon after the battle starts. The 3d, 29th, and 36th Divisions are in Army reserve. The mission is to cut the Metz-Sedan-Mézières railroad.

30 October. U.S. Divisions to British Sector. Ypres, Belgium.
As the Ypres-Lys Operation hits its stride, the 37th and 91st Divisions are sent to assist the Group of Armies of Flanders in the British Army sector. They fight in the Flanders region until the end of the war.

1 November. All-Out Effort is Launched.
The great Meuse-Argonne Offensive resumes at daybreak after a two-hour artillery preparation which pounds enemy positions. In the center V Corps speedily covers six miles and captures the Barricourt Heights. On the right, III Corps's advance protects the flank along the river line. On the left the I Corps

BATTLE OF BLANC MONT RIDGE

On 26 September 1918, the Allies launched a major offensive along the entire Western Front. The Belgians, British, and Americans all made significant gains. Only the French Army, exhausted by four years of war, failed to take their objectives. The French asked General John J. Pershing, AEF commander, for the loan of a fresh American division to support their offensive. Pershing acquiesced, offering the services of the veteran 2d Division, and as reserve the untried 36th Division, totaling some 54,000 men.

The 2d Division was a unique unit. At this time it was commanded by Major General John A. Lejeune, USMC, with two infantry brigades: the 3d Brigade with the Army's 9th and 23d Infantry Regiments, and the Fourth Brigade with the 5th and 6th Marines Regiments.

The division was to spearhead an attack against Blanc Mont Ridge, which dominated the Champagne region. The Germans had held the ridge for four years and it was heavily defended with trenches, barbed wire, pill boxes, and machine-gun positions, all covered by artillery. Taking the ridge would force the Germans to withdraw 30 miles to the Aisne River.

General Lejeune planned a converging attack, with the Fourth Brigade taking a knoll on the left of the ridge, and the 3d Brigade taking a similar height on the right near the Médéah Farm. The two brigades would join at the summit. A French division was to be on each of the division's flanks, with the one on the left assigned to take the key "Essen Hook" position.

On 3 October, with French light tanks in support, the 2d Division deployed on a three-mile front and began its assault behind a creeping artillery barrage. The 6th Marine's on the far left flank soon came under enfilade fire from the "Hook," which the French had failed to take. On the right, the 3d Brigade's was delayed. It had to recapture its jump-off point, which the Germans had taken the night before. The French division supporting the brigade advanced but left a gap, which the Germans exploited. Consequently, the 9th Infantry took heavy fire into its right flank. Despite severe casualties from murderous machine-gun and artillery fire, the division's brigades reached the crest of Blanc Mont and the Médéah Farm within roughly two hours.

The 23d Infantry passed through the 9th to continue the advance, while the 5th Marines passed through the 6th, which was bent back at a right angle to protect the brigade's open left flank. The Marines also took the "Hook" and turned it over to the French, who lost it again to a German counterattack. By day's end, the division had advanced nearly a mile and a half, passing over Blanc Mont ridge and nearly reaching the town of St. Étienne.

The division now held a precarious salient a mile and a half deep and only 500 yards wide at its front. Forced to defend its own flanks, the division tenaciously held its positions against heavy German counterattacks throughout 4 October. The 3d Brigade attempted to advance, but with both flanks unsecured it took heavy losses and fell back. On the left, the Marines suffered 1,100 casualties, their heaviest one-day losses of the war, but valiantly held their positions. By evening, the division had driven all enemy troops from the ridge.

The next day, the Americans consolidated their ground and waited for the French to link up. On 6 October, the division and the French pursued the retreating Germans until 7 October, when the 2d Division was relieved by the 36th Division.

Blanc Mont Ridge cost the 2d Division 4,075 casualties, of which 2,228 were Marines. The French heaped praise on the division, Marshal Pétain proclaiming, "The taking of Blanc Mont is the single greatest achievement of the 1918 campaign." By the end of the war the 3d Brigade had won four French decorations.

—*Vince Hawkins*

Above: *Doughboys and Leathernecks fought side by side in the 2d Infantry Division. ("Over the Top," George Harding, Army Art Collection, NMUSA)*

Left: *Germans surrender to charging doughboys who helped bring about an end to the stalemate in Europe by their valor and numbers. ("Kamerad," N. C. Wyeth, Farnsworth Art Museum, Rockland, ME)*

Opposite: *Once again, the ultimate price was paid by American soldiers who went "over there" in the defense of freedom. ("His Bunkie," W. J. Aylwald, Smithsonian Institution)*

gains a half-mile against the Hindenburg Line. The rapid advance causes the German High Command to issue orders (the night of 1–2 November) for a withdrawal from the 1st Army front west of the Meuse. The 1st Army continues to drive forward. On 4 November the enemy is in full retreat west of the Meuse. The 1st Division relieves the 80th and the 42d Division relieves the 78th. The pursuit continues until 7 November when units of the I Corps reach the heights overlooking the city of Sedan. Occupation of these heights effectively cuts the lateral railroad through Sedan, thus achieving the main objective of the Meuse-Argonne offensive.

1 November. **End-of-War Rumors Abound. Washington, D.C.**
High-ranking War Department officials obtain startling intelligence that the dominant political party in Germany is ready to sign an armistice, no matter the terms. Secretary of War Baker secretly decides to suspend further embarkations of U.S. troops headed for France. He puts the War Department to work on plans for bringing the AEF back to American shores.

4 November. **U.S. Corps Across the Meuse.**
The crossing of the Meuse by the III Corps begins with the establishment of bridgeheads by the 5th Division in conjunction with a major push by the

French. By 10 November the line of departure is established for a thrust toward Montmédy.

5 November. **Battle Focuses on Sedan.**
The U.S. I Corps is directed to capture the critical communications center at Sedan with V Corps to assist on the right flank. For reasons that are never fully explained the 1st Division crosses the zone of the 77th Division and enters that of the 42d Division. This results in a confusing situation, which envelops the 1st and 42d Divisions. Their advance regiments seize bridgeheads and the American front is established at Hill 252, the high ground in front of Sedan.

5 November. **The Second Army Alerted to Attack.**
General Pershing puts the 2d Army on alert to advance on a front between the Moselle River and Etang de Lachaussée. Bullard orders the Army to jump-off on attack early on 10 November with the VI Corps (Menoher), IV Corps (Muir), and French XVII Corps (Hellot). Second Army troops seize objectives and prepare to continue the advance on 11 November.

7–8 November. **Boundary Shift Sends French Into Sedan.**
The left boundary of 1st Army is changed to leave Hill 252 to the French. General Pershing makes the decision to permit French forces the honor of being

first into Sedan. 1st Army divisions wheel to the east and continue the attack toward Longwy and the Briey iron basin.

9 November. The End May Be Near.
Marshal Foch holds a conference with the enemy concerning an armistice but issues instructions to continue attacks to take full advantage of the demoralization of German forces..

10–11 November. Germany Surrenders to the Allies. Compiegne, France.
The 1st Army executes attacks as ordered and makes substantial gains to include forcing the crossing of the Meuse south of Mouzon and a 1-1/2-mile thrust east of Verdun. During the morning, word is flashed to all units that hostilities will cease at 11:00 a.m.

11 November. The Last Round is Fired, Then Guns Are Silent. Beaufort, France.
Battery E, 11th Field Artillery, a 6th Division unit now with the 89th Division, receives the mission to fire the last round of U.S. artillery in the war. At the 11th hour on the 11th day of the 11th month, Battery E's "Calamity Jane," roars for the last time. The guns fall silent all along the battlefront. The war is over.

11 November. The AEF Is a Mighty Force.
The strength of the American Expeditionary Force as armistice is announced is 2,057,675; actual available combat strength is 1,078,222. There are 646,000 U.S. infantrymen in the theater of war.

17 November. The Yanks Are Coming—to Germany!
Eight divisions strong—encompassing the 1st, 3d, 4th, 5th, 32d, 42d, 89th, and 90th Divisions—the American 3d Army breaks camp at 5:30 in the morning, starting out on its march to the Rhine. An observer writes in *Stars and Stripes*, "Whole platoons of American infantry can be seen in the parade, each head adorned with a spiked German helmet."

20 November. Prisoners to be Repatriated.
A final accounting shows that the AEF has taken 44,934 German prisoners. There are 2,082 Americans in German prisoner of war facilities.

21 November. Seven Hundred Miles in Four Hours. Mineola, N.Y.
Army Major E. J. Booth and Lieutenant Elmer J. Spencer complete a 700-mile non-stop flight, which originated at the Selfridge aviation field at Mount Clemens, Michigan. The flight, in a De Haviland military plane, takes four hours.

29 November. Homeward Bound. St. Nazaire, France
The 76th Division, a replacement division since its arrival in France, is to be the first division entity returned to the U.S. It will be followed by the 27th and 30th Divisions, which have the unusual distinction of never having served on the American front and not having taken part in the great November offensives. Both National Guard divisions fought with valor and distinction in the British sector where they helped to crack the Hindenberg Line and earned the admiration of British and Australian troops.

1 December. The Watch on the Rhine.
The U.S. Army of Occupation, designated the U.S. 3d Army with Major General Joseph T. Dickman in command, is ordered to move into Germany with nine battle-tested divisions to begin the "Watch on the Rhine."

6 December. Increase in Need for MPs.
As combat operations phase out, the AEF finds that it needs to organize 51 military police companies. Some will be detailed in the base sections; there is to be one MP company in each division, one to every army corps, and a battalion of four companies to each army.

8 December. Third Army on the Move. Coblenz, Germany.
Troops of the American 3d Army are beginning to establish the bridgehead into the area that is the focal

point of the U.S. occupation zone. The American bridgehead on the Rhine measures 35 kilometers on each side of the river and extends for a distance of 30 kilometers. U.S. troops are under orders to patrol and monitor key highways.

13 December. **President Wilson in France. Brest, France.**
The 139th Field Artillery regimental band of the 38th Division greets President Woodrow Wilson as he steps ashore in France from the liner S.S. *George Washington.* The entire artillery regiment is assigned to line both sides of the street running from the dock to the ramparts of the walled town. Wilson will work with heads of Allied nations to craft the peace treaty in Paris.

13 December. **Additional Troops for Occupation.**
American headquarters announces that the 2d, 7th, 28th, 33d, and 79th Divisions are being added to those divisions previously announced for the occupation army to move into Germany and Luxembourg. In the meantime, 100,000 troops are assembling in a camp set up at Brest, France, to allocate shipping for AEF elements heading back to the states.

Above: *After World War I's conclusion, Massachusetts National Guardsmen turn to another duty, the security of Boston during a strike by the city police. (National Archives)*

1919

3 January. **Center Established for Redeployment. Le Mans, France.**
The American Embarkation Center is set up to coordinate and facilitate the movement of units scheduled to return to the United States.

19 January. **Infantrymen Meet Bolsheviks. Shenkhursk, Northern Russia.**
U.S. forces in North Russian mount a strong defense against a major Bolshevik offensive in the Battle of Shenkhursk.

12 February. **Railway Mission to Northern Russia.**
President Wilson orders the organization of the "Murmansk Contingent" of U.S. Army railway troops for duty in Northern Russia.

15 March. **The American Legion Launched. Paris, France**
Assembled at the famed Cirque de Paris meeting hall, representatives of the units of the AEF create the American Legion, destined to become America's premier veterans organization. The first steering committee consists of a private, a sergeant, and three brigadier generals. One of the guiding lights of the new organization is Colonel Theodore Roosevelt, Jr., formerly of the 26th Infantry, 1st Division.

Right: *Army of Occupation Medal for duty in Germany or Austria-Hungary from 12 November 1918 to 11 July 1923. (American Military Insignia, Medals and Decorations, Chartwell Books, Inc.)*

Far Right: *The World War I Victory Medal with three campaign bars for service between 6 April 1917 and 11 November 1918, or in Russia 11 November 1918 to 5 August 1919, or Siberia 23 November 1918 to 1 April 1920. (American Military Insignia, Medals and Decorations, Chartwell Books, Inc.)*

28–29 March. **U.S. Troops Quit Italy. Genoa, Italy.**
The U.S. 332d Infantry assembles for its return to the United States after eight months in Italy. It is the only U.S. regiment with a battle streamer for Vittorio-Veneto. In addition to the infantrymen, 54 air service pilots (members of Italian bombardment squadrons) and 30 U.S. ambulance sections also are credited with service in Italy.

31 March–4 April. **Battling the Soviets. Bolshie Ozerki, Northern Russia.**
An all-out Soviet offensive gets underway as elements of the U.S. 339th Infantry fight alongside members of the Yorkshire Regiment in the face of overwhelming superior forces. The U.S. forces are alerted to prepare to turn over positions to the "new Northern Russian army" organized to fight the Bolsheviks—and destined for defeat.

17 April. **Commander Finds Troops Set to Leave. Archangel, Northern Russia.**
Brigadier General Wilds P. Richardson arrives to take command as the AEF in Northern Russia is preparing for departure.

1 May. **Bolsheviks Press Attack. Vaga River, Northern Russia.**
As they go about their preparations for exit from Russian soil, soldiers of the 339th Infantry find themselves fending off a strong offensive launched by Bolshevik troops.

30 May. **Last Formation. Archangel, Northern Russia.**
Troops of the Army Expeditionary Force Northern Russia parade through the streets and conduct Memorial Day ceremonies at the Archangel cemetery. This marks the last official appearance of American troops in Northern Russia.

12 June. **War Hero Heads Military Academy. West Point, New York.**
Douglas MacArthur, highly decorated combat hero of the 42d (Rainbow) Division, is named superintendent of his alma mater. At 39, Brigadier General MacArthur is the youngest "supe" in the academy's history. MacArthur's orders from General Peyton C. March, Army Chief of Staff: "Revitalize and revamp the Academy."

25 June. **Skirmish with Japanese. Sviyagino, Siberia.**
Patrolling U.S. troops are fired upon by Japanese "allies" and a heavy fire fight is reported. Lieutenant Sylvian G. Kindall, 27th Infantry, is hit and later enters his claim of being "the first American to qualify for the award of the Purple Heart for a wound received in a fight with the Japanese."

25 June. **Deadly Fire Fight with Bolsheviks. Romanovka, Siberia.**
Doughboys from Company A, 31st Infantry commanded by Lieutenant Lawrence D. Butler, encounter a force of Bolshevik irregulars (miners from Petrovka and Novo Rosskaya). American losses are

reported as 19 killed and 25 wounded, of whom five later die. This is one of the deadliest days in the Siberian campaign.

3 July. The Third Army Phased Out. Coblenz, Germany.
A new organization, American Forces in Germany (AFG), is created to replace the 3d Army. Lieutenant General Hunter Liggett returns to the United States.

3 July. Cavalry in Occupation. Coblenz, Germany.
The Mounted Detachment (later Provisional Cavalry Squadron) is organized, with Lieutenant Colonel Jonathan M. Wainwright as its first commander. The squadron gains renown for its sports program, with outstanding baseball, football, and polo teams.

7 July. Cross-Country Truck Convoy. Washington, D.C.
Formed to emphasize the transition to motorized rolling stock, the Army's First Transcontinental Motor Convoy departs for San Francisco. It is the first motor vehicle trip across the expanse of the nation and moving at an average speed of 6 m.p.h., will take nine weeks. The War Department assigns Lieutenant Colonel Dwight D. Eisenhower to accompany the column as an observer.

5 August. Goodbye Russia, Hello France! Murmansk, Northern Russia.
Two Army transportation companies, the last elements to leave, embark on movement to Brest, France, thus ending the U.S. military presence. Officials look the other way as doughboys take with them an array of Russian orphans who have been adopted as Army mascots. The "Headquarters AEF North Russia" goes out of existence. During the 11-month commitment, more than 400 casualties are sustained in combat with elements of the Bolshevik Seventh Army.

3 September. General Pershing Has New Military Rank.
With the passage of Public Law 45, the United States Congress appoints John J. Pershing the first General of the Armies of the United States. Although the title and five-star rank previously was on the books from 1797, Pershing is the only Army officer to actually assume this rank while on active duty. He is authorized to move the AEF Headquarters to Washington, D.C. but he never wears five stars.

11 September. Army Guard Protects City. Boston, Massachusetts.
When Boston city police strike, criminals begin assaulting citizens and looting stores. The governor

calls out the Army Guard to restore order and protect the city.

19 September. It's Official—Cavalry School. Fort Riley, Kansas.
The longtime Mounted Service School becomes The Cavalry School. The Commandant is Colonel George H. Cameron who, as a major general commanded the V Corps, 1st Army, in the 1918 AEF. In the Army's postwar retrenchment he and many others are returned to regular Army rank. The cavalry is ordered to train a team for the riding events at the Olympic Games at Antwerp in September 1920.

25 September. Service Schools Mission. Washington, D.C.
In a new, comprehensive long-range plan for its school system, the Army announces that there are to be (1) basic courses, (2) unit schools, (3) advanced courses, and (4) General service schools to help produce well-trained leadership for the future.

15 October. Trans-U.S. Air Race. Roosevelt Field, New York.
After three days en route, Lieutenant Belvin Maynard, flying a DH-4, reaches the end of a 5,400-mile round trip to San Francisco and the return to his point of origin. His flight to San Francisco took three days, six hours. This event would go into the record books as the first transcontinental flight.

9 October. Provisional Brigade Expedition Formed.
Brigadier General William H. Sage in command of the Provisional Brigade (5th and 50th Infantry Regiments) is ordered to prepare an expeditionary force to the Polish plebiscite region. These orders change in December 1919 when the brigade becomes part of American Forces in Germany.

18 November. Cavalry Saddles Up. Army of Occupation, Germany.
General Henry T. Allen, commander of Army Forces in Germany, orders the mounted cavalry squadron to alert status in response to reports of Germans assembling forces at Altenkirchen, Hachenburg, and Marienburg.

31 December. Army Ends Activity at Brest.
After more than two years of activity U.S. port operations at Brest, France, are discontinued. Antwerp, Belgium, is designated to handle all traffic for American Forces in Germany. S.S. *George Washington* leaves on its last departure from Brest with 3,000 troops from the rapidly thinning ranks of American Forces in France, successor to the once-mighty AEF.

BLACK JACK JOHN PERSHING: GENERAL OF THE ARMY

No American officer is more identified with World War I than John J. Pershing, commander of the American Expeditionary Force (AEF). He stubbornly refused to let the American force be broken up despite hard pressure from desperate Allied commanders. A disciplined task master, he honed a tough, aggressive army that turned the course of the war. This and his later service as Army chief of staff put an indelible stamp of high professionalism on the future Army. George C. Marshall, Douglas MacArthur, George S. Patton, Billy Mitchell, Fox Conner, and many lesser known officers developed as future leaders under Pershing's stern eye.

Graduating from West Point in 1886, Pershing went west to serve with the 6th and 10th Cavalry (Colored) Regiments. He acquired the nickname "Black Jack" because of his duty with the 10th, though no one ever said it to his face. He served in several Indian campaigns, including ones against Geronimo's Apaches and the Sioux. In 1891, he became a professor of Military Science and Tactics at the University of Nebraska, where he earned a law degree, taught mathematics, and trained a championship student drill team.

In 1898 he was teaching tactics at West Point when the Spanish-American War broke out. After repeated requests, he joined the 10th as its quartermaster. In Cuba, he found ways to be at the front and led a company of the 10th up Kettle Hill with the Rough Riders.

After the war, Captain Pershing was sent to the Philippines, where he saw action against the fanatical Moros. He impressed his superiors, but laws forced a strict seniority system of promotions. In 1906, President Roosevelt bypassed the system and promoted Pershing from captain to brigadier general over 862 senior officers. He returned to the Philippines three more times, where he finally destroyed the last major Moro stronghold in 1913. Pershing served as an observer during the Russo-Japanese War and in the Balkans.

After most of his family died in a fire in 1915, Pershing devoted himself to the Army. A year later he led the Mexican Punitive Expedition to capture Mexican bandit Pancho Villa. Although the operation was unsuccessful, Pershing gained invaluable experience and promotion to major general. He was the first to use automotive cars, trucks, and airplanes in action.

With his experience and proven leadership, Pershing was chosen to lead the AEF in Europe. While planning, he constantly defended independent

use of American troops with his Allied counterparts. His determination kept the AEF intact. Pershing enforced military courtesy, field sanitation, and dress. He set up schools to train the arriving men, but he preferred more mobile maneuver tactics to the trench war he saw. By early 1918, the AEF had its own front.

After several successes by American divisions, Pershing created the American 1st Army, which won the battle of St. Mihiel and took part in the Meuse-Argonne offensive. When more divisions arrived, he formed the 2d Army and later 3d Army and moved up to army group command. When the fighting ended on 11 November 1918, Pershing commanded more than 1.3 million men in 29 divisions.

Congress made Pershing General of the Armies in September 1919. He went on to serve as the Army chief of staff. His memoirs, *My Experiences in the World War*, won a Pulitzer Prize. Always a mentor, he died in 1948.

—*Kevin M. Hymel*

Above: *General of the Armies John J. Pershing commanded the AEF during World War I. Pershing epitomized the modern combat leader, combining tactical and strategic thinking along with political acumen. (U.S. Army Military History Institute, Carlisle Barracks, PA)*

PEACETIME SOLDIERING

1920–1940

PEACETIME SOLDIERING

1920–1940

Major General Bruce Jacobs, AUS (Ret)

The lowering and removal of the American flag that had been flying above Fort Ehrenbreitstein in the German city of Coblenz marked the end of the U.S. role in the occupation of Germany. The quiet ceremony on 24 January 1923 was a fleeting reminder of the Army that once had been; soon the last evidence that this Army had ever existed would be relegated to furled battle flags and the memories of the nation's nearly 4 million war veterans.

The advent of the postwar period truly came to pass as General of the Armies John J. Pershing relinquished his post as Army Chief of Staff to Major General John L. Hines, the first of Pershing's wartime lieutenants to be named to lead the peacetime Army to the eve of World War II. Following Hines would be Generals Charles P. Summerall, Douglas MacArthur, and Malin Craig—each in his own right a distinguished combat leader during the glory days of the American Expeditionary Force.

Despite the hopes expressed by Pershing and others that a strong Army would be maintained in recognition of the leadership role that was being assumed by the United States in the postwar period, it was soon starkly clear that this was not to be. The Army, it was quickly established, would henceforth exist on short rations. Its principal backup force, the National Guard, never was funded to exceed half-strength units.

The stringent budgets of 1924–1940 were strained to the breaking point by the expensive—but clearly important—maintenance of forces, garrisons, and outposts in the Panama Canal Zone, the Philippines, China, and the Hawaiian Islands.

As the war years gave way to the 1920s and as the 1920s made way for the 1930s, painfully slow progress

was made in the mechanization of the Army despite the fact that tank warfare had started to come into its own during the latter stages of the war and despite the reality that wheeled transportation had started to prevail as replacements for horses and mules.

Even as America enthusiastically embraced the automobile as its favorite mode of transportation and as farmers welcomed the advent of tractors, the Army was slow and even reluctant to adapt to the emerging technology. The struggle between the infantry and cavalry branches for control of tanks actually retarded the creation of viable armored forces. Initially, in the years after the war in France, control of tanks was given to the infantry. Although many cavalrymen sought to circumvent the problem by developing tanks called "cavalry cars," there were others in the cavalry who wanted no part of "stinking, gasoline-driven monsters."

When the experimental Seventh Cavalry Brigade (Mechanized) reached the maneuver area at Plattsburg, New York, in August 1939, it was recorded that "mounted cavalry would as soon discuss the devil as its rival on wheels, and the infantry has a low opinion of the mechanized brigade which it terms 'the men from Mars.'" But the brigade soon would win its "spurs" and transition into the soon-to-be-famed 1st Armored Division.

It would not be until 10 July 1940—virtually the end of this era—that the Armored Force officially came into being, roughly two months after the armored *blitzkrieg* that enabled Nazi Germany to race through the Low Countries, to rupture the French defense of their homeland, and to drive the forces of Great Britain from the continent of Europe. But it was also during these years of austerity and neglect

that the seeds were being nourished that would bring forth the great armored divisions that would form the spearhead for the success of American arms in the years to come.

The two decades after World War II were underscored by the gathering "push" for an air force independent of the Army. This was opposed not only by the Army leadership, but by the Navy as well. Even as the United States prepared for the possibility of participation in World War II, the Air Corps remained subordinate to the Army Chief of Staff and the War Department General Staff. Nevertheless, clearly some of the most notable achievements of the Army in the so-called interwar years were the accomplishments of the intrepid airmen who filled the cockpits and the ranks of the Army Air Corps and who wrote the playbook that would marshal American air power in the next decade.

It was through the extraordinary foresight of those associated with Army aviation that the vision came into focus of the airplane—and the parachute—as a means of transporting troops and delivering troops to the battlefield. The first, halting steps toward airborne

and airmobile warfare were actually taken during these years of austerity and meager resources.

The tiny, resource-deprived Army of the interwar years enjoyed one great attribute, and it made the most of it. The size of the army, the relative simplicity of its missions, the isolationism of the United States, the isolated condition of the Army, and its low visibility on the national scene led to an Army whose future leaders, with great introspection, wittingly or unwittingly converted the peacetime Army into a great ongoing school for officers, noncommissioned officers, and specialist soldiers. This, in the long run, would produce the standards of excellence that would stand the Army in good stead.

Pages 592-593: *A GI on guard duty in front of Diamond Head on Oahu in 1938, while the Hawaiian Territory still was a tranquil haven. (U.S. Army Museum, Hawaii)*

Above: *Although metal had replaced wood and canvas, biplanes of the 1920s and early 1930s Army Air Corps resembled their World War I predecessors in many ways. ("20th Pursuit Squadron," Konrad F. Hack)*

PEACETIME SOLDIERING
1920–1940

"When war is over, the country at large thinks no more of the means and methods of making war. Its object is to lick its wounds and recover its loss in life and money. The natural tendency is to put aside the weapons with which the last war had been fought as the main supply for the next."

—Colonel Adna Romanza Chaffee, U.S. Army
Fort Leavenworth, Kansas, 1919

1920

January. **Army Nurse School Consolidated.**
During the year, the entering students of the Army School of Nursing are consolidated at Letterman General Hospital, San Francisco, and Walter Reed General Hospital, Washington, D.C. By the time 512 nurses graduate in 1921, 21 student nurses have died while in service, most due to the flu epidemic.

1 January. **Army Exits England and France.**
The Provisional District of Great Britain is discontinued and remaining administrative functions in France become the responsibility of the Military Attaché, American Embassy, Paris. One week later Headquarters of the U.S. Army in France is closed out. Brigadier General William D. Connor and members of his staff sail from the port of Antwerp,

Above: *After World War I, expansion of Army medical resources included the establishment of a School of Nursing at Letterman General Hospital, Presidio of San Francisco. These nursing students were in attendance in 1920–1921. (William K. Emerson, ASMIC)*

Belgium, headed for home. Only Occupation forces in Germany remain in Western Europe.

16–19 January. **Wolfhounds on the Gobi Desert. Verhnudinsk, Siberia.**
Elements of the 27th Infantry prepare to recross the Gobi Desert to Vladivostok, a distance of 2,000 miles, as its commander learns the regiment will soon leave Siberia. When a Russian armored car detachment attacks, the regiment, now nicknamed "Wolfhounds," fights back with rifles and hand grenades. The last elements will reach Vladivostok on 25 February.

17 January. **AEF Siberia Winds Down. Vladivostok, Siberia.**
Six companies from the 27th Infantry are in the vanguard of U.S. troops exiting from Siberia. An ice-breaker is pressed into service to cut a passage for the Army transport, which sails for Manila as the combat elements of American Expeditionary Force (AEF) Siberia start the withdrawal from the Asian mainland. Other troop departures, to include the 31st Infantry Regiment, are scheduled for 15 February and 10, 21, and 31 March.

1 April. **Siberian Venture Ends. Vladivostok.**
After 18 months of a strange adventure, the U.S. colors come down to signal the final closing of Headquarters AEF in Siberia. The command post with all remaining units of the expeditionary force sails to Manila.

14–16 May. **Big Turnout for Air Show. Bolling Field, Washington, D.C.**
During a three-day period more than 10,000 enthusiasts flock to the Army's Bolling Field for the first Army Air Tournament, an aerial show of unprecedented scope as the Army Air Service struts its stuff. A first-day highlight that captures the crowd's attention is Lieutenant Fred Nelson in a German

attention is Lieutenant Fred Nelson in a German Fokker. Nelson leaves Middletown, Pennsylvania (a distance of 133 miles), and roars down the runway at Bolling 59 minutes later—a new speed record.

25 May. **First Tankers in Guard. Duluth, Minnesota.**
The 34th Tank Company, 34th Division—the first tank unit in the National Guard—is organized. The War Department plans to have one tank company assigned to each of the divisions to be reorganized in the National Guard.

4 June. **Postwar Army Sets Course.**
Following months of controversy during congressional hearings, the National Defense Act of 1920 is approved and the Army's course is set for the immediate postwar years. The U.S. "peace establishment" will have three components—the Regular Army, the National Guard, and the Organized Reserve. The act reiterates that when in the service of the United States the National Guard is part of the Army of the United States; stipulates that the Chief of the Militia Bureau will in the future be a National Guard officer; and directs that the names,

Above: *The Army Mine Planter Service (1918–1948) was responsible for protecting harbors and other key waterways in the U.S. and overseas. ("Let Go," Don Stivers)*

Below: *For a brief period after the Versailles Treaty, U.S. Army troops served in Germany as part of the Allied occupation force. (National Archives)*

U.S. ARMY WARRANT OFFICERS

The term "warrant officer" first appeared on 20 July 1918, when the Army Mine Planter Service was established as a part of the Coast Artillery. However, the function, if not the actual title, can be traced to the Army's 1896 "Headquarters Clerk" position, redesignated "Field Clerk" in 1916.

Warrant officers in the Mine Planter Service were given the grades of Master, First Mate, Second Mate, Chief Engineer, and Assistant Engineer. On 4 June 1920, Congress expanded the role of warrant officers to the whole Army, approving an additional 1,120 warrant officers for service in administrative and clerical duties in both headquarters and large tactical units. One of the primary motives for this expansion was to retain the experience and reward enlisted men of long service and former officers of World War I who were being forced out by the Army's strength reductions.

From 1922 to 1935 the number in the Warrant Officer Corps fluctuated, and in 1936 the Army initiated examinations to fill the vacancies. The Congressional Act of 1941 established two grades, Chief Warrant Officer and Warrant Officer Junior Grade. The Secretary of the Army designated warrant officers' duties and gave them the same powers as commissioned officers when performing similar duties. In 1942, the rank order of warrant officers was established immediately below commissioned officers and above all enlisted ranks.

In World War II warrant officers served in some 40 occupational areas. As no clear policy was established, thousands of warrant officers were appointed, trained, and assigned at the discretion of the major Army commands. In January 1944, the appointment of women was authorized. By war's end, of some 57,000 warrant officers, 42 were women.

Demobilization reduced the number of warrant officers and appointments ceased, but in 1946 the Corps occupations were incorporated into those used by all commissioned officers. In 1948, a long-range career plan was instituted that led to an increase in the Corps. This plan restructured units to include warrant officer positions. By 1949, a further 6,000 warrant officers had been appointed and two more pay grades created. Control of warrant officer appointments returned to the major commanders in 1951, and the occupational specialties increased to 60.

In 1968, the Regular Army, closed to them since 1948, was reopened to warrant officer applicants. By 1972, a trilevel education program was established that provided training for 59 entry-level, 53 mid-career-level, and 27 advanced-level occupational specialties. The Total Warrant Officer System, adopted in 1987, increased and defined the powers of warrant officers. It was followed in 1991 by the Warrant Officer Management Act, which established a system of personnel management. In January 1999, the Warrant Officer Leader Development Council was formed to direct warrant officer issues to the lowest levels of resolution. A "Warrant Officer Advisor to the CSA" was created as an additional duty within the office of the Army Chief of Staff in 2002.

The Army currently defines a warrant officer as "an officer appointed by warrant by the Secretary of the Army based on a sound level of technical and tactical competence. The warrant officer is the highly specialized expert and trainer who, by gaining progressive levels of expertise and leadership, operates, maintains, administers, and manages the Army's equipment, support activities, or technical systems for an entire career." Today's warrant officers continue to provide specialized service of significant importance to the functioning of the U.S. Army.

—*Vince Hawkins*

Above: *Traditional Warrant Officer Insignia cap and collar insignia. Recent changes to Army Regulations permit Warrants to wear the branch, limiting the old Eagle to Warrant Officer Candidates. (U.S. Army Institute of Heraldry)*

Right: *In 1919, the Tank Corps at Camp Meade, Maryland, was a small part of the post–World War I Army, but the force would grow in importance under young officers such as George S. Patton, Jr. (Patton Family Collection)*

Below: *The unique regimental insignia of the 9th Infantry Regiment is the "Manchu Dragon." (William K. Emerson ASMIC)*

subordinate elements that served in the World War shall be preserved and continued.

4 June. Tank Corps Abolished.

Chiefs of Infantry, Artillery, and Cavalry are created to head the combat arms. The Army's Tank Corps is ordered disbanded and the tanks placed under the infantry. Tank tactics will be based on the expectation that the future tank will be employed strictly as a close support weapon for the infantryman. The Tank School, however, is continued at Camp (later Fort) George G. Meade, Maryland, until 1931, when it is moved to Fort Benning, Georgia.

1 July. New Army Takes Shape.

As the new Army evolves from its wartime structure, new special-purpose organizations are needed. The Army Chemical Corps and the Army Finance Department are established.

20 October. Record Alaska Flight. Mineola Field, New York.

Led by 27-year-old Captain St. Clair Streett, an already legendary aviator, the Army's famed "Arctic Squadron" of four aircraft completes an epic 9,000-mile roundtrip flight from New York to Alaska. The mission originated on 15 July and encompassed 112 flying hours. Streett would subsequently be awarded the Distinguished Flying Cross and would be one of the pioneer Army airmen destined to wear a general's stars in World War II.

1921

12 February. "Model" Airway Set in Place. Bolling Field.

Under the watchful eye of aviation pioneer Orville Wright, a troop of Boy Scouts lays the cornerstone for the nation's first airway—a ground marker 20 feet long composed of white-washed stones spelling out the letters "DC-1" for "District of Columbia—Stop Number 1." The event marks the beginning of an undertaking to mark and chart the nation's sky highways.

15 February. Occupation Army Training. Engers, Germany.

Honing their skills while awaiting word as to when Occupation duties will come to an end, the machine gun companies of the 2d Brigade, Army Forces Germany, are brought together for training. Soldiers are told that availability of ammunition is not an issue.

MAJOR GENERAL FOX CONNER

In his time, he was considered one of the top intellects in the Army. He was both mentor and friend to young officers such as Dwight Eisenhower. The consummate professional, he was greatly admired and respected by all who knew him.

Fox Conner was born 2 November 1874 in Slate Spring, Mississippi. He graduated from West Point in 1898 and was commissioned a second lieutenant in the 2d Artillery. He was assigned to the U.S. occupation forces in Cuba. Over the next several years, Conner gradually rose through the ranks, becoming a "serious soldier and a technically proficient artillerist." In 1900, he returned to the United States to command a coastal artillery company at Fort Hamilton, New York, and from 1901 to 1905 he was detailed to the Army General Staff.

Conner graduated from the Army Staff College at Fort Leavenworth in 1907, then served as an instructor at the Army War College. Following this, Conner was sent as an exchange officer to the French army, where he was able to observe and worked closely with many of their officers. Conner was then assigned to the Inspector-General's Department as inspector of field artillery fire. In 1917, Conner received temporary promotions to lieutenant colonel and colonel.

General Pershing requested Conner for his American Expeditionary Force staff, assigning him as assistant chief of staff for operations. Conner was responsible for the Army's artillery requirements, and as most of the American artillery was French, Conner's previous experience proved invaluable. On 23 August 1918, Conner was promoted to brigadier general, and became AEF's G-3, chief of operations. Conner assembled a team of capable officers, setting a high standard for detailed planning. He predicted the German offensive in the Meuse-Argonne and advised Pershing on the first American offensive at St.-Mihiel. After the war, Conner wrote the AEF's official after-action report in which he discussed the future development of the Army. Pershing later told Conner, "I could have spared any other man in the AEF better than you."

On 27 April 1921, Conner became a Regular brigadier general and was then given brigade command in Panama. He requested as his executive officer Major Dwight D. Eisenhower, whom he had met a few years earlier. Conner, a skilled instructor and intellectual, became Eisenhower's mentor. The two men developed a friendship that would last throughout their lives.

Recalled to the United States in 1925, Conner was promoted to major general on 20 October and appointed Deputy Chief of Staff. From 1928 to 1930, he commanded the Hawaiian Department, and then was commander of the First Corps Area until he retired. In 1933, President Franklin D. Roosevelt assigned Conner the duty of mobilizing some 24,000 men needed to fill 125 companies of the Civilian Conservation Corps.

In 1938, Conner retired from active duty, but during World War II he continued to give advice to those who sought his counsel. On 13 October 1951, Fox Conner died. Although virtually unknown today, he was both revered and respected by many of the Army's greatest soldiers. Eisenhower said, "In sheer ability and character, he was the outstanding soldier of my time."

—*Vince Hawkinsa*

Above: *Major General Fox Conner standing next to a horse in Panama, 1924. (John S. D. Eisenhower)*

25 February. **Pineapple Soldiers. Schofield Barracks, Hawaii.**
Combat elements of the Army in the Hawaiian Islands are organized as the Hawaiian Division. Twenty years later this will become the Army's 24th Infantry Division.

5 March. **John W. Weeks Appointed Secretary of War.**
Former Navy Reserve Rear Admiral John W. Weeks is appointed as the 48th Secretary of War. He will serve under two Presidents, establish the Industrial War College, and work to improve the officer corps.

8 June. **Division in Philippines. Manila, Philippine Islands.**
The Army activates the Philippine Division as its major combat force stationed in the Far East. The division will include U.S. Army and Philippine Scouts elements.

1 July. **AEF Leader Heads the Army. Washington, D.C.**
General John J. Pershing, wartime commander of the Army Expeditionary Force in France, is named Army Chief of Staff, replacing his old rival, Major General Peyton C. March.

20 July. **Mitchell's Airmen "Attack" Navy Targets. Vicinity of Chesapeake Bay.**
The issue of whether naval vessels are vulnerable to attack from the air is put to the test as Army bombers from Langley Field, Virginia, launch an aerial attack on a naval force consisting of three captured German

vessels, including the battleship *Ostfriesland.* All three ships are sunk, and Brigadier General William (Billy) Mitchell jubilantly greets the airmen on their return to base. Navy officials derided the demonstration as "Mitchell's fool luck."

1 August. **Civilian Training Program. Camp Devens, Massachusetts.**
The charter members of the Citizens Military Training Camp (CMTC) program report here and to other military posts throughout the nation to begin a one-month course of training under Army auspices. CMTC is designed to be completed in four yearly segments of one month each. Graduates will be eligible to apply for Army Reserve commissions.

1 September. **Military District in Nation's Capital.**
The District of Washington is established to be responsible for all Army activity within the national capital region. In time (1942) it will be replaced by the "Military District of Washington."

Above: *General of the Armies John J. Pershing became Chief of Staff of the Army on 1 July 1921. (Sir William Orpen, National Portrait Gallery, Washington, D.C., Art Resource/NY)*

Left: *Company C, 45th Infantry, was part of the Philippine Scouts that were formed after the Spanish-American War. (Raymond S. Johnson, Company of Military Historians)*

16 September. Wear of Regimental Insignia.
Army Circular 244 authorizes wear of distinctive regimental insignia. Designs must be submitted for approval. One of the most unusual insignia is the belt buckle approved for the 9th Infantry.

11 November. A National Treasure. Arlington National Cemetery, Arlington, Virginia.
The Tomb of the Unknown Soldier is dedicated and the symbolic "unknown" war casualty is buried. The casket had been selected in Europe by Sergeant Edward F. Younger, 2d Battalion, 50th Infantry. Three Army Medal of Honor heroes—Charles Whittelsey, Alvin York, and Samuel Woodfill—are pallbearers. In later years and following future wars, this will be renamed "The Tomb of the Unknowns."

14 November. Road Commission Named.
The age of the American highway takes shape for the future, and the newly formed Army Road Commission takes over all territorial public works relating to the nation's roads.

17 November. The Old Guard's Long March. Fort Snelling, Minnesota.
The 3d U.S. Infantry Regiment ("The Old Guard") arrives at its new home station after a 950-mile trek from Camp Sheridan, Ohio. Recorded as one of the

Army's longest hikes, it was necessitated by a shortage of funds in the War Department budget. Toward the end of the march the infantrymen, carrying full field equipment, consistently covered nearly 30 miles each day, often despite snow and ice on the route of march.

22 December. Guard Division Headquarters. Harrisburg, Pennsylvania.
The Headquarters of the 28th Division is granted federal recognition by the War Department. The all-Pennsylvania division is the first of 18 to be created in the postwar National Guard. For the most part these will be divisions created in the Guard for field service in the World War.

1922

25 January. Strike Up the Band.
The U.S. Army Band is established in accordance with orders signed by the Army Chief of Staff, General Pershing. The band willl be known in perpetuity as "Pershing's Own."

Above: *Participants in the Citizens Military Training Camps (CMTC) received one month of training annually for four years. Here, CMTC candidates fire machine guns at Camp Del Monte, California, in 1925. (U.S. Army)*

30 June. **Congress Slashes the Army.**
Congress announces reduction of the Army to 175,000 officers and men. This results in the immediate loss of 600 line officers and more than 100,000 soldiers. All promotions are halted until 1 January 1923.

1 July. **Army Leadership Protests.**
In expressing his opposition to the Army cutbacks, Secretary of War John W. Weeks states: "My conclusions are not entirely welcome at this time, when people have been hoping that nations had learned to avoid conflict of force. My conclusions are, nevertheless, that we shall continue to prepare for such conflicts." General Pershing says: "It is my conviction that our Regular force is cut too much for safety."

September. **Rock of the Marne Finds a Home. Camp Lewis, Washington.**
With its elements scattered in a number of western locations, the 3d ("Rock of the Marne") Division headquarters moves to Camp Lewis, where it will remain through the end of the 1930s. The 1st Division has its headquarters at Fort Hamilton, New York, and the 2d Division sets up shop at Fort Sam Houston, Texas.

1923

24 January. **U.S. Occupation in Germany Ends. Coblenz, Germany.**
The Army's role in Europe comes to a close as Occupation duties in Germany are closed out. The U.S. flag flying over Fortress Ehrenbreitsen at Coblentz is lowered as U.S. Major General Henry T. Allen turns over command of the American area to the commander of French troops. The last remnant of the American Army of Occupation prepares to return home.

23 March. **American Battle Monuments Commission.**
Congress creates the American Battle Monuments Commission to be the federal agency responsible for honoring American service members who died overseas in the country's service. The first chairman is General Pershing, former AEF commander. He will remain head of the commission until 1948.

1 April. **Command in China.**
"American Forces in China," soon to be renamed "U.S. Army Forces in China," is created as the senior headquarters for U.S. Army troops protecting foreign

residential areas at Tientsin and guarding the line of communications to Peking. Army elements include two battalions of the 15th Infantry Regiment.

3 May. **Peacetime Work for Chemical Troops.**
The Chemical Warfare Service demonstrates a possible peacetime use for wartime techniques as an airplane is used to deploy a liquid spray for crops, orchards, and fields.

2–3 May. **Coast-to-Coast Flyers. Rockwell Field, California.**
Proving that troops and supplies can be moved from coast to coast in one day, two Army Air Service lieutenants, Oakley T. Kelly and John A. Macready, fly their upgraded T-2 Fokker monoplane from Roosevelt Field, New York, in a pioneering nonstop transcontinental flight which takes 27 hours. Their average speed over the 2,520-mile distance is 94 miles per hour. Macready makes the first in-flight engine repair in Army Air Service history when he replaces a defective voltage regulator en route to the west coast.

Above: *Members of Brigadier General Billy Mitchell's 1925 military court–martial board included Douglas MacArthur. (MacArthur Memorial and Archive, Norfolk, VA)*

Right: *Secretary of War Davis was a World War I veteran and oversaw the Army's first experiments in mechanization. ("Dwight Filley Davis," Douglas Chandor, Army Art Collection, NMUSA)*

Opposite, bottom: *2d Field Artillery Regiment (Mountain), as depicted circa 1927–1932. (James T. Jones, Company of Military Historians)*

1924

21 February. **Higher Education. Washington, D.C.**
The first class of the new Army Industrial College is convened as this institution is launched, destined to start a long run as one of the senior service schools operating under the direction of the War Department for the Army as a whole.

19 May. **Congress approves Army Bonus Bill.**
Congress approves $2 billion in 20-year annuities for Great War (World War I) veterans.

20 May. Babe Ruth Joins the Guard. New York, New York.

George Herman (Babe) Ruth joins the New York National Guard as a private in the 104th Field Artillery. The oath of enlistment is administered by regimental commander Colonel James E. Austin to help kick off a recruiting drive.

7 June. Army Takes on Boll Weevils. Washington, D.C.

Congress approves $25,000 for use by the Chemical Warfare Service to deploy newly-developed techniques which hopefully will destroy boll weevils threatening cotton crops.

July. Philippine Scout Mutiny.

Members of the Philippine Scouts mutiny in protest of inequity in pay and allowances with the Regular Army units. More than 200 are arrested, and most are discharged dishonorably.

22 July. Mitchell Predicts Future Conflict.

Following a Pacific area tour encompassing Hawaii, the Philippines, China, India, and Japan, the Army's controversial hero of the World War, Brigadier General Billy Mitchell, predicts the inevitability of a future attack by the Empire of Japan to be aimed at the U.S. naval bastion at Pearl Harbor in the Hawaiian Islands. He is ignored. Soon he is demoted to colonel; his controversial views on airpower will result in a court-martial.

13 September. Pershing Retires.

After 42 years in uniform—including cadet days at West Point, his heroic role in the Philippines, his command of forces on the Mexican Border, and command of the Army Expeditionary Force in France in the World War—General John J. Pershing retires from the Army and from his post as Army Chief of Staff. He is succeeded by Major General John L. Hines, one of his top battlefield lieutenants.

28 September. Army Pilots Around the World. Seattle, Washington.

Flying specially designed Douglas aircraft bearing the names *Boston, Chicago, New Orleans,* and *Seattle,* eight Army airmen complete a mission started on 6 April 1924—the first successful flight around the world. Five other countries, including France and Great Britain, were unsuccessful in similar efforts. *Seattle* and *Boston* crashed along the route, but the two remaining ships triumphantly finish the long grind.

Above: *On 14 September 1924, AEF veteran Major General Hines succeeded Pershing as Chief of Staff of the Army. ("John Leonard Hines," Joyce Ballantyne Brand, Army Art Collection, NMUSA)*

THE SOLDIER'S MEDAL

Established in 1926, the Soldier's Medal recognizes members of the armed forces who distinguished themselves by heroic actions not involving actual combat. There were 352 awards of the Soldier's Medal by 7 December 1941. The following is a sampling of incidents that resulted in its award.

First Lieutenant Henderson W. Allen, Philippine Scouts. When a fire broke out at the Fort William McKinley, Philippine Islands, gasoline station on 27 July 1928, Lieutenant Allen was 200 yards from the site when he saw the flames. He dashed to the station, where he succeeded in extinguishing the fire in the funnel through which gasoline was pouring into the tank. His heroic action prevented a serious explosion.

Private First Class Edward J. Woodfire, Battery A, 12th Coast Artillery. At Fort Monroe, Virginia, on 4 April 1931, an explosion occurred on board the U.S. Public Health Service ship, *Heron*. The vessel was engulfed in flames. Private Woodfire, serving as coxswain of a gasoline yawl, together with an engineer, took a line from *Heron* and towed the ship into deep water, away from other vessels and government property. He then assisted in bringing the yawl alongside the burning ship and removing its pilot to a place of safety. He exhibited great courage and skillful handling of the yawl in the face of danger of further explosion of gasoline tanks on board the *Heron*.

Captain Eduardo Andino, 27th Infantry Regiment. On 20 January 1932, south of Pohakea Pass, Oahu, Territory of Hawaii, a fellow officer fell from a steep mountaintop while on a training reconnaissance. He plunged a distance of 300 feet, breaking one leg and both shoulders. Captain Andino and eight soldiers from Company M, 27th Infantry, voluntarily descended the mountain to rescue the officer. They administered first aid and used their shirts to improvise a litter; they used other personal clothing to keep the injured officer warm. For more than four hours, Captain Andino and his party hacked out a trail through heavy jungle underbrush and carried the injured officer down this precarious trail to a hospital, thereby saving him from probable fatal effects of his injuries.

Private Millard Pugh, Medical Detachment, 32d Division Special Troops, Michigan National Guard. On 14 July 1932, while riding his horse into a lake to drink, Private Thomas Pobanz, who was unable to swim, was thrown by his mount. After struggling in the water, he lapsed into unconsciousness and sank to the bottom of the lake. Private Pugh swam out from the shore and succeeded in bringing the unconscious man to the surface. Pugh helped get Pobanz into a boat, where he was revived.

Private Eugene W. Banks, Company A, 24th Infantry Regiment. On 3 April 1936, when a fire engulfed a building at the Infantry School at Fort Benning, Georgia, Private Banks heard that an officer was trapped inside. With disregard for his own safety, Private Banks entered the building, where he was overcome by smoke and heat and temporarily blinded. After being evacuated he reentered the building and helped to save it from destruction.

Master Sergeant Benjamin Roth, U.S. Army Air Corps, for heroism while serving as airplane mechanic with the 1928–30 Byrd Antarctic Expedition. Just prior to the collapse of the Barrier Cliff, Sergeant Roth, with exceptional bravery and devotion to duty, continued with his work on the materiel stored on that portion of the cliff that was in constant danger of giving way. His fearlessness and dedication was of great importance to the expedition.

— *Vince Hawkins*

Above: *The Soldier's Medal authorized by an act of Congress on 2 July 1926. (Quintet Publishing Ltd., London)*

14 October. **Davis Appointed Secretary of War**
A World War I veteran of the 35th Division, Dwight F. Davis is approved to be the 49th Secretary of War. He supervises the Army's efforts at creating a mechanized force, and later serves as governor general of the Philippines.

28 October. **Mitchell Before Court-Martial. Washington, D.C.**
The court-martial of Colonel (former brigadier general) Billy Mitchell begins. He is accused of "conduct prejudicial to good order and military discipline" exacerbated by his outspoken style in promoting his advocacy of increased emphasis on military airpower. A prophet before his time, he is found guilty on 17 December; two months later he resigns from the Army, leaving behind a long and distinguished career.

21 November. **Summerall Replaces Hines as Chief of Staff.**
Lieutenant General Charles P. Summerall becomes the 12th Army Chief of Staff. Most of his career has been in the artillery. He served in China, the Philippines and as a brigade, division and corps commander in World War I.

Above: *Secretary of War Hurley brought wide military experience to the job and was recalled to active duty as a brigadier in 1942. ("Patrick Jay Hurley," Frank Townsend Hutchens, Army Art Collection, NMUSA)*

Below: *General Charles Summerall served as Army Chief of Staff from 21 November 1926 to 20 November 1930. (Ray Edward Goodbred, Army Art Collection, NMUSA)*

1926

28 May. **Remembering Cantigny. Upstate New York.**
Soldiers of the 28th Infantry Regiment at Fort Porter, Fort Ontario, and Fort Niagara (New York) commemorate the first organized offensive by U.S. forces in the battle of Cantigny, France, in the World War (28 May 1918). The 28th checks its morning reports and finds that it has 16 survivors of the battle among the 109 AEF veterans serving on active duty in the regiment.

21 June. **Graduation Day. Fort Leavenworth, Kansas.**
The class of 1926, consisting of 245 Army officers, completes the prestigious course at the Command and General Staff School. An infantry officer, Major Dwight D. Eisenhower, is named the honor man of the class.

2 July. **Army Air Corps Established.**
In an important recognition of the need to emphasize the role of aviation, the Army Air Corps is established as a separate branch of the Army. It is thus severed

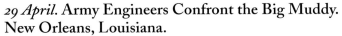

from its long-standing status under the Signal Corps. No longer is it to be known as the "Air Service."

2 July. The Soldier's Medal.

Congress authorizes recognition for heroism by military personnel in noncombat action. The first soldier to be awarded The Soldier's Medal is Staff Sergeant Arlie L. Downey, Finance Department, U.S. Army, for his heroism during explosions at the Lake Denmark Naval Ammunition Depot near Dover, New Jersey, on 10 July 1926.

31 December. Soldiers' "New Look."

The "choker" collar of the soldier's service coat—introduced during the war years—is replaced by a notch-lapel collar. The Army's "new look" uniform will, however, remain a single-breasted sack coat of the now-familiar olive drab wool. Many soldiers will continue to wear the old-style collars until new uniforms can be furnished.

29 April. Army Engineers Confront the Big Muddy. New Orleans, Louisiana.

Army engineer troops use dynamite to explode a large section of Mississippi River levee 15 miles below New Orleans, carrying out a dramatic plan to divert flood waters and secure large parts of the city under threat of destruction.

2 May. Pan-American Goodwill Flight. Bolling Field, D.C.

Weary after a spectacular 20,500-mile flight from San Antonio, Texas, by way of stops in Central and South American countries, eight Army pilots receive the new Distinguished Flying Cross medals from President Calvin Coolidge. The Army fliers made their 133-day odyssey, the "Pan American Goodwill Flight," in brand new Loening OA-1A airplanes. They were led by Major Herbert A. Dargue as they braved unknown terrain and hostile weather conditions to complete the mission.

20–21 May. Historic Solo Flight Across the Atlantic.

Captain Charles A. Lindbergh, a Missouri National Guard pilot, receives the Army's Distinguished Flying Cross (actually presented 11 June) for his daring solo flight across the Atlantic from New York City to Paris, France, 20–21 May. Lindbergh is on leave from the 110th Observation Squadron, Missouri National Guard. He is presented the Medal of Honor (December 1928) and rewarded with a commission as a colonel in the Army Air Corps Reserve.

28 June. Mainland-to-Hawaii Flight. Oahu, Territory of Hawaii.

In a daring trans-Pacific flight, two Army fliers—Lieutenants Lester J. Maitland and Albert F. Hegenberger—in a Fokker C-2 trimotor monoplane *Bird of Paradise* make landfall in Hawaii after a trail-blazing flight that originated in Oakland, California.

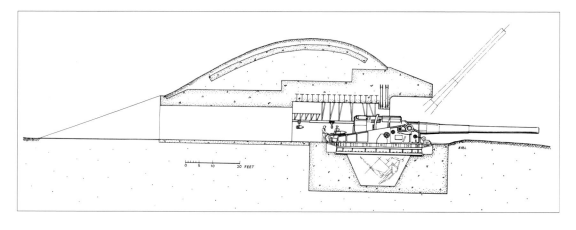

Left: *The U.S. coastal defenses included this sophisticated design for Battery Davis, with its impressive 16-inch guns that were installed to defend San Francisco Bay. (Emanuel R. Lewis)*

The Army Chief of Staff, Lieutenant General Summerall, declares that "the flight has made the reinforcement of the islands from a point on the mainland a matter of assurance and a few hours."

1928

23 February. **Army Chief to Wear Four Stars. Washington, D.C.**
Congress approves the four-star rank of general for the position of Army Chief of Staff. The first beneficiary of the new law is the incumbent Chief, Charles P. Summerall.

18 August. **Randolph Field "in the Army now." San Antonio, Texas.**
"West Point of the Air" launched as Randolph Field is formally turned over to the Army by city officials. Army airmen express confidence that operations will start 25 October 1931. Randolph is soon recognized as one of the world's finest military aviation schools.

28 September. **Parachute as Troop Transportation. Brooks Field, Texas.**
A closely watched demonstration said to hold important implications for the future takes place at this air base near San Antonio. Eighteen soldiers and three containers of equipment are successfully dropped by parachute for the first time.

1929

1–7 January. **Endurance Record Set by Army Fliers. Los Angeles, California.**
Air-to-air refueling techniques enable an Army Air Corps team flying a Fokker C-2 trimotor monoplane, *Question Mark*, circling aloft over Los Angeles, to set a new endurance record. The crew consists of Major Carl ("Tooey") Spaatz, Captain Ira C. Eaker, and Lieutenants Harry Halveson and Elwood ("Pete") Quesada. Engine trouble forces Spaatz to land after 150 hours, 40 minutes in the sky. The flight uses 5,205 gallons of fuel and 202 gallons of oil. Critical to the success of the mission: 37 efficient mid-air transfers of fuel from a pair of Douglas C-1Cs. The four intrepid airmen would go on to important roles in military aviation in future years.

Left: *Training at Pinecamp, New York, during August 1935 included infantry and light armor working in tandem, a tactic that would be employed a few years later in World War II. (National Archives)*

Below: *The adoption of the Army General Staff Badge indicated the growing prestige of the general staff from its origins early in the twentieth century. (U.S. Army Institute of Heraldry)*

4 March. **President Hoover Inaugurated**
Herbert C. Hoover becomes the 31st President and Commander-in-Chief of the Armed Forces.

6 March. **Good Appointed Secretary of War**
President Hoover appoints James W. Good to be 51st Secretary of War. Good dies after only nine months in office.

March–April. **Tension at the Mexican Border.**
As American lives and American property are in jeopardy, there is bad blood all along a troubled border with Mexico. Army troops are dispatched to several critical points and air patrols are widely used. Critical negotiations are conducted by Brigadier General George Van Horn Moseley.

1930

20 January. **Dry Days for the Army Worldwide.**
The War Department issues instructions stating that the nation's Prohibition Laws (the Volstead Act) banning the sale of liquor products applies to U.S. military forces throughout the world.

1931

3 March. **"Star-Spangled Banner" Adopted.**
Congress approves an act designating "The Star-Spangled Banner" as the national anthem of the United States. The song refers to the successful defense by soldiers of Fort McHenry against a British fleet attempting to capture Baltimore during the War of 1812. (See Chapter IV.)

31 March. **Engineers in Central America. Managua, Nicaragua.**
Members of the U.S. Army engineer battalion engaging in relief work here as a result of the disastrous earthquake and fire cope with enormous problems. The city's water supply is reported

Right: *In the fall of 1933, Maryland National Guardsmen took to the streets of Salisbury to secure four suspects from a lynch mob. (Washington Post, AP/Wire World Photo)*

destroyed, leaving only scant means of stopping the fire that is rapidly consuming the area. As the engineers deploy demolition charges to block the spread of the fire, the city continues to be shaken with tremors that cause walls and roof tiles to rain down on unsheltered personnel.

1932

21 January. Airborne Mercy Mission. Winslow, Arizona.
Six Army bombers drop five tons of supplies to snowbound Navajo Indians. Many lives are saved.

1 February. 31st Infantry to Shanghai. China.
As Japanese attack Chinese troops in the Shanghai area, the United States reinforces the 4th Marine Regiment. To ensure that adequate forces are available to protect U.S. interests, the 31st Infantry Regiment is ordered from the Philippines to assist in the defense of the International Settlement. The 31st trades its tropical khaki for winter wool taken out of World War I stocks. After four months in China, the 31st will return in June to the Philippines—and its date with destiny on Bataan ten years in the future.

22 February. Purple Heart Reestablished.
The Army designates the Purple Heart Medal—based on George Washington's Badge of Military Merit—to

be the decoration soldiers are to receive in recognition of wounds sustained in combat operations.

9 May. Solo Flight by Instrument.
Captain Albert F. Hegenberger, Army Air Corps, completes the first solo flight entirely by instruments. Hegenberger, already well known for his part in the 1927 flight to Hawaii, made a takeoff, maintained flight for 15 minutes and then completed the mission with a safe landing in an aircraft "hooded" to prevent any visual observation.

July. Army Pay Reduced.
To meet budget shortages, Congress reduces the pay of all officers and soldiers by 10 percent.

28 July. Bonus March Veterans Dispersed. Washington, D.C.
Secretary of War Patrick J. Hurley issues an executive order to Army Chief of Staff General Douglas MacArthur to remove the Bonus March veterans from the public areas and abandoned buildings where they have set up camp. The veterans have come to Washington seeking accelerated payment of the annuity bonus promised by Congress, and violence has occurred with D.C. police. Accompanied by his senior aide, Major Dwight D. Eisenhower, MacArthur uses four horse-mounted troops of the 3d Cavalry and four companies from the 16th Infantry Brigade accompanied by six Renault tanks to push the veterans back. Presidential orders not to enter the main camp

do not reach MacArthur until his men are already there. Angry veterans set fire to the camp as soldiers and police move them and their families out.

9 August. Reorganization Creates Field Armies.
The War Department creates four field armies for management of training and administration of forces within the continental limits of the United States: First Army (Governors Island, New York), Second Army (Chicago, Illinois), 3d Army (Atlanta, Georgia, and Fort Sam Houston, Texas), and Fourth Army (Omaha, Nebraska).

1933

4 March. Franklin Roosevelt Becomes President.
Franklin Delano Roosevelt is inaugurated as 33rd President and Commander-in-Chief. He immediately appoints George H. Dern as 53rd Secretary of War. Dern will die in office in August 1936.

7 April. First To Enroll in CCC. Alexandria, Virginia.
Henry Rich of Alexandria is officially first in line to enroll in the Civilian Conservation Corps (CCC). The newly created agency is designed to combat effects of the Depression by establishing programs for unemployed young men and war veterans who will work in forests, parks, and range lands. The Army is to run the camps. Reserve officers will play an important role as the nationwide program takes shape.

15 June. "Dual Status" for Guard Members.
As a result of the new National Defense Act, the Militia Bureau in the War Department is now the National Guard Bureau. Members of the National Guard now have "dual status" as members of their state's military force and of a new entity, "the National Guard of the United States." The President gains authority to call the Guard into active federal service as needed. (The Guard in its entirety was "drafted" in 1917.)

1934

9 February. Army Delivers the Mail.
President Franklin D. Roosevelt orders the Army to provide airmail service on 26 vital air routes because of concerns regarding commercial contract fraud claims.

5 July. Guard on Alert. San Francisco, California.
The California National Guard sends troops to the waterfront Embarcadero to maintain law and order, and a high-ranking officer warns that "law and order will be maintained at any cost."

Above: *Secretary of War. ("Harry Hines Woodring," Tino Costa, Army Art Collection, NMUSA)*

Below, left: *The Purple Heart Medal was based upon the Revolutionary-era Badge of Merit and approved for presentation to Army personnel wounded or killed in action. (Quintet Publishing Ltd., London)*

Below, right: *The Silver Star Medal was adopted to recognize Army personnel for gallantry in action. (Quintet Publishing Ltd., London)*

29 July. Up, Up, and Away. Black Hills, South Dakota.
Army airmen aboard the balloon *Explorer* set a new altitude record of 60,613 feet (14 miles), but misfortune overtakes them during descent as the bag tears and an explosion follows. Major William Kepner and Captain Orvil Anderson, future Air Force generals, and Captain Albert Stevens (head of the Army Air Corps photo lab at Wright Field, Ohio) bail out of the gondola and land by parachute in a Nebraska cornfield.

7–8 September. Disaster at Sea. Asbury Park, New Jersey.
The cruise ship S.S. *Morro Castle*, bound for New York from Havana, Cuba, founders offshore between Asbury Park and Sea Girt. Four aircraft from the New Jersey National Guard 44th Division's 119th Observation Squadron are dispatched to make a reconnaissance to determine what kind of help is needed. The Guardsmen will be used to direct surface vessels to survivors in the choppy waters.

Above: *Warrant officers filled many specialized positions in the increasingly technical Army. ("The Quiet Professional," Don Stivers)*

1935

1 March. Air Corps Gains Status.
A "General Headquarters for the Air Forces" is created within the War Department to provide control over all tactical air units in the Continental United States. The commander reports directly to the Army Chief of Staff rather than to the Chief of the Army Air Corps.

21 March. Highest Award To Greely.
The second award of the Medal of Honor for peacetime achievement is presented to Major General (Retired) Adolphus W. Greely for his long career in public service, which began on 26 July 1861 when he enlisted as a private in the U.S. Army. His career led him to promotion to major general on 10 February 1906. (The other peacetime award of the Medal of Honor was to Charles A. Lindbergh in 1928.)

GEORGE C. MARSHALL: ORGANIZER OF VICTORY

For his service during World War II, Winston Churchill called him "the true organizer of victory," while President Harry Truman stated he was "the greatest military man that this country has ever produced."

George Catlett Marshall, Jr., was born on 31 December 1880 in Uniontown, Pennsylvania. Graduating from the Virginia Military Institute in 1901, Marshall was commissioned a second lieutenant on 3 February 1902 and the next year became a company officer in the Philippines. He attended the Infantry-Cavalry School at Fort Leavenworth in 1906, then serving as an instructor there from 1908 to 1910.

From 1913 to 1917, Marshall served as an acting chief of staff, a general's aide, and a chief of operations. Captain Marshall joined the 1st Infantry Division in 1917, serving first as training officer and then as chief of operations. Selected for General John J. Pershing's AEF staff, Marshall was instrumental in planning the St. Mihiel and the Meuse-Argonne offensives. In 1920, he was promoted to major and served the next four years as Pershing's aide.

In 1923, Lieutenant Colonel Marshall was posted to the 15th Infantry Regiment in Tientsin, China. After teaching at the National War College, he became assistant commandant at the Infantry School at Fort Benning. Over the next five years Marshall revolutionized the Army's officer training program, rewriting the training manuals to emphasize simplicity, realism, innovation and mobility, and leadership.

In 1932, Marshall was promoted to colonel and for the next four years worked closely with National Guard units and helped develop camps for the Civilian Conservation Corps. He was given command of the Fifth Infantry Brigade when he was promoted to brigadier general in 1936. Recalled to the Army General Staff in 1938, Marshall became head of the War Plans Division, then in April 1939, acting Chief of Staff. On 1 September 1939, Marshall was promoted to general and appointed Army Chief of Staff. Marshall quickly began bringing the Army up to its authorized strength and preparing for war. He visited training camps, advised on instruction, culled the officer corps, and repeatedly applied to Congress to develop a large, well-balanced military force. By late 1941, the strength of the Army had increased from 225,000 to 1.4 million, and by 1945 to 8.3 million men.

In 1942, Marshall reorganized the War Department and became the key figure in both the U.S. Joint Chiefs of Staff and the Anglo-American Combined Chiefs of Staff as Roosevelt's primary military advisor.

Marshall retired on 18 November 1945. He was promoted to general of the Army (five-star rank) in December 1944. Within 48 hours, President Truman asked Marshall to become special emissary to China. In January 1947, he returned and was appointed Secretary of State. Over the next two years Marshall reorganized the State Department to deal with the Cold War and devised the European Recovery Program, or "Marshall Plan."

In 1949, for health reasons, Marshall resigned again, but the outbreak of the Korean War in 1950 caused Truman to recall Marshall to duty as Secretary of Defense. Marshall helped rebuild the Army and increase the resources to fight in Korea.

In September 1951, Marshall retired as Secretary, and in 1953 he became the first professional soldier to receive the Nobel Peace Prize. He died in Walter Reed Army Hospital on 16 October 1959.

—*Vince Hawkins*

Above: *General George C. Marshall assumed the duties of the Army Chief of Staff on 1 September 1939. ("Ernest Hamlin Baker," The George C Marshall Foundation, Lexington, VA)*

Right: *Brigadier General Adna R. Chaffee, dubbed the "father of armor," led pioneer efforts to develop that branch in the interwar years. ("The American Soldier, 1938," H. Charles McBarron, Army Art Collection, NMUSA)*

1 October. **MacArthur Departs for Manila Post. Washington, D.C.**

After five years in the top Army job, General Douglas MacArthur leaves the post of Chief of Staff. He is named military advisor to the president of the Philippines, Manuel Quezon. MacArthur selects Major Dwight D. Eisenhower to be his chief of staff in Manila.

2 October. **Malin Craig becomes New Chief of Staff**

Major General Malin Craig is promoted to general to serve as the 14th Army Chief of Staff. He is a veteran cavalryman with service in Cuba, China, France, Germany and Panama.

11 November. **Army Balloonists Aloft in Record Flight. Rapid City, South Dakota.**

Taking historic photographs which for the first time show the earth's curvature, the Army balloon *Explorer II* reaches 72,395 feet, setting a world altitude record that will endure for 21 years. The crew, reduced to Captains Anderson and Stevens since the July 1934 flight, employ the first helium balloon for the eight-hour, 13-minute odyssey.

1936

25 September. Woodring Selected to Replace Dern.
Assistant Secretary Harry H. Woodring is approved to serve as the 54th Secretary of War. Woodring was an enlisted man and officer in the tank corps in World War I. He serves until 20 June 1940.

27 October. Marshall Takes Command. Vancouver Barracks, Washington.
Newly promoted Brigadier General George C. Marshall, one of Pershing's principal staff officers in the AEF during World War I, takes command of the 3d Division's 5th Infantry Brigade. The assignment also entails responsibility for 35 CCC camps and the CMTC in the northwest. The promotion evokes praise from retired General Pershing, Marshall's commander in World War days.

9 December. Safety Record Earns Trophy.
The Columbian Trophy is awarded to the 3d Attack Group, Army Air Forces, for having achieved the best flying safety record for the year.

1937

1 March. Army's "Bomber of Future." Seattle, Washington.
The Boeing Company delivers the Army's first B-17, which is quickly dubbed the "Flying Fortress." The big four-engine airplane is acclaimed as the first to meet the Army's specifications for high-speed, long-range, and high-altitude capabilities. It will prove to be the workhorse bombardment aircraft of World War II.

21 September. AEF Relives Glory Days. New York City, New York.
The American Legion—150,000 strong, wearing uniforms and insignia reminiscent of the World War

era, and carrying battle flags—marches down Fifth Avenue to City Hall in one of the greatest patriotic outpourings in the nation's history. The marathon event lasts nearly 18 hours and 3.5 million onlookers barter choice vantage points to cheer the veterans.

1938

7 January. **Uniform Modernization.**
Soldiers express mixed feelings as yet another item in the Army inventory goes by the wayside. The use of spiral khaki, wrap-around leggings is discontinued, and the Army adopts more practical canvas leggings, long a prerogative of the cavalry, as a standard item for the field uniform.

2 March. **Out of China. Tientsin, China.**
The role of foreign forces in China under old treaty agreements is no longer viable as a result of Japanese aggression in northern China. The United States withdraws the 15th Infantry Regiment after 26 years in and around Tientsin. Thus ends the mission of the command known as "U.S. Army Troops in China" and a presence dating back to the Boxer Rebellion. The 15th Infantry heads for Fort Lewis, Washington, and soon is assigned to the 5th Brigade, 3d Division.

29 September. **"Hap" Arnold Heads Air Corps.**
Major General Henry H. (Hap) Arnold, pilot certificate No. 29, circa 1911, is named the chief of the Army Air Corps, and he starts the task of building the team that will in time became the world's greatest air power.

1939

9 January. **Garand is New Army Rifle.**
The Army adopts the .30-caliber M-1 semi-automatic Garand (named for inventor John Garand) as its standard rifle. This will be the principal weapon for the individual soldier in the U.S. Army and the armies of many allies in and after World War II, and it will remain in production until the 1950s. Selection of the Garand brings to an end a protracted competition in which the Marine Corps lobbies for adoption of the Johnson semi-automatic rifle. The Garand can fire an eight-round clip in 20 seconds.

12 January. **Bigger Army Air Corps.**
A presidential message to Congress indicates that production of aircraft will be a major national priority. This marks the start of significant growth of the Army Air Corps.

Opposite: *During the Depression some Army Regular and Reserve officers gained leadership experience by directing projects, such as bridge building, with the Civilian Conservation Corps. (Office, Chief of Army Reserve)*

Above: *In its many years of presence in China, the 15th U.S. Infantry had a number of future generals assigned to it. ("15th Infantry, American Barracks, Tientsin, China, 1925," Frederic E. Ray, Jr., Company of Military Historians)*

1 April. **Last Coast Artillery Chief.**
Major General Joseph A. Green is named the chief of Coast Artillery; he will be the last officer to serve in this assignment as the position is destined to be eliminated in an Army reorganization that takes place soon after Pearl Harbor.

8 August. **Cavalry Brigade Mechanized. Plattsburg, New York.**
The 7th Cavalry Brigade (Mechanized) arrives in this upstate New York location following a triumphal journey from Fort Knox, Kentucky. The unique,

HORSESHOES TO BRAKESHOES: MECHANIZATION OF THE ARMY

At the start of the twentieth century the U.S. Army was a horse-mobile force, depending on horses for transport, reconnaissance, and offensive mobility. Creation of a reliable internal-combustion engine mounted on wheels caused heated debates as to whether motor transport had its place. A prevailing opinion among Army officers was that nothing ever could—or would—replace the horse.

Experimentation with motor transport took place slowly. In 1902, the Ordnance Department purchased a battery wagon, probably the first truck in Army service. In 1903, the Surgeon General requested several companies to design a motorized ambulance for use as a test vehicle. By 1911, the Army owned a total of 12 trucks of various sizes and manufacture.

On 8 February 1912, the Army's first cross-country motor transport field test was conducted with four one-ton trucks driving from Washington, D.C., to Fort Benjamin Harrison, Indiana. Despite primitive road conditions and crude vehicles, the convoy successfully completed the 1,500-mile journey, arriving on 28 March. A second test using seven one-ton and six three-ton trucks to supply a regiment on a field march also proved successful. These tests clearly indicated that motor transport had a viable future.

General Pershing's Mexican Expeditionary Force in 1916–1917 provided the first combat field test of motor transport. Although the Army's inventory listed only 1,000 motorized vehicles of all types and manufacture, Pershing requested five motorized supply trains, each of 27 vehicles. His request was granted and by the end of the campaign over 500 vehicles were employed in the expedition. When the United States entered World War I on 6 April 1917, the number of Army trucks had increased to 2,400.

Pershing estimated the AEF's motor transport needs in the "first mechanized war" at 50,000 trucks. The Motor Transport Corps was established to provide these vehicles for the AEF. The Corps had several truck companies, each comprising 33 trucks and 70 men. By 1918, 294 American manufacturers had produced some 227,000 trucks for service. The horse Remount Service was also enlarged, providing some 571,000 horses and mules during the war. By war's end the ratio of horses and mules to motor vehicles in the AEF was still 2.8 to 1.

In 1919, the Army Transport Corps was created and the improvements in motor transport were tested by a coast-to-coast military convoy. The convoy completed the journey in two months, the same time it had taken the 1911 convoy to cover half that distance. In 1928, a major change took place with the creation of the Experimental Mechanized Brigade. This unit had tanks as well as truck-towed artillery and truck-borne infantry. The experiment failed due to outdated equipment, but in 1930 a Mechanized Force was created that employed better equipment and, with certain organizational changes, evolved into the 7th Cavalry Brigade (Mechanized). This unit was the start of the Armored Force in 1940.

When the Army prepared for war in 1940, it was estimated that it would require 200,000 horses. As mobilization proceeded, however, most units converted to motor transport, leaving the Remount Service to spend the war disposing of horses instead of procuring them.

World War II forced the Army to undergo a rapid dismounting program. The 1st Cavalry Division dismounted in April–May 1943, followed by the 2d Cavalry Division in March 1944. The Army horse had become a memory, replaced by the truck, tank, and airplane.

—*Vince Hawkins*

Above: *A squad from the 6th U.S. Infantry dismount from a truck during the Punitive Expedition in Mexico, 1916. (National Archives)*

Right: *Soon after World War I, the 9th Airship Company was organized to man observation balloons and other airships at Fort Omaha, Nebraska, where a balloon school was formed. (George M. Langellier, Jr., Collection)*

experimental unit under Brigadier General Adna R. Chaffee participates successfully in 1st Army maneuvers.

30 August. World's Fair Crowds Hail "Iron" Cavalry. Flushing Meadows, New York.

The Seventh Cavalry Brigade (Mechanized) arrives at the New York World's Fair, having been sent by the War Department to represent the Army. The newly mechanized cavalry unit is soon recognized as one of the outstanding attractions at the fair.

1 September. President Roosevelt Picks New Army Chief. Washington, D.C.

On the very day that war erupts in Europe, General George Catlett Marshall—the first Army Chief of Staff commissioned from a civilian college training program—takes office. Marshall is an alumnus of the Virginia Military Institute (VMI). The Army consists of 174,000 men—soon to be increased to 210,000—scattered over 130 different locations.

1 September. Panzers Roll into Poland—World War II Starts.

Germany invades Poland and is challenged by Great Britain and France in response to treaty obligations. World War II is underway as the United States announces a policy of neutrality but starts to focus on the status of military preparedness.

8 September. Limited National Emergency.

President Roosevelt reviews the war "now unhappily existing between certain nations" and calls for "strengthening of the national defense within the limits of peace-time authorizations." The Army, as well as the Navy, is put on notice that training and increased "preparedness" are now the order of the day in a time of "a limited national emergency."

16 September. Divisions Streamlined for Modern Battlefield.

Following field testing by the provisional 2d Division under the command of Major General Walter Krueger, the Army decides upon the "triangular" structure of the new division as the backbone of the emerging fighting force. The new division structure is built around three combat infantry regiments with appropriate field artillery as well as service and support elements. The 2d Division is the first to convert to the new structure, quickly followed by the 1st and 3d Divisions.

23 September. A Legend is Born. Camp Holabird, Maryland.

After an emergency call to U.S. industry, the American Bantam Car Company delivers a prototype vehicle for testing. The Army soon finds this to be the answer to its search for a new vehicle to replace its aging fleet of motorcycles and light trucks. Officially to be known as the "truck, one-quarter ton" and soon to be mass produced by the Willys-Overland Company and Ford, this is the Army's, and the world's, introduction to the "jeep." There would be approximately 650,000 produced in the next five years, and the "jeep" would become the soldier's favorite vehicle.

1 October. Army War College.

Fort Humphreys, District of Columbia, takes on a new name—the Army War College. This name will, after World War II, give way to the name by which the famed waterfront Army post is still known: Fort Lesley J. McNair.

2 October. **Army Buildup in Progress.**
The 5th Division, formed at Fort McClellan, Alabama, returns to the active rolls—the first of a series of reactivated Regular Army divisions scheduled to take shape as the Army expands to increase preparedness. Next to be formed is the 6th Division, on 12 October at Fort Lewis, Washington. The new divisions, formed in accordance with new divisional doctrine, will feature a trimmed-down strength of approximately 15,000 in contrast to the 28,105 required to man the old "square" divisions.

1 November. **Army Rations Modernized.**
The infamous "corned willy" is to be a thing of the past as newly designed "C-rations" are adopted as standard for Army in the field. (In 1944 important changes are made to the makeup of C-rations.)

1940

18 January. **Luke Trophy Awarded. Selfridge Field, Michigan.**
The Frank Luke Trophy for the highest gunnery average of the year in the General Headquarters (GHQ) Air Force is presented to the 94th Pursuit Squadron. The trophy is named for the World War hero. Luke is credited with 18 victories in 17 days but lost his life when, severely wounded, he refused to surrender and continued to fire his pistol until he was killed. The 94th Pursuit is the successor to the 94th Aero ("Hat in the Ring"). Eddie Rickenbacker was among its many World War aces. As the 94th Fighter Squadron it will serve with distinction in World War II.

23 January. **Pioneering Troop Airlift. Hamilton Field, California.**
The Army tests the feasibility of movement of units by air. A battalion of the 65th Coast Artillery is loaded into 38 bombers and flown 500 miles to a test destination.

Opposite, top: *After a long absence from the post, Henry Lewis Stimson was called upon again to serve as Secretary of War. (Fred W. Wright, Army Art Collection, NMUSA)*

Opposite, bottom: *Sergeant "Red" King was a member of the Test Parachute Platoon, Fort Benning, GA, that was the Army's early effort to establish an airborne capability. (U.S. Army)*

Above: *A display of Army weaponry and readiness, circa 1940. (National Archives)*

26 February. **First Continental Air Defense Command.**

The Army establishes the Air Defense Command to plan and supervise the U.S. air defenses. The capabilities of modern aircraft make it necessary for the first time to consider air attacks on North America possible.

21 April. **U.S. Officer Casualty in Europe. Oslo, Norway.**

Confirmation is received that Captain Robert M. Losey, an Army Air Corps military attaché in Norway, has been killed in a German air raid. He is the first American military officer to die in World War II. The 31-year-old New Jersey native graduated from West Point in 1929.

3 June. **Divisions Return to Rolls.**

After an absence from the rolls of the Army since the end of the World War, the 4th Division is activated at Fort Benning, Georgia. It is joined in the burgeoning active duty force by the 8th Division (1 July at Fort Jackson, South Carolina), the 7th Division (7 July at Fort Ord, California), and the 9th Division (1 August at Fort Bragg, North Carolina).

10 June. **Italy Enters the War.**

Italy declares war alongside Nazi Germany. Dictator Benito Mussolini states that Italy considers herself at war with France and Great Britain, fulfilling pledges he made to German Chancellor Adolph Hitler.

14 June. **Plattsburg Revisited?**

Corps Area commanders are given authority to conduct pre-World War I-style special training courses concurrently with CMTC in 1940. In the tradition of the 1915–1916 "Plattsburg Camps," this is designed to attract 3,000 business and professional men who will pay their own way to don olive drab. The camps are underway when it is announced on 24 July 1940 that the program is to be terminated.

14 June. **German Troops Enter Paris.**

France appeals to the United States for help as the German Army marches into Paris. "Our divisions are decimated. Generals are commanding battalions. France will go under like a drowning man and disappear after having cast a last look towards the land of liberty from which she awaited salvation."

6 July. **Guard Ready for Service. Washington, D.C.**

Major General John F. Williams, chief of the National Guard Bureau, reports to the War Department that the Guard, manned by 235,000 men, is ready for active service when and if needed. He notes that Guard divisions and observation squadrons will participate in August maneuvers on a record scale. (President Roosevelt recently asked Congress to grant to him authority to order the Guard to the colors to stimulate the national defense effort.)

10 July. **Stimson Becomes Secretary.**

Former Ambassador and Secretary of State Henry L. Stimson becomes the 55th Secretary of War. Stimson is a veteran of World War I. He was Governor General of the Philippines and a brigadier general in the Organized Reserve Corps.

10 July. Request for Defense Funding.
President Roosevelt announces that the administration is seeking equipment for a land force of 1,200,000, "though, of course, this total of men would not be in the Army in time of peace." He also calls for procurement of 15,000 airplanes for the Army.

10 July. Tankers Gain Identity.
No longer required by law to keep its tanks under the infantry branch, the Army forms the Armored Force and announces that it is to be led by Adna R. Chaffee. General Chaffee will go down in Army lore as the "Father of the Armored Force."

15 July. First Two Armored Divisions.
A scant two months after the Nazi panzer forces overrun France, the Army forms its first two armored divisions. With the Seventh Cavalry Brigade (Mechanized) as its core element, the 1st Armored Division (eventually to earn fame as "Old Ironsides") is activated at Fort Knox, Kentucky. On the same date the 2d Armored Division is activated at Fort Benning, Georgia.

18 July. Parachute Soldiers. Fort Benning, Georgia.
With 48 enlisted volunteers from the 29th Infantry Regiment, the parachute test platoon is established. It is headed by Lieutenants William T. Ryder and James A. Bassett, with Warrant Officer Harry M. Wilson as the jump technique instructor. Ryder and Bassett are recent West Point graduates.

25 July. McNair Heads Training. Army War College, Washington, D.C.
For the first time in 20 years the Army opens a General Headquarters much like the GHQ that directed World War I field operations. The new

command, under Brigadier General Lesley J. McNair, is concerned only with enhancement of training as the War Department seeks increased emphasis on readiness. McNair reports directly to General Marshall, Army Chief of Staff.

16 August. Parachute Platoon Hits Silk. Fort Benning, Georgia.
Putting airborne warfare theories into practical terms, the Army Parachute Test Platoon, established on 18 July, makes its first parachute jump. The jump is led by the 26-year-old Ryder, who is destined to command a parachute infantry regiment in European combat. Later in the month, the test platoon is moved to a special training field near Hightstown, New Jersey, where two 125-foot parachute jump towers (similar to those at the New York World's Fair) have been constructed by a retired naval officer.

6 September. Patton Takes Command. Fort Benning, Georgia.
Brigadier (soon to be Major) General George S. Patton, Jr., is named acting commander of the 2d

Above: *In 1933 the Army signed a contract with Boeing for 111 P-26A "Peashooter" fighters in a move to upgrade air power capabilities. (John H. Batchelor)*

Opposite, top: *In the 1930s, the new Army Air Corps used a shoulder sleeve insignia with a stylized three-bladed propeller. (American Society of Military Insignia Collectors)*

Opposite, bottom: *The second version of the U.S. Army Air Corps (and the subsequent Army Air Forces) shoulder sleeve insignia was adopted in March 1942 featuring upswept wings and a star below. (American Society of Military Insignia Collectors)*

EAGLE'S WINGS: THE ARMY AIR CORPS

While the Army traces its aviation history to the balloons used during the Civil War, the first major step in modern aviation came 1 August 1907, when the Aeronautics Division of the Army Signal Corps was created. Tasked with "ballooning, air machines, and all kindred subjects," the Aeronautics Division began with one officer, two enlisted men, and one civilian.

On 23 December 1907, the Army issued Specification No. 486, for a "Heavier-than-air Flying Machine." The Wright brothers delivered their plane, built under contract, to Fort Myer, Virginia, on 20 August 1908. After several trials and one crash fatality, the Wrights returned with an improved version of the plane, and on 2 August 1909, the Wright Flyer was designated Signal Corps Airplane No. 1, the world's first military airplane. Also in August, the Corps accepted the Baldwin dirigible, designated Signal Corps Dirigible No. 1.

In 1911, Congress approved the first budget for military aviation, $125,000, and by 1913 the Signal Corps Aviation School was established at North Island in San Diego Bay, California. On 18 July 1914, the Signal Corps established an Aviation Section with the 1st Aero Squadron comprising 12 officers, 54 enlisted men, and six airplanes.

In March 1916, the squadron became the Army's first "tactical air unit" and gained experience supporting the Mexican Expedition. On 21 May 1918, the Aviation Section was reorganized and renamed the Army Air Service. When the United States entered World War I on 6 April 1917, the Air Service had 131 officers, 1,087 enlisted men, and some 300 airplanes. At war's end, the Air Service had 45 aerial squadrons (including pursuit, observation, and bombing units) and 33 balloon companies serving in Europe—more than 190,000 personnel and 11,000 aircraft.

Following the war, the Air Service was reduced to 10,000 personnel, but air officers, most notably Brigadier General William Mitchell, lobbied for an independent air force. The Air Corps Act of 2 July 1926 changed the Air Service to a separate Army branch, the Army Air Corps, and set a five-year expansion goal. By June 1932, the Air Corps had 1,709 planes and 14,705 personnel. In the 1930s aircraft technology developed better engines and all-metal aircraft.

The Army created General Headquarters (GHQ) Air Force in March 1935 under Major General Henry Arnold, placing all combat aviation under one command. The Air Corps would manage material and training, while GHQ Air Force (later Air Force Combat Command) directed operational units. GHQ Air Force went beyond the established mission of supporting ground troops to include long-range bombardment, observation, and defense from sea attack.

With the outbreak of war in Europe in 1939, President Roosevelt called for the production of 50,000 planes a year. On 20 June 1941, the Army Air Forces (AAF) was created to provide unity of command over air activities. By December 1941 the AAF had 354,000 personnel and 2,846 airplanes, but only 1,157 planes were combat ready. In June 1942, the Army placed separate air capability within some units, such as artillery. During the war, the AAF provided transport, ground support, coastal defense, and strategic bombing missions. By August 1945, it numbered 2,253,000 personnel, roughly 31 percent of the Army's strength.

On 26 July 1947, President Truman signed the National Security Act, providing for an independent U.S. Air Force and leaving the Army with the aviation assets organic to its units. From this has developed the modern Army aviation program.

—*Vince Hawkins*

Left: *The Curtiss P-6E Hawk was adopted by the Army to improve its air arm. (John H. Batchelor)*

Opposite: *Men of the 189th Field Artillery depart in 1940 for what was to be one year of training. It would be five years before the survivors returned. ("Goodbye, Dear, I'll Be Back in a Year," Mort Künstler, National Guard Heritage Print)*

("Hell on Wheels") Armored Division, and in December the assignment is made permanent. He leads the division to acclaim in the 1941 Tennessee Maneuvers. For Patton this command is the first major step along the road that leads him to high command in wartime.

16 September. **President Roosevelt Signs Draft Law.**
President Roosevelt signs the first peacetime Selective Service and Training Law. In addition to draftees, the Army gets authority to mobilize National Guard units and to call up members of the Officers Reserve Corps. The plan is that drafted men, mobilized Guardsmen, and Reservists will spend one year on active duty.

16 September. **"Goodbye, Dear, I'll See You in a Year . . ."**
The 30th (Tennessee, Georgia, North Carolina), 41st (Washington, Oregon), 44th (New Jersey, New York), and 45th (Oklahoma, Arizona, Colorado, New Mexico) Divisions, composed of National Guardsmen, are in the first increment of units called to the colors for "one year of training."

27 September. **New Generals for Key Jobs. Washington, D.C.**
Evidence of the Army's burgeoning responsibilities in national defense, President Roosevelt creates 84 new brigadier generals and promotes 29 to two-star rank. The list of new brigadier generals includes many destined to play significant roles in next few years: Colonels George S. Patton, Robert L. Eichelberger, William H. Simpson, Leonard T. Gerow, Lewis H. Brereton, John C. H. Lee, and Carl Spaatz. Among the new two-stars are Jacob L. Devers, Jonathan Wainwright (en route to the Philippines), Joseph W. Stilwell, and Lesley J. McNair.

27 September. **Japan Signs On with Axis.**
Japan officially signs the Berlin Treaty, aligning itself with Germany and Italy in the war against the Allies.

2 October. **Parachute Battalion Debuts. Fort Benning, Georgia.**
With Major (later Major General) William M. Miley in command, the 501st Parachute Battalion (forerunner of the future 501st Regiment) is formed. Early training is conducted with specially rigged T-4 air corps parachutes from B-18s and C-33s, the latter being the military version of a DC-1 airliner.

27 September. **CMTC Closes Doors. Washington, D.C.**
The announcement is made that "Citizens Military Training Camps will be suspended during the summer of 1941." It is indicated that the War Department favors development of an officer candidate school program in its place. This brings to a close the training experiment inaugurated in 1921, which at its peak enrolled 40,000 trainees at 54 Army posts.

16 October. **Young Americans Enroll for Draft.**
Approximately 16,400,000 men register for possible military service in accordance with the Selective Service Act. The Army rushes to prepare camps and training areas for the influx of new soldiers.

16 October. **More Guardsmen Mobilized.**
The second increment of mobilized National Guardsmen includes the 27th Division (New York), 37th Division (Ohio), and 32d Division (Michigan and Wisconsin); nearly 100,000 National Guardsmen and thousands of Reserve officers are now on active duty.

**29 October. And the Lucky Number Is . . . ?
Washington, D.C.**
The military service "lottery" begins as the sequence for induction is established by numbers drawn from a fishbowl. Secretary of War Henry Stimson draws the first—No. 158—as families across the nation anxiously await results and young men prepare to embark upon temporary military careers.

25 November. The Army Continues Buildup.
The 31st (Alabama, Mississippi) and 36th (Texas) Divisions report for active duty as does the 192d Tank Battalion (Wisconsin, Illinois, Ohio, and Kentucky tank companies). This is one of two National Guard tank battalions destined to fight to the bitter end on Bataan.

18 December. Army Air Corps Commands.
As the outline begins to emerge of the Army Air arm that will take shape in the months and years to come, new commands are established by the Army Air Corps: Northeast Air District (future First Air Force), Northwest Air District (future Second Air Force), Southeast Air District (future Third Air Force), and Southwest Air District (future Fourth Air Force).

23 December. Christmas Greetings.
The 35th Division (Missouri, Kansas, Nebraska) reports for duty and is quickly headed to Camp Robinson, Arkansas. It is under the command of Major General Ralph Truman, cousin of a World War I veteran of the Division, U.S. Senator Harry S Truman. By this date 13 National Guard observation squadrons are on active duty with the Army Air Corps.

29 December. "Emergency As Serious As War."
President Roosevelt calls for "the same spirit of patriotism and sacrifice as we would show were we at war." He tells the U.S. public: "We must be the great arsenal of democracy. For us this is an emergency as serious as war itself." The tiny preemergency Army of 172,000 is now projected to encompass an Army of the United States of 1,400,000, comprising 500,000 Regular Army, 270,000 from the National Guard, and 630,000 draftees.

31 December. Reservists on Board.
As the year ends the Army's overall strength includes 104,000 members of the Officers' Reserve Corps. Also in the ranks are 8,000 mobilized enlisted Reserve members. National Guardsmen called to the colors total 147,700 officers and men.

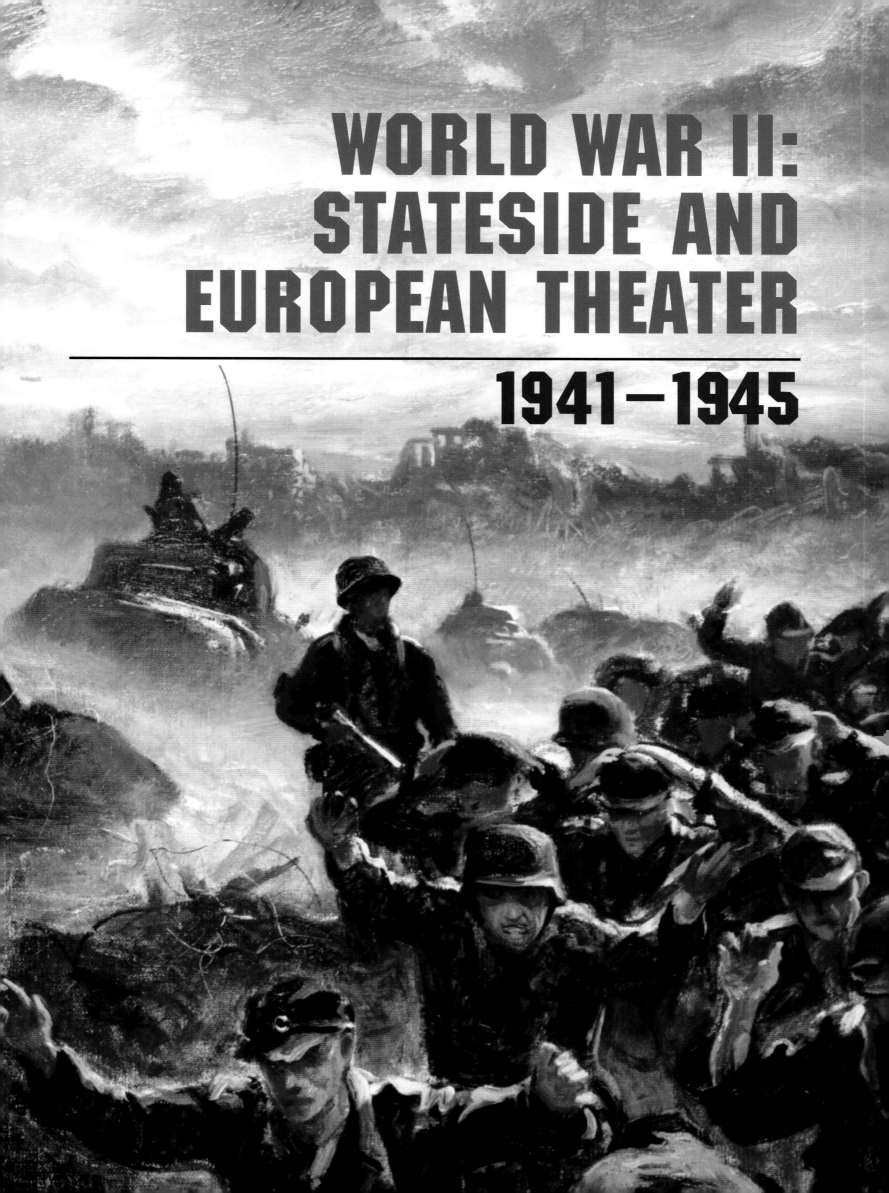

WORLD WAR II: STATESIDE AND EUROPEAN THEATER

1941–1945

WORLD WAR II: STATESIDE AND EUROPEAN THEATER

1941–1945

Major General Bruce Jacobs, AUS (Ret)

The Japanese attacks in the Pacific on 7 December 1941 and the subsequent declaration of war on the U.S. by Nazi Germany and the Axis nations roused the sleeping giant. More than 23 years had elapsed since the guns had fallen silent on the western front, but once again U.S. forces would be called upon. This would be a truly global effort and it would be known as World War II. It would require the greatest manpower mobilization in the history of the United States. The Army would grow in size to truly epic proportions, and by the time it was concluded more than 12 million men and women would have served in khaki, olive drab, or in herringbone twill fatigues.

This chapter concentrates upon the events of the Middle East–North African–European Theater of Operations. It also touches upon events within the continental United States as the Army expanded its training base, developed its organizational structure for deployment, built its great logistical base, and worked with the nation's industrial capacity to foster the greatest production lines of war equipment the world has ever known. For it fell to the U.S. industrial base to fulfill President Franklin D. Roosevelt's vision of America as "the arsenal of democracy."

The chronology of the war in the Asiatic-Pacific Theater of Operations is told in Chapter 14. The major wartime allies—Great Britain, the United States and the Soviet Union—agreed upon a master strategy that was based on defeating Germany first. The war in the European Theater of Operations was consistently influenced by the need to open a second front in the west to reduce Germany's capability to maintain the momentum of its attack against the Soviet Union. It became a major Allied objective to force the Nazi armies to fight on multiple fronts.

For this new, wartime United States Army, it would mean cutting its teeth in the campaigns in North Africa starting 8 November 1942. Here it would encounter success and failure, absorb lessons learned, and finally achieve victory. It would go on to seize Sicily and take the battle to the mainland of Europe with the invasion of Italy and the start of the long trek north, a campaign that would last more than a year.

Meanwhile, the huge bulk of the future battle army was assembling in the United Kingdom. While the ground forces trained and rehearsed, the Eighth Air Force from humble origins essentially took control of the skies over Europe and wrote the book on strategic bombardment as it took the fight to the German homeland. The Ninth Air Force also played an important role in bombardment but concentrated on the development of tactical air support that would lead to a unique partnership between the soldiers on the ground and the airmen in the skies overhead.

Even today—more than 60 years after the event—the enormous undertaking in the European Theater of Operations in World War II is best remembered for the D-Day assault on the Normandy coast of France. This is the high-water mark, which, for many Americans, is the historic epicenter of the long and convoluted road that the United States Army traveled in pursuit of the sometimes elusive objective of victory.

This was, in the very finest sense, a great crusade. Rarely have events in the background of a war so clearly delineated the forces of good and bad. There was no question in anyone's mind—once the U.S. entered the war—that there would be no cessation of hostilities until Germany's Nazi Empire was toppled.

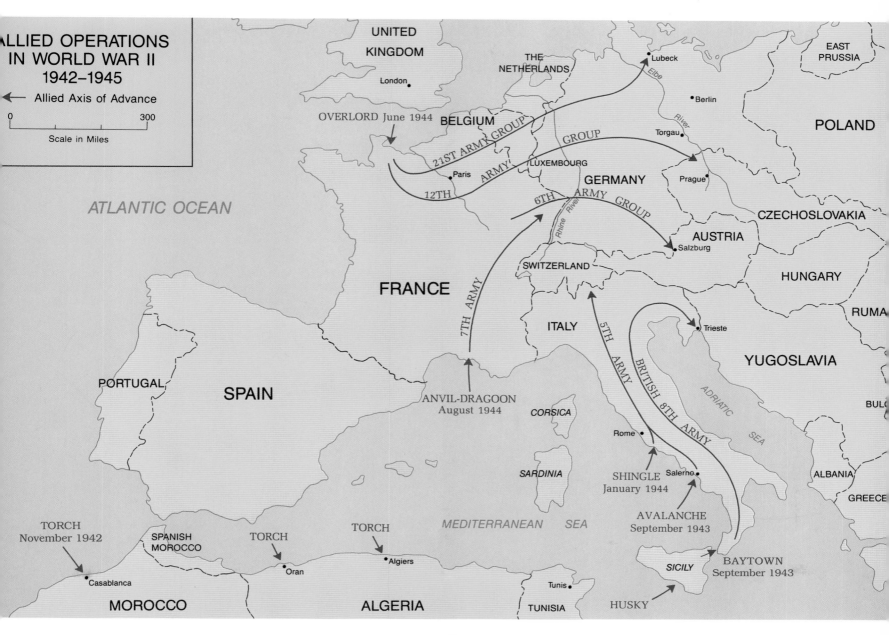

ALLIED OPERATIONS IN WORLD WAR II 1942–1945

← Allied Axis of Advance

0   300

Scale in Miles

ATLANTIC OCEAN

UNITED KINGDOM

London

THE NETHERLANDS

Lubeck

Elbe River

Berlin

EAST PRUSSIA

OVERLORD June 1944

BELGIUM

21ST ARMY GROUP

ARMY GROUP

LUXEMBOURG

Torgau

Paris

12TH

6TH ARMY GROUP

GERMANY

Prague

POLAND

Rhine River

Salzburg

AUSTRIA

CZECHOSLOVAKIA

FRANCE

SWITZERLAND

ITALY

HUNGARY

7TH ARMY

5TH ARMY

BRITISH 8TH ARMY

Trieste

RUMA

YUGOSLAVIA

ADRIATIC SEA

PORTUGAL

SPAIN

ANVIL-DRAGOON
August 1944

CORSICA

SARDINIA

BUL

Rome

SHINGLE
January 1944

Salerno

AVALANCHE
September 1943

ALBANIA

GREECE

MEDITERRANEAN SEA

TORCH
November 1942

SPANISH MOROCCO

TORCH

TORCH

Algiers

Casablanca

Oran

MOROCCO

ALGERIA

Tunis

TUNISIA

HUSKY

SICILY

BAYTOWN
September 1943

There was also never any doubt as to the tough, fighting quality of the enemy; there was never any doubt that it would be a fight to the finish. And it was.

This chronology traces the growth and evolution of what would prove to be a great wartime army, one unique in America's history. From the humble origins characteristic in peacetime, a great citizen army of 12 million American men and women would come into being, and in the end it would be the most powerful army ever assembled. And then—even more quickly than in the years and months of its creation—it disappeared into the pages of history once the job was done.

It was an army worthy of its creator, General George C. Marshall, and of its most illustrious combat commander, General Dwight D. Eisenhower. Like the men who shaped its destiny it was an army lacking in grandiloquence but never lacking in courage or imagination. It was, in retrospect, America at its very best.

Pages 626–627: *After the Normandy landing on 6 June 1944, Allied forces moved inland to St.-Lô, France, and other objectives in the drive to topple Hitler's fortress Europe. ("Sherman Tanks Passing Streams of German Prisoners," Ogden Pleissner, Army Art Collection, NMUSA)*

Above: *Major Allied operations in the European Theater. (U.S. Army Center of Military History)*

WORLD WAR II: STATESIDE AND EUROPEAN THEATER
1941–1945

"You are about to embark upon the great crusade, toward which we have striven these many months. The eyes of the world are upon you."

—General Dwight D. Eisenhower,
In His Orders of the Day Message to the Troops, 6 June 1944.

1941

January. **Status of the Army.**
Mobilization is now bringing over 140,000 men per month into the active Army. However, draftees and Guardsmen have only a one-year tour. Army GHQ is expanding the training while the General Staff plans for the organization of the forces. In various stages are 15 infantry, six armored, and two cavalry divisions, plus 11 sets of corps support troops. The Army Air Force has expanded to 6,180 officers, 7,000 flying cadets, and 88,000 enlisted men.

29 January. **High-Level British-American Military Meetings.**
Major General Stanley D. Embick heads the U.S. delegation to the British-American staff talks (the "ABC meetings"). The U.S. team includes Brigadier Generals Leonard T. Gerow and Sherman Miles and

Colonel Joseph T. McNarney, Air Corps. Under discussion is a strategy for possible future coalition warfare. Talks conclude after the 14th session on 29 March. An important outgrowth of these meetings is the establishment of the U.S. Joint Chiefs of Staff (JCS).

8 April. **Italy Ousts the U.S. Military Attaché. Rome.**
The Italian government requests the withdrawal of the American military attaché. Lieutenant Colonel Normal E. Fiske, the U.S. attaché, is the author of a report that comments on the Italian Army's "disaster" in Albania; he describes Italians as unprepared for winter or mountain warfare.

3 May. **U.S. Army Senior Commanders.**
With the assignment of Lieutenant General Walter Krueger to command the Third Army, all four of the U.S.-based field armies are commanded by non-West Pointers. The others are Lieutenant Generals Hugh A. Drum (First Army), Ben Lear (Second Army) and John L. DeWitt (Fourth Army). All four are Spanish-American War veterans and all except Lear served in France in World War I.

19 May. **Army Observers Abroad. London, England.**
Major General James E. Chaney is designated the Special Army Observer, London, reporting directly to the Army Chief of Staff. Chaney, an Army Air Corps officer, has been in England since the fall of 1940 to study British air defenses.

Left: *An Army bugler sounds a call through a megaphone for inductees at the 41st Cantonment Area, Fort Lewis, Washington, one of many marshalling locations that sprang up around the United States as the nation prepared for war. (Jeffery Ethell Collection)*

ARMY BATTLE STREAMERS—1941–1945

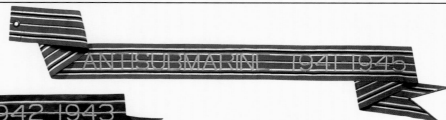

Europe, Africa, Middle East
Egypt-Libya, 1942–1943
Air Offensive, Europe, 1942–1944
Algeria-French Morocco, 1942
Tunisia, 1942
Sicily, 1943
Naples-Foggia, 1943–1944
Anzio, 1944
Rome-Arno, 1944
Normandy, 1944
Northern France, 1944

Southern France, 1944
North Apennines, 1944–1945
Rhineland, 1944–1945
Ardennes-Alsace, 1944–1945
Central Europe, 1945
Po Valley, 1945

American Theater
Antisubmarine, 1941–1945

---

27 May. **The Nation is in Unlimited National Emergency.**
President Roosevelt declares that "what started as a European war has developed, as the Nazis always intended it should develop, into a world war for world domination." The President proclaims an unlimited national emergency.

29 May. **Command Established for Ferry Missions.**
The Air Corps Ferrying Command is formed in an attempt to assist the British in the delivery of aircraft built in the U.S. The major task is to create an organization capable of ferrying aircraft across the Atlantic. This is the forerunner of the future Air Transport Command.

4 June. **Aviation Cadets Grade is Approved.**
The grade of Aviation Cadet is created in the Army Air Corps, replacing the designation of Flying Cadets. Fledgling fliers will become commissioned officers once they pin on pilot's wings.

9 June. **Tin Hats Soon Out of Style. Fort Benning, Georgia.**
Plans are underway to introduce a new style combat helmet to replace the World War I–era British-style "tin hat" helmet. Produced through the efforts of the Infantry Board, the "helmet, steel, M-1" is influenced by newly developed plastic football helmets with suspension systems to cushion weight and impact. The new helmet is a steel shell with a fiber (soon to be plastic) helmet liner adjusted to the individual soldier's head size. Production of the M-1917 helmet is terminated, but the old helmet will be worn by troops until the new "steel pot" is available in quantity.

20 June. **Consolidation Creates Army Air Forces.**
To achieve essential unity of command in periods of explosive expansion, the Secretary of War directs all air elements to be organized under a single command. This results in the establishment of the Army Air Forces. This new headquarters supersedes the "GHQ Air Force" as an element of the Army staff. Major General Henry H. (Hap) Arnold is designated Chief of the Army Air Forces and reports directly to the Army Chief of Staff. Arnold also retains his position as a deputy chief of staff. The existing GHQ Air Force becomes reorganized as First, Second, Third, and Fourth Air Forces.

1 July. **Officer Candidate Schools Ready To Train Lieutenants.**

With the Citizens Military Training Camps (CMTC) phased out, opening day for four of 10 new Officer Candidate Schools is at hand. All will be in operation by 15 September. Schools are to produce new officers for the Signal Corps, Medical Administrative Corps, Ordnance, Engineers, Coast Artillery, Quartermaster, Infantry, Armor, Cavalry, and Field Artillery. The initial goal is 10,000 new second lieutenants each year.

1 July. **Army Rapidly Growing in Size.**

Having experienced eight-fold growth, the Army now has 1,400,000 in uniform. Ground forces in the continental U.S. are organized into four armies with nine corps and 29 divisions, four armored divisions (soon to be six), and an Army Air Force of 54 combat groups.

3 July. **Army Agency To Supervise Lend-Lease to China.**
General Marshall approves a plan to create the American Military Mission to China (AMMISCA) to monitor lend-lease distribution and to provide a basis for strategic cooperation with China in the event of war. The Army looks for a hand from China to head the mission and selects Major General John Magruder, 54, who is summoned to Washington from Fort Devens, Massachusetts.

7 July. **U.S. Forces Occupy Iceland.**
At the request of the government of Iceland, U.S. Navy and Marine Corps forces start to establish a

U.S. presence in anticipation of the withdrawal of British forces. The Army is alerted to ready a divisional force to take over this mission and ensure an adequate defense.

7 July. **Greenland Force Makes Appearance. Narsarssock, Greenland.**
Greenland is regarded as a special U.S. interest due to its location in the western hemisphere. A force of 469

Right: *The Army Air Forces expanded rapidly after Pearl Harbor, requiring great numbers of air cadets such as these men who parade at Randolph Field, Texas. (National Archives)*

officers and men under Army Air Corps Colonel Benjamin F. Giles arrives to begin work on "Bluie West," the first major Army and Navy base in the subpolar region. The Army is ordered to develop a plan for organization of antiaircraft installations.

11 July. Special Purpose Divisions.
With the fielding of the first U.S. armored divisions accomplished and the prospects of still other special purpose divisions (airborne, motorized, jungle) in the offing, the standard Army division is redesignated infantry division (i.e., 1st Infantry Division replaces 1st Division).

5 August. Air Command for the Caribbean. Panama Canal Zone.
The Panama Canal Air Force is designated the Caribbean Air Force. It becomes the 6th Air Force on 5 February 1942 and is later redesignated Sixth Air Force. Its initial primary task is the defense of the Panama Canal.

6 August. Army Air Squadron Flies Off Navy Carrier. Reyjkavik, Iceland.
The 33d Pursuit Squadron (Interceptor) flies its 30 P-40s off the deck of U.S.S. *Wasp*, to set up its new base in Iceland. A 1,100-man U.S. task force also includes two infantry companies, an aviation engineer regiment, aircraft warning elements, and quartermaster port troops.

18 August. Army General Gets Iceland Command.
Major General Charles H. Bonesteel, one month after being named commander of the 5th Infantry Division, is informed that he is to command the "Indigo Force," destined to become the main Army component in Iceland. The goal is to relieve U.S. Marines and to make it possible for the British to redeploy its garrison to the Middle East.

10–15 August. Fourth Army on Maneuvers. State of Washington.
Deployed on the Olympia Peninsula between Olympia and Shelton in the western part of the state, the Fourth Army under Lieutenant General John L. DeWitt initiates a major field exercise pitting the 3d and 41st Divisions (IX Corps) and the 7th and 40th Divisions (III Corps) against a mythical invading "oriental" army.

11 September. Pentagon Building Construction Starts. Arlington, Virginia.
Ground is broken as construction begins on a new headquarters building to house the War Department. The five-sided design soon leads to its being known as "the Pentagon." Under the direction of Brigadier General Brehon B. Somerville, USA, the job is completed in just 16 months at a cost of $83 million and the lives of eight construction workers. It remains the largest office building in the world and was rapidly repaired after the devastating terrorist airplane attack exactly 60 years later—11 September 2001.

15–16 September. **Indigo Force Reaches Destination. Reykjavik, Iceland.**

Major General Charles H. Bonesteel's 5th Division task group ("Indigo Force") arrives to start development of the future Iceland Defense Command. The force includes 10th Infantry Regiment, 5th Engineers, 46th Field Artillery Battalion, and support elements. The unloading of men and equipment starts in the face of high winds, heavy seas, and a pouring rain.

15–30 September. **Army Forces in Massive Maneuver. Louisiana.**

The Second (Red) Army (Lieutenant General Ben Lear) is pitted against the Third (Blue) Army (Lieutenant General Walter Krueger) in the largest maneuver ever held during peacetime in the United States. Over 350,000 troops in 22 divisions (including two armored) and four Army Air Corps wings take part in the two-phase exercise in an area 30,000 square miles in size. Many Guardsmen and draftees

Above: *Trainees drilling at Fort Lewis, Washington, in the early morning light. (Jeffery Ethell Collection)*

Right: *One of the Army's first paratroopers participates in the Louisiana Maneuvers that were conducted just prior to America's entry into the Second World War. (U.S. Army)*

anticipate release from active duty after completion of the "army versus army" maneuver.

26 September. **Cops in Khaki a Separate Branch.**

A "Corps of Military Police" is established for the first time since 1918. All officers and men performing MP duties as a principal function become members of the military police. During the World War II era a total of 150 MP battalions and more than 900 other types of MP units are organized.

Right: *New recruits of the 186th and 162d Infantry Regiments receive training with the Springfield M-1903 rifle, still in use at the outset of World War II. (Jeffery Ethell Collection)*

27 September. **Infantry OCS Graduates Its First Class. Fort Benning, Georgia.**
Brigadier General Omar N. Bradley, commandant of the Infantry School, presides over the first graduating class of infantry officer candidates.

1 October. **Supplies and Troops for MacArthur.**
The Army searches for shipping to transport 500,000 tons of supplies and 20,000 troops earmarked as reinforcements for the Philippines garrison, causing a hasty conversion of passenger ships. Eleven sail between 21 November and 6 January 1942. Six troop ships and nine cargo vessels are at sea when word of Pearl Harbor is received.

10–28 November. **Two-Phased GHQ Maneuvers in the Carolinas.**
The First Army (Major General Hugh Drum) is pitted against a force composed of the IV Corps (Major General Oscar W. Griswold), reinforced by the I Armored Corps. Drum and Griswold employ 13 divisions including the 1st and 2d Armored Divisions fresh from the Louisiana maneuvers. All three major maneuvers of 1941 (State of Washington, Louisiana, the Carolinas) are influenced by requirements of peacetime safety regulations, shortages of equipment, the short supply of aviation, and armored elements.

15 November. **The Mountain Infantry Joins the Army. Fort Lewis, Washington.**
The Army activates its first unit designed specifically to fight in mountain terrain. The 1st Battalion, 87th Mountain Infantry, is destined to find its way to the future 10th Mountain Division.

27 November. **Tank Destroyer Training Gets Emphasis.**
Quickly adapting to "lessons learned" in the 1941 maneuvers, the Tank Destroyer and Firing Center is activated at Fort Meade, Maryland. It is under direct War Department control. Orders are issued for the activation of 53 tank destroyer battalions. Division antitank battalions are redesignated tank destroyer battalions and placed under GHQ.

30 November. **Pioneer Army Airman Retires.**
Frank P. Lahm (West Point, 1901), age 64, the Army's oldest pilot and first military aviator (1909), retires with the rank of brigadier general.

7 December. **Attack on Pearl Harbor, Army Installations. Hawaii.**
At 1:20 p.m. (Washington time) Japanese naval aviation strikes Pearl Harbor while diplomatic negotiations are still underway. (See details in chapter 14.)

8 December. **Congress Declares War.**
War against Japan is declared. Subsequent action is taken to declare war on Germany and Italy. Immediate action is taken by the Army to halt the discharges of draftees who have completed their year of training; Guard units due to be returned to state status are retained under federal control.

8 December. **West Coast Defenses. Los Angeles, California.**
In preparation for war, the U.S. west coast defenses are beefed up. An Army Air Corps pursuit group from Michigan arrives.

AMERICA'S GHOST ARMY

14th Army   XXXI Corps   XXXIII Corps

6th Airborne Division

9th Airborne Division   11th Division

14th Division   17th Division

18th Airborne Division

21st Airborne Division   22nd Division   46th Division

46th Division (variation)   48th Division   50th Division   55th Division   59th Division   108th Division

119th Division   119th Division (variation)   130th Division   135th Airborne Division   141st Division   157th Division

As early as 1942, U.S. Army planners began using nonexistent units to deceive Axis intelligence as to the real size and location of U.S. forces. To give credibility to the "ghosts," the Institute of Heraldry designed shoulder sleeve insignia that were shown in the press. Some were actually produced in limited quantities and worn by soldiers pretending to be members of the fictional units. To protect Operation Overlord in 1944, a "ghost" army was organized under First U.S. Army Group (FUSAG)—whose personnel later became the real Twelfth Army Group under General Omar Bradley. Composed of the 14th Army, three corps, and 20 divisions (many of the insignia shown above), FUSAG was depicted as the main invasion force destined for Pas de Calais. As part of the real 100-Division Plan proposed in 1942, a different set of 10 infantry divisions were planned but were not activated. Although numbered, official insignia were never designed for them.
(Association of Military Insignia Collectors)

Right: *Missouri National Guardsmen of the 203d Coast Artillery practice an antiaircraft drill with their unwieldy .50-caliber water-cooled machine guns during the Louisiana Maneuvers. (National Archives)*

11 December. Axis Principals Declare War.
Germany and Italy declare a state of war with the United States.

11 December. The Coastal Command is Upgraded.
The Western Defense Command is designated a theater of operations. Nine additional antiaircraft regiments are rushed from various parts of the U.S.

14 December. Army Corps Moves West.
With the U.S. west coast engulfed in uncertainty and amid rumors of Japanese naval forces offshore, the Army hurriedly moves a corps of two infantry divisions (27th and 35th) with other corps troops. By 17 December the War Department declares that major parts of both coasts have "to a reasonable degree" protection against possible sea or air attack.

14 December. Marshall Approves Wartime Army Plan.
General George C. Marshall, now a wartime chief of staff, gives his approval to a plan for a 2-million-man army with 100 divisions over the next two years. This soon gives way to a blueprint for a strength of 3.6 million and 69 new divisions within one year. (Three years later the Army numbers 8 million men and women and 89 combat divisions).

1942

1 January. Status of the Growing Army.
The Army has 36 divisions under arms—29 infantry, 5 armored, 2 cavalry. Production and procurement in 1941 includes 600 howitzers; 1,461 medium tanks (exceeding the goal of 1,030); and a shortfall in 37mm AA guns as only 504 of 837 are delivered.

15 January. School to Train MPs. Fort Myer, Virginia.
The Army opens the new Military Police School to help standardize training and techniques for soldiers detailed or assigned to the Corps of Military Police.

14 January. Looking to the Future.
The Army Air Corps awards the first contract to build a helicopter designed to meet military requirements.

26 January. First GI Sets Foot in ETO. Belfast, Northern Ireland.
Private First Class Milburn H. Henke from Hutchinson, Minnesota, tramps down the gangplank—the first American soldier of World War II to set foot in the European Theater of Operations. Henke and his fellow soldiers of Company B, 133d Infantry Regiment, 34th (Red Bull) Infantry Division, wear World War I–style helmets, OD blouses with ties, full field packs, gas masks, and canvas leggings. The company is a mobilized National Guard unit from Waterloo, Iowa.

28 January. Eighth Air Force Headquarters Created. Savannah, Georgia.
The Eighth Air Force is created with a headquarters and headquarters squadron under the command of Brigadier General Asa Duncan, an old-time Army Air Corps flier. Duncan's small headquarters group includes Colonel Leon V. Johnson, who is destined to earn the Medal of Honor in the epic Ploesti Raid.

1 February. **School To Convert Civilians to Chaplains. Fort Benjamin Harrison, Indiana.**
To help civilian religious leaders understand what is expected of a chaplain, the Army Chaplain School is established.

9 February. **First Formal Meeting of the Joint Chiefs of Staff. Washington, D.C.**
The U.S. Joint Chiefs of Staff evolves from the leadership group assembled for 1941 meetings with the British. The actual functions and duties of the JCS are not formally defined until the National Defense Act of 1947. During the war era the Army is represented by General George C. Marshall. The wartime JCS becomes the principal agency for coordination between the Army and Navy and eventually replaces the Army and Navy Joint Board, which dates back to 1903.

2 March. **The Army Adopts the New Structure for Wartime. Washington, D.C.**
A Presidential order reorganizes the wartime army into three principal divisions—Army Air Forces (AAF), Army Services Forces (ASF), and Army Ground Forces (AGF). Respective commanders are Lieutenant General Henry H. (Hap) Arnold,

Above: *The shoulder sleeve insignia of the Tank Destroyer Force. (American Military Insignia, Quintet Publishing Company)*

Right: *During amphibious training at Fort Ord, California, troops clamber down a cargo net while a 37mm antitank gun is lowered. (Jeffery Ethell Collection)*

Lieutenant General Brehon B. Somervell, and Lieutenant General Lesley J. McNair. They also function as staff officers reporting to Chief of Staff General Marshall.

9 March. **Antiaircraft Artillery Command is Created. Washington, D.C.**
With Major General Joseph Green as commander, the Antiaircraft Command is activated as an element of the Army Ground Forces. Concurrently the Antiaircraft Artillery School is established at established at Camp Davis, North Carolina. After being organized in Washington, D.C., Antiaircraft Command headquarters moves to Richmond, Virginia, on 23 March 1942.

13 March. **First War Dogs Unleashed. Front Royal, Virginia.**
The first war dogs join the Army as Under Secretary of War Robert P. Patterson approves a plan submitted by the quartermaster general. This Army branch quickly becomes the "K-9 (canine) Corps." In addition to Front Royal, reception and training centers are soon set up at Camp Rimini, Montana; Fort Robinson, Nebraska; San Carlos, California; and Cat Island off the Mississippi coast. In months to come, 20,000 dogs are "recruited," of which 10,526 are accepted for service; most serve overseas and 2,290 are killed in action.

Right: *African-American Military Police (MPs) were tasked with maintaining order and discipline among increasing numbers of black soldiers serving in the still segregated Army. (National Archives)*

8 April. **Future Ninth Air Force on the Books. Bowman Field, Kentucky.**

The 5th Air Support Command (organized 2 September 1941) is redesignated the 9th Air Force, subsequently renamed the Ninth Air Force.

25 April. **Relocation of Japanese-Americans is Ordered. San Francisco, California.**

The Army begins implementing orders to gather and confine Japanese-Americans into relocation camps in the western U.S. The Army's Western Defense Command removes 109,427 persons of Japanese ancestry from the West Coast in 1942. Despite controversy the U.S. Supreme Command initially upholds the constitutionality of the action, which is ultimately repudiated.

11 May. **The First Echelon of Eighth Air Force. High Wycombe, England.**

The vanguard—39 officers and 384 enlisted men—of what will in time become "the Mighty Eighth" arrives and prepares for the arrival of flying units. An early arrival (14 May) is the A-20-equipped 15th Bombardment Squadron (Light).

14 May. **Women in the Army. Washington, D.C.**

Congress approves and the President signs "An Act to establish a Women's Army Auxiliary Corps for service with the Army of the United States." This is soon nationally known as the "WAAC."

15 May. **V-Mail to Speed Up Mail to Overseas Troops.**

The Army Postal Service working with the Army Signal Corps hits upon a photographic concept to improve mail delivery time to overseas troops and to save precious cargo space in ships and airplanes as it institutes "V-Mail." Senders are encouraged to write letters on V-Mail forms, which are photographed and reduced to reels of film that are flown to V-Mail stations. At the receiving end the film is developed, enlarged, and printed as 4-1/2 x 5-inch reproductions for distribution to recipients. Peak volume will be 63 million letters processed in April 1944.

15 May. **Activation of School to Train Paratroopers. Fort Benning, Georgia.**

The Army's Parachute School is activated as a separate entity apart from the Infantry School activities.

16 May. **Mrs. Hobby of Texas Heads the WAAC. Washington, D.C.**

Mrs. Oveta Culp Hobby takes the oath of office as director, WAAC, and is awarded silver eagles symbolic of her "equivalent grade" as an Army colonel. Her swearing-in is witnessed by Secretary of War Stimson, Army Chief of Staff Marshall, Congresswoman Edith Nourse Rogers, and the new director's husband, former Texas governor William P. Hobby.

Left: *General George Marshall and Secretary of War Henry Stimson witness the swearing in of Mrs. Ovetta Culp Hobby as the director of the Women's Army Auxiliary Corps (WAAC). (U.S. Army)*

12 June. **Egypt-Based B-24s Strike Oilfields. Fayid, Egypt.**
A secretly trained detachment of Army Air Corps B-24 bombers commanded by Lieutenant Colonel Harry Halverson carries out the first raid on Axis oil fields from a base in the Egyptian desert near the Suez Canal. Designated the HALPRO mission, the force consists of 13 aircraft, which conduct a largely symbolic high-level bombing raid that accomplishes little.

16 June. **U.S.-Canadian Light Infantry Team. Camp Hale, Colorado.**
Originally codenamed the "Plough Project," the First Special Service Force comes into being and brings U.S. and Canadian soldiers together to form a unique and deadly light infantry combat team ostensibly destined for cold weather operations. Their collar

Right: *An Army Air Force aerial gunner serving in England, home of thousands of American airmen during the war in Europe. ("Aerial Gunner," Peter Hurd, Army Art Collection, NMUSA)*

Opposite: *A U.S. Coast Artillery crew prepares to fire their 155mm gun. In addition to fighting overseas, personnel assigned to such units had to maintain homeland defenses against the threat of possible German or Japanese attack by sea. (National Archives)*

insignia takes the form of crossed arrows in place of crossed rifles.

19 June. **First U.S. Rangers Step Forward. Carrickfergus. Northern Ireland.**
The U.S. V Corps organizes the 1st Ranger Battalion with Major William O. Darby as commander; 520 officers and men—mostly volunteers from the 34th Infantry Division and 1st Armored Division—head for training at the British Commando School in Scotland.

ARMY WOMEN IN THE ETO

During World War II many women in the Army were assigned to the European Theater of Operations (ETO). Sixty Army nurses of the 48th Surgical Hospital landed on the beaches of North Africa only hours after the first U.S. troops. When the nurses of the 77th Evacuation Hospital learned that the Germans had broken through the Kasserine Pass, they helped move 150 patients 60 miles. Within 12 hours, they received 500 new patients from the battlefield.

After the invasion of North Africa, Lieutenant General Dwight D. Eisenhower quickly requested WAAC officers be assigned to his headquarters in Algiers. In December the ship carrying the women was torpedoed 70 miles off the coast of Africa. Two of the women were rescued from the sinking ship by a British destroyer; the three others got aboard a life raft and were eventually picked up. One of the officers, Captain Louise Anderson, was the only woman at the Casablanca Conference in January 1943, where she recorded in shorthand conversations between President Roosevelt and Prime Minister Churchill. That month, the 149th WAAC Post Headquarters Company arrived in Algiers, where they worked as switchboard operators, teletypists, high-speed radio operators, and cryptographic clerks.

The first battalion of WACs reached England in July 1943. The 557 enlisted women and 19 officers were assigned to duty with the Eighth Air Force. A second detachment of 300 WACs was assigned to the Supreme Headquarters, Allied Expeditionary Force (SHAEF). They assisted in the planning for D-Day and subsequent operations against Germany.

Army nurses, meanwhile, were in the forefront of the invasions of Sicily, Salerno, and Anzio. Lieutenant Deloris Buckley was one of 103 Army nurses aboard the British hospital ship *Newfoundland* en route to Salerno on 13 September 1943 when it was bombed by enemy aircraft. She recalled, "Just before dusk . . . I heard the sound of an airplane motor . . . the first bomb landed off the port side and the explosion almost lifted the ship out of the water. The second bomb landed squarely in the middle of the Red Cross that was painted on deck. There was a mighty blast . . . a solid sheet of flame shot skyward." Four nurses were wounded in the attack.

On 8 November 1943 a C-54 ferrying 13 flight nurses and 13 medical corpsmen of the 807th Medical Air Evacuation Transport Squadron to Bari, Italy, crash landed in the Albanian mountains far behind German lines. Led by pro-Allied guerrilla fighters, the survivors hiked 800 miles to the safety. The group was

forced to hide from enemy patrols several times before reaching the coast and being evacuated.

In early 1944, 200 nurses working at Anzio experienced months of enemy bombardment. Six died and several were wounded. Lieutenant Deloris Buckley, who had been aboard *Newfoundland* when it was bombed, was hit in the leg. Buckley was putting a dressing on an abdominal case when she heard a plane. Suddenly "there was a mighty roar. I remember thinking in a detached way that it was strange for me to be lying on the floor. . . . I saw blood spurting through a pair of holes in my thigh. . . . shrapnel had entered through one side and gone clear through it."

During the invasion of Normandy, the first nurses arrived on D-Day plus four. Elizabeth Marshall Edwards of the 91st Evacuation Hospital wrote, "We were only a 1/2 mile from the front line and received casualties directly off the battlefield." During the Battle of the Bulge, many medical units were close to the lines. Army nurse Genevieve Wing, badly wounded during the Bulge, said, "We kept on operating. We had to, because there were so many wounded. When the shelling was close, we were taught to throw ourselves over the patient on the operating table. It was just second nature after a while. He was helpless during surgery and we had to do what we could to protect him."

A total of 17,345 Army Nurses and 7,600 WACs served in the ETO during the war.

—*Judi Bellifaire*

Above: *Women's Army Corps (WAC) members of the 6888th Central Post Directory Battalion on parade in France. They were the only African-American women serving overseas during World War II. (National Archives)*

Right: *Troops of the 34th Division were the vanguard of U.S. forces to train in Ireland. They still wear a version of the old-style helmet first issued in World War I instead of the new M1 helmet, which replaced this outmoded pattern. (Hulton Getty)*

24 June. **Eisenhower, a New Face on the European Scene.**
Major General Dwight D. Eisenhower arrives and replaces Major General James E. Chaney as commanding general European Theater of Operations USA (ETOUSA). Nicknamed "Ike," he is 52 and formerly held the post of assistant chief of staff for operations in the War Department. He is a 1915 graduate of West Point; unlike many of his contemporaries, he did not serve in France during World War I.

24 June. **Army Middle East Agency to Help U.S.S.R. Basra, Iraq.**
The United States Military Iranian Mission is redesignated the Iran-Iraq Service Command with the mission to expedite the flow of war materials to the Soviet Union from Persian Gulf ports. This is soon (13 August) redesignated the Persian Gulf Service Command.

25 June. **Mark Clark Reports for Duty with Eisenhower. England.**
Major General Mark W. Clark, recently promoted to two-star rank, becomes the chief of staff for U.S. ground forces in Europe and commander of II Corps. He decides to set up the corps command post at Tidworth, near Salisbury.

1 July. **First of the Heavies Safely Across the Atlantic. Polebrook, England.**
The first B-17 Flying Fortress of the 97th Bombardment Group completes the hazardous journey across the Atlantic Ocean. The remainder of the group straggles in over next 26 days.

4 July. **First Army Air Strike At Europe. Molesworth, England.**
Generals Eisenhower, Spaatz, and Eaker come out to cheer on the 15th Bombardment Squadron fliers scheduled to take part in an Independence Day attack by 12 RAF Boston bombers including six U.S. crews on a low-level raid against enemy-held airfields in Holland. Results are not considered encouraging. One lost pilot is the first U.S. airman taken prisoner in Europe.

20 July. **WAAC Officer Candidates In Training. Fort Des Moines, Iowa.**
The first women's OCS program starts with 440 members. The goal is to have 1,300 trained officers before the enlistment of "enrolled personnel." 436 new WAAC officers pin on gold bars following graduation on 29 August. The WAAC insignia is not yet available.

22 July. **Coastal Fort Takes Fire. Fort Stevens, Washington.**
A coastal Army post is shelled by a Japanese submarine, the first hostile attack against U.S. soil since the War of 1812.

20 July. **Female Troops Start Training. Fort Des Moines, Iowa.**

The first WAAC training begins. Eventually the Army will operate five locations for the training of female enrollees.

22 July. **Stateside Army is Reorganized.**

The Army's old Corps Areas are renamed "Corps Service Commands" as the Army's corps are now tactical commands.

31 July. **The Transportation Corps is Established. Washington, D.C.**

The Transportation Corps is officially formed, taking on many of the missions formerly handled by the Quartermaster Corps. Major General Charles P. Gross, as the head of the Transportation Corps, is the chief transportation officer of the Army. General Gross, a veteran of the AEF, graduated near the top of his West Point class in 1914. By the end of the war this global activity will employ 23,356 officers and 243,115 enlisted troops. General Gross heads the Transportation Corps until 30 November 1945.

7 August. **1st Division Is Overseas. England.**

Following in the footsteps of the 1st Division, which was first overseas in World War I, the 1st (Big Red One) Infantry Division is the first U.S. division to reach England. Its newly assigned commander is the colorful ex-cavalryman, Major General Terry de la Mesa Allen. Its assistant commander is Brigadier General Theodore Roosevelt, Jr., a reserve officer who served with the division in World War I.

16 August. **101st Airborne Division Activated. Camp Claiborne, Louisiana.**

A second airborne division, the 101st, is activated pursuant to War Department orders. Prophetically, its first commander, Major General William C. Lee, notes that, "The 101st Airborne Division . . . has no history, but it has a rendezvous with destiny." The division becomes the famed "Screaming Eagles."

19 August. **U.S. Rangers Accompany British Commandos. Dieppe, French Coast.**

Fifty Army Rangers participate with British Commandos in a raid on the German-held port. They are the first U.S. troops to fight in France in World War II. The senior Army observer is Colonel Lucian K. Truscott, Jr., a future three-star army commander.

17 September. **Super Secret "Manhattan Project" is Underway.**

Newly promoted Army Engineer Brigadier General Leslie R. Groves is placed in command of the super secret Manhatan Project. Its Mission: to build a devastating weapon, the atomic bomb.

21 September. **The B-29 Joins the AAF Team. Renton, Washington.**

The Army Air Force announces the launch of the B-29 bomber. Soon after the first test flight of the XB-29, the Army Air Force approves the B-29 for production. The future super-bomber of the U.S. strategic forces is 99 feet long and has a 140-foot wing span. (Boeing makes its first delivery of seven planes in July 1943. By the end of August 1945 AAF inventories show 2,132 B-29s on hand, of which 1,000 belong to the Marianas-based Twentieth Air Force. By the end of the war forty B-29 groups are organized and 21 of them have reached combat destinations.)

11 October. **Blue and Gray Division Deploys. England.**
A mobilized National Guard unit with troops predominantly from Virginia, Maryland, and the District of Columbia, the 29th (Blue and Gray) Infantry Division arrives in England. Its predecessor served in France in World War I. The division is under the command of Major General Leonard T. Gerow, a veteran Regular Army soldier.

22 October. **Conference Behind Enemy Lines. Algeria, North Africa.**
Major General Mark W. Clark leads a small party ashore at night from a submarine with the hope of negotiating with French officials to ensure an unopposed landing for the soon-to-be-launched allied invasion of North Africa. They are unable to obtain the promise that French troops will not open fire on their old allies.

8 November. **Eisenhower Commands Amphibious Operations in North Africa.**
With Major General Eisenhower in overall command, three Army invasion task forces operating in conjunction with British forces conduct Operation Torch, the amphibious landings against the Axis in North Africa.

8 November. **Army Task Forces Hit the Beach.**
The Eastern Task Force (Major General Charles Ryder), composed of forces launched from Great Britain, lands on Algerian beaches. The Central Task Force (Major General Lloyd Fredendall) lands at Oran on 10 November. On 11 November the Western Task Force (Major General George S. Patton, Jr.), composed of forces directly from the U.S., lands at three places along the coast of Morocco—Port Lyautey, Safi, and Casablanca. The 2d Battalion, 509th Parachute Infantry (formerly 2d Battalion, 503d Parachute Infantry), makes the first U.S. combat airborne assault to assist in the capture of an airfield. Aircraft of the 31st Fighter Group launch from the deck of a Navy carrier to start operations ashore at an airfield 15 miles south of Oran.

12 November. **Brereton Activates Ninth Air Force. Cairo, Egypt.**
Lieutenant General Lewis H. Brereton receives authority to activate the Ninth Air Force. His new command is to include the Ninth Bomber Command (Brigadier General Pat Timberlake) and the Ninth Air Service Command (Brigadier General Elmer E. Adler).

13 November. **V Corps Headquarters to the United Kingdom. Bristol, England.**
The V Corps headquarters moves from Northern Ireland to a new location at Clifton College, Bristol. It becomes, for the time being, Ground Forces headquarters for U.S. combat forces in the United Kingdom (under ETOUSA) with the departure of the

Right: *Troops laden with gear and weapons board their transport ships for Europe. ("Embarkation," Barse Miller, Army Art Collection, NMUSA)*

Left: *Men of the 1st Ranger Battalion secure an enemy bunker at Arzew, North Africa, on 8 November 1942. Rangers continued to serve with great success as a shock force throughout the remainder of the war. (U.S. Army)*

II Corps for North Africa. As they set up training camps in the UK, troops of the 29th and 5th Infantry Divisions come under V Corps. V Corps continues to share responsibility for helping to protect England from the threat of invasion

27 November. **Introducing the K Ration.**
Destined to be famous, or infamous, the Army's ubiquitous K ration is put into the distribution system—three packages designated breakfast unit, dinner unit, and supper unit.

1943

January. **The Call for Japanese-American Volunteers.**
While many Japanese-Americans are languishing in Civilian Relocation Centers, the Army calls for volunteers to make up an all-Nisei combat unit. This is greeted with great enthusiasm in Hawaii, where no civilian re-locations have taken place. Thousands clamor to join the 100th Battalion, soon to be followed by the 442d Infantry Regiment. Fewer than 1,300 volunteers are from the internment camps.

5 January. **New Fifth Army Headquarters. Oujda, Morocco.**
Lieutenant General Mark W. Clark, first commander of the U.S. Fifth Army, opens his headquarters. His new field command includes the I Armored Corps

(Patton) and VI Corps (Major General Ernest J. Dawley).

14 January. **FDR Makes a Long Journey. Casablanca.**
Army elements place a heavy security screen around the location where President Franklin D. Roosevelt participates in a critical Anglo-American Conference. FDR uses the occasion to present the Medal of Honor to Colonel William H. Wilbur for his exploits in the Western Task Force during the North Africa campaign.

15 January. **New Army Headquarters Opens Ahead of Schedule. Arlington, Virginia.**
The five-sided office building to house the War Department—The Pentagon—built in 16 months under the direction of the Army Corps of Engineers, opens ahead of schedule. It is the largest office building in the world.

27 January. **The Eighth Air Force Hits Germany.**
Army Air Force heavy bombers carry out the first full-scale attack on the Nazi homeland, striking at Wilhelmshaven.

27 January. **First WAAC Unit Overseas. Algiers, North Africa.**
The 149th Post Headquarters Company, the first WAAC unit deployed overseas, arrives in Algiers, North Africa.

Right: *A youthful Army Air Force B-17 pilot at one of the many bases that dotted the English countryside. ("Lt. Thomas Borders, Pilot, U.S. Air Force," Peter Hurd, Army Art Collection, NMUSA)*

Below: *Although never provided all of the resources he requested, Lieutenant General Mark Clark successfully commanded the Fifth U.S. Army during the difficult campaign in Italy. (National Archives)*

3 February. **Tragic Saga of the Four Chaplains.**
While crossing the Atlantic, SS *Dorchester* is torpedoed by a German submarine. The ship is carrying 902 troops headed for the U.S. base on Greenland. Four Army chaplains—Lieutenants George L. Fox (Methodist), Alexander D. Goode (Jewish), John P. Washington (Catholic), and Clark V. Poling (Dutch Reformed)—remove their own lifebelts and give them to others. The four chaplains go down with the ship.

19 or 20 February. **Germans Counterattack, Army Suffers Setback. Kasserine Pass, Tunisia.**
The U.S. II Corps is hit by a massive German counterattack and its lines are penetrated. Heavy

losses are suffered. The Allies recover the pass five days later.

26 February. **Kasserine Pass, Tunisia.**
U.S. troops retake the Kasserine Pass.

5 March. **Patton Takes Command of II Corps in North Africa.**
Major General George S. Patton, Jr., takes command of the U.S. II Corps. Major General Lloyd R. Fredendall is relieved.

17 March. **Rejuvenated II Corps On the Attack. Tunisia.**
The U.S. II Corps now fighting under the command of Major General Patton with the 1st Infantry Division on the point, attacks and seizes El Guettar; hard fighting continues. Patton soon earns a new assignment; on 16 April Major General Omar N. Bradley is named to command II Corps.

26 April. **U.S. II Corps Resumes Tunisian Offensive.**
The U.S. II Corps (Bradley) hurriedly moves 100,000 men an average distance of 150 miles in deployment from southern to northern Tunisia to launch what is destined to be final phase of the campaign. Bradley orders four U.S. divisions into action—the 1st Infantry, 9th Infantry, 34th Infantry, and 1st Armored. He has the 3d Infantry Division ready to assist as needed.

3 May. **First Phase of Tunisian Attack a Success.**
U.S. II Corps elements force the enemy to retreat to a line east of Mateur and the Tine Valley on the last hills protecting the roads to Bizerte and Tunis. The

second phase of the campaign begins on 4 May as the II Corps breaks through to seize Bizerte and Chouigui, working with British and French forces to destroy the Axis forces left in its zone of action.

9 May. Fifth Panzer Army Surrenders. Ferryville, Tunisia.

The beginning of the end of the battle for North Africa is marked by the arrival of German staff officers at the command post of the 1st Armored Division southeast of Bizerte, to arrange the surrender of the once-proud Fifth Panzer Army. Three days later the Italian First Army surrenders to the British Eighth Army, marking the end of the battle for North Africa.

11 June. Pantelleria, Italy.

Following an intensive bombardment campaign, the enemy signals surrender of the Italian island between Sicily and North Africa.

21 June. Army Nurse Earns Recognition. Yuma, Arizona.

Nurse Lieutenant Edith Greenwood receives the first

Above: *Army troops faced a formidable German enemy in Tunisia. ("Hill 609," Fletcher Martin, Army Art Collection, NMUSA)*

Soldiers Medal awarded to a woman for heroism in saving patients during a hospital fire.

25 June. New Field Ration Makes Appearance.

The Army quartermaster corps announces the "Ten-in-One" ration, a package that contains complete food supplies for ten men for one day—or for one man for ten days.

1 July. WACs. They're In the Army Now! Washington, D.C.

To remove all restrictions on employment of women soldiers overseas and to provide the women with benefits and protection similar to those provided male soldiers, the President signs a bill to establish the Women's Army Corps (WAC) as a component of the Army of the United States. The Army has 90 days to dissolve the WAAC—and to determine how many of the enrolled women and commissioned officers will opt for the new WAC.

10 July. The Seventh Army is Created on Shipboard. At Sea, Off Sicily.

The U.S. Seventh Army (Patton), the first U.S. field army in action in World War II, is activated on shipboard en route to the invasion of Sicily. The new Army is created by redesignation of the Headquarters I Armored Corps, which saw action in North Africa.

EYEWITNESS: THE SICILY CAMPAIGN

On 9–10 July 1943 Allied forces invaded Sicily. The U.S. Seventh Army advanced on the west toward the city of Messina in an effort to cut off the enemy. Traveling with the Army was war correspondent Ernie Pyle, who reported:

"When the 45th Division went into reserve . . . I moved on with the Third Division which took up the ax and drove the enemy on to Messina.

"I am still doing engineers and it was on my very first day with the Third that we hit the most difficult and spectacular engineering job of the Sicilian campaign.

"You've doubtless noticed Point Calava on your maps. . . . The coast highway is tunneled through this big rock, and on either side of the tunnel the road sticks out of the sheer rock wall like a shelf.

"Our engineers figured the Germans would blow the tunnel entrance to seal it up. But . . . (t)hey picked a spot about 50 feet beyond the tunnel mouth and blew a hole 150 feet long in the road shelf.

"We were beautifully bottlenecked. You couldn't by-pass around the rock. You couldn't by-pass over the mountain. All you could do was bridge it, and that was a hell of a job. But bridge it they did, and in only 24 hours.

"It was around 2 p.m. when we got there and in two hours the little platform of highway at the crater mouth resembled a littered street in front of a burning building. Air hoses covered the ground. Three big air compressors were parked side by side, their engines cutting off and on . . . and jack hammers clattered their nerve-shattering din. They had drilled and blasted two

holes far down the jagged slope. These were to set uprights into so they wouldn't slide down the hill when weight was applied. The far side of the crater had been blasted out and leveled off. . . . Steel hooks had been embedded into the rock to hold wire cables.

"At about 10 a.m., the huge uprights were slid down the bank . . . and their ends worked into the blasted holes. Then they were brought upright by men on the banks, pulling on ropes tied to them.

"A half-naked soldier doing practically a wire-walking act, edged out over the timber and bored a long hole down through two timbers . . . Then he hammered a steel rod into it, tying them together. Others added more bracing, nailing them together with huge spikes driven in by sledge hammers.

"Now came . . . 20 shirtless, sweating soldiers to each of the long-spliced timbers carried them and slid them out across the chasm. . . . Big stringers were bolted down, heavy flooring was carried on and nailed to the stringers. Men built up the approaches with stones. The bridge was almost ready.

"Around 11 a.m., jeeps had begun to line up at the far end of the tunnel. Around dusk of the day before, the engineers told me they'd have jeeps across the crater by noon of the next day. . . . But even they will have to admit it was pure coincidence that the first jeep rolled cautiously across the miracle bridge at high noon, to the very second.

"In that first jeep was General Truscott and his driver, facing a 200-foot tumble into the sea if the bridge gave way. The engineers had insisted they send a test jeep across first. But when he saw it was ready, the General just got in and went. . . . It showed that the 'Old Man' had complete faith in his engineers. I heard soldiers speak of it appreciatively for an hour.

"The tired men began to pack their tools into trucks. Engineer officers who hadn't been to sleep in 36 hours went back to their olive orchard to clean up. They had built a jerry bridge, a comical bridge, a proud bridge, but above all the kind of bridge that wins wars. And they had built it in one night and a half. The General was mighty pleased."

—Vince Hawkins

Above: *General Truscott makes the first drive across a bridge built by engineers of the Third Infantry Division along a mountain pass on Sicily. (National Archives)*

15 July. **New Commander, Home Base for V Corps. Somerset, England.**
Major General Leonard T. Gerow, formerly commander of the 29th Infantry Division, assumes command of V Corps. Corps headquarters moves to Taunton in Somerset and is assigned to the First U.S. Army with the mission to prepare for a major role in the invasion. V Corps reverts to a traditional corps activity as buildup grows.

9 July–17 August. **The U.S. Seventh Army Launches Operation Husky. Sicily.**
Elements of the 82d Airborne Division conduct the first major U.S. parachute assault in the war, followed by amphibious landings conducted by the U.S. Seventh Army (Patton) and British forces. The new Army amphibious truck DUKW ("duck") makes its appearance in combat operations for the first time. The battle for Sicily lasts six weeks.

Above: *A U.S. M3 Medium tank moves through Kasserine Pass in Tunisia. Nearly half the tanks deployed from the 1st Armor Division during this battle fell prey to German panzers on 14 February 1943. (National Archives)*

13 July. **The OSS is Activated for Special Operations.**
With Brigadier General William "Wild Bill" Donovan designated to take charge, the President orders creation of the Office of Strategic Services (OSS) for special operations behind enemy lines. This is the forerunner of the future Central Intelligence Agency (CIA).

21 July. **A First for a Black Aviator. Castelvetrano, Italy.**
While flying escort for B-25 bombers on his eighth mission, Charles B. Hall from Brazil, Indiana, becomes the first black fighter pilot to down an enemy aircraft. He tangles with two Fw-190s trying to intercept bombers.

23 July. **Capture of Palermo. Sicily.**
The Seventh Army captures Palermo, then swings east to seize Messina.

1 August. **Liberators Bomb Vital Oilfields. Ploesti, Romania.**
In a 2,400-mile flight B-24 Liberator Bombardment Groups of the Ninth Air Force make a daring, low-level strike at the Ploesti oil fields from desert bases in Africa. Five airmen are awarded the Medal of Honor.

Right: *B-24s of the 93d Bombardment Group (Heavy), 9th U.S. Air Force, attack oil refineries in Ploesti, Romania, on 1 August 1943. Both the pilot and copilot of the bomber leading the attack received Medals of Honor posthumously. ("Fire Over Ploesti," Roy Grinnell, National Guard Bureau)*

Below: *Lieutenant General George Patton and Brigadier General Theodore Roosevelt, Jr., in Sicily, 4 August 1943. (U.S. Army)*

2 August. **Air Strike Slams Naples.**
The campaign that is to culminate in the invasion of Italy gets underway with a heavy bombing raid on Naples.

7 August. **Amphibious Landings. Sicily.**
Sicily's north coast sees a series of amphibious landings.

17 August. **Troops Enter Messina. Italy.**
Patton's troops enter Messina, disappointed to find that Axis troops have evacuated successfully and have crossed the strait to the Italian mainland.

1 September. **50,000 Choose to Stay with the WAC.**
All eligible WAAC officers are sworn into the Army of the United States in military grade equivalent to WAAC grade; all WAAC units are redesignated part of the WAC. The conversion of status for the 50,000 (more than 75 percent of the force) who have volunteered for Army status is underway. Director Hobby is now Colonel Hobby. Renewed recruiting is underway as overseas commands request assignment of WAC units. On 30 September the old WAAC ceases to exist.

4 September. **Nisei Battalion Joins the Red Bull Division. Near Oran, North Africa.**
The Nisei 100th Infantry Battalion, composed of Hawaii-born Japanese-American volunteers, joins the 34th (Red Bull) Infantry Division and is quickly assigned to take the place of the 3d Battalion, 133d Infantry, which has been sent on a special security mission to guard General Eisenhower's headquarters. The 100th is soon en route to Italy with the division.

5 September. **The Ninth Air Force Moves to England.**
The books are closed on the Ninth Air Force mission in the Middle East under Lieutenant General Brereton. Since its activation in November 1942 the

Ninth has 1,060 missions under its belt. Its aircraft have dropped over 36 million pounds of bombs, destroyed 666 enemy aircraft, and sunk 109 ships.

9 September. **The Fifth Army Lands in Italy. Salerno, Italy.**
The Fifth U.S. Army under Lieutenant Mark Clark lands near Naples and launches the Battle of Salerno. Meanwhile, British under Montgomery are in action at Taranto to the south. The Fifth Army consists of VI Corps (Major General John P. Lucas) and British X Corps, with a total of eight divisions.

9–16 September. **Troops Battle Stubborn Defenders. Salerno Beachhead, Italy.**
VI Corps battles to dislodge enemy defenders. The 3d, 34th, 36th, and 45th Infantry Divisions, the 82d Airborne Division, the 13th Field Artillery Brigade, and Rangers are committed to the battle. Enemy counterattacks almost overwhelm the beachhead. On 7 September, near Salerno, the Allied forces in southern Italy link up.

Above: *WACs clean their mess kits during field training. ("Necessary Evil," Manuel Tolegian, Army Art Collection, NMUSA)*

18 September. **Italy Surrenders. Rome, Italy.**
Italy surrenders to the Allies; Italian forces not under German command and control re-enter the war on the Allied side.

14 September. **Strategic Strike by Bombers. Schweinfurt, Germany.**
Eighth Air Force heavy bombers conduct an important strike against roller and ball bearing factories.

23 September. **Slow Going from Salerno.**
The U.S. and Allies advance from Salerno. In the Fifth Army's VI Corps sector the 3d and 45th Infantry Divisions are slowed by demolitions. Engineers are called upon to keep routes of advance open. British forces move on Naples and Foggia, both of which are soon in Allied hands.

15 October. **Ninth Air Force Pre-Invasion Missions. Sunninghill Park, England.**
General Brereton reassembles his staff from the Middle East and reorganizes the Ninth Air Force for demanding missions in support of the coming invasion of the European mainland.

27 October. **Infantry Singled Out for Recognition. Washington, D.C.**
A War Department decision establishes two special

badges to provide special recognition for the infantry: the Combat Infantryman badge (CIB) and the Expert Infantryman badge (EIB). Higher standards are outlined for the CIB, which requires "duty in action against the enemy."

1 October. **82d Airborne Division Goes Into City. Naples, Italy.**
The 82nd Airborne Division enters Naples. On 5 October patrols are at the Volturno River and by 7 October VI Corps troops are at the Volturno in force preparing for further offensive operations. The 3d, 36th, and 45th Infantry Divisions man the portion of the Fifth Army sector at the boundary with the British Eighth Army.

12–15 October. **The Attack Toward Liri Valley. Volturno River, Italy.**
Fifth Army units begin assault crossings over the river on a 40-mile front, slogging into the Upper Volturno Valley against stiff resistance. During 26 October– 4 November, the VI Corps divisions make a third crossing of the twisting Volturno as the 34th and 45th Infantry Divisions maneuver to help the 3d Infantry Division take the Mignano Gap. By noon on 4 November the VI Corps is across the upper Volturno in force at the entrance to the Liri Valley.

5–15 November. **Fifth Army Meets The Winter Line. Near Mignano Gap, Italy.**
With terrible weather conditions enveloping the area, the decision is made to make an all-out effort to get into the Liri Valley before heavy flooding becomes an issue. VI Corps sends the 3d Infantry Division in an effort to penetrate the Mignano Gap as far as Cassino. It meets stiff enemy defenses at Mt. la Difensa, where one regiment is stymied for ten days. The Fifth Army directs VI Corps to pull out of the la Difensa stalemate; this is accomplished by 15 November. To the right, the 45th Division is having better luck taking the high ground flanking the Mignano Gap. Its efforts are reinforced by the 1st Ranger Battalion and the 509th Parachute Infantry. In the U.S. II Corps sector (Major General Geoffrey Keyes), the 36th Division is bolstered with attachment of the "Force"—the First Special Service Force, a regimental-size, light infantry combat team of Canadians and Americans under Colonel (later Major General) Robert T. Frederick.

16 November. **Combat Boot Approved.**
Responding to suggestions from troops in the field, the Army approves a standard combat boot to replace the field shoe worn with canvas leggings for field wear.

18 November. **Factories Bombed. Norway.**
Bombers strike at factories in German-held Norway.

2 December. **Chemical Surprise Follows Air Raid. Italy.**
Hundreds of burn casualties following destruction of the *John Harvey* in an enemy air raid against allied shipping in the harbor of Bari includes the loss of the Army's 701st Chemical Maintenance Company. Army

Right: *LSTs (Land Ship Tanks) proved indispensable to Army amphibious operations in all theaters of combat. ("Unloading LSTs," Gary Sheahan, Army Art Collection, NMUSA)*

medic Lieutenant Colonel Stewart F. Alexander finds casualties are due to mustard vapor. The transport was carrying the dreaded toxic agent, to be used only if the enemy used chemical agents first.

2 December. **An Obstacle on the Road to Rome. Near Mount la Difensa, Italy.**

II Corps (Keyes) initiates operations to deceive the Germans, intended to keep the enemy from using his reserves effectively. The 36th Division with the 1st Special Service Force attached, carries out an attack on the Difensa-Maggiore complex in rain and cold. By 8 December this complex, a key obstacle on the road to Rome, is in U.S. hands. During a two-day period the Fifth Army fires 206,929 artillery rounds weighing 4,066 tons against caves and entrenched positions. The 34th Division finds slow going on the slopes of Mt. Marrone.

Above: *In the Salerno area during the Italian Campaign, GIs encountered stubborn German defenders in a series of clashes fought at close quarters within caves. ("Battle of the Caves," Robert Benney, Army Art Collection, NMUSA)*

Right: *An Army L-4 "Cub" artillery-spotting plane takes off from one of the two LSTs that underwent conversion to miniaircraft carriers by the 3d Infantry Division prior to the invasion of Italy. This concept was used in all subsequent Mediterranean invasions. (National Archives)*

8–11 December. **The First Battle for San Pietro. Ceppagna, Italy.**

After several probes by the Rangers, 36th Infantry Division troops move up the slope of Mount Sammucro with the village of San Pietro as the objective. After three days of bitter fighting the attack is called off. A second attack is launched 15 December. The division is reinforced with the 504th Parachute Infantry and a battalion of tanks. By 17 December San Pietro is in U.S. hands. For the next two months both VI Corps and II Corps will engage in heavy action along a 15-mile front.

10 December. **Persian Command is Upgraded. Teheran, Iran.**

The Persian Gulf Service Command is redesignated the Persian Gulf Command. It is relieved from

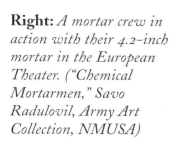
Right: *A mortar crew in action with their 4.2-inch mortar in the European Theater. ("Chemical Mortarmen," Savo Radulovil, Army Art Collection, NMUSA)*

assignment to the Army Forces in the Middle East and placed directly under the War Department. Work nears completion on a permanent, all-weather, two-lane highway from Khorramshahr to Andimeshk to facilitate movement of supplies to Russia.

15 December. **First All-Draftee Division in Theater. Casablanca, French Morocco.**
The first division composed almost entirely of draftees, the 88th Infantry Division, arrives and quickly prepares for movement to Magenta, Algeria, for intensive training. The division, commanded by Major General John E. Sloan, is ordered to prepare for combat service in Italy. The division reaches Naples, Italy, on 6 February 1944.

24 December. **General Eisenhower Commands Forces for Invasion.**
President Roosevelt announces General Dwight D. Eisenhower as Supreme Commander of the Allied Expeditionary Force for the future invasion/liberation of France.

30 December. **Black Parachute Unit is Formed. Fort Benning, Georgia.**
The Army activates the 555th Parachute Infantry Company, the first black airborne unit. This becomes the core of the future 555th ("Triple Nickel") Parachute Infantry Battalion at Camp Mackall, North Carolina, 25 November 1944.

1944

8 January. **Germans Withdraw Across the Rapido River. Near Mt. Trocchio, Italy.**
As the fight to break the Winter Line continues, in the U.S. II Corps area, Task Force B, 36th Infantry Division outflanks and captures Hill 1109. The enemy withdraws back to Mt. Trocchio and nearby high ground to defend approaches to the Liri Valley, which leads to Rome.

20–22 January. **River Crossing Meets Fierce Opposition. Rapido River, Italy.**
As the 34th Infantry Division feints toward Cassino, the 36th Infantry Division attempts a crossing of the Rapido River in the San Angelo area. A fragile hold on the far bank is achieved, but advance elements lose contact with the main body as German counterattacks hit the bridgehead, resulting in heavy U.S. casualties.

22 January. **Fifth Army Troops in Surprise Assault. Anzio-Nettuno, Italy.**
U.S. VI Corps (Major General John P. Lucas) spearheads Operation Shingle, an effort to surprise the Germans, ease the pressure at the Rapido, and open the road north to Rome. Three simultaneous landings initially stun defenders, and landing forces quickly advance to the initial beachhead line. Here the enemy rallies and bitter fighting ensues.

24 January–11 February. **Stalemate at the Rapido and at Anzio. Italy.**

In the II Corps area 34th Infantry Division elements are unsuccessful in their efforts to cross the Rapido. Red Bull Division troops make a river crossing upstream as the First Battle for Monte Cassino starts to develop. In the Anzio Beachhead a U.S. attack to recover lost ground is beaten back. During 29–30 January, the 1st and 3d Ranger Battalions are surprised by waiting German armor units and suffer crippling casualties while leading a night attack to capture Cisterna in an effort to break out of the beleaguered beachhead that is now being pounded by enemy artillery.

24 January. **"Old Ironsides" Joins the Fray. Anzio Beachhead, Italy.**

The 1st Armored Division (Major General Vern E. Prichard), which first saw action in North Africa, lands at Anzio, where it repels counterattacks and maintains defensive positions until the breakout 23 May. Divisional elements have already seen action at Salerno and near the Rapido River.

Above: *The U.S. Army Band ("Pershing's Own") plays at the Mosque of the Fisheries, Algiers, Algeria, 1943. (U.S. Army Band)*

9 February. **The Bronze Star Medal is Approved. Washington, D.C.**

The new Bronze Star Medal is authorized by the President to be awarded "for heroic or meritorious service against the enemy not involving aerial flight." It is noted that the ribbon will be issued until the medal is available.

11 February. **Armored Divisions in Buildup of Forces. United Kingdom.**

The arrival of the 5th and 6th Armored Divisions highlights the continuing pre-invasion buildup in the United Kingdom. Over one million U.S. troops have been transported across the Atlantic. Divisions are now training in England, Northern Ireland, and Scotland.

15 February. **Beachhead Defense Stiffens, Awaits Counterattack. Anzio, Italy.**

Major General Lucas reshuffles VI Corps defenses in anticipation of a counterattack by enemy forces. II Corps troops meanwhile continue efforts to establish a bridgehead across the Rapido, south of Cassino, but the attack fails. General Clark approves air and artillery to destroy the Benedictine Abbey of Monte Cassini, which is found to be a major base for enemy offensive operations.

DWIGHT D. EISENHOWER: GENERAL "IKE"

From humble beginnings in Kansas to Supreme Commander, Allied Expeditionary Force, and then two terms as President, Dwight David Eisenhower embodied the qualities of humility, sincerity, and hard work in everything he did. Despite his positions of great authority, throughout his career he was affectionately known to all as "Ike."

Born 14 October 1890 in Denison, Texas, Eisenhower early on demonstrated a keen interest in history. In 1911, at age 21, he was accepted at the U.S. Military Academy, graduating in 1915. Eisenhower rose steadily through the Army's slow promotion system, making temporary lieutenant colonel in October 1918. World War I ended before Eisenhower could join the AEF in France. Like many others, he reverted to his Regular rank of captain, but he was promoted to major in December 1920.

In 1922, Eisenhower went to the Panama Canal Zone as executive officer to Brigadier General Fox Conner. Conner became Eisenhower's mentor. Through Conner's efforts, Eisenhower attended the General Staff School, where he graduated at the top of his class, and the War College.

Transferred to Washington, D.C., in 1930, Eisenhower worked for the assistant secretary of war, and in 1933, for the chief of staff, General Douglas MacArthur. When MacArthur went to organize the new Philippine Army in 1935, Lieutenant Colonel Eisenhower was his chief of staff. In 1939, Eisenhower was concerned about missing a major war again and requested a transfer to the United States. As the Army expanded, temporary promotions were used again. In March 1941, Eisenhower was promoted to colonel and then in September to brigadier general for his performance as chief of staff, Third Army, during the summer maneuvers.

After Pearl Harbor, Eisenhower worked in the Army General Staff War Plans Division, under Chief of Staff General George C. Marshall. Temporary promotions to major general and lieutenant general came in 1942. In June, Marshall sent Major General Eisenhower to England, appointing him Commander of the European Theater of Operations and Commander of U.S. forces in Europe. In November 1943 Eisenhower commanded the Allied invasion of North Africa and retaking of Tunisia. He then commanded the Allied invasions of Sicily and then mainland Italy. Recalled to London, Eisenhower began planning the Allied cross-channel invasion of Europe. By December 1943, he was a temporary four-star general and Supreme Commander of the Allied Expeditionary Force.

Commanding the huge D-Day invasion force was the greatest military achievement of Eisenhower's career. The successful landings were due in large part to Eisenhower's decisions and meticulous planning of the operation. In December 1944 Eisenhower was promoted to temporary rank of General of the Army (it became permanent in 1946). Eisenhower's firm, but fair, hand eventually led the Allies to victory on 8 May 1945. He continued to command the Allied occupation forces in Germany until November, when he was recalled to Washington to replace General Marshall as Chief of Staff.

On 2 May 1948, Eisenhower retired from the active Army to become president of Columbia University. His retirement was short-lived as he was recalled to duty by President Truman in December 1950 to serve as the first Supreme Allied Commander Europe and commander of NATO forces. In 1952 Eisenhower retired again to enter politics as the Republican presidential candidate, easily winning the election. He served two consecutive terms in the White House (1952–1958), and his presidency was notable for several major achievements. Suffering from illness, Eisenhower retired from public life in January 1961. After a long hospitalization at Walter Reed Army Hospital, Eisenhower died on 28 March 1969.

—*Vince Hawkins*

Above: *During World War II, Eisenhower rose from lieutenant colonel to become the supreme commander of Allied forces in Europe. (Army Art Collection, NMUSA)*

16–19 February. **Another Powerful Counterattack. Anzio, Italy.**

Allied airpower is diverted to support Anzio beachhead forces (instead of hitting Cassino targets) as the Germans unleash yet another powerful and well-coordinated counterattack to batter VI Corps positions held by the 3d and 45th Infantry Divisions and British 56th Division. After heavy losses by Allied forces, the action subsides in the struggle for Monte Cassino.

18 February. **Soldier-Students Leave Campus Life Behind.**

As the shortage of infantrymen becomes apparent throughout the Army, orders are issued to drop 110,000 (of 140,000) soldier scholars from college classrooms by 1 April. This marks the virtual disbandment of the Army Specialized Training Program (ASTP), but General Marshall explains (to the Secretary of War) that the alternative is disbanding undermanned units. Approximately 80,000 ex-ASTP are soon headed to the ground forces. Remaining in ASTP status are 30,000 soldiers enrolled in advanced medicine, dentistry, and engineering.

23 February. **Truscott Commands VI Corps. Anzio Beachhead, Italy.**

Major General Lucian K. Truscott, Jr., gives up command of the 3d Infantry Division as he is put at the helm of the faltering VI Corps effort. Major General John P. Lucas is relieved. Enemy counterattacks are resumed during 28 February through 3 March. On 29 February alone, the 3d Division beats back three determined counterattacks by the enemy.

28 February. **Allied Commanders Look Ahead. Caserta, Italy.**

Senior allied commanders meet to plan for the drive on Rome. In the II Corps sector elements of the newly arrived 88th Infantry Division (Sloan) relieve 36th Infantry Division troops on Mount Castellone.

2 March. **Patch is to Command Operation Anvil.**

Lieutenant General Alexander M. Patch is advised that as commander of U.S. Seventh Army he will command "Anvil"—the invasion of Southern France. At this point it is anticipated that Anvil will be carried out simultaneously with the cross-channel invasion of Normandy. Anvil is later renamed Dragoon.

3 March. **Final Action in Anzio Defense. Ponte Rotto, Italy.**

In the Fifth Army's VI Corps sector, troops of the 3d Infantry Division successfully hold off a German counterattack, which proves to be the last major enemy effort to break the allied hold on the Anzio beachhead. Now enemy forces are organizing for defense.

Right: *Winter made Italy a frozen battleground as American artillery troops discovered while fighting their way northward. ("Artillery Position Above Loilano," Savo Radulovic, Army Art Collection, NMUSA)*

Below: *Maintaining communications remained the Signal Corps' primary mission in Africa and Europe. ("Signal Corps," Mead Schaeffer, Army Art Collection, NMUSA)*

4 March. **U.S. "Heavies" First Strike at Nazi Capital. Berlin, Germany.**
The capital of Nazi Germany experiences its first bombardment by the U.S. as the VIII Bomber Command dispatches 238 B-17 Flying Fortress aircraft on a daylight foray. Bad weather forces a recall of the

mission, but the 95th Bombardment Group presses on and bombs targets from 28,000 feet. It is later learned that the "recall" message came from an enemy transmitter.

15 March. **Monastery is Target of Air Strikes. Monte Cassino, Italy.**
In greatest effort to-date, U.S. Army aircraft help to level Cassino with 1,200 tons of bombs followed by an intense artillery barrage. The Third Battle of Cassino is underway on the ground as allied forces grind their way toward Monastery Hill. The 85th Infantry Division (Major General John B. Coulter) joins the Fifth Army after the completion of training in Algeria. Cassino defies Allied efforts for nearly four months. The battle-weary 36th Infantry Division is withdrawn for rest and refitting.

4 April. **Twentieth Air Force Activated. Washington, D.C.**
Created to exploit the capabilities of the B-29 Superfortress, the Twentieth Air Force is created to carry the air war to the Japanese home islands. It is initially under the direct control of the Joint Chiefs of Staff through General Henry H. Arnold, Army Air Force chief.

5 April. **The 90th, an "All-Draftee" Division, is Overseas. Liverpool, England.**
The 90th (T/O for Texas-Oklahoma) Infantry Division is the first of the "draftee" infantry divisions

Left: *Tankers and infantrymen of the 1st Armor Division and 1st Armored Infantry break out from the Anzio beachhead to move inland. ("Into the Shadow," James Dietz)*

DIETZ

deployed to the United Kingdom. Later the "T/O" on its insignia is defined as "Tough Ombres."

26 April. **Invasion Rehearsal Disrupted by E-Boats. Slapton Sands, England.**
German E-boats attack a convoy of Army troops practicing for D-Day. Almost 750 soldiers and sailors die in the tragedy off Slapton Sands in the southwest of England. The incident long remains classified. Rehearsals resume in early May.

11 May. **The 88th and 85th Divisions Lead the Attack. Near the Gulf of Gaeta, Italy.**
Under cover of artillery fire, the Fifth Army jumps off to break through German's Gustav Line, in the drive on Rome. The U.S. II Corps (Keyes) attacks with the 85th Infantry Division on the left and the 88th on the right. By 16 May both divisions are advancing rapidly through the Formia corridor. On 19 May a drop by the 509th Parachute Infantry Battalion north of Mt. Romano helps speed the II Corps advance.

18 May. **36th Division Displaces to Beachhead. Anzio, Italy.**
After its draw-down following the Rapido campaign and the protracted assault on Cassino, the 36th Infantry Division makes an amphibious landing at

Anzio where the 3d and 45th Infantry Divisions are preparing for an attack toward Cisterna. Allied troops learn during day that a Polish division has finally secured Monte Cassino.

22 May. **New Ninth Army in the United Kingdom. Bristol, England.**
Ten days after its arrival in the United Kingdom the original U.S. Eighth Army Headquarters is redesignated the U.S. Ninth Army. General Eisenhower requests the change to forestall any possible confusion with the British Eighth Army of desert fame. The new Ninth is under the command of Lieutenant General William Hood Simpson, a 1909 West Point graduate awarded the Distinguished Service Medal and Silver Star in World War I.

23 May. **Breakout from the Beachhead. Anzio, Italy.**
After more than four months under fire, the reinforced VI Corps breaks out of the Anzio beachhead and resumes the attack north toward Rome. The Fifth Army issues a plan for VI Corps to link up with II Corps and join forces for the push north.

4 June. **Rome Falls to the Allies. Rome, Italy.**
The Fifth Army forces converge on Rome. Troopers of the 88th Reconnaissance Troop, 88th Infantry

Right: *The invasion of France began with an assault by paratroopers of the 82d and 101st Airborne Divisions. Once on the ground, the scattered paratroopers regrouped to attack the German rear. ("Hours of Liberation," Larry Selman)*

Division are "officially" the first U.S. troops to enter the city limits. Other units join in the race; many enter claims to being "first" of the U.S. forces into the Eternal City. General Clark designates the 3d Infantry Division (less one regiment) to garrison Rome and revert to Army reserve.

6 June. The Longest Day: Invasion/Liberation is Launched. Normandy, France.

Operation Overlord (D-Day), the Allied invasion of France, begins with predawn airborne landings followed by a seaborne assault with U.S., British, and Canadian forces in the vanguard. The two U.S. landing sites are designated Omaha Beach (V Corps) and Utah Beach (VII Corps). German resistance is heaviest on Omaha Beach, where units of 1st and 29th Infantry Divisions land. The 2d Ranger Battalion scales cliffs at Point-de-Hoc to seize German coastal guns. On Utah Beach, the soldiers of the 4th Infantry Division are led ashore by Brigadier Theodore Roosevelt, Jr., son of the former President. A World War I veteran, he is assigned as a "spare" general officer because of his experience in amphibious landings in North Africa and Sicily. He succumbs to a heart attack on 13 July and is posthumously awarded the Medal of Honor.

7 June. Troop Ship Hits Mine, All on Board Are Saved. Near Reuville, France.

Headed for Utah Beach the transport *Susan B. Anthony* hits a mine and sinks in less than two hours. The ship is carrying an advance party of the 90th Infantry Division headquarters and 2d Battalion, 359th Infantry. Decisive action by Brigadier General Samuel T. Williams results in no loss of life. The bulk of equipment and weapons are lost.

8 June. U.S. and British Troops in Contact. Bayeux, France.

Contact is established between the U.S. First Army and the British Second Army near the village of Port-en-Bessin. In the First Army area the U.S. VII Corps (Major General J. Lawton Collins) begins on all-out drive to gain the important port city of Cherbourg with elements from the 82d Airborne Division and 4th Infantry Division. On VII Corps' south flank the 101st Airborne Division develops the battle for control of the Carentan area, the key to a linkup with V Corps (Major General Leonard Gerow) moving inland from Omaha Beach objectives. Elements of the 29th Infantry Division (Major General Charles Gerhardt) relieve the hard-pressed 2d Ranger Battalion at Pointe du Hoc. The 2d Infantry Division (Major General Walter M. Robertson) is in action in the V Corps zone.

10 June. **Nisei Regimental Combat Team at the Front. Civitavechchia, Italy.**

A few miles north of Rome the newly arrived 442d Regimental Combat Team, mostly Hawaiian Japanese-Americans, is attached to the 34th Infantry Division and is joined by the 100th Battalion, which has been in combat with the Red Bull since Salerno. After some reorganization the old 100th becomes the 1st Battalion of the 442d as they hit the road to Belvedere with the Rome-Arno campaign underway.

10 June. **VI Corps Out of Italy. Highway Marker 136, North of Rome.**

The U.S. IV Corps (Major General Willis D. Crittenberger) assumes control as the VI Corps (Truscott) headquarters pulls out to start planning for its role in the forthcoming invasion of southern France. As several combat-experienced divisions depart to prepare for the next VI Corps campaign, II Corps (Major General Geoffrey Keyes) and IV Corps will command the 34th, 85th, 88th, 91st, and 92d Infantry Divisions, 10th Mountain Division, and 1st Armored Division.

15 June. **The Army Celebrates Infantry Day. Fort McClellan, Alabama.**

As the Army celebrates "Infantry Day," this Infantry

Above: *Coming ashore under heavy attack by German defenders, men of the 4th U.S. Infantry Division were among the first to storm ashore at the hotly contested Utah Beach on 6 June 1944. ("Overlord, Utah Beach," James Dietz)*

Replacement Training Center welcomes the 200,000th man to arrive for infantry basic training—Private Norman W. Crew of Brookline, Massachusetts.

17–18 June. **Troops Battle Through the Night. Barneville-sur-mer, France.**

In the VII Corps area, the 9th Infantry Division (Major General Manton S. Eddy) breaks through to the west, sealing off the Cotentin Peninsula, trapping German defenders. Other units continue to press north and east out of the beachhead as the 82d Airborne Division at Pont l'Abbé comes under VII Corps control. In the XIX Corps (Major General Charles H. Corlett) zone of action the efforts of the 29th Infantry Division to advance are contained in the vicinity of Villiers-Fossard.

22 June. **"GI Bill" Gets Final Approval. Washington, D.C.**

In a moment that will have far-reaching effects for many years to come, President Franklin D. Roosevelt signs the "GI Bill," giving broad benefits to veterans.

23 June. **Outer Defenses Penetrated. Cherbourg, France.**

In VII Corps sector, the 9th Infantry Division breaks into the defenses of the port city with all three of the division's infantry regiments committed to the effort. It will take another three days of fighting to clear the city and start to exploit its harbor facilities. Progress is slow elsewhere in the corps sector by the 4th and 79th Infantry Divisions.

EYEWITNESS: D-DAY

On 6 June 1944 the largest amphibious-air assault force in history landed in Normandy, France. Among the thousands of men who struggled ashore on Omaha Beach, one of two American objectives, was Bob Slaughter, 116th Infantry Regiment, 29th Division. He recalled:

"The Channel was extremely rough, and it wasn't long before we had to help the craft's pumps by bailing with our helmets. . . . As the sky lightened, the armada became visible. The smoking and burning French shoreline also became more defined. At 0600, the huge guns of the Allied navies opened up with what must have been the greatest artillery barrage ever.

"A few thousand yards from shore we rescued three or four survivors from a craft that had been swamped and sunk . . . About two or three hundred yards from shore we encountered artillery fire. Near misses sent water skyward and then it rained back on us. About 150 yards from shore I raised my head despite the warning 'Keep your head down.' I saw the boat on our right taking a terrific licking from small arms. Tracer bullets were bouncing and skipping off the ramp and sides as the enemy zeroed in on the boat. Great plumes of water from enemy artillery and mortars sprouted close by. We knew then this was not going to be a walk-in. No one thought the enemy would give us this kind of opposition at the water's edge. We expected A and B Companies to have the beach secured by the time we landed. In reality, no one had set foot in our sector. The coxswain had missed the Vierville church steeple, our point to guide on, and the tides also helped pull us 200 yards east.

"The location didn't make much difference. We could hear the 'p-r-r-r-r-, p-r-r-r-r' of enemy machine guns to our right, towards the west. It was obvious someone was catching that hell, getting chewed up where we had been supposed to come in.

"The ramp went down while shells exploded on land and in the water. Unseen snipers were shooting down from the cliffs, but the most havoc came from automatic weapons. I was at the left side of the craft, about fifth from the front. . . . The ramp was in the surf, and the front of the steel bucked violently up and down. Only two at a time could exit.

"When my turn came, I sat on the edge of the bucking ramp, trying to time my leap on the down cycle. I sat there way too long, causing a bottleneck and endangering myself and the men to follow.

"When I did get out, I was in the water. It was very difficult to shed the 60 pounds of equipment, and if one were a weak swimmer he could drown before he inflated his Mae West. Many were hit in the water and drowned, good swimmers or not. There were dead men floating in the water and live men acting dead, letting the tide take them in. Initially, I tried to take cover behind one of the heavy timbers and then noticed an innocent-looking Teller mine tied to the top. I crouched down to chin deep in the water as shells fell at the water's edge. Small-arms fire kicked up sand. I noticed a GI running, trying to get across the beach. He was weighted down with equipment and having difficulty moving. An enemy gunner shot him. He screamed for a medic. An aidman moved quickly to help him and he was also shot. I'll never forget seeing that medic lying next to that wounded soldier, both of them screaming. They died in minutes.

"Boys were turned into men. Some would be very brave men; others would soon be dead men, but any who survived would be frightened men. Some wet their pants, others cried unashamedly. Many just had to find within themselves the strength to get the job done. Discipline and training took over."

—*Vince Hawkins*

Above: *D-Day at Omaha Beach, where American troops of the 1st and 29th Divisions and Rangers gained the beachhead with bravery and blood. ("Omaha Beach," Gary Sheahan, Army Art Collection, NMUSA)*

3 July. **Offensive Encounters Normandy Hedgerows.**
The U.S. First Army launches a general offensive into what is soon described as "the Battle of the Hedgerows." VIII Corps, in a driving rain that prevents air support and hampers movement, attacks down the west coast of the Cotentin Peninsula with the 79th Infantry Division, 82d Airborne Division, and 90th Infantry Division abreast from west to east.

13–14 July. **Hedgerow Cutter Demonstration. Normandy, France.**
Invited to a demonstration at the 2d Infantry Division command post, Generals Bradley and Gerow see the first demonstration of a hedgerow-cutting device improvised by members of the 102d Cavalry Reconnaissance Squadron, 102d (Essex Troop) Cavalry Group (Mechanized). The V Corps Ordnance officer soon has production lines cranking them out for attachment to light and medium tanks scheduled to take part in Operation Cobra. In the meantime the 4th Armored Division comes ashore to join the fight.

15–18 July. **End of Hedgerows Campaign, Liberation of St.-Lô.**
The First Army deploys elements for the attack, which finally gets them out of the hedgerow country. The 29th and 35th Infantry Divisions engage in the battle for St.-Lô. When a 35th Division unit seizes the slopes of Hill 122 it is within 2,000 yards of the city limits. With the capture of St.-Lô by XIX Corps troops on 18 July the Army concludes the Battle of the

Hedgerows and readies First Army elements for the launching of Operation Cobra.

18 July. **U.S. Forces Take Leghorn, Patrol to the Arno. Near Pisa, Italy.**
In Fifth Army's IV Corps sector the 34th Infantry Division begins its final assault on Leghorn with an RCT attached from the 91st Infantry Division (Task

Right: *Infantrymen of the 88th Infantry Division found street fighting in a Northern Italian town a dangerous undertaking. Urban warfare then and now poses a hazardous challenge to the American soldier. (Center of Military History)*

Force Williamson under Brigadier General Raymond Williamson). The attack reaches the city's outskirts. Other 91st Infantry Division elements reach the Arno River at Pontadera. On 19 July Leghorn falls to the Red Bull division. The 88th Infantry Division joins the 91st Infantry Division in patrolling to the Arno. By 20 July the 34th Infantry Division has elements nearing Pisa. Troops prepare to assault the enemy's Gothic Line.

22 July. Army Group is Under Bradley's Command. Colombières, France.

The headquarters of the U.S. 12th Army Group (originally formed in the U.K. as the First United States Army Group) moves to the continent and Lieutenant General Omar N. Bradley (already in France with First Army) open his first Group Command Post in a Normandy apple orchard. Bradley's command is operational 1 August 1944 and exercises command and control of the First Army (Hodges) and Third Army (Patton).

25 July. First Army Launches Breakout. Normandy, France.

The First Army initiates Operation Cobra, a breakout from Normandy. During a bombing strike, munitions land on U.S. positions. Lieutenant General Lesley J. McNair, the Army Ground Forces commander in France on a special mission, is killed. On the other side of the world, his son, Colonel Douglas C. McNair, is killed in action on Guam with the 77th

Infantry Division on 6 August (see Chapter 14.) General McNair is the highest ranking American officer to die as a result of "friendly" fire. Cobra continues and the VIII Corps joins V Corps and VII Corps in the drive.

1 August. Hodges Moved Up to Army Command.

Lieutenant General Courtney H. Hodges, until now serving under Bradley as the First Army deputy commander, is announced as Army commander. Although corps are attached and detached in accordance with tactical needs, the V Corps and VII Corps remain under the First Army from Normandy to the end of ETO action, 337 days in combat. Hodges remains in command throughout the war.

1 August. The Third Army's Secret is Out. Patton is Named Commander.

After a "secret existence" for many months, the U.S. Third Army is identified as being in the field. Lieutenant General George S. Patton, Jr., whose role was under wraps to mislead Germans, is now openly named as commander of the army he will now lead to the end of World War II combat. Patton is now "operational" with VIII, XII, XV, and XX Corps under his wing.

1 August. New Sixth Army Group in Wings. Bastia, Corsica.

The headquarters of the U.S. Sixth Army Group is organized under the command of General Jacob L.

Left: *A quartermaster laundry platoon performs a mundane but critical mission that promoted the health and comfort of American fighting men in the field. (National Archives)*

Below: *The "soldier's general," Omar Bradley, provided important high-level leadership in the European Theater of Operations. He particularly enjoyed the full confidence of his commander, Dwight Eisenhower. (National Archives)*

Devers. Its mission is to provide overall operational control for the U.S. Seventh Army (Patch) and the future French First Army (General Jean de Lattre de Tassigny), the major command elements in charge of the planned invasion of southern France. The southern France landing is delayed (see 15 August) due to an acute shortage of landing craft.

4 August. **The High Command Alters the Attack on the Gothic Line.**
The plan for attack on the Gothic Line is revised. The new plan calls for the Fifth Army to be strengthened by the attachment of British 13 Corps, to make a subsidiary attack north from Florence to Bologna. The D-Day for offensive is delayed to 19 August. The main effort is to be by II Corps, while IV Corps maneuvers in the Pontedera-Cascina area.

8 August. **Besieged Port is Objective. Vicinity Brest, France.**
In the Third Army area the VIII Corps demand for the surrender of Brest is ignored. The 6th Armored Division prepares for an all-out assault until a threat to the rear area forces a change in plans. An enemy division is intercepted moving toward Brest. Bitter fighting continues on the outskirts of St. Malo where elements of the 83d Infantry Division meet heavy opposition as they advance on Dinard. Le Mans is

overrun by XV Corps with the French 2d Armored Division attached. General Eisenhower moves his headquarters from England to France.

Right: *Operation Anvil-Dragoon was the Allied invasion of Southern France. Once again, airborne elements, including glider infantry, formed the leading elements of the invasion force. ("Glider Landing in Southern France," Tom Craig, Army Art Collection, NMUSA)*

14–15 August. **D-Day in the South of France. Riviera Coast, France.**
U.S. and French Divisions under the U.S. Seventh Army land in southern France. Launching Operation Dragoon, VI Corps (Truscott) lands a three-division force against moderate resistance and quickly expands the beachhead. The forerunner of the French First Army joins the Seventh Army in the seizure of the Riviera and for the drive up the Rhone River valley.

21 August. **The Falaise-Argentan Gap is Secured.**
The closure of the Falaise Gap results in a big bag (50,000) of German soldiers captured. This brings the Battle of Normandy to a conclusion and U.S. commanders turn their attention to the east—and Paris. The French 2d Armored Division is alerted to liberate the French capital. The 4th Infantry Division is transferred to V Corps from VII Corps and instructed to support the French division as needed.

25 August. **The French Capital is Liberated from the Nazis. Paris, France.**
The fabled capital city is liberated after three years of occupation by the Nazis. The honor of leading the way is given to the U.S.-equipped French 2d Armored Division (Major General Leclerc) supported closely by the soldiers of the U.S. 4th Infantry Division (Major General Raymond O. Barton). The advance is screened by the 102d Cavalry Group (Mechanized).

27 August. **Troops Parade. Into Combat. Paris, France.**
General Eisenhower and members of his staff arrive in Paris. In response to the French request, an impromptu parade is arranged. Troops of the 28th (Keystone) Infantry Division are diverted for a march down the Champs Elysées and continue through streets of Paris toward the frontlines.

21 August. **Transportation Corps Reveals "Red Ball" Plan. St.-Lô, France.**
The Army Transportation Corps announces its "Red Ball Express," a unique fast-delivery system using over 6,000 Quartermaster and Transportation Corps trucks and one-way road traffic to speed supplies to the advancing U.S. forces. The original Red Ball route is to Paris from St.-Lô and back. Other "express" routes are soon in operation. Red Ball convoys operate through 13 November 1944, traveling 1,504,616 ton-miles. Nearly 75 percent of the truck companies in the Motor Transport Service, ETO, were manned by black troops.

30 August. **Canadian-American Force Seizes Riviera Centerpiece. Nice. France.**
The 1st Airborne Task Force (General Robert T. Frederick) drives through this Riviera landmark to Beaulieu. Meanwhile the main body of the Seventh Army moves up the Rhone Valley (via Avignon). VI Corps, after action at Montelimar, races on toward Lyon. General Patch aims for an early linkup with U.S. forces moving east from Normandy.

GENERAL GEORGE S. PATTON, JR.

General George S. Patton, Jr., loved war. From his days sitting on his father's knee listening to stories of his heroic ancestors until the day he died, Patton relished the excitement of battle.

After spending a year at the Virginia Military Institute, he entered West Point and graduated in 1909 with a commission in the cavalry. He served at western outposts before representing the United States in the modern pentathlon at the 1912 Olympic Games.

He won approval to serve as one of Brigadier General John J. Pershing's staff in the 1916 expedition to Mexico, during which he became known as a tough fighter and a strict disciplinarian. He was again with Pershing in the AEF during World War I. On the battlefields of France he trained and led solders to use a new weapon, the tank, in the AEF's Tank Center. As a temporary lieutenant colonel, Patton commanded the 304th Tank Brigade in two battles and was wounded in one of them, ending the war as a temporary colonel.

After the war Patton reverted to his permanent rank of captain, holding several assignments with the cavalry, writing numerous articles on tanks and tactics, and attending the Army Staff College and War College. The approaching war brought back temporary promotions, and in 1940 he was made a brigadier and sent to the newly formed 2d Armored Division, which he took over in April 1941 as a major general. He trained this division, and then the I Armored Corps, hard and to high standards.

Patton was selected in 1942 to command the Western Task Force of the invasion of North Africa. On 8 November he led it in the amphibious attack on Morocco and then became the military administrator of the country. When the Germans smashed the American II Corps at Kasserine Pass in February 1943, Patton took command and within weeks his revitalized and reinforced II Corps checked the Germans at El Guetar, bringing Patton his third star in April.

Patton next commanded the Seventh Army in the invasion of Sicily on the left flank of the British 8th Army. He was unhappy with his supporting role and instead sent elements of his army blazing north to capture Palermo. He then headed to Messina, reaching the city a few hours before the British, proving that American soldiers were more than equal to any troops in the world.

During the campaign, Patton slapped two hospitalized soldiers who were suffering from battle fatigue. His behavior prompted rebukes from his superiors and he was moved aside until called to London in January 1944 to take command of the Third Army.

The Third Army would become Patton's own. After breaking out of the Normandy beachhead at St. Lo, Patton drove his units in three directions, capturing ports, knifing into France and cutting off retreating Germans. He raced across France until supplies ran low in September. He spent the next two months fighting along the German border, keeping the Germans off balance and preventing them from launching any major counterattacks in his sector.

But the Germans did launch a massive assault north of the Third Army on 16 December 1944, starting the Battle of the Bulge. Patton anticipated an attack and had been considering his actions. In one of the most remarkable maneuvers in military history, Patton had the Third Army disengage from the Germans to its front and turn north. Led by Lieutenant Colonel Creighton Abrams' 37th Tank Battalion, Patton's men fought through tough opposition and heavy snows to relieve Bastogne.

The Third Army next turned east and pushed into Germany, finally ending the war in Czechoslovakia. After the surrender, Patton became the military governor of Bavaria, but he ignored the American political policy for occupation. He was relieved in October, given command of the Fifteenth Army, and tasked with preparing a history of the war. He died on 21 December 1945 shortly after a car accident.

—*Kevin M. Hymel*

Above: *General George Patton's nickname—"Blood and Guts"—characterized his tenacity in battle. (National Archives)*

1 September. The Fifth Army Moves To Hit The Gothic Line. Italy.

General Clark orders IV Corps patrols across the Arno in pursuit of withdrawing enemy forces. Task Force 45 patrols to the Serchio River, crosses additional elements, and clears the northern part of the ancient city of Pisa. CCA, 1st Armored Division clears Mt. Pisano. In the II Corps area 88th Infantry Division patrols make contact with the British at Sesto. Later, the 88th Infantry Division relieves the 442d RCT for shipment to France. On 5 September, the CCA, 1st Armored Division, takes the walled town of Lucca.

2 September. Corps Advance Elements Enter Belgium.

In the First Army area, XIX Corps advance elements drive into Belgium and push toward Tournai. VII Corps units also pursue the enemy into Belgium, crossing the border in several places. The 3d Armored Division pushes to the vicinity of Mons; the 9th Infantry Division swings northeast to positions near Charleroi. V Corps releases the French 2d Armored Division, which, for the time being, remains in the Paris area.

2 September. Truscott Gains Star, Will Return to Italy.

Lucian K. Truscott, Jr., VI Corps commander since the breakout from the Anzio Beachhead in Italy, is promoted to three-star rank. He is told he will give up his command for a new assignment and soon learns he is to return to Italy to take command of U.S. Fifth Army. Truscott's place at the head of VI Corps is taken by Major General Edward H. Brooks.

5 September. The Ninth Army is Operational in France.

The U.S. Ninth Army (Simpson) is officially operational, taking over the mission of containing the besieged city of Brest and other enemy forces in the port cities of Lorient and St. Nazaire while protecting the south flank of the 12th Army Group on the Loire river.

5 September. Stars & Stripes Returns. Paris, France.

The Army newspaper *Stars & Stripes* reappears in the French capital 25 years after its publication was suspended with the end of World War I. Since D-Day, attempts have been made to resume publication in France with little success except in Rennes, where a modern printing plant was found. The Paris edition will use the equipment and offices of the *New York Herald Tribune*. *YANK*, the Army weekly, is already in business using captured German paper and ink.

7 September. The Enemy Withdraws to Gothic Line Positions. North of Florence, Italy.

As II Corps completes preparations for an attack, the enemy withdraws during night of 7–8 September to the Gothic Line itself. This makes the first phase of the planned offensive unnecessary.

10 September. The Long-Awaited Attack on Gothic Line.

II Corps opens the long-awaited drive toward the Gothic Line at 5:30 a.m. with two divisions—the 34th, and 91st Infantry Divisions—abreast. British 13 Corps

Left: *Facing a German counterattack in Mortain, France, men of the 30th Infantry Division dig in, determined to repel the enemy onslaught. ("Battle of Mortain," Keith Rocco, National Guard Bureau)*

Below: *WACs staff a radar site at Camp Griffs, England. Women filled many roles that previously had been assigned to male personnel prior to the war. (National Archives)*

attacks with three divisions in support of II Corps. In the IV Corps sector TF 45 gets additional elements across the Serchio at Vecchiano and the CCA, 1st Armored Division, also advances. On 12 September rapid advance comes to an end as II Corps encounters outer the defenses of the Gothic Line.

11 September. First into Germany.
In the V Corps sector, a dismounted patrol of the 85th Reconnaissance Squadron, 5th Armored Division, is the first Allied unit to cross the border into Germany. In the Third Army area the 90th Infantry Division element clear the heights of Thionville and reach the Moselle River at several points.

12 September–27 October. Troops Find the Gothic Line is Stoutly Defended.
The Fifth Army in attack phase hits the Gothic Line in the west and penetrates toward Bologna, taking heavy losses. Gothic Line defenders resist until the spring of 1945. (See entry for 25 April 1945.)

12–16 September. V Corps Meets the West Wall. Bastogne, Belgium.
General Hodges (First Army) authorizes V Corps (Gerow) to launch a reconnaissance in force toward the Schnee Eifel with an eye to the penetration of the German West Wall defensive position. Gerow dispatches his 5th Armored Division and the 4th and 28th Infantry Divisions, with the 102d Cavalry Group to maintain contact with the cavalry of the VII Corps on its left flank. The Corps front is about 30 miles. V Corps attacks on 14 September. It soon finds the terrain

of the Schnee Eifel discourages employment of armor. After early successes, the enemy reinforces defenses; the drive ends short of its objective on 16 September.

13 September. Into the Forest Primeval. Vicinity Roetgen, Germany.
The 3d Armored ("Spearhead") Division (Major General Maurice Rose) is committed to an initiative by the VII Corps (Collins) to exploit an axis of advance known as the Monschau corridor through the heavily wooded terrain on the border of Germany. On 14 September, the veteran 9th Infantry Division enters

Right: *During Operation Market Garden, paratroopers of the 502d Parachute Infantry Regiment, 82d Airborne Division, prepare to secure a bridge over the Maas River, Grave, Holland. ("Making It Happen," James Dietz)*

the battle that goes into the history books as the battle for the Huertgen Forest. The 9th (now under Major General Louis A. Craig) advances against stubborn resistance through October, when it is relieved by the 28th Infantry Division.

17 September. Joint Airborne Offensive in The Netherlands.
Joining with the British, the U.S. 82d and 101st Airborne Divisions conduct a daylight parachute assault as part of Operation Market Garden at Eindhoven and Arnhem in Holland. The plan is to seize key bridges as a part of a larger Allied operation to secure a route of advance for British armored forces.

4 October. Front Line Mission for the Ninth Army. Arlon, Belgium.
Displaced from its previous command post location at Rennes, France, the Ninth Army (Simpson) assumes responsibility for the sector between Bollendorf and St. Vith in order to establish a new presence in the Luxembourg-Southern Belgium region in order to enable First and Third Armies to concentrate in narrow fronts for offensive action. Initially, only VIII Corps is available to Simpson.

5 October. McLain Takes Reins of XIX Corps.
Major General Raymond S. McLain, after successfully leading the 90th Infantry Division in Normandy, is named to command XIX Corps in Patton's Third Army. The former Oklahoma banker is the first National Guard officer in modern times to command a corps in combat. He is nominated for a third star. (He is promoted 6 June 1945).

5–9 October. The First Struggle for Schmidt.
Adverse weather conditions hamper the 9th Infantry Division in the First Army's VII Corps sector in its attack at Schmidt, an important objective commanding the Roer River and the Schwammenauel Dam. On 6 October the division launches two regiments into the Huertgen Forest toward Schmidt against tenacious opposition. Advance elements make gains on 7 October but the main body fails to catch up. On 8 October tanks and tank destroyers arrive to extricate the 9th Infantry Division elements in the Huertgen. On 9 October 9th Division troops break out of Huertgen in two places. The V Corps attack on the West Wall is postponed to 11 October.

19–20 October. Enemy Garrison Surrounded, Collapses. Aachen, Germany.
In First Army's VII Corps sector, German resistance at Aachen is diminishing rapidly. Efforts to break out of encirclement by U.S. forces are abandoned as the garrison is told to fight to the end. Troops of the 1st Infantry Division clear the city and take Salvator Hill; the Big Red One is assisted by troops from the 28th (Keystone) Infantry Division forcing enemy troops toward the western and southwestern suburbs of the city. Task Force Hogan, 3d Armored Division gains Lousberg Heights and is given task of cutting the Aachen-Laurensburg highway.

1–3 November. **Second Attack on Schmidt by V Corps.**
V Corps (Gerow) adjusts the corps boundary north of Huertgen and launches an attack to clear the Vossenack-Schmidt-Lammersdorf triangles to the headwaters of the Roer. A regiment of the 28th Infantry Division crosses the Kall River and takes Kommerscheidt and Schmidt despite the lack of progress on its flanks. Schmidt is on the enemy's main supply route in the Lammersdorf Corridor.

3 November. **The 92d Division Enters Combat. Serchio Sector, Italy.**
With all of its elements under divisional control, the 92d Infantry Division (Major General Edward M. Almond) starts operations in the Serchio River Valley. Previously its 370th RCT had been attached to the 1st Armored Division. The 92d Infantry Division is composed predominantly of black troops, but many of its officers are white.

Above: *On 2 November 1944 troops of the 110th Infantry, 28th Division, move into the Huertgen Forest, where the enemy, severe weather, and dangerous terrain created a nightmare environment. (National Archives)*

Right: *By 1944 Army field uniforms had evolved into a set of functional and comfortable clothing and web gear. ("The American Soldier, 1944," H. Charles McBarron, Army Art Collection, NMUSA)*

16 November. **First Army on the Point. Schevenhuette, Germany.**
The First Army's VII Corps, in the farthest point of penetration yet made into Germany, launches the main effort toward Cologne and the Roer river. Collins sends the 104th and 4th Infantry Divisions into action.

21 November. **V Corps Rejoins the Fight in Huertgen.**
V Corps joins the offensive with orders to take Huertgen and Kleinhau. The reserve combat command (CCR) of the 5th Armored Division is attached to the 8th Infantry Division (Major General Donald A. Stroh) as the attack is launched through rain, fog, and mud. The 121st Infantry RCT registers only modest gains against positions defended by German guns in the Huertgen thickets. Tanks sever the Huertgen-Kleinhau highway. At 6:00 p.m. on 27 November the 121st RCT reports the fall of Huertgen village.

29 November. **Armor Lends a Hand in Huertgen Forest.**
The Combat Command Reserve (CCR), 5th Armored Division, under 8th Division command, seizes Kleinhau. The nine-day fight for Huertgen and Kleinhau costs the 121st Infantry, CCR 5th Armored Division, and the 1st Battalion, 13th Infantry, over 1,200 casualties. The 8th Infantry Division is ordered

Left: *M10 Tank Destroyers of the 893d Tank Destroyer Battalion move along a muddy road in the Huertgen Forest to challenge menacing German armor. (National Archives)*

to continue the attack toward the Brandenburg-Bergstein ridge. On 7 December the 2d Ranger Battalion joins the fight. The Rangers capture the critical Castle Hill, and hold it for two days against German counterattacks, suffering over 25 percent casualties The 8th Infantry Division is soon on the west bank of the Roer licking its wounds from the brutal fight in the Huertgen forest.

6 December. **Huertgen Forest Campaign is Over.**
The 83d Infantry Division relieves the battered 4th Infantry Division as the Huertgen Forest campaign comes to a close. Since 14 September, when elements of the 9th Infantry Division enter the fringes of the forest near Roetgen, five U.S. infantry divisions—the 1st, 4th, 8th, 9th, and 28th, along with the 2d Rangers and elements of the 5th Armored Division—suffered a terrible toll. Including losses from all causes, casualties reach 5,000 per division.

15 December. **Musical Legend is Lost Over the English Channel.**
Major Glenn Miller, director of the Army Air Force Band, disappears on a flight between England and France. The plane is never found but his music lives on.

16 December. **Clark To Command Army Group. Futa Pass near Florence, Italy.**
A change of command ceremony marks the departure of Lieutenant General Mark W. Clark from the Fifth Army for command of the new 15th Army Group.

Lieutenant General Lucian Truscott, Jr., takes over the Fifth Army.

16 December. **Congress Reactivates 5-Star Rank.**
General George C. Marshall, the Army's chief of staff, is the first of four veteran soldiers awarded the five-star rank of General of the Army. In the next few days the others receive five-star commissions: Douglas MacArthur (18 December), Dwight D. Eisenhower (20 December), and Henry H. Arnold (21 December).

16 December. **The Battle of the Bulge Begins. Ardennes Forest, Germany.**
Striking under cover of darkness, two German Panzer armies launch a surprise attack on U.S. First Army front line units, battering the 28th Division and the 14th Cavalry Group, surrounding—and virtually destroying—the green 106th Infantry Division and forcing back the 4th Infantry and 9th Armored Divisions. The battle will be one of the most intensely fought in the long history of the U.S. Army.

18–19 December. **German Panzer Army in Counterattack. Bastogne, Belgium.**
The 101st Airborne Division with elements of the 9th and 10th Armored Divisions and other units establishes a defensive perimeter around this vital crossroads town. Efforts to reach the 28th and 106th Infantry Divisions are abandoned as the German Panzer columns advance swiftly, hoping to seize the Ardennes, the city of Liege (Belgium), and the port of

Antwerp. Soon the 106th Division ceases to exist as a functioning element as thousands of inexperienced soldiers are taken prisoner.

20 December. Efforts to Block German Penetration. Ardennes Region, Belgium.

Army engineers frustrate advancing Germans by destroying bridges and creating roadblocks, while U.S. reinforcements attempt to stem the German tide.

20 December. Patton Rallies Troops to Break Enemy Hold on Bastogne.

Patton rapidly moves his Third Army headquarters from Metz in the Alsace region of France to Arlon, Belgium, and assembles the 4th Armored Division and 26th and 80th Infantry Divisions for rapid movement over icy roads to the Bastogne area.

22 December. The Enemy Completes Encirclement. Bastogne, Belgium.

The attacking Germans surround Bastogne; the 101st Airborne Division and the other U.S. units man the perimeter in freezing weather. Brigadier General Anthony McAuliffe, acting commander of the 101st ("Screaming Eagles") Airborne Division, replies to a German demand to surrender with the exclamation "Nuts!" (The division commander, Major General Maxwell Taylor, is in Washington attending a conference.) Although their supplies are scarce and bad weather prevents aerial resupply, the defenders are determined to hold out.

24 December. Troopship Disaster in the Channel. Off Cherbourg, France.

The troopship SS *Leopoldville* en route to Cherbourg, France, on a Christmas Eve crossing from England is torpedoed by the German submarine *U-486*. The Belgian-crewed ship carries troops of the 262d and 264th Infantry regiments, 66th (Panther) Infantry Division, plus some men from other units. Unaware of the seriousness of the damage, the men form in orderly ranks on the deck. The crew panics and the soldiers are never given the command to abandon ship. Stormy seas, confusion on shore, and communications problems compound the situation. When the ship goes down, more that 500 men die in the frigid water or trying to reach rescue ships that finally come to help. It is the worst ship disaster suffered by the Army in the war.

26 December. Black Troops Can Volunteer for Infantry. United Kingdom.

Troops in the Communications Zone (Lieutenant General John C. H. Lee) are advised that soldiers may request assignment to units "where assistance is most needed" without regard to color or race. This opens the door for black soldiers serving in all-black service and support units in England and France to serve alongside white soldiers in undermanned combat units. Men selected are to report to the 16th Reinforcement Depot at Compiegne, France, by 10 January 1945.

Right: *Although outnumbered and outgunned, the beleaguered paratroopers of the 101st Airborne Division, with artillery and elements of other units, stubbornly held Bastogne, Belgium. ("Stopped Dead in Their Tracks," James Dietz)*

26 December. **Armored Column Reaches Beleaguered Area. Bastogne, Belgium.**
In the Third Army's III Corps sector, Lieutenant Colonel Creighton Abrams' 37th Tank Battalion task force from the 4th Armored Division breaks through German lines from the south to relieve the Bastogne defenders. At 6:45 a.m. the first Sherman tank enters the U.S. positions and the siege is over.

28 December. **The Secondary Enemy Offensive in the Saar.**
Outside the Ardennes "bulge" in the Saar region, Patch's Seventh Army is attacked by Blaskowitz's Army Group G as a secondary German counteroffensive is launched. The Seventh Army initially yields a triangle-patch west of the Rhine.

29 December. **Offensive Toward Bologna Delayed. Italy.**
Reversals in the Serchio River Valley, combined with the onset of a bitterly cold winter, delays the Fifth Army's planned offensive north toward Bologna. By the end of the year most of the ground lost is regained, but U.S. positions are about the same as at the end of October.

31 December. **Execution of a Deserter.**
A 28th Division soldier, Private Eddie Slovik, guilty of desertion in the face of the enemy, is shot by a firing squad. He is the only U.S. soldier so punished in the entire war period, and is the first U.S. soldier executed for desertion since the Civil War.

1 January. **After Ship Disaster, 66th On Dry Land. St. Nazaire, France.**

Still recovering from the effects of the grim events of the *Leopoldville* sinking, the 66th Infantry Division (Major General Herman F. Kramer) takes over the 94th Infantry Division mission to contain 60,000 enemy troops in the St. Nazaire-Lorient area. The 94th Infantry Division heads for the Saar-Moselle Triangle facing the Siegfried Switch Line.

4 January. **Fighter-Bombers Disrupt Italy-Austria Traffic. Vicinity of the Brenner Pass.**

As the weather turns bad, the bombing campaign in the area of the Brenner Pass shifts to preventing enemy access to the pass by smashing open stretches of railroad tracks and hitting bridges to disrupt traffic between Austria and northern Italy.

8 January. **New Fifteenth Army Sets up Headquarters. Ferme de Suippes, France.**

Having displaced its headquarters elements from Le Havre, but with no combat mission assigned, the U.S. Fifteenth Army becomes operational under Major General Ray E. Porter. On 15 January Lieutenant General Leonard T. Gerow leaves V Corps to take command. The Army's immediate mission is the rehabilitation and refitting of the 12th Army Group losses in the Battle of the Bulge.

13 January. Ardennes Battle Front is Restored.

In the Third Army's VIII Corps sector, advance elements of the 87th Infantry Division reach the Ourthe river and make contact with the British. In the First Army XVIII Airborne Corps area the reconstituted 106th Infantry Division attacks alongside the 30th Infantry Division near the Salm River. Elements of the 12th Army Group gradually restore the front to its status just before the German Ardennes offensive started on 16 December 1944. During the bitter campaign the U.S. casualties are 19,000 KIA and 15,000 taken prisoner. Now "the Bulge" is gone and troops prepare to continue the advance.

Above: *The bodies of American prisoners of war shot by Germans at Malmedy, Belgium, during the Battle of the Bulge. (U.S. Army)*

Right: *General Courtney H. Hodges (1887–1966) replaced Omar Bradley as commander of the First U.S. Army. (U.S. Army)*

15 January. Black Volunteers Report for Duty. Compiegne, France.

The first 2,800 (of 4,562) black volunteers for combat duty report to the 16th Reinforcement Depot where they become members of the 47th Reinforcement Battalion, 5th Retraining Regiment, under the command of Colonel Alexander George, a combat veteran. The goal is to have the first detachment ready for assignment to units by 1 March.

17–18 January. The First Army Back Under U.S. Command.

At midnight the U.S. First Army (Hodges), which has been under British Field Marshal Montgomery's command during Battle of the Bulge, reverts back to 12th Army Group (Bradley) control.

21 January. New U.S. Divisions Head Toward the Front. Le Havre, France.

The 65th Infantry Division (Major General Stanley E. Reinhart) arrives and starts its precombat training at Camp Lucky Strike. Since September 1944, 22 new U.S. divisions, including six armored divisions, have reached France; the 65th is the first of yet another increment of seven new divisions.

Right: *In winter camouflage, ski-borne men of the 10th Mountain Division begin a combat patrol in Northern Italy, where the division ended the war. (Jeffery Ethell Collection)*

20 January. **President Signs Son's Promotion. Washington, D.C.**
Colonel Elliott Roosevelt, one of three of FDR's sons serving in the armed forces, is among 103 names on the Army list for promotion to brigadier general.

20 January. **New Defense Line for the Seventh Army. Drusenheim, France.**
In the U.S. Seventh Army area the VI Corps starts an orderly withdrawal to a new defensive line in the face of heavy enemy pressure. The 45th Infantry Division is unable to reach an encircled battalion of the 157th Infantry. Elements of the 314th Infantry (79th Infantry Division) escape the enemy trap but many members of the 2d Battalion are MIA.

22 January. **Offensive to Destroy Colmar Pocket. Guemar, Germany.**
In the French 1st Army area, two U.S. divisions—the 3d Infantry and 5th Armored—start a southward drive on Colmar with the objective of enveloping and destroying the Colmar Pocket. The 3d Infantry Division leads the attack. To the west the 28th (Keystone) Infantry Division, briefly serving with the Seventh Army, conducts raids on 22–23 January. On 5 February the Pocket is cut in two as U.S. XXI Corps (Major General Frank W. Milburn) and French 1st Corps make contact as the final phase of the difficult operation is underway.

28 January. **First, Third Armies Drives Toward West Wall.**
As the drive starts toward West Wall and Euskirchen, the First Army sends the 1st Infantry Division and 82d Airborne Divisions to lead the XVIII Airborne Corps advance. The 7th Armored Division concludes the St. Vith (Belgium) drive with the seizure of stubbornly held positions in Bois de St. Vith. The Third Army's 87th Infantry Division takes over the St. Vith sector. The Third Army attack deploys VIII, III, XII, and XX Corps.

9 February. **Germans Play Trump Card on the Roer.**
With U.S. forces poised to resume the offensive, German Army engineers deliberately open the discharge valves to unleash 111 million cubic meters of Roer River water contained in the Schwammenauel and Urfttalsperre reservoirs. The enemy ploy creates a great water barrier between themselves and the oncoming forces of the Ninth Army and First Army's VII Corps. This stalls the proposed offensive for two weeks and complicates plans for crossing the Roer.

9 February. **Colmar Pocket Campaign Ends. Chalampé, France.**
Operations on the Alsatian plain of eastern France comes to a close as U.S. forces operating with the French 1st Army completes the reduction of the Colmar Pocket and in the process virtually destroys

the German 19th Army. The U.S. XXI Corps, with significant support from U.S. XII Tactical Air Command, contributed significantly to the success. The 254th Infantry, relieved from its attachment to the 3d Infantry Division, returns to its parent 69th Infantry Division control.

15 February. **Enemy POW Strength in U.S.**
The Army reporting system accounts for 172,879 enemy prisoners of war under Army control in the U.S. This includes 7,598 officers. By the end of the war there are almost 400,000 German prisoners in detention in the U.S.

18 February. **Mountain Troops Surprise Defenders. Sarasiccia-Campana, Italy.**
In preparation for a forthcoming main attack on Mount Belvedere, soldiers of the 86th Infantry, 10th Mountain Division (Hays), moving under cover of darkness, scale a steep cliff to surprise and defeat German defenders. During 18–19 February the division's main assault force moves to Belvedere-Gorgolescu to prepare for the attack.

22–23 February. **Air Campaign Strikes Multiple Targets Simultaneously.**
Having patiently awaited a clear day, American and British heavy bombers and fighters launch Operation Clarion, a long-standing plan to utilize virtually all available aircraft to hit multiple targets over the Reich simultaneously. An estimated 9,000 airplanes take part, flying from Allied bases in England, France, Holland, and Belgium. U.S. Eighth Air Force (Lieutenant General James H. Doolittle) and Italy-based Fifteenth Air Force (Major General Nathan F. Twining) hit over 100 target sites in the two-day operation.

22 February. **Mount Belvedere is Taken. La Serra, Italy.**
The 10th Mountain Division reports all of its objectives are secure and division elements are moving to seize Mount Torraccia, which is taken two days later. The U.S. 92d Infantry Division (Major General Edward M. Almond), with the attached 473d Infantry Regiment, extends its zone to take responsibility for half of IV Corps zone of action.

Right: *Soldiers of the 27th Armored Infantry, 9th Armored Division, are shown as they race to secure the lone bridge still standing over the Rhine River at Remagen. Their success will speed the advance into Germany and the final drive to destroy the Third Reich. ("Bridge at Remagen," H. Charles McBarron, Army Art Collection, NMUSA)*

23 February. **Over the River, Into the Woods. Germany.**

Operation Grenade (the drive from the Roer River to the Rhine) is underway in the U.S. Ninth Army (Simpson) sector as fast-moving troops of the XIII (Major General Alvin C. Gillem) and XIX (McLain) Corps successfully conduct river crossings over the Roer River. XVI (Major General John B. Anderson) Corps stages a demonstration to mislead the enemy. Combat-experienced 29th, 30th, 35th, 79th, 83d, 84th, and 102d Infantry Divisions lead the way. Meanwhile, the 75th Infantry Division, which has been fighting in the Colmar region, moves north for temporary duty with the British Second Army on the right flank of the Ninth Army that continues under British 21st Army Group (Montgomery). On 2 March advance elements of the Ninth Army reach the Rhine south of Neuss. Deployed along the Rhine and scouting out crossing sites, the Ninth Army concludes Operation Grenade on 5 March.

28 February. **Successful Jet Fighter is Revealed. Washington, D.C.**

General of the Army H. H. Arnold, commanding general of the Army Air Force, announces the successful arrival of the revolutionary new P-80, the Army's first jet-propelled combat aircraft. It is nicknamed "Shooting Star."

1 March. **Black Volunteers Ready for Assignment. Compiegne, France.**

Organized into 37 platoons, the first graduates of the black combat volunteer program are deemed ready for assignment. Twenty-five platoons go to 12th Army Group divisions; 12 to the 6th Army Group. Some go to the veteran 1st and 9th Infantry Divisions. Others go to newer divisions, including the 12th and 14th Armored Divisions and the 69th, 78th, 99th, and 104th Infantry Divisions. In most cases they serve as members of all-black platoons integrated into line companies composed of white soldiers.

1 March. **Attack Continues Toward Cologne.**

The First Army's VII Corps attacks toward Cologne and expands its bridgeheads over the Erft as the 3d Armored Division and the 99th Infantry Division make gains. The 104th, 8th, and 1st Infantry Divisions have elements across Erft pushing toward Moedrath. In the Third Army's XX Corps sector, the 10th Armored Division enters the important communications center of Trier and clears it. The campaign that began in the Eifel on 29 January ends with the seizure of Trier. To the south the Detachment d'Armée des Alpes is established under the 6th Army Group (Devers) with responsibility for the Alpine sector along the French-Italian border from point of junction of France, Switzerland, and Italy to the Mediterranean. A French general

commands the new force, which includes French and American soldiers.

7 March. **GIs Find Bridge, Cross the Rhine. Remagen, Germany.**
In a lightning move that takes the enemy by surprise, the U.S. 9th Armored Division, III Corps, First Army, captures the damaged but usable Ludendorff railroad bridge over the Rhine River. First to fight their way across are the infantrymen of the 27th Armored Infantry Battalion, with other units close behind. By nightfall five infantry and tank battalions are on the east bank. Rapid exploitation results in encirclement and seizure of the Ruhr region.

8 March. **Devers Gains Fourth Star.**
The Sixth Army Group Commander, Jacob L.

Above: *American armor and infantry units prepare to close in on the enemy during the final phases of the European Campaign. ("Into Germany," James Dietz)*

Devers, is promoted to full general. His command includes the Seventh Army and the First French Army. Devers is a 1909 West Point graduate.

8–12 March. **Troops Poised on the North Bank of the Moselle. Vicinity Trier.**
In the northern part of Third Army's XII Corps zone, the 80th Infantry Division is pinched out of line by spearhead elements of the 11th Armored Division and 90th Infantry Division striking east toward the Rhine. The 10th Armored Division (Morris) and 4th Armored Division (Hoge) clear the north bank of the Moselle River with assistance of the 5th Infantry Division (Major General Stafford L. Irwin). The 90th Infantry Division passes from VIII Corps to XII Corps control.

10 March. **The Ninth Army Displaces its Headquarters. Munchen-Gladbach, Germany.**
As it marks the completion of its critical role in the drive from the Roer to the Rhine, the command post of the Ninth Army displaces from its winter-long

Right: *Soldiers of the 89th Division duck low in their fragile assault boat as they cross the Rhine River under enemy fire near Oberwesel, Germany, 26 March 1945. The enemy's resolve remained strong even as the final days of the war in Europe approached. (National Archives)*

Below: *Jacob L. Devers (1887–1979), seen here as a lieutenant general, commanded the Sixth U.S. Army Group, leading it in the invasion of Southern France. (National Archives)*

location at Maastricht, Holland, to this German city, a rail center with a population of 90,000—and a frequent Eighth Air Force target.

12 March. **Bradley Promoted to Full General.**
Omar Nelson Bradley, commander of the U.S. 12th Army Group, is promoted to four-star rank. Like Eisenhower, he is a member of the West Point Class of 1915.

15 March. **Two Armies Set out to Conquer the Saar-Palatinate.**
The Third (Patton) and Seventh (Patch) Armies team up to attack German forces in the Saar-Palatinate—a triangular land island bounded by the Rhine on the east, the Moselle on the northwest, and the Lauter-Sarre River on the south and west.

17 March. **Honors to The Screaming Eagles. Washington, D.C.**
The Army announces the presentation of the Presidential Unit Citation to the 101st Airborne Division for "extraordinary heroism and gallantry" in the defense of Bastogne during the Battle of the Bulge. It is the first time this award, the highest Army unit decoration, has been given to an entire division. Previously, the Army restricted the award to regimental level and below.

17 March. **Ludendorff Bridge Collapses. Remagen, Germany.**
Army engineers have pontoon bridges in place as the bridge at Remagen collapses as a result of enemy damage before it can be restored for rail service.

Engineers accelerate work on a 1,752-foot single-track bridge to span the Rhine near Wesel, Germany.

17 March. **D-Day Regimental Commander Now Leads a Corps.**
As III Corps advances under the Third Army, Major General James A. Van Fleet takes command. He relieves Major General John Millikin. Van Fleet was a colonel in command of an infantry regiment on D-Day.

17 March. **Supreme Commander Visits Field Commanders. Luneville, France.**
As the Third and Seventh Armies battle through Palatinate en route to the Rhine, General Dwight D. Eisenhower arrives at the airfield near the Seventh Army CP. With him is General George S. Patton, Jr., Third Army commander. Visitors are greeted by Generals Jacob L. Devers (Sixth Army Group) and Patch (Seventh Army). Army boundaries for the drive to the Rhine are discussed.

18–21 March. **Armored Divisions Spearhead the Race to Rhine.**
In the Third Army, a powerful XII Corps effort with four infantry and two armored divisions on the attack rocks the enemy back on his heels and seals the fate of enemy forces defending the Palatinate. The 4th Armored Division and 90th Infantry Divisions head for Mainz and Worms. Seventh Army frontline divisions smash through the Siegfried Line defenses.

22–23 March. **A Bold Assault Crossing of the Rhine. Oppenheim, Germany.**
In the Third Army sector, XII Corps (Eddy) caps its drive with an assault crossing of the Rhine near Mainz by the 5th Infantry Division, which bolts across in a bold night move using rafts and small boats until engineers construct crossings. In the Seventh Army area the XXI Corps (Milburn) takes command of the 71st and 100th Infantry Divisions near Bitche and covers the right flank of XV Corps (Haislip), which has the 3d and 45th Infantry Divisions at the Rhine looking for crossing sites. The First Army, meanwhile, attacks east from its bridgehead in the Remagen area and attacks toward Kassel.

24 March. **Airborne Drop Near the Rhine. Wesel, Germany.**
Under operational control of the British Second Army, the U.S. 17th Airborne Division and 6th British Airborne Division launch Operation Varsity, a daylight parachute and glider assault into landing zones east of the Rhine River north and northwest of Wesel. The mission is to secure bridgeheads for other units to cross. Of 1,305 gliders employed, only 172 are salvageable. The insufficient remaining airlift cancels the proposed drop of the U.S. 13th Airborne Division, which continues its training mission in the Oise section of France.

25 March. **Palatinate Triangle is Flattened.**
The six corps of the Third and Seventh Armies

Left: *After more than a year of combat, veterans of the 101st Airborne Division advance into Germany during the last days of the war in Europe. (U.S. Army)*

complete the reduction of the Saar Palatinate triangle. In the ten-day campaign the two German armies comprising Army Group G (the enemy's First and Seventh Armies) are decimated with a loss of 81,692 prisoners of war; a huge amount of combat equipment including critically needed artillery is abandoned east of the Rhine River. The banks of the Rhine River as far south as Speyer are cleared of enemy troops. The VI Corps, the southernmost element in Seventh Army's push, completes the clearing of northern Alsace as all elements enter Germany.

26–27 March. Armored Task Force in Failed Prison Raid. Hammelburg, Germany.
Under orders from General Patton, the 4th Armored Division sends a task force commanded by Captain Abraham Baum, S-3 of Lieutenant Colonel Creighton Abrams' Combat Command B, to attempt the rescue of allied prisoners at the Oflag XIIIB in the vicinity of Schweinfurt. With fewer than 300 troops, 16 tanks, 27 half-tracks, and three self-propelled guns, Task Force Baum is severely mauled. Nearly all go missing in action; briefly liberated prisoners are rounded up and returned to confinement. Patton is widely criticized when it is learned that his son-in-law is among U.S. POWs held in the camp.

28 March. Ruling the Rhineland.
The 12th Army Group assigns the Fifteenth Army (Gerow) the two-fold mission of containing bypassed enemy at Lorient and St. Nazaire in coastal areas of France and of governing the Rhineland sector of Germany. XXII and XXIII Corps are put under Gerow's command. As rear area responsibilities are readjusted, the First and Third Armies effect a juncture north of Idstein as 4th Armored Division spearheads (Third Army) moving north join forces with the 9th Armored Division (First Army). Both armies advance steadily to the east as Germans fall back.

28 March. Taking Berlin is Left to the Russians.
General Eisenhower redirects the final advance of the Allied forces and reorients toward Leipzig rather than Berlin as a terminal objective. His decision leaves the Russians to take the Nazi capital. The altered plan gives the 12th Army Group (Bradley) rather than the 21st Army Group (Montgomery) responsibility for the main effort.

30 March. Division Commander is KIA. Germany.
In the First Army's VII Corps (Collins) area, Major General Maurice Rose, commander, 3d Armored Division, becomes the second U.S. Army division commander to be killed in action in the war. He and his command group are surprised by German tanks while moving in jeeps along a wooded trail in the advance on Paderborn. The 104th Infantry Division (Allen), advancing behind armor, takes Paderborn, while the 78th Infantry Division relieves the 4th Cavalry Group and continues the attack north.

Right: *Battery A, 4520th Antiaircraft Artillery Battalion, provides protection against some of the last vestiges of the once mighty Luftwaffe. (National Archives)*

1 April. **U.S. Forces Trap Enemy in Pincers Move. Lippstadt, Germany.**

The U.S. Ninth (Simpson) and First (Hodges) Armies join forces, trapping two German Army Groups while sealing off the rich industrial Ruhr. In the XIII Corps sector the 5th Armored Division spearheads the drive toward the Weser; the 17th Airborne Division prepares to assault Muenster; and the 84th Infantry Division (Major General Alexander R. Bolling) begins to assemble east of the Rhine.

4 April. **The Third Army Reports Finding Cash and Stolen Property. Merkers, Germany.**

XII Corps (Eddy) troops from the 90th Infantry Division uncover a treasure trove in the vast underground cave that is part of an industrial salt mine. On investigation, this proves to be the German gold bullion reserve. An inventory ordered by Patton finds 4,500 twenty-five-pound gold bars and millions more in Reichsmarks. There was also a cache of foreign currency and art treasures looted by the

Germans in captured lands. Art experts are summoned from the U.S. to organize the recovery.

5 April. **Diversionary Attack in Coastal Sector. Italy.**

Under direct control of the Fifth Army, the 92d Infantry Division begins a diversionary attack in the Ligurian coast sector. The division's advance toward Massa and La Spezia meets heavy resistance after a one-mile advance. The attached 442d RCT takes Mt. Fragolito and Mt. Carchio and prepares to attack heavily defended Mt. Belvedere. During the next several days the 92d Infantry Division continues its drive up the Serchio River valley.

11 April. **Tankers Probe to the Elbe River. Germany.**

Lead elements of the 2d Armored Division are the first of the U.S. elements to reach the Elbe River 80 miles west of Berlin where the line of separation has been drawn for Soviet troops advancing from the east and allied forces moving from the west.

0 April. **Concentration Camps Liberated. Germany.**
The Third Army overruns the Ohrdruf site of an
infamous Nazi death camp. In the Seventh Army
sector, elements of the XX ("Ghost") Corps (Walker)
cross the Saale and advance toward Weimar. Troops
soon liberate concentration camps at Buchenwald,
Erla, Belsen, and Dachau. More joyful is the situation
when they find an Allied POW camp in the Bad Sulz
area. Other camps soon fall to Allied forces as
Germany is overrun.

12 April. **ETO Troops Learn of FDR's Death.**
At the brink of victory in Europe troops are saddened
to learn of the death of President Franklin D.
Roosevelt in Warm Springs, Georgia. Harry S.
Truman, a World War I veteran, takes the oath of
office as the new President and Commander-in-Chief.

Above: *The American First Army's eastward advance
and the Russian movement westward brought the forces of
the U.S. and U.S.S.R. together near Torgau, Germany.
("Meeting with the Russians at Torgau," Olin Downs,
Army Art Collection, NMUSA)*

Left: *Sergeant Bill Mauldin, cartoonist for* Yank *magazine, created the quintessential American GI infantrymen—Willie and Joe. (Army Art Collection, NMUSA)*

14 April. **The Army Attacks After Postponements. Po Valley, Italy.**

After two postponements blamed on bad weather, the U.S. Fifth Army gets the go-ahead to launch its final offensive—the Po Valley campaign. The IV Corps sends the 10th Mountain Division toward the Po Valley as the 1st Armored Division on the corps right flank battles for Vergato on Highway 64. There is heavy fighting in both II Corps and IV Corps sectors. On 18 April the Fifth Army moves the boundary between the corps west to enable the 10th Mountain Division troops in the center to concentrate on a rapid pursuit. Mountain troops reach the Lavino Creek and bag nearly 3,000 prisoners.

17 April. **Nuremburg Falls and Patch Races Toward Swiss Border.**

Shifting to the south from its southeasterly course, the Seventh Army (Patch) orders the 45th and 3d Infantry Divisions (XV Corps) to converge on Nuremburg. In the XXI Corps area the 42d Infantry Division pursues the enemy toward Fuerth, working closely with the 14th Armored Division. The 4th Infantry Division's motorized 8th Infantry task force races toward Ansbach. VI Corps picks up the 44th Infantry Division in a drive toward the Swiss border to block enemy escape routes out of the Black Forest. The 10th Armored Division (Major General William H. H. Morris, Jr.), 63d (Major General Louis E.

Below: *The four-wheel drive "Jeep" gained a reputation as the Army's workhorse in all types of circumstances, including the Italian mountains, where American troops push the lightweight vehicle up a particularly steep slope. (National Archives)*

Hibbs) and 100th (Major General Withers A. Burress) Infantry Divisions speed down the Neckar Valley.

19 April. **V Corps Troops Seize Leipzig, Roll On.**

In the First Army's V Corps area, the 2d and 69th Infantry Divisions complete the capture of Leipzig. In the VII Corps sector, moving against crumbling resistance the 1st Infantry Division advances in the Harz Mountains and reaches the corps northern boundary where it makes contact with adjacent friendly units. In the XVIII Airborne Corps sector the 13th Armored and 97th Infantry Divisions prepare to join the Third Army. The 104th Infantry Division elements capture Halle and move on.

25 April. **The First Army To Transfer to the Far East from Germany.**

After virtually continuous battle action since the Normandy landings, the U.S. First Army is taken out of action to prepare for transfer to the Far East. This affects only the Army headquarters as troop elements are distributed to the Ninth and Third Armies.

25 April. **The Gothic Line is Finally Overcome.**

In the U.S. Fifth Army area, the Gothic Line— initially attacked by U.S. forces on 12 September 1944—ceases to exist as a barrier to the Army's advance as the 92d Infantry Division completes its reduction with the capture of Aulla in the Ligurian coastal sector.

25 *April.* **The U.S. Links Up With the Russians. Torgau, Germany.**

Patrols from the 69th Infantry Division make first contact along the Elbe River with Soviet forces advancing from the east. Meanwhile a Russian army has surrounded the German capital, Berlin.

26 *April.* **Darby, Former Ranger, Leads Task Force. Verona, Italy.**

Task Force Darby (Colonel William O. Darby, former Ranger commander, now assistant division commander), 10th Mountain Division, enters Verona at 6:00 a.m. and finds elements of the 88th Infantry Division in control. TF Darby proceeds along the east side of Lake Garda to cut off enemy escape routes as the 88th Infantry Division turns east toward Vicenza. Darby is killed in action during fight at Lake Garda and is posthumously promoted to brigadier general. The 85th Infantry Division gains a bridgehead across the Adige River in the Verona area. The 1st Armored Division elements race toward Lake Como.

Above: *The rugged P-47 fighter-bomber could carry out escort missions or serve as ground attack aircraft. ("A Wolfpack Salute," Roy Grinnell)*

28 *April.* **The Fifth Army Gaining Control of Northern Italian Cities.**

The 92d Infantry Division, under the Fifth Army, seizes Alessandria on Highway 10; the 10th Mountain Division, also directly under Army control, clears the east shore of Lake Garda. In the IV Corps sector, the 34th Infantry Division rounds up enemy remnants west of Brescia as the 1st Armored Division reaches Lake Como near the Swiss border. Troops learn that ousted Italian dictator Benito Mussolini, intercepted by partisans in a Lake Como village, is executed by a firing squad. In the II Corps sector the 88th Infantry Division clears Vicenza; the 91st Infantry Division elements cross the Brenta river, driving toward Treviso.

29 *April.* **Troops Enter the Infamous Death Camp. Dachau, Germany.**

Third Army troops of the 45th and 42d Infantry

Divisions batter down the gates of the Dachau concentration camp to liberate surviving prisoners held by the Nazis.

29 *April.* Surrender of the German Army in Italy. Caserta, Italy.

As the U.S. 1st Armored Division (Prichard) takes up positions near Milan, the U.S. 91st Infantry Division (Major General William G. Livesay), which is operating with the South African 6th Armored Division, crosses the Brenta river, driving toward Treviso. Commander of the German Army Group Southwest agrees to unconditional surrender effective 2 May.

30 *April.* U.S. and Soviet Army Commanders Meet. Eilenburg, Germany.

General Courtney Hodges, commander of the U.S. First Army, greets the commanding general, Soviet 5th Guard Army on the east bank of the Mulde River to mark the junction of U.S. and Soviet forces in the sector. Headquarters First Army relinquishes its duties, turns over its units to adjacent U.S. armies, and prepares for its return to the U.S. and redeployment to the Pacific.

30 *April.* Fifth Army Troops Nearing the End of the Road in Italy.

As the long, grinding war in Italy winds down, the U.S. 92d Infantry Division (Almond) reaches Turin, which it finds undefended. The 473d Infantry Regiment, containing many soldiers from disbanded antiaircraft artiller units, links up with French troops on the Franco-Italian border. The 10th Mountain Division (Hays) puts down enemy resistance in the vicinity of Lake Garda and deploys elements to take Gargnano and Riva. IV Corps (Crittenberger) formally occupies Milan and II Corps (Keyes),

Right: *Wounded Americans proceed to a hospital ship for their return voyage to the United States. ("All Aboard for Home," Joseph Hirsch, Army Art Collection, NMUSA)*

reinforced with the addition of the 85th and 91st Infantry Divisions takes Treviso, north of Venice. Milan is taken by the 1st Armored Division This ends the eastward drive of IV Corps.

1 May. U.S. Forces Fan Out in Northern Italy.
In the IV Corps sector of the Fifth Army (Truscott), the 34th Infantry Division relieves troops of the 1st Armored Division northwest of Milan. In the II Corps sector, the 85th Infantry Division in the Piave Valley relieves the 88th Infantry Division, which now concentrates on clearing the Brenta Valley. II Corps is directed to clear Highway 49 in preparation for the drive through Brenner Pass to Austria.

2 May. Hostilities Cease in Italy.
Berlin falls to the Soviet Army. The surrender of German forces marks the end of 604 days in continuous combat for Fifth Army troops since the Salerno landing in southern Italy in September 1943.

3 May. The Seventh Army Seeks Juncture With the Fifth. Augsburg, Germany.
In the Seventh Army's VI Corps sector, the 103d Infantry Division's (Major General Anthony C. McAuliffe) 411th Regimental Combat Team dispatches a motorized force from Mittenwald, across the Austrian border, down the Sill River valley toward the Brenner Pass to establish contact with Fifth Army

troops advancing from northern Italy. The main body of the 103d Infantry Division negotiates the surrender of Innsbruck. 44th Infantry Division troops also head toward the Innsbruck area. XV Corps are moving toward Salzburg; troops under XXI Corps cross the Austrian border and advance toward Hitler's retreat at Berchtesgaden.

4 May. Forces From Italy Meet the Seventh Army Troops. Vicinity of Vipiteno, Italy.
The motorized column from the 411th RCT, 103d Infantry Division (Seventh Army), advances through Brenner Pass, enters Italy, and at 1:50 a.m. makes contact with the Intelligence and Reconnaissance Platoon, 349th Infantry, 88th Infantry Division (Fifth Army), and with VI Corps (Seventh Army) troops between Vipiteno and Colle Isarco on the Austro-Italian frontier.

4 May. Germans Routed, U.S. Troops Encounter Russian Allies.
In the Ninth Army area, the U.S. XIII Corps commander (Major General Alvan C. Gillem, Jr.) meets with the Soviet III Cavalry Corps commander following the juncture of 113th Cavalry Group, 83d, 29th and 84th Infantry Division patrols with Soviet forces. In the Seventh Army's XV Corps sector, 3d Infantry Division elements crossing into Austria advance through Salzburg to Hitler's retreat at Berchtesgaden. In the Third Army area, with V Corps

now transferred from the departing First Army to Patton's command, 5th and 90th Infantry Divisions start to clear passes into Czechoslovakia through which the 4th Armored Division plans its attack toward Prague. But Soviets protest and Patton is cautioned not to advance beyond Pilsen.

7 May. **Victory in Europe Proclaimed. Reims, France.**
A modest school building takes center stage as the German High Command surrenders all land, sea, and air forces unconditionally to the Allies effective 9 May. President Truman declares 8 May as "V-E Day"—for Victory in Europe.

8 May. **Ninety Divisions in Eisenhower's Command.**
Stars & Stripes headline says it all: "VICTORY!" As the ETO war comes to a close, General Eisenhower has under his command a total of 90 divisions—60 U.S., 13 British, five Canadian, 10 French, and one Polish. Ground forces include three Army groups; also First Allied Airborne Army, First Tactical Air Force, U.S. Ninth Air Force, and Second British Tactical Air Force. Some elements are quickly alerted for shipment to the Pacific.

9 May. **Combat in Europe is Terminated.**
All hostilities in the European Theater of Operations are officially terminated as the surrender of Germany

goes into effect. The Occupation phase of the Army's service in Europe begins. It is D-Day plus 338.

21 May. **The First Army Starts Redeployment. Le Havre, France.**
Headquarters, First U.S. Army, embarks under orders to proceed, via the U.S., to the Pacific area to prepare for a major role in the forthcoming invasion of Japan. (See Chapter 14.)

2 June. **Haislip Commands the Seventh Army.**
Major General Wade H. Haislip assumes command of the U.S. Seventh Army as General Patch departs for the United States.

14–15 June. **Mission Complete, the Ninth Army Leaves. Braunschweig, Germany.**
The Ninth Army is directed to turn over its occupation area and all troops to the Seventh Army as it returns to the U.S. for redeployment to the Pacific. Lieutenant General William Hood Simpson commanded the Army during its entire operational period in the ETO.

15 June. **Occupation Armies Are Designated. SHAEF Headquarters, Germany.**
It is announced at the Supreme Headquarters of the Allied Expeditionary Forces that the Third (Patton)

and Seventh (Haislip) Armies are designated as the major command headquarters for U.S. forces in the occupation of the captured territory.

30 June. **Wartime Production Enormous. Washington, D.C.**
Munitions recap shows that between July 1940 and July 1945 U.S. industry produced 17.4 million rifles, carbines, and pistols, 315,000 artillery weapons (including mortars), 86,338 tanks, and 297,000 aircraft.

1 July. **New Commander for the AGF. Washington, D,C.**
General Jacobs L. Devers, wartime commander of the Sixth Army Group, assumes command of the Army Ground Forces.

14 July. **Wartime Top Headquarters Phases Out. Frankfurt, Germany.**
With its mission accomplished, Supreme Headquarters Allied Expeditionary Force (SHAEF) is discontinued. General Eisenhower ceases to be an "Allied commander" and sends his final message of thanks to the entire command. Eisenhower is now commanding general, United States Forces in Europe (USFET) and Military Governor of the U.S. Occupied Zone in Germany. Later in the year he will return to the U.S. to serve as the Army's 16th Chief of Staff.

17 July. **President Truman in Europe for Conference. Potsdam, Germany.**
President Harry S. Truman arrives in Germany to participate in the critical Big Three Conference on postwar issues and means to conclude the war against Japan in the Far East. During the conference, he visits the 84th Infantry Division (Bolling), whose chief of staff is his cousin, Colonel Louis Truman. During Potsdam, Truman is advised of the atomic bomb test success at the New Mexico test site.

31 July. **The 12th Army Group Mission is Over.**
General Omar N. Bradley's great wartime command, the 12th Army Group, is dissolved as operational control of all American forces in Germany passes to USFET—United States Forces, European Theater. During most of the ETO war the 12th Army Group commanded the First, Third, and Fifteenth Armies. Bradley returns to the U.S. soon to take charge of the Veterans' Administration.

25 August. **First of the ETO Divisions is Inactivated. Belluno-Agordo Region, Italy.**
The 85th Infantry Division, a veteran of three Italian campaigns since its arrival in the theater on

23 December 1943, is inactivated—the first inactivation of the many combat divisions organized for World War II. Soldiers not eligible for return home are reassigned. As the news spreads of the Japanese surrender in the Far East (see Chapter 14) the Army responds to the public clamor "to get the boys home." By 31 December, 42 of the ETO divisions are off the Army's rolls.

8 September. **Command Change at the Seventh Army. Heidelberg, Germany.**
Lieutenant General Geoffrey Keyes, wartime II Corps commander in the Italian campaign, takes command of the Seventh Army, which remains in Germany as an occupation army. Twelve U.S. infantry divisions, five armored divisions, two airborne divisions, as well as seven French divisions fought at different times under the Seventh Army.

21 September. **Stimson Steps Down. Washington, D.C.**
After more than five years in office during a turbulent period in history, the Hon. Henry L. Stimson retires from office as Secretary of War. He is replaced by his wartime deputy, Judge Robert P. Patterson, a World War I combat veteran.

1 October. **Change in Persian Gulf Status, Mission. Khorramshahr, Iran.**
The Persian Gulf Command is deactivated and replaced by the Persian Gulf Service Command under control of U.S. Army Forces, Africa-Middle East

Left: *In anticipation of a full-scale invasion of the Japanese mainland, GIs stationed in France were to be relocated to the Pacific. Troops leave France bound for a massive task force that never came into being. (National Archives)*

Opposite: *American Liberty ships unload supplies and equipment at a port in Iran. The materiel is destined for the Soviet Union as part of the Lend-Lease Program. ("Unloading Liberty Ships," Richard H. Jansen, Army Art Collection, NMUSA)*

Theater (MET). Its principal task now is the liquidation of U.S. installations and activities in the region.

2 October. **The Wartime Fifth Army Is Discharged.** Thirty-four months after its activation in Morocco, the Fifth Army is inactivated.

7 October. **Patton Relieved From Third Army Command. Bad Tolz, Germany.** Lieutenant General Lucian Truscott, Jr., is appointed commanding general of the Third Army and Eastern

Military District (Bavaria) to replace General George S. Patton, Jr., who is relieved after a conflict with General Eisenhower over occupation policies.

10 October. **The Ninth Army is Inactivated. Fort Bragg, North Carolina.** With the surrender of Japan, redeployment planning is terminated and the Ninth Army is inactivated.

18 November. **Marshall Leaves His Post. Washington, D.C.** After six years and three months in office, the

architect of the wartime Army, General of the Army George C. Marshall, retires from his post as Chief of Staff. His place is taken (19 November) by General of the Army Dwight D. Eisenhower.

21 November. **Patch Dies. San Antonio, Texas.**
Lieutenant General Alexander M. Patch, wartime Seventh Army commander, dies at the age of 56, at Fort Sam Houston, Texas. He is posthumously promoted to four-star rank.

26 November. **McNarney is Last USFET Commander. Frankfurt, Germany.**
General Joseph T. McNarney succeeds to command of the United States Forces, European Theater (USFET). The post was held by General Dwight D. Eisenhower from 1 July 1945 to 11 November, when it was briefly assumed by General George S. Patton, Jr. McNarney will command the USFET until 10 March

1947. USFET tasks include implementation of occupation policy in response to directives from the Joint Chiefs of Staff.

9 December. **General Patton is an Accident Victim. Near Mannheim, Germany.**
Starting off on an early morning hunting trip, General George S. Patton, recently appointed commander of the U.S. Fifteenth Army, is critically injured when his 1939 model 75 Cadillac sedan collides with an Army vehicle.

21 December. **General Patton Dies. Bad Neuheim, Germany.**
General George S. Patton, Jr., famed wartime commander of the U.S. Third Army, one of the architects of the victory in Europe, dies as a result of the injuries suffered in an automobile accident 11 days earlier.

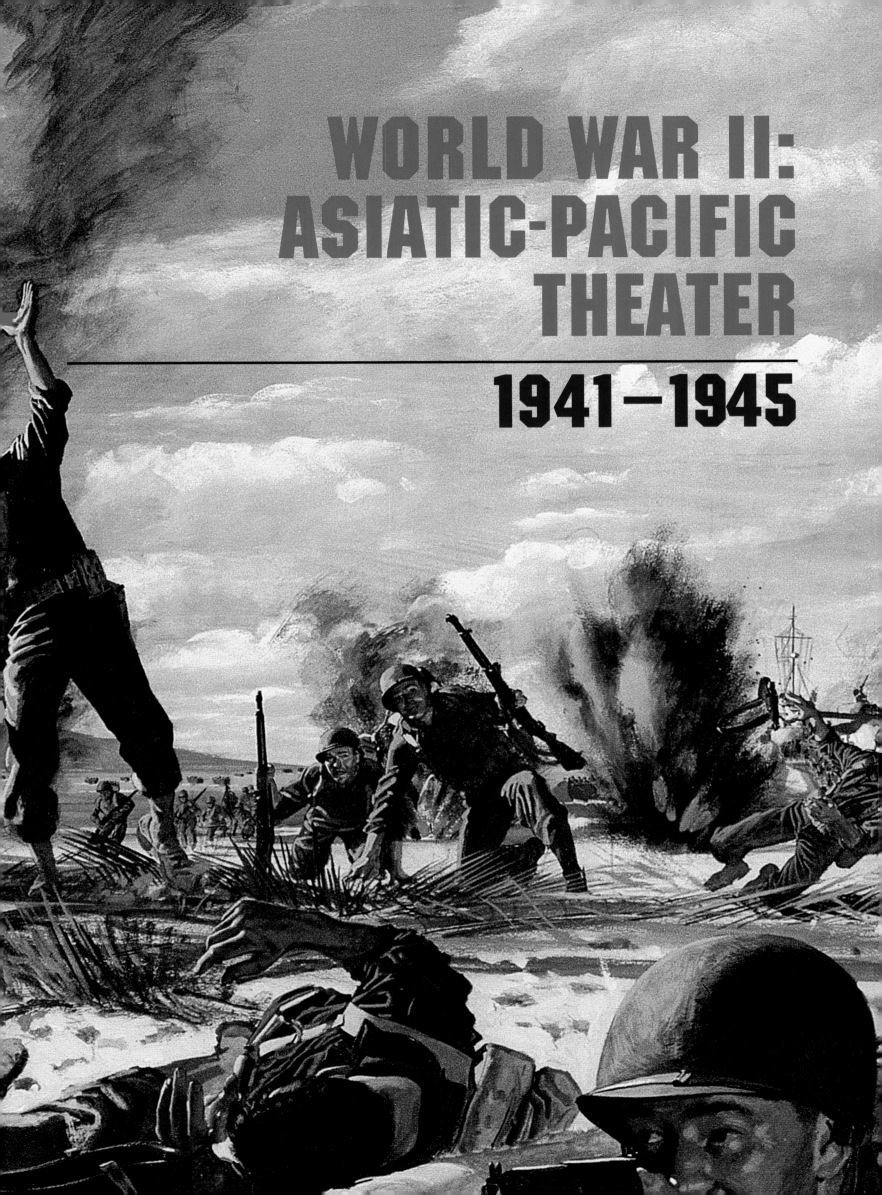

WORLD WAR II: ASIATIC-PACIFIC THEATER

1941–1945

WORLD WAR II: ASIATIC-PACIFIC THEATER

1941–1945

Major General Bruce Jacobs, AUS (Ret)

It is a strange dichotomy that the war in the Pacific, which most Americans looked upon with far more passion than the war on the far side of the Atlantic, was nevertheless destined to be of secondary consideration.

Although the heaviest initial blow in the opening hours of the conflict fell upon the Navy, which suffered cruel losses in manpower and warships at Pearl Harbor, the picture that would linger in the public memory would be the tattered columns of U.S. soldiers in the infamous march from Bataan to prison camps, where they would be hidden from public view but subjected to barbaric indignity during 41 frightful months.

Nevertheless, the U.S. and British leadership agreed upon a "Germany first" strategy before turning the full effort of the allies against Japan. The Quebec Conference in 1943 established the objective—"to strike at the heart of Germany and to destroy her military forces!"—as the first and primary goal.

There were a variety of wars in the Asiatic-Pacific Theater—the official name given by the Army—to the 21 "official" campaigns recognized with battle streamers.

There would be the campaigns in the Southwest Pacific, fought by soldiers and marines from the forces allocated to General Douglas MacArthur. MacArthur, certainly the senior U.S. flag officer in the region, if not in the entire war (certainly in terms of age and total active service), carried the designation as Allied Supreme Commander, Southwest Pacific. Under MacArthur were two battle-tested Armies—the Sixth, led by Lieutenant General Walter Krueger, and the Eighth, led by Lieutenant General Robert L. Eichelberger. The new Tenth Army, under Lieutenant General Simon Bolivar Buckner, fought valiantly in "the last battle"—the Okinawa campaign.

There were also the war campaigns of the Central Pacific region, conducted largely by Hawaii-based forces. This would include campaigns under Army control but closely correlated with supporting naval action; these were campaigns commanded by the Navy's CINCPAC, Admiral Chester W. Nimitz. These were usually predominantly conducted by Marine divisions but often with Army participation or follow-up. These operations, as might be expected, occasionally led to controversy, which, since the Army and Marines frequently differed on operational concepts, sometimes made the headlines.

And then there was the corner of the Asiatic war where neither MacArthur nor Nimitz exerted any influence—the geographically enormous but meagerly supported China-Burma-India area (CBI). This region found the U.S. playing second fiddle in many ways to the British (especially in India and Burma) but determined to be the dominant partner of Chiang Kai-shek, the wily president of China. But to the disappointment of Lieutenant General Joseph W. Stilwell, who was sent by the U.S. to "command" in the CBI, no U.S. divisions could be spared to engage the enemy in this critical vortex. Much of Stilwell's combat would be on the political and diplomatic fronts, and the tough old infantry soldier likely breathed a sigh of relief when he was recalled toward the end of 1944.

Lastly—but no less importantly—there was the air war conducted by the Army often in conjunction with naval aviation. Starting very modestly, U.S. air assets gradually overtook, matched, and then by far exceeded what the enemy could put into the skies. The U.S. organization for the air war against Japan followed closely the variety of wars described above. With MacArthur were the Fifth and Thirteenth Air Force in the Southwest Pacific. The Seventh Air Force

operated in the Central Pacific. The Tenth Air Force operated out of India. The Fourteenth, under Major General Claire L. Chennault, was mainly China-based. The Eleventh Air Force was responsible for Alaska and environs. The Twentieth Air Force, which with its B-29 Superfortress fleet would become the strategic air command of the theater, had the task of carrying the air war to the Japanese homeland. It operated initially out of bases in India and China before moving its venue to the Marianas Islands (Guam, Saipan, and Tinian) in the later stages of the war.

The long war in the Pacific—from December 1941 through August 1945—was a war fought on the proverbial shoestring. Of the 89 combat divisions in the Army's World War II inventory, only 20 were available in the 21 Pacific campaigns. Two divisions sent from the European war arrived in the theater after the Japanese surrender. Equipment and materiel shortages were commonplace throughout the 44 months of combat activity. Fortunately, superb and innovative logisticians were on the job.

The sheer vastness of this area, with its sprawling landmasses, its endless ocean, and its chains of islands and archipelagos, challenged the conventional techniques for supplying an army in the field. The enormity of the battle area encouraged joint operations long before the word "joint" became commonplace in the military vocabulary. Nowhere is this more succinctly stated than on the Army's Asiatic-Pacific Campaign Medal, which depicts a tropical scene with a battleship, aircraft carrier, submarine, and airplane in the backdrop with landing troops in the foreground.

If any one individual can be said to "personify" the war in a theater of operations in the Asiatic-Pacific campaigns, that man was General Douglas MacArthur. Throughout the war years in the Pacific there was an underlying competition for command pitting General MacArthur against Admiral Nimitz for the predominant leadership role in the theater.

Many historians contend—with no disrespect to Admiral Chester W. Nimitz—that it was General Douglas MacArthur who personified—and orchestrated—the long comeback from abject defeat in 1941 and early 1942 to the total victory that is captured in the photos of the surrender ceremony aboard U.S.S. *Missouri* in Tokyo Bay, Japan, on 2 September 1945, followed by MacArthur's understated but triumphant entry into Tokyo on 8 September 1945 in the vanguard of a powerful occupation army.

What makes the story of the war America's army fought in the Pacific so compelling is its completeness. It has a beginning, which is largely recorded in ignominy and tragedy. It has a main body, which is richly detailed with determination and continuity. It has an ending, which is a story of triumph and final victory. It covers a span of just under five years; and in the end it is a proud moment in the long history of the United States Army.

Pages 696–697: *Colonel Aubrey "Red" Newman leads the men of his 34th Infantry on RED Beach during the 1944 landing at Leyete, Philippine Islands. His command of "Follow me!" and his example of courageous leadership brought his battalion off the exposed beach. The colonel's words became the motto of the American infantry. ("Follow Me," H. Charles McBarron, Army Art Collection, NMUSA)*

Above: *Even before Pearl Harbor, the American countryside was being crossed by crowded troop trains as the Army mobilized. Men moved by rail to training stations and then to a port of debarkation, where they boarded ships for duty in the Pacific. ("Tokio Express," Edward R. Lanning, Army Art Collection, NMUSA)*

WORLD WAR II: ASIATIC-PACIFIC THEATER
1941–1945

"General Eichelberger, have our country's flag unfurled, and in Tokyo's sun let it wave in its full glory as a symbol of hope for the oppressed and as a harbinger of victory for the right."

—General Douglas MacArthur to Lieutenant General Robert L. Echelberger,
8 September 1945, at the U.S. Embassy, Tokyo, Japan.

1941

4 February. **Far to the North, New Defense Command. Fort Richardson, Alaska.**
The Alaska Defense Command is established under the Western Defense Command. Brigadier General (later lieutenant general) Simon Bolivar Buckner, Jr., is designated commander.

7 February. **New Army Commander in Hawaii. Fort Shafter, Hawaii.**
Walter C. Short is promoted to lieutenant general and is appointed the commanding general of the Hawaiian Department.

5 March. **Army Completes Call-Up of Guard Divisions. Camp Forrest, Tennessee.**
With the call-up of the Illinois' 33d Division, the Army completes the mobilization of the National Guard's 18 combat divisions, although many nondivisional units are still to be called as training sites become available. The 33d is among the nine Guard divisions destined to see combat in the Pacific.

17 March. **Regional Command for the West. San Francisco, California.**
A new regional headquarters, the Western Defense Command, is established, co-located with Headquarters, Fourth U.S. Army. Lieutenant General John L. DeWitt commands both organizations. Western Defense Command includes Alaska.

15 April. **Secret Order Gets Flying Tigers Off the Ground.**
An unpublished executive order is signed by President Roosevelt that authorizes Reservists on active duty to resign from the Army Air Corps (and other services) to sign up with the American Volunteer Group (the Flying Tigers), forming in China under Claire L. Chennault to fly P-40's in an effort to help China fend off Japan.

13–14 May. **Remarkable Long Distance Over-Water Flight. Hickam Field, Oahu.**
In what is termed "a remarkable feat of navigation," the U.S.-based 19th Bombardment Group delivers 21 B-17Ds to the Hawaiian Air Force (later Seventh Air Force) without a single mechanical failure. All 21

Left: *Frequent inspections ingrain the discipline necessary in combat. During a January 1941 exercise, infantrymen on Oahu receive a full field inspection. (National Archives)*

ARMY BATTLE STREAMERS—PACIFIC AND ASIA

PHILIPPINE ISLANDS 1941-1942

Philippine Islands, 1941–1942
Burma, 1941–1942
Central Pacific, 1941–1943
East Indies, 1942
India-Burma, 1942–1945
Air Offensive, Japan, 1942–1945
Aleutian Islands, 1942–1943
China defensive, 1942–1945
Papua, 1942–1943
Guadalcanal, 1942–1943
New Guinea, 1943–1944

Northern Solomons, 1943–1944
Eastern Mandates, 1944
Bismarck Archipelago, 1943–1944
Western Pacific, 1943–1944
Leyte, 1944–1943
Luzon, 1944–1945
Central Burma, 1945
Southern Philippines, 1945
Ryukyus, 1945
China Offensive, 1945

aircraft land within 30 minutes of each other, in the order in which they had taken off.

26 July. MacArthur Recalled to Army. Manila, Philippines.

Douglas MacArthur is recalled to active duty as a U.S. major general to command U.S. Army Forces in the Far East (USAFFE). Since his retirement in 1937 he has been serving in an advisory capacity as field marshal of the Philippine Army. He is instructed to "report assumption of command by radio." On 29 July he is promoted to three-star rank in the U.S. Army.

26 August. Hawaiian Division Renamed, Reorganized. Schofield Barracks, Hawaii.

The Hawaiian Division, which dates back to 25 February 1921, trades its name for a number and is reorganized as the 24th Infantry Division.

28 August. Bombers En Route to Reinforce the Philippines.

The 19th Heavy Bombardment Group (Lieutenant Colonel Eugene L. Eubank) begins the deployment of its 35 B-17 "Flying Fortress" bombers to Clark Field in the Philippines. The long trans-Pacific route is via Hawaii, Midway and Wake Islands to a staging point in Australia or New Guinea before the final leg north to the Philippines. By the first week in November all 35 B-17s have completed the long journey from the U.S. west coast.

31 August. FDR Mobilizes Philippine Forces.

President Roosevelt issues a proclamation mobilizing the ten reserve divisions of the Philippine National Army and authorizes General MacArthur to equip them from U.S. resources.

20 September. Air Headquarters is Formed. Nichols Field, Luzon.

The Philippines Department Air Force is established, the forerunner of the future Fifth Air Force. Since 4 August the fledgling Philippines Air Force, a token force of 210 obsolete aircraft, is under U.S. command.

26 September. Reinforcements for Far East Forces. Manila, Philippines.

S.S. *President Coolidge* arrives with long-awaited reinforcements. Arrivals include the 200th Coast

Artillery (Antiaircraft) Regiment from the New Mexico National Guard. Also, the 194th Tank Battalion, a GHQ light-tank battalion of National Guard tank companies (Minnesota, California) arrives with accompanying 17th Ordnance Company (armored). The 194th has 54 new M3 light tanks and 23 late-model half-tracks.

1 October. Supplies, Troops for MacArthur.

The Army searches for shipping to transport 500,000 tons of supplies and 20,000 troops earmarked as reinforcements for the Philippines garrison. Passenger ships are hastily converted—11 to sail between 21 November and 6 January 1942. Six troop ships and nine cargo vessels are at sea when word of Pearl Harbor is received.

10 October. New Division is Formed. Schofield Barracks, Hawaii.

Built around two regiments and a cadre from the 24th Infantry Division (former Hawaiian Division), the 25th Infantry Division is formed. In addition to the 27th and 35th Infantry Regiments it will later add the 161st Infantry from the Washington National Guard. The new division is destined to earn fame as the "Tropic Lightning" division.

10 October. Mission Chief Reaches Destination. Chungking, China.

Major General John Magruder, after a stopover in Manila to confer with General MacArthur, assumes his post as chief of the American Military Mission to China. Magruder's arrival coincides with "10-10" (i.e., 10 October), the 30th anniversary of the Chinese

Above: *Men of the 19th Bomb Group arrive as part of Army reinforcements for the Philippine Islands barely a month before the attack on Pearl Harbor. ("They Fought With What They Had," John D. Shaw, Liberty Studios)*

Republic. Magruder soon sends Washington a gloomy report on the status of China's armed forces.

23 October. Mission of Philippine Department Downgraded. Manila, Philippines.

The Philippine Department (a U.S. army command since 1913) becomes a service command under USAFFE, and its commander, Major General George Grunert, returns to the U.S. for reassignment.

3 November. Brereton Takes Over New Command. Nielsen Field, Philippines.

Leaving command of the stateside Third Air Force, Major General Lewis H. Brereton arrives to assume command of the newly formed Far East Air Force (FEAF). The Philippines garrison now boasts the largest concentration of U. S. Army aircraft outside of the continental U. S., including 107 P-40 fighters and 35 B-17 bombers. Brereton orders all post, group, and squadron commanders to be prepared for emergency service. FEAF (V Bomber Command, V Interceptor Command) is officially activated 16 November.

20 November. Reinforcements for MacArthur. Manila, Philippines.

The 192d Tank Battalion arrives (Kentucky, Illinois, Ohio; also a company from Wisconsin, which goes to the understrength 194th Battalion). The two tank battalions form the new 1st Provisional Tank Group (with 108 light tanks). The transport *H. L. Scott* (formerly S.S. *President Pierce*) returns to the U.S. mainland loaded with military family members and other civilians, the last who would leave the Philippines. *Scott* is the last ship to bring reinforcements to MacArthur's command. The Philippine garrison now numbers 31,095—a 40 percent increase in 120 days.

Right: *At Wheeler Field on Oahu, Army anti-aircraft crewmen man a .50-caliber water-cooled machine gun. As relations between the United States and Japan deteriorate, they will be reassigned to antiriot duties in response to pro-Japanese demonstrations that were predicted by local authorities but never materialized. (National Archives)*

1 December. **MacArthur Organizes Forces. Manila, Philippines.**

With most of ten undermanned and poorly equipped Philippine Army (PA) divisions now incorporated with U.S. forces, General MacArthur reorganizes for the possibility of ground combat in defense of the Philippines. The Northern Luzon Force (NLF) is under Major General Jonathan M. Wainwright; the Southern Luzon Force (SLF) is under Brigadier General George M. Parker, Jr.; the Visayan-Mindanao Force is commanded by Brigadier General William F. Sharp; Major General George F. Moore commands the Harbor Defense forces; and the command's Reserve is directly under MacArthur. .

5 December. **Alternate Bomber Base Established. Del Monte Field, Mindanao.**

Despite incomplete facilities, General Brereton moves two B-17 squadrons (16 aircraft) to Del Monte to initiate a dispersion plan. The 14th and 93d Squadrons from the 19th Bomb Group, commanded by Majors Emmett O'Donnell, Jr., and Cecil Combs, find no natural cover to camouflage airplanes and use a single spray gun to convert the shining silver finish of the aircraft to olive drab.

7 December. **Attack on Pearl Harbor, Army Installations. Hawaii.**

At 1:20 p.m. (Washington time) Japanese naval aviation strikes Pearl Harbor while diplomatic negotiations are still underway. The nation is stunned by the news of Japan's surprise attack launched from aircraft carriers against targets in the Hawaiian Islands. The greatest damage is done at the naval base at Pearl Harbor. Army troops scramble to man beach defense

positions as Schofield Barracks, Hickam Field, and other Army targets sustain damage. The Army reports 233 soldiers and airmen killed and 364 wounded.

7 December. **Army Fliers Respond Quickly. Oahu, Hawaiian Islands.**

As the Naval Base at Pearl Harbor and the Army's Schofield Barracks and Wheeler Army Air Field are under attack, two Army pilots, Second Lieutenants Kenneth Taylor and George Welch, of the 47th Pursuit Squadron at Haleiwa Airfield, get their P-40 Tomahawk fighters into the air and go after the intruders. Together they earn credit for shooting down six Japanese aircraft. Other soldiers use rifles and machine guns to engage the enemy. The Army sustains the loss of 96 aircraft.

8 December. **Philippine Reinforcements, Supplies Diverted.**

Six troop transports and nine cargo vessels sailing toward the Philippines are ordered to proceed to the nearest friendly port and to observe radio silence. Four troop ships return to San Francisco; two continue on to Brisbane, Australia.

8 December. **Japanese Hit Clark Field. Luzon, Philippines.**

The U.S. 19th Bombardment Group (Lieutenant Colonel Eugene L. Eubank) suffers devastating losses as Japanese airplanes strike Clark Field and other bases in the Philippines. The first "return fire" is by gunners of the 200th Coast Artillery, a former cavalry regiment from New Mexico. It is learned that Japanese forces are invading Thailand and occupying the International Settlement at Shanghai.

DOUGLAS MACARTHUR: GENERAL OF THE ARMY

Born on 26 January 1880 in Little Rock, Arkansas, to a military family, Douglas MacArthur graduated from West Point in 1903 with an exceptionally high academic record. As a officer in the Corps of Engineers, MacArthur spent the next ten years serving as an engineer, an aide to his father, Lieutenant General Arthur MacArthur in the Philippines, a presidential aide, and Army school instructor. In 1914 he took part in the ocupation of Vera Cruz, Mexico.

With America's entry into World War I, MacArthur, now an infantry colonel, helped organize the 42d "Rainbow" Division, then served as its chief of staff. He was promoted to temporary brigadier general in June 1918 and commanded the 84th Infantry Brigade with distinction during the St. Mihiel and Meuse-Argonne offensives, being twice wounded and receiving several decorations for bravery.

From 1919 to 1922, MacArthur was superintendent at West Point, being promoted to Regular Army brigadier general in January 1920. He revitalized the curriculum and helped West Point become one of the world's premier military academies. He had two tours of duty in the Philippines and at age 45 became a major general. In November 1930 he was selected as Army Chief of Staff and promoted to temporary general. MacArthur worked to improve and modernize the Army, promoted mechanization, and established an Army Air Force headquarters. On leaving that post in 1935, he was appointed military advisor to the Philippines. He retired in December 1937 but continued to serve as military advisor to the Philippine government. Roosevelt recalled MacArthur to active duty in July 1941 as a lieutenant general and Commander of U.S. Forces in the Far East.

In December 1941 MacArthur was again promoted to general—he led the defense against Japanese forces invading the Philippines until ordered to Australia by Roosevelt in March 1942. MacArthur was awarded the Medal of Honor and appointed commander of the Southwest Pacific Area. With limited men and resources MacArthur struck back in the Papuan Campaign, stopping a Japanese thrust toward Port Moresby and destroying the Japanese force. The high casualties made MacArthur determined to avoid such battles, and he devised a successful strategy of island-hopping across the Pacific, bypassing Japanese strong points. His forces covered more ground with fewer losses than any other army in the Pacific Theater. In December 1944 MacArthur was promoted to General of the Army (five stars) and made commander of all U.S. Forces in the Pacific in April 1945.

As Supreme Commander, Allied Powers, MacArthur presided over Japan's surrender and postwar occupation. His administration in Japan was both notable for the major political, economic, and social reforms it enacted. In 1946 MacArthur was made head of the Far East Command, and when the Korean War broke out in June 1950, he became Commander in Chief, United Nations Command. Despite initial North Korean successes, UN troops managed to hold at Pusan, South Korea, while troops and materiel built up for a counterattack. On 15 September MacArthur launched a daring landing at Inchon. Taking the enemy completely by surprise, MacArthur's troops dashed across the North Koreans' rear, cutting their supply lines and linking up with forces advancing from Pusan. The North Koreans fled north with UN troops in pursuit. Inchon became MacArthur's greatest, and final, military triumph.

Disagreements with President Truman over the prosecution of the war finally resulted in MacArthur's relief from command on 11 April 1951. He returned to a hero's welcome in the U.S, and although poised for public office, MacArthur retired to private life. He died at Walter Reed Hospital on 5 April 1964.

—*Vince Hawkins*

Above: *Brilliant West Point-trained engineer-turned-Pacific commander Douglas MacArthur. (MacArthur Memorial and Archive, Norfolk, VA)*

10 December. **First Landings by the Japanese Army. Northern Luzon, Philippines.**

Defense forces are unable to mount resistance in the first Japanese landings at Aparri and down-coast at Vigan. Japanese troops also land on island of Guam, a U.S. territory between Wake Island and the Philippines. Guam, overrun in a few hours, is the first U.S. possession to fall into Japanese hands.

12 December. **Landing on Luzon East Coast. Legaspi, Philippines.**

Southeast of Manila, in the sector defended by the Southern Luzon Force (Major General Parker), Japanese land at Legaspi, are initially unopposed, and move north on the coastal road.

16 December. **First Army Ace. Nichols Field, Luzon, Philippines.**

An Army pilot, Lieutenant Boyd D. (Buzz) Wagner, and since May the commander of the 17th Pursuit Squadron, becomes the first U.S. Army Air Corps ace of World War II as he downs his fifth enemy plane in action near the Japanese landing site at Vigan.

19-20 December. **Japanese Into Southern Philippines. Davao, Mindanao.**

The Japanese begin landing operations in the northern sector of Davao. They encounter a Philippine Army battalion commanded by U.S. Army Lieutenant Colonel Roger B. Hilsman. The Japanese soon use Davao as a launching point for attack, which results in the capture of Jolo on Christmas Eve. The enemy now has forces in position for an attack against Borneo.

20 December. **Northern Landing Forces Link-Up.**

Japanese Aparri and Vigan landing parties join forces and prepare to move south to the Lingayen Gulf area.

22 December. **MacArthur Gains Four-Star Rank. Philippines.**

Douglas MacArthur is promoted to full general in the wartime army as he deploys his battered forces to continue the fight in the face of overwhelming odds, with no prospects of reinforcement in sight.

22-24 December. **Main Enemy Force Landings in Progress. Luzon, Philippines.**

The main assault of the Japanese 14th Army (Lieutenant General Masaharu Homma) is underway as 76 army transports and nine navy transports, with 43,110 troops, enter Lingayen Gulf with a strong naval escort. Major General Wainwright maneuvers elements of the North Luzon Force (NLF) to meet the enemy. But by 24 December one enemy column is in Baguio; the main thrust south toward Manila reaches Binalonan and is driving toward the Agno River.

23 December. **Attempt to Save Manila from Destruction.**

Hoping to stave off civilian casualties, General MacArthur declares Manila an open city. He evacuates troops from the city and orders American and Filipino

Above: *A flight of 12 unarmed B-17D bombers of the 38th and 88th Reconnaissance Squadrons arrives in the midst of the 7 December attack on Oahu. All 12 planes broke through to land, although several were badly damaged. ("Flying into War," Stan Stokes, Stokes Collection)*

units to fight a delaying action as he withdraws the Army into the Bataan Peninsula, where it is hoped that defensive positions will deter the enemy attack.

23 December. Philippine Corps in Withdrawal.
Major General Albert M. Jones (Commander, I Philippine Corps) orders the withdrawal of troops from the Bicol Peninsula as another Japanese invasion (the Lamon Bay Force) task force appears off Atimonan on the east coast.

24 December. Cavalry Into the Fray. Binalonan, Philippines.
In the retrograde action toward Bataan, Colonel Clinton S. Pierce's 26th Cavalry, Philippine Scouts, makes a mounted charge in an effort to stem the Japanese tide.

24 December. Japanese Launch Secondary Landing. East Coast, Luzon.
With the Southern Luzon Force (SLF) badly dispersed and hampered by the absence of artillery, the Japanese Lamon Bay Force encounters little resistance as it lands at three points and opens a drive north-westward in the direction of Manila. General Homma moves his headquarters ashore as both the Lingayen Gulf and Lamon Bay assault forces continue to advance.

24 December. No Help for MacArthur.
The Pensacola convoy, with critically needed supplies, reaches Australia, but no way can be found to

transport its troops or cargo north to the Philippines. As the year comes toward an end, General MacArthur has not received a single piece of equipment or any additional soldiers to reinforce his beleaguered army.

24 December. "WPO-3 Is In Effect!" Manila, Philippines.
The prewar plan anticipating the possibility of a withdrawal of U. S. and Philippine forces into the Bataan Peninsula is activated. The Bataan Defense Force is created, with Major General George M. Parker in command of II Philippine Corps.

24 December. Bomber Operations No Longer Possible. Fort McKinley, Luzon.
Brereton closes down his headquarters and on orders from General MacArthur leaves by Navy PBY to join his bombers at Batchelor Field near Port Darwin, Australia. MacArthur informs Washington: "Operations heavy bombardment no longer possible from bases here." Surviving B-17s are in Australian or Netherlands East Indies bases.

25–31 December. Fighting Withdrawal From the North.
The Northern Luzon Force withdraws below the Agno River and starts a phased retrograde action, fighting from a series of D-lines to the final and most southerly position, D-5, stretching from Bamban in front of Mt. Arayat, across Route 5 to Sibul Springs. D-5 is organized for a protracted defense to enable the

Right: *Men of the 26th Cavalry (Philippine Scouts) formed part of the Philippine Division who bravely faced superior Japanese numbers. Even in the face of overwhelming enemy ground troops they made several mounted counterattacks led by their American officers before having to dispose of their horses. One of the final attacks was led by Lieutenant Edwin Ramsey. (Blandford Press)*

Below: *Tough former cavalryman Major General Jonathan "Skinny" Wainwright (left) and Lieutenant General Douglas MacArthur were charged with the daunting responsibility of defending the Philippines. (MacArthur Memorial and Archive, Norfolk, VA)*

South Luzon Force to slip into San Fernando and into Bataan before the closure of the NLF.

31 December. Army Role in Establishing New Trans-Pacific Route.
As a consequence of the Pearl Harbor attack and increased Japanese naval presence, a new trans-Pacific

route has to be developed after the loss of Wake Island and Guam. Army task forces are organized to move rapidly to secure Christmas and Canton Islands and to establish U.S. facilities in the Society Islands (Bora Bora), Fiji, and New Caledonia.

31 December. Tankers Cover Withdrawal. Calumpit Bridge, Luzon.
In the withdrawal into Bataan the NLF withdrawal is covered by the tanks of Brigadier General James R. N. Weaver's Provisional Tank Group of National Guard light tanks. In the extrication of the SLF, a brisk action involving the 192d Tank Battalion and six of Lieutenant Colonel David S. Babcock's self-proppelled 75mm guns make a shambles of the portion of Baliuag in Japanese hands. When the action breaks off, eight Japanese tanks are destroyed with only negligible damage to the U.S. force. The last of the U. S. tanks crosses the Calumpit bridge at about 2:30 a.m. on 1 January. By 5:00 a.m. Generals Jones, Stevens, and Weaver assure General Wainwright that all their units are safely across. Final preparations are made for demolition of the bridge. MacArthur's Army is in Bataan.

1942

1 January. **Brett Commands New Army Effort. Port Darwin, Australia.**
Newly promoted Lieutenant General George H. Brett, a veteran airman, arrives from a special mission to Chungking, China, to take command of U.S. Army Forces in Australia (USAFIA), initially created as a support base for General MacArthur's army in the Philippines. He is subsequently named a principal deputy and commander of the Fifth Air Force.

2 January. **Withdrawal into Bataan is Completed.**
With the passage of all U.S. and Filipino units into Bataan, the 26th Cavalry (PS) covers the left flank of the new defensive line anchored at the town of San Jose. Japanese are reported crossing the Pampanga river and moving toward San Fernando. Occupation forces move into Manila; enemy aircraft start daily attacks on the island bastion of Corregidor.

Above: *Desperate fighting occurred at close quarters as MacArthur's American and Filipino soldiers attempted to hold defensive positions blocking the Japanese advance against the last stronghold on Bataan. (Army Art Collection, NMUSA)*

5 January. **New Defensive Line on Bataan.**
In the face of heavy enemy pressure, a new defense line, manned by battered Philippine army divisions, is established along the base of the Bataan peninsula.

7 January. **Army Girds for Japanese Siege of Bataan.**
U.S. and Filipino forces are reorganized to defend the Bataan Peninsula as the Northern Luzon Force becomes I Philippine Corps. Bataan Defense Force is renamed II Philippine Corps. The combined force has 47,500 troops. I Corps is responsible for the western sector, II Corps for the Eastern sector. A provisional infantry unit is formed near Marivales composed of Air Corps personnel, many of whom are pilots without planes to fly.

9 January. **Enemy Force Launches Assault. Bataan, Philippines.**
An attack is launched by three Japanese regimental combat teams with artillery support. On the II Corps front, the Abucay Line is set up from Mabatang on Manila Bay to Mt. Natib. Demolitions are used in an effort to slow the enemy on I Corps' Mauban line.

10 January. **Enemy Surrender Demand is Spurned.**
Japanese make their first surrender demand with a message dropped by aircraft. During the day, General MacArthur makes an inspection of Bataan defenses.

11 January. **Artillerymen Land in Pacific Hot Spot. Surabaya, Java.**

Detached from a convoy diverted to Darwin, Australia, with six artillery battalions intended to reinforce the army in the Philippines, the 2d Battalion, 131st Field Artillery, Texas National Guard, debarks from USS *Republic* and is assigned to join a mixed defense force of Dutch, British, and Australian troops.

12 January. **First Medal of Honor Hero. Abucay, Bataan, Philippines.**

Wounded three times in a desperate counterattack, 2d Lieutenant Alexander R. (Sandy) Nininger, 57th Infantry, Philippine Scouts, succumbs in hand-to-hand fighting. He is posthumously awarded the first Army Medal of Honor in World War II. He is a 1941 graduate of West Point.

16 January. **Major Breakthrough Jeopardizes Defense. Moron, Luzon.**

The U.S. 31st Infantry Regiment enters the fight near the Abucay Hacienda as the enemy launches an encirclement hoping to turn the left flank of the II Corps. I Corps engages the enemy for the first time as Japanese cross the Batalan river to engage Filipino infantrymen and cavalrymen of the 26th Cavalry (PS). Lieutenant Edwin P. Ramsey leads his platoon of 26 men on horseback in an effort to secure Moron—possibly the last horse cavalry charge by the U.S. Army. The cavalrymen are withdrawn after taking heavy losses, and remaining horses are soon destroyed.

22 January. **A Final Defensive Position is Set-Up. Bataan, Luzon.**

General MacArthur orders the withdrawal of the Mauban-Abucay line southward to a final defense position behind the Pilar-Bagac road as the enemy starts an attack that regains ground lost in the II Corps counteroffensive of 16 January. In I Corps area, infantry elements supported by cavalry scouts and tanks are unsuccessful in their efforts to reduce a roadblock held by the enemy. During the night Japanese forces undertake a series of amphibious operations to establish a position below Bagac.

23–24 January. **Japanese Army Extends Its Control.**

Japanese troops in land at Rabaul (New Britain) and Kavieng (New Ireland). The Australian garrison at Rabaul is quickly overwhelmed and Kavieng is undefended. The enemy can now strike at New Guinea targets and menace Australia. Other Japanese move toward the east coast of Borneo at Balikpapan. U.S. Army field artillerymen, with the Dutch forces, prepare to meet the oncoming enemy.

27 January. **"Bobcat" Troopers Start Journey To War. Charleston, South Carolina.**

One of the early deployment task forces formed hastily by the War Department, BOBCAT sets sail in a six-ship convoy to construct a U.S. base at Bora Bora in the French Society Islands; the Task Force includes the 102d Infantry Regiment and the 198th Antiaircraft Regiment. These regiments are, respectively, from the the Connecticut and Delaware Guards.

Right: *Sergeant First Class Emil Morello, Company C, 194th Tank Company, crashes through a Japanese roadblock in an effort to break the assault on Bataan. Inadequate numbers of tanks contributed to the American defeat during the desperate efforts to repel the massive enemy assault. ("At a Roadblock on the Road to Bataan," D. Millsap, Army Art Collection, NMUSA)*

29 January. Pursuit Squadron to the South Pacific. Suva, Fiji.
The 70th Pursuit Squadron, with supporting elements for a total personnel of 725, sets up its base to help provide a link between New Caledonia and Samoa. Redesignated the 70th Fighter Squadron on 15 May 1942, it will later operate from Guadalcanal.

31 January. Task Forces to Establish Pacific Bases. San Francisco, California.
Infantrymen, coast artillerymen, air corps elements, and supply troops man Army task forces destined for Christmas Island (Birch) and Canton Island (Holly). Two thousand troops sail on board the transport, the *President Taylor*.

5 February. Air Arm in Central Pacific. Hickam Field, Hawaii.
The 7th Air Force succeeds the Hawaiian Air Force and is subsequently redesignated the Seventh Air Force (18 September 1942). It is under the command of Major General Clarence L. Tinker. The first mission of the "Pineapple Air Force" is the defense of the Hawaiian Islands.

10 February. Task Force Sets Up Base. Christmas Island, Central Pacific.
Task Force Holly lands and sets up base camp.

12 February. Tenth Air Force Organized. Patterson Field, Ohio.
The Tenth Air Force is activated and earmarked for service, with General Stilwell in the CBI.

13 February. Incident Mars Task Force Arrival. Canton Island, Central Pacific.
Entering the lagoon of this remote location, the *President Taylor* goes aground short of the pier. Task Force Birch troops land without any loss of life, set up camp, and start a survey of area to begin construction of an airstrip. The *Taylor* is never refloated.

17 February. Bobcat Force is in Place. Bora Bora, Society Islands.
Army Task Force Bobcat arrives and sets to work to develop a base at this a critical spot on the vital supply line between the U.S. west coast and Australia. Bora Bora is 2,000 miles south of Pearl Harbor and 4,000 miles west of Panama.

23 February. Australia-Based Bombers In Action. Townsville, Australia.
Six B-17s, survivors of the Philippines campaign, make their first strike by the Fifth Air Force against Japanese installations at Rabaul, New Britain.

24 February. Brereton Leaves for New Assignment. Bandoeng, Java.
General Brereton is ordered to turn over his command as the defense of the region is assumed by the Dutch. He leaves for a new assignment as commander of U.S. Air Forces in India and Burma. Four days later he arrives in New Delhi, India. He is soon (5 March) in command of the Tenth Air Force. Its immediate duties are to defend the ferry route over the Hump. Initially it is also responsible for the Kunming-based China Air Task Force under Major General Claire L. Chennault.

4 March. CBI Commander Reaches Destination. Chungking, China.
After consultations in India, Lieutenant General Joseph W. Stilwell (promoted to three-star rank on 25 February 1942) arrives to establish headquarters of his new command, the China-Burma-India (CBI) theater of operations. He is welcomed by Chinese president Chiang Kai-shek.

Opposite: *Lieutenant Alexander R. Nininger, 57th Infantry (Philippine Scouts), was the first Army recipient of the Medal of Honor in World War II. President Franklin D. Roosevelt personally bestowed the medal in recognition of Nininger's heroism at Bataan. (National Archives)*

Right: *Rebounding after the fall of the Philippines, U.S. troops began to gather and train in Australia in preparation for the hard-fought island-hopping war that was intended to topple the Japanese empire. (Library of Congress)*

9 March. **Texas Artillerymen Trapped in Surrender. Surabaya, Java.**

After fighting under Dutch command, the 2d Battalion, 131st Field Artillery, is swept up in the Japanese conquest of Java. Elements of the battered 19th Bombardment Group manage to evacuate to Broome, Australia, as Japanese now control the Dutch East Indies. The ill-fated "lost battalion" of artillerymen will be among the prisoners forced to labor on the bridge over the River Kwai and remain imprisoned until 29 August 1945.

10 March. **27th Division Deploys. San Francisco, California.**

The 27th (New York) Infantry Division is the first full division deployed from stateside to a Pacific area destination following the attack on Pearl Harbor. After duty in defense of the West Coast, the leading elements of the division depart the port of embarkation. The urgency of this movement results in the 27th being the only unit to go overseas in the configuration of a "square" division. It is to be reconfigured to the new divisional structure after it arrives in the Hawaiian Islands.

11 March. **General MacArthur to Australia. Corregidor, Manila Bay.**

Under Presidential order, General Douglas MacArthur, his family and some staff depart the

Philippines by PT boat and, later, B-17 aircraft to Australia, where the four-star general is designated to command U.S. forces in the Southwest Pacific area.

12 March. **U.S. Occupies Key French Island. Nouméa, New Caledonia.**

At the end of long trip, which originated at the Boston Port of Embarkation, and after a brief stop in Australia, Army Task Force 6814 (17,500 troops) under Major General Alexander M. Patch reached their destination. The local government aligns itself with General De Gaulle and distances itself from the Vichy regime, easing the political situation confronting U.S. troops. TF 6814 troops provide the core for the future Americal Division.

17 March. **MacArthur in Australia Pledges to Return to the Philippines.**

After a harrowing journey by PT Boat and a rescue flight from Mindanao by daring Australia-based B-17 bomber crews, General MacArthur arrives and sets up his new headquarters. He promises those left behind in the Philippines, "I shall return."

18 March. **Troops Occupy Island Needed for Air Base. Efate, New Hebrides.**

A small force of infantrymen and engineers from units located in New Caledonia occupy this island so work can be started to build an airstrip.

25 March. Highest Honor to MacArthur. Washington.
Citing heroic leadership against invading Japanese forces in the Philippines, the War Department announces the Medal of Honor is awarded to General Douglas MacArthur. Five days later, in a joint announcement with the Australian government, MacArthur is appointed Allied Supreme Commander, Southwest Pacific.

9 April. Bataan Campaign Ends in Surrender. Marivales, Philippines.
Bataan falls after a heroic and desperate defense against overwhelming Japanese forces. With food and ammunition gone, Major General Edward P. King, Jr., surrenders the surviving "Battling Bastards of Bataan," 75,000 American and Filipino soldiers. The six-day Bataan Death March begins 10 April. 76,000 allied POWs, including 12,000 Americans, make the 60-mile forced march under brutal supervision of their captors; many die even before they reach the infamous prison camps.

Above: *Hefting denim bags, troops headed for combat in the Pacific Theater make their way up the gangplank in uniforms reminiscent of the World War I. ("Blue Duffle Bags," Barse Miller, Army Art Collection, NMUSA)*

9–11 April. APO 41 Sets Up Its New Camp, Far From Home. Seymour, Australia.
Joyfully welcomed by Aussies after a long odyssey across the Pacific, the advance elements of the 41st Infantry Division (Washington, Oregon, Idaho, Montana, and Wyoming), now designated APO 41 c/o Postmaster, San Francisco, reach the land Down Under. The division assembles at a training base 65 miles inland from Melbourne. The last of the 41st arrives in Melbourne 13 May with advance elements of the 32d Infantry Division from Wisconsin and Michigan. The 32d is initially outside Adelaide until moved to Camp Cable near Brisbane in July 1942. The 32d and 41st Divisions are charter members of U.S. I Corps (Major General Robert L. Eichelberger).

18 April. Audacious B-25 Raid Strikes Japan. USS *Hornet*, Pacific Ocean.
Army fliers led by Lieutenant Colonel James H. Doolittle make a surprise retaliatory attack on Tokyo, Nagoya, and Yokohama. The raid is largely symbolic but a huge boost for U.S. morale. Doolittle's army fliers use 16 Army B-25 bombers modified for launch off an aircraft carrier.

Right: *Manhandling a 37mm gun into position, men of the Philippine Scouts of the American-Filipino Philippine Division practice deployment on a field training exercise. (U.S. Army)*

Below: *Lieutenant General Joseph "Vinegar Joe" Stilwell trudged out of Burma with his small group of American advisors and Chinese just ahead of the advancing Japanese. He too would return. ("Vinegar Joe Stilwell," Mort Künstler)*

2 May. **Stilwell's Long Trek Out of Burma.**
With a party that includes 26 Americans, 13 British, 16 Chinese, and a number of Chinese nurses from the Seagrave ("Burma Surgeon") military hospital, Lieutenant General Stilwell starts the trek toward allied territory in the wake of the Anglo-Chinese collapse in northern Burma.

5 May. **Beginning of the End on The Rock. Corregidor, Philippines.**
Japanese forces start to land on this island harbor defense center at the entrance to Manila Bay.

6 May. **Wainwright Surrender Ends Doomed Campaign. Corregidor, Philippines.**
Lieutenant General Jonathan M. Wainwright surrenders all U.S. and Philippine Army forces in the Philippines. Among thousands of American and Filipino soldiers taken prisoner are 19 U.S. Army generals.

20 May. **End of the Long March. Imphal, India.**
With the stragglers that joined his footsore column, Stilwell reaches India and leads 114 weary soldiers and civilians at the end of long trek through mountains and jungle. The undiplomatic Stilwell declares, "We got a helluva beating." The Japanese seizure of Burma effectively cuts the CBI into two sectors (i.e., China and India) with a tenuous "air connection" operating out of bases in northeastern India (Assam). Stilwell learns that the Japanese have launched a major invasion of China.

27 May. **New Division is Formed in Pacific. New Caledonia.**
The Americal Division (Major General Alexander M. Patch) is formed from the elements of Army Task Force 6814—three National Guard regiments from the states of Illinois, Massachusetts, and North Dakota. It is the only U.S. division in World War II with a name instead of a number. (In postwar years it becomes, briefly, the 23d Infantry Division).

28 May. **Important Base for the Solomons Offensive. Espiritu Santo, New Hebrides.**
Soldiers and Marines from the garrison on Efate occupy Espiritu Santo to accelerate airfield development needed for forthcoming operations in the Solomons.

EYEWITNESS: THE FALL OF BATAAN

On 8 December 1941 the Japanese launched an attack against the Philippines. For the next five months, American and Filipino troops fought a tenacious battle against superior enemy forces. Pushed back to the last few strongholds, running out of food and ammunition, and with no help in sight, U.S. forces grudgingly faced the inevitable. Lieutenant Madeline Ullom, Army nurse, witnessed the final desperate days on Bataan:*

"Fresh carabao meat sometimes supplemented the diet. Fresh fruits and vegetables were occasionally obtained from markets. The time eventually arrived when the usefulness of the cavalry horses passed. . . . A radio was the center of communication, to listen to the Voice of Freedom broadcasts from Corregidor. Mimeograph news dispatches were distributed. . . .

"The supply of plasma for blood transfusion was soon exhausted. Doctors and enlisted men donated blood. The influx of many orthopedic cases used up the supply of traction ropes. Jungle vines were substituted. Backs ached from long dawn-to-dusk hours of changing dressings of patients on beds about one foot from the ground. Amputees without hope of prosthesis tried to learn balance and move in their weakened condition. Gauze was washed, sterilized, and reused. Amputees spent long hours stretching and folding gauze.

"On 29 March, a bomb dropped at the hospital entrance. The Japanese apologized for the accident. The hospital was bombed at 10:17 on 30 March. A direct hit landed on the ward which Hattie Brantly had left. . . . Traction ropes and jungle vines were slashed to permit patients to slide under beds. . . . A second wave of bombardment hit. Devastation was everywhere. Trees were uprooted. Fragments of clothing and parts of bodies were in the tree branches. Roofs were pulverized. Sides of buildings were splintered. Beds were twisted, dead and wounded were partially buried in debris. Many died of shock.

"By five in the evening on the next day (4 April) shells were raining. Word was that the Japanese had landed at Cabcaben which was only two kilometers away. Beds were assigned before those who occupied them were discharged prematurely to return to combat. Front lines seemed to vanish. Most of the patients suffered from gunshots and Hospital Number Two sent buses, trucks and ambulances to transfer patients.

"Around eight on the evening of 8 April nurses at Hospital Number One and Number Two were ordered to take a small bag and be ready to depart immediately. It evoked mixed feelings from the nurses. Many were reluctant to go. They felt an obligation to nurse the seriously and critically ill patients. But they knew orders must be obeyed. The doctors came to see them leave. Goodbyes were hasty with promises to see each other again.

"About midnight, the nurses from Hospital Number One were in a small open boat. It tossed about in the water as blasts hit nearby. Guns on Corregidor were hitting the Japanese on Bataan. Shells whizzed overhead repeatedly. Men on all sides were attempting to swim to Corregidor. At 3:30 the (island) pier was reached finally, amidst flashes of gunfire and blast of bombs.

"(6 May) A corpsman stopped to gravely inform us he saw the white flag at the tunnel entrance. We heard the time of a broadcast was set. We gathered around Major Richardson's radio in the dental clinic. A desolate, numb, unbelievable feeling engulfed one. We listened to the words we had pushed to the backs of our minds. Tears came to our eyes. No one spoke. We walked away as though we were in an unrealistic situation."

Lieutenant Ullom survived three years in a Japanese camp before being liberated in 1945.

—*Vince Hawkins*

Above: *Army staff inside the Malinta Tunnel continue to hold out against the Japanese onslaught of 1942. (National Archives)*

Right: *After discovery by a Japanese scout plane, Lieutenant Colonel James Doolittle's crews were forced to make a premature takeoff on 18 April 1942 for their daring attack against the Japanese mainland. While this raid had little tactical value, the mission presaged the coming destruction of the Japanese empire by American military might. ("Early Launch," James Dietz)*

3–6 June. **Flying Forts Join in Battle of Midway Island.**
Nine of the Seventh Air Force's Midway-based B-17s attack the Japanese invasion force of 45 ships 570 miles to the southwest of the island and strike the first blow as naval task forces race to intercept enemy would-be invaders. On the following day, as the battle develops, other B-17s from Barking Sands, Kauai, join the fray and attack another enemy task force approaching Midway from the north and already within 145 miles of the island. With the assistance of the AAF's B-17s, the Navy scores a major victory at Midway. Later U.S. intelligence learns that after Midway the Japanese have cancelled proposed invasions of Fiji and Samoa.

6 June. **Air Force Commander Lost in Action. Near Midway Island.**
Major General Clarence L. Tinker, commander of the Hawaii-based Seventh Air Force, disappears while leading a bombing raid. He is the first Army air force general to die in action in World War II. After a brief period under Brigadier General Howard C. Davidson, on 20 June 1942, Major General Willis H. Hale takes command of the Seventh.

6–7 June. **Japanese Move Into the Western Aleutians. Bering Sea, Alaska.**
Japanese invade the western Aleutians, landing 1,800 men on Attu and Kiska. On 11 June reconnaissance confirms Japanese garrisons have been established on both islands. Reconnaissance landings 26–27 August fail to disclose any enemy on Adak Island.

22 June. **Stilwell Units in New Status. Washington, D.C.**
By War Department order all units under General Stilwell's command are assigned to "American Army Forces in India, China, and Burma." This is regarded as the first step in the evolution of a U.S. "theater of operations" on the Asiatic mainland.

25 June. **Brereton Departs From Tenth Air Force. New Delhi, India.**
With the Allies facing a critical situation in the Middle East, Major General Brereton is ordered to proceed immediately to Egypt "with all available heavy bombers." He turns over command of the Tenth Air Force to his deputy, Brigadier General Earl L. Naiden; in August command goes to Major General Clayton L. Bissell.

2 July. **JCS Issues Orders for Pacific Action. Washington, D.C.**
General MacArthur receives a directive from the Joint Chiefs of Staff (JCS), which prescribes the New Britain-New Ireland-New Guinea offensive, which is to be conducted in three phases with 1 August as target date. (This is later changed to 7 August). Boundaries between South Pacific (Navy) and Southwest Pacific (Army) commands, as altered, place the lower Solomons within the South Pacific zone.

22-25 July. **Heavy Bomber Group Joins South Pacific Forces. New Caledonia.**
Four bombardment squadrons of the B-17-equipped 11th Bombardment Group (Colonel LaVerne G. Saunders) complete deployment from Hawaii. Two squadrons are based in New Caledonia; one is at Efate, the other in Fiji.

26 July. **Harmon Commands New Headquarters. Auckland, New Zealand.**
Major General Millard F. Harmon, a senior army airman, takes command of the newly created U.S.

Army Forces in the South Pacific (USAFISPA) under Navy Vice Admiral Robert L. Ghormely. Harmon plans to transfer his command post to Noumea, New Caledonia, as planning for offensive operations in the Solomons gets into high gear.

3 August. **Fifth Air Force Commander Reassigned. Brisbane, Australia.**
Lieutenant General George H. Brett, a principal deputy to General MacArthur and commander of the Fifth Air Force, is recalled to the United States for reassignment.

6–7 August. **Air Hero Awarded Medal of Honor. Rabaul, New Britain.**
Although he is not scheduled to fly, Captain Harl Pease, Jr., leads a strike by the 93d Squadron, 19th Bomb Group, survivors of the Philippines campaign. Flying an aircraft deemed "unserviceable for combat" and with only three hours' rest, Pease leads a foray that is intercepted by 30 enemy fighters. He is lost on mission. Earlier in year Pease played a prominent role in the rescue of MacArthur from Mindanao.

Above: *Those American and Filipinos who survived the brutal battle of Bataan suffered even more on the infamous death march as prisoners of the Japanese. Years of captivity took the lives of many of those who made the brutal trek. ("Bataan Death March," James Dietz)*

1 September. **Army Seizes Island Base at Adak Island.**
4,500 troops move ashore rapidly in the occupation of Adak Island, to be used as an advanced air base from which to attack Kiska, some 250 miles distant. Army plans are to have 10,000 or more troops on Adak by mid-October. On 11 September a runway is completed to permit stepped-up air offensive against Kiska targets.

3 September. **Kenney Commands Air for MacArthur. Brisbane, Australia.**
After a month in-theater and nearly a month after General Brett's departure, Major General George C. Kenney officially takes command of the Fifth Air Force. He is promoted to three-star rank.

14 September. **Air Attacks Launched at Kiska. Adak, Western Aleutians.**
Kiska is attacked for the first time by a force of 12 B-24 Liberator bombers accompanied by 28 fighters (42d and 54th Fighter Squadrons) from Adak. Meanwhile, the enemy completes the transfer of his Attu garrison, including antiaircraft elements to Kiska. Despite heavy antiaircraft fire, bombers drop more than 100 tons of bombs in September and 200 tons in October. In November the onset of bad weather restricts further air operations against Kiska. In late October the Japanese reinforce the garrison in the Kuril islands and reoccupy Attu.

15 September. **Red Arrow Troops In Pioneer Airlift. Amberly Field, Brisbane.**

As hard-pressed Australian forces are pushed back to about 32 miles from Port Moresby, the capital of Papua, General MacArthur orders the 32d Infantry Division (MG Edwin F. Harding) to New Guinea. Urgency results in one regiment moving by air—a pioneer effort by the Fifth Air Force (Kenney). At dawn, 230 soldiers of the 126th Infantry Regiment climb aboard a mixture of Douglas and Lockheed transports and by late afternoon they land at Port Moresby. Adding 12 transports from the Australian civil airlines, the entire 128th Infantry is airlifted to the Seven-Mile Strip near Port Moresby. By 29 September all of the division elements, less the rear echelon, are in Port Moresby, quickly poised for offensive action against the Japanese.

24 September. **I Corps First Pacific Command Post. Rockhampton, Australia.**

U.S. I Corps, inactivated in Europe in 1919 after World War I, opens its first Pacific command post under Major General Robert L. Eichelberger. He notes with some astonishment that the 32d Infantry Division is assigned to the I Corps for offensive training and to the Australian II Corps for defensive training. This anomaly is resolved as the Red Arrow division heads for New Guinea. The 41st Infantry Division is also under I Corps. In October, Eichelberger is promoted to three-star rank.

7 October. **Rugged Trail Through Mountains. Port Moresby, New Guinea.**

Captain Alfred Medendorp sets out with a small force ahead of 2d Battalion, 126th Infantry, on a difficult march that leads across the Owen Stanley Mountain Range. Starting from Kalikodobu, southeast of Moresby, Medendorp heads for Jaures. On 10 October the main body of the 2d Battalion follows. The rugged march over the Kapa Kapa Trail takes until 24 October. After Jaure, the Medendorp force protects the battalion rear along the remaining distance to Buna via Natunga and Bofu.

13 October. **Army Reinforces Marines. Guadalcanal Island.**

The 2,852 soldiers of 164th Infantry (Colonel Bryant E. Moore), Americal Division, arrive to join the Marines in battle. They quickly go into action near Henderson Field.

19 October. **Army Division Alerted for Guadalcanal. Schofield Barracks, Hawaii.**

The 25th Infantry Division (Major General J. Lawton Collins) is ordered to prepare for deployment to the South Pacific. The plan is to stage through New Caledonia en route to Guadalcanal.

Right: *The 206th Coast Artillery (Antiaircraft) was on hand at Dutch Harbor, Alaska, when the Japanese attacked in June 1942. Although a diversionary attack, the enemy did capture Kiska and Attu, which they occupied briefly before being driven out of the Aleutians. ("Defense of the Aleutians," Domenick D'Anrea, National Guard Bureau)*

Above: *Army and Marine ground troops found Guadalcanal a grueling experience as they pushed the Japanese out of their strong defenses. (Sergeant "Mike" Levine, Army Art Collection, NMUSA)*

Opposite: *At Nelson's Bay, New South Wales, Australia, the 32d Infantry Division practices amphibious landings, a key to Pacific operations. During the course of the war the Army will conduct the most and largest amphibious operations. (National Archives)*

4 November. **Buckeye Infantrymen Diverted to Guadalcanal.**

The 147th Infantry, "squared-out" of its parent 37th ("Ohio") Infantry Division in streamlining of infantry divisions, has its scheduled move to Ndeni Island canceled; instead, the 147th (Colonel W. B. Tuttle) heads to Guadalcanal. With support from a provisional artillery battery out of the Americal division, the regiment makes an amphibious landing near Lunga. By the end of November two battalions of the 147th are operational with Army forces on Guadalcanal.

6 November. **MacArthur Moves Advance CP. Port Moresby, New Guinea.**

The advance echelon of General MacArthur's General Headquarters (GHQ) opens; MacArthur arrives to direct operations.

12 November. **Americal Division Deployment. Guadalcanal, Solomons.**

The 182d Infantry (Colonel Daniel W. Hogan) is the second major element of the Americal to land in Guadalcanal. The arrival of troops fresh from the States makes possible the relief of Americal from the defense of New Caledonia. During December, remaining elements of the Americal (16,196 troops) join the Division in the frontlines.

16 November. **Forces Assemble for Buna Drive. Natunga, New Guinea.**

The 32d (Red Arrow) Division's 126th and 128th Infantry Regiments initiate an attack toward Buna in concert with an advance by the Australian infantry. During a tragic incident, a fleet of small barges with sorely needed supplies is attacked and destroyed by 18 enemy aircraft. The division turns to the Army Air Force for emergency resupply by air. The attack is resumed on 19 November. As the division confronts an immense swamp, the Warren Force attacks from one side of swamp; elements formed as Urbana Force attack on the other side. The division commander (Major General Harding) receives a message from General MacArthur to press the attack "regardless of cost."

20 November. **Engineers Finish Alaskan Highway. Soldier's Summit, Canada.**

The 1,422-mile Alaska Military (ALCAN) Highway, built mostly by seven Army Corps of Engineer regiments, opens nine months after the project began. The strategic road connects Alaska with Dawson Creek, Canada.

1 December. **Eichelberger is Ordered to Take Buna. Port Moresby, New Guinea.**
Due to an unusual command arrangement, the I Corps troops—such as the 32d Infantry Division—fall under Australian control when they reach New Guinea. I Corps' CP remains in Australia as Lieutenant General Eichelberger, accompanied by his chief of staff, reports to General MacArthur in Port Moresby. He is told to relieve the 32d Division commander (Harding) and to "take Buna or not come back alive." On
2 December Eichelberger proceeds to the front. On 14 December Buna Village is taken, but the worst of the campaign lies ahead in the push to Buna Mission.

9 December. **Army Commands Campaign on Guadalcanal.**
Responsibility for command of the campaign is passed to Major General Patch as the 1st Marine Division prepares to depart after continuous combat since
7 August. Patch's American Division headquarters finds itself in the role of a Corps headquarters.

15 December. **Army Launches a December Offensive. Guadalcanal, Solomons.**
Despite the lack of sufficient troops on hand, the Army undertakes a limited offensive with its objective to dislodge Japanese forces entrenched in the Mount Austen area. High command contends Henderson

Field cannot be secure until Mount Austen is in U.S. hands. The mission is given to the 132d Infantry, last of the America's regiments to reach the battlefront. By 31 December the bitter fight is bogged down. After 22 days the 132d Infantry succeeds in controlling part of Mount Austen; observation of the U.S. perimeter is now denied to the enemy.

17 December. **Harmon Rushes 25th Division to the Front. Guadalcanal.**
Hard pressed for troops as the 1st Marine Division departs, General Harmon (Commander, USAFISPA), makes the decision to forego scheduled reloading at New Caledonia and orders the Hawaii-based 25th Infantry Division (Major General J. Lawton Collins) directly to Guadalcanal. The 35th Regimental Combat Team is first to land and is quickly pressed into perimeter defense.

17–19 December. **Army Ponders Amchitka Island as Objective.**
A reconnaissance party lands on the island and reports to Western Defense Command (DeWitt) that a fighter strip could be constructed in two to three weeks and a main airfield in three to four months. DeWitt recommends to the War Department that an Amchitka landing be made as soon as practicable.

23 December. **Planning Underway for Proposed Amchitka Move.**

The War Department concurs in the Amchitka seizure and agrees on the 7th Infantry Division (Major General Albert E. Brown) in lieu of a proposal to build a landing force around the 35th Infantry Division. The 7th Division at Fort Ord, California, is alerted to begin special mission training. Major General Charles H. Corlett is advised he is to command the task force. The 184th Infantry Regiment (ex-California National Guard) becomes the 7th Division's third regiment.

24 December. **Infantry Breaks Through. Buna, New Guinea.**

Driving through enemy lines to reach a critical objective, the lead platoon encounters heavy fire from two enemy pillboxes. Sergeant Kenneth E. Gruennert, of Company L, 127th Infantry, 32d Infantry Division, advances alone to put the enemy position out of action. He is shot by snipers as his platoon is first to attain the objective that splits the enemy position. He is awarded the Medal of Honor.

31 December. **Urbana Force Starts Encirclement. Buna Mission, New Guinea.**

As the year ends, the 32d Infantry Division "Urbana Force" attacks eastward from Buna Village and Musita Island to begin the encirclement of Buna Mission. Meanwhile, advance elements of the arriving 41st Infantry Division are flown to Dobodura and Popondetta from Port Moresby.

1943

2 January. **Allied Forces Score Success. Buna Mission, New Guinea.**

A coordinated attack by the Urbana and Warren Forces is launched. The Warren Force is spearheaded by tanks and the Urbana Force surrounds Buna Mission. By nightfall the coastline is in U.S. hands and organized resistance ceases on 3 January, although mopping-up operations will take another three weeks. General Eichelberger comments, "The 32d which 'failed' at Buna was the same 32d that won the victory there."

2 January. **South Pacific Has New Corps Command. Guadalcanal, Solomons.**

To relieve the American Division headquarters of excessive command and control burdens, General Harmon activates the XIV Corps under the command of Major General Patch. Brigadier General Edmund B. Sebree takes the helm of the American Division. The XIV Corps consists of the American, 25th Infantry Division, the 147th Infantry Regiment, the 2d Marine Division, and other Marine ground troops.

4 January. **Collins Has Entire Division Ashore. Guadalcanal, Solomons.**

With the 27th Regimental Combat Team already on hand (since 1 January), the 161st RCT lands to complete the arrival of the 25th Infantry Division (Collins) and is ordered by XIV Corps to relieve the

132d Infantry to complete the seizure of Mount Austen. Collins gives this mission to the 35th RCT.

5 January. Bomber Commander Dies Leading Attack. Rabaul, New Britain.
Brigadier General Kenneth N. Walker, commander of V Bomber Command, leads a daring daylight bombing attack against harbor shipping with hits scored on nine enemy vessels. His aircraft is disabled and forced down by an attack of enemy fighters. Walker's heroism is later recognized with the award of the Medal of Honor.

11 January. U.S. Force Occupies Amchitka Island. Western Aleutians.
A small security detachment is landed from the destroyer *Worden*, followed on the morning of 12 January by the landing of a combat team of 2,000 troops under Brigadier General Lloyd E. Jones, commander of the 76th Field Artillery Brigade. The landing meets with no opposition. By 16 February a fighter strip is ready for limited operations as eight P-40s arrive and are soon running patrols over Kiska.

13 January. Army Names New Air Command. Noumea, New Caledonia.
The 13th Air Force (later the Thirteenth) is activated for the air defense of Guadalcanal, to hit enemy shipping, and to strike at Japanese airfields in the region. Brigadier General Nathan F. Twining, assigned as commander, is promoted to two-star rank.

25 January. Sixth Army is Activated. Fort Sam Houston, Texas.
With a cadre drawn from the Third Army, the new U.S. Sixth Army is activated to become the major field command in the Southwest Pacific. Lieutenant General Walter Krueger, who had been Third Army commander, takes command on 13 February, eight days after the departure of the advance party to Australia.

9 February. Link-Up Marks End of Campaign. Tenaro Village, Guadalcanal.
Troops of the American Division and 25th Infantry Division link up to mark the end of organized fighting on the island. But through skill and cunning, the enemy succeeds in evacuating troops to Buin and Rabaul. Admiral William F. "Bull" Halsey sends a congratulatory message to General Patch.

28 February. Priority Task for Engineers. China-Burma-India Theater.
Army engineers begin construction of the Ledo Road over the mountains from India through Burma to China. Two Army engineer outfits are soon joined by 6,000 troops sent from the United States Brigadier General Lewis A. Pick is to command the enormous undertaking.

Right: *During December 1942, on Papua, New Guinea, the American 32d Infantry Division and two Australian divisions were pitted against a well-entrenched Japanese force. Fighting raged for four months before the Allies prevailed. ("Red Arrow at War: 32d Infantry Division at Buna," Michael Gnater, Jr., National Guard Bureau)*

2 March. **Air Power Success in Bismarck Sea.**
The air battle of the Bismarck Sea is launched after a B-24 detects a well-protected Japanese convoy from Rabaul en route to Huon Gulf. U.S. aircraft launch a series of damaging raids on enemy shipping. Land-based aircraft are given major credit for the air battle, which ends on 4 March.

10 March. **Chennault Command Has New Name. Kunming, China.**
The 14th (later Fourteenth) Air Force is activated and replaces the China Air Task Force. Legendary Flying Tiger commander Major General Claire L. Chennault is recalled to active duty and remains in command throughout the war.

26 March. **Air Medal is Awarded to an Army Nurse.**
Second Lieutenant Elsie S. Ott, an Army nurse, receives the first Air Medal awarded to a woman in the military for gallantry in escorting patients more than 10,000 miles from India to the U.S.

18 April. **P-38s Intercept, Down Japanese C-in-C. Bougainville, Solomon Islands.**
Using information gained by breaking Japanese codes, U.S. Army Air Force P-38s intercept and shoot down a plane carrying Japanese Admiral Isoruku Yamamoto, Commander in Chief Combined Fleet.

11 May. **U.S. Lands in Western Aleutians. Attu Island.**
Landing at widely separated points, the 7th (Hourglass) Infantry Division finds initial resistance light, but mud immobilizes tracked vehicles. As troops progress inland, the division encounters stiff enemy defenses. After heavy fighting, Attu is secured on 30 May. Shemya Island is occupied with no resistance.

SKETCHED THIS PIX OF PVT. MERLIN MURRAY AS HE SAT ON RIDGE GUARDING THE NATIVE SUPPLY BEARERS FROM JAP SNIPERS —

ARMY WOMEN IN THE PACIFIC

When the Japanese first attacked the U.S. in the Pacific in December 1941, nurses were the only women in the Army. An earlier proposal to establish a Women's Army Auxiliary Corps (WAAC) had not been approved by Congress, and it was still not accepted until May 1942. Even then the WAAC was not given status as a military organization, and initially was not granted equal military pay. For the first year of the war, Army nurses served alone.

On 7 December 1941 there were 187 Army nurses in Hawaii serving the hospitals at Fort Shafter, Schofield Barracks, and Hickam Army Airfield. They performed magnificently under the Japanese attack, and several awards were made for heroism and "extraordinary fidelity." Fortunately, none of the nurses were injured or killed in the attack.

Army nurses were also assigned in the Philippines. When the Japanese attack came on 8 December, there were 88 Regular Army and Reserve nurses working in the islands. The Japanese invasion progressed rapidly, and the first nurses were captured on Christmas Day. When Manila was evacuated, Army nurses established two open-air hospitals on the Bataan Peninsula for American and Filipino soldiers.

Hospital # 1, near Limay, was bombed twice by the enemy, and nurses were wounded in each attack. Eventually the nurses were ordered to move to Malinta Tunnel Hospital on the island of Corregidor. The Japanese shelled the hospital constantly, and the nurses struggled to care for increasing numbers of patients in the close, dusty air. Major General Jonathan Wainwright arranged for 20 nurses to leave aboard two Navy planes and another ten to escape aboard a submarine. When American forces finally surrendered to the Japanese, the remaining nurses were taken to Santo Tomas, a prisoner of war camp for allied civilians, where they were joined by ten Army nurses whose plane had crashed in Mindanao. The women remained prisoners for more than two and one-half years.

Army nurses went to Australia with U.S. troops and followed them into New Guinea and eventually back to the Philippines. Nurses on New Guinea dealt with frequent Japanese air raids and learned how to find their way to open-trench shelters in blackout conditions. A transport ship bringing Army nurses to Leyte on 2 December 1944 was attacked by a Japanese torpedo bomber. During their first night on Leyte the nurses had three air raids, and later in the week enemy paratroopers landed on the beach near the hospital and engaged in a battle with Allied troops.

Even after the WAAC was created and manpower shortages were acute, Army commanders in the Pacific Theater were reluctant to request WAACs, believing the conditions were too harsh and primitive, although Army nurses were handling conditions without complaint. By mid-1944, however, the need for soldiers of both sexes in the front areas was critical. WAAC units were stationed first at Hollandia and Oro Bay in New Guinea, and later at Leyte and Manila in the Philippines. Approximately 5,500 WAACs were assigned to the Southwestern Pacific Theater, with 70 percent of the women working in administrative and office positions. They requisitioned and tracked supplies and equipment for soldiers in the field, identified and sent properly trained and equipped personnel to combat forces as needed, and worked as cryptographers and mail censors. A unit of WAAC cryptographers discovered and decoded sections of a Japanese codebook that provided the Allies with valuable information on the Japanese Air Force in the China-Burma-India Theater.

The women did not escape death. On 28 April 1945 a Japanese suicide plane bombed the hospital ship USS *Comfort* off Leyte Island. In the attack, six Army nurses were killed and four others wounded, making it the largest single loss of Army women in the war.

—*Judi Bellafaire*

Above: *Four of the first Army nurses to arrive on Okinawa, 3 May 1945. These nurses are already veterans, with more than 14 months service in Africa and Italy. (U.S. Army)*

Right: *While the war in the Pacific is usually associated with steaming jungles, some Army personnel faced a far colder climate in the northern Aleutians, an important American island chain near Alaska that was attacked by the Japanese in an effort to secure forward bases against the United States. ("Chow Line," Ogden Pleissner, Army Art Collection, NMUSA)*

21 June–25 August. **New Georgia Campaign is Underway. Solomon Islands.**
The campaign to seize New Georgia starts with an attack at Segi Point. The 43d and 37th Infantry Divisions begin operations on New Georgia Island.

29 June. **MacArthur Orders CARTWHEEL.**
The Operation Cartwheel offensive is launched against Rabaul, the main Japanese base in the area. This involves an air offensive to keep enemy shipping out of Rabaul harbor, to pin down enemy air, and to clear the Solomons—including Bougainville and New Georgia.

25 July. **Attack is Renewed. Munda, New Georgia.**
XIV Corps opens the final offensive to take the Munda Airfield. There is slow progress, as the 37th and 41st Infantry Divisions get support from tanks and flame throwers. The Corps commander relieves Major General John H. Hester. On 5 August the airfield is taken, and by 7 August it is ready for emergency use.

31 July. **Hero in Jungle Fighting. New Georgia, Solomon Islands.**
Wounded as his platoon is forced to withdraw, Private Rodger Young, 148th Infantry, 37th Infantry Division, strikes back at the enemy with hand grenades until he is cut down. His action earns the Medal of Honor and inspires "The Ballad of Rodger Young," a popular "hit parade" song in World War II.

15 August. **Strike Force Takes Kiska. Aleutians.**
A 34,000-man force under Major General Charles H. Corlett lands, only to find the Japanese have fled. Major troop elements include the U.S. 7th Infantry Division and the 1st Special Service Force, a light infantry brigade composed of U.S. and Canadian soldiers who are specially trained for cold weather and mountain warfare.

15 August. **Tropic Lightning Strikes. Vella Lavella, Solomons.**
Regimental Combat Team 35 from the 25th (Tropic Lightning) Infantry Division quickly establishes a beachhead.

17–18 August. **Air Strike is Launched From Secret Base. Near Lae, New Guinea.**
A force of more than 200 airplanes from an airfield constructed 60 miles west of Lae makes a surprise strike on enemy airstrips in the Lae-Salamaua area and wipes out all but a few of the remaining Japanese airplanes.

28 September–2 October. **Enemy Evacuates Under Fire. Kolombangara, Solomons.**
Caught in a pincers as fighting heats up on Vella Lavella and New Georgia, Japanese forces leave Kolombangara. Meanwhile the U.S. 503d Parachute Infantry jumps northwest of Lae, New Guinea, to support the offensive by the Australian 9th Division.

1 November. **Invasion of Bougainville.**
After several feints toward smaller islands late in October, Army troops of the 37th (Major General Robert S. Beightler) and 43d Infantry Divisions and Marine elements start a large-scale invasion of Bougainville in the northern Solomon Islands, where a strong enemy garrison promises to offer a determined defense. On 7–8 November the enemy launches a counterattack.

20–23 November. **Troops From Hawaii Seize an Enemy Base. Makin Atoll.**
A task force of the 165th (Fighting Irish) Infantry from the 27th (New York) Division makes the Army's first amphibious landing in the Central Pacific command and soon reports "Makin Taken." The objective, 2,000 miles southwest of Oahu, is in conjunction with the assault of the 2d Marine Division 105 miles away at Tarawa. Disputes between the Army commander, Major General Ralph C. Smith, and the Marines' General H. C. Smith presages a bitter interservice conflict, which rears its head again when the 27th Division fights under "Howling Mad" Smith's command in the Saipan campaign in July 1944. The last 27th Division elements depart from Makin after Christmas.

Above: *Munda airfield in New Georgia was important for American advances in the Southwest Pacific. Infantrymen patrol the dense jungle nearby. Camouflage uniforms were used by several Army units but were usually discarded after a short time. ("Marching Through New Georgia," Aaron Bohord, Army Art Collection, NMUSA)*

25 December. **Americal Division Enters Fight. Bougainville, Solomon Islands.**
In order to assist Marine units, the Americal Division (Sebree) arrives and deploys forces to enlarge the beachhead. On 28 December the Americal takes command of the eastern sector of the beachhead and relieves the 3d Marine Division.

26 December. **Krueger Moves CP Closer to Action. Near Finschafen, New Guinea,**
Headquarters Sixth Army's command post closes out of Brisbane, Australia, and opens a new location at Cape Cretin. It is joined by Headquarters Alamo Force in order to continue to train selected soldiers in reconnaissance and raider work. Graduates are eligible to become Alamo Scouts.

1944

2 January. **Red Arrow Troops Surprise Enemy. Saidor, New Guinea.**
A successful landing under cover of smoke enables the capture of an important port and airfield by troops of the 126th Infantry, 32d (Red Arrow) Infantry Division.

6 January. **Merrill Commands Marauders. Burma.**
Brigadier Frank D. Merrill assumes command of the 3,000-man 5307th Composite Unit, soon to win renown as "Merrill's Marauders." Merrill, West Point 1929, was U.S. military attaché in Tokyo 1938–1941.

EYEWITNESS: MERRILL'S MARAUDERS

The China–Burma–India Theater held nearly impregnable terrain and jungle, necessitating the formation of special units designed for the conditions. The 5307th Composite Unit (Provisional), nicknamed "Merrill's Marauders," after their commander, Brigadier General Frank D. Merrill, was such a unit. In February 1944 the Marauders set out to capture Myitkyina, the main transportation terminal in northern Burma, cut off enemy forces in the area, and reopen the Burma Road. Edward McLogan, 2d Battalion, describes his experience:

"It was probably 10:00 when we got into the village of Nhpum Ga and Merrill was there. He and (Colonel) McGee (battalion commander) laid out a defensive perimeter for us. Later that night, the Japanese hit the southern part of our perimeter. We were dug in our foxholes on the north end, which was a bare hill. We sent out patrols to make contact with our other battalions. It was day three that we were surrounded by a Japanese regiment. It turned out to be about 3,000 men. Our strength was about 700, down from about 850.

"Every day they made attacks or probes. The mules were tethered . . . here and there. And each morning we'd experience artillery. We'd hear a 'plunk,' and the animals would fall over after they were hit. We were in foxholes; they weren't. After about three or four days, the odor was just unbelievable. In addition, there were dead Japanese bodies. The odor was so intense you had to breathe through your mouth instead of your nose . . . The water hole was contaminated. We had to get our water from swampy areas before the water (parachute) drop. There was never enough water.

"That night I could hear this rumbling . . . (Japanese) were mumbling a couple hundred feet from the hill . . . I told McGee and he said, 'Send Matsumoto down there.'

"Roy Matsumoto listened but couldn't understand anything, so he handed me his ammo belt and carbine and said, 'I'm going to crawl out there.' It was maybe 10:00 at night. We figured out a password and off he went. I guess maybe he was gone twenty to thirty minutes and said, 'You're not going to like what I'm going to tell ya. They're going to concentrate and attack this portion of the hill.'

"I got McGee on the radio. He said, 'Keep Matsumoto with you and vacate your foxholes, booby-trap them, and move back on the hill 100 feet or so

and dig in. That will give you a better field of fire.' In the morning . . . (we) could sense they were gathering, and then they were yelling and screaming at the top of their lungs and running forward.

"More than half of the platoon was on the top of the hill. We had a dozen foxholes. We held our fire, and they started coming. They never quite reached the line. There were a couple of Japanese officers, and they retreated back down the hill and all was quiet...and then they launched a second charge, and this time they jumped into our foxholes. I'm not sure if any of the booby traps made a difference. That's when Matsumoto called out to them Charge! Charge! in Japanese, and we mowed them down again. Then Colonel McGee came up to tell us what a good job we had done. The Japanese opened up with small-arms fire of such magnitude that I had never believed was possible . . . We jumped in our foxholes. The bullets . . . were popping and cracking when they'd go right over your head. You could see them literally hitting the trees and bushes . . .

"The next day was Easter Sunday, and we were told that they were gone and the 3d Battalion had fought their way into us. What a joy that was. Then we disposed of the dead. We put lime on the dead bodies, and the flame throwers burned the bodies as best they could. We gathered up the wounded. We had a lot of men wounded and killed."

—*Vince Hawkins*

Above: *Men of the 5307th Composite Unit take a break on a trail near Nhpum, Burma. Composed of volunteers, the unit was organized into three battalions, with 700 pack animals. (U.S. Army)*

31 January. **Attack on Key Central Pacific Atoll. Kwajalein, Marshall Islands.**

The 7th Infantry Division lands and overcomes fierce Japanese resistance. The small atoll at the crossroads of the Pacific sealanes is secured on 4 February. Troops also seize smaller islands in the group, including Roi and Namur.

18–23 February. **Central Pacific Expeditionary Force Strikes. Eniwetok Atoll.**

An Army cannon company assists Marines in the Eniwetok atoll landing; a regimental combat team from the 27th Infantry Division lands on 19 February. The island is secured in four days.

29 February. **MacArthur Forces on the Move. Admiralty Islands.**

Following a reconnaissance by Alamo Scouts from the Sixth Army, the 1st Cavalry Division, with the 112th Cavalry RCT attached, makes an amphibious landing on the principal island of Manus and begins clearing out the Japanese defenders.

5 March. **Engineers Jump Into Burma Combat. Near Indaw, Burma.**

In a drop organized by Air Commandos under Colonel Philip G. Cochran, U.S. Army engineers parachute in to assist British forces working with long-range penetration forces.

4 April. **Twentieth Air Force Activated. Washington.**

Created to exploit the capabilities of the B-29 Superfortress, the Twentieth Air Force is created to carry the air war to the Japanese home islands. It is initially under the direct control of the Joint Chiefs of Staff through General Henry H. Arnold, Army Air Force chief.

9 April. **Marauders in Debilitating Campaign. Nhpum Ga, Burma.**

In the NCAC area of Burma, the 1st and 3d Battalions, Merrill's Marauders, break through to relieve the 2d Battalion, which had been holding out against Japanese attacks for ten days. In addition to 59 KIA and 314 wounded, Marauders lose 379 soldiers to illness.

9 April. **New Army Corps for Pacific Area. Schofield Barracks, Hawaii.**

The XXIV Corps enters the rolls of the Amy under the command of Major General John R. Hodge, until recently the commanding general of the Americal Division in the South Pacific. XXIV Corps staff anticipates command of the 7th, 27th, 77th, and 96th Infantry Divisions in forthcoming major operations. XI Corps is formed in the Southwest Pacific under Major General Charles P. Hall.

17 April. **China Air Operations Interrupted. South China.**

Many bases of the 308th Bombardment Group (B-24s) are in the path of a Japanese offensive, which

threats the loss of Fourteenth Air Force bases in south China. The 308th, which uses specially equipped aircraft to track enemy shipping in the South China Sea, is the only U.S. heavy bomber unit in China.

17 May. Marauders Take Vital Airfield. North Burma
After a well-executed tactical operation, Merrill's Marauders seize the airfield at Myitkyina, but stubborn resistance combined with heavy U.S. casualties preclude the capture of the town.

17 May. Islands on the Road to the Philippines. Wakde and Biak.
The Sixth Army launches the first of two important island invasions with an operation to take Wakde (Netherlands New Guinea); on 27 May General Krueger sends a 41st Infantry Division task force to Biak, a volcanic island formerly under Dutch administration, with two airfields of potentially significant importance to U.S. forces.

29 May. Rare Tank Battle in Island Campaign. Biak Island, New Guinea.
The first tank battle of any consequence in the Southwest Pacific occurs as Japanese armor clashes with American medium tanks in support of the 162d Infantry. The encounter results in the destruction of eight enemy light tanks. As the battle grows more intense, the 34th Infantry from the 24th Infantry Division enters the fight. During the campaign

Brigadier General Jens A. Doe replaces Major General Fuller as commander of the 41st Division. The difficult campaign comes to an end on 9 July.

15 June. B-29 Superfortresses Hit Japan Mainland. Chabua, India.
India-based B-29s of the Army Air Force XX Bomber Command, staging through forward area bases in China, bomb the steel works at Yawata, Japan—the first attack on Japanese main home islands since the Doolittle raid in April 1942. Attacks aimed at aircraft factories, oil refineries, ordnance plants, and war industry facilities continue until March 1945, when XX Bomber Command transfers to the Marianas Islands.

15 June. Campaign Starts to Seize Marianas Islands.
Saipan, the first of the strategically important islands representing a gateway to the northern Pacific and the Japanese home islands, is invaded by the V Amphibious Corps (Lieutenant General Holland M. Smith, USMC). By end of the day, two Marine divisions hold a beachhead 10,000 yards long and 1,000 yards deep. The Army 27th Infantry Division (Major General Ralph C. Smith), in VAC reserve, is en route. Another amphibious task force under Marine command heads for the island of Guam.

Above: *Men of the 162d Infantry, 41st Division, land on Wake Island. This May 1944 action retook the base that had been lost to the Japanese early in the war. (U.S. Army)*

16–17 June. Army Elements Start Ashore. Saipan, Marianas Islands.

An advance party of the Army XXIV Corps Artillery (Brigadier General Arthur M. Harper) and first units of the 27th Infantry Division land and prepare to join the fighting.

19 June. Battle Enters a New Phase. Saipan, Marianas Islands.

The 27th Infantry Division is given the task of clearing Nafutan Point and the south coast as Marines clear north. On 21 June the 27th Division assembles in corps reserve; its artillery is placed under XXIV Corps Artillery. By 23 June the division's mission is broadened to include clearing critical Purple Heart Ridge and Death Valley. An inability to advance results in a gap between Army troops and the 4th Marine Division.

21 June. Buckner Establishes New Command. Schofield Barracks, Hawaii.

Lieutenant General Simon Bolivar Buckner, Jr., a

Above: *B-29 bombers of the 20th Air Force head for Japan with lethal loads. Capture of the islands of Guam, Iwo Jima, and Tinian permitted forward bases for these planes. ("Valor in the Pacific," Robert Taylor, Military Gallery)*

Right: *Troops descend cargo nets into landing crafts at Empress Augusta Bay, Solomon Islands, in November 1943. (National Archives)*

former commander of the Alaskan Department, arrives with orders to organize and command the new U.S. Tenth Army. It is tentatively planned that Buckner will head the force to seize Formosa (Taiwan).

24 June. Command Controversy Mars Campaign. Saipan, Marianas.

The festering controversy over tactics leads to the relief of Army Major General Smith. The 27th Division is temporarily under Major General Sanderford Jarman who, earlier, was designated commander of the Saipan

Right: *Time and time again troops boarded frail landing crafts of all types to strike at strongly held Japanese positions throughout the Pacific. These many "D-Days" brought ultimate victory, but at considerable sacrifice. A determined foe had to be defeated on each of these fiercely fought operations. ("Amphibious Operations," Aaron Bohrod, Army Art Collection, NMUSA)*

army garrison. On 27 July Major General George W. Griner arrives from the 98th Infantry Division in Hawaii to take command of the 27th, which he leads until the end of the war. On 9 July, as final mop-up continues, Saipan is declared secure. The U.S. now has a site within bombing range of Japan.

21 July. **Invasion of Former Island Territory. Guam, Marianas Islands.**
The Army's 77th Infantry Division (Major General Andrew D. Bruce) is initially in III Amphibious Corps (Marine Lieutenant General Roy S. Geiger) reserve as Marines carve out the beachhead. The 305th Regimental Combat Team lands to help hold the beachhead.

24 July. **Stubborn Resistance is Encountered on Guam.**
As an effort is made to link two beachheads, the 77th Division completes the relief of the 1st Provisional Marine Brigade in the south beachhead with the 305th and 306th Infantry Regiments driving abreast. By the end of month the 77th Division and 3d Marine Division are moving rapidly to the north. On 8 August the campaign comes to an end as Army troops clear Mt. Santa Rosa. Surviving enemy stragglers retreat into the hills.

26 July. **U.S. Brigade Force Activated. Headquarters, CBI.**
The 5332d Brigade (Provisional) is activated to provide a command headquarters for two U.S. and one Chinese Army combat component. Brigadier General Thomas S. Arms is named commander. Major U.S. elements are the 475th Infantry, which is to be formed from the remnants of Merrill's Marauders; and the 124th Cavalry Regiment (dismounted), en route from the U.S. The 124th is a mobilized Texas National Guard outfit.

27 July. **Key Airstrip in Burma Falls to U.S. Troops. Myitkyina, Burma.**
After weary infantrymen of Merrill's Marauders take the airstrip at Myitkyina, it becomes necessary to press the 209th and 236th Engineer Battalions into service as riflemen to defend it from Japanese counterattacks.

27–29 July. **President's Only Trip to Pacific. Honolulu, Hawaii.**
In his only trip to the Pacific theater of operations, President Franklin D. Roosevelt conducts high-level strategy meetings ("The Waikiki Conference") with General Douglas MacArthur and Admiral Chester Nimitz. They discuss whether to bypass the Philippines in favor of an invasion of Formosa

(Taiwan). On 27 July the Commander-in-Chief reviews the 7th (Hourglass) Infantry Division; on 28 July he visits the Army's jungle warfare training center. He also visits soldiers and Marines wounded in the fighting on Saipan.

30 July. Continuing Action in New Guinea. Sansapor, Vogelkop Peninsula.

Landing without bombardment of the beaches to attain surprise, troops of the 6th Infantry Division (Major General Franklin C. Sibert) launch a successful attack against objectives on the New Guinea northern coast. But at Aitape, 32d Infantry Division troops (Major General William H. Gill) meet heavy enemy fire in an attempt to seize high ground. On 9 August the Corps commander is advised there is no further resistance along the Driniumor river line.

1 August. Reorganization of Pacific Army Forces. Fort Shafter, Hawaii.

Newly named U.S. Army Forces, Pacific Ocean Areas (Lieutenant General Robert C. Richardson, Jr.), supersedes U.S. Army in Central Pacific Area and now includes all Army elements of the South Pacific area as well. Army Air Forces, Pacific Ocean Areas, comes into being under Lieutenant General Millard F. Harmon.

3 August. Victory in North Burma. Myitkina, Burma.

With the arrival of Chinese Army reinforcements, the town of Myitkina is finally in Allied hands. The capture of Myitkina signals the end of the North Burma Campaign.

5 August. Marauders Are Core of New Regiment. Myitkina, Burma.

The 475th Infantry Regiment is formed as a unit specially organized to engage in long-range penetration missions. It is immediately assigned to the 5332d Brigade (Provisional). (The Brigade is soon better known as the Mars Task Force [MTF]. In this chronology the abbreviation MTF will be used to denote activities of the brigade.) The MTF is assigned to the Northern Combat Area Command (NCAC) in Burma. On 16 September the 5307th Composite Group, better known as Merrill's Marauders, is officially disbanded.

6 August. **General's Kin is KIA. Guam, Marianas Islands.**
Twelve days after the death of General Lesley J. McNair in Normandy, France (25 July 1944, see Chapter 13), his son, Colonel Douglas C. McNair, chief of staff, 77th Infantry Division, is killed in action.

4 September. **Eighth U.S. Army is Formed. Hollandia, New Guinea.**
As command and control of far-flung elements of the U.S. Sixth Army (Krueger) becomes complex, the U.S. Eighth Army is established. On 7 September Lieutenant General Robert L. Eichelberger, a former superintendent of the U. S. Military Academy, is named to command. Command of the I Corps passes to Major General Innis P. Swift, recently commander of the 1st Cavalry Division. Newly arrived X Corps is to be commanded by Major General Franklin A. Sibert.

17 September. **Baptism of Fire for Wildcat Division. Angaur Island, Palaus.**
81st (Wildcat) Infantry Division troops move ashore while Marines continue their advance at Peleliu as U.S. forces begin the defeat of enemy forces in the Palau Islands in the Western Pacific. In the Southwest

Pacific area, 32d Infantry Division elements are winding up the campaign on Morotai.

30 September. **Palaus Islands In U.S. Hands.**
The commander of U.S. Western Attack Force declares Peleliu, Angaur, Ngesebus, and Kongarur successfully occupied by U.S. soldiers and marines. Meanwhile, the Wama airdrome on Morotai is ready for use if needed. The 81st Infantry Division and attached units count more than 3,275 casualties, including 542 KIA.

19 October. **Ax Falls on Stilwell. Chungking, China.**
In the culmination of a tumultuous relationship with Chiang Kai-shek, General Stilwell is "recalled." The CBI theater is split, with Major General Albert C. Wedemeyer to command U.S. troops in China; Major General Daniel Sultan is named to temporary command in India. After 32 months of frustrating duty, Stilwell leaves China on 26 October.

20 October. **Back to the Philippines, Ormoc Bay, Leyte, Philippines.**
With the 6th Ranger Battalion striking island targets prior to H-Hour, General Walter Krueger's Sixth

Opposite: *The sleek, fast, twin-tailed Lockheed P-38 became one of the main Army Air Forces' fighters in the Pacific. ("P-38 'Lightning' Jumps a Japanese Zero," Echelon Publishing Co.)*

Right: *Often laboring in the most primitive of conditions, Army medical personnel performed near miracles to save the lives of wounded soldiers. At times they could be called upon to work around the clock. Often located near the front lines, they were no less subject to an enemy attack than the casualties they treated. (Robert Benney, Army Art Collection, NMUSA)*

GENERAL "VINEGAR JOE" STILWELL

As the Japanese Army advanced through Burma in 1942, a small team of advisors and native officers led by an American general marched just ahead of them to keep out of harm's way. After a 140-mile trek through the jungles and out of the closing Japanese pincers, Lieutenant General Joseph W. Stilwell went before cameras and microphones to discuss his experience. When asked what happened he said bluntly, "I claim we got a hell of a beating. We got run out of Burma and it is humiliating as hell. I think we ought to find out what caused it, go back, and take it."

Stilwell did not mince words. One of the Army's best corps commanders before the war, he had come to the attention of General George C. Marshall at Fort Benning's Infantry School. Marshall considered him farsighted and highly intelligent. He had a short temper, though, and spoke without mincing words, earning him the nickname "Vinegar Joe."

Born in March 1883 in Palatla, Florida, Stillwell grew up in New York and attended West Point. He graduated in 1904 as an infantry lieutenant and served two tours in the Philippines, where he saw action against Moro insurgents. In World War I he served with British and French forces before moving to the American IV Corps as the chief of staff for intelligence. He finished the war as a temporary colonel but like others went back to his Regular rank after the war. After studying Chinese at the University of California, he served in China first as an intelligence

officer, then with the 15th Infantry in Tientsin, and finally, as a colonel, the military attaché to China and Siam (Thailand). He attended the Infantry School and Army Staff College in between these tours.

The 1939–1940 Army expansion brought promotions to temporary brigadier and major general. He activated the 7th Infantry Division, then became commander of III Corps. After the Pearl Harbor attack, Stilwell came to the Army Staff for the task of planning and leading the invasion of North Africa, but his experiences in China led Marshall to send him back to China to take command of the American forces, oversee shipments of Lend-Lease materials, and train the Chinese Nationalist Army.

Stilwell's job was exceedingly difficult. After withdrawing from Burma he had to train a Chinese army to retake the country. He had frequent disagreements with Chiang Kai-shek, China's Nationalist leader, who was more interested in fighting Communists than the Japanese. Stilwell also had difficulty with Chinese commanders who would not engage the Japanese for fear their American-supplied weapons might get destroyed. He also encountered problems with his air commander, Major General Claire Chennault, who believed airpower alone could defeat the Japanese.

In early 1944 he lead two Chinese divisions to retake Myitkyina, Burma, a vital town along the Ledo Road and land supply route through Burma to China. He took the town, after almost seven months of heavy fighting, with the help of the 5307th Composite Unit (Provisional)—better known as "Merrill's Marauders."

In August 1944 Stilwell was promoted to temporary general. President Roosevelt urged Chiang to give full command of the Chinese forces to Stilwell. Chiang refused and Stilwell was recalled in October to be Chief of Army Ground Forces in the U.S.

The death of Lieutenant General Simon Bolivar Buckner, commander of Tenth U.S. Army on Okinawa, opened that position for Stilwell. Stilwell was preparing plans to invade Japan when the atomic bomb ended the fighting. After the war Stilwell commanded the Western Defense Command and finally the Sixth Army before he died in March 1946. He had been a dedicated soldier for more than 40 years.

—*Kevin M. Hymel*

Above: *"Vinegar Joe" Stilwell led his haggard group out of Burma, then returned with a force of Americans and Chinese that drove the Japanese out. (National Archives)*

Army starts the return to the Philippines. Troops of X Corps (1st Cavalry Division, 24th Infantry Division) and XXIV Corps (7th and 96th Infantry Divisions) establish the beachhead. A fleet of more than 700 ships helps put 160,000 troops ashore. Testing an idea developed jointly by Army and Navy amphibious warfare experts, the landing gets close-support from two groups of "mortar boats," each consisting of four Landing Craft Infantry (M) armed with 4.2 heavy mortars manned by troops from the Hawaii-based 98th (Iroquois) Infantry Division. On 24 October elements of the 1st Cavalry Division establish beachheads on the Samar Island. By 2 November much of Leyte is in U.S. hands, as General Krueger's staff watches for indications of an enemy counterattack.

31 October. New Commanders in Mars Task Force. Camp Landis, Burma.

Readying for a push to the Burma Road the MTF organizes 12 miles north of Myitkyina. Brigadier General John P. Willey takes command. In other important changes, Colonel Ernest F. Easterbrook takes command of the 475th Infantry and Colonel Thomas J. Heavey heads the 124th Cavalry. The MTF now includes the 612th and 613th Field Artillery Battalions (pack, mule).

15 November. Eighth Army Amphibious Campaigns. Mapia Island, Pacific.

After consolidation of its operational areas in New Guinea, New Britain, and the Admiralties (in October), the Eighth Army begins combat operations with amphibious landings on Mapia and Asia islands by elements of the 31st (Dixie) Infantry Division.

22 November. Inland Fighting is Tough on Leyte.

In the X Corps sector, the 112th Cavalry Regiment and the 32d Infantry Division are heavily engaged; in the XXIV Corps sector, the 11th Airborne Division enters the fight. The 77th Infantry Division is landing and preparing to move into the XXIV Corps lines. Work on airfields is halted as troops fend off counterattacks.

24 November. Tokyo is Target. Marianas Islands.

Operating from bases on Guam, Saipan, and Tinian, B-29 Superfortresses of the XXI Bomber Command begin the air campaign aimed at the enemy's capital of Tokyo. This is the beginning of a sustained campaign that results in U.S. domination of the sky over Japan.

5 December. End Run Leads to Capture of Ormoc.

The Sixth Army opens its offensive to capture Ormoc on Leyte's west coast. On 7 December the 77th Infantry Division, under XXIV Corps command, makes a waterborne end run from Leyte's east coast and makes an unopposed landing at Deposito, south of Ormoc. On 10 December the 77th Division takes Ormoc. Elements of newly arrived 38th Infantry Division fight alongside the 11th Airborne Division to seize Buri airfield area. When the 7th Infantry Division joins the 77th Division, the enemy force is divided. By 21 December, with juncture of X and XXIV Corps, U.S. forces are in control of the Ormoc Valley.

Above: *Four Army divisions struck from Leyte Gulf in October 1944 to begin the liberation of the Philippine Islands from the Japanese occupation. It was the largest amphibious operation to date in the Pacific Theater. ("Red Beach," Paul Sample, Army Art Collection, NMUSA)*

14 December. Terrible Prison Camp Atrocity. Puerto Princesa Prison. Palawan.
In one of the cruelest atrocities of the war, 139 Army prisoners of war (from Bataan and Corregidor) die on the island of Palawan at a narrow strip of land in the Sulu and South China Seas off the west coast of the Philippines. Japanese captors herd 150 POWs into three covered trenches, where they are doused with fuel and set afire. Those who try to escape are shot down, but 11 survive to tell the story.

15 December. Task Force Lands on Mindoro Island.
A task force with troops from the 24th and 77th Infantry Divisions on Leyte lands unopposed on the island of Mindoro.

17 December. Bomber Group Formed for Secret Mission. Wendover Field, Utah.
Veteran airman Colonel Paul W. Tibbets, Jr., activates the super-secret 509th Composite Group, whose principal combat element is the 393d Bombardment Squadron (VH), equipped with B-29s. The 393d is commanded by Major Charles W. Sweeney.

Above: *An M7 self-propelled howitzer crosses a stream in the Philippines as Sixth Army units push to liberate Manila. As the war progressed, improvements in American armor and artillery far outstripped the Japanese equivalents. (U.S. Army)*

18 December. MacArthur Joins Very Elite Company.
Two days after the promotion of General George C. Marshall, Douglas MacArthur is advanced to five-star rank and is designated the new rank of General of the Army.

25 December. Eighth Army Commands Leyte-Samar.
As organized resistance winds down, the U.S. Eighth Army (Eichelberger) relieves the Sixth Army of responsibility in the Leyte-Samar area. This frees the Sixth Army to prepare for the invasion of Luzon. Engineers race to complete airfields at Tacloban, Dulag, and Tanauan. The tedious mop-up of stragglers goes on until 8 May 1945.

31 December. Troops In Action Throughout Region at Year's End.
In Burma, the Mars Task Force starts a march toward Mong Wi, where it is to join up with a Chinese brigade forming in the Northern Combat Area Command (NCAC). Troops on Mindoro find themselves under attack from the air as Japanese strike at coastal shipping. Enemy counterattacks are launched on Leyte as the 77th Infantry Division starts to relieve the 1st Cavalry Division. On Saipan, the 24th Infantry Regiment, transferred from Bougainville to join the island garrison, takes over the mop-up of Japanese holdouts.

THE BATTLE FOR MANILA

At 9:30 a.m. on January 9, 1945, 68,000 men of Lieutenant General Walter Krueger's U.S. Sixth Army began landing at Lingayen Gulf on Luzon. The landings were unopposed. I Corps advanced north, toward Luzon's mountain ranges, while XIV Corps turned south toward the capital city of Manila.

Although XIV Corps advanced steadily, it was not fast enough to suit General Douglas MacArthur, who wanted to occupy Manila's vital port facilities and liberate Allied prisoners. On 31 January MacArthur told Major General Verne Mudge, commanding the 1st Cavalry Division, "Go to Manila, go around the Nips, bounce off the Nips, but go to Manila." Mudge organized two mechanized "flying columns," under Brigadier General William Chase, and sent them toward Manila early the next morning. Chase's forces covered the 100 miles to the city in 66 hours, reaching the eastern outskirts of Manila on 3 February. That evening, the 8th Cavalry Regiment rolled into the city, its tanks crashing through the gates of Santo Tomás University and liberating some 3,500 internees. Meanwhile, the 37th Infantry Division was approaching from the north and the 11th Airborne Division parachuted southwest of Manila, both reaching the city's defenses on 4 February.

The city was defended by the 20,000-man Manila Naval Defense Force (MNDF). The 14th Area Army commander, General Yamashita, had ordered Manila evacuated and declared it an open city, as MacArthur had done in 1942, but Admiral Iwabuchi disobeyed, following navy orders to defend the city at all costs. Using weapons and materials stripped from ships and planes, demolition charges, and barricades of overturned trolley cars and trucks, the MNDF turned several administrative sections of Manila into small fortresses.

On 4 February the 37th Division rescued 1,330 internees from the Old Bilibid Prison. By 7 February, U.S. troops controlled the town north of the Pasig River, which divided Manila in half. To delay the Americans, the Japanese set several buildings afire and destroyed all the river bridges. By 8 February the 37th Division completed an amphibious crossing of the Pasig despite heavy enemy fire. Fighting intensified as the division encountered Japanese strongpoints, which had to be cleared street by street, building by building. MacArthur had restricted artillery to fire only on observed enemy positions, but with such fierce resistance and the Japanese already destroying large parts of the city, he

now allowed artillery to blanket any area of advance.

On 12 February the 1st Cavalry Division completed the city's encirclement and began closing in. Tanks used pontoon bridges to cross the Pasig on 14 February to support the infantry assaults. The fighting became vicious and desperate, a battle of "submachine guns, bazookas, flame throwers, demolitions, and hand grenades." By 23 February U.S. troops had fought their way to the Intramuros, an old Spanish stone fortress. A massive artillery bombardment was followed by three days of bitter, close-quarter fighting through every room and subterranean tunnel before the fortress fell on 25 February. With Intramuros taken, Admiral Iwabuchi and his staff committed suicide. The solidly built and heavily defended Agricultural, Finance and Legislative Buildings held the last major Japanese positions. Point-blank tank and artillery fire was required to reduce them one at a time, then troops with flame throwers and phosphorous grenades were sent in to mop up. The last Japanese defenders were cleared on the morning of 3 March.

The fight for Manila was the only U.S. battle for a major city in the Pacific Theater. The cost was high: U.S. forces suffered 6,576 killed, wounded, and missing; the Japanese lost 16,665 dead. There were also some 100,000 civilian casualties, and Manila itself suffered extensive damage and lay largely in ruins.

—*Vince Hawkins*

Above: *Soldiers of the 129th Infantry, 37th Infantry Division, fire a 37mm gun at Japanese positions in Manila as Americans close on the city from several directions. (U.S. Army)*

1945

4–8 January. **Mars Task Force Moves to Assembly Area. Mong Wi, Burma.**
Heading into action, the elements of the Mars Task Force, after a long march from the Myitkyina area, cross the Shweli River and make the two-day march to Mong Wi.

8–16 January. **MTF Mission Prepares to Attack Enemy on Burma Road.**
In the NCAC area of Burma, the Mars Task Force leaves Mong Wi and marches through rugged jungle and mountain terrain to get into position for an attack on the Burma Road between Hsenwi and Wanting. On 17 January MTF troops clear the enemy from Namhkam village and move to within three miles of Burma Road. On 18 January MTF troops gain hold on Loi-kang ridge, overlooking the road. MTF artillery craters the road to harass the enemy.

9 January. **MacArthur's Pledge is Redeemed. Lingayen Gulf, Luzon, Philippines.**
Lieutenant General Walter Krueger's Sixth Army puts the 40th, 37th, 6th, and 43d Infantry Divisions ashore to launch the drive for the return to Luzon and the liberation of Manila. Army Air Force B-29s lend support.

12 January. **Convoy to Kunming Hits the Ledo Road. Ledo, India.**
A U.S.-Chinese convoy starts along the newly opened Ledo Road toward a juncture with Burma Road. Its destination is Kunming, China. On 15 January the convoy is halted at Myitkyina, Burma. On 22 January the Ledo Road links with the Burma Road and the long-closed supply line from India to China is reopened.

20 January. **LeMay To Pacific, XXI Bomber Command. Guam, Marianas Islands.**
Major General Curtis E. LeMay, noted for his exploits with the England-based Eighth Air Force, transfers to the Pacific and takes command of XXI Bomber Command.

21–30 January. **West Side of Burma Road is Secured. Hpa-pen Area, Burma.**
The MTF establishes its perimeter along the west side of the Burma Road and prepares a joint attack with Chinese troops to seize the hills overlooking the road. On 2 February the MTF's 124th Cavalry takes the Hpa-pen heights in a sharp battle.

26 January. **Troops Retrieve Former Air Base. Clark Field, Luzon.**
In the U.S. Sixth Army area, XIV Corps elements, in addition to securing the former U.S. air base at Clark Field, cross the Pampanga at Calumpit. 40th Infantry Division troops start to envelope the enemy near

Bamban. Attacking I Corps troops probe toward Cabanatuan.

27 January. Major Reinforcements Ashore. Mabilao, Lingayen Gulf.

The Sixth Army receives major reinforcements as the 1st Cavalry Division and the 112th Cavalry RCT, along with the 32d (Red Arrow) Infantry Division, arrive.

31 January. Two Divisions in Race to Manila. Luzon, Philippines.

With the 37th Infantry Division moving on a parallel route, the 1st Cavalry Division launches its 5th and 8th Cavalry Regiments, organized into "flying columns" in the race to be first into Manila. Meantime, the 188th and 187th Glider Infantry Regiments, 11th Airborne Division, come ashore on Luzon's west coast.

2 February. The Hero of Knight's Hill. Near Hpa-pen, Burma.

First Lieutenant Jack L. Knight, commanding a troop of 124th Cavalry from Mineral Wells, Texas, goes after a series of four pillboxes on high ground held by the enemy. Both he and his brother, First Sergeant Curtis Knight, are wounded. Despite his wounds, Lieutenant Knight retains command and continues to attack the enemy. He is killed advancing toward Japanese lines. He is posthumously awarded the only Medal of Honor to a soldier in the CBI.

Above: *Recently promoted Corporal Bruce Jacobs pulls guard duty in the Pacific in khaki shorts and a lightweight summer helmet. (Jacobs Collection)*

Left: *The Sixth Army's Alamo Scouts performed dangerous reconnaissance behind Japanese lines, providing invaluable information prior to full-scale landings. (Company of Military Historians)*

3–8 February. **Mars Task Force Concludes Mission. Loi-kang, Burma.**
The 475th Infantry finishes clearing the Loi-kang ridge and enters the town of Loi-kang, the first significant penetration east of the Burma Road. U.S. and Chinese forces are now in control and enemy traffic is no longer free to use the road. The Mars Task Force moves into an administrative bivouac one month after its departure from Mong Wi.

3 February. **Cavalry Claims First Into Manila.**
Cavalrymen claim victory in the race to the capital city of the Philippines. Both the 1st Cavalry Division and 37th Infantry Division encounter brutal urban combat as the Japanese commander decides to try to fend off U. S. liberation forces. Civilian casualties are high. In the Eighth Army zone, near Tagaytay Ridge, the 511th Parachute Infantry jumps in and links up with the 188th Glider Infantry.

3 February. **LeMay Sends B-29s to Strike Kobe, Japan.**
The XXI Bomber Command launches a 129-plane offensive, but only 69 manage to get through to the target, where they drop 159.2 tons of incendiaries and 13.6 tons of fragmentation bombs despite being challenged by 200 enemy fighters. 1,039 buildings were destroyed or seriously damaged. Through February, 29 B-29s are lost to enemy fighters.

4 February. **Buckeyes Release POWs. Manila, Philippines.**
Moving to link-up with 1st Cavalry, troops of the 37th (Buckeye) Infantry Division battle at the Quezon Bridge in northern Manila and reach the infamous Bilibid prison to rescue prisoners held by the Japanese since early 1942. Meanwhile, air action against Corregidor is intensified.

4 February. **End of the Road is Hailed. Kunming, China.**
Led by Brigadier General (soon to be major general) Lewis A. Pick of the Army engineers, the first convoy from Ledo, India, makes a triumphal entry into Kunming, China. The convoy left Ledo on 12 January; it crossed into Chinese territory on 28 January, prompting President Chiang Kai-shek to rename it "The Stilwell Road" in honor of the former CBI commander.

13 February. **Way Being Cleared to Bataan. Manila Bay Area, Luzon.**
In the XI Corps zone of action, the bombardment of Corregidor begins to set the stage for landings. The 38th Infantry Division finishes clearing the Zigzag Pass defenses, except for a final stronghold between the 152d and 149th Regiments. Corps elements are clearing the way to the Bataan peninsula as 6th Infantry Division elements help clear the coastal area of Manila Bay.

14 February. **Aloha Greetings for Liberated Army Nurses. Hickam Field, Oahu.**
After a long imprisonment in Manila's Santo Tomas University, 54 liberated Army nurses are welcomed as heroes. They arrive in two Air Transport Command C-54 aircraft and are welcomed by Lieutenant General Robert C. Richardson, Jr., commander of the Army's Pacific Ocean Areas Command. The homeward-bound nurses enjoy a day of Hawaiian hospitality before continuing on stateside.

Opposite: *The first convoy moves out on the newly completed Ledo Road, a vital supply route in the CBI Theater that connected to the Burma Road and into China. It later was renamed the Stilwell Highway. (U.S. Army)*

Right: *The parachutes of the men and equipment of the 503d Parachute Infantry, 11th Airborne Division, are seen as paratroopers land to retake Corregidor. Navy PT boats stand by to rescue men blown off course into Manila Bay. (Navy Art Collection)*

16 February. **U.S. Force Hits The Rock. Corregidor, Manila Bay.**

With the 3d Battalion, 34th Infantry (6th Division), striking from the sea as two battalions of the 503d Parachute Infantry drop from air transports, the U.S. launches the recapture of Corregidor Island, which fell to the Japanese in May 1942. On 2 March the American flag is raised over the battered fortress island.

17 February. **Bataan With a Different Ending.**

The reinforced 151st Regimental Combat Team, 38th Infantry Division, secures the southern tip of Bataan and soon links up with the 1st RCT, 6th Infantry Division. With the seizure of Bagac, organized resistance comes to an end. Sixth Army troops put the finishing touch to the recapture of Bataan.

23 February. **Airborne Troops Rescue Endangered Prisoners. Los Banos, Luzon.**

Employing airborne and amphibious techniques, a battalion task force from the 511th Parachute Infantry, led by a Wyoming rancher, Lieutenant Colonel Henry A. Burgess, strikes behind enemy lines to rescue endangered prisoners of war held at the Los Banos prison camp.

28 February. **Objectives Taken in Southern Philippines. Puerto Princesa.**

Palawan Task Force seizes the island, the site of the massacre by Japanese troops (see 14 December 1944), and establishes radar sites. On Samar, an Americal Division battalion and 1st Filipino Infantry make progress. The attack force leaves Mindoro.

3 March. **Manila is Secured After Bitter Fight.**

The 37th Infantry Division, after house-to-house urban warfare that results in heavy military and civilian casualties, declares the city to be secure. The 11th Airborne Division puts an end to resistance in the Manila Bay sector. 25th Infantry Division elements work along Highway 5.

4 March. **First B-29 Lands on Newly Won Airstrip. Iwo Jima, Bonin Islands.**

A damaged B-29 returning to base from a raid on Tokyo requests permission to make an emergency landing to repair a damaged fuel line. The huge bomber lands at Motoyama airstrip No. 1 as Seabees scurry to remove grading and construction equipment. Nearby, Marines battle the enemy. After repairs are done, the pilot hurriedly takes off for the return to home base. An additional 35 B-29s use Iwo as an emergency landing site in the days to come.

9–10 March. **First "Fire Raid" Against Japan Devastates Tokyo.**

A force of 300 B-29 Superforts from bases in the Marianas launches the first major incendiary strike in the capital of Japan. Two thousand tons of incendiary bombs destroy a quarter of the city, with very high casualties. In the following days the B-29s hit Nagoya, Osaka, and Kobe.

10 March. **Japanese Are Attacked, Overrun in Southern Philippines.**

In the Eighth Army zone, Romblon and Simara attack

forces sail from Mindoro. Following air bombardment and naval gunfire, 41st Infantry Division troops land on Zamboanga Peninsula virtually unopposed. They take Wolfe airfield and quickly drive to Mindanao City. By 15 March, 24th Infantry Division troops have Romblon and Simara under control.

14 March. **Commander is KIA. Luzon, Philippines.**
Major General Edwin D. Patrick, Commander, 6th Infantry Division, is mortally wounded and dies the following day after taking part in an action near the Japanese "Shimbu" defense line. He is the first of two Army division commanders to die in World War II as a result of enemy action.

17 March. **Army Regiment Relieves Marines. Iwo Jima, Bonin Islands.**
The Army's 147th Infantry Regiment, including many Guadalcanal veterans, lands to relieve Marines

Above: *Men of the 37th Division engage in desperate street fighting against Japanese defenders intent on keeping Manila in their control. (". . . Manila Would Do," Keith Rocco)*

Opposite: *American forces raise the same Stars and Stripes above Corregidor that had been flying during the Japanese attacks four years earlier. (National Archives)*

fighting cave-to-cave at the northern end of the island. Forty-four Army men are killed and 89 wounded in early hours of 26 March as the Japanese launch a banzai attack. Most of casualties are air corps and service troops. Major General James E. Chaney, Army Air Force, is named commander of the Army Garrison Force on Iwo.

1 April. **Easter Sunday is Okinawa L-Day. Ryukyus Islands.**
The U. S. Tenth Army, under the command of Lieutenant General Simon Bolivar Buckner, Jr., lands in the Ryukyus Islands. The Army XXIV Corps (Major General John Hodge) and the Marines' III Amphibious Corps (Major General Roy S. Geiger) hit the Higashi beaches virtually unopposed.

3 April. **Planning for Japan Invasion.**
The Joint Chiefs of Staff tell General MacArthur and Admiral Nimitz to initiate planning for the invasion of Japan. MacArthur's forces are now at 1,500,000; Nimitz has 6,000 ships. Army and naval aviation totals more than 35,000 aircraft in theater.

4 April. **Strong Defensive Positions Encountered. Okinwa, Ryukyus.**
XXIV Corps (Major General John Hodge), attacking to the south, makes contact with heavy Japanese defenses.

The Corps has the 7th, 27th, 77th, and 96th Infantry Divisions in action. Heavy fighting slows the advance.

6 April. **MacArthur in New Command. Manila, Philippines.**
United States Army Forces in the Pacific (AFPAC) is created to conclude the campaign in the Philippines and make preparations for the invasion of Japan. General of the Army Douglas MacArthur is named commander. General Headquarters (GHQ) remains in Manila until 25 March 1946, when it is transferred to Tokyo. Lieutenant General William D. Styer is named commanding general of U.S. Army Forces in the Western Pacific (WESPAC).

12 April. **President Franklin D. Roosevelt Dies. Warm Springs, Georgia.**
Soldiers and other U.S. service personnel at battle stations learn the sad news of President Franklin D. Roosevelt's death. Harry S. Truman is the new Commander-in-Chief.

16–21 April. **Attack on Islands Near Okinawa.**
Troops of the 77th Infantry Division land on the south and southwest coasts and fan out to seize Ie Shima Island. The enemy puts up stiff resistance. The 77th Division troops hold off a heavy counterattack to end the battle on 21 April. On Okinawa, III Amphibious Corps secures the northern half of Okinawa.

Above: *Lieutenant General Simon B. Buckner, commander of the Tenth Army, observes the fierce fighting on Okinawa just minutes before he is killed by a Japanese shell. (National Archives)*

17 April. **Mindanao is Eighth Army Objective.**
Lieutenant General Robert L. Eichelberger, Eighth Army commander, sends soldiers of the U.S. X Corps (Major General Franklin C. Sibert) to seize Mindanao, the principal island of the southern Philippines. This turns out to be a tough task that takes until 30 June.

18 April. **Ernie Pyle Killed in Action. Ie Shima, Ryukyu Islands.**
War Correspondent Ernie Pyle, beloved by the GIs, is killed by a Japanese sniper while accompanying soldiers of the 77th Infantry Division. A veteran of North Africa and the European Theater of Operation's toughest battles, Pyle focused his war coverage on the fighting men of all branches of the service.

4 May. **Army Division Takes Over in the North. Nago, Okinawa.**
Marines start displacing toward the scene of battle in the south; the 27th Infantry Division takes over the sector vacated by the 6th Marine Division. In the XXIV Corps area, a Japanese counterattack is a costly failure.

22 May. **Slowdown at the Shuri Line. Southern Okinawa, Ryukyus.**
As weather conditions reduce ability to conduct offensive operations, the U.S. forces consolidate gains. The enemy begins withdrawing supplies and wounded from the Shuri sector. On 24 May Marines enter Naha. The Army 7th Infantry Division advances in the Yonabaru valley.

18 May. **Special Mission B-29 Unit Completes Deployment. North Field, Tinian.**
The advance air echelon of the 509th Composite Group, equipped with specially modified B-29s, arrives and promptly starts to fly training missions that are shrouded in mystery.

25 May. **Planning for the Invasion of Japan Home Islands. Washington, D.C.**
U.S. Joint Chiefs receive plan for the invasion of Kyushu (Olympic) on 1 November, and for the follow-up invasion of Honshu (Coronet) around 1 March 1946.

26 May. **First Army Commander and Staff Arrives. Manila, Philippines.**
Lieutenant General Courtney Hodges and members of his First Army staff arrive to start development of plans for the First Army role in the forthcoming assault against targets in the Tokyo Bay area in Operation Coronet.

Right: *The 96th Division needed "Zippo" Sherman tanks fitted out with flame throwers to overcome some of the last Japanese defenses during the bitter final fighting on Okinawa during June 1945. ("Taking the Big Apple," David Pentland)*

10 June. Enemy Spurns Surrender Demand. Okinawa, Ryukyus.

General Buckner offers surrender terms to Lieutenant General Ushijima Mitsuru, commander of the Japanese 32d Army. No acknowledgment or response is received.

18 June. Tenth Army Commander Killed at an O.P. Okinawa, Ryukyus.

Lieutenant General Buckner, Tenth Army commander, is killed by an enemy shell while at a Marine Corps forward observation post. He is the senior U.S. Army officer to die in action in the Pacific. Major General Roy Geiger (USMC) assumes command of Tenth Army, the first Marine officer to command a field army in combat.

23 June. Link-Up with Guerrilla Fighters. Near Aparri, Luzon, Philippines.

The reinforced 1st Battalion, 511th Airborne Infantry, parachutes behind enemy lines to link up with Filipino guerrilla units and push toward link-up with the 37th Infantry Division (Beightler) on 27 June. At the end of its campaign in the Cagayan Valley, the 37th Division captures the last major towns still in the hands of the Japanese.

30 June. Japanese Beaten in Southern Philippines.

The capture of Mindanao is accomplished by the 24th Infantry Division; all major tasks in the main islands of the Philippines are completed. On Mindanao, X Corps continues the mop-up to the end of the war.

1 July. Luzon Campaign is Over, Forces Regroup.

The Luzon campaign officially ends at midnight. The Sixth Army turns over the task of wrapping up operations to the Eighth Army as it starts to regroup for Operation OLYMPIC, the invasion of Japan. The Eighth Army takes control of XXIV Corps for the final mop-up, with the 6th, 32d, 37th, and 38th Infantry Divisions.

20 July. First Combat Strikes by Mystery Outfit. North Field, Tinian.

The 509th Composite Group B-29s begin a series of combat strikes over Japan to familiarize crews with target areas and contemplated tactics to include lulling the enemy into becoming accustomed to small formations flying at very high altitudes.

23 July. Stilwell Commands Tenth Army.

Looking forward to closing out the Okinawa campaign and getting ready for the land battle in the invasion of Japan, Lieutenant General Joseph W. Stilwell assumes command of the U. S. Tenth Army.

2 July. The Long Battle Comes to An End. Okinawa, Ryukyus.

The U.S. Tenth Army, under General Stilwell, mops up Japanese defenders and brings the costly Ryukyus campaign to a close. Army and Marines suffer 12,520

Above: *Danger and privation were always present as American foot soldiers waged war in Okinawa through July 1945. ("Messing in the Open in Okinawa," John A. Ruge. Army Art Collection, NMUSA)*

KIA and 36,631 wounded—the price of a foothold in the southernmost of Japan's home islands. On 1 August Stilwell, 40 years and six weeks after graduation from West Point, is promoted to four-star rank. He is the last of 17 army officers to serve as a full general in World War II.

16 July. **Project Manhattan Reports Blast. Alamogordo, New Mexico.**
The super-secret Project Manhattan reports to President Truman the successful detonation of the nation's first atomic bomb at the top secret Trinity Site. President Truman, aboard a naval vessel returning from the Potsdam Conference, is briefed on the A-Bomb test and on future war plans in the conflict with Japan.

16 July. **LeMay, Twining Command Strategic Force. Harmon Field, Guam.**
Major General Curtis LeMay is officially in command of the Twentieth Air Force; on 1 August Lieutenant General Nathan F. Twining is named commander.

1 August. **Record Bombardment by B-29s Hits Japan. Marianas Islands.**
A force of 825 Marianas-based B-29s dispatched by the Twentieth Air Force drops 6,520 tons of incendiary and demolition bombs on Japanese industrial targets in a series of night raids.

6 August. **A New Era of Warfare. Hiroshima, Japan.**
The first operational atomic bomb is dropped from 31,000 feet over Hiroshima by the U.S. Army Air Force B-29 *Enola Gay* from the 509th Composite Group. The pilot is Colonel Paul W. Tibbets, Jr., a veteran of heavy bombardment in Europe. The bomb, nicknamed "Fat Boy," packs the power of 20 thousand tons of TNT.

9 August. **Second A-Bomb Dropped. Nagasaki, Japan.**
A U.S. Army Air Force B-29, *Bock's Car*, flown by Major Charles W. Sweeney, drops a second atomic bomb as the U.S. seeks to force the surrender of the Japanese Empire. The U.S. awaits word from the Imperial Palace.

Right: *Paul Tibbets pilots the B-29* Enola Gay, *named in honor of his mother, to drop the first atomic bomb. Days later a second atomic bomb followed, and soon after the Japanese capitulated. ("Beginning of the End," William S. Phillips)*

10 August. **New Air Commander in China.**
As the war winds down, the earlier decision to relieve Major General Chennault is finalized and Major General Charles B. Stone arrives to take command of the Fourteenth Air Force. Plans to move the Tenth Air Force to China are dropped.

10 August. **Japan Seeks Peace Terms.**
With only the stipulation that the Allies impose no "prejudice to the Emperor's position," the Japanese Government offers to surrender. On 11–12 August the U.S. and Allies reply to the Japanese with requested assurance. On 13 August surrender documents approved by President Truman are sent to General MacArthur.

14 August. **Imperial Japan Surrenders. Tokyo, Japan.**
An announcement from the Imperial Palace confirms the unconditional surrender of the Japanese Empire. The 11th Airborne Division (Major General Joseph M. Swing) moves by air from the Philippines to Okinawa to be ready for rapid transfer to Japan. The formal surrender ceremony is set for 2 September.

15 August. **General MacArthur is Supreme Commander. Manila, Philippines.**
General of the Army MacArthur receives official word that he is designated Supreme Commander of the Allied Powers for the surrender and occupation of Japan. All offensive action against Japan is terminated.

19 August. **Surrender Party Arrives From Tokyo. Manila, Philippines.**
The Japanese surrender delegation arrives to plan for the movement of U.S. troops starting the occupation of Japan.

20 August. **Hero of Bataan Located in POW Camp. Sian, Northeast Manchuria.**
American OSS agents locate and liberate Lieutenant General Jonathan M. Wainwright, the last commander of American forces in the Philippines. He is rescued from a Japanese prison camp about 100 miles from Mukden. The OSS teams parachute into Japanese-controlled territory to accomplish the rescue mission. In addition to Wainwright, they also free four U.S. "Doolittle raiders" held since 1942.

20 August. **Beightler Heads Luzon Island Command.**
Major General Robert S. Beightler is designated to head the Luzon Island Command. As POWs stream into collection points, Buckeyes erect a sign: "Japanese Army Demobilization Center conducted by the 37th Infantry Division." The Buckeye division continues the task of the collection and processing of POWs until November, when it leaves for the U.S. and demobilization after 41 months of overseas service. The 31st Infantry Division (Major General Clarence A. Martin) takes the surrender of all Japanese forces remaining in Mindanao.

Left: *Aboard the "Might Mo" (USS* Missouri*) in Tokyo Bay, General of the Army Douglas MacArthur countersigns the Japanese surrender documents. Standing to the right rear of the general is Lieutenant General Wainwright, only recently released from a Japanese prison camp, where he had been held for more than three years. (National Archives)*

28 August. **Vanguard of Army Starts Japan Occupation. Atsugi, Japan.**
After a two-delay delay due to a typhoon in the Ryukyus, the 11th Airborne Division (Swing), which has been poised on Okinawa, is airlifted into Atsugi airfield near Yokohama. It is quickly followed by the 27th Infantry Division (Major General Joseph W. Griner, Jr.) as the Army Air Force assembles a mighty fleet of modern C-54 four-engine Skymaster transport planes. The decision is made that the flow of troops into Japan will generally conform to the order of battle for Olympic and Coronet, the two major invasion plans.

30 August. **General Eichelberger With Eighth Army Advance Elements.**
General Robert L. Eichelberger arrives at Atsugi Airfield outside of Tokyo with advance elements of his U.S. Eighth Army at the end of his long "Jungle Road to Tokyo." Instead of Operation Coronet, Eichelberger prepares to take over the northern part of Honshu including Tokyo. On 1 September, General MacArthur arrives and is escorted to quarters at the New Grand Hotel in Yokohoma.

2 September. **The Instruments of Surrender. Tokyo Bay, Japan.**
The official document of surrender is signed on the deck of USS *Missouri* by Japanese and witnessing Allied officials. General Douglas MacArthur is designated to take the surrender of his former enemy. Lieutenant General Wainwright, former senior POW and former commander of U.S. and Filipino Forces in 1941–1942, learns that he has been awarded the Medal of Honor.

2 September. **Cavalry Heads for Tokyo. Yokohama, Japan.**
After its long campaign in the Philippines, the 1st Cavalry Division (Major General William C. Chase) is waterborne to Japan. The division's troopers formally occupy Tokyo on 8 September; the division, which describes itself as "The First Team," earns the distinction of being the first U.S. division to enter the Japanese capital.

3 September. **Wainwright's Turn. Baguio, Philippines.**
Fresh from the surrender ceremonies in Tokyo Bay, Lieutenant General Jonathan M. Wainwright, in a bittersweet moment, takes the surrender of General Tomoyuki Yamashita, commander of the Japanese Fourteenth Area Army, the former "Tiger of Malaya." He is the senior commander of the Imperial Japanese Army in the Philippines. He is placed under arrest and is later tried by an American Military Court in Manila. Yamashita is found guilty of permitting brutal atrocities and other high crimes against Americans and Filipinos. Major charges include responsibility for the brutalities at Pasay School and the Palawan Massacre. He is sentenced on 7 December 1945. Execution by hanging is carried out on 23 February 1946.

8 September. **Triumphant Entry Into Tokyo.**
Flanked by Admiral William Halsey and Lieutenant General Robert L. Eichelberger, General MacArthur makes the 22-mile journey from Yokohama to Tokyo. In the former enemy capital MacArthur is saluted by an honor guard from the 1st Cavalry Division on the grounds of the U.S. Embassy. At hand is the flag—sent from Washington—which flew over the U.S. Capitol on the day of Pearl Harbor. General

MacArthur turns to his Eighth Army commander: "General Eichelberger, have our country's flag unfurled, and in Tokyo's sun let it wave in its full glory as a symbol of hope for the oppressed and as a harbinger of victory for the right."

8 September. **Army Corps Enters Korea. Inchon.**
Mindful of a demarcation line established at the 38th Parallel to separate U.S. and U.S.S.R. military forces, the U.S. Army XXIV Corps (6th, 7th, and 40th Infantry Divisions), under Lieutenant General John C. Hodge, arrives to begin occupation duty. First to arrive is the 7th Division under Major General A. V. Arnold. Brigadier General J. L. Ready takes command of the division as General Hodge designates General Arnold to head the U.S. Army Military Government in Korea (USAMGIK). The U.S. Military Government of Korea will remain in place until
15 August 1948, when the Republic of Korea (ROK) is formed. The 40th Infantry Division (Brigadier General Donald J. Myers) is returned home for inactivation in March 1946; the 6th and 7th Divisions continue to train Korean troops until they are withdrawn in 1948.

September–October. **Eighth Army Elements Assume Occupation Tasks. Japan.**
General Eichelberger avails himself of the Olympic/Cornet planning of the invasion to deploy and disperse Eighth Army elements in Japan under the IX (Major General Charles W. Ryder), XI (Lieutenant General Charles P. Hall), and XIV (Major General Joseph M. Swing) Corps. He soon has on the ground—in addition to divisions previously identified, above—the Americal Division, the 43d, 77th, and 81st Infantry Divisions and the 112th Cavalry and 158th Infantry Regimental Combat Teams.

10 September. **Search Teams Seek U.S., Allied POWs in Japan.**
Army search-and-rescue teams fan out to locate known prison camps and to find many ex-POWs who are on their own after leaving detention centers

Left: *With the war's end, American forces uncovered the Japanese silver reserves hidden in Atomi, Japan. Such treasure had allowed the enemy to sustain a prolonged, hard-fought war. (U.S. Army)*

following news of the Japanese surrender. Rescue and roundup is completed in 18 days. Before the end of the month more than 35,000 former prisoners are repatriated—including many captured on Bataan and Corregidor in the darkest days of World War II.

19 September. Sixth Army Headquarters In Occupation. Western Honshu, Japan.

Thirty-one months after its arrival in Australia, the advance party of General Walter Krueger's Sixth Army headquarters lands at Wakayama to start its tour of occupation duty. The main body of the headquarters arrives on 25 September. Under Sixth Army control for this final major troop movement of the war: the Army's I Corps (Major General Innis P. Swift), X Corps (Sibert), and the V Amphibious Corps (Major General Harry Schmidt, USMC). Later, Headquarters Sixth Army is established in the Daiken Building in Kyoto.

22 September. Sixth Army Occupation Elements on the Move. Sasebo, Japan.

After staging in the Marianas Islands, the V Amphibious Corps (USMC) puts the 2d and 5th Marine Divisions ashore to occupy Nagasaki-Sasesbo

and Shimoneseki-Fukuoka. In a last-minute change the 32d Infantry Division is substituted for the 3d Marine Division; its elements, coming from Luzon, reach Sasebo on 15 October.

23 September. Division From ETO Arrives. Yokohama, Japan.

After a brief stop in Leyte, a second major element redeployed from Europe, the 97th Infantry Division (Major General Herman F. Kramer), arrives to join Eighth Army occupation forces. The 97th, with 41 combat days in the ETO, is ordered to relieve the 43d Infantry Division from locations in and around Yokohama.

25 September. I Corps Elements Land. South of Osaka, Japan.

Moving from Luzon, the I Corps lands in Japan with the 6th, 25th, and 33d Infantry Divisions, taking control of the Wakayama area about 50 miles south of Osaka. It takes over the area that encompasses Osaka-Kyoto-Kobe in western Honshu. Its newly assigned 98th ("Iroquois") Infantry Division, from Hawaii, lands in Japan on 27 September.

3 October. **X Corps Occupation Movement. Hiro Wan, Japan.**
With its elements from Mindanao, the X Corps deploys its major units in the Kure-Hiroshima sector of western Honshu, where it also occupies the Okama area with the 24th and 41st Infantry Divisions.

12 October. **American Patrol Strikes Silver. Honshu, Japan.**
The Americal Division (Major General William H. Arnold) lands in Japan with occupation duties in the Yokohama-Kawasaki-Yokosuka area and reports a startling discovery. A division patrol searching the Atomi city hall finds clues that lead to a stash of 2,660 silver ingots, about 103.4 tons, with an estimated value of $1.3 million.

5 October. **First of the Pacific Divisions Inactivated. Yokohama, Japan.**
With three major campaigns against the Japanese under its belt, the 43d Infantry Division is the first of the Asiatic-Pacific veteran divisions to be returned home to be inactivated. The division's overseas duty started 2 October 1942. On 26 October its colors are furled at Camp Stoneman, California. Despite occupation demands, the Army expedites the return to the U.S. of soldiers who have served the longest. By 31 December seven of the Asiatic-Pacific divisions are off the Army's rolls.

19 November. **Americal Division Gets Honorable Discharge. Seattle, Washington.**
The first elements of the Americal Division, fresh from occupation duties in Japan, lands on the U.S. west coast. By 1 December the movement of the division to its final assembly point at Fort Lawton is completed. The division—the successor to TF 6814—born on foreign soil (New Caledonia in the South Pacific), is mustered out of the service on 12 December, after an existence of 43 months.

24 December. **Guadalcanal Army Corps Is Closed Out.**
XIV Corps (Major General Joseph M. Swing) returns to the United States after wartime service which began on Guadalcanal. It is inactivated 31 December.

31 December. **End-of-War Casualties.**
As the region welcomes its first peacetime, post-war New Year, the costs of war are counted in over 300,000 killed in action or wounded in the campaigns of the Asiatic-Pacific theater of operations. U.S. Army battle casualties on all fronts is pegged at 936,259—or, about 9% of the 10,420,000 men and women who served in the U.S. Army and Army Air Forces.

Above: *Left to Right—American Defense Medal, Asiatic Pacific Campaign Medal, and World War II Victory Medal were authorized for the millions of GIs who served during the war. (U.S. Army Institute of Heraldry)*

DEFENDING FREEDOM'S FRONTIER

1946–1960

DEFENDING FREEDOM'S FRONTIER

1946-1960

Matthew Seelinger

When World War II ended on 2 September 1945 with the unconditional surrender of the Japanese Empire, the United States emerged as the most powerful nation in the world. In addition to its tremendous industrial capacity, the United States possessed the world"s most powerful armed forces, led by the Army, which numbered more than eight million men in 1945. Furthermore, America had a monopoly on the devastating power of the atom, in the form of the atomic bomb, which wrought destruction on the Japanese cities of Hiroshima and Nagasaki and finally brought the war to a conclusion. In fact, much of America's overall postwar military posture would eventually be based on the concept of nuclear deterrence, much to the Army's detriment.

It took America less than five years to build and equip such a magnificent army. It took far less time, however, to demobilize it. Unlike previous wars, international commitments and the uncertainty of the post–World War II era required the United States to maintain the largest peacetime army in its history to date. Still, the demobilization of the Army began in earnest; the Army discharged an average of 1.2 million men a month from September 1945 to January 1946. By the time demobilization officially ended in June 1947, the Army had been reduced from more than eight million soldiers to 684,000, and from 89 divisions to 12. With the end of the draft in March 1947, a decrease in voluntary enlistments, and the creation of an independent Air Force in July 1947, the Army would drop to fewer than 600,000 soldiers and a total of ten active divisions in 1948.

With the increase in tensions with the Soviet Union, stemming from the Communist overthrow of Czechoslovakia's democratic government and the Russian blockade of West Berlin, the United States reinstated Selective Service in June 1948. Even with the draft, the increase in the Army's ranks was minimal. Furthermore, budget constraints left little funding for weapons development and procurement or large-scale live-fire training exercises. Many units were far below their authorized strengths in men and equipment.

As a result, the Army was woefully unprepared for the Korean War. The first combat unit thrown into the conflict, the ill-fated Task Force Smith, forever became a symbol of American unpreparedness. The Korean War also marked the United States' first experience with a new concept for warfare in the atomic age—limited war. During three years of war in Korea, the Army acquitted itself well, pushing the North Koreans to their northern border before the Chinese intervened, and then fighting the Chinese Communists to a standstill despite their seemingly endless supply of soldiers. By the time the Korean War ended in July 1953, the Army had deployed eight divisions and hundreds of smaller units (including dozens of National Guard and Reserve units) to Korea, and the Army had grown to 1.5 million officers and enlisted men.

With the inauguration of retired General Dwight D. Eisenhower to the presidency in 1953, however, the Army began a period where it nearly reached a point of irrelevancy. The Eisenhower administration's "new look" defense posture stressed the concept of "massive

retaliation," emphasizing more cost-effective nuclear weapons as the cornerstone of America's defense— "more bang for the buck." As a result, the Air Force secured the largest portion of the defense budget.

Yet, during this era, the Army also obtained its own nuclear arsenal, developing a variety of tactical nuclear weapon systems, including rockets, missiles, artillery, and even land mines. The Army was assigned the mission of ground-based continental air defense and established dozens of surface-to-air missile sites around the country, some of them armed with nuclear-tipped rockets. The Army even reorganized many of its divisions to fight on the nuclear battlefield and began to increasingly explore the potential and versatility of the helicopter. Yet, the Army's budgets decreased and its ranks continued to drop through the 1950s. As a result, many within the Army's senior leadership became increasingly frustrated with the

Army's role in the nation's defense, leading to resignations and public criticism of the Eisenhower administration. Some of this criticism would eventually be an important issue in the presidential election of 1960 and serve as the basis for the defense policy later called "flexible response."

Pages 752–753: *Artist James R. Ryan captures the tension of a vigilant combat patrol in Korea. (Raytheon Systems Co., Burlington, MA)*

Above: *General of the Army Douglas MacArthur and other U.S. commanders meet their counterparts in the Republic of Korea Army, 1950. ("We Can Go Together," Don Stivers)*

DEFENDING FREEDOM'S FRONTIER
1946–1960

"There will be no more retreating, withdrawal, or readjustment of the lines or any other term you choose. There will be no Dunkirk, there will be no Bataan. . . . We must fight until the end. . . . We will fight as a team. If some of us must die, we will die fighting together."

—Lieutenant General Walton H. Walker, Commander, 8th U.S. Army, 29 July 1950

1946

January. Status of the Army.

With the conclusion of World War II in September 1945, the Army continues its rapid demobilization into 1946. After reaching peak strength of more than eight million soldiers in 1945, the Army now numbers 1,891,011 officers and enlisted men. Unlike the end of previous conflicts, the Army will not be reduced to the point of ineffectiveness as it has been in years past. Occupation duty in Germany, Italy, Japan, and Korea, along with other international commitments and tensions with its former ally, the Soviet Union, will require the United States to maintain a sizeable peacetime army. At the same time, however, some begin to question whether large armies like those deployed in World War II are now necessary with the development of atomic weapons.

4–15 January. Demonstrations Over Demobilization.

On 4 January the War Department releases a confusing statement indicating that the demobilization of the armed forces would be "slowed down." This appears to many to be a reversal of the policies announced previously and sets off a series of peaceful protests by GIs, thousands of letters to Congress, and media outrage, just as Secretary of War Robert P. Patterson is making a global visit to military units. Confusion persists until 20 January when General Dwight D. Eisenhower gives a congressional address in which he clearly explains there is no policy change and the Army is ahead of its plans.

26 January. 1st Experimental Guided Missiles Group Formed. Eglin Field, Florida.

The Army activates the 1st Experimental Guided Missiles Group to oversee the development of guided missiles and drones.

Left: *Linked arm-in-arm, GIs stationed in Paris protest the slowdown in World War II demobilization brought about by the Cold War. These soldiers were anxious to return to peacetime activities back home in the United States. (AP/World Wide Photo)*

ARMY BATTLE STREAMERS—KOREA

UN DEFENSIVE 1950

UN Defensive, 27 June–15 September 1950

UN Offensive, 16 September–2 November 1950

CCF Intervention, 3 November 1950–24 January 1951

First UN Counteroffensive, 25 January–21 April 1951

CCF Spring Offensive, 22 April–8 July 1951

UN Summer-Fall Offensive, 9 July–27 November 1951

Second Korean Winter, 28 November 1951–30 April 1952

Korea Summer–Fall 1952, 1 May–30 November 1952

Third Korean Winter, 1 December 1952–30 April 1953

Korea Summer 1953, 1 May–27 July 1953

---

3 March. **Army Officer Killed. Berlin, Germany.**
First Lieutenant James Wilson, an ordnance officer, is shot and killed by a Soviet sentry in Berlin.

15 April. **First Army Flight Test of V-2 Rocket. White Sands Proving Ground, New Mexico.**
The Army conducts its first flight test of the German-developed V-2 rocket. The test is part of Operation Paperclip, a program that brings captured German technology and scientists, including Dr. Wernher von Braun, to the United States. More than 40 tests will be conducted over the next two years.

27 April. **Gillem Board Report. Washington, D.C.**
The War Department releases the Gillem Board Report (War Department Circular 124), a study of the status of African-Americans within the armed forces. While the report calls for the armed forces to "eliminate, at the earliest possible moment, any special considerations based on race," many of the report's recommendations are ambiguous, and the study does little to improve the standing of blacks in the military.

14 May. **Army Reorganization. Washington, D.C.**
The Army announces a major postwar reorganization with the release of War Department Circular 138. The Army Ground Forces and Army Air Forces continue as

Above: *The U.S. Constabulary was a "spit and polish" symbol of America in occupied countries of Europe. (Fritz Kredel,* Soldiers of the American Army, 1775–1954*)*

separate commands, with the understanding that the Army Air Forces will eventually become an independent service. The wartime corps area and field force organizations in the continental U.S. are replaced by six army areas. Furthermore, the Army Service Forces are eliminated; the traditional and administrative and technical agencies employed before World War II return as separate agencies within the War Department.

25 June. **Selective Service Extended. Washington, D.C.**
Congress extends Selective Service to 31 March 1947, for men ages 19 to 34. Fathers and those under age 19 are exempt, and the length of service is reduced to 18 months.

1 July. **U.S. Army Constabulary Becomes Operational. Bamberg, Germany.**
To fulfill the requirements for highly mobile, multi-capable security and border forces for occupied Germany and Austria, the Army organizes the U.S. Constabulary. Comprising elements from the 1st and 4th Armored Divisions, along with several separate armored infantry and cavalry units, the U.S. Constabulary consists of a headquarters, special troops, three Constabulary Brigades, and ten Constabulary Regiments. Equipped with jeeps, light armored cars, motorcycles, and horses, it is the Army's last mounted tactical unit. Major General Ernest Harmon is named the first commanding general.

12 July. **Firefight at Ursina. Italian-Yugoslav Border.**
A squad from L Company, 351st Infantry Regiment, 88th Infantry Division, is ambushed by Yugoslav partisans. The Americans kill two partisans while suffering no casualties.

12 August. **U.S. Troops Captured by Soviets. Yohyon, Korea.**

Three soldiers from the 32d Infantry Regiment, 7th Infantry Division, part of the U.S. occupation forces in Korea, are taken prisoner by Soviet troops occupying the northern part of Korea. The Americans are held for 13 days before being released.

30 September. **Battle with Filipino Communists. Fort McKinley, Philippine Islands.**

A small force of American military policemen clash with 35–40 Filipino Communists guerrillas known as Huks near Manila. One soldier is killed and another wounded.

2 October. **Universal Military Training Plan Announced. Washington, D.C.**

As a proposal to replace Selective Service, the War Department announces a plan to provide six months of universal military training (UMT) to all young men at special training centers. Trainees will be separate from the Army and will not be subject to regular military justice. Furthermore, the plan calls for nonmilitary phases of training, which will be supervised by a civilian advisory board. While popular with many in the Army, the federal government, veterans organizations, and civic groups, UMT is never implemented, forcing a continuation of the draft.

16 October. **Nazi War Criminals Executed. Nuremberg, Germany.**

Before dawn, Army executioner Master Sergeant John C. Woods performs his official duty to impose the sentence of death by hanging on the ten surviving Nazi war criminals condemned by international court.

31 December. **World War II Officially Ends.**

President Harry S Truman declares hostilities terminated against the former Axis Powers.

1947

January. **Status of the Army.**

By the beginning of 1947, the strength of the Army stands at 991,285 officers and enlisted men. Ongoing demobilization and the establishment of an independent Air Force will significantly reduce the Army's personnel strength in 1947.

13 January. **Successful Drone Flight. Eglin Field, Florida, and Washington, D.C.**

The 1st Experimental Guided Missiles Group conducts a successful drone flight from Eglin Field to Washington, D.C. The test simulates a long-range bombing mission.

15 March. **Clay Appointed Military Governor of Germany.**

General Lucius D. Clay is named Military Governor of Germany and Commander-in-Chief, Europe (CINCEUR). He replaces General Joseph McNarney.

31 March. **Selective Service Expires.**

With voluntary enlistments remaining high, and the assumption that UMT will be adopted, the War Department does not ask for an extension of Selective Service, marking the first time since 1940 that the United States does not have a military draft.

16 April. **Army-Navy Nurses Act of 1947.**

President Truman signs legislation establishing the Army Nurse Corps as a part of the Regular Army. The act also creates the Women's Medical Specialist Corps, an organization for medical specialists such as dieticians and physical/occupational therapists. The Corps is renamed the Army Medical Specialist Corps in 1955 as more men take up those medical specialties.

22 May. **Corporal E Missile Launched. White Sands Proving Ground, New Mexico.**
The Army launches the Corporal E missile; this is the first successful launch of a U.S.-developed ballistic missile.

24 May. **U.S. Army Military Group-Greece Created.**
The U.S. Army Military Group-Greece (USAMGG) is formed as part of President Truman's policy to stop Communist attempts to seize control of several countries (Truman Doctrine). Most of the men are involved in coordinating the delivery of the new weapons and equipment sent to the Greek army.

18 June. **First Regular Army Commission for a Female.**
Colonel Florence Blanchfield, Army Nurse Corps, becomes the first woman to receive a Regular Army commission.

30 June. **World War II Demobilization Ends.**
With the discharge of the last wartime draftee on 30 June, World War II Army demobilization officially ends.

19 July. **Royall Becomes Last Secretary of War. Washington, D.C.**
Kenneth C. Royall succeeds Robert P. Patterson as Secretary of War. He will be the last man to hold the position, and the first to be Secretary of the Army.

26 July. **National Security Act of 1947.**
President Truman signs the National Security Act of 1947 into law. The act creates a "National Military Establishment" consisting of three military departments—Army, Navy, and Air Force (an independent Air Force)—with a Secretary of Defense to serve as the President's chief advisor for national security issues. James F. Forrestal is named the first Secretary of Defense. The act also provides statutory recognition for the Joint Chiefs of Staff (JCS) and creates the Central Intelligence Agency and the National Security Council.

4 August. **Medical Service Corps Established.**
In an effort to consolidate the ancillary organizations

Opposite: *Korea's rugged terrain and harsh weather made movement difficult. Here, troops use a Sherman M4A3 tank and a "pack" cow to move through Waegwan, Korea. (U.S. Army Center of Military History)*

Above: *General Omar Bradley serves only one year as Army chief before being appointed as the first Chairman of the Joint Chiefs of Staff and promoted to five-star rank. (Clearance L. MacNelly, Army Art Collection, NMUSA)*

Left: *In the three decades immediately after World War II, the WACs remained a part of the Army's permanent organization. (U.S. Army Center of Military History)*

Left: *Japanese culture placed U.S. Army personnel in Japan in a unique status while serving there as an occupation force. ("Respect for New Emperors," Robert MacDonald Graham, Jr., Army Art Collection, NMUSA)*

Opposite, top: *J. Lawton Collins was the Army Chief of Staff during the Korean War and creation of NATO. ("Joseph Lawton Collins," Lloyd Bowers Embrey, U.S. Army Art Collection, NMUSA)*

of the Medical Department, the Army establishes the Medical Service Corps consisting of four sections: Pharmacy, Supply, and Administration; Medical Allied Sciences; Sanitary Engineering; and Optometry.

15 September. **Occupation of Italy Ends.**
A friendly Italian government is in place and the Army-led occupation of the country ends. As a part of the NATO military force, however, U.S. forces will retain several bases.

17 September. **Royall Named Secretary of the Army. Washington, D.C.**
With the creation of the Department of the Army as part of the National Military Establishment, Kenneth C. Royall becomes the first Secretary of the Army.

1948

January. **Status of the Army.**
With creation of an independent Air Force, the end of Selective Service, and a steep decrease in enlistments in late 1947, the Army's ranks have dropped to 554,030. Furthermore, the Army is saddled with an arsenal that is becoming increasingly obsolete.

7 February. **Omar N. Bradley Becomes Chief of Staff, USA.**
After serving as Administrator of the Bureau of Veterans' Affairs since August 1945, General Omar N. Bradley is appointed the 17th Chief of Staff, USA, replacing General-of-the-Army Dwight D. Eisenhower.

19 February. **Van Fleet Heads Greek Advisory Group.**
Lieutenant General James A. Van Fleet is appointed director of the Joint U.S. Military Advisory and Planning Group (JUSMAPG), which replaces the earlier USAMGG. The group will provide expanded operational and logistical support to the National Greek Army in its battle against communist insurgents. Of the 400 personnel, 182 are Army advisors; most posted at the division level. The conflict ends in victory on 16 October with no American losses.

10 March. **Army Field Forces Established.**
Army Field Forces replaces the Army Ground Forces (AGF), with responsibility for Army forces within the United States. AGF commander General Jacob L. Devers becomes commander of Army Field Forces.

11–14 March. **Key West Agreement. Key West, Florida.**
In an attempt to decrease interservice friction over service functions, especially nuclear warfare planning, Secretary of Defense Forrestal meets with the Joint Chiefs of Staff at Key West, Florida. The resulting agreement establishes a framework for resolving disagreements but does little to eliminate the underlying sources of interservice rivalry.

10 May. **Army Takes Control of U.S. Railroads.**
Under orders from President Truman, the Army assumes control of the U.S. railroads during a nationwide rail strike. Army operation of the railways will last until 9 July.

12 June. **Women's Army Corps Established as Permanent Branch of the Army.**
After a difficult, two-year struggle, Congress passes the Women's Armed Services Integration Act giving the Women's Army Corps both Regular and Reserve status as a branch of the Army. Colonel Mary A. Halloran remains as WAC Director.

24 June. **Selective Service Act Signed. Washington, D.C.**
As tensions mount with the Soviet Union, President Truman signs the Selective Service Act of 1948, reinstating the draft.

24 June. **Berlin Airlift Begins.**
When the Soviet Union suspends all ground and air travel in and out of West Berlin, U.S. and British forces

begin operations to supply the city with food and fuel from the air. Army engineers and logisticians provide major support to the operation. The Soviets eventually end the blockade in May 1949; the airlift officially ends on 30 September 1949. One soldier and one Army civilian die in accidents during the operation.

26 July. **President Truman Orders Integration of Armed Forces. Washington, D.C.**
President Truman issues Executive Order 9981, which calls for the end of segregation in the armed forces. The process of integrating the armed forces will take time—the Army's last segregated units will not be disbanded until 1954.

Right: *American personnel serving with the Korean Military Advisor Group (KMAG) withdraw from Seoul in 1950. (National Archives)*

Above: *Each ridge became a defensive line as American forces sought to stop the North Korean invaders. ("From the Crest of Hill 233," Howard Brodie)*

Below: *Soon after KMAG came into being in July 1950 its Army members were authorized a shoulder sleeve insignia. (Quintet Publishing Ltd., London)*

15 August. **Military Advisory Group Formed in Korea.**
The Army establishes the Provisional Military Advisory Group (PMAG), with 100 officers and enlisted men, to provide training and logistical support to the constabulary forces of the newly formed Republic of Korea. PMAG is later renamed the Korean Military Advisory Group (KMAG).

20 November. **New Balloon Altitude Record.**
An Army Signal Corps balloon sets a new altitude record when it reaches a height of 26.5 miles.

10 December. **Soldiers Captured. Ceska Kubie, Czechoslovakia.**
Two soldiers from the 6th Armored Cavalry Regiment are captured by Communist troops and held prisoner until February 1949.

1949

January. **Status of the Army.**
With the draft and an increase in enlistments, the Army has grown to 660,473 officers and enlisted men. Budgetary constraints, however, will plague the armed forces, especially the Army, and the Army's numbers will actually decrease during the year.

24 February. **Missile Reaches Outer Space. White Sands Proving Ground, New Mexico.**
A modified Army Corporal missile becomes the first man-made object to reach outer space, attaining an altitude of 244 miles.

ARMY WOMEN DURING THE KOREAN WAR

Army nurses first arrived in Korea with the 8054th and 8055th Mobile Army Surgical Hospital (MASH) units on 6 July 1950, one day after Task Force Smith. Nurses assigned to Korea faced primitive conditions and severe supply shortages. The operating tents often had dirt floors and operating tables on wooden platforms. Overhead lights hung from wooden crossbars with tin cans as reflectors. Captain Cathy Boles of the 8076th MASH reported that nurses ripped up sterilized bedsheets to make bandages. Her chief nurse, Captain Elizabeth N. Johnson, washed sheets and blankets by hand to keep her unit supplied. The two biggest supply problems, wrote chief nurse Eunice Coleman, were blood and blankets. Nurses donated their own blood and gave up their own blankets.

As mobile and evacuation hospitals followed the fluid battle lines, Army nurses found themselves close to the front lines. On 9 October 1950 the 1st MASH was attacked as it convoyed from Inchon to Pusan, and the nurses spent the night in a roadside ditch. About sun-up the nurses began treating the wounded. Coleman said, "All that day . . . we worked on the roadside: operating, treating for shock, and putting the wounded in the ambulances for care. We lost eight men."

Members of the Women's Army Corps (WACs) at headquarters in Japan helped the Army transport, supply, care for, and evacuate troops in the Far East Theater. WAC clerks typed and filed paperwork while telephone and teletype operators kept the lines of communication functioning. Servicewomen were also research analysts, draftsmen, and mapmakers. Approximately one-quarter of the enlisted WACs in Japan were laboratory and pharmacy technicians, nursing assistants, and medical record specialists. As the war continued, WACs were assigned as ward masters in Army hospitals, traditionally a supervisory role of male noncommissioned officers (NCOs).

Army nurses and medical specialists at hospitals in Japan coped with large numbers of sick and wounded. At Tokyo Army Hospital, Private Muriel Scherrar Wimmer said that during peak combat the wards filled and beds were in the hallways. The WACs worked 12-hour days six days a week doing whatever was necessary to help patients, which included many Ethiopian, Turkish, Colombian, and Greek soldiers.

WAC Corporal Janet Preston was assigned to the mail section of the casualty reporting office at MacArthur's headquarters. Her office rerouted letters addressed to injured soldiers, tracking the wounded down by calling each hospital and then forwarding the mail. If an individual could not be located, an indication he was missing in action or dead, his mail was kept until confirmation that the next of kin had been notified.

In Europe, the developing Cold War kept American forces on alert. WACs at NATO and Supreme Headquarters Allied Powers Europe (SHAPE) relayed classified messages among the Army commands, American embassies, and Washington. WACs also worked at military hospitals and in intelligence, public information, finance, and personnel positions.

Servicewomen in the United States also were directly involved in the war effort. Sergeant 1st Class Elizabeth Darwin, a reservist, was recalled to active duty and assigned to the 373rd Transportation Major Port unit at Hampton Roads, Virginia, where she was responsible for coordinating the delivery of supplies. Sergeant Dorothy J. VandenOever, a blood bank technician at Letterman Army Hospital in San Francisco, kept the hospital's blood supply updated. Sergeant VandenOever volunteered several times for overseas posting but was told that her job at Letterman was critical. Wherever the Army was, WACs were there, playing a vital role in the Army's success.

—*Judi Bellefaire*

Above: *Both Army nurses and members of the WACs served with distinction in Korea and suffered the same severe conditions as their male counterparts. (National Archives)*

Left: *Not one to be shy, 8th U.S. Army commander Lieutenant General Walton H. Walker became known for his distinctive jeep. (National Archives)*

Below: *A U.S. M-4 tank of the 5th Regimental Combat Team moves forward past a Russian-manufactured T-34 tank near the Kum Chun front lines in Korea, 10 June 1950. (National Archives)*

4 April. **North Atlantic Treaty Organization Created. Washington, D.C.**

In response to the Soviet Union's belligerence, the United States, the United Kingdom, Canada, France, Norway, Belgium, the Netherlands, Denmark, Luxembourg, Portugal, Iceland, and Italy sign a treaty establishing the North Atlantic Treaty Organization (NATO). The treaty commits the signatories to the mutual defense of Western Europe. The U.S. Senate quickly ratifies the treaty 83–12, marking the first time the United States has entered a military alliance in peacetime.

20 June. **Gordon Gray Appointed Secretary of the Army. Washington, D.C.**

Under Secretary of the Army Gordon Gray is named Secretary of the Army, replacing Kenneth C. Royall.

29 June. **Army Occupation of Korea Ends. South Korea.**

A national election is scheduled in August and U.S. Army X Corps forces that demobilized the Japanese and maintained the security of the southern half of Korea begin to depart. Responsibility to build the Republic of Korea (ROK) military will be left to a small advisory detachment. Hostile incidents along the "temporary" line of the 38th parallel quickly begin.

30 June. **Last U.S. Occupation Troops Leave South Korea.**

The last U.S. Army unit, the 5th Regimental Combat

Team, withdraws from the Republic of Korea. The 472 advisors from the Korean Military Advisory Group (KMAG) remain.

1 July. **Philippine Scouts Disbanded.**

After serving the Army for 48 years against insurgents in the early 20th century and the Japanese in World War II, the Philippine Scouts are disbanded.

Right: *Despite President Harry S. Truman's 1948 executive order to desegregate, the 24th Infantry regiment remained an African-American unit during the first part of the Korean War. (National Archives)*

10 August. **Amendment to National Security Act Signed. Washington, D.C.**
President Truman signs legislation amending the National Security Act of 1947. The amendment replaces the National Military Establishment with the Department of Defense (DoD), a new executive department, and enhances the power of the Secretary of Defense. The Departments of the Army, Navy, and Air Force lose their executive department status and become military departments within DoD. The amendment also increases the size of the Joint Staff from 100 to 210 officers.

16 August. **General Bradley Named Chairman, Joint Chiefs of Staff. Washington, D.C.**
After Eisenhower declines the job, General Bradley is named the first Chairman of the Joint Chiefs of Staff. General Joseph Lawton Collins replaces Bradley as Chief of Staff.

1950

January. **Status of the Army.**
Drastic budget cuts have reduced the Army's strength to 593,167 and ten active divisions. Furthermore, a lack of large-scale live-fire exercises and a drastic decrease in weapon development and procurement severely reduce the Army's combat effectiveness.

12 April. **Frank Pace Becomes Secretary of the Army.**
Frank Pace, former director of the Bureau of the Budget, is named the third Secretary of the Army.

5 May. **Congress Enacts Uniform Code of Military Justice. Washington, D.C.**
Congress replaces the Articles of War with the Uniform Code of Military Justice as the judicial regulations for the U.S. armed forces.

25 June. **Korean War Begins.**
The Korean War begins when an estimated 135,000 North Korean People's Army (NKPA) troops, supported by 150 tanks and artillery, cross the border and attack the Republic of Korea. Within days, the United Nations adopts a resolution calling for member nations to aid South Korea.

27 June. **First Efforts to Coordinate Defense of South Korea.**
The General Headquarters, Advance Command and Liaison Group team, led by Brigadier General John H. Church, arrives at Suwan to begin coordination of military activities on the Korean peninsula. After quickly assessing the chaotic situation, Church radios General Douglas MacArthur, Commander-in-Chief, U.S. Far East Command, that only U.S. troops can stem the invasion. (Beginning of the United Nations Defensive Campaign—it ends 15 September.)

29 June. **First American Casualties. Suwon, South Korea.**
A day after Seoul, the ROK capital, falls, the United States armed forces suffer their first casualties of the Korean War when five soldiers of the 507th Anti-Aircraft Artillery Battalion are wounded.

Left: *An American infantryman moves cautiously through a burning village in Korea. (National Archives)*

Opposite, top: *A sketch of an infantryman outfitted for a harsh Korean winter. ("Yea, Though I Walk Through the Valley of the Shadow of Death," Howard Brodie)*

Opposite, bottom: *Korean War–era American M-1 helmet with a combat–inflicted fragment hole and improvised burlap cover. (Kevin Mahoney)*

30 June. **The United States Commits Ground Forces to Korea.**

President Truman commits U.S. ground troops to enforce the United Nations resolution. The closest Army units, those of the Eighth U.S. Army in Japan, however, are greatly undermanned—combat units are at less than 50 percent of authorized strength, and there is a great shortage of heavy weapons, tanks, and ammunition. On the same day, Truman signs legislation extending Selective Service until 9 July 1951 and authorizes the call-up of National Guard and Reserve forces for up to 21 months of federal service.

1 July. **First U.S. Combat Troops Deployed to Korea.**
Task Force Smith, comprising the 1st Battalion, 21st Infantry Regiment, 24th Infantry Division, plus artillery and a medical platoon, and named for its commander, Lieutenant Colonel Charles B. Smith, arrives in South Korea and quickly advances north to take up positions at Osan. Though few of the task force's soldiers have combat experience, most are confident that the NKPA forces will break and run when confronted by American soldiers. The remaining elements of the 24th Infantry Division, commanded by Major General William F. Dean, will arrive in the following days.

4 July. **Planning for Amphibious Operation. Tokyo, Japan.**
General MacArthur directs his staff to begin preparing plans for an amphibious operation along the west coast of South Korea at Inchon. Called Operation Bluehearts, the plan is overly ambitious and is soon canceled. MacArthur, however, still believes that an amphibious landing at Inchon will succeed, and planning continues for what will become Operation Chromite.

5 July. **Battle of Osan.**
In the first ground action against American and NKPA forces, Task Force Smith clashes with the NKPA 4th Division at Osan. The Americans fight bravely, disabling or destroying four T-34 tanks, inflicting significant casualties, and delaying the NKPA advance for seven hours. Eventually, Smith has no choice but to withdraw his men in the face of overwhelming numbers. Task Force Smith loses 181 men killed, wounded, and missing; NKPA losses are estimated at 130 killed and wounded.

6–12 July. **Elements of the 24th Infantry Division Clash with NKPA.**
On 6 July, the 34th Infantry Regiment battles the

advancing North Koreans at Pyongtaek, delaying the enemy before withdrawing south. The 21st Infantry Regiment also delays the North Koreans at Chochiwon before withdrawing. While suffering significant casualties in the process, the 24th Infantry Division's actions buy time to allow reinforcements to be rushed to Korea. During the fighting, a number of Americans are taken prisoner and later executed by the NKPA. During the war, hundreds of American prisoners of war (POWs) are either executed by the Communists or die in captivity. Furthermore, United Nations forces will later discover the bodies of thousands of South Korean civilians who have been brutally murdered by the North Koreans.

7–8 July. **United Nations Command Established.**
On 7 July, the UN Security Council asks the United States to serve as its executive agent for the conflict in Korea and to organize a United Nations Command. On 8 July, Truman appoints General MacArthur to head United Nations Command (UNC).

10 July. **25th Infantry Division Lands at Pusan.**
Advance elements of the 25th Infantry Division, commanded by Major General William B. Kean, begin arriving from Japan.

13 July. **Eighth U.S. Army Headquarters Established in Korea. Taegu, South Korea.**
Lieutenant General Walton H. Walker, commander of 8th Army, establishes his headquarters at Taegu and assumes command of all U.S. ground forces in Korea.

14–26 July. **Battle of Kum River.**
Beginning on 14 July, Dean's overstretched 24th Infantry Division clashes with NKPA forces along the Kum River. The North Koreans cross the river and, after heavy fighting, push American forces south. Intense fighting takes place in and around the

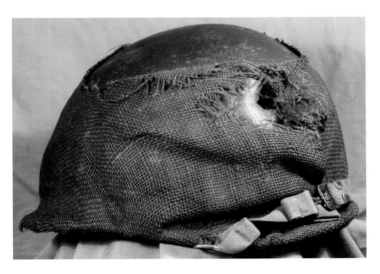

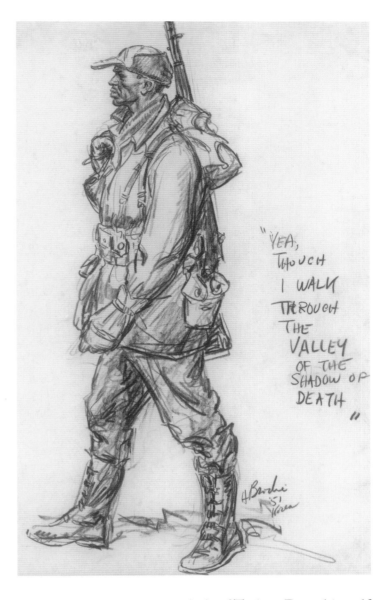

"YEA, THOUGH I WALK THROUGH THE VALLEY OF THE SHADOW OF DEATH"

important communication hub of Taejon. Dean himself becomes personally involved in the street fighting and assists in knocking out an enemy tank as part of a bazooka team. During the chaotic withdrawal from Taejon, Dean is injured and becomes separated from his troops on 20 July. He wanders through enemy-held territory for more than a month before being captured on 25 August and held as a POW until the end of the war. (On 9 January 1951, the President presents the Medal of Honor to Dean.) The delay along the Kum River allows Walker to establish a defense line along the Naktong River that becomes known as the Naktong Perimeter (sometimes called the Pusan Perimeter). Brigadier General Church assumes command of the 24th Infantry Division on 22 July.

18 July. **1st Cavalry Division Lands at Pohang.**
Lead elements of the 1st Cavalry Division, commanded by Major General Hobart R. ("Hap") Gay, arrive from Japan and make an unopposed landing at Pohang along the east coast of South Korea.

THE ARMY NATIONAL GUARD IN KOREA

In October 1945, War Department policy stated that the Army National Guard (ARNG) would remain in the nation's first line of defense and retain its unique, dual status as a federal and state force. The ARNG moved quickly to rebuild itself following World War II. The first postwar unit was organized in June 1946, and thereafter, the ARNG's reorganization was rapid and widespread.

The National Security Act of 1947 split the National Guard into the Army National Guard and the Air National Guard, all under the central administration of the National Guard Bureau. By the end of 1948, 288,427 Army Guardsmen were organized into 4,646 units, and within two years, the ARNG reached a peak strength of nearly 325,000. Twenty-one states and Hawaii completed their Guard reorganizations by 1950, and the ARNG's force structure included 27 divisions and 20 regimental combat teams (RCTs).

The ARNG's first test came in the summer of 1950 when, in response to the outbreak of the Korean War, President Harry S Truman announced a partial mobilization of Guardsmen for 21 months. The Army transferred large numbers of Guardsmen from their units and shipped them to Korea as individual replacements. ARNG units were also rushed to Korea, providing desperately needed field artillery, engineer, and transportation support. On New Year's Day 1951, the 231st Transportation Truck Battalion, an all-black unit from Baltimore, Maryland, was the first ARNG unit to arrive in Korea. Two months later, Arkansas's 936th Field Artillery Battalion became the first Guard unit to enter combat. After extensive training,

California's 40th and Oklahoma's 45th Infantry Divisions arrived in Korea in late 1951.

Other mobilized Guard units performed important missions. Pennsylvania's 28th and New England's 43d Infantry Divisions deployed to Europe to deter against a possible Soviet attack. Army units in Europe stripped of personnel for duty in Korea received individual guardsmen. Four other ARNG divisions—the 31st, 37th, 44th, and 47th—were called up in January 1952 to form a ready reserve. Guardsmen serving stateside bolstered the Army's training base and prepared for possible overseas duty. In addition, Guardsmen not ordered to active duty constituted a reserve of manpower for other emergencies. Before the Korean War ended, 138,600 Army Guardsmen— nearly one-third of the entire ARNG—had answered the call to arms. The Korean mobilization was the ARNG's largest and most significant contribution during the Cold War.

The Korean War validated concerns that the Cold War would continue for an indefinite period. However, the ARNG was still geared for the slow, deliberate mobilizations of the World Wars and unprepared to provide combat-ready units on short notice to trouble spots around the globe. To increase its effectiveness, the ARNG implemented a series of sweeping reforms under the Regular Army's supervision. The Regular Army took responsibility for providing basic training to all ARNG volunteers so that Guard commanders could focus more on unit training. Drill activities were concentrated on a single weekend each month instead of weekly, and weekend drill became mandatory in 1966. The ARNG reduced the number of units, increased personnel manning, and received more modern weapons and equipment. Altogether, these changes resulted in a much-improved ARNG for the remainder of the Cold War.

—*Michael Doubler*

Above: *Cannoneers of the 300th Armored Field Artillery, Wyoming National Guard, provide support fire during a seven-day engagement in May 1951, earning a Presidential Unit Citation. ("Cowboy Artillery at Soyang," Mort Künstler, National Guard Heritage series)*

Right: *A squad of 2d Infantry Division soldiers moves forward in Korea with the support of a half-track. ("The American Soldier, 1950," H. Charles McBarron, Army Art Collection, NMUSA)*

20 July. **Army Reorganization Act of 1950. Washington, D.C.**

Congress passes the Army Reorganization Act of 1950, which removes size limits on the Army General Staff; firmly establishes the Secretary of the Army as the immediate superior to the Chief of Staff; creates a Comptroller of the Army; merges field, coast, and anti-aircraft artillery into a single Artillery branch; merges tanks and mechanized cavalry into the Armor branch; and recognizes 14 services: Chemical Corps, Corps of Engineers, Military Police Corps, Ordnance Corps, Quartermaster Corps, Transportation Corps, Adjutant General Corps, Finance Corps, Women's Army Corps, Army Medical Service, Chaplain Corps, Inspectors General, and Judge Advocate General Corps.

25 July. **29th Infantry Regiment Committed to Combat.**

The two battalions of the 29th Infantry Regiment, recently arrived from Okinawa to reinforce the decimated 19th Infantry Regiment, are committed to combat at Chinju. On 27 July, the 29th's 3d Battalion is virtually massacred when attacked by the NKPA 6th Division, suffering more than 400 casualties, most of them killed. The 1st Battalion, 29th Infantry, suffers

Left: *Trenches along a ridge in Korea provide some protection against enemy fire. (1st Air Cavalry Division)*

another 200 casualties in fighting with the NKPA 4th Division. Both battalions will later be incorporated into the 25th Infantry Division.

27 July. Enlistments Extended.
President Truman signs legislation extending enlistments in the armed forces for 12 months. Furthermore, a draft call is issued ordering 50,000 inductees to report for training in September.

28 July. Military Police Established as a Permanent Service.
Congress establishes the Military Police Corps as a permanent organization within the Army.

29 July. Walker Issues "Stand or Die" Order.
With his army's back to the sea, 8th Army commander Lieutenant General Walker issues his "Stand or Die" order, declaring, "There will be no Dunkirk, there will be no Bataan."

31 July and 1 August. Reinforcements Arrive. Pusan, South Korea.
On 31 July, the 5th Regimental Combat Team (5th Infantry Regiment, 555th Field Artillery Battalion, and a tank company) arrives from Hawaii. The next day, advance elements of the 2d Infantry Division, commanded by Major General Laurence B. Keiser, begin arriving from Fort Lewis, Washington.

Right: *In 1951 the 187th Parachute Infantry made one of the few airborne assaults of the war. (U.S. Army Military History Institute, Carlisle Barracks, PA)*

Below: *Watchful troops in a night position observe flares that may mean fighting will erupt at any minute. (Army Art Collection, NMUSA)*

2 August. **I Corps Activated. Fort Bragg, North Carolina.**
I Corps is activated and ordered to Korea, with Major General John B. Coulter as its commanding officer.

3 August. **National Guard Units Called Up.**
One hundred thirty-four Army National Guard units receive orders to report for active duty.

3 August. **Naktong Perimeter Established.**
Walker's 8th Army establishes a perimeter measuring 100 miles north and south and 50 miles east and west, anchored along the Naktong River in the west and encompassing Pusan. The perimeter is defended by the 1st Cavalry Division, 2d, 24th, and 25th Infantry Divisions, First Provisional Marine Brigade, 27th British Brigade, eight ROK divisions, and air and naval support.

5–19 August. **First Battle of the Naktong Bulge.**
The 24th Infantry Division, reinforced by the 1st Marine Provisional Brigade and elements of the 2d and 25th Infantry Divisions, halts a North Korean penetration of the Naktong Perimeter, inflicting more than 8,500 enemy casualties and destroying large amounts of enemy vehicles and equipment. UN casualties number 1,800 killed, wounded, and missing.

10 August. **Units Activated.**
The Army activates IX Corps at Fort Sheridan, Illinois, and orders it to Korea with Major General Frank W. Milburn as its commander. On that same day, President Truman calls four National Guard divisions (28th Infantry, 40th Infantry, 43d Infantry, and 45th Infantry) and two regimental combat teams (196th and 278th) to active duty. The 40th and 45th will later serve in Korea, while the 28th and 43d will be sent to Europe to bolster NATO forces.

16 August. **X Corps Activated. Japan.**
X Corps is activated to oversee the upcoming Inchon

Left: *Members of the 8225th Mobile Army Surgical Hospital (MASH), whose frontline work in tandem with helicopters saved many GIs in Korea. (U.S. Army Military History Institute, Carlisle Barracks, PA)*

Below: *Company B, 2d Battalion, 7th Infantry, was engaged in the see-saw fighting in Korea. ("Radio Operator Pinned Down," Howard Brodie)*

Opposite: *The 57th Field Artillery Battalion was trapped with the rest of TF McLean east of the Chosin Reservoir. ("Chosin Fires," James A. Dietz)*

operation. Major General Edward M. Almond is named commander.

18–25 August. Battle of the Bowling Alley.
For nearly a week, NKPA forces attempt to penetrate the UN lines through a narrow valley (nicknamed the "Bowling Alley" by American soldiers) but are repulsed each time, first by the 27th Infantry Regiment, 25th Infantry Division, and then by the 23d Infantry Regiment, 2d Infantry Division. NKPA losses are estimated at 4,000 killed, wounded, and missing; American casualties are minimal.

25 August. Army Takes Over U.S. Railroads.
President Truman orders the Army to take control of the railroad system during a period of labor strife. The Army will retain control of the railroads until May 1952.

25 August. Japan Logistical Command Established.
The Army forms the Japan Logistical Command to manage supplies and equipment for the war in Korea and assume occupation duties for 8th Army.

31 August–9 September. Second Battle of the Naktong Bulge.
NKPA forces launch a powerful attack against the 2d Infantry Division's sector along the Naktong Perimeter, overrunning some units before counterattacks by Army and Marine units drive the Communists back. Losses on both sides are heavy, with NKPA casualties estimated as high as 10,000.

15 September. Operation Chromite. Inchon, South Korea.
Operation Chromite, MacArthur's daring amphibious landing of X Corps on the western coast of Korea, begins early on 15 September. The 1st Marine Division (with some attached Army units) conducts the initial operations. The 7th Infantry Division, led by Major General David G. Barr, will begin landing on 18 September. The operation is a great success and is carried out with few casualties. American and ROK forces quickly move inland toward Seoul

16 September. 8th Army Begins Breakout from Naktong Perimeter.
Following the landings at Inchon, 8th Army begins its breakout north from the Naktong Perimeter to link up with X Corps. With X Corps landed behind their lines, NKPA forces quickly withdraw north. On that same day, the 3d Infantry Division (minus the 65th Infantry Regiment), commanded by Major General

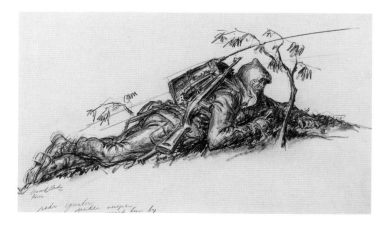

Robert H. Soule, arrives in Japan and forms the Far East Command reserve. (Beginning of the UN Offensive Campaign—it ends 2 November.)

19 September. **Creation of Logistical Commands.**
The Army establishes the Second Logistical Command, which replaces the Pusan Logistical Command. Its mission is to provide logistical support for 8th Army. The 3d Logistical Command is activated to support X Corps.

20 September. **Bradley Promoted to General of the Army. Washington, D.C.**
Congress promotes General Omar N. Bradley, who is serving as Chairman of the Joint Chiefs of Staff, to the rank of General of the Army (five stars). He is the first to be promoted to that rank since World War II and will be the last one to hold it.

21 September. **George C. Marshall Appointed Secretary of Defense. Washington, D.C.**
After Louis Johnson resigns on 19 September, Truman names former Army Chief of Staff and Secretary of State George C. Marshall as Secretary of Defense.

24–25 September. **187th Airborne Regimental Combat Team Arrives in Korea.**
The 187th Airborne RCT (187th Airborne Infantry Regiment, 674th Field Artillery Battalion), commanded by Colonel Frank S. Bowen, Jr., is airlifted from Japan to Kimpo Air Base near Seoul.

26 September. **UN Forces Link Up. Suwon, South Korea.**
After the landings at Inchon and the breakout at Naktong, elements of the 7th Infantry Division (X Corps) links up with the 1st Cavalry Division (8th Army) at Suwon.

27 September. **Seoul Falls to UN Forces.**
The 7th Infantry Division and 1st Marine Division capture Seoul.

27 September. **Operations North of 38th Parallel Authorized.**
Upon the recommendation of the Joint Chiefs of Staff, and with the concurrence of the Departments of Defense and State, President Truman authorizes operations north of the 38th Parallel and into North Korean territory. On 7 October, the UN passes a resolution authorizing UN troops north of the 38th parallel to establish a unified and democratic Korea.

9 October. **U.S. Forces Cross 38th Parallel.**
The 8th Army's I Corps, led by the 1st Cavalry Division, crosses the 38th Parallel near Kaesong and advances north toward Pyongyang, the North Korean capital, in pursuit of enemy forces.

11 October. **MacArthur Demands Surrender of NKPA.**
General MacArthur issues a demand calling for the immediate surrender of all NKPA forces. The North Koreans ignore the demand.

15 October. Truman and MacArthur Meet at Wake Island.

President Truman and MacArthur meet on Wake Island to discuss the Korean War. MacArthur denies the need for more troops and downplays the possibility of Chinese or Soviet intervention. The two depart on good terms, but relations between Truman and MacArthur become strained in the coming months.

14–17 October. 7th Infantry Division Redeploys.

The 7th Infantry Division is transported south from Seoul to Pusan for a landing on the northeastern coast of Korea.

19 October. Pyongyang Falls.

The 1st Cavalry Division and the 1st ROK Division capture Pyongyang

20 October. First Parachute Assault of Korean War. Sukchon and Sunchon, North Korea.

In an effort to cut off retreating NKPA forces north of Pyongyang and free UN prisoners, the 187th Airborne RCT carries out the first combat parachute assault of the Korean War. The action, however, fails to catch significant numbers of enemy troops. The drop does feature a number of firsts, including the first combat

jump from C-119 aircraft and the first successful drop of 105mm howitzers and jeeps.

25 October. First Contact with Chinese Forces. Unsan, North Korea.

ROK forces are attacked by elements of the Chinese Communist Forces' (CCF) 50th Field Army north of Unsan. On that same day, a Chinese prisoner captured near the Chosin (Changjin) Reservoir states that large numbers of CCF are nearby. CCF units have been infiltrating into Korea since shortly after UN forces crossed into North Korea, but UNC intelligence has failed to detect them. Furthermore, MacArthur has unwisely divided his forces on the Korean peninsula. The 8th Army and X Corps, acting as separate, independent commands, are operating on opposite sides of the rugged Taebaek Mountains and are unable to support each other.

29 October. 7th Infantry Division Lands at Iwon.

After embarking from Pusan, the 7th Infantry Division lands unopposed at Iwon along the eastern coast of North Korea and begins advancing north.

1 November. 8th Army Reaches Northernmost Point.

The 21st Infantry Regiment, 24th Infantry Division, reaches Chonggodo, 18 miles south of the Yalu River and the northernmost point reached by 8th Army.

5 November. **3d Infantry Division Lands at Wonsan.**
The 3d Infantry begins landing at Wonsan on the eastern coast of North Korea.

2–6 November. **U.S. Forces Clash with CCF. Unsan, North Korea.**
The 8th Cavalry Regiment, 1st Cavalry Division, is attacked by the CCF 116th Division. The regiment's 3d Battalion is virtually annihilated before the Chinese retreat into the hills. (3 November—beginning of the CCF Intervention Campaign—it ends 24 January 1951.)

21 November. **American Forces Reach Yalu River. Hyesanjin, North Korea.**
Elements of the 17th Infantry, 7th Infantry Division, reach Hyeasanjin along the Yalu River, which separates North Korea from China.

22 November. **Army Deploys First Helicopter Unit.**
After witnessing the successful use of helicopters by the Air Force and Marines, the Army deploys its first helicopter unit to Korea. The 2d Helicopter Detachment, equipped with Bell H-13 helicopters, is attached to the 8055th Mobile Army Surgical Hospital (MASH).

24 November. **Final UN Offensive.**
In northern North Korea, UN forces launch what is intended to be the final offensive of the war. MacArthur tells reporters the operation will "get the boys home by Christmas."

24 November. **Headquarters, U.S. Army Constabulary, Inactivated. Bamberg, Germany.**
With the occupation of Germany coming to an end, the Headquarters, U.S. Army Constabulary, is inactivated. Most of the units return to their traditional unit designations and become part of the U.S. Seventh Army. The last operational Constabulary units, the 2d Constabulary Brigade, comprising the 15th and 24th Constabulary Squadrons, remain on active duty in Europe until December 1952.

25 November. **CCF Launches Major Offensive Against 8th Army.**
A day after 8th Army launches what is to be the final offensive of the war, the CCF Thirteenth Army Group, consisting of 18 divisions plus NKPA units (approximately 180,000 soldiers), attacks 8th Army in northwest North Korea on the bitterly cold night of 25 November. The onslaught is devastating—many units of the 2d and 25th Infantry Division are overrun, and

Opposite: *General Matthew Ridgway gave a simple order to the demoralized 8th U.S. Army: find and destroy the enemy. ("Find 'Em, Fix 'Em, Finish 'Em," Rick Reeves)*

Right: *In one of the few bayonet charges in modern times, Captain Lewis Millet led the men of Company E, 27th U.S. Infantry Regiment (Wolfhounds), to seize Hill 180 from the Chinese. ("Cold Steel," Don Stivers)*

several ROK units are destroyed. Soon 8th Army is in full retreat south down the Korean peninsula.

27 November. Chinese Launch Second Phase of Offensive. Northeastern North Korea

As X Corps launches an offensive to ease pressure on 8th Army, the CCF 9th Army Group attacks with 12 divisions (120,000 men) in the Chosin Reservoir area.

27 November–1 December. Destruction of TF MacLean.

Late on 27 November, Task Force MacLean (also known as the 31st RCT), commanded by Colonel Allan D. MacLean, comes under attack by the CCF 80th Division along the eastern side of the Chosin Reservoir. Facing overwhelming numbers of Chinese troops, MacLean has no choice but to withdraw. Over the next five days, the task force fights a running battle with the Chinese, inflicting heavy casualties but suffering grievous losses themselves, not only from enemy fire but also from the bitterly cold weather. After MacLean is captured on 29 November (he later dies in captivity), Lieutenant Colonel Don Faith assumes command, and the task force becomes known as Task Force Faith. Two days later, as the task force continues the withdrawal under constant enemy fire, Faith is mortally wounded (he later receives the Medal of Honor posthumously), and the task force virtually ceases to exist. The Chinese reach the column and

slaughter many of the wounded lying in abandoned and disabled vehicles. Those still able to move flee onto the frozen reservoir and escape to the Marine lines at Hagaru-ri. Of 2,500 American soldiers in the task force, less than 1,000 make it to Marine lines, and only 385 are still capable of fighting. While suffering terrible losses, Task Force MacLean/Faith delays the Chinese advance and prevents the Marines from being cut off on the western side of Chosin. For their actions, the 31st RCT is later awarded a Navy Presidential Unit Citation.

28 November. Task Force Kingston Reaches the Yalu. Singalpajin, North Korea.

Second Lieutenant Robert C. Kingston leads a small task force from the 3d Battalion, 32d Infantry, 7th Infantry Division, that reaches the Yalu at Singalpajin. Kingston's force becomes the second, and last, American unit to reach the Yalu.

28–29 November. Battle of Kunu-ri, North Korea.

During 8th Army's retreat south, intense fighting occurs around Kunu-ri. The 2d Infantry Division, serving as 8th Army's rearguard, suffers horrific casualties, losing nearly 5,000 killed, wounded, and missing, almost a third of the division's strength. Two of the division's infantry regiments, the 9th and the 38th, are decimated.

Opposite: *Due to rough terrain, tanks played a minor but key role in Korea. (Army Art Collection, NMUSA)*

Right: *General of the Army Douglas MacArthur departs from Korea after his much-publicized relief by President Harry S. Truman. (Imperial War Museum, London)*

Below: *Colonel Paul Freeman's reinforced 23d Infantry held the line against the Chinese. ("Breakthrough at Chihyong-Ni," H. Charles McBarron, Army Art Collection, NMUSA)*

30 November. **X Corps Withdraws to Hungnam.**
Major General Almond orders X Corps (3d Infantry Division, 7th Infantry Division, 1st Marine Division, and ROK I Corps) to withdraw to the port city of Hungnam on North Korea's eastern coast. On 9 December, Almond receives orders to evacuate his corps to Pusan by sea. When the evacuation is completed on 24 December, UN forces destroy the port facilities.

15 December. **Defensive Line Established.**
Walker's 8th Army establishes a defensive line (Line B) along the Imjin River, just north of Seoul.

16 December. **Eisenhower Appointed Supreme Allied Commander, Europe.**
General Eisenhower, who retired in February 1948, is called out of retirement and named the first Supreme Allied Commander, Europe, to command NATO forces.

23 December. **Walker Killed. Ridgway Arrives. South Korea.**
8th Army commander Lieutenant General Walker is killed in a jeep accident near Uijongbu. He is replaced by Lieutenant General Matthew B. Ridgway on 26 December. Walker is posthumously promoted to general on 2 January 1951.

THE DEATH OF TASK FORCE MACLEAN/FAITH

In November 1950, soldiers of the 7th Infantry Division were pushing up the east side of the Chosin Reservoir while the 1st Marine Division moved on the west side. Leading the Army advance was a 3,000-man task force (TF)—2d and 3d Battalions and HQ, 31st Infantry, Colonel Allan D. MacLean commanding. On the night of 26 November, the 80th Chinese Division hit the task force, and for the next four days and five nights of sub-zero temperatures, snow, and ice, the men of TF MacLean, later TF Faith, fought a bloody and ultimately unsuccessful battle to withdraw south to the base of the reservoir. Army Lieutenant James O. Mortrude, already wounded in the head and wearing a Chinese soldier's coat for warmth, fought to take a hill to keep the road open for the retreating convoy:

"Someone initiated movement up the hill, which quickly became a spontaneous attack under the rallying cry of 'Come on, GI.' Somewhat recovered by this time, I salvaged an M-1 rifle from a wounded Korean auxiliary and followed the movements up the hillside, which was now dotted with our casualties. This attack carried to the crest of the hill into the very midst of the Chinese occupied positions. The Chinese broke under the pressure of our assault and ran down toward the saddle where the road crossed the high ground. Those that did not run were quickly killed in their holes and I have heard that at least one was choked to death by an enraged American. During this melee on the hill, we were struck again by U.S. Marine air support, this time by rocket fire. Fortunately we had the abandoned positions as refuge and I saw no casualties.

"With the line of trucks now moving across the valley and up the road to our rear, the movement of our troops continued south. Once down on the road again, I observed at least one disabled U.S. tank and several friendly KIAs as I followed the line of march down to the reservoir . . . it seemed to me that we converged into a sizable group of perhaps 50 or more people as we moved out on the ice of the reservoir. In recall, it seems we were led by a wounded officer who was familiar to me and that it was Capt. Bigger . . . as we moved across the ice, groups of Chinese would attempt to intercept us, but we would drive them back to shore with much shouting and shooting. Also, we came across one wounded U.S. soldier and one wounded and one dead Chinese, all literally frozen to the ice of a watering hole location. The U.S. soldier

said the Chinese had shot him after initially indicating friendship as they hosted him to a drink from the water hole. Subsequently, the wounded U.S. soldier had retaliated by shooting both of them.

"Just prior to darkness we observed a friendly air drop of supplies in what we assumed to be the Haragu-ri area and I was heartened by the assurance of our direction of our march.

"Sometime after darkness, it seemed to me that we were moving through a built-up area and in my state of exhaustion I wanted to fall out and rest in one of the houses. Fortunately, someone of more presence of mind convinced me my 'buildings' were merely rocks and that I must keep moving. Upon reaching Haragu-ri, my impromptu camouflage and again my expropriated Chinese gray coat occasioned some concern and curiosity among the Marines. I was, however, able to identify myself."

—*Kevin M. Hymel*

Above: *Colonel Allan D. MacLean and Lieutenant Colonel Don C. Faith, 1950. (Courtesy Colonel Erwin B. Bigger)*

Right: *The men of the 65th Infantry Regiment from Puerto Rico compiled an impressive record, earning four Distinguished Service Crosses and 125 Silver Stars. ("The Borinqueneers," D. Andrea, National Guard Heritage series)*

29 December. **Washington Issues New War Directive.**
The Truman administration informs MacArthur that the plan for the unification of Korea is being scrapped. MacArthur criticizes the decision as a loss of fighting spirit and demands a naval blockade of China, bombing of the Chinese mainland, and the use of Chinese Nationalist troops. He warns the JCS that if it turns down his demands, defeat and evacuation of UN troops from Korea will be his only alternative.

31 December. **Communist Forces Launch Offensive.**
Communist forces, including seven CCF armies and two NKPA corps, commence a general offensive, pushing UN forces farther south.

1951

January. **Status of the Army.**
With increased draft calls, mobilization of National Guard and Reserve units, and the recall of individual reservists, the Army's size has increased to 1,531,774 and 18 divisions (four of them federalized National Guard divisions). Nevertheless, with the war in Korea intensifying and U.S. troops committed to NATO, Army forces will be stretched thin.

4–5 January. **Seoul and Inchon Abandoned.**
The ROK capital of Seoul and the port of Inchon are abandoned by UN forces as Communist forces advance south.

7–14 January. **Lines Stabilize.**
Ridgway's 8th Army halts the Communist offensive and stabilizes the lines just south of the 38th Parallel.

15–17 January. **Operation Wolfhound. Western South Korea.**
Ridgway orders reconnaissance-in-force comprising 6,000 troops, supported by tanks and artillery, to find and destroy CCF units. In two days of fighting, UN forces inflict more than 1,800 casualties while suffering three killed and seven wounded.

16 January. **Additional National Guard Divisions Federalized.**
The 31st and 47th Infantry Divisions enter federal service, but both will remain in the United States.

25 January. **Operation Thunderbolt. Western South Korea.**
With the success of Wolfhound, Ridgway launches a similar but larger operation called Operation Thunderbolt with I and IX Corps. (Beginning of the First UN Counteroffensive Campaign—it ends on 21 April.) The attack is slow and methodical—the first use of Ridgway's so-called meat grinder tactics. The advance continues until UN forces reach the Han River just short of Seoul on 10 February. In the east, X Corps conducts a similar operation code-named Operation Roundup.

1 February. **Battle of the Twin Tunnels. Sinchon, South Korea.**
What begins as a probing attack turns into a significant action as elements of the 23d Infantry Regiment and the French Battalion (with support from Marine aircraft) rout the CCF 125th Division, inflicting nearly 5,000 casualties while losing 225 killed and wounded.

Left: *During January 1952, an artillery battery goes into action with their 105mm, providing support to infantry positioned forward in the Korean hills. Even under such strenuous conditions, heavy winter dress is needed for protection against the brutal Korean winters. (U.S. Army Reserve painting)*

Below: *The strain of combat and losing friends took a toll on all frontline troops. ("Rifleman Morgan Weeps," Howard Brodie)*

5–9 February. **Operation Punch.**
On the same day that X Corps begins Operation Roundup, Ridgway launches Operation Punch to capture the Hill 440 complex south of Seoul. By 9 February elements of the 25th Infantry Division, supported by artillery, armor, and air power, have taken their objectives and inflicted more than 4,200 casualties, while losing 70 killed and wounded.

11 February. **CCF Launch Fourth Offensive. Central Korea.**
Chinese forces launch a fourth offensive intended to destroy UN forces. Ridgway's troops respond quickly to thwart the enemy advance.

11–13 February. **Fighting at Hoengsong.**
The 2d Infantry Division suffers heavy casualties while withdrawing south through Hoengsong. Two battalions of the 38th Infantry are shattered. In addition, the 15th and 503d Field Artillery Battalions lose large numbers of men and most of their guns and vehicles. Determined resistance by the Dutch Battalion against the CCF allows the battered Americans to withdraw to Wonju.

13–15 February. **Battle of Chipyong-ni.**
In one of the most important battles of the war, Colonel Paul Freeman's 23d Infantry Regiment, supported by the French Battalion, Rangers, tanks, and artillery, form a perimeter around the village of Chipyong-ni and hold for two days despite being surrounded and attacked by six CCF divisions. Despite suffering heavy casualties—350 killed, wounded, and

missing—the UN forces refuse to surrender and are finally relieved by the 5th Cavalry Regiment. The 23d's stubborn resistance blunts the CCF offensive, and it eventually grinds to a halt on 18 February.

14–17 February. **Battle of Wonju.**
In heavy fighting around Wonju, elements of the 2d Infantry Division, 7th Infantry Division, 187th Airborne RCT, and large quantities of artillery inflict

GENERAL MATTHEW RIDGWAY: A SOLDIER'S GENERAL

Ridgway graduated from West Point in 1917 and served with the 3d Infantry in Texas before returning to West Point as an instructor and athletics officer. After the attack on Pearl Harbor, Ridgway was appointed deputy to Major General Omar Bradley, commander of the 82d Infantry Division, then succeeded Bradley and oversaw the 82d's conversion into an airborne division. He led them in combat on Sicily where, landing by boat, he met up with scattered elements of one of his regiments. Despite widely scattered drops, friendly-fire incidents, and heavy enemy resistance, his division took all its objectives.

On D-Day, Ridgway parachuted into Normandy with his men. As the battles of Normandy progressed, Ridgway was out front leading. In August 1944, he was given command of the XVIII Airborne Corps but was not in command of his two airborne divisions (82d and 101st) during Operation Market Garden, an offensive through Holland.

During the Battle of the Bulge, Ridgway proved himself as one of the U.S. Army's best corps commanders. When the German army broke through the American lines on 16 December 1944, he rushed to the front and took command of a handful of divisions on the northern side of the bulge. He effectively slowed the German advance with a strong defense of St. Vith until forced to retreat. He then worked to contain the German offensive and helped push it back into Germany.

After World War II, Ridgway served in various commands before becoming Deputy Chief of Staff of the Army in 1949. It was then he got the call to report as head of the 8th Army in Korea. Only four months after taking command, Ridgway received his fourth star and succeeded General MacArthur as head of Far East and United Nations Commands. Under his leadership, truce talks began for ending the war.

Ridgway went on to serve as the Supreme Commander, Allied Forces in Europe, and finally in 1953, as Chief of Staff of the Army, but he is best remembered for revitalizing a defeated army in the field and sending back it on the offensive.

—*Kevin M. Hymel*

In the winter of 1950–51, the Communist Chinese army broke through the UN lines and pushed them down the Korean peninsula. To make matters worse, Lieutenant General Walton Walker, U.S. 8th Army commander, was killed in a jeep accident. When things looked their bleakest for the UN effort, Lieutenant General Matthew B. Ridgway replaced Walker and showed what the leadership of one man could do.

On arrival in Korea, Ridgway took command of a shaken 8th Army and was shocked at what he found: poor discipline, bad tactics, and almost no morale. Ridgway set about changing all that. He told his subordinates to stop thinking about retreat and to begin planning offensive operations. He instituted training, restored discipline, improved the men's diet, and made sure mail was brought up to the front line. Within four months of his arrival, 8th Army was attacking and gaining ground.

Above: *General Matthew Ridgway wears his trademark hand grenade as he inspects the front lines as the new commander of the 8th U.S. Army in Korea. (National Archives)*

heavy casualties on Communist forces at Wonju. The battle becomes known as the "Wonju Shoot" because of the massive amounts of artillery expended in the battle.

21 February. Operation Killer.
Ridgway orders a counterattack by IX and X Corps to clear a salient in the UN lines. The operation, which lasts until 6 March, inflicts moe than 10,000 casualties on the enemy.

6–31 March. Operation Ripper.
Following on Operation Killer, Ridgway orders UN forces to advance north on a broad front. By 7 March, the 25th Infantry Division has crossed the Han River after a heavy artillery barrage and quickly reaches its phase line objectives with little resistance. The remainder of 8th Army advances and faces weak to moderate resistance. By 14 March, UN forces reach Seoul, and upon learning the CCF and NKPA have abandoned it, Ridgway orders the 3d Infantry Division and 6th ROK Division to occupy it. UN forces continue to advance north, and patrols eventually extend north of the 38th Parallel. While Seoul is taken without a fight, the operation is considered only partly successful as it falls short of inflicting significant casualties on Communist forces. Shortly after Operation Ripper is launched, State Department officials protest Ridgway's aggressive code names for his offensives; later operations will be given less menacing titles.

22–31 March. Operation Courageous.
Ridgway launches Operation Courageous to support Operation Killer, destroy Communist forces facing I Corps, and clear any remaining units from South Korea. While the operation fails to kill large numbers of CCF and NKPA troops, it does push 8th Army to the 38th Parallel. Operation Courageous marks a transition from offensive actions to ones focusing on active defense.

23 March. Operation Tomahawk.
The 187th Airborne RCT, with the 2d and 4th Ranger Companies attached, makes the second and final combat parachute jump of the war near Munsan-ni in an effort to cut off retreating Communist forces. The operation, however, fails to catch the main body of enemy troops. One American is killed and 18 wounded in the assault; 84 soldiers suffer jump-related injuries.

24 March. MacArthur Demands Communists Surrender.
General MacArthur unilaterally issues a demand for the surrender of Communist forces, scuttling a peace initiative from Washington to the Chinese. The Chinese refuse the demand.

5–9 April. Operation Rugged.
8th Army units advance and quickly cross the 38th Parallel, reaching objective lines Kansas and Utah. American forces suffer just over 1,000 casualties.

Opposite: *U.S. troops secure Compound 77, Koje Island POW Camp, in June 1952. (Courtesy John Langellier, photographer Warren Lee)*

Right: *With grenades, M-1 rifles, and M-1 carbines, the 5th Regimental Combat Team fight to take Objective Baker from the enemy in January 1951. ("How It Ought To Be Done," Rick Reeves)*

11–22 April. **Operation Dauntless.**
Units from I Corps (3d, 24th, and 25th Infantry Divisions, plus ROK units) push north and reach Lines Utah and Wyoming, then drive into the Iron Triangle, suffering minimal casualties in the process.

11 April. **MacArthur Relieved of Command.**
With MacArthur becoming increasingly insubordinate and defiant of official policy, President Truman relieves him of command of UN forces in Korea. The final straw comes when Representative Joseph Martin

(Republican-Massachusetts) reads a letter from MacArthur on the House floor in which he criticizes Truman's policy on limited war. MacArthur returns to the United States (his first time back in 14 years) to a hero's welcome and addresses a joint session of Congress on 19 April, where he gives his famous "Old Soldiers Never Die" speech.

11 April. **Ridgway Replaces MacArthur.**
After relieving MacArthur, President Truman names Ridgway commander of all UN forces in Korea,

Left: *In 1953, fighting in Korea at last came to a halt with the signing of an armistice by Lieutenant General William Harrison. (National Archives)*

Below: *During the Cold War, air defense batteries, such as this Nike unit in the San Francisco area, were built and manned to defend the U.S. from Soviet air and missile attacks. (U.S. Army, John P. Langellier Collection)*

commander of Far East Command, and supreme commander of Allied occupation forces in Japan.

14 April. James Van Fleet Named Commander of 8th Army.

Lieutenant General James A. Van Fleet, who had been commanding the 2d Army at Fort Meade, Maryland, assumes command of 8th Army.

22 April. Rotation Plan Announced.

The Army announces a troop rotation policy based on a point system. Soldiers who accumulate a total of 36 points, based on length of service in Korea (service in combat zones is worth more than service in rear echelon areas) will be rotated back to the United States and discharged. The policy is controversial—many officers feel that the system weakens unit cohesion with its high turnover rate.

22 April. CCF Launches Fifth (Spring) Offensive.

Communist forces launch a massive offensive with nine armies and 250,000 troops against 8th Army. (Beginning of the CCF Spring Offensive 1951 Campaign—it ends 8 July). While forced to withdraw, 8th Army establishes a defensive line (the "No Name Line") around Seoul and halts the Communist drive, inflicting more than 70,000 enemy casualties in the process. American forces suffer 1,900 killed and wounded during nine days of fighting.

3 May. Soldier Killed in Vienna, Austria.

A military policeman from the 796th Military Police Battalion is killed by Soviet troops.

16 May. CCF Launches Sixth Offensive.

Twenty Communist divisions, totaling 175,000 soldiers, attack down the center of the Korean peninsula, hitting X Corps, the ROK III Corps, and the right flank of 8th Army. While driven back by the initial force of the onslaught, UN units halt the offensive after a week with the support of air power and massive amounts of artillery. Communist forces suffer an estimated 90,000 casualties, while American losses are 1,200 killed, wounded, and missing.

3–12 June. Operation Piledriver.

In the last large-scale UN offensive of the war, Van Fleet orders 8th Army north to attack the Iron Triangle just above the 38th Parallel to strengthen UN defensive lines. UN forces run into unexpectedly heavy resistance and fail to attain all of their objectives. Following the operation, both sides begin to settle into defensive lines, with the Iron Triangle becoming a virtual no man's land.

Right: *Employing General Ridgway's "active defense" strategy, multiple rocket launchers in support of the 40th Infantry Division sector light up the night sky on 26 November 1951. (National Archives)*

19 June. **Universal Military Training and Service Act. Washington, D.C.**
President Truman signs the Universal Military Training and Service Act, which extends Selective Service until 1 July 1955, lowers the draft age to 18, and extends the length of service from 21 to 24 months. The act also endorses the idea of universal military training but provides no funds or statutory requirement for UMT.

9 July. **UN Summer-Fall Offensive 1951 Campaign.**
The UN Summer-Fall Offensive Campaign opens—it ends on 27 November.

18 August–5 September. **Battle of Bloody Ridge.**
After several weeks of heavy fighting, the 2d Infantry Division and ROK units seize a series of hills known as Bloody Ridge at the southeastern apex of the Iron Triangle. UN forces suffer 2,700 casualties, mostly American. Communist losses are estimated at 15,000.

13 September–15 October. **Battle of Heartbreak Ridge.**
Following the capture of Bloody Ridge, the 2d Infantry Division, supported by ROK units and the attached French Battalion, seizes Heartbreak Ridge but suffers nearly 3,700 casualties in the process. Communist losses are estimated at 25,000. During the battles for Bloody and Heartbreak Ridges, UN artillery fires so many rounds in support of the operations that it creates an ammunition shortage in Korea. (The 2d Division's 15th Field Artillery Battalion sets a record by firing 14,425 rounds in a 24-hour period.)

1 October. **Integration of 8th Army.**
8th Army becomes fully integrated when the all-black 24th Infantry Regiment and 159th Field Artillery Battalion, both assigned to the 25th Infantry Division, are disbanded. They are replaced by the 14th Infantry Regiment and the 69th Field Artillery Battalion.

3–9 October. **Operation Commando.**
Five divisions from I Corps, including the 1st Cavalry Division and 3d and 25th Infantry Divisions, advance to secure Line Jamestown in the Old Baldy Area. American forces suffer more than 2,600 casualties, with most coming from the 1st Cavalry Division.

12 November. **Ridgway Orders Active Defense Strategy.**
General Ridgway orders Lieutenant General Van Fleet to assume an "active defense" in which UN forces will suspend large-scale offensive operations. Instead, UN forces will remain in static defensive positions, employing patrols, raids, ambushes, and other small unit actions. In addition, UN forces will be supported by air power and massive amounts of artillery.

28 November. **Opening of Second Korean Winter 1951–1952 Campaign.**
The Second Korean Winter Campaign Begins—it ends 30 April 1952.

5–29 December. **45th Infantry Division Arrives in Korea.**
The 45th Infantry Division, a National Guard unit, arrives in Korea and replaces the 1st Cavalry Division on the front lines. The 1st Cavalry redeploys to Japan to become part of the Far East Command reserve.

1952

January. Status of the Army.
As the second year of the Korean War approaches, the Army has grown to 20 divisions and 1,596,419 officers and enlisted men.

31 January. 40th Infantry Division Arrives in Korea.
The 40th Infantry Division, a National Guard unit, arrives in Korea and replaces the 24th Infantry Division on the front lines. The 5th Infantry Regiment, which had been assigned to the 24th, will remain in Korea with the 555th Field Artillery Battalion as an independent RCT. The rest of the division redeploys to Japan.

17 April. Enlistments Extended.
President Truman issues Executive Order 10345, which extends enlistments for nine months.

27 April. End of Occupation of Japan.
U.S. forces end the military occupation of Japan as a civilian government takes control. However, extensive rights are retained for U.S. bases in Japan, and the Ryukyus Islands remain under U.S. control.

1 May. Korea Summer–Fall 1952 Campaign Opens.
The Korea Summer–Fall 1952 Campaign, the eighth campaign of the Korean War, begins—it ends 30 November.

7 May–10 June. POW Uprising. Koje-do Island, South Korea.
CCF and NKPA prisoners initiate an uprising at the Koje-do POW Camp, quickly capturing the camp's commander, Brigadier General Francis Dodd. The standoff continues even after Dodd is released on 11 May. On 10 June, the uprising is finally suppressed when American troops, including elements of the 187th Airborne RCT, clash with the prisoners, killing or wounding 150. One American is killed in the fighting.

12 May. Mark Clark Appointed as Commander, UN Forces.
General Mark Clark replaces Ridgway as Commander-in-Chief, UN Command/Far East Command. Ridgway is reassigned to Europe to become Supreme Allied Commander.

19 May. Harrison Becomes Senior UN Negotiator.
Major General William K. Harrison, Jr., Deputy Commander, Eighth U.S. Army, is appointed as the senior delegate to the Panmunjom armistice talks. He begins a policy of declaring a recess in the negotiations when the North Koreans or Chinese stall with propaganda speeches.

11 June. First Special Forces Unit Activated. Fort Bragg, North Carolina.
The Army activates its first Special Forces unit, the 10th Special Forces Group.

26 June. Fighting on Old Baldy.
Heavy fighting breaks out on Old Baldy, a bare hill defended by elements of the 2d and 45th Infantry Divisions. Old Baldy will see sporadic fighting for much of the remainder of the war, with control of the hill changing hands several times.

9 July. Armed Forces Reserve Act of 1952.
Congress passes the Armed Forces Reserve Act of 1952, which reorganizes the nation's reserve components. The act also eliminates the Officers' Reserve Corps and Enlisted Reserve Corps, and renames the Organized Reserve Corps the Army Reserve.

14 October–5 November. Battle of Triangle Hill.
In response to a CCF attack on White Horse Hill, Van Fleet orders the 7th Infantry Division to assault Triangle Hill. The attack is led by the 31st Infantry Regiment and supported by 16 field artillery battalions and Air Force fighter-bombers. In 12 days of fierce combat, the 7th suffers 2,000 casualties and fails to take the hill; CCF losses are estimated at more than

Opposite: *General Maxwell Taylor became Army Chief of Staff in 1955, then was recalled to serve as Chairman of the Joint Chiefs seven years later. (Bjorn P. Egeli, Army Art Collection, NMUSA)*

Right: *With bayonets fixed, Army Rangers charge forward to meet the enemy. ("At the Cutting Edge of Battle, James Dietz)*

Below: *A GI uses an artillery observer scope to keep watch at the DMZ. (1st Cavalry Division)*

19,000. Efforts to capture Triangle Hill are called off by General Clark on 5 November.

4 November. Eisenhower Elected President.
General Eisenhower is elected President of the United States, the first professional military officer to win election since Ulysses S. Grant in 1868. In early December President-elect Eisenhower honors his campaign pledge to go to Korea and visits U.S. forces in the Korean theater.

1 December. Third Korean Winter 1952–1953 Campaign Opens.
The Third Korean Winter Campaign 1952–1953 Campaign begins—it ends 30 April 1953.

1953

January. **Status of the Army.**
With an end to the war in Korea in sight, the Army's numbers decrease slightly to 1,533,815, though the number of divisions remains the same.

20 January. **Eisenhower Inaugurated as President. Washington, D.C.**
Dwight D. Eisenhower is inaugurated as the 34th President and Commander-in-Chief.

2–20 February. **Army Provides Flood Relief. The Netherlands.**
Army forces in Europe take part in relief operations after the Netherlands is struck by massive flooding.

4 February. **Robert Ten Broeck Stevens Named Secretary of the Army. Washington, D.C.**
President Eisenhower appoints Robert Ten Broeck Stevens as the fourth Secretary of the Army.

10 February. **Maxwell D. Taylor Named 8th Army Commander.**
Lieutenant General Maxwell D. Taylor, who had been serving on the Army Staff, is named commander of 8th Army, replacing James A. Van Fleet.

23 March. **CCF Capture Old Baldy.**
Chinese forces take Old Baldy after a heavy artillery and mortar bombardment. The 31st Infantry Regiment, supported by the Colombian Battalion, launches several counterattacks on 24–25 March but fails to retake the hill. UN forces withdraw on 26

Above: *The U.S. Army's flag bears 175 approved streamers representing the campaigns and major engagements fought since the American Revolution. (Association of the U.S. Army)*

March. Lieutenant General Taylor does not consider Old Baldy essential to UN defenses and cancels all further efforts to retake it.

20 April–3 May. **Operation Little Switch.**
Beginning on 20 April, the UN and the Communists begin an exchange of sick and wounded POWs at Panmunjom. By 3 May, the UN has repatriated 6,670 Communist prisoners; Communist forces return 684 UN prisoners, including 149 Americans.

1 May. **Korea Summer 1953 Campaign Opens.**
The final campaign of the Korean War, Korean Summer 1953, begins—it ends 27 July.

25 May. **Army Fires Nuclear Artillery Shell. Frenchman's Flat, Nevada Test Site.**
The Army's Artillery Test Unit from Fort Sill, Oklahoma, fires the first nuclear shell from a specially designed 280mm cannon. The shell is fired 10,000 meters and detonates 160 meters above the ground with a yield of 15 kilotons. It is the only nuclear artillery shell actually fired by the Army.

10–18 June. **Battle for Outpost Harry.**
In one of their last major assaults of the war, the CCF 74th Division attacks Outpost Harry, defended by the 15th Infantry Regiment and 5th RCT. The two regiments successfully defend the outpost, inflicting 4,200 casualties while losing 550 killed and wounded.

6–10 July. **Battle of Pork Chop Hill.**
On 6 July the Chinese attack and gain a foothold on Pork Chop Hill, located along the eastern side of the Iron Triangle. The 7th Infantry Division, which defends the hill, makes several counterattacks, supported by massive artillery fire, but fails to dislodge the Chinese. On 10 July, General Taylor decides that holding Pork Chop Hill, the scene of sporadic heavy fighting since March, is not worth the casualties and orders it abandoned. American forces lose 232 killed, 805 wounded, and nine missing; CCF casualties are estimated at 6,500.

13–20 July. **Battle of the Kumsong River.**
In the last CCF offensive of the war, the 2d, 3d, 40th, and 45th Infantry Divisions, supported by the 187th Airborne RCT and artillery, repel an assault by six Chinese divisions. American casualties number 243 killed, 768 wounded, and 88 missing; CCF casualties are estimated in the thousands.

27 July. **Korean War Ends.**
After nearly two years of negotiations, the Korean War comes to a close with the signing of an armistice at Panmunjom by UN, Chinese, and Korean officials. In just over three years of war, the Army incurs the most casualties of the U.S. armed services—29,856 killed and missing, 77,596 wounded. The 2d Infantry Division suffers the heaviest casualties of all Army units—7,094 killed, 16,575 wounded. CCF and NKPA losses are estimated to run as high as 1.5 million. Civilian casualties for both North and South Korea are estimated at two million.

5 August–23 December. **Operation Big Switch. Panmunjom, Korea.**
In the second and final release of prisoners from the Korean War, 12,773 UNC POWs, including 3,597 Americans, are returned at Freedom Village. The UNC repatriates 75,823 Communist prisoners. Twenty-three Americans choose to remain with the Communists.

16 August. **Ridgway Becomes Army Chief of Staff.**
General Ridgway becomes the 19th Chief of Staff, USA, replacing General Joseph Lawton Collins. Ridgway will later call his tenure as Army chief "the toughest, most frustrating job of my whole career."

20 August. **Launch of Redstone Missile. White Sands Proving Ground, New Mexico.**
The Army conducts its first successful flight test of the Redstone missile, which is capable of carrying a nuclear warhead 200 miles.

10 December. **Marshall Awarded Nobel Peace Prize. Oslo, Norway.**
Retired General and former Army Chief of Staff George C. Marshall is awarded the Nobel Peace Prize for his efforts to bring about the economic recovery of Europe while serving as Secretary of State under President Truman. He is the first professional soldier to win the award.

1954

January. **Status of the Army.**
With the Korean War over, the Army's strength drops to 1,404,598 officers and enlisted men. The six National Guard Divisions federalized during the war will revert to state control in the coming months. Under the fiscally conservative Eisenhower administration, the Army's numbers will decrease steadily over the next few years.

1 April. **Army Activates First Helicopter Battalion. Fort Bragg, North Carolina.**
The Army's first helicopter battalion, the Transportation Battalion (Helicopter), is activated at Fort Bragg. Commanded by Major Robert Kolb, the battalion consists of three helicopter companies and one maintenance company.

30 May. **First Nike Ajax Site Becomes Operational. Fort Meade, Maryland.**
The first Nike Ajax surface-to-air missile site becomes operational at Fort Meade, Maryland, about halfway between Baltimore and Washington, D.C. Over the next several years, the Army will construct dozens of sites for the Nike Ajax, and the more advanced Nike Hercules, to guard the nation's major cities, industrial centers, and military installations.

1 June. **Honest John Batteries Activated.**
Eight artillery batteries are equipped with the Honest John rocket, the Army's first tactical nuclear weapon.

3 September. **Army Advisors Killed. Quemoy Island, Republic of China.**
Advisors Lieutenant Colonels Alfred Medendorp and Frank Lynn are killed when Communist Chinese forces shell Nationalist Chinese positions on Quemoy Island.

1955

January. **Status of the Army.**
With demobilization from the Korean War winding down, Army strength drops to 1,109,296 and 19 divisions.

1 February. **Continental Army Command Established.**
U.S. Army Continental Army Command (CONARC) replaces Army Field Forces as the principal agency for Army forces and activities in the continental United States. General John E. Dahlquist, commander of Army Field Forces, becomes commander, CONARC.

5 May–27 July. **Occupation of Europe Ends.**
Establishment of a stable government and entry into NATO brings U.S. occupation of West Germany to an end on 5 May. Berlin, however, surrounded by Soviet and East German units, remains an Army enclave. On 27 July, Army units begin their withdrawal from Austria.

Above: *Aidmen help a wounded infantryman down from Pork Chop Hill during heavy fighting there in 1953. (National Archives)*

30 June. **Taylor Named Army Chief of Staff.**
General Maxwell Taylor becomes the 20th Chief of Staff, USA, replacing General Ridgway, who retired after battling the Eisenhower administration about the decreased Army role in American defense posture. Like Ridgway, Taylor will come into conflict with many of the Eisenhower administration's decisions on defense policy.

21 July. **Brucker Appointed Secretary of the Army.**
DoD General Counsel Wilber M. Brucker is named the fifth Secretary of the Army.

17 August. **Civil Affairs Branch Established.**
The Army creates the Civil Affairs/Military Government Branch in the Army Reserve. It will be redesignated the Civil Affairs Branch in 1959.

6 October. **First Male Commissioned Army Nurse.**
Edward L.T. Lyon, a nurse anesthetist, becomes the first male to receive a commission in the Army Nurse Corps.

1 November. **Military Assistance Advisory Group Vietnam Formed.**
With the creation of the Republic of Vietnam, the United States establishes the Military Assistance Advisory Group Vietnam (MAAG-Vietnam) to provide military aid to the new nation. MAAG-Vietnam replaces MAAG-Indochina, which provided advisory support to France in Vietnam, Laos, and Cambodia. Lieutenant General Samuel T. Williams is named the first commander of MAAG-Vietnam.

1956

January. **Status of the Army.**
The Army's ranks stand at 1,025,778 officers and enlisted men (in 20 active divisions), a 10 percent drop from the year before.

1 February. **Army Ballistic Missile Agency Established. Redstone Arsenal, Alabama.**
The Army Ballistic Missile Agency is activated to oversee the development of Army ballistic missiles. By the end of the year, however, Secretary of Defense Charles Wilson has restricted the range of Army missiles to 200 miles.

12 June. **Army Adopts an Official Flag. Philadelphia, Pennsylvania.**
After 181 years of existence, and an executive order issued by President Eisenhower, the Army finally adopts a flag in a ceremony in Independence Hall.

2 August. **Last Union Civil War Veteran Dies. Duluth, Minnesota.**
Albert Woolson, who served as a drummer boy with the 1st Minnesota Heavy Artillery, dies at the age of 109. The last Confederate veteran, Walter Williams, will die in Texas on 19 December 1959.

14 August. **First Aerial Refueling of Helicopter. Fort Rucker, Alabama.**
The Army conducts the first aerial refueling of a helicopter when a fixed-wing tanker aircraft transfers fuel to an H-21 helicopter. Less than two weeks later, an Army H-21 helicopter, with a crew of five, makes the first nonstop transcontinental helicopter flight. With the aid of several aerial refuelings, the Army pilots make the 2,610-mile flight from San Diego to Washington, D.C., in 37 hours.

21 September. **First Pentomic Division Organized. Fort Campbell, Kentucky.**
The 101st Airborne Division is reorganized into the Army's first pentomic division. Designed for the nuclear battlefield, the pentomic division replaces the basic triangle organization of three infantry regiments for five battle groups, each slighter larger than a battalion. Eventually, the remainder of the Army's infantry and airborne divisions will be reorganized as pentomic divisions. The Army makes no organizational changes to its armored divisions.

23 October. **Army Troops Placed on Alert. Germany.**
In response to the Hungarian Uprising, the 6th Armored Cavalry Regiment is placed on alert status and deployed along the German border.

1 December. **Army Inactivates Last Mule Unit.**
On 1 December, the Army announces it will inactivate its last mule unit and replace it with a helicopter unit. Three days later, the Army declares it will discontinue the use of carrier pigeons.

January. **Status of the Army.**
At the beginning of President Eisenhower's second term, the Army's ranks have dropped to 997,994 officers and enlisted men in 19 divisions.

29 April. **First Army Nuclear Reactor Dedicated. Fort Belvoir, Virginia.**
Secretary of the Army Wilber M. Brucker dedicates the Army's first nuclear reactor at Fort Belvoir, Virginia. The Army Corps of Engineers will use it to train nuclear power plant operators. The reactor, known as SM1, is also the first nuclear reactor to provide power to an electrical grid in the United States.

1 May. **Army Adopts M-14 Rifle.**
The Army adopts the M-14 rifle, which uses the new standard NATO 7.62mm round and is capable of full or semi-automatic fire. It replaces the M-1 rifle, the Browning Automatic Rifle, and M-1A1 and M-2 carbines.

31 May. **Successful Launch of Jupiter Rocket. Cape Canaveral, Florida.**
An Army-developed Jupiter missile launched from Cape Canaveral flies more than 1,500 miles and reaches an altitude of 300 miles.

24 September. **Eisenhower Orders Troops to Little Rock, Arkansas.**
President Eisenhower orders Arkansas National Guard troops and units of the 101st Airborne Division to Little Rock to enforce the federally mandated integration of the city's Central High School.

1958

January. **Status of the Army.**
The size of the Army stands at 898,925 officers and enlisted men in 17 active divisions.

31 January. **Army Launches First U.S. Satellite. Cape Canaveral, Florida.**
Using a Jupiter-C rocket, the Army successfully places the *Explorer I* into orbit. On 26 March, the Army places a second satellite, the *Explorer III,* into orbit.

30 May. **Unknown Soldiers Buried. Arlington National Cemetery, Virginia.**
The Unknown Soldiers of World War II and the Korean War are buried at the Tomb of the Unknowns in Arlington National Cemetery.

19 July. **Army Forces in Lebanon.**
Task Force 201, comprising largely the 187th Battle Group, 24th Infantry Division, arrives in Beirut to support Marine forces in Operation Blue Bat, which is intended to thwart a civil war in Lebanon. One soldier is killed and another wounded (another four die in accidents) before U.S. forces are withdrawn in October.

1959

January. **Status of the Army.**
Additional budget restrictions further reduce the size of the Army. At the beginning of 1959, the Army ranks boast 861,964 officers and enlisted men in 16 active divisions, the lowest totals since 1950, just before the outbreak of war in Korea.

1 July. **Lyman L. Lemnitzer Appointed Chief of Staff.**
Vice Chief of Staff General Lyman L. Lemnizter is appointed the 21st Chief of Staff, replacing General Taylor.

8 July. **First American Fatalities in Vietnam.**
U.S. Army advisors Major Dale Buis and Master Sergeant Chester Ovnard are killed by a Viet Cong rocket attack on the American base at Bien Hoa.

16 October. **George Marshall Dies.**
General of the Army George C. Marshall dies in Walter Reed Army Hospital after a period of declining health.

Opposite: *(Left to right) World War II Victory Medal; Women's Army Corps Service Medal; Army Occupation Service Medal (for both Japan and Germany); and Korean Service Medal. (Quintet Publishing Ltd., London)*

Right: *In 1959, the Army placed its first production order for a new main battle tank, the M-60, with its impressive 105mm gun. (Army Art Collection, NMUSA)*

1960

January. **Status of the Army.**
During the final year of the Eisenhower administration, the size of the Army slightly increases to 873,078; the number of active divisions drops to 15.

25 January. **Hawk Intercept of a Ballistic Missile. White Sands Missile Range, New Mexico.**
An Army Hawk surface-to-air missile downs an Honest John in the first successful kill of a ballistic missile. The Hawk, designed to defend against low-flying aircraft, has just entered the Army inventory.

25 February. **Launch of Pershing Missile. White Sands Missile Range, New Mexico.**
The Army launches the first Pershing missile from a mobile launcher. The solid fuel, nuclear-capable Pershing is designed to replace the Redstone missile.

20 April. **M60 Main Battle Tank Goes Into Production.**
The M60 tank, armed with a 105mm main gun, goes into production. With numerous upgrades, the M60 will serve as the Army's main battle tank into the early 1980s.

1 October. **General George Decker Appointed Chief of Staff.**
General George Decker becomes 22nd Chief of Staff, replacing General Lyman L. Lemnizter, who is appointed Chairman, Joint Chiefs of Staff.

THE ARMY IN THE
VIETNAM ERA

1961–1975

THE ARMY IN THE VIETNAM ERA

1961–1975

Dale Andrade

DAVID LEWIS
©1992

Despite the Cold War climate following World War II, the 1960s were marked by a shift away from reliance on nuclear deterrence to an increasing capability of "flexible response" to worldwide threats. Secretary of Defense Robert S. McNamara moved the U.S. military away from its reliance on strategic deterrence and saw the Korean War experience as a model of limited conventional wars that would be the shape of future conflicts. The Army discontinued its "Pentomic" division organization and replaced it with the more flexible ROAD (Reorganization Objectives Army Division) concept. A ROAD division used maneuver battalions as its basic unit with three brigade headquarters to command them plus supporting units. Army manpower grew from 875,000 to nearly 1 million soldiers, and the number of divisions rose from 11 to 16, along with new airlift capabilities.

Although the Army's main focus continued to be on a conventional war in Europe, the Kennedy administration believed it likely that "small wars" would become more likely, an idea given increased credence by Soviet Premier Nikita Khrushchev, who in January 1961 stated that the Communists would fully support "wars of national liberation." Thus Kennedy also turned his attention to potential unconventional conflicts against guerrillas, which were cropping up in places like the Philippines, Malaya, and Indochina. The Army's nascent Special Forces were increased by 150 percent in the first two years of the administration, and their training was expanded to include all aspects of unconventional warfare.

Southeast Asia proved to be the first major test of the new American doctrine, and the Army that arrived in Vietnam was the most advanced in the world, utilizing devastating firepower and exceptional mobility. Armored personnel carriers and troop-carrying helicopters—including a brand-new airmobile unit, the 1st Cavalry Division—made it easier and faster for the American soldier to move into battle, while new weapons brought increasing lethality to bear on the enemy. In addition to improved artillery and machine guns, infantrymen were armed with M14, and later M16, rifles, which gave each soldier a full-automatic fire capability, and the M79 grenade launcher hurled grenades out to 350 yards, a vast improvement over hand-thrown grenades.

Despite its technological prowess, the war in Vietnam was like no other faced by American

soldiers. Although it was a classic insurgency, it was simultaneously a main force war, with more than 150,000 Communist soldiers organized into 160 regiments facing the U.S. Army as it entered the war in the summer and fall of 1965. Increasing infiltration of North Vietnamese units over the coming years would raise the total to around 340,000 by 1968. This dual dynamic—combined with restrictions imposed by Washington that forbade crossing the borders to destroy enemy sanctuaries—prompted General William C. Westmoreland, the commander of U.S. forces in Vietnam, to choose to tackle the main enemy forces first.

Within two years American forces had stabilized the situation in South Vietnam, but it was not enough to win the war. Westmoreland's decision neglected pacification and other counterinsurgency tactics, which he felt were best left to the South

Vietnamese Army. The result was a difficult war that did not end in victory for the United States.

Through it all, the U.S. Army fought well and adjusted to adversity. In his memoir, Colin Powell wrote that "I am proud of the way American soldiers answered the call in a war so poorly conceived, conducted, and explained by their country's leaders."

Pages 796–797: *Depicted is the 7th Squadron, 17th Cavalry Regiment, in Pleiku Province, Vietnam, conducting an air assault on 15 January 1969 to secure a downed helicopter and protect the crew. ("Leave No One Behind," Joe Kline)*

Above: *An artistic impression of American infantry fighting in the highlands of Vietnam. ("Pop Smoke," David S. Lewis, Collection of Amy and Wade Hooper)*

THE ARMY IN THE VIETNAM ERA

1961–1975

"In the final analysis, it is their war.
They are the ones who have to win it or lose it.
We can help them . . . but they have to win it, the people of Vietnam"

—President John F. Kennedy, 1963

1961

January. Status of the Army.

With only four months on the job, General Henry Decker serves as Chief of Staff as conflict in Laos dominates headlines. The 12 teams of U.S. Special Forces advisors, in Laos as "civilian" contractors since July 1959, are working under the auspices of the Program Evaluation Office (PEO). There are also Army advisors in South Vietnam. As the year begins 800 Army personnel are serving in Military Assistance Advisory Group (MAAG)-Vietnam commanded by Lieutenant General Lionel C. McGarr.

24 January. Stahr Becomes Secretary.

Elvis J. Stahr, Jr., is sworn in as the sixth Secretary of the Army. A Reserve officer with service in the China-Burma-India Theater during World War II, Stahr oversees a major Army reorganization, restructuring of divisions, and expansion of Special Forces during his 18 months in office.

28 January. Kennedy Approves Counterinsurgency Plan.

Newly inaugurated President John F. Kennedy approves a "counterinsurgency plan" that will give South Vietnam $28.4 million in military aid and increase the Army of the Republic of South Vietnam (ARVN) from 150,000 to 170,000.

April. White Star Teams Established. Laos.

MAAG-Laos is created with 48 mobile training teams named "White Star." The 430 soldiers, initially under the command of Lieutenant Colonel Arthur D. Simons, provide unit advisors as well as training camp cadre.

26–29 April. Plan to Send Troops.

As President Kennedy and the National Security Council meet to decide whether to send troops to Laos, Deputy Secretary of Defense Roswell L. Gilpatric raises the specter of a North Vietnamese invasion through Laos and recommends sending 3,200 military advisors, including 400 Special Forces.

11 May. More Special Forces.

President Kennedy issues National Security Action Memorandum No. 52 directing the Secretary of

Left: *Secretary of the Army Elvis Jacob Stahr, Jr. (Irving Resnikoff (pseudonym C. J. Fox, Jr.), Army Art Collection, NMUSA)*

ARMY BATTLE STREAMERS—1961–1975

Vietnam War
Vietnam Advisory, 1962–1965
Vietnam Defense, 1965
Vietnam Counteroffensive, 1965–1966
Vietnam Counteroffensive, Phase II, 1966–1967
Vietnam Counteroffensive, Phase III, 1967–1968
Tet Counteroffensive, 1968
Vietnam Counteroffensive, Phase IV, 1968
Tet 69/Vietnam Counteroffensive, 1969
Vietnam Summer-Fall, 1969

Vietnam Winter-Spring, 1970
Sanctuary Counteroffensive, 1970
Vietnam Counteroffensive, Phase VII, 1970–1971
Consolidation I, 1971
Consolidation II, 1971–1972
Vietnam Cease-Fire, 1972–1973

Dominican Republic
Dominican Republic, 1965–1966

Defense to examine "increasing the counterguerrilla resources" of the Army. He also approves sending 400 additional Special Forces soldiers and 100 more military advisors to South Vietnam.

9 June. **Building the South Vietnamese Army.**
South Vietnamese President Ngo Dinh Diem requests help in expanding his army by an additional 100,000 men—to a total strength of 270,000. President Kennedy agrees to finance a 30,000-man buildup, but postpones sending the military advisors needed to train them.

18 October. **No U.S. Troops Needed.**
General Maxwell D. Taylor, a former Army Chief of Staff and now the newly named Military Representative to the President, visits Saigon and is told by Diem that there is no need for U.S. combat troops, only military aid.

1 November. **CIDG Program Begun.**
The Central Intelligence Agency starts up the Civilian Irregular Defense Group (CIDG), organizing indigenous ethnic tribesmen, known by the French word *montagnard*, into paramilitary groups in an attempt to extend South Vietnamese government influence and deny the Communists access to the border regions. Camps are organized into three companies of 132 men each—three reconnaissance platoons, a heavy weapons section with two 105mm howitzers, and a political warfare section. Total authorized strength is 530 men. Many of the advisors are Army Special Forces.

1–3 November. **General Taylor Recommends Sending a Task Force.**
General Taylor urges the formation of a "U.S. military task force" of between 6,000 and 8,000 troops as "essential to reverse the present downward trend of events" in South Vietnam. On 3 November President Kennedy rejects the proposal.

11 December. **Helicopters Arrive.**
The ship USNS *Core* arrives in Saigon with 33 U.S. Army Vertol H-21C Shawnee helicopters and 400 air and ground crewmen. The helicopters and crews will ferry South Vietnamese troops into combat.

26 December. **First U.S. Army Soldier Captured.**
Spec. 4 George Fryett, a clerk at the MAAG office in Saigon, is captured while riding a bicycle on the outskirts of the city on his way to a swimming pool. The Viet Cong do not know what to do with Fryett and release him the following June.

31 December. **American Casualties.**
U.S. Army casualties in South Vietnam are 14 killed and wounded during the year.

1962

January. **Status of the Army.**
Authorized Army strength remains at 16 divisions. U.S. Advisory teams continue in both Laos and South Vietnam with limited success. American manpower in South Vietnam stands at 3,200, of which 2,100 are U.S. Army personnel. Only two months earlier the authorized strength was 948.

4 February. **First U.S. Helicopter Shot Down.**
A group of 15 Army helicopters ferrying South Vietnamese troops south of Saigon is hit by enemy fire and one is shot down, killing four U.S. crew members. It is the first U.S. helicopter lost to enemy fire since the war began.

Above: *CH-21C Shawnee helicopters and their crews return from an operation. These helicopters were deployed with American crews and support personnel in 1961 to provide the Army of the Republic of Vietnam with air mobility. (Center of Military History, U.S. Army)*

8 February. **MACV Established. Saigon.**
The U.S. Military Assistance Command, Vietnam (MACV) is established under the command of General Paul D. Harkins, but MAAG remains in place for another two years in order to avoid disrupting its chain of command. MACV is a unified command subordinated to the Commander-in-Chief, Pacific, in Honolulu with authority over all U.S. military personnel and operations in South Vietnam.

Opposite bottom: *Army Chief of Staff General Earl Wheeler (left) and General Paul D. Harkins, commander of the newly established Military Assistance Command Vietnam (MACV), meet in Saigon during 1961. (Center of Military History, U.S. Army)*

Right: *An American advisor wearing the Military Assistance Advisory Group (MAAG) shoulder-sleeve insignia of the early 1960s plans a mission with a South Vietnamese Army captain. (U.S. Army)*

15 March. First Campaign of the War Begins.
The date marks the start of the Vietnam Advisory Campaign, the first official campaign streamer of the war.

22 March. Pilot Pacification Project. Binh Duong Province.
Operation Sunrise, later known as the Strategic Hamlet Program, begins. American advisors help build a fortified village north of Saigon in an attempt to move villagers away from the Viet Cong. The program, which hopes to move 39 percent of the rural population into protected villages, is ultimately unsuccessful, largely because the civilians resent being forced to move.

23 March. First U.S. Army Unit Arrives.
The 39th Signal Battalion arrives in South Vietnam. It will assume responsibility for all communications support under the command of the U.S. Army Support Group, Vietnam.

9 April. Two American Soldiers Killed.
Two U.S. soldiers die in a Viet Cong ambush. Combat deaths are still a rare occurrence in Vietnam.

22 April. Mekong Delta Operation. Kien Phong Province.
Twenty-nine U.S. helicopters lift some 600 South Vietnamese troops to reinforce units already engaged in combat against Viet Cong units of battalion size or larger.

12 May. First Medevac Mission. Tuy Hoa.
The 57th Medical Detachment (Helicopter Ambulance) flies its first evacuation mission. The 57th Medical Detachment—the first helicopter medical evacuation unit in Vietnam—arrived in April. One year later the unit begins using the term "Dust Off"—named for the dirt and debris churned up by the helicopters—to describe medical evacuations. The Detachment will remain in action for the rest of the war, and medical evacuation helicopters will carry almost 900,000 U.S. and allied casualties from the battlefield.

1 July. Military Intelligence Branch Formed.
General Orders 58 establishes an Army Intelligence and Security Branch, which is renamed the Military Intelligence Branch in 1967. This is the birthday of the branch.

5 July. Vance Replaces Stahr as Secretary.
Cyrus R. Vance assumes duties as seventh Secretary of the Army. He continues the Army restructuring plans, supervises Army support to authorities during the civil rights conflicts and the Cuban missile crisis.

25 July. First Armed Helicopter Unit.
The Army forms the Utility Tactical Transport Company. It the first armed helicopter unit.

18 July. Largest Helicopter Lift to Date.
South Vietnamese troops engaging Viet Cong forces north of the capital are lifted into battle by 18 Marine,

12 Army, and 11 Vietnamese Air Force helicopters—the largest such operation so far.

21 September. 5th Special Forces Group Activated. Ft. Bragg, North Carolina.
The U.S. Army's 5th Special Forces Group, 1st Special Forces, is activated. President Kennedy is impressed with the Special Forces' counterinsurgency capabilities.

30 September–1 October. Army Troops Sent to Restore Order. Oxford, Mississippi.
The Mississippi National Guard is federalized by President Kennedy. Regular Army troops on alert in Memphis are flown to Oxford to restore order when rioting and gunfire breaks out at the University of Mississippi by individuals protesting integration of the school.

1 October. Wheeler Becomes Chief of Staff.
General Earle G. Wheeler replaces General Decker and becomes the 23d Chief of Staff of the Army.

Above: *In 1962 General Earl G. Wheeler (1908–1975) became the Army's 23rd Chief of Staff. (Lloyd B. Embry, Army Art Collection, NMUSA)*

Right: *Secretary of the Army Cyrus Roberts Vance was a strong proponent of airmobile operations. (George Augusta, Army Art Collection, NMUSA)*

12 October. Green Beret Approved for Special Forces
At the request of the Special Forces commander, Brigadier General William P. Yarborough, President Kennedy authorizes its soldiers to wear the green beret.

6 October. White Star Ends. Laos.
Following the declaration of neutrality by Laos in July, the operation winds down. The last Army Special Forces White Team departs on 6 October.

19 October. Operation Morning Star. Tay Ninh Province.
Five thousand South Vietnamese troops, ferried by U.S. helicopters, engage Viet Cong guerrillas northwest of Saigon where an increasing number of guerrillas try to threaten the capital.

22 October–1 November. Army Air Defense Units Deploy. Florida
As the Cuban missile crisis deepens, President Kennedy orders Army air defense units in the U.S. to deploy to the southern Florida coast. Battery B, 1st Automatic Weapons Battalion, 59th Artillery, is among the first. It is armed with obsolete 40mm Dusters. Close behind are two HAWK battalions and a NIKE-Hercules battalion that are sent to key locations. Air defense units will remain active in the state until 1979. Many other Army units are alerted for a possible invasion of Cuba, but within a few weeks are released.

Right: *A Hawk Missile site at a permanent installation. Early models of this missile were deployed to Florida to defend against a Soviet air attack during the 1962 Cuban missile crisis. ("Hawk Missiles, Okinawa," Al Crull, Army Art Collection, NMUSA)*

Below: *One legacy of John F. Kennedy's presidency was the enhancement of the Army's Special Forces who gained fame as the "Green Berets." ("U.S. Special Forces, 1963," Fredrick T. Chapman, Company of Military Historians)*

31 December. **Eightfold Increase in American Casualties.**
One hundred and nine Americans were killed or wounded during 1962, almost eight times as many as in 1961.

1963

January. **Status of the Army.**
Army strength in Vietnam stands at 7,900. Army aviation units have flown more than 50,000 sorties, almost half of them into combat. The enemy is organizing larger units and is increasingly willing to engage in pitched battles.

7 January. **Experimental Air Assault Division.**
The Army authorizes an experimental air assault division, which is organized in February at Fort Benning, Georgia. Named the 11th Air Assault Division, its first commander is Brigadier General Harry O. Kinnard. The division is organized into eight infantry battalions (another is added later) in three brigades, two assault helicopter battalions, an aviation battery of light observation helicopters, and companies of UH-1B gunships (armed with M60 door guns and rockets). The division forms the basis of the 1st Cavalry Division, which will deploy to Vietnam in 1965.

24–26 February. **U.S. Helicopters Can Shoot First.**
A U.S. soldier was killed when Viet Cong ground fire brings down three Army H-21 helicopters airlifting South Vietnamese troops. New orders allow American helicopters ferrying South Vietnamese troops to fire at enemy soldiers on sight.

11 April. **Soldiers from the 25th Division Arrive. Saigon.**
One hundred soldiers from the 25th Infantry Division arrive from Hawaii to serve as machine gunners aboard Army H-21 helicopters.

Left: *The 11th Air Assault Division (Test) proved the viability of the airmobile concept during Exercise "Air Assault II" in October–November 1964. (1st Cavalry Division)*

1 July. **CIDG Program Placed Under Special Forces.**
The CIA's CIDG program comes under control of the 5th Special Forces Group. In October the CIA also turns over responsibility for border surveillance. At its height in 1964–1965, total CIDG strength will reach 45,000 men in dozens of camps.

30 August. **Two Helicopter Pilots Killed. Tay Ninh Province.**
Two Army pilots are killed and three others injured when Viet Cong ground fire brings down their helicopter northwest of Saigon.

22 October. **Operation Big Lift. Republic of Germany.**
In a demonstration of rapid response deployment, the entire 2d Armored Division is flown from Fort Hood, Texas, to Germany in 65 hours. It is the first time an entire armored division has been air lifted.

1 November. **Special Forces Takes Over Border Surveillance.**
The CIA turns over surveillance responsibilities along the Laotian and Cambodian borders to the Special Forces. By the following June, 18 border camps have been established.

22 November. **Commander-in-Chief Assassinated. Dallas, Texas.**
President Kennedy is assassinated. Vice President Lyndon B. Johnson assumes the presidency with little knowledge of Kennedy's planning or intentions for the war in Vietnam.

1964

January. **Status of the Army.**
Casualties for the past year are 489 with 45 of them killed in action. Of 16,300 servicemen in Vietnam, 10,100 are Army.

Right: *A Special Forces–led commando team of native Montagnards sets off on a mission in Quang, Ngai Province. (Center of Military History, U.S. Army)*

Below: *The unofficial insignia of the MACV Studies and Observations Group (SOG).*

16 January. MACV Special Operations.

The Joint Chiefs approve the formation of the MACV Studies and Observations Group (SOG), a highly classified joint organization composed of personnel from all services and aimed at secret

operations into Laos, Cambodia, and North Vietnam. On the Army side, specially selected Special Forces soldiers help train teams of South Vietnamese agents for covert missions in North Vietnam, and, beginning in 1965 and 1966, will lead small teams into Laos and Cambodia. Operations into North Vietnam had been ongoing since 1961 under the CIA, but were transferred to the military in late 1963.

28 January. Ailes Becomes Secretary of the Army.

Stephen Ailes replaces Vance as Secretary of the Army. As the eighth secretary, Ailes is involved in several international negotiations, deals with riots in Panama and dispatches the first Army combat units to South Vietnam.

3 February. Bombing in Kontum. Central Highlands.

Viet Cong sappers raid a U.S. advisory compound killing one American. It is one of the first times that Americans are specifically targeted in their own bases.

9–15 April. Battles in the Mekong Delta.

In the heaviest fighting to date, Viet Cong main forces attack several targets in the Mekong Delta. More than 250 South Vietnamese soldiers and militiamen are killed, along with four Americans.

15 May. MACV Reorganized.

MACV officially absorbs the MAAG and is increased in manpower and responsibility.

15 May. Project Leaping Lena/Delta.
The Joint Chiefs of Staff approve a long-range reconnaissance program called Leaping Lena. Originally a CIA-run program, it is transferred to MACV in October and renamed Project Delta. U.S. Army Special Forces train Vietnamese CIDG and Vietnamese Special Forces for combined reconnaissance operations, initially forming six teams of two Americans and eight Vietnamese. The teams operate throughout the country. Before deactivation on 31 July 1970, Project Delta gathers intelligence on more than 70 North Vietnamese units, locates several infiltration routes, and captures valuable documents.

20 June. Change of Command at MACV.
General Westmoreland replaces General Harkins as MACV commander.

3 July. Johnson Becomes New Chief of Staff.
General Harold K. Johnson assumes his duties as the 24th Chief of Staff of the Army. A survivor of the Bataan Death March and prisoner of the Japanese during World War II, Johnson had thought his military career was over when he was released.

Above: *A survivor of the Bataan Death March, General Harold K. Johnson became Army Chief of Staff in 1964. (Francis H. Beaugureau, Army Art Collection, NMUSA)*

Right: *Secretary of the Army Stephen Ailes. (Irving Resnikoff (pseudonym C.J. Fox, Jr.), Army Art Collection, NMUSA)*

4 July. Special Forces Camp Overrun. Central Highlands.
Viet Cong guerrillas overrun a Special Forces camp at Polei Krong killing 41 South Vietnamese soldiers. Two American Special Forces men are wounded.

6 July. Special Forces Camp Attacked. Nam Dong.
Captain Roger Donlon leads the eleven men of Detachment A-726 and their Vietnamese troops in the defense of their Central Highlands camp against a Viet Cong battalion.

27 July. Five Thousand More U.S. Troops for Vietnam.
The U.S. government announces that it will send 5,000 troops to Vietnam.

2 August. Tonkin Gulf Alert.
U.S. forces throughout Asia are placed on full alert after North Vietnamese gunboats attack the U.S. Navy destroyer *Maddox* in the Gulf of Tonkin.

21–28 September. Montagnard Revolt. Central Highlands.
Montagnard tribesmen revolt and demand autonomy from the South Vietnamese. Some 500 tribesmen seize five Special Forces camps in Darlac Province, killing 34 South Vietnamese and taking Vietnamese and Americans hostage. Special Forces at one camp prevent a massacre of South Vietnamese and invoke

Right: *Captain Roger Donlon led the defense of his Special Forces base camp on 6 July 1964 against a Viet Cong battalion. (John Witt, Army Art Collection, NMUSA)*

the close bond between the Montagnard and Americans. The rebels give in and the crisis is defused.

1 October. 5th Special Forces Group Arrives.
The 5th Special Forces Group officially establishes its headquarters. Many teams are understaffed, however, and duty tours are extended from six months to one year.

13 October. More Helicopters to South Vietnam.
The Army announces that it will send a third helicopter company to the Mekong Delta.

1 November. Attack at Bien Hoa.
Viet Cong guerrillas sneak into the perimeter of the U.S. air base at Bien Hoa, 12 miles northeast of Saigon, and launch a mortar attack, destroying or damaging 13 aircraft and killing four Americans and two South Vietnamese.

4 December. Viet Cong Offensive. Binh Gia.
Viet Cong units converge southeast of Saigon and begin a series of attacks that culminate at month's end in the defeat of South Vietnamese forces. Only after three additional battalions of marines and airborne troops are brought in are the Viet Cong driven off, but in the end more that 500 South Vietnamese are wounded or killed, and five American advisors are lost.

17 December. **First Medal of Honor Awarded.**
Captain Roger A. Donlon, a Special Forces officer, is awarded the first Vietnam War Congressional Medal of Honor for gallantry during the attack on his base camp in July.

23 December. **First Use of Riot Control Agents in Vietnam. An Xuyen Province.**
During an attempt to rescue American prisoners held by the Viet Cong in the Mekong Delta, Army advisors use CS riot control agents (a form of tear gas), but the mission turns up empty. In February, it becomes official MACV policy to allow advisors to use CS gas in self-defense, and kits containing gas masks and CS grenades are issued. Gas is used in limited situations throughout the war, especially against enemy tunnel complexes.

1965

January. **Status of the Army.**
The South Vietnamese Army seems incapable of staving off defeat. American troops are badly needed, but there are only 23,300 U.S. military personnel in country, 14,700 of them from the Army. During 1964, North Vietnam began sending troops down the Ho Chi Minh Trail, an event that persuades MACV that more must be done to halt Communist gains.

ORIGINS OF AIR ASSAULT WARFARE

Major General James M. Gavin's perception of military failures of armored cavalry in the Korean War started it all. In an influential 1954 article in *Harper's Magazine*, "Cavalry—And I Don't Mean Horses," Gavin wrote that armor units, even if called cavalry, were too heavy and road-bound to be so considered. On numerous occasions in Korea the Army had suffered because it lacked what true cavalry could provide. Gavin proposed to regain battlefield mobility and the mobility differential (the difference between cavalry's mobility and that of other land forces) by introducing an air cavalry element. Although he did not specify that the essential vehicle to achieve this goal was the helicopter, it turned out that no other would do.

Critical work to transform Gavin's concept into reality began at Fort Rucker in 1955. Over several years, a group under Brigadier General Carl I. Hutton proved the helicopter could effectively function as a weapons platform and developed tactical concepts for air assault warfare. In an inspired piece of conceptualizing, Colonel Jay D. Vanderpool saw a helicopter air assault organization as analogous to the Duke of Wellington's cavalry. With the horse and the helicopter as rough tactical equivalents, he saw light cavalry as armed reconnaissance helicopters, the dragoons as helicopter-borne infantry, and the horse artillery as aerial rocket artillery. In preliminary tests, this all seemed to work, adding a new dimension—vertical—to traditional attack and maneuver.

A new powerful helicopter, the UH-1, and a new Secretary of Defense, Robert McNamara, who was willing to push the staid Army establishment, gave birth to more serious but still limited tests in 1962. The sweeping conclusions that the Army should adopt the airmobile concept and create five air assault divisions to replace five conventional ones proved too radical. Instead, Secretary McNamara approved the creation of the 11th Air Assault Division (Test) to further evaluate the potential of a division that had exchanged hundreds of trucks for hundreds of helicopters. Throughout 1963 and 1964 the 11th Air Assault carried out numerous experimental exercises, culminating in Air Assault II from 12 October to 14 November 1964, when 35,000 soldiers maneuvered in four million acres of North Carolina and South Carolina countryside. Although emphasizing the

offensive, Air Assault II also included defensive actions and withdrawals. For example, a heliborne unit facing a superior force could easily slip away or, more aggressively, leapfrog over the opposition to concentrate and attack from the rear or the flanks. The ability to defy, in Major General Harry Kinnard's famous phrase, "the tyranny of terrain," made it easy to navigate difficult land barriers. In scenario after scenario, the opposing 82d Airborne Division found itself surprised, out-maneuvered, overwhelmed, and defeated. Vertical envelopment now became an exciting reality. The test director concluded that "the significant question is not whether we can afford such organizations, but whether this nation . . . can afford *not* to have them." After that, the unit's acceptance into the force structure of the Army came easy.

On 15 June 1965, McNamara approved the addition of an air assault division to the Army and on 1 July, the 11th Air Assault Division (Test) was redesignated the 1st Cavalry Division (Airmobile). Kinnard, the division's first commander, believed that the Vietnam War allowed the new division to become a reality. That American troops would have to fight in the almost roadless yet strategically significant central highlands of South Vietnam required a uniquely mobile unit. The era of air assault warfare had begun.

—*John M. Carland*

Above: *Airborne pioneer General James Gavin championed the use of helicopters for the Army. ("Instant Support," Burdell Moody, Army Art Collection, NMUSA)*

Right: *A first sergeant inspects men from one of the companies of the 82d Airborne Division, a unit that provided a ready reaction force capable of deployment on short notice. (Center of Military History, U.S. Army)*

Below: *A paratrooper from the 82d Airborne Division stands guard while fellow soldiers distribute food during the 1965 expedition to the Dominican Republic. (National Archives)*

7 February. **Viet Cong Target Americans. Central Highlands.**
Viet Cong guerrillas attack a helicopter base at Camp Holloway and blow up the barracks of U.S. military advisors at Pleiku, killing eight and wounding 126. President Johnson orders retaliatory air strikes against North Vietnam.

10 February. **Terrorist Bombing. Qui Nhon.**
Viet Cong guerrillas blow up an American barracks killing 23 military personnel.

22 February. **Protecting Danang.**
General Westmoreland asks for two battalions of Marines to protect the coastal city of Danang in northern South Vietnam. This is the first step in the American buildup, but it is not universally accepted. The U.S. ambassador to South Vietnam, Maxwell Taylor, argues this will widen the war and lull the South Vietnamese into thinking that Americans will fight their war for them. However, the Joint Chiefs agree with Westmoreland, and on 26 February the request is approved.

8 March. **Army Welcomes the Marines. Danang.**
The 9th Marine Expeditionary Brigade lands and is greeted by girls carrying flowers—and four U.S. Army soldiers carrying signs that read "Welcome Gallant Marines."

24 March. **Military Police Arrive.**
The 716th Military Police Battalion deploys to Saigon, the first Army unit to arrive after the buildup decision. Units are immediately sent to each of South Vietnam's four corps tactical zones.

2–5 April. **American Advisors Killed. Mekong Delta.**
Three days of combat take a heavy toll on the Viet Cong with only light South Vietnamese casualties, but six American advisors are killed.

30 April–September. **Intervention in Dominican Republic.**
Special Forces and elements of the 82nd Airborne Division are sent to the Dominican Republic at the request of its new government when fighting breaks out with supporters of the former leader, Juan Bosch. Troops depart in September when a provisional government is installed.

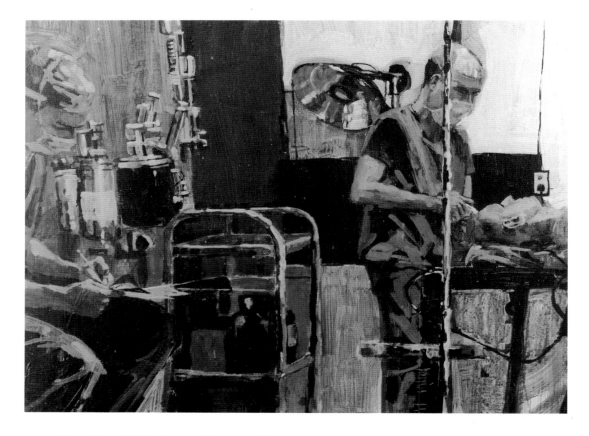

3–12 May. **First U.S. Army Combat Unit Arrives.**
The 173d Airborne Brigade deploys from Okinawa. Some the soldiers are assigned to Bien Hoa northeast of Saigon, and the remainder to Vung Tau, southeast of the capital. The 3,500-man force includes the 3d Battalion, 319th Artillery, the first U.S. artillery unit in South Vietnam.

10 May. **Main Force Battles Continue. Phuoc Long Province.**
The equivalents of two Viet Cong regiments overrun Song Be and hold it for most of the day. Five U.S. Army advisors and 48 South Vietnamese soldiers are killed.

7 June. **Westmoreland Asks for More Troops.**
General Westmoreland requests 44 battalions. When called to justify his request, Westmoreland argues that the increasing number of enemy main force attacks— and the mounting totals of North Vietnamese troops—demand a "substantial and hard-hitting offensive capability on the ground to convince the VC that they cannot win."

9–12 June. **Battle of Dong Xoai. Phuoc Long Province.**
Late on the night of 9 June, 1,500 Viet Cong attack a new Special Forces camp at Dong Xoai in northern III Corps. A CIDG force of Montagnard tribesmen and 24 Special Forces advisors push back four heavy assaults and hold out until morning. A South Vietnamese Ranger battalion sent as reinforcement is

ambushed and scattered. Air strikes keep the Viet Cong at bay and the exhausted Americans are finally evacuated. In the end eight Special Forces soldiers die in the fighting. Second Lieutenant Charles Q. Williams, the executive officer, is later awarded the Medal of Honor.

26 June. **Final Authority to Commit U.S. Troops to Battle.**
General Westmoreland receives final authority to commit U.S. troops to battle whenever he deems it necessary. The enclave strategy is no longer discussed.

2 July. **New Secretary of the Army Takes Office.**
The ninth Secretary of the Army, Stanley R. Resor, is sworn in by President Johnson. Resor is a combat veteran of World War II and has been Under Secretary. He oversees the commitment of major Army forces to Vietnam, the shift to Vietnamization, and planning for the first withdrawals of U.S. troops.

24 July. **Advances in Battlefield Medicine Saves Lives.**
The Pentagon reports that the number of Americans wounded in action since 1961 outnumbers the number killed by a ratio of 5-to-1, the highest ratio of any American war.

29 July. **Brigade of the 101st Airborne Division Arrives.**
The 1st Brigade, 101st Airborne Division, temporarily commanded by Colonel Joseph D. Mitchell, arrives in II Corps where it is to secure the coastal province of

Right: *A squad from the 1st Infantry Division (Big Red One) dismount from an M113 armored personnel carrier north of Saigon during October 1965. Note the heavy M-14 rifle and nonsubdued insignia still were in use. (Center of Military History, U.S. Army)*

Below: *Secretary of the Army Stanley Rogers Resor. (George Augusta, Army Art Collection, NMUSA)*

Phu Yen. General Westmoreland and Ambassador Taylor—both former commanders of the division—are present for a demonstration parachute jump.

2–11 August. **Fighting in the Central Highlands. Duc Co.**
A Special Forces camp only a few miles from the Cambodian border is attacked by 3,000 Viet Cong. South Vietnamese units bolster the defenses, but it is not until troops from the 173d Airborne Brigade arrive that the assault is turned back.

3 August. **Combat Dogs.**
Army Military Police units begin deploying sentry dogs, a program that dates back to 1961 when American instructors began training South Vietnamese to use dogs for combat scouting and sentry duty. The 25th Infantry Division employs a scout dog platoon near Cu Chi to sniff out tunnels and explosives, and the following year the Army forms the 212th Military Police Sentry Company (Sentry Dog), to be followed over the next two years by two additional sentry dog companies. By war's end the Army will have trained and deployed 2,220 dogs in sentry, scouting, and mine detection.

11 September. **1st Cavalry (Airmobile) Division Deploys. An Khe.**
The 1st Cavalry Division (Airmobile) arrives and establishes its headquarters in central II Corps. It is the first full U.S. Army division to deploy. The unit represents the beginning of a new battlefield concept—the airmobile division—that relies on helicopters for mobility.

20 September. **Project Shining Brass.**
The Joint Chiefs of Staff authorize Project Shining Brass, highly classified cross-border operations into Laos to conduct reconnaissance and sabotage missions along the Ho Chi Minh Trail. Shining Brass teams usually consist of three American Special Forces soldiers and nine Montagnard civilians controlled by MACVSOG. The project will be renamed Prairie Fire in 1968. Between 1965 and 1970 MACVSOG launches more than 1,200 missions into Laos.

2 October. The "Big Red One" Arrives. Bien Hoa.
The 1st Infantry Division arrives outside Saigon. The division will take up position north in III Corps as a barrier against Communist infiltration.

5 October. Debate Over Tear Gas.
After much debate the Johnson administration authorizes the use of tear gas. The decision came after press reports revealed U.S. troops were using smoke spread from crop dusters in an attempt to ferret out Viet Cong. The smoke was ineffective, however, and MACV advocates the use of tear gas.

10–14 October. 1st Cavalry Division's First Major Operation. Central Highlands.
The division joins South Vietnamese Marines in a major operation aimed at enemy troops near An Khe. Although poor coordination allows the North Vietnamese to escape, the allies manage to reopen the highway running from the coast to the city of Pleiku.

19–27 October. Communist Assault at Plei Me. Central Highlands.
The North Vietnamese attack the Special Forces camp at Plei Me for more than a week until South Vietnamese reinforcements arrive. Units from the 1st

Above: *There was bloody close-in fighting during the November 1965 Battle of LZ X-RAY. ("Ia Drang," David S. Lewis, 1st Cavalry Division Museum)*

Cavalry Division move west of the camp to intercept the enemy as he flees toward Cambodia.

14–20 November. Battle of LZ X-Ray. Pleiku Province.
In an attempt to gain control of the Cambodian border and harry the North Vietnamese, General Westmoreland sends the 1st Cavalry Division deep into enemy strongholds. Waiting are some 2,000 North Vietnamese regulars from the 66th Regiment, along with part of the 33d Regiment. On 14 November, 1st Battalion, 7th Cavalry, commanded by Lieutenant Colonel Harold G. Moore, air assaults into the Ia Drang Valley. The landing zone—dubbed X-Ray—appears to be unoccupied, but as the first helicopters land they are engaged by elements of the 66th Regiment. During intense fighting, one platoon from Company D is cut off and holds out against almost 200 North Vietnamese for more than 24 hours before being rescued. As artillery and air strikes hold off the enemy, elements of the 2d Battalion reinforce the beleaguered Americans. The following day the 2d Battalion, 5th Cavalry, joins the fight. The enemy finally breaks contact and flees across the border into Cambodia. The battle is the first major engagement between U.S. and North Vietnamese troops.

15 November. Field Forces Established. Nha Trang.
MACV establishes Field Force, Vietnam (FFV), a provisional headquarters for the II Corps. The field force concept is adopted instead of a normal corps headquarters because it will be operating side by side

EYEWITNESS: BATTLE OF LZ X-RAY

On 14 November 1965 the 1st Battalion, 7th Cavalry, under the command of Lieutenant Colonel Harold G. Moore, launched the first large-scale airmobile operation of the Vietnam War. Landing near the Chu Pong massif in the Ia Drang Valley, Moore's 450-man battalion was immediately attacked by a North Vietnamese Army division totaling some 2,000 men. Specialist 4 Bill Beck, Alpha Company, 1st Battalion, described the fighting.

"We moved toward the creek bed after chow. Suddenly (gun)fire was everywhere and Jerry Kirsch, three yards directly in front of me, got hit with machine-gun fire and dropped screaming, rolling on his back, yelling for his mother. I jumped to the left for cover, beside a soldier on the ground . . . He had a small hole in his forehead and he was dead.

"I jumped up as fast as I jumped down and ran forward toward Adams. We were in the open about 30 yards left of the creek bed, moving parallel to it toward Chu Pong. Nobody told us how far to go, so we kept moving. Adams, firing from the hip, blew away an NVA aiming his AK at us through the fork of a tree.

"As I was chasing after Adams, above the noise of automatic fire someone yelled 'Grenade!' and right in front of me, less than two yards away, one of those wooden-handled potato-masher grenades rolled to a stop. I started to go to ground, my knees bent; then came an explosion and flash of bright-white light. I never did hit the ground and continued to move, carrying my boxes of M-60 ammo.

"On the right, 20 yards away, was an anthill with a clump of trees on it, just outside the creek bed.

American GIs were on one side and two NVA soldiers were on the other side, not five yards away from each other. I don't think our men could see the enemy. I yelled at the top of my lungs but nobody could hear me because of the overall noise of the battle. It was deafening.

"All this time I had been jumping, dodging, hitting the dirt, and moving forward with Adams. Now I pulled my .45 and fired the entire clip of seven rounds at the left side of that anthill and both of the enemy dropped. Adams called for ammo, and I moved up with him beside a little tree. We were now the forward most position. I was feeding belt after belt of 7.62mm ammunition into the gun. We were prone and he was firing in front and to the right.

"I would spot movement to the front, point where, and Adams did the firing. This went on for several attacks. The enemy were zeroed in on Russ and me, their bullets hitting the tree trunk, the dirt around us, and crackling over our heads. Russ stopped those assaults and we started looking for our ammo bearer. He was gone. We were soaked with sweat and the sun was very hot as we lay in the brown grass, in the open with really no cover but the grass.

"Suddenly the M-60 jammed. We were being assaulted and I could see the enemy 25 yards out . . . Lying prone I opened the feed cover, flipped the gun over and hit it on the ground. It jarred the shells loose. Debris from the ground had caught in the ammo belt when Adams was hit. I flipped it right side up, slapped the ammo belt back in, slammed the feed cover closed, and began firing. It seemed like a lifetime, but wasn't more than five or ten seconds . . . I saw more movement to the front and right. I started firing again.

"There was no one on my left for a long time. I don't know what the hell's happening. I'm out there by myself. I'm only a twenty-year-old kid. I don't know what's going on. I followed Russell Adams; I'm his assistant gunner so I go where he goes. That's how I got up there."

—*Vince Hawkins*

Above: *Troopers of the 1st Battalion, 7th Cavalry, 1st Cavalry Division, fought a desperate battle for survival at Landing Zone X-RAY. (National Archives)*

with the South Vietnamese corps zones, which would cause confusion. Three field forces will eventually be established: I and II Field Forces (which operate in II and III Corps respectively) on 15 March 1966, and XXIV Corps (which was a slightly different structure under the command of III Marine Amphibious Force) on 15 August 1968.

17 November. Disaster at Landing Zone Albany. Ia Drang.

As the 1st Cavalry Division continues to chase the North Vietnamese, the 2d Battalion, 7th Cavalry, commanded by Lieutenant Colonel Robert McDade, leaves Landing Zone X-Ray and marches toward Landing Zone Albany, two miles to the northeast. Strung out and complacent, the battalion walks into a hasty ambush set by the North Vietnamese. The Americans are nearly overrun, but airstrikes and timely reinforcement by a company from the 1st Battalion, 5th Cavalry, save the day. Casualties are heavy: the 2d Battalion suffers 276 killed and wounded—60 percent of its force—while the North Vietnamese lose an estimated 400 dead.

27 November–December. Troop Strength Must Be Increased.

The year saw the buildup of the Army in Vietnam from 15,000 to 116,800 and a dramatic shift from an advisory effort to a direct combat role. The Army suffered 898 killed in action—up from 118 the previous year—the single largest annual percentage increase of

the entire war. The Defense Department informs the White House that General Westmoreland will need 400,000 men in order to pursue his strategy of seeking out and destroying the enemy.

1966

January. Status of the Army.

General Westmoreland plans the continuation of his strategy of finding and destroying enemy units before they can mass and attack populated areas. The North Vietnamese have sent increasing numbers of troops to the south, changing the conflict from primarily a guerrilla war to one with a greater emphasis on main forces. Although the emphasis is on American troops, the advisory effort with the South Vietnamese military also continues to grow.

28 January–6 March. Masher/White Wing. Binh Dinh Province.

In the war's first major "search and destroy" operation, Colonel Hal Moore's 3d Brigade, 1st Cavalry Division, along with a South Vietnamese division, an airborne brigade, and a South Korean division, moves into the Bong Son Plain, home of a North Vietnamese division and various Viet Cong main force units. On 4 February, at the White House's insistence, the operation name is changed from Masher to White Wing because of fears of adverse public opinion. White Wing ends 6 March with mixed results.

Although the North Vietnamese suffer some 1,300 dead, the enemy maintains their hold on much of the province.

16 March. **Special Forces Camps Fall. A Shau Valley**
The last of three Special Forces camps located in the valley are captured by the North Vietnamese.

28 March. **"Tropic Lightning" Comes to Vietnam. Cu Chi.**
The 25th Infantry Division arrives northwest of Saigon to help the 1st Infantry Division block infiltration across the Cambodian border. The division's 3d Brigade deployed the previous December to the Central Highlands, but now joins the rest of the division.

11–12 April. **1st Infantry Division Company Mauled.**
The 1st Infantry Division commanded by Major General William E. DePuy, moves into previously unmolested Viet Cong base areas in III Corps. Not all goes well, however. During Operation Abilene a company from 2d Battalion, 16th Infantry, finds itself surrounded by the Viet Cong 40 miles east of Saigon, and is badly mauled. The company loses 35 men killed and 71 wounded.

17 April–9 June. **Operation Lexington.**
In Operation Lexington III General DePuy sends the 1st Battalion, 18th Infantry, into the Rung Sat Special Zone, a tangled swamp southeast of Saigon that has long been a Viet Cong hideout. Hip-deep mud slows movement and the watery environment makes it necessary to rotate soldiers out every two days to prevent foot rot. Operation Lexington III fails to find many Viet Cong, and on 9 June DePuy recalls the battalion.

May. **Experimental Night Vision. Mekong Delta.**
Five UH-1C helicopter gunships equipped with low-light-level television cameras deploy to test the use of TV as a night-vision and target-detection aid. They achieve only limited success. However, the concept leads to more experimentation and the development in 1969 of more sophisticated night vision devices.

10 May–30 July. **Operation Paul Revere. Central Highlands.**
The 3d Brigade, 25th Infantry Division, and the 2d Brigade, 1st Cavalry Division, team up in a series of operations called Paul Revere I through IV.

Right: *A U.S. Air Force Phantom drops napalm in support of ground troops during combat in Southeast Asia. ("Phantom Strike," David S. Lewis)*

25 May. Aviation Management.
The 1st Aviation Brigade is activated to manage the increasingly large helicopter assets in South Vietnam. At its height in 1969 and 1970 the brigade will control more than 3,500 helicopters and 600 fixed wing aircraft.

2–20 June. Screaming Eagles in the Highlands. Kontum Province.
The new commander of the 1st Brigade, 101st Airborne Division, General Willard Pearson, begins Operation Hawthorne along the border near Dak To. In a classic spoiling attack, Lieutenant Colonel David H. Hackworth's 1st Battalion, 327th Infantry, and South Vietnamese troops from 22d Division, defeat the enemy and rescue a hilltop Special Forces position. Hackworth pursues the fleeing enemy, but has one company badly mauled when it runs into a North Vietnamese base camp. On 7 June the 2d Battalion, 502d Infantry, is sent in. North Vietnamese attacks against U.S. hilltop positions are repulsed, but on 9 June, Company C, commanded by Captain William Carpenter, is in danger of being overrun by the enemy. Carpenter calls in a napalm strike on his own position, burning friend and foe alike, but the North Vietnamese attack is stopped. Carpenter's men suffer 6 killed and 25 wounded. Operation Hawthorne is

Above: *In 1966 William O. Woolridge became the first Sergeant Major of the Army. (Center of Military History, U.S. Army)*

Right: *Military Police performed security checks and were frequent Viet Cong targets. ("Road Check," William F. Flaherty, Army Art Collection, NMUSA)*

reinforced by the 1st Cavalry Division's 1st Battalion, 5th Cavalry, and one company from the 101st Airborne Division's 2d Battalion, 327th Infantry. By 20 June the North Vietnamese have withdrawn.

2 June–13 July. Operation El Paso II. Binh Long Province.
General DePuy pushes the 1st Infantry Division to seek out the Viet Cong north and west of Saigon. On 8 June, elements of the division find a Viet Cong regiment near the Cambodian border and crush it. Other actions follow, and by 13 July almost 1,000 Viet Cong have died, while the Americans lose 200 dead and wounded.

11 July. First Sergeant Major of the Army Sworn In.
Sergeant Major William O. Woolridge is sworn in as the first Sergeant Major of the Army. The position was created by General Orders No. 29, dated 4 July 1966. Woolridge has over 25 years service including two wars and been decorated with two Silver Stars. The tenure of the individual in the position is the same as that of the Chief of Staff he serves.

26 August. 196th Infantry Brigade Deploys.
The 196th Infantry Brigade (Light) is rushed to Vietnam where it takes up operations northwest of Saigon.

8 September. **Blackhorse and MPs Arrive. Bien Hoa.**
The 11th Armored Cavalry Regiment (The
Blackhorse) arrives north of Saigon. As an
independent unit, the Blackhorse will operate both
alone and attached to other units throughout the war.
The regiment has 51 M48A3 tanks, 296 M113
personnel carriers, 18 155mm self-propelled howitzers,
9 M132 flamethrower vehicles, and 48 helicopters. The
same month, the 18th Military Police Brigade arrives.
It will secure the exterior of the U.S. Embassy, patrol
roads, and escort convoys.

13 September–12 February. **Operation Thayer. Binh
Dinh Province.**
The 1st Air Cavalry Division continues air assaults into
the province with the largest air assault to date. More
than 120 helicopters land five battalions near the Kim
Son Valley trying to trap a North Vietnamese regiment,
but most of the enemy slips away. The operation
continues as Thayer II with some of the heaviest
fighting on 27 December when the North Vietnamese
22d Regiment attacks half-strength Company C, 1st
Battalion, 12th Cavalry, at Landing Zone Bird. The
attackers creep to the perimeter undetected, then assault
with fixed bayonets. Battery B, 2d Batalion, 19th
Artillery, helps save the position by firing new "Beehive"
rounds into the attackers as they close to within 15 feet.

25 September. **4th Infantry Division Arrives. Central
Highlands.**
The 4th Infantry Division arrives at Pleiku. One
brigade, including the division's armor component, is
sent south to III Corps where it will temporarily

Above: *As the war progressed, new uniforms and
equipment suited to jungle warfare were introduced.("The
American Soldier, 1965," H. Charles McBarron, Army Art
Collection, NMUSA)*

Left: *An American advisor and a Vietnamese captain of
the ARVN take a break to share a C-Ration while in the
field with a battalion of the 47th Regiment, 22d ARVN
Division, near Tuy Hoa. (Collection of Ray Bluhm, Jr.)*

reinforce units around Saigon. It eventually becomes
part of the 25th Infantry Division, which in turn will
give up one of its brigades to the 4th Infantry Division.

14 September–3 November. **196th Brigade in Action.
Northwest of Saigon.**
The newly arrived 196th Infantry Brigade, under the
operational control of the 25th Infantry Division,
begins a series of patrols to test the unit in Operation
Attleboro. The target is the fringes of the Michelin
rubber plantation. Only light resistance is expected.
There is little contact for a month, but on 3
November, Major Guy S. Meloy's 1st Battalion, 27th
Infantry, runs headlong into a Viet Cong division near

the town of Dau Tieng. Over a 30-hour period, Meloy's men fight off six major enemy assaults. The battle prompts expansion of the operation into a full-blown, corps-level affair.

2 November. **Attack in the DMZ. South Korea.**
A patrol of the 23d Infantry, 2d Infantry Division, is ambushed by North Koreans. Six Americans are killed.

6-25 November. **Operation Attleboro Expands. Central Highlands.**
II Field Force commander Lieutenant General Jonathan O. Seaman commits the 1st Infantry Division and a brigade of the 25th Infantry Division, making Attleboro the first multi-divisional operation of the war. Viet Cong forces cannot stand against the expanding operation, and after several battles begin

Above: *Despite their weight and size, armored vehicles such as the M48A3 Patton tanks, shown here, were effective weapons against the enemy in many situations. (A. J. Alexander)*

retreating toward the Cambodian border. In the end, more than 300 enemy soldiers are killed, and several large weapons caches are captured. American losses are 155 killed and 494 wounded. Operation Attleboro convinces Westmoreland that the normally elusive enemy will fight to protect his base areas—making them a prime target for his search-and-destroy strategy.

2 December. **11th Armored Cavalry Regiment's First Fight. Suoi Cat.**
While patrolling the road, the Blackhorse Regiment's 1st Squadron is ambushed by the Viet Cong 275th Regiment. Firing canister rounds from the tank's 90mm guns, and calling in artillery from nearby firebases, the cavalry routs the enemy.

10 December. **199th Infantry Brigade Arrives.**
The 199th Infantry Brigade (Light) rushes to III Corps as part of an ever-increasing cordon of U.S. forces around Saigon. For the rest of the war, although the brigade will change location five times, it will continue to focus its operations near the capital.

16 December. **9th Infantry Division Deploys to Southern III Corps.**

The 9th Infantry Division arrives at Bear Cat, and within months is fighting in the Mekong Delta. The 1st Brigade remains at Bear Cat and the 3d Brigade deploys to Long An Province. The 2d Brigade becomes part of the Mobile Riverine Force which, along with a naval river boat component, is the first time since the Civil War that the Army uses an amphibious force existing and operating entirely afloat.

1967

January. **Status of the Army.**

There are now 485,300 U.S. troops in South Vietnam, 239,400 from the Army. General Westmoreland is optimistic and believes that this is enough to do more than simply stabilize the situation. Large operations aimed at destroying the enemy's main forces will mark this as the "year of the offensive."

1 January–5 April. **4th Division Begins Highland Campaign. Pleiku Province.**

Major General William R. Peers, commander of the 4th Infantry Division, begins a series of screening operations along the border aimed at preventing the North Vietnamese from pushing into the Central Highlands. From 1 January through 5 April, the 1st and 2d Brigades range along the western border fighting 11 major engagements.

8–26 January. **Operation Cedar Falls. Northwest of Saigon.**

Due to the success of Operation Attleboro, General Westmoreland decides to clear the Viet Cong from an area known as the Iron Triangle. Long a Communist stronghold, fortified and honeycombed with tunnels, it houses a major enemy headquarters and is home to a number of Viet Cong units. II Field Force commander General Seaman deploys elements of the 173d Airborne Brigade, the 1st and 25th Infantry Divisions, and a South Vietnamese division in a massive hammer and anvil movement. Although the Viet Cong do not stand and fight as expected, 750 enemy are killed and 280 captured plus large quantities of supplies and weapons. Seventy-two U.S. soldiers and 11 South Vietnamese are killed.

12 January. **Operation Fairfax. Gia Dinh Province**

Alarmed by the deteriorating security situation around Saigon, General Westmoreland orders the newly

Right: *M113 Armored Personnel Carriers and Patton tanks with 90mm main guns travel in column ready for combat. Armor could operate in most areas of Vietnam except the Delta. ("Route Red Clearance," David Lavender, Army Art Collection, NMUSA)*

arrived 199th Infantry Brigade, with the South Vietnamese 5th Ranger Group, to begin a year-long pacification operation around Saigon. Called Operation Fairfax, it succeeds in pushing the enemy main forces back, though guerrillas remain a problem. In December the Americans turn the operation over to the South Vietnamese.

11 February–21 January. **Operation Pershing. Binh Dinh Province.**
The 1st Cavalry Division begins a three brigade sweep of the province. Other American units join in the long-running operation, including the South Korean Capital Division and the South Vietnamese 22d Division. By the end more than 9,000 Communist soldiers are killed.

12 February. **Ambush in Korean DMZ. South Korea.**
North Koreans ambush a patrol of the 2d Divisions 23d Infantry, killing one American.

Above: *Paratroopers of the 2d Battalion, 503d Airborne Infantry, 173d Airborne Brigade, make the only full-scale combat jump of the Vietnam War in February 1967. (Time-Life, Inc.)*

Right: *Troops bring in suspected Viet Cong operatives in Binh Dinh Province. (Center of Military History)*

13 February. **Operation Enterprise. Long An Province**
The 3d Brigade, 9th Infantry Division, begins a long-running pacification operation aimed at clearing the area of Viet Cong. Although the hardest fighting is over by mid-April, Operation Enterprise continues until March 1968.

Right: *Artillerymen fire an M110 8-inch howitzer. ("Hip Pocket," David E. Graves, Army Art Collection, NMUSA)*

14 February. **Operation Kittyhawk. Long Khanh Province**

The 11th Armored Cavalry begins one of several long-running attempts to keep the roads north of Saigon open. Kittyhawk lasts until 21 March 1968. Ambushes are plentiful especially northeast of the capital, but the armored vehicles are well-suited to the task.

22 February. **Airborne Assault in War Zone C.**

The 173d Airborne Brigade's 2d Battalion, 503d Infantry, executes the only U.S. full-scale parachute assault of the war. In the opening move of Operation Junction City, 13 C-130 transport planes drop 778 paratroopers, including the brigade commander, Brigadier General John R. Deane, near Katum on the edge of War Zone C, a Communist stronghold near the Cambodian border.

22 February–14 May. **Operation Junction City. Northwest of Saigon**

In the second corps-sized operation of the war, Westmoreland sends 22 battalions from 1st, 4th, 9th, and 25th Infantry Divisions, the 11th Armored Cavalry, and the 196th Infantry and 173d Airborne Brigades. Operation Junction City has the mission to clear the enemy from its base areas. Three major battles occur—all of them initiated by the enemy. On 19–20 March, at Bau Bang Village, two Viet Cong battalions attack the night position of the 3d Squadron, 5th Cavalry, but are beaten back. On 21 March other enemy elements attack Firebase Gold

near the town of Suoi Tre, and on 1 April the Viet Cong attack 1st Battalion, 26th Infantry, commanded by Lieutenant Colonel Alexander M. Haig, at Firebase George. All the attacks are beaten back with terrible losses. Operation Junction City temporarily clears the enemy from War Zone C.

12 April. **Task Force Oregon. Chu Lai.**

Task Force Oregon, a provisional division-sized unit, deploys in southern I Corps to bolster the 1st Cavalry Division's operations in Binh Dinh Province. The task force is composed of units taken from various areas, including the 3d Brigade, 25th Infantry Division; 1st Brigade, 101st Airborne Division; and the 196th Infantry Brigade (Light).

29 April. **2d Division Strikes Back. Korean DMZ.**

A patrol of the 2d Division ambushes a party of North Korean infiltrators, killing one.

9 May. **Pacification Reorganization. South Vietnam.**

Civil Operations and Revolutionary Development Support (CORDS) is formed to support pacification. Placed within MACV, CORDS will oversee all civilian agencies in Vietnam and place them within the military command structure. Always headed by a civilian, CORDS has access to military resources and advisors. At its height in 1969, CORDS will have 6,464 military advisors—95 percent of them from the Army. CORDS is particularly effective in expanding territorial militia forces, which in early 1967 had only

108 U.S. advisors. One year later the number is 2,243, and militia strength climbs to 475,000 men.

11 May–2 August. Operation Malheur.
Operation Malheur I, a search and destroy sweep aimed at countering increased Communist activity in southern I Corps, is Task Force Oregon's first major test. After almost three months in the field, the Americans kill 869 enemy soldiers, but they also force the evacuation of almost 9,000 villagers and rely heavily on artillery to keep down U.S. casualties, resulting in large-scale destruction.

18–26 May. 4th Division Continues in Highlands
The 4th Infantry Division has a series of fights with two North Vietnamese regiments that came to be known as "Nine Days in May." Operations Sam Houston and Francis Marion kill more than 2,000 enemy, but the fighting also wears out the division. Most companies have less than 70 percent strength, prompting I Field Force commander, Lieutenant General Stanley R. Larsen, to ask MACV to transfer the 173d Airborne Brigade to the highlands. Westmoreland agreed, and in late May the 173d arrives in Kontum Province.

22 May. Project Daniel Boone.
The Joint Chiefs of Staff authorize a highly classified cross-border operation into Cambodia, codenamed Daniel Boone (changed to Salem House in December 1968), and placed under MACV-SOG. The operation is aimed at gathering intelligence, conducting reconnaissance, undertaking sabotage, and capturing prisoners in an area deemed off-limits to regular U.S. forces. Teams made up of two or three specially trained U.S. Special Forces and 10 to 12 indigenous soldiers—usually Cambodians—are inserted by helicopter along the border. Although the missions are confined by tight operational rules, over the course of four years the project launches 1,825 missions.

22 May. American Barracks Destroyed. South Korea.
North Korean raiders blow up an American barracks at Camp Greaves, just south of the DMZ. Several Americans are killed or wounded.

17 June. Operation Greely. Central Highlands.
Along with the 1st Cavalry Division's 3d Brigade, the 173d Brigade begins Operation Greeley in an attempt to prevent the North Vietnamese from attacking Dak To.

August. Rome Plow Introduced.
The Rome Plow, a 4,000-pound clearing blade attached to a bulldozer, is first used to clear Route 13 north of Lai Khe. This stretch of road is completely

controlled by the enemy, and Radio Hanoi claims that it will never be reopened. Engineers using Rome Plows and backed by security forces peel back the jungle for 200 yards on both sides of the road, denying the enemy cover. The road is open by 1 November.

9 August. Battle of LZ Pat. Central Highlands.
For the first time in several years American troops penetrate the Song Re River valley in a search for North Vietnamese units. The 2d Battalion, 8th Cavalry, 1st Cavalry Division, is given the task and Company A, under Captain Raymond K. Bluhm, Jr., is the first unit to be air assaulted in. Company A lands on LZ Pat, a high, narrow ridge overlooking the valley. As the helicopter flights approach, they are taken under fire by a North Vietnamese heavy weapons battalion and a supporting Viet Cong unit dug in overlooking the LZ. Isolated and outnumbered, Company A battles over four hours using air support, aerial guns ships, and artillery until it is able to penetrate the enemy's positions and cause them to flee. A Valorous Unit Award (equivalent to a Silver Star) is later presented to the unit and a streamer is placed on the company guidon.

10 August. Engineers Attacked. South Korea
A work party from the 13th Engineers is attacked by North Koreans in the DMZ, resulting in three American deaths.

1 September. Cobra Gunships Arrive.
The AH-1G Cobra helicopter gunship arrives in Vietnam. Although still experimental, the gunship performs well, and by October 1968 the Army orders 838. Almost twice as fast as the UH-1, the Cobra is armed with 7.62mm mini guns and rocket pods, making it a lethal platform.

Opposite: *In the field, troops loaded quickly into their helicopters as any lingering aircraft was an extremely inviting target for the enemy. ("Landing Zone," Augustine G. Acuna, Army Art Collection, NMUSA)*

Right: *Courageous pilots routinely risked their lives by bringing their helicopters into a firefight to deliver badly needed ammunition and evacuate wounded. ("Storm," David S. Lewis, Nam Knights of America M.C.)*

Left: *Army engineers carried out their dangerous assignment of clearing away bush and dense jungle that could possibly conceal enemy ambushes and mines along roadsides. ("Engineers Lead the Way," Dale Gallon, U.S. Army Engineer Association)*

Below: *The artist captures the tense caution of an Army patrol moving through the jungle. ("Patrol," Samuel E. Alexander, Army Art Collection, NMUSA)*

11 September. **Operation Wheeler/Wallowa.**
Task Force Oregon launches Operation Wheeler, in southern I Corps. On 11 November Operation Wheeler merges with the 1st Cavalry Division's Operation Wallowa, and the two units move into the Que Son Valley to tackle the North Vietnamese 2d Division. Operation Wheeler/Wallowa continues for a year, ending on 11 November 1968, and succeeds in decimating the North Vietnamese. However, the setback is only temporary for the enemy.

25 September. **Task Force Oregon Reinforced.**
It is announced that Task Force Oregon will receive two new independent units—the 11th Infantry Brigade and the 198th Infantry Brigade (Light)—and be redesignated as the 23d Infantry Division (American) commanded by Major General Samuel W. Koster.

7 October. **U.S. Patrol Boat Attacked. South Korea.**
A patrol boat from the 2d Infantry Division is attacked on the Imjim River by North Korean raiders.

21 October. **198th Infantry Brigade Arrives.**
The 198th Infantry Brigade (Light) is raised at Fort Hood, Texas, and scheduled to deploy to Vietnam to guard the "McNamara Line," a proposed barrier of mines and sensors along the Demilitarized Zone. When the project fails to materialize, the brigade joins the new American Division.

3 November–1 December. **Battle of Dak To. Central Highlands.**
Communist forces make a concerted attempt to overrun the Special Forces camp at Dak To, northwest

Right: *A soldier directs USAF gunships firing at night on a suspected enemy mortar position. ("Mortar Attack Counterfire," Ronald A. Wilson, Amy Art Collection, NMUSA)*

of Kontum. A large North Vietnamese presence detected in October prompted MACV to order a spoiling attack by the 4th Infantry Division's 3d Battalion, 12th Infantry. The battalion drives a North Vietnamese regiment from its positions on Hill 1338, while units from the 173d Airborne Brigade, the 4th Infantry Division, and the 1st Cavalry Division gradually force the enemy back toward the border. The North Vietnamese leave a regiment atop Hill 875 as a rear guard. On 19 November the 173d's 2d Battalion, 503d Infantry, is ordered to take the hill, but the paratroopers are stalled by the well-fortified positions. The battalion is relieved the following day by the 4th Battalion, 503d Infantry, and the hill is taken 22 November. Over 1,000 North Vietnamese die in the battles for Dak To, as do 115 Americans.

19 November. "Screaming Eagles" Gather.
The remaining two brigades of the 101st Airborne Division deploy to Bien Hoa. The 1st Brigade remains in II Corps. In April 1968 the entire division will move north to I Corps.

8 December. Operations Northwest of Saigon.
The 25th Infantry Division moves into War Zone C in Tay Ninh Province to root out enemy forces as part of Operation Yellowstone. At the same time, the 1st Infantry Division makes forays into the Iron Triangle in Binh Duong Province in an operation called Saratoga. The two operations are part of an attempt to prevent the enemy from massing for an offensive.

More than 5,000 enemy are killed in the two operations, both of which continue into the new year.

19 December. 11th Infantry Brigade Arrives.
The 11th Infantry Brigade arrives in Vietnam as part of an emergency deployment. In February 1969 it will join the Americal Division in southern I Corps, making it the Army's largest division with more than 20,000 men.

1968

January. Status of the Army.
MACV has 100 infantry and mechanized battalions and 54 artillery battalions totaling 331,098 soldiers and 78,013 marines—still not considered sufficient, but enough to maintain the offensive. Casualties are also mounting. The year 1967 saw 9,378 Americans killed in action, more than the total killed in all previous years. Between 1961 and the end of 1966 there were 6,872 killed in action.

6 January. First Medal of Honor for Dust Off.
Major Patrick H. Brady, a veteran pilot with the 54th Medical Detachment, flies into a fogbound valley west of Chu Lai in southern I Corps to evacuate some badly wounded soldiers from the 198th Infantry Brigade. Although one helicopter has already been shot down, Brady lands in the midst of heavy enemy fire to evacuate the wounded. He makes the trip four

times, picking up 39 men and taking several rounds in his helicopter. For his selfless bravery Brady is awarded the Medal of Honor on 9 October 1969.

22–29 January. **Outposts Under Attack. South Korea.**
North Korean raiders hit 2d Division outpost and defensive positions along the DMZ with a series of harassing attacks.

29–31 January. **The Tet Offensive Begins.**
MACV intelligence believes the enemy might launch some sort of an attack. Three hours past midnight on 31 January, the Communists launch an offensive that hits 36 of 44 provincial capitals and 64 of 242 district capitals, along with dozens of villages and military installations—including 23 airfields. In Saigon, a Viet Cong assault team breaches the wall of the U.S. Embassy before American Military Police stop them. In I Corps, North Vietnamese units capture the imperial capital of Hue and hold it for almost a month. In II Corps and in the Mekong Delta, enemy troops attack every major population center. During the crucial first nine days of the offensive, U.S. forces suffer 546 killed and more than 6,000 wounded, while the South Vietnamese lose almost 1,000 killed. Communist losses are estimated at more than 20,000 dead and wounded. Although the offensive ends in military defeat for the Communists—and the Viet Cong never quite recover from their losses—American political and public opinion turns against the war.

2–21 February. **Army Units at the Battle of Hue.**
As U.S. Marines and the South Vietnamese Army fight to retake the city, 2d Brigade, 101st Division, is hotly engaged to the south attempting to cut off North Vietnamese reinforcements. In the north, 1st Cavalry Division commander Major General John J. Tolson air assaults 2d Battalion, 12th Cavalry, northwest of the city where there they run into an enemy force. After three days of fighting Tolson sends the 5th Battalion, 7th Cavalry, in from the west in an attempt to link up, but they do not succeed until 9 February. Not until 21 February does the cavalry shut down enemy resupply efforts. Four days later Hue is liberated.

18 February. **82d Airborne Division Lands. Chu Lai**
The 3d Brigade, 82d Airborne Division, arrives in southern I Corps as part of an emergency reinforcement. Initially attached to the 101st Airborne Division where it helps defend Hue, the brigade moves south to Saigon in September, where it will secure the western approaches to the capital.

2 March. **9th Infantry "Manchu" Company Destroyed.**
In one of the worst American defeats of the war, 25th Infantry Division's Company C, 4th Battalion, 9th Infantry (Manchu), is ambushed and nearly annihilated, losing 49 killed and 29 wounded in a matter of minutes. The battalion was north of Tan

Right: *American advisors with Vietnamese forces shared the danger of their small outpost being attacked by a larger enemy force. ("Field Communications in a Fox Hole," Mort Künstler)*

Son Nhut looking for enemy rocket sites. For courageous action during the battle, Spec. 4 Nicholas J. Cutinha, Company C, is posthumously awarded the Congressional Medal of Honor. All three companies of the battalion continue operations in this area and take many more casualties until finally leaving on 11 March.

11 March–30 April. Allied Counteroffensive.

In an attempt to regain the initiative, Westmoreland orders II Field Force commander, Lieutenant General Frederick C. Weyand, to take a series of counteroffensives in III Corps. The first, Operation Quyet Thang (Resolve to Win) involves 50,000 troops from 22 U.S. infantry battalions from the 1st, 9th, and 25th Infantry Divisions, and 11 South Vietnamese battalions. Between 11 March and 7 April, the offensive claims 2,658 Communist soldiers killed. One hundred five Americans and 193 South Vietnamese are also killed. A second offensive, begun the next day, is even larger, involving 42 U.S. and 37 South Vietnamese battalions. By 30 April the operation killed an additional 3,542 Communist soldiers in the 11 provinces surrounding Saigon.

16 March. My Lai Massacre. Quang Ngai Province.

While on patrol in the coastal lowlands the 11th Brigade's Company C, 1st Battalion, 20th Infantry, commanded by Captain Ernest Medina, enters a cluster of hamlets named My Lai, but called "Pinkville" because of its well-known enemy connections. Americans often took casualties from mines sprinkled throughout the area. Expecting to encounter Viet Cong in the village, Company C is soon out of control, especially 1st Platoon, commanded by First Lieutenant William L. Calley, which rounds up and shoots men, women, and children. The slaughter is stopped when Warrant Officer Hugh Thompson, seeing the massacre, lands his helicopter between Calley's men and the fleeing Vietnamese and confronts the soldiers.

27 March. North Korean Infiltrators Hit. Korean DMZ.

A patrol from the 2d Division surprises a group of North Korean infiltrators and kills three of them.

1–15 April. Operation Pegasus. Khe Sanh.

The 1st Cavalry Division is ordered to relieve the Marines at Khe Sanh near the Laos border. Major General Tolson, the division commander, also has at his disposal two battalions of Marines and a South Vietnamese airborne task force, as well as operational control of the 26th Marines inside Khe Sanh—a total of about 30,000 troops. Operation Pegasus begins 1 April and immediately encounters stiff resistance from the two North Vietnamese divisions surrounding Khe Sanh. Tolson's aggressive, fast-moving operation

breaks through the North Vietnamese cordon and by 15 April the siege is over. It is the first full-division air cavalry raid in history.

5 April. **Army Helps Restore Order. United States.**
Racial tensions and anti-war hostility breaks out into violent riots and civil disorders in several cities following the assassination of Dr. Martin Luther King, Jr. National Guard and Army units are dispatched to help civil authorities restore order.

19 April–17 May. **Operation Delaware.**
MACV launches an operation into the A Shau Valley, a major infiltration corridor. On 19 April, the 1st Cavalry Division's 1st and 5th Battalions, 7th Cavalry, air assault into the valley's northern end, running into heavy anti-aircraft fire that downs 10 helicopters. The two battalions fight their way to the south where they will be resupplied. On 24 April the division's 1st Brigade, commanded by Colonel John E. Stannard, air assaults to the valley's southern entrance, near an abandoned village. Resistance is again heavy, but by 3 May the division has a logistics beachhead that can be used to resupply forays into the valley. On 29 April elements of the 101st Airborne Division and a South

Above: *General Creighton Abrams and Major General George Forsyth discuss MACV redeployment to III Corps. (Center of Military History, U.S. Army)*

Right: *General Westmoreland left Vietnam to become Army Chief of Staff. (Herbert E. Abrams, Army Art Collection, NMUSA)*

Vietnamese regiment deploy and fight several actions. When Operation Delaware ends on 17 May, most of the enemy have fled the valley, leaving behind dozens of weapons caches.

21 April. **DMZ Firefight. South Korea.**
A company of the 7th Division's 31st Infantry engage in a firefight with an estimated company of North Koreans while patrolling in the DMZ.

11–12 May. **The Fall of Kham Duc. Quang Tin Province.**
Only one Special Forces camp remains along the Laotian border in I Corps—Kham Duc. The camp is soon under attack by the North Vietnamese. Kham Duc is defended by 1,500 CIDG, U.S. Special Forces, and the 196th Infantry Brigade's 2d Battalion, 1st Infantry. On 12 May the base is evacuated, but the losses are heavy—689 CIDG killed or missing, and 24 U.S. personnel killed (including 12 U.S. Marines as part of an artillery battery stationed at the camp), 112 wounded, and 26 missing in action.

17 May–28 February. **Operation Nevada Eagle. Thua Thien Province.**
During the allied counteroffensive, the 101st Airborne Division moves against enemy forces in the mountains of central I Corps. Operation Nevada Eagle's main objective is to keep open major roads and protect the South Vietnamese rice harvest. The Communists are reluctant to fight, preferring to concentrate on luring helicopters into ambushes.

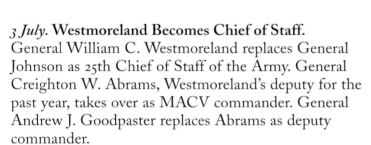

3 July. Westmoreland Becomes Chief of Staff.
General William C. Westmoreland replaces General Johnson as 25th Chief of Staff of the Army. General Creighton W. Abrams, Westmoreland's deputy for the past year, takes over as MACV commander. General Andrew J. Goodpaster replaces Abrams as deputy commander.

20 July. American Patrols Attacked. Korean DMZ.
Patrols from both the 2d and 7th Infantry Divisions are attacked by North Koreans while moving in the DMZ. There are no losses.

25 July. Mechanized Brigade Activated.
MACV wants to beef up forces in the north but cannot afford to move troops. Instead, the Defense Department reestablishes 1st Brigade, 5th Infantry Division (Mechanized), at Fort Carson, Colorado. It is sent to Quang Tri where its mechanized units patrol the region paralleling the Demilitarized Zone.

5 August. 38th Infantry Attacked. Korean DMZ
A patrol for the 38th Infantry is attacked by North Koreans in the DMZ.

28 August. Democratic National Convention Violence. Chicago.
Army Regulars and Illinois Guardsmen are deployed to Chicago to help restore order when anti-war demonstrations outside the convention site turn violent.

Above: *Official U.S. Army shoulder-sleeve insignia of divisions and other major commands serving in the Republic of Vietnam. (U.S. Army)*

WESTMORELAND: EMBATTLED GENERAL

During his long Army career William Childs Westmoreland distinguished himself in every assignment from World War II through Korea. As the senior American commander in Vietnam, he faced his most daunting challenge in what became America's longest and most difficult war.

Westmoreland was born in South Carolina, 26 March 1914. After briefly attending the Citadel, Westmoreland entered West Point, graduating in 1936 with a commission in the field artillery.

By 1942, Westmoreland was a temporary lieutenant colonel, serving as operations officer of the 34th Field Artillery Battalion, 9th Infantry Division, in Tunisia and Sicily. Westmoreland landed with the 9th Division at Normandy on 10 June 1944. He was promoted to colonel and made division chief of staff in July, then commanded the 60th Infantry Regiment on occupation duty in Germany before returning to the U.S. in 1946.

After parachute training in 1947, Westmoreland commanded the 504th Parachute Infantry Regiment until August when he was appointed chief of staff of the 82nd Airborne Division. From 1950 to 1952, Westmoreland was an instructor at the Command and General Staff School and at the Army War College. In August 1952, he was given command of the 187th Airborne Regimental Combat Team in Korea.

From 1953 to 1958, Westmoreland served on the Army General Staff as secretary to Army Chief of Staff General Maxwell Taylor, and became the Army's youngest major general in December 1956. From April 1958, Westmoreland commanded the 101st Airborne Division until appointed superintendent of West Point in July 1960, where he worked hard to double the size of the corps of cadets. In 1963, he moved to command of the XVIII Airborne Corps and was promoted to lieutenant general.

In June 1964, Westmoreland was named by President Lyndon Johnson as commander of the U.S. Military Assistance Command in Vietnam (MACV), and that August he was promoted to full general. Starting in 1965, Westmoreland began a gradual buildup of American forces in Vietnam in response to increasing enemy activity. Westmoreland pushed an aggressive strategy, using American units to fight a war of attrition against the Viet Cong (VC) and North Vietnamese Army (NVA) forces. His "search and destroy" tactics inflicted heavy losses on the enemy troops, but also caused American casualties.

Unable to defeat U.S. forces in conventional engagements, the North Vietnamese leaders directed a reversion to guerrilla warfare in the south, hoping to avoid encountering the American units until the most favorable conditions. During the Tet cease-fire in January–February 1968, the VC and NVA launched a massive surprise offensive, striking nearly every major city in South Vietnam. Caught off guard, U.S. forces quickly recovered and handed the enemy one of their worst military defeats of the war. Despite this victory, growing unrest in America over the war and an enemy that seemed impervious to losses caused President Johnson to work for a negotiated peace. He refused Westmoreland's request for 200,000 more troops, suspended air operations, and began withdrawing U.S. forces from Vietnam.

In June 1968, Westmoreland returned to the U.S. to become Army Chief of Staff. In that position he oversaw the U.S. withdrawal from Vietnam, the end of the draft, and worked to improve Army life and improve the public image of the Army. After 38 years in the Army, he retired from active duty in 1972. In his 1976 memoirs, *A Soldier Reports*, Westmoreland admitted his policy of gradual escalation was a strategic mistake, allowing the enemy time to adapt. He urged that hereafter, the country should strike quickly and decisively, to avoid "future Vietnams."

—*Vince Hawkins*

Above: *General William C. Westmoreland served four years, 1964–1968, as the MACV commander, overseeing the massive buildup of U.S. forces. (National Archives)*

Right: *As part of an innovative Riverine Force, troops of the 9th Infantry Division move in armored landing craft along a canal in the Dinh Toung Province to land at their objective. (Center of Military History, U.S. Army)*

29 August. **Riot at Long Binh Jail. Long Binh.**
U.S. military prisoners temporarily seize the stockade compound at Long Binh Jail. They go on a destructive rampage, beating any guard they can find before order is restored. Long Binh Jail (formal name is U.S. Army, Vietnam, Installation Stockade) was built in 1966 and housed military men convicted of crimes ranging from drug abuse to rape to black marketeering.

1 September. **First Black Brigade Commander.**
Brigadier General Frederic E. Davison replaces Brigadier General Franklin M. Davis as commander of the 199th Infantry Brigade. Davison is the first black officer to command a U.S. Army brigade in combat. He will command the unit until 28 May 1969.

13 September. **1st Infantry Division Commander Killed.**
Major General Keith L. Ware, commander of the 1st Infantry Division since March, dies in a helicopter crash. He is succeeded by Major General Orwin C. Talbot.

19 September. **Infiltrators Destroyed. Korean DMZ.**
Patrols and a quick reaction force isolate and destroy a North Korean infiltration detachment.

24 September. **Harassment and Interdiction.**
Artillery from the 25th Infantry Division, using newly acquired motion detection equipment, fires 175mm artillery at North Vietnamese troops on a known infiltration route in Tay Ninh Province. The division's 155mm and 105mm guns also join in, cutting off the enemy as they flee. The sensors enhance these "unobserved" artillery missions—called harassment and interdiction fire—that were previously determined on a map. During the war, harassment and interdiction fire accounts for approximately 50 percent of all missions fired by American field artillery units, and uses nearly 70 percent of all ammunition expenditures.

30 September. **Special Forces Apex.**
U.S. Army Special Forces in Vietnam reaches its highest strength with 3,542 assigned personnel.

11 October. **North Koreans Ambushed. Korean DMZ.**
A group of North Korean infiltrators skirmish with a 2d Division patrol that kills two of the Koreans.

27 October. **1st Cavalry Division Moves South.**
With troop reductions coming soon, General Abrams decides to concentrate his forces around Saigon. On 27

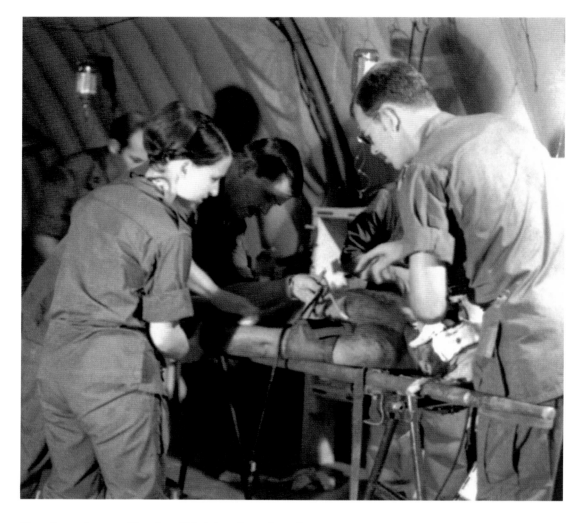

October, the 1st Cavalry Division is ordered to move south to III Corps where it will act as a screen along the border. Over the next 16 days, 437 C-130 sorties transport 11,550 passengers and almost 4,000 short tons of cargo. The U.S. Navy also ferries 4,037 men and 16,600 tons in 38 ships. By 9 November the division is moved. Its new job is to establish temporary firebases in a screen as the first line of defense against enemy infiltration toward the capital. The move proves to be an unqualified success.

16 November. Helicopter Crash Injures Americal General. Quang Ngai Province.

While flying to inspect a weapons cache uncovered by the 11th Infantry Brigade, a UH-1H helicopter carrying division commander Major General Charles M. Gettys and some of his staff crashes while trying to land. Despite a broken ankle, Major Colin Powell, General Getty's operations officer, drags the injured division commander from the wreckage. Colonel Jack L. Treadwell, the division chief of staff and a Medal of Honor winner in World War II, is killed in the crash.

19 November. First Sniper Kill.

The 9th Infantry Division's sniper unit records its first kill. The Army has no formal sniper program in Vietnam, but some units create their own. The most proficient belongs to the 9th Division, which began a sniper program in June 1968. Major General Julian J. Ewell, the division commander, assigns 72 snipers throughout the division, which he refers to as "our most successful ambush tactic." One of Ewell's snipers, Sergeant Adelbert F. Waldron, III, becomes one of the most successful snipers of the war, with 109 confirmed kills and winning two Distinguished Service Crosses for his skill and bravery.

1 December. Operation Speedy Express.

The 9th Infantry Division begins Operation Speedy Express, a seven-month affair conducted by seven of the division's battalions in the northern Mekong Delta. General Ewell's concept is to give the enemy no time to rest, using air mobility to land troops whenever an enemy troop concentration is discovered—a technique he calls "jitterbugging." The division claims to kill 10,899 enemy at a cost of 267 Americans—a "kill ratio" of 40.8-to-1—but only 748 weapons are captured, leading many to doubt the claims. Despite the controversy, the 9th Division operations have a serious effect on the Viet Cong. Speedy Express comes to a close on 1 June 1969.

Right: *Colonel George S. Patton, Jr.'s, 11th Armored Cavalry Regiment fought an aggressive and effective campaign to keep the main roads around Saigon clear of enemy forces. ("Find the Bastards, Then Pile On," James Dietz)*

1969

January. **Status of the Army.**
U.S. Army strength in Vietnam has reached 359,800, but within six months Army personnel will begin to leave. The enemy, still reeling from its losses during 1968, can launch no more spectacular offensives during the year, but the war goes on at a steady level. Although the Army will continue to seek out the enemy, emphasis will fall on "Vietnamization," training and equipping the South Vietnamese to fight the war themselves.

1 January. **Operation Rice Farmer. Mekong Delta**
The 9th Infantry Division and various South Vietnamese units launch Operation Rice Farmer. Aimed at Viet Cong guerrillas, Rice Farmer will last until 31 August and claim 1,860 enemy dead.

13 January–21 July. **Operation Russell Beach. Quang Ngai Province.**
In a long-running joint operation, Army and Marine Corps units thrust into the Batangan Peninsula. Previous efforts in the region had failed. Two battalions from the Americal Division and two Marine Corps battalion landing teams would rotate in and out of the operation. Operations consist mainly of cordon and searches of villages to separate the guerrillas from the civilians. Army losses at the end of Russell Beach are 56 killed and 268 wounded, most of them from mines and booby traps.

23 January. **DMZ Attacks Repulsed. South Korea.**
Several outposts manned by the 2d Division successfully turn-back probing attacks by North Koreans.

15 February. **Sheridan Fighting Vehicles See Action.**
An M551 Sheridan fighting vehicle from the 3d Squadron, 4th Cavalry, strikes a mine, destroying the vehicle. It is the first time a Sheridan has seen combat since its arrival the previous month. The Sheridan, with its 152mm main gun and .50 cal. machine gun, was originally designed as an anti-tank vehicle, but is sent to Vietnam as a lighter alternative to the M48A3 main battle tank. By the summer of 1969 there are 81 Sheridans distributed throughout the 11th Armored Cavalry.

1 March–14 April. **Operation Wayne Gray. Central Highlands**
The 4th Infantry Division steps up patrols in Kontum Province, killing 608 enemy soldiers.

1 March–8 May. **A Shau Valley Assault. Central Highlands.**
The North Vietnamese considered the A Shau Valley a crucial logistics corridor, and always fight hard to keep it open. On 1 March, the 101st Airborne Division launches Operation Massachusetts Striker in an attempt to cut this corridor. The paratroopers immediately encounter resistance. On the first day, the 1st Battalion, 502d Infantry, must be reinforced by four

more battalions. As enemy activity slackens, the paratroopers uncover massive supply depots. Throughout April the division destroys several weapons caches and a supply base complete with trucks and a hospital.

13 March. **Fence Crews Attacked. Korean DMZ.**
U.S. work parties repairing the southern fence of the DMZ are attacked but respond well and suffer no losses.

18 March–2 April. **Operation Atlas Wedge. South Vietnam.**
Enemy attempts to interdict traffic near the Michelin rubber plantation cause II Field Force to order the 1st Infantry Division, with the 11th Armored Cavalry Regiment, to run reconnaissance-in-force missions along Highway 13. The 11th Cavalry, commanded by Colonel George S. Patton, engages the enemy with its formidable firepower. U.S. forces kill more than 400 North Vietnamese, while suffering 20 dead and 100 wounded.

30 April. **Army Strength in Vietnam Peaks.**
U.S. military manpower in Vietnam reaches its highest point at 543,482. Army strength stands at 365,600.

Above: *The many canals and streams in the Mekong River Delta area made movement slow, difficult, and dangerous for the American GIs. ("Perimeter Patrol," Michael R. Crook, Army Art Collection, NMUSA)*

6 May. **Attack on Landing Zone Carolyn. War Zone C.**
One day after Major General Elvy B. Roberts takes command of the 1st Cavalry Division, Landing Zone Carolyn along the Cambodian border is attacked by a North Vietnamese regiment. The base is manned by Company C, 2d Battalion, 8th Cavalry; Battery A, 2d Battalion, 19th Artillery; and Battery B, 1st Battalion, 21st Artillery. Assaulted from two sides, the 422 defenders fight desperately, backed by AH-1G Cobra gunships. The North Vietnamese withdraw, leaving behind 172 dead. Carolyn's defenders lose 10 killed and 80 wounded.

10 May–7 June. **Operation Apache Snow and Hamburger Hill.**
General Abrams orders new operations into the A Shau Valley. On 10 May Colonel Joseph Conmy's 3d Brigade, 101st Airborne Division, along with U.S. Marine and South Vietnamese regiments attack. The 101st Division's 3d Battalion, 187th Infantry, commanded by Lieutenant Colonel Weldon Honeycutt, runs into two battalions of the North Vietnamese on Ap Bia Mountain—soon to be known as "Hamburger Hill." There is heavy fighting over the next ten days as the paratroopers inch their way up the hill, only to be pushed back. Three additional units—the 1st Battalion, 506th Infantry, and the 2d Battalion, 501st Infantry, plus a South Vietnamese battalion, join the fight on 20 May, and their combined forces carry hill. By the next day the North Vietnamese are fleeing for Laos. Fifty-six

Americans and five South Vietnamese are killed, and another 300 are wounded.

16 May–13 August. Operation Lamar Plain. Quang Tin Province

Elements of the 101st Airborne and Americal Divisions team up to sweep southern I Corps of enemy forces. The operation nets 524 enemy dead.

1 June. Working with the South Vietnamese.

American units concentrate on a continuing series of joint operations called Dong Tien (Progress Together). The object is to increase the skills of South Vietnamese units that will soon be taking over much of the combat load. Dong Tien operations will continue until U.S. Army units are gone.

5–7 June. Advanced Sensor Technology Wins the Day.

On the evening of June 5 seismic sensors alert the garrison at Firebase Crook that enemy forces are closing in. Early the next morning the Communists unleash a barrage of rockets, rocket propelled grenades, and mortar fire, followed by an infantry assault on the base by a Viet Cong battalion. The defenders—two companies from the 25th Infantry Division's 3d Battalion, 22d Infantry—stop the assault, but they are attacked again the following night. During the first few hours of 7 June, American artillery inside Firebase Crook fire flechette-filled beehive rounds toward the detected enemy, driving them off for good. The defenders' casualties were one dead and seven wounded.

8 June. Army Nurse Killed in Action. Chu Lai.

First Lieutenant Sharon A. Lane is killed by shrapnel when a rocket hits the 312th Evacuation Hospital. Lane is one of eight female nurses to die in Vietnam, and the only one killed by hostile fire. She is posthumously awarded the Bronze Star. Defense Department figures show that 7,465 women served in

ARMY WOMEN DURING THE VIETNAM WAR

Approximately 6,000 Army women received assignments to Vietnam between 1962 and 1973. More than 5,000 were nurses and medical specialists. Many, although not all, of these women volunteered for their assignment because they felt Vietnam was where they were most needed.

A nurse's experience in country depended on when and where she served in Vietnam. Nurses serving at the 85th Evacuation Hospital at Qui Nhon between 1965 and 1966 faced limited supplies and exposure to combat, which complicated patient care. Lieutenant Judy Dennis recalled, "We were originally in tents in a valley, but due to enemy fire we moved fully operational into the city of Qui Nhon." Lieutenant Louise Graul Eisenbrandt, stationed in Vietnam in 1970, remembers, "Three mornings in a row we grabbed flak jackets while racing to bunkers to avoid rounds of incoming mortars."

In Vietnam there were no front lines and no safe areas. Enemy forces could strike anywhere, but some areas were more dangerous than others. Yet, only one Army nurse, Lieutenant Sharon Lane, was killed by enemy fire. Lane died on 8 June 1969, when a 122mm rocket hit the 312th Evacuation Hospital in Chu Lai.

Although only small numbers of physical therapists and dietitians were assigned to Vietnam, their presence was important. Physical therapists were able to dramatically improve patients' medical prognoses with early intervention, reducing the extent of injuries and shortening rehabilitation time. Rather than remaining safely inside hospitals, dietitians accompanied food service equipment by landing ship from port to destination and supervised the construction of hospital mess halls.

Fifteen skilled WAC stenographers, E-5s and above, were assigned to MACV headquarters in Saigon in 1965. In 1967, a detachment of 100 WACs was assigned to the U.S. Army Vietnam (USARV) headquarters near Saigon. Most of the women had less than 12 months Army experience and were between 19 and 23 years old. Six months after the detachment arrived, the WACs and the entire USARV command moved to Long Binh, 27 miles northeast of Saigon. Because the ammunition depot at Long Binh was a major target of the enemy, WACs experienced incoming artillery fire and some were, on occasion, injured while diving for cover. By 1969, the WAC detachment peaked at 140 women. The last WACs and nurses left Vietnam in 1973.

The majority of Army women worked on bases in the United States where the Army was slowly expanding the number of jobs open to women. During ten months in 1972, the number of WACs training for jobs in the Signal Corps went from less than 100 to over 500. Many WAC assignments had a direct impact on the war. Specialist 5 Christine Jones was one of the first WAC computer operators at Fort Sam Houston, Texas, using a Burroughs 3500 system with "a large mainframe system that filled the entire room and ran by magnetic tape and key punch cards." Jones processed the records of men assigned to Vietnam. Colonel Alice M. Davis, a Russian linguist and Soviet specialist, was assigned to the Washington-Moscow "hotline" from 1972 to 1975. During the last year of her assignment, she served as Chief Presidential translator, providing direct support to President Gerald R. Ford. Staff Sergeant Judy Morgan Hoffmeister served as a clerk typist at Fort Dix, New Jersey, where she typed up the orders to "process out" troops from infantry training to Vietnam, often 500 or more soldiers in one day.

Army women were also directly involved in the end of the war. Master Sergeant Sharon Cooper was one of 100 women sent from Hawaii to Guam in April 1975 to participate in Operation New Life, assisting South Vietnamese refugees evacuated from Saigon. Wherever they were permitted, female soldiers served steadfastly side by side with their male comrades.

—*Judi Bellefaire*

Above: *U.S. Women's Army Corps advisors issuing uniforms to their South Vietnamese Army counterparts in March 1965. (Center of Military History, U.S. Army)*

the military in Vietnam—6,250 in the Army—
80 percent of them as nurses.

20 June. The "Green Beret Affair."
Special Forces soldiers murder a Vietnamese
informant because they believe he is a double agent.
The 5th Special Forces Group commander, Colonel
Robert B. Rheault, later admits to having approved
the killing, but claims his actions were justified.
General Abrams relieves Rheault of command on 21
July, and charges are brought against him and some of
his men, but political pressure prompts the Army to
dismiss them. Rheault is succeeded briefly by Colonel
Alexander Lemberes. In August Colonel Michael D.
Healy becomes the last commander of the 5th Special
Forces Group.

1 July. Change in Service Numbers.
In a change to the system of issuing military
identification numbers that started during World War
I, the Department of Defense now begins using the
soldier's Social Security Number (SSN).

1 July–31 August. Beginning to Draw Down.
The Army's withdrawal from Vietnam begins with the
departure of two brigades from the 9th Infantry
Division. This is Increment I, codenamed Keystone
Eagle, and will result in a reduction of 15,700 Army
personnel. The division's 3d Brigade remains to help
guard Saigon.

Above: *Pressing artillery ammunition containers into
service as a makeshift altar, an Army chaplain says Mass
for the gun crew during a lull in the fighting. ("The
Chaplain," John Wheat, Army Art Collection, NMUSA)*

17 August. North Koreans Down Helicopter. Korean DMZ.
A helicopter of the 59th Aviation Company strays over
the DMZ into North Korea and is shot down. Three
U.S. soldiers are captured.

27 August. CIDG Program Phased Out.
General Abrams orders the CIDG program phased
out, and Montagnard soldiers put under the control of
the South Vietnamese Army. A total of 38 light
infantry battalions are formed.

5 September. Army Charges Calley With Murder. Fort Benning, Georgia.
Lieutenant William Calley is charged with the
murders of "Oriental human beings," for his part in
the 16 March 1968 My Lai massacre, one day before
he is scheduled to be discharged.

18 September–15 December. Keystone Cardinal. South Vietnam.
Increment II of the troop withdrawals, called
Keystone Cardinal, sends the 3d Brigade, 82d
Airborne Division, back to the United States.

Left: *The U.S. Army Signal Corps station near An Khe on Hon Cong Mountain is an example of the extensive modern communication systems used during the war in Southeast Asia. (Center of Military History, U.S. Army)*

Below: *Brigadier General William Peers later headed the investigation into the My Lai incident as a lieutenant general. (U.S. Army)*

18 October. **U.S. Jeep Ambushed. Korean DMZ.**
Four soldiers are killed when a jeep from the 7th Infantry Division is ambushed by North Korean infiltrators.

11–15 November. **Troops Placed on Alert. Washington, D.C.**
Regular Army and National Guard units are placed on alert for possible riot control duty as two large anti-war demonstrations are held in the capital.

1970

January. **Status of the Army.**
The first troop draw downs further restricted the Army's offensive capabilities, but General Abrams will make good use of what he has left. Army strength in Vietnam is 330,300 (total U.S. military strength has dropped to 474,400). Army casualties are down to 6,710 soldiers killed in action the previous year.

1 February–15 April. **Keystone Bluejay.**
The 1st Infantry Division, a crucial lynchpin in blocking enemy infiltration in III Corps, leaves South Vietnam as part of Operation Keystone Bluejay. The 3d Brigade, 4th Infantry Division, soon follows.

14 March. **Peers Report Submitted.**
Lieutenant General William Peers submits his

preliminary report on the My Lai massacre. Since the statute of limitations on the offenses would run out the following day, the Army Judge Advocate General files charges against 11 officers, including Major General Samuel W. Koster, the Americal Division commander, and Colonel Oran K. Henderson, the 11th Brigade commander during the massacre. The charges against 10 of the officers will later be

Right: *The war was not restricted to Vietnam. An American combined helicopter and mechanized force finally moves into clean out the long-held enemy supply bases in Cambodia. (A. J. Alexander)*

dismissed, though Koster is demoted one grade and relieved of his command as superintendent at the U.S. Military Academy. Colonel Henderson is tried by general court martial and acquitted.

18 March. Americal Division Commander Injured.
Major General Lloyd B. Ramsey, commander of the Americal Division, is seriously injured when his helicopter crashes while surveying operations in southern I Corps. He is replaced by Major General Albert E. Milloy.

23 March. Troops Sent to Restore Order. New York.
Army National Guard troops are sent to help restore calm when a labor dispute threatens to become violent.

1 April. Defense of Firebase Illingsworth. Tay Ninh Province.
Elements of a Viet Cong regiment attack Firebase Illingworth, less than three miles from the Cambodian border. The base is manned by Lieutenant Colonel

Michael J. Conrad's 2d Battalion, 8th Cavalry, backed by two eight-inch howitzers from Battery A, 2d Battalion, 32d Artillery; three 155mm howitzers from Battery A, 1st Battalion, 30th Artillery; and six 105mm howitzers from Battery B, 1st Battalion, 77th Artillery. The assault comes in the morning and is repelled with the enemy leaving more than 75 dead. American losses are 24 killed and 54 wounded. The fight ends the enemy's offensive against the 1st Cavalry Division's screen along the northern and western borders.

1 April. 199th Brigade Commander Killed in Action. Binh Tuy Province.
The 199th Infantry Brigade's Troop D, 17th Cavalry, is ambushed while accompanying a resupply convoy. Watching the action from his helicopter, Brigadier General William R. Bond, the brigade commander, lands near the battle, then helps his men check enemy bodies for documents. A North Vietnamese soldier fires a round into General Bond's chest, killing him. Colonel Robert W. Selton, the brigade deputy

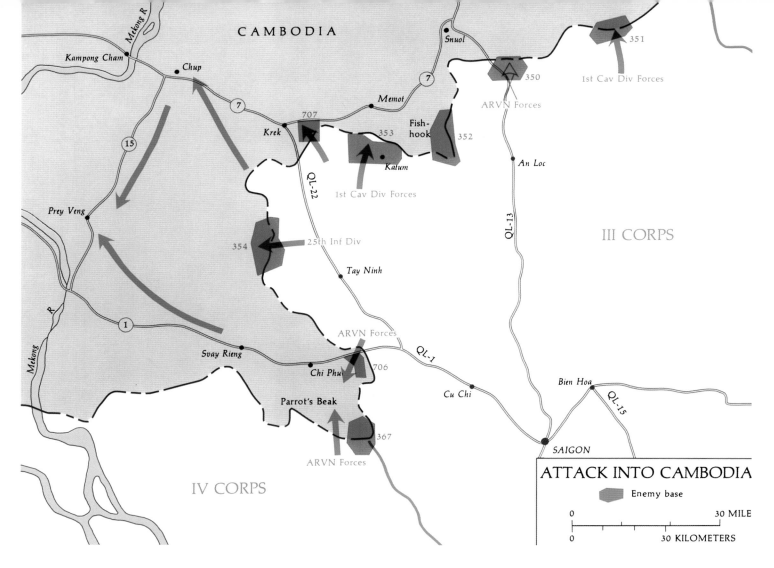

Kampong Cham
Mekong R.
Chup
7
15
707
Krek
Prey Veng
354
25th Inf Div
QL-22
Katum
1st Cav Div Forces
353
Fish-hook
352
Memot
7
Snuol
350
ARVN Forces
351
1st Cav Div Forces
An Loc
QL-13
III CORPS
Tay Ninh
Mekong R.
1
Svay Rieng
ARVN Forces
Chi Phu
706
Parrot's Beak
367
ARVN Forces
IV CORPS
QL-1
Cu Chi
Bien Hoa
QL-15
SAIGON

ATTACK INTO CAMBODIA

⬡ Enemy base

0   30 MILE

0   30 KILOMETERS

commander, assumes command until 18 July, when Colonel Joseph E. Collins arrives to take over the 199th Infantry Brigade.

26 April. Planning for Cambodia.

II Field Force commander Lieutenant General Michael S. Davison orders Major General Roberts, to prepare the 1st Cavalry Division for an operation into the Fishhook region of Cambodia, a major enemy stronghold, and reputedly the home for the elusive Central Office for South Vietnam (COSVN), the North Vietnamese command for all of southern South Vietnam. Roberts has 72 hours to plan and prepare.

29 April. "Total Victory" in the Parrot's Beak.

The South Vietnamese launch Operation Toan Thang 42, a six-phase affair that will eventually involve American units as well. Three task forces consisting of 8,000 men strike into a salient of the Cambodian border called the Parrot's Beak.

1 May. Cambodian Incursion Steps Off.

For the first time during the war, U.S. forces cross the border and strike at previously inviolate enemy sanctuaries in Cambodia. The operation is aimed at

Above: *Map of the 1970 incursion into Cambodia. (Center of Military History, U.S. Army)*

the Fishhook region north of the Parrot's Beak. The American part of the operation is named Rockcrusher, with the main thrust involving Task Force Shoemaker, named after its commander, Brigadier General Robert M. Shoemaker, the 1st Cavalry deputy commander. The task force consists of 10,000 troops from the 1st Cavalry Division, the 11th Armored Cavalry Regiment, and 5,000 South Vietnamese. The North Vietnamese mostly retreat from the operation, prompting General Davison to order the 11th Armored Cavalry Regiment to swing northward to capture the Communist-held town of Snoul. The goal is easily achieved.

3–4 May. Finding "The City."

The 1st Cavalry Division's 1st Squadron, 9th Cavalry, flying north of the main spearhead, discovers an enemy truck park that leads the following day to uncovering a massive supply base spanning almost a square mile, which the Americans dub "The City."

4–16 May. Northern Prong of the Cambodian Incursion.

As the main thrust of the Cambodian Incursion is moving across the border from III Corps, MACV orders a four-stage operation against enemy base areas in the northeastern corner of Cambodia. On 4 May, the 4th Infantry Division, commanded by Major General Glen D. Walker, and the South Vietnamese

THE ARMY NATIONAL GUARD IN VIETNAM

By most accounts, the outcome of the Vietnam War was determined in the streets and cities of America as much as in the rice paddies and jungles of Southeast Asia. While Regulars and draftees bore the burden of fighting a determined, elusive enemy in Vietnam, the ARNG had the divisive task of confronting angry crowds of civil rights activists and anti-war protesters at home.

In the summer of 1965, the U.S. committed 20,000 combat troops to South Vietnam. Against the recommendations of his top advisors, President Lyndon B. Johnson refused to mobilize the National Guard. The president had no desire to provoke a major war in Southeast Asia, and calling out the Guard, he believed, might escalate the war. At the same time, numerous educational and professional deferments permitted young men to evade the draft. Anyone entering the Guard could avoid the draft but had to serve for six years. As the war dragged on, young men increasingly sought Guard service. By the end of the war, many Americans considered the ARNG a haven for draft dodgers, a notion that frustrated and angered career Guardsmen. Denied the opportunity to serve in Vietnam, individual Guardsmen volunteered. Approximately 2,000 ARNG volunteers fought in Vietnam, half of them officers. In all, they provided distinguished service, and 23 were killed.

To aid the war effort, the Defense Department created the Selected Reserve Force, a 150,000-man composite force of ARNG and U.S. Army Reserve units. Its mission was to act as a strategic hedge against threats in Korea, Europe, and elsewhere. The ARNG provided nearly 120,00 troops to the Selected Reserve Force in three composite infantry divisions, six separate brigades, and an armored cavalry regiment.

An aura of crisis prompted by the seizure of USS *Pueblo* and the Tet Offensive in early 1968 finally prompted a reserve component mobilization. On 13 May 1968, 13,633 Army Guardsmen reported to their armories. Two ARNG infantry brigades were called up—Hawaii's 29th and Kansas' 69th. Though the brigades never deployed, 4,000 Guardsmen from their ranks volunteered for Vietnam. Thirty-one combat support and combat service support units served on various Army posts for extended active duty. Eight ARNG units went to war. Alabama's 650th Medical Detachment was the first unit to reach Vietnam. The only ARNG ground maneuver unit sent to Vietnam was Company D (Ranger), 151st Infantry, from Indiana. In December 1969, the last mobilized Army Guardsman returned home. All together, over 9,000 ARNG soldiers served in Vietnam, either in units or as individual volunteers and replacements.

Between 1957 and 1970, the ARNG acted as a domestic constabulary to quell race and anti-war riots throughout America. Guardsmen were thrust onto the national scene in 1957 when the governor of Arkansas attempted to use them to block court ordered integration in Little Rock. President Dwight D. Eisenhower countered by ordering Guardsmen to active duty with instructions to enforce racial integration. The Arkansas Guard followed the commander in chief's orders and established the ARNG as a reliable instrument of federal power in enforcing civil rights laws. In the Watts section of Los Angeles in 1965, and three years later in Detroit, thousands of Guardsmen were deployed on riot control duty. After the surprise Tet Offensive and the assassination of Dr. Martin Luther King, Jr., in 1968, 105,000 Guard soldiers were called up to face civil rights and anti-war protesters all across the nation. Perhaps the ARNG's most infamous moment occurred in May 1970 on the campus of Kent State University in Ohio, where Guardsmen opened fire on student anti-war protesters, killing four and wounding nine others.

—*Michael Doubler*

Above: *Only one Army National Guard unit, Company D, (Ranger), 151st Infantry, was deployed for combat duty in South Vietnam. ("Indiana Rangers," Mort Künstler, National Guard Bureau)*

Left: *Son Tay raiders are shown in their helicopter on the way to attack a North Vietnamese prison believed to hold American POWs. The facility is empty, but the raiders escape without loss. (John F. Kennedy Special Warfare Museum)*

Below: *Colonel Arthur "Bull" Simons delivers a final briefing before the Son Tay raiders set out on their rescue operation. (Benjamin F. Schemmer)*

22d Division launch Operation Binh Tay (Tame the West), but the move is slow and disorganized, angering General Abrams. The 4th Infantry Division is badly overextended in a vast and rugged region, as are the South Vietnamese. On the eve of the incursion there are few forward bases along the border and logistic lines are long. Despite the problems, the allies move forward, only to be hit hard by enemy forces entrenched in the dense jungle. For several days they are heavily engaged, but on 6 May units discover a North Vietnamese base camp and hospital complex. The 4th Infantry Division withdraws from Cambodia on 16 May leaving the rest of the operation to the South Vietnamese.

4 May. **Guard Fires on Students. Ohio.**
Ohio Army National Guardsmen, acting as state troops, open fire on student anti-war demonstrators at Kent State University, killing four and wounding nine others. Demonstrations take place at a number of other colleges across the nation.

6–14 May. **The Dog's Head.**
The Cambodian incursion expands to include the 1st and 3d Brigades of the 25th Infantry Division moving into the Dog's Head region west of Tay Ninh Province. Another thrust, this one by elements of the 3d Brigade, 9th Infantry Division, attacks the Parrot's Beak.

9–24 May. **Opening the Mekong River.**
U.S. Army advisors accompany the South Vietnamese 9th and 21st Divisions to clear the banks of the

Mekong River as they move upstream to open a river path to Phnom Penh, the Cambodian capital.

28 May. **New Rules on War Crimes.**
In response to the Peers Inquiry into the My Lai massacre, the Army implements Regulation 350-216, regarding an individual soldier's responsibilities for reporting war crimes, the procedure to follow when given an illegal order, and what to do when his commander is accused of a war crime.

11 June. **First Female General Officers**
Colonel Anna M. Hayes, Chief of Army Nurse Corps, and Colonel Elizabeth P. Hoisington, Director of WAC, are promoted to brigadier general, making them the Army's first female generals.

30 June. **Cambodian Incursion Ends.**
All U.S. forces cross the border back into South Vietnam. Although South Vietnamese troops will continue limited operations into December, this is the last time the allies will move in strength into Cambodian territory. At its height, the incursion involved 30,000 U.S. and 48,000 South Vietnamese troops. American losses are 338 killed and 1,525 wounded; the South Vietnamese lose 638 killed and 4,009 wounded. COSVN headquarters is not captured, but Communist losses are severe. Enemy manpower losses were thought to be more than 11,000 killed, with an additional 2,328 captured, but it was the Communist logistical system that suffered most.

1 July–31 December. **Keystone Robin.**
MACV executes Increments IV and V of the draw down and redeploys the 3d Brigade, 9th Infantry Division, the last major U.S. Army unit south of Saigon; the 199th Infantry Brigade; the 1st and 2d Brigades, 4th Infantry Division; and the 1st and 3d Brigades of the 25th Infantry Division. The withdrawal is a reduction in Army strength of almost 57,000 men.

1–23 July. **Siege of Firebase Ripcord. Thua Thien Province.**
As a part of Operation Texas Star launched in April to protect pacification gains in the lowlands, the 101st Airborne Division builds a handful of firebases west of

Hue. On 1 July, the North Vietnamese attack Ripcord. Manned by two companies from 2d Battalion, 506th Infantry, and 2d Battalion, 319th Artillery, Ripcord holds its own until 18 July when a Chinook helicopter is hit by enemy antiaircraft fire and crashes into the ammunition dump. Thousands of rounds explode, destroying six howitzers, two recoilless rifles, and the base counter-mortar radar unit. Major General John J. Hennessey, division commander, decides to evacuate and on the morning of 23 July sends in 14 Chinooks to pick up the defenders. One helicopter is shot down and eight are damaged by North Vietnamese gunners. The base is successfully evacuated, leaving the remaining artillery and other heavy equipment behind. Losses at Ripcord are 61 killed and 325 wounded.

7 July. **1st Cavalry Commander Killed in Crash.**
The new commander of the 1st Cavalry Division, Major General George W. Casey, is killed in a helicopter crash. He is replaced by Major General George W. Putnam, Jr., who will remain with the division until it leaves Vietnam.

5 September–8 October. **Last Major U.S. Ground Operation. Thua Thien Province.**
The 101st Airborne Division steps up pacification protection operations with Operation Jefferson Glen. The objective is to aggressively patrol to prevent enemy forces from disrupting the government's new programs in the countryside. Jefferson Glen lasts for 399 days and accounts for 2,026 enemy dead.

21 November. **Operation Kingpin. Son Tay Raid.**
A joint Army and Air Force special operations team flies deep into North Vietnam, landing by helicopter at Son Tay prison 20 miles northwest of Hanoi. The

56 raiders, led by Colonel Arthur D. "Bull" Simons, kill some 25 North Vietnamese defenders but the American prisoners had been moved a few weeks earlier. The "Son Tay Raiders," as they come to be known, return to Thailand without losing a man.

22 December. Congress Halts Advisory Efforts.
Congress prohibits the use of U.S. combat forces or military advisors in either Laos or Cambodia.

1971

January. Status of the Army.
The U.S. Army in Vietnam is deteriorating. Ongoing troop withdrawals combined with continued fighting have undermined morale, causing a surge in drug use, insubordination, and lax combat discipline. The military mission has reached an impasse: Army strength is at 250,700 out of a total of 385,800 U.S. military personnel. During the year General Westmoreland approves creation of the Board for

Above: *The UH-1 "Huey" became the workhorse of airmobile operations. Keeping these craft flying required dedicated ground crews. ("Chopper Maintenance," Stephen H. Sheldon, Army Art Collection, NMUSA)*

Dynamic Training under Colonel Paul F. Gorman. His mission is to find ways to improve combat arms training. From this study will come the Combat Arms Training Board which will have a major impact on future Army training.

1 January. 1st Cavalry Division Redeploys.
The 1st and 2d Brigades of the 1st Cavalry Division, along with the 11th Armored Cavalry Regiment and the 2d Brigade, 25th Infantry Division, leave South Vietnam as the last segment of Keystone Robin.

30 January–7 February. Operation Dewey Canyon II.
Armored personnel carriers from the 1st Brigade, 5th Infantry Division, move west on Route 9 just below the Demilitarized Zone toward the old U.S. Marine base at Khe Sanh, opening the road on 5 February. At the same time, elements of the 101st Airborne Division move into the A Shau Valley in a feint to distract the North Vietnamese from the real target—a North Vietnamese base in Laos.

8 February–6 March. Operation Lam Son 719.
A South Vietnamese force of 16,000 moves into Laos along Route 9, aiming to raze a major North Vietnamese supply center and cut the Ho Chi Minh Trail. U.S. Army forces can only provide helicopter

Right: *In Class "A" uniforms, smiling troops from the 101st Airborne Division return from their tour of duty in Vietnam. (National Archives)*

Below: *Secretary of the Army Robert F. Froehlke assumed his post in July 1971. (Everett Raymond Kinstler, Army Art Collection, NMUSA)*

support. Some 2,600 Americans serve as crews for 700 helicopters flying into Laos, all under the command of XXIV Corps commander Lieutenant General James W. Sutherland. The North Vietnamese do not expect the attack, but the area is well-defended and directly to the south are bases with 22,000 troops. The South Vietnamese make strong headway for a few days, but

by 10 February they are bogged down and additional North Vietnamese units are closing in. The enemy overruns two outposts north of Route 9, but the incursion continues and the South Vietnamese reach the town of Tchepone, a key enemy command center, on 6 March.

1 March. **5th Special Forces Group Departs.**
The 5th Special Forces Group ceases all operations and departs Vietnam. Some Special Forces personnel remain in country as instructors to the South Vietnamese as part of the Special Advisory Group.

4 March–6 April. **Withdrawing From Laos.**
After reaching Tchepone, the South Vietnamese declare the operation a success and begin to withdraw. But the enemy is closing in, and Route 9—the only way back to South Vietnam—becomes a gauntlet. American helicopters help evacuate the fleeing troops in the face of intense enemy fire. By operation's end, 108 helicopters are shot down and 618 damaged. The last South Vietnamese forces reach the border on 6 April with heavy losses. American aircrews suffer 1,402 casualties, 215 of them killed.

15 March. **A Rise in "Fraggings."**
During the night a grenade rolls into officers' barracks at Bien Hoa, killing two lieutenants and wounding a third. A black soldier known for his anti-war

activities, Private Billy Dean Smith, is accused of the murders and arrested, but the evidence is inconclusive and he is found not guilty. The case highlights two increasingly troublesome trends in Vietnam—worsening race relations and an increase in attacks by soldiers against their own officers, called "fraggings" because they were often carried out by throwing grenades into sleeping quarters. During the war there are reported to be a total of 788 cases, resulting in 86 deaths and 714 wounded.

28 March. Attack on Firebase Mary Ann. Quang Tin Province.

In the early morning hours some 50 North Vietnamese creep through the wire surrounding Firebase Mary Ann, a remote outpost of the Americal Division's 196th Infantry Brigade in the highlands. The defenders—231 Americans from Company C, 1st Battalion, 46th Infantry, along with artillery and a reconnaissance platoon—are surprised by the attack and can put up only limited opposition. When it is over, 30 Americans are dead and 82 wounded. An investigation into the attack finds that the defenders were lax in their duties, and the Americal Division commander, Major General James L. Baldwin, and 196th Infantry Brigade commander Colonel William S. Hathaway, are relieved.

29 March. Calley Guilty of Murder.

A jury finds Lieutenant William Calley guilty of the premeditated murders of 22 people at My Lai. The 45-day trial is one of the longest military courts-martial in American history. Two days later the judge sentences Calley to life in prison at hard labor, but the sentence will later be reduced to 10 years, and in November 1974 Secretary of the Army Howard Callaway paroles Calley.

30 April. New Command Arrangements.

With most U.S. forces now withdrawn from Vietnam, the command structure is changing. I and II Field Forces stand down and are replaced by the Second and Third Regional Assistance Commands (SRAC and TRAC respectively). In addition, the Delta Regional Assistance Command (DRAC) is formed in the Mekong Delta. The new regional commands will oversee the remaining U.S. advisors.

1 May–30 November. Keystone Oriole.

Three increments of withdrawals, named Keystone Oriole, result in the departure of most of the Americal Division, the 173d Airborne Brigade, and several independent units—a total of almost 71,000 Army troops.

1 July. **Froehlke Becomes Secretary.**
Robert F. Froehlke replaces Resor to become the tenth secretary. Froehlke supervises the final withdrawal of the Army from Vietnam and implements the All-Volunteer (VOLAR) Army plan with the end to the draft.

7 August. **Last U.S. Army Medal of Honor Action. Quang Tri Province.**
A small reconnaissance team led by First Lieutenant Loren D. Hagen runs into a large North Vietnamese force and is pinned down. The enemy tries to overrun the small team, but Hagen rallies his men, directing fire, distributing ammunition, and firing his own weapon. When a rocket-propelled grenade wounds some of his men, Hagen crawls through enemy fire to get to them. He almost reaches his objective before being killed in a hail of bullets. Lieutenant Hagen is posthumously awarded the Medal of Honor.

1 December. **101st Airborne Division Redeploys.**
After 1,573 days in Vietnam, the "Screaming Eagles" begin redeploying to their home base at Fort Campbell, Kentucky. The move, called Keystone Mallard, will take until 31 January 1972.

1972

January. **Status of the Army.**
Troop strength is down to 133,000, with the Army's portion at 109,000. Most soldiers are advisors—a return to the earliest days of the war—who have volunteered for duty in Vietnam. And despite the continuing troop withdrawals, MACV intelligence clearly sees a massive enemy offensive on the horizon. As MACV watches the enemy move men, tanks, and artillery down the Ho Chi Minh Trail, General Abrams is convinced of a coming offensive, but the Army withdrawal continues unabated.

19 March. **First Regional Assistance Command Established.**
The First Regional Assistance Command (FRAC) takes over for XXIV Corps and assumes control of American advisors remaining in the five northernmost provinces. Major General Frederick J. Kroesen, Jr., becomes the first FRAC commander.

30 March. **The Easter Offensive Begins.**
The Communists launch the largest assault of the war. The North Vietnamese take aim at three major targets—Quang Tri near the Demilitarized Zone,

Opposite: *Outposts in the jungle were subject to attack at any hour. ("Night Battle," John Wheat, Army Art Collection, NMUSA)*

Right: *In the foreground Army Bell H-1 Cobra gunships fly a mission ready to attack the enemy with swift, deadly fire. ("Heading for Trouble," William S. Phillips)*

Kontum in the Central Highlands, and An Loc just north of Saigon. American intelligence sees the attack coming, but does not realize the extent to which armor and artillery will play a role. Fourteen Communist divisions and 26 separate regiments of some 120,000 men will take part in the offensive, along with some 1,200 tanks and armored vehicles. The U.S. Army presence consists of advisors stationed with South Vietnamese combat units and air cavalry gunships, both of which will play crucial roles.

30 March–1 May. Battle for Quang Tri. Quang Tri Province.

North Vietnamese forces make their quickest gains in northernmost I Corps. Attacking across the Demilitarized Zone and from the Laotian border, they swallow up most of the South Vietnamese firebases in northern Quang Tri Province, all but destroying Saigon's 3d Division. A brand new unit, the 3d Division, has the largest U.S. Army divisional advisory team of the war, called Team 155. Commanded by Colonel Donald J. Metcalf, Team 155 attempts to hold the 3d Division together, but by the end of April what

Above: *Before becoming Chief of Staff of the Army, General Bruce C. Palmer served as II Corps Field Force commander in Vietnam. (Herbert E. Abrams, Army Art Collection, NMUSA)*

Right: *Former armor officer Creighton W. Abrams, Jr., became the Army's 27th Chief of Staff. (Herbert E. Abrams, Army Art Collection, NMUSA)*

is left of the unit is holed up in Quang Tri City. Air Force helicopters rescue the American advisors on the morning of 1 May, and the North Vietnamese capture their first provincial capital since Hue fell in 1968.

5 April–12 May. The Battle of An Loc. Binh Long Province.

On 5 April the North Vietnamese attack north of Saigon. North Vietnamese tanks roll over the town of Loc Ninh, killing two American Army advisors and capturing four, and then turn on An Loc. With three divisions they virtually surround the town, which is defended by one South Vietnamese division and a handful of American advisors. A savage mortar and artillery barrage starts on 12 April and the next day a ground assault spearheaded by PT-76 and T-54 tanks is made. The senior advisor to III Corps, Major General James F. Hollingsworth, orders massive airstrikes in support of the besieged town. Hand-to-hand fighting rages for three days, but continued air support—particularly Cobra helicopter gunships—keeps the enemy at bay. A second attack opens 11 May with two armored forces. They come close to breaking through, but increased airstrikes—including B-52—bombers stave off defeat. The worst of the fighting is over, but desultory combat continues into July.

21 April. TOW Helicopters Sent to Vietnam.

Two UH-1B helicopters armed with an experimental anti-tank missile system called the TOW (tube-launched, optically tracked, wire-guided) arrive for the 1st Aviation Brigade at Tan Son Nhut Airbase. For the next two months the helicopters assist South

CREIGHTON W. ABRAMS: GENERAL "ABE"

Despite being featured as a 30-year-old, World War II tank battalion commander in 1945 in *Life* magazine, and as a 47-year-old division commander in *Time* magazine in1961, Creighton W. Abrams is far better known inside the Army he loved than he is to the American public. He was the consummate professional, whose skills and wisdom grew apace with his responsibilities. Known primarily as a field commander—of two tank battalions, an armored cavalry regiment, an armored division, a corps, and the Military Assistance Command, Vietnam (MACV)—General Abrams also served four separate tours and over nine years in the Pentagon.

Born and raised in Agawam, Massachusetts, "Abe" entered West Point three years into the Great Depression, was commissioned in 1936 as a cavalry officer, and, after marrying his lifelong partner Julie, went to his first post, the 1st Cavalry Division at Fort Bliss, Texas. One of the techniques he studied there was how to defeat tanks while on horseback.

Within seven years, however, he was trained as a tanker, promoted four times, and put in command of the 37th Tank Battalion of the 4th Armored Division. In nine months of combat in Europe, the 4th Armored Division, led by the 37th Tank Battalion, was credited with the relief of the 101st Airborne Division at Bastogne and became known as Patton's favorite division. Sixteen years later, when Cold War tensions were high and the Berlin Wall had just been erected, Major General Abrams was in command of the 3d Armored Division, the unit deemed most likely to be sent to relieve the American forces in Berlin.

A year and a half later on the Army Staff in the Pentagon, he dealt with major incidents involving school desegregation and the civil rights movement. Thrust into one particularly difficult situation when tempers were short, he had to tell Attorney General Robert Kennedy to wait while he took another incoming phone call from "his brother." Just shy of his 50th birthday, he became the Army's Vice Chief of Staff.

Abrams' 10 years as a full general encompassed the Vietnam War. First as Vice Chief of Staff preparing the Army to go to war, then as Deputy to General Westmoreland, and finally as the commander of MACV. He shifted the American strategy to emphasize pacification and Vietnamization and supervised the return of American forces. During his two years, 1972–1974, as the Army Chief of Staff, Abrams set about the task of rebuilding the Army.

When he talked to his superiors or testified before Congress, his reputation for integrity and leadership gave him enormous credibility. In the summer of 1974, when he knew he was dying of cancer, Abrams convinced Congress that the Army should be allowed to increase active Army divisions from 13 to 16 without increasing the number of soldiers in the active Army. The plan was carried out after he died and resulted in fundamental changes in the structure of the total Army.

Despite his bluff exterior, "Abe" was hard to pigeonhole. He was undeniably charismatic and inspirational to those he led, but also to those he worked for. If there is an Abrams legacy, it is one that really started with our first Commander, George Washington. It is this: the best Army officers and soldiers are needed most when the mission and the times are the most difficult and demanding; and their commitment to the best that is America and her Army must be total.

—*Brigadier General Creighton, W. Abrams, Jr., USA (Ret)*

Above: *General Creighton Abrams made a special effort to visit commanders in the field to obtain first-hand information on the situation. (National Archives)*

Above: *World War II Pacific veteran General Frederick C. Weyand followed General Abrams as the MACV's commander. (Bjorn Egeli, Army Art Collection, NMUSA)*

Vietnamese troops besieged at Kontum. By the time the TOW crews depart on 22 June, they are credited with destroying two dozen tanks, four armored personnel carriers, seven trucks, and two artillery pieces during its short tour of duty.

30 April. **MACVSOG Deactivated.**
MACV deactivates the Studies and Observations Group (SOG), the organization responsible for clandestine operations into Laos, Cambodia, and North Vietnam. SOG is replaced by Advisory Team 158, which will support the South Vietnamese side of SOG, the Strategic Technical Directorate.

1 May–30 June. **Last of the 1st Cavalry Division Departs Vietnam.**
The last major U.S. combat units, the 3d Brigade, 1st Cavalry Division, and most of the 196th Infantry Brigade, depart Vietnam as part of the Increment XII drawdown, dubbed Keystone Pheasant.

14 May. **Fighting in the Highlands. Central Highlands**
The North Vietnamese open the third prong of their offensive with a thrust at Kontum. The South

Vietnamese 23d Division is defending the town, along with a determined group of U.S. Army advisors, and air support is controlled by the corps senior advisor, John Paul Vann, a former U.S. Army advisor and the only civilian to hold such a position. By early June the attack is blunted and the North Vietnamese retreat.

9 June. **John Paul Vann Killed.**
John Paul Vann is killed in a helicopter crash while flying to survey the fighting at Kontum. Vann is the civilian equivalent of a major general, making him the highest-ranking American official killed during 1972.

29 June. **Weyand Replaces Abrams at MACV.**
General Abrams turns over command of MACV to his deputy, General Frederick C. Weyand, and returns to Washington.

30 June. **Westmoreland Steps Down As Chief.**
General Bruce Palmer, Jr., is appointed as acting Chief of Staff to replace General William C. Westmoreland, who retires in July. Controversy on the conduct of the war in Vietnam causes the senate to delay approval of General Abrams to the position.

9 July. **Army General Killed at An Loc.**
Brigadier General Richard Tallman, the deputy commander of TRAC, the U.S. advisory command in III Corps, is killed by North Vietnamese mortar rounds as he surveys the damage at An Loc.

10 August. **Cheyenne Helicopter Cancelled. Washington, D.C.**
The Army announces cancellation of the contract to build a new modernized helicopter named Cheyenne. Cost and concerns about whether it fits the future needs of the Army caused the decision. However at the same time the Army said it is moving ahead with development of a new Advanced Attack Helicopter (AAH), a concept under consideration for several years.

11–26 August. **Last Army Combat Ground Force Departs.**
Commander, Lieutenant Colonel Rocco Negris, retires the battalion colors of Task Force Gimlet, a force made up of 3d Battalion, 21st Infantry, along with remnants of other recently inactivated units. The task force headquarters closes down on 11 August and leaves Vietnam. The American unit ground war in Vietnam comes to an end, but Army advisors remain.

12 October. **Abrams Confirmed as Chief, Washington.**
General Creighton W. Abrams, Jr., is sworn in as the 27th Chief of Staff of the Army. He faces the

challenge of renewing the Army's spirit and rebuilding it in the face of reduced manpower and budget, and a widespread anti-military sentiment after the war.

24 December. **Bob Hope's Last Show. Saigon.**
Comedian Bob Hope gives his last Christmas show to U.S. troops in Vietnam. It is his ninth consecutive holiday appearance there.

25 December. **Army Strength Drops.**
U.S. military strength in Vietnam is reduced by another 700 men, bringing the total to 24,000 (16,100 Army), the lowest number since early 1965. Of the 300 men killed in 1972, 172 of them were Army.

1973

January. **Status of the Army.**
The Army begins the long rebuilding of its NCO Corps. The Sergeant Major Academy approved in 1972, opens its doors to the first class. Other steps are being taken to put in place a pyramid of professional education courses and schools for more junior NCOs.

In Vietnam U.S. military attention returns to ensuring that the South Vietnamese armed forces are outfitted and equipped to fight alone. Operation Enhance, as it is called, will have scheduled for delivery 70,767 individual and crew-served weapons, 383 artillery pieces, 622 tracked vehicles, and 2,035 wheeled vehicles. Meanwhile, in Cambodia, a handful of American advisors work as the Military Equipment Delivery Team (MEDTC) stationed in Phnom Penh.

23 January. **Paris Agreement.**
President Nixon announces that the United States and North Vietnam have initialed an agreement in Paris.

23 January–3 February. **"Landgrab 73."**
MACV reports the North Vietnamese are trying to expand their holdings. The South Vietnamese fight hard to keep their territory, and MACV believes that they can hold their own.

27 January. **Last Soldier Killed in Action. An Loc.**
Army advisor Lieutenant Colonel William B. Nolde is killed by an artillery round. Nolde's death comes 11 hours before the ceasefire, making him the last U.S. serviceman to die in combat during the war.

27 January. **Ceasefire Takes Effect.**
The ceasefire is in effect. Saigon controls about 75 percent of South Vietnam's territory and 85 percent of

Above: *Secretary of the Army Howard H. Callaway oversaw the Army's reorganization after Vietnam. (George Augusta, Army Art Collection, NMUSA)*

the population. The South Vietnamese army is well-equipped with weapons, and the United States promises that aid will continue.

28 January. **Defense Attaché Office Established.**
The Defense Attaché Office (DAO), commanded by Major General John E. Murray, is established to take over residual U.S. military activities. With an authorized strength of 50 military and 1,200 civilians, much of the DAO's responsibilities focus on maintaining the South Vietnamese military and closing down remaining American facilities.

12–27 February. **Operation Homecoming Begins.**
As per the Paris Agreement, Hanoi begins releasing the 591 acknowledged American prisoners of war. Claiming that the U.S. has violated the Paris Agreement, the North Vietnamese halt the releases, but on 29 March the last 67 POWs are released. During Operation Homecoming 117 Army prisoners are released, out of a total of 164 captured during the war.

16 March. **Longest Held POW Released.**
Army Captain Floyd J. Thompson is finally released after being a prisoner of the Viet Cong for nine years.

28 March. Aviation Brigade Departs.

The 1st Aviation Brigade is deactivated and the men depart Vietnam.

29 March. MACV Closes Down.

MACV is disestablished after more than a decade of military presence in South Vietnam. In his final report MACV commander General Weyand warns that South Vietnam's future depends on "the continuation of adequate levels of U.S. military and economic assistance." The DAO assumes control of the few remaining military functions.

29 March. Military Police Depart Vietnam.

The 18th Military Police Brigade becomes the last major Army unit to leave. In addition to normal police activities, the brigade had tactical responsibility for a 22-square-mile area around Long Binh. At the height of the war there were about 30,000 military police serving in Vietnam.

14 May. Callaway Becomes New Secretary of The Army.
After a short gap, Howard H. Callaway is sworn in as the 11th Secretary of the Army. He completes Army adjustment to phase out of the draft and oversees reorganization of the Army command and staff structure.

19 June. Case-Church Amendment.
The U.S. Senate passes a bill to bar appropriations from being used to finance U.S. military operations in Southeast Asia unless specifically authorized by Congress. Critics argue that the amendment paves the way for North Vietnam to violate the Paris Accords and invade the South without fear of American retaliatory action.

August. Powell Takes Battalion Command. South Korea.
Lieutenant Colonel Colin Powell begins his tour as commander of a battalion of the 2d Infantry Division under Major General Henry Emerson, division commander. Emerson has put together an extensive program to restore morale and discipline in the division.

24 October. Hanoi Continues Buildup.
U.S. intelligence reports that, since the ceasefire, the North Vietnamese presence in South Vietnam has increased by 70,000 men, 400 tanks, and 200 artillery pieces. There are also 12 enemy airfields inside South Vietnam, along with several new all-weather roads, stretching from Quang Tri Province south to the Mekong Delta.

1974

January. Status of the Army.
As part of its rebuilding, the Army activates the 75th Infantry Regiment (Ranger) with three battalions. The unit is later redesignated the 75th Ranger Regiment. In Vietnam, only a small group of advisors with the Defense Attaché Office remain. Major General Murray, the DAO commander, can do little except attempt to manage the diminishing supplies going to the South Vietnamese Army.

4 June. First Female Army Pilot. Fort Rucker, Alabama.
Second Lieutenant Sally W. Murphy graduates from Army flight school, becoming the Army's first female helicopter pilot.

9 August. A New President.
President Richard Nixon resigns. His vice president, Gerald R. Ford, takes office and becomes the new commander-in-chief.

4 September–3 October. General Weyand Replaces Abrams.
After a relatively short illness, General Abrams, Army Chief of Staff, dies of cancer and General Frederick C. Weyand, vice chief of staff becomes acting chief. He is confirmed on October 3 and becomes the 28th Chief of Staff of the Army. Among other things he works to increase the Army and improve readiness.

1975

January. Status of the Army.
American military aid and advice to South Vietnam has all but ceased. Observers mostly watch as battles continue to rage throughout the country and the North Vietnamese prepare for the final offensive.

27 March. General Weyand Goes to Vietnam.
Army Chief of Staff General Frederick Weyand goes to Saigon to make a personal assessment of the situation. He concludes the South Vietnamese cannot withstand a major Communist offensive without U.S. air support and he predicts that without it South Vietnam will soon fall.

31 March. Clemency Program Ends.
President Ford's program to grant clemency to military deserters and draft evaders ends. A total of 22,500 men applied for return out of a possible 124,400.

5 April. Evacuation of Phnom Penh. Cambodia.
The Cambodian army is unable to resist the advance of the Khmer Rouge and its North Vietnamese and Viet Cong allies. Operation Eagle Pull, the evacuation of the American personnel including the Army advisors of MEDTC under Brigadier William Palmer, is implemented by helicopters as the city begins to fall.

29–30 April. Evacuation of Saigon. South Vietnam.
Operation Frequent Wind, the largest helicopter evacuation in history, removes the last Americans from the U.S. Embassy. In 19 hours, 81 helicopters carry 978 Americans and almost 1,100 Vietnamese to ships

Above: *Even as the United States makes its withdrawal from Vietnam, an Army artillery crew maintains readiness, training at Fort Sill, OK. ("Target Practice," Joseph Santoro, Army Art Collection, NMUSA)*

offshore. Two U.S. Marines are killed when their helicopter crashes—the last American servicemen to die in the war. North Vietnamese forces take Saigon on the morning of 30 April. At the war's end 58,148 Americans had died: 6,598 officers, 1,276 warrants, and 50,274 enlisted.

5 August. Hoffman Becomes Secretary of the Army.
Martin R. Hoffman assumes his duties as the 12th secretary. As a Reserve OCS graduate, he has extensive active duty experience and will serve under two presidents. A major focus of his efforts will be to help rebuild the Army following the Vietnam War.

8 October. U.S. Military Academy Opens to Women.
The Army announces that the U.S. Military at West Point will accept women as cadets for the first time for the next academic year.

***Fall.* Army Begins Testing New Attack Helicopters.**
As the year draws near a close, the Army renews testing of competing models of advanced attack helicopters, moving along a development track that will ultimately result in the selection of the AH-64 Apache.

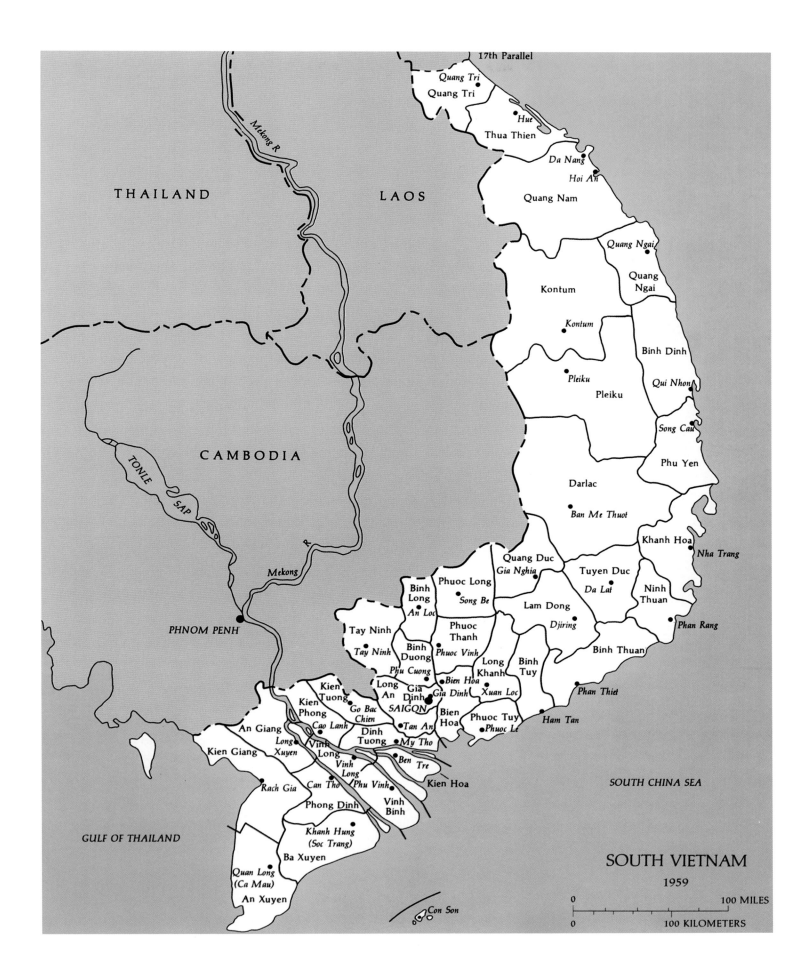

17th Parallel

THAILAND

LAOS

Mekong R.

Quang Tri
Quang Tri

Hue
Thua Thien

Da Nang
Hoi An
Quang Nam

Quang Ngai
Quang
Ngai

CAMBODIA

Kontum

Kontum

Binh Dinh

Pleiku
Pleiku

Qui Nhon

TONLE
SAP

Song Cau

Phu Yen

Darlac

Ban Me Thuot

Khanh Hoa

Nha Trang

Mekong

PHNOM PENH

Quang Duc
Gia Nghia

Tuyen Duc
Da Lat

Ninh
Thuan

Phan Rang

Binh
Long
An Loc

Phuoc Long
Song Be

Lam Dong
Djiring

Tay Ninh

Phuoc
Thanh

Binh Thuan

Tay Ninh

Binh
Duong
Phuoc Vinh

Long
Khanh

Binh
Tuy

Phu Cuong

Phan Thiet

Kien
Tuong

Kien
Phong

Long
An

Gia
Dinh
Bien Hoa
Gia Dinh

SAIGON
Tan An

Bien
Hoa

Xuan Loc

Phuoc Tuy
Phuoc Le

Ham Tan

*Go Bac
Chien*

An Giang

Cao Lanh

Dinh
Tuong
My Tho

Long
Xuyen

*Vinh
Long*

Kien Giang

Vinh
Long
Phu Vinh

Ben Tre

Kien Hoa

SOUTH CHINA SEA

Rach Gia

Can Tho

Phong Dinh

Vinh
Binh

GULF OF THAILAND

Khanh Hung
(Soc Trang)

Ba Xuyen

*Quan Long
(Ca Mau)*

An Xuyen

Con Son

SOUTH VIETNAM

1959

| 0 | | 100 MILES |

| 0 | | 100 KILOMETERS |

Above: *Map of South Vietnam delineating its
provinces and their capitals. (Center of Military
History, U.S. Army)*

REFORGING THE SWORD

1976–1990

REFORGING THE SWORD

1976—1990

Matthew Seelinger

In the years following the Vietnam War, the United States Army began a process of rebuilding and reorganization to heal the wounds it had suffered during the long conflict in Southeast Asia. In addition to substantial changes in its force structure, doctrine, and training, the Army began to develop and field several new and modern weapons systems superior to anything the Soviet Union possessed. Slowly, the Army would emerge from the shadow of Vietnam, and led by many veterans of that trying conflict, proudly reestablish itself as the world's most powerful and professional ground force.

The Army of the immediate post-Vietnam era faced several problems, including budget constraints, outdated doctrine, aging weapons, public apathy, and a number of personnel problems, such as drug use, low quality of recruits, and racial strife. Symbolic of the Army's—and the rest of the U.S. armed services'—problems in the years after Vietnam was the disastrous April 1980 attempt to rescue American hostages in Iran. This aborted joint service operation never came close to achieving its goal and ended in an accident that killed eight American servicemen.

Despite these and other problems, Army leaders continued or implemented new reforms designed to overhaul and improve the Army, now composed completely of volunteers. In addition, a core of dedicated officers and senior noncommissioned officers opted to stay to rebuild the Army they loved.

Changes in the Army's force structure, built around the late General Creighton W. Abrams' "Total Army" concept, continued. As a result of General Abrams' vision, the Army's reserve components, the Army National Guard and Army Reserve, were more fully integrated into the Army's overall force structure by the late 1980s, particularly in the combat support and combat service support elements.

During this period, the Army's senior leadership reexamined the Army's warfighting doctrine and released several revised editions of Field Manual 100-5, *Operations*, which advocated concepts such as Active Defense, and later AirLand Battle, for fighting a war in Europe against Warsaw Pact forces. The Army also placed renewed emphasis on education and training with the opening of the School of Advanced Military Studies at Fort Leavenworth, Kansas, and the National Training Center at Fort Irwin, California.

Saddled with an aging array of weaponry, the Army of the post-Vietnam era undertook a massive weapons development program to reequip its forces. Among the most important weapon systems that emerged during this era were the UH-60 Black Hawk helicopter, the M1 Abrams main battle tank, the M2/3 Bradley Fighting Vehicle, the AH-64 Apache helicopter, and the Patriot Air Defense Missile System. All of these systems would eventually play major roles in the Army's combat actions of the future, and each would perform its assigned missions effectively.

The presidency of Ronald Reagan (1981–1989) undoubtedly had a profound impact on the Army and the rest of the nation's armed forces. Reagan kept his campaign promise to increase defense spending, and consequently, the Army was able to buy the numbers of improved weapons it had spent many years developing. Furthermore, with increased defense spending, the Army's ability to attract higher quality recruits, and an overall rise in national pride, morale within the Army reached levels that had not been seen since before the Vietnam War.

During the 1980s, American soldiers were deployed around the world to participate in a number of operations. In addition to peacekeeping assignments in the Sinai Peninsula and Lebanon, U.S. forces, led by the Army, conducted two significant

1st Special Forces Group (Airborne)

Practice Jumping — Yomitan Airfield, Okinawa
27 May 1971

combat operations. The first of these, Operation Urgent Fury—the invasion of the Caribbean island nation of Grenada in October 1983—was the largest American military operation since the Vietnam War. While ultimately successful, Operation Urgent Fury was not devoid of problems, and it provided a number of lessons in conducting joint military campaigns.

The second major operation of the 1980s, Operation Just Cause—the invasion of Panama in December 1989—was a much larger and more complex joint service campaign, largely consisting of Army units, that again proved highly successful. Much of the success of Just Cause can be attributed to the lessons learned from Grenada, rigorous training and increased professionalism of the Army, improved weapons, and various organizational reforms, such as the Goldwater-Nichols Act of 1986 and the creation of U.S. Special Operations Command, which helped to ease the problems of joint operations. Additionally, American soldiers during this period were deployed around the world in advisory roles, supporting allied governments against Communist insurgencies. In some cases, particularly in Central and South America, American advisors became combatants, and a number of American soldiers were killed or wounded in these brush-fire wars.

By late 1989, however, with the collapse of communism in Eastern Europe, the Cold War effectively came to an end. As a result, American military planners began to draw down U.S. forces now deemed unnecessary in the post-Cold War era. But just as the United States prepared to reap the rewards of the peace dividend, a new threat to world peace and economic stability emerged with Iraq's invasion of neighboring Kuwait. The United States, under a United Nations mandate, began organizing an armed international coalition, first to protect Saudi Arabia, then to oust Iraqi forces from Kuwait. Unlike Grenada and Panama, however, Iraq had a powerful military, hardened by a long war with Iran and equipped with a modern, largely Soviet-designed arsenal that included large numbers of tanks, armored vehicles, and artillery pieces. The coming war with Iraq would provide the first serious test for the post-Vietnam War Army, its largely unbloodied All-Volunteer Force soldiers, and its rebuilt arsenal.

Pages 858–859: *An M1A1 Abrams tank and M2 Bradley Fighting Vehicle of the 2d Battalion, 8th Cavalry, 1st Cavalry Division, take part in maneuvers at Fort Hood, Texas. (Center of Military History)*

Above: *Soldiers from the 1st Special Operations Group (Airborne) practice parachute assaults at a base on the island of Okinawa. ("Practice Jumping," Al Crull, Army Art Collection, NMUSA)*

"I won't be happy until I see his tanks destroyed. I want to leave their tanks as smoking kilometer fence posts all the way back to Baghdad."

—General Colin Powell, Chairman, Joint Chiefs of Staff,
Pentagon briefing, 11 August 1990 (quoted in *The Generals' War: The Inside Story of the Conflict in the Gulf,*
Boston: Little, Brown, 1995)

1976

January. Status of the Army.
As the Army continues to reorganize and rebuild after the Vietnam War, its strength stands at 779,412 officers and enlisted soldiers in 16 active divisions. The Army faces a number of problems—budgetary constraints, an arsenal growing in obsolescence, the nation's general apathy toward the military following the divisive Vietnam War, the low quality of recruits, and drug problems and racial tensions among the enlisted ranks.

7 May. **First Female Commissioned Through Army ROTC.**
Martha Hahn, a student at South Dakota State

University, becomes the first female to be commissioned as a second lieutenant through the Army ROTC. Three other women—Lois Stensby, Lynn M. Simpson, and DeEtte A. Stenson—are also commissioned through South Dakota State's ROTC program. The commissioning ceremony is conducted by General William E. DePuy, commander of U.S. Army Training and Doctrine Command (TRADOC), which oversees Army ROTC. DePuy had received his commission through ROTC at South Dakota State in 1941.

21 May. **SAM-D Missile System Renamed Patriot.**
The Surface-to-Air Missile, Development (SAM-D), which the Army has been developing since the 1960s, is renamed the Patriot.

1 July. **Army Issues New Edition of Field Manual 100-5. Fort Monroe, Virginia.**
TRADOC issues a new edition of Field Manual 100-5 *Operations.* Largely the work of TRADOC's commander, General DePuy, the new manual stresses the concept of "Active Defense," which emphasizes rigorous training, along with heavy firepower and concentration tactics to wear down numerically superior Warsaw Pact forces on the European battlefield. The manual soon spurs debate among Army planners that leads to new thinking. Later editions of FM 100-5 will focus on the concept of AirLand Battle, which emphasizes the interplay of air and ground forces and calls for attacking an enemy's attacking forces as well as follow-on echelons to disrupt their arrival to the battlefield.

7 July. **First Female Cadets Enroll at West Point.**
The first female cadets arrive at the United States Military Academy. The Class of 1980 includes 119 women.

12 July. **Army Retains Chemical Corps.**
With intelligence reports indicating that the Soviet Union is greatly increasing its chemical warfare

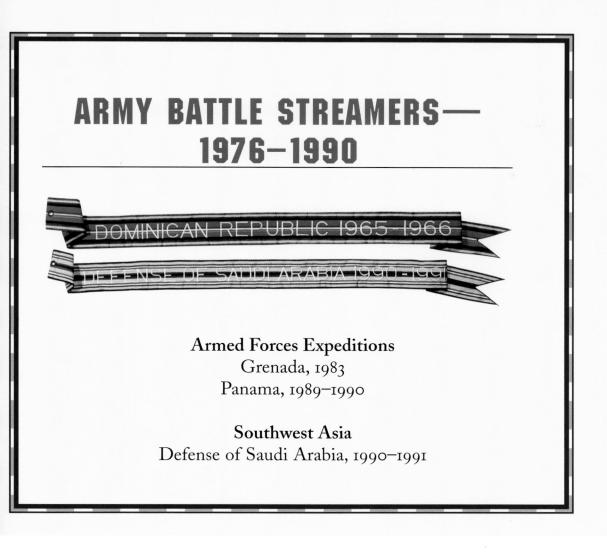

ARMY BATTLE STREAMERS—1976–1990

DOMINICAN REPUBLIC 1965–1966

DEFENSE OF SAUDI ARABIA 1990–1991

Armed Forces Expeditions
Grenada, 1983
Panama, 1989–1990

Southwest Asia
Defense of Saudi Arabia, 1990–1991

Opposite: *In the years following the Vietnam War, women joined the Army's ranks in significant numbers and played an increasingly important role in the Army as more opportunities became available to them. ("Recondo," Elzie Ray Golden, Army Art Collection, NMUSA)*

Below: *North Korean soldiers attack a U.S. work detail in the Korean DMZ on 18 August 1976, killing two American officers and escalating tensions between the United States and North Korea. (U.S. Army)*

capabilities, Secretary of the Army Martin R. Hoffmann overturns an earlier Army decision to eliminate the Chemical Corps and shift its missions and personnel to the Ordnance Corps. As a result, the Chemical Corps remains a separate branch of the Army. Three months later, the Army resumes commissioning officers in the Chemical Corps.

18 August. **Soldiers Killed Along the Korean DMZ. Panmunjom, South Korea.**
A small party of American and South Korean soldiers is attacked by a larger group of North Koreans as they attempt to prune a large tree that obscures observation of the Demilitarized Zone (DMZ). Captain Arthur Bonifas and First Lieutenant Mark Barrett are killed and four other soldiers wounded. American troops in Korea are placed on full alert.

21 August. **UN Troops Reenter Panmunjom.**
American and South Korean troops, supported by fully armed soldiers and air power (including Army attack helicopters and Air Force B-52 bombers), conduct Operation Paul Bunyan and finish pruning the tree. Bonifas is posthumously promoted to major, and the United Nations Command compound at Panmunjom is renamed Camp Bonifas.

23 August. **Army Secretary Announces Amnesty for Cadets.**
Secretary of the Army Hoffmann announces that the 149 West Point cadets implicated in the March 1976 cheating scandal can be readmitted to the academy in the summer of 1977 after a one-year "period of reflection." The scandal resulted from a number of cadets collaborating on a take-home exam. Hoffmann's decision draws severe criticism from West Point leaders, including Lieutenant General Sidney B. Berry, the Superintendent of West Point, and

Brigadier General Walter R. Ulmer, West Point's Commandant. Eventually, 93 of the 149 cadets caught up in the affair return to the academy as members of the Class of 1978.

1 October. **Rogers Appointed Chief of Staff.**
General Bernard W. Rogers, who had been commanding U.S. Army Forces Command, becomes the 28th Chief of Staff of the Army. The last veteran of World War II to be chief, he has also served in the Korean and Vietnam Wars.

23 November. **Final Performance of Silver Eagles. Fort Rucker, Alabama.**
Budgetary constraints cause the Army to disband the Silver Eagles, the Army's precision helicopter demonstration team. It performs for the last time at Knox Field. In its four years of existence, the Silver Eagles team flew OH-6A Cayuse and OH-58A Kiowa helicopters.

15 December. **Report on West Point Cheating Scandal. West Point.**
The Borman Commission, formed to investigate the

Above: *General Bernard Rogers, the 28th Chief of Staff of the Army. (Robert Clark Templeton, Army Art Collection, NMUSA)*

Right: *Clifford L. Alexander, Jr., the 13th Secretary of the Army. (Harrison Edward Benton, Jr., Army Art Collection, NMUSA)*

cheating scandal at West Point and named for the commission's leader, Frank Borman (a former astronaut and a 1950 graduate of West Point), issues its final report. The commission concurs with the decision to allow cadets to be readmitted but also makes several recommendations, including an end to any ongoing investigations and retention of the Honor Code ("A cadet will not lie, cheat, or steal, nor tolerate those who do") in its present form. The Army will eventually concur with most of the recommendations made by the Borman Commission.

1977

January. **Status of the Army.**
As the nation enters a new era with Jimmy Carter as president, the Army's strength stands at 782,246 officers and enlisted personnel (a slight increase from the previous year) and 16 Regular divisions.

1 January. **Intelligence and Security Command Formed. Arlington Hall, Virginia.**
The U.S. Army Intelligence and Security Command (INSCOM) is activated in an effort to consolidate Army intelligence activities. The U.S. Army Security Agency, U.S. Army Intelligence Agency, and other Army intelligence assets are incorporated into INSCOM. Brigadier General William I. Rolya is named its first commander.

20 January. **Jimmy Carter Inaugurated.**
Jimmy Carter is inaugurated as the 39th President and Commander-in-Chief.

21 January. **Vietnam War-Era Draft Evaders Pardoned.**
One day into his presidency, President Carter provokes controversy when he pardons the approximately 13,000 men who fled to Canada and other nations to avoid the draft during the Vietnam War. The decision angers many veterans.

14 February. **Alexander Appointed Secretary of the Army.**
Clifford Alexander, Jr., a corporate lawyer who held a number of government posts in previous Democratic administrations, is named the 13th Secretary of the Army. He is the first African-American to hold that position. His military experience is a short period as an enlisted man in the New York National Guard.

10 June. **Army Restores Medal of Honor.**
Secretary Alexander restores the Congressional Medal of Honor to Dr. Mary Walker, a contract surgeon for the Union Army during the Civil War who endured four months in Confederate captivity in 1864. Walker's Medal of Honor, originally awarded to her on 11 November 1865, was rescinded for "unusual circumstances" in the "Purge of 1917" (the federal government's attempt to correct errors that had been made in issuing medals). Walker remains the only female to have earned the Medal of Honor.

12 July. **President Carter Requests Funding for Neutron Bomb.**
Two months after the Energy Research and Development Administration acknowledges to Congress the development of enhanced radiation weapons, President Carter announces his decision to request funds for further development of what becomes more commonly known as the neutron bomb. The neutron bomb is a nuclear weapon, but with a lower yield and reduced blast and heat effects. Plans call for building enhanced radiation warheads for the Army's Lance battlefield support missile and eight-inch and 155mm howitzers. Eventually, further development is terminated, and no enhanced radiation warheads are deployed.

14 July. **Army Helicopter Downed. Demilitarized Zone, Korea.**
A CH-47 Chinook helicopter from the 17th Aviation Group is shot down by North Korean forces after it strays into North Korean airspace. Three U.S. soldiers are killed and one is wounded; the American dead and wounded are returned at Panmunjom several days later.

Left: *After 36 years of service, the Women's Army Corps (WAC) was abolished on 20 October 1978. Since then women have been integrated into the branches of the Army in which they are permitted to serve. ("The Retreat Ceremony," H. Charles McBarron, Army Art Collection, NMUSA)*

28 September. **Last WAC Officers Orientation Course. Alabama.**
The final Women's Army Corps (WAC) Officers Orientation Course graduates 129 women at Fort McClellan.

18 November. **Pershing II Missile Launch. White Sands Missile Range, New Mexico.**
The Army conducts the first flight test of the Pershing II battlefield support missile. The Pershing II, which is being developed in response to the Soviet deployment of the SS-20 missile, will replace the Pershing 1a in Europe.

21 November. **Army Creates Delta Force. Fort Bragg, North Carolina.**
The Army creates the 1st Special Forces Operational Detachment-Delta (1st SFOD-D) and names Colonel Charles Beckwith as commanding officer. Better

known as Delta Force, the 1st SFOD-D is largely conceived as an overseas counterterrorist unit specializing in hostage rescue, barricade operations, and reconnaissance. Delta Force's operations are highly classified, and the Army never publicly acknowledges the detachment's existence.

20 December. **Combat Exclusion Policy for Women.**
Secretary Alexander announces that women can serve in most officer and enlisted specialties or units except those involved in direct combat, such as infantry, armor, cannon field artillery, combat engineers, and low-altitude air defense units of battalion size or smaller.

Right: *Soldiers of the 2d Armored Cavalry Regiment patrol the German border during the late 1970s near Hof, West Germany. Note the soldier's black berets, which were not authorized for soldiers at that time. (U.S. Army)*

1978

January. Status of the Army.
While the number of active divisions remains at 16, the personnel strength of the active Army falls to 771,624 officers and enlisted personnel—10,622 fewer soldiers than in the pervious year.

January. Soldiers Help Dig Out After Blizzards.
Thousands of soldiers are mobilized to help dozens of communities after blizzards strike. Nearly 5,600 Guardsmen are called up to help clear snow and rescue stranded citizens. In addition, Regulars from the 20th Engineer Brigade and Reservists from 83d Army Reserve Command provide assistance in Ohio. A week later, approximately 7,500 Guardsmen and additional engineer units are called up when 30 inches of snow blanket parts of New England.

24 January. 761st Tank Battalion Receives Presidential Unit Citation.
Nearly 33 years after it fought its last battle in Europe, the 761st Tank Battalion, an armored unit comprising mostly black personnel, is awarded the Presidential Unit Citation for its combat service against the German Army in World War II.

26 June. Army Adopts New Helmet.
After several years of development and testing, the Army adopts a new helmet to replace the M1 "steel pot." Largely made of Kevlar, the new helmet is nicknamed the "Fritz" because of its resemblance to the German Army helmet of World Wars I and II. The Army also develops new body armor.

25 September. First Test Fire of Hellfire Missile. Redstone Arsenal, Alabama.
The Army test fires the first AGM-114 Hellfire laser-guided missile. The Hellfire is an air-to-ground missile for helicopters to use against enemy armor.

17 October. North Korean Tunnel Under Demilitarized Zone. Korea.
U.S. and South Korean soldiers discover a tunnel four miles from Panmunjom and running along the main invasion route to Seoul. The tunnel, which measures two meters wide by two meters high, can accommodate the passage of thousands of North Korean troops; it is the third such tunnel discovered since 1974.

20 October. Women's Army Corps Abolished.
President Carter signs legislation abolishing the Women's Army Corps as a separate corps within the Army. On the same day, the Department of the Army issues General Orders 20, which discontinues the Women's Army Corps. Women will be integrated into the noncombat branches in which they are permitted to serve. The final WAC director, Brigadier General

Mary E. Clarke, is reassigned as Commander, U.S. Army Military Police and Chemical Schools/Training Center, Fort McClellan, Alabama. Clarke becomes the first female commanding general in Army history. Less than two weeks later, she is promoted to major general, making her the first female two-star general in the Army.

1 November. Men and Women Integrated into Training Units.

Male and female recruits begin training in the same basic training units at Fort McClellan, Alabama; Fort Jackson, South Carolina; Fort Dix, New Jersey; and Fort Leonard Wood, Missouri.

1979

January. Status of the Army.

The personnel strength of the Army reaches its lowest level since 1950, with 758,852 officers and enlisted, a drop of 12,772 soldiers from the previous year.

Above: *A drill sergeant instructs two female soldiers in the use of the M-60 machine gun at Fort Gordon, Georgia, in 1979. (Center of Military History)*

Right: *General Edward C. Meyer, the 29th Chief of Staff of the Army. (Everett Raymond Kinstler, Army Art Collection, NMUSA)*

1 January. Ban on Unauthorized Headgear and Clothing.

Due to a "seemingly ever increasing number of unauthorized items," General Rogers orders a ban on nonstandard headgear and clothing. Under Rogers' directive, the only nonstandard headgear allowed to be worn are the Special Forces green beret, the Rangers' black beret, the women's beret, white covers for military police, and specialized headgear for honor guards and bands. In 1981, Chief of Staff General

Right: *In the decades following the Korean War armistice, American soldiers regularly patrolled the southern edge of the DMZ and occasionally exchanged fire with North Korean forces. ("Mini-Tower, DMZ ROK," William H. Steel, Army Art Collection, NMUSA)*

Edward C. Myers overturns the ban and allows airborne troops to wear the maroon beret.

April. Army Receives First UH-60 Black Hawk Helicopters. Fort Rucker, Alabama.

The first production UH-60 Black Hawk helicopters are delivered to the U.S. Army Aviation Center at Fort Rucker, Alabama. The Black Hawk, built by Sikorsky Aircraft, replaces the Bell UH-1 Huey. The UH-60 is faster, can carry more troops and cargo, and is designed to be far more survivable for the crew in a crash. On 19 June, the 101st Airborne Division (Air Assault) at Fort Campbell, Kentucky, becomes the first unit to be equipped with the Black Hawk.

22 June. General Edward C. Meyer Appointed Chief of Staff.

General Edward C. Meyer, whose previous assignment was deputy chief of staff for operations and plans, becomes the 29th Chief of Staff of the Army. He initiates studies to examine the organization of the Army's divisions and tasked General Donn A. Starry, commander of Training and Doctrine Command, to find ways to make the Army's forces more easily deployable.

25 June. Assassination Attempt on General Haig. Belgium.

General Alexander Haig, Supreme Allied Commander in Europe, narrowly misses assassination when a bomb explodes in the roadway after his motorcade passes.

The Red Army Faction, a German ultra-left terrorist group, claims responsibility.

1 September. First Female African-American General Officer.

Colonel Hazel W. Johnson is promoted to brigadier general and named Chief, Army Nurse Corps. Johnson becomes the first female African-American general officer.

1 October. Enlistment Qualifications Standardized.

Secretary Alexander orders that enlistment qualifications be made the same for men and women.

November. Army Adopts Camouflage Battle Dress Uniform.

The Army changes its standard field uniform from solid green fatigues to the camouflage Battle Dress Uniform (BDU). Soldiers of the 82d Airborne Division, 75th Rangers, and Special Forces already wear camouflage uniforms.

4 November. American Embassy Seized. Tehran, Iran.

The U.S. Embassy in Tehran is overrun and seized by a group of militant Islamic students. Two soldiers, Colonel Charles W. Scott, head of the U.S. Military Assistance Advisory Group to Iran, and Master Sergeant Regis Ragan are among those taken hostage. Scott, Ryan, and 50 other Americans will be held for 444 days until released on 20 January 1981.

Left: *Two UH-60 Black Hawk helicopters lift off, each carrying a 105mm howitzer. The Black Hawk, designed to replace the venerable UH-1 Huey, was one of the Army's key weapons development programs of the 1970s. (U.S. Army)*

7 December. **Soldier Killed Along Demilitarized Zone. Korea.**
A patrol from the 2d Infantry Division wanders into a North Korean minefield in the DMZ. One soldier is killed and two others are wounded.

14 December. **U.S. Army Chemical School Reopens. Alabama.**
The Army abandons plans to disestablish the Chemical Corps and merge its soldiers into the Ordnance Corps. The Chemical School reopens at Fort McClellan.

1980

January. **Status of the Army.**
As international tensions, sparked by the Iranian hostage crisis and the Soviet Union's invasion of Afghanistan, increase, Army personnel strength grows slightly—777,036 officers and enlisted personnel. However, no new divisions are proposed.

28 February. **Army Receives First M1 Abrams Tanks.**
The first M1 Abrams main battle tanks are delivered to the Army. Named for the late Chief of Staff of the Army, General Creighton W. Abrams, the M1 replaces the M60, which has been in service since the early 1960s. The original model is armed with an M68A1 105mm main gun; the improved M1A1, delivered in 1985, will incorporate a more powerful 120mm gun. Additional upgrades will be made over the years, including more advanced electronics and heavier armor.

1 March. **Rapid Deployment Joint Task Force Established.**
President Carter orders the creation of the Rapid Deployment Joint Task Force (RDJTF or RDF). Elements of the 82d Airborne Division will comprise the bulk of the RDF's forces.

2 April. **Women's Army Auxiliary Corps Service Recognized.**
Secretary of Defense Harold Brown announces that under Public Law 95-202, Women's Army Auxiliary Corps (WAAC) service during World War II will be considered active military service for all laws administered by the Veterans Administration.

24 April. **Iran Hostage Rescue Mission (Operation Blue Light). Iran.**
Led by Army Colonel Charles Beckwith, Operation Blue Light, a joint military service effort to rescue American hostages held at the U.S. Embassy in Tehran, is aborted when a number of the mission's helicopters suffer mechanical failure. As the rescue team, which includes Delta Force operators, Special Forces soldiers, and Rangers, prepares to depart the assembly area in the Iranian desert, a CH-53 helicopter and C-130 airplane collide, killing eight Americans and injuring several more.

25 May. **Army Guard Assists After Mount St. Helens Erupts. Washington.**
Army National Guard troops are mobilized to provide disaster relief when Mount St. Helens, a volcano in the Cascades Range in Washington State, erupts, killing dozens of people and causing widespread

Right: *A drill sergeant, wearing the Army's new camouflage battle dress uniform, conducts a barracks inspection of new soldiers undergoing basic training. (Center of Military History, U.S. Army)*

damage. Oregon Army National Guard aviators fly OV-1 Mohawk aircraft equipped with sensors and side-looking airborne radar to assess the volcano's condition.

28 May. First Female Cadets Graduate from West Point.
Andrea Hollen, ranked tenth in the United States Military Academy's Class of 1980, becomes the first female to graduate and receive a commission from West Point. Another 61 females also graduate in the same class.

June. Army Adopts Meals-Ready-to-Eat.
The Army awards a contract to American Pouch Foods, Inc., for new field rations known as Meals-Ready-to-Eat, or MREs. The new rations, consisting of dehydrated foods packaged in airtight pouches, will replace C-rations. They are much lighter, require no refrigeration, and have a much longer shelf life than C-rations.

10 September. Myers Approves Test of New Division Concept.
General Meyer approves testing of a new lighter division with only 17,773 soldiers, as proposed by General Starry. The 9th Infantry Division at Fort Lewis, Washington, is selected as the test bed for this concept. Within two years, however, the focus of the 9th Division's effort is shifted from testing technical equipment to testing a new innovative "motorized" organizational concept.

16 October. National Training Center Activated. Fort Irwin, California.
The National Training Center (NTC), encompassing more than 1,000 square miles in the Mojave Desert, is officially activated. Utilizing extensive computer and laser equipment to monitor and simulate combat, the NTC becomes the Army's premier training range for large-scale maneuvers involving armor and mechanized infantry units.

5 November. Civilian Hiring Freeze.
The federal government orders a hiring freeze for civilian Army employees, forcing many soldiers into jobs usually held by civilians.

1981

January. Status of the Army.
The strength of the Army stands at 781,419 officers and enlisted personnel, organized into 16 active divisions. The Army also launches a new recruiting campaign centered on the slogan, "Be All You Can Be." Largely conceived by Major General Maxwell R. Thurman, commander of U.S. Army Recruiting Command, the campaign proves to be extremely successful in bringing high-quality young men and women into the Army's ranks and is later named one of most successful advertising campaigns of the 20th century.

20 January. Ronald Reagan Inaugurated as President.
Ronald Reagan is inaugurated as the 40th President of the United States and Commander-in-Chief. Reagan, a member of the Army Reserve, served as a captain in the Army's 1st Motion Picture Unit (a unit that produced training films in World War II), before being honorably discharged in December 1945.

22 January. Haig Appointed Secretary of State.
General Alexander M. Haig, USA (Ret.), becomes President Reagan's Secretary of State. He is only the second professional soldier to hold the position. Haig will resign on 5 July 1982, over disagreements with the Reagan Administration's foreign policy decisions. In 1988 he will make an unsuccessful bid for President.

29 January. Marsh Appointed Secretary of the Army.
John O. Marsh, Jr., who served as an assistant secretary of defense during the Nixon Administration, is named the 14th Secretary of the Army. Marsh, a graduate of Infantry Officer Candidate School (OCS), served in the occupation of Germany and in the Army Reserve. He will be the longest-serving Army Secretary to date.

24 February. Ray Benavidez Awarded Medal of Honor.
President Reagan awards the Congressional Medal of

Above: John O. Marsh, the 14th and longest serving Secretary of the Army. (Sylvia Rogers Barnes, Army Art Collection, NMUSA)

Honor to retired Special Forces Master Sergeant Ray Benavidez nearly 13 years after his heroic combat actions in the rescue of a Special Forces reconnaissance team in Vietnam. Benavidez, who was seriously wounded in the 2 May 1968 operation, was originally awarded the Distinguished Service Cross.

27 February. Stinger Missile System Becomes Operational. Germany.
The Stinger shoulder-fired air defense missile system becomes operational as the first Army Stinger missile teams are deployed to Europe. The supersonic, heat-seeking Stinger replaces the Redeye missile system, which has been fielded since the late 1960s but has significant limitations.

3 April. Vietnam War Study Published. Carlisle Barracks, Pennsylvania.
The Strategic Studies Institute of the Army War College publishes *On Strategy: The Vietnam War in Context*, by Colonel Harry G. Summers. The study contends that U.S. forces should have focused on fighting a conventional war against North Vietnamese regulars. Summers is also critical of the lack of internal political support for the war. *On Strategy* becomes one of the most influential studies on the Vietnam War.

8 April. General Bradley Dies. New York.
General of the Army Omar N. Bradley, the Army's senior officer and last surviving five-star general, dies at the age of 88 in New York City.

15 September. Assassination Attempt on General Kroesen. West Germany.
General Frederick J. Kroesen, Commander, U.S. Army, Europe, and his wife are attacked by German Red Army Faction terrorists with rocket-propelled grenades (RPGs) while driving near Heidelberg. The attack severely damages the general's armored automobile, but he and his wife escape with minor injuries.

20 October. New Fighting Vehicles Named For General Bradley. Virginia.
In a ceremony at Fort Myer, the Army officially names its new M2/3 fighting vehicles after the late General of the Army Omar N. Bradley.

17 December. Army General Kidnapped by Italian Terrorists. Verona, Italy.
Brigadier General James L. Dozier is kidnapped from his apartment by members of the Red Brigades, an Italian ultra-left terrorist group.

VOLAR: THE ALL-VOLUNTEER ARMY

With the growing unpopularity of the draft and the winding down of the war in Vietnam, American military planners began to examine an end to conscription and a return to armed forces raised and maintained with voluntary enlistments. On 27 March 1969 President Richard M. Nixon appointed an advisory commission on an all-volunteer armed force with former Secretary of Defense Thomas S. Gates, Jr., as its chairman.

The Gates Commission submitted its report on 27 February 1970, which said that a smaller volunteer force, supported by an effective stand-by draft, would be more effective than a mixed force of conscripts and volunteers and would not jeopardize national security. Furthermore, the commission contended that labor market dynamics would make it economically feasible to raise a volunteer army.

Congress then took steps to implement the All-Volunteer Force (AVF) by raising the pay of first-term enlisted soldiers by 61 percent in 1972 and refusing to extend the Selective Service Act. With the expiration of the Act on 30 June 1973, the AVF was born on 1 July 1973.

Initially, the AVF was a success. With the high unemployment, particularly among young men and women, the Army and the rest of the armed forces attracted large numbers of recruits with pay for new enlistees comparable to, or better than, many entry-level jobs. The numbers of African-Americans and women joining the military increased significantly during this period. As the 1970s continued, however, the AVF faced serious problems when Congress cut recruiting budgets and let the GI Bill, an important recruiting tool, expire in 1976. Overall, the quality of recruits declined and problems with morale, discipline, and drug abuse increased. In 1979 the Army fell 17,000 soldiers short of its recruitment goals, the worst shortfall in the post-World War II era. Personnel issues combined with equipment and readiness problems led many military analysts of the era to characterize the Army as a "hollow force."

The defense build-up by the Reagan administration gave the AVF a significant boost. In January 1981 the Army launched a new recruiting campaign around the slogan, "Be All You Can Be."

This effort, combined with new benefits from Congress, such as a revised GI Bill, the Army College Fund, and better pay, attracted large numbers of quality recruits to meet the Army's higher standards. By 1991 98 percent of enlistees had a high school diploma and 75 percent scored in the upper brackets in aptitude tests. Unauthorized absences dropped by 80 percent, courts-martial declined by 64 percent, and drug use fell to negligible levels, while training and professionalism intensified. Unlike the draft-era conscripts, who stayed in for two years and then left the Army, the soldiers of the AVF stayed longer, allowing them to become more thoroughly trained in operating increasingly advanced weapons and equipment, as well as effectively managing the Army's support elements.

The proof of the AVF's effectiveness has been demonstrated on several occasions. American forces quickly achieved their objectives in Operation Just Cause, the invasion of Panama in December 1989, with a minimum of casualties and collateral damage. In February 1991 an allied coalition comprised largely of U.S. Army troops needed fewer than five days to defeat the larger Iraqi Army in Operation Desert Storm. Most recently, U.S. troops quickly neutralized Iraqi forces in Operation Iraqi Freedom and effectively battled Taliban and al-Qaeda forces in Afghanistan in Operation Enduring Freedom.

The future for continuing the All Volunteer Army is an open question. With the Army conducting two major combat operations and several smaller ones in the Global War Against Terrorism as well as other stability and peacekeeping assignments, the Army has been stretched to the point of deep concern. The Army today has a large married population, some families with both parents in the active or reserve military. The impact of frequent and repeated family separations on recruiting and retention of volunteers for the Regular Army as well as for the increasingly committed ARNG and Army Reserve remains to be seen.

—*Matthew Seelinger*

1982

January. Status of the Army.
Army personnel strength is 780,391 officers and enlisted personnel in 16 Regular divisions.

January. Troops as U.N. Peacekeepers. Sinai Peninsula.
Soldiers from the 82d Airborne Division are the first American troops to serve as U.N. Multinational Force and Observers (MFO) between Egypt and Israel in the Sinai Peninsula. The mission continues today as the Army's longest-running participation in a peacekeeping mission.

13 January. Army Assists After Airliner Crash.
After Air Florida Flight 90 crashes into the icy Potomac River, killing 78 people, soldiers from various units in the Military District of Washington (including the 3d Infantry and the U.S. Army Corps of Engineers Baltimore District) assist in the recovery of victims and wreckage.

Above: *The heavily armed M2/3 Bradley Fighting Vehicle, another of the Army's weapons development programs of the 1970s, provides the Army with a powerful vehicle for both mechanized infantry and cavalry units. (U.S. Army)*

18 January. Army Officer Assassinated. Paris, France.
Lieutenant Colonel Charles R. Ray, an assistant military attaché at the U.S. Embassy in Paris, is assassinated by an unknown gunman.

28 January. Dozier Rescued. Italy.
Brigadier General Dozier is safely rescued from his captors by Italian antiterrorist forces. The Army's Delta Force plays an advisory role in the rescue operation.

3 May. Army Reverts to Same-Sex Basic Training.
After nearly three years of training men and women together, the Army returns to separate basic training, keeping men and women in single-sex training units.

18 June. General John W. Vessey Appointed Chairman, Joint Chiefs of Staff.
General John W. Vessey, the Army's Vice Chief of Staff, is appointed to serve as the 10th Chairman of the Joint Chiefs of Staff. Vessey served as a National Guard enlisted man in World War II and received a battlefield commission. He is the fifth Army general officer to serve as chairman

30 August. First African-American Four-Star General.
Lieutenant General Roscoe Robinson, Jr., commander of U.S. Army, Japan, is promoted to full general,

making him the first African-American four-star general in Army history. He later serves as the U.S. representative to the NATO Military Committee before retiring in 1985.

13 November. **Vietnam Veterans Memorial Dedicated. Washington, D.C.**
The Vietnam Veterans Memorial, designed by Yale architecture student Maya Lin, is dedicated at the National Mall. Of the 58,000-plus names of American servicemen killed or missing in the Vietnam War that are etched on the memorial's panels, 38,205 are Army soldiers. The effort to raise funds for the memorial's construction was led by Jan Scruggs, a Vietnam War veteran who served in the Army's 199th Light Infantry Brigade.

1983

January. **Status of the Army.**
Army personnel strength stands at 779,643 officers and enlisted men.

1 January. **U.S. Central Command Established. Florida.**
The Rapid Deployment Joint Task Force, established during the Carter era, becomes the U.S. Central Command (CENTCOM). The new command at MacDill Air Force Base has responsibility for U.S. military operations in 25 countries throughout Northeast Africa, Southwest and Central Asia, and portions of the Indian Ocean. Lieutenant General Robert C. Kingston is named its first commander. To support this new unified command, the Army reactivates the Third Army at Fort McPherson, Georgia, with Lieutenant General Marion C. Ross as commanding general. Third Army will serve as the command element for Army forces assigned to Central Command.

22 March. **Army Awards High Mobility Multipurpose Wheeled Vehicle Contract.**
After several years of rigorous competition and testing, the U.S. Army Tank-Automotive and Armaments Command awards a contract for 55,000 High-Mobility Multipurpose Wheeled Vehicles (HMMWV). Known as the "Humvee," it is intended to replace several Army vehicles, including the M151 utility vehicle ("jeep.") The HMMWV comes in several versions, including models armed with the M60 7.62mm machine gun, the M2 .50-caliber machine gun, and the TOW (Tube-Launched, Optically Tracked, Wire-Guided) missile launcher.

31 March. **Army Fields First MLRS Battery. Fort Riley, Kansas.**
The first M270 Multiple Launch Rocket System (MLRS) battery is assigned to the 1st Infantry Division. Each M270 launcher, derived from the Bradley Fighting Vehicle, can fire 12 M26 rockets,

Right: *From 1953 through 1999, the Army's Jungle Operations Training Center at Fort Sherman, Panama, trained thousands of soldiers in jungle warfare. ("Alert," Al Sprague, Army Art Collection, NMUSA)*

each containing dozens of submunitions, to a range of 19 miles. The MLRS marks the first development of an Army multiple-rocket system since the Korean War. On 1 September, the first MLRS battalion to be deployed overseas is attached to the 8th Infantry Division in Germany.

April. **First Bradley Fighting Vehicles Arrive.**
The first Bradley Fighting Vehicles are assigned to mechanized infantry and armored cavalry units. The M2 Bradley Infantry Fighting Vehicle, designed to replace the M113 armored personnel carrier in a number of roles, is armed with a 25mm cannon, a coaxial 7.62mm machine gun, a TOW missile launcher, and firing ports for assault rifles. In addition to a crew of three, it carries a squad of six infantrymen. The M3 Cavalry Fighting Vehicles are assigned to armored cavalry units for flank protection and reconnaissance duties. While largely similar to the M2, the M3 carries more main gun ammunition and additional TOW rounds, but only two dismounts.

12 April. **Aviation Branch Established.**
In recognition of the growing importance of aviation, especially helicopters, in Army doctrine and operations, the Army establishes a separate aviation branch for the first time since World War II.

18 April. **U.S. Embassy Bombed. Beirut, Lebanon.**
The U.S. Embassy in Beirut is virtually destroyed by a truck bomb. Seventeen Americans are killed, including three soldiers.

June. **School of Advanced Military Studies Opens. Kansas.**
The School of Advanced Military Studies (SAMS) opens at Fort Leavenworth, home of the Command and General Staff College and several other academic centers. The school trains its students with a rigorous curriculum of military history, military theory, and execution-based practical exercises.

23 June. **Wickham Appointed Chief of Staff.**
General John A. Wickham, Jr., who had been serving as the Army's Vice Chief of Staff, becomes the 30th Chief of Staff of the Army. Wickham is a wounded veteran of the Vietnam War, where he served with the 1st Cavalry Division (Airmobile). General Wickham continues initiatives started under his predecessor, General Meyer, to change the Army's division structures with an eye to making units more easily and quickly transportable to trouble spots around the world. Wickham's reforms become known as "The Army of Excellence."

1 October. **2d U.S. Army Activated. Georgia.**
The 2d U.S. Army is activated at Fort Gillem after 17 years on inactive status. The 2d Army will oversee Army Reserve units in Kentucky, Tennessee, North Carolina, South Carolina, Mississippi, Alabama, and Georgia.

23 October. **Soldiers Killed in Attack on Marines. Lebanon.**
Three soldiers are among the 241 U.S. servicemen killed when a suicide truck bomb destroys the headquarters for U.S. Marine peacekeeping forces in Beirut. By the time American forces are withdrawn in February 1984, five other soldiers there have died in accidents.

25 October. **Operation Urgent Fury. Grenada.**
American forces, including Army Special Forces, 75th Rangers, and units of the 82d Airborne Division, make a hastily planned invasion of the Caribbean nation of

Above: *General John A. Wickham, Jr., the 30th Chief of Staff of the Army. (Margaret Holland Sargent, Army Art Collection, NMUSA)*

Opposite: *Paratroopers from the 82d Airborne Division prepare to board transport aircraft for Operation Urgent Fury, the invasion of Panama, in October 1983. (Center of Military History)*

Grenada. The operation begins before sunrise on 25 October with a daring parachute assault by the 1st and 2d Ranger Battalions, 75th Infantry, onto the Port Salines airstrip. In addition to stabilizing the country, U.S. troops rescue some 600 American medical students on the island. The country is largely secured within the next two days, but sporadic fighting with Grenadian and Cuban troops continues until 2 November. Army casualties are 12 killed and 120 wounded.

December. **U.S. Forces Withdraw from Grenada.**
Operation Urgent Fury ends and U.S. forces withdraw from the island. Urgent Fury marks the first time the UH-60 Black Hawk helicopter and the Kevlar helmet are used in combat. In addition, more than 100 female soldiers participated, including four female military police (MPs).

15 December. **First Pershing IIs Deployed. West Germany.**
The 56th Field Artillery Brigade becomes the first unit to receive the Pershing II battlefield support missile. The Army eventually deploys 108 Pershing IIs to Germany. The missile has a range of more than 1,000 miles and improved accuracy over its predecessor. The Pershing II is also equipped with a new nuclear warhead, the W85, which has a smaller yield (five to 50 kilotons) but can penetrate the ground to destroy underground targets.

1984

January. **Status of the Army.**
Following a year in which the Army fields a number of new weapon systems and participates in its largest operation action since the Vietnam War, personnel strength still stands at only 780,180 officers and enlisted soldiers. However, Army plans are being developed for a new "light" division, and during the year the 7th Division begins the transition. To fill out the new divisions planned for activation with three brigades, Army National Guard brigades are identified as "roundout" units to serve with a selected Regular division.

26 January. **Army Receives First Apache Helicopters. Alabama.**
The first AH-64 Apache attack helicopters are delivered to Army Aviation Center at Fort Rucker. The Apache replaces the Bell AH-1 Cobra attack helicopters, which date back to the Vietnam War. The AH-64 carries a crew of two (pilot and gunner) and is armed with a 30mm chain gun, Hydra 70 2.75-inch rockets, and TOW missiles. The Apache is also designed to carry the Hellfire laser-guided missile, still in development.

3–11 February. First Army Astronaut in Space.
Lieutenant Colonel Robert L. Stewart becomes the
first Army astronaut in space as a part of the crew of
the space shuttle *Challenger* flight STS-41B. The
mission ends on 11 February. He is the first soldier
astronaut to serve on a shuttle mission.

15 April. Army Attaché Killed. Oshakati, Namibia.
The Army attaché in Namibia and a U.S. diplomat
are killed when their vehicle hits a mine planted by
Marxist guerrillas.

10 June. Antimissile System Test. Pacific Ocean.
The Army conducts a successful test of the anti-
ballistic missile system when a rocket fired from
Kwajalein Atoll intercepts and destroys a ballistic
missile launched from Vandenberg Air Force Base,
California.

August. Army Divisions Reorganize.
The key issue is to find the right balance among all
the Army's forces, including the National Guard and
Reserve. As plans to "lighten" some Regular divisions
are implemented, the Army National Guard's 35th
Division is reactivated as a heavy mechanized division.
Plans are made to activate the 6th Infantry Division
and the 10th Mountain Division as light divisions, and
the 25th Division is selected to transition to a light
organization. To provide manpower for the new 6th

Division, the 172d Infantry Brigade is inactivated and
a National Guard brigade is also selected to serve with
the 6th. Changes continue for the next two years.

**30 September. School of the Americas Relocates.
Georgia.**
In accordance with the 1977 Panama Canal Treaty, the
U.S. Army School of the Americas at Fort Gulick,
Panama Canal Zone, moves to Fort Benning. The
school, established in 1946, is intended to foster better
cooperation between the United States and its Latin
American neighbors by providing training to soldiers
and police officers from that region.

1 October. 4th U.S. Army Activated. Illinois.
The Army activates the 4th U.S. Army at Fort
Sheridan. The 4th Army will oversee Army Reserve
units in Ohio, Michigan, Illinois, Indiana, Iowa,
Minnesota, and Wisconsin.

**23 November. Firefight Along Demilitarized Zone.
Korean DMZ.**
U.S., South Korean, and North Korean troops engage
in a sharp firefight when a Communist defector makes
a break for freedom at the Panmunjom Truce
compound. One U.S. soldier is wounded.

THE APACHE HELICOPTER

The AH-64A Apache entered service in 1984 as the U.S. Army's primary attack helicopter and quickly became the mainstay of Army ground-support capabilities. Designed as a quick-reaction, airborne weapons system with high-combat survivability, the Apache can fight during day or night, in adverse weather conditions, in any part of the world. Capable of close engagement and deep penetration, the Apache's primary mission is the destruction of high-value targets such as tanks and armored vehicles.

Designed and built by Hughes Helicopters (later McDonnell Douglas, now Boeing), the Apache incorporates several advances in both flight and weapons systems development. The Apache has four main rotor blades and twin T700 engines, the same engines used in the UH-60 Blackhawk and SH-60 Seahawk, giving it a cruising airspeed of 145 miles per hour, a flight endurance of three hours, a combat radius of approximately 150 kilometers, and attack speeds of up to three kilometers a minute. The Apache's two crewmen have several potent weapons systems at their command, including a 30mm chain gun with 1,200 rounds of ammunition, up to 16 Hellfire laser-designated missiles, and 76 2.75-inch folding-fin rockets. The Apache can also carry Sidearm anti-radar and Sidewinder Air-to-Air missiles. By April 1996, 827 Apaches were in Army service, and to date some 1,000 export versions have been sold internationally.

The Apache first saw combat in December 1989 during Operation Just Cause in Panama. Used primarily in night actions, the Apache aptly demonstrated its advanced sighting and sensor systems. The Apache fully proved its combat capabilities during Operation Desert Storm in 1990. Apaches not only destroyed Iraq's early warning radar sites, which allowed the UN coalition forces to initiate their battle plan, but were also responsible for destroying more than 500 Iraqi tanks and hundreds of armored personal carriers, trucks, and other vehicles. Apaches are used in peace-keeping missions in Bosnia, Turkey, and Kosovo, and combat-ready AH-64A units are deployed in the U.S., Germany, and Korea. Apaches are also flown by Army National Guard units in North and South Carolina, Florida, Texas, Arizona, Utah, and Idaho.

In 1997 Boeing produced an upgraded model, the AH-64D Longbow Apache. The Longbow, named for the Longbow Hellfire fire-and-forget air-to-ground missiles it can carry, possesses several improvements over the AH-64A. The Longbow is more lethal than the AH-64A, with the ability to radar scan, detect, and classify over 128 targets, prioritize the 16 most dangerous, and launch a precision attack in less than 30 seconds. The Longbow can also engage more than one enemy at a time. More heavily armored than the AH-64A, the Longbow is more survivable, being able to continue fighting for up to 30 minutes after sustaining hits by 12.7mm rounds. The main rotor blades, cockpits, and other sections of the Longbow are rated to withstand hits from 23mm rounds. The Longbow's advanced target acquisition system allows it to acquire and hit moving or stationary targets in all weather conditions at ranges exceeding seven kilometers.

The first unit equipped with the Longbow was the 1st Battalion, 227th Aviation Regiment. The Longbow demonstrated its effectiveness in Afghanistan during Operation Anaconda in 2002 and Operation Iraqi Freedom in 2003. Presently, there are more than 300 Longbows in service with plans for 501, including upgrades to some AH-64As. The Army plans to upgrade all AH-64As to Longbows by 2010.

—Vince Hawkins

Above: *The AH-64A Apache attack helicopter, designed to replace the aging AH-1 Cobra, proved to be an effective weapon against tanks and other Iraqi targets in Operation Desert Storm. (U.S. Army)*

22 December. **Army Football Wins First Postseason Bowl Game. Michigan.**
The United States Military Academy football team wins its first postseason bowl game ever by defeating Michigan State 10-6 in the Cherry Bowl at Pontiac.

1985

January. **Status of the Army.**
Army personnel strength is 780,787 officers and enlisted personnel in 16 Regular divisions; however, plans are being made to expand the force structure by two divisions organized under a new "light" division organization as money becomes available.

31 January. **Army Adopts New Pistol.**
The Army decides to replace the Colt-Browning M1911 .45-caliber pistol and the .38-caliber revolver with the Beretta M-9 9mm pistol. The M1911 has been in service with the Army since 1911, when it was adopted for use against fanatical Moro insurgents in the Philippines. While still effective, no new Colt-Browning pistols had been manufactured since 1945, and replacement parts, such as slides and barrels, are becoming increasingly expensive and difficult to find.

March. **Army Ends Support of Modern Pentathlon. Fort Sam Houston, Texas.**
Due to budget constraints, the Army announces that it is phasing out its support of athletes training for the modern pentathlon, an Olympic event comprising running, swimming, fencing, shooting, and horseback riding. The Army has had a long affiliation with the sport—in 1912, Lieutenant George S. Patton, Jr., represented the United States at the Olympic Games finishing fifth.

24 March. **Army Officer Killed. East Germany.**
Major Arthur D. Nicholson, Jr., assigned to the U.S. Military Liaison Mission, is shot and killed by a Soviet sentry while on an observation trip in Ludwiglust. Nicholson, considered the last American killed in action in the Cold War, is posthumously awarded a Purple Heart and the Legion of Merit.

27 August. **Sergeant York Air Defense Gun Terminated.**
Secretary of Defense Caspar W. Weinberger stops purchase of the Army's M988 Sergeant York Division Air Defense Gun after only 64 systems out of 146 are delivered. The Sergeant York, a self-propelled air defense gun system built on the M48A5 tank chassis, utilizes twin 40mm L/70 Bofors guns. It is designed to

M-9 Pistol
Type: Semiautomatic pistol
Entered Army service: 1990
Specifications:

Above: *In January 1985, the Army selected the Beretta M9 9mm pistol as a replacement for the Colt-Browning M1911 .45-caliber pistol, which was first used by the Army in the early 1900s against Moro insurgents in the Philippines. (U.S. Army)*

replace the aging M163 self-propelled 20mm Vulcan air defense gun system. In several live-fire tests, however, the Sergeant York suffers a number of embarrassing setbacks. Furthermore, its dated chassis has difficulty keeping up with the new M1 tanks and M2/3 fighting vehicles it is designed to protect.

1 October. **Army Eliminates Specialist Grades.**
The Army eliminates the enlisted ranks of Specialist Five and Specialist Six, believing soldiers at that level were more than technical specialists and performed normal noncommissioned officer duties. The Army had used these ranks since 1958.

12 October. **Army Activates 10th Mountain Division. New York.**
The Army activates the 10th Mountain Division at Fort Drum. The Army National Guard's 29th Infantry Division, comprising National Guard units from Virginia and Maryland, is also reorganized as a light infantry division. The light infantry division is designed for rapid deployment and for operating in terrain unsuitable for heavy armor or mechanized infantry forces.

8 November. **Prisoner of War Medal Authorized.**
President Reagan signs the 1985 Defense Authorization Act, which includes an amendment (sponsored by Senator William V. Roth, Jr.) providing for the creation and awarding of a Prisoner of War (POW) Medal for U.S. service members. The medal, authorized to any American servicemember taken prisoner from 5 April 1917 to the present, was not requested by the Army or any other U.S. armed service.

12 December. **Military Aircraft Crash. Gander, Newfoundland.**

While returning to the United States after performing peacekeeping duty in the Sinai Peninsula, 248 members of the 3d Battalion, 502d Infantry, 101st Airborne Division, perish when their chartered DC-8 aircraft crashes shortly after takeoff in Gander, Newfoundland. It is the worst U.S. military aviation disaster in history.

1986

January. **Status of the Army.**

Army personnel strength stands at 780,980 officers and enlisted personnel now in 17 Regular divisions. Other changes in the force structure are planned to generate the troops to fill the new units without increasing the overall manpower.

3 February. **Ranger Units Reorganized. Fort Benning, Georgia.**

The 75th Infantry Regiment (Ranger), activated in 1984, is redesignated as the 75th Ranger Regiment, and all Ranger units are consolidated into three battalions. The 75th Ranger Regiment, commanded by Colonel Wayne A. Downing, is assigned to the 1st Special Operations Command, with its headquarters at Fort Benning.

15 April. **ROTC Cadet Command Activated. Fort Monroe, Virginia.**

The Army activates the U.S. Army ROTC Cadet Command as a major subordinate command of the Training and Doctrine Command (TRADOC), replacing the Office of the Deputy Chief of Staff for ROTC. The new command will oversee ROTC programs at more than 400 colleges and universities, along with more than 800 high school Junior ROTC programs. ROTC provides the Army with more than 70 percent of its commissioned officers. Major General Robert E. Wagner is named Cadet Command's first commanding general.

Opposite: *Soldiers of the 10th Mountain Division take part in training exercises in winter conditions. The division, which saw action in the mountains of northern Italy during World War II, was reactivated as a light infantry division in October 1985 and based at Fort Drum, New York. (U.S. Army)*

Right: *Soldiers from the 75th Ranger Regiment, the Army's elite light infantry unit, tackle the Ranger obstacle course at the Ranger School, located at Fort Benning, Georgia. (U.S. Army)*

1 October. **Goldwater-Nichols Act. Washington, D.C.**
President Reagan signs the Goldwater-Nichols Act into law. This legislation, cosponsored by Senator Barry Goldwater (R-AZ) and Representative Bill Nichols (D-AL), introduces the most significant changes in the nation's defense establishment since the National Security Act of 1947. The act centralizes operational authority through the Chairman of the Joint Chiefs of Staff, rather than the service chiefs, and establishes the chairman as the principal military advisor to the President, the National Security Council, and the Secretary of Defense. Furthermore, the act establishes the position of vice chairman and streamlines the operational chain of command from the President to the Secretary of Defense to the unified commanders.

4 December. **U.S. Army South Activated. Panama Canal Zone.**
The Army activates U.S. Army South to better support the joint-service U.S. Southern Command through a single Army headquarters. Its first commander, Major General James R. Taylor, also commands the 193d Infantry Brigade, headquartered at Fort Clayton in the Panama Canal Zone.

1987

January. Status of the Army.
Army personnel strength remains steady at 780,815 officers and enlisted soldiers, but the number of Regular divisions has increased to 18. These are the 1st–9th, 24th and 25th Infantry Divisions, 10th Mountain Division, 82d and 101st Airborne Divisions, 1st–3d Armored Divisions, and the 1st Cavalry Division. Four of the divisions are light, and several have only two Regular brigades and a third National Guard round-out brigade. It is the largest number fielded by the Army since 1968 at the height of the Vietnam War.

31 March. Soldier Killed in El Salvador.
Special Forces Staff Sergeant Gregory Fronius, an advisor to El Salvador's army, is killed in a firefight with Marxist Farabundo Marti Liberation National (FMLN) guerrillas near El Paraiso.

9 April. Special Forces Branch Established.
As the result of renewed emphasis on special operations in the 1980s, the Army establishes the Special Forces as a basic branch of the Army.

Above: *General Carl E. Vuono, the Army's 31st Chief of Staff, led the Army during Operation Just Cause and Operation Desert Shield/Storm. (Ned Bittinger, Army Art Collection, NMUSA)*

23 June. Vuono Becomes Chief of Staff.
General Carl E. Vuono, who has been serving as the commander of Training and Doctrine Command, becomes the 31st Army Chief of Staff. Vuono is an artilleryman and a veteran of the Vietnam War.

August – October. Army Helicopters Escort Convoys. Persian Gulf.
On 8 August, Army MH-6 Little Bird helicopters begin escorting merchant ships transiting the gulf to protect them from attacks by Iranian gunboats. An Iranian mine-laying boat is attacked on 21 September and captured. Again, on 8 October, three Iranian gunboats are surprised at night and sunk. The escort mission continues until the Iran-Iraq war ends in July 1988.

1 November. Ranger Training Brigade Established. Fort Benning, Georgia.
The Army reorganizes the Ranger Department as the Ranger Training Brigade and establishes four Ranger Training Battalions. The Ranger Training Brigade's mission is to conduct the Ranger and Long-Range Surveillance Leader courses.

8 December. Army's Pershing II Missile Eliminated.
The United States and the Soviet Union sign the Intermediate-Range Nuclear Forces (INF) Treaty, which calls for the elimination of intermediate-range nuclear weapon systems in Europe. Among the weapons to be eliminated by the treaty is the Pershing II missile.

1988

January. Status of the Army.
After remaining steady for several years, the number of soldiers in the Regular Army drops to 771,847 in 18 divisions.

17–18 March. Operation Golden Pheasant. Honduras.
In response to provocations by Nicaraguan troops along the Nicaragua-Honduras border, the 1st and 2d Battalions, 504th Infantry, 82d Airborne Division, parachute into Honduras, where they are met by elements of the 7th Infantry Division (Light). American troops then engage in extensive training exercises in the region. Nicaraguan forces soon pull back, ending the crisis.

26 April. First Flight Test of ATACMS. New Mexico.
The Army conducts the first flight test of the Army Tactical Missile System (ATACMS) at White Sands

Missile Range. Originally a joint Army and Air Force program (the Air Force withdrew in 1984), the ATACMS is fired from the M270 MLRS launcher and is designed for deep attack of enemy tactical surface-to-surface missile sites, air defense positions, and command, control, and communication centers. Early versions of the ATACMS have a range of just under 40 miles; later variants can hit targets more than 100 miles away.

1 June. **Army Engineer School Relocates. Missouri.**
After 68 years at Fort Belvoir, Virginia, the U.S. Army Engineer Center and School moves to Fort Leonard Wood. Also relocated there will be the Chemical School and the Military Police School.

9 September. **First Pershing II Missile Destroyed. Texas.**
The first Pershing II missile is destroyed under the INF Treaty at Longhorn Army Ammunition Plant in Karnack, Texas. The missile is first static fired, then crushed in a hydraulic press.

1989

January. **Status of the Army.**
At the beginning of a year that will see tremendous changes in Europe, the Army's strength is 769,741 officers and enlisted personnel.

20 January. **George H. W. Bush Inaugurated as President.**
George H.W. Bush becomes the 41st President of the United States and Commander-in-Chief.

21 April. **Army Officer Assassinated. Philippines.**
Colonel James N. Rowe, chief of the Army branch of the Joint United States Military Advisory Group (JUSMAG), which provides counterinsurgency training for the Philippine military, is assassinated by Marxist guerrillas in Quezon City.

14 August. **Stone Named Secretary of the Army.**
Michael P. W. Stone, an Under Secretary of the Army and concurrently Under Secretary of Defense for Acquisition, becomes the 15th Secretary of the Army. The first foreign-born Secretary of the Army, he served as a pilot in the Royal Navy during World War II.

1 October. **General Colin L. Powell Named Chairman, Join Chiefs of Staff.**
General Colin L. Powell, who was serving as the commander of U.S. Army Forces Command, is appointed to be the 12th Chairman of the Joint Chiefs of Staff by President Bush. He is the sixth Army officer and first African-American to serve in that position.

9 November. **The Berlin Wall Comes Down. Germany.**
With the movement for democracy growing in East Germany and throughout Soviet-dominated Eastern Europe, the East German government collapses. Citizens of both East and West Berlin begin tearing down the Berlin Wall, which has divided the city for nearly 30 years and has come to symbolize the Cold War. The fall of the Berlin Wall effectively marks the end of the Cold War.

20 December. **Operation Just Cause. Panama.**
President Bush orders American forces to invade Panama and arrest its president, Manuel Noriega, on drug-trafficking charges. Led by General Maxwell R. Thurman, commander of U.S. Southern Command, forces include XVIII Airborne Corps, 7th Infantry Division (Light), 193d Infantry Brigade, 75th Ranger Regiment, Special Forces, and elements of the 5th Infantry and 82d Airborne Divisions. Heavy fighting

Above: *Michael P. W. Stone, the 15th Secretary of the Army, was a pilot in the Royal Navy in World War II and the first foreign-born Army Secretary. (John Boyd Martin, Army Art Collection, NMUSA)*

takes place at Rio Hato, Torrijos/Tocumen Airport, Tinajitas, Paitilla, and the Panamanian Defense Headquarters. Most military objectives are taken by the end of the first day, but sporadic fighting continues until 23 December. During an assault on a Panamanian installation, Captain Linda Bray, commander of the 988th Military Police Company, becomes the first female to lead soldiers in combat. More than 600 other women serve in Panama in various roles.

1990

January. Status of the Army.
With the Army still engaged in the largest American military operation since Vietnam, but with the Cold War all but over, personnel strength stands at 732,043 officers and enlisted soldiers (a personnel decrease of

Above: *Soldiers from the 75th Ranger Regiment make a night combat parachute assault from 500 feet on Torrijos Airfield, Panama, during the opening hours of Operation Just Cause, 20 December 1989. ("Jump Into Night, Torrijos Airport," Al Sprague, Army Art Collection, NMUSA)*

nearly 38,000 from the year before). The number of Regular divisions remains at 18.

3 January. Operation Just Cause. Noriega Taken. Panama.
Former President Noriega, who has taken refuge in the Vatican diplomatic mission compound, surrenders on 3 January. Hostilities officially end on 31 January. Eighteen soldiers are killed and 255 wounded. Operation Just Cause marks the first use of the AH-64 Apache attack helicopter in combat. Apache helicopters also fire the first Hellfire laser-guided missiles employed in combat operations.

21 February. Helicopter Crash Kills Soldiers. Panama.
Eleven soldiers from the 7th Infantry Division are killed when two helicopters crash in a blinding rainstorm while conducting mopping-up operations in Colon Province.

1 March. Last German Border Patrol, West Germany.
The 11th Armored Cavalry Regiment performs the last patrol of the border in the Fulda Gap between East and West Germany.

EYEWITNESS: OPERATION JUST CAUSE

On 20 December 1989 a U.S. combined force initiated Operation Just Cause in Panama. The mission was to capture Panamanian dictator Manuel Noriega for trial in the U.S. and to free American hostages held by Noriega's Panamian Defense Force (PDF). First Lieutenant Clarence E. Biggs III, executive officer of Bravo Company, 3d Battalion, 504th Parachute Infantry Regiment, 82d Airborne Division, recalls his company's combat landing.

"We loaded the aircraft. (Sgt.) Crittenden and I were the last on and would be the first out at Cerro Tigre. The chopper shuddered and the motors roared with ear-shattering intensity. It was dark, very dark. My right hand gripped my weapon while my left wrapped around an unseen steel protrusion from the ceiling. Sweat poured from my face and my gut was in a knot as I observed streaks of light slice across the ground below in odd patterns. A firefight was taking place, I realized, as I watched the intermingling dance of red and green tracers.

"The two Hueys came in first, while the Cobras launched rockets that streaked through the sky and exploded on the ground. Our CH-47 descended rapidly, the ramp dropped open, and we charged out. The odor of ground burning from the rockets filled our nostrils. The chopper took off immediately as we sprinted forward in two files to link up with the other CH-47 chalk.

"Somehow we started to move toward the edge of the golf course, where First Platoon was securing the linkup site. We crawled ahead slowly, crouching in the shadows. Third Platoon broke off and moved to the left to attack and secure the northern position of the objective, the PDF logistics site. Somehow I managed to get everybody in the correct order of movement. We stopped just outside the fence.

"The guard spotted us and fled. First Platoon moved through the breach. . . . Crittenden and I followed. When we arrived at the corner of the warehouse, the M60 (machine-gun) team that was supposed to cover the rear while the rest of the platoon cleared the warehouse was not there. . . . We were crouched at the corner of the warehouse when suddenly gunfire and a stream of tracers seemed to surround us. Both of us slammed to the ground and assumed the prone position. Tracers flew everywhere.

"I yelled, 'Cover me!' and rushed to the building opposite the warehouse. Now we could interlock fires and observe more of the area. We were ten meters apart when tracers yammered against the wall of the warehouse. Over to our left we spotted movement in the shadows. Someone was firing at the building. I took out my grenades and laid them in front of me and switched my weapon off safe.

"Again the tracers flew. This time I fixed on the source. We spotted soldiers crossing the road. I drew a bead and was about to fire when I heard, 'Hurry up, and get across the f—g road!' Immediately I put my weapon back on safe and cautiously breathed a sigh of relief. It was Third Platoon, taking out the guardhouse.

"By this time, the attack was in full swing, and the roar of AT4's and the blast of grenades reverberated through the night. The minutes turned into hours and the battle subsided in the distance. Our eyes became heavy from stress and fatigue. I reached into my pocket, pulled out a packet of dehydrated coffee and unceremoniously consumed it. The bitter stimulant counteracted my body's demand for sleep, which was gnawing away at my consciousness. By the time the initial attack was over, we had suffered two casualties.

"Panama was being enveloped by American soldiers, and everywhere unsung heroes were performing deeds of valor and determination. Our experience was by no means unique and other units were probably engaged in actions that were similar to, or even more severe, than ours."

—*Vince Hawkins*

Above: *During the assault on the Commandancia, soldiers from the 4th Battalion, 6th Infantry, 5th Infantry Division (Mechanized), dismount from an M113 armored personnel carrier. ("Attack on the Commandancia," Al Sprague, Army Art Collection, NMUSA)*

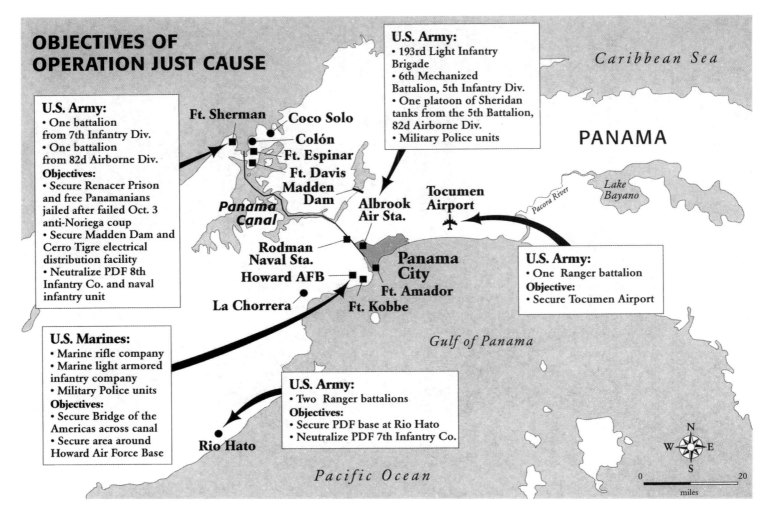

OBJECTIVES OF OPERATION JUST CAUSE

U.S. Army:
• 193rd Light Infantry Brigade
• 6th Mechanized Battalion, 5th Infantry Div.
• One platoon of Sheridan tanks from the 5th Battalion, 82d Airborne Div.
• Military Police units

Caribbean Sea

PANAMA

U.S. Army:
• One battalion from 7th Infantry Div.
• One battalion from 82d Airborne Div.
Objectives:
• Secure Renacer Prison and free Panamanians jailed after failed Oct. 3 anti-Noriega coup
• Secure Madden Dam and Cerro Tigre electrical distribution facility
• Neutralize PDF 8th Infantry Co. and naval infantry unit

Ft. Sherman Coco Solo
Colón
Ft. Espinar
Ft. Davis
Madden Dam
Panama Canal
Albrook Air Sta.

Tocumen Airport

Pacora River Lake Bayano

Rodman Naval Sta.
Howard AFB

Panama City
Ft. Amador
Ft. Kobbe

La Chorrera

U.S. Army:
• One Ranger battalion
Objective:
• Secure Tocumen Airport

Gulf of Panama

U.S. Marines:
• Marine rifle company
• Marine light armored infantry company
• Military Police units
Objectives:
• Secure Bridge of the Americas across canal
• Secure area around Howard Air Force Base

U.S. Army:
• Two Ranger battalions
Objectives:
• Secure PDF base at Rio Hato
• Neutralize PDF 7th Infantry Co.

Rio Hato

Pacific Ocean

N
W E
S

0   20
miles

---

2 August. **Iraq Invades Kuwait.**
Under orders from Saddam Hussein, Iraqi forces invade and quickly conquer the neighboring country of Kuwait. The U.N. Security Council immediately issues Resolution 660, condemning the invasion and demanding an immediate Iraqi withdrawal.

4 August. **General Schwarzkopf Briefs National Security Council.**
General H. Norman Schwarzkopf, commander of U.S. Central Command, briefs the National Security Council on the military options available. Schwarzkopf states that it will take several weeks to establish effective ground defenses to thwart an Iraqi invasion, and at least 17 weeks to gather sufficient forces to drive the Iraqis out of Kuwait. Contingency plans are also discussed in case Iraq uses chemical weapons.

Above: *Map showing the objectives of Operation Just Cause, 20 December 1989. (From* America's Splendid Little Wars, *Peter Huchtausen, Courtesy of Viking)*

Opposite: *Rangers quickly advanced and attacked their objectives after parachuting into Panama, 20 December 1989. ("Energetically…Rangers in Panama," James Dietz)*

4 August. **ARCENT Staff Begins Planning. Georgia.**
At Fort McPherson Lieutenant General John Yeosock, Commander, Army Central Command (ARCENT) and 3d Army, and Major General William G. Pagonis, Director of Logistics, and several staff officers begin planning for operations in the Persian Gulf region.

6–7 August. **American Ground Troops Ordered to Saudi Arabia.**
Following a request for troops from Saudi Arabia, the first Army units receive orders for deployment to Saudi Arabia. On 6 August, the 82d Airborne Division (commanded by Major General James H. Johnson) and the 24th Infantry Division (commanded by Major General Barry McCaffrey) receive orders from Lieutenant General Gary Luck, commander of XVIII Airborne Corps, to begin deployment. On the following day, the 1st Cavalry Division; the 1st (Tiger) Brigade, 2d Armored Division; 101st Airborne Division (commanded by Major General J. H. Binford Peay III); and the 3d Armored Cavalry Regiment (commanded by Colonel douglas H. Starr) are alerted. This troop deployment and the defense of Saudi Arabia is named Operation Desert Shield; General Schwarzkopf serves as operational commander.

8 August. **24th Infantry Division at Port. Georgia.**
The 2d Brigade, 24th Infantry Division, arrives in Savannah from Fort Stewart for deployment by sea to Saudi Arabia. The first ships carrying the division's equipment set sail on 13 August. Most of the division's combat elements arrive in theater by 12 September.

8–9 August. **First Ground Troops. Saudi Arabia.**
Troops from the 2d Brigade, 82d Airborne Division (commanded by Colonel Richard Rokosz), reach Dhahran, Saudi Arabia. The brigade had been on short-notice, stand-by status as the division's "ready brigade" when it was alerted to deploy. Staff officers from the XVIII Airborne Corps also arrive.

11 August. **7th Transportation Group Arrives.**
The 7th Transportation Group (commanded by Colonel David Whaley) arrives from Fort Eustis, Virginia, to begin managing the tremendous influx of men and materiel.

Top, left: *Lieutenant General Gary E. Luck, a Vietnam War veteran and former commander of U.S. Army Special Forces Command, led XVIII Airborne Corps during Operation Desert Shield/Storm. (U.S. Army)*

Top, right: *Lieutenant General John J. Yeosock, an advisor during the Vietnam War and former commanding general, 1st Cavalry Division, concurrently led the Third U.S. Army and Army Component Central Command during Operation Desert Shield/Storm. (U.S. Army)*

13 August. **First Patriot Unit Arrives.**
The first air defense artillery unit equipped with the PAC-2 Patriot surface-to-air missile (SAM)—Battery B, 2d Battalion, 7th Air Defense Artillery, 11th Air Defense Artillery Brigade—arrives. The PAC-2 variant has a software upgrade that allows it to engage and intercept tactical ballistic missiles such as the Soviet-designed Scud, of which Iraq has hundreds in its arsenal.

12–14 August. **Operations Desert Dragon I and II.**
The 2d Brigade, 82d Airborne Division, establishes defensive positions around the port of al-Jubayl. Two days later, elements of the same brigade set up positions to defend the port and air facilities at Dhahran and ad-Damman. In all, the 2d Brigade has 4,575 paratroopers supported by a company of M551 Sheridan light tanks, a battalion of 105mm howitzers, and an MLRS platoon.

14 August. **Army Satellite Employed for Desert Shield.**
An Army satellite begins supplying images of Iraqi troop deployments for XVIII Airborne Corps.

15 August. **Two Brigades of 82d Airborne Arrives.**
The 1st and 3d Brigades, along with other divisional units of the 82d Airborne Division, arrive in Saudi Arabia.

17 August. **101st Airborne Division Deploys. Kentucky.**
One brigade of the 101st Airborne Division begins

11 NOV 1990 SH90
C BATTERY 343 ADA
PATRIOT MISSILE SITE
SAUDI

deploying by air from Fort Campbell. The division's two other brigades travel to Saudi Arabia aboard ready-reserve ships from Jacksonville, Florida. Most of the division and its equipment are in theater by 22 September.

22 August. **Reservists Called Up.**
President Bush signs Executive Order 12727 authorizing the call-up of 200,000 reservists for 180 days. Reservists man much of the Army's combat service support units. It is the largest mobilization of reserve forces since the Korean War.

23 August. **Troops Deployed to the Desert. Saudi Arabia.**
The 2d Brigade, 82d Airborne Division, is redeployed to the desert to establish initial battle positions in case of an Iraqi offensive. Temperatures exceed 100 degrees Fahrenheit, but casualties due to the intense heat are few.

31 August. **5th Army Special Forces Arrive. Saudi Arabia.**
The 5th Special Forces Group (commanded by

Colonel Jesse Johnson) arrives to provide training and support to Saudi and other Arab ground forces. Eventually the 3d and 10th Special Forces Groups also deploy, along with elements of Delta Force.

1 September. **101st Airborne Division Units Deployed.**
Elements of the 101st Airborne Division relieve 82d Airborne troops at Forward Operating Base (FOB) Essex, which is renamed FOB Bastogne.

3 September. **Operation Desert Dragon III.**
The 101st Airborne Division establishes two additional forward operating bases, FOB Normandy and FOB Carentan, north and west of FOB Bastogne.

Above: *Patriot missile batteries were among the first Army units deployed to Saudi Arabia in August 1990 to defend allied forces against potential ballistic missile attacks from Iraq. Patriots would eventually see action against Iraqi Scud missiles soon after hostilities began on 17 January 1991. ("Patriot Missile Site," Sieger Hartgers, Army Art Collection, NMUSA)*

7 September. **Units of 24th Infantry Division and Army Reserve Deploy.**
The 1st and 2d Brigades of the 24th Infantry Division are deployed to the Saudi desert, along with the 12th Aviation Brigade. The first U.S. Army Reserve units also begin arriving in theater.

14 September. **197th Infantry Brigade Arrives.**
The 197th Infantry Brigade arrives from Fort Benning, Georgia. The 197th is attached to the 24th Infantry Division after it is determined that the 24th's round-out brigade, the 48th Infantry Brigade (Georgia), cannot be ready with the rest of the division. The 48th will not be called to active duty until 30 November.

14 September. **82d Airborne Division Establishes Base Camps.**
The 2d Brigade, 82d Airborne Division, establishes Camps Red, Gold, and White at Ab Qaiq.

16 September–22 October. **1st Cavalry Division Begins Deployment. Texas**
Brigadier General John Tilleli, Jr., begins deploying the 1st Cavalry Division from Fort Hood. Like the 24th Infantry Division, the 1st Cavalry's round-out brigade, the 155th Armored Brigade (Mississippi), is

not ready. Instead, the 1st (Tiger) Brigade, 2d Armored Division, is attached. The final elements of the 1st Cavalry arrive on 22 October. The 155th will be ordered into active service on 7 December.

6 November. **M1A1 Tank Replacement Begins. Saudi Arabia.**
The Army begins replacing M1 Abrams tanks deployed to Saudi Arabia with the M1A1 model. The M1A1 has heavier armament than the M1—a 120mm main gun as opposed to a 105mm gun—and is equipped with a nuclear-biological-chemical (NBC) overpressure protective system to protect the crew from chemical or biological attack.

8 November. **VII Corps Receives Deployment Orders. West Germany.**
President Bush announces that the allied coalition in Saudi Arabia will be reinforced and orders an additional 200,000 U.S. troops to the Persian Gulf region. VII Corps, commanded by Lieutenant General Frederick M. Franks, consisting of the 1st Armored Division, 2d Armored Division's (Forward), 3d Armored Division, 2d Armored Cavalry Regiment, and other units, receives orders to begin deployment. The 1st Armored Division's 1st Brigade will be replaced by the 3d Brigade, 3d Infantry Division, which has more modern equipment. Additional units such as the 1st Infantry Division, and Army National Guard units, such as the 142d Field Artillery Brigade (Arkansas/Oklahoma Army National Guard), deploy from the United States and join the corps in theater. VII Corps includes more than 6,000 tracked combat vehicles, 59,000 wheeled vehicles, and 200,000 soldiers. VII Corps' deployment will stretch from December 1990 to mid-February 1991.

8 November. **1st Infantry Division Ordered to Saudi Arabia. Fort Riley, Kansas.**
Major General Thomas G. Rhame's 1st Infantry Division (Mechanized) is ordered to commence deployment. Two of the division's brigades will come from Fort Riley; the 2d Armored Division's forward brigade will become the 1st Division's third brigade. Major non-divisional units deploying with the 1st include the 937th Engineer Group, 541st Maintenance Battalion, and 716th Military Police Battalion. The 1st Division will eventually be assigned to VII Corps.

13 November. **Reserve Call-Up Extended.**
President Bush extends the length of service for Rreservists activated in support of Operation Desert Shield for an additional 180 days by issuing Executive

Opposite: *Lieutenant General Frederick M. Franks, who lost part of a leg in the Vietnam War, commanded the powerful VII Corps during Operation Desert Shield/Storm. VII Corps, which contained several heavy armor divisions, had been stationed in West Germany for many years to counter a possible Soviet invasion of Western Europe. (U.S. Army)*

Right: *Soldiers from the 101st Airborne Division (Air Assault), assigned to the XVIII Airborne Corps, begin deploying to Saudi Arabia as part of Operation Desert Shield. (U.S. Army)*

Order 12733. On the following day, Secretary of Defense Richard B. Cheney authorizes the Army to call up an additional 80,000 Reservists and National Guardsmen.

27 November. **Reorganization of Army Special Forces. North Carolina.**
The Army reorganizes the U.S. 1st Special Operations Command at Fort Bragg and redesignates it as the U.S. Army Special Operations Command (Airborne). The U.S. Army Reserve Special Operations Command is redesignated as the U.S. Army Civil Affairs and Psychological Operations Command.

1 December. **Army Reserve Call-Up Increased.**
Secretary of Defense Cheney increases the Army Reserve call-up to 115,000 personnel.

22 December. **2d Armored Cavalry Regiment Arrives. Saudi Arabia.**
The 2d Armored Cavalry Regiment, commanded by Colonel Don Holder, becomes the first VII Corps unit to arrive.

27 December. **War Plans Briefing. Riyadh, Saudi Arabia.**
General Schwarzkopf briefs Secretary Cheney, General Powell, and others on his plans for a flanking movement by VII Corps and XVIII Airborne Corps to the west. The maneuver, which will bypass the strongest Iraqi defensive lines along the Saudi-Kuwaiti frontier, becomes known as the "Hail Mary" or "Left Hook."

SHIELD OF FREEDOM

1991—2004

SHIELD OF FREEDOM

1991–2004

Matthew Seelinger

With the Cold War over, the United States prepared to reap a financial "peace dividend" by severely cutting its military. But as many Army units prepared to leave Europe, a new threat emerged. Iraq, led by brutal dictator Saddam Hussein, used its powerful armed forces to invade neighboring Kuwait on 2 August 1990. An allied coalition led by the United States began deploying troops and equipment to Saudi Arabia to drive Saddam's forces from Kuwait. By 1 January 1991, the Army had nearly 200,000 soldiers in the Persian Gulf Region, including thousands from the Army Reserve and Army National Guard.

Army helicopters fired the first shots of the war on 17 January 1991, when several AH-64A Apaches destroyed two Iraqi early-warning radar stations, allowing coalition aircraft to easily penetrate Iraqi air space. During the ensuing six-week air campaign, Army units conducted several artillery raids and armed reconnaissance missions by helicopter. As Army Special Forces operated in Iraq's western desert areas, hunting Scuds and raiding selected targets, the Army's VII Corps and XVIII Airborne Corps moved to their jumping-off positions.

Finally, on 26 February, G-Day, the ground war commenced. In a 100-hour whirlwind war, the U.S.-led allied coalition routed the Iraqi Army in one of the most decisive engagements in military history. In battles such as 73 Easting, Objective Norfolk, and Medina Ridge, American armored and attack helicopter units annihilated several divisions of the elite Iraqi Republican Guard. American technology—in the form of the M1A1 Abrams tank, the M2/3 Bradley fighting vehicle, and other weapons—proved to be far superior to the Iraqis' Soviet-supplied arsenal. Fewer than 100 American soldiers were killed in action.

The billions of dollars spent on weapons in the 1980s, coupled with the superior training of American soldiers, had paid off with a victorious Army, but in 1992 that Army was still on the chopping block. The need for large, heavy forces designed to fight a conventional war appeared gone. Older weapon systems were retired, unneeded posts were closed, and the Army's ranks steadily dropped. By 1997, the Army had fewer than 500,000 active soldiers and only ten divisions, its lowest numbers since the eve of the Korean War in 1950.

Despite this, the Army was ordered to conduct a number of operations around the world. While many of these were peacekeeping or humanitarian missions, American soldiers sometimes engaged in combat against local forces. During the 1990s, American soldiers were in Somalia, Haiti, Croatia, Bosnia-Herzegovina, Kosovo, Macedonia, Sinai, Latin America, and many other locations where they continue to serve today.

U.S. troops were also dispatched to Kuwait after Iraqi forces twice made threatening moves. With Regular Army resources stretched thin, the 1990s also saw the first large-scale foreign deployments of Army National Guard units in peacetime. As the 1990s drew to a close, the Army formulated plans to become a leaner, more deployable force for overseas missions. In particular, the Army started development of a lighter class of armored vehicle, named the "Stryker," to be deployed in reconfigured brigade combat teams

The horrific terrorist attacks of 11 September 2001 on New York City and the Pentagon ushered in a new era for the Army. Large numbers of soldiers, especially from the reserve components, were called up for extended tours within the continental United States in support of homeland security and what

became know as the Global War on Terrorism. By mid-October, U.S. and allied forces had struck back in Afghanistan with Operation Enduring Freedom to destroy al Qaeda and its Taliban allies. In less than three months, the Taliban were driven from power and hundreds of al Qaeda fighters killed or captured. Today, the Army continues operations to hunt down remaining terrorist elements and to bring stability to that war-torn nation.

On 19 March 2003, American and allied forces launched Operation Iraqi Freedom to depose Saddam Hussein and liberate the Iraqi people from his oppressive regime, seize and destroy Iraqi weapons of mass destruction, and eliminate terrorist elements within Iraq. In just over three weeks of intense combat, the 3d Infantry Division was in Baghdad after a dramatic thrust that broke the Iraqi military with a minimum of casualties.

On 1 May, President George W. Bush declared that major military operations were over, but within weeks the Army found itself embroiled in a widening guerrilla war with Iraqi insurgents, most of them loyal to the ousted Saddam regime. To date, more than 700

American servicemen have died in Iraq, and as in America's earlier wars, the Army bears the majority of the casualties. While the eventual outcomes of Operation Iraqi Freedom and Operation Enduring Freedom are not in doubt, it will be some time before Iraq is secure and redeveloped. As an unfortunate result, American soldiers will continue to make the ultimate sacrifice as they serve as the shield of freedom for the United States and other nations and peoples with similar ideals.

Pages 894–895: *Two M1A1 Abrams tanks roll past destroyed Iraqi armor during the ground phase of Operation Desert Storm. ("Night Attack," Mario Acevedo, Army Art Collection, NMUSA)*

Above: *An American soldier distributes newspapers to Somali citizens. American soldiers and marines arrived in Somalia in late 1992 to assist in a humanitarian relief mission for famine-plagued Somalia. ("The Somalian Update," Jeffery T. Manuszak, Army Art Collection, NMUSA)*

SHIELD OF FREEDOM

1991–2004

"We promised this [the Persian Gulf War] would not be another Vietnam. And we kept that promise. The specter of Vietnam has been buried forever in the desert sands of the Arabian Peninsula."

—President George H. W. Bush, radio address, 2 March 1991

1991

January. Status of the Army.
With the United States at the brink of war, the strength of the Army is 710,821 officers and enlisted personnel in 18 divisions. Seven of the Army's divisions (from the VII Corps and XVIII Airborne Corps) are either in Saudi Arabia or in the process of deploying to the Persian Gulf region. In addition to seven divisions, the Army has also deployed two armored cavalry regiments and hundreds of smaller units, many of them from the Army National Guard and Army Reserve, as part of the allied coalition to expel Iraqi forces from Kuwait. As of 1 January, the Army has deployed approximately 200,000 soldiers to Saudi Arabia, with more on the way.

1 January. Elements of 1st Armored Division Arrive. Saudi Arabia.
Infantry units of the 1st Armored Division, VII Corps, commanded by Major General Ronald H. Griffith, begin arriving at Tactical Assembly Area (TAA) Thompson, northeast of King Khalid Military City, to establish defensive positions. As the division's armored units begin to reach TAA Thompson over the next few days, the 1st Armored begins extensive training, including map reading, maneuvers, and gunnery.

7 January. Estimate of Iraqi Troop Strength.
U.S. Central Command's (CENTCOM's) intelligence section estimates Iraqi strength in the Kuwaiti Theater at 542,000 troops organized into 35 divisions, along with 4,300 tanks and 3,100 artillery pieces.

8 January. Operation Quick Silver. Riyadh, Saudi Arabia.
In response to a terrorist threat to the Saudi capital, the 3d Brigade, 82d Airborne Division, is ordered to Riyadh.

10 January. Tiger Brigade Reassigned to the Marines.
The 1st Brigade, 2d Armored Division ("Tiger Brigade"), commanded by Colonel John B. Sylvester and attached to the 1st Cavalry Division, is reassigned to the 2d Marine Division to provide the Marines with heavier firepower. Unlike the Marines, who are equipped with older M60A3 tanks, the Tiger Brigade's armament includes 196 M1A1 tanks and 59 Bradley fighting vehicles. Tiger Brigade replaces the British 7th Armoured Brigade, which is reassigned to the British 1st Armoured Division, a unit of VII Corps.

14 January. Reconnaissance of Area West of Iraqi Defenses.
Major General Griffith of the 1st Armored Division makes a visual reconnaissance of the area west of the Iraqi defensive line along the Saudi-Iraqi border and determines the area to be passable for tanks and armored vehicles. Later, Griffith and VII Corps commander Lieutenant General Frederick M. Franks

ARMY BATTLE STREAMERS— 1991–2004

DEFENSE OF SAUDI ARABIA 1990–1991

KOSOVO AIR CAMPAIGN 1999

Southwest Asia

Liberation and Defense of Kuwait, 17 January–11 April 1991

Cease-Fire, 12 April 1991–30 November 1995

Kosovo

Kosovo Air Campaign, 24 March–10 June 1999

Kosovo Defense Campaign, 11 June 1999–Today

Opposite: *A soldier from the Florida Army National Guard says farewell to his family before deploying for Operation Desert Shield, the largest overseas deployment of Guardsmen since the Korean War. (U.S. Army)*

Below: *Soldiers of the 24th Infantry Division (Mechanized), wearing desert camouflage uniforms, prepare to deploy to the Saudi desert. Operation Desert Storm was the largest deployment of female soldiers since World War II. ("24th Infantry Division Soldiers," Peter G. Varisano, Army Art Collection, NMUSA)*

study film from U-2 reconnaissance aircraft and find the terrain 60 miles north to Al Bussayah, Iraq, capable of handling military vehicle traffic. This information allows the 1st and 3d Armored Divisions to be deployed further west and prevents crowding with other units of VII Corps when ground operations commence.

15 January. **Soldiers Prepare for Chemical Warfare.** As the possibility of hostilities becomes more likely, soldiers of XVIII Airborne Corps are ordered to Mission Oriented Protective Posture (MOPP) Level I and begin taking antinerve-agent pills.

16 January. **Allied Units Begins Deploying West.** A convoy carrying troops and equipment from VII Corps and XVIII Airborne Corps begins moving west along the Tapline Road in northwestern Saudi Arabia. By the end of the day, the convoy is 120 miles long. Convoy operations will continue well into February to transport coalition troops, equipment, and supplies to their jumping-off positions before the anticipated ground war.

17 January. **Operation Desert Storm Begins.** Task Force Normandy, commanded by Lieutenant Colonel Richard A. Cody and comprising AH-64A

Apache attack helicopters from the 1st Battalion, 101st Aviation Regiment, 101st Airborne Division (Air Assault), and Air Force Special Operations MH-53J Pave Low helicopters, fires the opening shots of the conflict, successfully destroying two Iraqi early-

warning radar sites with Hellfire laser-guided missiles and 2.75-inch rockets. The destruction of the radar sites clears a path that allows coalition aircraft to strike targets deep into Iraq. This is the beginning of the Liberation and Defense of Kuwait Campaign; it will end 11 April.

17 January. **Rehearsal for Ground Operations.**
The 1st Infantry Division's 2d Battalion, 34th Armor, begins practice on clearing Iraqi trenches quickly by using tank plows and armored combat earthmovers.

18 January. **Reserve Call-Up Extended. Washington, D.C.**
President Bush signs an executive order authorizing the extension of active duty service for reservists beyond 180 days. The order also authorizes a call-up of an additional one million reservists if needed.

18 January. **Scud Missile Intercepted. Dhahran, Saudi Arabia.**
Battery A, 2d Battalion, 7th Air Defense Artillery, 11th Air Defense Artillery Brigade, engages and intercepts an Iraqi Scud missile. On the same day, Saddam Hussein orders Scud missiles launched against Israel. Six missiles strike Tel Aviv while another two hit Haifa. Since the Israeli Defense Force's Patriot batteries have not reached operational status, the Israeli government requests American Patriot units. The Army sends Task Force Patriot Defender,

consisting of two batteries from the 4th Battalion, 43d Air Defense Artillery, 10th Air Defense Artillery Brigade, from Germany to Israel. The Patriot batteries become operational on 22 January. The Army later deploys Batteries A and B, 1st Battalion, 7th Air Defense Artillery, 94th Air Defense Artillery Brigade, to Israel on 25–26 January.

18 January. **First Combat Use of ATACMS. Kuwait.**
Battery A, 1st Battalion, 27th Field Artillery, destroys an Iraqi SA-2 missile site 30 kilometers inside Kuwait with an Army Tactical Missile System (ATACMS) round fired from a multiple-launch rocket system (MLRS) launcher. The action marks the first use of the ATACMS and MLRS in combat.

20 January. **Scud Missiles Intercepted. Saudi Arabia.**
Batteries A and B, 2d Battalion, 7th Air Defense Artillery, intercept three of four Scud missiles fired at Dhahran.

22 January. **Iraqi Troops Captured.**
A patrol from the 3d Armored Cavalry Regiment captures six Iraqi prisoners.

23 January. **American Troops Begin Reconnaissance of Iraqi Positions.**
Scouts from the 1st Battalion, 325th Infantry, 82d Airborne Division, begin nightly reconnaissance missions of Iraqi positions near Objective Falcon.

Opposite: *Soldiers from the XVIII Airborne Corps train among a series of trenches and obstacles designed to replicate the Iraqi defensive lines in southern Kuwait that extended west into Iraq. (U.S. Army)*

Right: *As part of its deception plan in Operation Desert Shield, the Army used various types of decoys, including inflatable helicopters, fuel cells, and vehicles. (U.S. Army)*

28 January. **Successful Missile Intercept Experiment. Kwajalein Atoll.**

The Army conducts a successful test of an antiballistic missile system when an exoatmospheric reentry interceptor system (ERIS) launched from the Army's Kwajalein Atoll test range in the Marshall Islands intercepts a dummy warhead fired from Vandenberg Air Force Base, California, some 4,200 miles away. The intercept takes place 160 miles above the earth.

31 January. **American Soldiers Taken Prisoner. Iraq.**

Two soldiers from the 233d Transportation Company travelling by truck become lost and accidentally run into Iraqi forces, who take them prisoner. One of the prisoners, Specialist Melissa A. Rathbun-Nealy, becomes the first female POW of the conflict.

31 January. **Special Forces to Hunt Scuds.**

The Joint Special Operations Task Force (JSOTF), commanded by Major General Wayne A. Downing, is organized to prevent Scud launches against Saudi Arabia and Israel. By the time operations begin on 7 February, JSOTF will consist of two Delta Force squadrons, a reinforced company from 1st Battalion, 75th Ranger Regiment, a small number of Navy SEALs, and elements of the Army's 160th Special Operations Aviation Regiment (SOAR), also known as the "Night Stalkers." Based at Ar Ar, Saudi Arabia, the task force will operate largely in the western Iraqi desert near the Syrian border ("Scud Alley"). The mobile Scud launchers prove to be extremely difficult to locate, and very few, if any, are actually destroyed. In addition to hunting mobile Scud launchers, Special Forces troops will conduct reconnaissance missions, attack specially selected targets, and rescue downed pilots.

1 February. **Firefight with Iraqi Soldiers. Saudi-Iraqi Border.**

Paratroopers from the 4th Battalion, 325th Infantry, 2d Brigade, 82d Airborne Division, engage Iraqi forces in a 15-minute firefight at Phase Line Blue along the frontier, forcing the Iraqis to flee. No casualties are reported.

3 February. **Allied Ground Units Complete Movement to Assembly Areas.**

Both the VII Corps (minus elements of the 3d Armored Division) and the XVIII Airborne Corps complete their deployments to their forward assembly areas in northwestern Saudi Arabia in preparation for the ground phase of Operation Desert Storm. The remaining units of VII Corps will reach their assembly areas by 18 February.

6 February. **Last Units of VII Corps Arrive. Saudi Arabia.**

The final elements of VII Corps—the last units from the 3d Armored Division, commanded by Major General Paul E. Funk—reach Saudi Arabia.

7 February. **Army Conducts Artillery Raids. Kuwaiti-Iraqi Border.**

VII Corps and 1st Cavalry Division artillery units launch the first artillery raids of the war near Wadi al-Batin, a dry riverbed. During the raids, an artillery unit from the 1st Cavalry fires a laser-guided Copperhead round at an Iraqi observation tower and destroys it. The action marks the first use of a Copperhead in combat. One result of the raids is that Iraqi military leaders believe the major allied ground attack will come through the Wadi al-Batin, and they order the area reinforced with artillery and antitank weapons.

THE M1 ABRAMS TANK: BATTLE CHAMPION

The M1 Abrams Main Battle Tank (MBT) in its various models is the backbone of the U.S. heavy armored force and is unquestionably the best tank in the world. Named after General Creighton W. Abrams, World War II commander of the 37th Armored Battalion and 27th Army Chief of Staff, the Abrams MBT represents major advances in tank design.

The Cold War design concept behind the Abrams MBT program was to combine the three major components of firepower, mobility, and protection, thus creating a tank with such tactical superiority as to offset the numerical inferiority of U.S. and NATO forces against Soviet and Warsaw Pact Forces. Designed by General Dynamics Corporation, the first M1 Abrams tanks were delivered to the U.S. Army on 28 February 1980. It featured a stabilized 105mm gun, composite armor, advanced sensors and fire control system, and a turbine engine that made the M1 more maneuverable, faster—with a top speed of 45 mph—and quieter than other tanks, earning it the nickname, "Whispering Death." The stabilized gun enabled the M1 to fire and hit a target while traversing even the roughest terrain, while the composite armor gave greater protection against antitank rounds. A new type of kinetic energy ammunition with a rod of very dense, depleted uranium, could penetrate any enemy tank at ranges up to 3,500 meters. The aiming and thermal imaging systems allowed the M1 to find targets regardless of weather or light conditions, thereby giving it the tactical advantage of engaging the enemy first. Early concerns over performance of the engine air filter in dusty conditions were overcome, though the high gas consumption rate is still a concern for logistical planners.

Since the M1's introduction, two upgraded versions have also entered service, the M1A1 in 1985, and the M1A2 in 1998. The M1A1's improvements include a 120mm gun, depleted uranium armor, nuclear-biological-chemical warfare protection system, and an increased range to 290 miles. The M1A1 first saw combat in 1991 during Operation Desert Storm, where enemy tanks proved no match against the Abrams. Outranged by the M1A1 on an average of 1,000 meters, Iraqi tanks, even when they did manage to hit an Abrams, could not penetrate its armor, while the depleted uranium rounds of the Abrams usually only had to hit once to destroy an Iraqi tank. Of the 1,848 M1A1s fielded by the Army and Marine Corps, only 18 were removed from service due to battle damage. Of these, nine were considered permanent losses, while the other nine were repairable. Not a single Abrams crewman was lost to enemy fire and there were few reported breakdowns. During the conflict, U.S. armored forces maintained an unprecedented 90 percent operational readiness for the Abrams.

By 1993 production of the M1/M1A1 series was complete, with more than 8,800 tanks in service. Of these, 3,273 M1s and 4,796 M1A1s were produced for the U.S. Army, 221 M1A1s for the Marine Corps, and 555 for Egypt. To date, the Army has received 77 of the M1A2 version and a further 1,000 M1s are being upgraded to the M1A2 configuration. The first M1A2s were delivered to the 1st Cavalry Division in 1998. The large size and heavy weight of the tank does limit its air mobility to only the largest aircraft, leaving the Army dependent on sea lift to move its heavy armored units.

Of the M1A1s currently serving in Operation Iraqi Freedom only 14 have been reported damaged, most of these to mechanical breakdown, and two destroyed. While some M1A1s have sustained damage from mines, antitank rockets, and roadside bombs, to date, no Abrams tank has ever been destroyed by enemy tank fire.

—*Vince Hawkins*

Above: *The M1A1 Abrams tank, an upgraded version of the original M1, first entered Army service in 1985. During Operation Desert Storm, the M1A1 decimated Iraqi armored formations. (U.S. Army)*

Right: *While legally barred from direct combat positions, female soldiers provided invaluable service to front line units in dangerous support missions during Operations Desert Storm and Desert Shield. ("2LT Ellen Ainsworth," Dennis Uciba, Army Art Collection, NMUSA)*

9 February. **Timetable for Ground Operations.**
General H. Norman Schwarzkopf, CENTCOM commander, recommends that the ground phase of Operation Desert Storm begin between 21 and 25 February. President Bush approves.

13 February. **Additional Artillery Raids.**
Three MLRS batteries (two from the 42d Field Artillery Brigade and one from the 1st Cavalry Division) attack Iraqi artillery positions. The three batteries fire a total of 216 rockets, dropping an estimated 140,000 bomblets on the enemy. Iraqi soldiers call MLRS attacks "steel rain."

14 February. **1st and 3d Armored Division in Position.**
The 9,000 vehicles of the 1st Armored Division begin moving towards TAA Garcia, a staging area just south of the 2d Armored Cavalry Regiment's positions. The 3d Armored Division will take up positions just to the west of the 1st Armored.

15 February. **CENTCOM Briefing on Iraqi POWs.**
General Schwarzkopf receives a briefing on the condition of Iraqi POWs. Interrogation of the prisoners has found that most of them are veterans of the Iran-Iraq War and are tired of fighting. CENTCOM also learns that many more Iraqi soldiers are willing to surrender, but that the extensive minefields between the combatants' lines, probable execution at the hands of the Republican Guard, and threats to their families back home prevent most from doing so. All of the prisoners agree that large numbers of their comrades will quickly surrender once the ground war starts.

16 February. **Soldiers Killed by Friendly Fire.**
While on a night mission, an AH-64A Apache helicopter from the 1st Infantry Division (Mechanized) mistakenly fires Hellfire missiles at an M113 armored personnel carrier and a Bradley fighting vehicle. The vehicles are from the 1st Division's Task Force Iron, which had earlier cut through a sand berm along the Iraqi border in twenty locations and advanced three miles into Iraq. Two soldiers are killed and six are wounded.

17 February. **Air Assaults on Iraqi Positions.**
AH-64A Apaches from the 2d Battalion, 229th Aviation Regiment, 101st Airborne Division (Air Assault), attack an Iraqi bunker near what becomes Main Supply Route (MSR) New Market. Ten Iraqi soldiers surrender. Another group of Apaches from the same unit, supported by Company C, 3d Battalion, 502d Infantry, attack elements of the Iraqi 45th Infantry Division, taking another 30 prisoners.

17 February. **VII Corps Launches Largest Artillery Raid to Date.**
VII Corps conducts the largest artillery raid to date with five battalions of artillery. The barrage destroys Iraqi air defenses, opening an air corridor for Apaches from the 2d Squadron, 6th Cavalry, 11th Aviation Brigade, commanded by Lieutenant Colonel Terry Branham. The Apaches target and destroy numerous Iraqi communications facilities.

18 February. **XVIII Airborne Corps Units Attack Iraqis.**
Helicopters from the 1st Battalion, 82d Aviation Regiment, 82d Airborne Division, conduct an armed

reconnaissance and attack the Iraqi 45th Infantry Division at Objective Rochambeau. On the same day, 12 Apaches from the XVIII Airborne Corps' 12th Aviation Brigade hit Iraqi troops at Objective White.

18 February. **Special Forces Soldiers Rescue Downed American Pilot.**
An American F-16 pilot shot down 40 miles north of the Saudi border is rescued by an MH-60 Black Hawk from the 3d Battalion, 160th Special Operations Aviation Regiment.

19 February. **24th Infantry Division (Mechanized) Attacks Iraqi Positions.**
The 24th Infantry Division's Aviation Brigade attacks several Iraqi positions across the border. In addition to air attacks, Battery B, 4th Battalion, 41st Field Artillery, destroys an Iraqi border post with a Copperhead round.

20 February. **1st Cavalry Division Units Clash With Iraqis. Wadi al Batin, Kuwait.**
The 1st Battalion, 5th Cavalry, 1st Cavalry Division, commanded by Lieutenant Colonel Michael Parker, pushes north through two cuts in the border sand berm with orders to probe Iraqi positions. After

Above: *MLRS launchers from the 158th Field Artillery Brigade (Oklahoma Army National Guard) fire on Iraqi positions. Iraqis soon referred to MLRS attacks as "steel rain." ("Steel Rain," Frank M. Thomas, Army Art Collection, NMUSA)*

advancing six miles and capturing a handful of Iraqi prisoners, the battalion comes under heavy fire from enemy artillery, mortars, and a number of expertly camouflaged antitank guns. After an hour-long battle, the battalion pulls back, suffering three dead and nine wounded. Iraqi casualties are unknown.

20 February. **Helicopter and Artillery Strikes on Iraqi Positions.**
Helicopters from the 101st Airborne Division (Air Assault) strike Iraqi positions and gather more than 400 Iraqi POWs. Additional helicopters from the 82d Airborne Division, supported by the 1st Battalion, 201st Field Artillery, a West Virginia Army National Guard unit, attack the Iraqi 45th Infantry Division.

23 February. **Eve of Ground War.**
President Bush addresses the nation on television and states that he has directed General Schwarzkopf "to use all forces available, including ground forces, to eject the Iraqi Army from Kuwait. . . . The liberation of Kuwait has entered a final phase."

23 February. **Special Forces Teams Deployed in Iraq. Euphrates River Valley, Iraq.**
Several Special Forces teams are deployed in Iraq to provide information on Iraqi troop movements. One team, deployed six miles west of Oawam al Hamzah and Highway 8 and commanded by Master Sergeant Jeffrey Sims, is discovered. The three-man team battles hundreds of Iraqi soldiers for two hours before

Right: *AH-64A Apache helicopters from the 11th Aviation Brigade fly over the smoldering wreckage of an Iraqi tank. By the end of Operation Desert Storm, Apaches were credited with destroying hundreds of Iraqi tanks, armored vehicles, and artillery pieces. ("11th Aviation Brigade in the Attack," Mario H. Acevedo, Army Art Collection, NMUSA)*

being rescued by an MH-60 Black Hawk from the 160th SOAR. Seven other teams remain undiscovered, and for the next five days the Special Forces manning the sites report no large Iraqi troop movements along Highway 8.

24 February. G-Day Ground Attack Begins.

At 4:00 a.m. local time Lieutenant General Gary E. Luck's XVIII Airborne Corps moves into Iraq. Supported by the 2d Brigade, 82d Airborne Division, the French 6th Light Armored Division meets little resistance and quickly achieves its objectives. By the early evening, the 82d and the French, supported by the 18th Field Artillery Brigade, are deep into Iraqi territory. Meanwhile, the 101st Airborne Division begins an air assault into Iraq. The first operation involves airlifting the division's 1st Brigade, commanded by Colonel Tom Hill, from TAA Campbell to Forward Operating Base Cobra, approximately 95 miles away. Using 66 UH-60 Black Hawk and 30 CH-47 Chinook helicopters in three lifts, the brigade lands and secures Foreword Operating Base (FOB) Cobra, taking 340 prisoners. Additional troops, equipment, fuel, and supplies are flown in, but increasingly deteriorating weather halts the airlifts late in the day. Meanwhile the Marine divisions, supported by the Army's Tiger Brigade and units from several Arab nations, plunge directly into Kuwait.

24 February. VII Corps Ordered to Attack.

Intelligence indicates disarray among the Iraqis, and no significant resistance has been encountered. General Schwarzkopf orders VII Corps to begin its attack a day early. With the 2d Armored Cavalry Regiment as advance guard, the attack begins around 3:00 p.m. A massive 30-minute artillery bombardment pounds the Iraqi defenses with 11,000 artillery rounds and 414 MLRS rockets. Using tank plows and armored combat earthmovers, the 1st Infantry Division breaches the Iraqi defenses, collapsing enemy field fortifications and burying dozens of Iraqi soldiers. Instead of the expected 18 hours, the breaching operation is accomplished in two. At the same time, the 2d Armored Cavalry engages and destroys small numbers of Iraqi T-55 tanks. The 1st Armored Division advances behind the 2d Armored Cavalry in a wedge formation.

25 February. VII Corps Ordered to Turn East.

Concerned that the Iraqi Republican Guard is trying to escape, General Schwarzkopf orders VII Corps to accelerate its attack. VII Corps commander Lieutenant General Franks orders his divisions to swing east into Kuwait toward the Republican Guard units.

25–26 February. 101st Airborne Division Assaults Deep into Iraq.

The 3d Brigade, 101st Airborne Division, commanded by Colonel Robert Clark, is airlifted 150 miles into Iraq. The air assault, the longest in the history of warfare, effectively cuts Highway 8, the main route for Iraqi resupply and reinforcements.

25 February. Scud Strikes Barracks in Dhahran. Saudi Arabia.

A Scud missile fired at the Saudi port city of Dhahran strikes a warehouse serving as a U.S. Army barracks, killing 28 soldiers, including the first female enlisted soldier killed in action. Another 97 soldiers are wounded. Thirteen of those killed come from the 14th Quartermaster Detachment, an Army Reserve water purification unit. Patriot batteries defending Dhahran experienced a software problem and were unable to intercept the missile. Furthermore, several studies after the conflict question the Patriot's actual effectiveness against the Scuds. After the war, the Patriots will be upgraded to better deal with such missiles.

26 February. Helicopters from 1st Armored Division Attack. Iraq.

AH-64A Apaches from the 3d Battalion, 1st Aviation Regiment, commanded by Lieutenant Colonel William Hatch, attack the Iraqi Adnan Infantry Division, destroying 38 T-72s, 14 BMP fighting vehicles, and 70 trucks.

26 February. Battle of 73 Easting.

Beginning in the late afternoon, the 2d Armored Cavalry Regiment engages the 18th Mechanized Brigade of the Republican Guard Tawakalna Division. The regiment destroys 28 Iraqi tanks, mostly T-72s, and 16 other armored vehicles, while losing three soldiers killed. The American M1A1 tank guns prove to have far greater range, and the M1A1s can fire effectively on the move with thermal sights that allow their crews to detect the enemy in darkness, fog, smoke, and dust storms.

26 February. Engineers Killed in Accident. As Salman Airfield, Iraq.

Seven soldiers from 1st Platoon, Company A, 27th Engineer Battalion, 20th Engineer Brigade, are killed while clearing unexploded cluster bomb submunitions at As Salman Airfield.

26–27 February. Battle of Objective Norfolk.

After passing through the 2d Armored Cavalry Regiment, the 1st Infantry Division's 1st and 3d

Opposite: *With visibility hampered by burning oil wells, M1A1 Abrams tanks of Task Force 1-32 Armor, 1st Cavalry Division, breach the Iraqi sand berm and begin an attack up the Wadi al Batin. ("Bermbusters," Jody Harmon)*

Right: *Soldiers of the 1st Brigade, 101st Airborne Division (Air Assault), take up positions at Forward Operating Base Cobra after a 95-mile airlift into Iraqi territory. ("Lightning of Desert Storm," James Dietz)*

Brigades fight a chaotic battle against the 18th Brigade of the Republican Guard Tawakalna Division and 37th Brigade of the 12th Armored Division. Both Iraqi brigades are destroyed, with hundreds killed or taken prisoner. Several Abrams and Bradleys are destroyed by American fire, killing six soldiers. Another 30 are wounded during the battle.

27 February. Battle of Medinah Ridge.
In the biggest tank battle of the war, the 1st Armored Division engages the Republican Guard's Medinah Division and surviving elements of the 12th Armored Division. The main battle focuses on fighting between the 1st Armored's 2d Brigade, under Colonel Montgomery Meigs, and the Medinah Division's 2d Brigade. Meigs' 200 M1A1 Abrams and M2 Bradleys devastate the Iraqi formations. Divisional artillery and attack helicopters, along with Air Force close support aircraft, add to the carnage. By the time the battle ends in the late afternoon, more than 300 Iraqi armored vehicles have been destroyed. American losses are one soldier killed and a handful of vehicles destroyed or damaged.

27 February. Black Hawk Shot Down During Rescue Mission.
While attempting to reach a downed Air Force pilot, a UH-60 Black Hawk from the 2d Battalion, 229th Aviation Regiment, is shot down. Five of the eight soldiers on board are killed and the rest taken prisoner. Among the prisoners is flight surgeon Major Rhonda Cornum, the second female American captive of the war.

27 February. Jalibah Air Base Captured.
After capturing Tallil Air Base and swinging east toward Basrah, the 24th Infantry Division (Mechanized), led by Major General Barry R. McCaffrey, attacks and secures Jalibah Air Base, destroying 14 MiG fighters in their hangars. The 24th then continues down Highway 8, capturing enemy supply depots and encountering scattered elements of the al-Faw, Nebuchadnezzar, and Hammurabi Republican Guard Divisions. The 24th halts its advance at 5:00 a.m. on 28 February but continues to pound the Iraqis with artillery right up to cease-fire at 8:00 a.m.

28 February. Cease-Fire Announced.
With Kuwait liberated and Iraqi forces all but routed, President Bush calls for a unilateral cease-fire after 100 hours of ground combat, effective at 8:00 a.m. local time. Since 17 January, 98 soldiers have been killed in action or died of wounds, 21 of them in friendly-fire incidents; 126 soldiers were killed in nonhostile incidents in both Operation Desert Shield and Desert Storm. Another 354 soldiers were wounded. Casualties are unexpectedly light—prewar estimates ran as high as 20,000. In total, the Army deployed 227,800 soldiers to the Persian Gulf area. Of these, 37,692 came from the Army National Guard. Another 35,158 soldiers from the Army Reserve served in Operation Desert Shield/Desert Storm.

2 March. 24th Infantry Division Engages Iraqis.
When elements of the fleeing Hammurabi Division fire on the 24th Infantry Division, the 24th's helicopters, tanks, and artillery engage them. More than 185 Iraqi armored vehicles, 400 trucks, and

ARMY WOMEN: SOLDIERS OF THE DESERT

Operation Desert Shield/Storm was the largest overseas deployment of military women in U.S. history. Together, the two operations were the first major test of the Army under the All Volunteer Force concept, which had come into existence at the end of the Vietnam War.

In the post-war period the Army had competed for the best of those who volunteered to serve, regardless of race, sex, or quotas. Commanders quickly realized that the recruitment of women was essential to the success of the All Volunteer Force, because of the limited number of available high-quality male recruits. Between 1973 and 1990 the number of women in the Army grew steadily, and by 1990 women comprised 11 percent of the Regular Army, 21 percent of the Army Reserve, and 7 percent of the National Guard. Minority women represented 56.4 percent of enlisted women and 25.6 percent of women officers in the Army.

When the Army mobilized for Operation Desert Shield in August 1990, 26,000 Army women deployed to the Persian Gulf. Women comprised 8 percent of Army Regulars and 20 percent of Army Reservists in the Gulf. Army women were eligible for assignment in 52 percent of all Army positions and served as integral members of their units. Although Army policy prevented women from serving in positions with high probability of direct combat, women served in combat support and combat service support jobs.

In Operation Desert Storm female pilots of the 101st Airborne Division flew Black Hawk and Chinook helicopters loaded with supplies and troops 50 miles into Iraq as part of the largest helicopter assault in military history. Throughout the operation, women served in air defense artillery, military police, medical search and rescue, graves registration, civil affairs units, and Patriot missile battalions. They worked as traffic controllers, truck drivers, ammunition technicians, ordnance specialists, and communications radio operators. Women truck drivers hauled supplies and equipment and transported enemy prisoners of war to holding facilities.

Operation Desert Storm was in many ways a test case for Army women. The desert conditions were tough and Army women worked side by side with their male counterparts. Some Army women in the Gulf were required to deal with special restrictions imposed on their clothing and activities by Saudi cultural expectations. In Dhahran, an area known for its high humidity, women soldiers were required to keep their winter-weight fatigues rolled down over elbows, while male soldiers simply removed their shirts. Some restrictions prevented Army women from doing their jobs. Women soldiers were not allowed to drive vehicles. Women passengers in uniform were not allowed to give civilian bus drivers directions; the drivers would listen only to a male. Some Saudi officers and civilian officials would not talk directly to American women soldiers. They would not accept anything a servicewoman said without verification from a male soldier.

Women soldiers in the Gulf received media attention disproportionate to their numbers because of their news value in a situation where "hard" news was tightly controlled. The American media latched onto the image of servicewomen working side by side with male soldiers and broadcast home to American viewers stories of women mechanics working on the engines of aircraft, of women standing guard, women tracking aircraft on radar, and women flying helicopters. The public responded favorably, granting to servicewomen a level of acceptance, respect, and approval that would eventually be translated into political action. In 1991 Congress lifted the ban on servicewomen flying in aircraft engaged in combat missions. In 1993 the ban on women serving aboard combat vessels was removed and the next year the Army opened more positions to women.

Eleven Army women lost their lives in Saudi Arabia. Five of the 122 U.S. troops killed in action were Army enlisted women. Two Army women, a truck driver and a flight surgeon, were among the 25 U.S. personnel held prisoner of war by Iraq; both were among 19 women who received Purple Hearts for combat injuries.

—Judi Bellifaire

Right: *M1A1 Abrams tanks and M2/M3 Bradley fighting vehicles of the 2d Armored Cavalry Regiment destroyed dozens of tanks and other armored vehicles of the Iraqi Republican Guard Tawakalna Division. The engagement become known as the Battle of 73 Easting. ("Battle of 73 Easting," David Pentland)*

34 artillery pieces are destroyed, and hundreds of Iraqis killed or captured.

3 March. **Cease-Fire Talks. Safwan, Iraq.**
General Schwarzkopf and other allied coalition leaders meet with Iraqi representatives at Safwan Air Base in southern Iraq. The Iraqis accept all the cease-fire terms and agree to repatriate allied prisoners in a few days. After the cease-fire, U.S. Army Civil Affairs units, mostly from the Army Reserve, lead the efforts to provide food, shelter, and medicine to the masses of refugees. Engineer and Explosive Ordnance Disposal units also begin clearing the thousands of mines laid by Iraqi forces, as well as eliminating the tons of unexploded ordnance littering the battlefield. In the weeks following the war, 29 American servicemen are killed by mines and unexploded ordnance.

4–12 March. **Iraqi Bunker Complex Destroyed. Khamisiyah.**
Engineers from the 82d Airborne Division destroy dozens of Iraqi bunkers and weapons caches at a massive depot complex. Unknown to the engineers, some of the bunkers contain chemical weapons, primarily nerve agents. During later investigations of what becomes known as Gulf War Syndrome (a number of common chronic illnesses suffered by significant numbers of Desert Storm veterans), the Department of Defense estimates that as many as 100,000 servicemen may have been exposed to low levels of nerve agents.

5 March. **Coalition POWs Released.**
Thirty-five coalition prisoners are repatriated. Five soldiers are among those released, including two women.

8 March. **Army Units Begin Returning Home.**
The first soldiers who served in Operation Desert Shield/Desert Storm begin returning to the United States.

12 March. **Southwest Asia Service Medal Authorized.**
President Bush issues an executive order authorizing the Southwest Asia Service Medal for all military personnel who served in Operations Desert Shield and Desert Storm.

31 March. **Last Pershing II Missiles Removed. Europe.**
The last Pershing II missiles are removed under the terms of the 1987 INF Treaty. The missiles are transported back to the United States to be destroyed.

6 April. **Operation Provide Comfort. Northern Iraq.**
To bring humanitarian assistance to nearly 1.5 million Iraqi Kurdish refugees who have fled to northern Iraq, the United States forms Joint Task Force Provide Comfort at Incirlik Air Base, Turkey. The task force, which includes elements of the 3d Infantry Division (Mechanized), provides food, water, shelter, and medicine, as well as protection from Iraqi attacks. Lieutenant General John M. Shalikashvili assumes

command of the task force on 17 April. By the time Operation Provide Comfort ends on 24 July, allied forces have delivered 17,000 tons of relief supplies. As Operation Provide Comfort ends, Operation Provide Comfort II commences, with the second operation intended more as a show of force against the Iraqis than as a humanitarian mission.

11 April. Liberation of Kuwait Complete.
The cease-fire officially takes effect, ending the Liberation and Defense of Kuwait 1991 Campaign. The United States declares a final end to conflict on 31 July 1991. The Southwest Asia Cease-Fire 1991–1995 Campaign begins the following day. It will conclude 30 November 1995.

23 April. Powell, Schwarzkopf Awarded Congressional Gold Medal.
Congress approves Congressional Gold Medals for General Colin L. Powell, Chairman of the Joint Chiefs of Staff, and General Schwarzkopf for their leadership in Operation Desert Storm. There is also discussion to promote both generals to five-star rank, but no action is taken. President Bush presents Powell and Schwarzkopf with their medals on 10 December 1992.

Above: *With ground operations nearly over, an M1A1 tank and a dismounted infantryman advance through the Rumayiah Oil Field while several oil wells destroyed by Iraqis still burn. ("Final Push Through Rumayiah Oil Field," Mario H. Acevedo, Army Art Collection, NMUSA)*

24 April. Corporal Freddie Stowers Awarded Medal of Honor.
Corporal Freddie Stowers, who served with the all-black 371st Infantry Regiment in France in World War I, is posthumously awarded the Congressional Medal of Honor by President Bush. Stowers receives the medal for his heroic actions while leading a squad against the Germans on 28 September 1918 and suffering a mortal wound. He becomes the first black soldier of either World War I or II to be presented with the Medal of Honor.

16 May. 11th Armored Cavalry to Kuwait. Germany.
The 11th Armored Cavalry Regiment is ordered to deploy to Kuwait as part of Operation Positive Force—the continued presence of U.S. forces. On 13 June, the regiment relieves the 1st Brigade, 3d Armored Division, and assumes responsibility for the defense of Kuwait.

8 June. Parade for Troops of Desert Storm.
Led by General Schwarzkopf, thousands of soldiers, sailors, airmen, and marines who participated in Operation Desert Storm march in a victory parade in the nation's capital. Two days later, New York City holds a ticker-tape parade in Manhattan in honor of the troops.

21 June. Gordon R. Sullivan Becomes Chief of Staff.
General Gordon R. Sullivan, who had been serving as the Army's Vice Chief of Staff, is named the 32nd Chief of Staff, United States Army. Sullivan,

SCHWARZKOPF: COMMANDING THE STORM

As commander of U.S. Central Command (USCENTCOM), General H. Norman Schwarzkopf led the allied coalition against the Iraqi Army that had invaded Kuwait in early August 1990. He was the right man for the job. After a 43-day air campaign starting 17 January 1991, Schwarzkopf's ground force of American, British, French, and Arab units routed the Iraqis in a 100-hour ground campaign. With the victory, Schwarzkopf emerged as a national hero. He also came to represent how his generation of professional soldiers persevered during the difficult years of the post-Vietnam era and rebuilt the U.S. Army.

Born on 22 August 1934 in Trenton, New Jersey, Herbert Norman Schwarzkopf was the son of an Army officer who later left the service to command the New Jersey State Police. He followed in his father's footsteps and entered the United States Military Academy in 1952. At graduation in June 1956, he was commissioned in the Infantry. His early Army career included the 101st Airborne Division, a tour in Berlin, and at West Point as an engineering instructor.

In 1965 Schwarzkopf requested his first of two tours to Vietnam. He served as an advisor to South Vietnamese airborne troops, earning two Silver Stars and a Purple Heart. After attending Army Command and General Staff College, he returned to Vietnam in 1969 to command the 1st Battalion, 6th Infantry, Americal Division. He was awarded a third Silver Star and another Purple Heart for rescuing wounded soldiers trapped in a minefield.

After Vietnam, Schwarzkopf served as deputy commander, 172d Infantry Brigade, in Alaska and commander, 1st Brigade, 9th Infantry Division, at Fort Lewis, Washington. Selected as a brigadier general in June 1978, he served on the staff of the U.S. Pacific Command, then returned to West Germany as assistant division commander, 8th Infantry Division (Mech). As a major general in 1983, Schwarzkopf took command of the 24th Infantry Division (Mech) at Fort Stewart, Georgia. Later that year, he was named deputy commander of the invasion of Grenada.

After a tour in the Pentagon, Schwarzkopf was promoted to lieutenant general in 1986 and appointed I Corps commander. He returned to the Pentagon in 1987 as Deputy Chief of Staff for Plans and Operations. In 1988, he received his fourth star and assumed command of USCENTCOM.

Iraq's invasion of Kuwait in August 1990 was not a surprise to Schwarzkopf who had envisioned such a scenario—USCENTCOM was actually conducting an exercise on Iraqi military actions at the time of the invasion. Schwarzkopf immediately put his staff to work planning first for the defense of Saudi Arabia (Operation Desert Shield), then for the eventual expulsion of Iraqi forces from Kuwait (Operation Desert Storm).

Tagged by the media and soldiers as "Stormin' Norman" for a sometimes ferocious temper, Schwarzkopf commanded the largest coalition of allied forces since the Korean War with over 700,000 troops from 29 nations, 541,000 of them from the United States. By December, Schwarzkopf and his staff had formulated a strategy to drive Iraq out of Kuwait. Nicknamed the "left hook" or "Hail Mary," the plan called for allied troops to deceive Iraqi forces with demonstrations along the coast while sending the inland main attack from Saudi Arabia into Iraq to cut off and destroy Iraqi forces.

Ground operations commenced on G-Day, 24 February 1991. What resulted was one of the most decisive military campaigns in history. By 1 March the Iraqis' were in flight and the Allies declared a cease-fire. Two days later, Schwarzkopf met with Iraqi leaders at Safwan to discuss terms.

The desert victory made Schwarzkopf an international figure and capped a distinguished 35-year Army career. He received numerous U.S. and foreign decorations, including a Congressional Gold Medal, and reviewed his soldiers in victory parades in Washington, D.C., and New York City, before retiring 30 August 1991.

In the years following his retirement, Schwarzkopf authored a best-selling autobiography, *It Doesn't Take a Hero*, in addition to speaking around the country. He has also narrated a number of military history programs and makes frequent appearances on television news as a military affairs commentator.

--Matt Seelinger

Right: *Generals H. Norman Schwarzkopf and Colin Powell ride with Mrs. Schwarzkopf in a victory parade held for soldiers returning from Desert Storm. Parades for the victorious troops were held in Washington, D.C., New York City, and many other American cities and towns. (U.S. Army)*

Below: *An armor officer and veteran of the Vietnam War, General Gordon R. Sullivan, the 32d Army Chief of Staff, would lead the Army in its transition from a Cold War fighting force to a high-tech army of the twenty-first century. ("General Gordon R. Sullivan," Ned Bittinger, Army Art Collection, NMUSA)*

commissioned through Norwich University's ROTC program in 1959, is the first non-West Point graduate to be named to that position since General Frederick C. Weyand.

3 July. **Powell, Schwarzkopf Awarded Presidential Medal of Freedom.**
President Bush awards Generals Powell and Schwarzkopf the Presidential Medal of Freedom for their leadership in Operation Desert Storm.

1992

January. **Status of the Army.**
With the Cold War effectively over, the Army's personnel strength is significantly reduced, to 610,450 active duty officers and enlisted personnel. At the beginning of 1992, the Army retains 18 divisions, but this number will soon drop.

1–10 May. **Troops Dispatched to Quell Rioting. Los Angeles, California.**
In response to massive rioting and looting, soldiers from the 7th Infantry Division (Light) and the California Army National Guard's 40th Infantry Division (Mechanized) are ordered to Los Angeles to restore order. By the time the rioting ends, 54 people have been killed, 2,383 injured, and more than 13,000 arrested. Property damage is estimated at $700 million.

August–October. **Soldiers Conduct Relief Operations. South Florida.**

After Hurricane Andrew devastates South Florida on 24 August, soldiers from the 82d Airborne Division, 10th Mountain Division (Light), and Florida Army National Guard units are deployed to assist in disaster relief operations, particularly in and around the city of Homestead.

3 December. **Operation Restore Hope. Somalia.**

The headquarters of the 10th Mountain Division (Light) is designated as the headquarters for all Army forces in Operation Restore Hope, a humanitarian relief mission to provide assistance to famine-plagued Somalia. Major General Steven L. Arnold, the 10th's commanding general, has the mission of providing safe passage of relief supplies. Through the efforts of American soldiers and Marines and troops from other nations, humanitarian aid agencies can soon call an end to the food emergency. As a result, the numbers of American troops in Somalia are gradually reduced in mid-February.

1993

January. **Status of the Army.**

The Army's active duty personnel strength continues to drop, to 572,423 officers and enlisted soldiers. Force structure is cut from 18 to 16 divisions.

15 January. **Firefight with Somali Militiamen. Baledogle, Somalia.**

Soldiers from Company E, 2d Battalion, 87th Infantry, 10th Mountain Division (Light), engage a group of Somali militiamen, killing six while suffering no casualties.

20 January. **Bill Clinton Inaugurated as President.**

William Jefferson Clinton is inaugurated as the 42nd President and Commander-in-Chief of the United States. Clinton is the first President born after World War II and the first without military service since Franklin Delano Roosevelt. Documents appearing during the presidential campaign showed Clinton avoided the draft during the Vietnam War era and disparaged the military. Clinton's relationship with the military grows more tense as a result of his campaign pledge to open military service to homosexuals.

25 January. **Army Helicopters Engage Somalis. Kismaayo, Somalia.**

AH-1 Cobra attack helicopters from the 3d Squadron, 17th Cavalry, destroy six Somali pickup trucks carrying automatic weapons called "technicals," killing eight militiamen.

24–26 February. **Firefights in Kismaayo. Somalia.**

The 2d Battalion, 87th Infantry, 10th Mountain Division (Light), clashes with Somali militiamen in Kismaayo. At least 23 Somalis are killed. No American casualties are reported.

4 May. **Operation Continue Hope. Somalia.**
The United Nations' Operation Continue Hope in Somalia assumes control of the peacekeeping and humanitarian mission. American troops continue to provide logistics, communications, and intelligence support, a Quick Reaction Force, and transportation elements. In addition to infantry and combat service support units, more than 60 Army aircraft and 1,000 aviation personnel will serve in Operation Continue Hope. Army forces operate under the tactical control of Major General Thomas M. Montgomery, Commander, U.S. Forces Somalia.

21 June. **First Female Army Astronaut in Space.**
Major Nancy Currie, an Army aviator, becomes the first female Army astronaut in space as part of space shuttle mission STS-57 aboard *Endeavour.* Currie will later serve on three additional missions through 2002.

8 August. **Four GIs Killed in Medina, Somalia.**
Four soldiers are killed when a land mine destroys their humvee.

28 August. **Task Force Ranger Deployed. Somalia.**
Task Force Ranger, comprising Company B, 3d Battalion, 75th Ranger Regiment, Delta Force soldiers, elements of the 160th SOAR, Air Force Special Operations personnel, and Navy SEALs, arrives. Task Force Ranger, commanded by Major General William F. Garrison, has the mission of capturing senior

Somali leader Mohamed Farah Aidid and his lieutenants. The task force conducts six missions, none of which results in Aidid's capture, but they do limit his movements.

26 September. **Black Hawk Shot Down. Mogadishu, Somalia.**
Somali militiamen shoot down a UH-60 Black Hawk helicopter with a rocket-propelled grenade, killing the three-man crew. Three more soldiers are wounded trying to reach the crash site.

3–4 October. **Battle of Mogadishu, Somalia.**
After receiving a tip that several of Aidid's lieutenants are meeting in the Olympic Hotel, Task Force Ranger launches an operation to capture them. A combined force of Delta Force soldiers and Rangers, flown in by 160th SOAR MH-6 Little Bird and MH-60 Black Hawk helicopters, conducts the raid in the late afternoon. The prisoners are quickly rounded up and placed aboard trucks and humvees for the trip to Task Force Ranger headquarters at the Mogadishu Airport. Thousands of Somali militia, interspersed with women and children, converge on the American convoy. The situation becomes worse when two Black Hawks are shot down by rocket-propelled grenades. Rangers and Delta Force soldiers quickly secure one crash site, but the other is not as accessible. Two Delta Force snipers, Master Sergeant Gary Gordon and Sergeant First Class Randall Shugart, land near the second crash site

Right: *Rangers and Delta Force soldiers defend the crash site of a 160th Special Operations Aviation Regiment MH-60 Black Hawk ("Super 61") against Somali militiamen during the bloody "Battle of the Black Sea" in Mogadishu, Somalia, 3–4 October 1993. ("I Will Never Leave Behind a Fallen Comrade," Jeanine Mosher)*

and defend the downed helicopter and its surviving pilot, Chief Warrant Officer Michael Durant. Gordon and Shugart are eventually overwhelmed by a Somali mob and killed. Both are later awarded the Congressional Medal of Honor posthumously. They are the first soldiers to be awarded the Medal of Honor since the Vietnam War. Durant is taken prisoner and held until 14 October. Meanwhile, the convoy makes it out, carrying a number of dead and wounded. Nearly 100 Rangers and Delta troops remain trapped in the city. Assisted by helicopters firing 7.62mm miniguns and 2.75-inch rockets, the trapped soldiers hold off the Somali militia. A rescue force comprising Rangers, the 2d Battalion, 14th Infantry, and Pakistani and Malaysian armored units fights its way to the trapped Americans just after midnight. The column then fights its way out, with the last soldiers reaching safety around 6:30 a.m. In the longest and bloodiest firefight involving American troops since Vietnam, 19 soldiers are killed and nearly 100 wounded; Somali casualties are estimated to be as high as 1,000. The casualties create significant public outcry against American involvement in Somalia, and American forces are withdrawn from Somalia by March 1994.

6 October. Special Forces Soldier Killed. Mogadishu.
Hours after the Battle of Mogadishu, Sergeant Matt Rierson, a Special Forces soldier, is killed in a mortar attack on the American base at Mogadishu Airport. He is the last American serviceman killed in action in Somalia.

25 October. **Shalikashvili Appointed Chairman, Joint Chiefs of Staff.**
General John M. Shalikashvili, the Supreme Allied Commander in Europe, becomes the 13th Chairman, Joint Chiefs of Staff, and the seventh Army officer to hold that position. Shalikashvili, who first entered the Army as an enlisted soldier, is also the first foreign-born soldier to serve as Chairman.

22 November. **West Named Secretary of the Army.**
Togo West, Jr., who has previously held positions within the Department of Defense and the Department of the Army, becomes the 16th Secretary of the Army.

1994

January. **Status of the Army.**
The Army's strength stands at 541,343 officers and enlisted personnel. A reduction of another two divisions leaves the Army with 14 active divisions.

1 January. **Army Historical Foundation Reactivated. Arlington, Virginia.**
After several years of inactivity, a decision is made to reactivate the foundation under retired Colonel Raymond K. Bluhm, Jr., as executive director. With the mission to promote and preserve the history and heritage of the American soldier, the foundation is the

Left: *American soldiers continue the longtime mission of military and humanitarian assistance in Latin America, such as Joint Task Force-Bravo in Honduras. ("MP Formation–Joint Task Force-B," George Banagis, Army Art Collection, NMUSA)*

Opposite, top: *A soldier from the 24th Infantry Division (Mechanized) watches for Iraqi activity. ("On Guard at Sunset," Peter G. Varisano, Army Art Collection, NMUSA)*

Opposite, bottom: *General Dennis J. Reimer became the 33d Army Chief of Staff in June 1995. (U.S. Army)*

only organization chartered to support the building of a national Army museum.

8 March. Army Modernization Plan Announced.
General Sullivan announces the Army's Force XXI project, which will incorporate the latest digital equipment into Army weapon systems and other equipment and into Army training, to bring the Army into the 21st century.

12 March. Last American Combat Troops Leave Somalia.
The last Army combat unit in Somalia, 2d Battalion, 22d Infantry, 10th Mountain Division, leaves Somalia to return to its home base at Fort Drum, New York. During the Somalia operations, 27 American soldiers were killed in action, another four died in accidents, and more than 100 were wounded.

14 April. Black Hawks Shot Down in Friendly Fire Incident. Northern Iraq.
Two Army UH-60 Black Hawk helicopters flying in support of Operation Provide Comfort II are mistakenly identified as Iraqi Mi-24 Hind helicopters violating the Northern No Fly Zone and are shot down by two U.S. Air Force F-15C fighters. All 26 people aboard the two helicopters are killed, including six soldiers.

8 September. Berlin Brigade Inactivated.
The Army's Berlin Brigade is inactivated, ending the U.S. Army presence in Berlin that first began in 1945 after the defeat of Nazi Germany.

19 September. Operation Uphold Democracy. Haiti.
As part of an American-led multinational force led by Army Lieutenant General Henry H. Shelton, U.S. forces, land unopposed in Haiti to restore the constitutionally elected government. Army units include the XVIII Airborne Corps, 10th Mountain Division (Light), 3d Special Forces Group, 25th Infantry Division (Light), and dozens of other units. Three soldiers are killed in nonhostile incidents. Uphold Democracy ends on 31 March 1995, when it is replaced by the United Nations Mission in Haiti. A substantial number of U.S. troops continue to serve until March 1996, when the 2d Armored Cavalry Regiment (Light) returns to its home base at Fort Polk, Louisiana.

10 October. Operation Vigilant Warrior. Kuwait.
Elements of the 24th Infantry Division (Mechanized) are deployed along the Kuwait-Iraq border in response to aggressive actions by Iraqi forces.

January. **Status of the Army.**
With further reductions to the Army's personnel numbers, the Army has 508,559 active duty officers and enlisted soldiers in its ranks. One more division is cut, leaving 13 divisions.

20 June. **Reimer Named Army Chief of Staff.**
General Dennis J. Reimer, who had been serving as Commander, Forces Command, becomes the 33rd Chief of Staff, United States Army.

30 June. **Gene C. McKinney Named Sergeant Major of the Army.**
Gene C. McKinney becomes the 10th Sergeant Major of the Army. McKinney, who had previously served as Command Sergeant Major, U.S. Army Europe, is the first African-American soldier to hold the position.

27 July. **Korean War Veterans Memorial Dedicated.**
In a ceremony attended by President Clinton and South Korean President Kim Young Sam, the Korean War Veterans Memorial is dedicated along the National Mall in Washington, D.C.

13 November. **Army Personnel Killed in Terrorist Attack. Riyadh, Saudi Arabia.**
One soldier and four civilians assigned to U.S. Army Materiel Command are killed when a car bomb explodes at a Saudi National Guard facility in Riyadh.

14 December. **U.S. Soldiers Deployed to Balkans. Bosnia-Herzegovina.**
After the signing of the Dayton Peace Accords, which end the civil war in Bosnia-Herzegovina, the 1st Armored Division is deployed as part of Task Force Eagle, the U.S. element of NATO's Operation Joint Endeavor force sent to Bosnia-Herzegovina as peacekeepers.

21 December. **First Patriot PAC-3 Missiles Deployed. Fort Bliss, Texas.**
The 2d Battalion, 7th Air Defense Artillery, receives the first Patriot PAC-3 missiles, which have improved capabilities against tactical ballistic missiles such as the Scud.

31 December. **Engineers Complete Record Pontoon Bridge. Bosnia-Herzegovina.**
Engineers from the 1st Armored Division complete a 620-meter pontoon bridge—the longest assault float bridge in military history—over the swollen Sava River, allowing the division to move into its area of responsibility.

Left: *The AH-64D Longbow Apache attack helicopter, which entered the Army's inventory in March 1997, included a number of upgrades to an already powerful weapon system, such as a new weapons aiming system, more powerful engines, and improved avionics. (U.S. Army)*

1996

January. **Status of the Army.**
The Army has a personnel strength of 491,103 officers and enlisted soldiers. Only 12 active duty divisions remain—1st, 2d, 3d, 4th, 24th, and25th Infantry, 10th Mountain, 1st Cavalry, 82d and 101st Airborne, and 1st and 2d Armored.

3 February. **Soldier Killed In Bosnia-Herzegovina.**
Sergeant First Class Donald A. Dugan of Troop A, 1st Squadron, 1st Cavalry, 1st Armored Division, is killed by a mine at a checkpoint near Gradacac. He is the first American soldier killed in Operation Joint Endeavor.

15 November. **24th Infantry Division Inactivated. Fort Stewart, Georgia.**
The 24th Infantry Division (Mechanized) is inactivated. With the earlier inactivation of 2d Armored division, the Army now has 10 active divisions, the lowest number since 1950, just prior to the Korean War.

1997

January. **Status of the Army.**
The Army's personnel strength remains steady at 491,707 officers and enlisted soldiers, although the number of active duty divisions has been reduced to ten—1st, 2d, 3d, 4th, and 25th Infantry, 10th Mountain, 82d and 101st Airborne, 1st Cavalry, and 1st Armored. A 2.4 percent pay raise brings a private's basic pay to $900/month, a sergeant's to about $1,500/month, and a second lieutenant's to $1,725/month.

2 April. **First Female Three-Star General. Washington, D.C.**
Major General Claudia J. Kennedy is promoted to the rank of lieutenant general; she is the first female in Army history to attain three-star rank. She will serve as the Deputy Chief of Staff for Intelligence.

21 March. **Delivery of First AH-64D Apache Longbow. Mesa, Arizona.**
The Army accepts delivery of the first AH-64D Apache Longbow helicopter at the Boeing helicopter manufacturing facility. The new Apache includes several upgrades, including a millimeter-wave fire

Right: *Troopers from the 2d Battalion, 505th Parachute Infantry, 82d Airborne Division, land in Kosovo as part of NATO's Operation Joint Guardian, in June 1999. ("Panthers On Point for the Nation: 2-505 in Kosovo," Rick Reeves)*

Below: *Louis Caldera, a 1978 graduate of the United States Military Academy, is sworn in as the 17th Secretary of the Army in July 1998 by Secretary of Defense William Cohen. He was the first Hispanic-American to serve as Army Secretary. (U.S. Army)*

control radar, more powerful engines, and improved avionics. On 2 June 1998, the 1st Battalion, 227th Aviation Regiment, based at Fort Hood, Texas, becomes the first unit to be equipped with the Apache Longbow.

21 October. **Robert E. Hall Becomes Sergeant Major of the Army.**
Robert E. Hall is sworn in as the 11th Sergeant Major of the Army. Hall's most recent assignment was as command sergeant major of CENTCOM.

1 October. **Hugh Shelton Appointed Chairman, Joint Chiefs of Staff.**
General Hugh Shelton, who has been serving as the commander of U.S. Special Operations Command, becomes the 14th Chairman, Joint Chiefs of Staff. He is the eighth soldier to serve as Chairman and the third consecutive soldier to hold that position.

1 October. **Army Modernization Program.**
The 4th Infantry Division (Mechanized), headquartered at Fort Hood, Texas, is selected to be the Army's test unit for the conversion of all of its electronic equipment to digital format.

1998

January. **Status of the Army.**
The Army's personnel strength stands at 480,698 officers and enlisted soldiers. The number of active divisions remains at ten.

Above: *General Eric K. Shinseki, a 1965 graduate of West Point, armor officer, and combat-wounded veteran of Vietnam, became the Army's 34th Chief of Staff in June 1999. Shinseki was the first Japanese-American soldier to serve as Chief of Staff. (U.S. Army)*

11 November. **Operation Desert Thunder. Kuwait.**
The 1st Brigade, 3d Infantry Division (Mechanized), is deployed to Kuwait to counter threatening moves by Iraqi forces.

2 July. **Louis Caldera Appointed Secretary of the Army.**
Louis Caldera, a lawyer and 1978 graduate of West Point, becomes the 17th Secretary of the Army.

1999

January. **Status of the Army.**
The Army's strength at the beginning of 1999 is 477,501 officers and enlisted soldiers, and ten active divisions.

25 February. **Disaster Relief Operations. Austria.**
Army helicopters and medical personnel in Europe are ordered to Austria after a series of avalanches bury dozens of people in the Austrian Alps.

24 March. **Operation Allied Force. Yugoslavia.**
In response to Serbian aggression in Kosovo, NATO aircraft begin an air campaign against Yugoslav and local Serbian forces. The campaign is under the operational control of the Supreme Allied Commander in Europe, General Wesley K. Clark. This is the start of Kosovo Air Campaign; the campaign ends on 10 June.

31 March. **American Soldiers Taken Prisoner. Macedonia.**
Three American soldiers, Staff Sergeant Christopher Stone, Staff Sergeant Andrew Ramirez, and Specialist Steven Gonzalez, are taken prisoner by Serbian forces while patrolling the Macedonian-Serbian frontier. The three soldiers are beaten and held prisoner until 1 May.

21 April. **Task Force Hawk Deployed to Albania.**
As part of Operation Allied Force, the Army deploys Task Force Hawk to Tirane, Albania. The 5,100-man Task Force Hawk consists of 24 AH-64 Apache, eight CH-47 Chinook, and 22 UH-60 Black Hawk helicopters from the 11th Aviation Brigade; the 1st Battalion, 6th Infantry, 1st Armored Division, with two companies of M2 Bradley fighting vehicles and a company of M1A1 Abrams tanks; the 2d Battalion, 505th Infantry, 82d Airborne Division; three MLRS batteries; a battery of M109A6 Paladin self-propelled howitzers; a battery of M119 105mm towed howitzers; and a battery of Avenger air defense systems. While Task Force Hawk never fires a shot in anger, its Q-37 firefinder radars locate the positions of several Yugoslav artillery and mortar positions in Kosovo. In addition, the task force's UH-60 Quick Fix helicopters and RC-12 Guardrail electronic warfare aircraft gather large amounts of electronic intelligence.

5 May. **Fatal Crash of Task Force Hawk Apache. Albania.**
A week after a Task Force Hawk AH-64 Apache crashes while on a training flight, injuring the two-man crew, another Apache goes down, killing both crewmen.

4–5 June. **Activation of Integrated Divisions.**
At Fort Carson, Colorado, the Army reactivates the 7th Infantry Division (Light) as the first of two divisions that will include both Regular and Army National Guard units. Called Integrated Divisions (IDIV) they will consist of a Regular active duty headquarters and three Army National Guard brigades. The 7th has the 39th Separate Infantry Brigade (Arkansas), 41st Separate Infantry Brigade (Oregon), and 45th Separate Infantry Brigade (Oklahoma). The next day the Army reactivates

the 24th Infantry Division (Mechanized) at Fort Riley, Kansas, as a second IDIV. In addition to its headquarters and an active duty forward headquarters at Fort Jackson, South Carolina, the 24th Division includes the 30th Heavy Separate Brigade (North Carolina), 48th Separate Infantry Brigade (Georgia), and 218th Heavy Separate Brigade (South Carolina).

11 June. **Operation Joint Guardian. Kosovo.**
NATO ground troops move into Kosovo. The American contingent of the NATO-led force is Task Force Falcon, comprising the 2d Battalion, 505th Infantry, 82d Airborne, and the 26th Marine Expeditionary Unit. Elements of the 1st Infantry Division (Mechanized) will soon follow. This is the beginning of the Kosovo Defense Campaign; the campaign is ongoing.

21 June. **Shinseki Appointed Chief of Staff.**
General Eric K. Shinseki, who has been serving as the Army's Vice Chief of Staff, becomes the 34th Chief of Staff, U.S. Army. A wounded combat veteran of Vietnam, Shinseki is the first Japanese-American to serve as Chief of Staff.

23 July. **Crash of Army Reconnaissance Aircraft. Putumayo Province, Colombia.**
Five soldiers from the 204th Military Intelligence Battalion are killed when their RC-7 aircraft slams into a mountain while supporting antinarcotic operations in Colombia.

13 August. **U.S. Army South Moves. Puerto Rico.**
In anticipation of Panama's assuming control of the Panama Canal Zone at the end of 1999, U.S. Army South transfers its headquarters to Fort Buchanan, Puerto Rico. The departure of U.S. Army South from Panama marks the beginning of the end of a U.S. military presence in Panama that dates back to the early 20th century.

12 October. **Major Army Reorganization Announced.**
General Shinseki announces plans to reorganize and reequip the Army from a heavy force to a more balanced and deployable strategic ground force. In particular, Shinseki calls for a new class of wheeled armored vehicles. Two brigades at Fort Lewis, the 3d Brigade, 2d Infantry Division, and the 1st Brigade, 25th Infantry Division (Light), are selected for the initial changes.

Above: *Re-enlisting soldiers of the 1st Battalion, 15th Field Artillery, 2d Infantry Division, wear the Army's new black beret with light blue "flash." The 15th Field Artillery's unit insignia is pinned in the flash's center. (U.S. Army)*

2000

January. **Status of the Army.**
Army strength stands at about 480,000 Regular officers and soldiers, and 208,000 Reservists with 232,000 Army civilians. There are about 91,000 soldiers stationed overseas.

21 January. **Medals of Honor Awarded to Asian-American Soldiers.**
President Clinton awards the Congressional Medal of Honor to 21 Asian-American soldiers from World War II. The awards are the culmination of a four-year investigation by the Army to determine whether the soldiers' bravery was not properly recognized because of anti-Japanese sentiment during the World War II era. Most of the soldiers honored served in the legendary 442d Regimental Combat Team, a unit largely comprising Japanese-Americans. Among those honored is Senator Daniel K. Inouye (D-HI).

February. **49th Armored Division Deploys. Bosnia.**
The 49th Armored Division (Texas) deploys to Bosnia

as the first Army Guard unit to command the U.S. Task Force Eagle in support of the NATO forces in Bosnia. The division remains until October.

April. **Exercise New Horizons. Nicaragua.**
Army National Guard units from Mississippi, Ohio, California, and Alabama deploy to Nicaragua to assist in recovery from hurricane damage.

23 June. **Tilley Becomes Sergeant Major of the Army.**
Jack L. Tilley is sworn in as the 12th Sergeant Major of the Army. Tilley, whose previous assignment was Command Sergeant Major, U.S. Central Command, has mostly served in cavalry and armor units during his career.

2 July. **Franks Takes Over Central Command. MacDill Air Force Base, Florida.**
General Tommy Franks takes command of U.S. Central Command at its Florida headquarters.

16 October. **New Headwear Announced.**
In a move to improve the Army's *esprit de corps*,

General Shinseki announces that a black beret will become the standard headwear for soldiers. The decision is initially unpopular, particularly with the Rangers, who have worn a black beret as a mark of distinction for a number of years. Eventually, after much discussion, the Rangers adopt a tan beret as their distinctive headwear; Special Forces wear green; and Airborne maroon.

Above: *On 11 September 2001 in United Flight 77 slammed into the Pentagon in Arlington, Virginia, killing everyone on the plane and 125 in the building, including 74 Army personnel. (U.S. Army)*

Right: *Thomas E. White, a 1967 West Point graduate, Vietnam veteran, and retired brigadier general, became the 18th Secretary of the Army on 31 May 2001. (U.S. Army)*

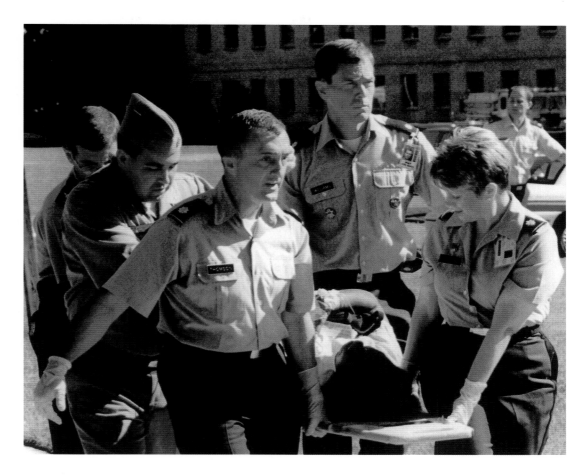

Right: *Following the 11 September 2001 terrorist attack on the Pentagon, four soldiers and a sailor help carry an injured worker to a waiting ambulance. Soldiers from the Pentagon and nearby Fort Myer played an important role in rescuing and treating personnel injured in the attack. (U.S. Army)*

27 October. **William Clark Promoted to Captain.**
Nearly 200 years after he left the Army, Congress approves legislation promoting Lieutenant William Clark, coleader of the Lewis and Clark expedition (Corps of Discovery) to captain, Regular Army, backdated to 26 March 1804.

29 November. **Destruction of Chemical Weapons. Johnston Atoll, Pacific.**
The Army announces that it has safely eliminated the last of the chemical weapons stored on Johnston Atoll, located 825 miles southwest of Hawaii. In the past ten years, Army personnel have destroyed more than 400,000 chemical weapons including mines, rockets, artillery and mortar rounds, bombs, and more than 2,000 tons of nerve and blister agents.

2001

January. **Status of the Army.**
With continuing emphasis on quality recruits and generous reenlistment bonuses, education programs, and improved family living to retain career soldiers, the Army is able to maintain its Regular strength at 487,780 active duty officers and enlisted soldiers. The same ten divisions remain active, with two of them integrated Regular-Guard divisions. More than 114,000 soldiers are deployed outside the continental United States.

11 January. **New Recruiting Campaign Debuts.**
The Army's new recruiting campaign—centered on the theme "An Army of One"—debuts. The campaign is created through the combined efforts of the Army's senior leadership, Army Recruiting Command, and a commercial advertising firm.

16 January. **Theodore Roosevelt Awarded Medal of Honor.**
Theodore Roosevelt is awarded the Congressional Medal of Honor 104 years after he led the 1st U.S. Volunteer Cavalry in a dramatic dismounted charge during the Battle of San Juan Heights in the Spanish American War. Roosevelt's great-grandson, Tweed Roosevelt, accepts the medal in a ceremony at the White House.

20 January. **George W. Bush Inaugurated President.**
George W. Bush, son of President George H. W. Bush, is inaugurated as the 43rd President of the United States and Commander-in-Chief.

20 January. **Powell Appointed Secretary of State.**
General Colin L. Powell, USA (Ret), who served as Chairman, Joint Chiefs of Staff, under two Presidents, is named Secretary of State. He is the third professional soldier to be selected to serve in this position.

31 May. **White Named Secretary of the Army.**
Thomas E. White, a 1967 graduate of West Point, retired Army brigadier general, Vietnam veteran, and business executive, becomes the 18th Secretary of the Army.

14 June. **Army Dons New Beret.**
On the Army's 226th birthday, its soldiers don the new black beret unless authorized to wear a different color. If a soldier's unit does not have a beret flash, the soldier will wear a light blue flash with white stars, styled after George Washington's flag.

11 September. **Terrorists Attack. New York City and the Pentagon.**
Islamic terrorists linked to Osama bin Laden's al Qaeda terrorist network hijack four American airliners, crashing two into the World Trade Center towers in New York City and another into the Pentagon in Arlington, Virginia. A fourth airliner crashes in rural Pennsylvania after passengers fight to regain control of the aircraft. More than 3,000 people are killed in the attacks, most of them in the World Trade Center. New York Army National Guard units are quickly called up to restore order and provide disaster relief. The Army Corps of Engineers also plays a major role in the recovery operations. At the Pentagon, 125 military and civilian personnel are killed, 74 of them from the Army. Among the dead is Lieutenant General Timothy J. Maude, the Army's

Deputy Chief of Staff for Personnel and the highest-ranking soldier killed by enemy action since World War II. Soldiers from the Pentagon itself, along with personnel from the 3d U.S. Infantry (The Old Guard) posted at nearby Fort Myer, Virginia, rescue and treat people injured in the attack. General Franks, who is travelling to Pakistan, immediately returns to his Central Command headquarters. Al Qaeda and its Taliban allies are based in Afghanistan, part of his area of responsibility.

15 September. **Operation Noble Eagle.**
President Bush authorizes a partial mobilization of the Army Reserve and Army National Guard. The initial order calls approximately 10,000 soldiers to active duty in support of various missions, including airport and border security, intelligence, engineering, search and rescue, civil affairs, logistics, and medical support. By December, more than 17,000 soldiers from the reserve components are mobilized for various homeland security functions. The Department of Defense calls this collective effort Operation Noble Eagle.

28 September. **Army Reserve Colonel Sentenced for Espionage. Tampa, Florida.**
After his conviction on espionage charges on 26 June, retired Army Reserve Colonel George Trofimoff is sentenced to life in prison without parole for spying for the Soviet Union for 25 years. He is the highest-ranking Army officer ever convicted of espionage.

Left: *A soldier from the 4th Battalion, 31st Infantry, 10th Mountain Division (Light), takes a break while on patrol in the rugged mountains of Afghanistan. Elements of the 10th Mountain Division first arrived in Afghanistan in late November 2001. (© 2003 Dennis Steele, Association of the United States Army)*

Right: *During Operation Anaconda in early March 2002 in Afghanistan's Shah-i-Kot Valley, elements of the 10th Mountain Division and 101st Airborne Division, along with Special Forces troops and Rangers, battled hundreds of Taliban and al Qaeda fighters. ("Brothers in Battle," Don Stivers)*

7 October. **Operation Enduring Freedom Begins. Afghanistan.**

Operation Enduring Freedom begins with objectives that include the destruction of the terrorist camps and infrastructure within Afghanistan, the capture of al Qaeda leaders, and the overthrow of the Taliban regime, which rules Afghanistan and supports al Qaeda. While the early military operations largely consist of air strikes, Army Special Operations soldiers are deployed to Afghanistan to advise Northern Alliance forces fighting the Taliban and coordinate bombing missions against enemy targets. At the same time, 1,000 soldiers from the 10th Mountain Division (Light) are deployed to neighboring Uzbekistan to protect an airfield used by U.S. forces for search and rescue operations. It is the first deployment of American troops into former Soviet territory.

20 October. **Rangers, Delta Force Raid Taliban Bases. Southern Afghanistan.**

Early on the morning of 20 October, more than 100 men of the 75th Ranger Regiment parachute into a Taliban-held airfield 60 miles southwest of Kandahar. As the Rangers search the airfield and adjacent buildings, they find it all but deserted. Several Rangers suffer jump injuries, but there are no casualties from hostile fire. Later that morning, another force of Rangers and a reinforced Delta Force squadron raid an enemy complex near Kandahar that includes a house used by a key Taliban leader.

26 November. **Five Special Forces Soldiers Wounded. Mazar-e Sharif, Afghanistan.**

While assisting Northern Alliance forces to suppress a prisoner uprising, five Special Forces soldiers are wounded by a bomb dropped by U.S. Air Force aircraft. The soldiers are evacuated to Uzbekistan, then flown to the Army hospital at Landstuhl, Germany.

28 November. **10th Mountain Division Arrives. Afghanistan.**

Elements of the 10th Mountain Division arrive in Mazar-e Sharif from Uzbekistan. Their arrival marks the first deployment of conventional U.S. troops to Afghanistan.

5 December. **Special Forces Killed by Friendly Fire. Afghanistan.**

Three Special Forces soldiers are killed and 20 others wounded when a 2,000-pound bomb dropped from a B-52 bomber mistakenly strikes their command post instead of a Taliban position. The three soldiers are the first Army personnel killed in action during Operation Enduring Freedom.

22 December. **New Afghan Government Installed. Kabul, Afghanistan.**

General Franks travels to Kabul to attend inauguration ceremonies for Afghanistan's interim government. The ceremonies take place 78 days after the opening of Operation Enduring Freedom.

EYEWITNESS: OPERATION ENDURING FREEDOM

In March 2003, as part of Operation Enduring Freedom, elements of the 4th Battalion, 31st Infantry Regiment (Polar Bears), 10th Mountain Division, were deployed into the Shah-e-Kot Valley in Afghanistan. Lieutenant Andrew Exum's, 3d Platoon, A Company, was among those assigned to clear caves and bunkers of Al-Qaeda terrorists and weapons. He describes the operation:

"My platoon, as the main effort, was the last to land. The other platoons had been given the mission of clearing our route to suspected cave sites south of the landing zone. As we landed, we heard explosions in the distance.

"We began to climb the steep ridge. Eventually we crested the ridge and advanced toward our objective, the suspected cave . . . We were about 300 meters from our objective when we spotted the first of many enemy bunkers.

"With a wave of my left hand, my men launched an anti-tank rocket into the bunker. Then with the wave of my right hand, 40mm grenades rained down on the bunker's roof. I saw the anti-tank rocket burst into flames on impact, showering the bunker with its smoke and gases. I watched as the grenades fired from tubes 300 meters away ripped full-grown trees in half.

"Once the dust had settled, I quickly scanned the bunker for movement.

"The bunker remained silent. Either the enemy had already gone, they were dead, or they had decided not to answer our call to join battle.

"We continued down the ridge, spotting another bunker . . . and giving it the same treatment. Finally we arrived within 100 meters of our suspected objective. After 30 minutes of searching the area where the cave was supposed to be, we had found nothing.

"We had worked our way up into some rough, rocky terrain when we spotted the bunker. We weren't sure if it was manned or not. It wasn't one of the positions we had fired an anti-tank rocket at earlier. 'Sir, I think there's a position behind us.' To our rear and up a steep hill, a poncho hung in the trees above what looked to be a fighting position. Suddenly McCauley whispered, 'Sir, I see feet to the right! Feet to the right!' In less than a second, I lowered the muzzle of my weapon . . . I fired two shots.

"After I fired the first two shots, the man sat up 12 meters directly in front of me, swinging a machine gun in our direction. I released four more rounds, sending them into his chest. McCauley and I ran up with our weapons at the ready.

"As I looked down on the man I had just killed, I took stock of his clothes: North Face jacket, Mountain Hardware pants, and synthetic long underwear. By his clothes he looked more like a Vail ski bum than a terrorist. I then saw his weapon, an American-made M249 light machine gun.

"I . . . told two of my soldiers to begin searching the dead man. Strewn among all the American equipment was a collection of Soviet-type small arms. Also mixed in were assorted American gadgets usually belonging to special operations soldiers . . . I put two and two together and realized we had discovered a cache of equipment stolen (days earlier) from the dead SEALs and Rangers atop Takur Ghar.

"Before we headed out, McCauley produced a "death card" from his pocket. He had taken a deck of . . . American playing cards and written the name of our unit on each of the cards. McCauley dropped a nine of spades onto the motionless corpse.

"It read, '3d Platoon, A Company. Jihad this . . .'"
—*Vince Hawkins*

Above: *Soldiers provide security for fellow members of the 82d Airborne Division during a search for Taliban and al Qaeda fighters in Afghanistan. (U.S. Army)*

Right: *CENTCOM Commander General Tommy R. Franks and his deputy, Lieutenant General John P. Abizaid, listen to a briefing on the progress of Operation Iraqi Freedom at CENTCOM's forward headquarters in Qatar. (CENTCOM Public Affairs)*

2002

January. **Status of the Army.**
The Army's Regular strength is held at 479,026 officers and enlisted personnel in ten active divisions. Another 17,000 soldiers from the reserve components have been activated.

10 January. **American Soldiers Arrive in the Philippines.**
An advance team of American soldiers arrives in the Philippines as part of the U.S. effort to aid the Philippine armed forces in their battle against Abu Sayyaf, a local Muslim guerrilla organization with ties to al Qaeda. Another 100 soldiers will arrive later in the month. Some 600 American soldiers will be deployed to the Philippines in the following months.

29 January. **101st Airborne Division Replaces Marines. Afghanistan.**
The 3d Brigade, 101st Airborne Division (Air Assault), replaces marines at Kandahar Airport. Named Task Force Rakkasan, it has three battalions of the 187th Infantry Regiment (Rakkasan is the regiment's nickname) plus other attached units.

21 February. **Army Helicopter Crashes. Basilan Island, Philippines.**
An Army MH-47E Chinook helicopter from the 160th SOAR crashes just off the north coast of Basilan Island in the southern Philippines, killing

eight soldiers and two Air Force personnel. The helicopter had been transporting U.S. Special Operations soldiers who were taking part in joint U.S.-Philippine training exercises.

27 February. **Army Names New Armored Vehicle. Fort Lauderdale, Florida.**
The Army formally names its new Interim Armored Vehicle the "Stryker." Named for two Army Medal of Honor recipients—Private First Class Stuart S. Stryker (World War II) and Specialist Robert F. Stryker (Vietnam War)—the Stryker will serve as the primary weapons platform for the Army's newly structured Stryker Brigade Combat Teams (SBCTs). Army plans call for four additional SBCTs: 172d Infantry Brigade; 2d Armored Cavalry Regiment; 2d Brigade, 25th Infantry Division (Light); and 56th Brigade, 28th Infantry Division (Mechanized) (Pennsylvania National Guard).

2–10 March. **Operation Anaconda. Shah-i-Kot Valley, Afghanistan.**
In the largest Army operation to date, American and coalition soldiers, including the 1st Battalion, 87th Infantry, 10th Mountain; the 3d Brigade, 101st Airborne Division; and elements of the 1st Battalion, 75th Rangers, battle Taliban and al Qaeda fighters in eastern Afghanistan. In just over a week of intense combat, coalition forces kill an estimated 500 enemy personnel. Eight American servicemen are killed and another 40 are wounded.

15 April. **Soldiers Killed in Explosion. Kandahar, Afghanistan.**
Four Explosive Ordnance Disposal (EOD) soldiers are killed and another injured when a booby-trapped cache of 107mm rockets explodes near Kandahar.

8 May. **Crusader Artillery Program Cancelled.**
Secretary of Defense Donald H. Rumsfeld orders the cancellation of the Army's Crusader artillery system, an armored, self-propelled 155mm gun with accompanying resupply vehicle.

31 May. **Combined Joint Task Force 180 Created. Bagram, Afghanistan.**
General Franks creates Combined Joint Task Force 180 (CJTF-180) to provide a headquarters in Afghanistan. Lieutenant General Dan K. McNeill, commanding general of XVIII Airborne Corps, is appointed commander, with responsibility for most coalition forces operating in Afghanistan.

18–26 August. **Operation Mountain Sweep. Southeastern Afghanistan.**
Elements of the 82d Airborne Division, 75th Rangers, and Army aviation units conduct Operation Mountain Sweep, capturing several suspected Taliban guerrillas and weapons caches.

7–11 September. **Operation Champion Strike. Bermel Valley, Afghanistan.**
The 1st Battalion, 504th Parachute Infantry (82d Airborne), sweeps through the Bermel Valley, 175 miles south of Kabul. In addition to seizing weapons and documents, the troopers detain several individuals, including one suspected of being a key financier of al Qaeda.

29 September. **Operation Alamo Sweep. Southeastern Afghanistan.**
In the largest operation since Operation Anaconda,

EYEWITNESS: OPERATION IRAQI FREEDOM

O n 20 March 2003 U.S. and coalition forces intiated *Operation Iraqi Freedom, the military campaign to remove Saddam Hussein and liberate Iraq. While Special Forces and Rangers penetrated Iraq in the north and west, a pincer maneuver composed of two armored columns, one on each side of the Euphrates River closed in on Baghdad from the south. A third column built around the high-tech 4th Infantry Division that was supposed to enter Iraq from the north never materialized. That plan was frustrated by Turkish refusal to approve transit, and after days of waiting, the division was to land in Kuwait. By the time the 4th arrived, Baghdad was captured and the soldiers of the division mistakenly thought they had missed all the action. Lieutenant Colonel Steve Russell, commander, 1st Battalion, 22nd Infantry Regiment, 1st Brigade, 4th Infantry Division, describes his unit's operations:*

"Our soldiers operate in the city and surrounding villages of Tikrit, Iraq. Tikrit was the birthplace and hometown of Saddam Hussein . . . (where) there are many 'die hard' loyalists to the old regime. Our operations target hostile forces trying to prevent the efforts of U.S. soldiers and the Iraqi local government and police.

"This phase of the war in my mind seems to be an insurgency. The Iraqi army had no formal surrender. Instead the Iraqi soldiers simply dissolved into a hundred cities, towns, and villages. A small minority appears to cling to the past. These are the ones that are attacking our soldiers.

"On the night of 5 June (2003), a Bradley from . . . [B] company hit an anti-tank mine on the left front side of the vehicle. The blast ripped a hole through the driver's compartment. The resulting laceration in the hull was almost big enough for me to climb through. The driver, a young private, endured the shock of the blast, instantly suffering two broken legs and a broken arm. His body armor and equipment saved him from more severe injuries. This brave young man kept his head and immediately hit the fuel shut-off valve and dropped the ramp door, allowing his fellow Infantrymen to escape from the vehicle. His comrades came to his aid, as he was trapped in the vehicle.

"That same night our C Company also had a Bradley hit by an RPG. The cone of the warhead hit a case of water, causing the warhead to malfunction. Miraculously, the warhead did not explode and we

were able to render the explosive safe. Our men suffered no injuries.

"Two sisters played in front of their house . . . near one of the city laundry shops in Tikrit. Two women and a man walked along the street about mid-morning. One of the ladies carried a black plastic sack, the kind that is so common among all of the shops and food stands. The 7-year-old sister noticed that the lady forgot her sack on the road. She and her 12-year-old sister went over to pick up the bag and carry it to the lady. The 7-year-old made it only a few steps when she was ripped apart by a powerful blast. Her sister was mangled and blinded. She could not walk. She struggled to pull herself to her house, leaving bloody handprints on the concrete and the gate where she lived. The gutless attackers blended into the daily bustle of the city.

"We can never lose sight of just how evil that regime and the thousands . . . that supported it in Iraq were. Their viewpoint is extremely narrow, . . . barbaric and uncivilized. We found this type of activity good for bullets, and that's what we use to deal with it. There will never be dancing Iraqis on our equipment. We will kill everyone of them that tries."

On 28 May 2004, Iraq was returned to an Iraqi government, but American Army forces remain to assist in training and maintain security.

—*Vince Hawkins*

Above: *Soldiers from the 3d Battalion, 15th Infantry, 3d Infantry Division, engage Iraqi forces at Objective Curly. (Dennis Steele, Association of the United States Army)*

Left: *An M1A1 Abrams tank leads a column of armored vehicles through a driving sandstorm during the 3d Infantry Division's advance towards Baghdad. (© 2003 Dennis Steele, Association of the United States Army)*

elements of the 82d Airborne Division, along with Rangers and other Army units, are airlifted to areas near the Afghan-Pakistani border in southeastern Afghanistan to combat Taliban and al Qaeda forces. Operation Alamo Sweep will last into November.

2 October. **Ammunition Cache Discovered. Central Afghanistan.**
Working on a tip from a local Afghan, Special Forces soldiers discover an enemy cache of 500,000 rounds of small arms ammunition in Central Afghanistan.

31 December. **Provincial Reconstruction Team Formed. Gardez, Afghanistan.**
The first provincial reconstruction team (PRT) is organized as part of a civil-military project intended to help Afghan citizens build and repair damaged

infrastructure such as roads, schools, and wells. The PRTs are also designed to broaden security by extending the reach of the newly formed central Afghan government throughout the country.

2003

January. **Status of the Army.**
The Army has 484,628 officers and enlisted personnel in its Regular ranks. The number of Regular divisions remains at 12, but two are composed of National Guard brigades. As the United States moves closer to war with Iraq, 10,000 soldiers are already in the Persian Gulf region, including the 2d Brigade, 3d Infantry Division (Mechanized), several Patriot missile batteries, and various support units.

Opposite: *During a sweep of an Afghan village, two paratroopers from the 504th Parachute Infantry, 82d Airborne Division, search for caches of weapons along with Taliban and al Qaeda suspects. (U.S. Army)*

Right: *In a scene repeated numerous times around the United States since September 11, National Guardsmen say goodbye to their families after their unit received activation orders. ("Freedom Isn't Free," James Dietz)*

Left: *An Illinois National Guardsman mans a security checkpoint at a U.S. base in Germany. He is one of thousands of soldiers from the Army's reserve components mobilized to secure military and civilian installations in the U.S. and overseas following September 11. (U.S. Army)*

3 January. **3d Infantry Division Receives Deployment Orders. Fort Stewart, Georgia.**
The entire 3d Infantry Division receives deployment orders to Kuwait. There, the division's units will join its headquarters and 2d Brigade, which recently completed live-fire exercises.

14 January. **Air Defenders Arrive for Exercises. Israel.**
Several hundred U.S. air defense artillery soldiers from the 5th Battalion, 7th Air Defense Artillery, based in Hanau, Germany, arrive for joint exercises to test air defense capabilities.

28 January. **Operation Mongoose. Spin Boldak, Afghanistan.**
Soldiers from Special Forces, 82d Airborne Division, and the Afghan militia conduct operations to clear caves in the Adi Gahr Mountains of suspected al Qaeda fighters. American and allied forces kill 18 enemy with no losses to themselves. Several other caves are marked with lasers for Air Force F-16 fighter-bombers to destroy with laser-guided bombs.

16 January. **Special Forces Arrive. Colombia, South America.**
Sixty members of the 7th Special Forces Group arrive in Colombia to train Colombian troops, who are battling leftist rebels. The Green Berets join ten Special Forces advisors already in Colombia.

20 January. **4th Infantry Division Receives Deployment Orders. Fort Hood, Texas.**
The 4th Infantry Division (Mechanized) receives

deployment orders to the Middle East. The headquarters and three brigades are at Fort Hood; a fourth brigade is at Fort Carson, Colorado. Classified plans call for the 4th, the Army's most technologically advanced division, to deploy through Turkey to open a northern front in Iraq.

2 February. **Columbia Recovery. Southwest U.S.**
Army National Guardsmen from Texas, Oklahoma, Arkansas, New Mexico, and Louisiana are called up to assist in the recovery of the space shuttle *Columbia*, which disintegrated on 1 February over Texas during reentry, killing all seven crew members.

6 February. **101st Airborne Receives Orders. Fort Campbell, Kentucky.**
The 101st Airborne Division (Air Assault) receives deployment orders "to support possible future operations in the global war on terrorism." The division will deploy by air and sea to the Central Command area of operations.

14 February. **3d Armored Cavalry Receives Deployment Orders. Fort Carson, Colorado.**
The 3d Armored Cavalry Regiment is ordered to begin deployment to Kuwait.

16 February. **Army Enters NASCAR Racing. Daytona Beach, Florida.**
To improve its recruiting efforts and connections with the American public, the Army enters into a sponsorship deal with NASCAR and MB2 Motorsports. In its first race, the #01 "Army of One"

stock car, driven by Jerry Nadeau, finishes 28th at the Daytona 500. Eventually, the Army National Guard will have its own NASCAR sponsorship deal. The Army will later expand its racing program by sponsoring a dragster ("The Sarge") and pro-stock motorcycles.

19 February–3 March. Operation Viper. Baghran Valley, Afghanistan.
Paratroopers from the 2d Battalion, 504th Parachute Infantry, 82d Airborne, conduct an air assault into the valley to search for Taliban and al Qaeda forces and enemy weapon caches. The battalion meets little resistance and suffers no casualties.

1 March. Turkey Denies Use of Territory.
The Turkish parliament rejects deployment of the 4th Infantry on its soil. After a couple of weeks of failed negotiations, the 4th redeploys to Kuwait, and the 30

ships carrying the division's equipment are diverted through the Suez Canal to the Persian Gulf.

15 March. Eve of Military Operations Against Iraq.
As war with Iraq becomes imminent, the Army has two divisions, the 3d Infantry and the 101st Airborne, and elements of the 2d Brigade, 82d Airborne Division, deployed in Kuwait. The 4th Division (Mechanized) is on its way to Kuwait after being diverted from Turkey. On the eve of war, 57,500 soldiers are in the Persian Gulf region. The 3d U.S. Army (the Army component of Central Command) is commanded by Lieutenant General David D. McKiernan, who also holds the title of Coalition Force Land Component Commander.

19 March. Operation Iraqi Freedom Begins.
Less than two hours after a deadline expires for Iraqi dictator Saddam Hussein to leave Iraq, coalition forces move against Iraq. Early attacks are air strikes, mainly

Above: *A Bradley fighting vehicle and a Humvee from the 3d Infantry Division cross a pontoon bridge built by Army engineers over the Euphrates River during the march on Baghdad. (Dennis Steele, AUSA)*

Left: *Soldiers from the 502d Infantry, 101st Airborne Division, air assault into landing zones around Karbala, Iraq, and link up with the 3d Infantry Division prior to attacking the town. (James Dietz)*

against Baghdad, although some Special Forces soldiers are already operating in Iraq, providing targeting information and working with Kurdish opposition forces in the north and other opposition elements. Special Forces soldiers are also sent into the western Iraqi desert to prevent Scud missiles from being fired at Israel. President Bush announces the objectives for Operation Iraqi Freedom, including the ouster of the current regime, elimination of Iraqi weapons of mass destruction (WMDs), and destruction of terrorist elements.

20 March. Ground Forces Cross into Iraq.
Army ground forces, consisting of the 3d Infantry Division (commanded by Major General Buford C. Blount III) and other units under the operational control of V Corps (commanded by Lieutenant General William S. Wallace), cross into Iraq from Kuwait. Division artillery and AH-64 Apache helicopters quickly eliminate a series of Iraqi outposts.

Above: *A medic from the 3d Battalion, 15th Infantry, 3d Infantry Division, bandages a wounded comrade who continues to fight during the highway intersection battle at Objective Curly. (© 2003 Dennis Steele, AUSA)*

Right: *Three soldiers from the 3d Infantry Division, battle Iraqi and foreign fighters at "Objective Curly," a highway intersection on their route into Baghdad. (© 2003 Dennis Steele, Association of the United States Army)*

In the late afternoon, the 3d Squadron, 7th Cavalry (3d Division), becomes the first Army unit to engage Iraqi forces. Shortly after this initial contact, the 3d Battalion, 15th Infantry (3d Division), destroys several Iraqi armored vehicles, along with a command post and an observation post. The division is advancing at the rate of 24 miles per hour.

20 March. Patriots Intercept Missiles. Kuwait.
Patriot Advanced Capability 3 (PAC-3) missiles, fired by Battery D, 5th Battalion, 52d Air Defense Artillery, successfully intercept at least two missiles fired from Iraq against the 101st Airborne Division headquarters at Camp Thunder. Iraq will fire a total of 28 missiles at coalition forces during Operation Iraqi Freedom. Each missile alert sends soldiers dressed in chemical protective gear scrambling for bunkers.

20 March. Operation Valiant Strike. Southern Afghanistan.
About 600 soldiers from the 2d Battalion, 504th Parachute Infantry (82d Airborne), led by Lieutenant Colonel Charles A. Flynn, move against Taliban and al Qaeda forces in the Sami Ghar Mountains, approximately 100 miles east of Kandahar. By the time the operation ends on 27 March, American soldiers have captured several weapons caches.

21 March. 101st Airborne Division Advances. Iraq.
Elements of the 101st Airborne Division (Air Assault), commanded by Major General David H. Petraeus, cross into Iraq, employing both helicopters and ground vehicles.

21 March. 3d Infantry Division Penetrates Deep. An Nasiriyah, Iraq.
After a 100-plus mile dash through southern Iraq, the 3d Division's 3d Brigade comes under artillery fire. With the support of air strikes, the brigade destroys

Right: *After reaching the Iraqi capital, armored vehicles of Task Force 1-64, 3d Infantry Division, pass through central Baghdad's war memorial. ("Through the Hands of Victory, Baghdad, Iraq, 7 April 2003," David Pentland)*

the Iraqi 11th Infantry Division and seizes Talil Airfield, along with copies of the Iraqi war plan. The 1st Brigade seizes the Jalibah Airfield, then hands it over to the Marines.

23 March. **Attack at 101st Airborne Camp. Kuwait.**
A disgruntled soldier from the 101st lobs several hand grenades into tents at Camp Pennsylvania, killing an intelligence officer and an Air National Guard officer. Fourteen others are wounded. The soldier is charged with two counts of premeditated murder and 14 counts of attempted murder. Prosecutors will eventually seek the death penalty against the soldier.

23 March. **Army Convoy Ambushed. Iraq.**
An 18-vehicle convoy of the 507th Maintenance Company makes a navigational error and is ambushed by Iraqi forces near An Nasiriyah. Of the 33 soldiers in the convoy, 11 are killed and six taken prisoner; several are wounded, and some are missing. The remaining 16 soldiers manage to reach friendly forces.

23 March. **Apache Helicopter Shot Down. Karbala.**
During a night attack on Republican Guard forces, an AH-64D Apache Longbow is shot down, and several more are badly damaged by intense ground fire. The crewmen of the downed Apache—Chief Warrant David S. Williams and Chief Warrant Officer Ronald Young, Jr.—from Company C, 1st Battalion, 227th Aviation Regiment, evade capture for several hours before being taken prisoner by Iraqi forces. Both later appear on Iraqi television.

23 March. **Friendly Fire Incidents with Patriot Missiles.**
A Royal Air Force GR4 Tornado fighter-bomber is mistakenly shot down by an American Patriot missile, killing both crewmen. On the same day, a U.S. Air Force F-16 fighter fires on a Patriot battery in Iraq after the battery's radar locks on to it. No one is injured in the incident. The Patriot is involved in a third friendly-fire incident on 2 April, when a missile downs a Navy F/A-18 Hornet, killing the pilot. Months later, studies determine that a software error misidentified the planes as Iraqi missiles, causing the largely automated Patriot batteries to lock on to targets and fire missiles.

Operation Noble Eagle.
With the nation's threat level at Code Orange, coinciding with the start of military operations against Iraq, several Army National Guard and Army Reserve units are deployed to strengthen security forces along the U.S. border, at nuclear facilities, and at other critical domestic sites. The California Army National Guard's 9th Weapons of Mass Destruction Civil Support Team is ordered to support the Los Angeles Police Department at the 75th Academy Awards presentation. By April, 1,148,450 soldiers from the Army National Guard and Army Reserve have been activated.

24 March. **3d Division Battles Iraqi Irregulars. An Najaf, Iraq.**
After its 1st Brigade establishes blocking positions along Highway 9, Iraqi irregulars make suicidal attacks

Left: *An Army Reserve unit brings fuel to a helicopter refueling point. In both Operation Desert Storm and Operation Iraqi Freedom, Transportation and Quartermaster units performed many unglamorous but critically important and often dangerous assignments supporting the combat forces. ("Saudi Arabia, 1991," James Dietz)*

after nightfall. Bradley fighting vehicles and Abrams tanks destroy several vehicles. At one point, troopers from the 3d Squadron, 7th Cavalry, run so low on ammunition that they resort to using captured Iraqi weapons.

25 March. Advance Slowed by Sandstorms.
Powerful sandstorms slow the coalition's advance toward Baghdad. Elements of the 3d Infantry Division, including the 3d Squadron, 7th Cavalry, and the 2d Battalion, 69th Armor, begin crossing the Euphrates River at As Samawah. Intelligence begins picking up signals indicating that Iraqi forces may use chemical weapons once coalition forces reach Baghdad.

26 March. 3d Division Surrounds Najaf.
Two brigades of the 3d Division complete the encirclement of Najaf. Two M1A1 Abrams tanks and one M2 Bradley fighting vehicle are disabled during the fighting, killing one tank crewman. Iraqi casualties are estimated at 1,000. Soldiers of the 101st Airborne are transported north by truck to reinforce the advance. The division's helicopters, however, remained grounded by the intense sandstorms.

26 March. 173d Airborne Makes Combat Jump. Northern Iraq.
1,000 paratroopers from the 173d Airborne Brigade conduct a combat drop to seize the Bashur Airfield and open a northern front. It is the 173d's first combat parachute drop since the Vietnam War. Approximately 160 Special Forces soldiers from the 10th Special Forces Group (Airborne) are in the area,

helping to direct air strikes against enemy positions. No casualties are reported.

27 March. Patriot Intercepts Iraqi Missile. Kuwait.
A Patriot missile successfully engages and destroys an Iraqi tactical ballistic missile fired at coalition installations in Kuwait.

27 March. American Forces Advance. Iraq.
With the weather improving, lead elements of the 3d Division advance on Karbala, while other units continue fighting Iraqi regular forces and paramilitaries in the encircled city of Najaf.

27 March. Operation Desert Lion. Afghanistan.
Soldiers from the 2d Battalion, 505th Parachute Infantry (82d Airborne), conduct an air assault into the Kohe Safi Mountains near Bagram Air Base. During sweeps of the area, the paratroopers seize large amounts of 107mm rockets, mortar rounds, and machine gun ammunition.

28 March. Apaches Strike Republican Guard. Iraq.
AH-64D Apache Longbow helicopters from the 101st Airborne strike at the Republican Guard Medina Division around Karbala.

29 March. Suicide Bomber Attack. Najaf, Iraq.
Five soldiers from the 1st Brigade, 3d Division, are killed by a suicide bomber at a checkpoint in Najaf.

29 March. 3d Division Continues Advance.
Units of the 3d Division assemble between Najaf and

Karbala in anticipation of a battle with the Republican Guard Medina Division. Significant numbers of 3d Division soldiers are increasingly tied up in dealing with paramilitary forces, especially the Saddam fedayeen who fire from schools, hospitals, and mosques, dress in civilian clothing, and use women and children as human shields.

30–31 March. Army Closes On Baghdad.
American units are within 50 miles of Baghdad. The 2d Brigade, 3d Division, captures a bridge over the Euphrates at Al Handiyah. Engineers clear the explosives on the bridge. The division captures 150 prisoners and destroys several armored vehicles, air defense systems, and weapons caches. The 101st Airborne seizes an airfield at An Najaf, destroying two T-55 tanks along with an artillery battery. The division takes 70 enemy prisoners. At Samawah, artillery from the 2d Brigade, 82d Airborne, commanded by Colonel Arnold Neil Gordon-Bray, fires counterbattery missions against Iraqi artillery, destroying several enemy guns. The primary mission of the 82d Airborne troops is to keep V Corps' lines of communications open, allowing the 3d Division to focus its combat power on the advance to Baghdad.

31 March. Redesigned Class A Uniform Rejected.
Chief of Staff General Shinseki rejects three redesigns of the Army's green Class A uniform. In November 2001, Shinseki had ordered the Army Uniform Board to come up with new designs. The current uniform was first adopted in the late 1950s.

1 April. American POW Rescued. Iraq.
U.S. Special Operations troops, including 75th Rangers, rescue Private First Class Jessica Lynch, a captive survivor from the 507th Maintenance Company. Seriously injured, Lynch is held in a hospital in Nasiriya. The bodies of several missing soldiers from the 507th are found in shallow graves around the hospital.

1 April. Patriot Intercepts Missile in Iraq.
A Patriot missile successfully intercepts a tactical ballistic missile fired at coalition troops in Iraq. This is the first Patriot intercept in Iraq—all previous missiles have been fired at targets in Kuwait.

2 April. Air Defenders Killed by Air Force. Iraq.
Three soldiers from the 1st Battalion, 39th Field Artillery, are killed near Karbala when an Air Force F-15E Eagle fighter-bomber misidentifies their MLRS launcher as an Iraqi surface-to-air missile vehicle and drops a GBU-12 laser-guided bomb on it.

3 April. 3d Division Reaches Baghdad.
After moving through the Karbala Gap and seizing a bridge over the Euphrates at Yasin al Khudayr, the 1st Brigade, 3d Division, reaches Saddam International Airport. Tanks from Task Force 3-69 (3d Battalion, 69th Armor, with infantry) and other units from the brigade surprise Republican Guard units defending the airport as artillery and aircraft pound Iraqi positions. To the south of Baghdad, the 101st Airborne and the 2d Brigade, 82d Airborne, fight Iraqi regular and paramilitary forces bypassed in the 3d Division's advance.

Right: *A finance officer from the 82d Airborne Division displays some of the $650 million in U.S. and Iraqi currency found by soldiers hidden behind a wall in a residence. Coalition soldiers have found several similar caches of cash and weapons hidden in homes all over Iraq. (U.S. Army)*

Left: *Newly appointed Army Chief of Staff General Peter J. Schoommaker (center) tours Iraq with 101st Airborne Division (Air Assault) commander Major General David Petraeus (right). (U.S. Army)*

4 April. **Fighting at Saddam International Airport.** Elements of the 1st Brigade, 3d Division, secure the airport in the early morning hours of 4 April from Special Republican Guards. In the 12-hour battle, American forces suffer one killed, eight wounded; Iraqi losses are estimated at 250 killed, and large amounts of equipment destroyed or captured. During the heavy fighting, Sergeant First Class Paul R. Smith of Company B, 11th Engineer Battalion, mans an exposed .50 caliber machine gun on an M113 armored personnel carrier, breaking up several Republican Guard counterattacks and allowing the evacuation of wounded American soldiers. Smith's bravery, however, costs him his life. Hit in the throat, he dies minutes later. Smith is recommended for the Congressional Medal of Honor.

5 April. **American Forces Reach Downtown Baghdad.** Two battalion task forces from the 3d Division conduct raids ("thunder runs") into downtown Baghdad, reaching the central district of palaces and government buildings before withdrawing to the west to link up with the 1st Brigade. On the same day, Central Command announces that coalition forces have captured 6,500 POWs to date.

6 April. **Artillery Pounds Iraqi Positions. Northern Iraq.** Artillery attached to the 173d Airborne Brigade bombards Iraqi forces west of Irbil.

6 April. **Outnumbered Special Forces Troops Hold Off Iraqis. Northern, Iraq.** Thirty-one Special Force soldiers, aided by Kurdish forces, hold off a larger force of Iraqi infantry, supported by armor and artillery, along a plateau near the northern Iraqi towns of Irbil and Makhmur. The Special Forces soldiers destroy a number of enemy vehicles with Javelin missiles. Navy close air support aircraft also assist. An errant bomb, however, kills 19 Kurdish fighters and wounds 40 more.

7 April. **3d Infantry Division Pushes into Baghdad.** The 3d Division's 2d Brigade advances into central Baghdad and occupies several buildings, including the Republican Palace, the official seat of power for Saddam's regime. Resistance is heavy at times—Task Force 3-15 (3d Battalion, 15th Infantry) engages in a ferocious firefight at a series of overpasses along Highway 8. Four U.S. soldiers are killed and at least 30 are wounded. Iraqi losses are estimated at 600 killed, along with dozens of vehicles destroyed.

8 April. **3d Infantry Division Consolidates Positions in Baghdad.** Elements of the 3d Division move into downtown Baghdad and consolidate their positions along the west bank of the Tigris River. When the Iraqis counterattack from the east bank, traveling in trucks, buses, and armored personnel carriers, the 3d Division, with the help of Air Force close air support, destroys many of the vehicles, killing hundreds of Iraqi soldiers and paramilitaries. During the fighting two journalists are killed and several wounded when an M1A1 Abrams tank fires on the Palestine Hotel after soldiers report there are Iraqi fighters within the hotel firing on them.

9 April. Baghdad Falls.
Marines advance into Baghdad and link up with the 3d Division, which is holding the central part of the capital. In a scene transmitted around the world, a huge statute of Saddam is pulled down while crowds of enthusiastic Iraqis watch.

10 April. American Forces Continue Operations.
American Special Forces soldiers, serving as advisors to Kurdish troops, enter the city of Kirkuk. Troopers from the 173d Airborne Brigade soon follow. Resistance from Iraqi army units is minimal. The 173d also secures four gas-oil separation plants and several oil wells. Elements of the 101st Airborne continue operations against pockets of resistance bypassed by the 3d Division, especially in the region around Karbala. The 2d Brigade, 82d Airborne, conducts similar operations in As Samawah, Ar Rumaythah, and Ad Diwaniyah.

11 April. Army Starts Postconflict Operations. Iraq.
In an effort to halt widespread looting in Baghdad and Kirkuk, Army and Marine forces begin conducting patrols in both cities. Army Special Forces arrange a cease-fire with the commander of the Iraqi V Corps near Mosul. Many Iraqi soldiers abandon their equipment and return to their garrisons, while others discard their uniforms and go home. At a

border crossing near the Syrian frontier at Highways 10 and 11, an Iraqi colonel surrenders the border control point to Special Forces troops. In Baghdad, Army patrols begin uncovering caches of Iraqi weapons, including tactical ballistic missiles, surface-to-air missiles, and other heavy weapons.

11 April. First Army Space Unit Formed. Colorado.
The Army Space Command activates the 1st Space Brigade at Peterson Air Force Base.

12 April. Sporadic Fighting and Looting Continue. Iraq.
Widespread looting continues in Baghdad, Kirkuk, and Mosul. Soldiers from the 3d Division clash with armed militiamen, with no American casualties. Soldiers also take General Amir Saadi into custody. Saadi is the highest-ranking Iraqi official captured by the coalition to date.

13 April. American POWs Found. Samarra, Iraq.
Seven American POWs are found walking along a road by U.S. marines in the area. They are five soldiers from the 507th Maintenance Company and two Apache helicopter crewmen.

14 April. Organized Iraqi Resistance Ends.
General Franks announces that all major Iraqi towns

Right: *Lieutenant Colonel Tony Carr, U.S. Army Southern European Task Force, talks to Liberian children while assigned to Joint Task Force Liberia. The task force successfully ended its mission in October 2003, one of many generally unnoticed missions ongoing by the Army around the world. (U.S. Army)*

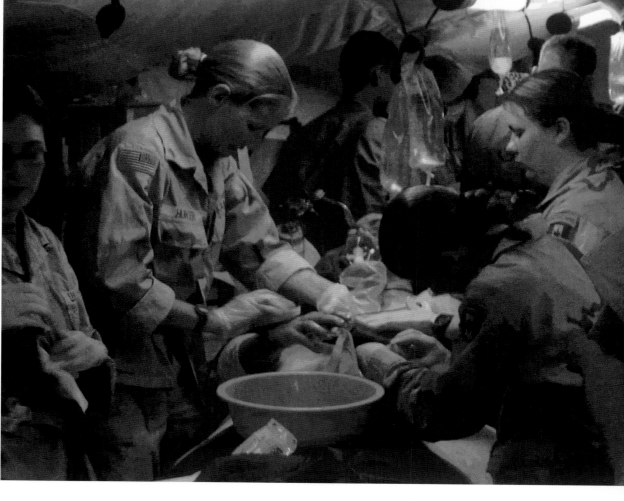

Opposite: *An AH-64D Apache Longbow attack helicopter hovers menacingly during a training mission. (Ted Carlson, Photodynamics)*

Right: *Medical personnel of the 86th Combat Support Hospital, Camp Udairi, Kuwait, provide life saving medical support to a wounded soldier. (U.S. Army)*

and cities are now under coalition control and that organized resistance by Iraqi armed forces has all but ceased. The main effort now switches to rounding up government officials and finding Iraq's weapons of mass destruction. Army engineers begin the long and difficult task of restoring electricity and water to Iraq's major cities, in addition to working on various other infrastructure projects. Special Forces soldiers and troops from the 3d Division conduct an operation in southern Baghdad that results in the capture of Mohammed Abas, better known as Abu Abbas, the secretary general of the Palestinian Liberation Front and mastermind of the 1985 *Achille Lauro* hijacking.

14 April. 4th Division Moves into Iraq.
Elements of the 4th Infantry Division (commanded by Major General Raymond T. Odierno) cross into Iraq from their assembly areas in Kuwait. The division will provide the core of Task Force Iron Horse, a combination of various combat units.

17 April. 4th Division Elements in Firefight. Taji Airfield.
As elements of the 4th Division reach Taji Airfield, they engage in a brief firefight with Iraqi forces occupying the area. The 4th's soldiers kill or wound several enemy soldiers, destroy two T-72 tanks, and take 100 prisoners.

19 April. Clashes with Iraqi Paramilitaries.
As it advances north, the 4th Division runs into pockets of resistance between Taji and Samara,

destroying eight technicals and capturing 30 prisoners. Later in the day, armored elements from the division attack an airfield after an unmanned surveillance drone transmits images of 20 to 30 fedayeen guerrillas loading ammunition into trucks. No American casualties are reported.

19 April. 3d Division Seizes Currency. Baghdad.
While patrolling an exclusive neighborhood that is home to many high-ranking Baghdad officials, soldiers from the 3d Division find a stash of American currency totaling $656 million in $100 bills.

20 April. Missile Threat Declared Over. Israel.
Soldiers from the 5th Battalion, 7th Air Defense Artillery, who manned Patriot batteries around Tel Aviv, begin returning to their home base at Hanau, Germany.

25 April. Secretary White Resigns.
After months of increasingly difficult relations with Secretary of Defense Rumsfeld, Thomas White resigns as Secretary of the Army. Under Secretary Leslie Brownlee assumes duties as Acting Secretary.

1 May. President Bush Declares End to Major Military Operations.
After landing in a Navy S-3B Viking aircraft on the deck of USS *Abraham Lincoln* off the West Coast of the United States, President Bush declares an end to major combat operations in Iraq.

Left: *Acting on a tip from a local Iraqi, soldiers from the 22d Infantry, 4th Infantry Division, locate the hiding place of Saddam Hussein about 10 miles from his home town of Tikrit and capture him. (Associated Press)*

Below: *The allied coalition taking part in Operation Iraqi Freedom established a most wanted list of Iraqi leaders and used a deck of playing cards to identify them. Highest on the list was Saddam Hussein, who was designated the "Ace of Spades." (U.S. Army)*

4 May. **National Guardsmen Assist in Disaster Relief. Southeast United States.**
Hundreds of Army National Guardsmen are called up to assist in relief efforts after tornadoes and flooding hit Missouri, Kansas, Tennessee, and Alabama.

7 May. **Roche Nominated to be Army Secretary.**
Air Force Secretary James G. Roche is nominated by President Bush to become the Secretary of Army.

13 May. **Army Announces Laser Incident. South Korea.**
The Army publicly announces that North Korean forces fired a laser in early March at two AH-64 Apache attack helicopters on patrol near the Demilitarized Zone (DMZ). Intelligence analysts believe the laser came from a Chinese-developed system designed to injure human eyes.

14 May. **Redeployment of 3d Division Halted.**
With violence continuing in Baghdad and other parts of Iraq, the 3d Division is ordered to stop sending troops home. The security of Baghdad is now the official responsibility of the 1st Armored Division, commanded by Major General Ricardo S. Sanchez, and 3d Division soldiers will now remain to assist the 1st Armored.

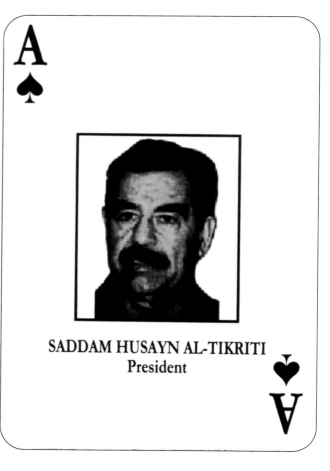

SADDAM HUSAYN AL-TIKRITI
President

Right: *Troopers from the 1st Battalion, 505th Parachute Infantry, 82d Airborne Division, screen civilian traffic in Fallujah, Iraq, during Operation Market Sweep, one of the many operations conducted to ferret out insurgents and weapons. (U.S. Army)*

15 May. **Operation Planet X. Northern Iraq.**
In one of its first sizeable operations, soldiers of the 1st Brigade, 4th Division, raid a village 11 miles south of Tikrit. The operation nets 260 suspected Baath Party members and militants, including General Mahdi Adil Abdallah, who is on the coalition's most wanted list.

1 June. **American Soldiers Detained. Iran.**
Four soldiers from the 1092d Engineer Battalion are detained, blindfolded, and interrogated by Iranian forces while traveling by boat on the Shatt al Arab waterway. The soldiers are released the following day.

3 June. **Army Engineers Search for Saddam's Remains. Baghdad.**
Army engineers begin excavating a bomb crater in the hopes of finding the remains of Saddam Hussein and his sons. On 7 April, an Air Force B-1B bomber destroyed a building in the Mansur district of Baghdad following a tip that Saddam, his sons, and other government loyalists were meeting there.

9–13 June. **Operation Peninsula Strike. Balad.**
Soldiers of Task Force Iron Horse, including the 3d Brigade, 4th Division; 173d Airborne Brigade; and 3d Squadron, 7th Cavalry (3d Division), conduct raids to eliminate Baath Party loyalists. Approximately 400 people are detained. On 13 June, the 3d Squadron kills 20 Iraqi insurgents in a firefight. Several Americans are wounded during Peninsula Strike, but no fatalities are reported.

14 June. **Sanchez Assumes Command of V Corps.**
Ricardo Sanchez is promoted to lieutenant general and assumes command of V Corps. Sanchez had previously served as commander of the 1st Armored Division. Brigadier General Martin E. Dempsey succeeds Sanchez on 16 June as commander of the 1st Armored Division.

18 June. **4th Division Soldiers Capture Currency.**
In raids on two farmhouses north of Baghdad, soldiers from the 4th Division seize $8.5 million in U.S. dollars and nearly $400 million in Iraqi dinars. In addition to capturing money, the soldiers detain 20 men, including several of Saddam's personal security guards, and seize large amounts of weapons and $1 million in jewels.

29 June–7 July. **Operation Sidewinder.**
Units from the 4th Division secure Highways 1 and 2 north of Baghdad to stop insurgent attacks on military and civilian traffic. By the time the operation ends on 7 July, American soldiers have detained 282 Iraqis and seized hundreds of weapons and large quantities of ammunition.

7 July. **Abizaid Takes Central Command. Baghdad.**
General John P. Abizaid takes over as commander of Central Command after General Franks retires. General Abizaid had served as the Deputy Commander (Forward), Combined Forces Command.

12–17 July. **Operation Soda Mountain. Central and Northern Iraq.**
Coalition forces, including the 4th Division, 101st Airborne Division, and the 3d Armored Cavalry, conduct 141 raids in central and northern Iraq. The operation nets more than 600 prisoners, including 62 former regime leaders, and large amounts of munitions.

16 July. **Iraq Now a Guerrilla War. Pentagon.**
General Abizaid states that American forces in Iraq are engaged in a "classic guerrilla-type" war with insurgents loyal to deposed dictator Saddam Hussein, and that attacks against coalition troops are growing increasingly sophisticated. General Abizaid also addresses declining morale in the 3d Division, whose return home has been delayed several times, and promises that the division will be back at Fort Stewart, Georgia, by September.

22 July. **Uday and Qusay Hussein Killed. Iraq.**
Saddam Hussein's sons, Uday and Qusay, are killed in a battle with the 101st Airborne Division in the northern city of Mosul. Both Uday and Qusay were leading figures in Saddam's brutal regime and among the most highly sought individuals still remaining on the coalition's most-wanted list.

3 August. **Schoomaker Named Army Chief of Staff.**
General Peter J. Schoomaker is sworn in as the 35th Army Chief of Staff. Nearly three years after retiring from active duty, General Schoomaker is asked to return by the President. Prior to his retirement in November 2000, Schoomaker served as commander of U.S. Special Operations Command.

6–18 August. **Caches of Weapons and Explosives Uncovered. Iraq.**
Soldiers from the 4th Division uncover a cache of weapons consisting of large quantities of artillery shells, mortar rounds, rockets, and small arms ammunition. On 18 August, soldiers of the 2d Brigade, 1st Armored, discover another large stash of weapons and explosives, including 123 pounds of C-4 plastic explosive and 20 pounds of gunpowder, buried just outside their perimeter in Baghdad.

18 August. **Female Soldier Wins Shooting Competition. Camp Perry, Ohio.**
Specialist Liana Bombardier, a member of the U.S. Army Marksmanship Unit at Fort Benning, Georgia, becomes the first woman to win the Service Rifle National Long-Range Rifle Championship—and the Billy C. Atkins Trophy—in the 100-year history of the competition.

22 August. **3d Division Returns Home. Fort Stewart, Georgia.**
Major General Blount, the 3d Division's commander, returns to the division's home base of Fort Stewart with the last elements of the division. The 2d Brigade had been deployed in Saudi Arabia since September 2002, the longest overseas deployment for any Army unit during the Global War on Terrorism.

24 August. **Artillery Fights Wildfires. Montana.**
Soldiers of the 1st Cavalry Division's 82d Field Artillery are sent to assist in the fight to contain one of the largest wildfires of the season, near Missoula.

26 August. **Operation Ivy Needle. Khalis, Iraq.**
The 2d Brigade, 4th Division, led by Colonel David Hogg, launches Operation Ivy Needle against a gang

of organized criminals responsible for attacking coalition forces and Iraqi police. The operation nets 24 suspected gang members.

31 August. **Army Begins Burning Chemical Weapons. Anniston, Alabama.**
Workers at the Anniston Army Depot, site of the Army's newest chemical weapons incinerator, begin destroying 800 gallons of deadly sarin nerve agent in the facility's first bulk burn of chemical weapons. The sarin once filled 600 M55 rockets, which were drained, cut up, and burned on 8 August. The operation marks the first time the Army has destroyed chemical agents in a populated area.

10 September. **Chaplain Arrested. Guantanamo, Cuba.**
Chaplain (Captain) James Yee, one of the Army's few Muslim chaplains, is arrested and charged with espionage. Yee, a West Point graduate who left the Army for several years, is accused of aiding Islamic inmates and carrying classified information. Eventually all charges against Yee are dropped.

12 September. **3d Infantry Division Awarded Presidential Unit Citation.**
During a visit to Fort Stewart, Georgia, President Bush awards the 3d Division a Presidential Unit Citation, the highest Army unit award, for its service in Iraq. It is the first for this conflict and the first for the 3d Division since World War II.

30 September. **34th Infantry Division Begins Deployment. Bosnia-Herzegovina.**
Some 1,100 soldiers of the 34th Infantry Division, mostly from the Minnesota Army National Guard, deploy to Bosnia-Herzegovina to serve in the NATO-led Stabilization Force (SFOR). This marks the largest overseas deployment by the 34th Division since World War II, when it served in North Africa and Italy.

30 September. **U.S. Army South Moves. Texas.**
After four years in Puerto Rico, U.S. Army South transfers headquarters to Fort Sam Houston, San Antonio, Texas. On the following day, U.S. Army South transitions from a Major Army Command to Major Subordinate Command of U.S. Forces Command.

1 October. **Army Tests 15-Month Enlistments.**
In response to congressional passage of the National Call to Service Act in 2002, the Army begins a pilot program that allows new recruits to enlist for 15 months. Recruits can also continue to sign up for two, three, four, five, or six years.

2–5 October. **Army Personnel Commands Reorganized.**
On 2 October, the Army's Total Personnel Command

Above (left to right): *Kosovo Campaign Medal. Southwest Asia Service Medal. Global War on Terrorism Expeditionary Medal. Global War on Terrorism Service Medal (Institute of Heraldry)*

Left: *U.S. Army scouts in a M1025A Humvee patrol the back-country areas of Afghanistan in an ongoing search for Osama bin Laden and remaining al Qaeda and Taliban fighters. ("Tracking bin Laden," Elzie Golden, Army Art Collection, NMUSA)*

and the Reserve Personnel Command merge into the U.S. Army Human Resources Command. Three days later the U.S. Army Civilian Human Resources Agency is established.

2 November. **Chinook Helicopter Shot Down. Fallujah, Iraq.**
A CH-47 Chinook helicopter from the 12th Aviation Brigade is shot down by a shoulder-fired surface-to-air missile, killing 16 soldiers and injuring another 26. Many of the soldiers are members of the 3d Armored Cavalry going on leave.

5 November. **Army Announces Rotation Plan.**
The Army issues its unit rotation plan. III Corps, Fort Hood, Texas, will replace V Corps. The 1st Cavalry Division will replace the 1st Armored Division between January and April, while the 3d Brigade, 1st Infantry Division, based in Germany, will replace elements of the 4th Division. The 25th Infantry Division (Light) will deploy 4,500 soldiers to Iraq in February, while another 3,500 soldiers from the 25th will replace elements of the 10th Mountain Division in Afghanistan in April. Some 37,000 National Guard and Army Reserve troops also receive orders, including the 81st Armored Separate Brigade (Washington and California), the 39th Enhanced Separate Brigade (Arkansas), and the 30th Heavy Separate Brigade (North Carolina).

12 November. **First Stryker Brigade Arrives. Kuwait.**
The 3d Brigade, 2d Infantry Division, commanded by Colonel Michael E. Rounds, arrives in Kuwait en route to Iraq. The brigade is the first unit organized and equipped with the new wheeled Stryker vehicle to be deployed overseas. Many of the brigade's Strykers are equipped with recently developed slat armor as added protection from rocket-propelled grenades.

15 November. **Two Black Hawk Helicopters Crash. Mosul, Iraq.**
Two UH-60 Black Hawk helicopters from the 101st Airborne Division crash in the northern Iraqi city of Mosul, killing 17 soldiers and injuring five. Reasons for the accident are unclear.

27 November. **President Bush Visits Soldiers. Baghdad, Iraq.**
President Bush makes a secret trip to Iraq to visit U.S. troops on Thanksgiving Day. The President receives an enthusiastic welcome from soldiers of the 1st Armored and 82d Airborne Divisions who are enjoying a Thanksgiving dinner at Baghdad International Airport.

4 December. **Operation Bulldog Mammoth. Abu Ghurayb, Iraq.**
Soldiers from the 2d Battalion, 70th Armor (4th Division); 1st Battalion, 325th Airborne Infantry (82d Airborne); 709th Military Police Battalion; and an Estonian unit raid an apartment complex northwest of Baghdad. The soldiers detain 40 individuals and confiscate weapons and equipment. No shots are fired during the six-hour operation.

6 December. **Army Football Finishes 0-13. Philadelphia, Pennsylvania.**
The United States Military Academy football team

completes the worst season in its history with a 0-13 record after a 34-6 loss to Navy. Army becomes the first college football team in Division 1-A history to finish 0-13.

8 December. **First Casualties for 2d Division. Ad Duluyiyah, Iraq.**
Three days after two soldiers from the 3d Brigade, 2d Division, are injured in a grenade launcher accident, three soldiers from the same unit die when two Stryker combat vehicles roll down an embankment into a canal.

13 December. **Saddam Hussein Captured (Operation Red Dawn).**
After spending nearly eight months eluding coalition forces, Saddam Hussein is captured by soldiers from the 1st Brigade, 4th Infantry Division (Mechanized), about ten miles south of his hometown of Tikrit. The soldiers find him in a spider-hole beneath a hut. Saddam, bewildered and disheveled, surrenders without a struggle.

17 December. **3d Infantry Soldiers Deploy to Africa. Camp Lemonier, Djibouti.**
Company B, 3d Infantry, is deployed to Djibouti as part of Combined Joint Task Force-Horn of Africa. The task force's mission is to disrupt and defeat terrorist activities in the region. American soldiers also perform humanitarian assistance missions, such as medical and veterinary work. This is the first overseas deployment for the 3d Infantry since Vietnam. They join C

Company, 4th Battalion, 31st Infantry, 10th Mountain Division; the 478th Civil Affairs Battalion; and a detachment of the 463d Engineer Battalion, which deployed to the Horn of Africa earlier in the year.

29 December. **American Soldier Is Person of the Year.**
National news magazine *Time* names the American soldier its "Person of the Year" and features on its cover three soldiers from Headquarters Battery, 2d Battalion, 3d Field Artillery (1st Armored), serving in Iraq.

2004

January. **Status of the Army.**
Despite the heavy rate of deployments as the Army continues two major military operations in Iraq and Afghanistan, the Regular strength of the Army stands at 67,953 officers, 11,913 warrant officers, and 413,696 noncommissioned officers and enlisted soldiers. Force structure remains ten active divisions, two armored cavalry regiments, and numerous other units and organizations. Almost 213,000 officers, warrants, and enlisted soldiers serve in the Army Reserve. There are also 197,000 U.S. Army civilians. The Army starts the year with 394,000 soldiers in the United States and over 100,000 overseas in more than a dozen countries.

16 January. **Army to be Moved from DMZ. South Korea.**
The United States and South Korea reach an agreement to move U.S. forces away from the DMZ

Right: *The Army's increasingly sophisticated inventory of electronic equipment includes the Blue Force Tracking system, which marries digital technology with Global Positioning System to display the location of all friendly (blue) forces and is small enough to fit in a Humvee. (Tobyhanna Army Depot Public Affairs Office)*

and out of metropolitan Seoul beginning in 2005. Army units will be consolidated south of Seoul at Camp Humphreys.

2 January. Kiowa Warrior Helicopter Shot Down. Iraq.
An OH-58D Kiowa Warrior scout helicopter from the 1st Battalion, 82d Aviation Regiment, is shot down near Fallujah, killing its pilot, Captain Kimberly N. Hampton, and injuring the copilot. Hampton is the first female helicopter pilot killed in Operation Iraqi Freedom.

8 January. Medevac Black Hawk Crashes.
A medevac UH-60 Black Hawk helicopter from C Troop, 1st Squadron, 17th Cavalry, crashes in Fallujah, killing all nine on board. Witnesses claim a rocket hit the helicopter's tail rotor.

12 January. Special Forces Deploy to Mauritania and Mali.
A $100 million plan is announced to provide military assistance to Mauritania and Mali. Soldiers from the 1st Battalion, 10th Special Forces Group (Airborne), deploy in the following months as advisors.

15 January. Preston Becomes Sergeant Major of the Army.
Kenneth O. Preston, who has spent most of his Army career in cavalry and armor units, is sworn in as the 13th Sergeant Major of the Army. Preston's most recent assignment was command sergeant major of Combined Joint Task Force 7 in Baghdad.

19 January. 82d Airborne Division Returns Home. Fort Bragg, North Carolina.
Soldiers of the 82d Airborne Division's 2d Brigade begin returning to their home post after service in Iraq.

28 January. Army Announces New Organization Plan.
General Schoomaker briefs the House Armed Services Committee on the Army's plan to reorganize its divisions. The plan calls for retaining the Army's ten division headquarters but increasing each division's maneuver brigades from three to four. The brigade combat teams will be restructured into "units of action." One important difference between the brigade combat team and the unit of action is that assets that once supported the brigade (field artillery, signal, engineers) will be permanently assigned to the unit of action.

29 January. Soldiers Killed in Explosion. Gahzni, Afghanistan.
In one of the deadliest episodes of Operation Enduring Freedom, seven soldiers are killed when a weapons cache explodes.

1 February. 1st Infantry Division Deploys. Wuerzburg, Germany.
An advance party from the 1st Division led by Major General John R. S. Batiste leaves for Iraq. The remainder of the division will come to Iraq by the end of the month. Most of the division's heavy equipment will remain in Germany and the division will rely more on up-armored Humvees and small arms. The 1st Infantry Division will form Task Force Danger to replace Task Force Iron Horse (4th Division and 173d Airborne Brigade). Task Force Danger will also include soldiers from the 2d Brigade, 25th Infantry Division, and the 30th Heavy Separate Brigade.

6 February. Korean Service Medal Authorized.
The Defense Department authorizes a medal for all military personnel who served in Korea in the years following the Korean War.

12 February. General Abizaid Comes Under Hostile Fire. Iraq.
Iraqi insurgents open fire with rocket-propelled grenades and small arms at a Fallujah Iraqi civil defense post where General Abizaid is visiting. Soldiers from the 82d Airborne Division return fire. Abizaid is uninjured in the attack.

12 February. Soldier Arrested on Espionage Charges. Fort Lewis, Washington.
Specialist Ryan G. Anderson is arrested by undercover Army agents for attempting to pass information to al

Above: *A soldier models one of three new camouflage patterns that will be available for issue in 2005. The Army is developing the new camouflage uniform with many improvements in design and utility for better use with body armor. (U.S. Army)*

Above: *A soldier from the Army Reserve's 478th Engineer Battalion mans a Humvee-mounted Mk 19 automatic grenade launcher while pulling guard duty near Baghdad. (U.S. Army)*

Qaeda. Anderson is a member of Company A, 1st Battalion, 303d Armor, 81st Armored Brigade (Separate), which comprises California and Washington Army National Guard units.

14 February. **101st Airborne Division Returns Home. Fort Campbell, Kentucky.**
In a ceremony at Fort Campbell, Major General Petraeus uncases the 101st Airborne Division's colors, officially marking the division's homecoming. Fifty-eight soldiers from the 101st were killed in Operation Iraqi Freedom. The 101st Airborne was relieved in Iraq by Task Force Olympia, which includes the 3d Brigade, 2d Infantry Division.

16 February. **Army Begins Tests of New Rifle. Fort Benning, Georgia.**
The Army begins testing the prototype XM-8 rifle at the Infantry Center as a possible replacement to the M-16, which the Army has used since the Vietnam War.

23 February. **Comanche Program Cancelled.**
General Schoomaker cancels the RAH-66 Comanche helicopter program. The aircraft was designed to eventually replace the AH-64 Apache and OH-58D Kiowa Warrior helicopters. The Comanche has been in development for 20 years, and the Army has invested nearly $8 billion in the program.

26 February. **War on Terrorism Medals Approved.**
Two medals are approved for military personnel serving in the Global War on Terrorism. The Global War on Terrorism Expeditionary Medal is to be awarded to any service member deployed to

Afghanistan (Operation Enduring Freedom) or Iraq and Kuwait (Operation Iraqi Freedom). Military personnel eligible for the Global War on Terrorism Service Medal include anyone participating in homeland security activities (Operation Noble Eagle).

4 March. **3d Infantry Division to Return to Iraq. Fort Stewart, Georgia.**
The 3d Infantry Division, which spearheaded the American advance into Iraq in March–April 2003, is notified that it will be redeployed to Iraq as early as November 2004.

6 March. **Special Forces Clash with Taliban Fighters. Afghan-Pakistani Border.**
Special Forces snipers kill nine Taliban fighters after a group of 40 Taliban guerrillas attempt to flank the position held by the Americans and a small group of allied Afghan soldiers.

10 March. **Roche Withdraws His Name.**
After almost a year of delay by the Senate to consider his nomination to be Secretary of the Army, James Roche requests his name be withdrawn. In the meantime, Brownlee continues as Acting Secretary.

10–23 March. **Shield of Hercules 2004. Greece.**
Army personnel are among 400 U.S. Special Operations troops taking part in exercises in Athens to test Greek security measures for the 2004 Olympics.

14 March. **U.S. Troops Exchange Fire with Iranians. Northeastern Iraq.**
A patrol from the 4th Division exchanges shots with Iranian border guards. No casualties are reported.

ARNG: DEFENDERS OF THE HOMELAND

Even before the tragic events of September 11, 2001, the ARNG had started to focus on new and unexpected dangers. A series of national strategic reviews concluded that rogue nations and terrorist groups armed with weapons of mass destruction constituted a serious, credible threat to the country. In the late 1990s, the ARNG created several regional Civil Support Teams located around the country. These special units were capable of assessing the extent of a chemical, biological, radiological, or nuclear attack, providing state and local governments with technical advice, and expediting the flow of federal and state assets toward emergencies.

Meanwhile, overseas deployments and domestic crises increased the knowledge and experience of ARNG units to respond to unexpected situations on short notice. Major peacekeeping deployments throughout the 1990s imparted valuable training and honed operational skills. Large domestic events, such as Hurricane Andrew, the Los Angeles riots, the Midwestern floods, the Oklahoma City bombing, and the 1996 Summer Olympics focused Guard soldiers on domestic emergencies and associated security concerns.

On September 11th, the nation's first military responders were the men and women of the New York ARNG. Citizen-soldiers in New York City reacted to the attack on the World Trade Center in the same manner as the colonial minutemen who instantly abandoned their plows to take up arms at the sound of an alarm. Without waiting for orders, New York Guardsmen rushed to the scene of the crisis. In the hours following the attack, large numbers of citizen-soldiers assisted policemen, firefighters, and emergency medical personnel.

The first organized military unit to arrive at the World Trade Center was New York's ARNG 2nd Civil Support Team. Authorities feared that the hijacked airliners might have carried harmful chemical-bio-radioactive agents, but the unit was able to assure rescuers that the smoldering debris of the Center towers was free of deadly toxins. Meanwhile, New York Guard leaders quickly organized their citizen-soldiers into a security zone around the debris field to limit public access. In the days following the attack, ARNG members worked alongside firefighters and policemen in the search for survivors, manned first aid stations and makeshift morgues, and deployed equipment that sustained non-stop recovery operations.

Since September 11th, the ARNG has been a key participant in Operation Noble Eagle, the homeland defense portion of the war on terrorism. On any given day, as many as 25,000 Guard soldiers are on duty across the nation. In the weeks following the attack, over 9,000 citizen-soldiers helped to improve security at commercial airports across the country. After a series of anthrax attacks delivered through the postal system, Civil Support Teams conducted over 100 inspections of suspicious letters and packages. Army Guard troops augmented customs agents at the busiest crossing sites on the Canadian and Mexican borders and increased security at a number of ports of entry. Guard men and women have served on extensive security details at the World Series, the New York City Marathon, the Super Bowl, and the 2002 Winter Olympics.

Homeland defense is not new to the ARNG. The modern concept of citizen-soldiers contributing to homeland defense began after the Spanish-American War when enemy battle fleets posed a threat to American shores. Starting in 1907 and lasting until World War II, a significant portion of the National Guard manned heavy defensive positions along the nation's extensive coastline. At the beginning of both World Wars, Guard units protected dams, water reservoirs, industrial centers, and utilities from sabotage. During the early Cold War, ARNG missilemen occupied Nike Missile launcher sites that protected centers of population and industry against attacks from Soviet heavy bombers. Whether at home or abroad, the men and women of the ARNG will continue to play a significant role in winning the war on terrorism.

—*Michael Doubler*

Above: *Following September 11, a California National Guardsman patrols an area around the Golden Gate Bridge at San Francisco, California, during a heightened terrorism alert. (U.S. Army)*

Right: *The National World War II Memorial was dedicated on 30 May 2004. The plaza is flanked by two arches, representing the Atlantic and Pacific theaters of war, honoring its 16 million veterans and more than 400,000 casualties. (Robert C. Lautman, Courtesy of the Chief Architect, GSA)*

26 March–10 April. **Unit of Action Tested. California.**
The Army begins testing the new brigade unit of action organization at the National Training Center, Fort Irwin. The 2d Brigade, 3d Division, is selected to be the first unit to be reorganized into the new structure. It will deploy to Iraq later in the year.

28 March. **Weapons Caches Seized. Afghanistan.**
After a PRT in Ghazni receives a tip from local Afghans, soldiers from the 10th Mountain Division (Light) seize a cache of grenades, mines, and mortar rounds. On the same day, soldiers from the 3d Battalion, 6th Field Artillery, 10th Mountain Division, locate a cache of 2,000 rifles and various types of ammunition while searching a house in Kandahar.

31 March. **Unit Rotations Continue. Iraq.**
Elements of Major General Peter W. Chiarelli's 1st Cavalry Division arrive in Iraq to replace the 1st Armored Division in Baghdad. The 39th Brigade Combat Team will be placed under the operational control of the 1st Cavalry Division. The 1st Brigade, 1st Division, and the Army National Guard's 81st Armored Brigade are attached to the 1st Marine Expeditionary Force in the Iraqi insurgent strongholds of Fallujah, Ramadi, and western Iraq.

2 April. **Army Meets Retention/Recruiting Goals.**
Despite the ongoing conflicts in Iraq and Afghanistan, the five divisions that have been deployed in either Operation Enduring Freedom or Iraqi Freedom have all achieved, or nearly achieved, their reenlistment goals. Furthermore, the Army announces it met its recruiting goals for the previous fiscal year and is on pace to meet its goals in the current year.

4 April. **1st Cavalry Soldiers in Firefight. Iraq.**
Soldiers from the 1st Brigade, 1st Cavalry Division, engage Iraqi insurgents in a fierce firefight in Baghdad. Seven American soldiers are killed and 51 are wounded. Iraqi casualties are unknown.

9 April. **Soldier Taken Prisoner.**
Two soldiers from 724th Transportation Company (Army Reserve) are unaccounted for after their convoy is ambushed west of Iraq. Several days later, one of the missing soldiers, Private First Class Keith M. Maupin, appears on videotape as a prisoner of Iraqi insurgents. The body of the second soldier is found two weeks later.

9 April. **First Female National Guard Soldier Killed.**
Specialist Michelle Witmer, a military policewoman with the 32d Military Police Company (Wisconsin) is killed by an improvised explosive device in Baghdad. She is the first female Army National Guard soldier to be killed in action in Army history, and the first Wisconsin National Guard member to die in combat since World War II.

15 April. **Tours in Iraq Extended for 20,000 Soldiers.**
A sudden increase in violence causes 20,000 soldiers due to rotate home to have tours extended by 90 days, with an additional month for restaging out of Kuwait. Soldiers from the 1st Armored Division, 2d Armored Cavalry Regiment, and several Army National Guard and Army Reserve units are affected by the order.

22 April. **Last Units of 4th Infantry Division Return Home. Fort Hood, Texas.**
After a year in Iraq and Kuwait, the last elements of the 4th Infantry Division (Mechanized) return to Fort Hood, completing the 4th Division's homecoming. The 4th lost 79 soldiers during its tour in Iraq.

29 April. **National World War II Memorial Opens to the Public. Washington, D.C.**
The National World War II Memorial, located on the National Mall and constructed at a cost of $172 million, opens to the public. The memorial's official dedication will take place a month later, on 29 May over Memorial Day weekend.

ACKNOWLEDGMENTS

Completion of this massive volume was a true team effort. I should like to thank all my colleagues, in particular authors MG Bruce Jacobs, AUS Ret., LTC Clayton Newell, USA Ret., Matt Seelinger, John Langellier, Dale Andrade, and Sandi Daugherty. Judi Bellifaire, Kevin Hymel, and COL Michael Doubler, USA, Ret., provided sidebars, while Vince Hawkins did yeoman work with both sidebars and image research. Randy Yasenchak pitched in with captions.

A special note of thanks is made to General Peter J. Schoomaker, who took time from his many demanding duties as a wartime Army Chief of Staff to provide the foreword.

In addition to the many talented artists who generously consented to the use of their work in the book, the cooperation of the Company of Military Historians, Association of the U.S. Army, National Park Service, National Guard Bureau, Soldiers Magazine (U.S. Army), West Point Museum, U.S. Army Institute of Military History, and the U.S. Marine Corps in use of their art and photo collections was key. There were many others whose kindness and assistance is most appreciated. These include Renee Klish and Henrietta Snowdon (Army Art Collection) and the knowledgeable and always helpful members of the National Archives Still Picture staff. I am sure there are others whom I have overlooked. My apologies, and sincere thanks.

Finally, sustaining me through the long two-year journey with the patience and support that only another "book widow" can understand was my wife, Tena. Her encouragement, keen reviewer's eye, and thoughtful suggestions were invaluable.

AUTHOR BIOGRAPHIES

EDITOR-IN-CHIEF

Colonel Raymond K. Bluhm, Jr., USA, (Ret.) received his Army commission from the University of Illinois ROTC Program in July 1963. After 30 years of service as an Infantry officer, he retired in October 1993. His varied service included two tours in Korea, 18 months in combat in Vietnam, two tours in Europe, senior positions on both the Army and Secretary of Defense staffs, and Defense and Army Attaché to Belgium. His final position was as a division chief with the Center of Military History. He has led battlefield tours in Europe, co-authored a book on the Army, and contributed to several historical articles and reviews. After retirement he served six years as the first Executive Director of the Army Historical Foundation (1994–2000),was Director of Institute for Land Warfare, AUSA, and one of the editors of *The Army*. He continues today as an officer of the foundation.

General Peter J. Schoomaker, USA, was recalled to active duty to serve as Chief of Staff, U.S. Army. General Schoomaker retired in December 2000 with more than 30 years of service. Before retirement, he commanded the United States Special Operations Command from 1997 to 2000. As Commander-in-Chief, he was responsible for all special operations forces of the Army, Navy, and Air Force special operations units, active, guard, and reserve. He commanded special operations units and organizations at every rank from captain to general and participated in numerous combat operations, including the 1980 Iranian hostage rescue attempt known as Desert One, Urgent Fury, in Grenada, Just Cause in Panama, Desert Shield, and Desert Storm in Southwest Asia, Uphold Democracy in Haiti, and other special operations throughout Central and South America, Africa, the Middle East, Europe, and Asia. General Schoomaker is a director of the Special Operations Warrior Foundation and the Chairman of the Special Operations Memorial Foundation, and authored a chapter for *U.S. Special Operations Forces*.

Dale Andrade is a senior historian at the U.S. Army Center of Military History, where he is writing a volume in the official Vietnam War combat history series. He is also the author of *America's Last Vietnam Battle: Halting Hanoi's 1972 Easter Offensive*, *Ashes to Ashes: The Phoenix Program and the Vietnam War*, and co-author of *Spies and Commandos: How America Lost the Secret War Against North Vietnam*.

Major General Bruce Jacobs, AUS (Ret.) was commissioned in the Army Reserve following enlisted service in World War II. He was detailed as a combat historian in the Marianas, Iwo Jima, and Okinawa. He transferred to the Army National Guard in 1957. He served with the U.S. Army in Vietnam, 1968–1969, and after a detail to the White House in 1970, was appointed Chief of Public Affairs, National Guard Bureau, 1971–1974. He was Secretary of the Army Reserve Forces Policy Committee, 1975–1979. He joined the staff of the National Guard Association of the U.S. in 1979 and was Chief Historian when he retired in 1995. He is the author of books and articles on military topics and served as an editor and author of *The Army*. He earned an M.A. in diplomatic history at Georgetown University. He became an adviser to the Army Historical Foundation in 1983, joined the Board of Governors in 1995, and has served two terms as its secretary.

John Phillip Langellier received his B.A. and M.A. in history and historical archeology from the University of San Diego, and his Ph.D. in military history from Kansas State University. In addition to being the author of more than 30 books and monographs as well as dozens of articles on a wide range of historical topics, Dr. Langellier also serves as a consultant to motion pictures and television. He spent a dozen years with the Department of the Army, serving variously as a museum director and historian, and four years with the U.S. Navy before his transfer to the National Archives and Records Administration, where he now is the assistant director of the Ronald Reagan Presidential Library.

Lieutenant Colonel Clayton R. Newell, USA (Ret.) retired in 1992 after 27 years of active duty, which included tours in Germany and Vietnam. While on the faculty of the Army War College, he held the John J. Pershing Chair of Military Planning and Operations. He frequently contributes to the analysis of Army operations in the Balkans, is a research fellow of the Institute for Land Warfare, and has served on the Army Historical Foundation board of directors since 1994. His books include *Lee vs. McClellan: The First Campaign* and *The Historical Dictionary of the Persian Gulf War*. He has written articles for the *Encyclopedia of the American Military*, *The D-Day Encyclopedia*, the *Reference Guide to the United States Military*, numerous professional journals, and served as an author for *The Army*.

Matt Seelinger, a native of Falls Church, Virginia, holds a B.A. in History from James Madison University and an M.A. in History from Ball State University. He began working for the Army Historical Foundation in 1997 and is currently the foundation's historian, with much of his work focusing on AHF's public inquiry research program. He is also the editor of *On Point: The Journal of Army History*, the Army Historical Foundation's quarterly magazine. He serves on the advisory committee of the National Guard Memorial Museum in Washington, D.C., and has made several presentations on Army history and the Army Historical Foundation.

Stambaugh, Charles B., 1stLt., 455
Stance, Emanuel, Sgt., 454
Standish, Miles, 13
Stanley, D.S., Col., 458-459, 461
Stannard, John E., Col., 830
Stansbury, Howard, Capt., 333, 333
Stanton, C. E., Col., 522
Stanton, Edwin M., 382-384, 385, 392, 416, 433-434, 442
Stanton, Henry W., Capt., 351
Starh, Elvis Jacob, Jr., 800, 803
Stark, John, 42, Col., 59-60, 63, 78, BrigGen., 82, 84, Maj.Gen., 122, 127
Starr, Douglas H., Col., 888
Starry, Donn A., Gen., 869, 871
State Milita/Guard Units:
1st California Cavalry, 406, 429; 1st California Volunteers, 338, 346, 498; 1st Illinois Infantry, 547; 1st Illinois Light Artillery, 407; 1st Illinois Regiment, 296, 307; 1st Kansas Colored Volunteered Infantry, 401; 1st Louisiana Native Guards, 401; 1st Maine Heavy Artillery, 425; 1st Maryland Artillery Regiment, 195; 1st Michigan Cavalry, 396; 1st Minnesota Heavy Artillery, 793; 1st Mississippi Regiment, 306-307, 313; 1st Missouri Mounted Volunteers, 296, 303, 309, 312-313; 1st Nebraska Volunteer Infantry, 506; 1st New Mexico Cavalry, 380; 1st New Mexico Infantry, 338, 351; 1st North Dakota Volunteers, 507; 1st Texas Rifle Volunteers, 362; 1st Veteran Volunteer Corps, 414; 1st Washington Infantry, 355; 2nd California Cavalry, 364; 2nd Illinois Regiment, 296, 307; 2nd Indiana Regiment, 307, 2nd Iowa Cavalry, 2nd Kentucky Regiment, 307; 2nd Michigan Cavalry, 389; 2nd Missouri Mounted Rifles, 299; 2nd Oregon Infantry, 498; 2nd Virginia Infantry, 426; 2nd Wisconsin Infantry, 503; 3rd Illinois Infantry, 503; 3rd Indiana Regiment, 307;
3rd Maryland Brigade, 208, 215; 3rd Wisconsin Infantry, 503; 3rd Vermont Infantry, 415; 4th Illinois Regiment, 310; 4th Iowa Cavalry, 428; 4th Kentucky Infantry, 383; 4th Michigan Cavalry, 435; 4th Missouri Volunteer Cavalry, 418; 4th Ohio Infantry, 503; 4th Pennsylvania Infantry, 503; 5th Minnesota Infantry, 396; 5th New York Volunteers, 395; 6th Illinois Cavalry, 407; 6th Indiana Volunteers, 386; 6th Massachusetts Infantry, 375; 6th Michigan Cavalry, 471; 6th Minnesota Infantry, 396; 6th New York Volunteer, 381; 6th US Volunteers, 437; 6th Wisconsin, 373; 7th Illinois Cavalry, 407; 7th Iowa Cavalry, 437; 7th Illinois Volunteer Infantry, 519; 7th New York, 377, 379; 7th Pennsylvania Infantry, 418; 8th Minnesota Infantry, 429; 8th New York Cavalry, 397; 9th Massachusetts Battery, 415; 11th Kansas Cavalry, 437; 11th Minnesota Infantry, 476; 11th New York (Fire Zouaves), 376; 11th Ohio Cavalry, 437; 12th Pennsylvania Cavalry, 520; 13th Pennsylvania Reserves, 393; 13th Tennessee Cavalry, 419; 15th Iowa Infantry, 454; 16th Pennsylvania Infantry, 503; 17th Indiana, 404; 18th Kansas Volunteers, 447; 20th Kansas Volunteer Infantry, 506-507; 20th Maine, 412, 416; 21st Illinois Volunteer Infantry Regiment, 376, 422; 21st Maryland Regiment, 206; 21st Ohio Infantry, 417, 471; 22nd Iowa Infantry, 409; 24th Wisconsin Infantry, 417, 510; 29th Infantry Brigade, 843; 45th Illinois Infantry, 453; 48th Pennsylvania Infantry, 426; 54th Massachusetts Volunteers, 413, 446; 56th New York Volunteers, 389; 57th Indiana, 404; 72nd Indiana, 404; 75th Indiana, 404; 77th Missouri Infantry, 488; 81st Pennsylvania Infantry, 457; 83rd Pennsylvania Volunteers, 394; 92nd Illinois Infantry, 404; 95th Illinois Infantry, 392; 98th Illinois Infantry, 404; 123rd Illinois, 404; 124th New York Infantry, 448; 153rd New York State Volunteers, 392;Arkansas Mounted Volunteers, 296; California Battalion, 298, 303, 306, 308, 314; California Volunteers, 365; Chihuahua Rangers, 305; Creek Volunteer Regiment, 255-257, 260, 267; Florida Volunteers, 260; Georgia Volunteers, 260, 262; Independent Company of Kentucky Mounted Volunteers, 296; Indiana Vounteers, 292, 307; Kentucky Volunteers, 307; Leclede Rangers, 296; Macon Volunteers, 263;
Missouri Volunteers, 262, 272, 296, 307, 375; Mormon Battalion, 299, 301, 303, 305; Mormon Volunteers, 296; New York National Guard, First AeroCompany, 542, 547, 566; Pennsylvania Volunteers, 375; Philadelphia City Cavalry, 237;
Rhode Island Detached Militia, 381; St Augustine Guards, 250; St Louis Volunteer Artillery, 296; Tennessee Brigade, 256-258; Tennessee Volunteeers, 263; Texas Rangers, 287, 289, 291, 296, 306, 317-318; Texas Volunteers, 297; United States Colored Troops (USCT), 411, 419, 423, 437, 444, 448; United States Colored Volunteers, 411; West Tennessee Militia, 200
Stearns, George L., Maj., 411
Steele, Frederick, Col., 449
Steen, Enoch, Maj., 356, 358
Steinberger, Justus, Col., 355
Stensby, Lois, 2ndLt., 862
Stenson, DeEtte A., 2ndLt., 862
Stephen, Adam, MajGen., 79-80
Steptoe, Edward J., Maj., 356, LtCol., 363
Sternberg, George N., Maj., 476, BrigGen., 489
Sternberg, Sigismund, Lt., 447
Stevens, Albert, Capt, 613, 615
Stevens, Edward, Col., 103
Stevens, Isaac, BrigGen., 397
Stevens, Phineus, Capt., 35
Stevens, Robert Ten Broeck, 789
Stevenson, Carter, L., Capt., 337
Stevenson, Hugh, 64
Stevenson, John D., Col., 447
Stevenson, Thomas G., BrigGen., 446
Stewart, George H., Capt., 355
Stewart, Joseph, Capt., 355
Stewart, Robert L., LtCol., 879
Stillman, Isaiah, Maj., 243
Stilwell, Joseph W., BrigGen., 624, LtGen., 710, 712, 712, 715, 733-734, 734, 740, 741, 745-746
Stimson, Henry L., 529, 530, 532, 621, 621, 625, 639, 640, 693
Stockton, Robert, Commodore, 253, 297-298, 303-305, 364
Stoddard, Amos, Capt., 152
Stone, Christopher, SSgt., 920
Stone, Michael P.W., 885, 885
Stoneman, George, 2ndLt., 291, MajGen., 406, 409
Stowers, Freddie, Cpl., 910
Streight, Abdel D., Col., 407
Strickler, John, BrigGen., 208, 210, 215
Stone, Charles P., BrigGen., 381
Streett, St Clair, Capt., 599
Stroh, Donald A., MajGen., 672
Stone, Charles B., MajGen., 747
Strong, David, LtCol., 137
Strong, George S., BrigGen., 413
Stryker, Robert F., Specialist, 927
Stryker, Stuart S., PFC, 927
Stuart, J.E.B., Lt., 351-352, 366, Confederate BrigGen., 382, 391, 396, 402, 411-412, 413, 421
Sturgis, Samuel D., 2ndLt., 291, Maj., 380, LtCol., 447, Col., 470, BrigGen., 423
Stuyvesant, Peter, 22
Styer, William D., LtGen., 744
Sullivan, Gordon R., Gen., 910, 912, 916
Sullivan, John, Maj., 51, BrigGen., 7-73, 77, MajGen., 80, 89, 94-95
Sultan, Daniel, MajGen., 733
Summerall, Charles P., Lt., 513, BrigGen., 555, LtGen., 561, 607, 607, Gen., 609
Summers, Harry G., Col., 872
Sumner, Edwin V., Capt., 247, 287, LtCol., 334, 337-338, Col., 300, 340, 351-352, 355, 360, MajGen., 385, 394, 398-399, 402, 406
Sumter, Thomas, BrigGen., 60, 98-99, 101-102, 107
Supreme Headquarters Allied Powers Eurpoe (SHAPE), 765
Surrat, Mary, 437
Sutherland, James W., LtGen., 847
Sweeney, Charles W., Maj., 736, 746
Sweeney, Thomas, Lt., 337
Swift, Alexander, J., Capt., 290
Swift, Innis P., MajGen., 733, 750
Swift, Joseph G., Lt., 150, Col., 215, BrigGen., 204
Swift, William H., Capt., 295
Swing, Joseph M., MajGen., 747-749, 751
Sykes, George, 2ndLt., 275, Col., 412, 457
Sylvester, John B., Col., 898
Taft, Alphonso, 464-465, 465
Taft, William Howard, 521, 521, 524, President, 464, 527
Talbot, Orwin C., MajGen., 833
Talcott, George H., Maj., 297
Tallmadge, Benjamin, Maj., 103
Tallmadge, George, Lt., 331
Tallman, Richard, BrigGen., 852
Tarleton, Banastre, LtCol., 97, 106, 110-111
Task Forces:
1-32 Armor, 907; 1-64, 935; 3-15, 938; 3-69, 937; 201, 794; 6814, 711-712, 751; B, 655; 1st Airborne Task Force, 667; Baum, 685; Birch, 710; Bobcat, 709-710; Central Task Force, 645; Combined Joint Task Force-Horn of Africa, 947; Danger, 948; Darby, 689; Eagle, 917, 922; Eastern Task Force, 645; Faith, 778, 780; Falcon, 921;
Gimlet, 852; Hawk, 920; Hogan, 671; Holly, 710; Indigo Force, 633-634; Iron, 903; Iron Horse, 941, 943, 948; Joint Special Operations Task Force, 901; Joint Task Force 7, 948; Joint Task Force 180, 928; Joint Task Force Bravo, 916; Joint Task Force Liberia, 939; Kingston, 778;
Mars, 732, 735-736, 738; McLean, 774, 778, 780; Normandy, 899; Olymipia, 949; Oregon, 823-824, 826; Palawan, 741; Patriot Defender, 900; Provide Comfort, 909; Rapid Deployment Joint Task Force, 870, 875; Rakkasan, 927; Ranger, 914; Shoemaker, 842; Smith, 765, 768; Western Task Force, 645-646, 668; Williamson, 664-665
Taylor, Daniel, Lt., 269
Taylor, Issac, 170
Taylor, James R., MajGen., 883
Taylor, Kenneth, 2ndLt., 703
Taylor, Maxwell D., MajGen, 675, LtGen., 789, 789, 790, 792, 794, 801, 811, 813, 832
Taylor, Oliver Hazard Perry, 1stLt., 363
Taylor, Richard, Confederate MajGen., 419, LtGen., 435
Taylor, Zachary, Lt., 164, Capt., 177, 180, Maj., 201, 211, 207, 217, 224-225, 232, LtCol., 233, 240-241, Col., 242-243, 245, 256, 260-265, 268-269, BrigGen., 283-284, MajGen., 285, 285, 287-292, 292, 294, 296-297, 299-302, 302, 303-304, 306-307, 312-313, 315, 318, 322, 332 President, 323, 328, 330, 419
Tecumseh, 169, 171, 179-180, 188, 191-192
Terrazas, Joaquin, Col., 476
Terrett, John C., Lt., 338
Terry, Alfred H., BrigGen., 430, 464-465
Thayer, Sylvanus, Lt., 179, Capt., 201, 226-227, 229
Thomas, Evan, Capt., 460
Thomas, George H., Lt., 299, 307, BrigGen., 383, 388, MajGen., 401, 404-405, 415-417, 417, 419, 425, 430, 471
Thomas, John, MajGen., 59, 71-72
Thompkins, William H., Pvt., 500
Thompson, Floyd J., Capt., 853
Thompson, Hugh, Warrant Officer, 829
Thompson, Seth B., Capt., 291
Thompson, Stephan W., Lt., 563
Thompson, Wiley, 249
Thompson, William, BrigGen., 72
Thorn, Herman, 1stLt., 346
Thornburgh, Thomas T., Maj., 475, 477
Thoughts of a Freeman, 85
Through the Western Parts of Louisiana, 165
Thurman, Maxwell R., MajGen., 871, 885
Tibbetts, Paul W., Jr., Col., 736, 746, 747
Tilleli, John, Jr., BrigGen., 892
Tilley, Jack L., SgtMaj., 922
Tilton, James Dr., 198
Timberlake, Pat, BrigGen., 645
Ting, Chia Cer, 528
Tinker, Clarence L., MajGen., 710, 715
Titus, Calvin, 513, 513
Tolson, John J., MajGen., 828-829
Tomb of the Unknown Soldier, 602, 794
Tompkins, Sally, 392
Torrey, Robert A., Capt., 455
Totten, Joseph G., Capt., 181-182, Maj., 206, Col., 290, 336, 372, BrigGen., 446
Tower, Zealous B., Lt., 314, 334
Towson, Nathan, Capt., 181
"Trail of Tears," 264, 276
Treadwell, Jack L., Col., 834
Treaties:
of Aix-la-Chapelle, 36; of Brest-Litovsk, 565; of Dancing Rabbit Creek, 241; Dayton Peace Accords, 917; of Fort Wayne, 169; of Ghent, 213; of Greenville, 141, 155; of Guadalupe-Hidalgo, 318, 328; Intermediate Range Nuclear Forces Treaty, 884-885, 909; Jay's Treaty, 141; Laramie Treaty of 1868, 442-443, 449;
of Paris, 123; of Paris (1898), 505; of Ryswick, 28; of Utrecht, 29; of Versailles, 597
Trembley, William B., Pvt., 507
Trescott, Lemuel, Maj., 110
Trofimoff, George, Col., 924
Trotter, John, Col., 129, 131
Trueman, Alexander, Capt., 136
Truman, Harry S., 1stLt., 570, Senator, 625, President, 614, 623, 657, 687, 692-693, 704, 744, 746-747, 759, 761, 763, 767, 767, 768-770, 772-776, 779, 781, 785, 787-788, 791
Truman, Louis, Col., 693
Truman, Ralph, MajGen., 625
Trumbull, Jospeh, 65
Truscott, Lucian K., Jr., Col., 644, MajGen., 649, 658, 662, 667, LtGen., 669, 674, 691, 694
Tryon, William, 49
Tubman, Harriet, 392
Tucker, Spephen S., Capt., 333
Tudor, William, Col., 64
Tupper, Tullius C., Capt., 477
Turner, Edward, Capt., 153
Tuttle, W.B., Col., 718
Twiggs, David E., Maj., 227, 237-238, LtCol., 254, Col., 263, 268, 282, 284, 289-290, 292, 297, BrigGen., 303-304, 307-308, 310, 313, 323, 347, MajGen., 373
Twining, Nathan F., BrigGen., 721, MajGen., 680, LtGen., 746
Tyler, Charles H., 2ndLt., 329
Tyler, John, President., 270-271, 284
Ullom, Madelaine, Lt., 714
Ulmer, Walter R., BrigGen., 864
Underhill, John, Capt., 17
Underwood, Edmund, Capt., 363
Uniform Code of Military Justice, 130, 767
United Colonies of New England, 17, 19, 69
United Nations Command, 769
United States Air Force Bases:
MacDill AFB, 875, 922; Peterson AFB, 939; Vandenberg AFB, 901
United States Air Force Special Operations, 899
United States Army Band, 602, 603, 656
United States Army Publications:
Army Register, 189; *Coast Artillery Journal*, 517; *Field Artillery Journal*, 529; *Field Manual 100-5 Operations*, 862; *Infantry Journal*, 489; *Instruction of Field Artillery, Horse and Foot*, 284; *Journal of the United States Artillery*, 488;*Military Policy of the United States*, 454;*On Strategy: The Vietnam War in Context*, 872; *Rules and Regulations for the Field Exercise and Maneuvers of the Infantry*, 215, 284; *Regulations of the Army of the United States*, 356; *Rules and Regulations of the Army of the United States*, 188; *Rules for the Exercise and Manuevers for US Dragoons*, 253; *Saber Regulations, 1914*, 541; *Stars and Stripes*, 563, 587, 669, 692; *System of Exercise and Instruction of Field Artillery*, 239; *US Infantry Drill Regulations*, 239; *YANK*, 669
United States Army Schools:
Antiaircraft Artillery School, 638; Army Chaplain School, 638; Army Chemical School, 870, 885; Army Engineer School, 885; Army Industrial College, 604; Army Infantry School, 614, 734; Army School of the Americas, 879; Army School of Nursing, 596, 596; Army Signal School, 522; Army War College, 511, 517, 520, 522, 538, 544, 600, 614, 619, 622, 657, 668, 832, 872; Artillery School, 448, 488; Artillery School of Practice, 235; Cavalry School, 590; Cavalry and Light Artillery School, 483, 489; Command and General Staff College, 467, 558, 600, 607, 668, 734, 832, 876, 911; Field Artillery School, 530; First Army Tank School, 558, 599; General Staff School, 657; Infantry Officer Candidate School,635, 872
Infantry School of Arms, 533, 556, 635; Infantry School of Practice, 236-237; Military Police School, 637, 885; Mounted Service School, 541, 590; Parachute School, 639; Quartermaster School, 526;
School of Advanced Military Studies, 876; School of Application of Infantry and Cavalry, 476; School of Fire, 530; School of Instruction for Light Artillery, 452; School of the Line, 522; School of Musketry, 533; Second Corps Aeronautical School, 564; Second Corps Artillery School, 564; Signal School of Instruction, 449; Staff College, 522; Tank Destroyer and Firing Center, 635; US Army Medical School, 489; US Infantry and Cavalry School, 476, 522
United States Army Units:
Commands
American Expeditionary Force, (AEF), 481, 549, 551, 551, 552-557, 557, 558, 558, 560-563, 563, 564-566, 571-572, 574, 575, 576-577, 581, 581, 582, 584-588, 590-591, 591, 600-601, 603, 605, 605, 607, 614, 616, 618, 644, 657, 668; American Expeditionary Force-North Russia, 589-590; American Expeditionary Forces-Siberia, 576-577, 596; Bataan Defense Force, 706, 708; Northern Luzon Force, 703, 705-708; Southern Luzon Force, 703, 705-707; US Army Forces in China, 603, 617; First Army Group, 636; Sixth Army Group, 665, 681-682, 683, 684, 693; Twelfth Army Group, 636, 665, 669, 677-678, 681, 683, 685, 693; Fifteenth Army Group, 674; Twenty-first Army Group, 685; Army of the Center, 179, 182-183; Army of the Constitution, 141;
Army of Cuban Occupation, 524, 527; Army of the Cumberland, 401, 403-404, 415-416, 425, 430;
IV Corps (Granger), 415; XIV Corps (Thomas), 404, 415; XX Corps, 415; XXI Corps, 415;
Army of the Frontier, 402; Army of the James, 421; Army of the Mississippi, 388, 399, 405; Army of the North, 198; Army of the Northwest, 177-178; Army of Observation, 283, 287; Army of Occupation, 288; Army of the Ohio, 386, 388, 401, 416, 430;
I Corps, 401;
Army of the Potomac, 379, 383, 383, 385, 391, 393-395, 398, 402, 405-407, 409, 411, 413, 414-415, 419-420, 422-423, 427, 437;
I Corps, 385, 399, 400, 406, 411; II Corps (Hancock), 385, 391, 394, 399, 406, 412, 414, 416, 419-421, 423; III Corps, 385, 391, 394, 406, 412, 416; IV Corps, 385, 391; V Corps (Warren), 385, 391, 393, 399, 406, 412, 419, 426; VI Corps (Sedgwick), 399, 406, 409, 420; VI Corps (Wright), 423-425, 428; IX Corps (Burnside), 399, 406, 421, 426; XI Corps (Howard), 398, 406, 409, 411, 415; XII Corps (Slocum), 398-399, 406, 412, 415; XVIII Corps (Smith), 423; XIX Corps, 425;
Army of the Shenandoah, 428; Army of the South, 270; Army of the Southwest, 384; Army of the Tennessee, 386, 387, 389, 407, 410, 416, 422, 425;
XII Corps, 416; XIII Corps, 405, 410; XIV Corps, 416; XV Corps, 410, 425; XVII Corps, 407, 409-410; XIX Corps, 410; Army of Virginia, 393, 396, 398;
I Corps, 393, 397-398; II Corps, 393, 396, 398; III Corps, 393, 398; IX Corps, 399;
Army of the West, 253; Army of the West, 296, 298-299, 299; Army of the West, 380, 383; North Western Army, 181, 193, 199; "Provisional Army," 146;
US Army South, 883, 945; US First Army, 576-579, 581-582, 584, 586-587, 590-591, 630, 635, 650, 661, 664, 665, 670-672, 674, 678, 678, 679, 681-682, 684-686, 687, 688, 690, 692-693, 744; US Second Army, 581, 586, 591, 630, 634, 786, 876; US Third Army, 587, 590-591, 603, 630, 634, 665-666, 668, 671, 675-676, 678-679, 681-685, 687, 688-689, 691-695, 721, 875, 888, 890, 933; US Fourth Army, 630, 633, 700, 879; US Fifth Army, 630, 646, 647, 652-655, 658-660, 664, 666, 669-670, 674, 676, 686, 688-689, 691, 694; US Sixth Army, 721, 726, 728-729, 733-734, 736, 737-739, 739, 745, 750; US Seventh Army, 648-649, 650, 658, 666-668, 676, 679, 682-685, 687-688, 691-693, 695, 777; US Eighth Army, 660, 733, 736, 740-741, 744-745, 748-750, 756, 766, 768-769, 772-777, 777, 778-779, 781, 783, 783, 784, 786-789; US Ninth Army, 660, 669, 671, 679, 681-682, 686, 688, 691-692, 694; US Tenth Army, 730, 734, 742, 744, 745; US Fourteenth Army, 636; US Fifteenth Army, 677, 685, 693, 695; Corps of Discovery," 143, 150, 151-153, 153, 154, 154, 156-159, 159, 161, 161-163, 167, 923
I Corps, 562, 572-573, 577, 579-581, 584, 586, 712, 717, 719, 733, 737, 739, 750, 773, 775, 781, 784-785, 787; I Philippine Corps, 708-709; II Corps, 560, 566, 571, 578-579, 581-582, 646-648, 654-656, 658, 660, 662, 666, 668-670, 688-691; II Philippine Corps, 708-709; III Corps, 572, 578-581, 584, 586, 633, 676, 679, 682, 684, 734, 946; IV Corps, 576-578, 586, 662, 664, 666, 680, 669-670, 688-691, 734; V Corps, 499, 501, 572, 578-581, 584, 590, 645-646, 650, 661, 665, 667, 669-672, 677, 688, 691, 937, 946; VI Corps, 574, 586, 646, 652-656, 658, 660, 662, 664, 667, 669, 679, 685-688, 691, 735; VII Corps, 502, 661-662, 665, 667, 669-672, 679, 681, 685-688, 892-893, 893, 898-899, 901, 903, 905; VIII Corps, 498, 503-504, 506, 508-509, 664-666, 671, 678-679, 682, 735; IX Corps, 633, 749, 773, 775, 781, 784; X Corps, 733, 735, 744-745, 750-751, 766, 773-776, 778-779, 781-782, 784, 786; XI Corps, 679, 728, 740, 749; XII Corps, 665, 682, 684-686; XIII Corps, 681, 685-686, 691; XIV Corps, 681, 720, 725, 737, 742, 749, 751; XV Corps, 665-666, 684, 688, 691; XVIII Corps, 688; XIX Corps, 662, 664, 671, 681, 738; XX Corps, 665, 679, 681, 687; XXI Corps, 679-680, 684, 691; XXIV Corps, 728, 735, 744-745, 749;
Infantry Units:
1st Division, 506, 550, 552-556, 558, 560, 566, 568, 572-574, 576-580, 584, 586-588, 603, 614, 619, 633, 644, 647, 661, 663, 671, 674, 679, 681, 688, 813-814, 817-818, 820, 823, 827, 829, 833, 836, 840, 875, 884, 892, 900, 903, 905-906, 918, 921, 946, 948; 2nd Division, 498, 500, 506, 556, 560, 565, 568, 570-576, 584-585, 585, 588, 603, 619, 661, 664, 688, 771-774, 777-778, 782, 787-788, 790, 820-821, 823, 826, 828-829, 831, 833, 835, 855, 870, 884, 918, 921, 921, 944, 946-947, 949; 3rd Division, 564, 565, 568, 570, 572-575, 579-582, 584, 587, 603, 616-617, 619, 633, 647, 649, 652-653, 654, 658, 660-661, 679-680, 684, 688, 691, 700, 774, 777, 779, 784-785, 787, 790, 884, 892, 909, 918, 920, 929, 931, 931, 932-933, 933, 934, 934; 4th Division, 572, 574-575, 578, 580, 587, 621, 661, 662, 667, 670, 672, 674, 688, 819, 821, 823-824, 827-828, 835, 840, 842, 844-845, 884, 918-919, 928, 929, 932-933, 941, 942, 943-944, 946-949, 951;
5th Division, 556, 567, 581-582, 584, 586-587, 620, 633-634, 646, 682, 684, 692, 831, 846, 884, 887; 6th Division, 582, 584, 587, 620, 732, 738, 740-742, 745, 749-750, 879, 884; 7th Division, 581, 588, 621, 633, 720, 722, 725, 728, 728, 732, 734-735, 744, 749, 759, 774, 775-780, 782, 788, 790, 830-831, 840, 878, 884-886, 912, 920;
8th Division, 576, 621, 672, 674, 681, 876, 884, 911; 9th Infantry Division, 647, 662, 669-671, 674, 681, 821-822, 829, 832, 833, 834-835, 837, 839, 844-845, 871, 884, 911; 10th Mountain Division, 635, 662, 679, 680, 686, 687-690, 879, 881, 883, 884, 913, 913-914, 916, 918, 924, 925, 925, 926, 927, 946-947, 951; 23rd Division, (Americal), 711-712, 717-721, 726, 728, 741, 749, 751, 826-827, 835, 837, 840-841, 848, 911; 24th Division, 601, 621, 701-702, 729,735-736, 742, 745, 751, 768-769, 773, 785, 788, 794, 884, 888, 890, 892, 899, 904, 907, 911, 916, 916, 918, 921; 25th Division, 702, 717, 719-721, 725, 741, 750,769, 772-774, 777, 782, 784-785, 787, 805, 813, 817, 819-821, 823, 827, 829, 833, 837, 844-846, 879, 884, 916, 918, 921, 927, 946, 948; 26th Division, 543, 554, 557, 560, 563, 566, 572-575, 577-578, 581-582, 675; 27th Division, 571, 579-581, 587, 624, 637, 702, 711, 726, 728-731, 744, 748; 28th Division, 543, 572-577, 579-581, 588, 602, 667, 669, 670-672, 672, 674, 676, 679,770, 773, 927;
29th Division, 578-579, 581-582, 584, 645-646, 650, 661-663, 663, 664, 681, 691, 881; 30th Division, 571, 578-581, 587, 624, 670, 678, 681; 31st Division, 625, 735, 747, 770, 781; 32nd Division, 543, 560, 563, 566-567, 575-576, 579-580, 582, 584, 587, 624, 712, 717-718, 718, 719-720, 721, 726, 732-733, 735, 738, 745, 750; 33rd Division, 572, 578, 580, 581, 588, 750; 34th Infantry Division, 597, 637, 640, 643, 647, 651-652, 654-656, 662, 664-665, 669, 689, 691, 945; 35th Division, 570, 579-580, 607, 625, 637, 664, 664, 681, 702, 720, 879; 36th Division, 570, 584-585, 625, 652-655, 658-660; 37th Division, 579, 581, 584, 624, 718, 725-726, 737, 737, 738-742, 742, 745, 747, 770; 38th Division, 543, 564, 588, 735, 740-741, 745; 40th Division, 633, 720, 738, 749, 770, 773, 788, 790,